STEFAN R. LANDSBERGER
AND MARIEN VAN DER HEIJDEN

CHINESE POSTERS

THE IISH-LANDSBERGER COLLECTIONS

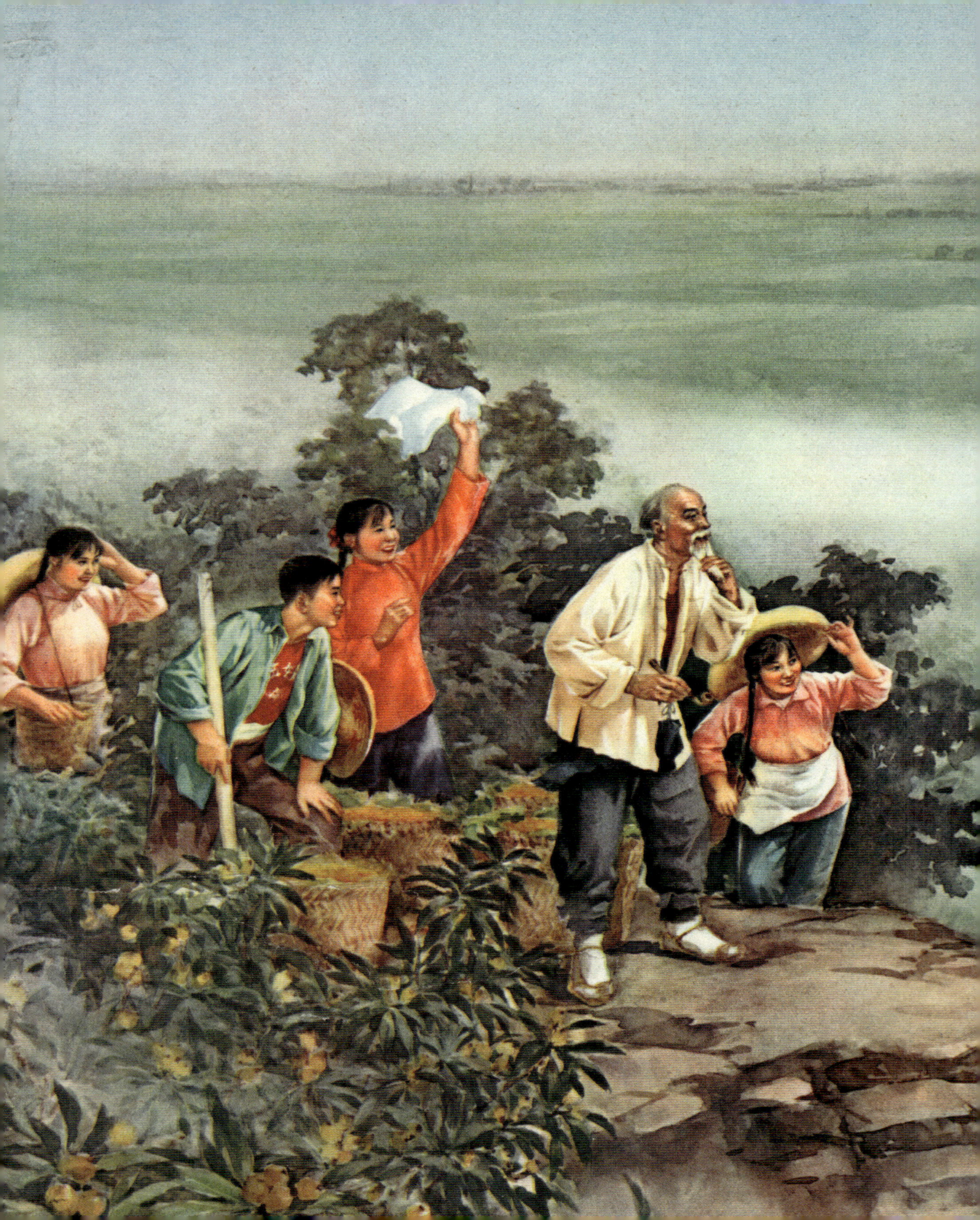

CONTENTS

PREFACE

MARIEN VAN DER HEIJDEN
AND STEFAN R. LANDSBERGER

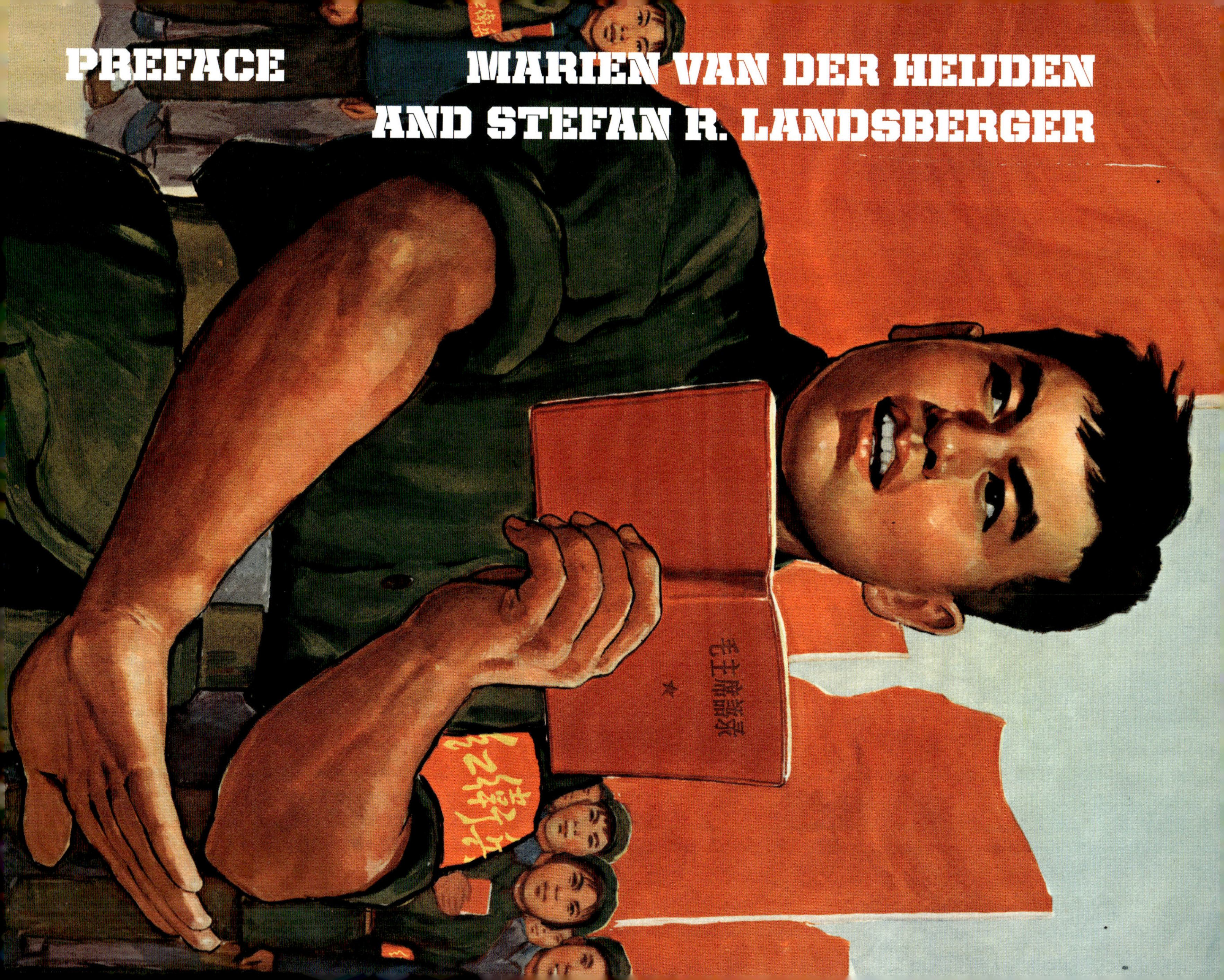

For over half a century, staggering quantities of propaganda posters were produced in China. Since the proclamation of the People's Republic of China in 1949, tens of thousands of different posters have been produced, printed in billions of copies. They cover a vast panoply of subjects and styles, and reflect every change in the country's official ideology. The widest possible range of emotions is conveyed, from sweet sentimentality to brutal aggression. All together, the posters form a visual chronicle of arguably the most turbulent half century in the long history of China. The country shown on the posters is of course an imagined China, the China of the Communist Party's propaganda. But even in this distorting mirror, many aspects of reality can be perceived.

The posters in this book were selected from the collections of the International Institute of Social History (IISH) and Stefan R. Landsberger. The IISH, based in Amsterdam, the Netherlands, is one of the world's largest documentary and research institutions in the field of social history, holding important archival, library, visual, and digital collections (among which over 100,000 posters). The IISH was founded in 1935 in order to rescue collections endangered by the rise of totalitarian ideologies in large parts of Europe. Stefan R. Landsberger (Leiden University, University of Amsterdam) started to collect Chinese propaganda posters in the 1970s. He considered them as rich primary sources for research on contemporary Chinese developments, and used them as the basis for his Ph.D. research, which focused on materials published in the 1980s. In 1995 he entrusted his collection to the IISH as a standing loan.

Since then, the IISH and Landsberger have joined forces and together built up a large and representative collection of Chinese propaganda posters, consisting of some 4,500 pieces at present. The collection is accessible to the general public and specialized researchers through the Institute's online catalog and a special website, chineseposters.net.

The combined IISH/Landsberger collection may be not just the largest, but also the most comprehensive collection of Chinese propaganda posters in the West. The whole era of the People's Republic is covered, even stretching back to the years before 1949, and continuing into the present. Different genres of posters are included: from propaganda posters in the strict sense of the word, to New Year pictures and reproduced paintings: genres with political messages and significance as well. While some themes and subjects may be represented better than others, the collection aims to cover all aspects.

With the selection of posters shown in this book, striking images in themselves, we hope to show the reader the quality, diversity, and intensity of Chinese visual propaganda. At the same time the reader will gain an insight into the extraordinary developments that have taken place in the country over the past decades. Knowing where the country has come from may help us to understand better what is happening in China today.

PROPAGANDA POSTERS IN CHINA

KUIYI SHEN

Production of propaganda posters in their unique form lasted in China for more than half a century. The introductory statement to the authoritative compilation *Ten Years of Propaganda Posters* of 1960 clearly defines the function of this mass art form: "The propaganda poster is an art form filled with militancy [*zhandouxing*] and mass character [*qunzhongxing*] that directly serves politics, production, the workers, peasants, and soldiers. It is a powerful tool of the party's propaganda agenda. It carries out the mission of publicizing and agitating for political movements and economic production. Propaganda posters, with their simple, lively forms and bright, powerful images, as well as their high volume printing and circulation throughout the whole nation, publicize the principles and policies of the party and government to the multitude of the masses. This unique form of art, the propaganda poster, enables the policies of the party and government to open the door to the hearts of the people and inspire their utmost efforts."[1] The Shanghai editor who wrote those words described the achievements of Chinese propaganda posters as the fruit of "Mao Zedong Thought" on Literature and the Arts, but combined with study of the experience of fraternal socialist countries, especially the Soviet Union. The writer characterizes it as a new genre.

Propaganda art was actually not new to China. Both Communists and Nationalists had very successfully deployed woodblock printed posters in their struggle against the Japanese between 1937 and 1945, and continued to use them against each other in the civil war of the late 1940s. Nevertheless, the rapid development of the propaganda poster into the most widespread form of Chinese visual art, the one that totally changed the aesthetic standards of an entire generation, is extraordinary. The New Woodblock Print Movement promoted by Lu Xun (1881–1936) in the early 1930s, now considered the foundation of political art in China, was originally very much associated with reform-minded intellectuals, and like most reform programs of the period, its models were Western. It adopted the style of German Expressionist art, aimed to arouse the social conscience of the viewer, was critical of social ills, and sought to portray faithfully the essence of everyday life. But its politically leftist stance and its criticism of current social issues offended the Nationalist government and led to its suppression. After the outbreak of the anti-Japanese war in 1937, many young woodcut artists of the suppressed movement went to Yan'an or southern Anhui and Jiangsu, the base areas of Communists throughout the anti-Japanese war and civil war periods. The black-and-white woodblock print, an economical and convenient medium for art, merged with traditional modes of New Year prints, and gradually became a successful visual tool for the propaganda of the Communist Party.[2] Meanwhile, some artists joined the Nationalists' Third Bureau of the Political Department to produce propaganda posters, especially in the beginning of the anti-Japanese war when the bureau was under the leadership of Guo Moruo (1892–1978).

After the establishment of the People's Republic of China (PRC) government in 1949, a tremendous effort was made to consolidate the Communist victory and create a new socialist world. Mao's famous talk at the Yan'an Conference on Literature and Art in 1942 was reintroduced as the infallible law of the art world: "Literature and art (must) become a component part of the whole revolutionary machinery, so they can act as a powerful weapon in uniting and educating the people while attacking and annihilating the enemy, and help the people achieve solidarity in their struggle against the enemy." Gaining control of the commercial publishing industry, which was based mainly in Shanghai, made it possible for the party, perhaps for the first time, to print full-color pictures in large runs.

It is against this background that the propaganda poster became institutionalized in China.[3] Although the propagandistic nature of many forms of visual art in post-1949 China, and especially that produced during the Cultural Revolution, may lead to the label of "propaganda poster," for all such printed matter, in practice the propaganda poster, or *xuanchuanhua*, was produced in different circumstances, on different schedules, and for different functions from other kinds of printed posters, such as the New Year's picture [*nianhua*] or reproductions [*huapian*]. The designs for *xuanchuanhua* were painted in gouache on paper and combined the bright colors of traditional Chinese New Year's pictures with the use of light and shade, perspective, and bold but simple propaganda slogans typical of Soviet propaganda posters. Propaganda posters reflected virtually every political movement and social program. In the 1950s, for example, they included the Establishment of the People's Republic of China, the War to Resist American Aggression and Aid Korea, the Movement to Suppress Counter-revolutionaries, the New Marriage Law, the Increase Production and Practice Economy Movement, the Patriotic Public Health Campaign, the Rural Cooperative Movement, the Party's General Line, the Great Leap Forward, the People's Communes, and the Preserve World Peace Movement. More than two million copies of Ha Qiongwen's famous *Long Live Chairman Mao*, which was commissioned in 1959 to celebrate the tenth anniversary of the PRC, were printed. Propaganda posters were usually ordered by work units [*danwei*] in response to particular events or ideological movements and were displayed in public spaces, in meeting rooms and hallways, or on propaganda bulletin boards. Issued on an irregular schedule, as deemed necessary by developing political events, the function of propaganda posters may be distinguished from that of a New Year's picture. The latter was usually bought at the end of the year by ordinary people to decorate their homes or paste on outside doors or gates. Artists of New Year's pictures were thus busy with annual deadlines to assure that a plentiful supply would reach bookstores and other distributors well before the New Year.

By contrast, *huapian*, a general term that includes full-color reproductions of oil paintings or ink paintings, were available all year round, and were purchased by both individuals and work units for decorative or inspirational purposes. Dong Xiwen's famous oil painting, *Founding Ceremony of the Republic*, created for Beijing's newly established Central Museum of Revolutionary History in 1952–53, was widely distributed as a *huapian* soon after its completion. An oil painting of 1961 by Wu Biduan and Jin Shangyi, *Chairman Mao Standing with the People of Asia, Africa and Latin America*, painted in praise of China's leadership of the Third World, was also widely distributed in poster reproduction. Although most *huapian* from the Maoist years are reproductions of oil or ink paintings that are propagandistic in subject matter, the circumstances of their production, marketing, and use are somewhat different from those of the other two major genres of full-color single-sheet publication.

Professional artists were involved in design of both New Year's pictures and propaganda posters from the early days of the PRC. Revolutionary New Year's prints were very successfully promoted by the party during the 1940s because they easily reached a large part of the population. During the early 1950s, they received a great deal of support from the government and developed further in the full-color format. Artists who specialized in all media, including oil painters, woodcut artists, traditional-style painters, cartoonists, and illustrators participated in creating this new form of New Year's picture. The Ministry of Culture sponsored New Year's picture competitions in 1950 and 1952. In 1950, 400 New Year's picture designs were published; in 1952, 570 new pictures were issued in 40 million copies.[4] Most of these pictures were executed in traditional formats, with recognizable thematic links to folk art. The two predominant pre-1949 techniques in Shanghai New Year's pictures were

gongbi (a meticulous technique using fine lines to contour figures and objects; the contours are then filled with bright colors) and *cabi* (rubbed charcoal and watercolor, as used in yuefenpai calendar prints). The post-1949 New Year's pictures followed the old styles but modified them with new revolutionary themes. They remained popular with their consumers, who were primarily rural, until large color photo-calendars were introduced in the mid-1980s.
In the early 1950s, on the other hand, before dedicated propaganda poster units were established within the state publishing industry, painting of propaganda posters also largely relied on professors at select national art academies, especially those of Beijing, Shanghai, Tianjin, and Hangzhou. Some of these artists had no prior experience in the commercial publishing industry; but, with greater or lesser degrees of enthusiasm, they joined propaganda painting teams that produced large quantities of such posters. Prominent participants included the director of the newly established Central Academy of Fine Arts, Xu Beihong (1895–1953), oil painting professors Wu Zuoren (1908–1997), Li Binghong (1913–1986), Ai Zhongxin (1915–2003), Dong Xiwen (1914–1973), and Yu Yunjie (1917–1992), and revolutionary printmakers Li Hua (1907–1990) and Zhao Yannian (b. 1924), and even ink painters Li Keran (1907–1989) and Li Kuchan (1898–1983). The oil painter Wu Guanzhong (b. 1919), who had just returned from studying modernist art in France, immediately threw himself into propaganda painting activities. The production of propaganda posters and new New Year's paintings absorbed the energies of most artists, particularly those in the academies, during the first half of the 1950s. The posters of this period reflect the atmosphere of enthusiasm that was widespread among the Chinese population of the time, despite the numerous political campaigns organized to consolidate Communist rule. Later, during the Cultural Revolution period, when design studios of the publishing industry had been dismantled, their students, such as Jin Shangyi (b. 1938) and Hou Yimin (b. 1930), by that time professors themselves, found themselves in a similar position.

By 1953, the Chinese government had managed to rebuild much of the country's war-devastated infrastructure, bring hyperinflation under control, and orient the population towards a degree of mutual cooperation not previously known. Intent on building a socialist state, it now entered the period of intensive industrialization, as well as organization of agricultural cooperatives. The first Five-Year Plan was set up as a basic structure for the state-planned economy, on the model used in the Soviet Union. Thus, the establishment of a formal, professional poster design team, intended as an important means of conveying party ideology, was explicitly listed on the party's agenda.

The first professional propaganda poster team in China was organized in 1954 at the East China People's Art Publishing House in Shanghai, the pre-liberation center of China's publishing industry.[5] Its staff was expanded in 1958, as part of the centralization of industry, when it was merged with the New Year's picture team from the old Shanghai Art Print (*Shanghai huapian*) Press, and reorganized as the New Year's Picture and Propaganda Poster Editorial Department of the new Shanghai People's Fine Arts Publishing House. The team was primarily formed by two groups of artists. One group of artists had originally been commercial artists, who worked in various advertising agencies and design studios before 1949. Their works are usually quite colorful and rather decorative in the so-called *yuefenpai* manner. The other group tended to be art school graduates of the late 1940s or early 1950s. They received formal training in oil painting rather than in commercial art and were often highly skilled at figurative rendering in an academic manner. By 1966, on the eve of the Cultural Revolution, there were many teams in the nation's major art publishers who were dedicated to designing propaganda posters and to publishing *huapian*. To take only a few examples, the Shanghai team published more than 2,000 different poster designs, issued in more than 40 million prints, between 1954 and 1966; Beijing People's Fine Arts Publishing House published more than 500 poster designs and printed about 28 million copies between 1951 and 1959;[6] and Tianjin Fine Arts Publishing House published 267 varieties of posters in 16,760,000 copies.[7]

Despite government complaints of the shortage of paper, the peak of propaganda poster production was during the Great Leap Forward, a movement officially launched by Mao Zedong in 1958 shortly after the conclusion of the Anti-Rightist campaign. According to a report made in the national conference on propaganda posters held in 1959, Beijing People's Fine Arts Publishing House published 241 poster designs and issued 11,340,000 copies in twelve months between 1958 and 1959, which were more than two-thirds of the output since it started to publish posters in 1950. The Tianjin Fine Arts Publishing House published 130 poster designs and printed 13,200,000 copies, which was almost a hundred times the number of copies they issued in 1957.[8] A great number of professional artists who were not poster designers participated in the production of Great Leap Forward posters. New designs were created in a few hours and sent directly to the printing factory, where the entire process was monitored by editors on press. Posters of particular importance could be produced in about ten hours, starting from conception and design to final printing. The poster thus became an almost instantaneous expression of party policy, reflecting the smallest changes in the thinking of the leadership almost as quickly as did official statements.[9]

During the Great Leap Forward campaign, with its calls for "more, faster, better, [and] cheaper" production, propaganda posters conveyed idealistic expectations for agricultural and industrial production that were inspired by the Communist party's utopian slogans (right). One slogan was "Surpass Great Britain's industrial production within fifteen years." With this target, the State Planning Committee established in 1957 the ambitious goal

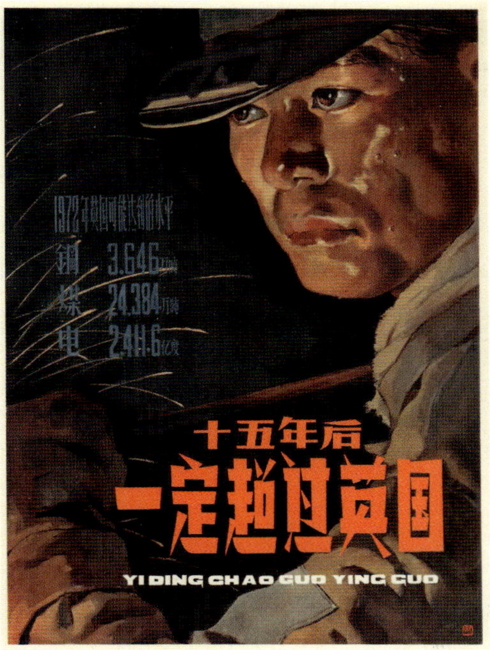

In fifteen years we will certainly have surpassed England, 1958.
In fünfzehn Jahren werden wir England mit Sicherheit überholt haben, 1958.

of producing 5.3 million tons of steel for the following year. Mao arbitrarily doubled the quota to 10.7 million tons, a figure that is celebrated in a 1958 poster by Shanghai artists Lu Xinchen and Shen Lin.

In posters about agricultural production, the output of grain might be exaggerated to ten times, or even a hundred times, the actual figures. Qian Daxin's poster *Zhengqu gengda de fengshou, xiangei Shehuizhuyi* [Fighting for a Bigger Harvest, Presenting it to Socialism], which portrays an old peasant with a very happy face holding a tray of grains and fruits, implied that "the general line of the party" created the bounty in agriculture. In 1958, 8,230,000 copies were sold.

The communist government's passion for control and for ideological brainwashing reached its zenith in Mao Zedong's Cultural Revolution. During the ten years of the Cultural Revolution period (1966-1976), all art became entirely propagandistic, and the functions and production process of the three genres, propaganda poster (*xuanchuanhua*), New Year's picture (*nianhua*), and reproduction (*huapian*), completely merged thematically and stylistically.

One of the best examples of a Cultural Revolution *huapian* is *Chairman Mao Goes to Anyuan*, by Liu Chunhua, a student at the prestigious Central Academy of Arts and Crafts. The work was first exhibited on October 1, 1967, in an exhibition called "Mao Zedong Thought Illuminates the Anyuan Worker's Movement," at the Chinese Museum of the Revolution. The oil painting portrays the young Mao with a kind of magical illumination, as though he were a god descended to earth, and thus goes beyond documenting his political credentials for leadership of the party and nation, which were considered beyond question, and takes a step even further to suggest a divine mandate. The choice of subject, Mao Zedong travelling to Anyuan, moreover, was intended to demolish the reputation of Mao's rival Liu Shaoqi, famed for his success in organizing the 1922 Anyuan Coal Miners' strike, as leader of the workers' movement. By July 1, 1968, Mao's powerful wife, Jiang Qing, had hand-picked Liu Chunhua's painting, along with the piano version of the modern opera *Red Lantern*, as model achievements of the Cultural Revolution. The painting was reproduced for the first time as a

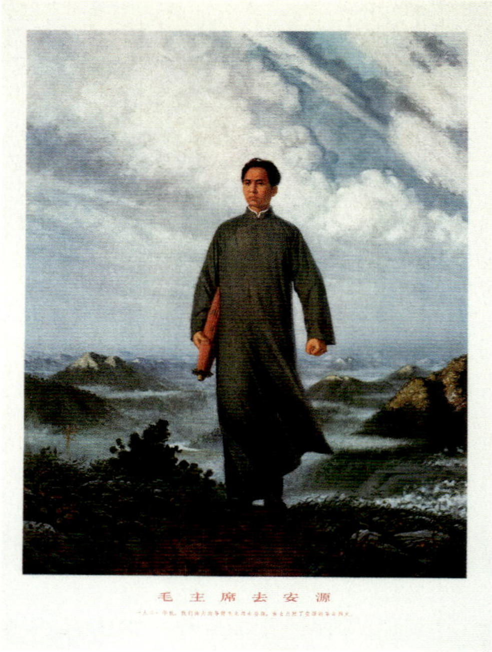

Chairman Mao going to Anyuan, 1968.
Der Vorsitzende Mao auf dem Weg nach Anyuan, 1968.

color supplement [*huapian*] to the most important publications in China, *People's Daily, PLA Daily*, and *Red Flag* magazine, to celebrate the July 1 anniversary of the founding of the Chinese Communist Party. This poster guaranteed widespread popular familiarity with the image and inspired further reproduction. According to the artist, Liu Chunhua, the painting was subsequently reproduced in various forms, from posters to Mao badges to postage stamps, nine hundred million times (above).[10]

A similar example from southern China was *Chairman Mao Inspects the Whole Nation*, an oil painting created by a group of young instructors and students at the Zhejiang Academy of Fine Arts in Hangzhou, led by Zheng Shengtian. This painting, which was later destroyed, survives in the form of large *huapian*, or posters, that were widely disseminated throughout the country.[11] In poster form, with slogans added, it becomes virtually indistinguishable from a *xuanchuanhua*, or propaganda poster (right).

When the Cultural Revolution began in 1966, however, most design studios of the publishing industry were dismantled. The Red Guard art movement swept the nation, replacing the official arts developed in the previous seventeen years. To show their loyalty to Mao and his revolutionary tradition, they looked back to the simple but strong black, white, and red color scheme of the Yan'an woodcut as a symbol of revolutionary purity. At the same time, in the absence of professional designers in the publishing industry, reproductions of oil paintings temporarily, but only partially, filled the gap left by the absence of specialized propaganda poster designs.

By the end of 1968, when Mao had reestablished his political power in most parts of China and had irrevocably removed his political rivals from power, the function of the Red Guard became superfluous. To solve the problem of employing the millions of college, high-school, and middle-school graduates, including the Red Guard, in the context of the dismantled academic and economic system, Mao launched a so-called Reeducation of Educated Youth movement that sent millions of graduates to poor villages in the countryside, state and military farms in remote regions, and

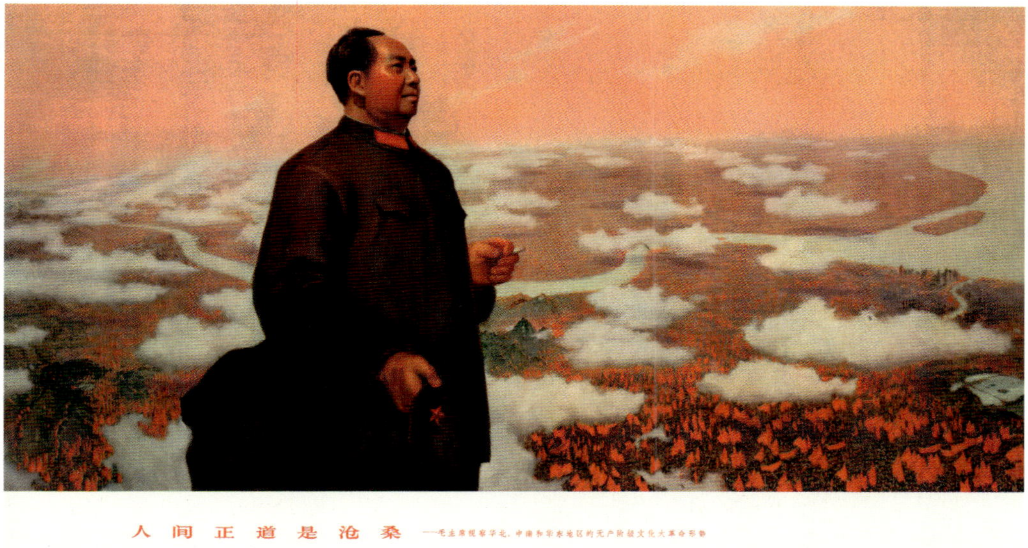

The correct way among the people is bringing great change to the world, 1967.
Der richtige Weg der Menschen ist, die Welt einem umfassenden Wandel zu unterziehen, 1967.

factories in the cities. The Red Guard movement officially ended. The former Red Guard now became workers, peasants, and soldiers themselves.

Especially after the demise of Mao's appointed successor and comrade-in-arms, Lin Biao, who apparently was killed attempting to flee the country on September 13, 1971, an effort was made by a small group of surviving central bureaucrats to return the nation to normalcy by beginning to reestablish some economic, political, and cultural institutions. Beginning in 1972 many local and national exhibitions were held in response to instructions from the central government. The Cultural Revolution leadership vigorously promoted the participation of the "workers, peasants, and soldiers" as artists in these exhibitions.

The art of the second half of the Cultural Revolution reflects the change in Mao's political policy and in the socio-political status of the artists. In addition to the former Red Guard, who had been so active during the Red Sea movement, those who emerged as "Educated Youth" painters in the early 1970s included many who had learned art in the urban Children's Palace system, which offered after-school artistic training, or in middle-school art classes. These urban young people now, as worker-peasant-soldier artists, participated in local and national artistic activities as representatives of the masses.

With Sunlight in Our Hearts We are Fearless; We Willingly Give Our Young Lives to the People, depicting eleven educated youths who died in a flood while trying to protect the property of their state farm, was painted in gouache in 1969 by the seventeen-year-old Shanghainese middle-school graduate, Liu Borong, who had been sent to live in a village in Jiangxi, thus becoming part of the rusticated youth. This image of martyred heroes was shown in the 1972 National Exhibition to celebrate the thirtieth anniversary of Mao's Yan'an talks, and was reproduced later as poster and widely disseminated in China.[12]

An even more famous example from the same period, *Chairman Mao's Red Guard: Learn from the Model of Revolutionary Youth Jin Xunhua*, was painted by another rusticated youth, Xu Chunzhong, who was then working as a farmer in the Shanghai suburbs. Jin Xunhua was a Shanghai high-school graduate sent to a village in Heilongjiang in May 1969. On August 15 of that year, attempting to prevent an electricity pole from being lost to floodwaters, he was swept away and drowned. After this heroic self-sacrifice was highly praised in the Communist Party journal *Red Flag*, the Shanghai newspaper *Liberation Daily* recruited a number of young artists to paint illustrations of the glorious deed. Xu Chunzhong, who had learned to paint at the Shanghai Children's Palace before the Cultural Revolution and had some reputation as a painter among local rusticated youth, composed a draft for this poster. A talented young graduate of Shanghai Art College, Chen Yifei, who then worked at the Shanghai Painting Institute, was assigned to help the amateur artist complete a work of professional caliber. After its first publication in color by *Liberation Daily*, it caught the attention of the central authorities, who praised it as a model painting, leading to numerous reproductions in poster form, and even its issue as a postage stamp.

Most of the posters published in the second half of the Cultural Revolution were reproductions of paintings selected from the major exhibitions. Some new characteristics appeared in art during this period. One is a style based upon the model theatrical works promoted by Mao's wife Jiang Qing, which are characterized as "red, shiny, and bright," and subject matter based upon the "three prominences." The latter formulation dictates: "Among all characters, give prominence to the positive character. Among positive characters, give prominence to heroic characters. Among heroic characters, give prominence to major heroes." In practice, in painting and in the theater, this meant that the heroic character was placed in the center of the composition or at center stage and brightly illuminated with a spotlight.

Pan Jiajun's oil painting, *I am "Petrel"* of 1972, illuminates the heroic face of the female soldier as she checks the telephone lines in a pounding rainstorm. The girl's red, shiny, bright face and dramatic lighting is a perfect example of Jiang Qing's aesthetic. The code name by which the girl calls herself is taken from Gorky's 1901 short story, *Petrel*, that concludes with the defiant sentence, "Let the thunderstorm hit with even more force !" The second new aspect of this period is a thematic expansion to incorporate in particular the activities of the Maoist triad of the workers, peasants, and soldiers, now reinterpreted, often with local flavor, to include the many new people produced by the Cultural Revolution, such as rusticated youth and worker/peasant/soldier college students.[13] Chen Yanning's *New Doctor in the Fishing Village* exemplifies both characteristics: the barefoot doctor is depicted in the red-bright-shiny heroic manner, and the setting clearly reflects the semi-tropical home province of the artist, a 1965 graduate of the Guangzhou Art Academy. The latter part of the Cultural Revolution is particularly notable for its many images of heroic young women, echoing Mao's words that "women hold up half the sky." The same aesthetic could be applied to ink painting, as in the case of Yang Zhiguang's *New Soldier of the Coal Mine* of 1972, and even achieved in black-and-white woodblock printing, as in Xu Kuang's *Poem on the Grassland* of 1976.

Portraits of a virile, active Mao Zedong from this period exemplify the same theatrical aesthetic. Tang Xiaohe's *Strive Forward in Wind and Waves* of 1971 is centered on an image of Mao waving after he completed his famous swim in the Yangzi River at the beginning of the Cultural Revolution. Although in the actual event he swam with his bodyguards and a couple of high officials, here he is depicted surrounded by Red Guards, workers, peasants, and soldiers. In Chen Yanning's painting of 1972, Chairman Mao's brightly illuminated figure forms the apex of a pyramid composed of Guangdong villagers. All these paintings were soon reproduced as posters and distributed to schools, work units, army camps, and communes nationwide. In addition, they were selected for publication in *Model Images of the Worker-Peasant-Soldier*, a how-to-paint book for amateur artists to carry out their propaganda duties, such as decorating billboards, blackboards, and newsletters. Such images became ubiquitous.

The third characteristic of late Cultural Revolu-tion art is that the worker/peasant/soldier triad is not only the subject of the painting, but also the producer of the artwork. Almost all the artists mentioned above were rusticated youth, and thus officially became workers, peasants, or soldiers, depending upon where they were sent. The professional artists who were trained in the art colleges before the Cultural Revolution mainly worked in supporting roles, to facilitate the conversion of amateur paintings into something that could be exhibited. The case of Xu Chunzhong and Chen Yifei is typical.

One of the hallmarks of the Cultural Revolution was that everyone had to participate in visual art, music, theater, or "culture" in some way, and all art was propaganda. Propaganda posters, as a "powerful tool to attack the enemy, to eradicate the enemy, to unite the people, and to educate the people," to quote Mao Zedong, served a very important role during this period. Red Guard posters helped Mao achieve his goal of overthrowing his enemies in the early years of the movement, and of glorifying the Cultural Revolution and his own achievements later on. In the latter years

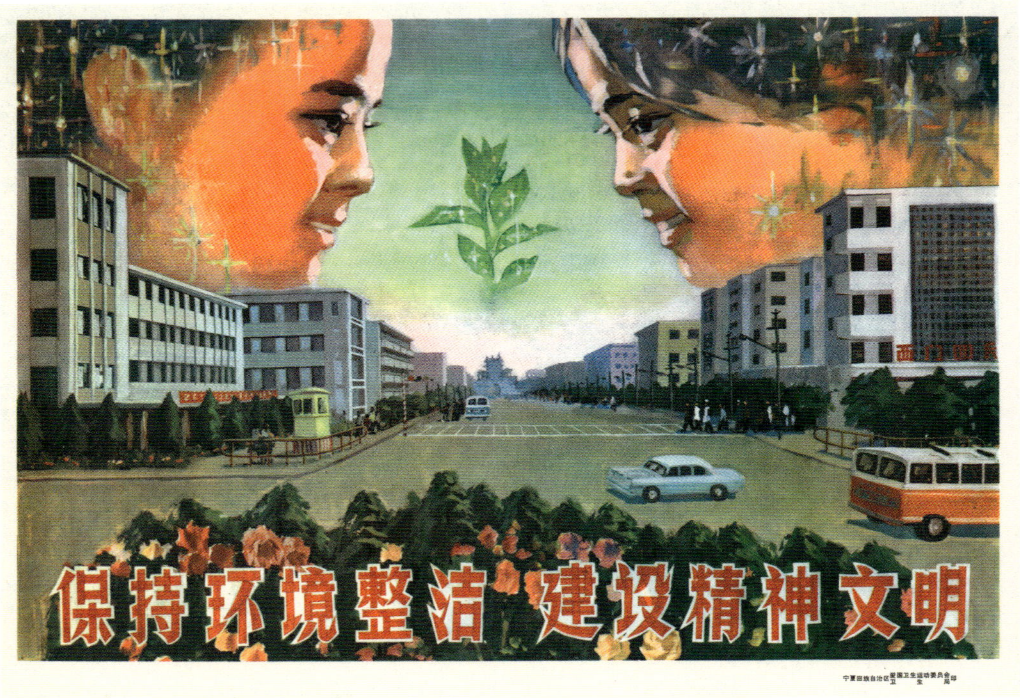

Keep the environment clean, create spiritual civilization, 1980s.
Haltet die Umwelt rein, erschafft spirituelle Zivilisation, um 1980.

of the movement, the many artificial images of model workers, peasants, and soldiers helped indoctrinate the people in their proper roles in Maoist society. Although many older people, including some of the artists themselves, thought privately that these pictures were ridiculous, they very effectively influenced any children who saw them.

Professional design teams in the publishing houses did not fully resume their activities until the end of the Cultural Revolution, when one important change returned the production of posters gradually to the hands of professional poster designers. As higher education resumed and there was renewed activity in professional art institutions, academic artists withdrew from poster-making. With artistic practice returned to the professionals, it slowly retreated to a more specialized realm, and society rediscovered differentiated labor and professions. In the 1980s, the function of propaganda posters was no longer limited to directly publicizing political ideology, focusing rather on promoting a more practical party agenda: the four modernizations, social morality, and public safety. The posters of the period featured campaigns against littering, rudeness, waste, and sloppy work, and promoted good customer service, planting trees, sanitation, and athletics, among other social goals, thus trying to soften the now meaningless revolutionary tone of propaganda posters (left).[14]

In the early 1990s, along with the rise of the new market economy and the depoliticization of ideology, the extremely ideologically oriented posters of the past lost their *raison d'être*. The demand for such posters dramatically declined and publishers could no longer justify their production. China's first propaganda poster team, established in 1954 at Shanghai People's Fine Arts Publishing House, was abolished in 1992. The last design to emerge from this department was by one of the founders of the team, Ha Qiongwen, author of the famous pre-Cultural Revolution image, *Long Live Chairman Mao*. The theme of his last work was praise for the new special economic zones in Shanghai's suburb of Pudong, which was heavily promoted by the economic reformers in the party and underwent a building boom in the early 1990s. Ironically, this anti-Maoist poster design won the first prize for creativity in the exhibition, *Celebrate the Fiftieth Anniversary of Mao's Yanan Talks on Art and Literature*, and was acquired for the permanent collection of the Shanghai Institute of Culture and History [*Shanghai wenshiguan*]. Even more ironically, because no advance orders were received from bookstores for this poster, it was never printed.[15] After the dismantling of the professional design teams in all the state publishing houses in the early 1990s, propaganda posters were still occasionally commissioned by the party or the government to satisfy their political or social agendas. The format of these new posters, affected by new mass-market commercial advertising, expanded to include photographs, digitally manipulated images, and new designs. Many functions of the poster have now been replaced by multi-media propaganda that uses electronic billboards, digital screens, light boxes, neon, and so forth, often subtly and effectively combining commercial and ideological advertising. "In a climate of possible swings in prevailing policies, which might make posters obsolete as soon as they appear on the market, it may be seen as more effective to present the message via the electronic media."[16]

The rise and fall of the production of propaganda posters, New Year's pictures, and *huapian* over the course of a highly politicized half-century paralleled the fate of China's people. The power of their imagery, even if produced by artists who were deceived, or who were aware of the deception they perpetrated, now survives to fill the minds of those who follow with questions and fantasies about an incomprehensible era. While memories of this recent past may have been forgotten or suppressed, these material traces can serve as a reminder of how easily an art form may be manipulated as a political tool.

Notes

1. "Editor's Words," *Shinian xuanchuanhua xuan* [Ten Years of Propaganda Posters]. (Shanghai: Shanghai People's Art Publishing House, 1960), n. p.

2. Julia Andrews and Kuiyi Shen, "The Modern Woodcut Movement," in *A Century in Crisis–Modernity and Tradition in the Art of Twentieth Century China*, (New York: Guggenheim Museum, 1998), pp. 213–25.

3. See Kuiyi Shen, "Publishing Posters before the Cultural Revolution," *Modern Chinese Literature and Culture*, vol. 12, no. 2. (Fall 2000): 177–201.

4. Ellen Johnston Laing quoting Yu Feng, "New Year Pictures," *People's China*, March 1, 1953, 14, and "'New Year Pictures,' An Old Custom Serves the New China," *China Reconstructs* (1953), 2: 26.

5. *Shinian xuanchuanhua xuan* [Ten Years of Propaganda Posters], (Shanghai: Shanghai People's Art Publishing House, 1960), n. p.

6. "Cujin xuanchuanhua chuangzuo de gengda fazhan–'Shinian xuanchuanhua zhanlan' zuotanhui [Promoting the Further Development of the Propaganda Posters–A Conference in Conjunction with the Exhibition of Propaganda Posters in Past Ten Years]," *Meishu 2* (1960): 8.

7. Ibid.

8. Ibid.

9. Maria Galikowski, *Art and Politics in China*, 1949–1984 (Hong Kong: Chinese University Press, 1998), p. 98.

10. Julia F. Andrews, *Painters and Politics in the People's Republic of China, 1949–1979*, (Berkeley: University of California Press, 1994), p. 339.

11. Author's interview with Zheng Shengtian, September 6, 2006.

12. Wang Mingxian and Yan Shanchun, *The Art History of the People's Republic of China, 1966–96*, (Beijing: Zhongguo qingnian chubanshe, 2000), pp. 81–82.

13. Zou Yuejin, *Art in the Era of Mao Zedong, 1942–1976*, (Changsha: Hunan meishu chubanshe, 2005), p. 13.

14. Kuiyi Shen, "Publishing Posters before the Cultural Revolution," *Modern Chinese Literature and Culture*, vol. 12, no. 2 (Fall 2000): 177–201.

15. Author's telephone interview with Ha Qiongwen, August 31, 1999.

16. Stefan R. Landsberger, *Chinese Propaganda Posters*, (Amsterdam: The Pepin Press, 1995), p. 206.

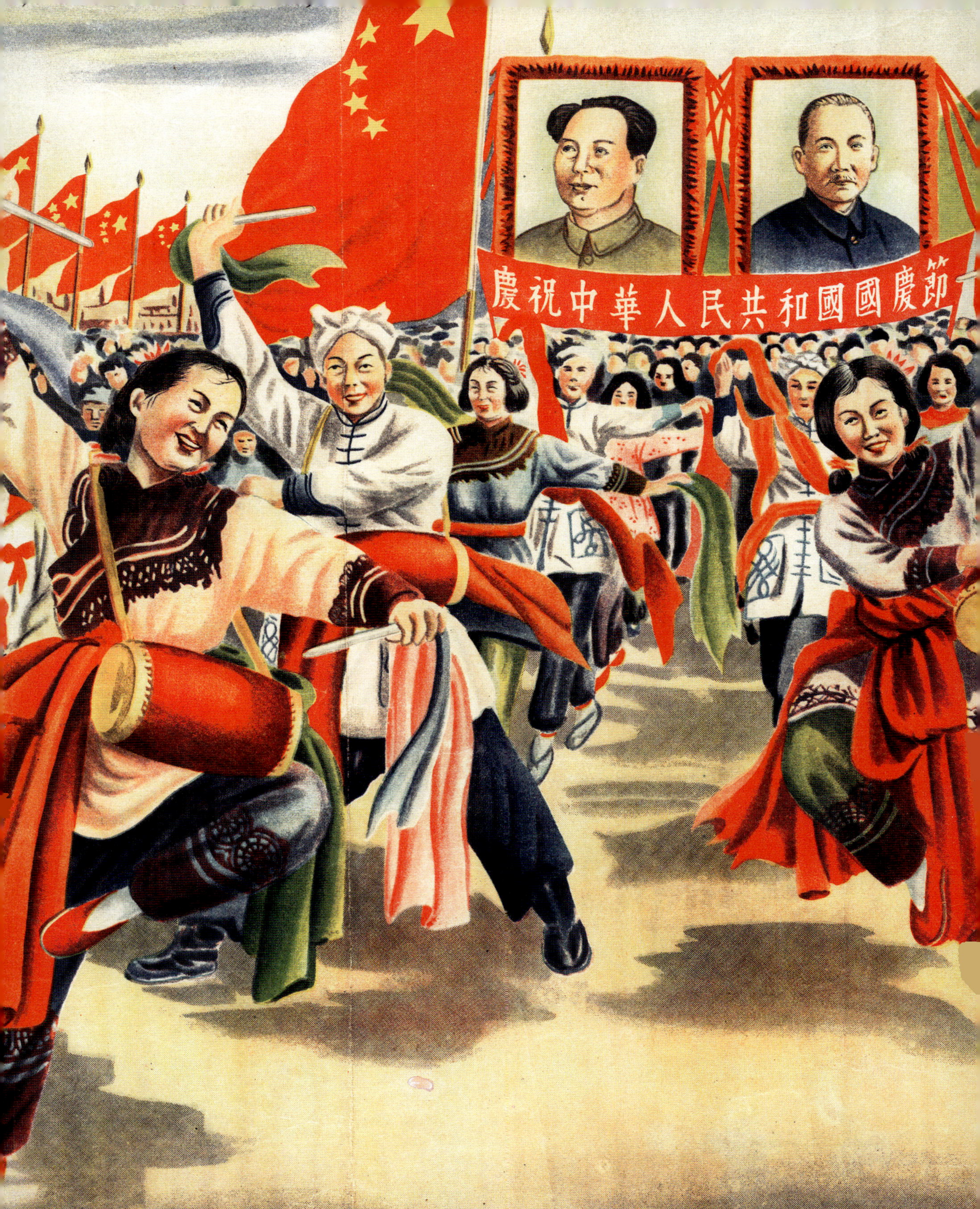

新華書店 東北總分店發行

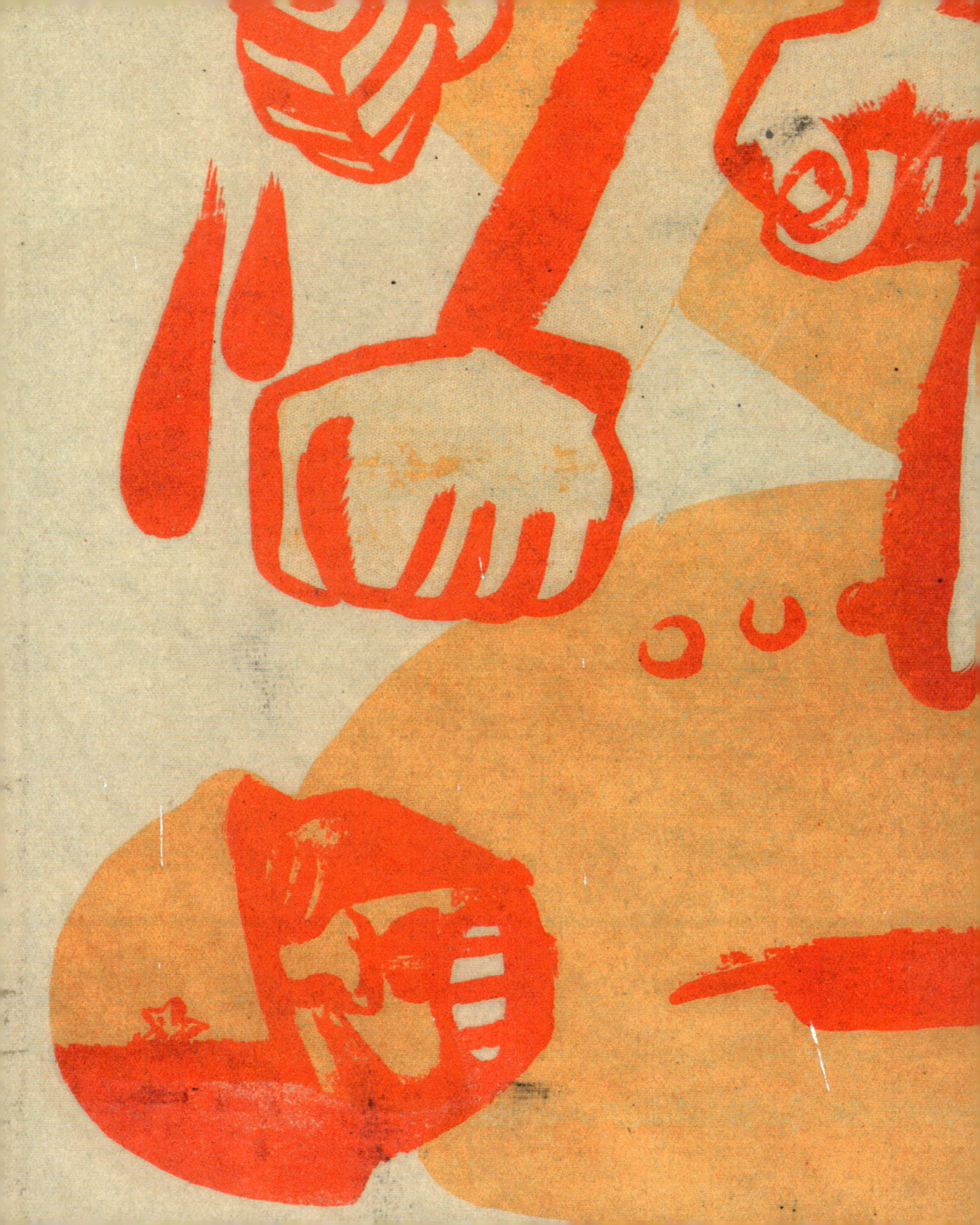

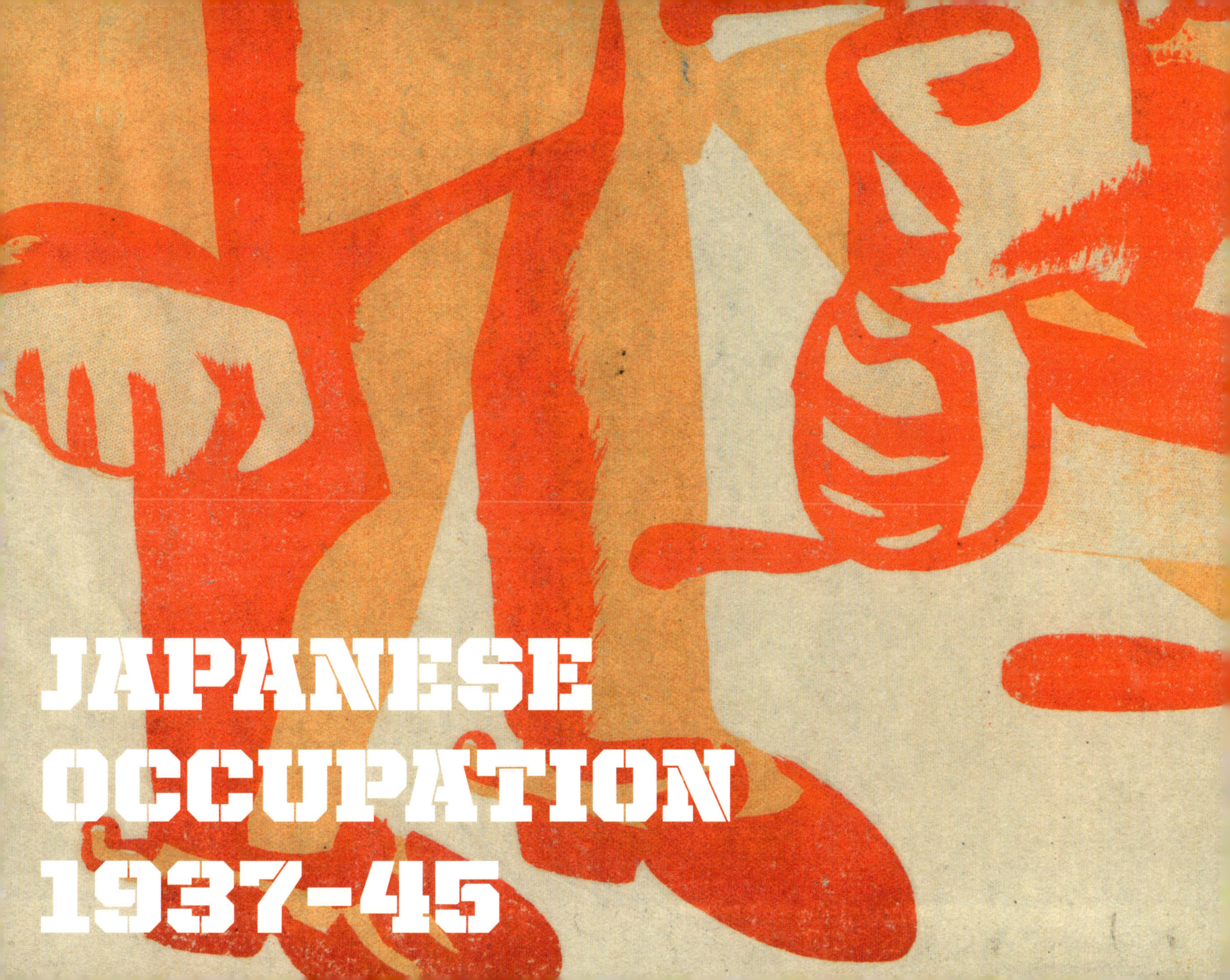

JAPANESE OCCUPATION 1937–45

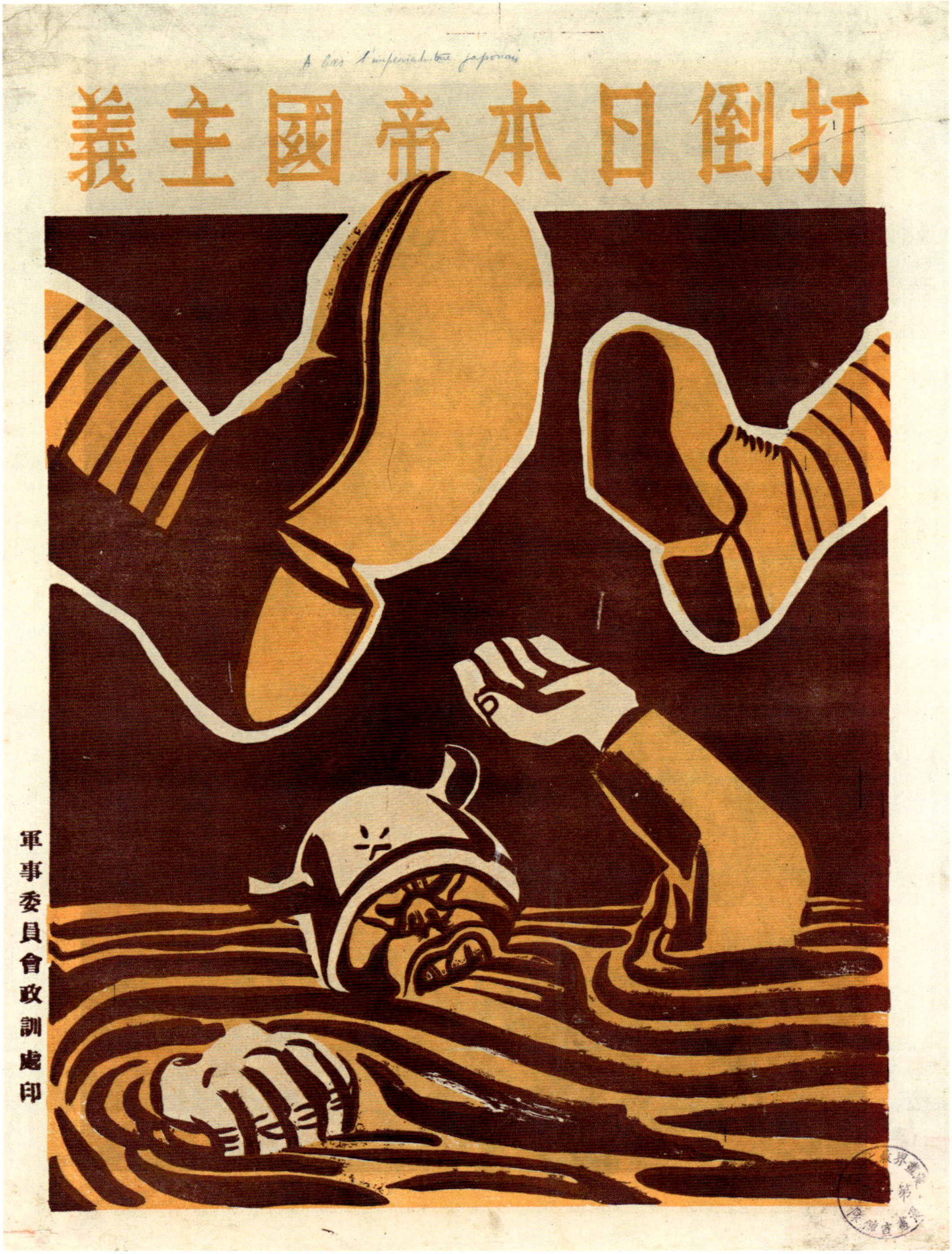

Defeat Japanese imperialism, c. 1937.
Besiegt den japanischen Imperialismus, um 1937.

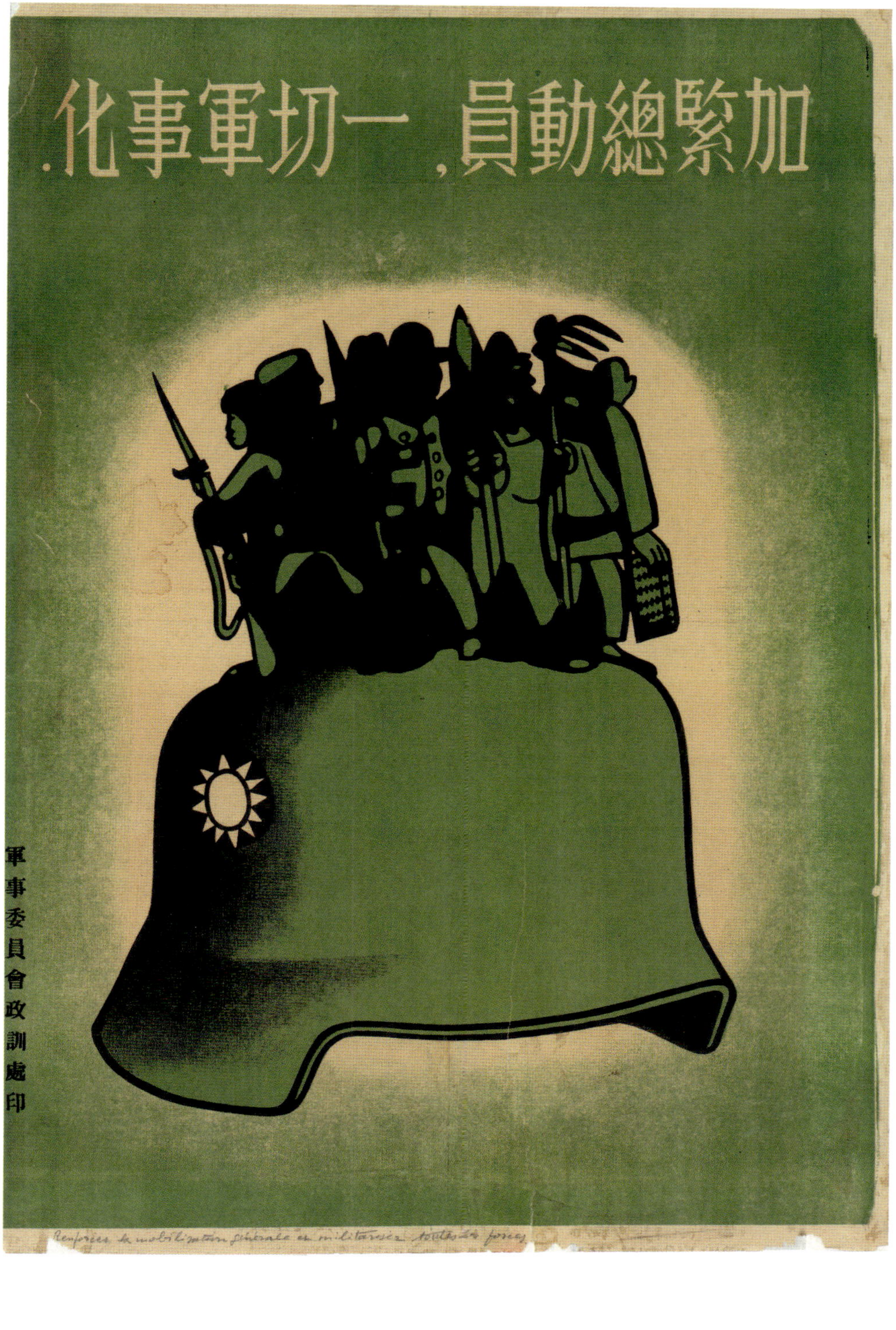

Step up general mobilization, towards total militarization, c. 1937.
Besiegt den japanischen Imperialismus, um 1937.

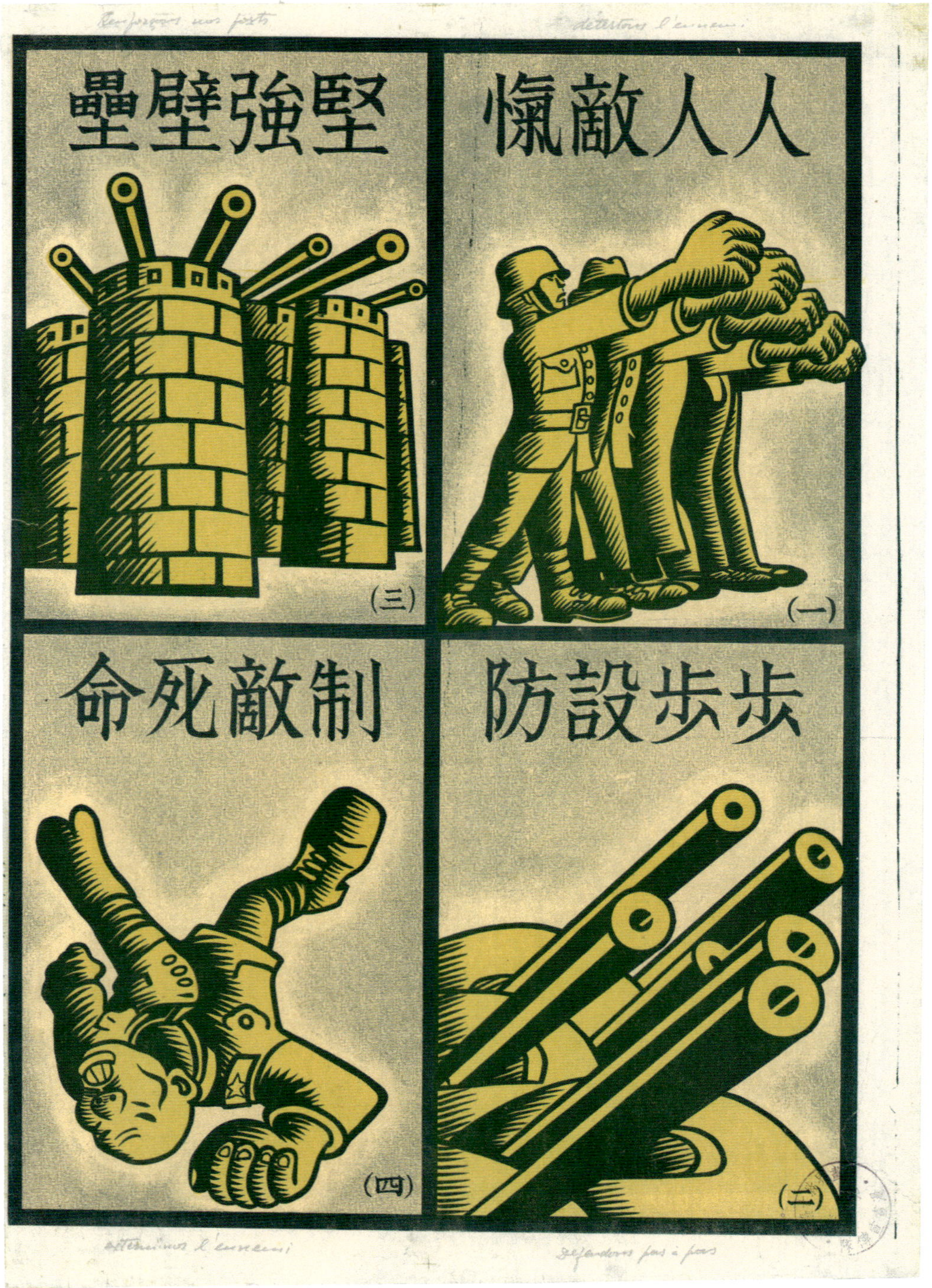

Everybody must hate the enemy, defenses must be constructed step-by-step, fortifications must be strengthened, the enemy must be exterminated, c. 1937.
Der Feind ist zu hassen, die Verteidigung ist Schritt für Schritt aufzubauen, die Befestigungsanlagen sind zu verstärken, der Feind ist zu vernichten, um 1937

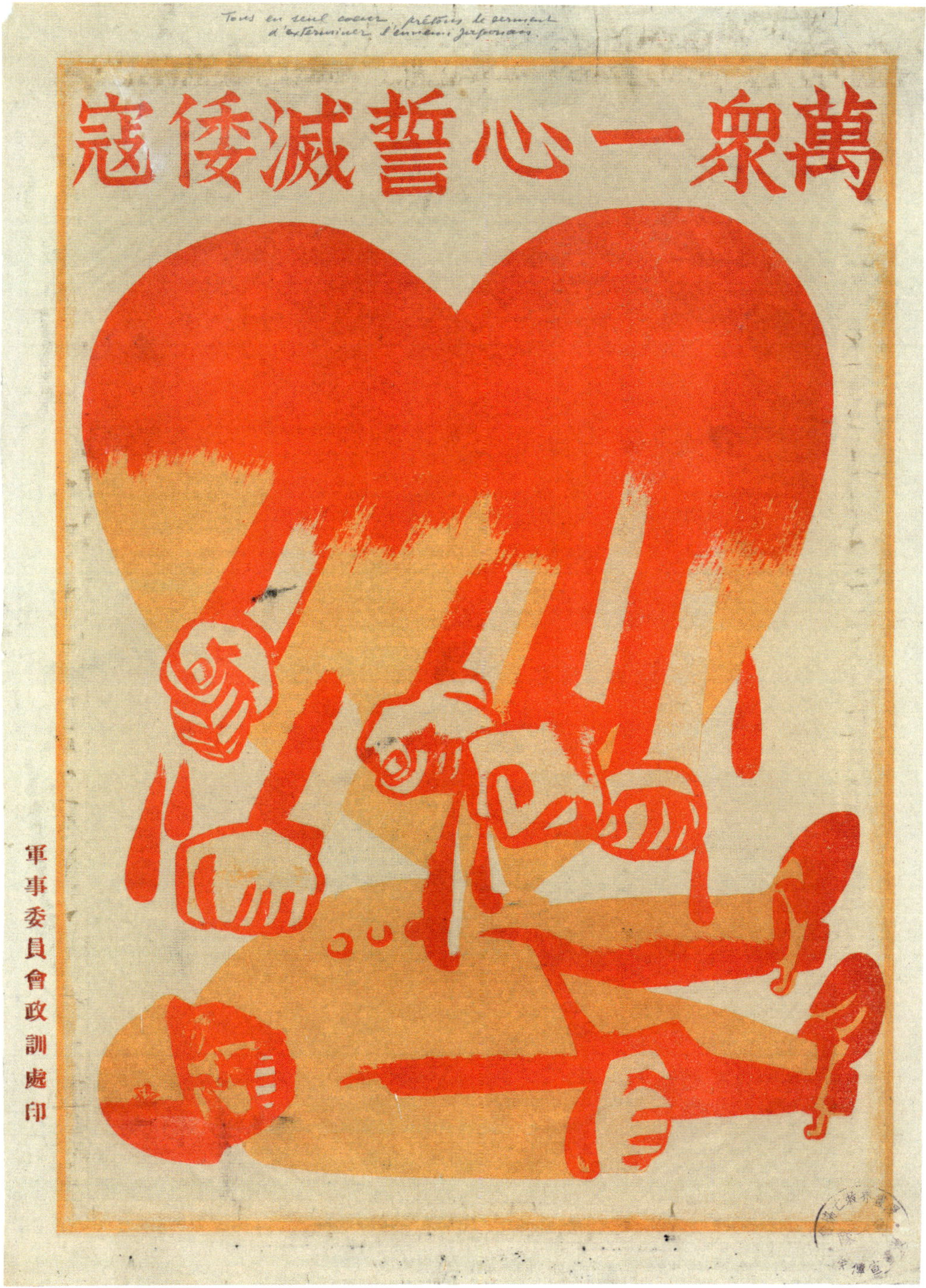

Millions of people all of one mind vow to exterminate the Japanese enemy, c. 1937.
Millionen von Menschen geloben einmütig den japanischen Feind zu vernichten, um 1937.

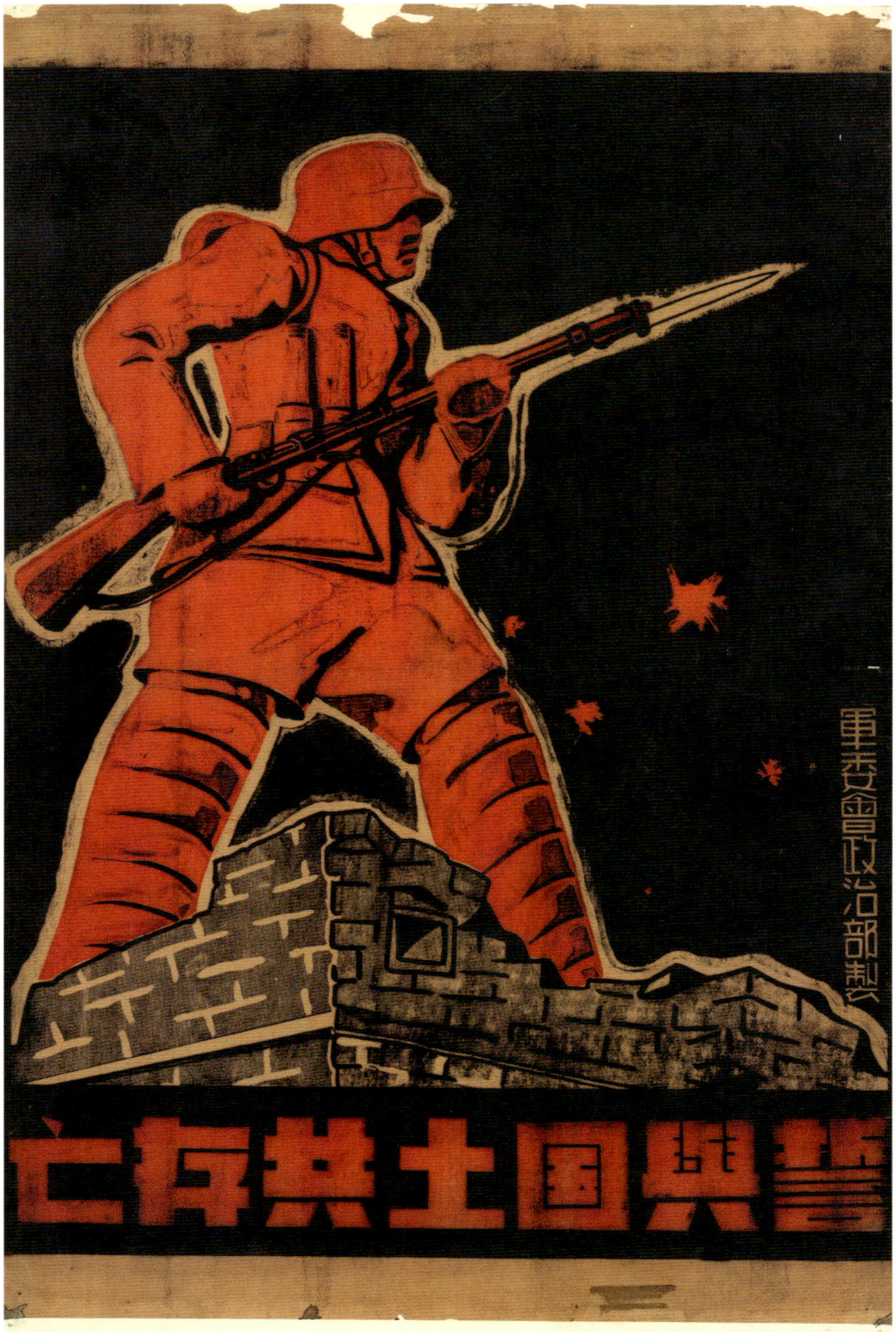

Swear to defend the nation to the death, c. 1937.
Gelobe die Nation bis in den Tod zu verteidigen, um 1937.

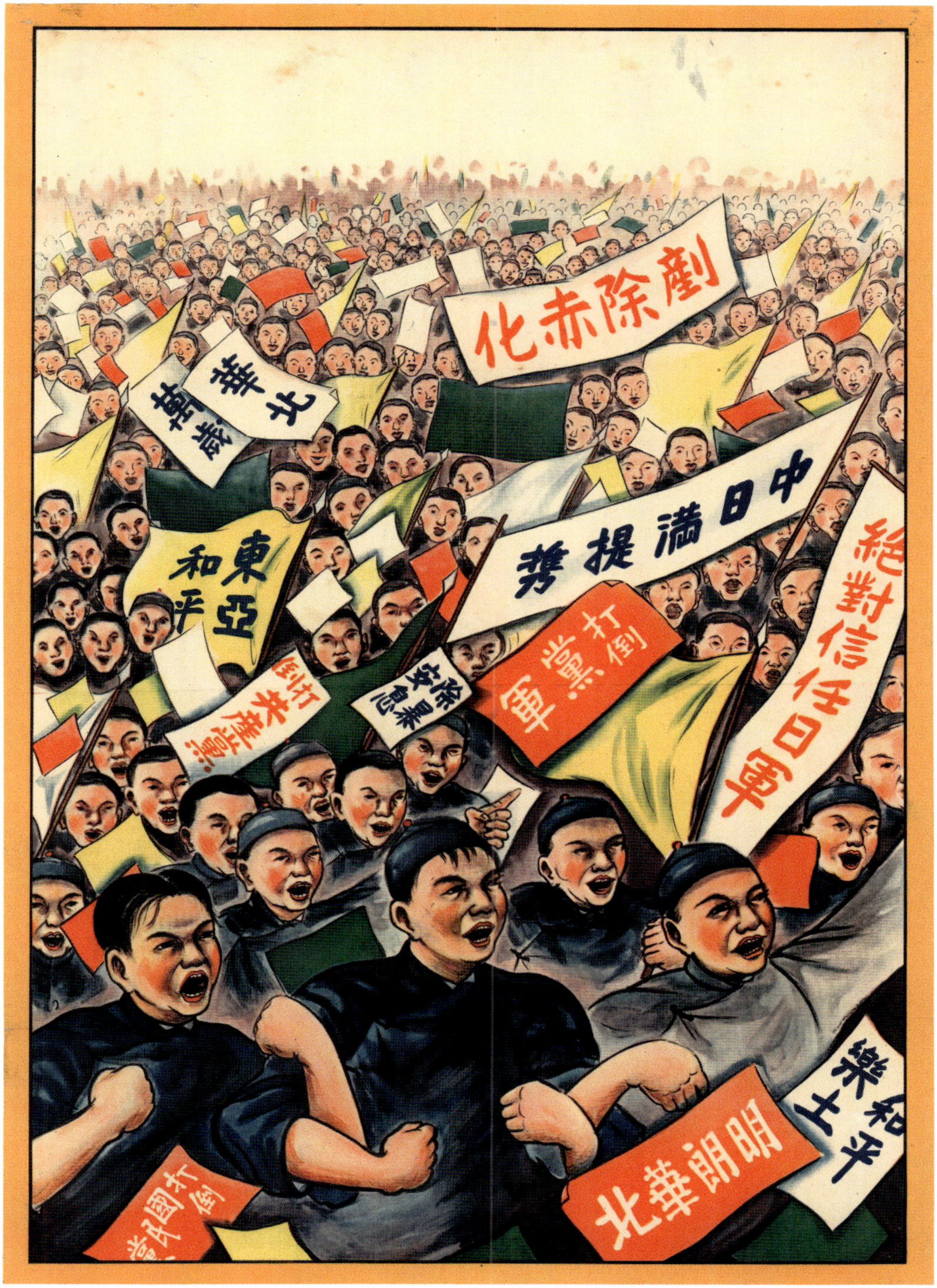

No Title, 1938.
Ohne Titel, 1938.

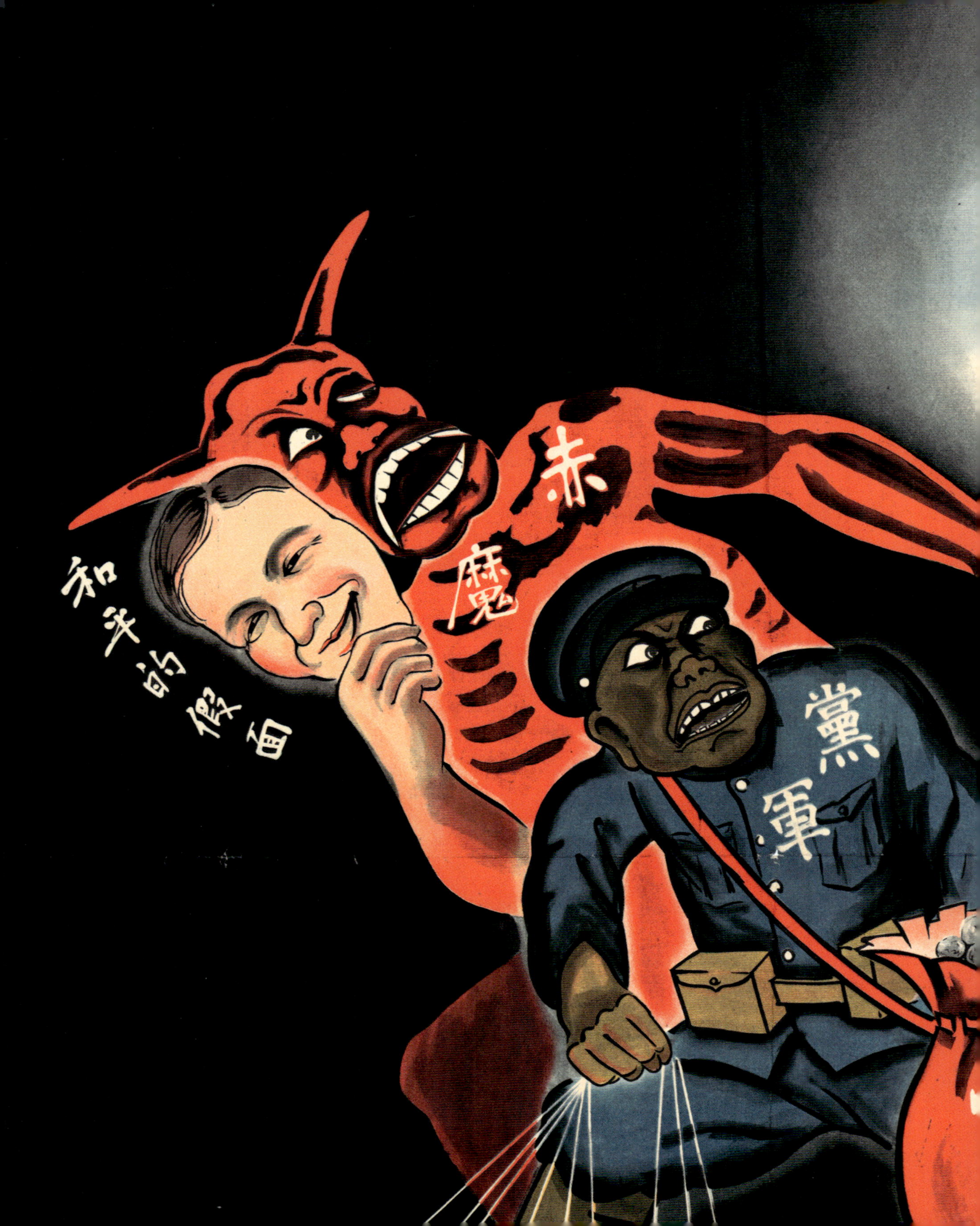

和平的假面
赤魔
黨軍

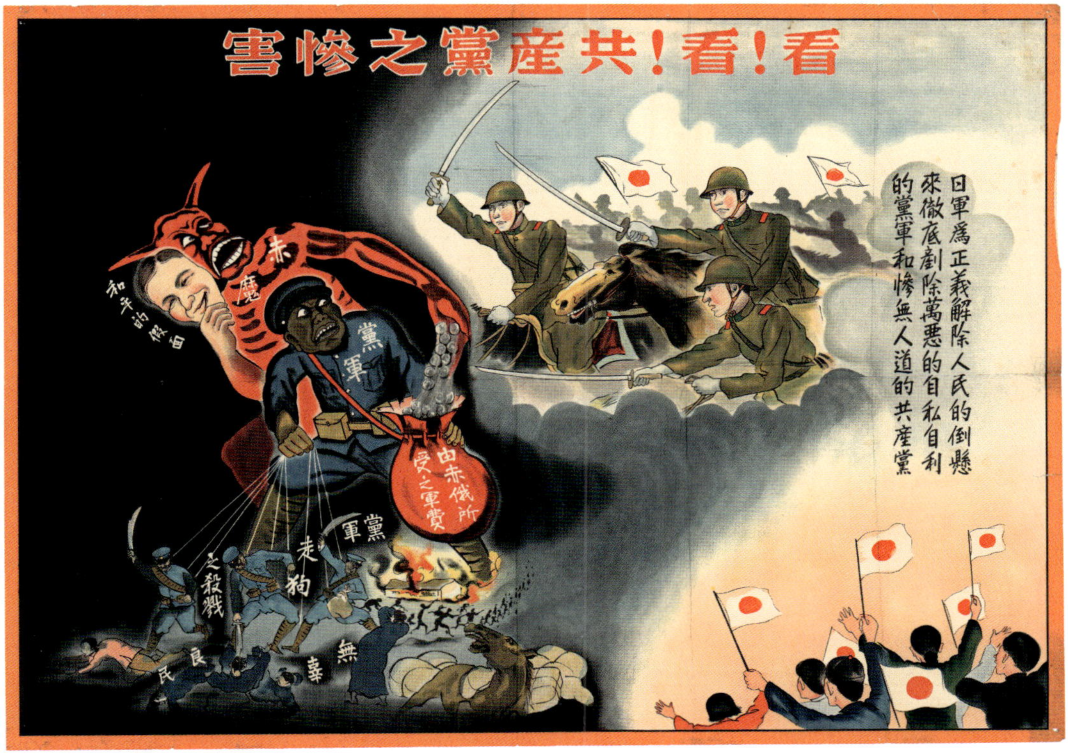

← Japanese propaganda. The Communist Party, in blue uniform, receives money from the red devil hiding behind a friendly Western mask.

Look! Look! The cruel injustice of the Communist Party, 1938.

Sieh hin! Sieh hin! Die grausame Ungerechtigkeit der Kommunistischen Partei, 1938.

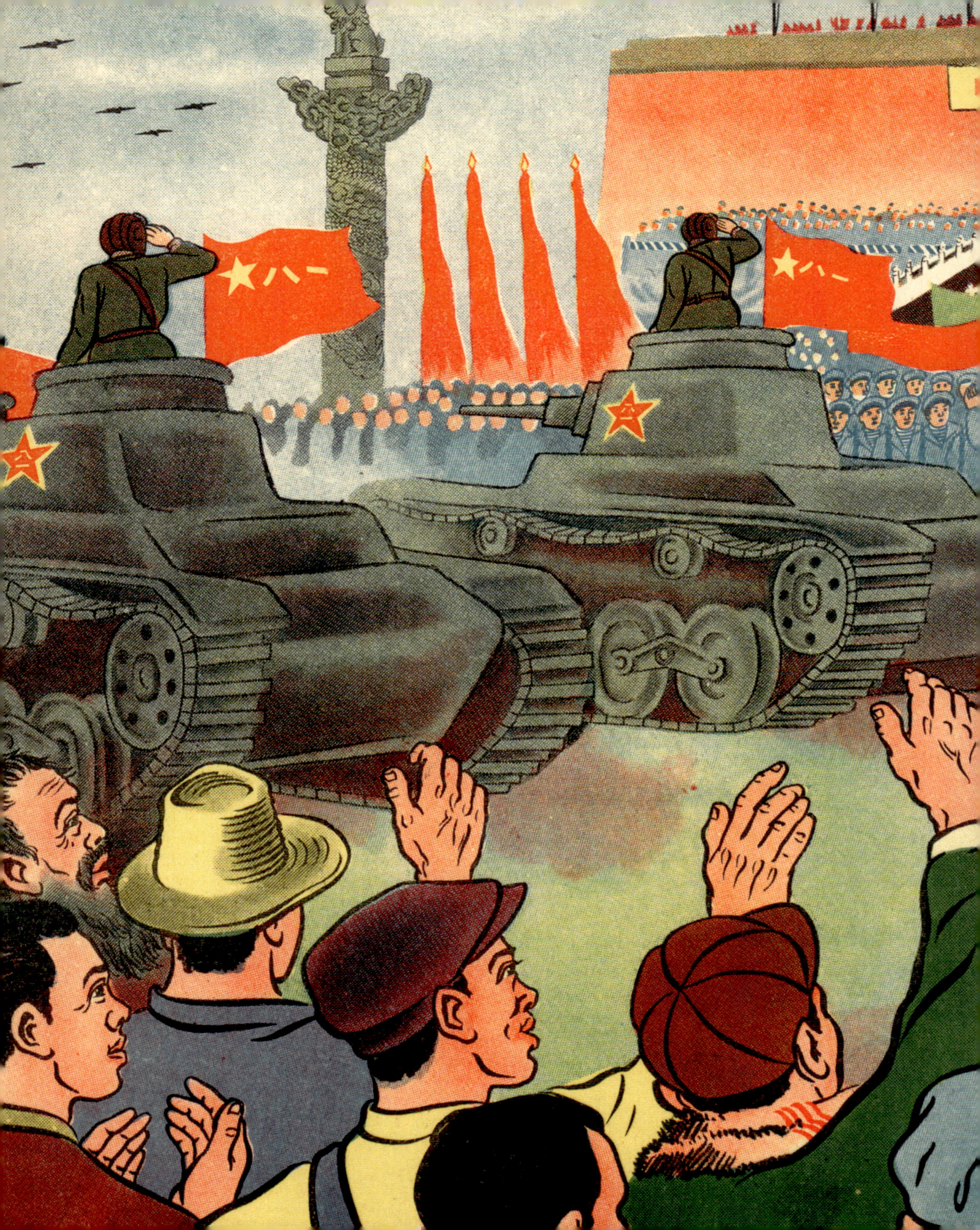
八一
八一

BUILDING THE PEOPLE'S REPUBLIC 1949–56

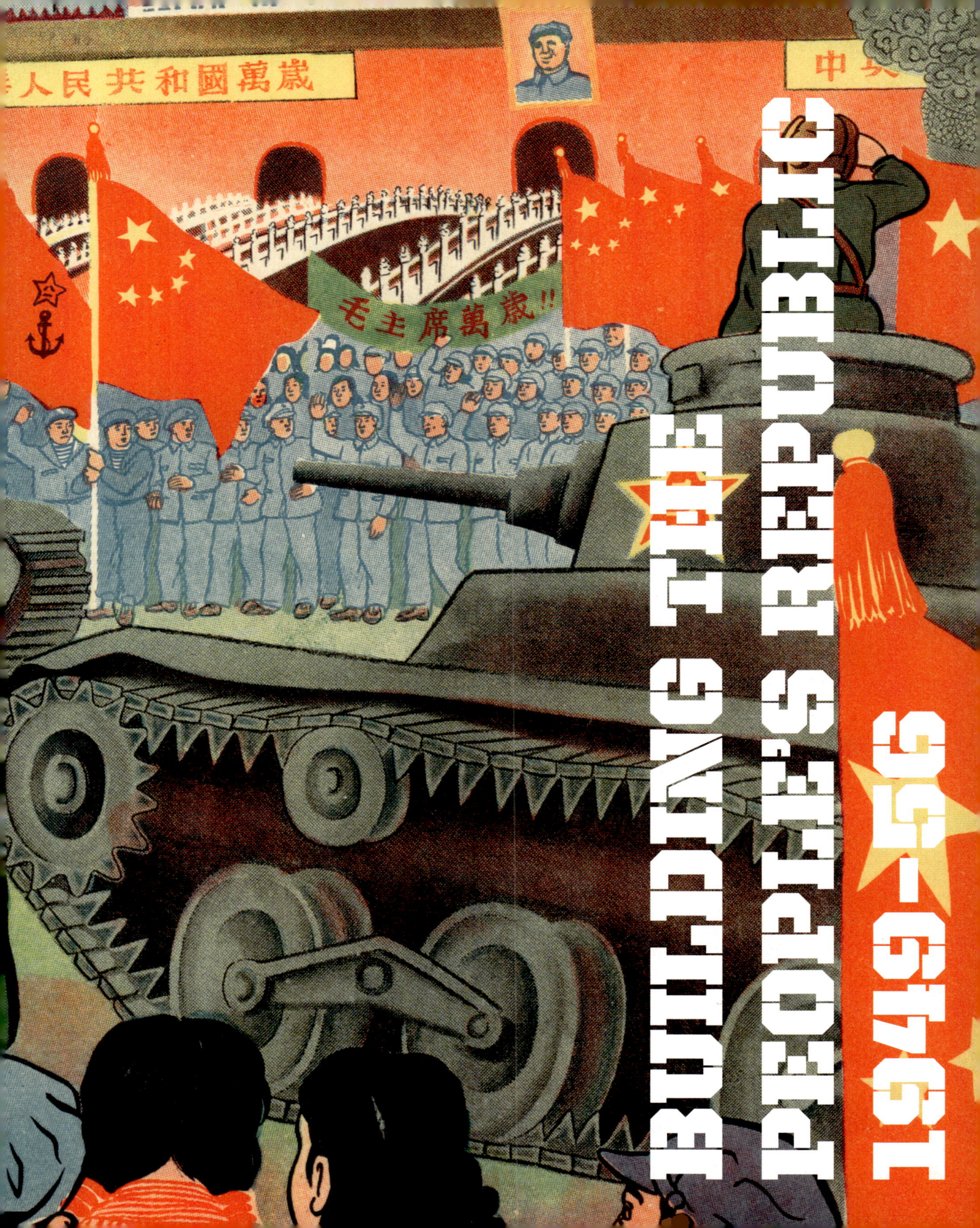

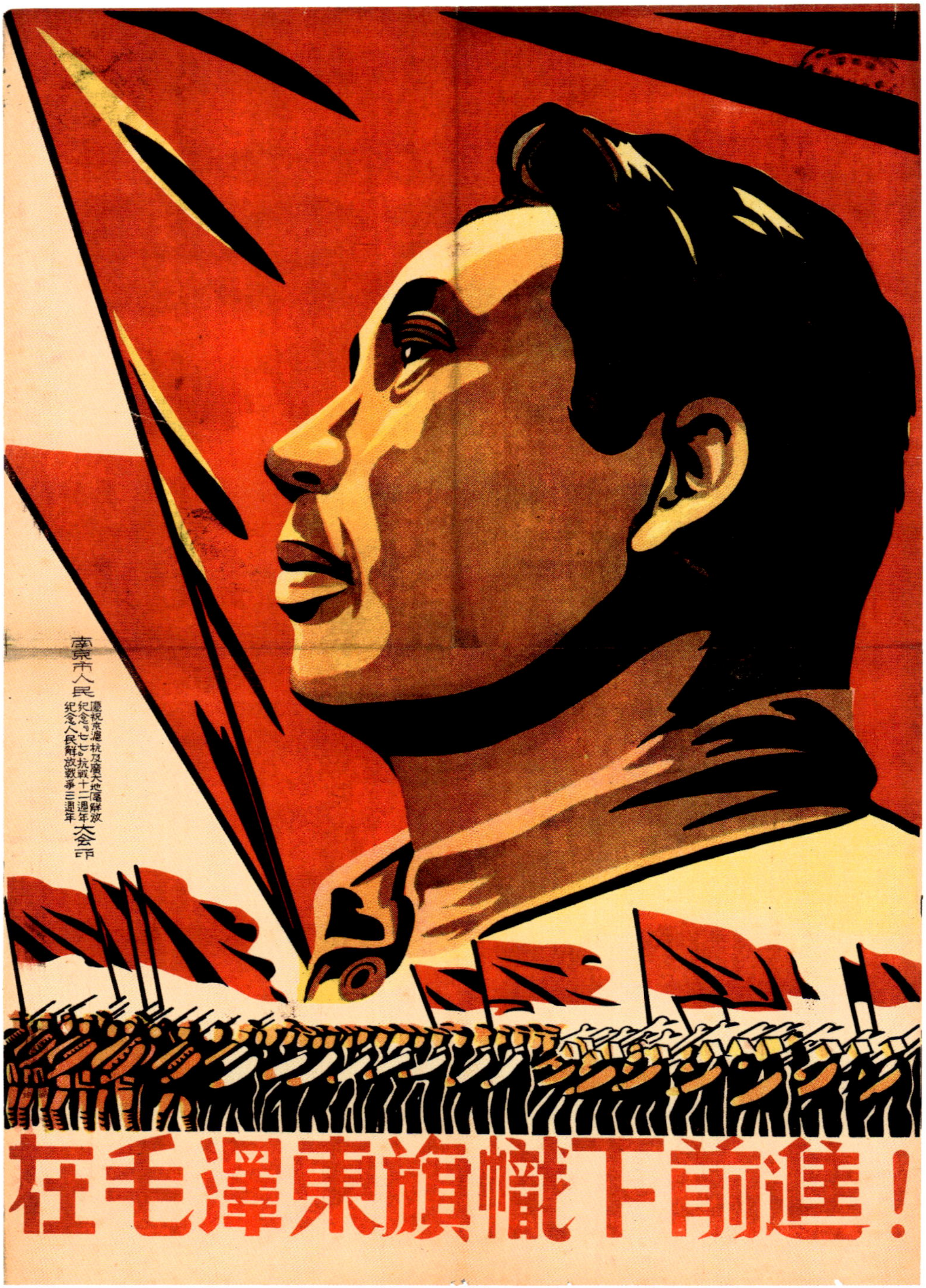

Advance under the banner of Mao Zedong! 1949.
Schreitet voran unter der Fahne Mao Zedongs! 1949.

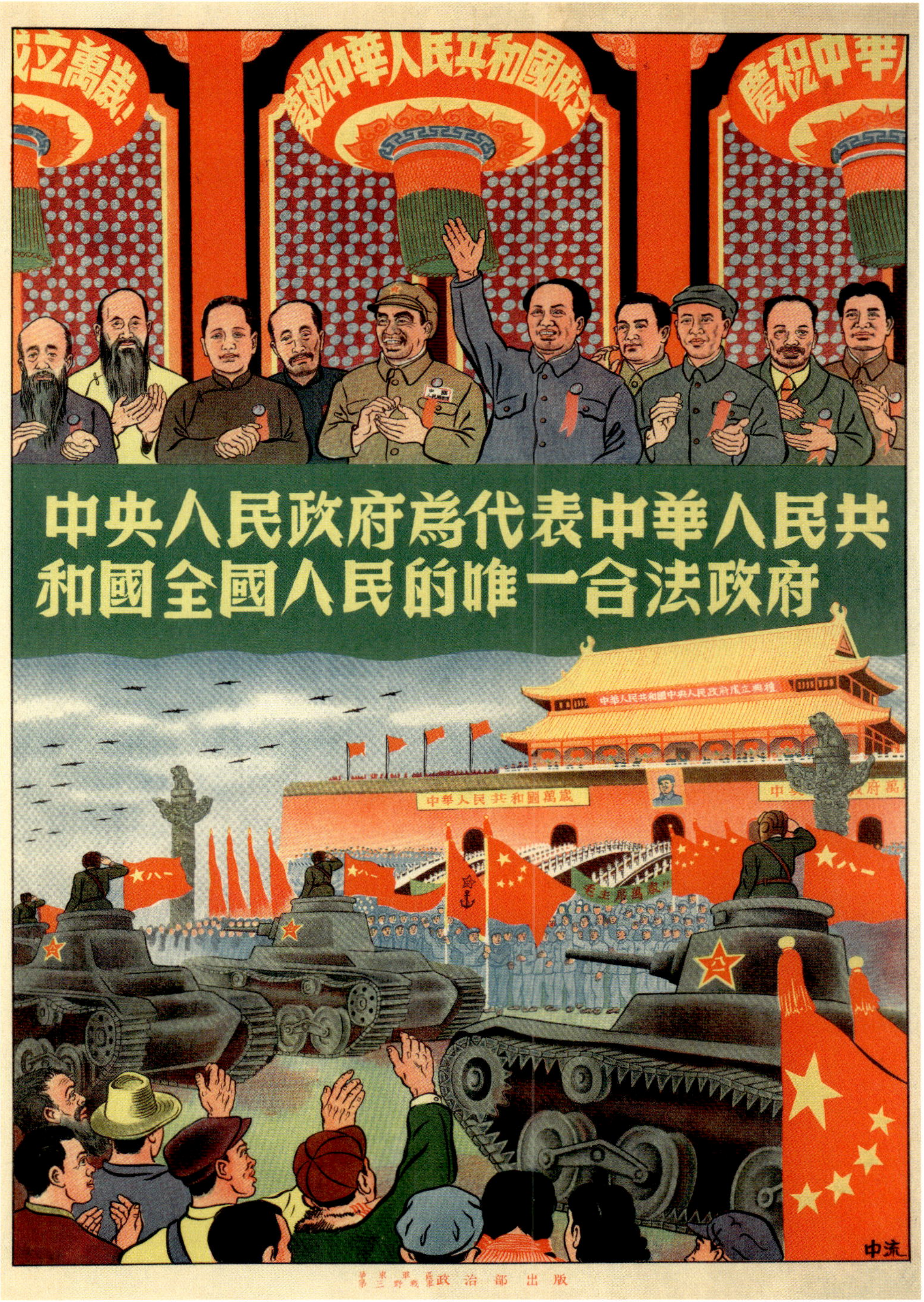

The central people's government constitutes the only legitimate government of all the people of the People's Republic of China, c. 1950.
Die Nationale Volksregierung ist die einzig rechtmäßige Regierung des chinesischen Volkes, um 1950.

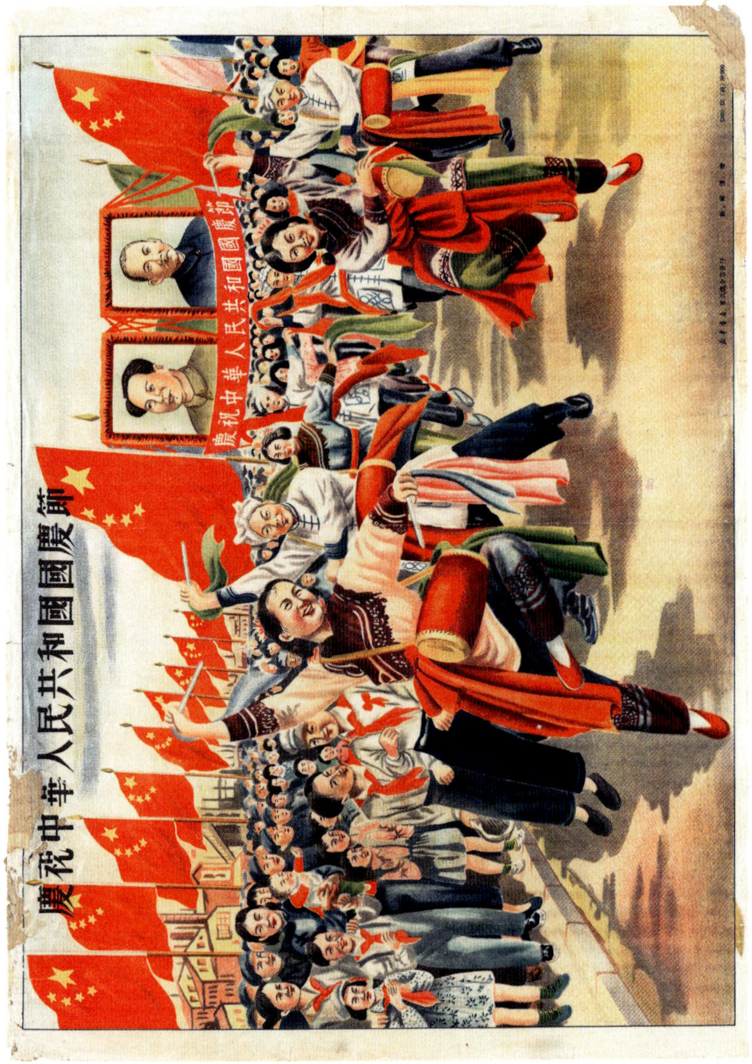

Celebrating the People's Republic of China's National Day, 1950.
Die Volksrepublik China begeht den Nationalfeiertag, 1950.

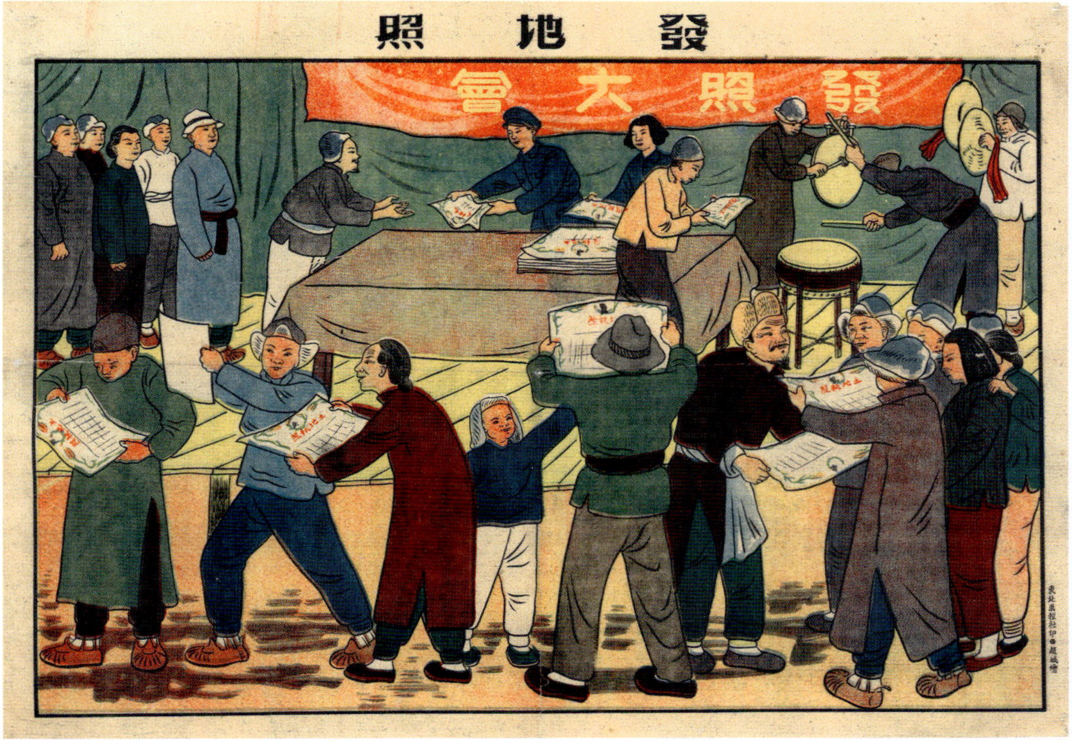

Distributing land, c. 1948.
Verteilung von Land, um 1948.

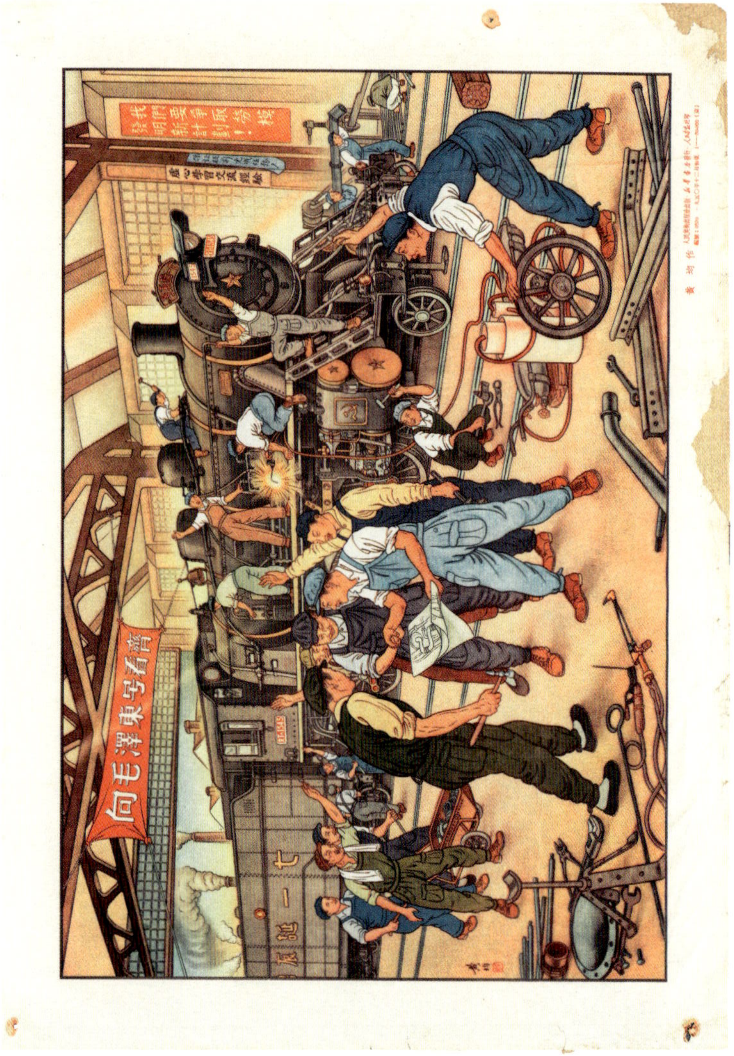

Emulate the Patriotic production campaign, 1950.
Eifert der patriotischen Produktionskampagne nach, 1950.

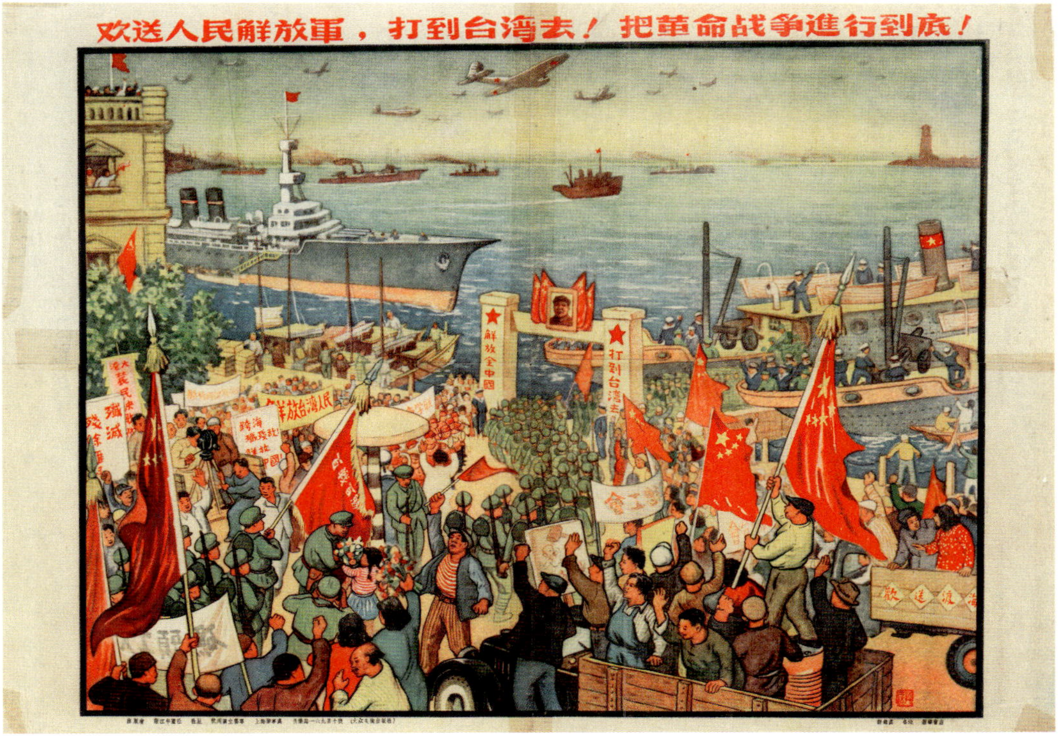

Sending off the People's Liberation Army to overthrow Taiwan! Carry out the revolutionary war to the end! c. 1950.

Entsendung der Volksbefreiungsarmee zum Sturz Taiwans! Führt den revolutionären Krieg zu Ende! um 1950.

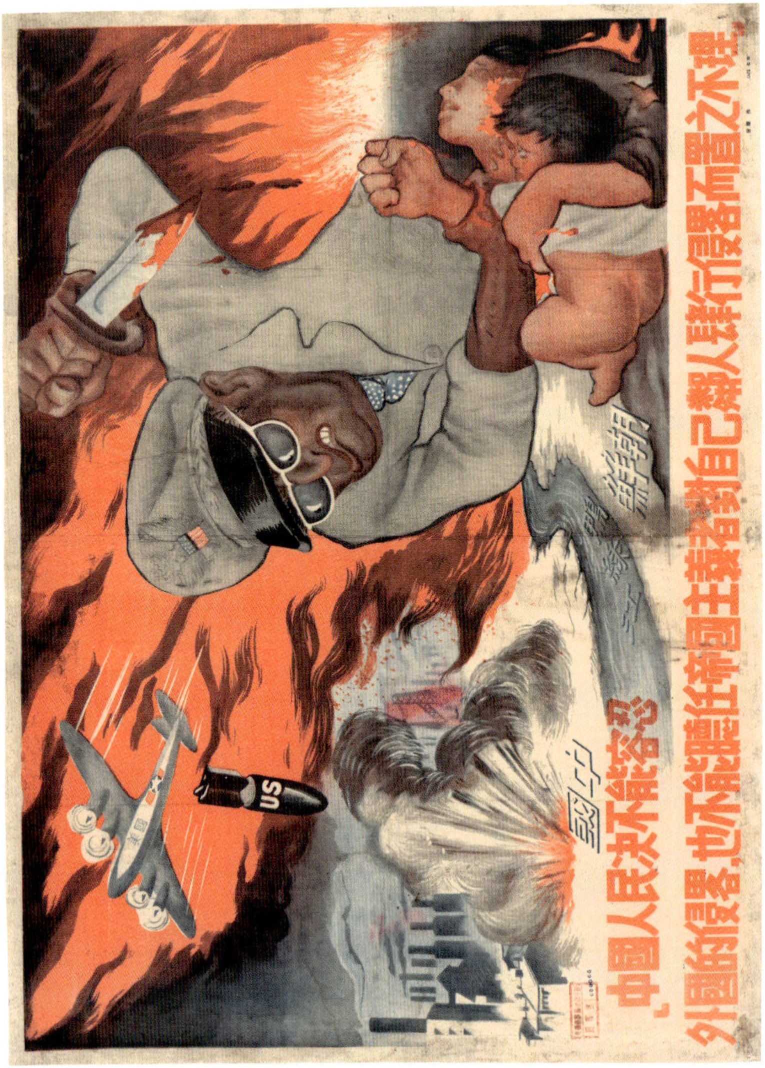

The Chinese people absolutely cannot condone the encroachment of other countries, and cannot listen to any imperialist who thinks that it can wantonly encroach on its own neighbors without action, c. 1950.
Das chinesische Volk kann Übergriffe auf andere Länder unter keinen Umständen dulden, und es hört nicht auf die Imperialisten, die denken sie könnten willkürlich auf ihre Nachbarn übergreifen... um 1950.

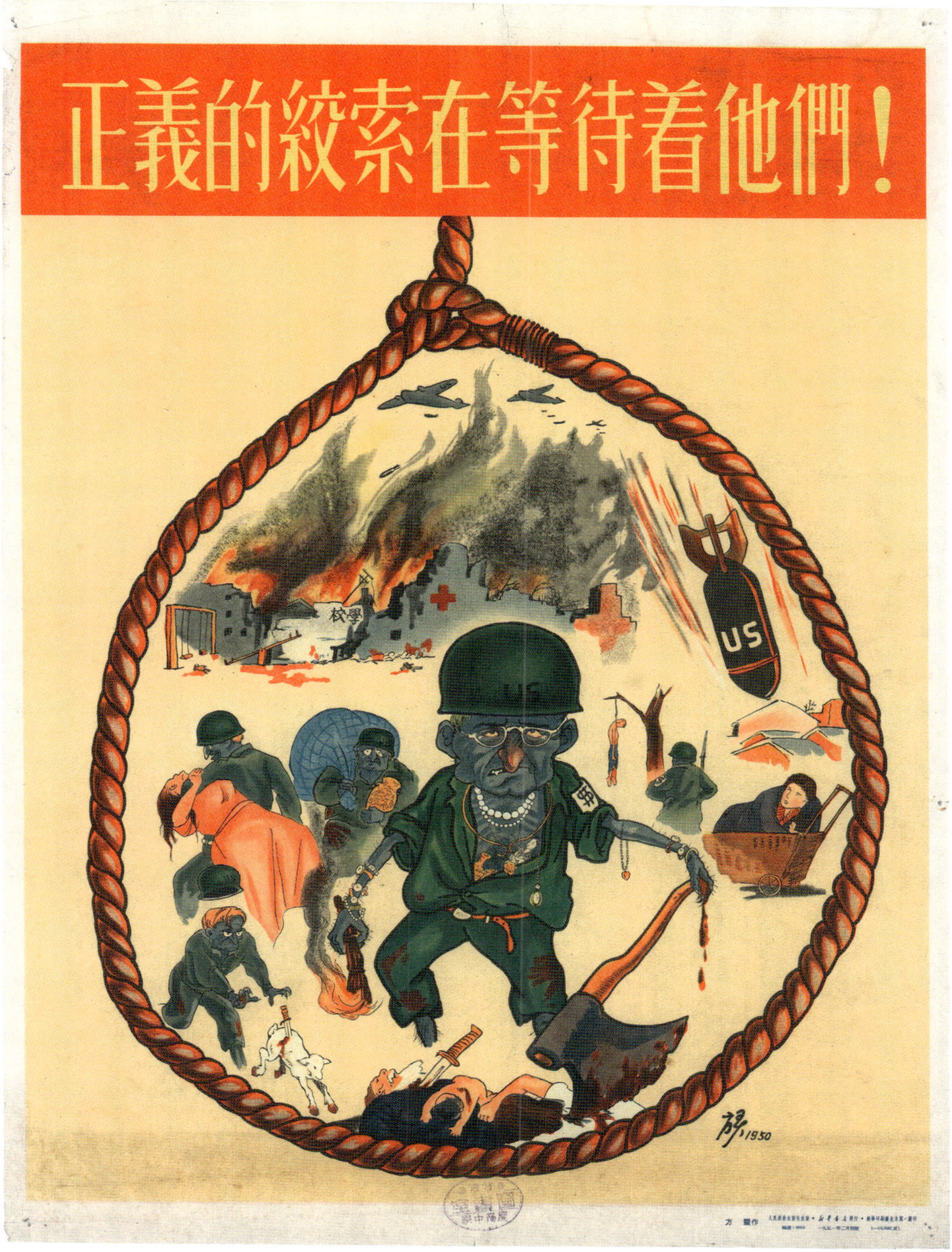

The justified noose awaits them! 1951.
Die gerechte Schlinge erwartet sie! 1951.

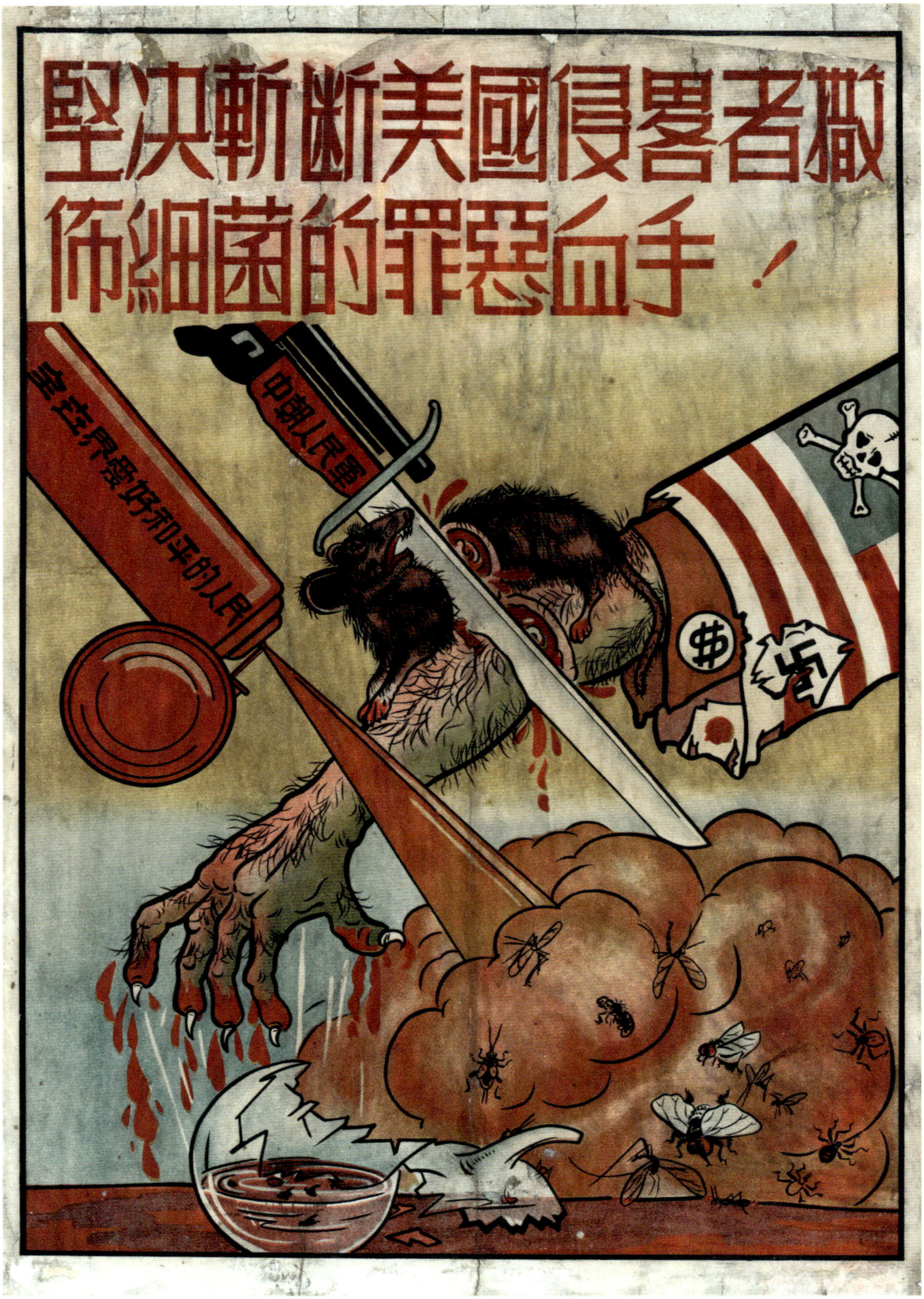

Resolutely cut off the bloody and criminal hand of the American aggressor that spreads germs! c. 1951.
Hackt entschlossen die blutige und verbrecherische Hand des amerikanischen Aggressors ab, die Krankheitserreger sät! um 1951.

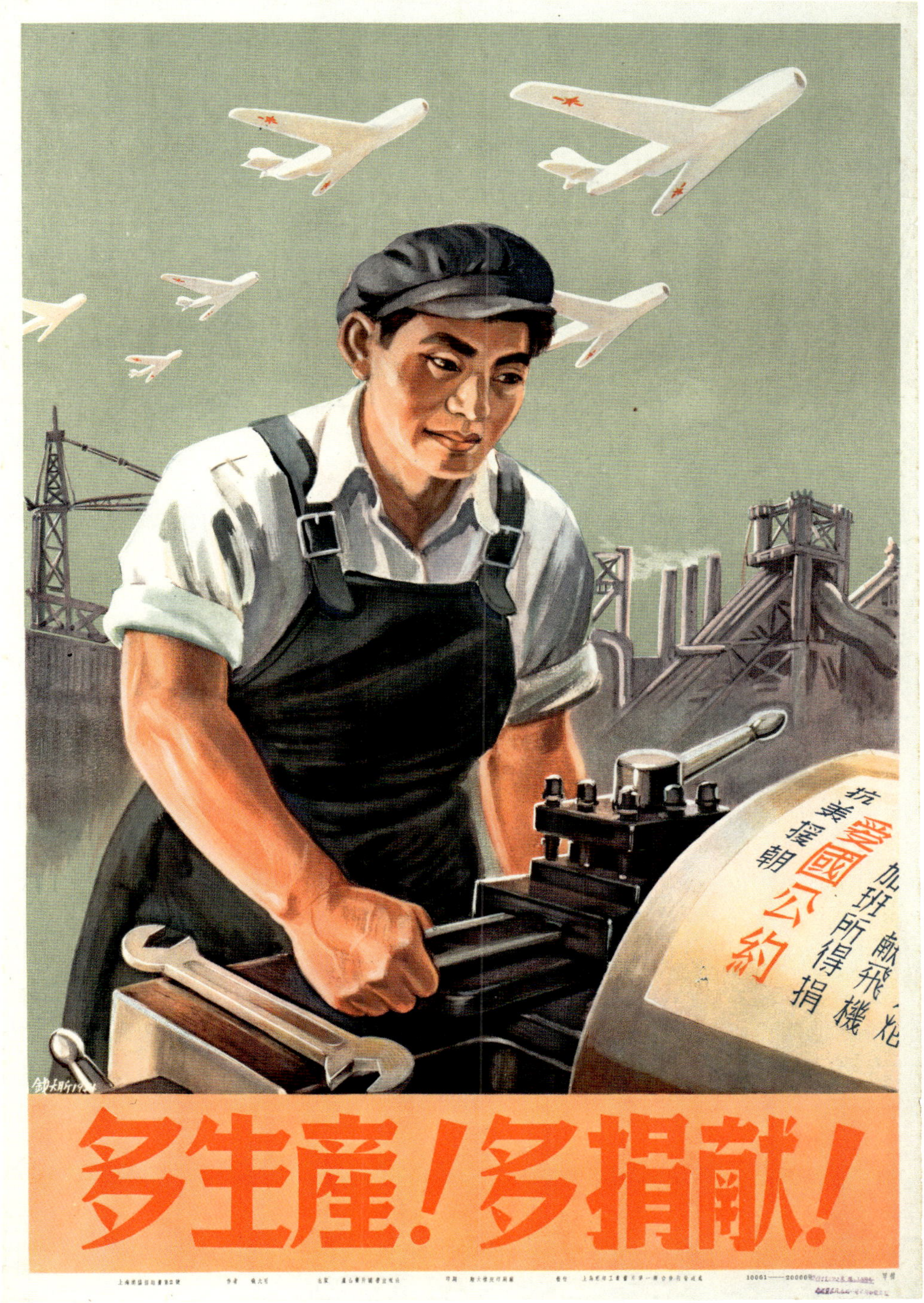

Produce more! Contribute more! c. 1951.
Produziert mehr! Tragt mehr bei! um 1951.

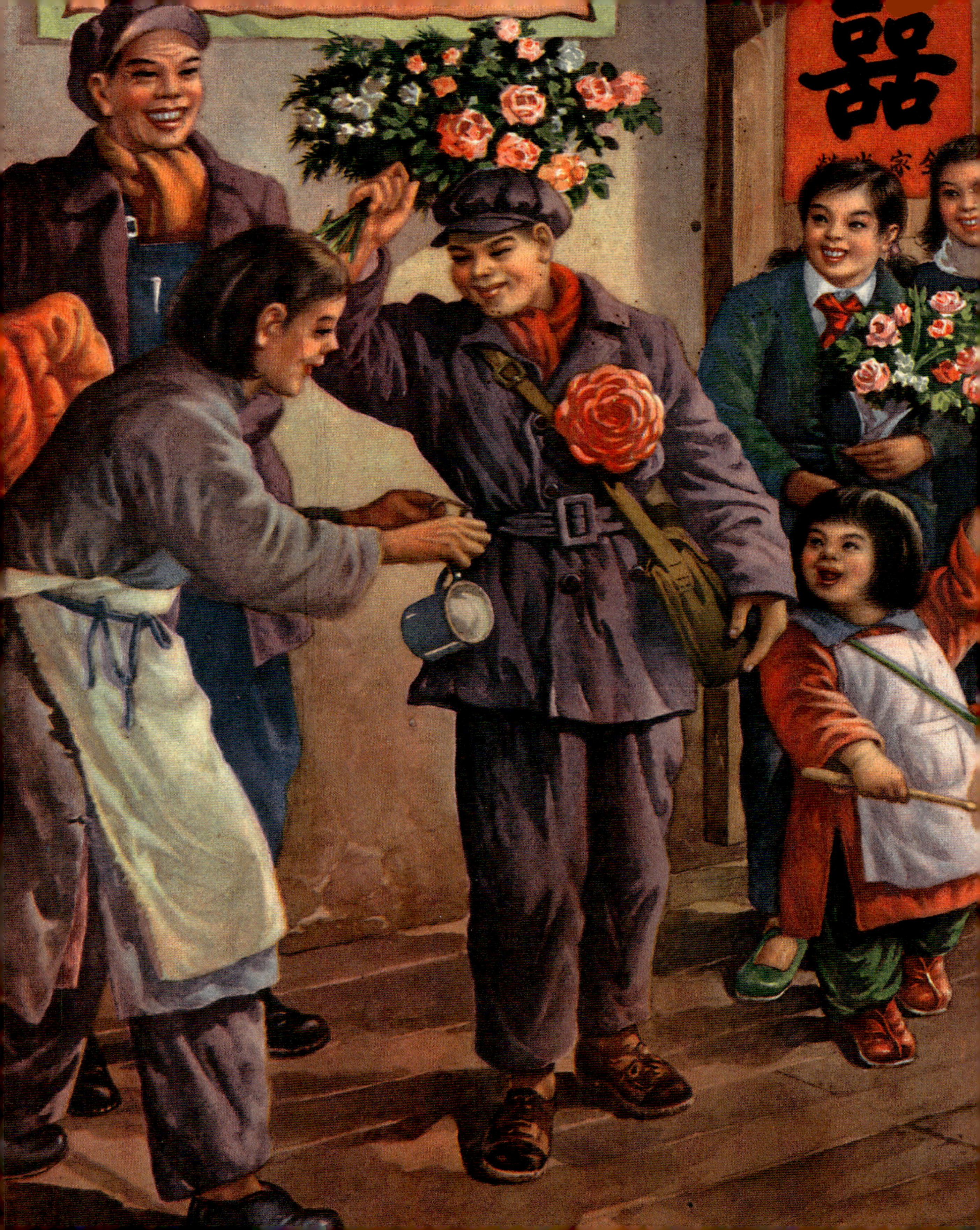
囍

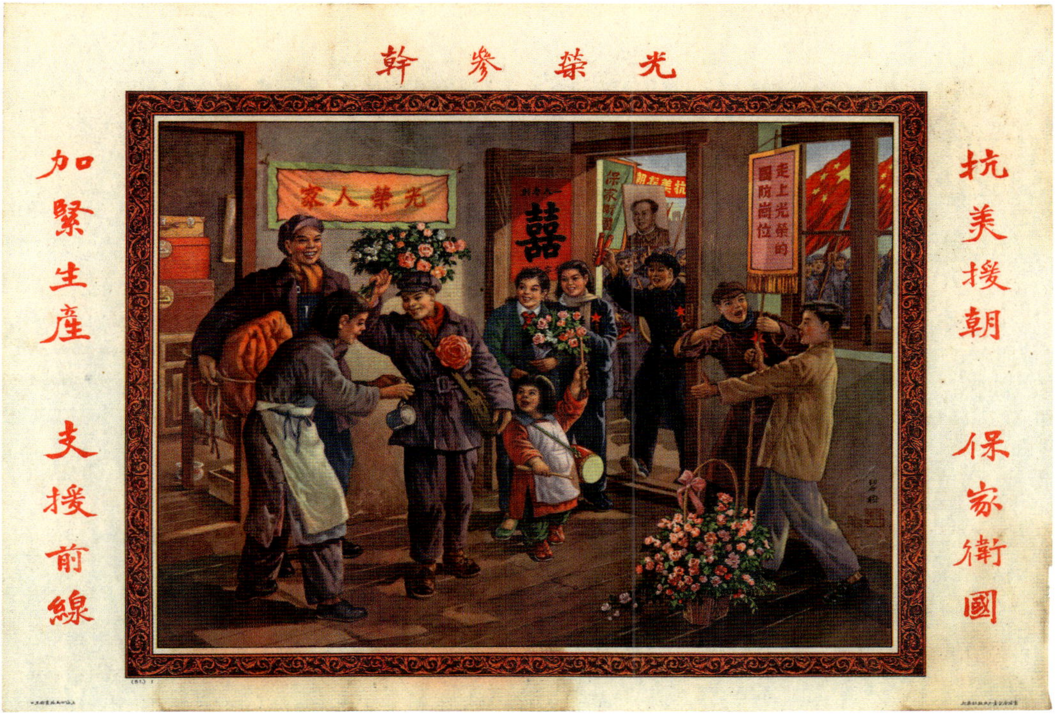

← Family and neighbors bidding farewell to a volunteer leaving for the Korean front. In the Korean War, the Chinese support the North, the USA the South. An estimated one million Chinese die in battle.

It's glorious to participate, to oppose America, to support Korea, and to protect the home and the nation, 1951.
Es ist ruhmvoll mitzuwirken, Amerika entgegenzutreten, Korea zu unterstützen, und Heimat und Nation zu beschützen, 1951.

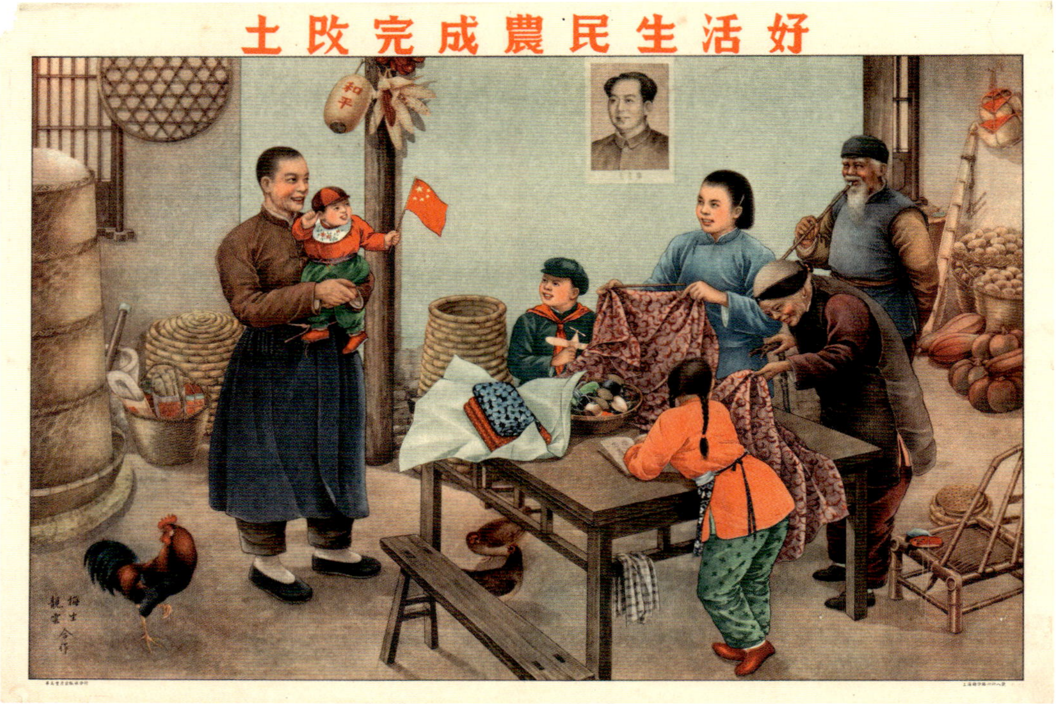

The life of peasants is good after the Land Reform, c. 1951.
Nach der Bodenreform ist das Leben der Bauern gut, um 1951.

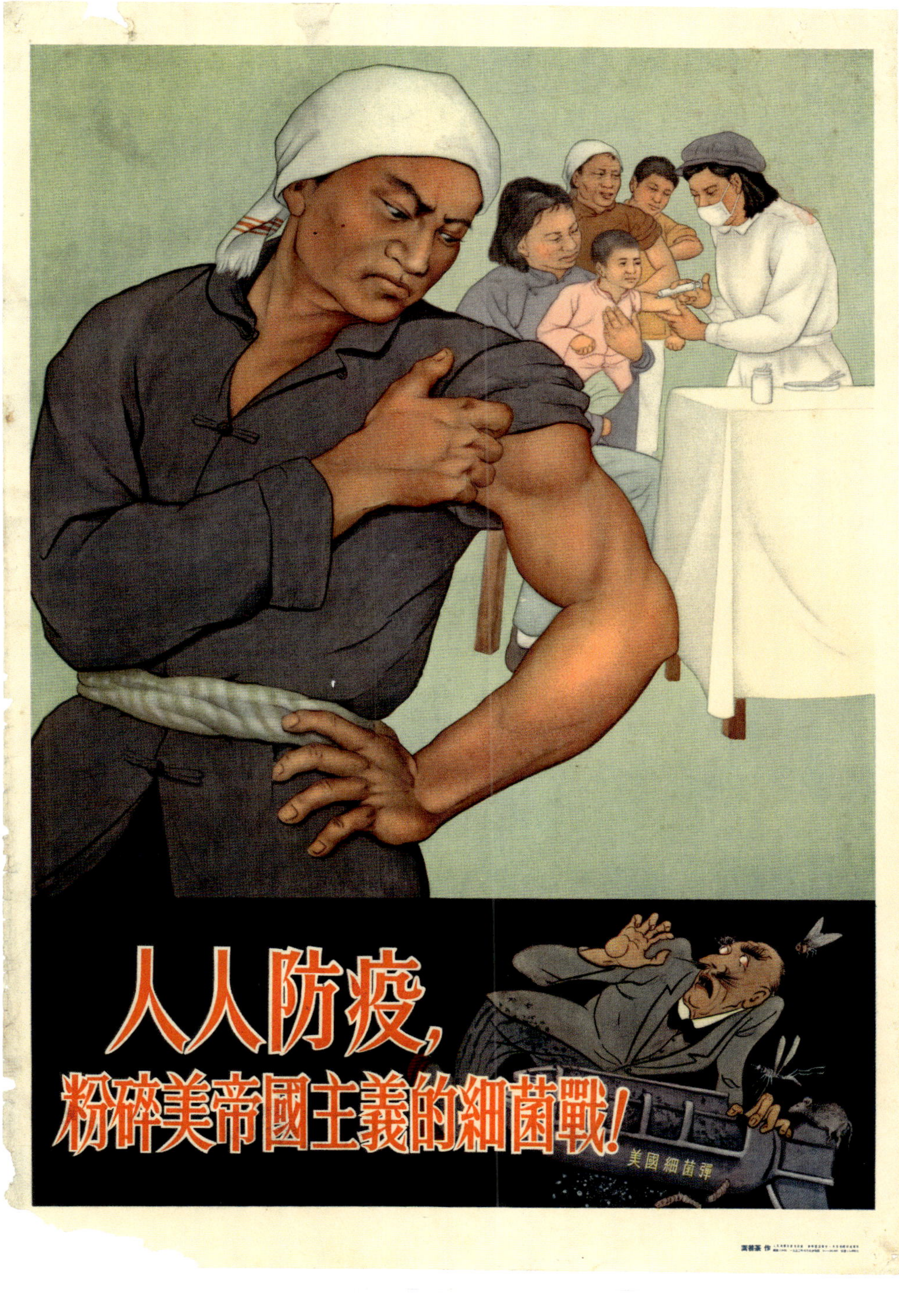

Everybody must take precautions against epidemics to smash the germ warfare of American imperialism! 1952.

Jeder muss Vorsichtsmaßnahmen gegen Seuchen ergreifen, um die biologische Kriegsführung des amerikanischen Imperialismus zu vereiteln! 1952.

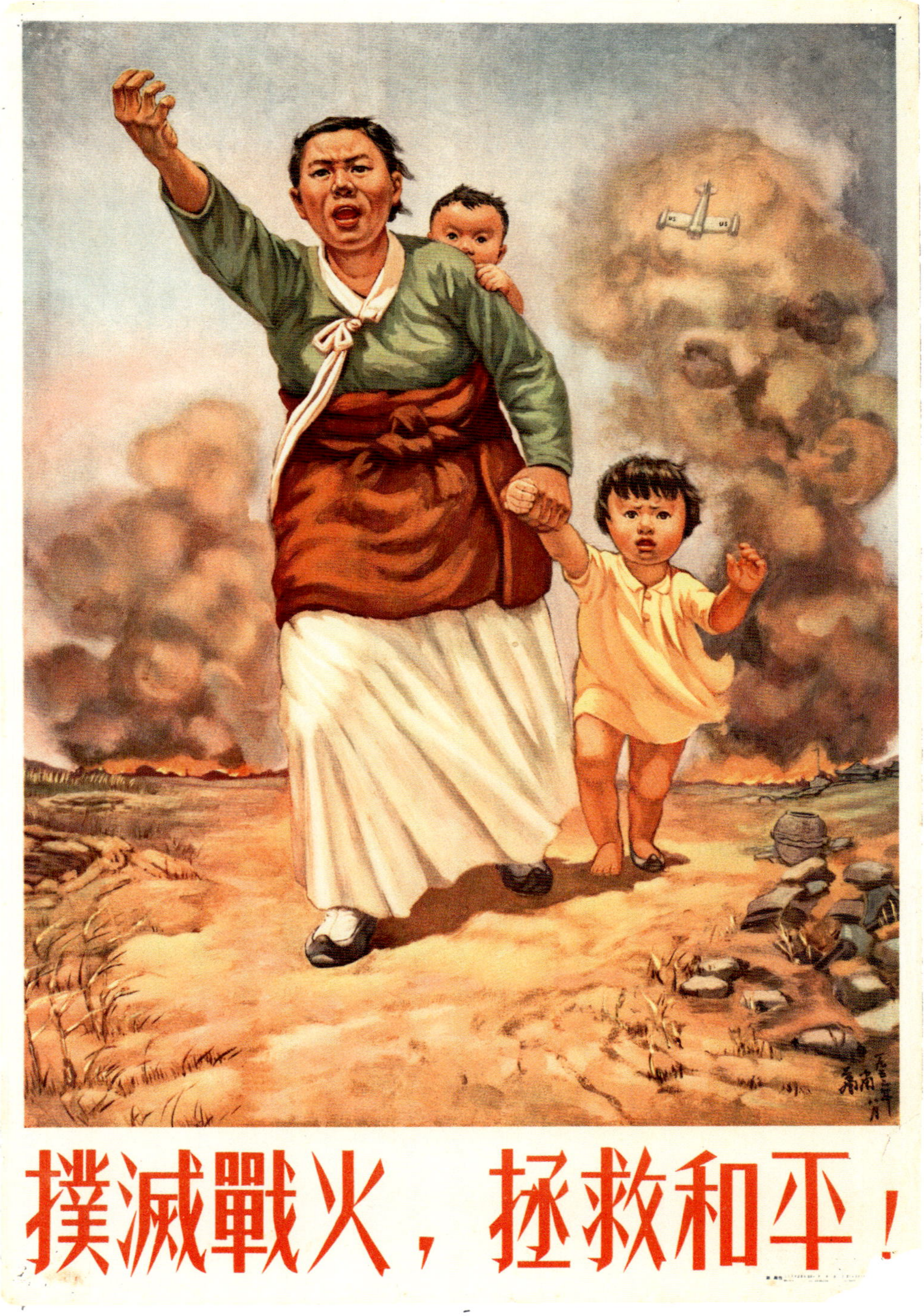

Stamp out the flames of war, save the peace! 1952.
Tretet die Flammen des Krieges aus, rettet den Frieden! 1952.

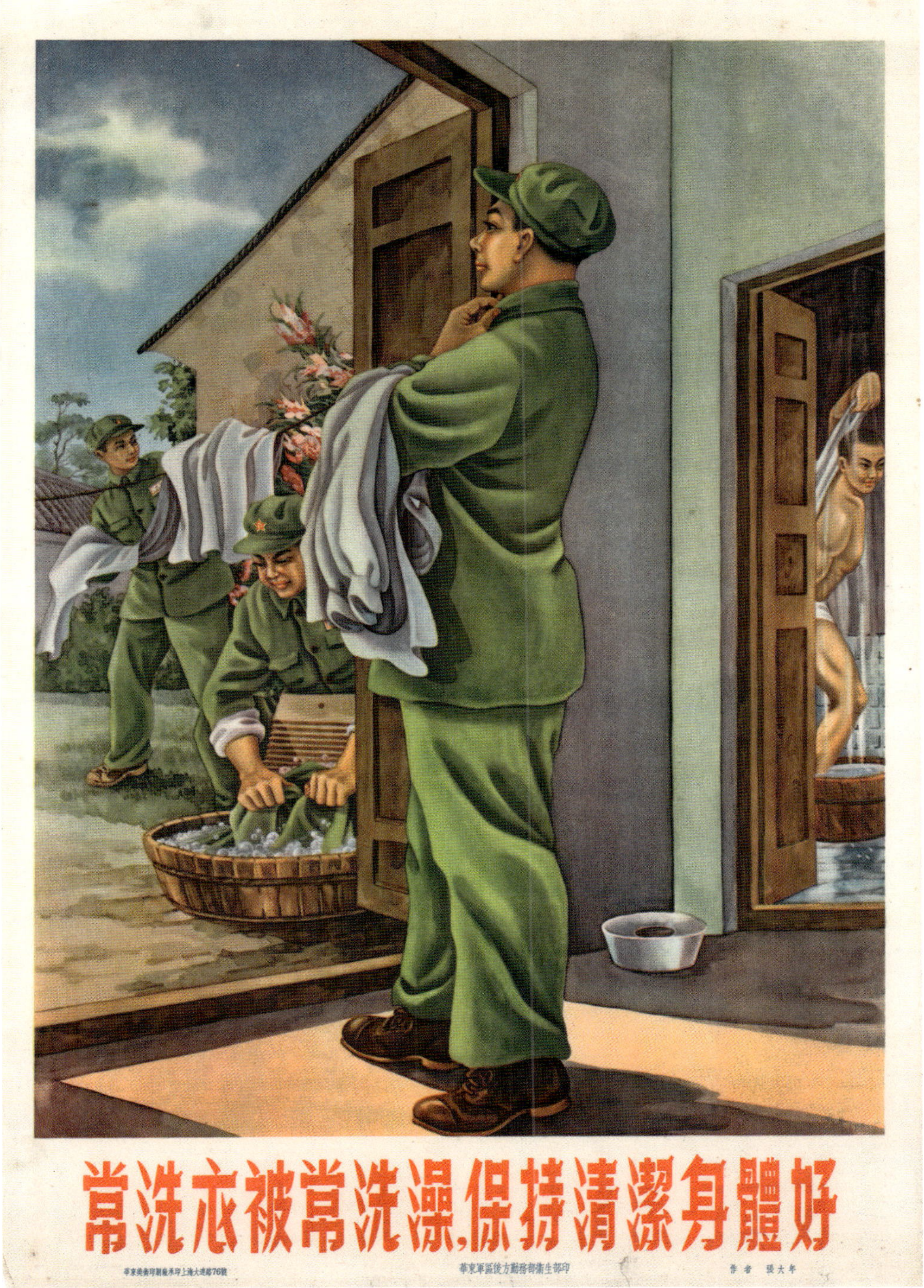

Regularly wash clothes and bedding, bathe often, and maintain cleanliness for good health, c. 1952.

Wasche regelmäßig Kleider und Bettwäsche, bade häufig, und erhalte die Reinlichkeit für eine gute Gesundheit, um 1952.

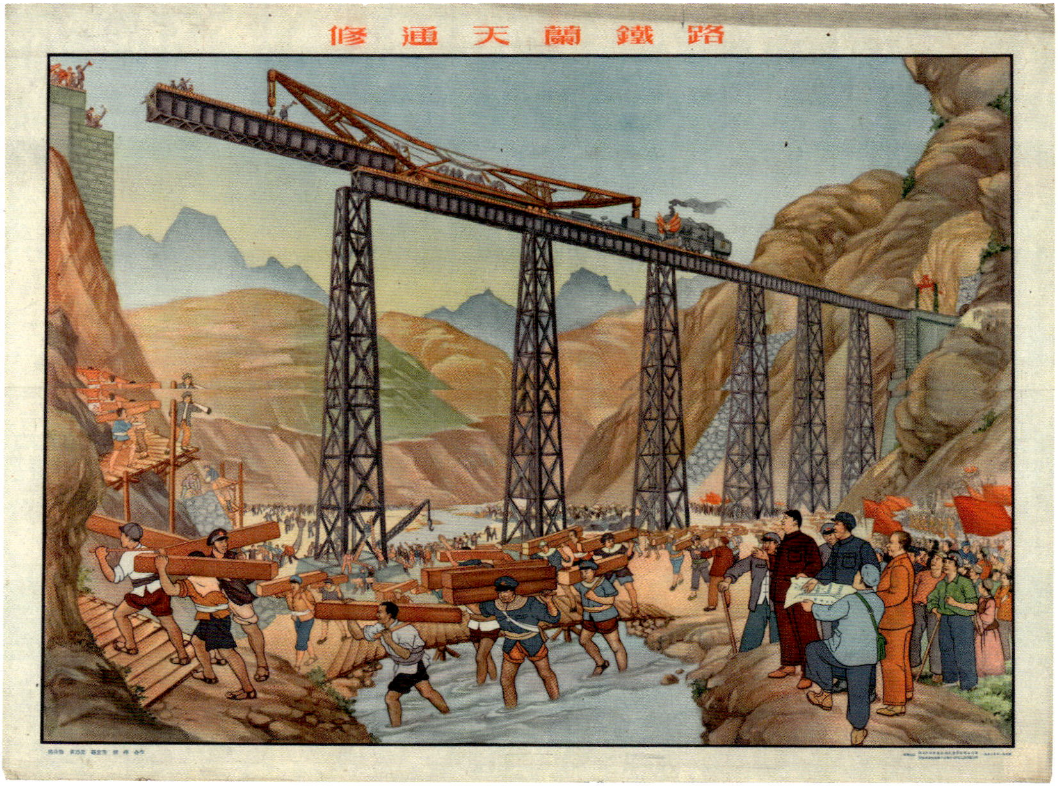

Building the Tianlan railway, 1952.
Beim Bau der Tianlan Eisenbahnstrecke, 1952.

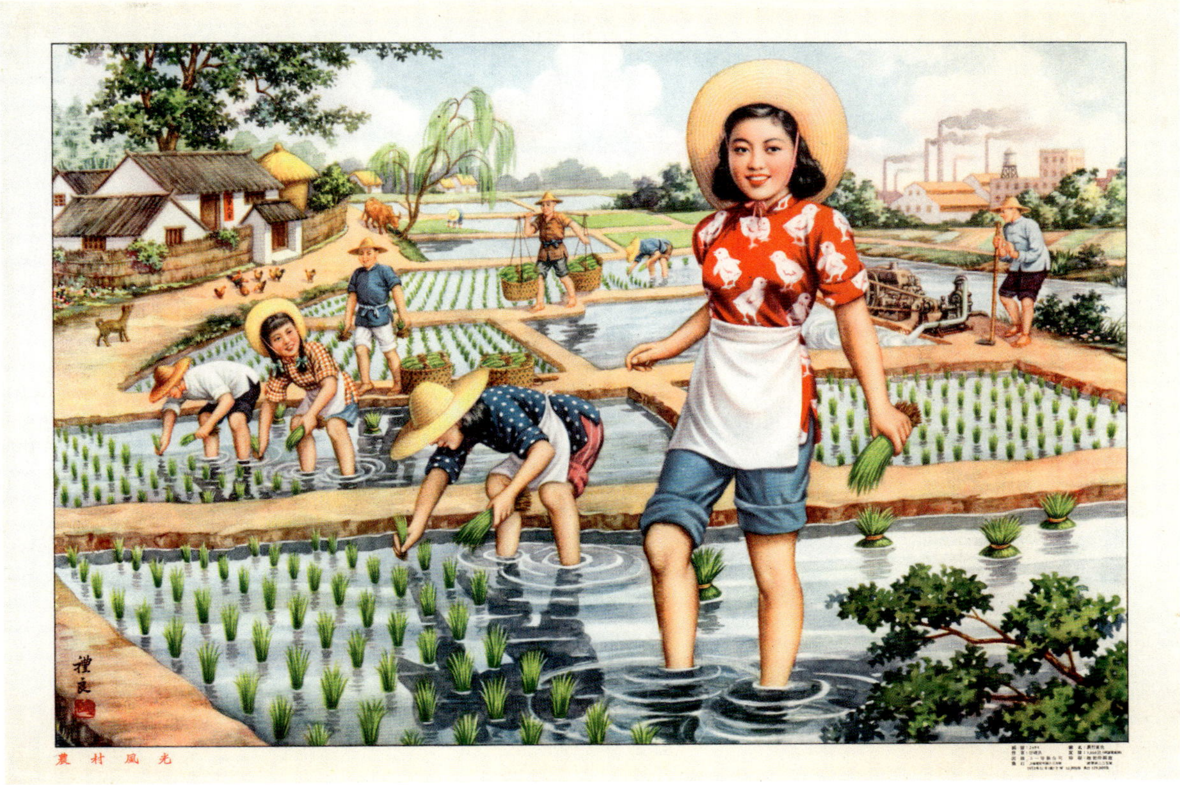

A new view of the rural village, 1953.
Ein neuer Anblick des bäuerlichen Dorfes, 1953.

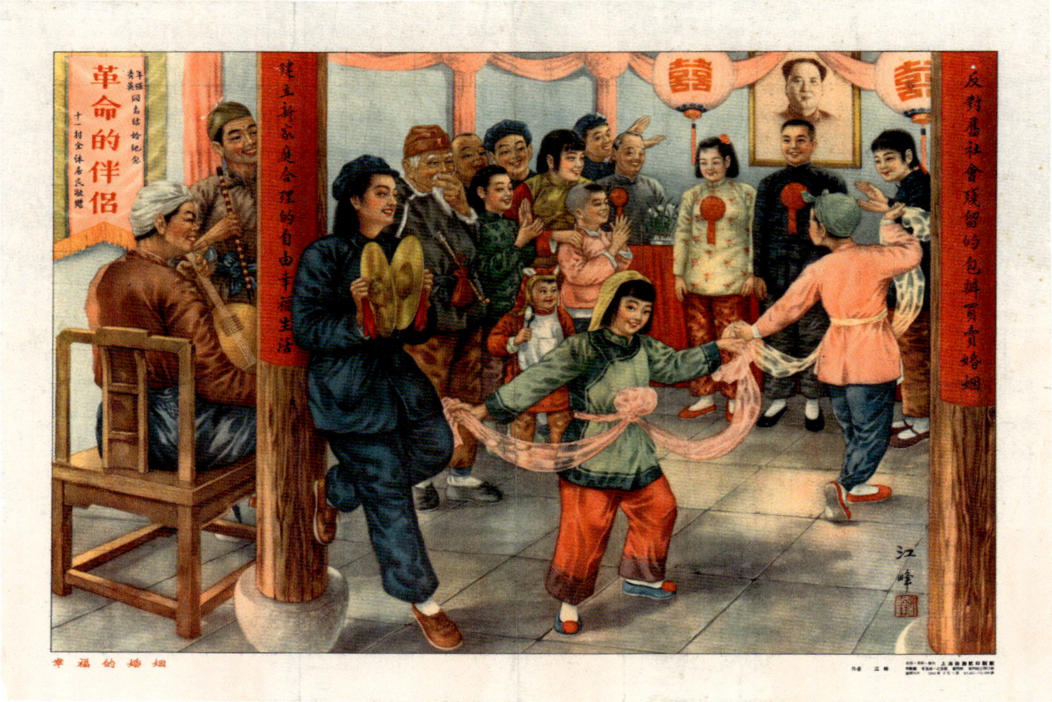

A happy marriage, 1953.
Eine glückliche Ehe, 1953.

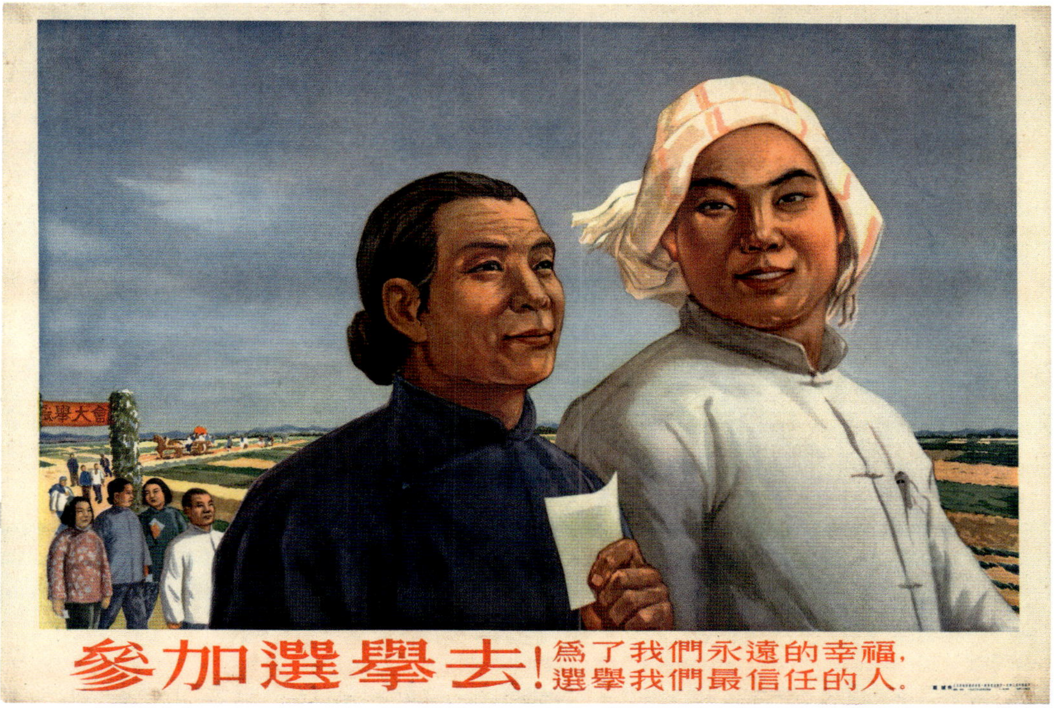

Go participate in the elections! 1953.
Nehmt an den Wahlen teil! 1953.

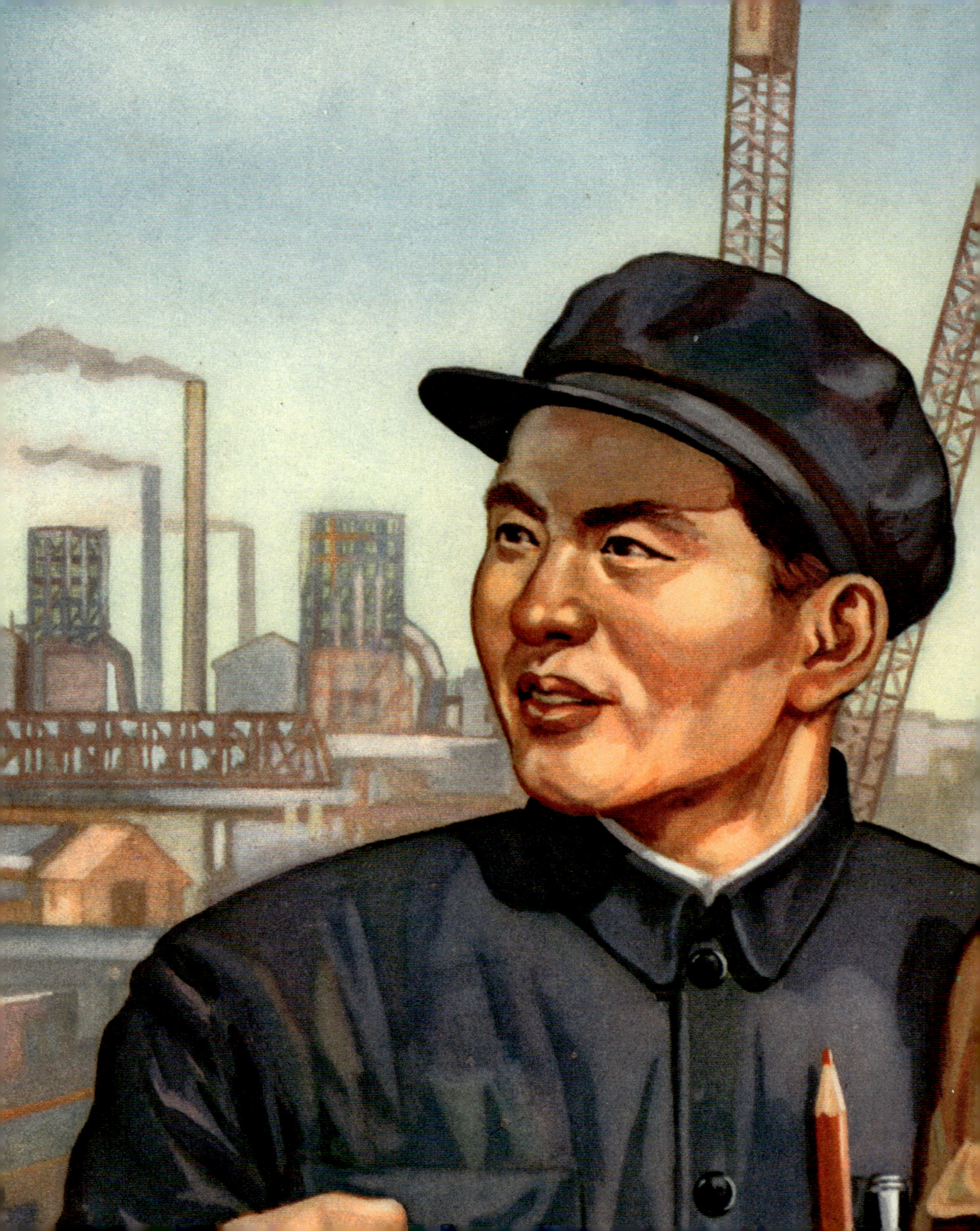

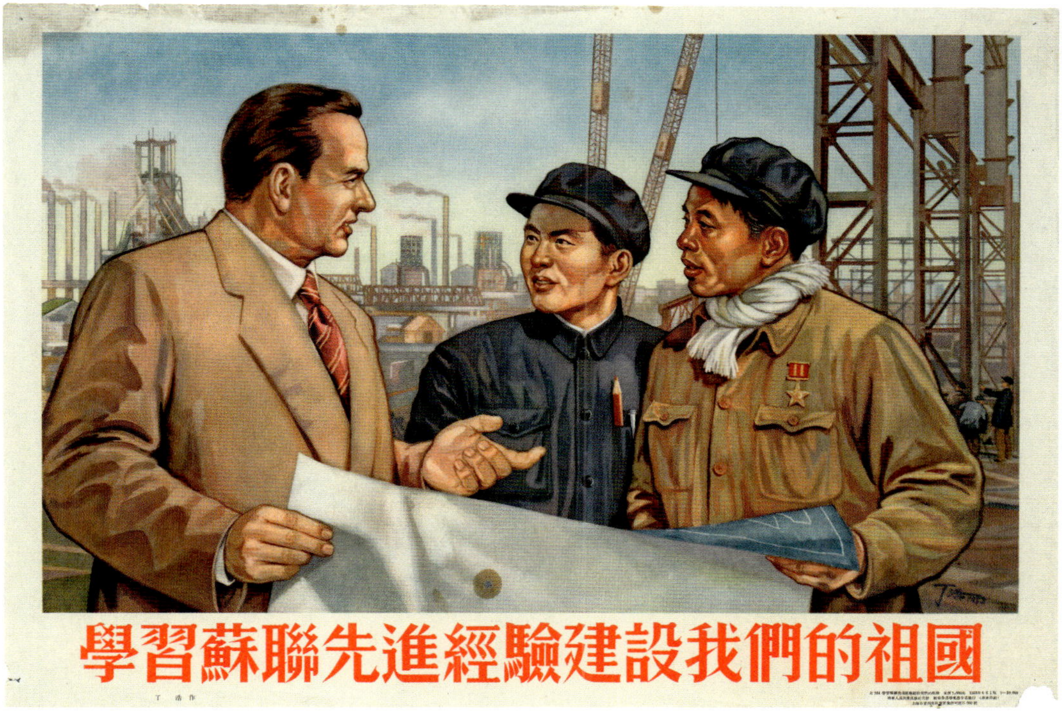

Study the Soviet Union's advanced economy to build up our nation, 1953.
Studiert die fortschrittliche Ökonomie der Sowjetunion, um unsere Nation aufzubauen, 1953.

The Soviet Union sends engineers and other advisors to China to help build up the infrastructure and industry. The arts are under Soviet influence also. Many poster designers of the 1950s were trained by Russian artists.

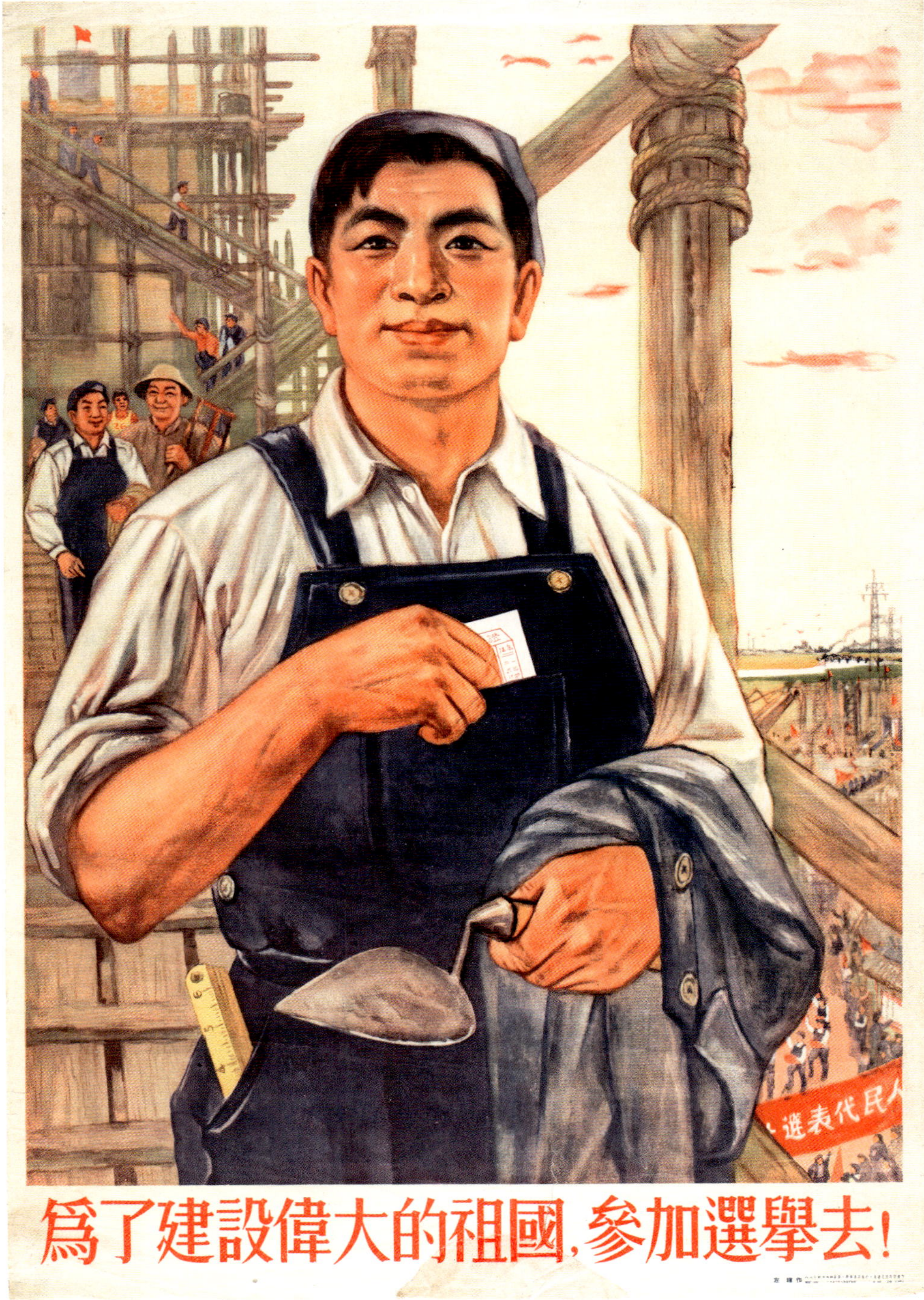

Participate in the elections to build up a great motherland! 1953.

Nehmt an den Wahlen teil, um ein großartiges Vaterland zu errichten! 1953.

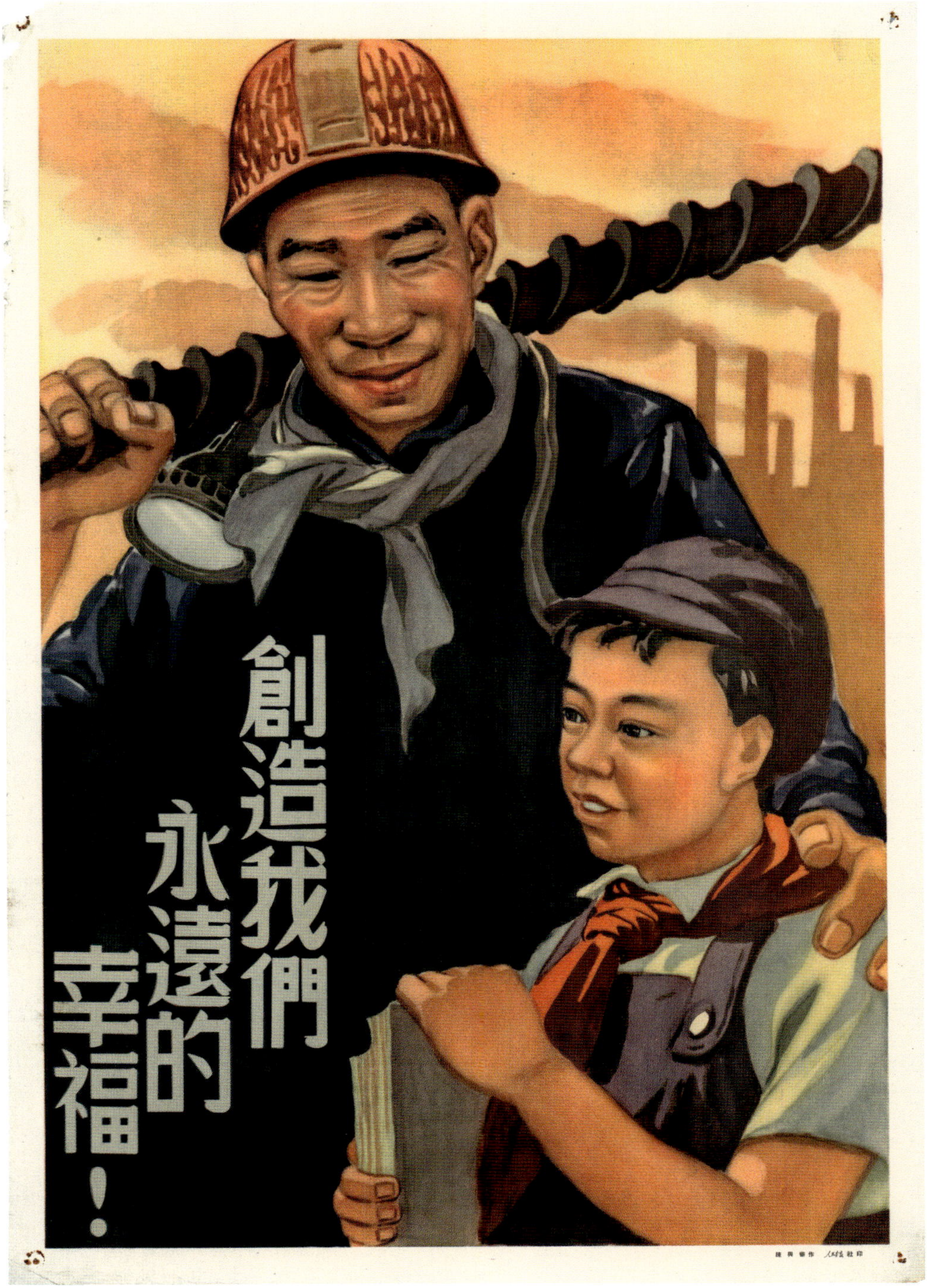

Create our eternal happiness! c. 1950.
Erschafft unser ewiges Glück! um 1950.

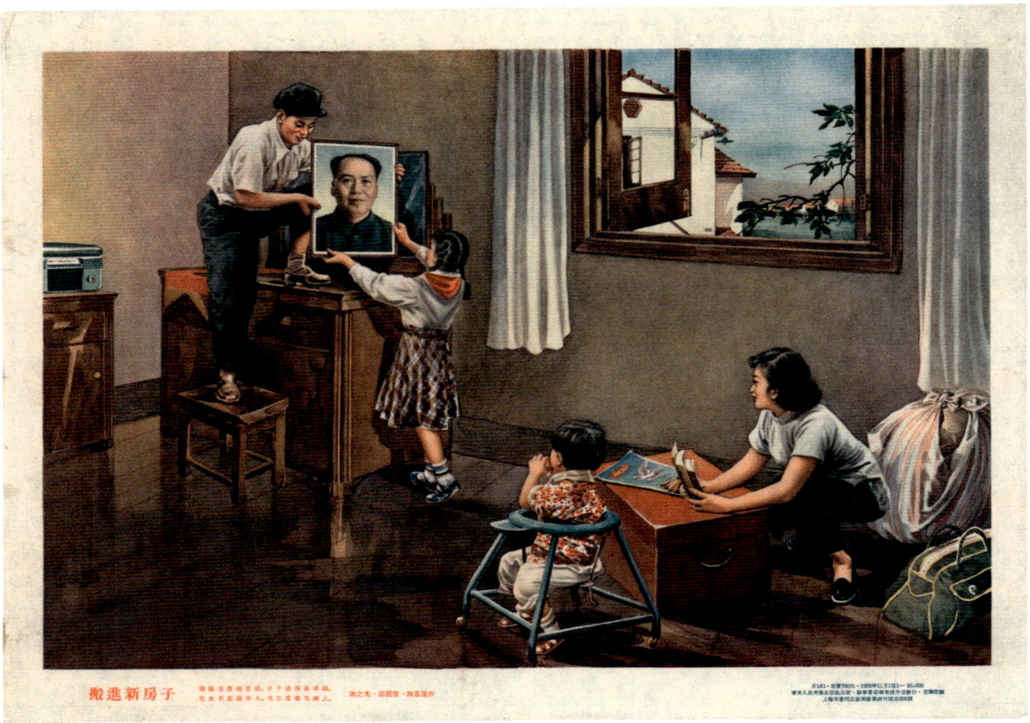

Moving into a new house, 1953.
Einzug in ein neues Haus, 1953.

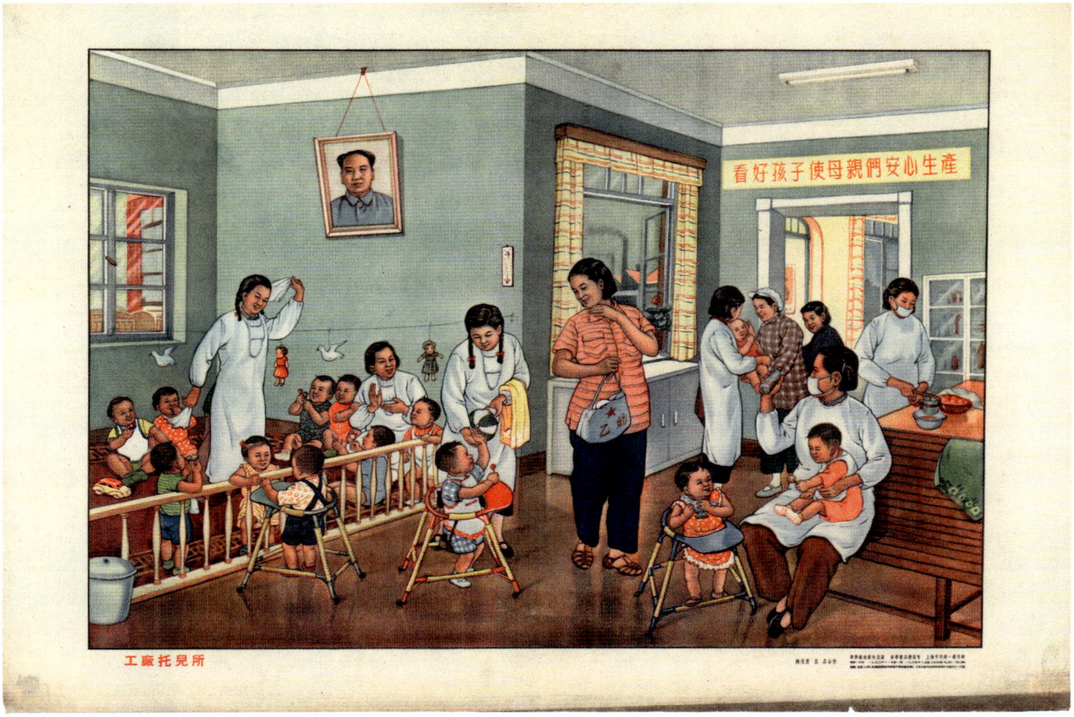

The kindergarten at the factory, 1953.
Der Kindergarten in der Fabrik, 1953.

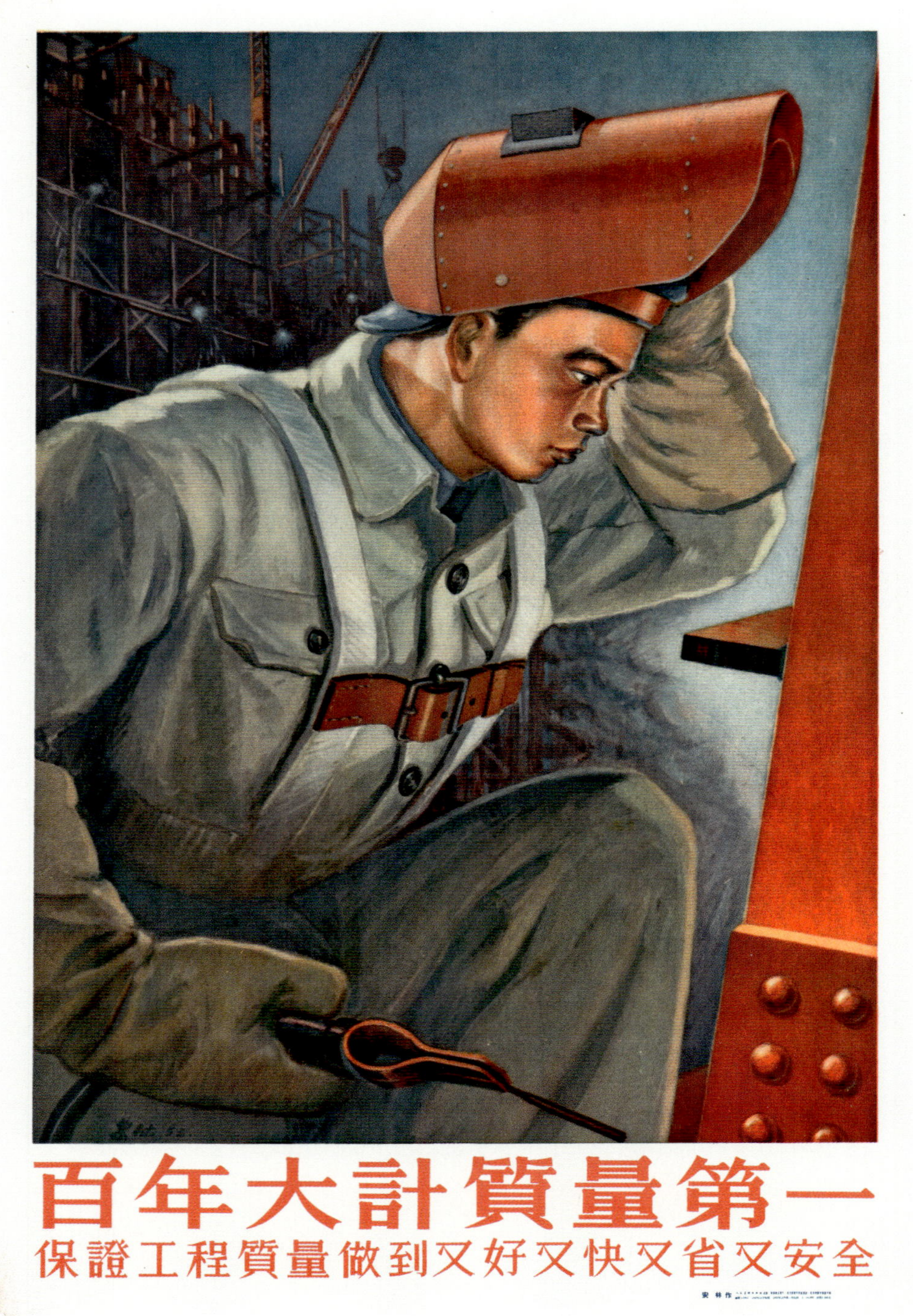

For projects of vital importance, quality is number one, 1953.
Bei lebenswichtigen Projekten steht Qualität an erster Stelle, 1953.

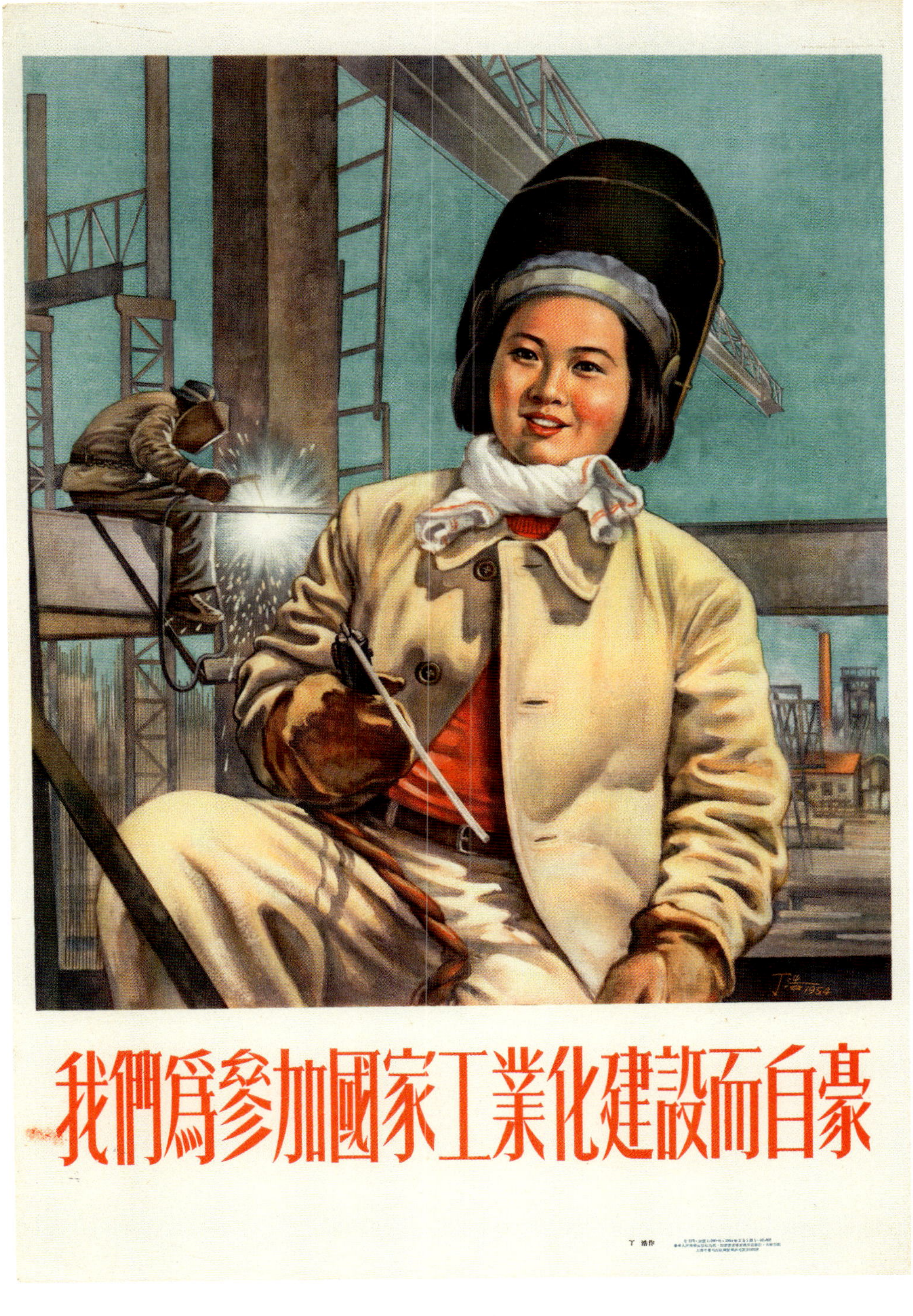

We are proud of participating in the founding of our country's industrialization, 1954.
Wir sind stolz darauf, am Aufbau der Industrialisierung unseres Landes teilzuhaben, 1954.

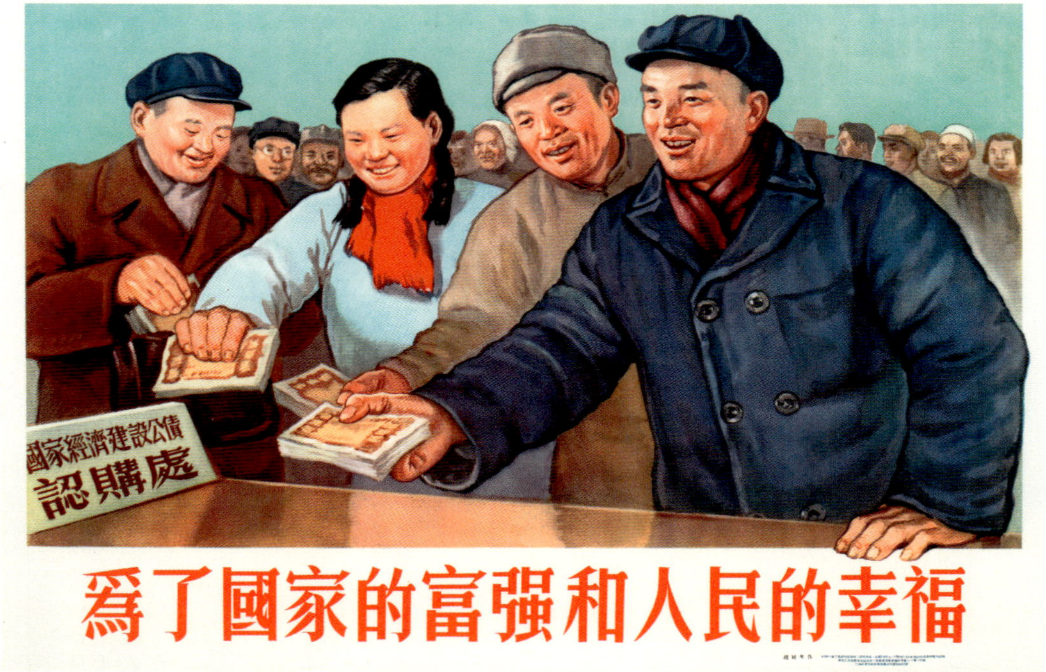

Make the nation rich and strong and the people happy, 1954.
Macht das Land reich und stark und die Menschen glücklich, 1954.

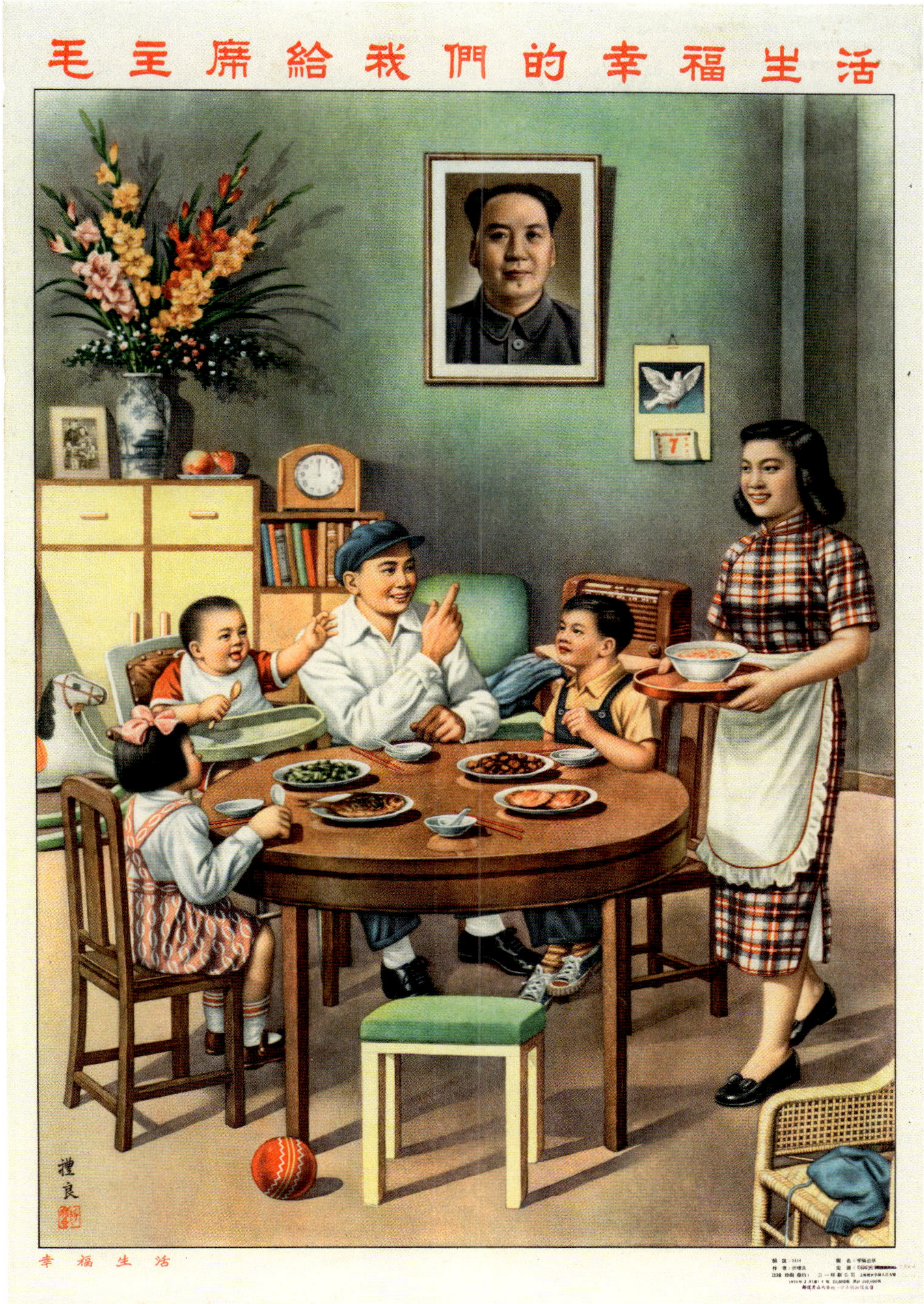

Chairman Mao gives us a happy life, 1954.
Der Vorsitzende Mao schenkt uns ein glückliches Leben, 1954.

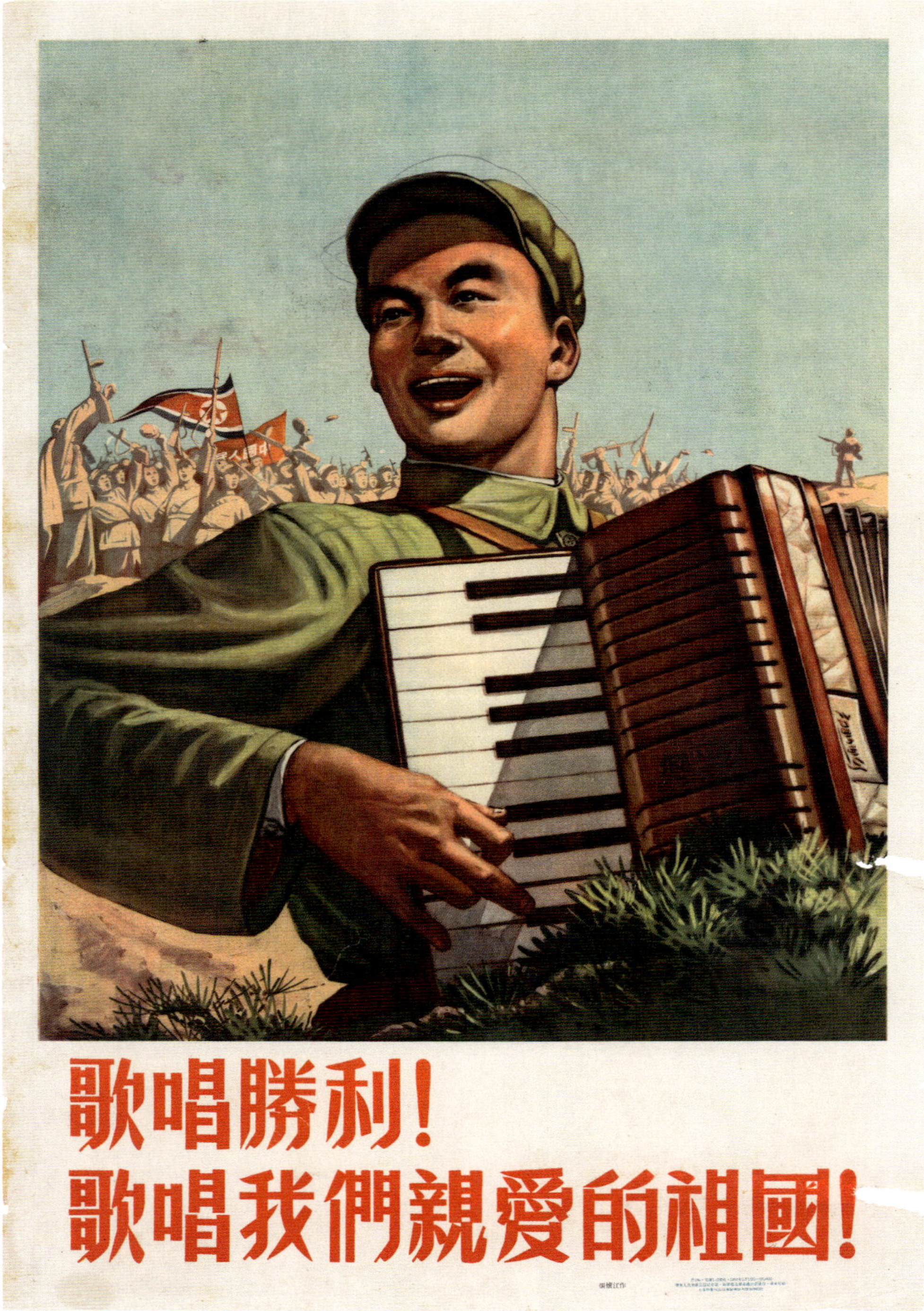

Sing about victory! Sing about our beloved nation! 1954.
Singt vom Sieg! Singt von unserer geliebten Heimat! 1954.

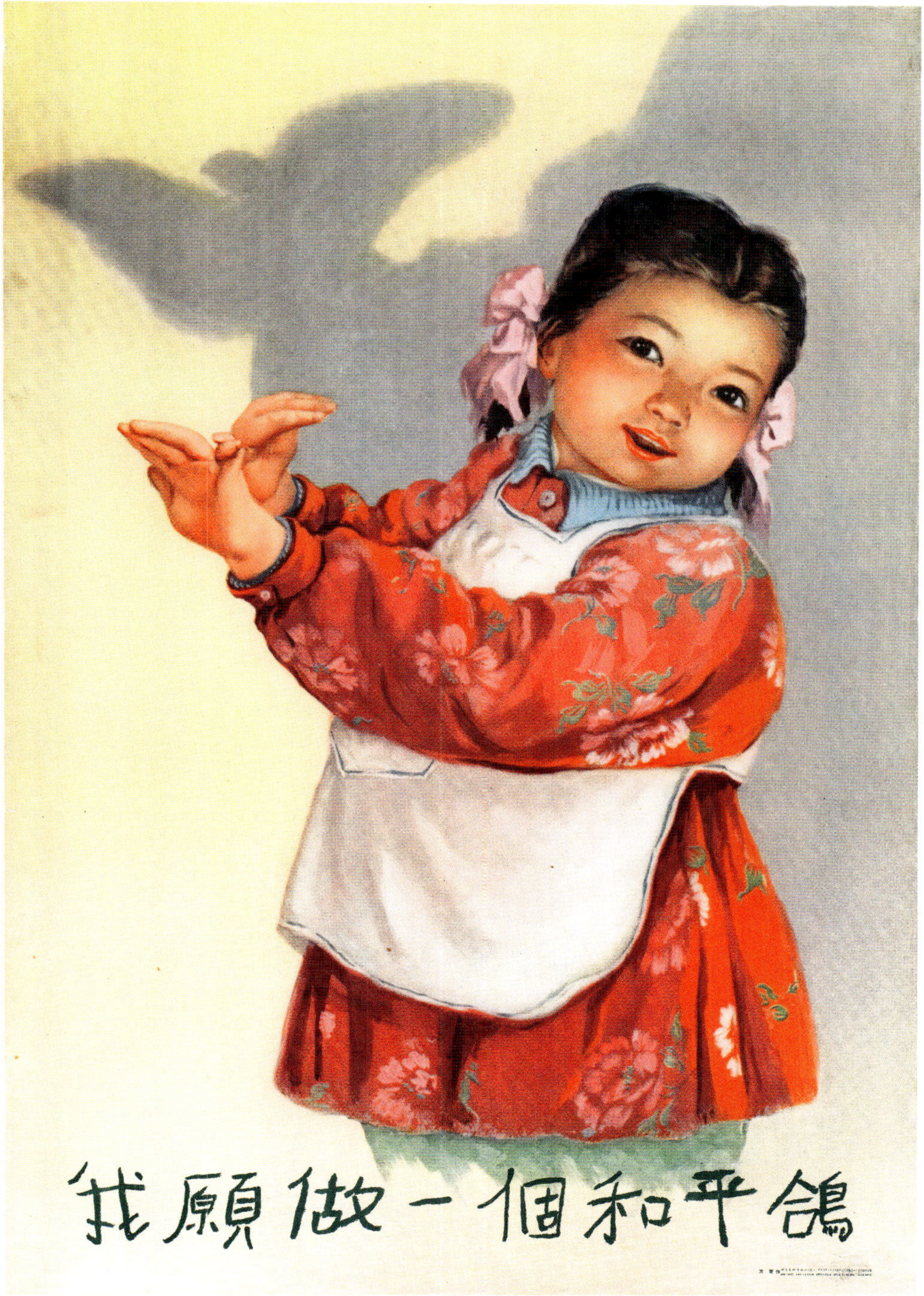

I want to make a dove of peace, 1954.
Ich möchte eine Friedenstaube machen, 1954.

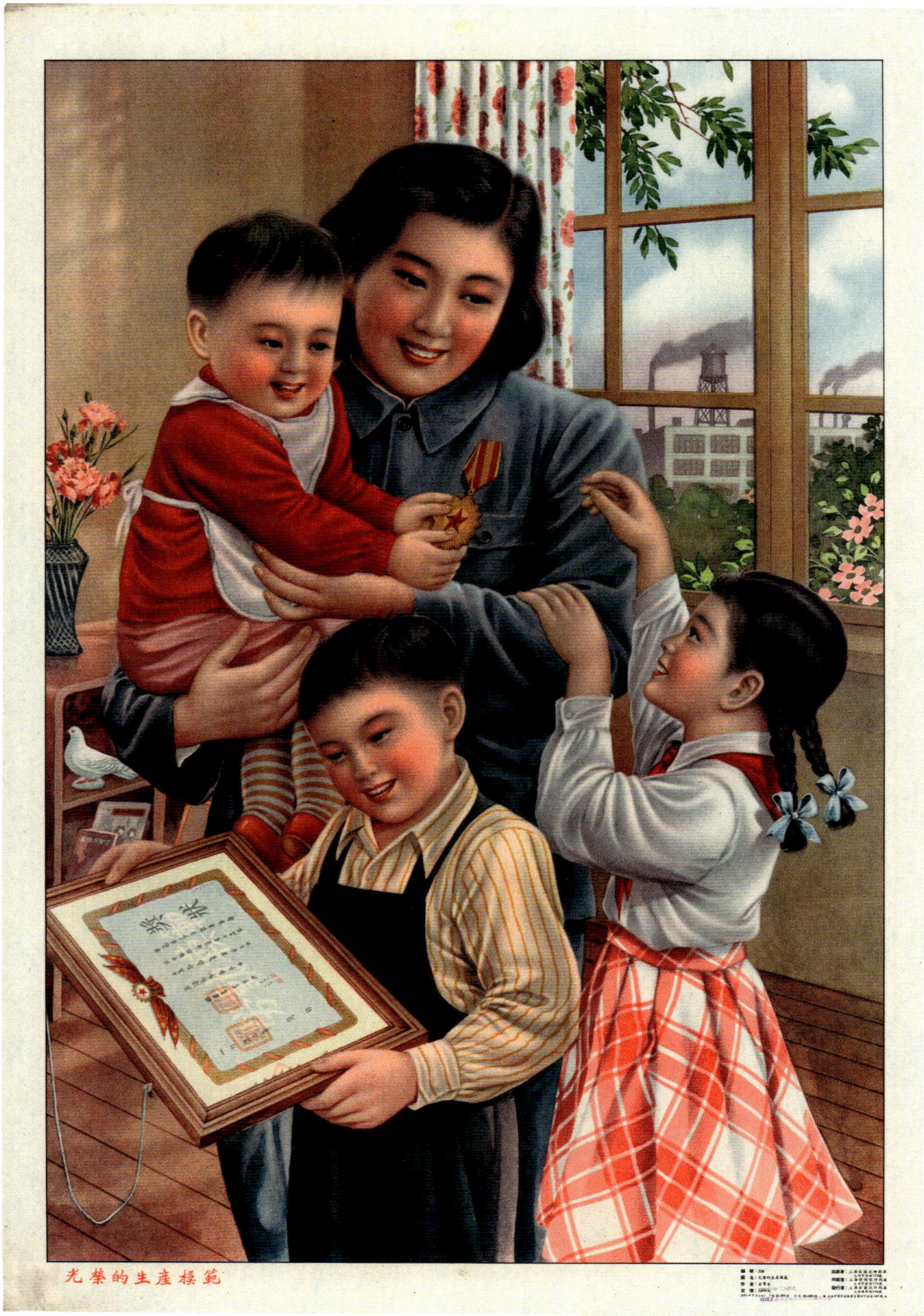

A glorious production model, 1954.
Ein prächtiges Produktionsmodell, 1954.

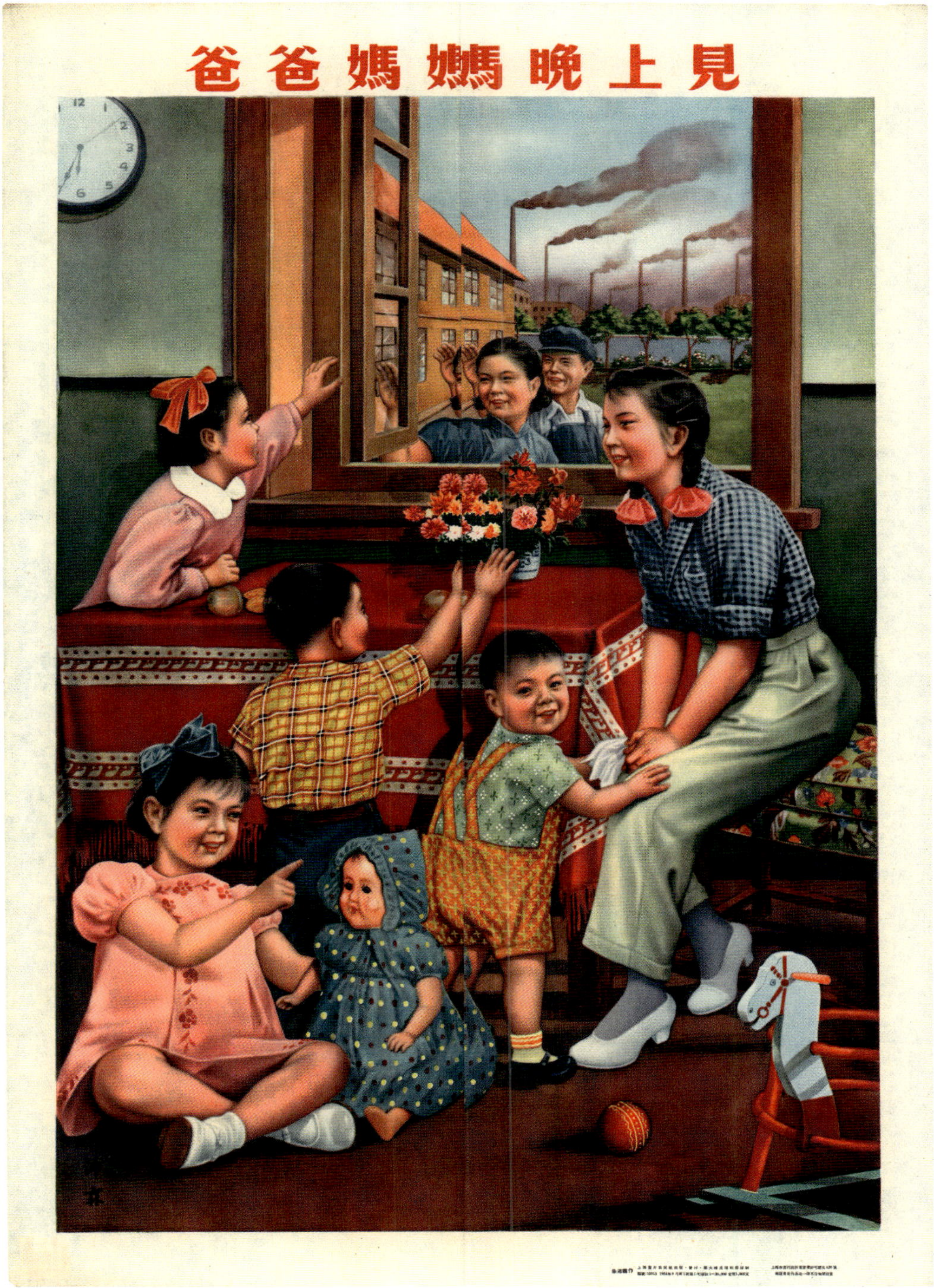

Daddy, mummy see you tonight, 1954.
Vati, Mutti, bis heute Abend, 1954.

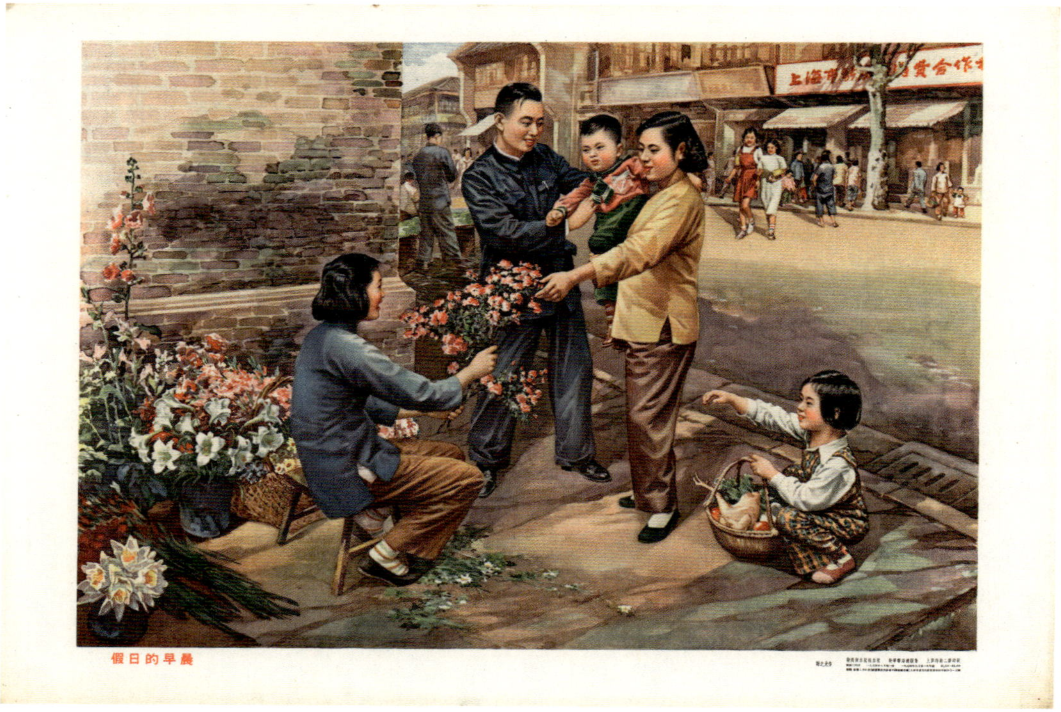

A morning off, 1954.

Ein freier Morgen, 1954.

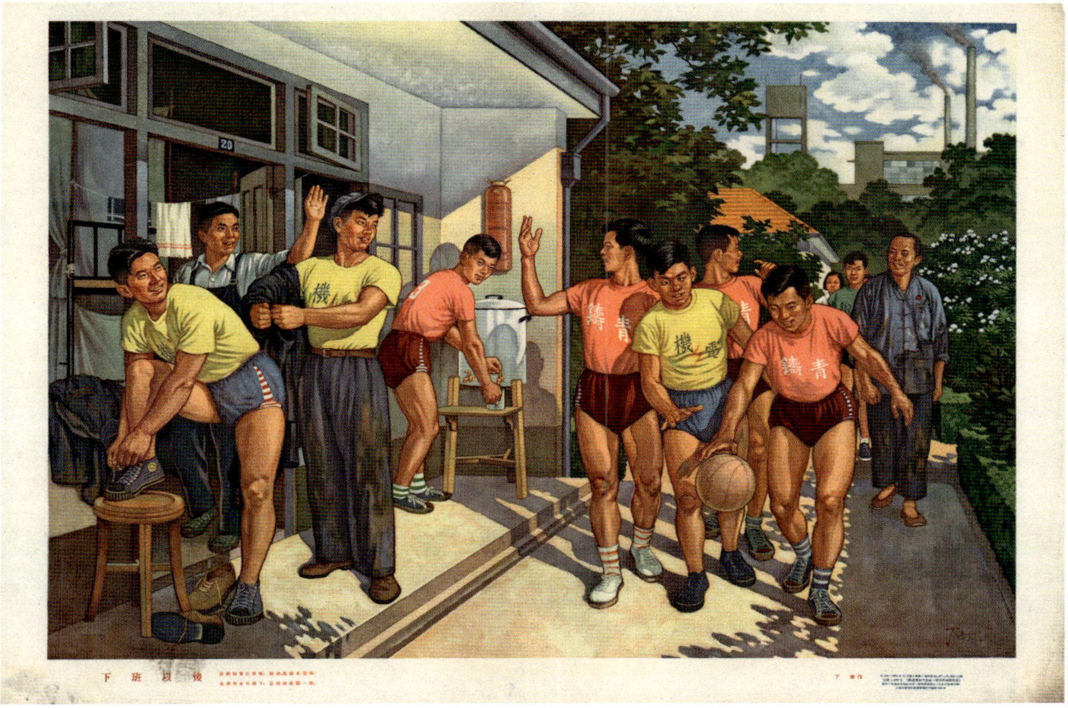

After work, 1954.
Nach der Arbeit, 1954.

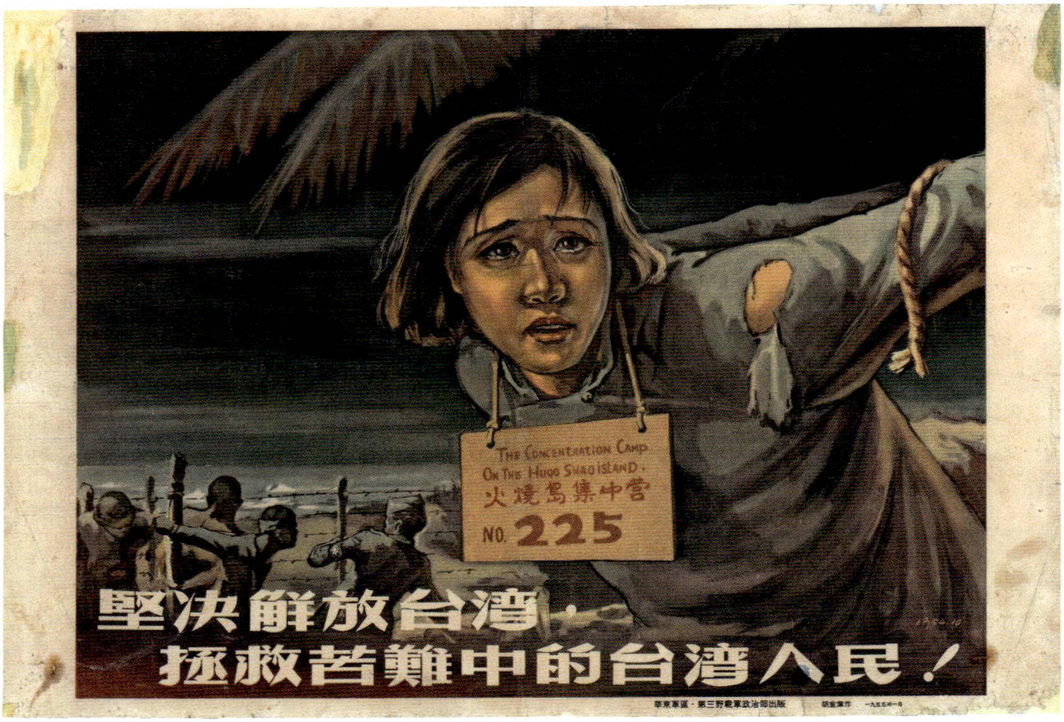

Resolutely liberate Taiwan, save the Taiwanese people from their misery! 1955.
Befreit Taiwan, errettet das taiwanesische Volk aus seinem Unglück! 1955.

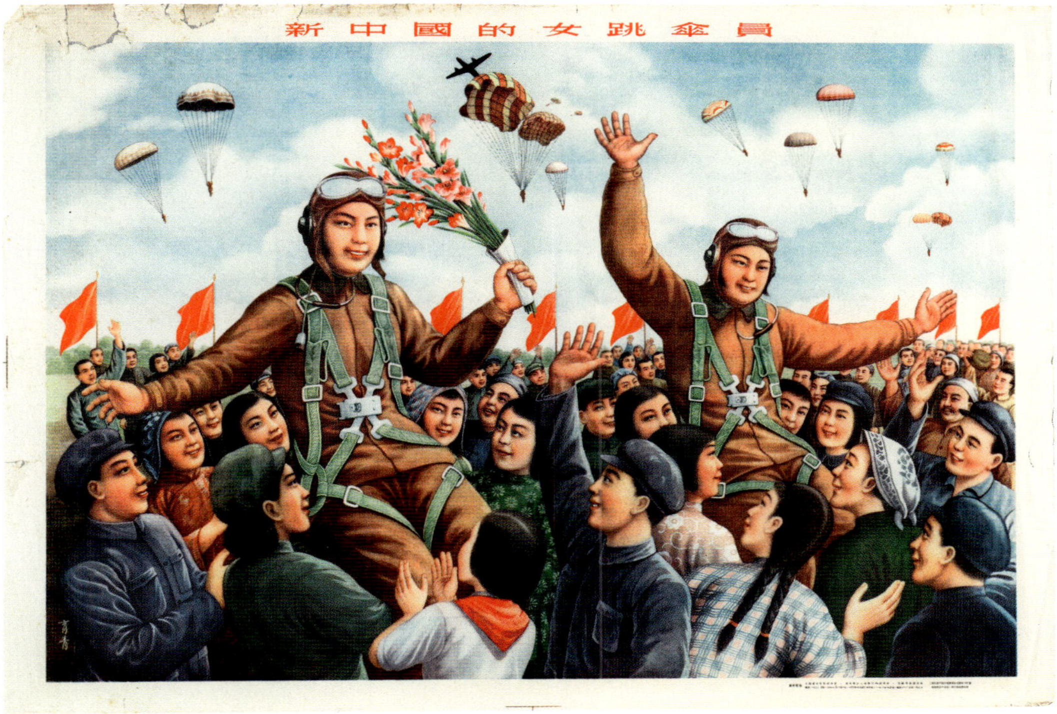

New China's female parachuters, 1955.
Die Fallschirmspringerinnen des neuen China, 1955.

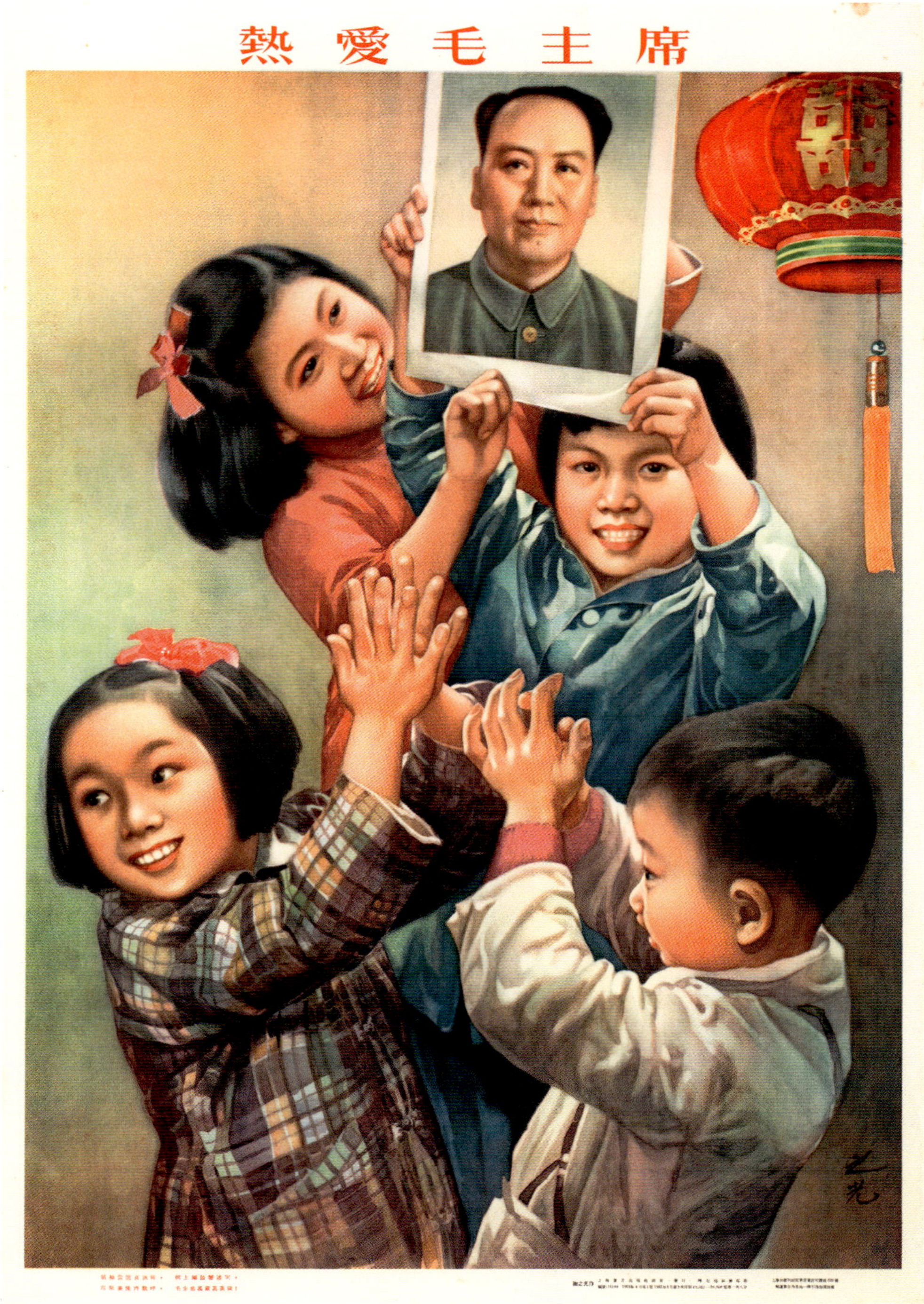

Lots of love for Chairman Mao, 1955.
Tiefe Zuneigung für den Vorsitzenden Mao, 1955.

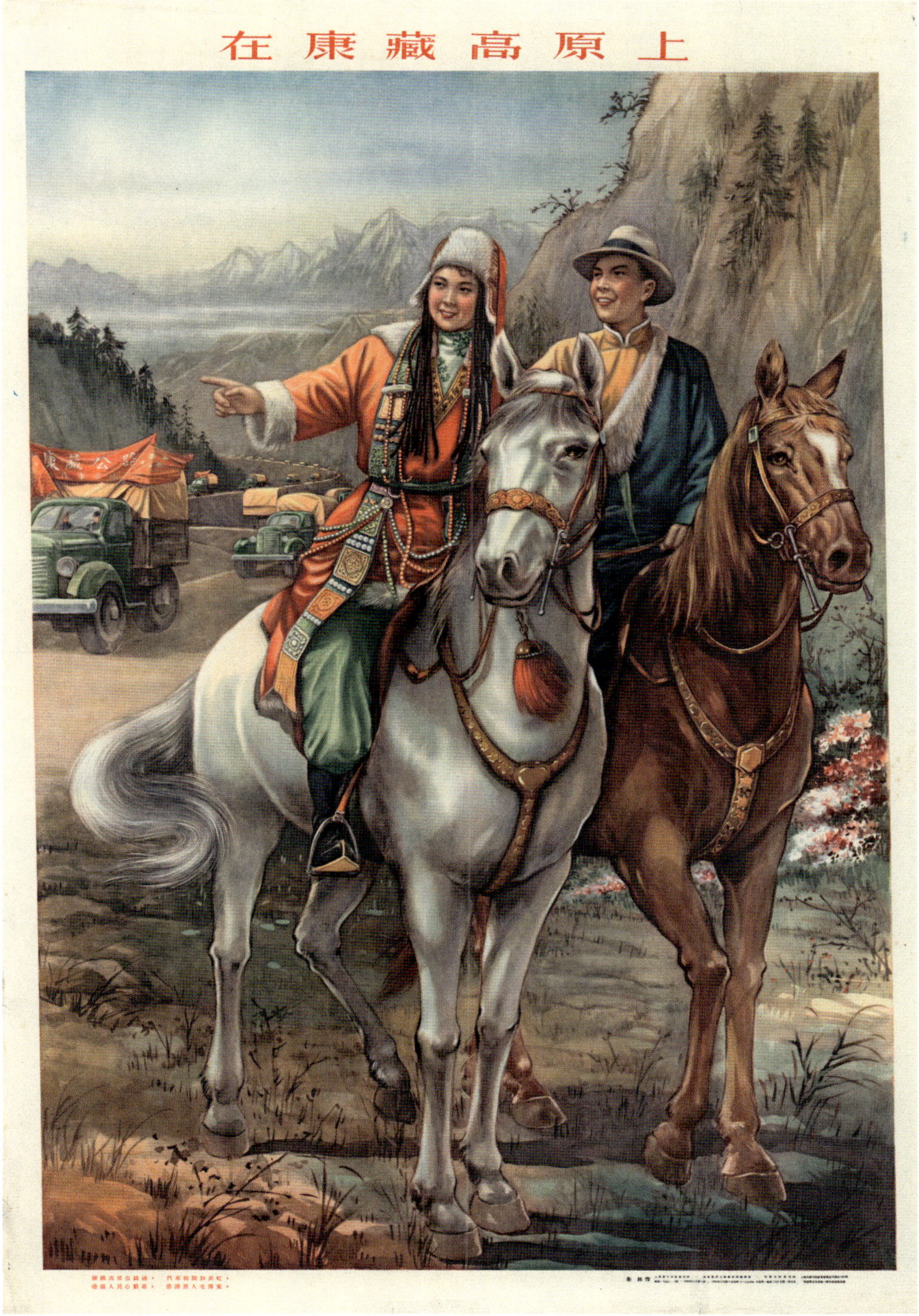

On the Kangzang Plateau, 1955.
Auf dem Kangzang Plateau, 1955.

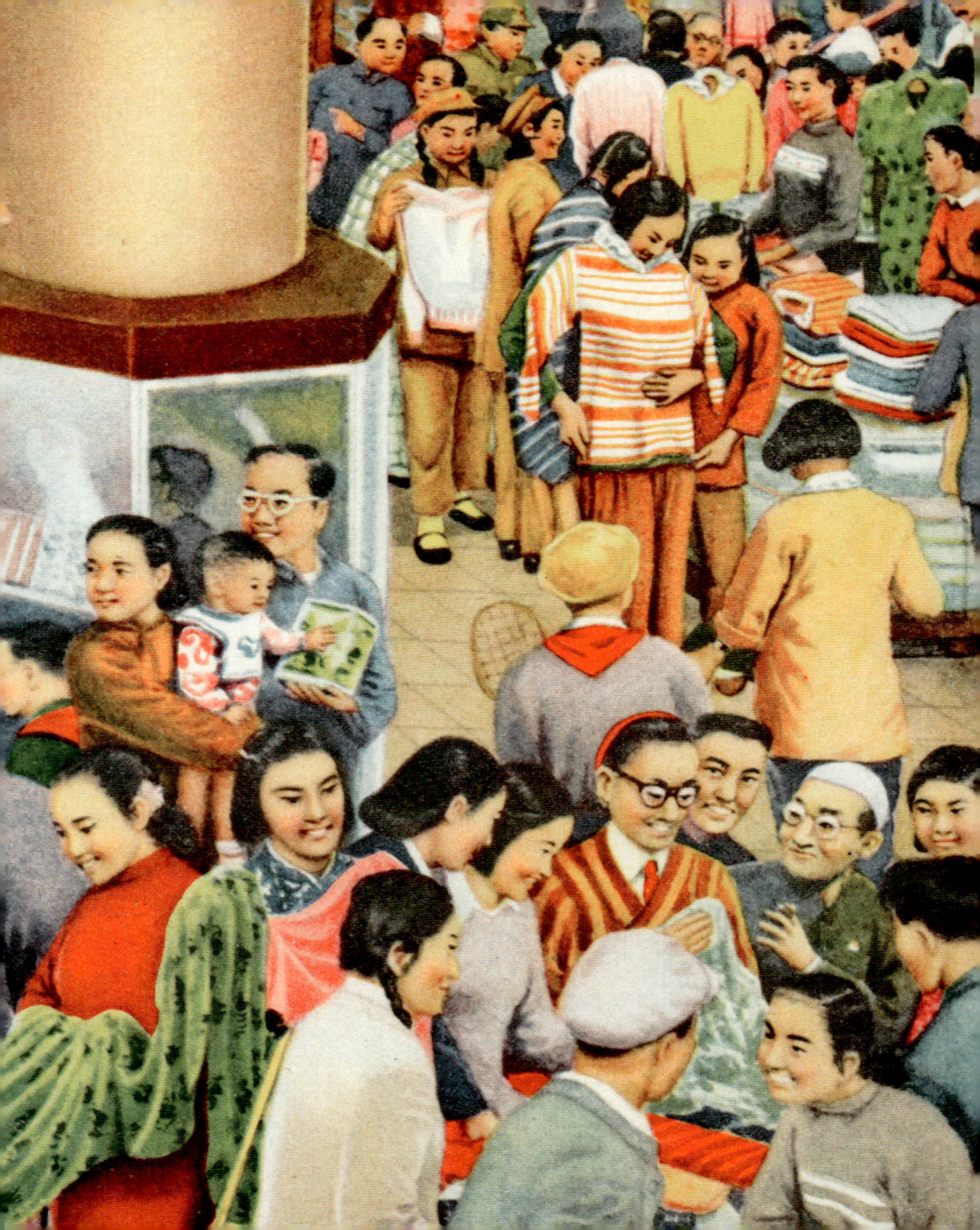

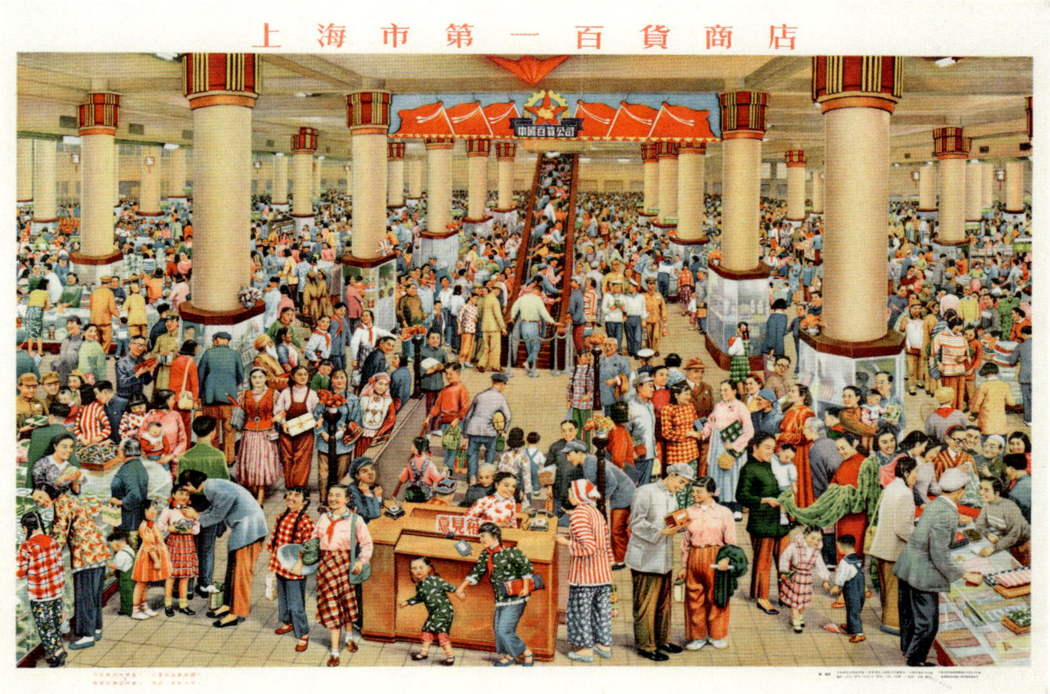

Shanghai's no. 1 Department Store, 1955.
Shanghais Nummer 1 Warenhaus, 1955.

For many years, this department store was the largest in Asia. The escalator was the only one in operation in all of China. The store still exists. The floor shown here now serves as the perfume department, selling expensive Asian and Western cosmetics.

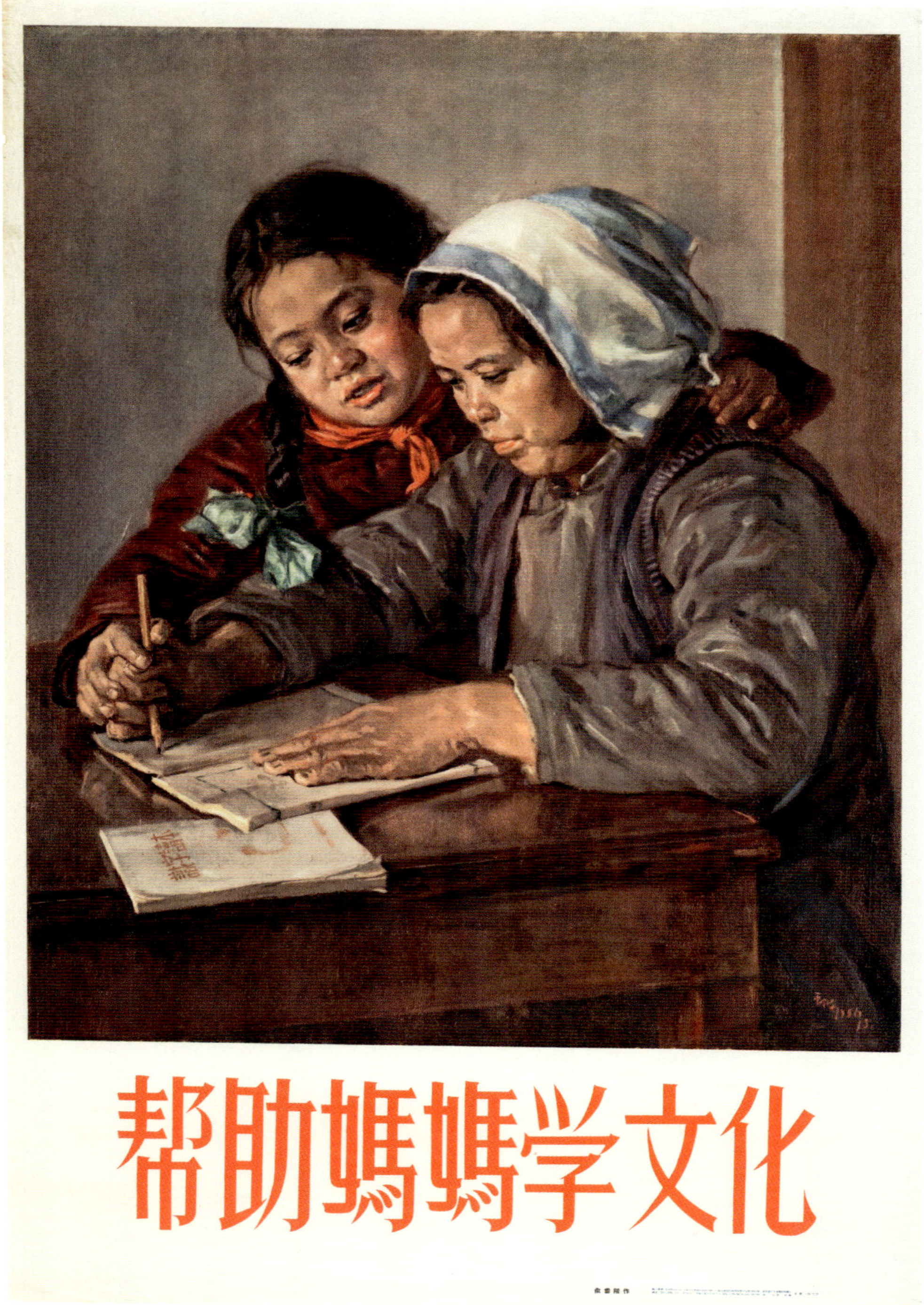

Helping mama study culture, 1956.

Ich helfe Mama bei der Weiterbildung, 1956.

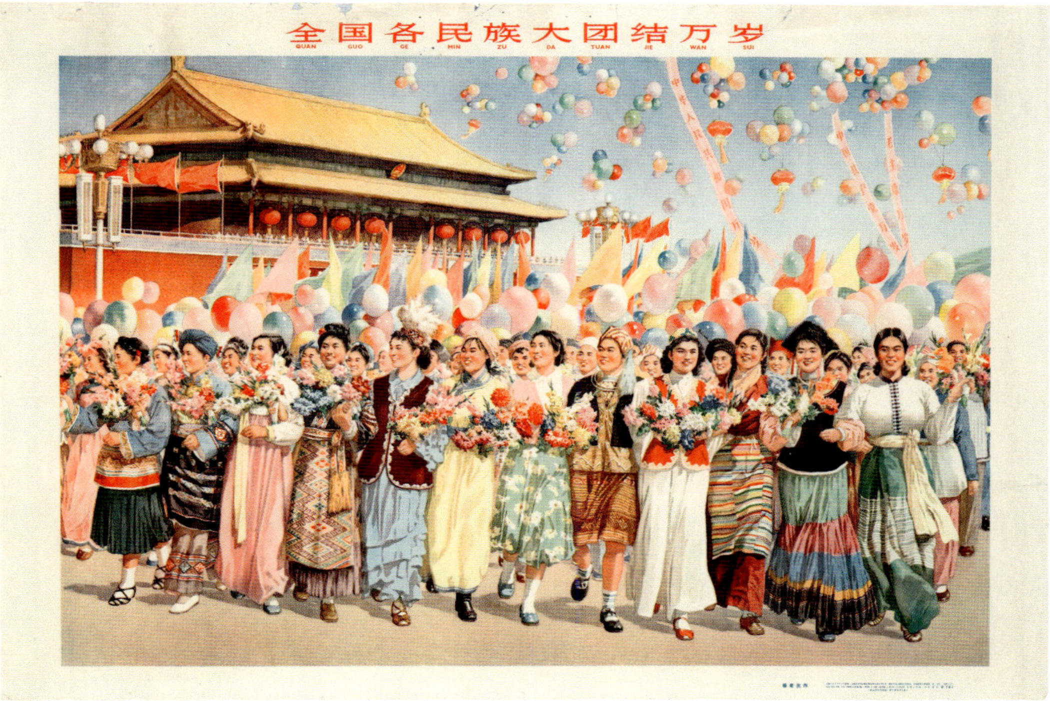

Long live the great unity of all the people of the whole nation, 1957.
Lang währe die große Eintracht aller Menschen dieser Nation, 1957.

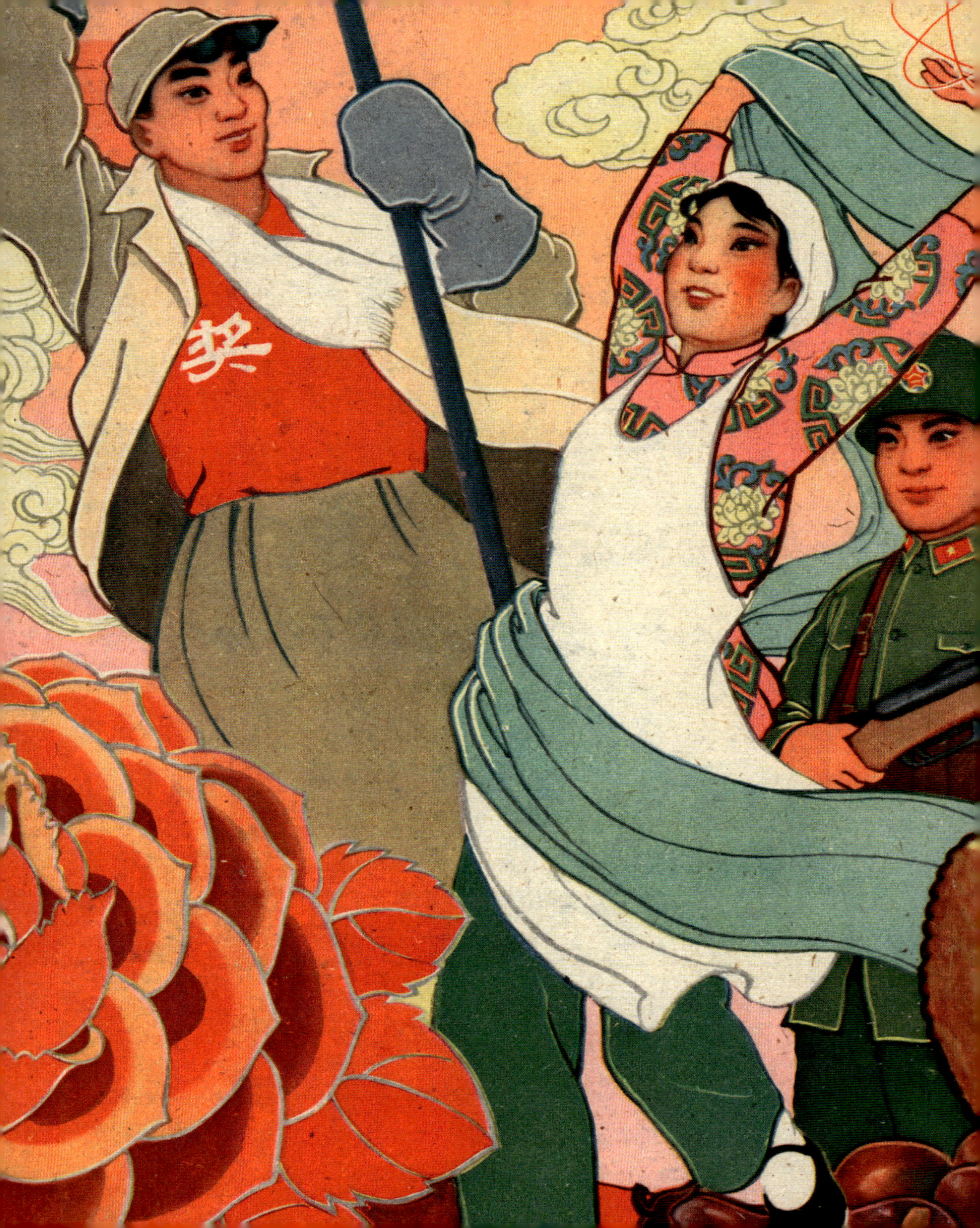
奖

THE GREAT LEAP FORWARD – AND BACK 1956–66

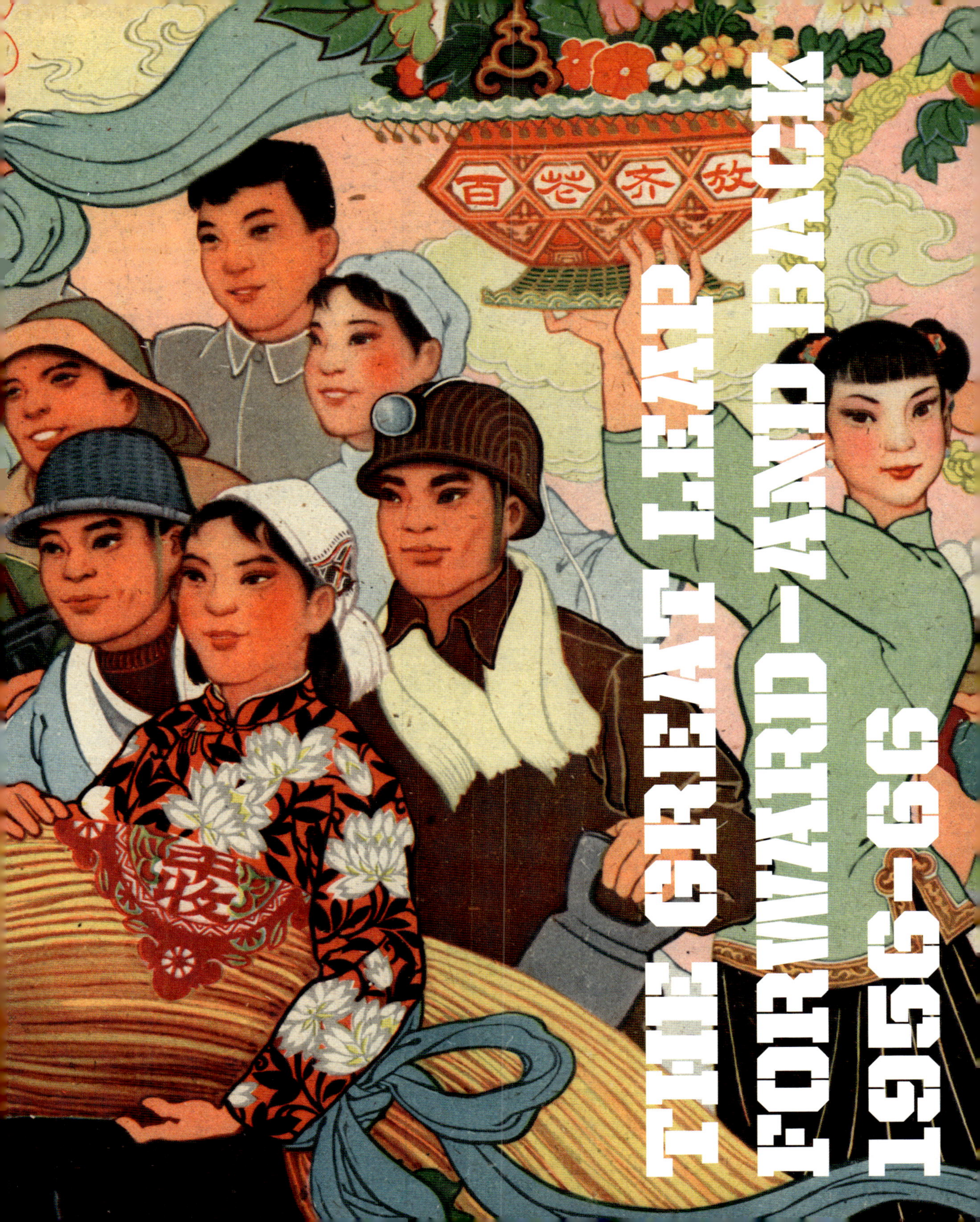

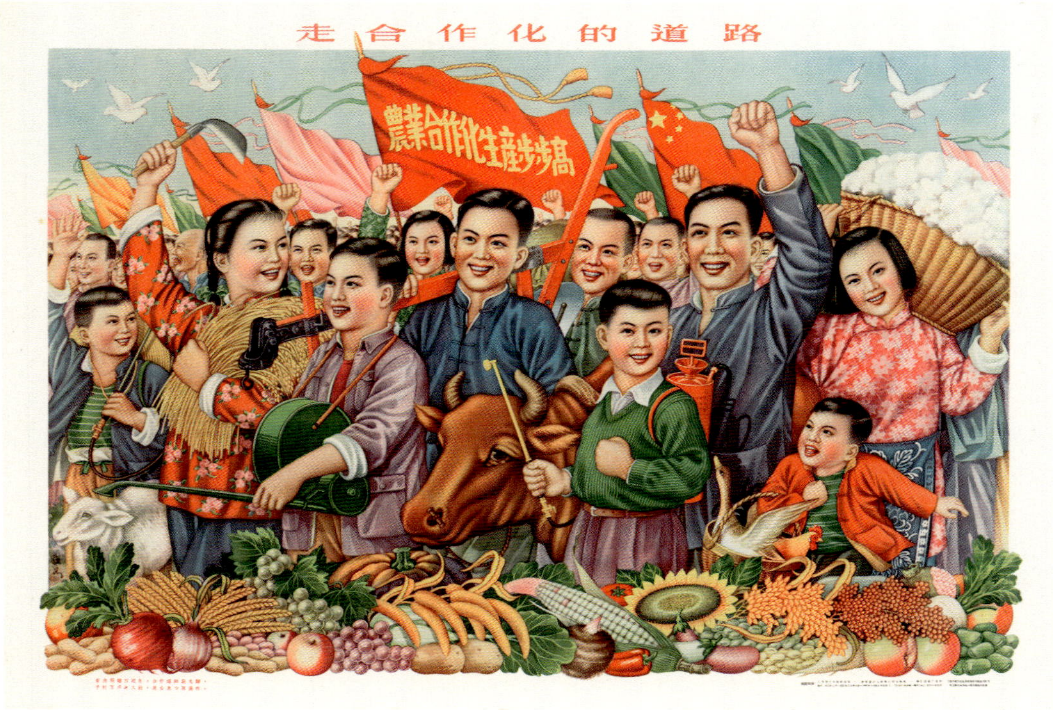

Walk along the road to cooperativization, 1956.
Geht den Weg der Kooperative, 1956.

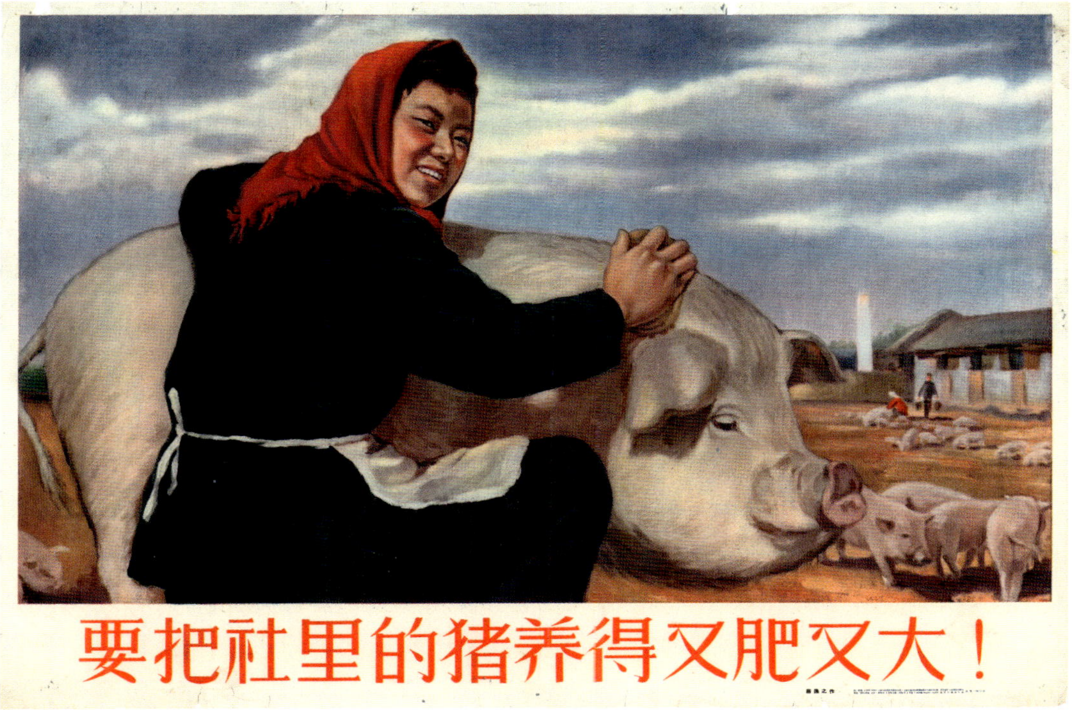

The hogs of the commune must be raised to be fat and big! 1956.
Die Schweine der Kommune müssen aufgezogen werden, bis sie dick und fett sind! 1956.

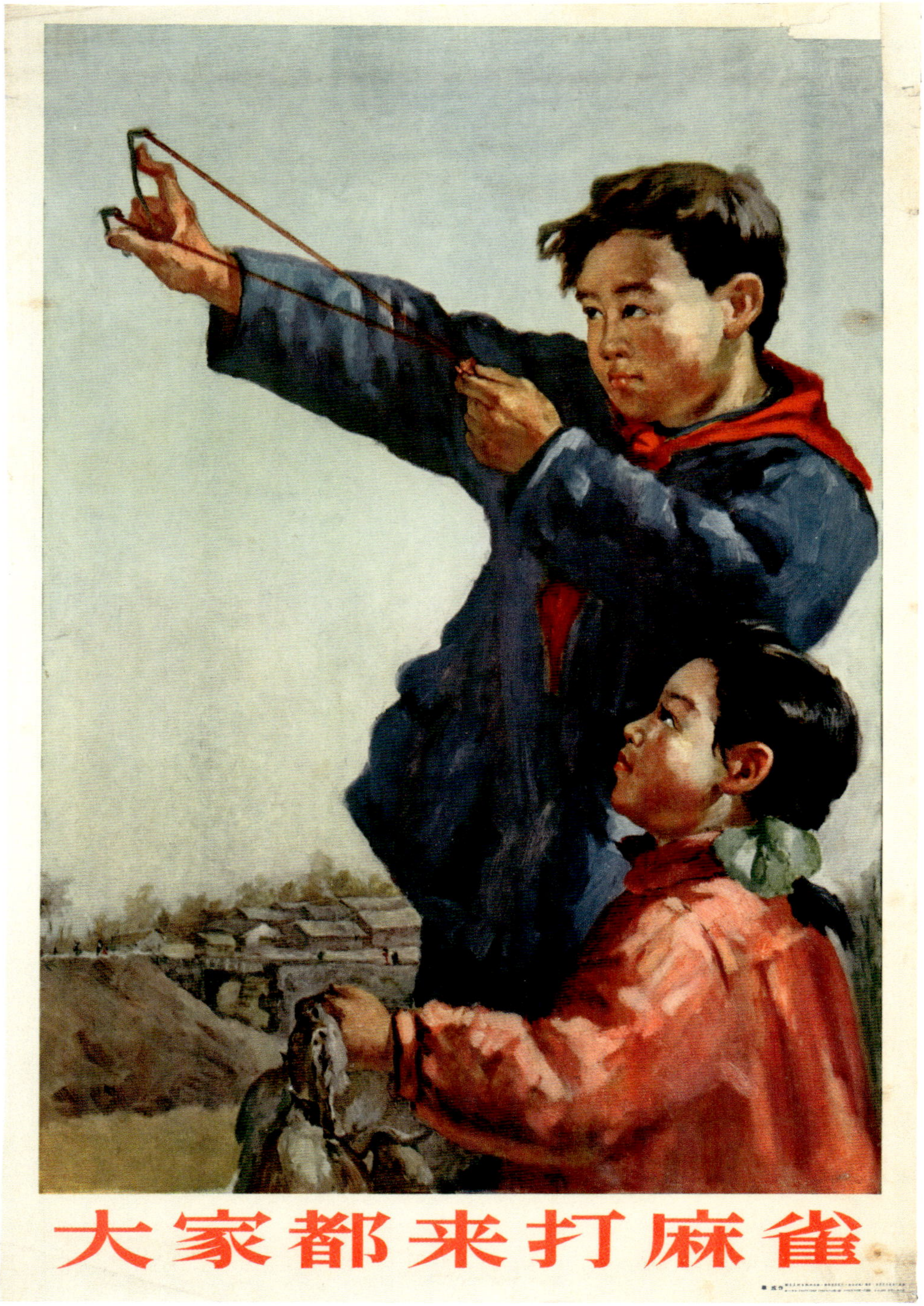

Everybody comes to beat sparrows, 1956.

Alle beteiligen sich am Abschuss der Spatzen, 1956.

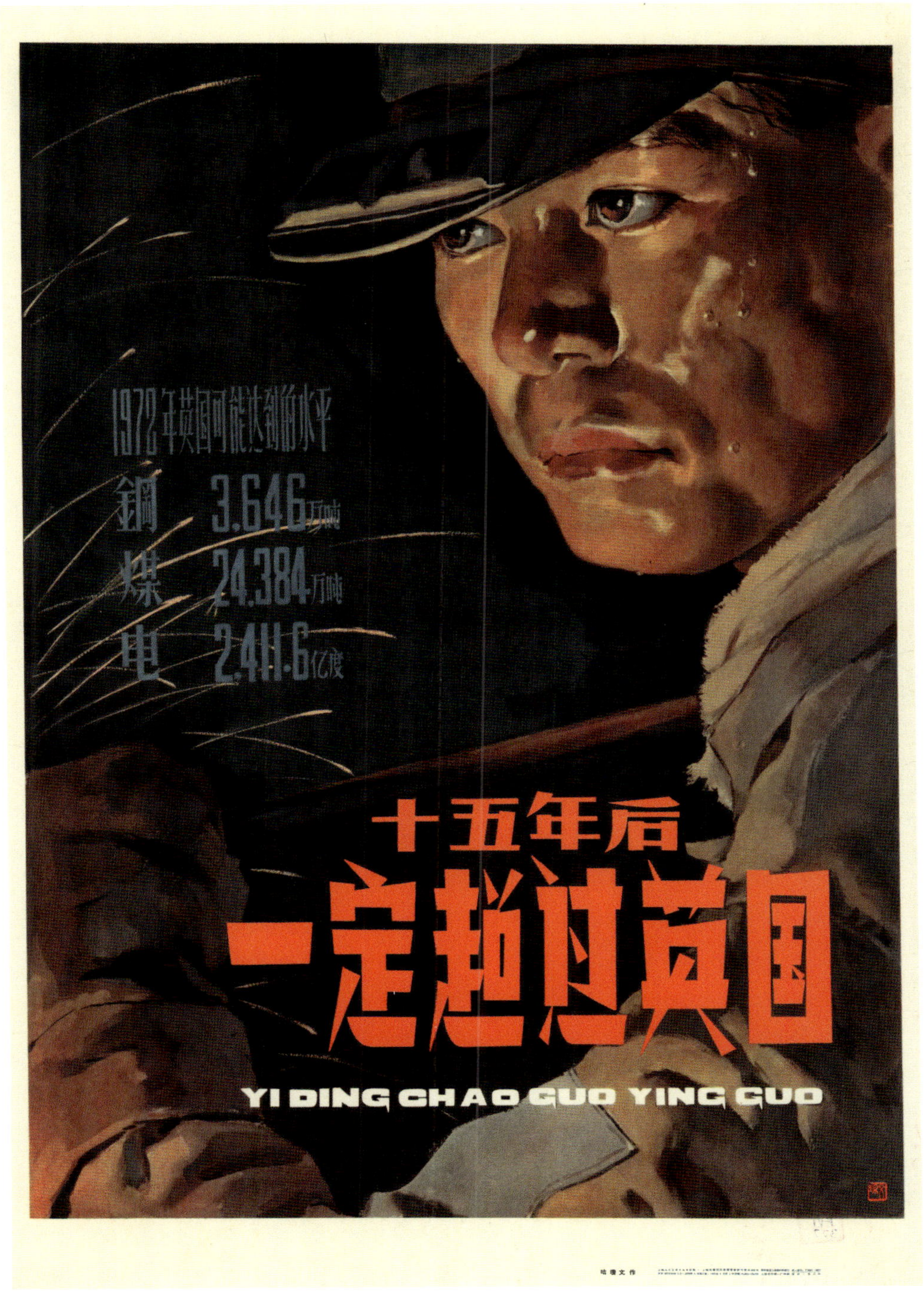

In fifteen years we will certainly have surpassed England, 1958.
In fünfzehn Jahren werden wir England mit Sicherheit überholt haben, 1958.

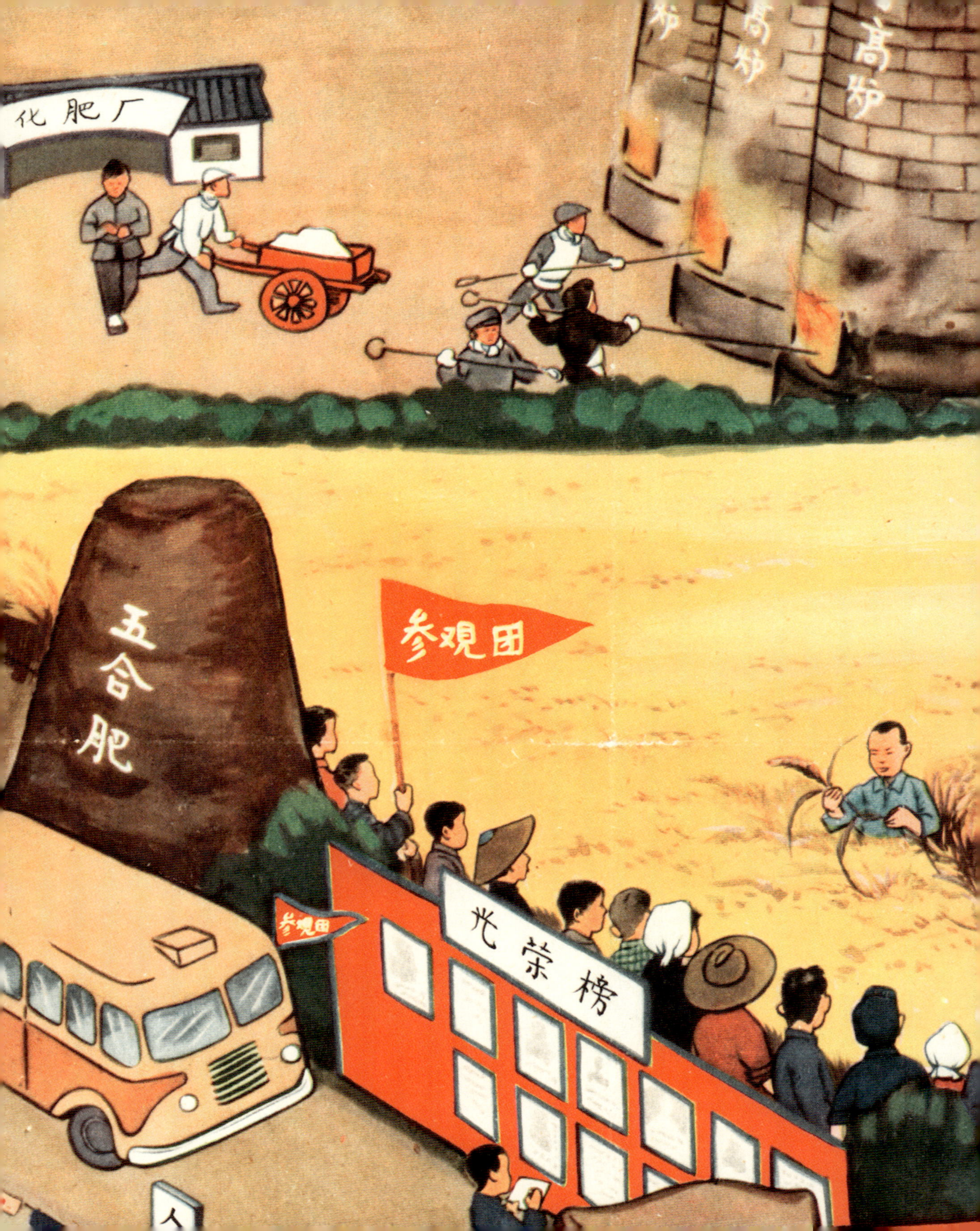
化肥厂
高炉
高炉
炉
五合肥
参观团
参观团
光荣榜

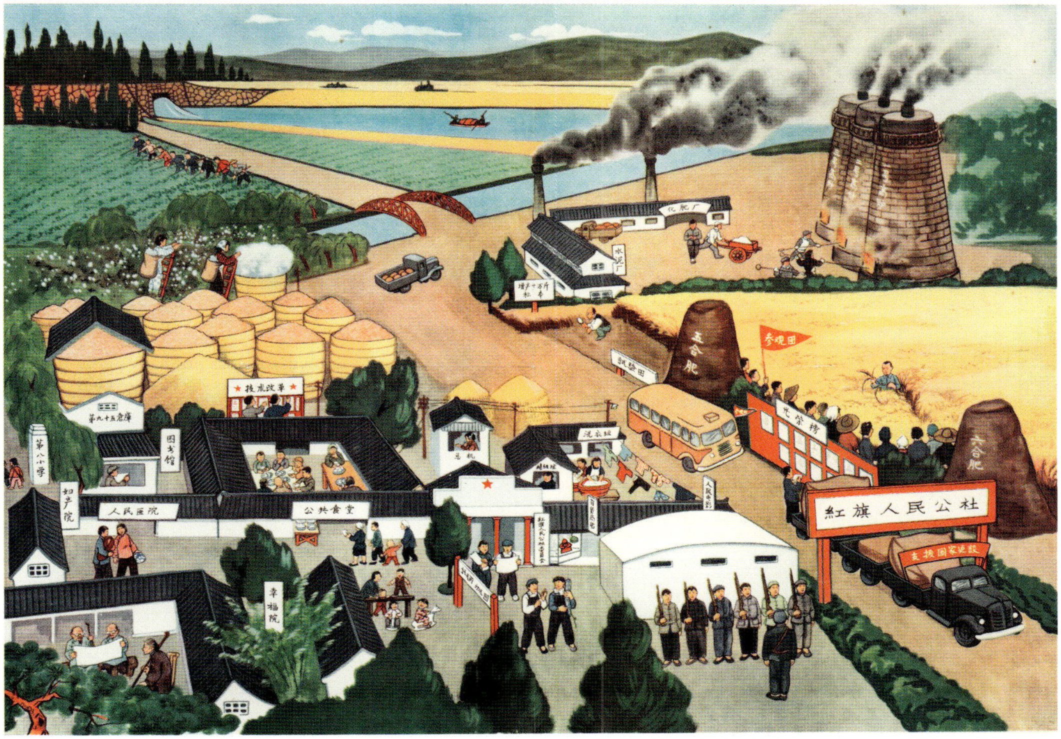

The people's communes are good, 1958.
Die Volkskommunen sind gut, 1958.

← This poster for schools shows the ideal people's commune, with a rich harvest, backyard furnaces for the production of steel, communal facilities for eating and washing, a center for the elderly, and the people's militia.

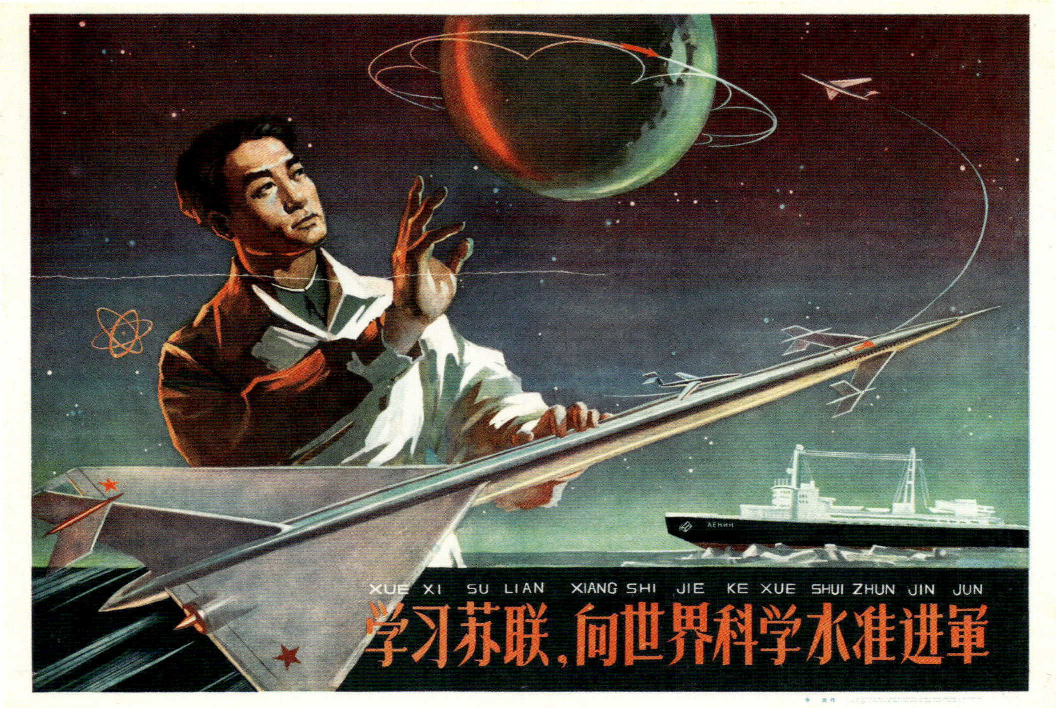

Study the Soviet Union, to advance to world-class levels of science, 1958.

Studiert das Vorbild der Sowjetunion, um in den Wissenschaften Weltniveau zu erreichen, 1958.

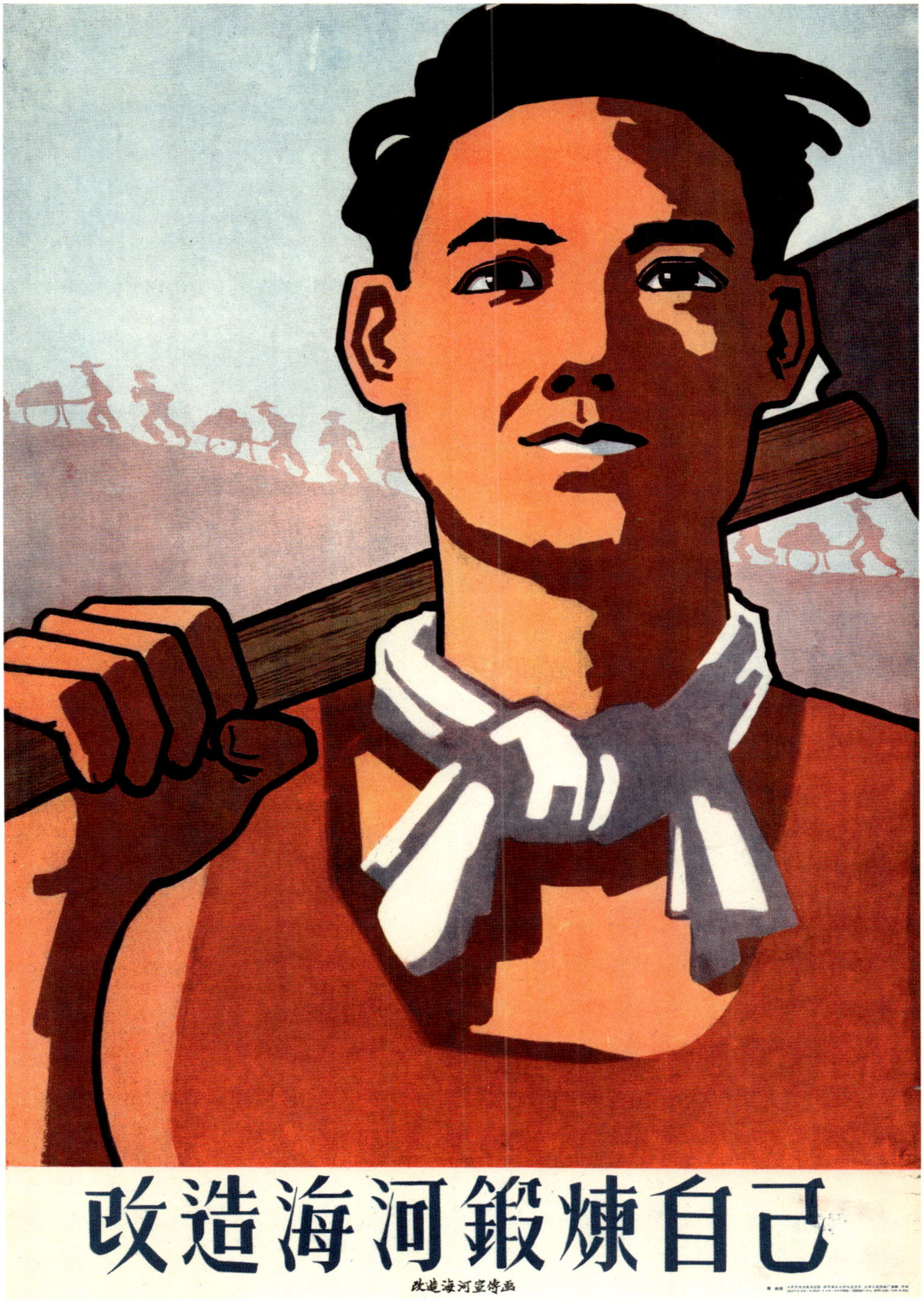

Transform seas and rivers, temper yourself, 1958.
Wandelt Meere und Flüsse um, mäßigt euch selbst, 1958.

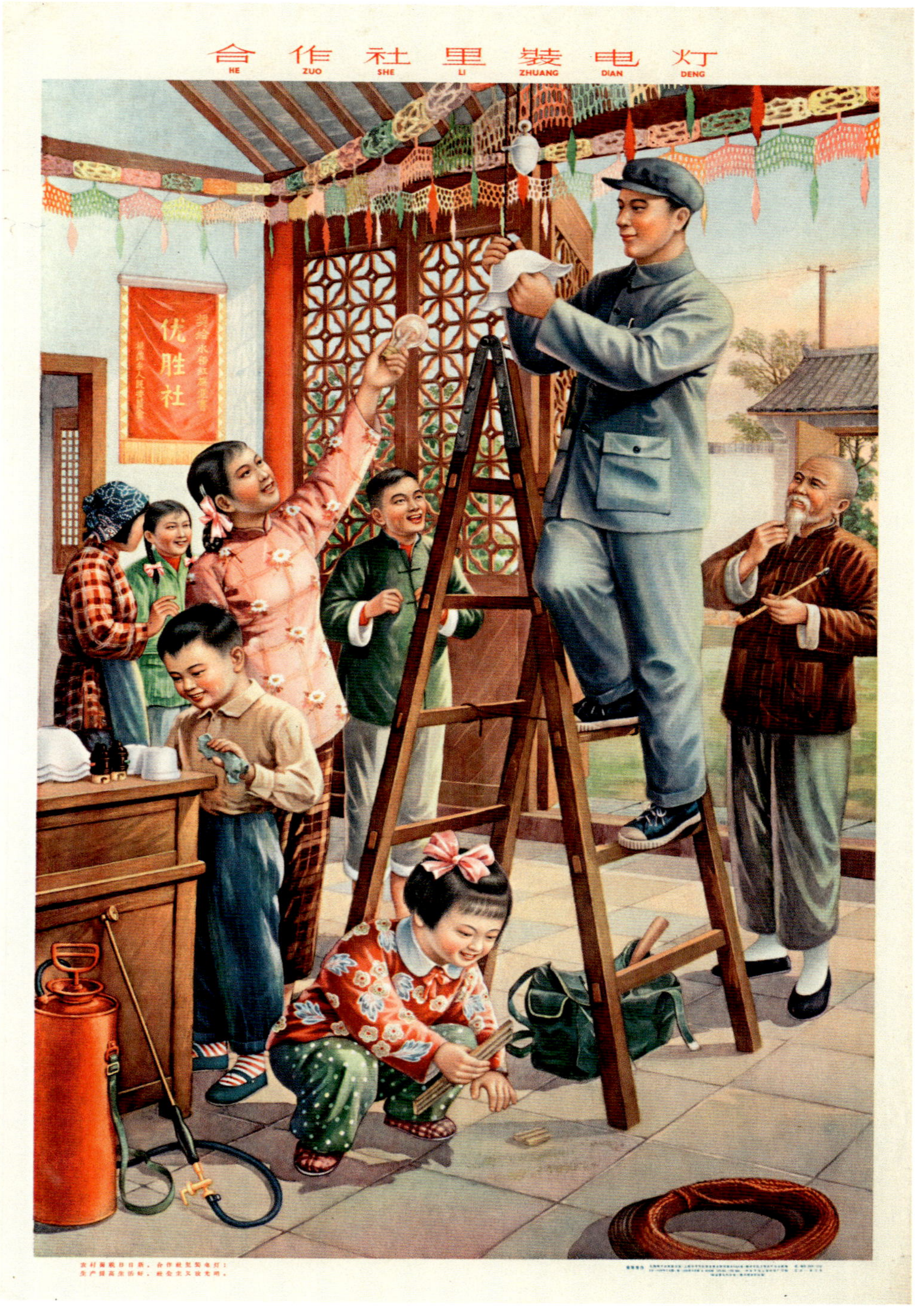

Installing electric lights in the cooperative, 1958.
Beim Installieren von elektrischem Licht in der Kooperative, 1958.

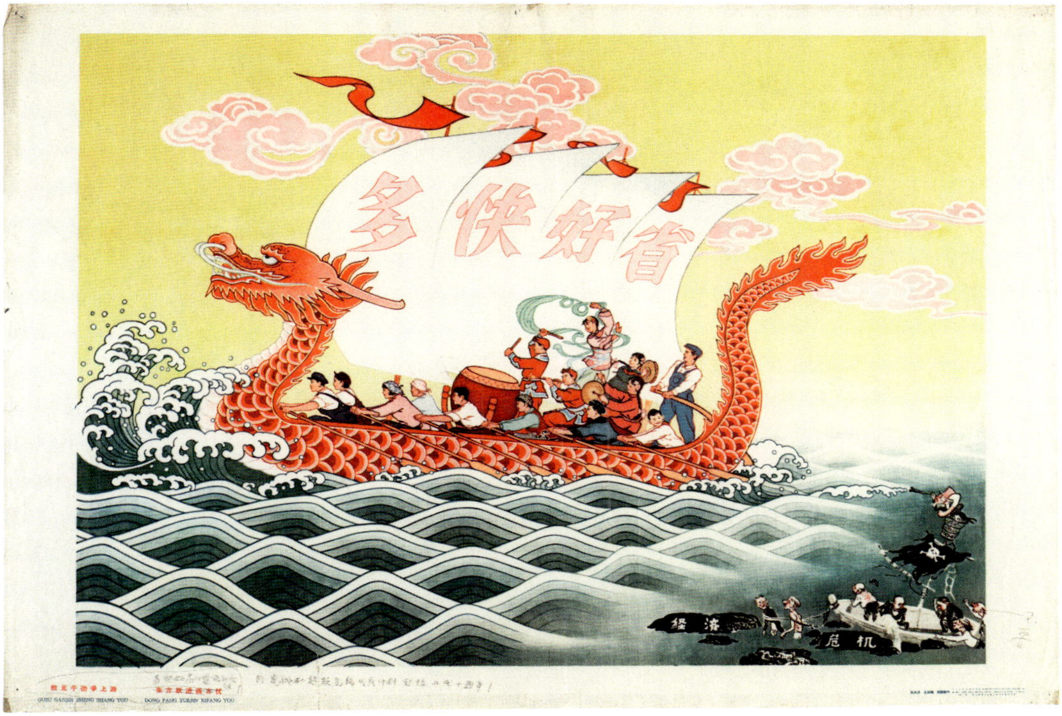

Go all out and aim high. The East leaps forward; the West is worried, 1958.
Geht hinaus und steckt euch hohe Ziele. Der Osten ist auf dem Vormarsch; der Westen ist beunruhigt, 1958.

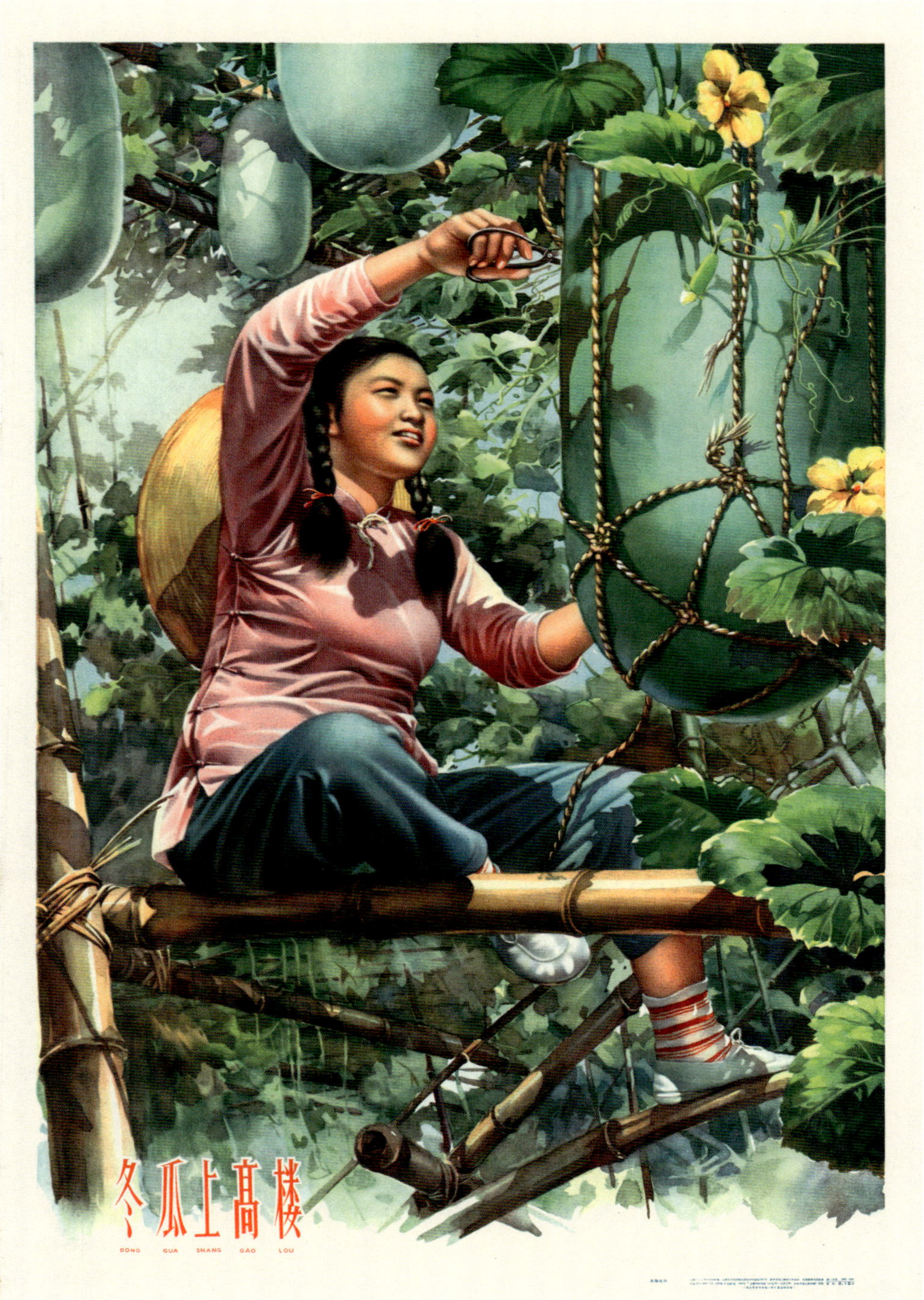

A high pile of winter gourds, 1959.
Hoch aufgetürmte Winterkürbisse, 1959.

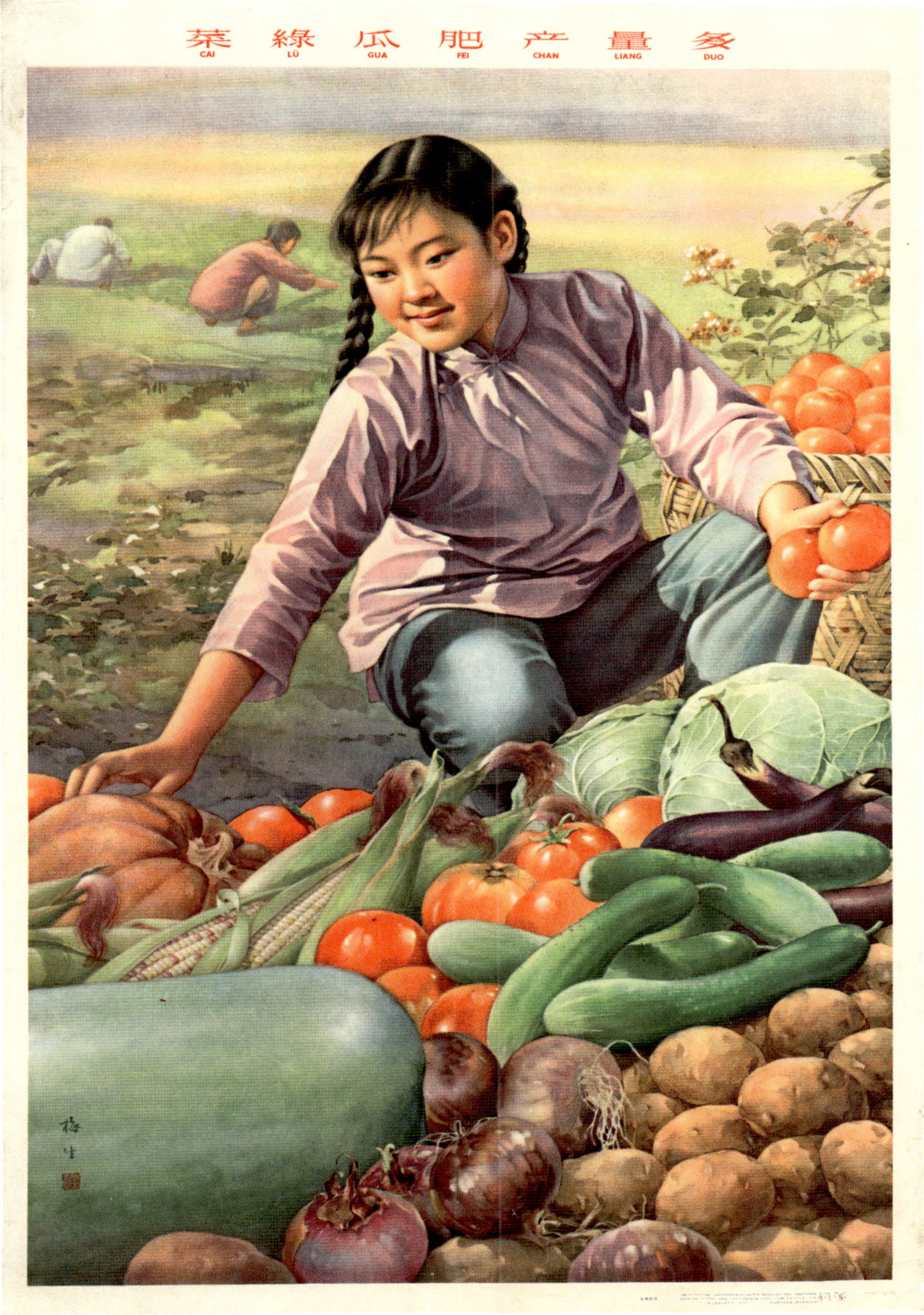

The vegetables are green, the cucumbers plump, the yield is abundant, 1959.
Das Gemüse ist grün, die Gurken sind dick, die Ernte ist reich, 1959.

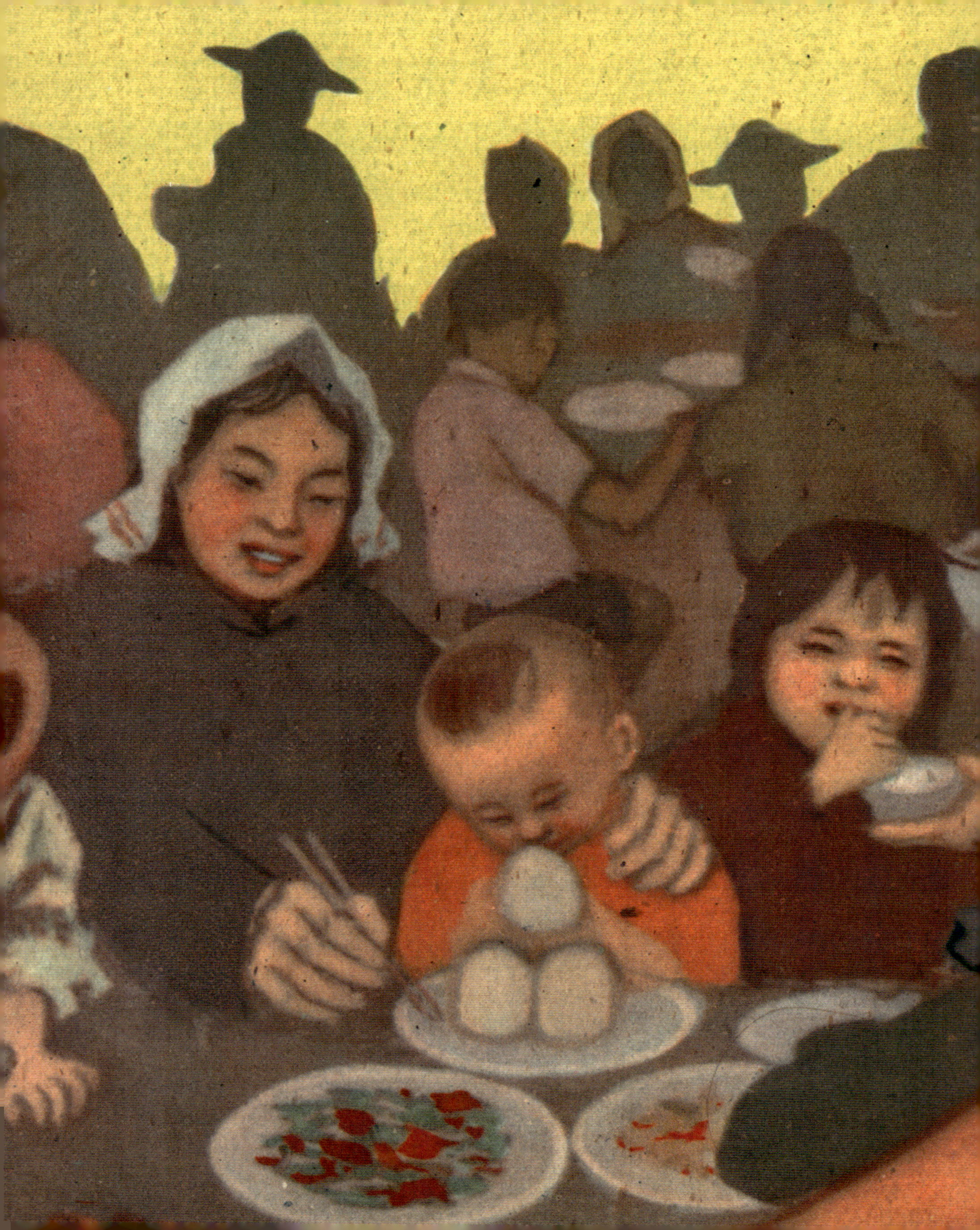

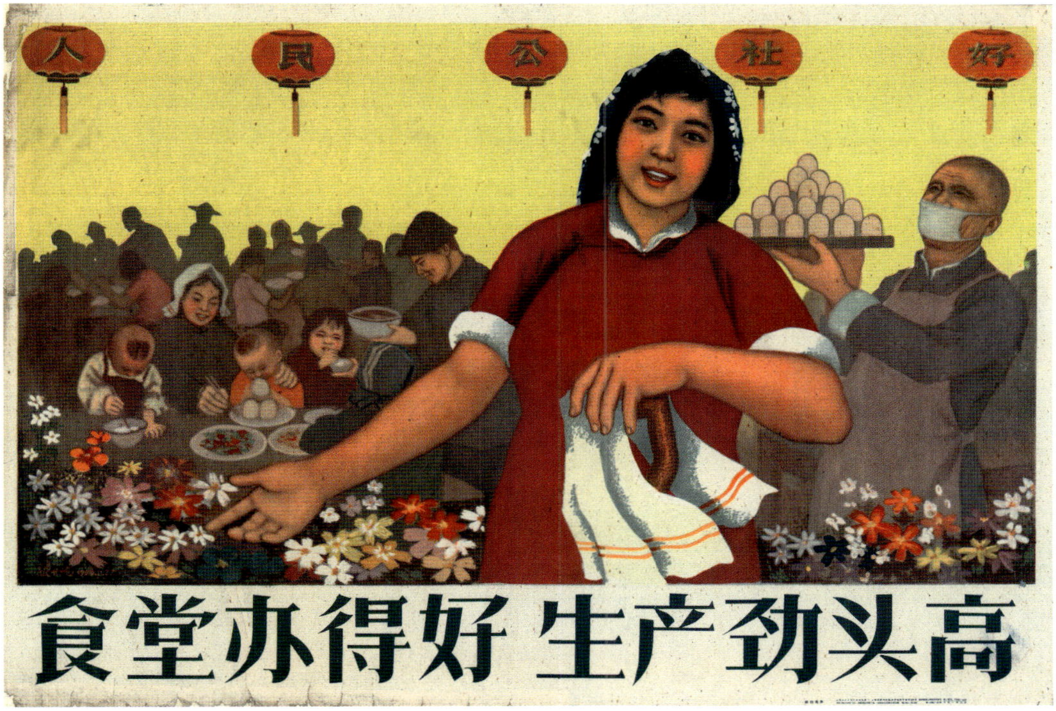

When the dining hall is well-run, the spirit of production will rise, 1959.
Wenn der Speisesaal gut geführt ist, steigt der Produktionsgeist, 1959.

The canteens of the people's communes serve free meals, but are compulsory. People are not allowed to eat with their families anymore: they must merge into the collective. Eating in the canteen also saves time that could be spent working.

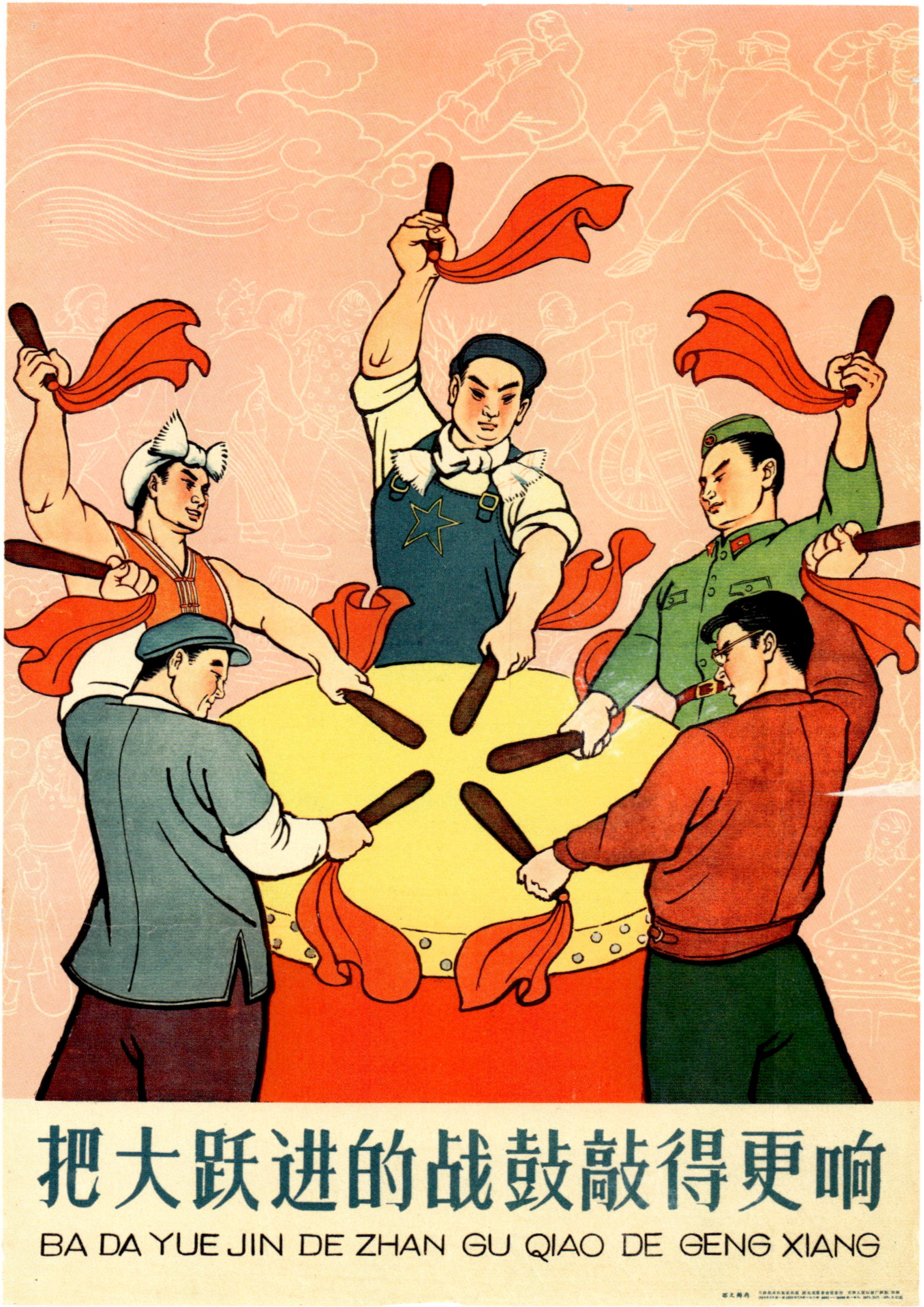

Strike the battle drum of the Great Leap Forward ever louder, 1959.
Schlagt die Kriegstrommel des "Großen Sprungs nach vorn" immer lauter, 1959.

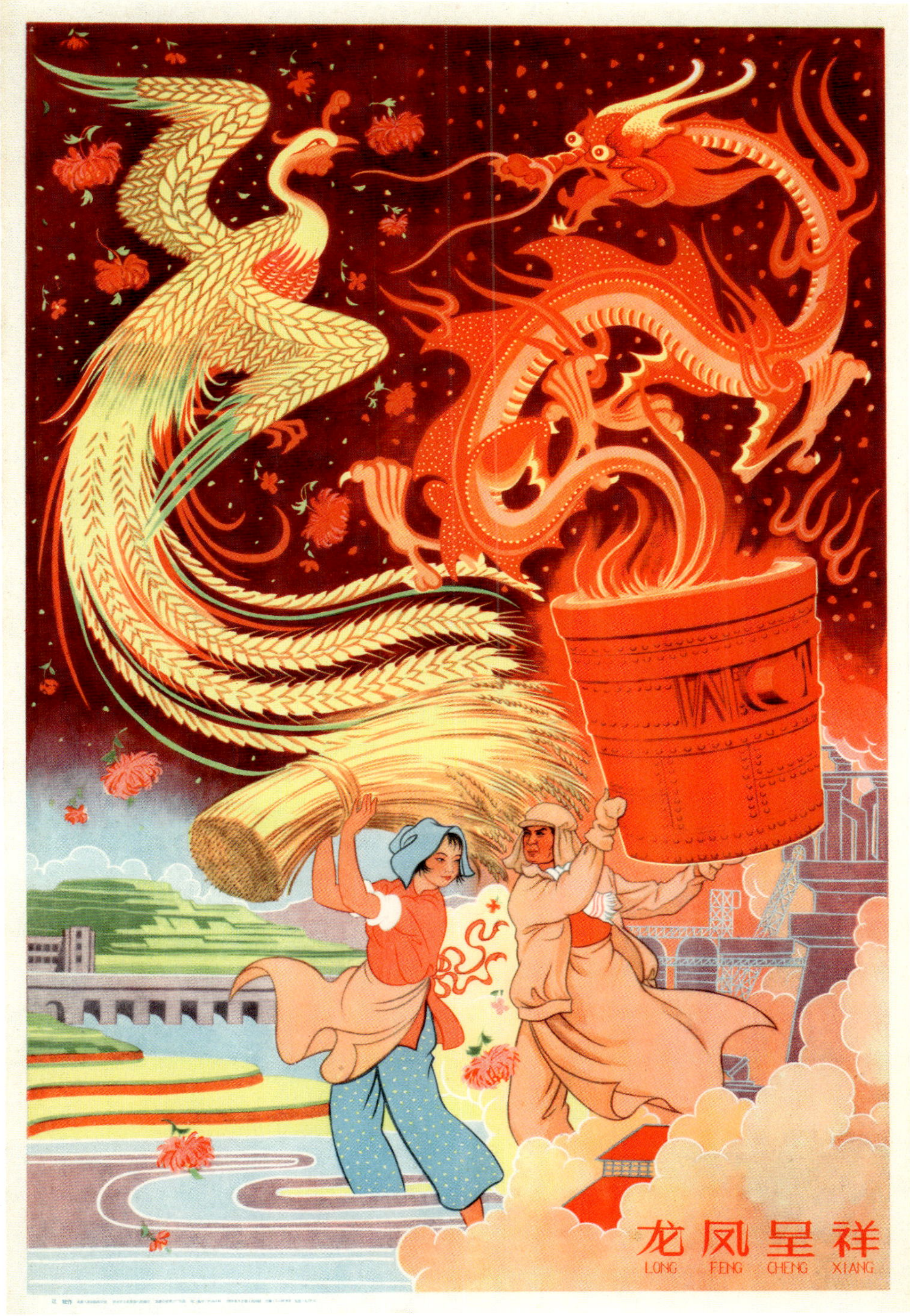

Prosperity brought by the dragon and the phoenix, 1959.
Drache und Phönix bringen Wohlstand, 1959.

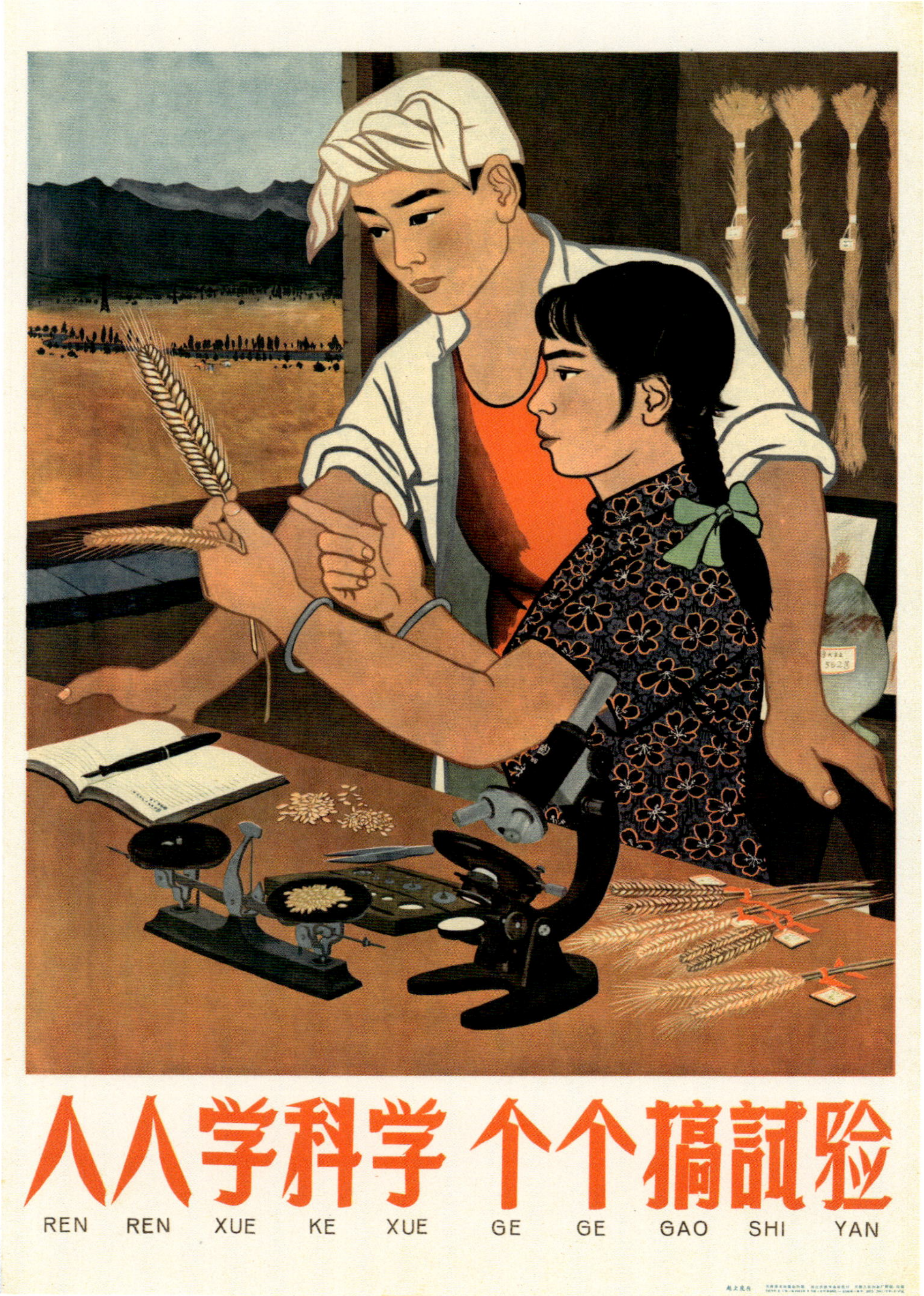

Everybody studies science, everybody does experiments, 1959.
Jeder studiert die Wissenschaften, jeder macht Versuche, 1959.

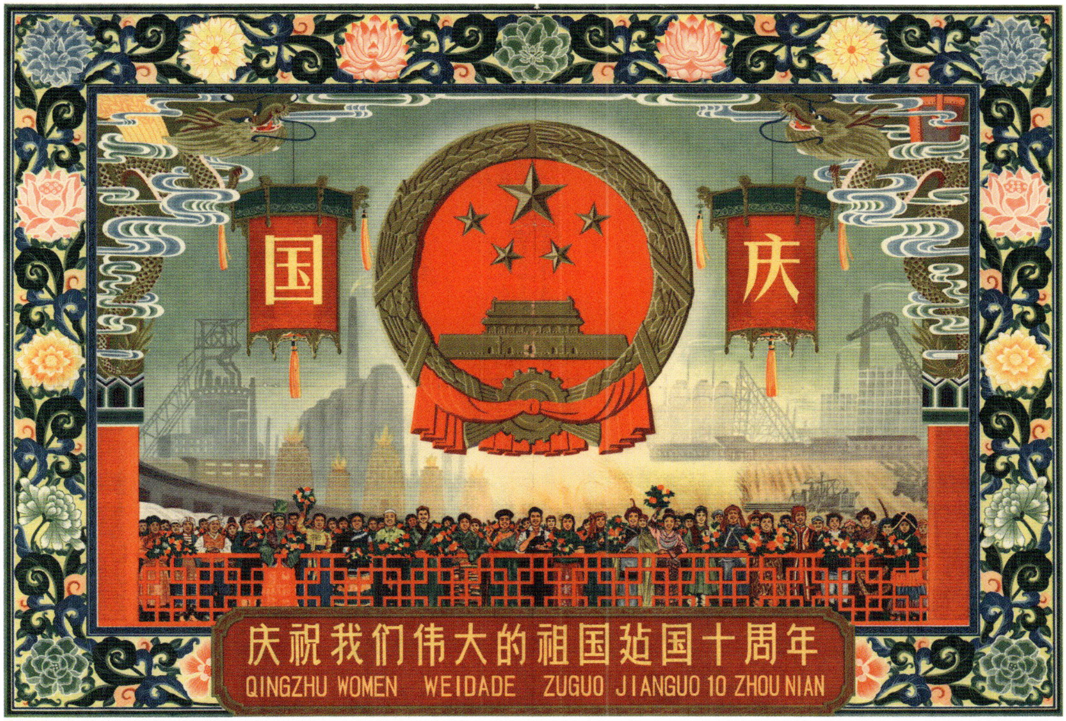

Celebrate the 10th anniversary of the founding of our great nation, 1959.
Feiert den zehnten Jahrestag der Gründung unserer großen Nation, 1959.

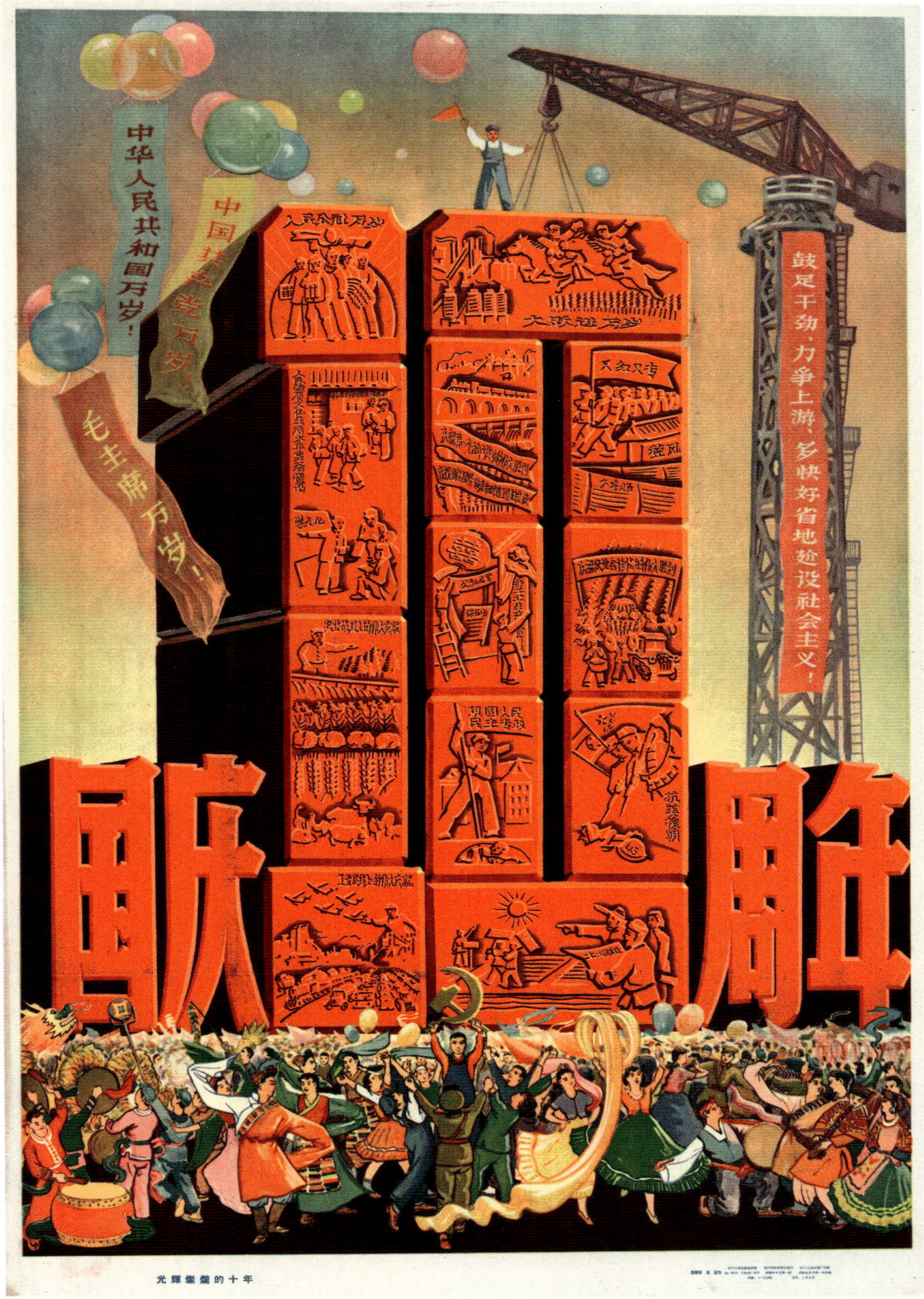

Ten gloriously bright years, 1959.
Zehn ruhmreiche und glanzvolle Jahre, 1959.

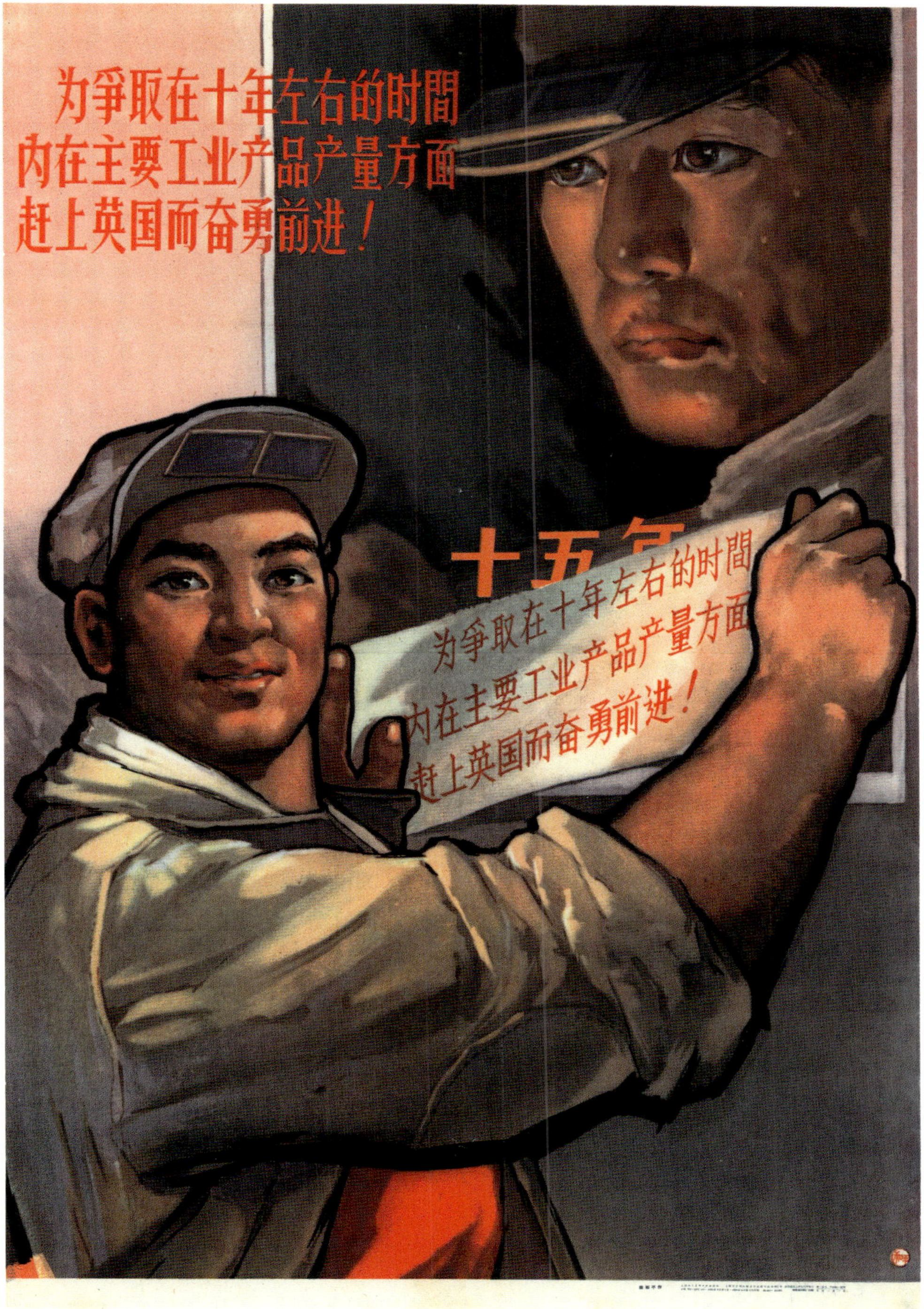

To catch up with England in the output of industrial products in about ten years time, we bravely forge ahead! 1959.

Um die industrielle Produktionsleistung Englands in etwa zehn Jahren zu erreichen, kämpfen wir uns mutig voran! 1959.

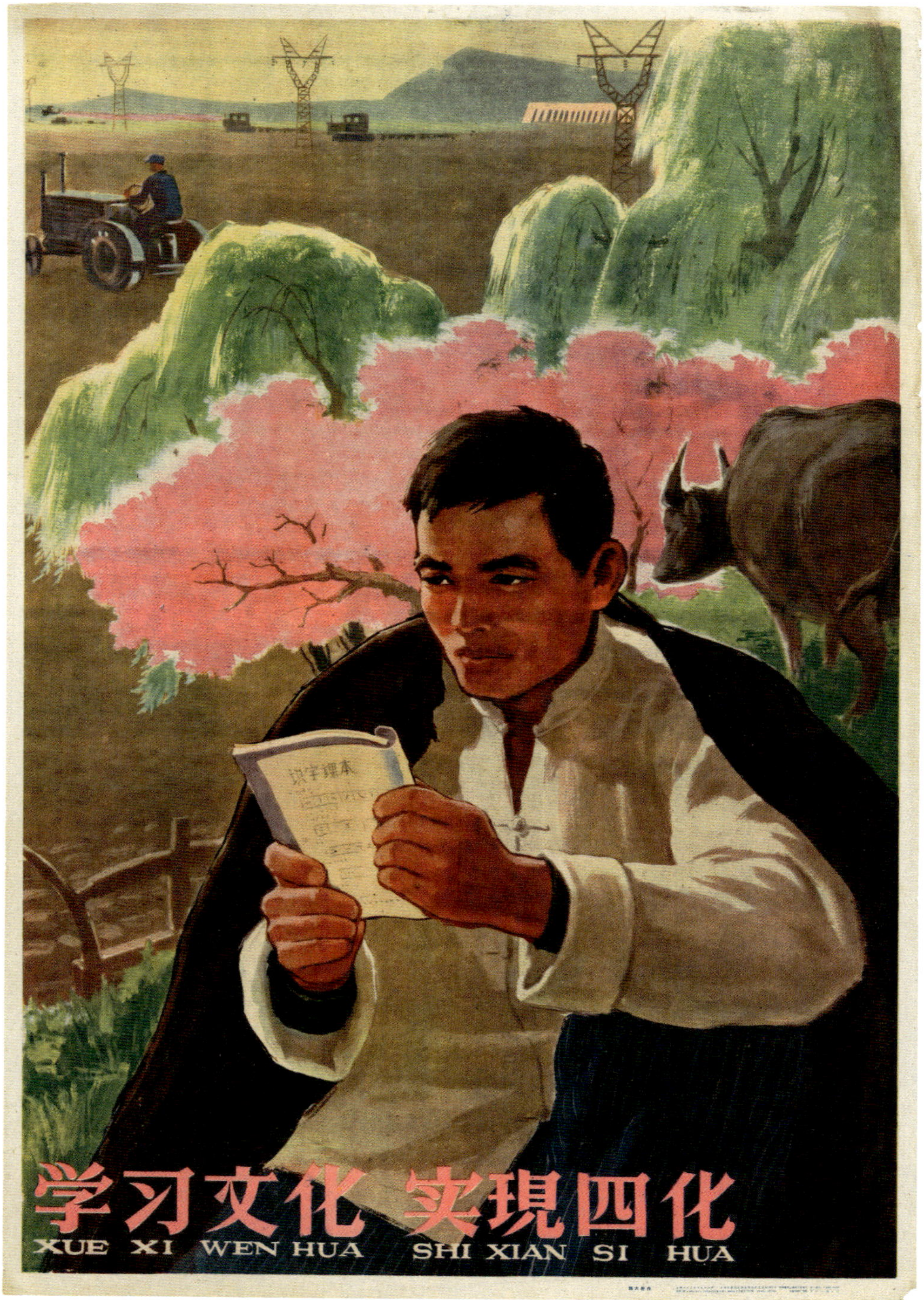

Study culture and realise the Four Modernizations, 1959.
Studiert die Kultur und vergegenwärtigt euch die "Vier Modernisierungen", 1959.

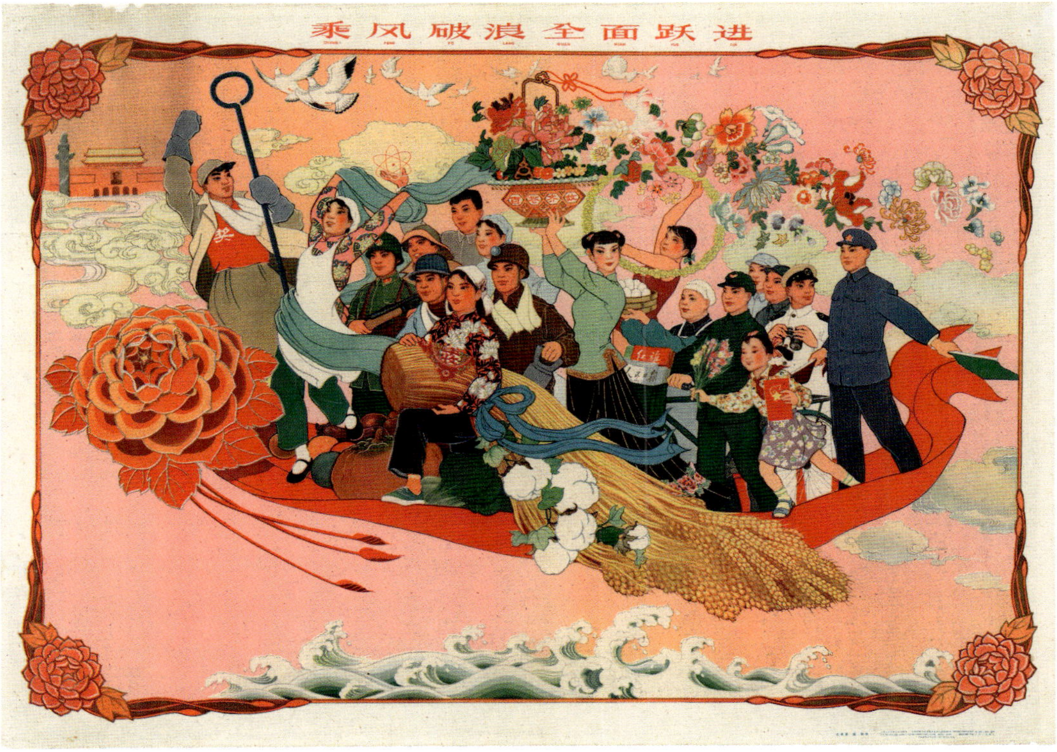

Ride the wind and part waves to realize a leap forward in all fields, 1960.
Reitet den Wind und teilt die Wellen, um auf allen Gebieten einen großen Sprung nach vorne zu machen, 1960.

Be indomitable in training, to strengthen the physique of officers and soldiers, 1960.
Seid im Training unbezwingbar und stärkt die Kräfte der Offiziere und Soldaten, 1960.

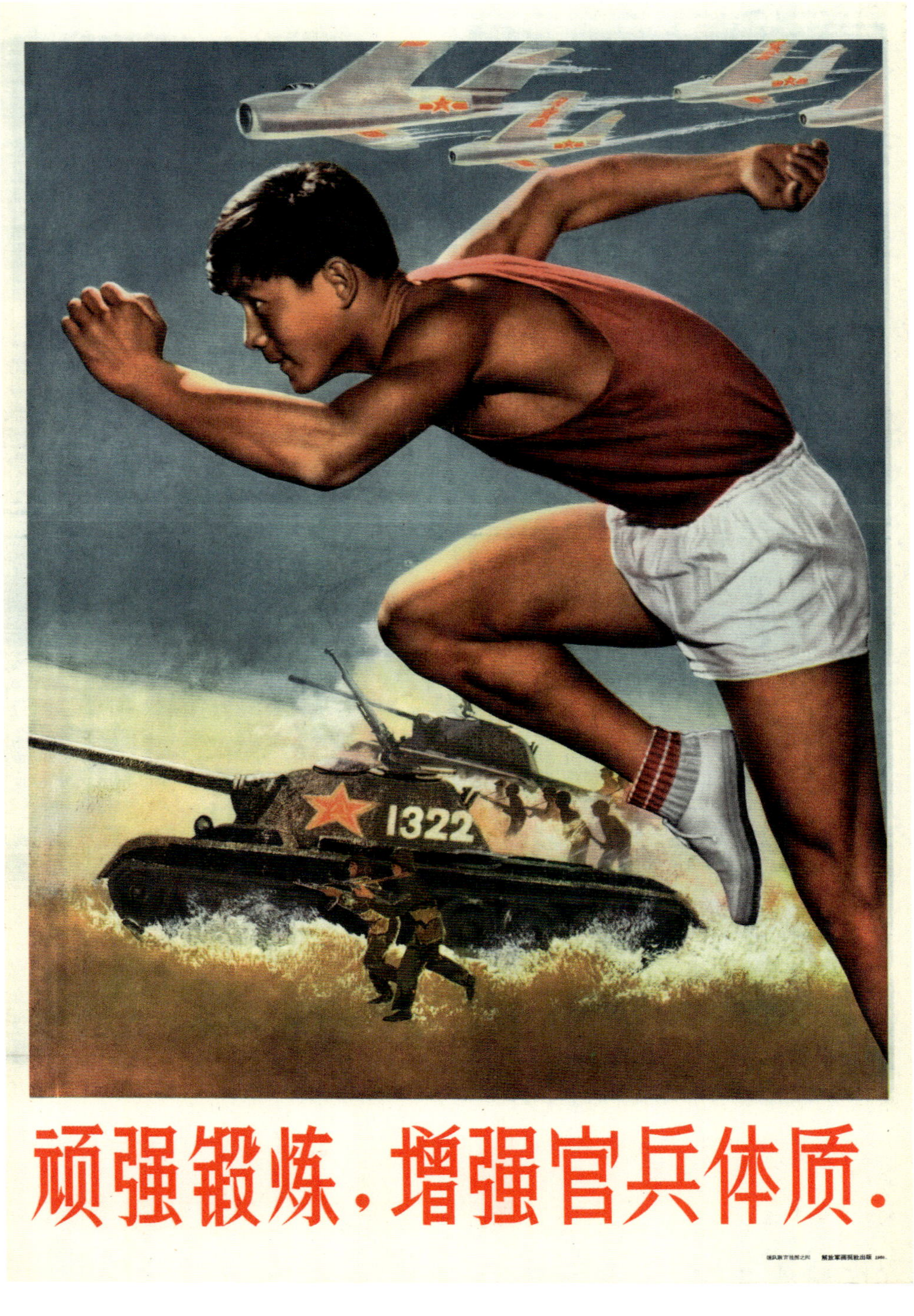

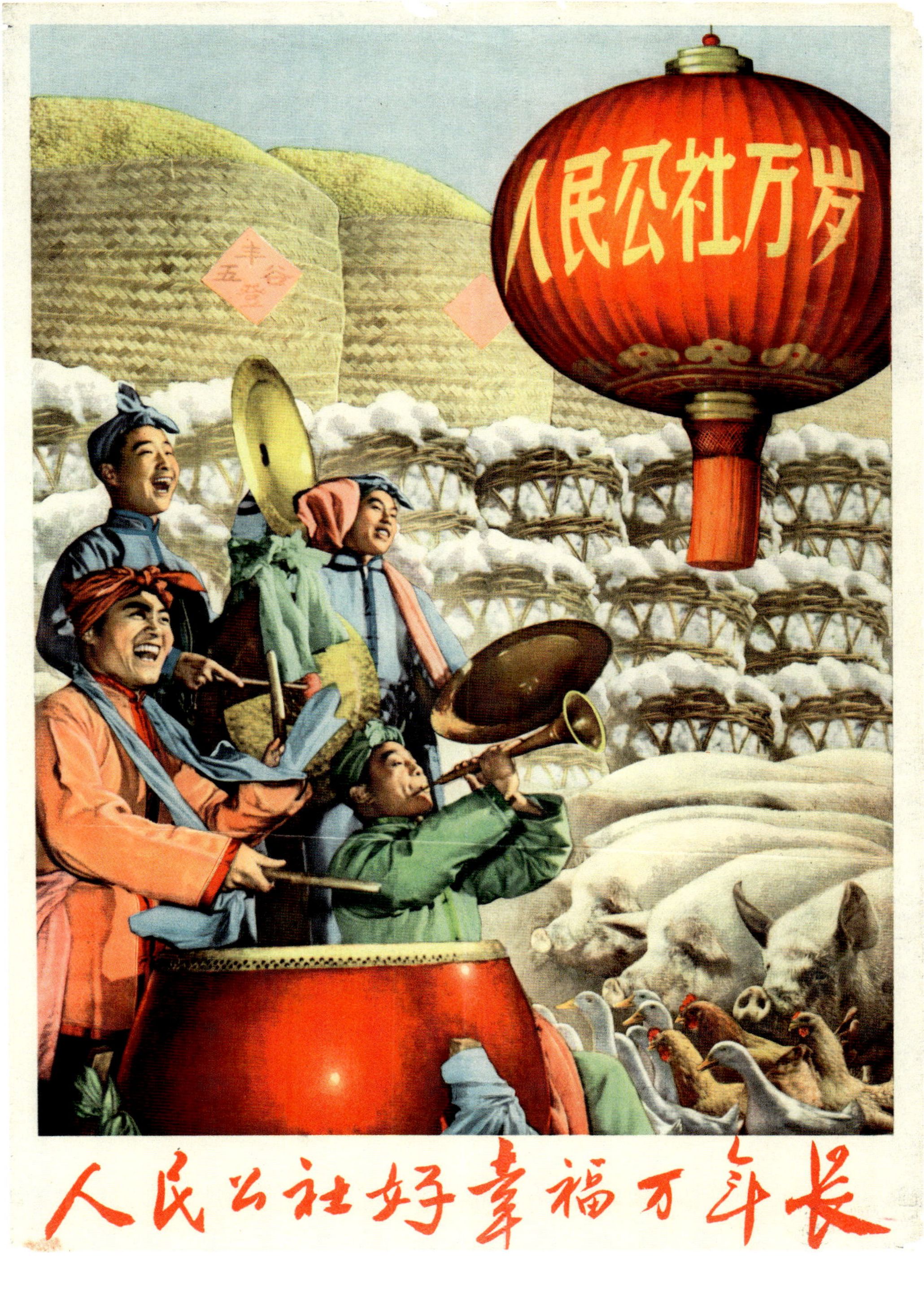

The people's commune is good; happiness will last for ten thousand years, c. 1960.
Die Volkskommune ist gut; die Glückseligkeit wird zehntausend Jahre währen, um 1960.

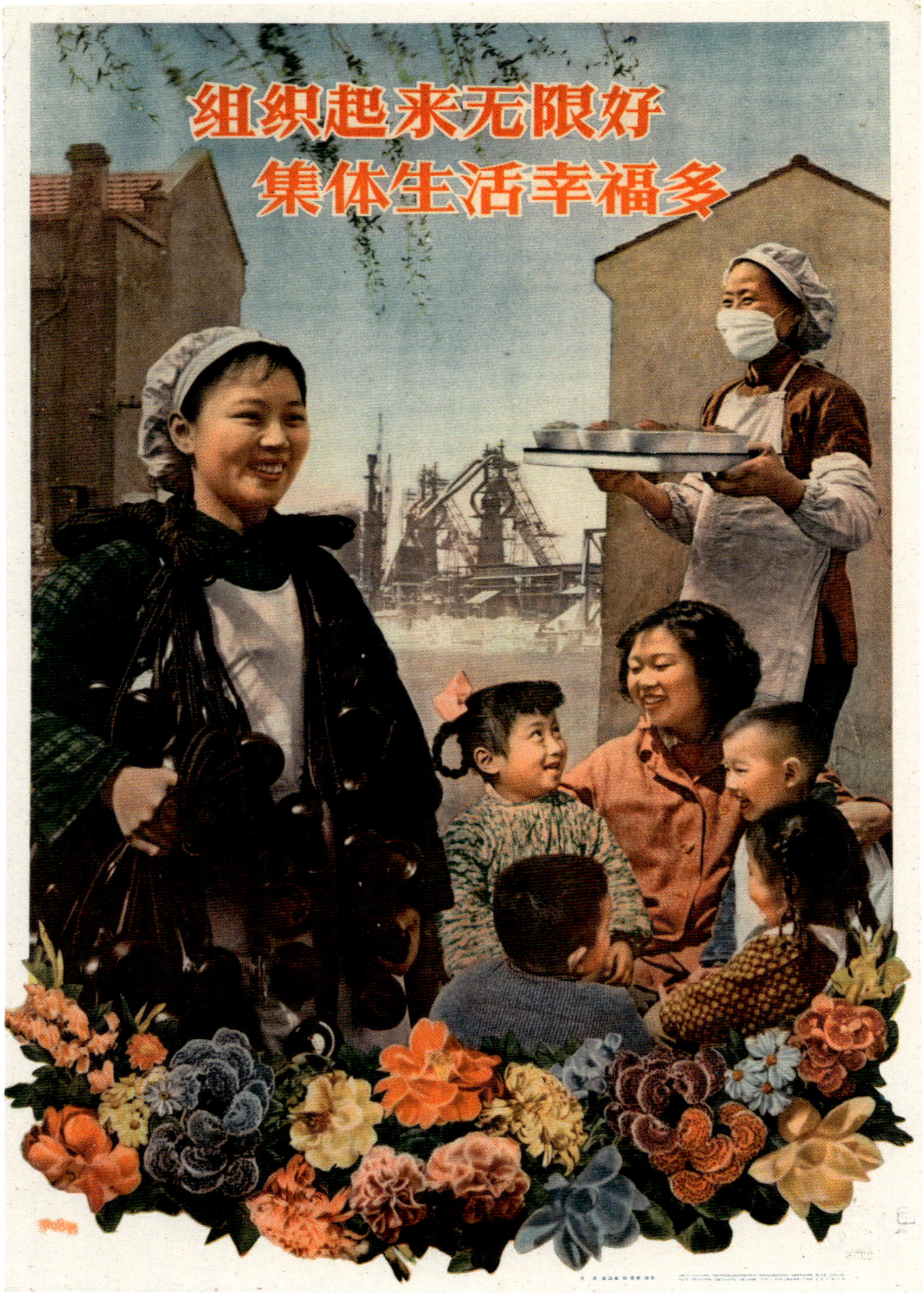

Getting organized is boundlessly good. Collective life brings a lot of happiness, 1960.
Sich zu organisieren ist uneingeschränkt gut. Das Leben in der Kollektive macht glücklich, 1960.

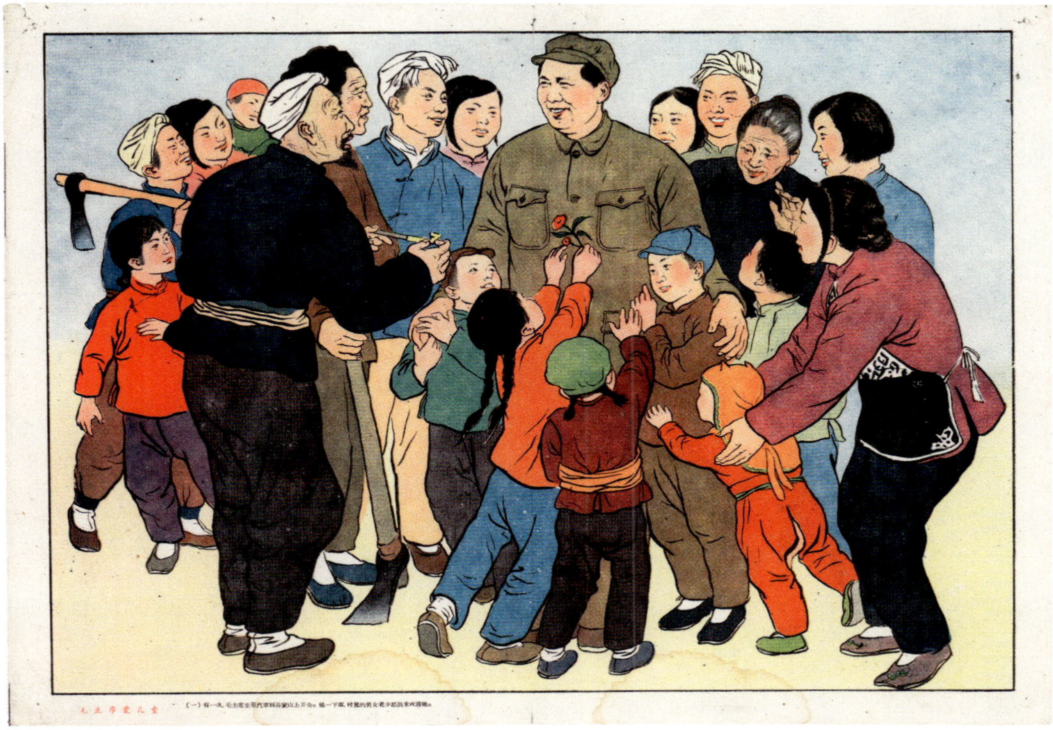

Chairman Mao loves children (1). Chairman Mao visits a peasant village, 1960.
Der Vorsitzende Mao liebt Kinder (1). Der Vorsitzende Mao besucht ein Bauerndorf. 1960.

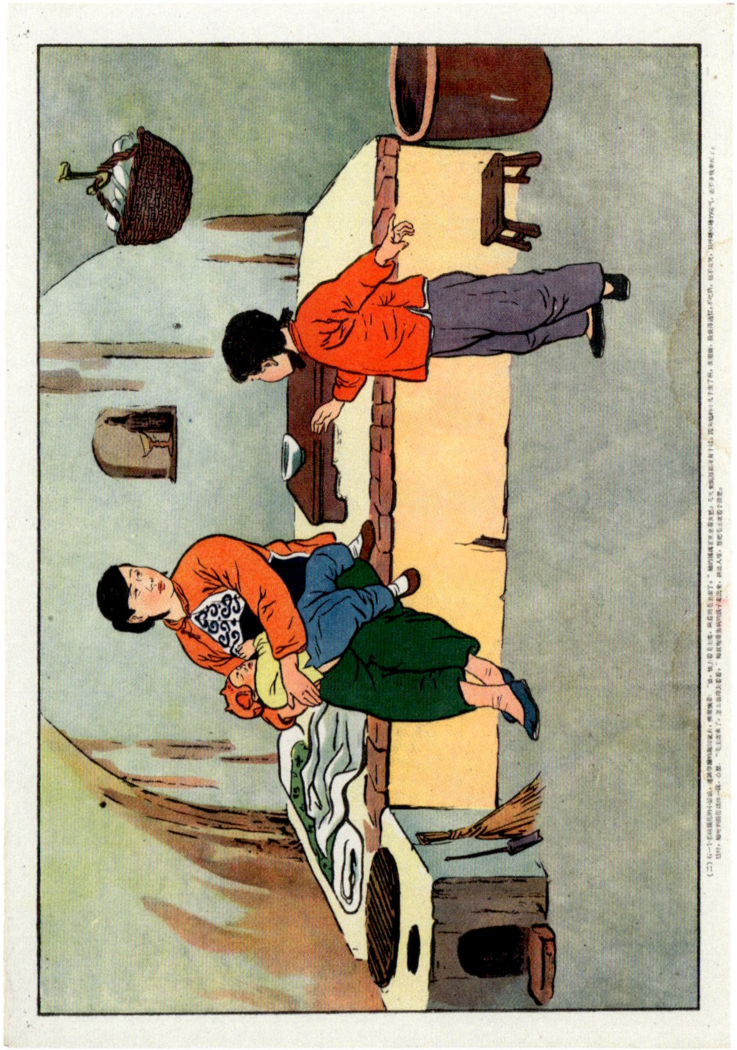

106

Chairman Mao loves children (2). A mother is unable to come and see the Chairman; her child is ill. Another child urges the mother to go and see Mao. 1960.

Der Vorsitzende Mao liebt Kinder (2). Eine Mutter ist nicht in der Lage zu kommen, um den Vorsitzenden zu sehen, denn ihr Kind ist krank. Ein anderes Kind drängt die Mutter zu gehen und Mao zu sehen. 1960.

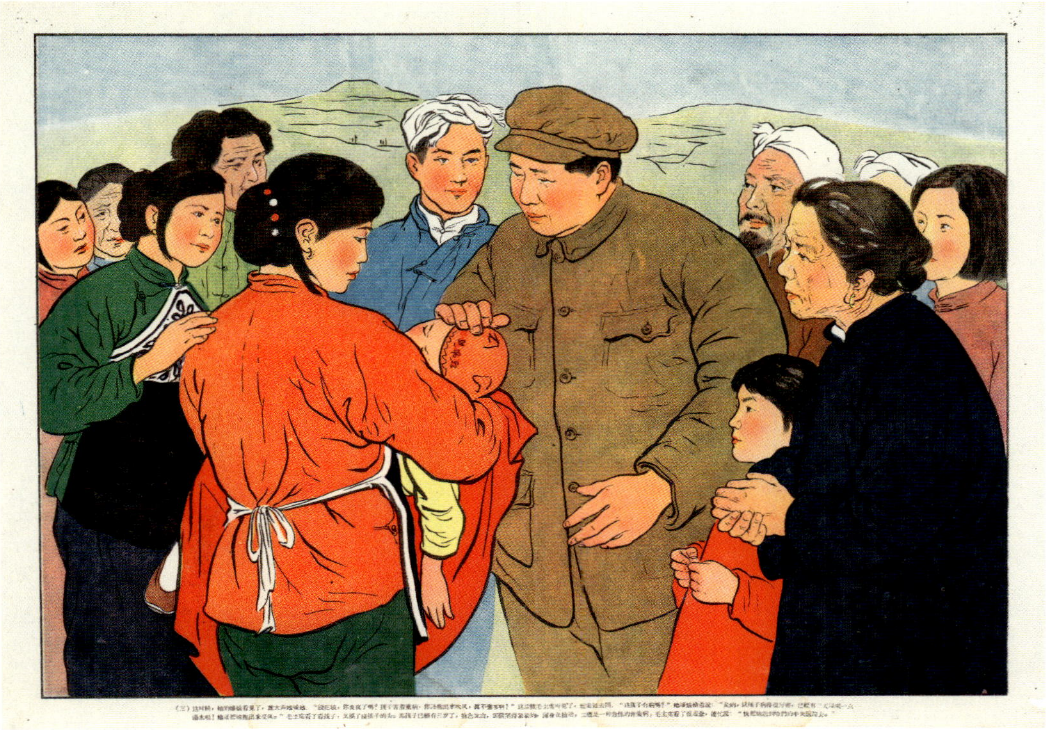

Chairman Mao loves children (3). Mao is informed of the situation. 1960.

Der Vorsitzende Mao liebt Kinder (3). Mao wird über die Situation in Kenntnis gesetzt. 1960.

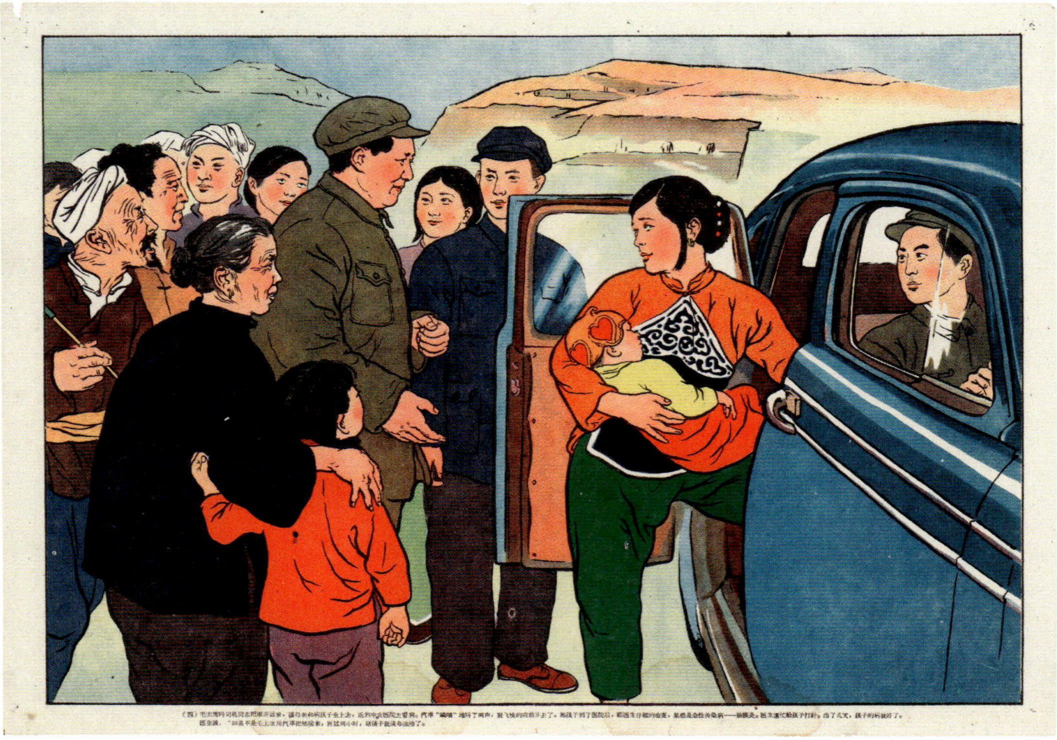

Chairman Mao loves children (4). Mao sends mother and child to a hospital in his car. 1960.

Der Vorsitzende Mao liebt Kinder (4). Mao schickt Mutter und Kind in seinem Auto zu einem Krankenhaus. 1960.

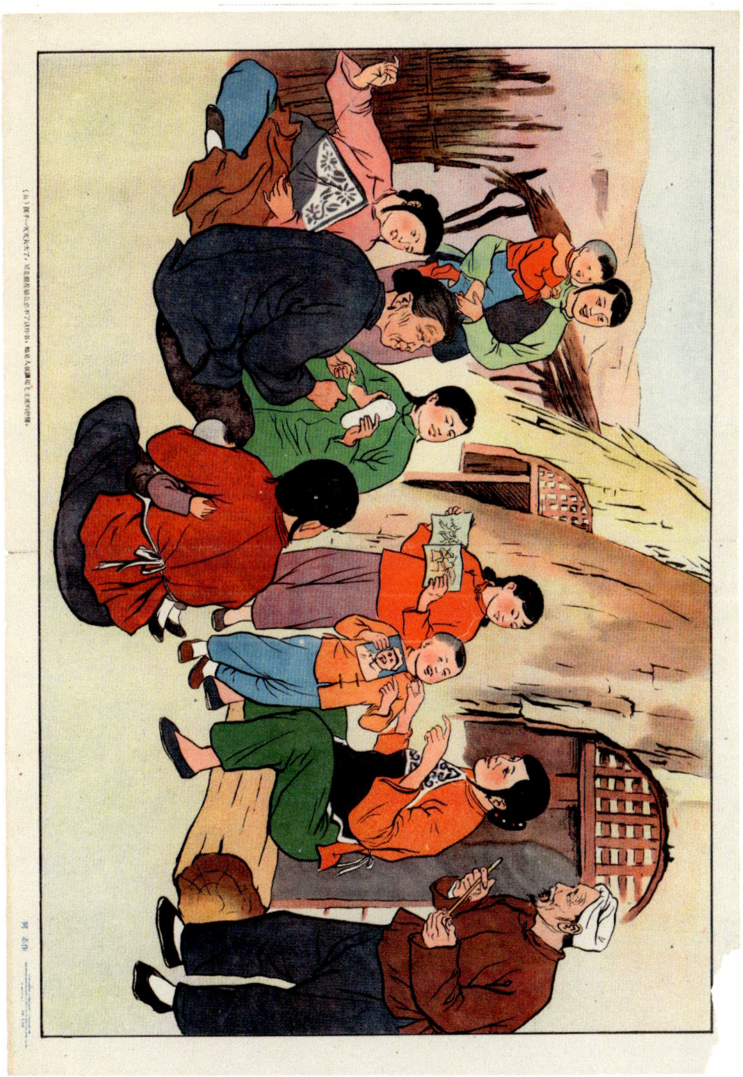

Chairman Mao loves children (5). The child recovers and tells the story of his salvation to the people of the village. 1960.
Der Vorsitzende Mao liebt Kinder (5). Das Kind ist wieder gesund und erzählt den Leuten aus seinem Dorf die Geschichte seiner Rettung. 1960.

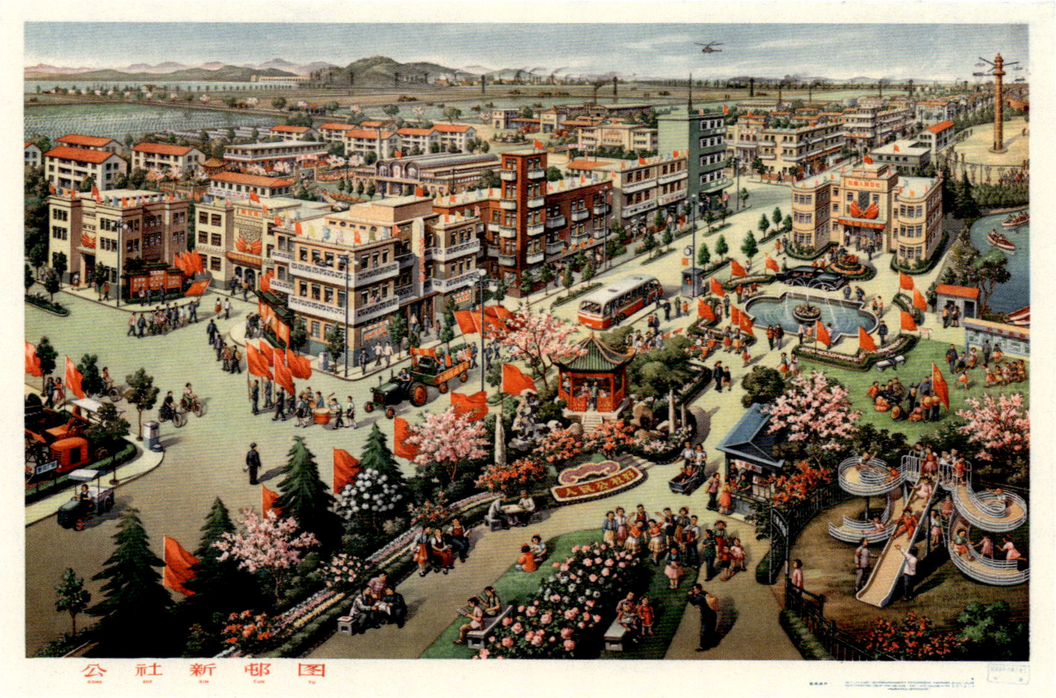

The new center of the commune, 1961.
Das neue Zentrum der Kommune, 1961.

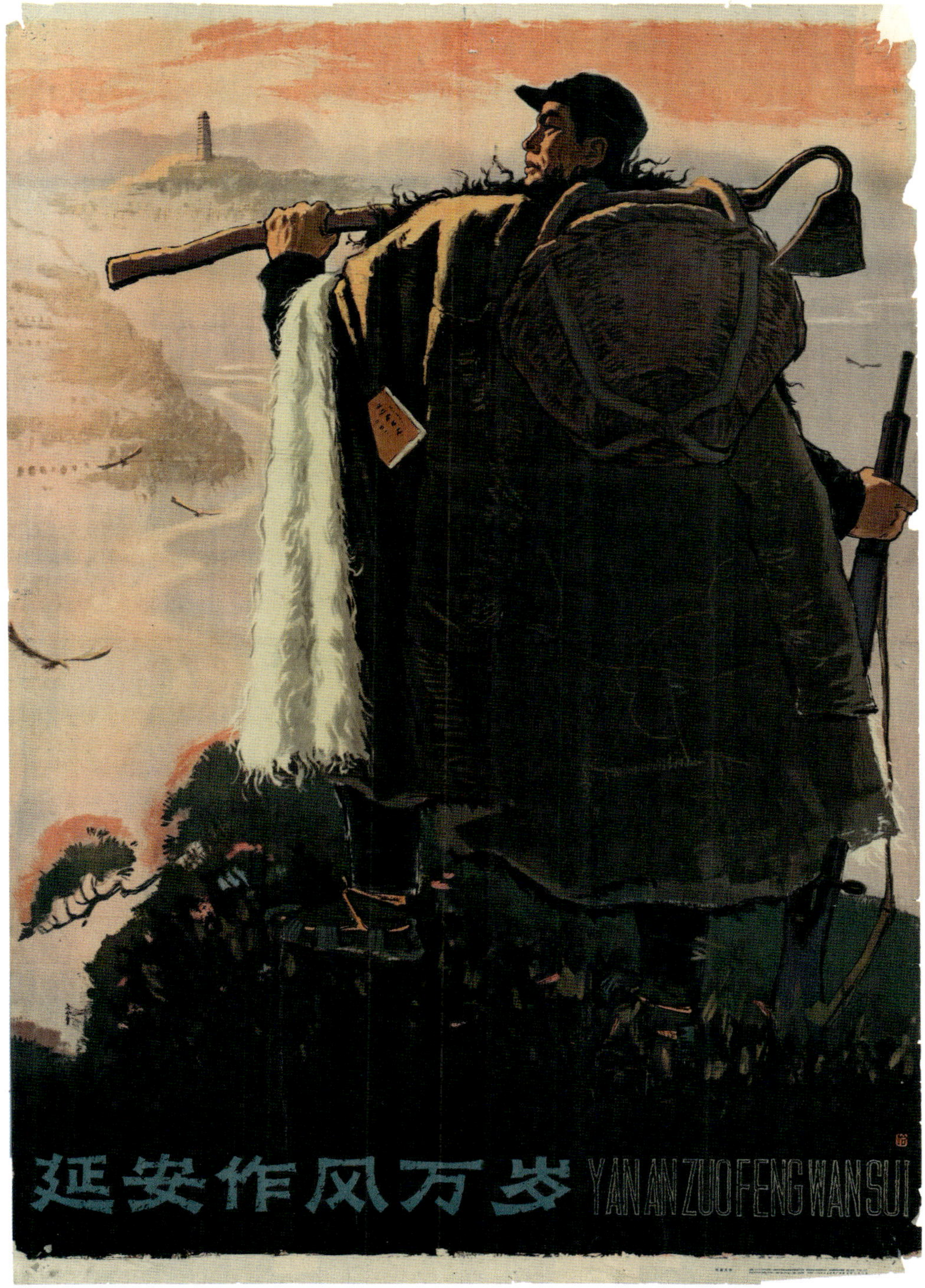

Long live the Yan'an spirit, 1961.
Lang lebe der Geist Yan'ans, 1961.

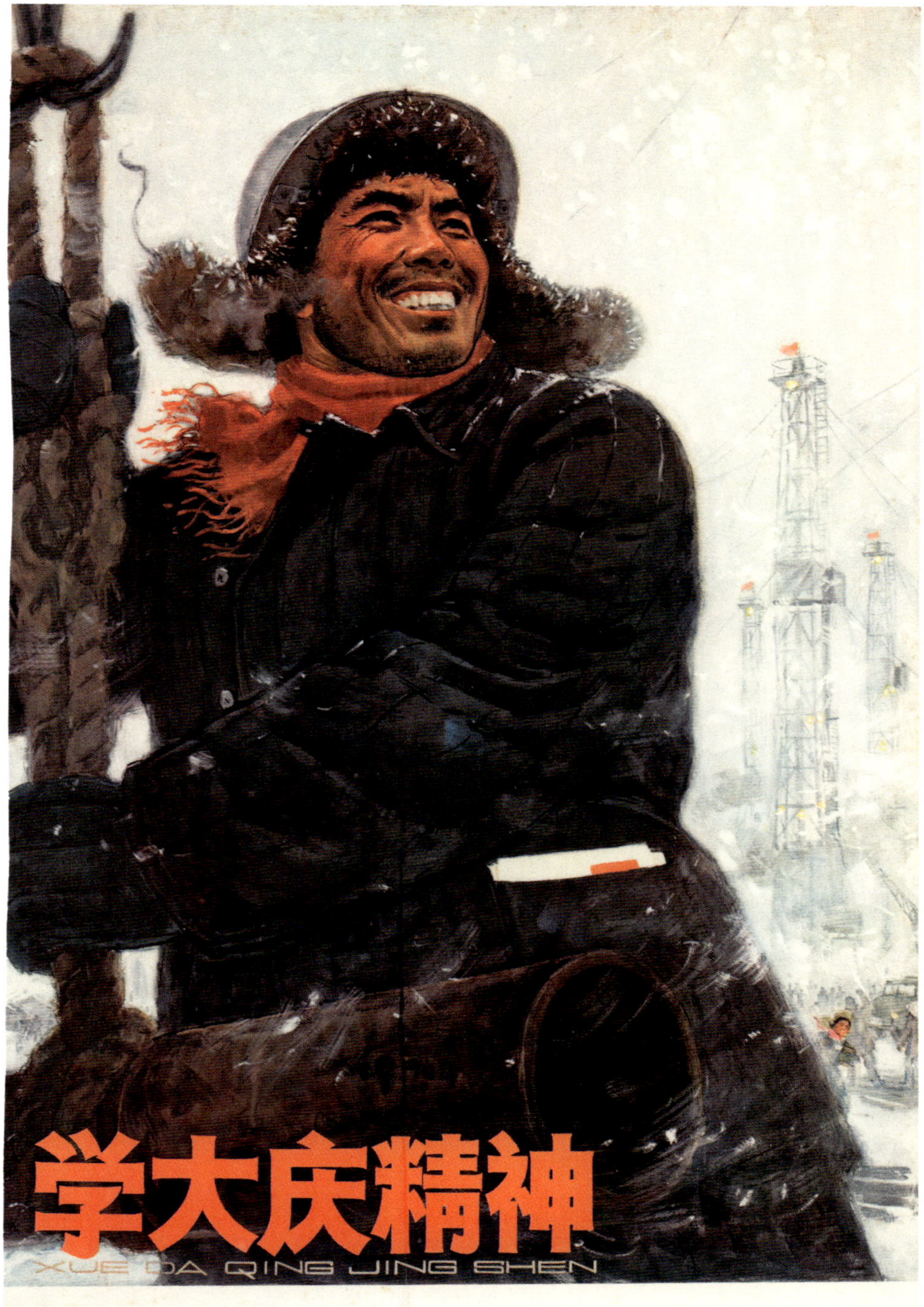

Study the spirit of Daqing, 1965.
Befasst euch mit dem Geist Daqings, 1965.

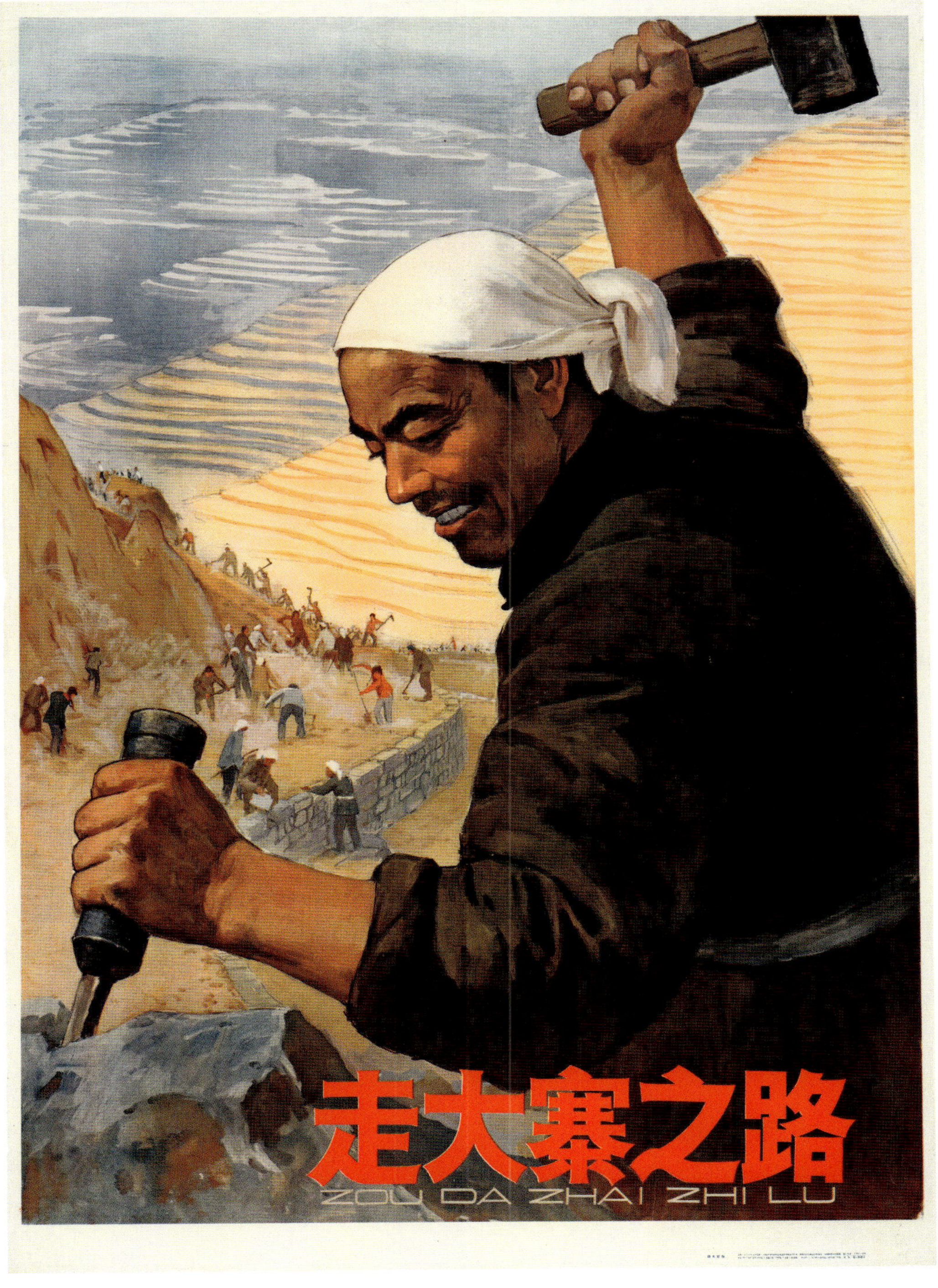

Walk the road of Dazhai, 1965.
Tretet in die Fußstapfen Dazhais, 1965.

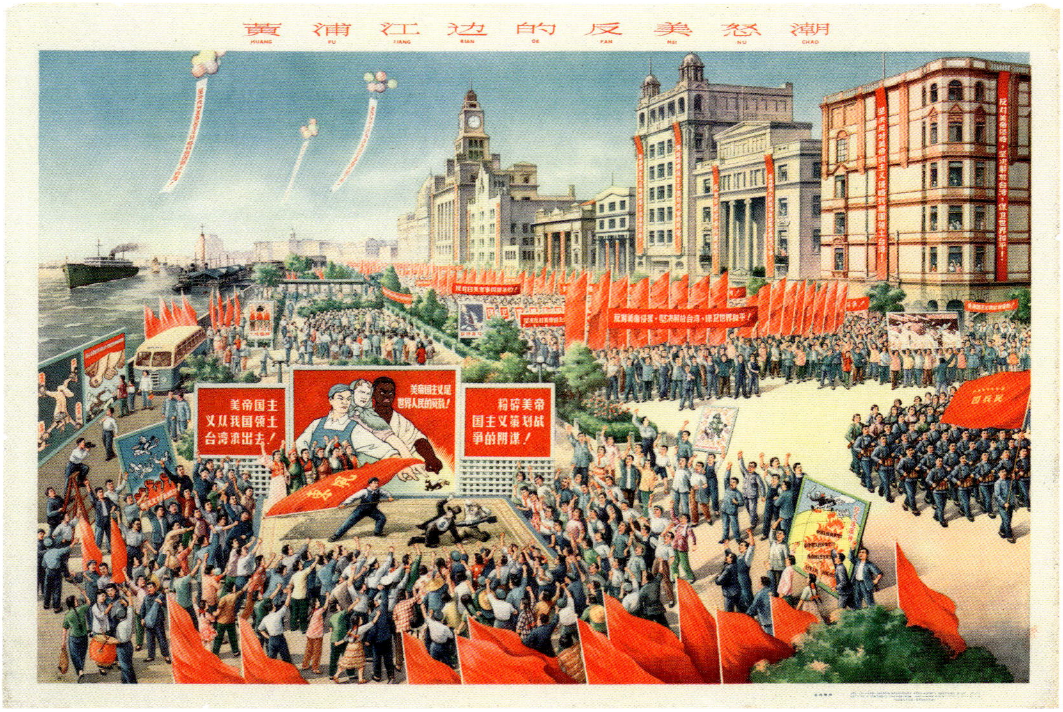

Anti-American wave of rage next to the Huangpu river, 1961.
Antiamerikanische Welle des Zorns am Ufer des Huangpu Flusses, 1961.

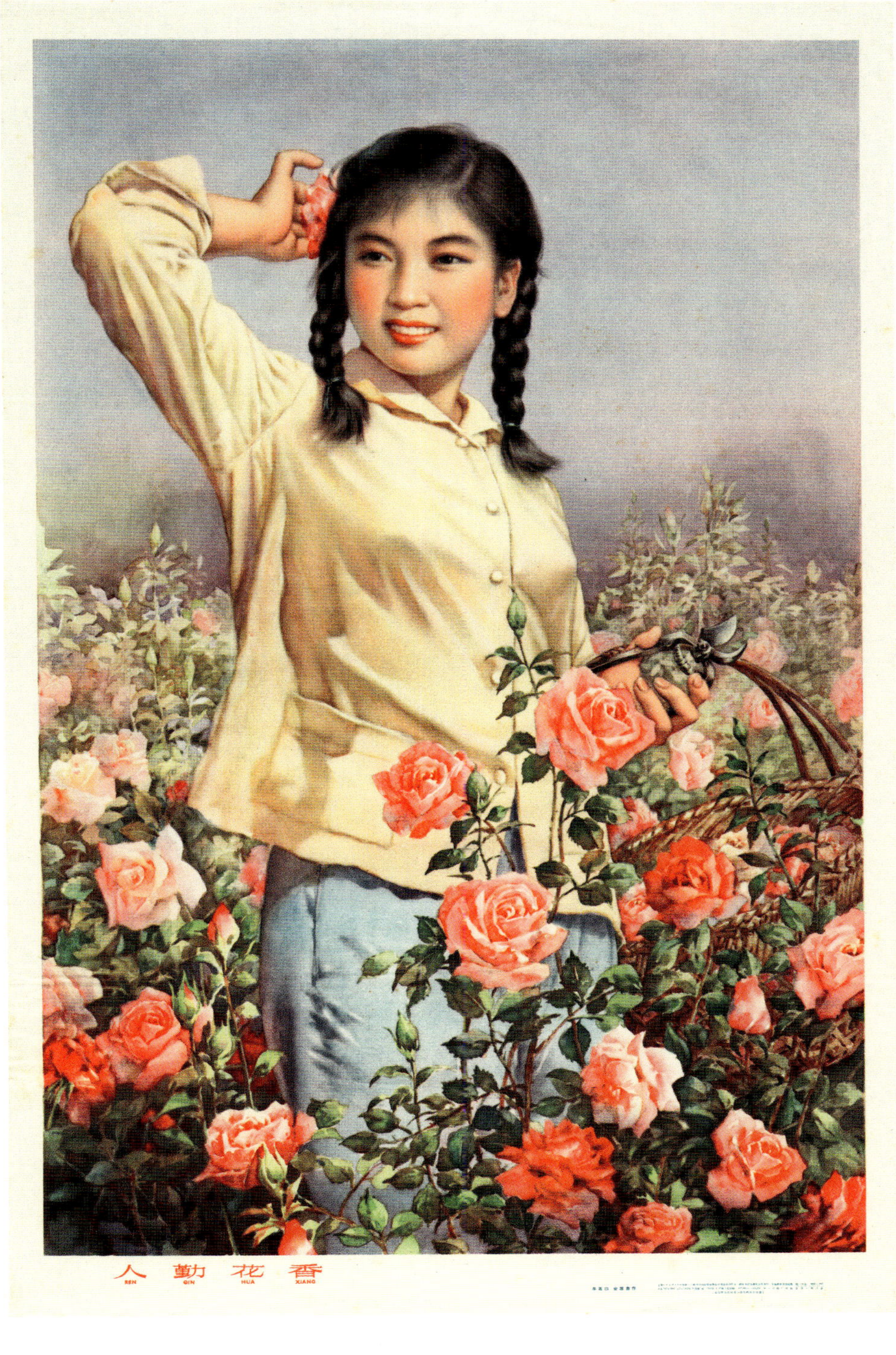

Man works hard; flowers are fragrant, 1962.
Die Menschen arbeiten hart; die Blumen duften, 1962.

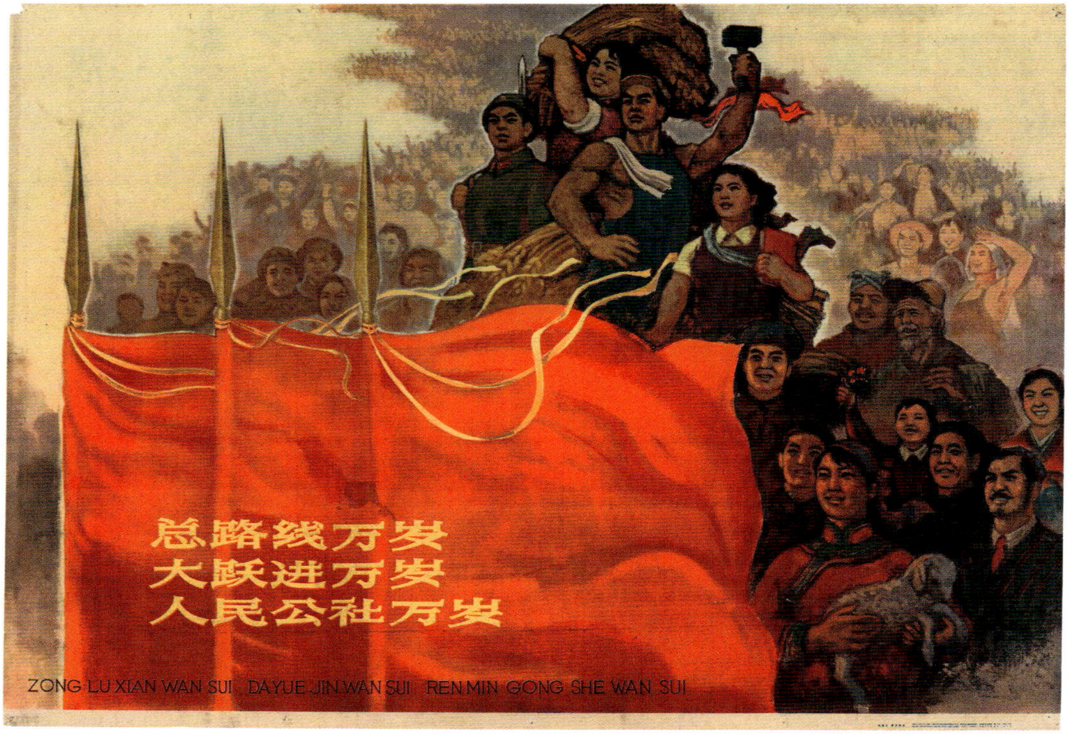

Long live the General Line, long live the Great Leap Forward, long live the People's Communes, 1963.

Lang lebe Generallinie, lang lebe der „Große Sprung nach vorn", lang mögen die Volkskommunen leben, 1963.

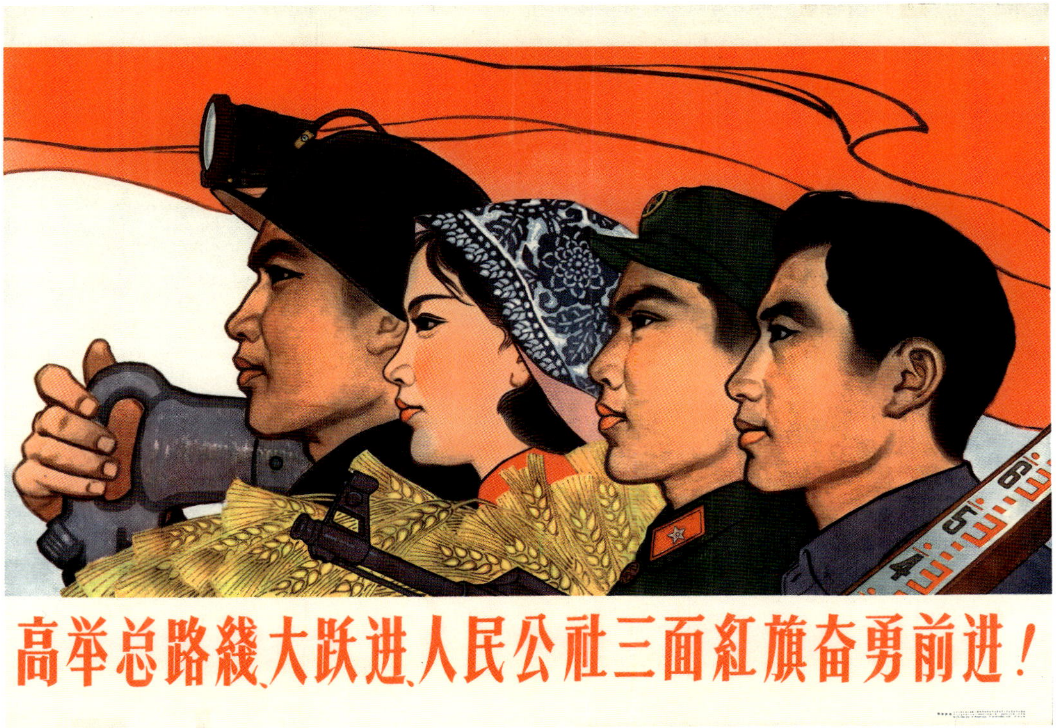

Hold high the banner of the General Line, the Great Leap Forward and the three aspects of the people's commune, and advance bravely! 1963.
Haltet hoch die Fahne des Generalline, des "Großen Sprungs nach vorn" und der drei Grundsäulen der Volkskommune und schreitet mutig voran! 1963.

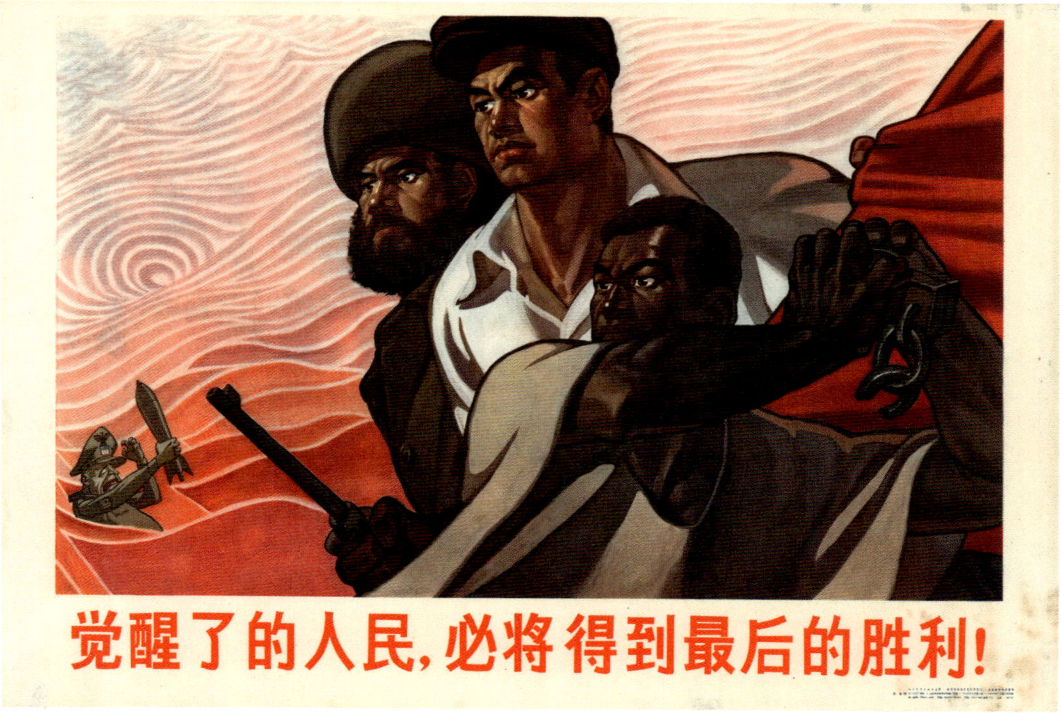

Awakened peoples, you will certainly attain the ultimate victory! 1963.
Erwachte Völker, ihr werdet den endgültigen Sieg erringen! 1963.

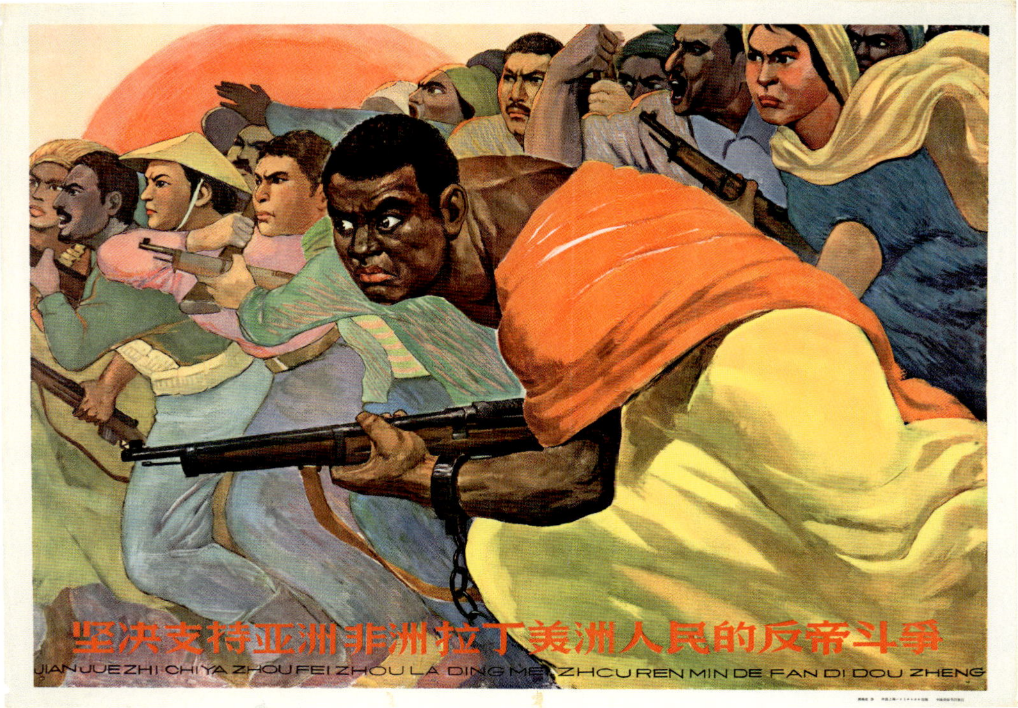

Vigorously support the anti-imperialist struggle of the peoples of Asia, Africa, and Latin America, 1964.
Unterstützt energisch den antiimperialistischen Kampf der Völker Asiens, Afrikas und Lateinamerikas, 1964.

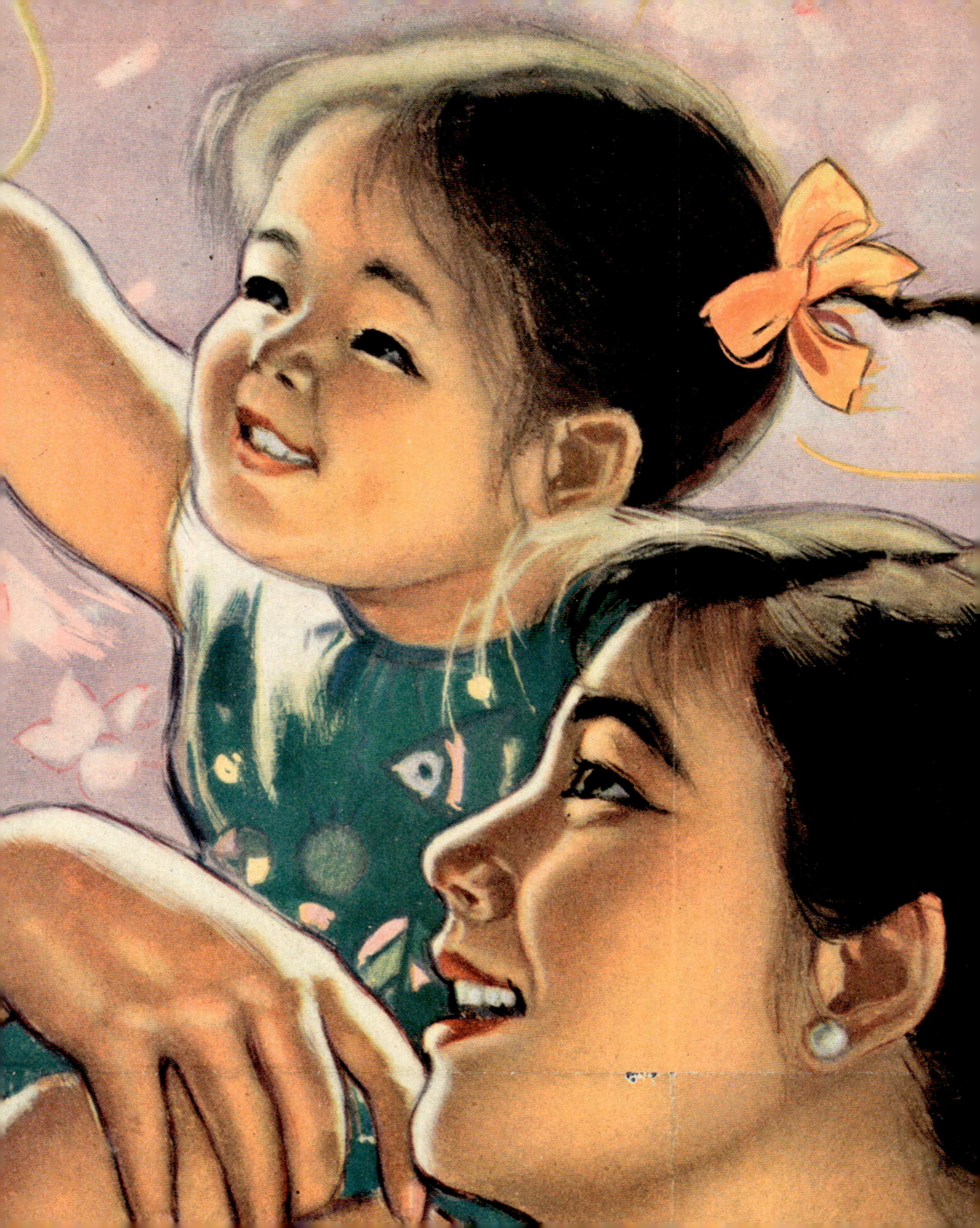

Each member of the Party must perform sincere criticism and self-criticism.
Jedes Mitglied der Partei muss wahre Kritik durchführen und selbstkritisch auftreten.

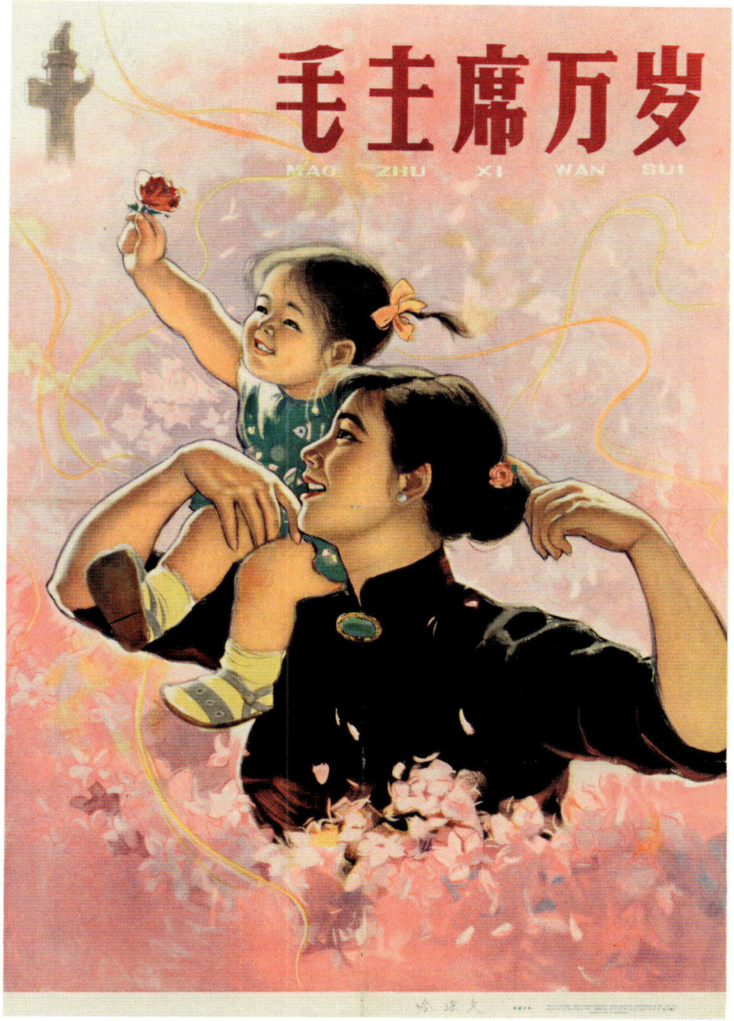

← A famous poster that will cause great problems for the designer during the Cultural Revolution: why did he not depict Mao? And why give prominence to such an elegant, bourgeois woman, instead of showing an ordinary worker?

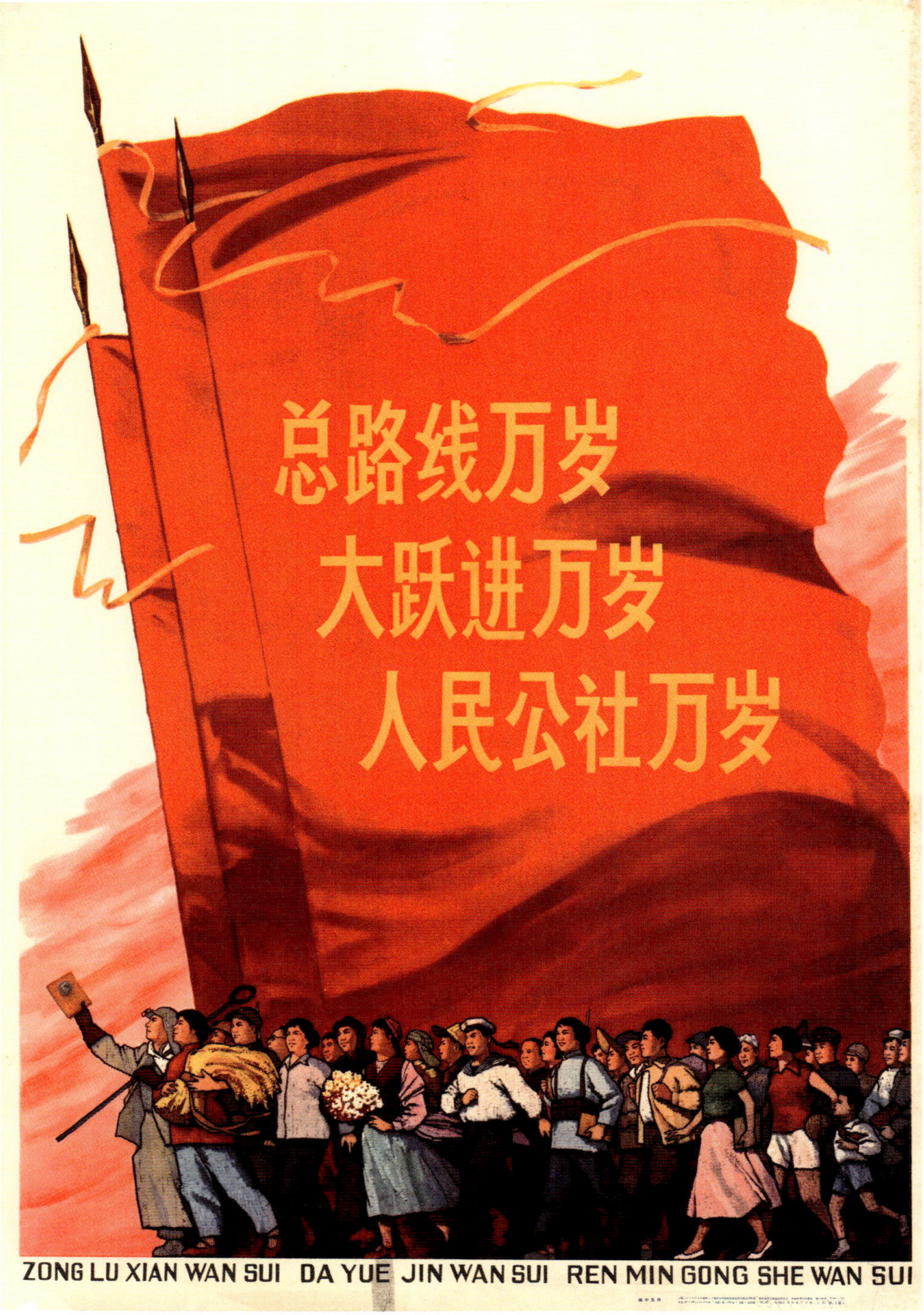

Long live the General Line, long live the Great Leap Forward, long live the People's Communes, 1964.

Lang lebe Generallinie, lang lebe der "Große Sprung nach vorne", lang mögen die Volkskommunen leben, 1964.

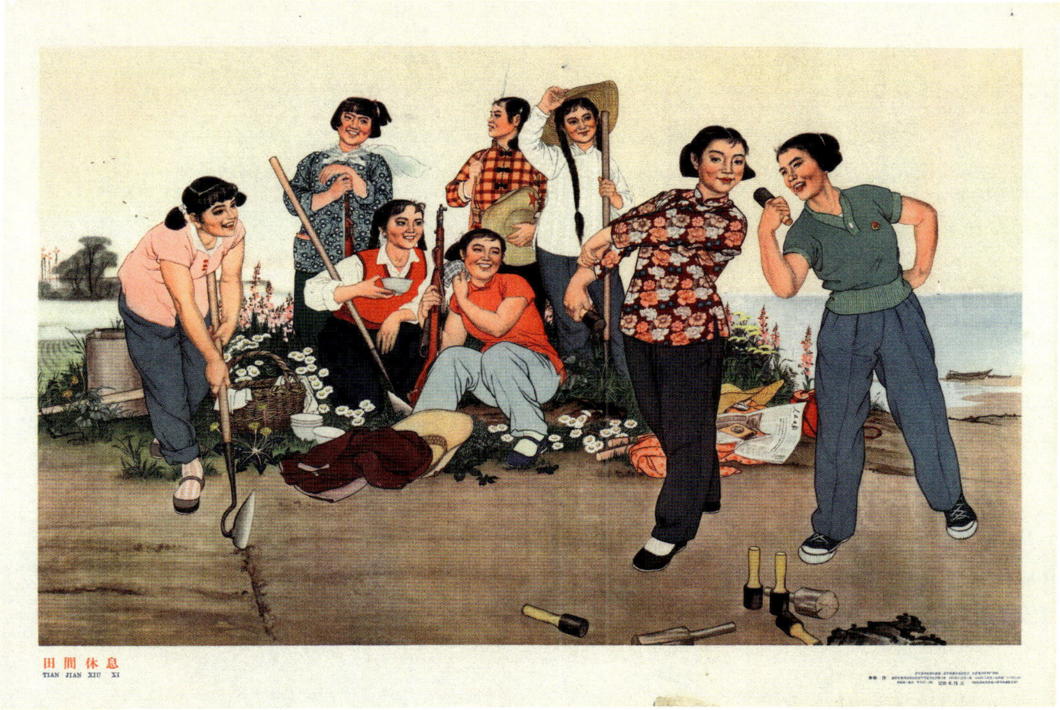

Resting between the fields, 1964.
Rast zwischen den Feldern, 1964.

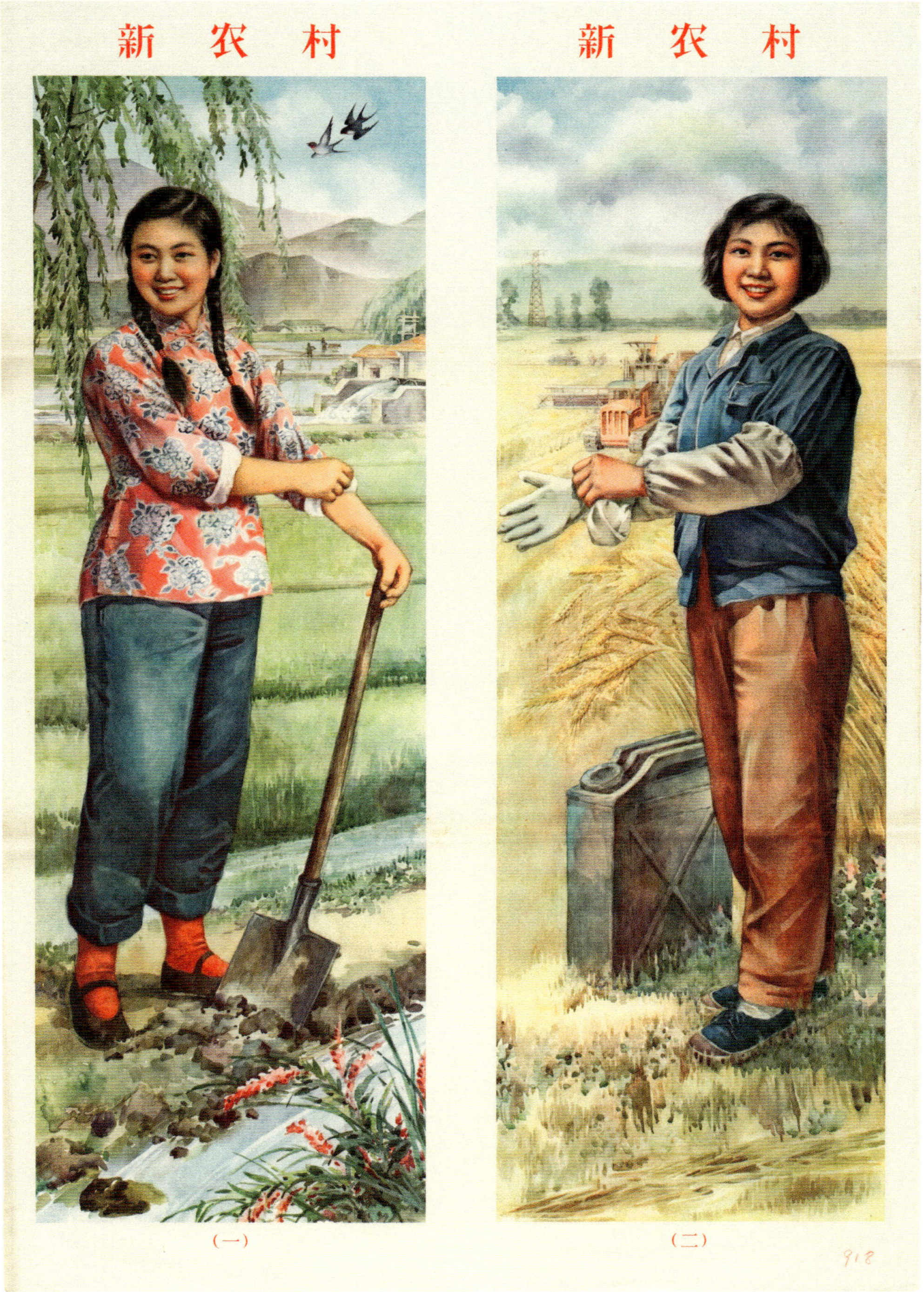

New village (1, 2), 1964.
Neues Dorf (1, 2), 1964.

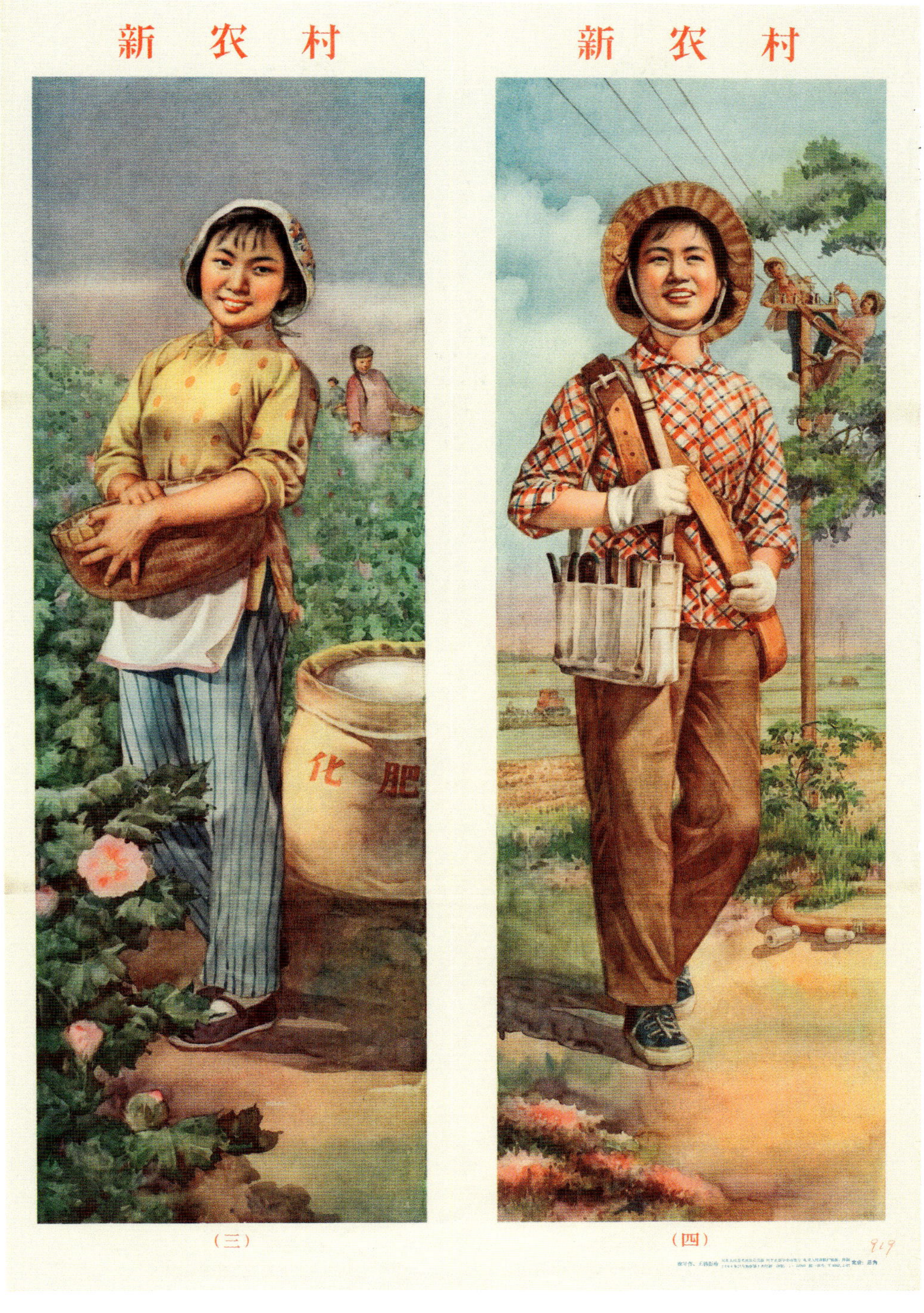

New village (3, 4), 1964.
Neues Dorf (3, 4), 1964.

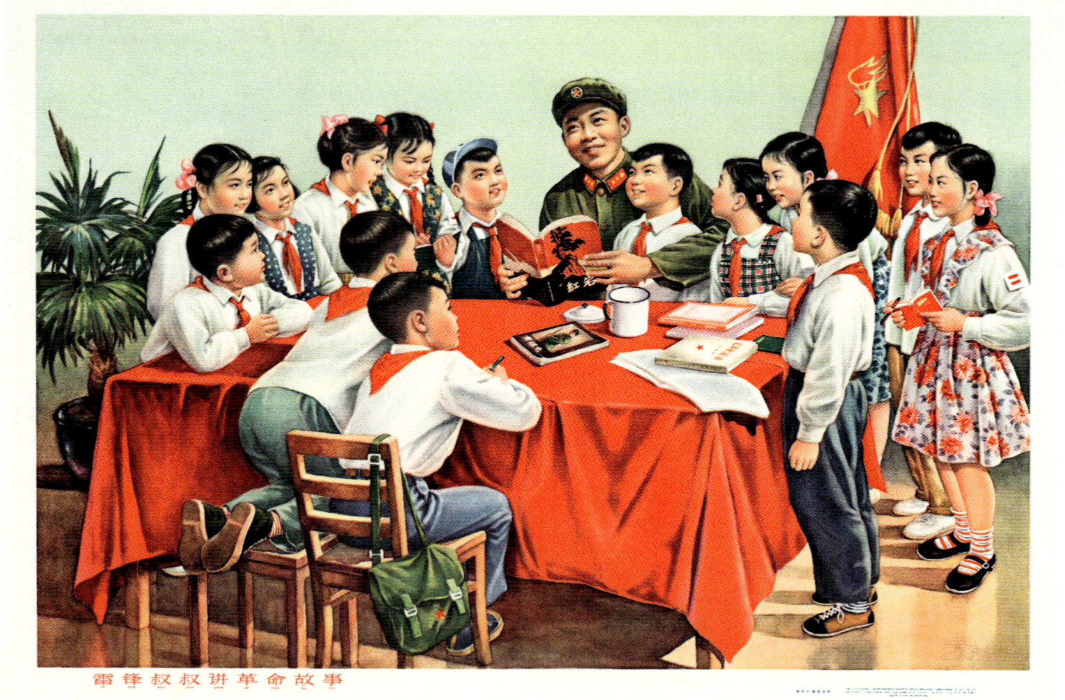

Uncle Lei Feng tells revolutionary stories, 1965.

Onkel Lei Feng erzählt Geschichten der Revolution, 1965.

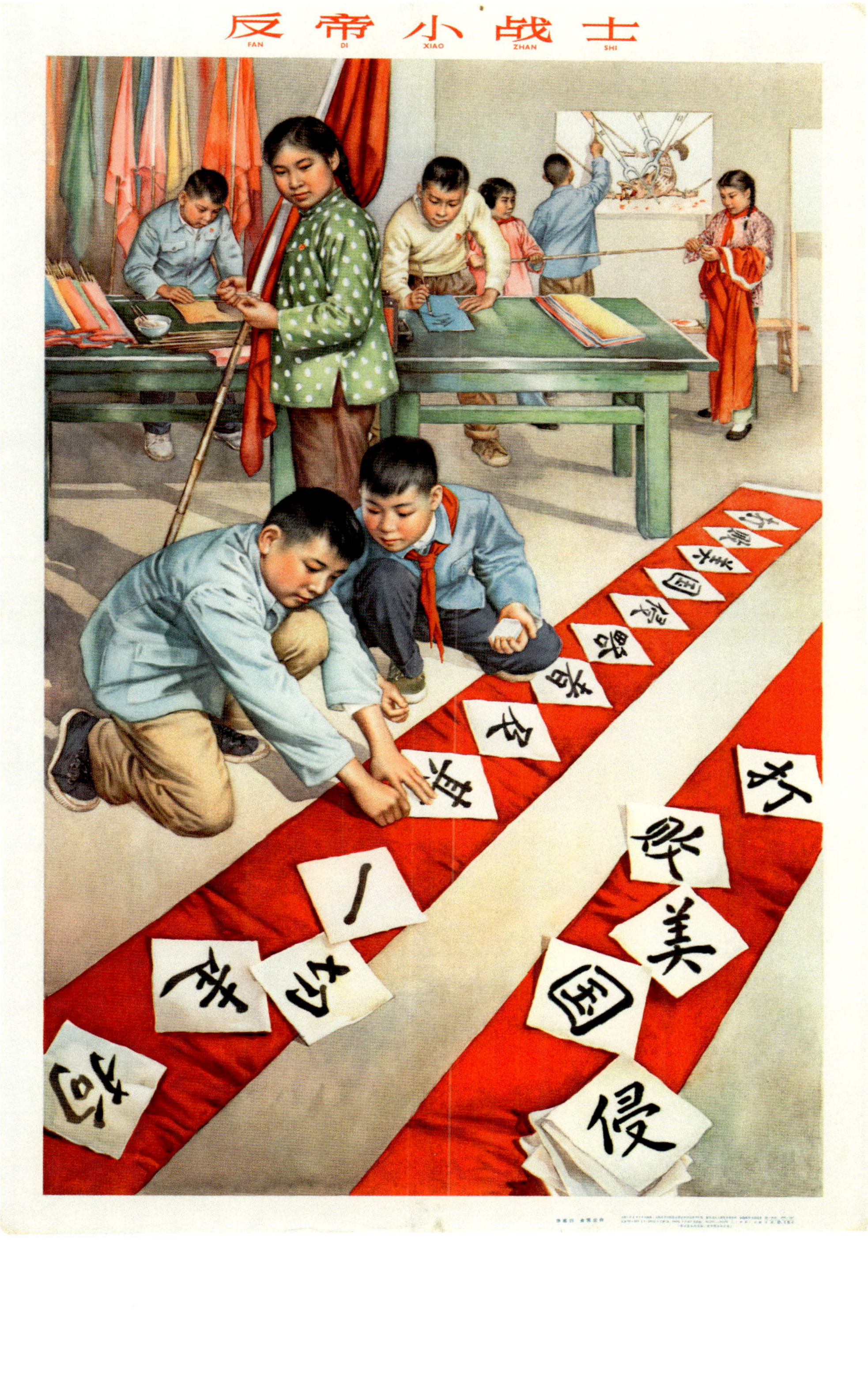

Little anti-imperialist warriors, 1965.
Kleine antiimperialistische Kämpfer, 1965.

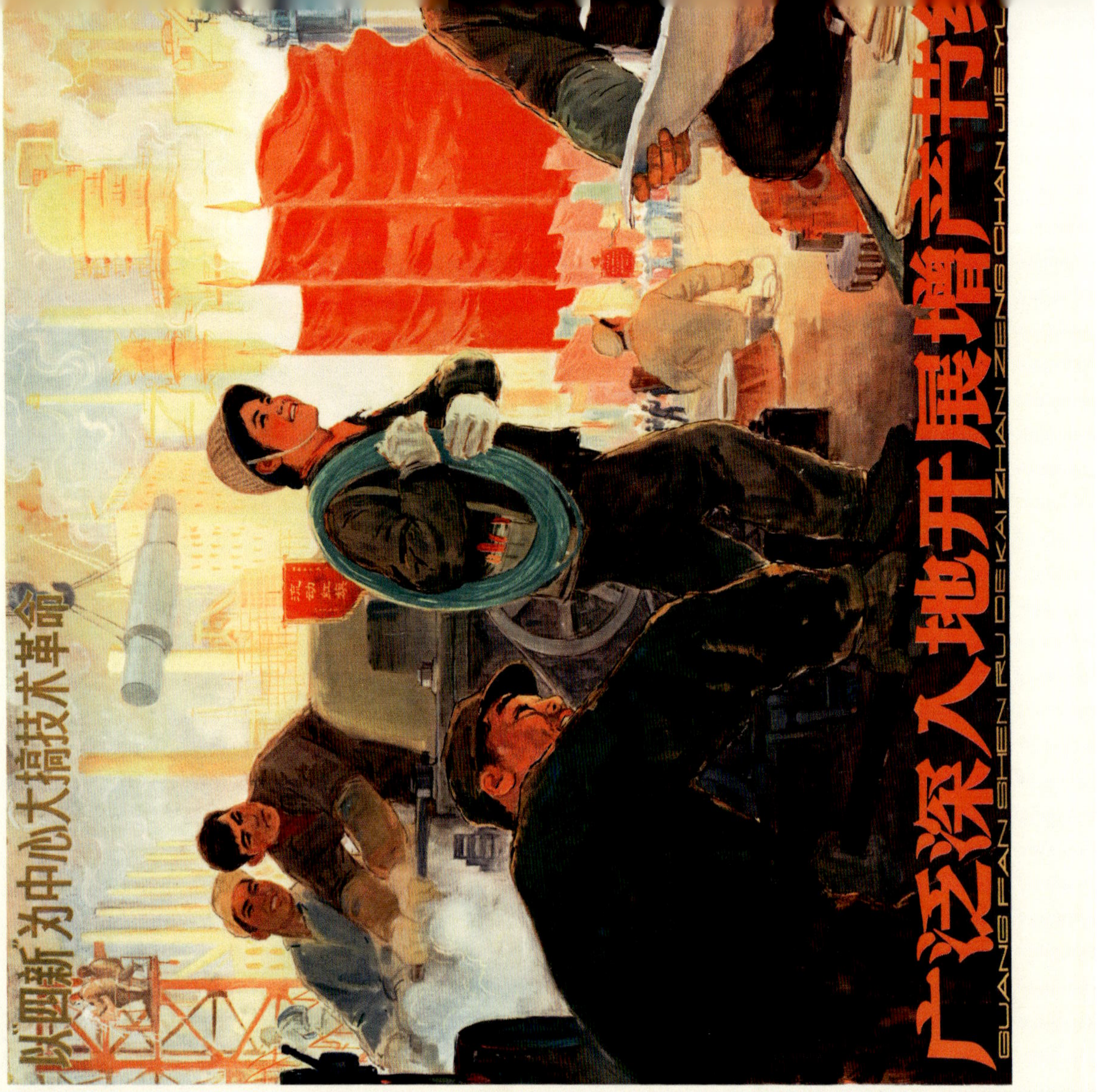

Fully engage in the movement to increase production and to practise economy to set off a new upsurge in industrial production, 1965.
Lasst euch voll und ganz auf die Bewegung ein, um die Produktion zu steigern und die Wirtschaft so zu betreiben, dass sie einen neuen Aufschwung erlebt, 1965.

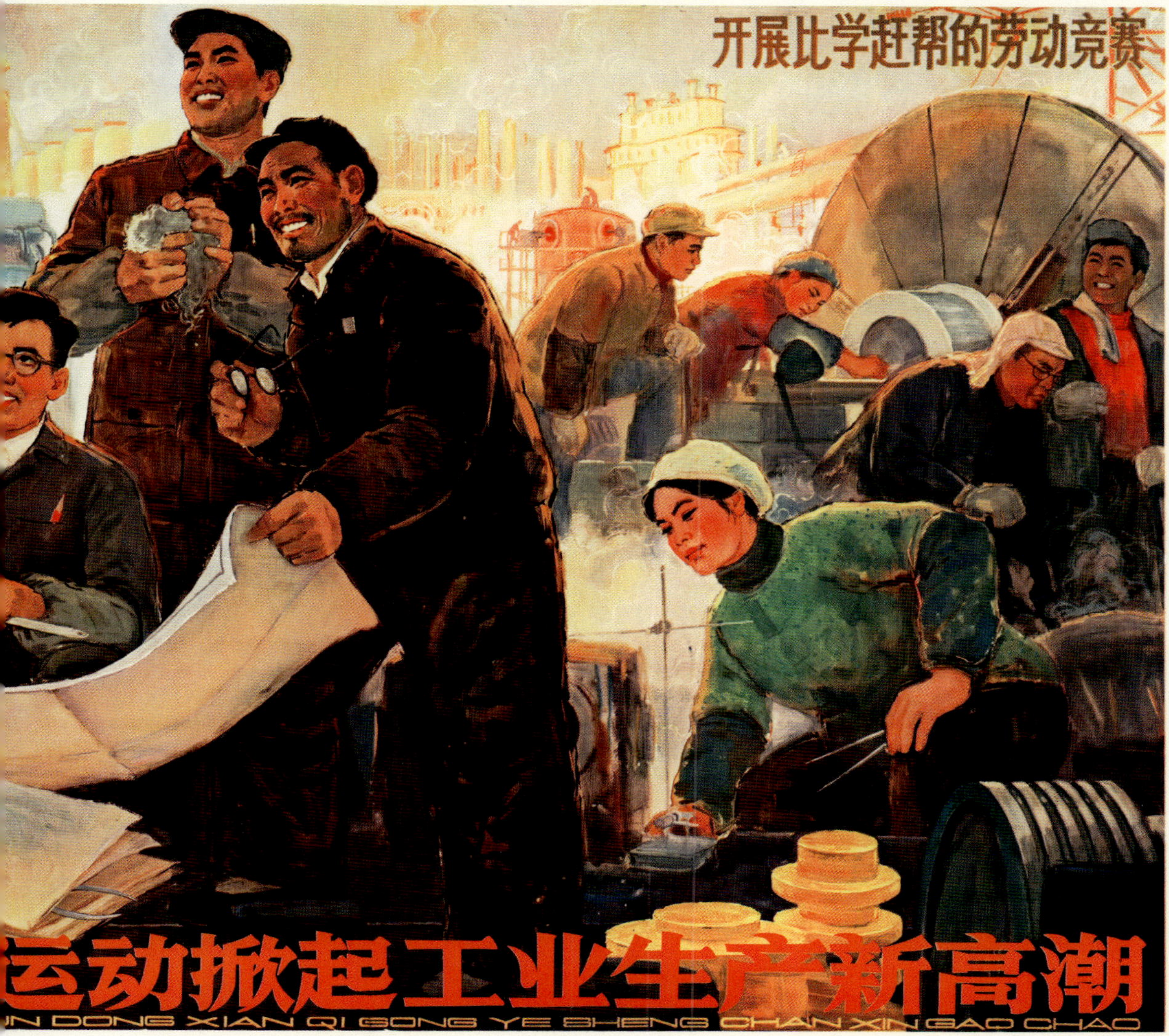
开展比学赶帮的劳动竞赛
运动掀起工业生产新高潮
N DONG XIAN QI GONG YE SHENG CHAN XIN GAO CHAO

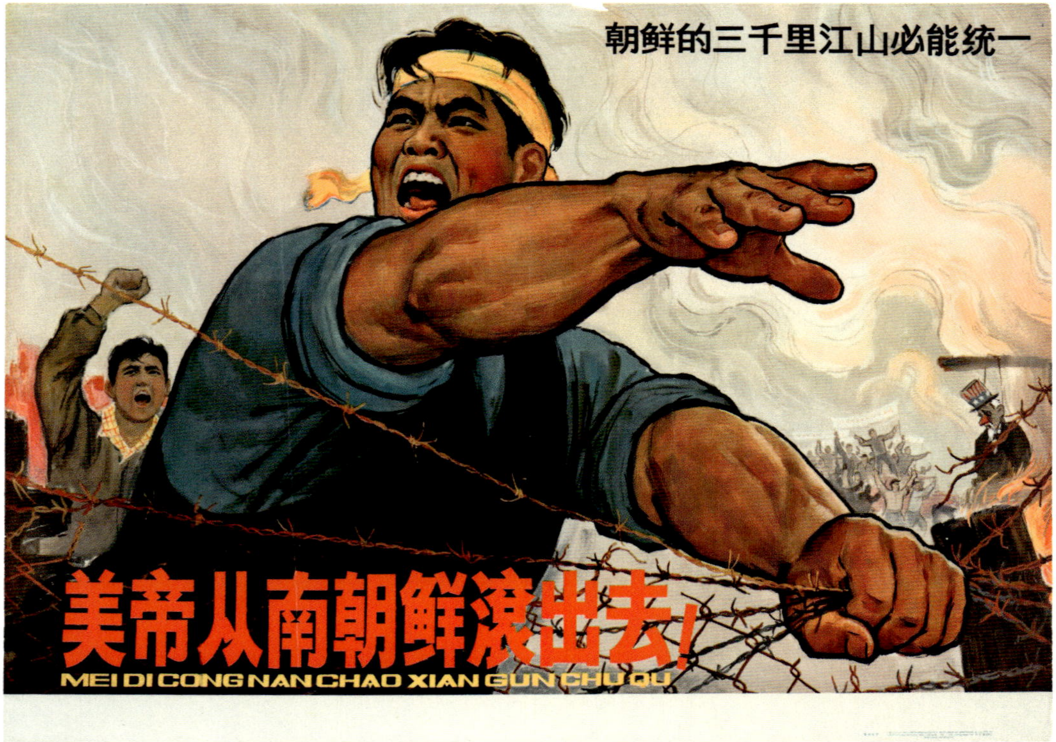

American imperialists, get out of South Korea! 1965.
Amerikanische Imperialisten, verschwindet aus Südkorea! 1965.

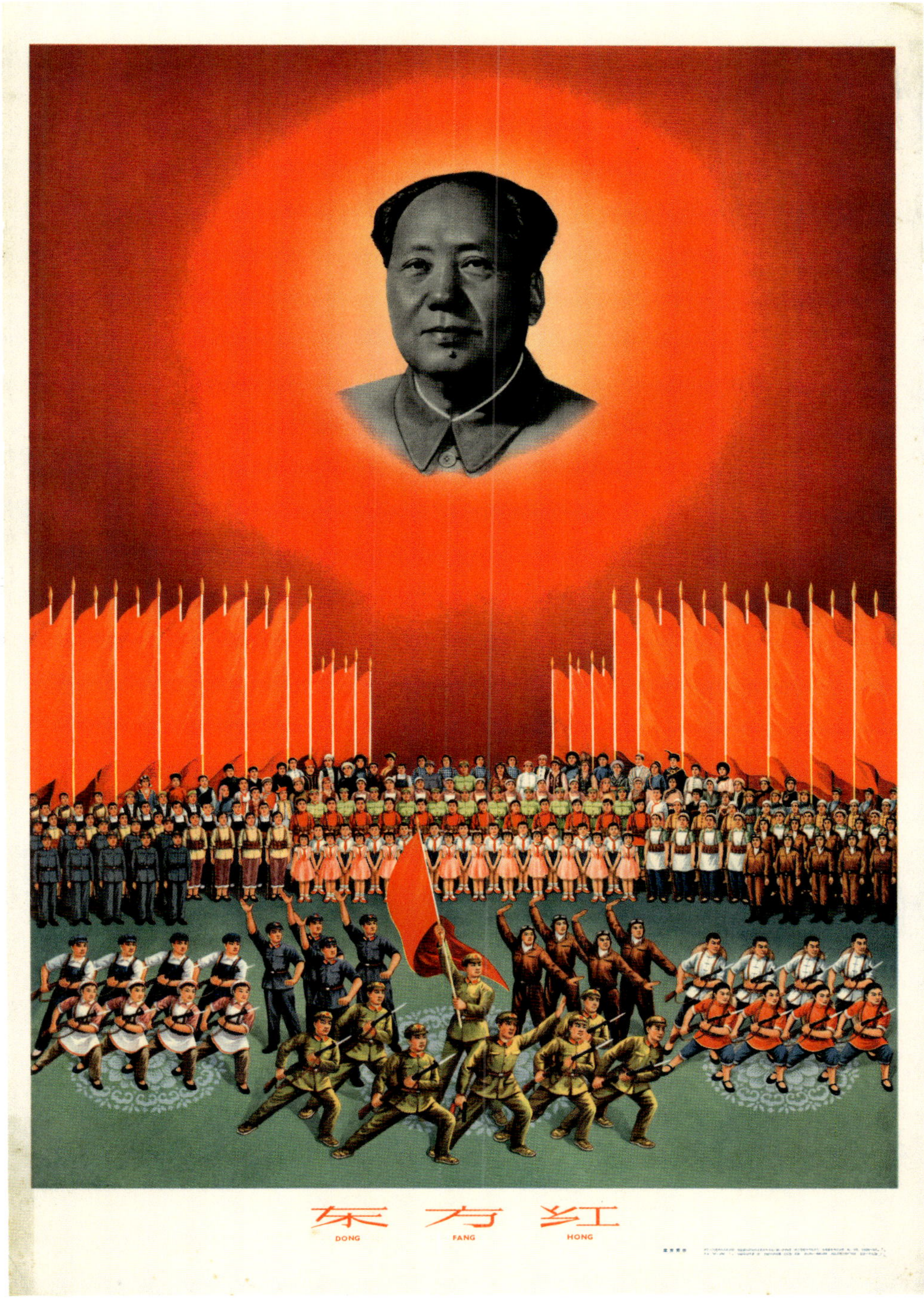

The East is red, 1965.
Der Osten ist rot, 1965.

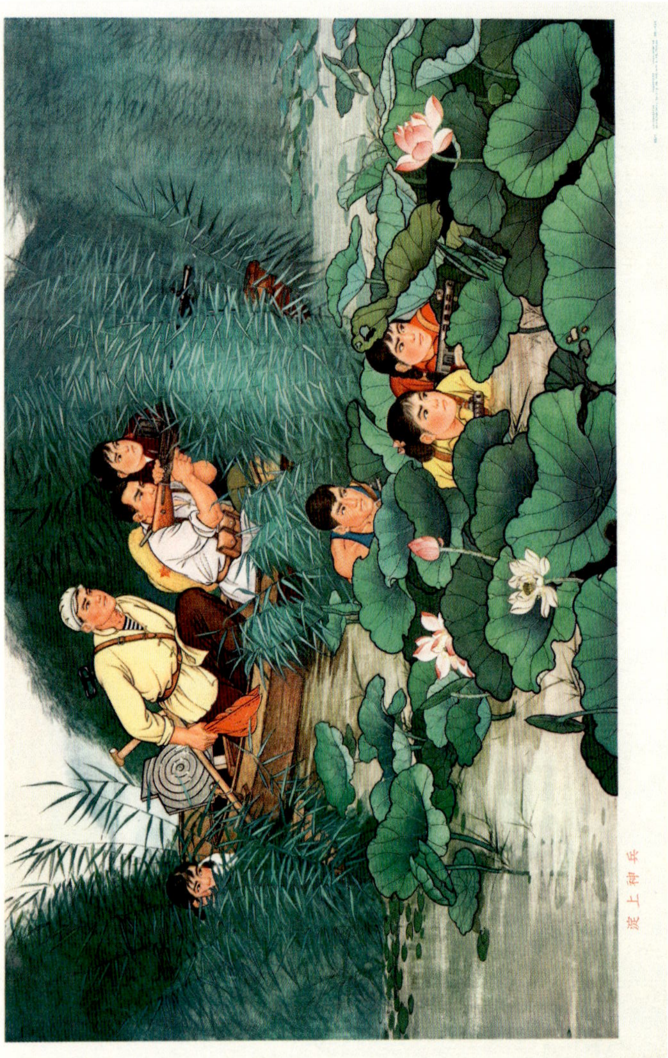

Miraculous soldiers on the shallow lake, 1966.
Übermenschliche Soldaten auf dem seichten See, 1966.

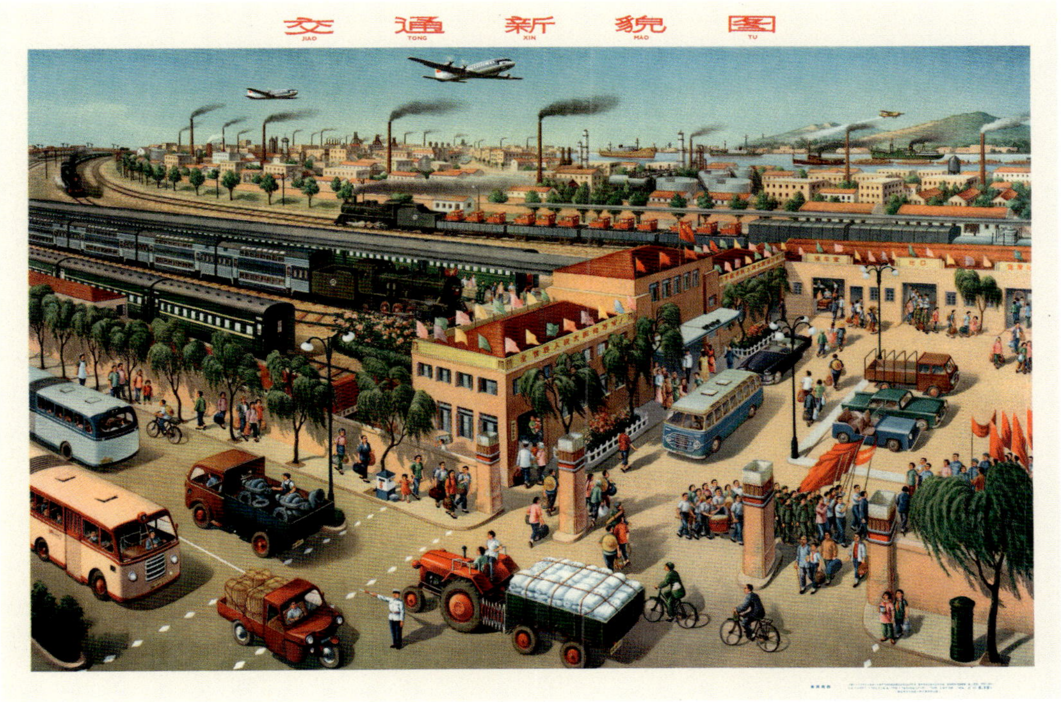

The new look of traffic, 1966.
Das neue Aussehen des Verkehrs, 1966.

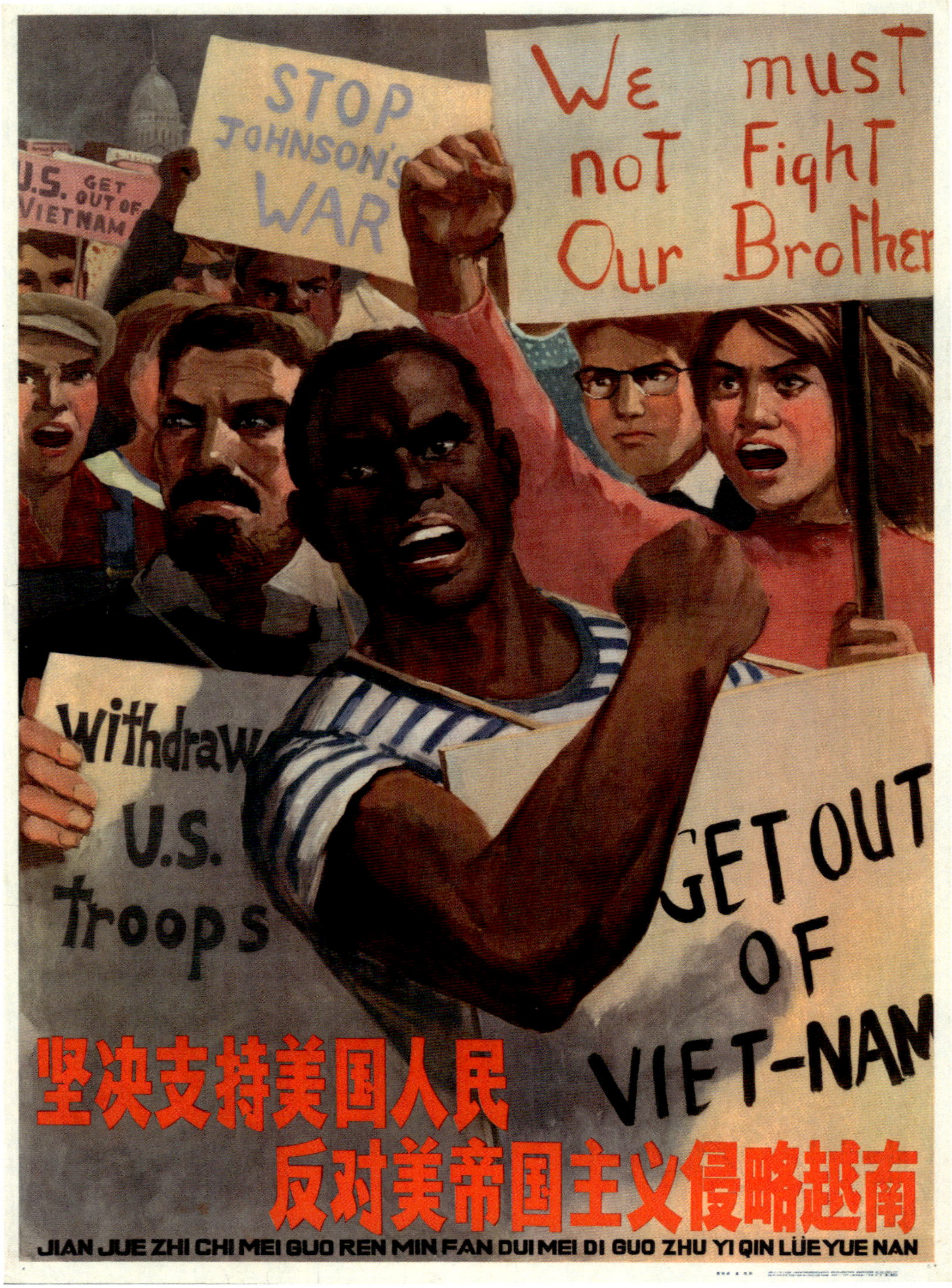

Resolutely support the American people in their resistance against American imperialist aggression in Vietnam, 1966.

Unterstützt energisch das amerikanische Volk in seinem Widerstand gegen den Angriff der amerikanischen Imperialisten auf Vietnam, 1966.

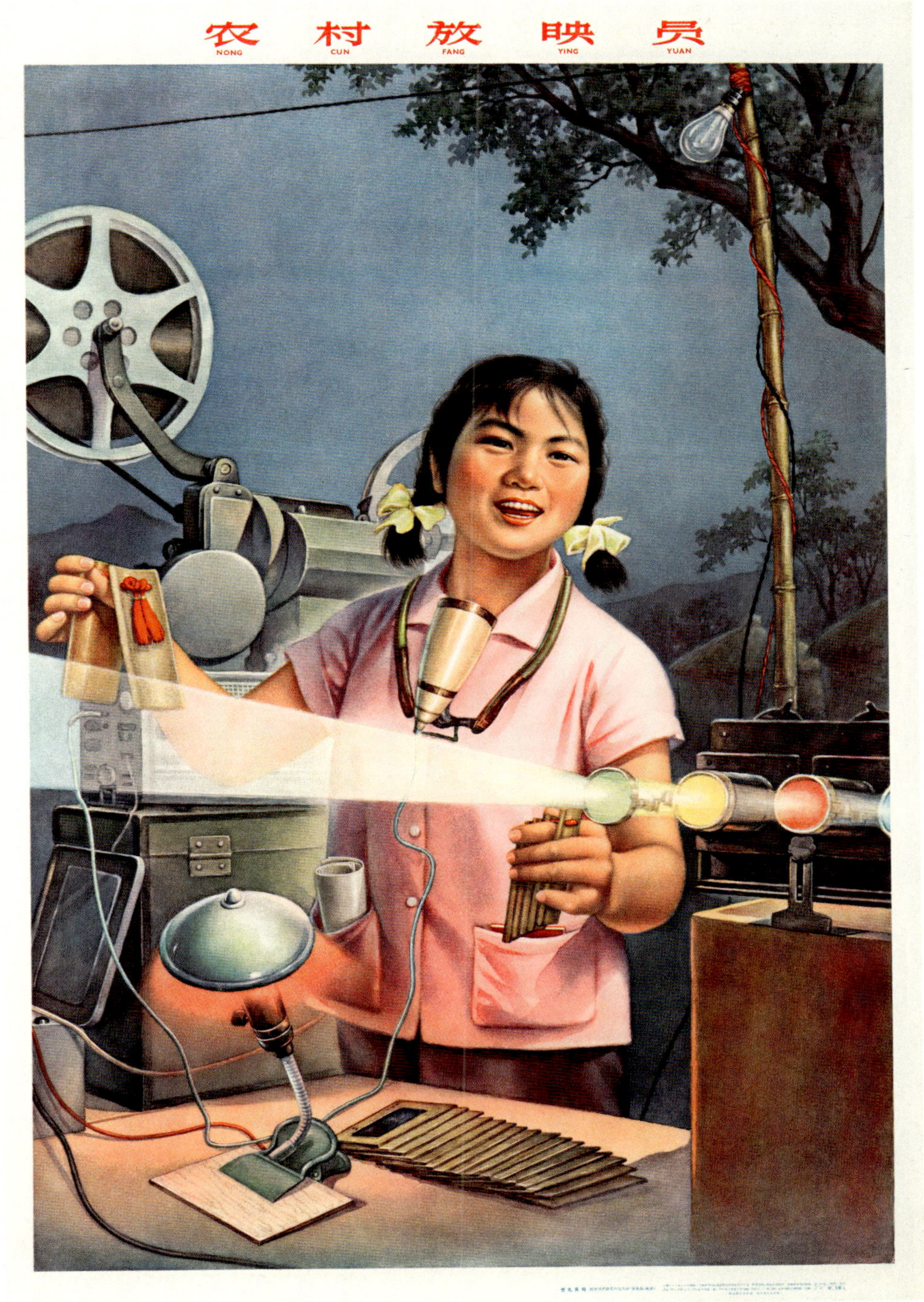

The projectionist of the village, 1966.
Die Filmvorführerin des Dorfes, 1966.

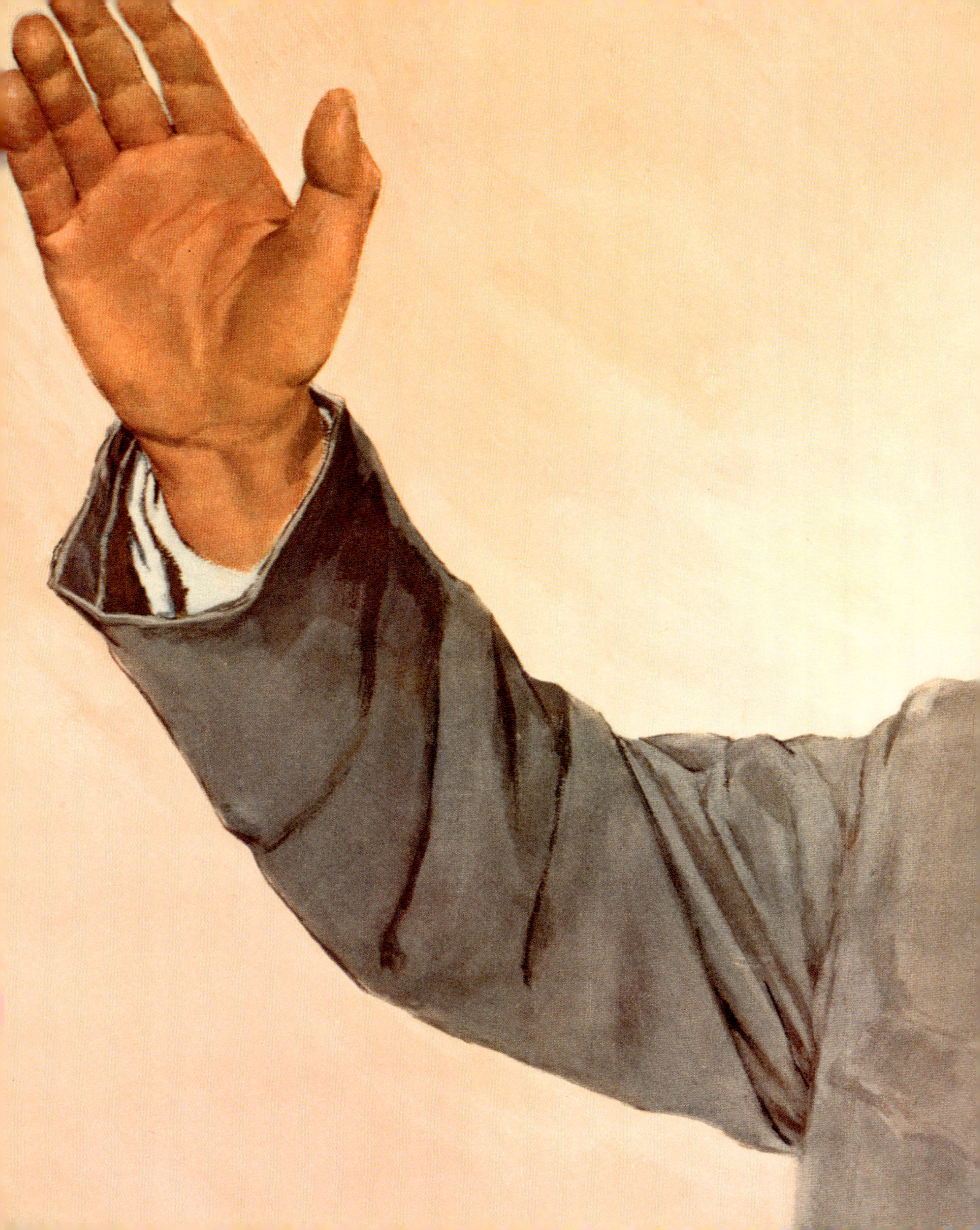

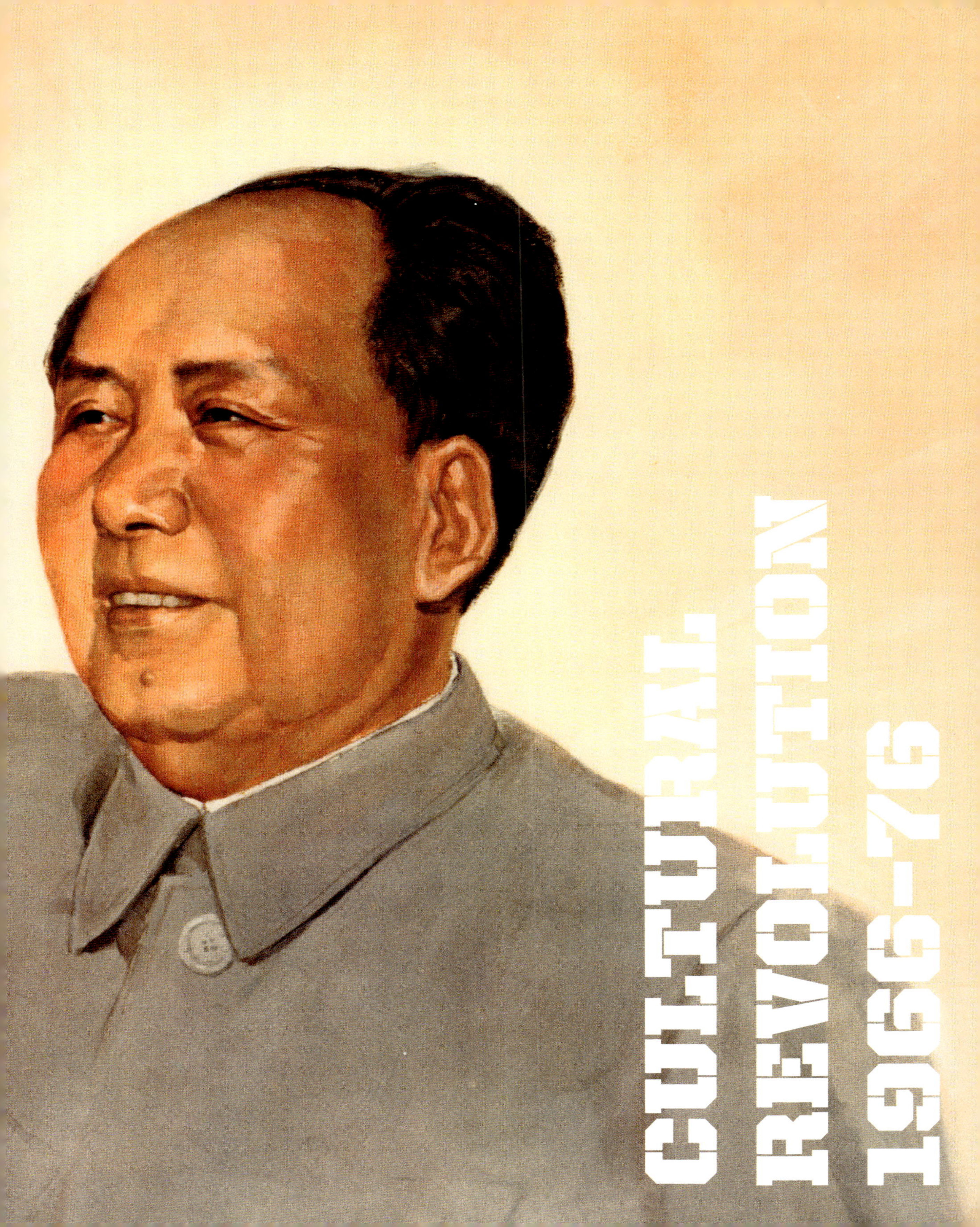
CULTURAL
REVOLUTION
1966–76

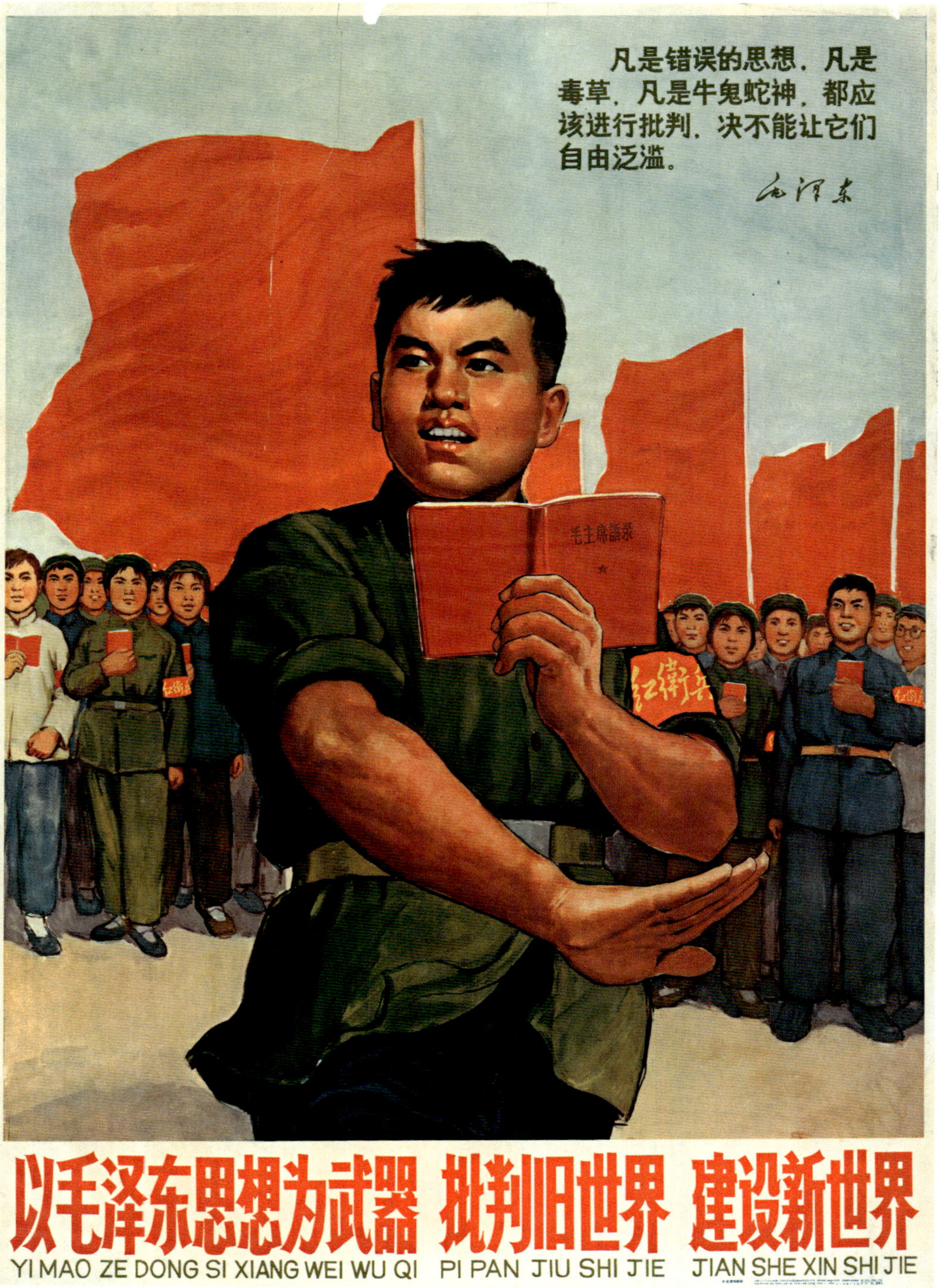

Criticize the old world and build a new world with 'Mao Zedong Thought' as a weapon, 1966.

Unterzieht die alte Welt der Kritik und baut eine neue Welt auf mit 'Mao Zedong Denken' als Waffe, 1966.

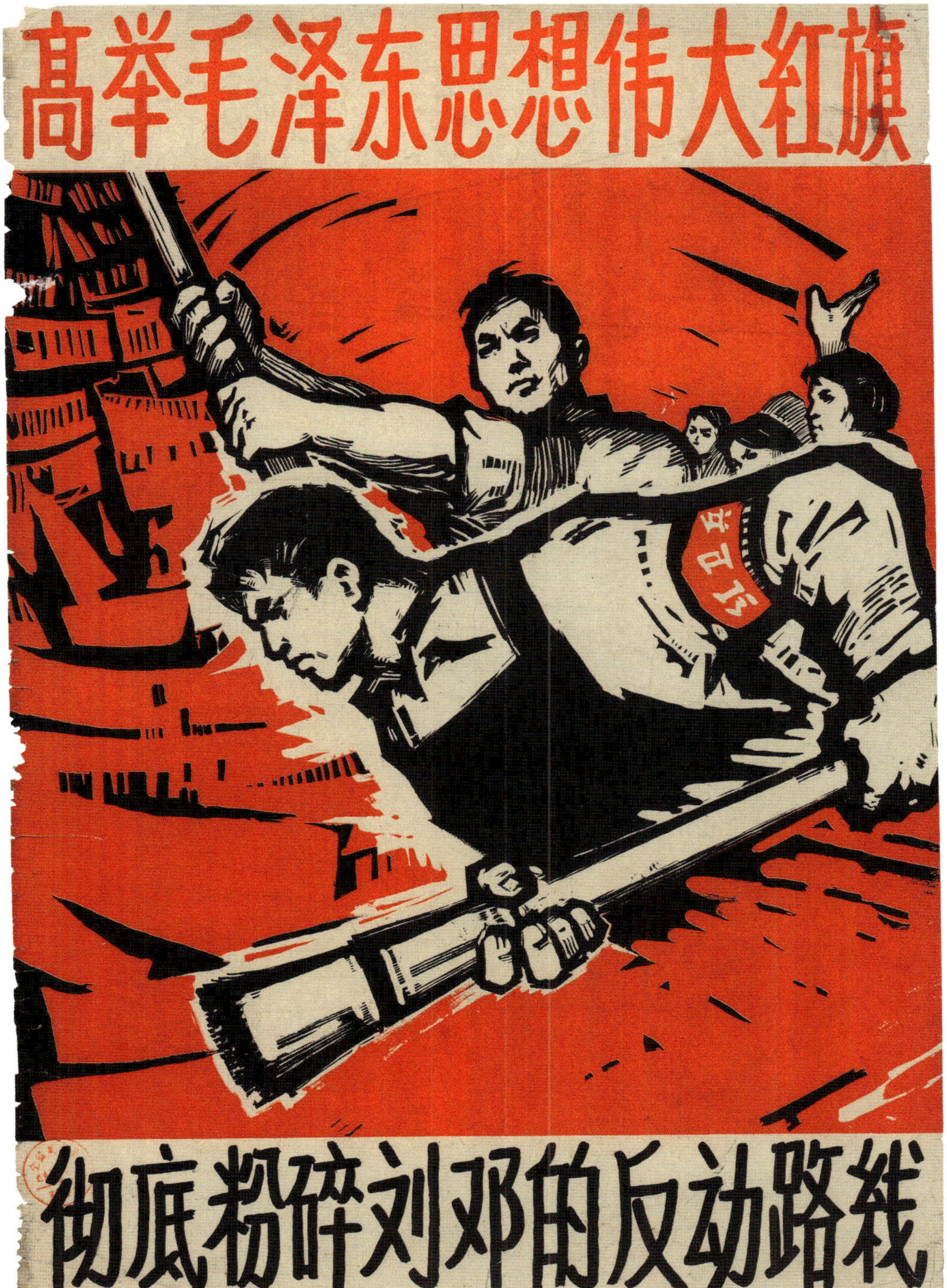

Hold high the great red flag of 'Mao Zedong Thought'; thoroughly smash the reactionary line of Liu and Deng, 1966.
Haltet hoch die große rote Fahne des 'Mao Zedong Denken'; durchbrecht die reaktionäre Front von Liu und Deng, 1966.

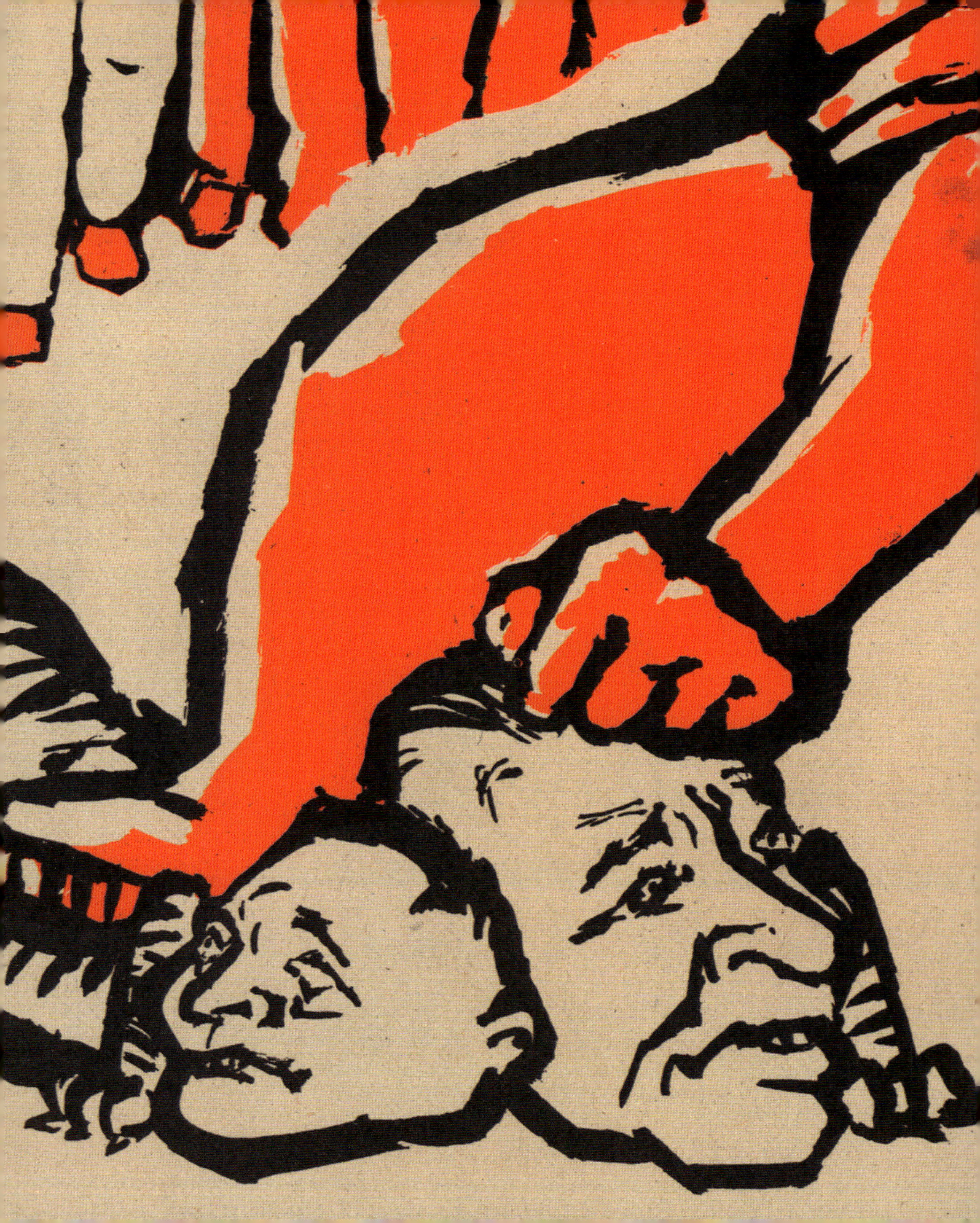

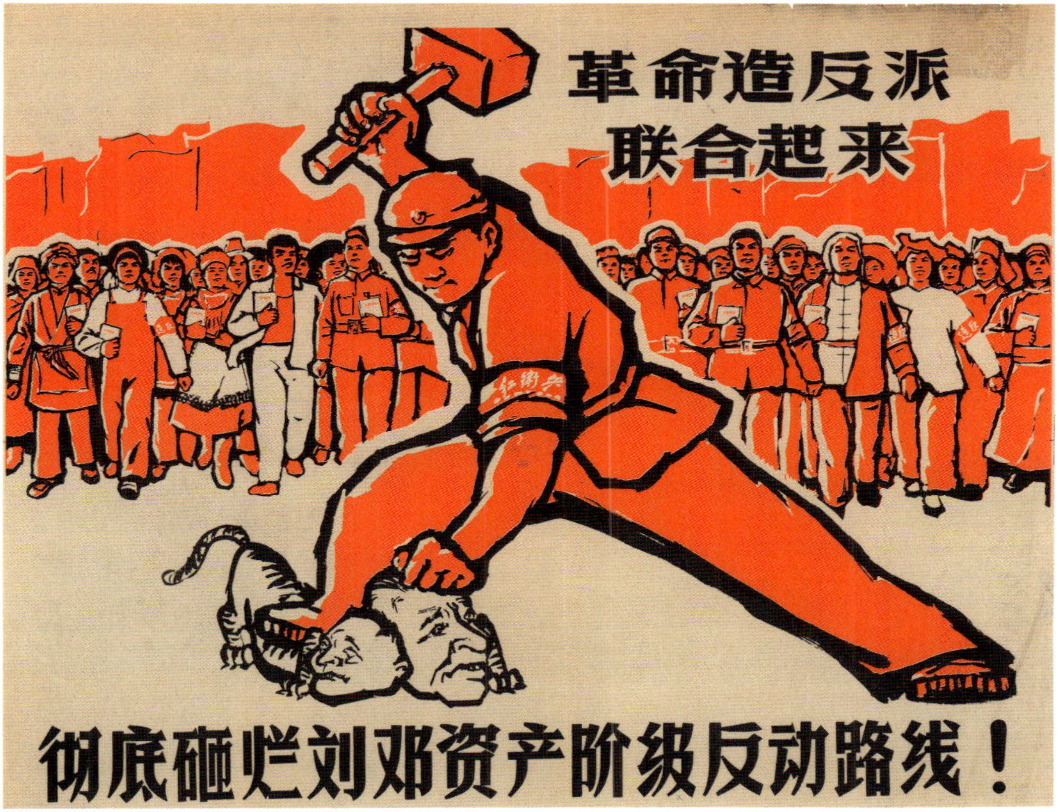

Completely smash the capitalist class and the reactionary line of Liu and Deng! c. 1967.
Zerstört die kapitalistische Klasse vollständig und durchbrecht die reaktionäre Front von Liu und Deng, um 1967.

← Liu Shaoqi and Deng Xiaoping are the most prominent victims of the Cultural Revolution. Liu, Head of State, is arrested and dies in captivity in 1969. Deng, General Secretary of the Communist Party, is exiled to the countryside. He is rehabilitated in 1974.

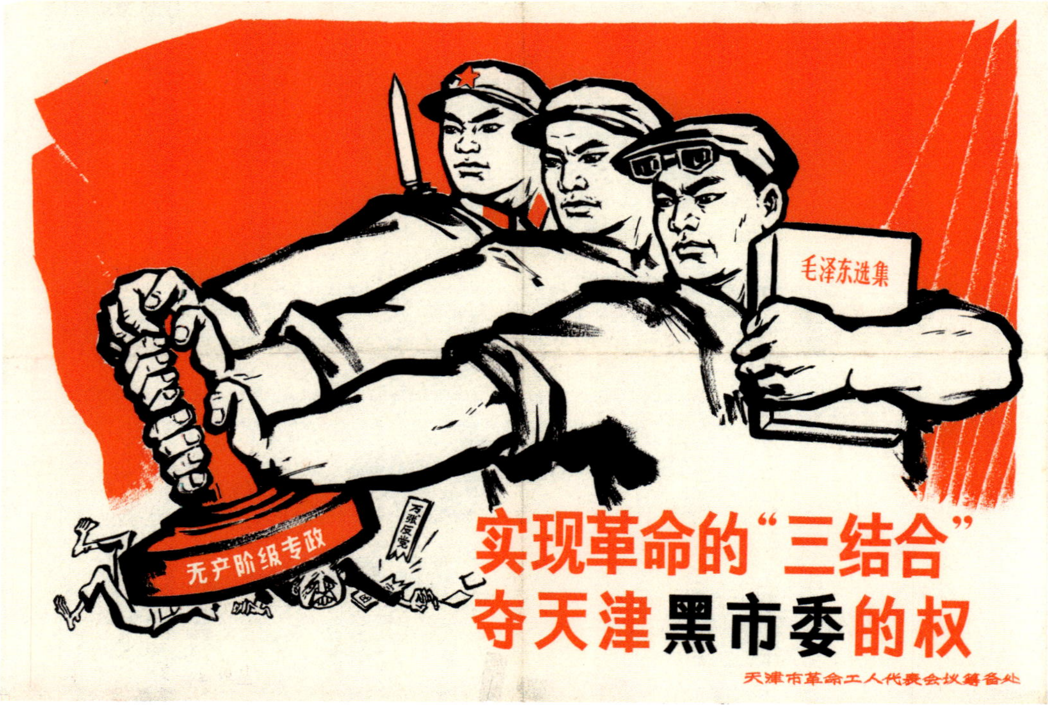

Carry out the revolutionary "integration of three"
take the power from Tianjin's black municipal Party committee, 1967.
Vollzieht den revolutionären „Zusammenschluss der drei", entzieht
Tianjin's schwarzem Stadtparteikomitee die Macht, 1967.

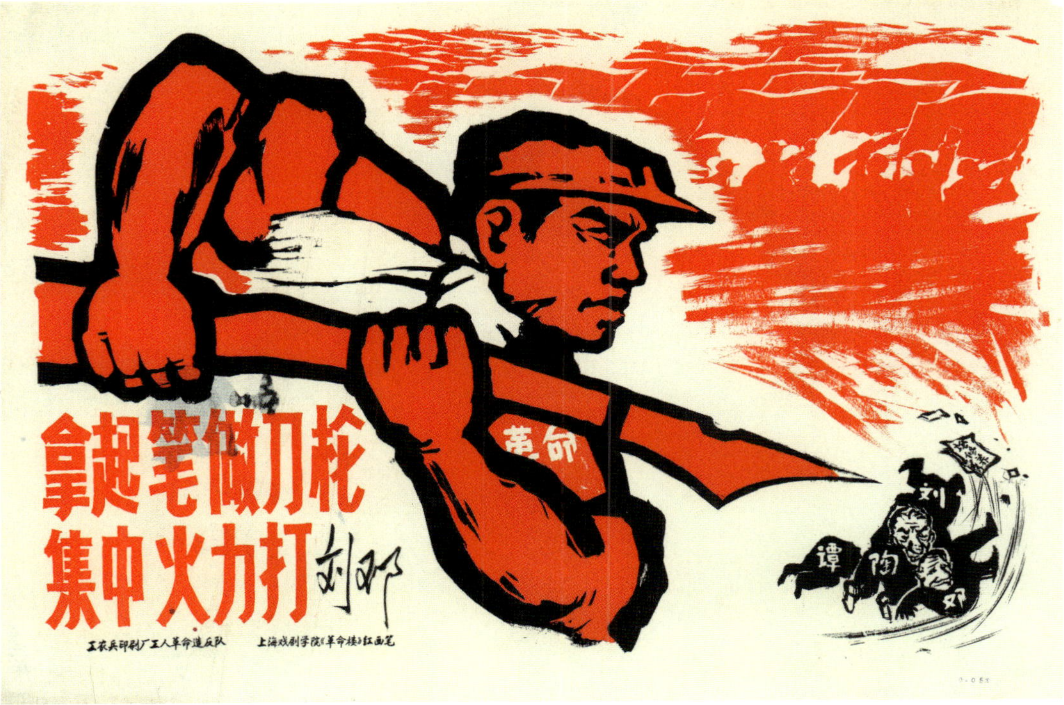

Take up a pen as a weapon and concentrate fire to hit Liu and Deng, c. 1967.
Nehmt den Stift als Waffe zur Hand und richtet das Feuer gegen Liu und Deng, um 1967.

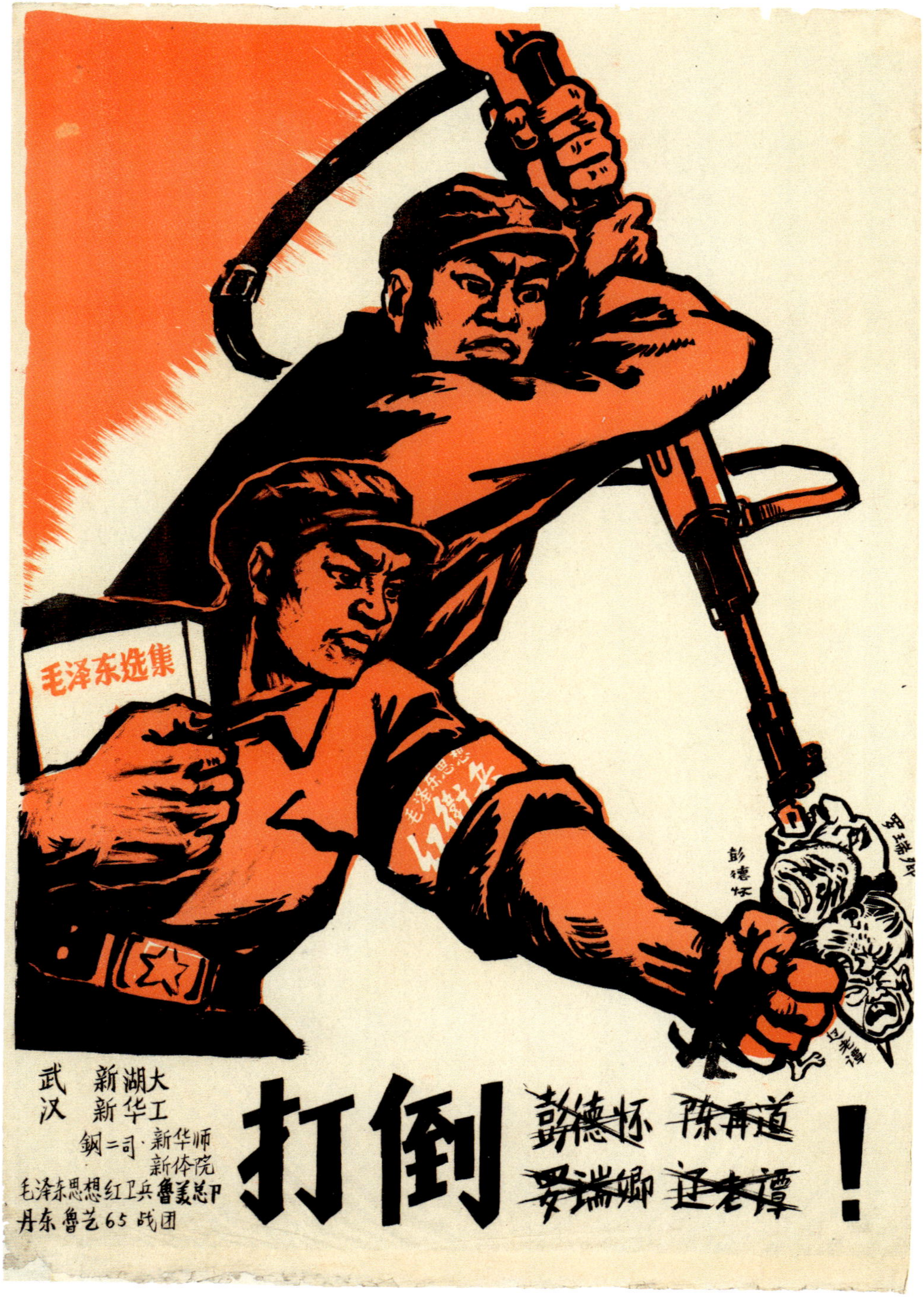

Overthrow Peng Dehuai, Luo Ruiqing, Chen Zaidao, Liao Laotan! c. 1967.
Stürzt Peng Dehuai, Luo Ruiqing, Chen Zaidao, Liao Laotan! um 1967.

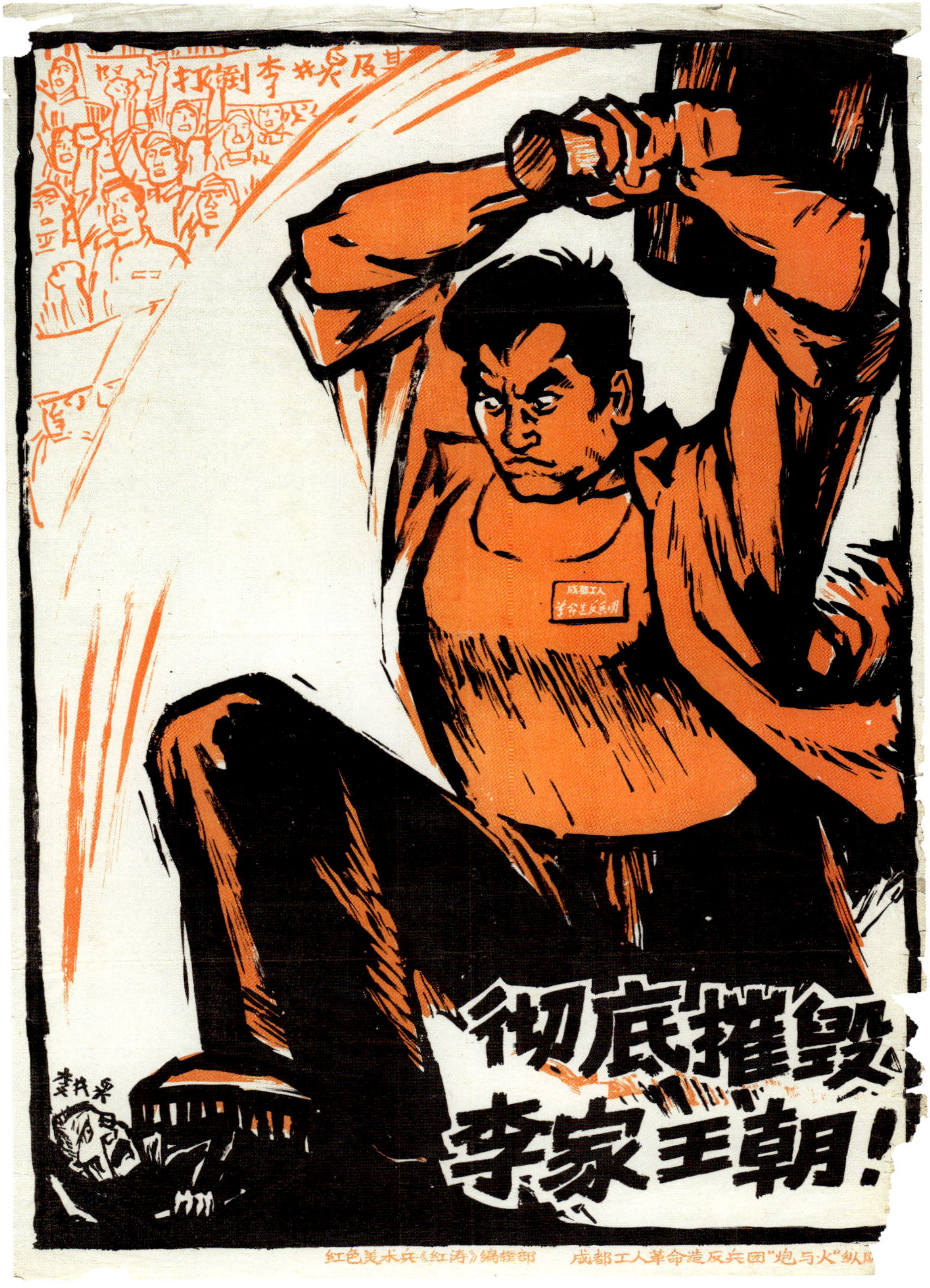

Thoroughly smash the dynastic Li family! c. 1967.
Zerstört die dynastische Familie Li vollständig! um 1967.

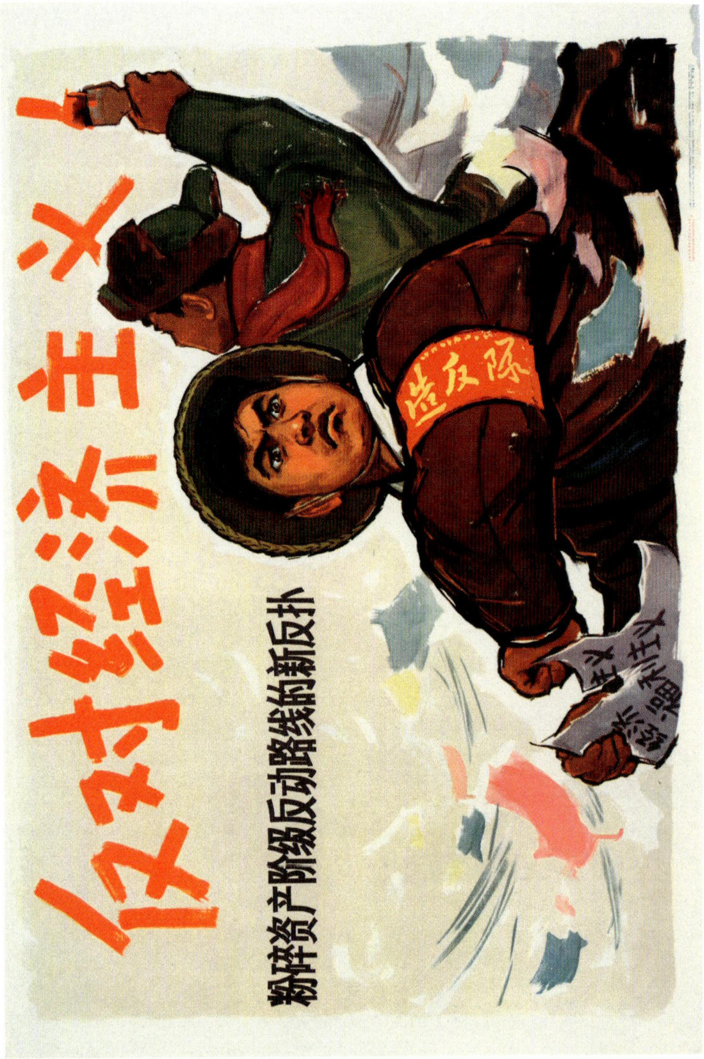

Oppose economism: destroy the new counter-offensive of the capitalist class reactionary line, 1967.

Widersetzt euch dem Ökonomismus: Schlagt die neue konterrevolutionäre Offensive der reaktionären Klasse nieder, 1967.

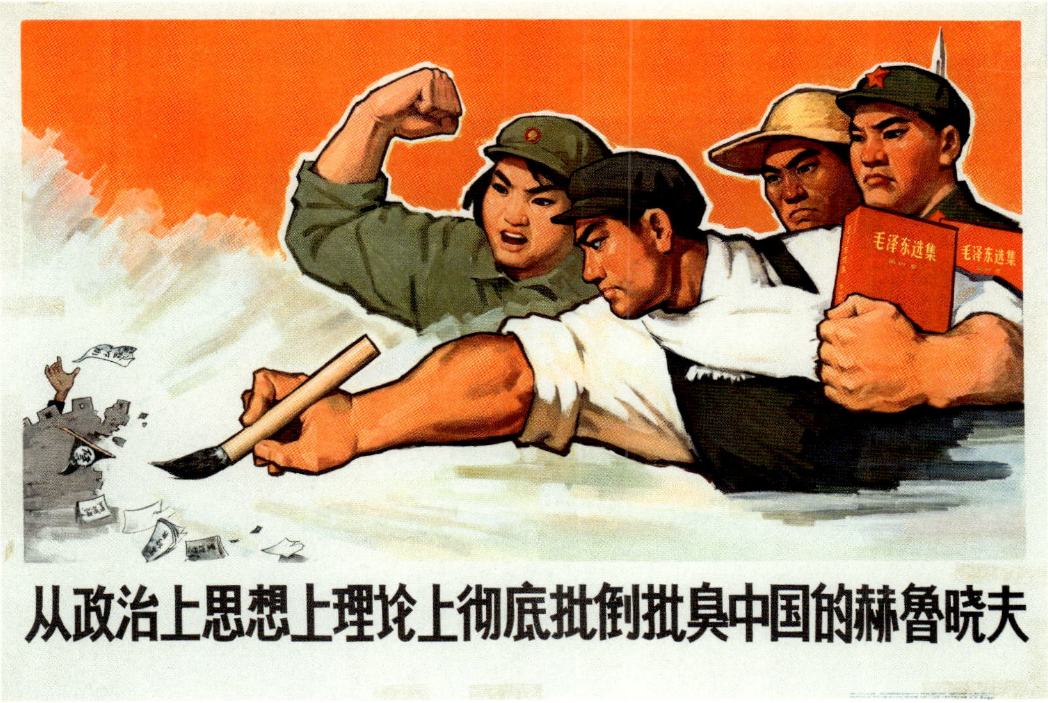

Fully criticize the Chinese Khrushchev from a political, ideological, and theoretical perspective, 1967.
Übt umfassende Kritik am chinesischen Chruschtschow – aus politischer, ideologischer und theoretischer Perspektive, 1967.

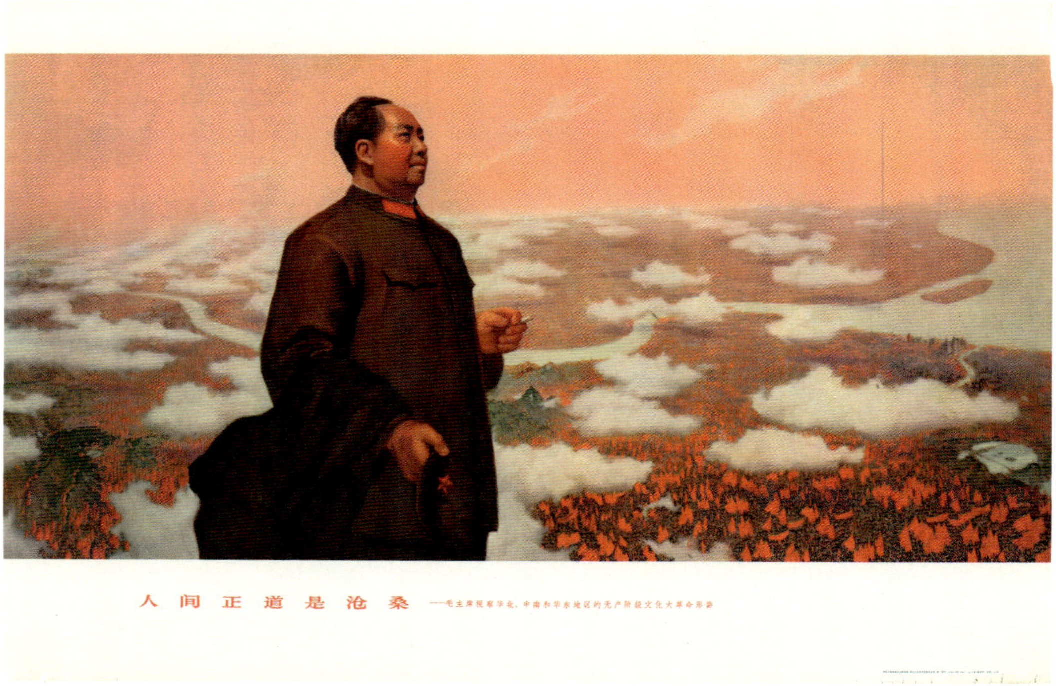

The correct way among the people is bringing great change to the world, 1967.

Der richtige Weg der Menschen ist, die Welt einem umfassenden Wandel zu unterziehen, 1967.

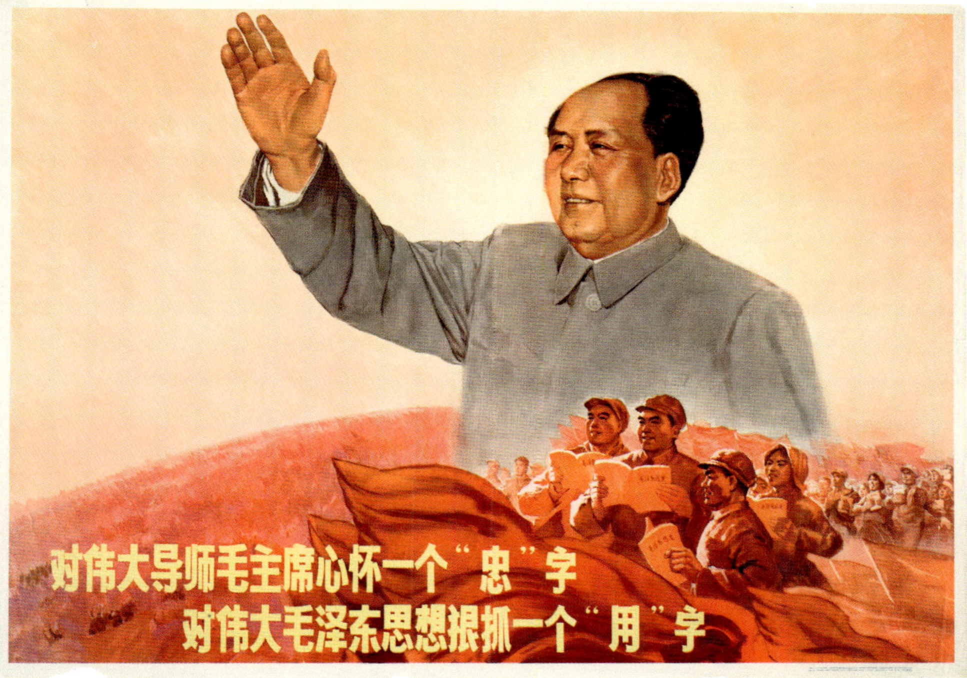

With regard to the great teacher Chairman Mao, cherish the word "loyalty."
With regard to the great "Mao Zedong Thought", vigorously stress the word "usefulness." 1967.
Erweist dem großen Lehrer Vorsitzenden Mao die Ehre und bewahrt die Bedeutung des Wortes "Loyalität".
Erweist dem 'Mao Zedong Denken' die Ehre und betont die Bedeutung des Wortes "Nützlichkeit", 1967.

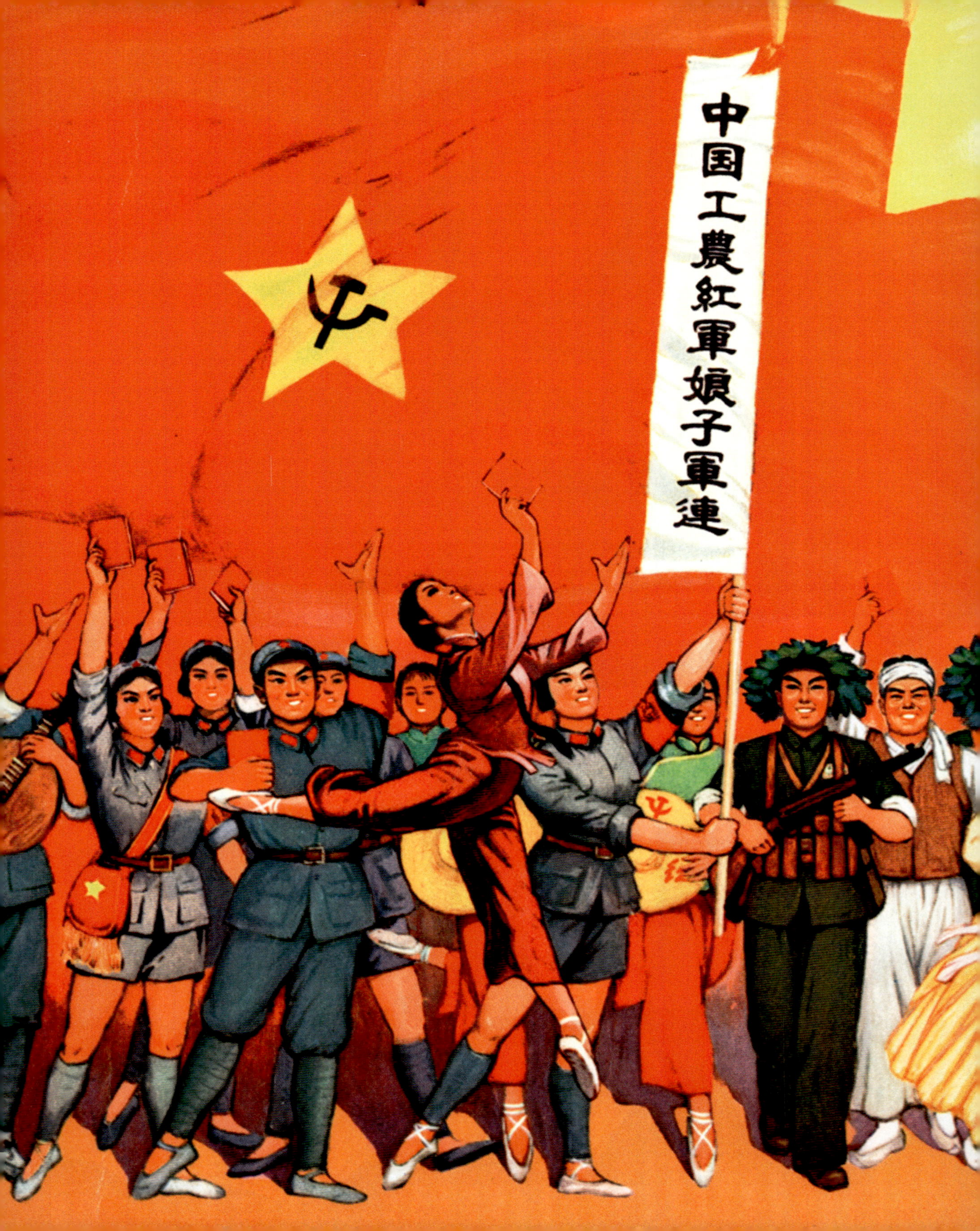
中国工農紅軍娘子軍連

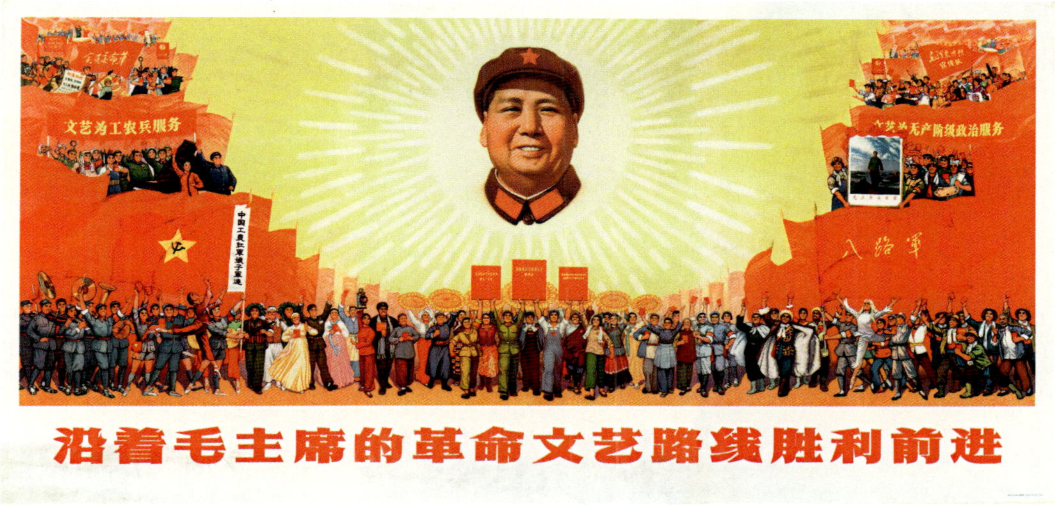

Advance victoriously while following Chairman Mao's revolutionary line in literature and the arts, c. 1968.
Schreitet siegreich voran und folgt der revolutionären Linie des Vorsitzenden Mao in der Literatur und den schönen Künsten, um 1968.

← At the height of Mao worship, Mao appears as radiant sun, high above the masses. The dancing figures are from the revolutionary model operas developed by Mao's wife Jiang Qing.

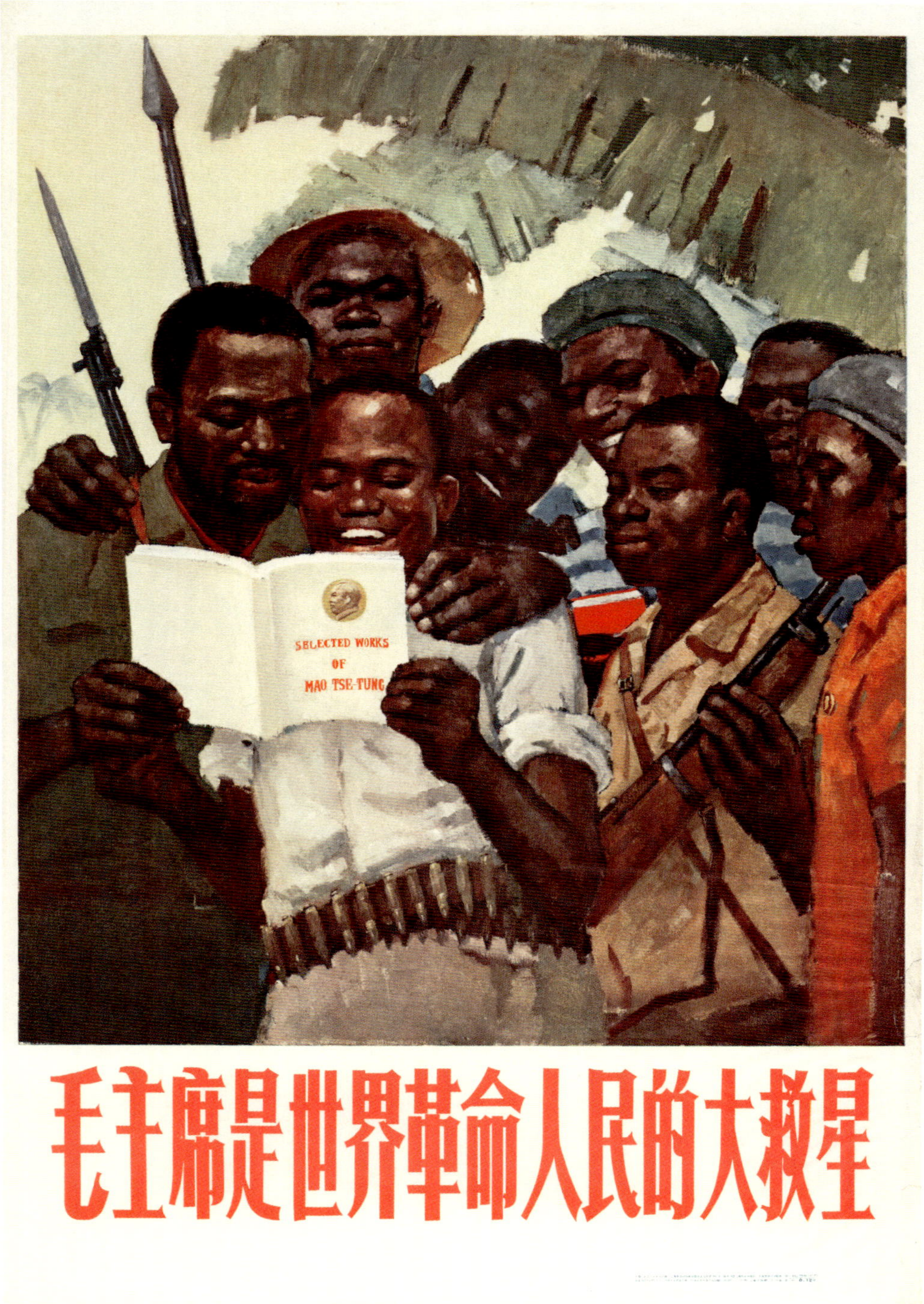

Chairman Mao is the great liberator of the world's revolutionary people, 1968.
Der Vorsitzende Mao ist der große Befreier der revolutionären Völker der Erde, 1968.

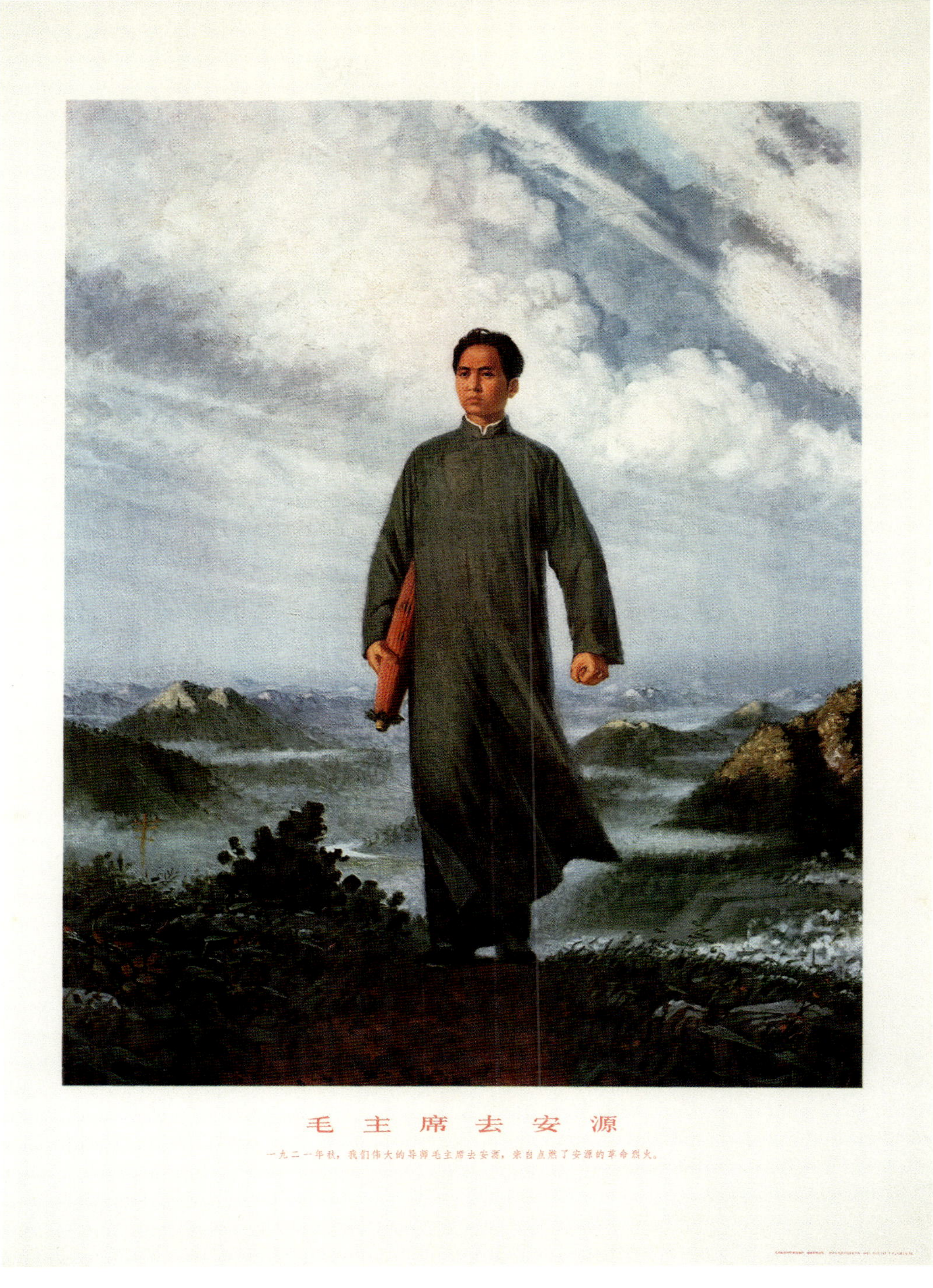

Chairman Mao going to Anyuan, 1968.
Der Vorsitzende Mao auf dem Weg nach Anyuan, 1968.

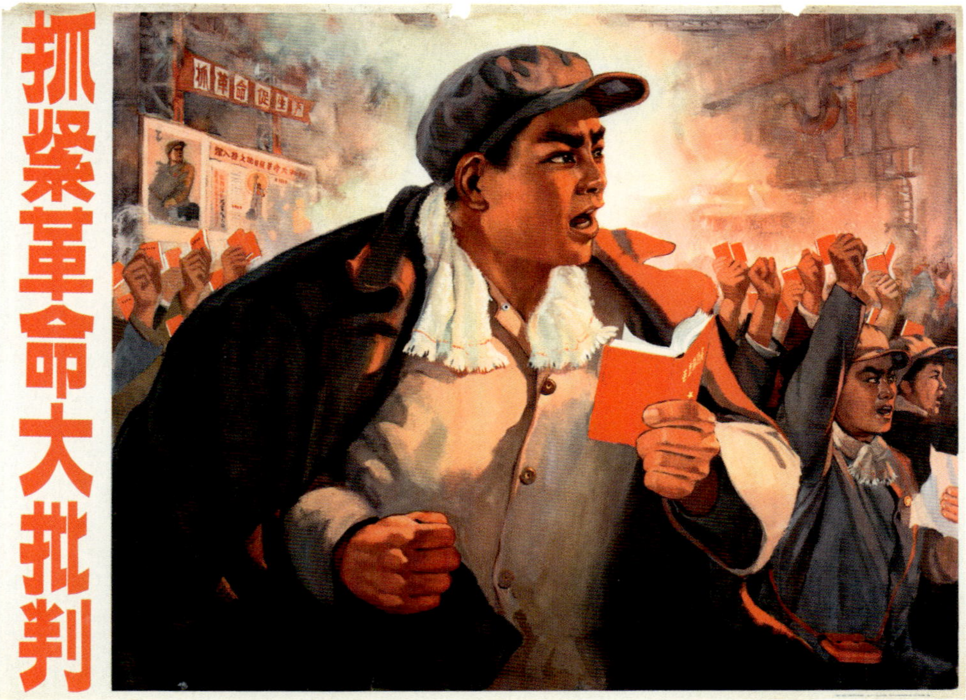

Firmly grasp large-scale revolutionary criticism, 1969.
Begreift die umfassende revolutionäre Kritik, 1969.

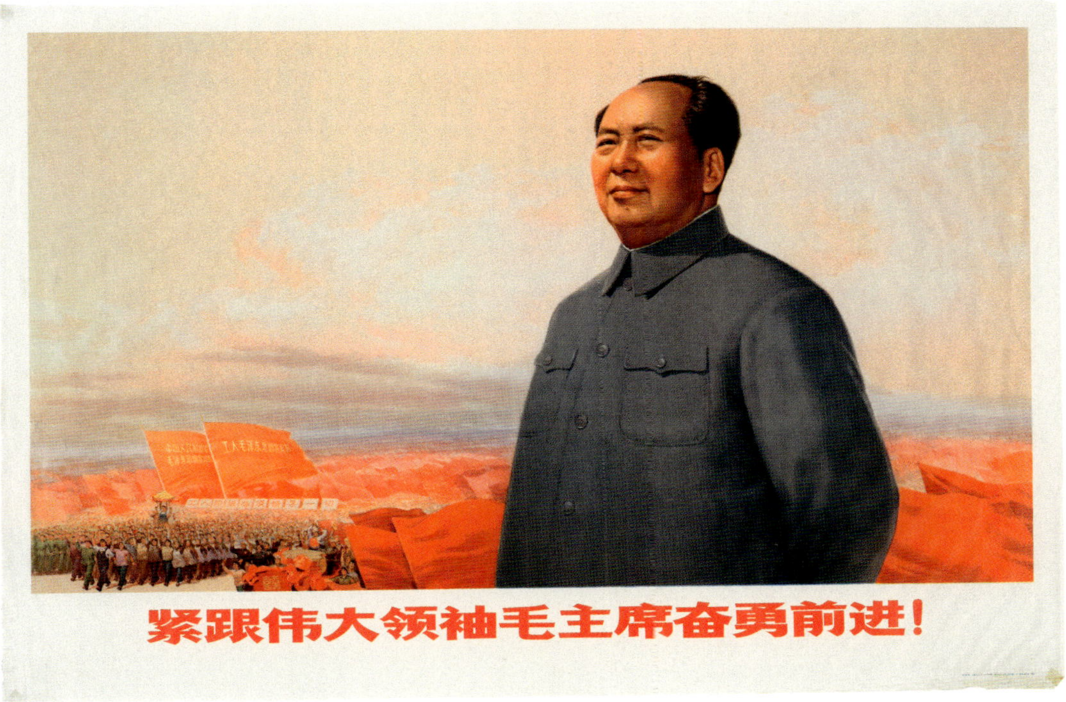

Forging ahead courageously while following the great leader Chairman Mao! 1969.
Wir schreiten mutig voran und folgen dem großartigen Führer, dem Vorsitzenden Mao! 1969.

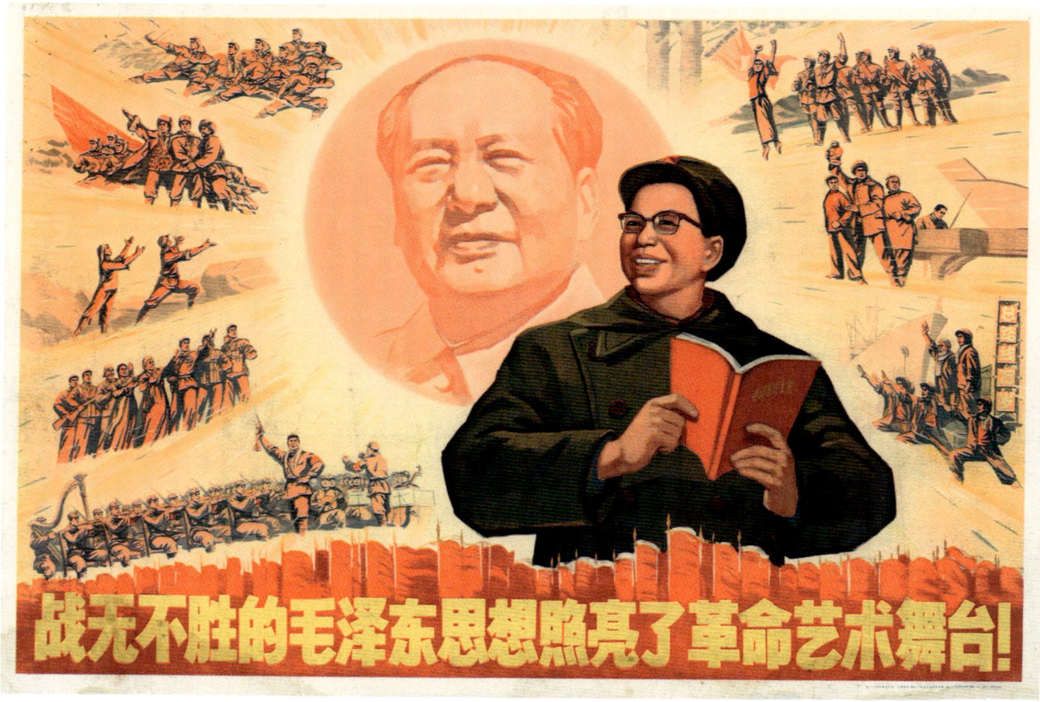

The invincible thought of Mao Zedong illuminates the stage of revolutionary art! 1969.
Der unbesiegbare Gedanke von Mao Zedong erleuchtet die Bühne der revolutionären Kunst! 1969.

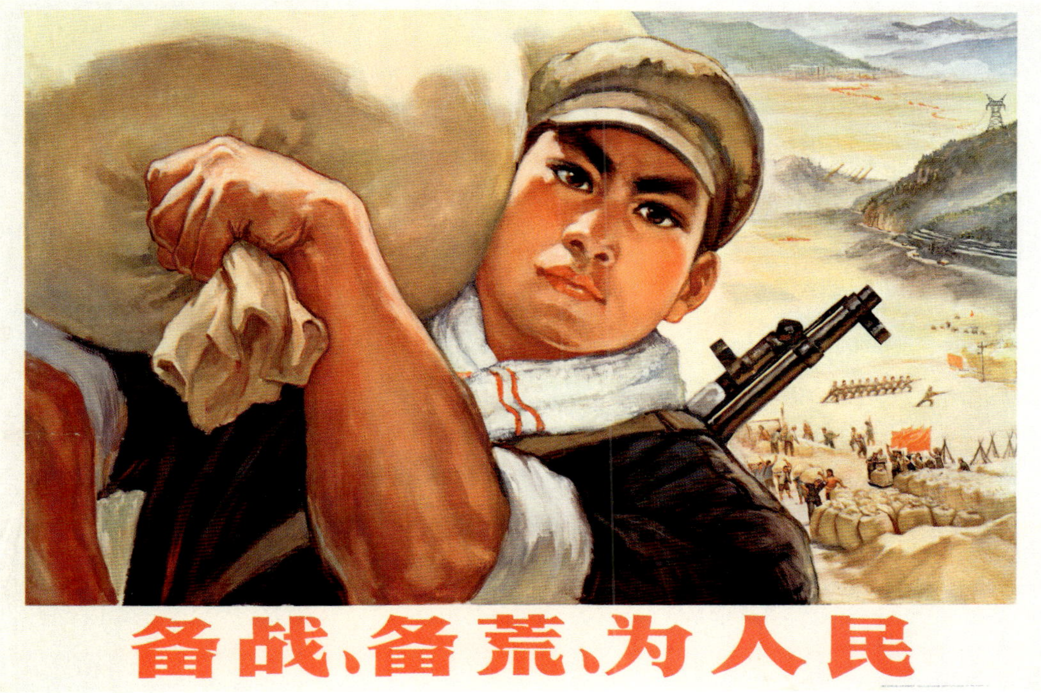

Prepare for struggle, prepare for famine, for the people, 1970.
Sei bereit zu kämpfen, sei bereit zu hungern, für das Volk! 1970.

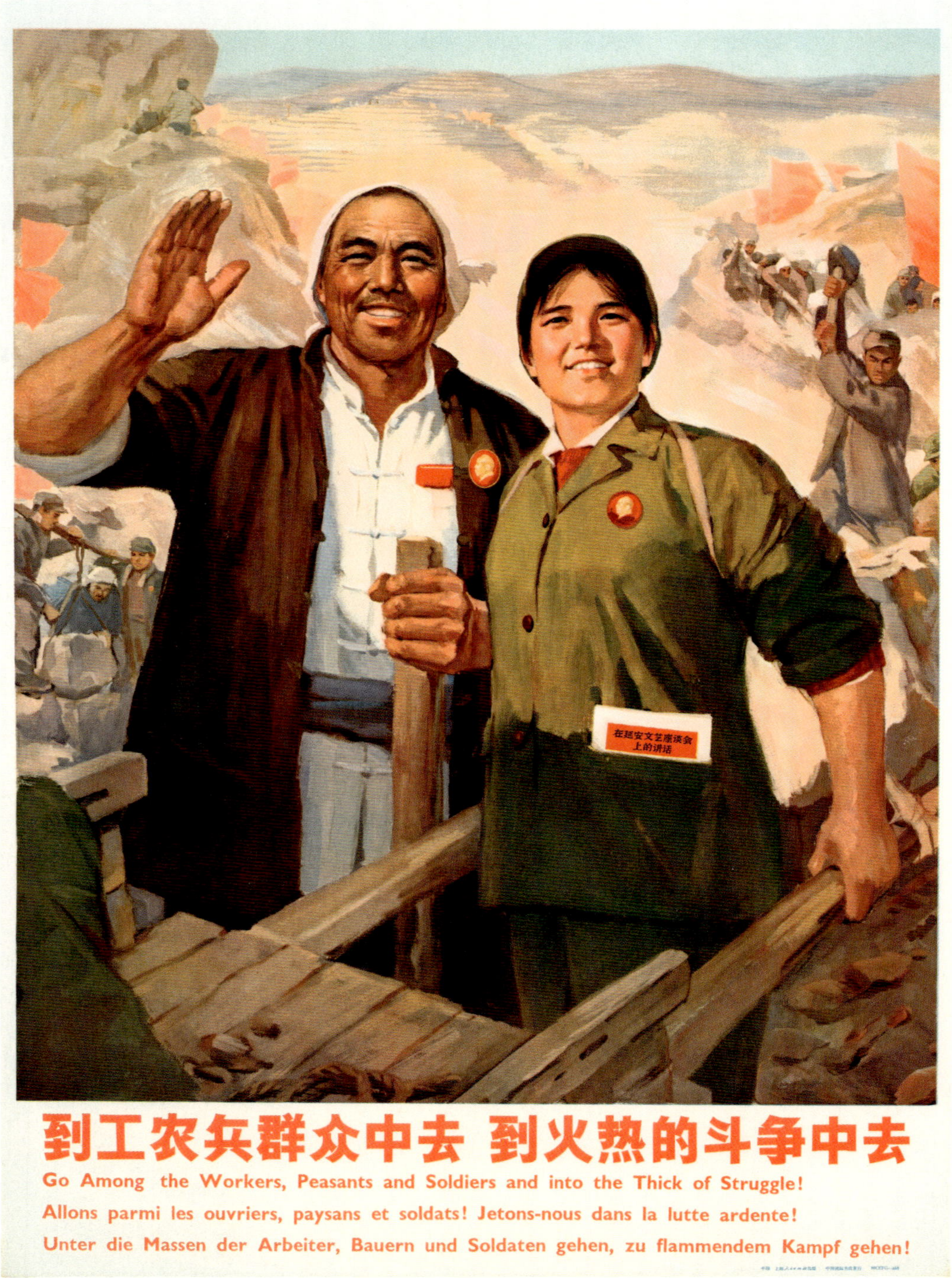

Go among the workers, peasants and soldiers and into the thick of struggle! c. 1970.

Unter die Massen der Arbeiter, Bauern und Soldaten gehen, zu flammendem Kampf gehen! um 1970.

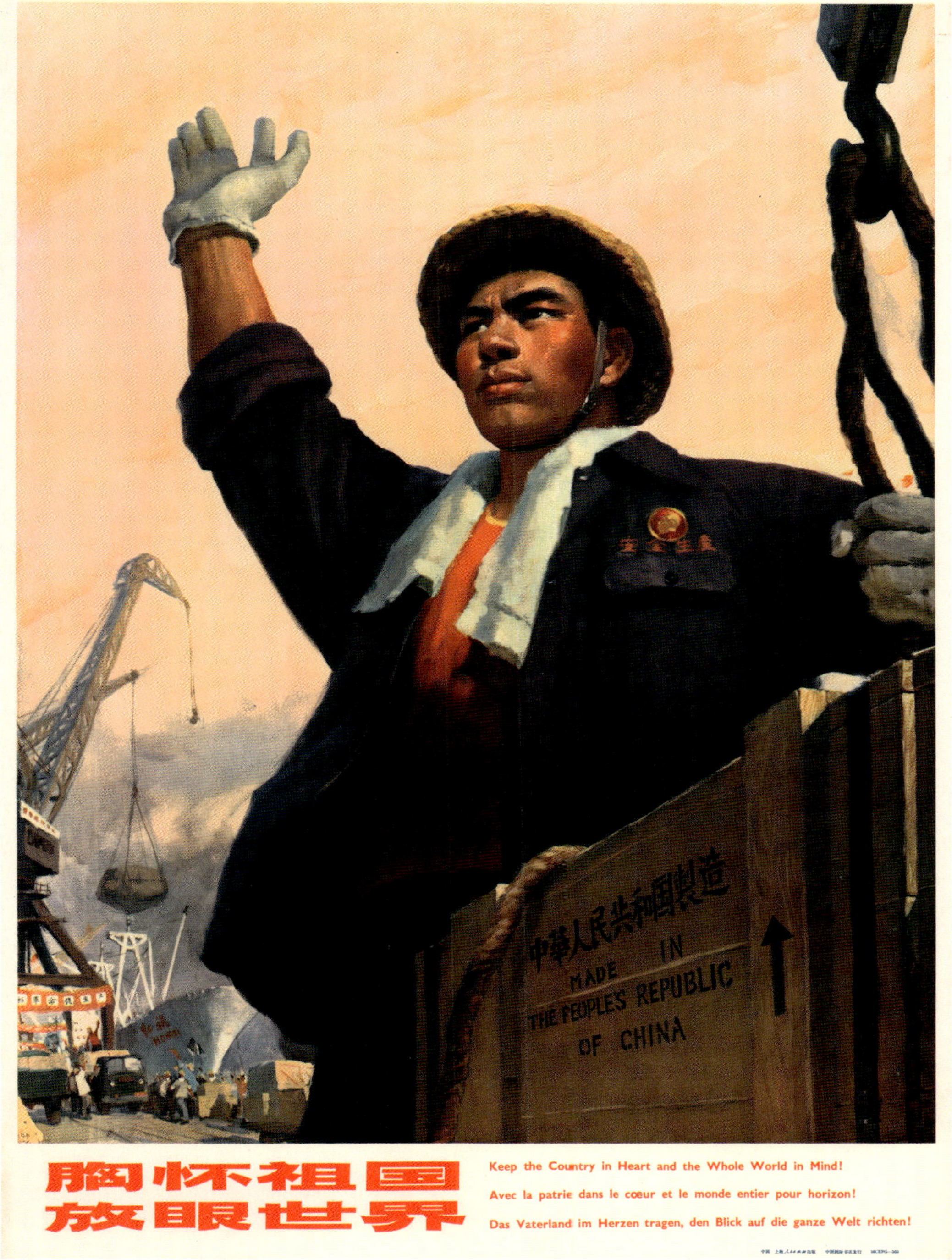

Keep the country in heart and the whole world in mind! c. 1970.
Das Vaterland im Herzen tragen, den Blick auf die ganze Welt richten! um 1970.

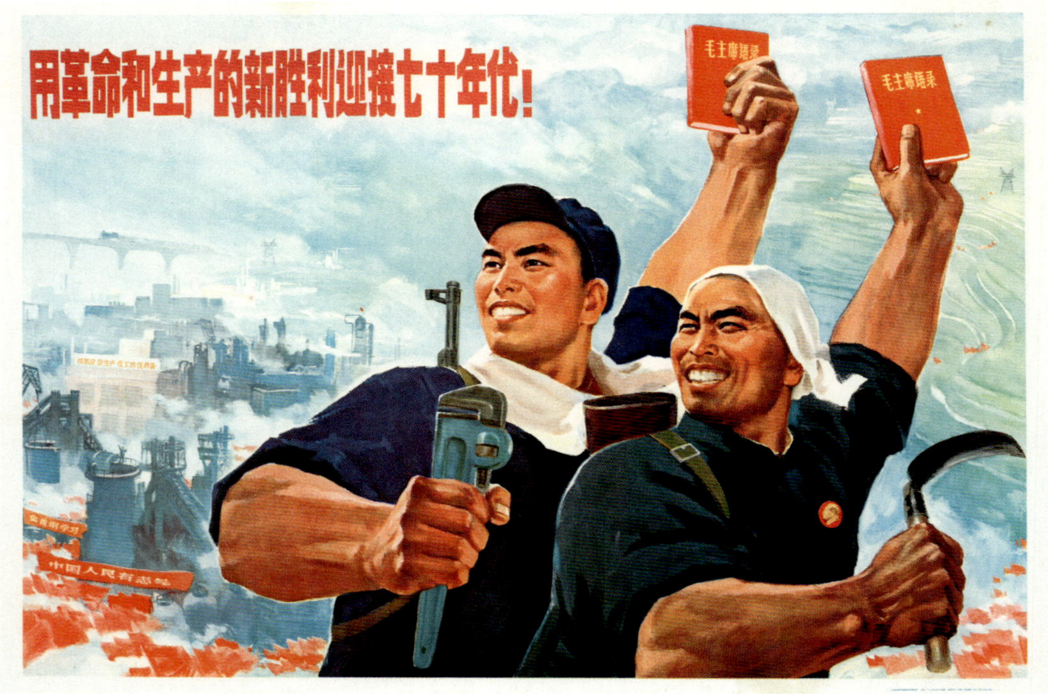

Greet the 1970s with the new victories of revolution and production! 1970.

Begrüßt die 1970er mit den neuen Errungenschaften der Revolution und der Produktion! 1970.

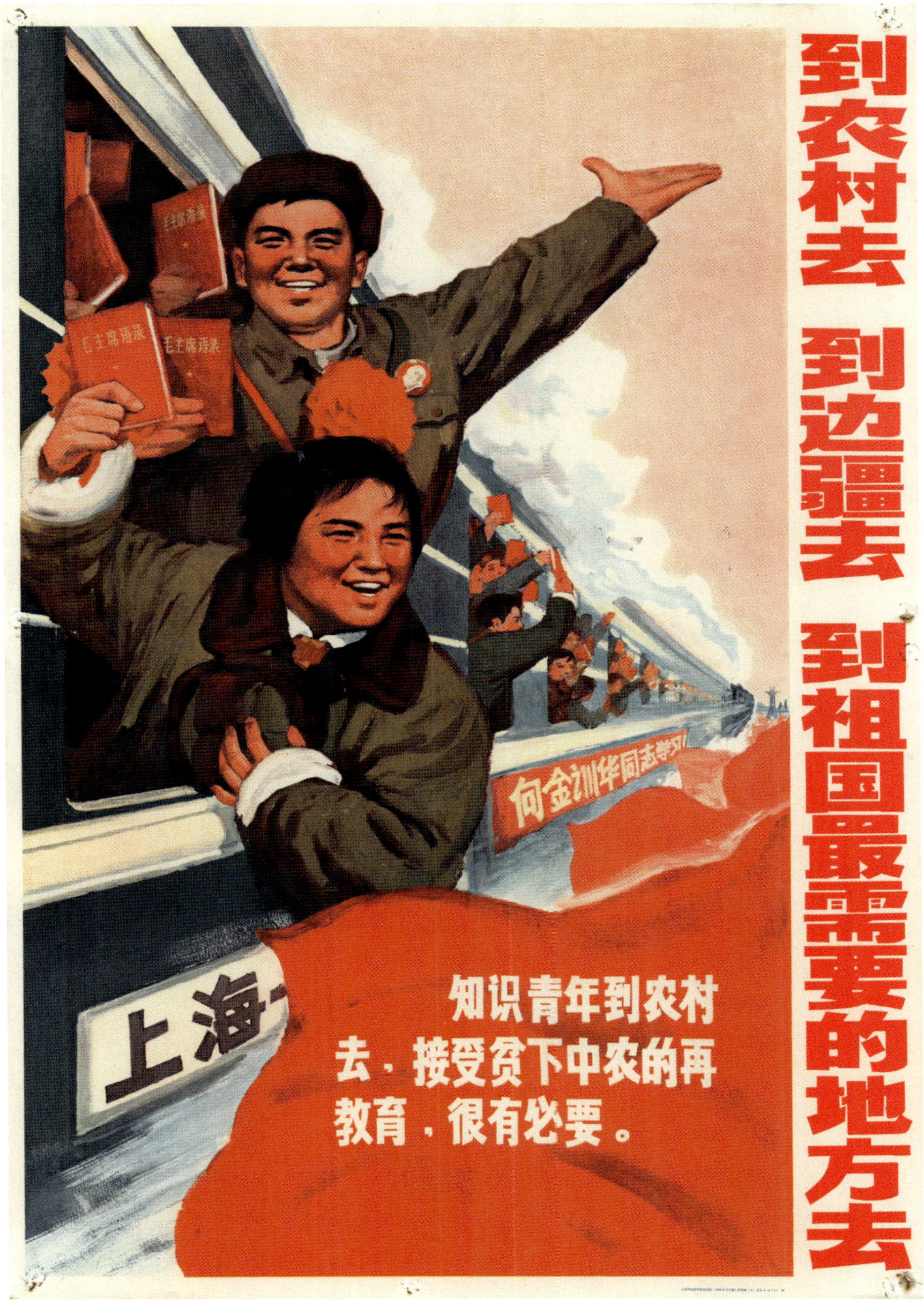

To villages we go, to the borders we go, to places in the fatherland where we are most needed, we go, 1970.
In Dörfer gehen wir, an die Grenzen gehen wir, an die Orte im Vaterland, wo wir am dringensten gebraucht werden, gehen wir, 1970.

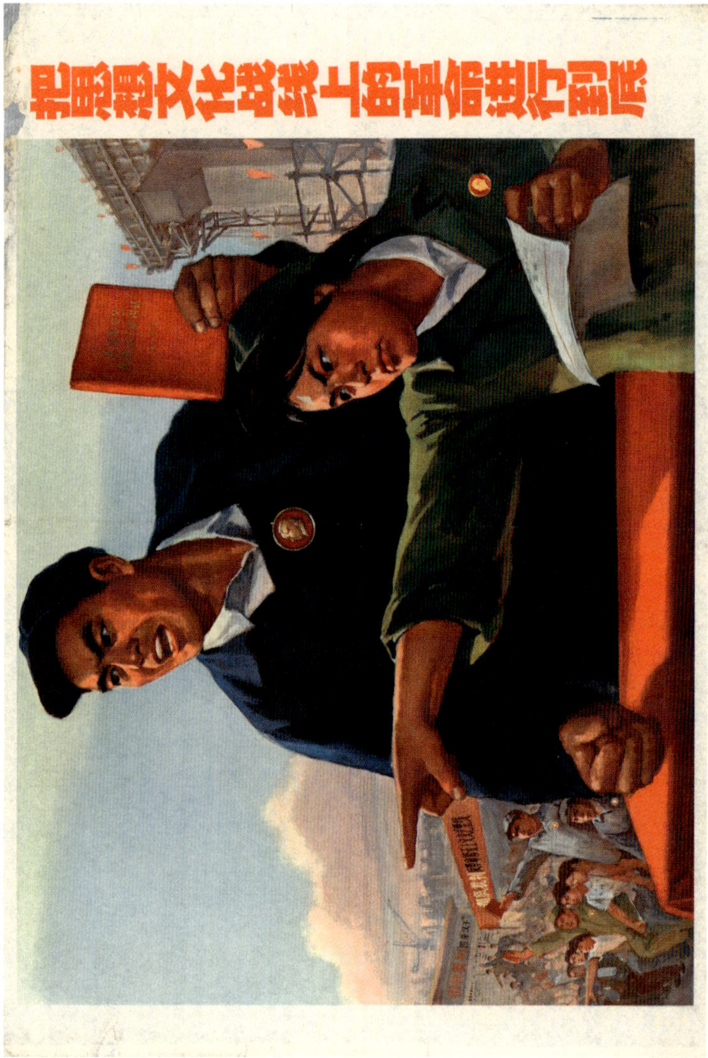

Fully carrry out the revolution on the line of thought and cultural struggle, 1970.
Tragt die Revolution auf der Ebene des Gedankens und des kulturellen Kampfes aus! 1970.

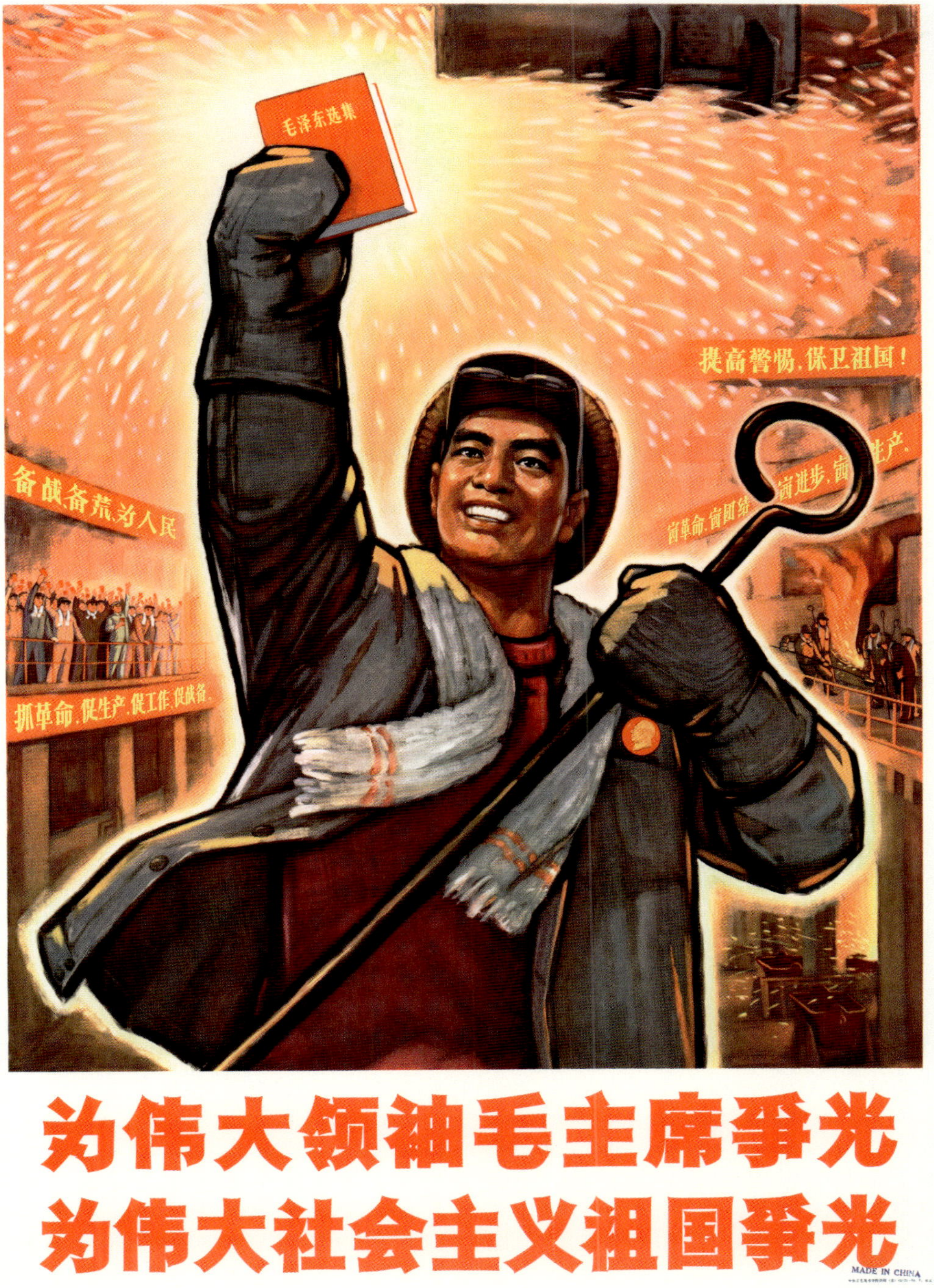

Win honor for our great leader Chairman Mao, bring credit to our socialist motherland, 1970.
Verdient Ehre für unseren großen Anführer Vorsitzenden Mao, bringt unserem sozialistischen Vaterland Anerkennung ein! 1970.

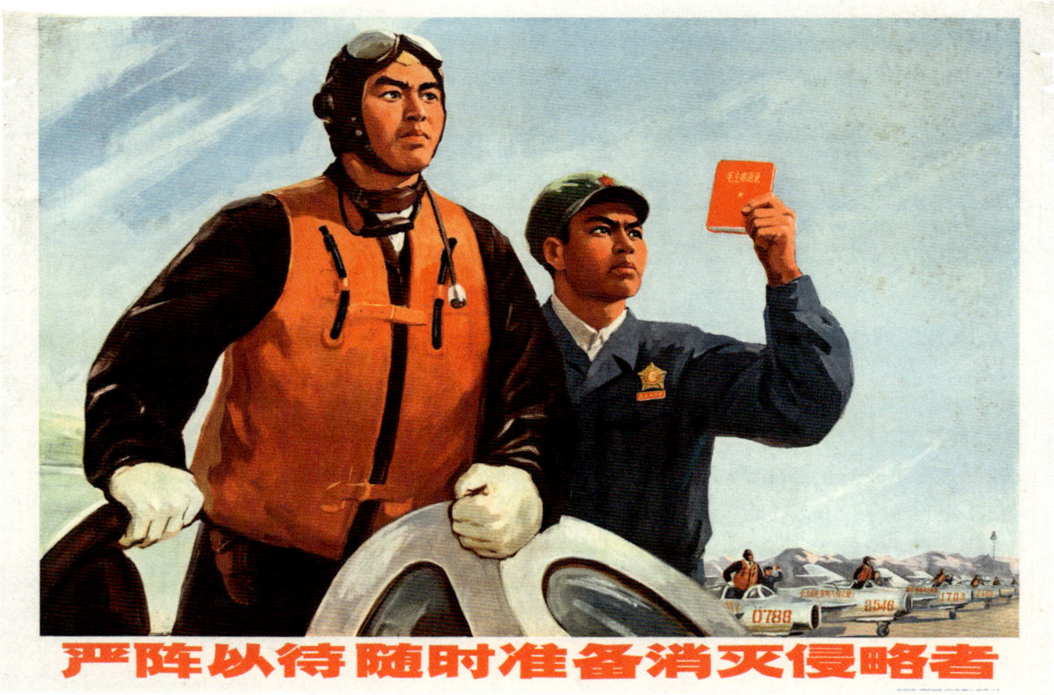

Stand in combat readiness, be always prepared to eliminate the aggressor, 1970.
Sei in Gefechtsbereitschaft, allzeit bereit den Angreifer auszulöschen, 1970.

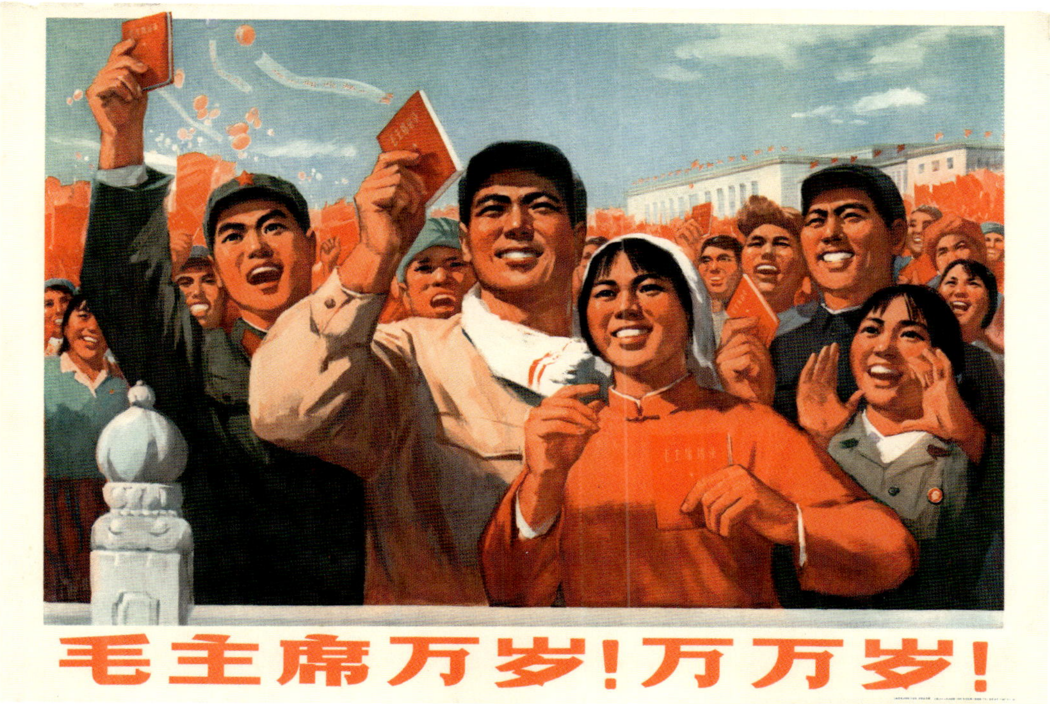

Long live Chairman Mao! Long long life! 1970.
Lang lebe Mao! Ein langes, langes Leben! 1970.

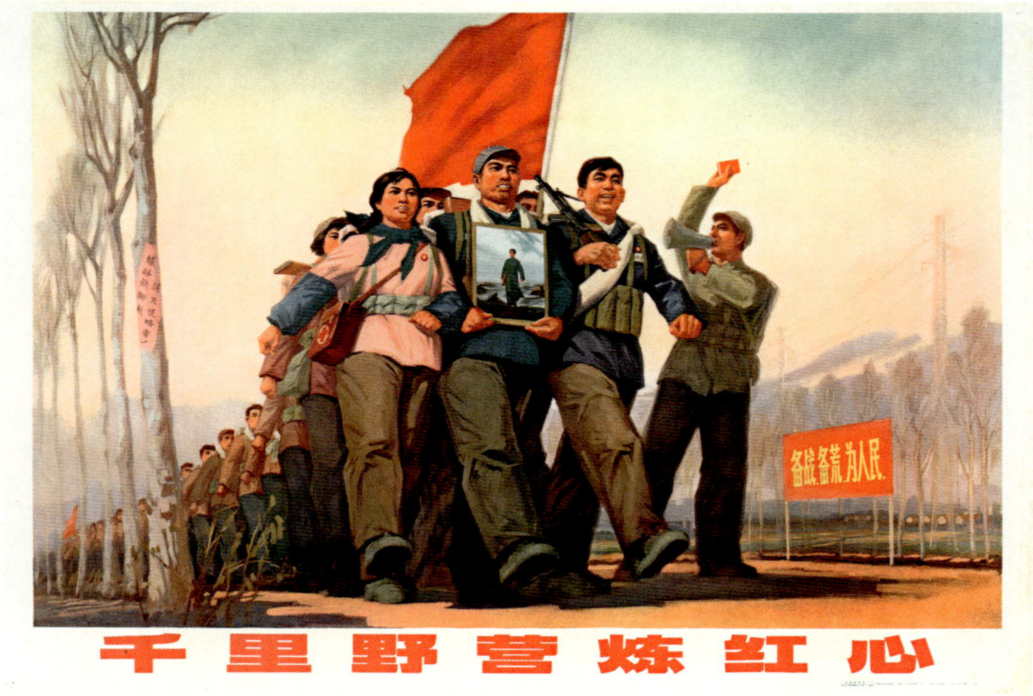

March a distance of a thousand li to temper a red heart, 1971.
Marschiere 1000 li, um ein rotes Herz glühen zu lassen, 1971.

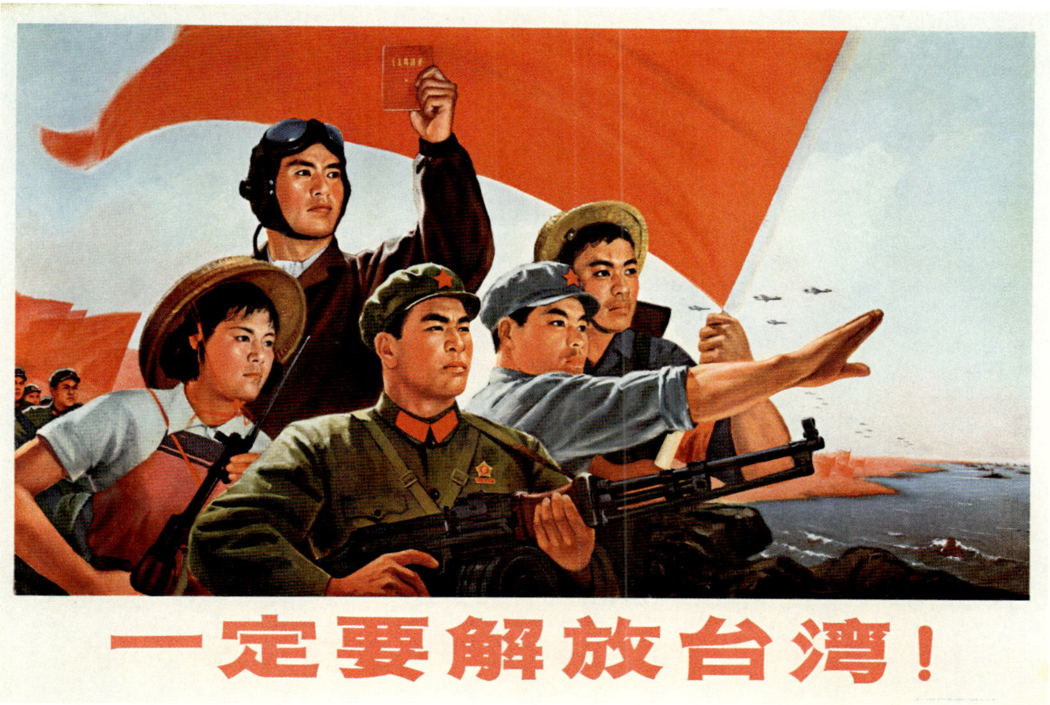

We will definitely free Taiwan! 1971.
Wir werden Taiwan endgültig befreien! 1971.

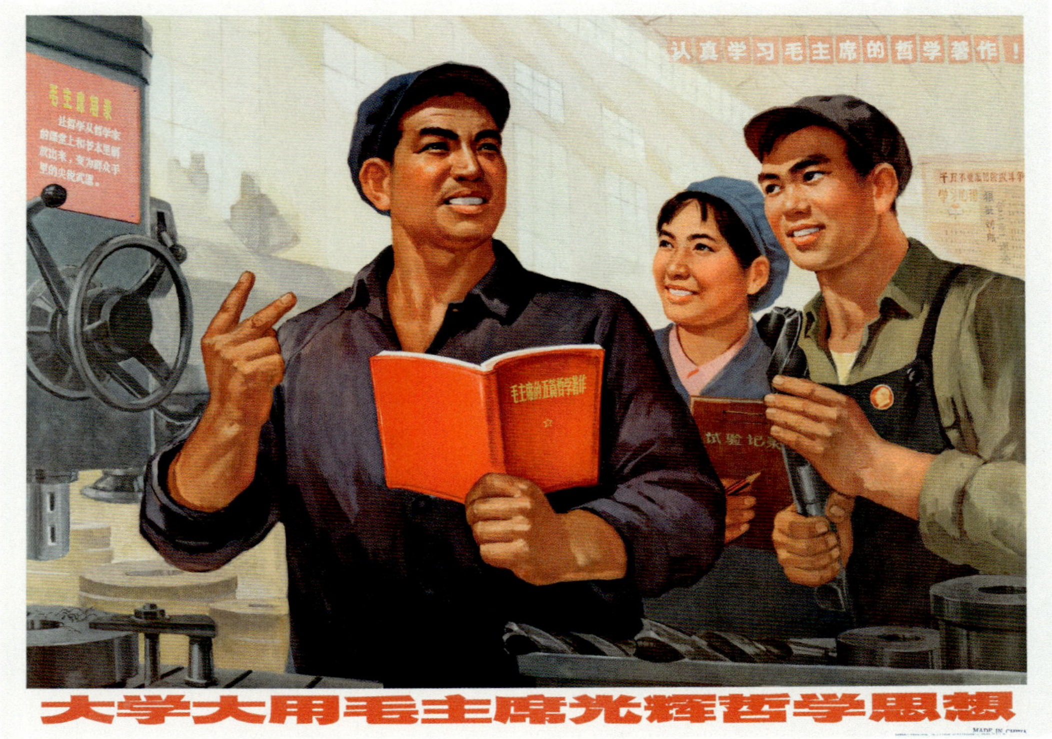

Use and study Chairman Mao's glorious philosophical thought in a big way, 1971.

Nutze und studiere das ruhmvolle philosophische Denken des Vorsitzenden Mao! 1971.

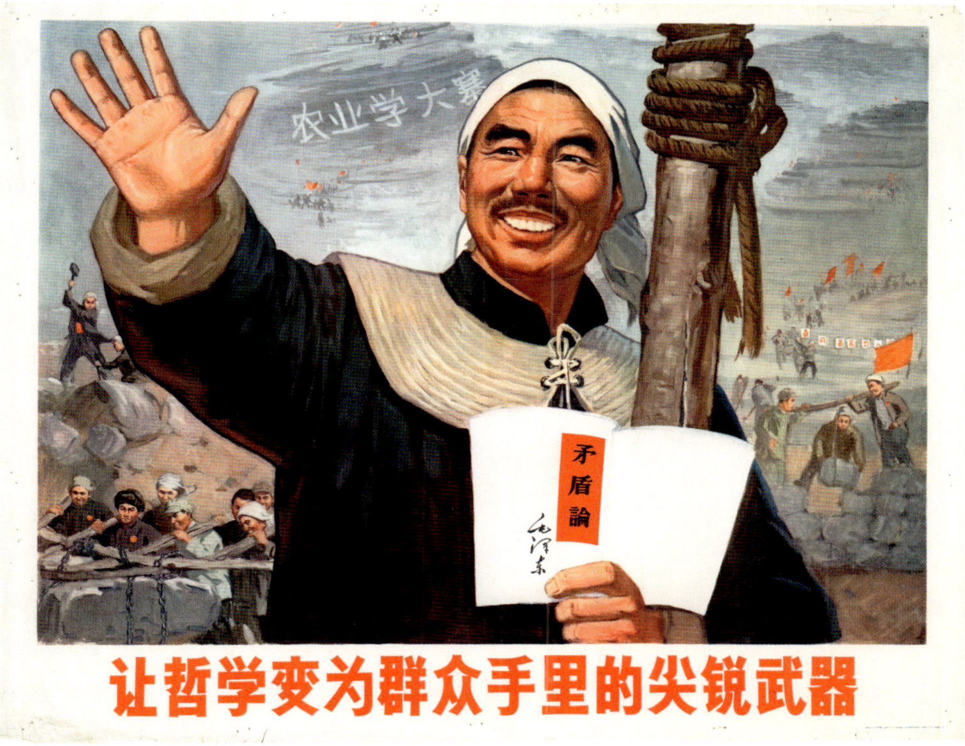

Turn philosophy into a sharp weapon in the hands of the masses, 1971.
Macht Philosophie zu einer scharfen Waffe in den Händen der Masse! 1971.

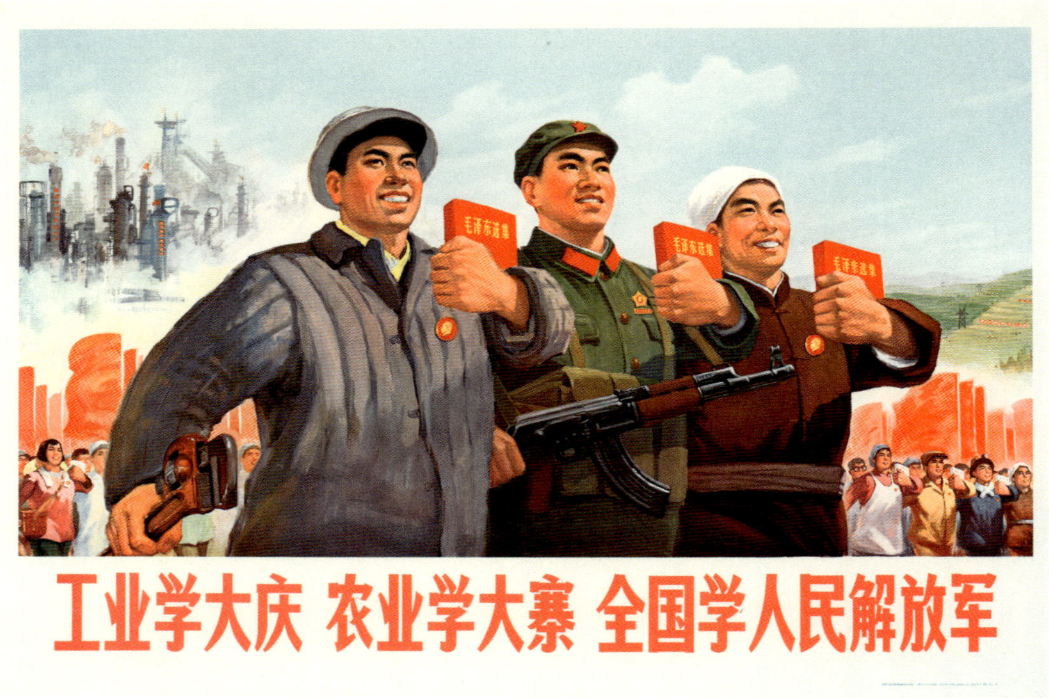

The industry learns from Daqing, agriculture learns from the village of Dazhai and the whole country learns from the People's Liberation Army, 1971.

Die Industrie lernt von Daqing, die Landwirtschaft lernt von dem Dorf Dazhai und das gesamte Land lernt von der Volksbefreiungsarmee, 1971.

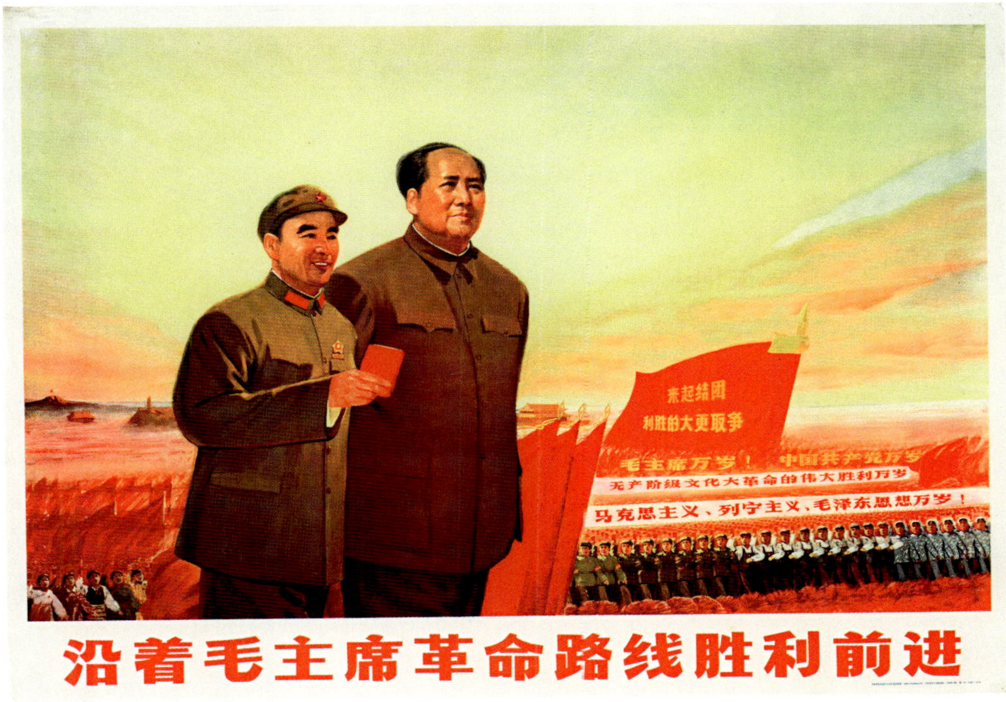

Advance victoriously while following Chairman Mao's revolutionary line, 1971.
Schreite siegreich voran und folge dabei der revolutionären Bewegung des Vorsitzenden Mao, 1971.

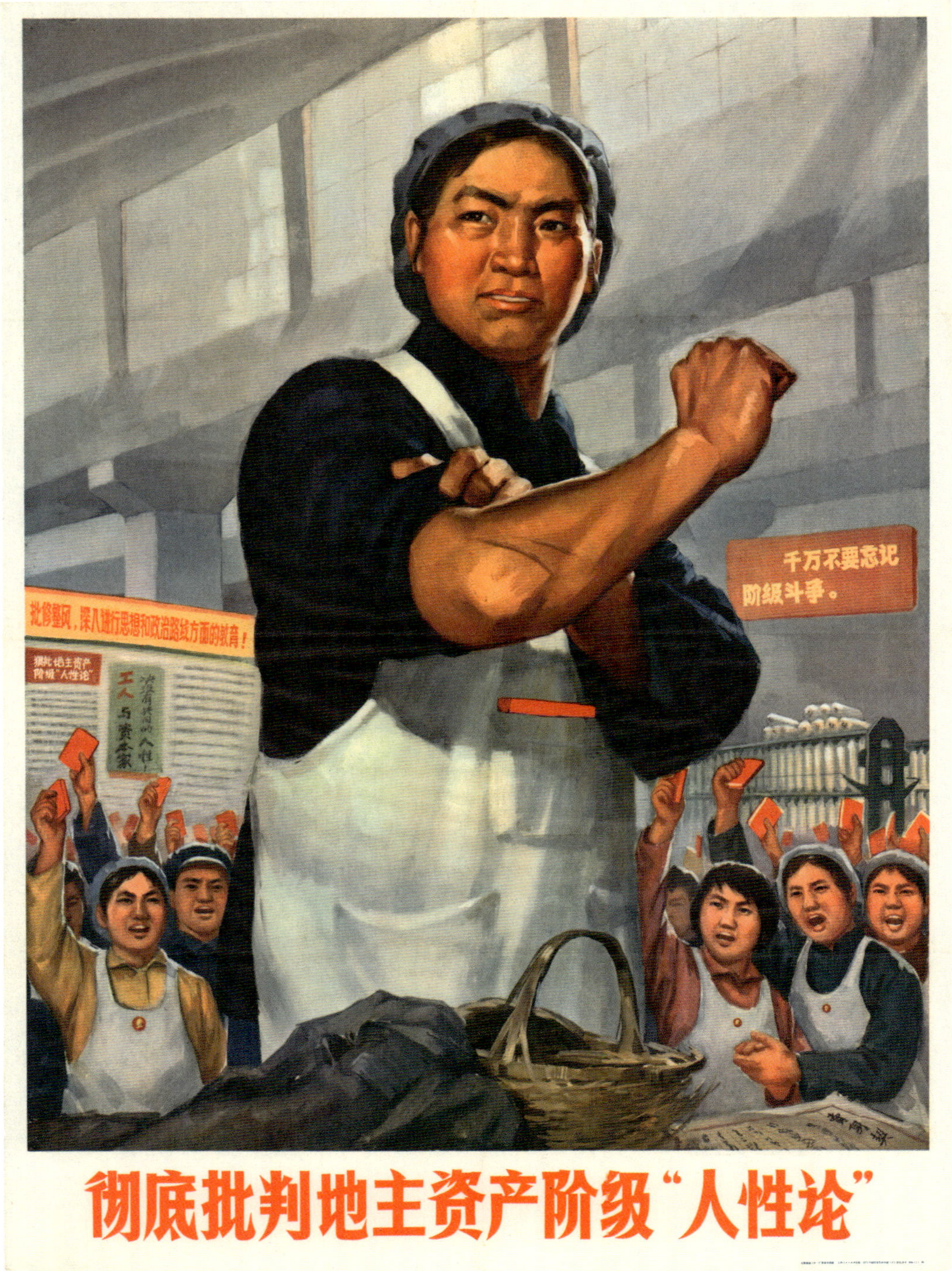

Thoroughly criticize the "theory of human nature" of the landlord and capitalist classes, 1971.

Kritisiere die "Theorie zur Natur des Menschen" der Grundbesitzer und der kapitalistischen Klassen durch und durch! 1971.

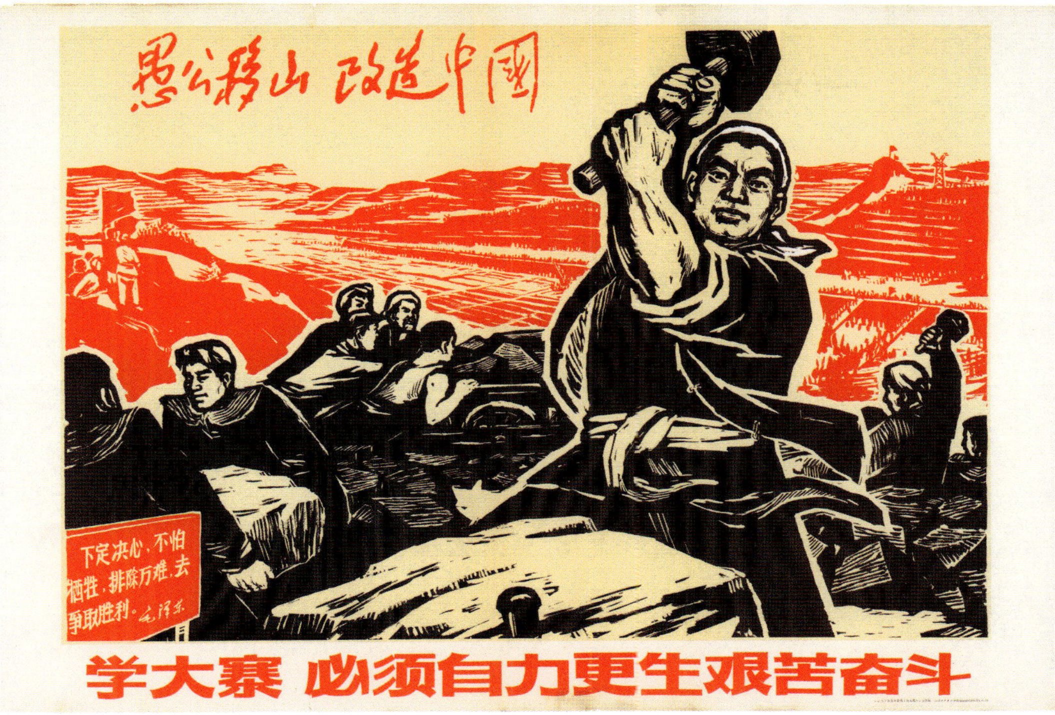

Study the village of Dazhai; we must rely on self sufficiency to wage the bitter struggle, c. 1972.
Befasse dich mit dem Dorf Dazhai; wir müssen uns auf Selbstversorgung stützen, um den bitteren Kampf zu führen, um 1972.

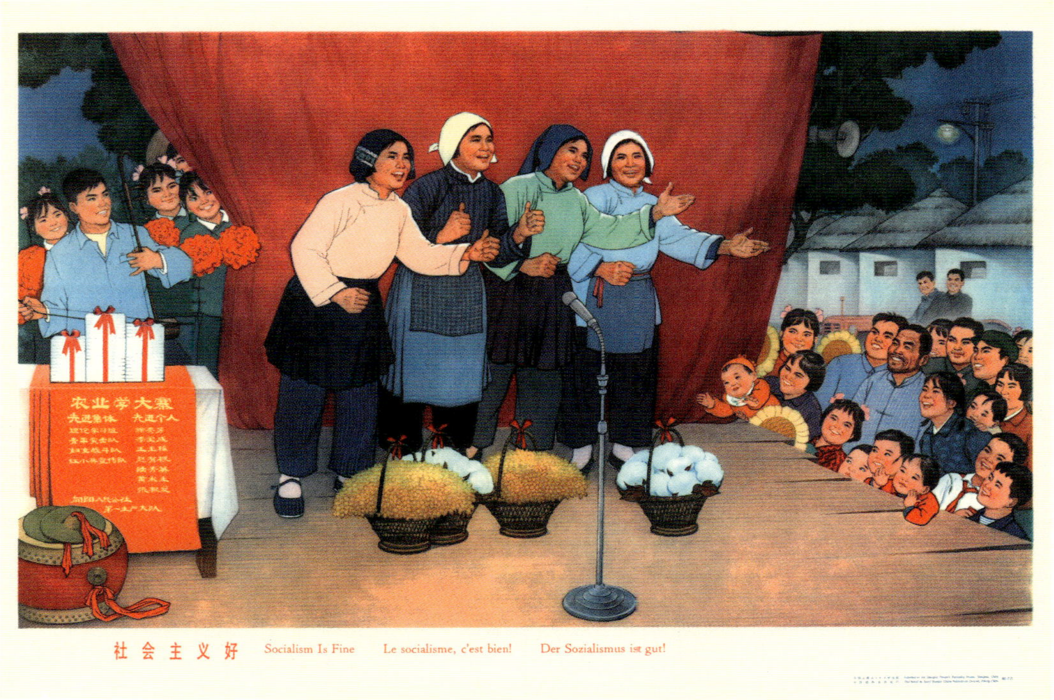

Socialism is fine, c. 1972.
Der Sozialismus ist gut, um 1972.

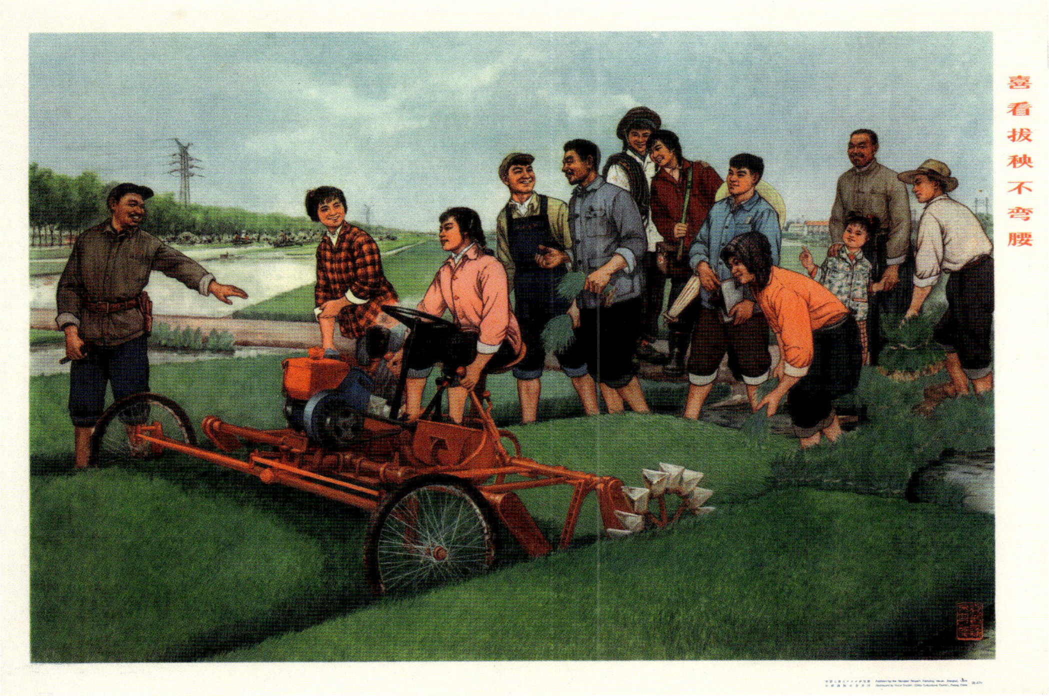

Happy that pulling up seedlings no longer means bending down, c. 1972.
Glücklicherweise bedeutet das Heranziehen von Setzlingen nicht mehr, dass man sich hinknien muss, um 1972.

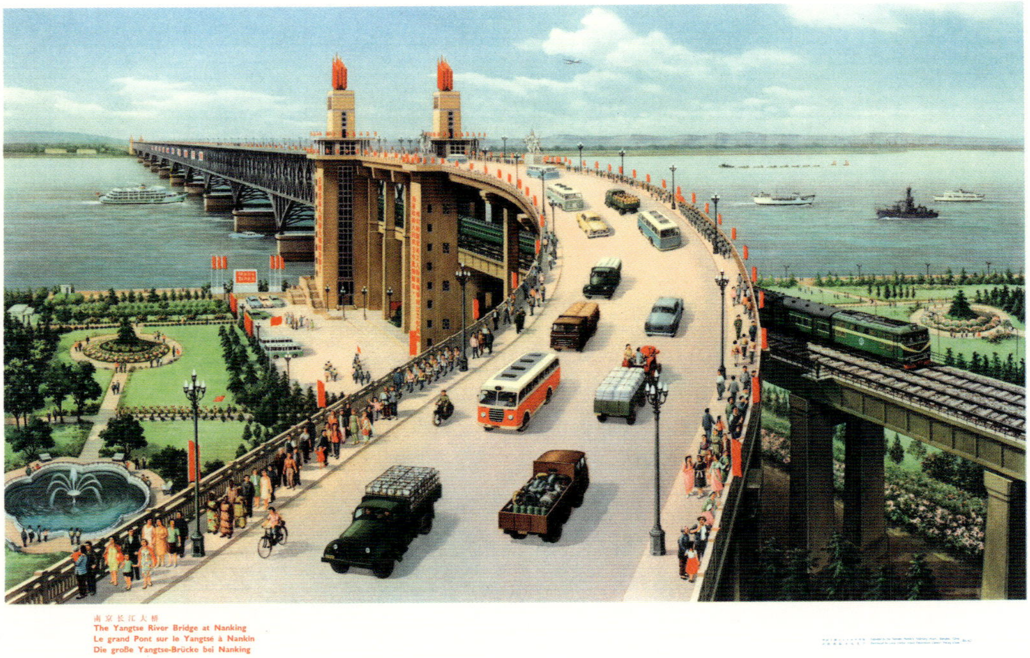

The Yangzi River Bridge at Nanjing, c. 1972.
Die große Brücke Yangzi in Nanjing, um 1972.

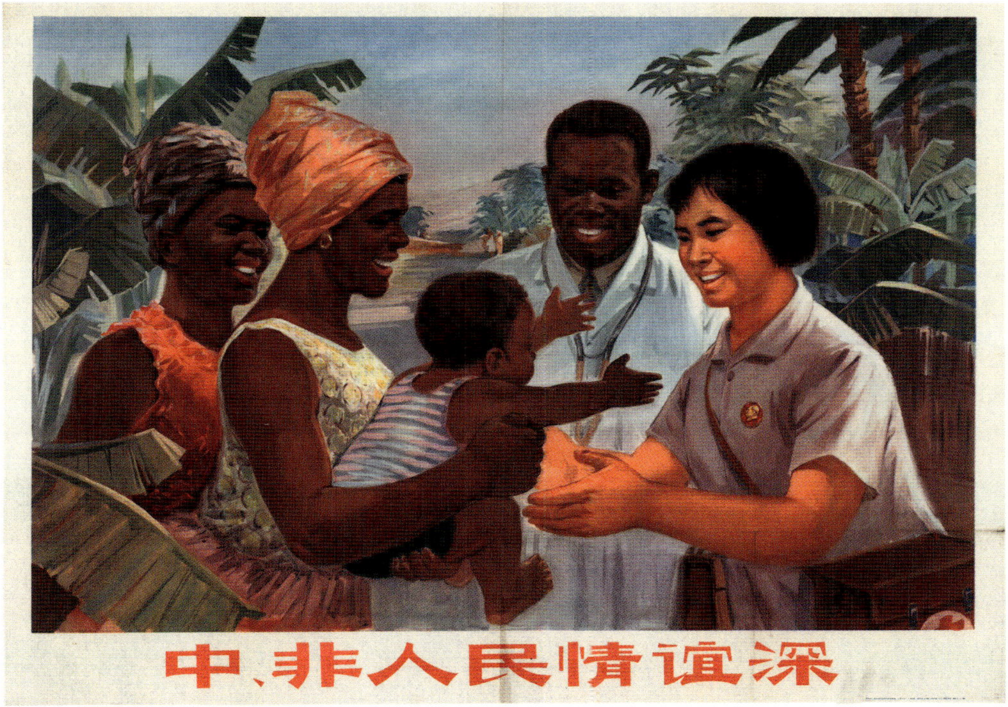

The feelings of friendship between the peoples of China and Africa run deep, 1972.
Die Freundschaft zwischen den Menschen von China und Afrika geht sehr tief, 1972.

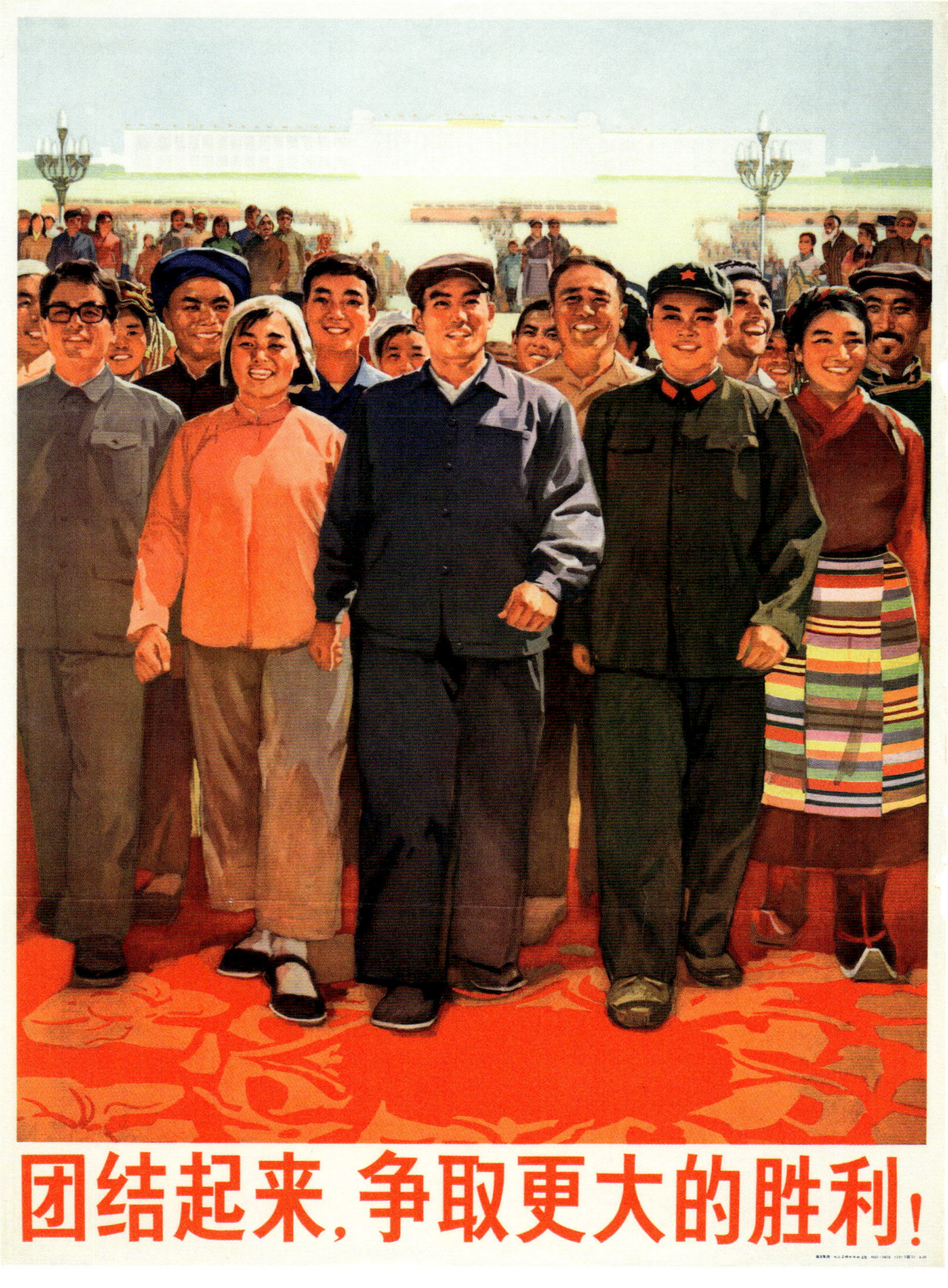

Unite to achieve an even greater victory! 1973.
Vereint Euch für einen noch größeren Sieg! 1973.

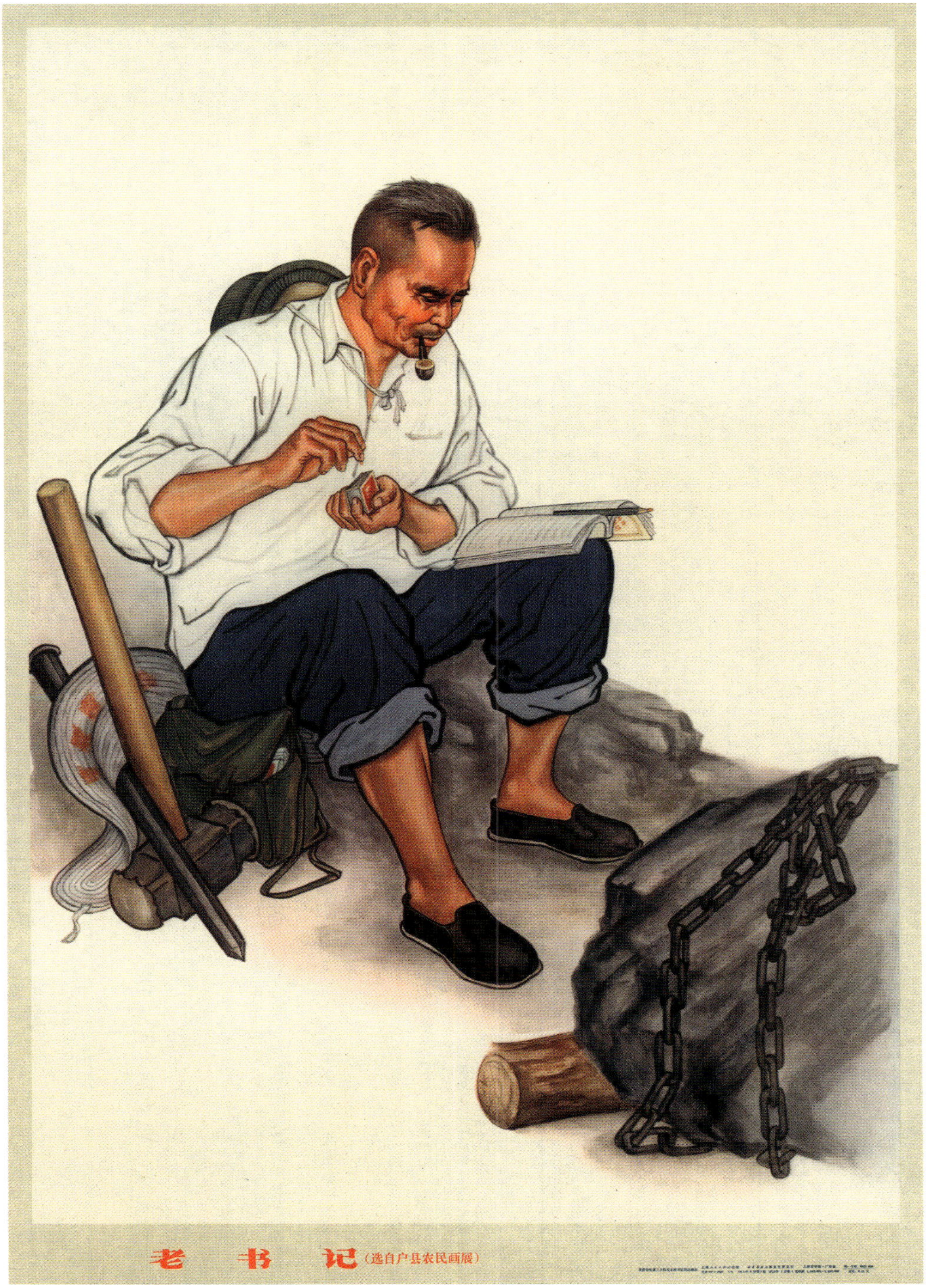

Old party secretary (Selected from the Huxian peasant painting exhibition), 1973.
Der alte Parteisekretär (ausgewählt aus der Huxian-Bauernmalerei Ausstellung), 1973.

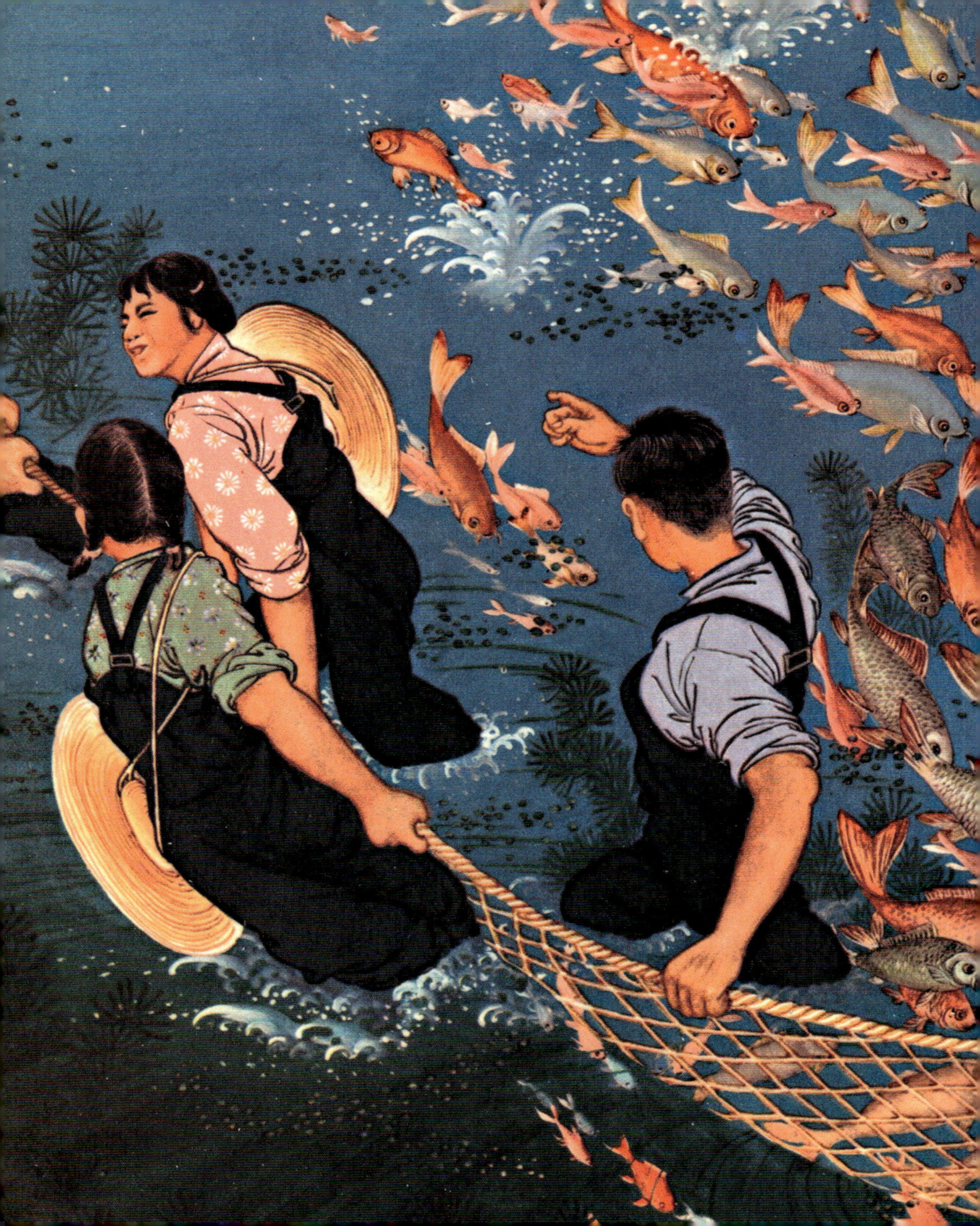

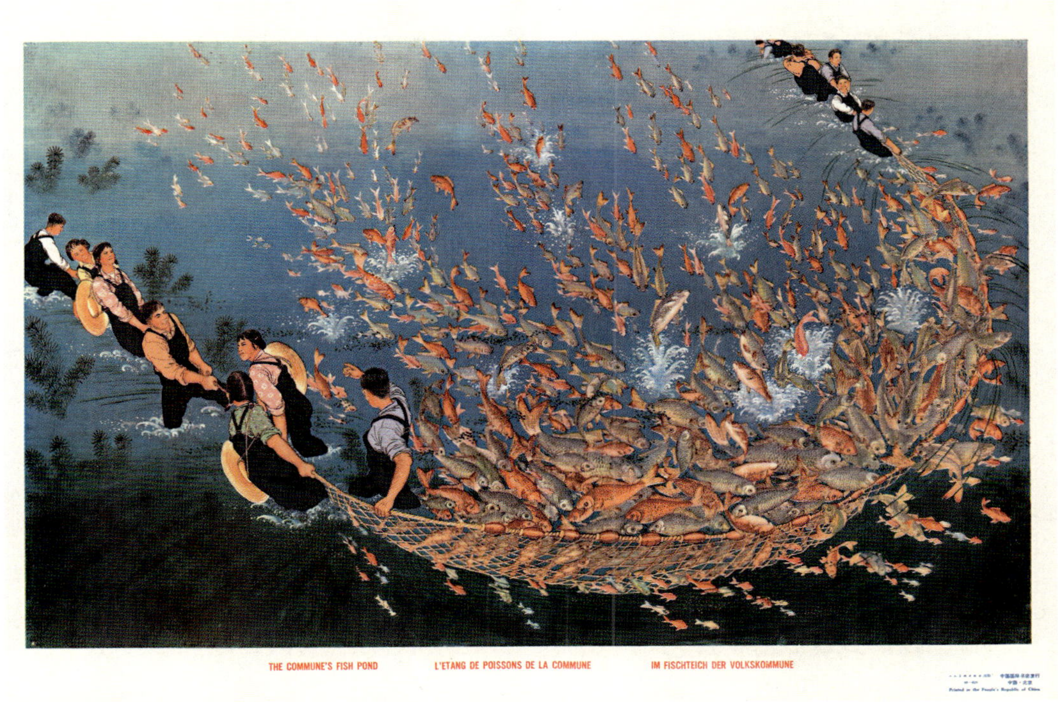

The commune's fishpond, 1973.
Der Fischteich der Volkskommune, 1973.

One of the most famous "Huxian peasant paintings," especially popular in the West. The peasant painters from rural Huxian district are extolled as examples of the innate genius of the people. In reality, these amateur artists are helped by professionals.

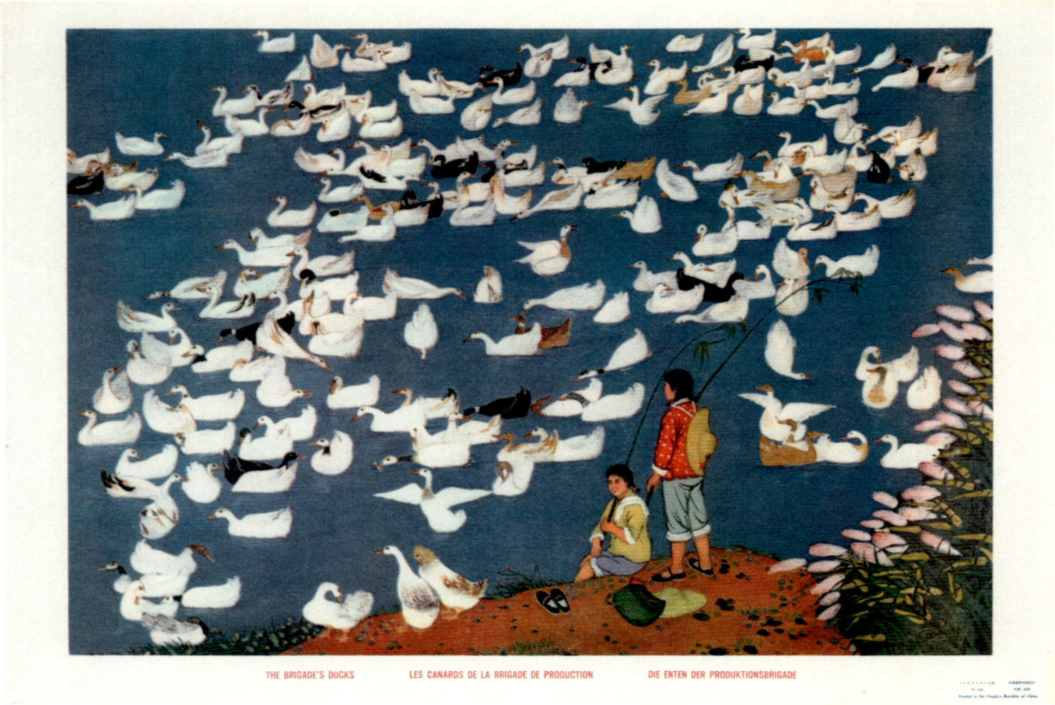

The brigade's ducks, 1973.
Die Enten der Produktionsbrigade, 1973.

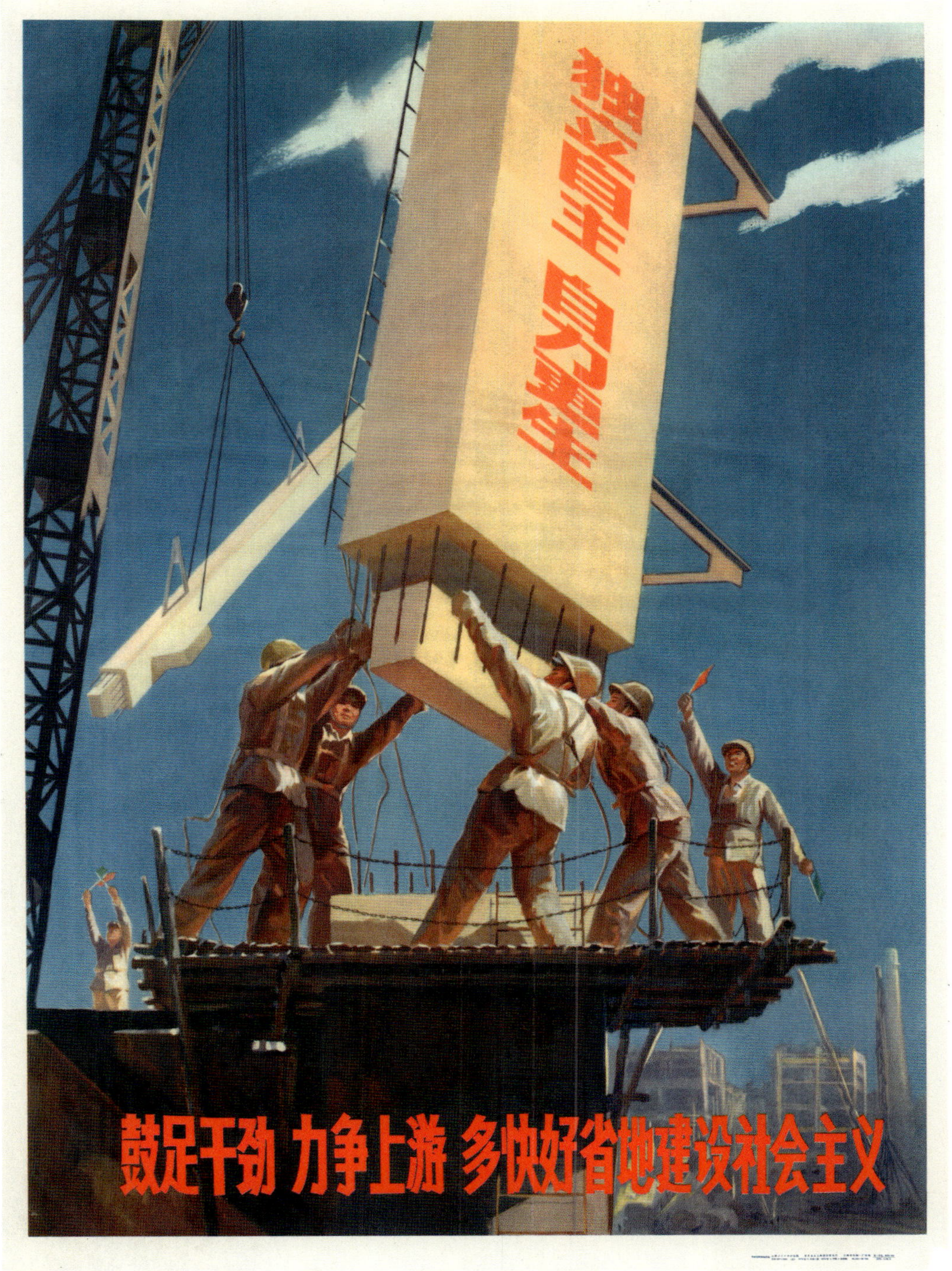

Go all out, aim high, and achieve greater, faster, better, and more economical results in building socialism, 1973.
Geht hinaus, setzt Euch hohe Ziele und erreicht größere, schnellere, bessere und ökonomischere Ergebnisse im Aufbau des Sozialismus, 1973.

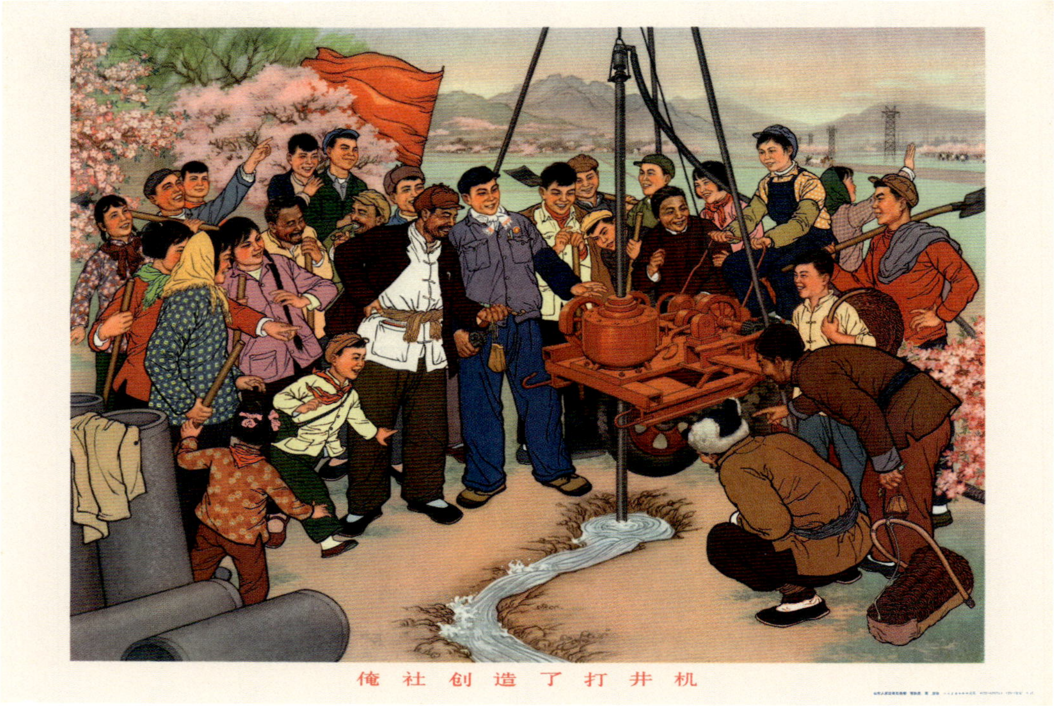

Our commune has constructed a well drilling machine, 1973.
Unsere Kommune hat eine Bohrmaschine konstruiert, 1973.

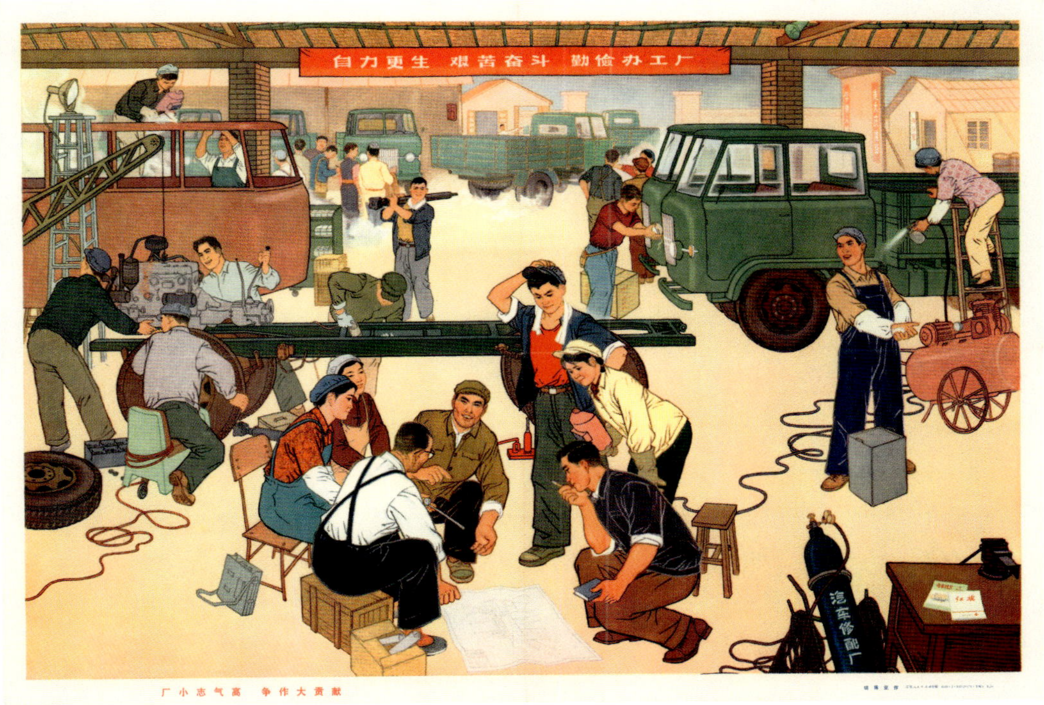

The factory is small, the aspirations high, striving to make great contributions, 1973.
Die Fabrik ist klein, das Bestreben ist hoch, man wetteifert um große Beiträge zu leisten, 1973.

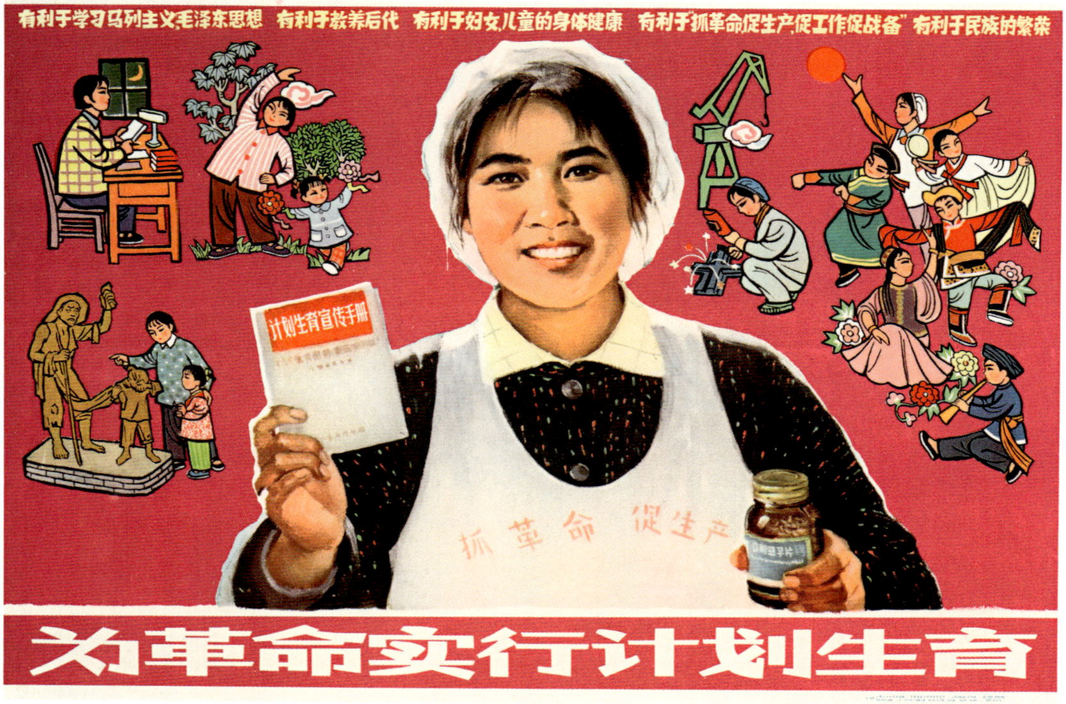

Carry out birth planning for the revolution, 1974.
Betreibe Geburtenplanung für die Revolution, 1974.

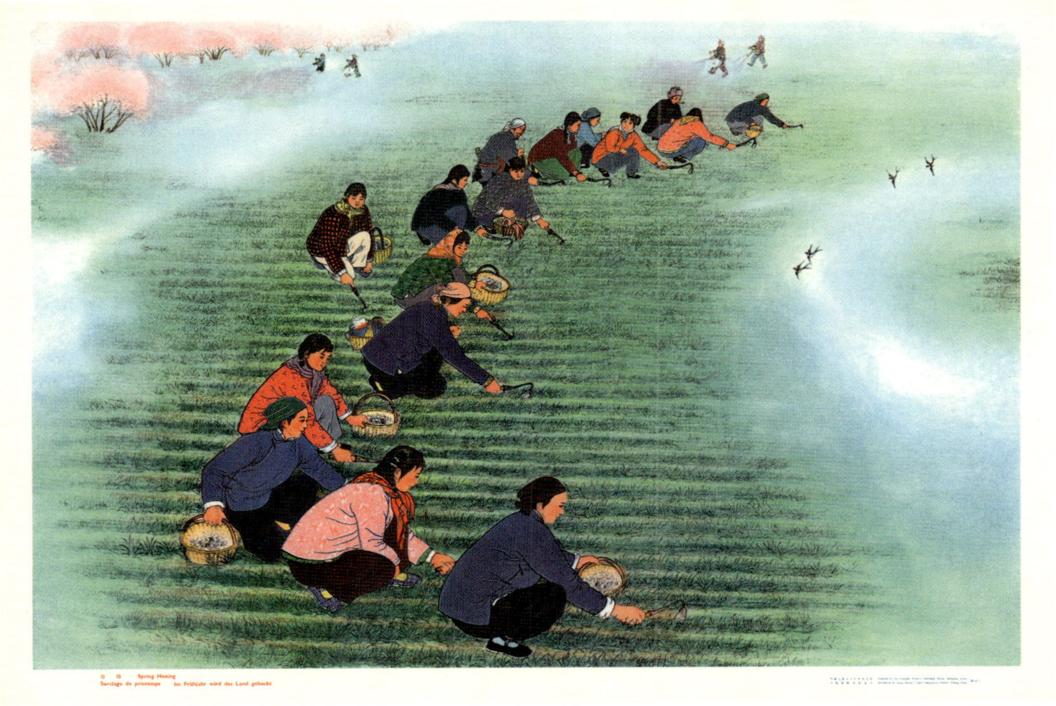

Spring hoeing, 1974.
Frühjährliches Aufhacken, 1974.

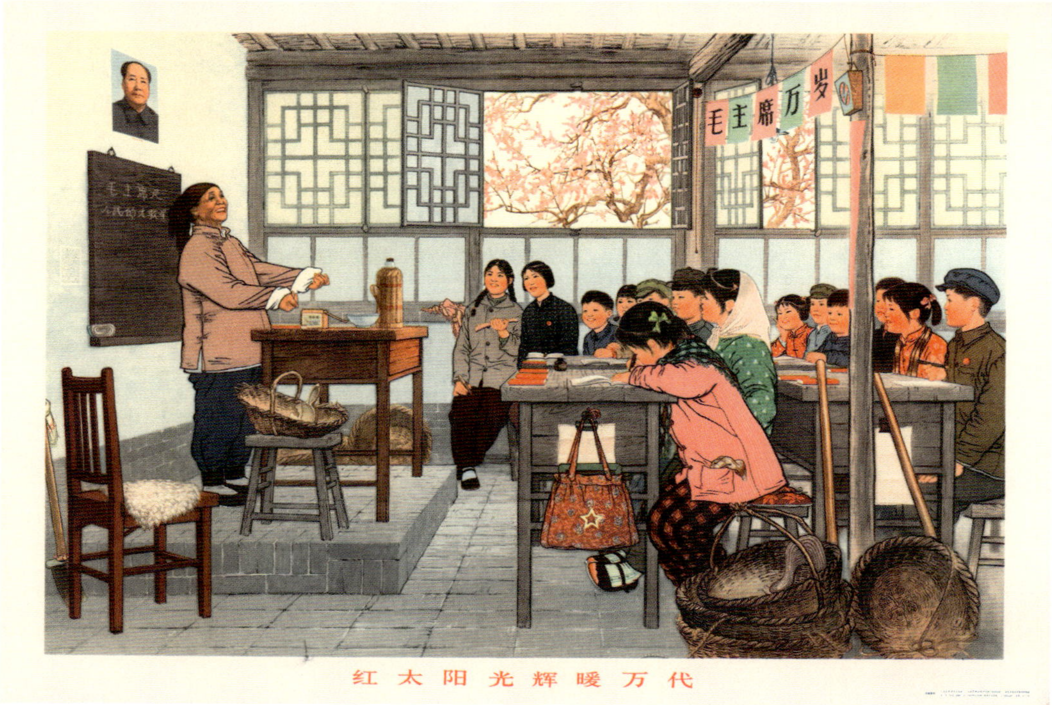

The glow of the red sun warms ten thousand generations, 1974.
Das Glühen der roten Sonne erwärmt zehntausend Generationen, 1974.

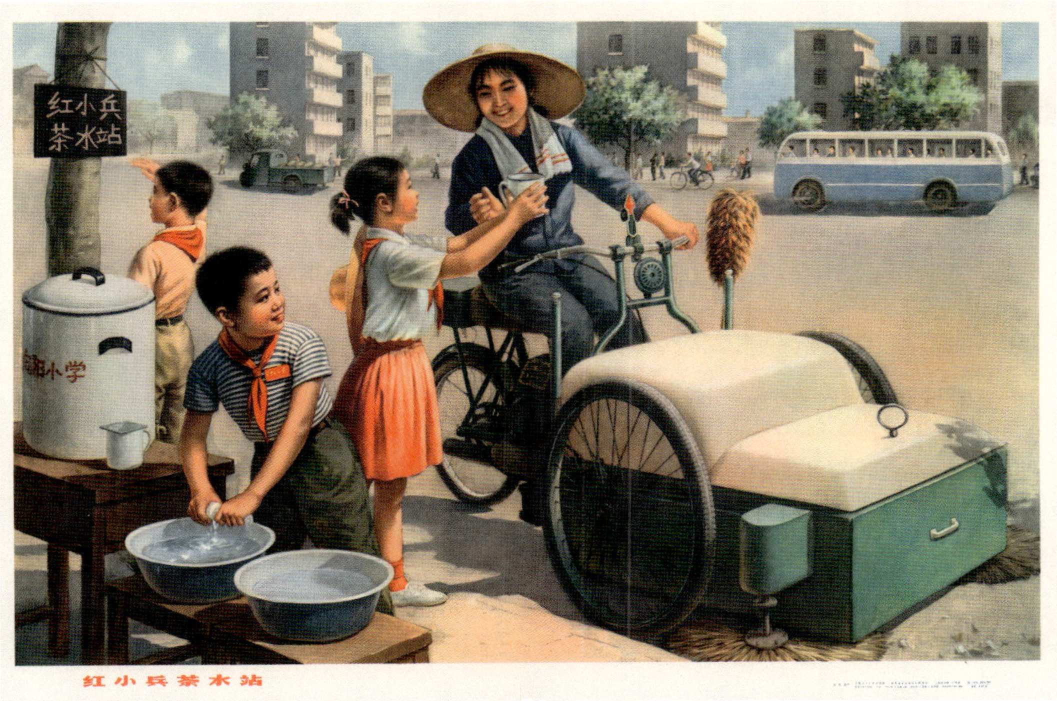

Little Red Guard tea stop, 1974.
Teeausschank der Kleinen Rote Garde, 1974.

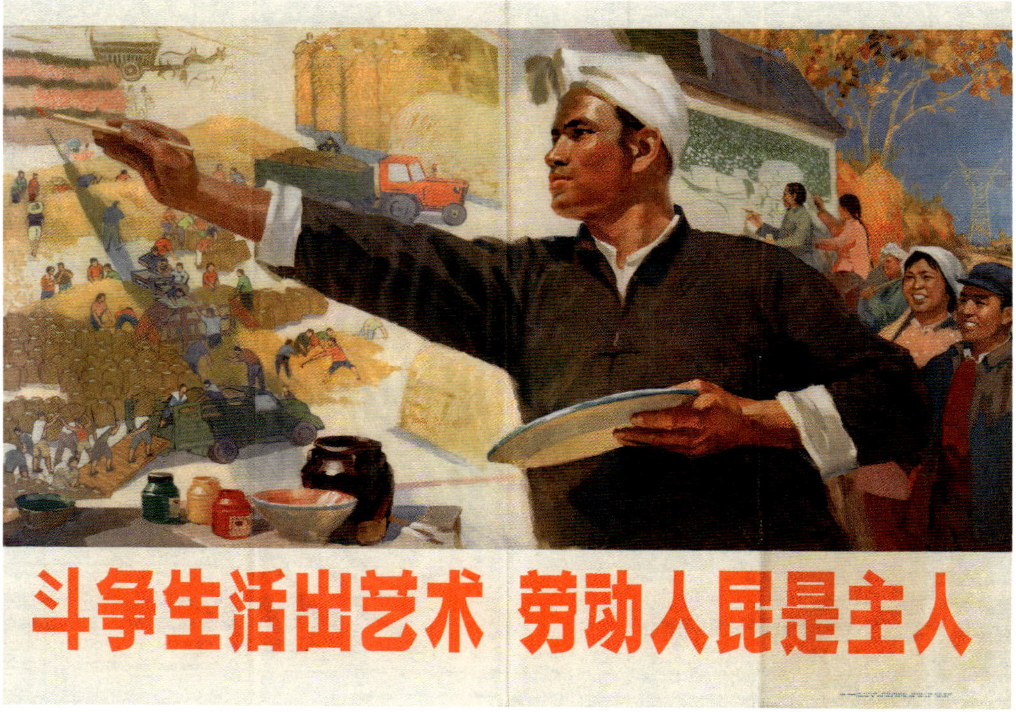

A life of combat produces art; the working people are in charge, 1974.
Ein Leben im Kampfe erzeugt Kunst, die Arbeiter sind tonangebend, 1974.

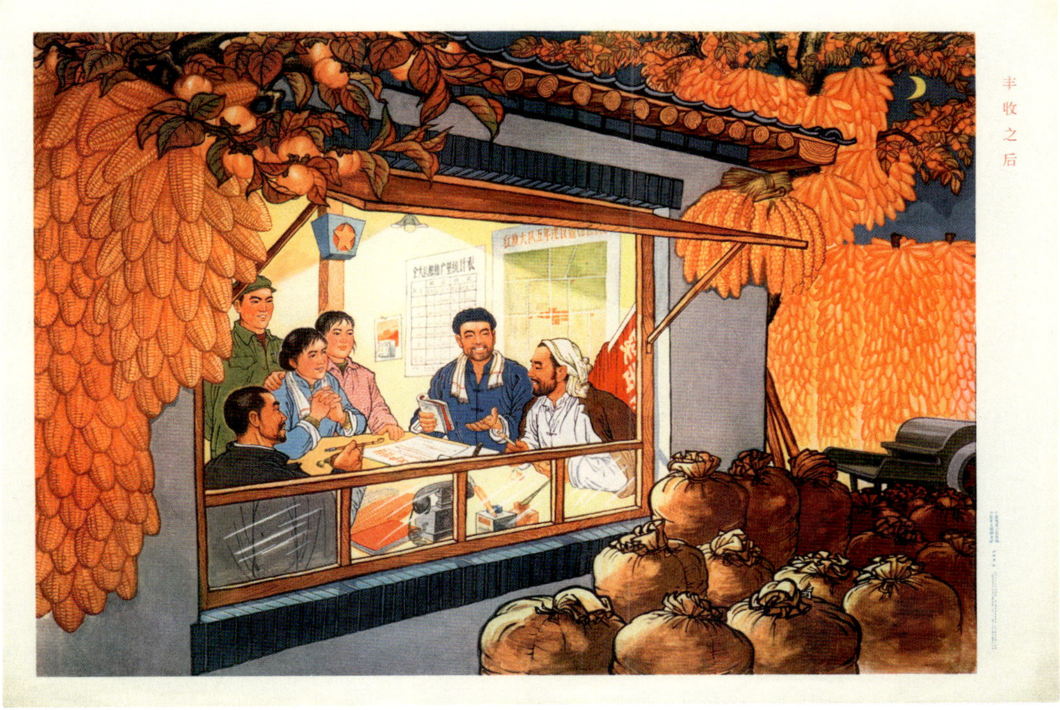

After the bumper harvest, 1974.
Nach der Rekordernte, 1974.

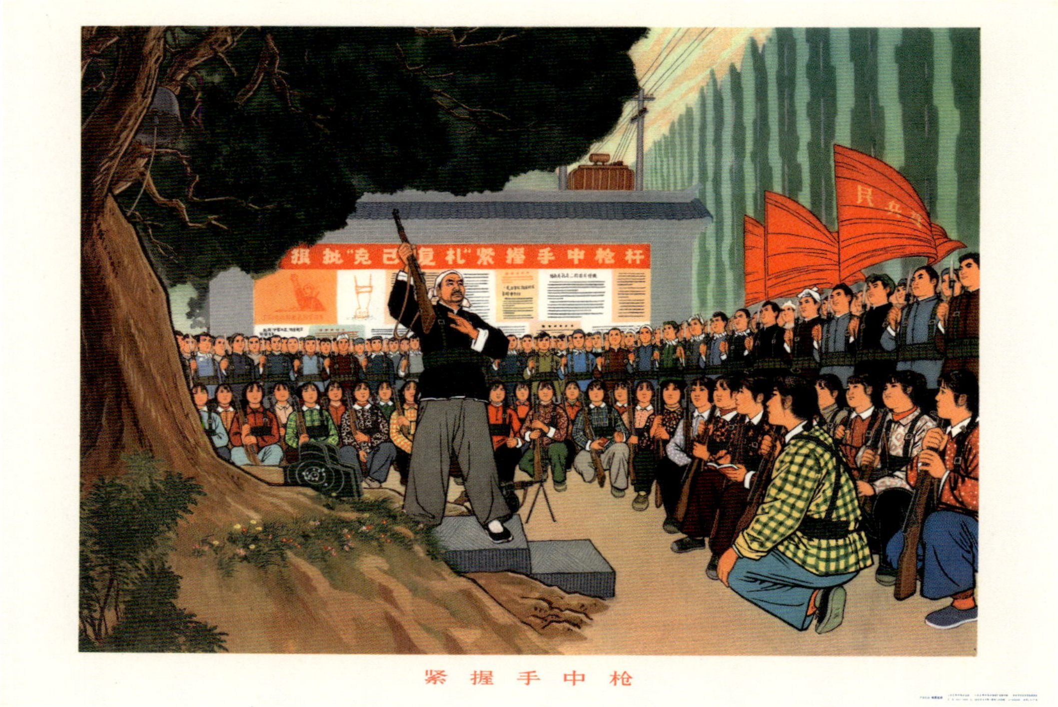

Hold the gun tight in one's hand, 1974.

Die Waffe fest in der Hand halten, 1974.

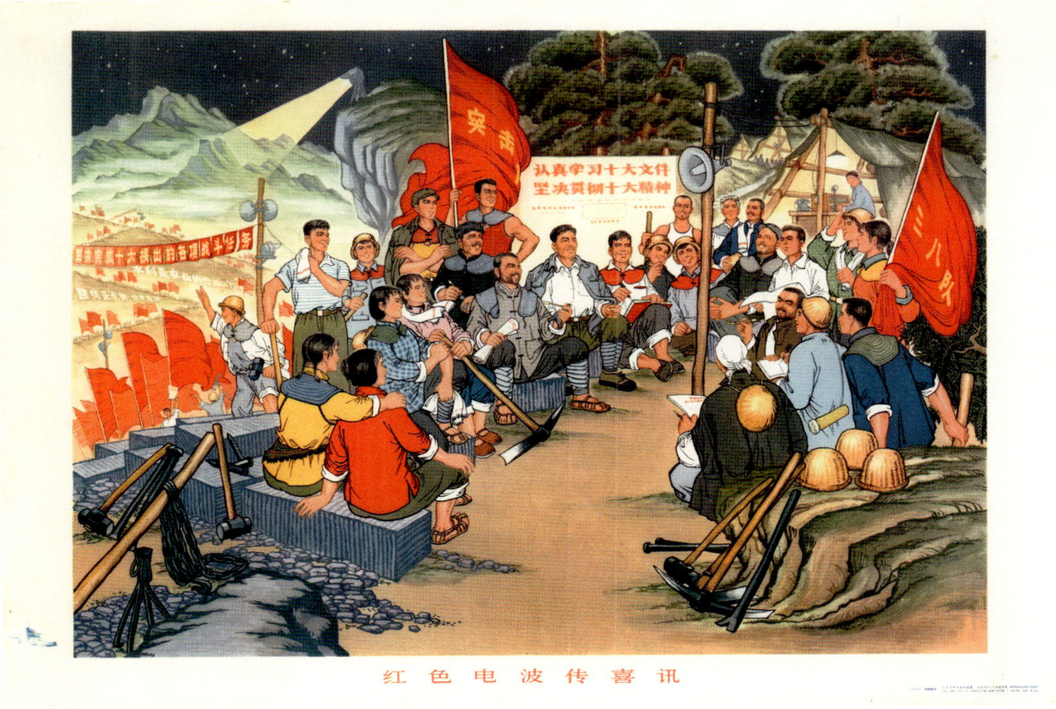

The red electromagnetic wave brings good news, 1974.
Die rote elektromagnetische Welle bringt gute Neuigkeiten, 1974.

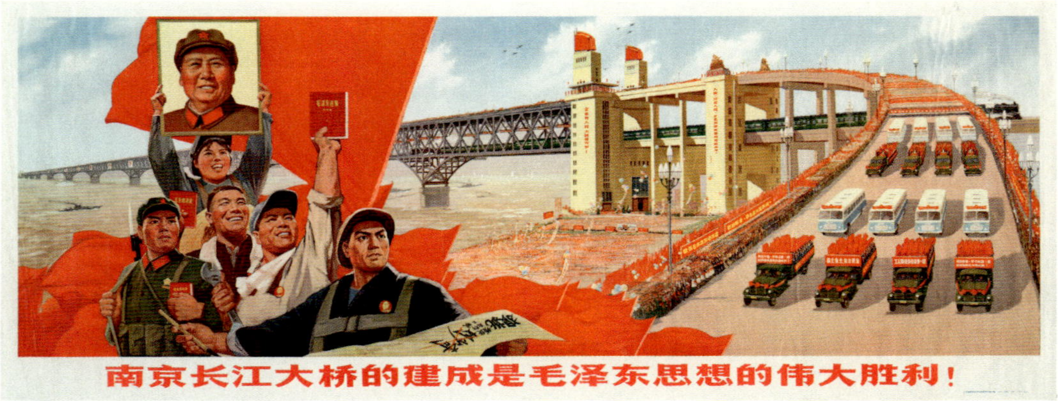

The construction of the bridge over the Yangzi River at Nanjing is a great victory for 'Mao Zedong Thought', c. 1975.

Der Bau der Brücke über den Yangzi Fluss in Nanjing ist ein großer Erfolg des 'Mao Zedong Denken', um 1975.

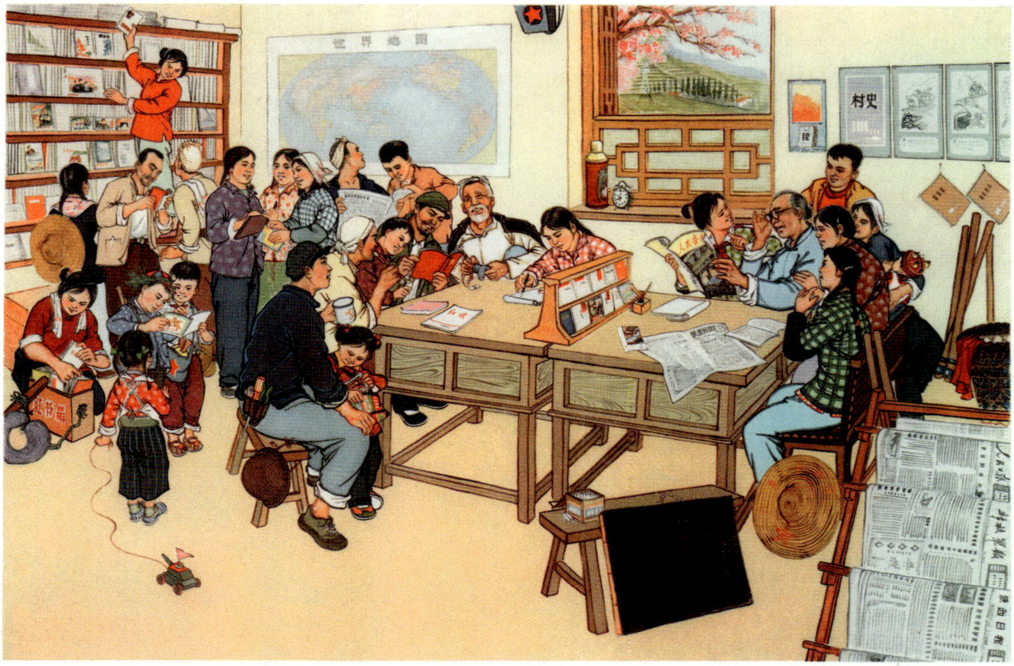

大队图书室（选自户县农民画展）

The production brigade's reading room
(Selected from the Huxian peasant painting exhibition), 1975.
Der Lesesaal der Produktions-Brigade
(aus der Huxian Bauernmalerei Ausstellung), 1975.

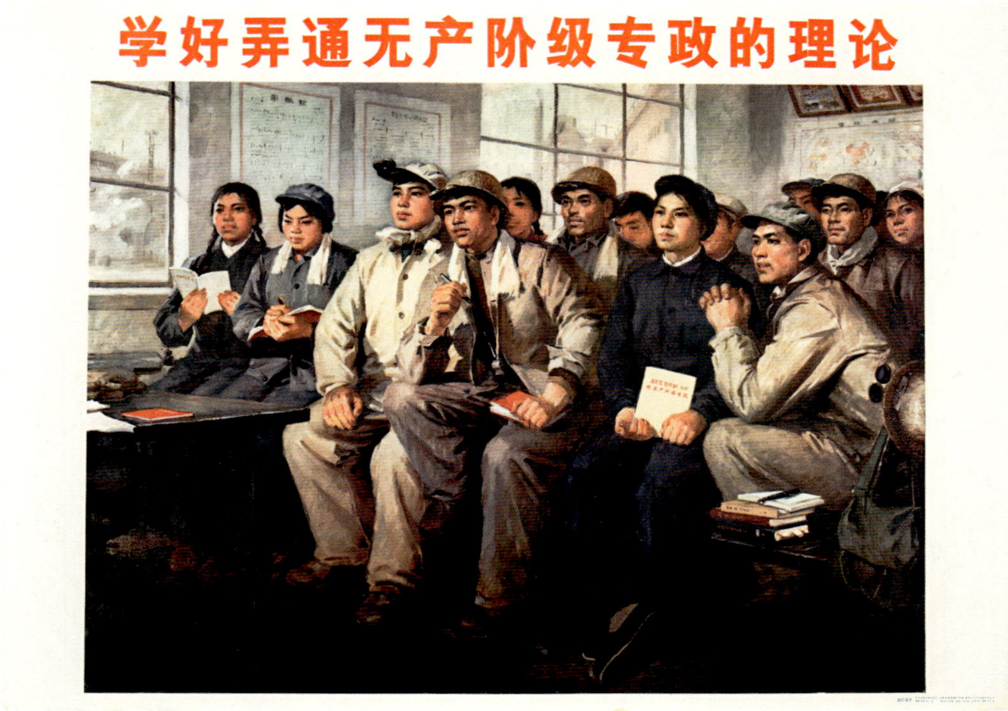

Study well and grasp the theory of the dictatorship of the proletariat, 1975.
Lerne fleissig und begreife die Theorie der Diktatur des Proletariats, 1975.

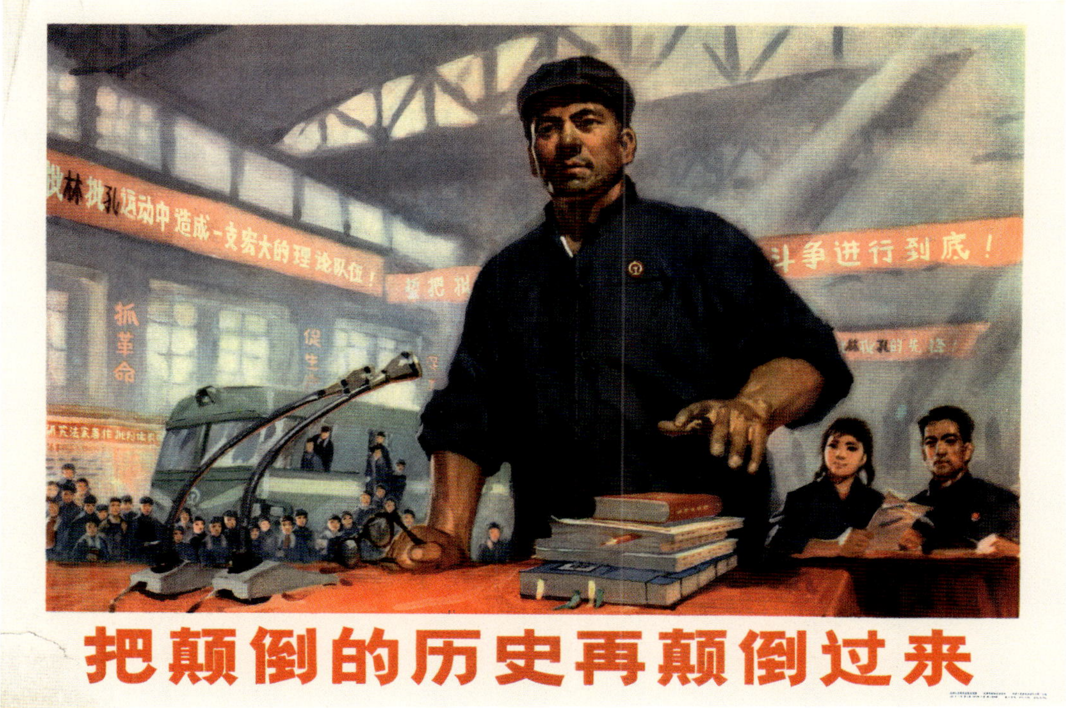

Set the record of history straight, 1975.
Berichtige die Geschichtsschreibung, 1975.

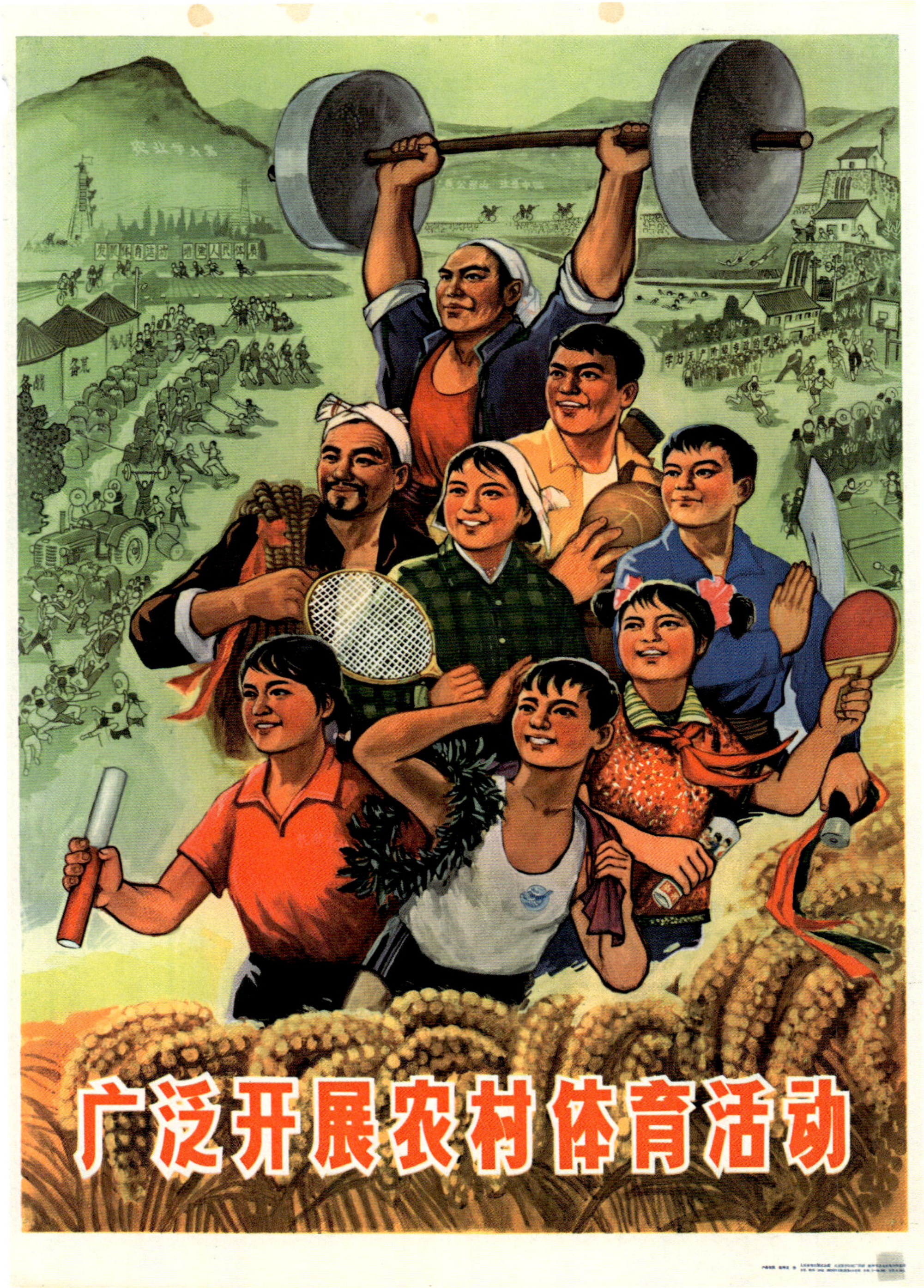

Develop physical education activities in peasant villages, 1975.
Schafft Möglichkeiten für Sportunterricht in den Dörfern, 1975.

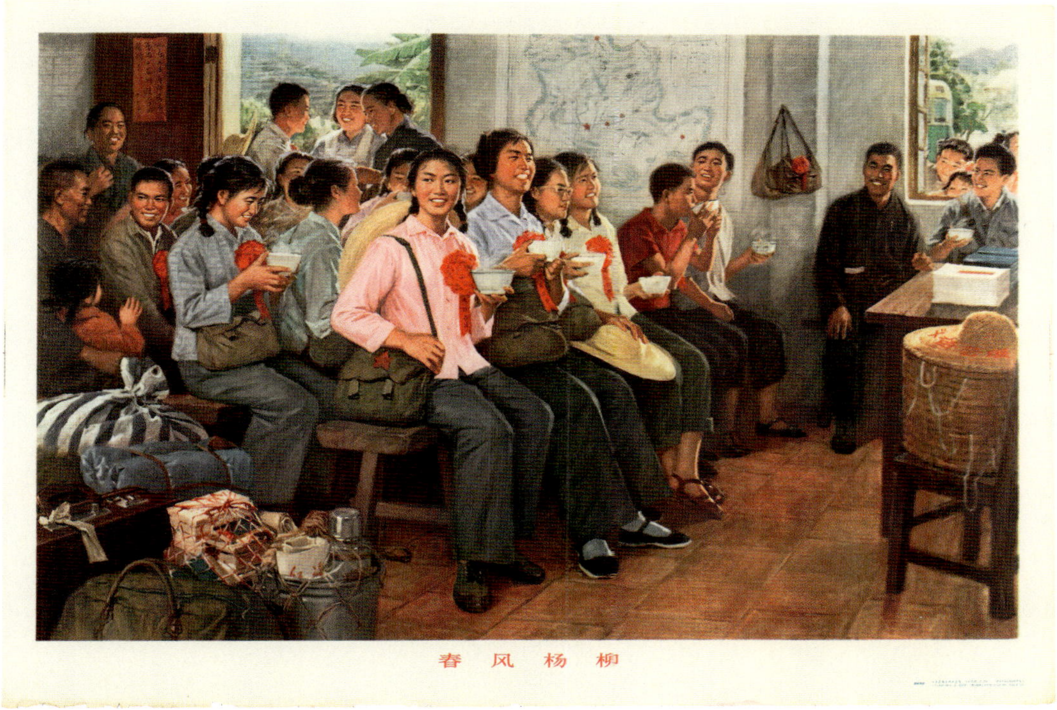

Spring breeze in Yangliu, 1975.
Frühlingsbrise in Yangliu, 1975.

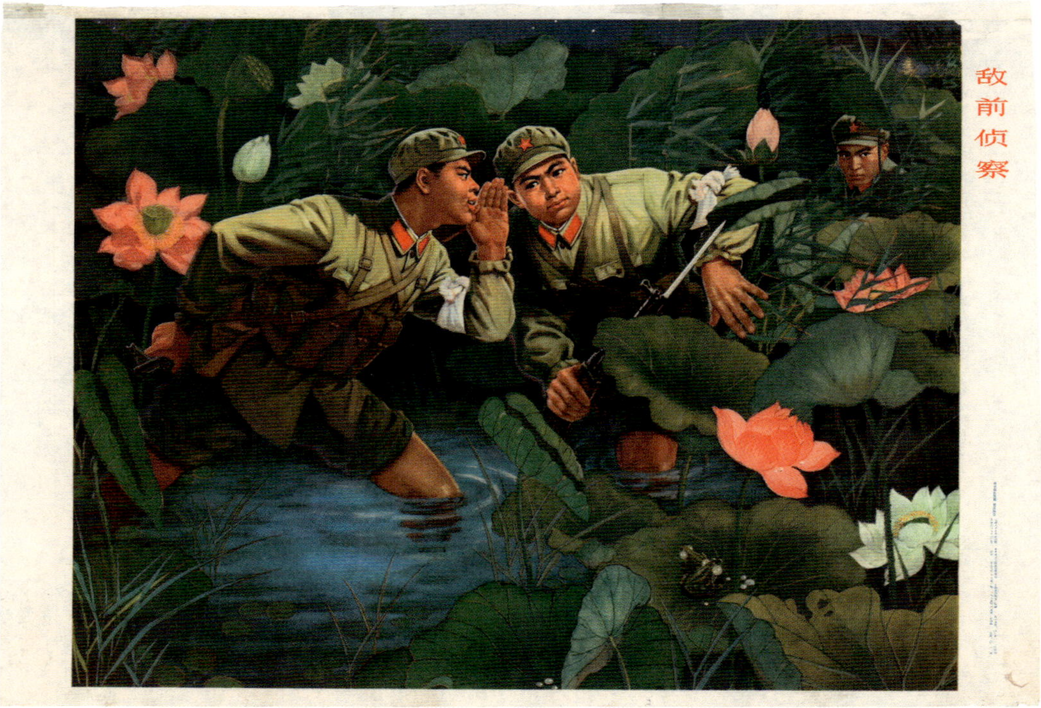

Reconnoitering the enemy's advance, 1975.
Das Vorrücken des Feindes ausspähen, 1975.

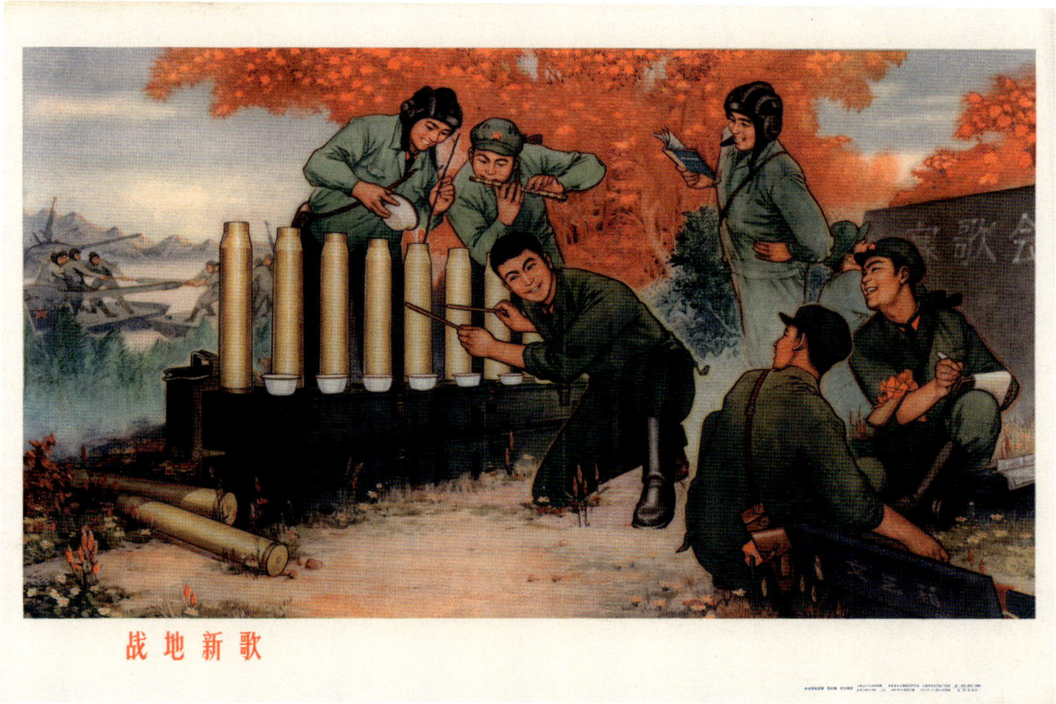

New songs on the battlefield, 1975.
Neue Lieder auf dem Schlachtfeld, 1975.

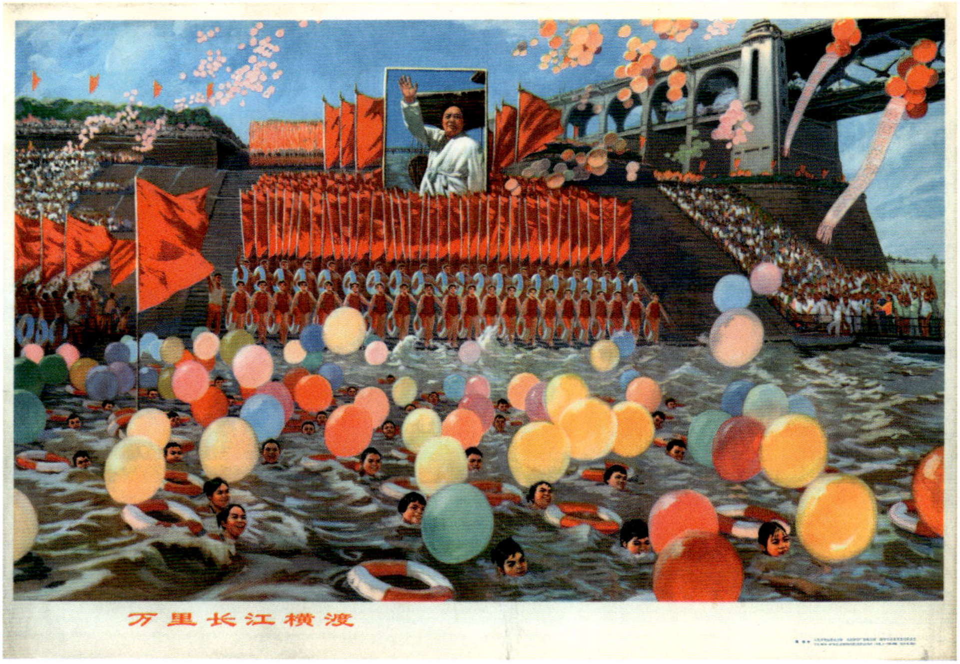

Crossing the 10,000 li long Yangzi River, 1976.

Das Überqueren des 10,000 li langen Flusses Yangzi, 1976.

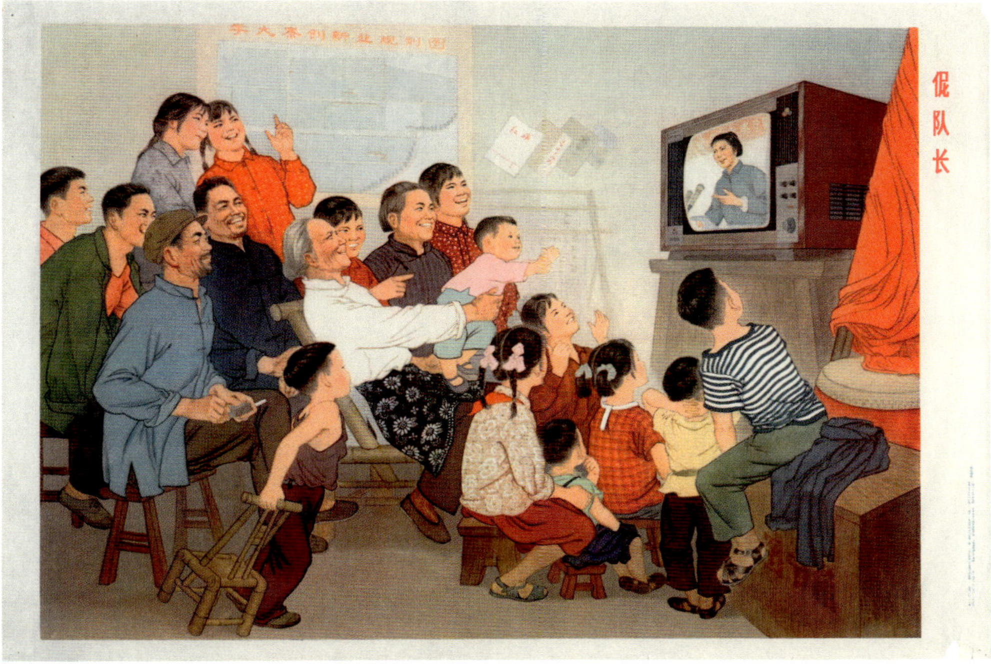

Our brigade leader, 1976.
Unser Gruppenführer, 1976.

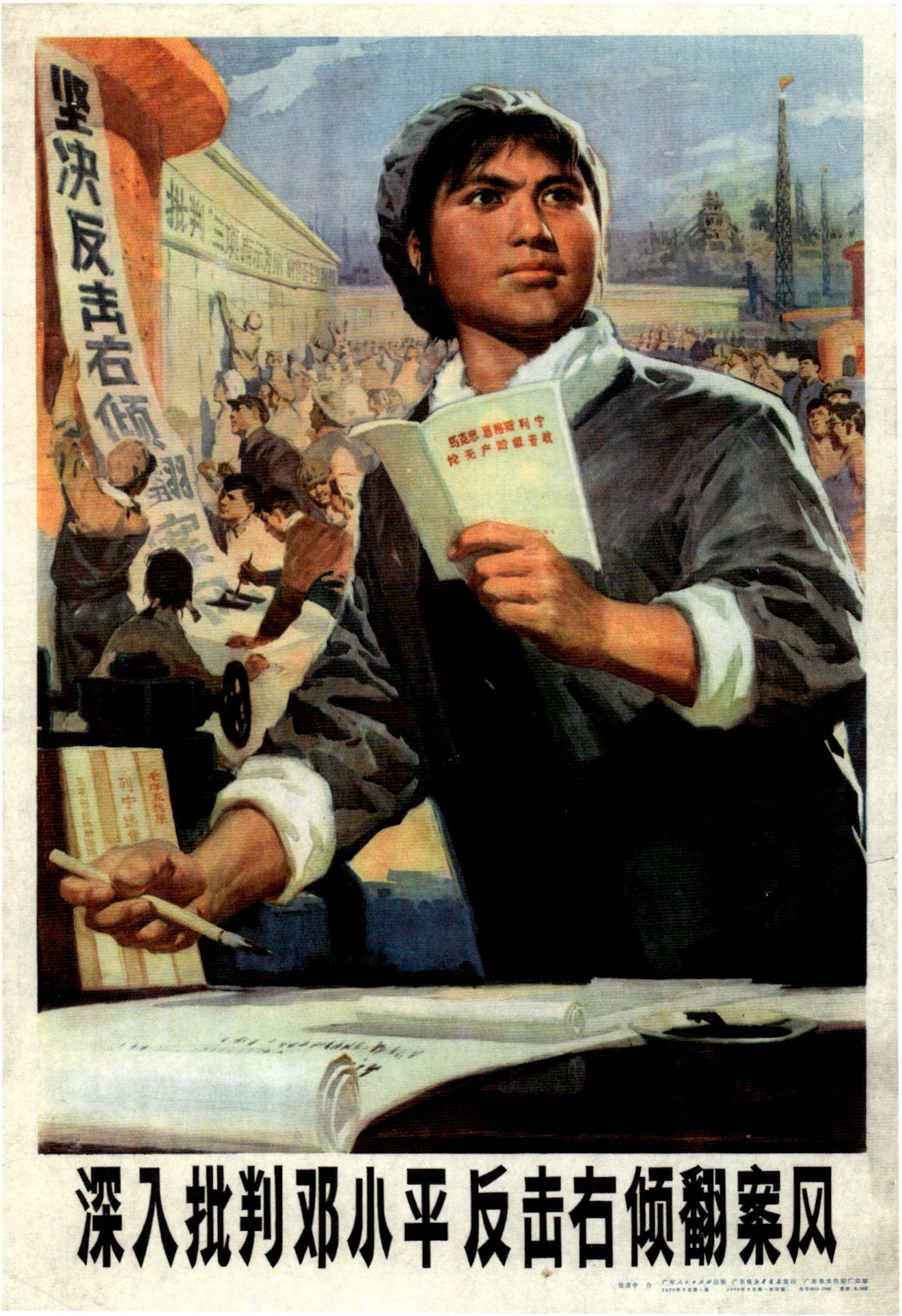

Deepen the criticism of Deng Xiaoping, strike against the right deviatonist wind of overturned verdicts, 1976.

Verstärkt die Kritik an Deng Xiaoping, schlagt gegen den rechten aufrührerischen Wind von verdrehten Ansichten, 1976.

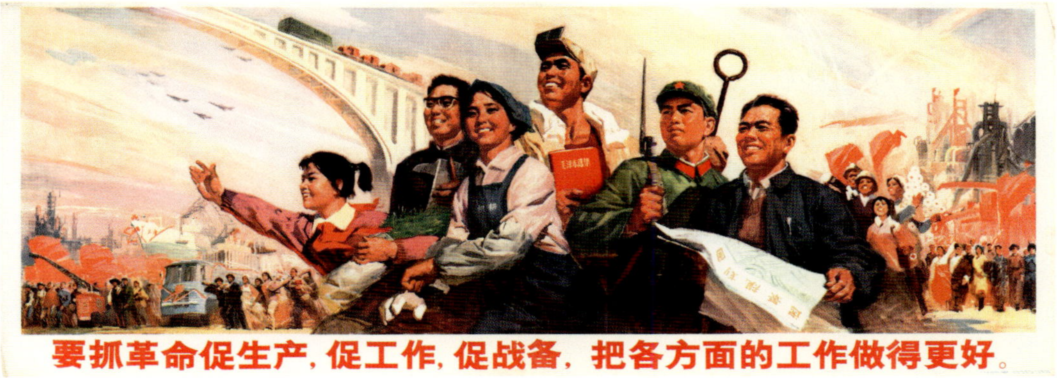

We must grasp revolution and increase production, increase work, increase preparation for struggle, to do an even better job, 1976.
Wir müssen die Revolution ergreifen und die Produktivität erhöhen, mehr Arbeit schaffen und die Vorbereitung auf den Kampf verstärken, um noch bessere Arbeit zu machen, 1976.

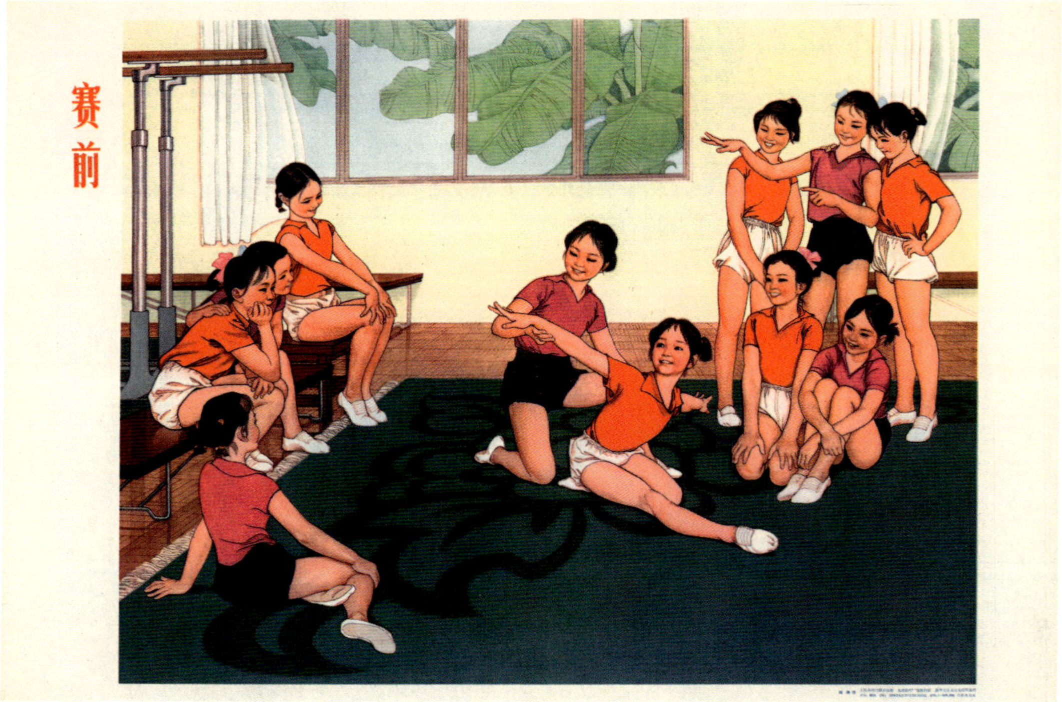

Before the contest, 1976.

Vor dem Wettkampf, 1976.

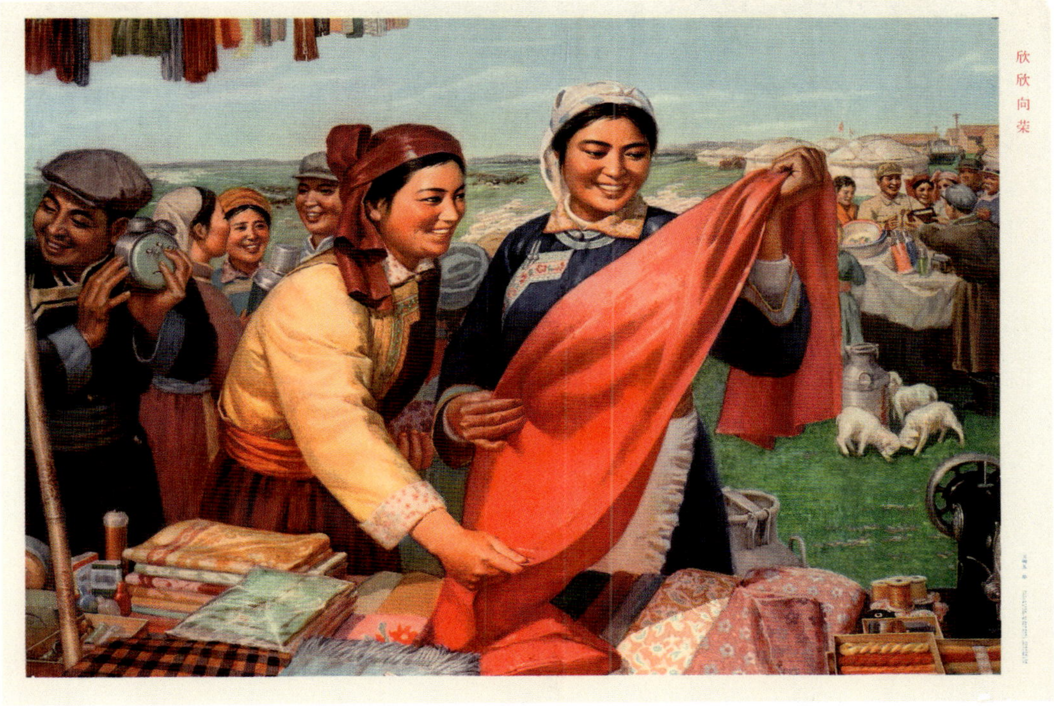

Prosperity, 1976.
Wohlstand, 1976.

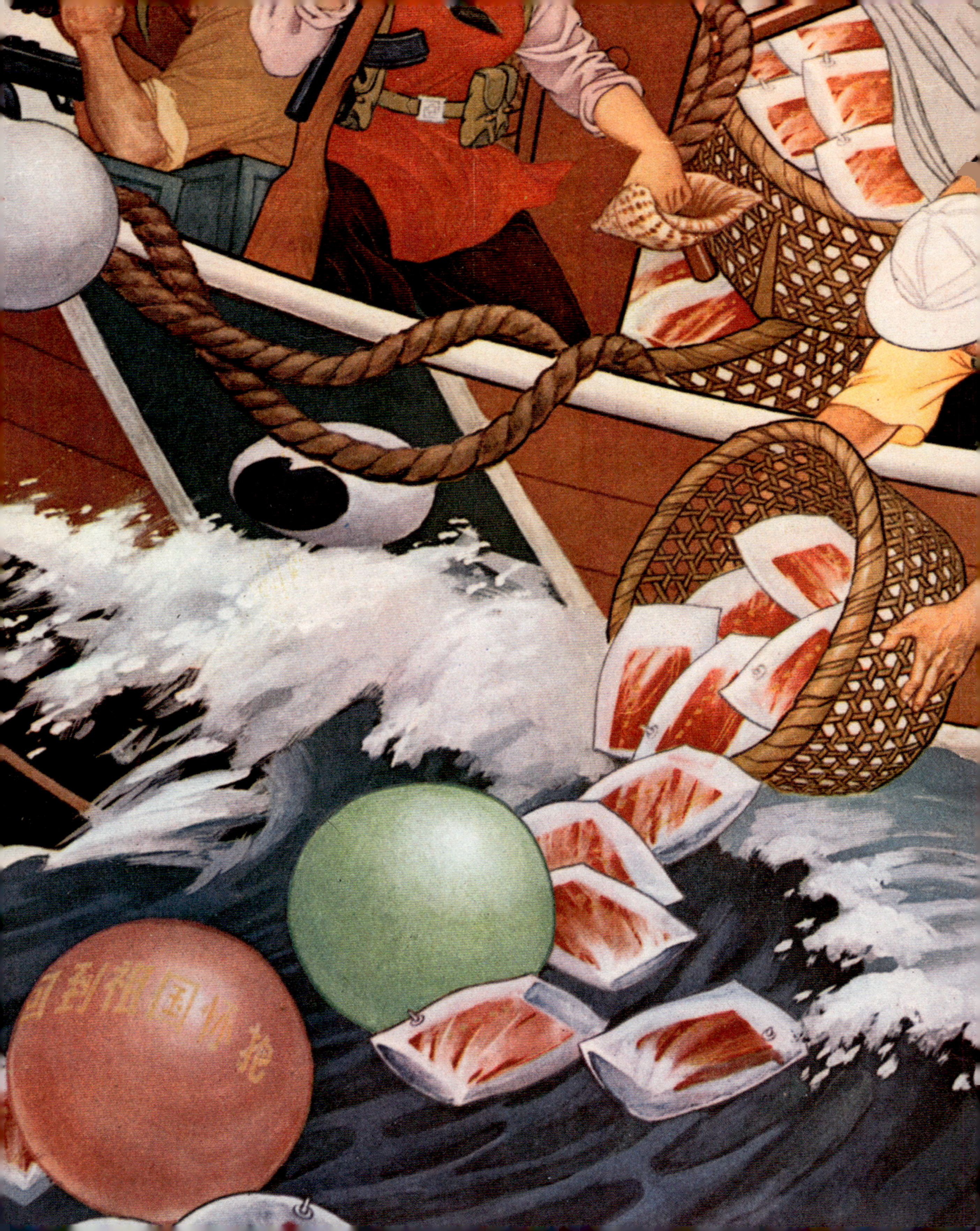
到祖国怀抱

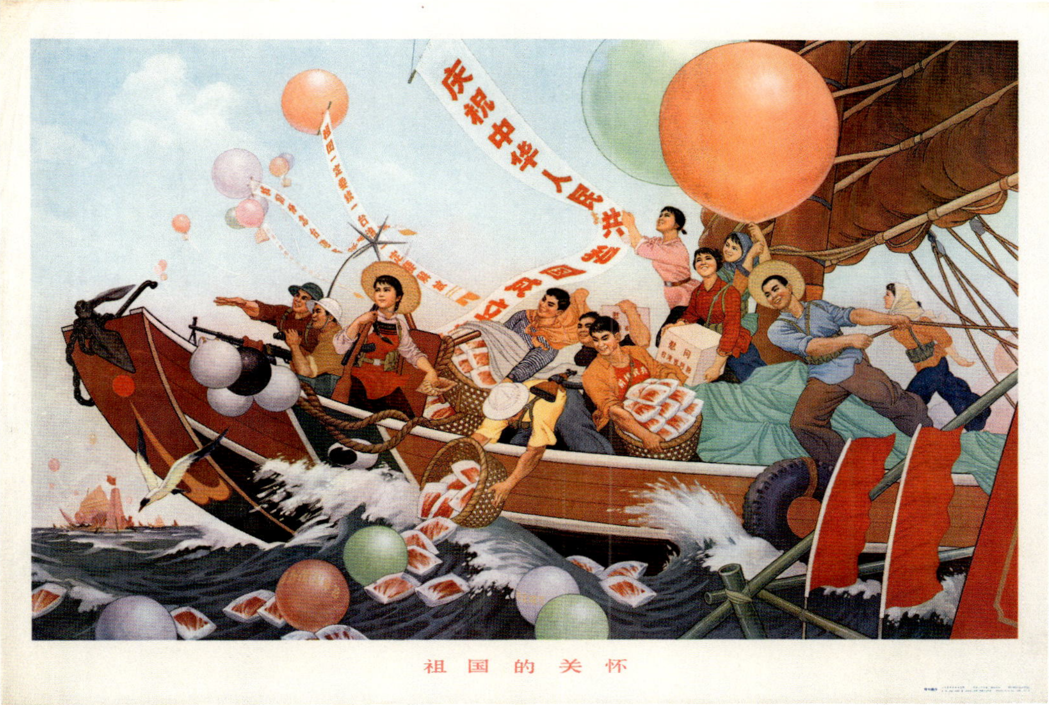

The loving care of the mother country, 1976.
Die Fürsorge des Vaterlandes, 1976.

← Little Red Books with Mao quotations in waterproof packing are thrown into the sea. They are meant to wash ashore in Taiwan, and to inspire the Taiwanese to "come back to the mother country."

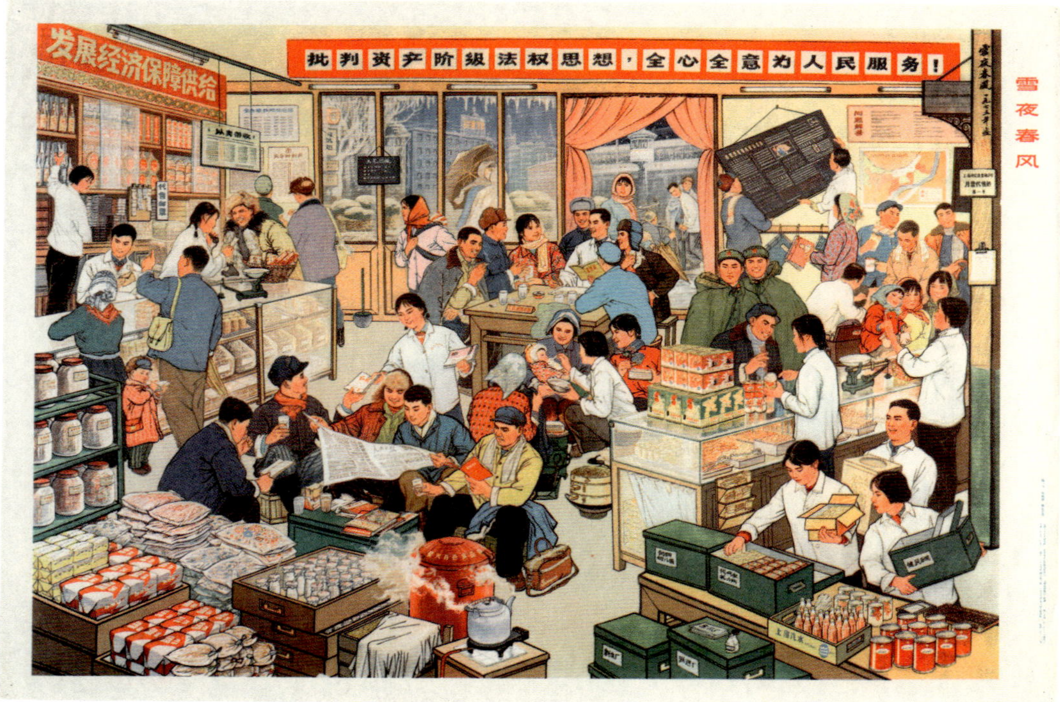

A spring breeze in a snowy night, 1976.

Eine Frühlingsbrise in verschneiter Nacht, 1976.

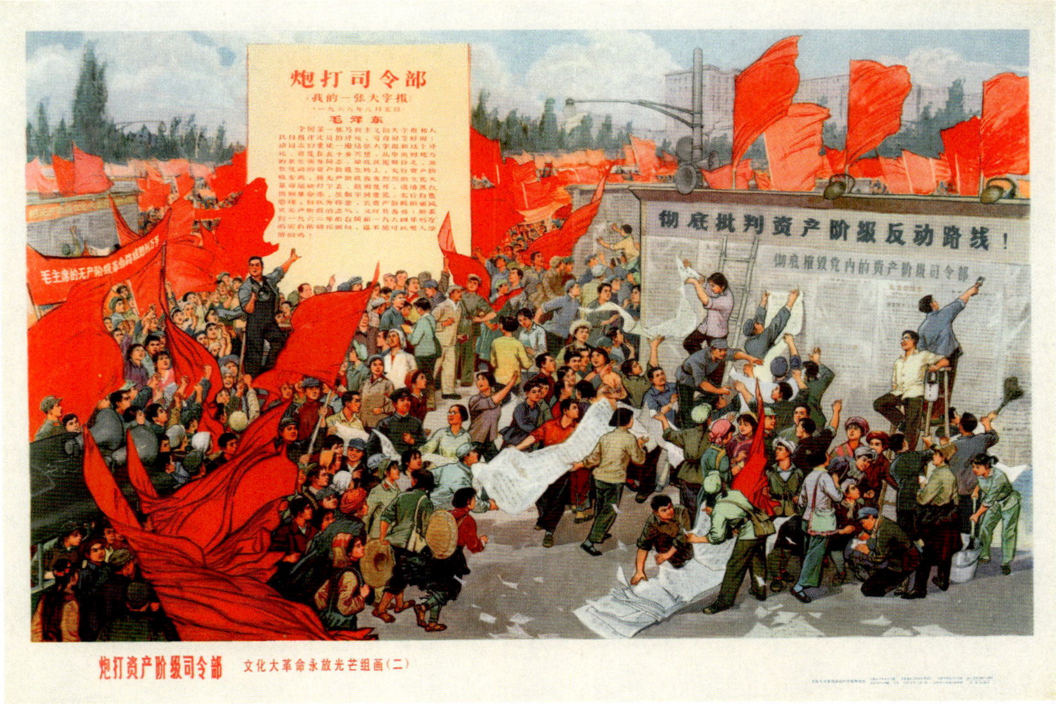

Bombard the capitalist headquarters, 1976.
Bombardiert die Hauptquartiere der Kapitalisten, 1976.

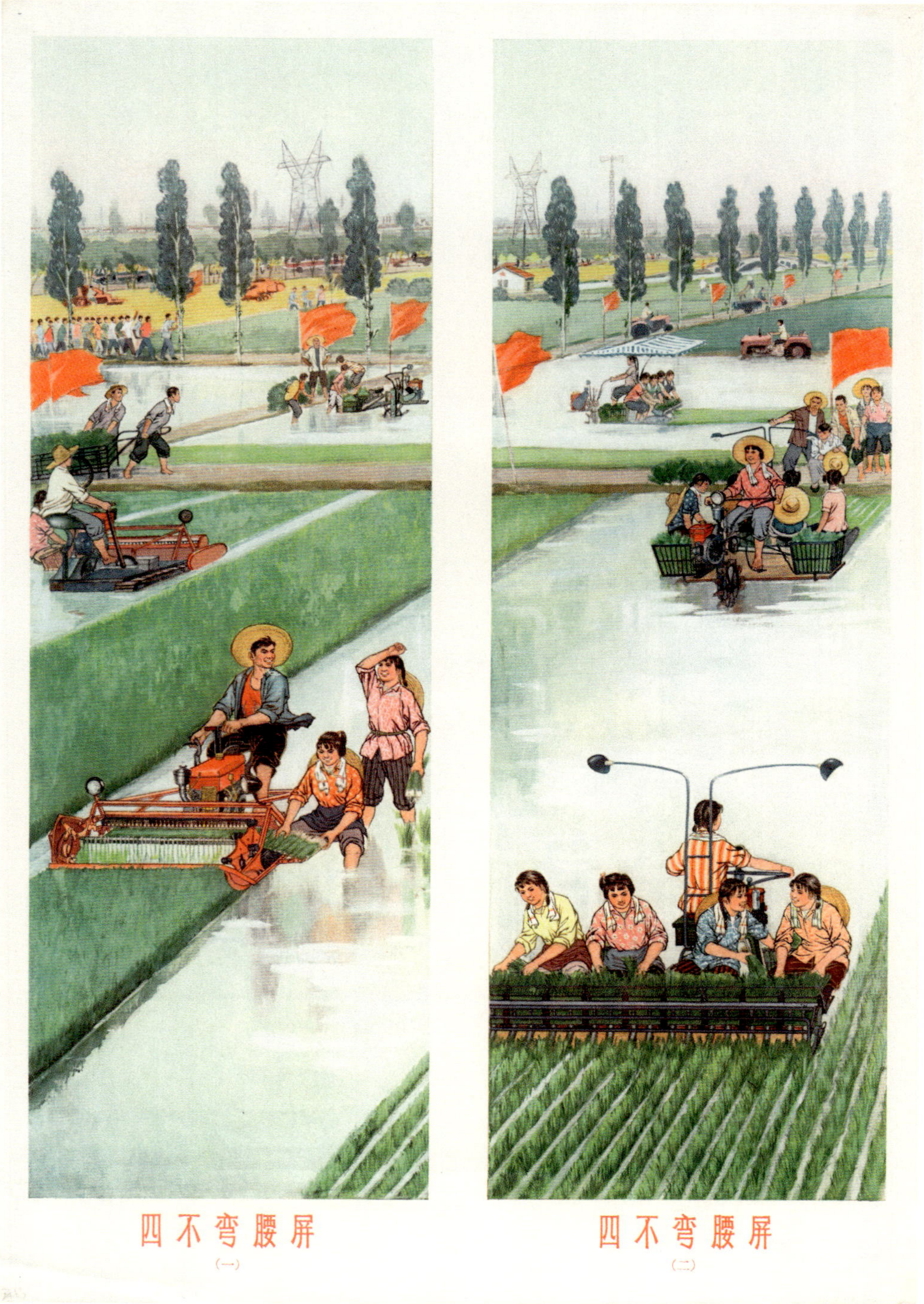

Four scrolls about not having to bend down (1, 2), 1976.
Vier Papierrollen über das Nicht-Bücken-Müssen (1, 2), 1976.

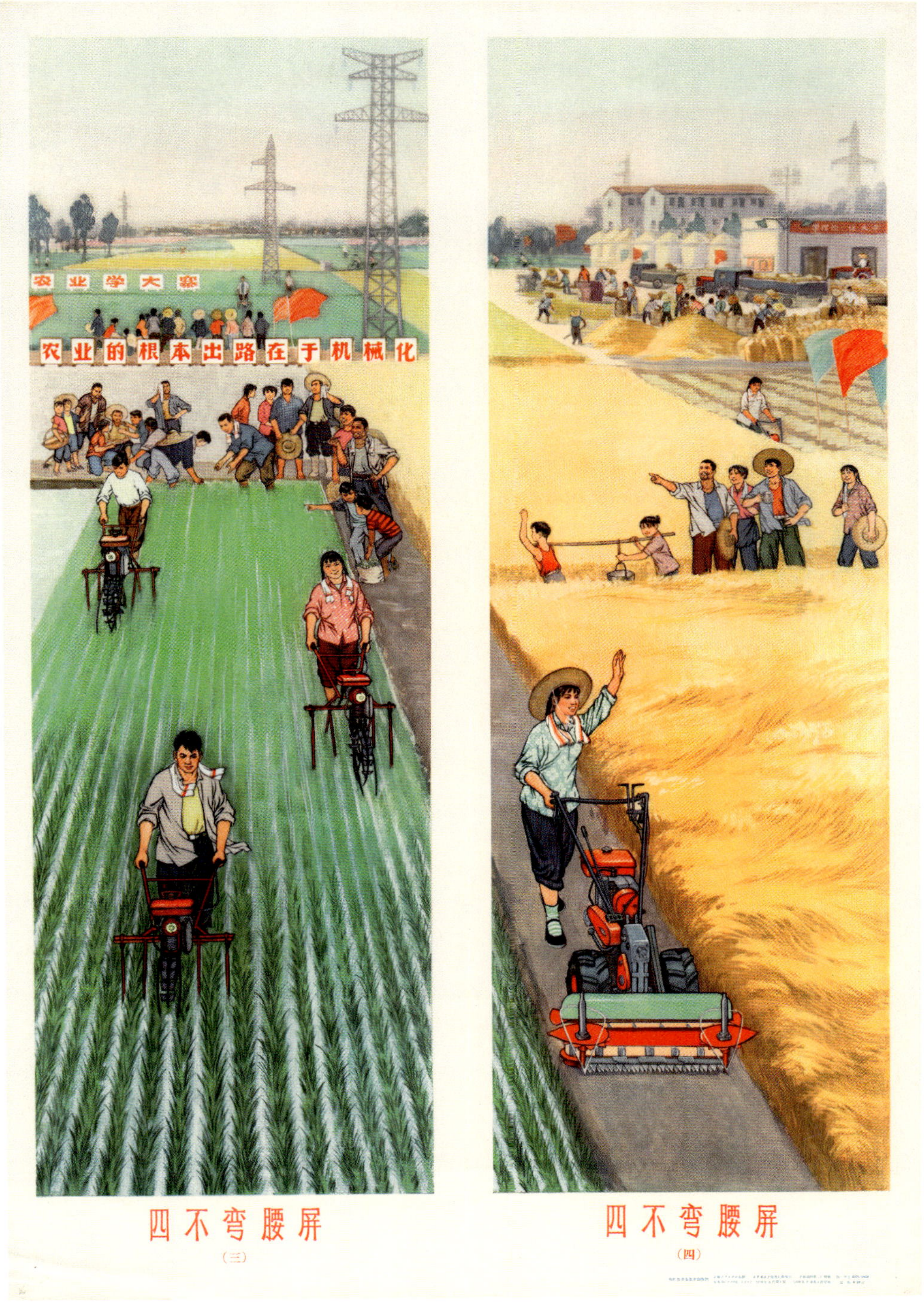

Four scrolls about not having to bend down (3, 4), 1976.
Vier Papierrollen über das Nicht-Bücken-Müssen (3, 4), 1976.

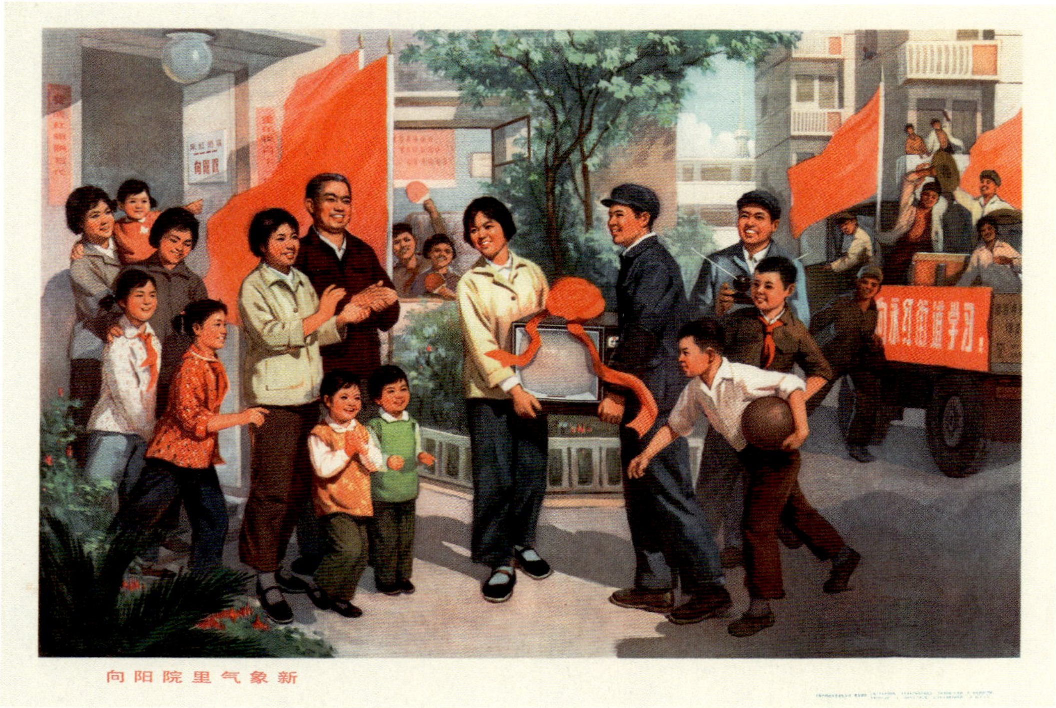

A new scene in Xiangyangyuan, 1976.
Eine neue Situation in Xiangyangyuan, 1976.

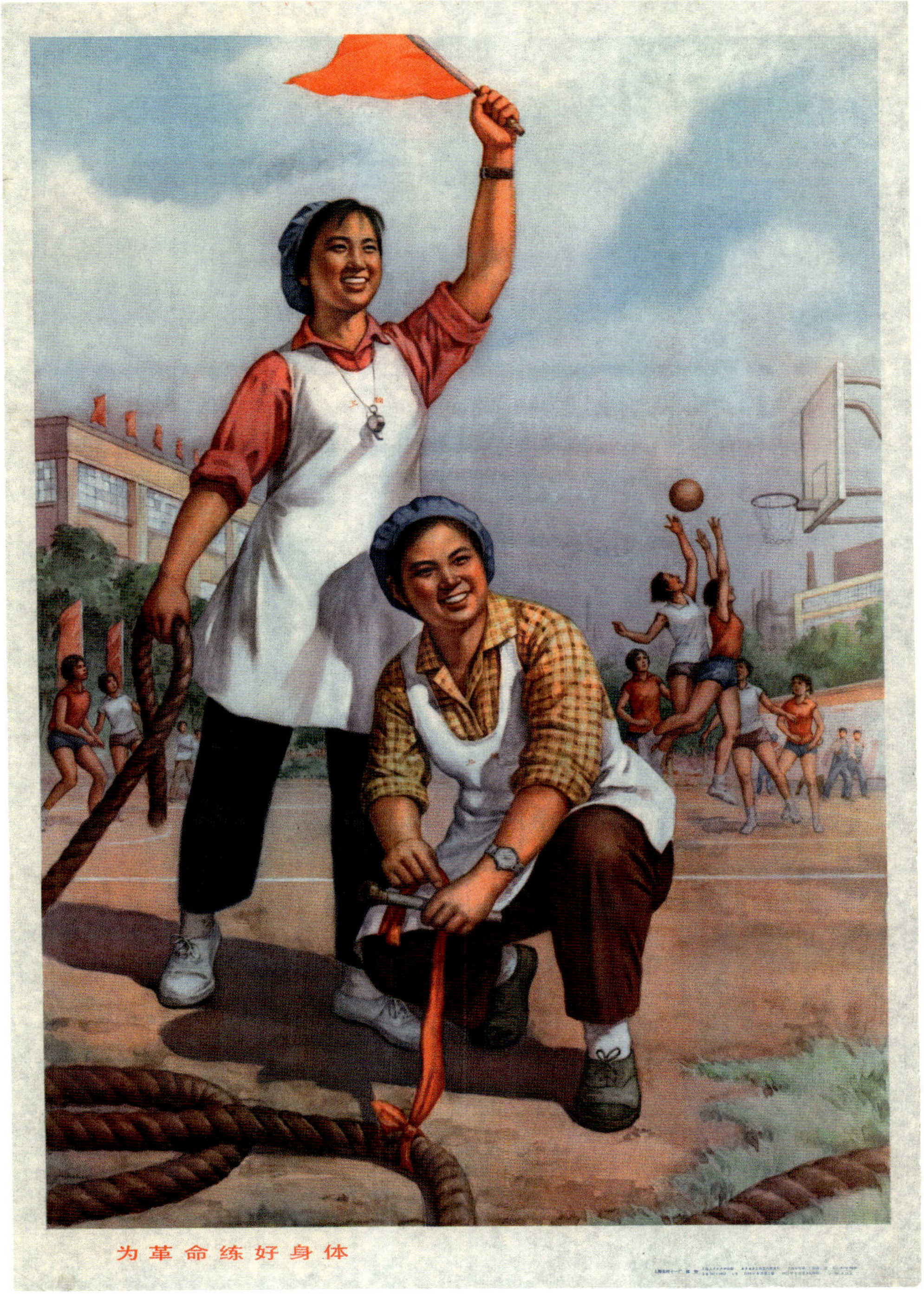

Training the body for the revolution, 1977.
Den Körper für die Revolution trainieren, 1977.

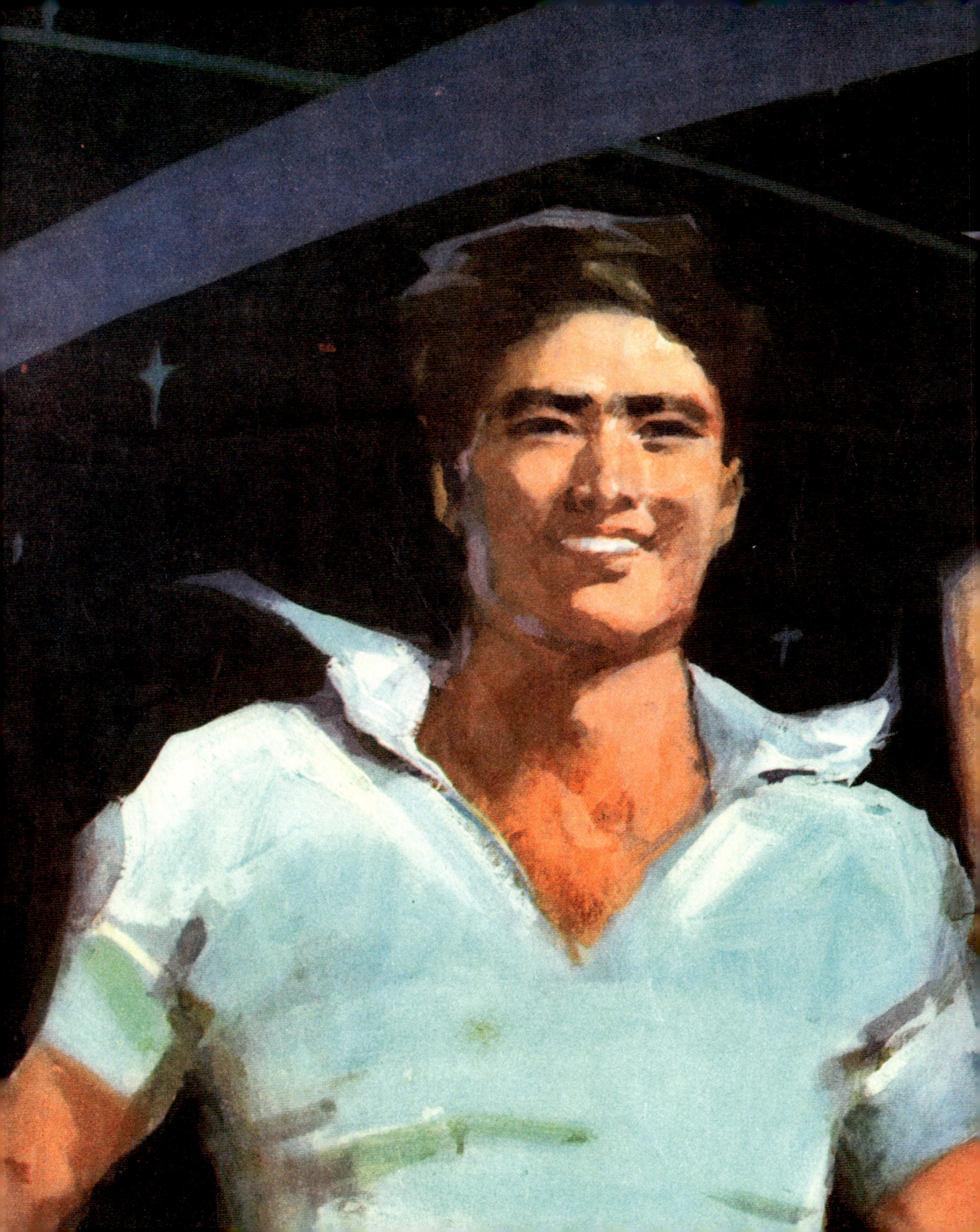

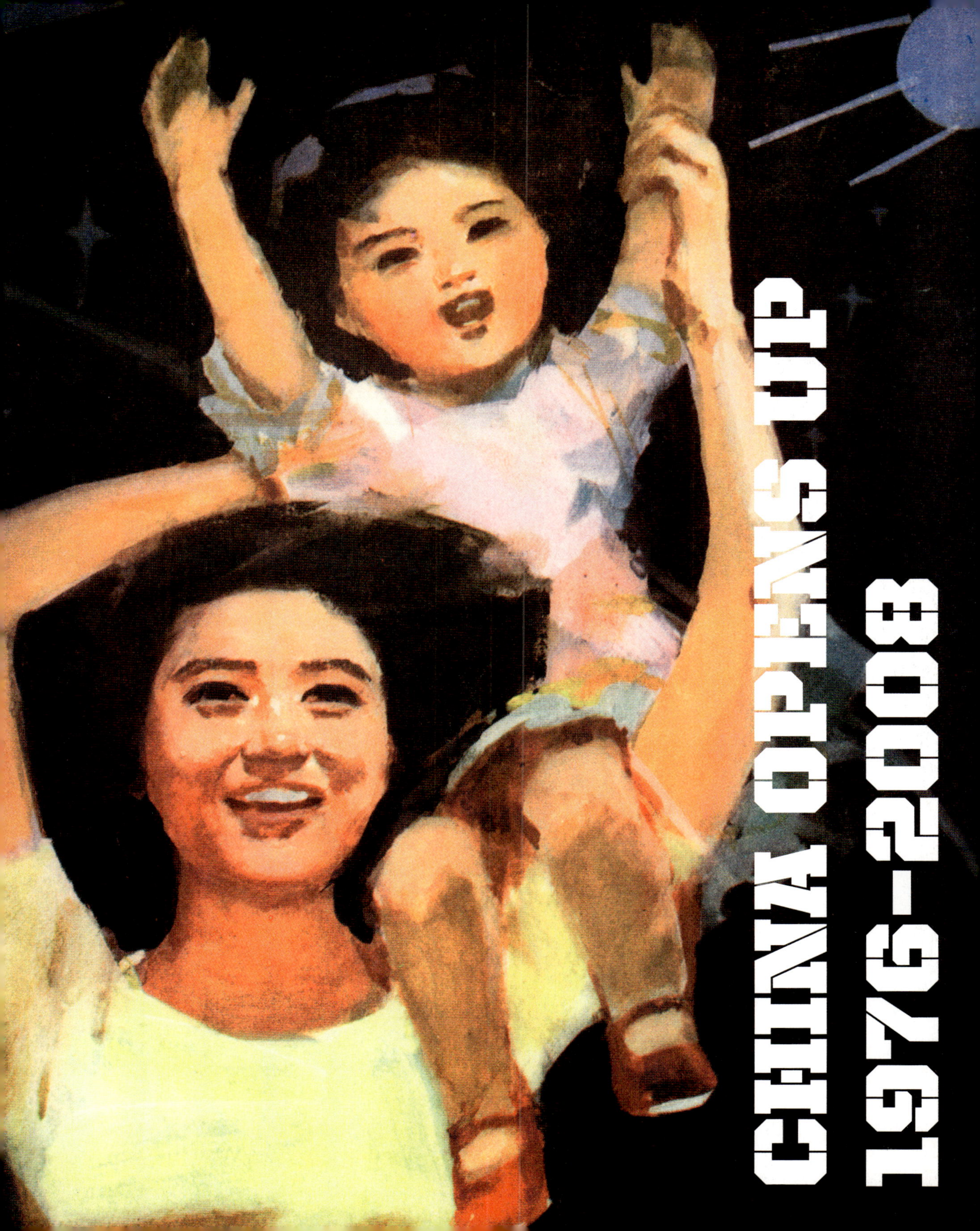

CHINA OPENS UP 1976–2008

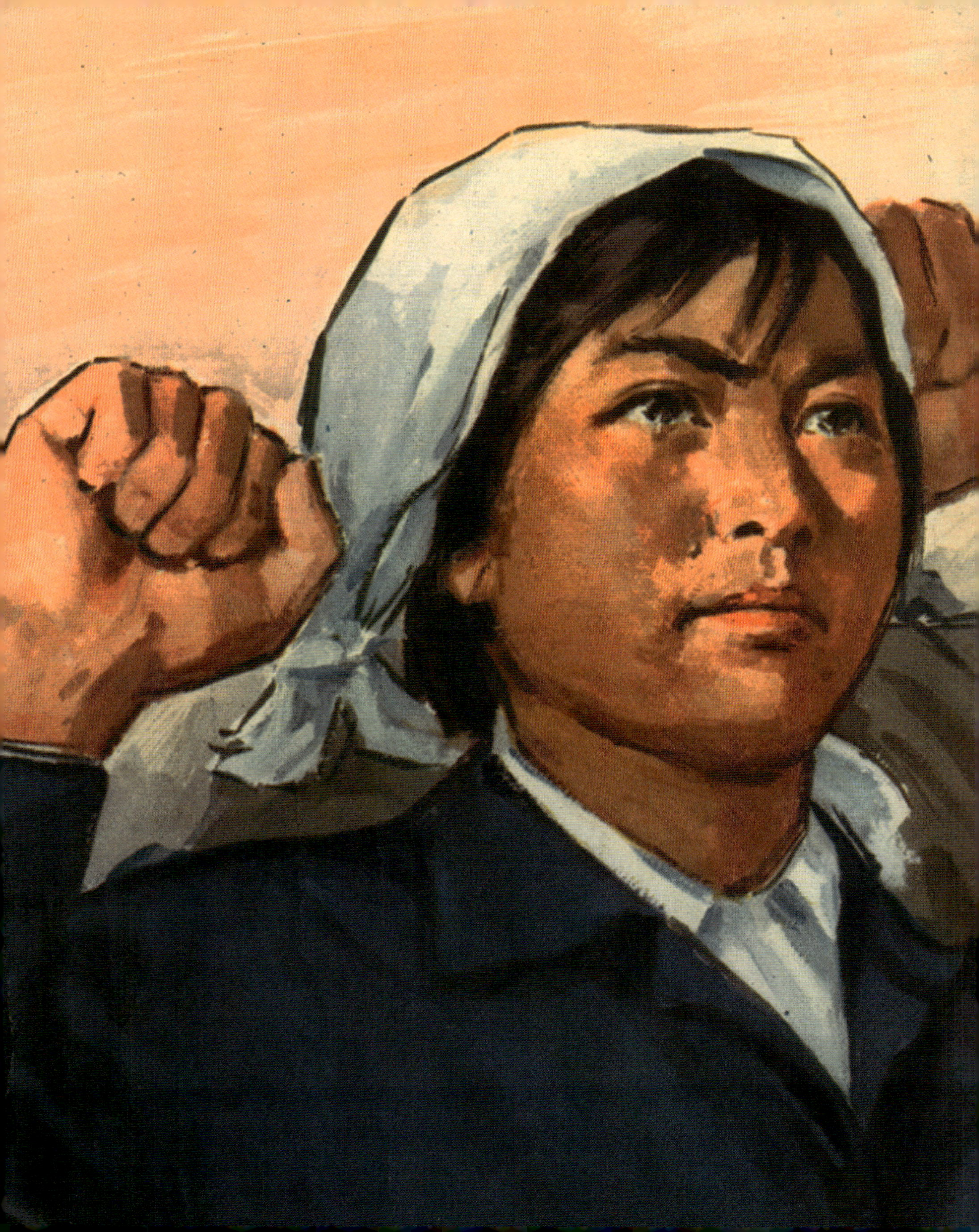

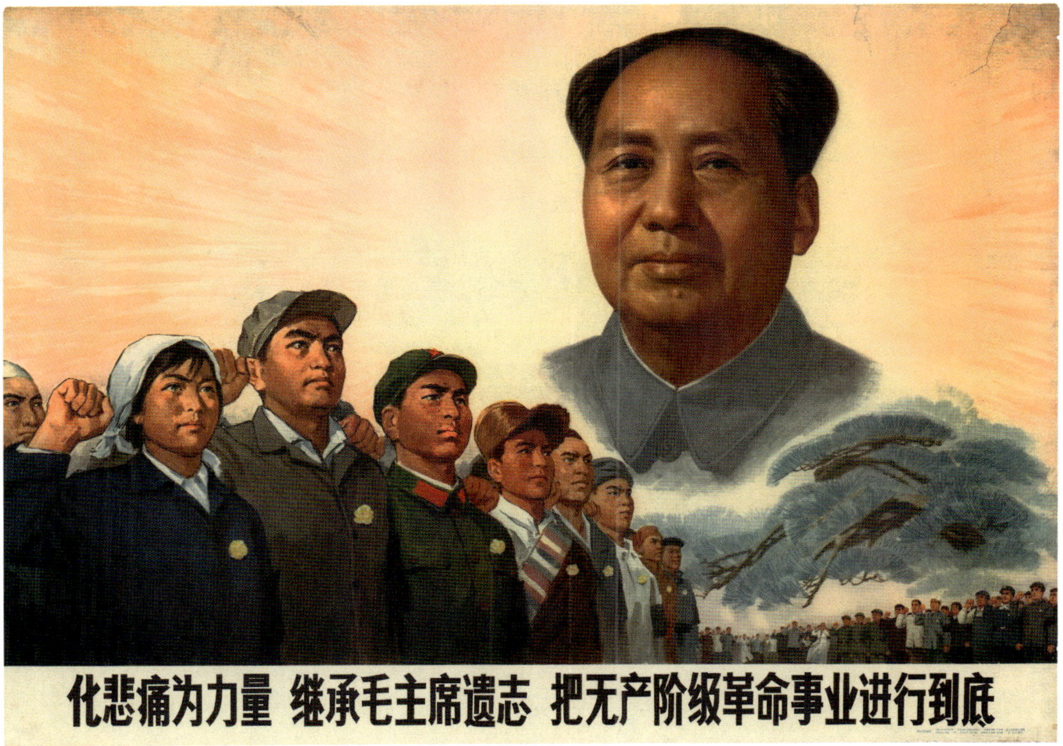

Turn grief into strength, carry out Chairman Mao's behests, and carry the proletarian revolutionary cause through to the end, 1976.
Verwandle Kummer in Stärke, folge dem Geheiß des Vorsitzenden Mao, und führe die proletarische Revolution zum Ende, 1976.

Mao dies on September 9, 1976. A power struggle ensues between Mao's widow Jiang Qing and her supporters, dubbed the "Gang of Four," and more moderate Party leaders around Hua Guofeng. Hua, who claims Mao has designated him as his successor, has the Gang ousted from power.

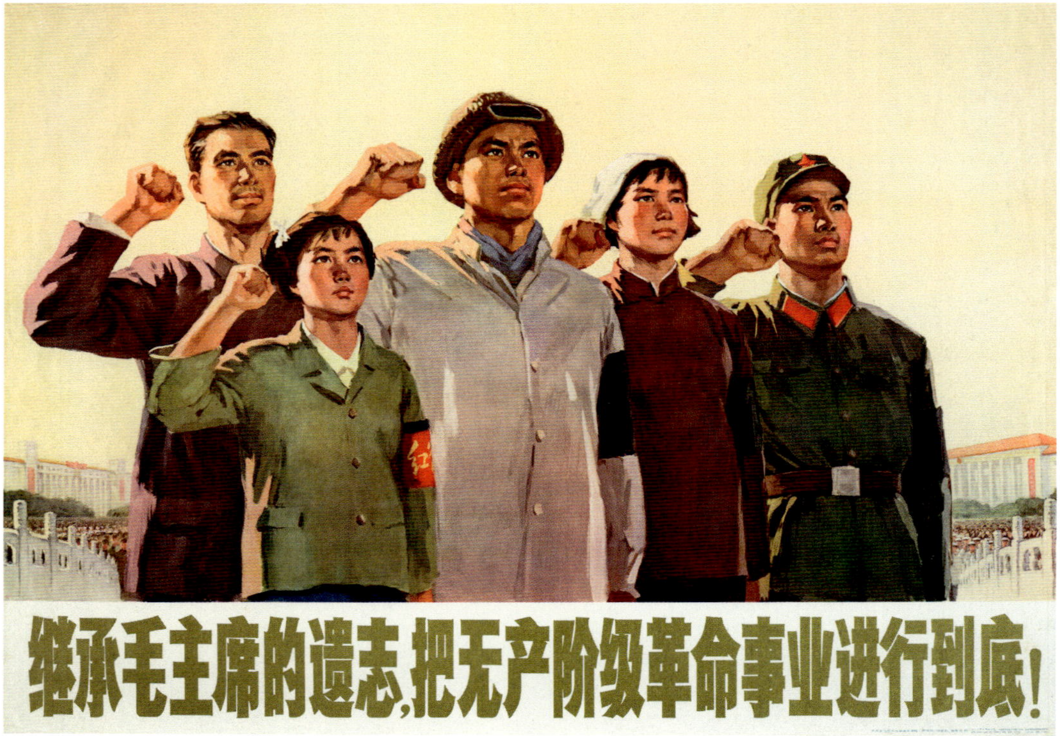

Carry out Chairman Mao's behests and carry the proletarian revolutionary cause through to the end! 1976.

Folge dem Geheiß des Vorsitzenden Mao und führe die Proletarische Revolution zum Ende! 1976.

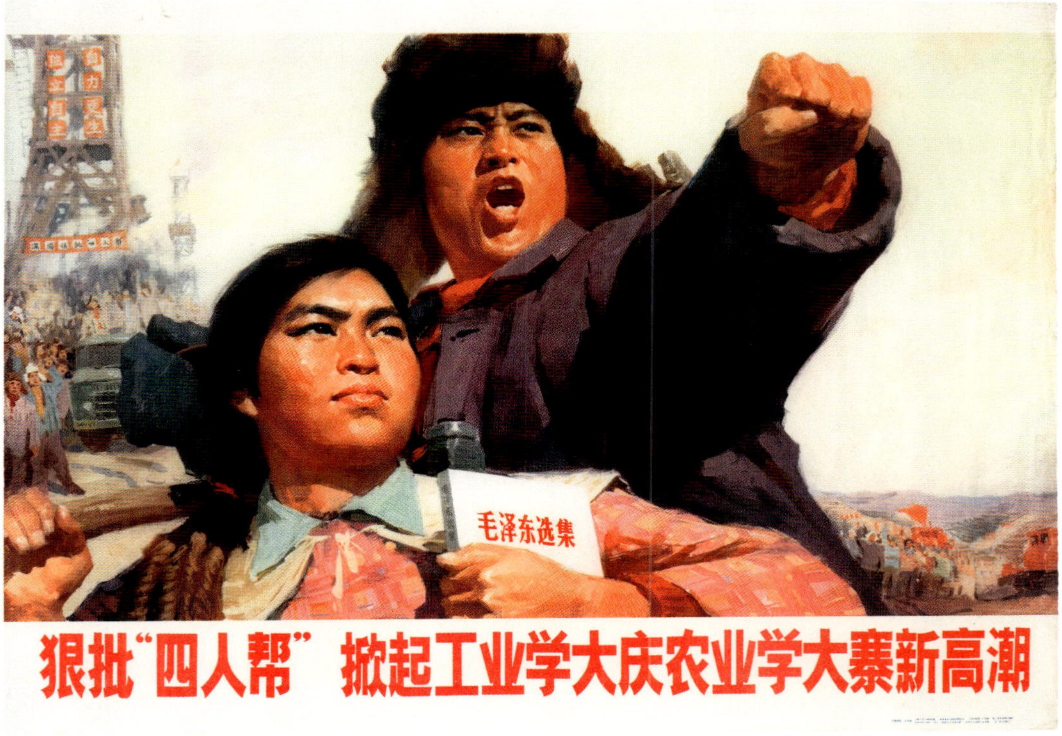

Relentlessly criticize the Gang of Four, set off a new upsurge of industry studying Daqing and agriculture studying Dazhai, 1977.
Kritisiert die Viererbande unerbittlich, leitet einen neuen industriellen Aufschwung ein, indem ihr Daqing und die Landwirtschaft von Dazhai als Vorbild nehmt, 1977.

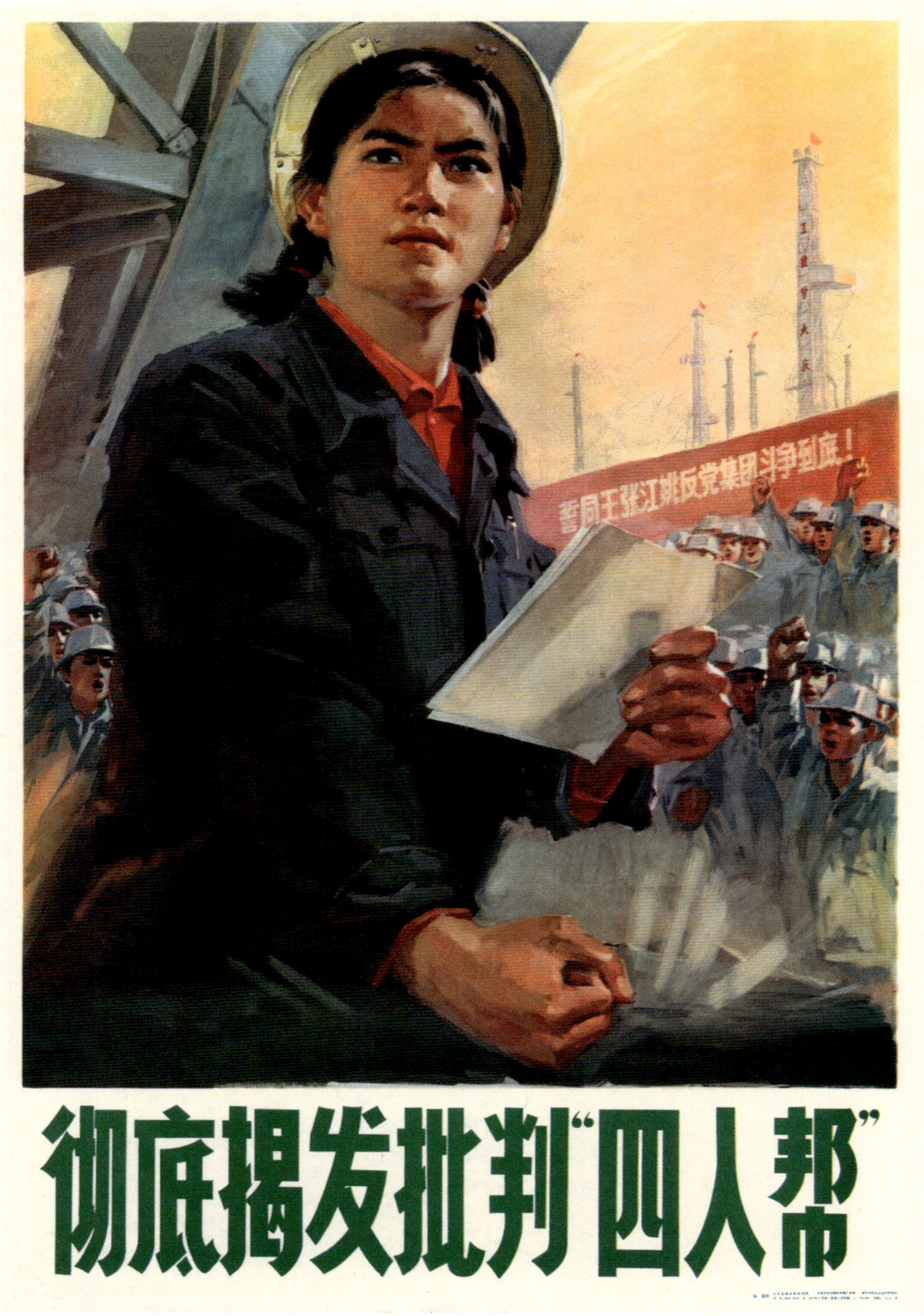

Thoroughly expose and criticize the Gang of Four, 1977.
Kritisiert die Viererbande und stellt sie gründlich bloß, 1977.

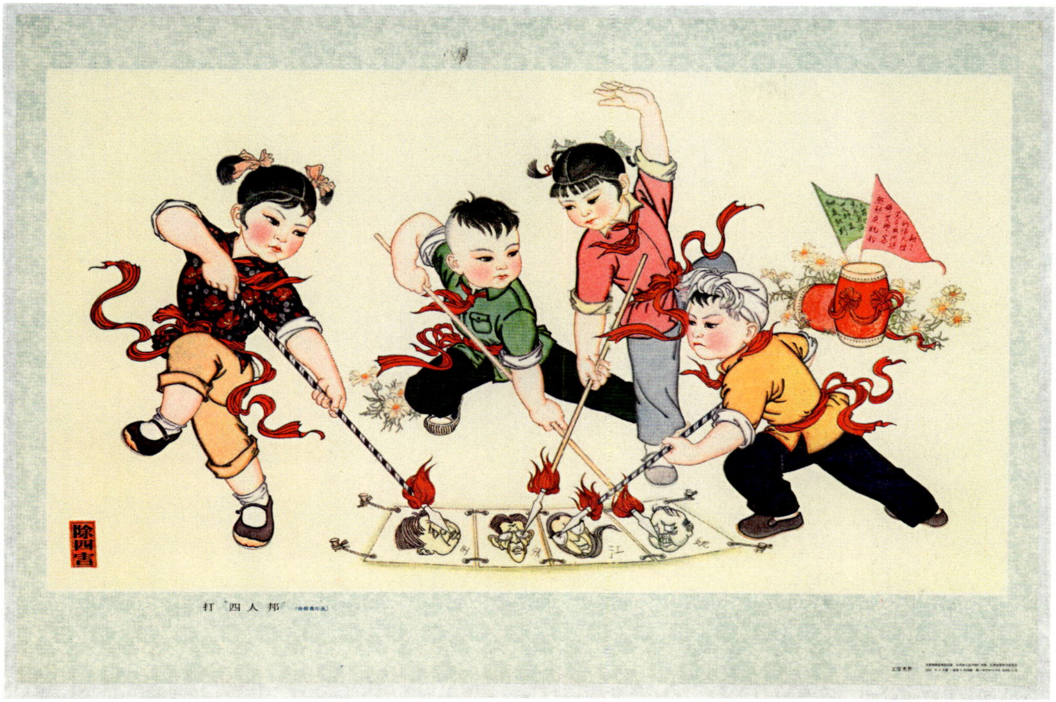

Smash the Gang of Four, 1978.
Zerschlagt die Viererbande, 1978.

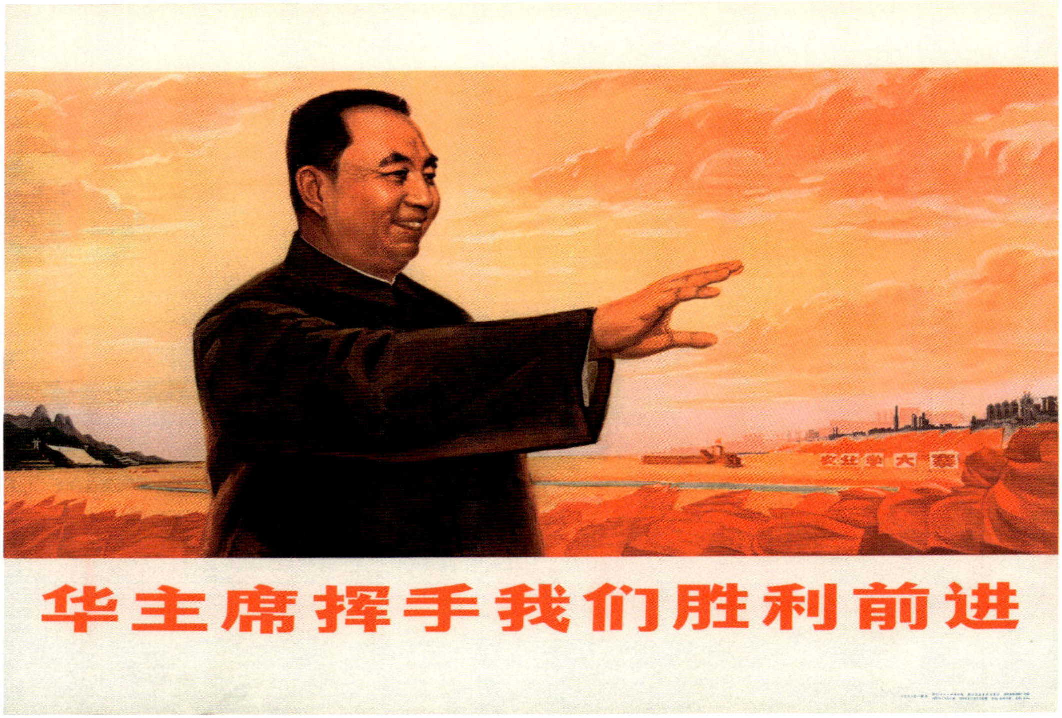

Chairman Hua waves his hand, we advance victoriously, 1977.
Der Vorsitzende Hua winkt, wir schreiten siegreich voran, 1977.

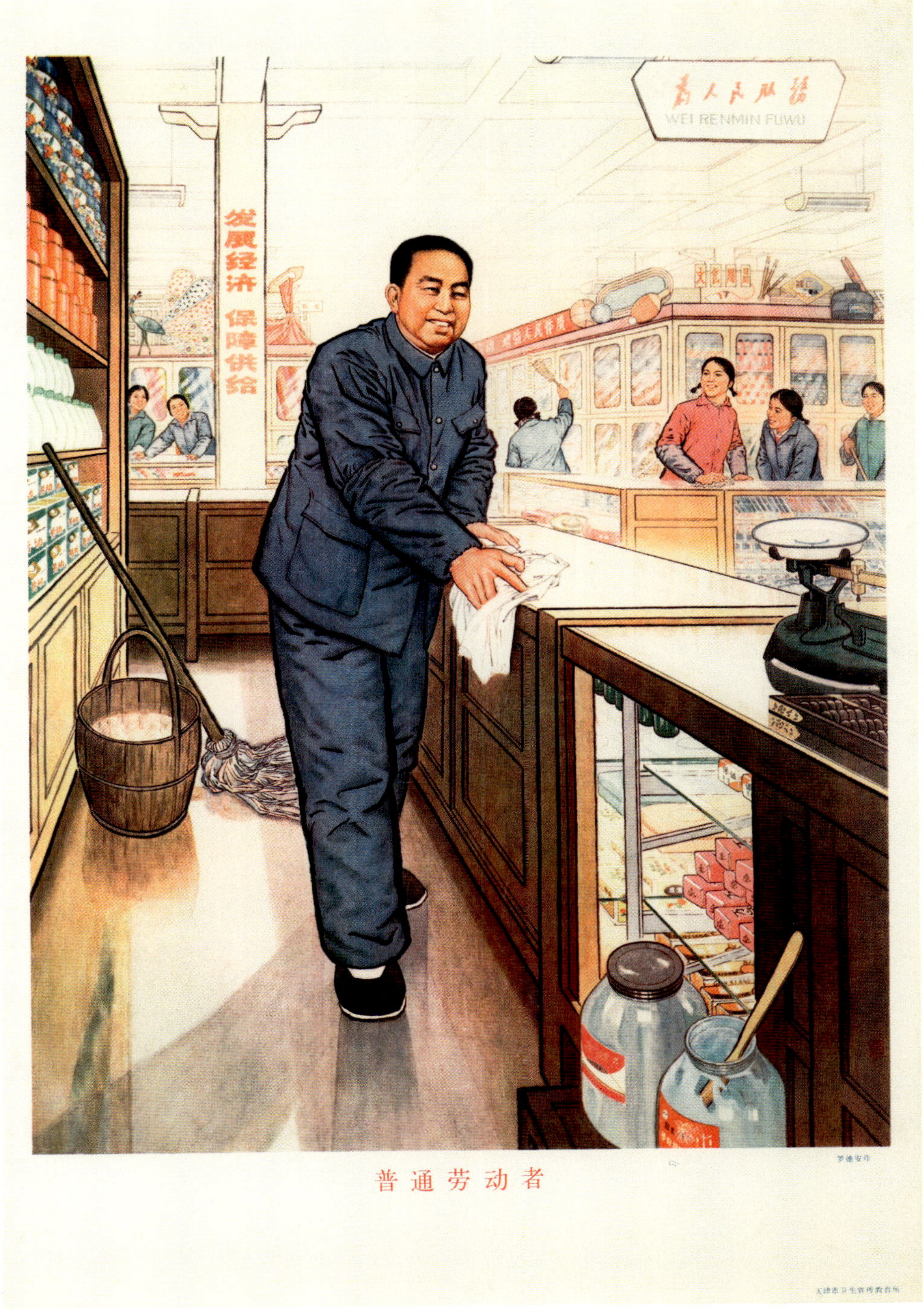

Ordinary worker (Hua Guofeng), c. 1977.
Einfacher Arbeiter (Hua Guofeng), um 1977.

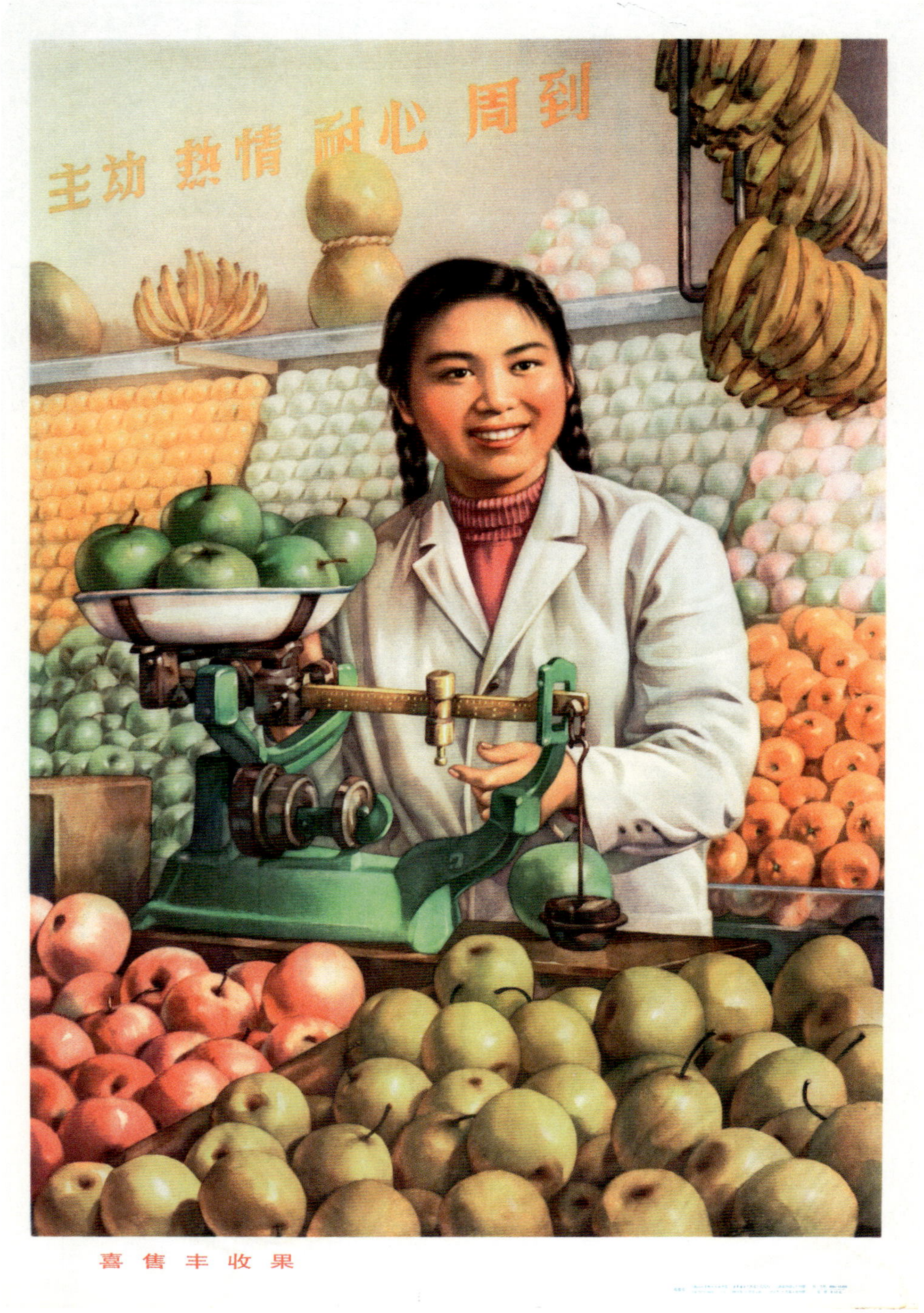

Selling the fruits of a bumper harvest in a friendly manner, 1978.
Die Früchte einer Rekordernte freundlich darbieten, 1978.

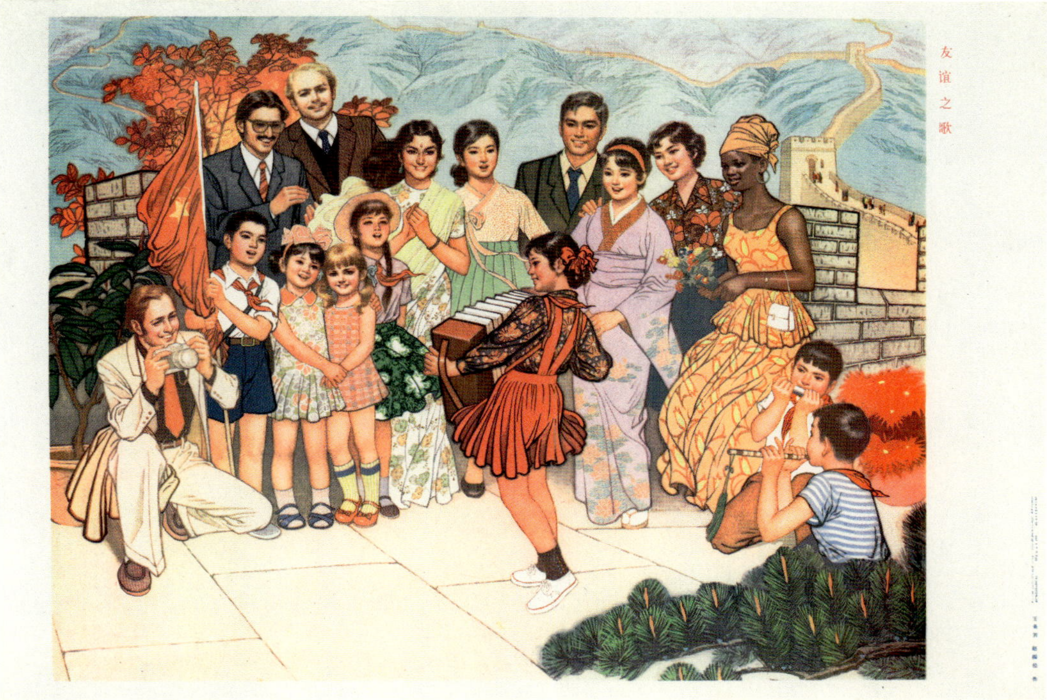

Song of Friendship, 1979.
Lied der Freundschaft, 1979.

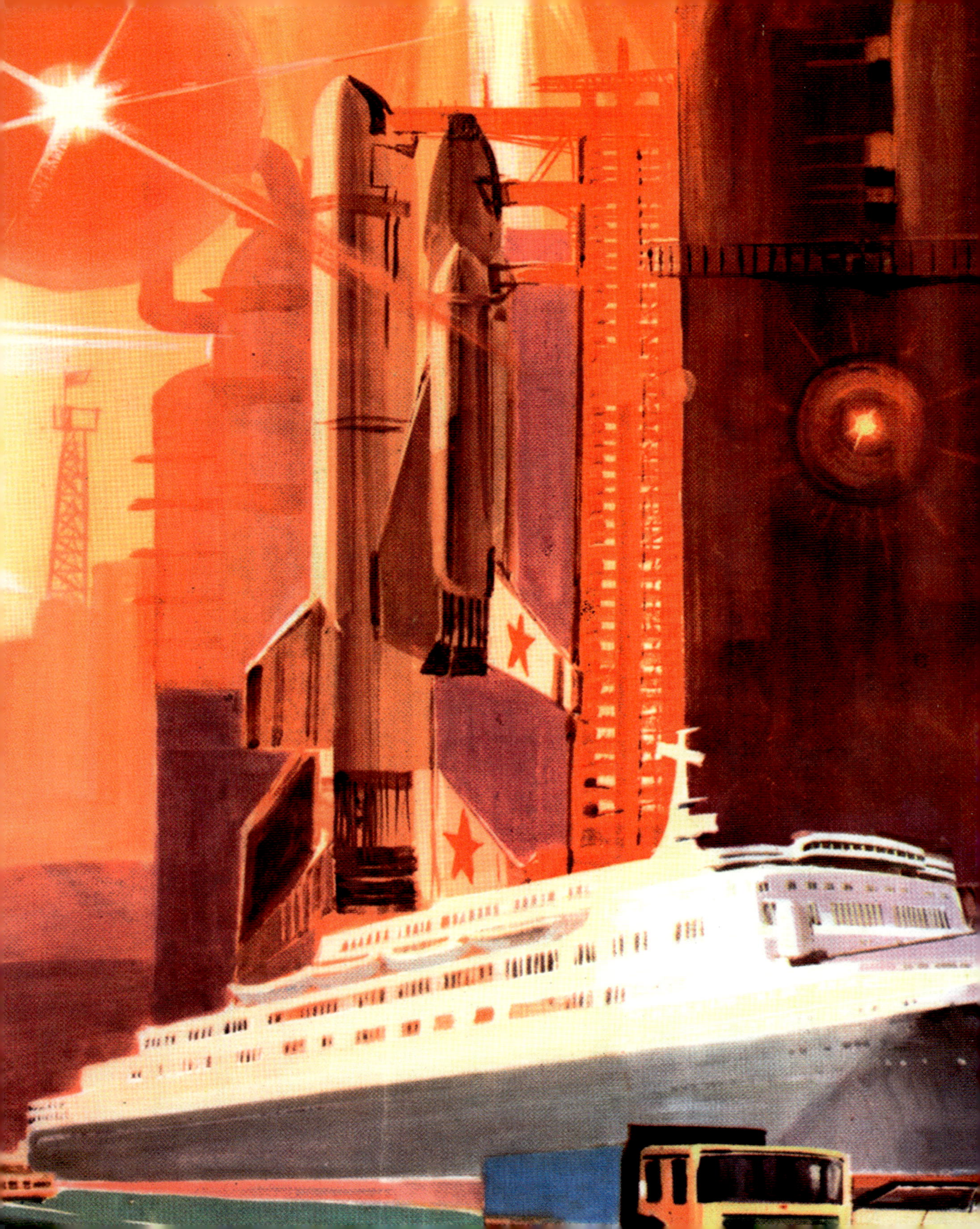

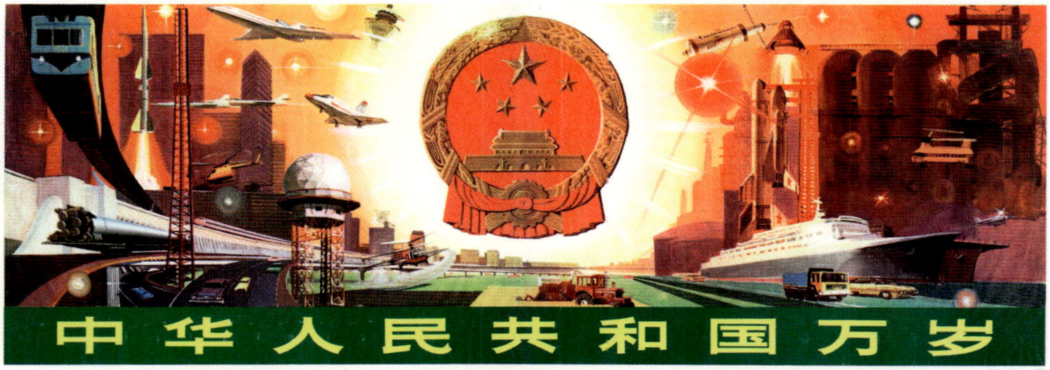

Long live the People's Republic of China, 1979.
Lang lebe die Volksrepublik China, 1979.

← Examples of modern technology around the emblem of the People's Republic. China's campaign for modernization has started. The absence of industrial and agricultural workers on the poster is conspicuous.

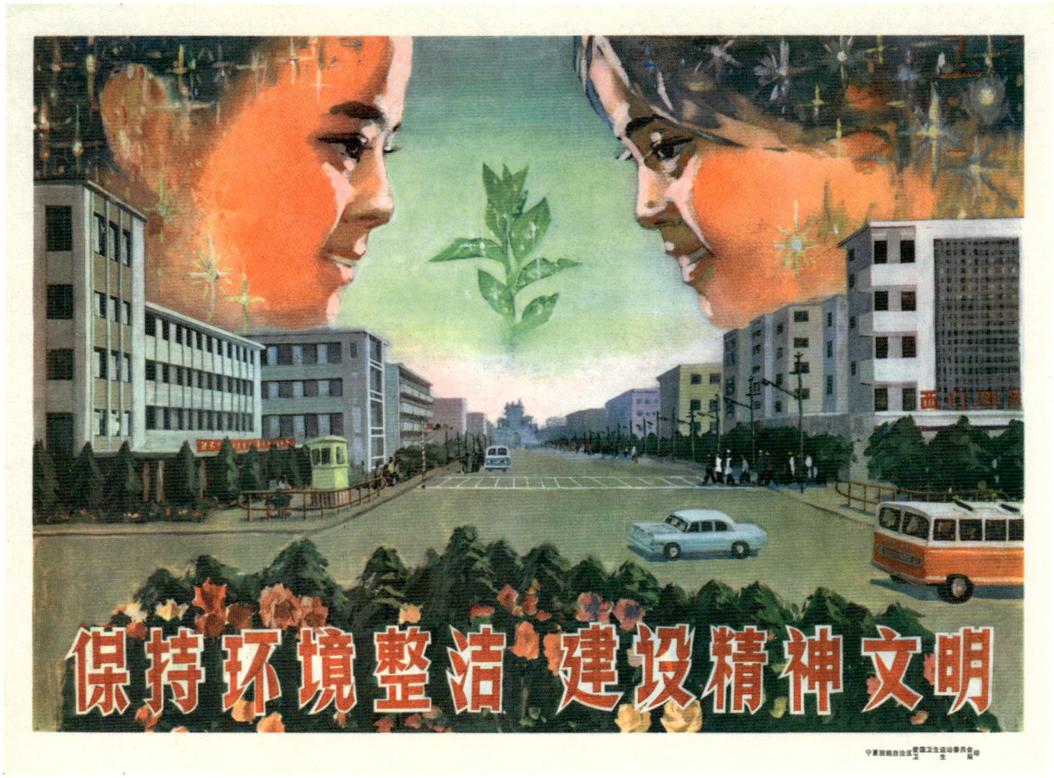

Keep the environment clean, create spiritual civilization, c. 1980.
Haltet die Umwelt rein, erschafft spirituelle Zivilisation, um 1980.

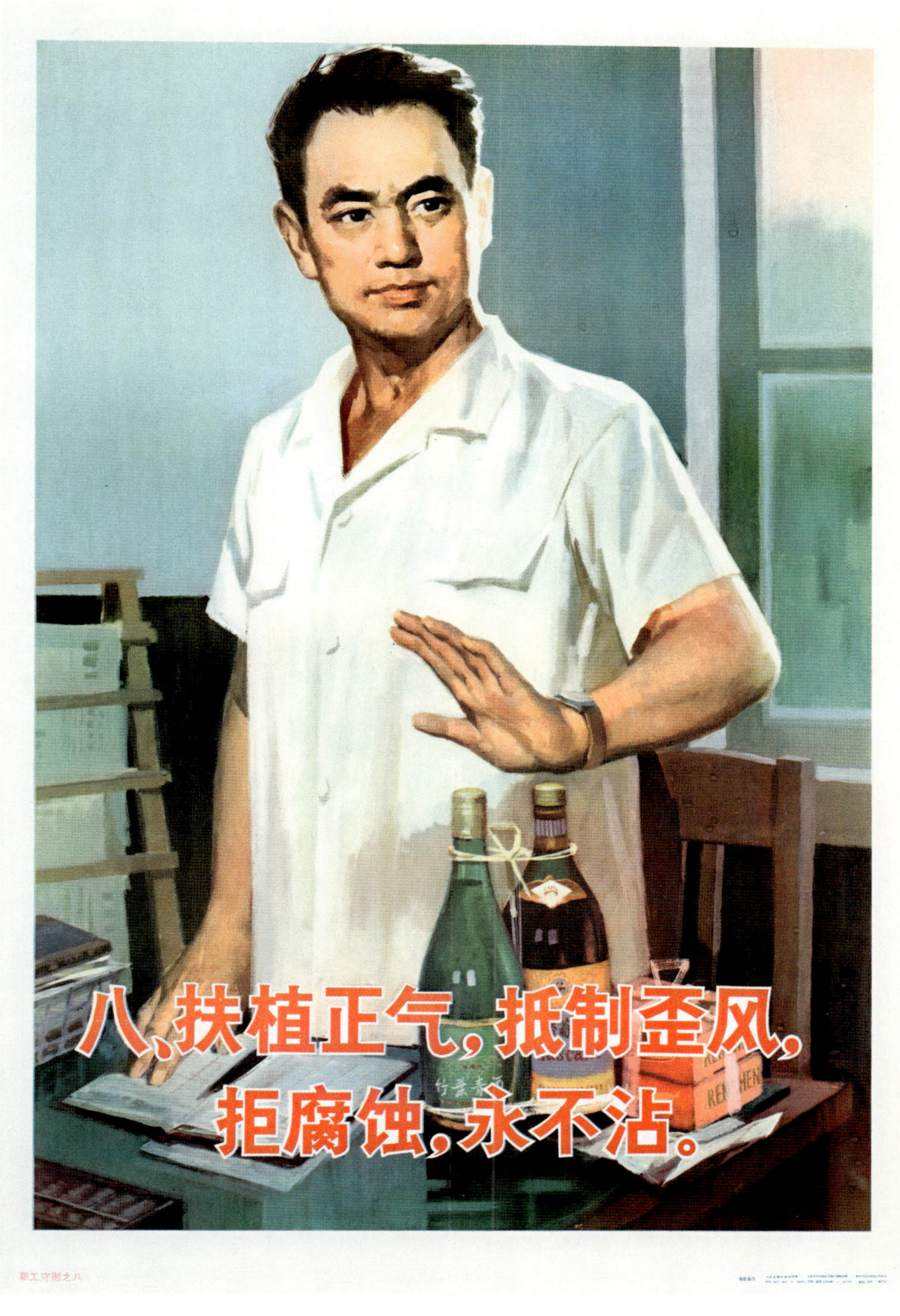

Foster a correct spirit, resist the evil spirit, resist corruption, never get involved with it, 1983.
Pflege einen gesunden Geist, widerstehe dem bösen Geist, widerstehe der Korruption, lass dich niemals darauf ein, 1983.

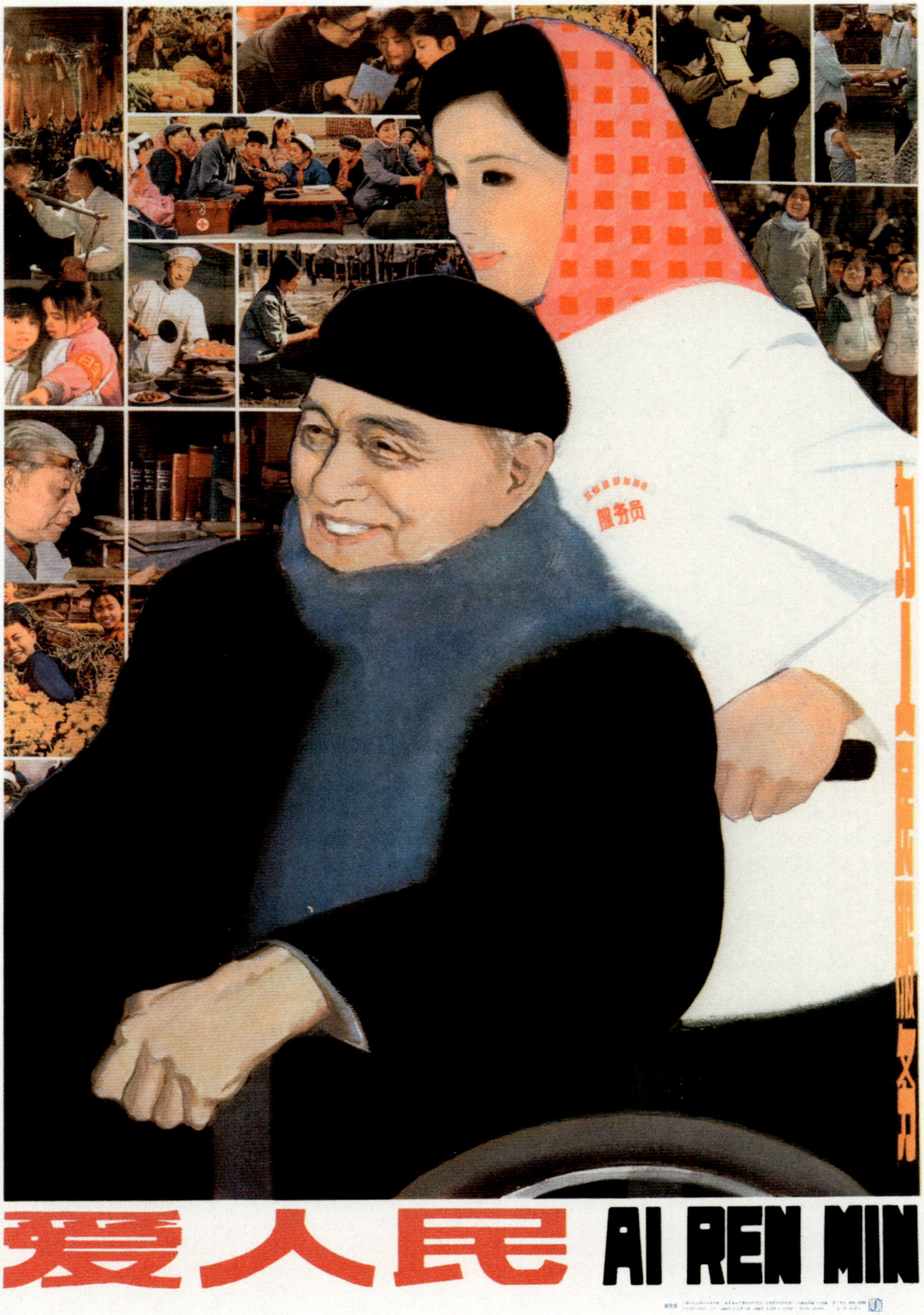

Love the people, 1983.
Liebe das Volk, 1983.

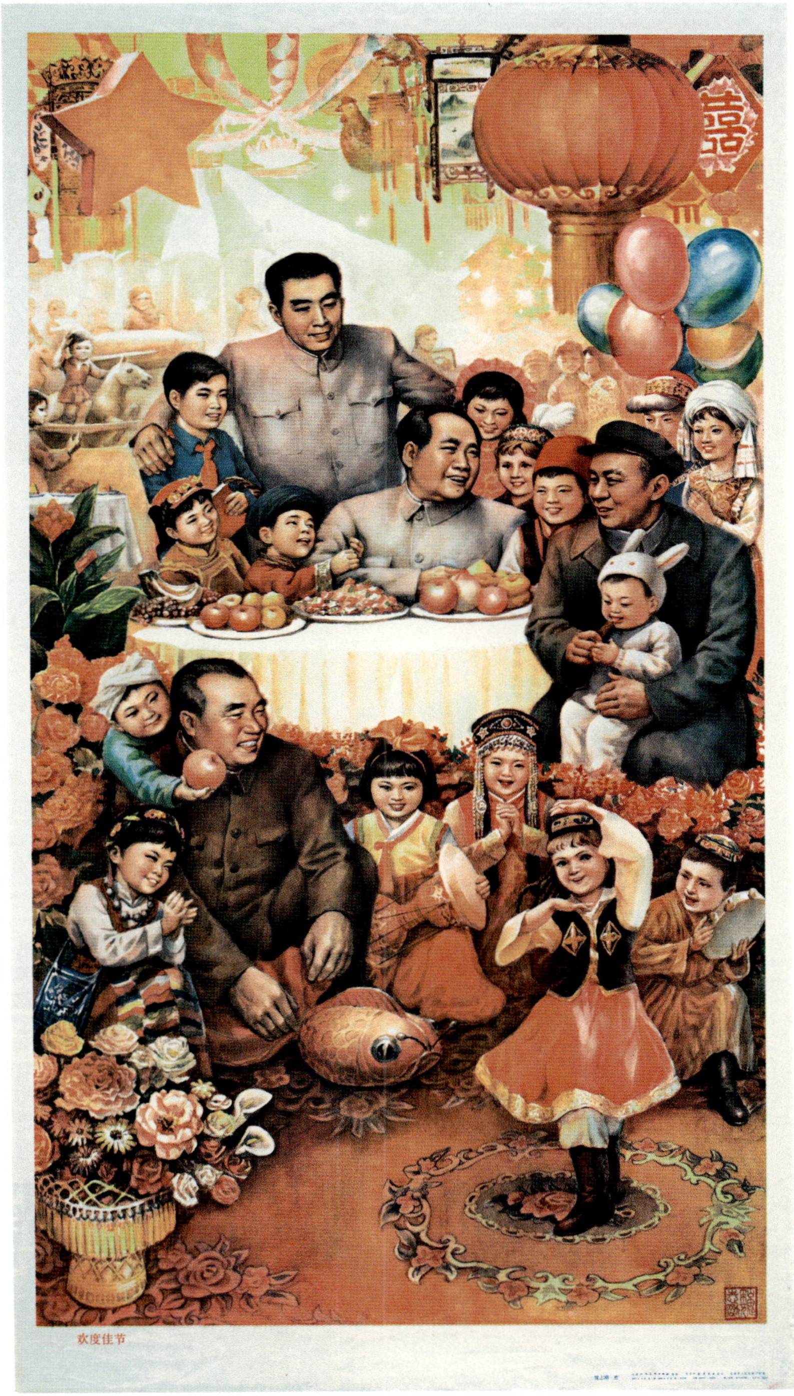

Celebrate a festival with jubilation, 1983.
Feiert ein Fest mit Jubel, 1983.

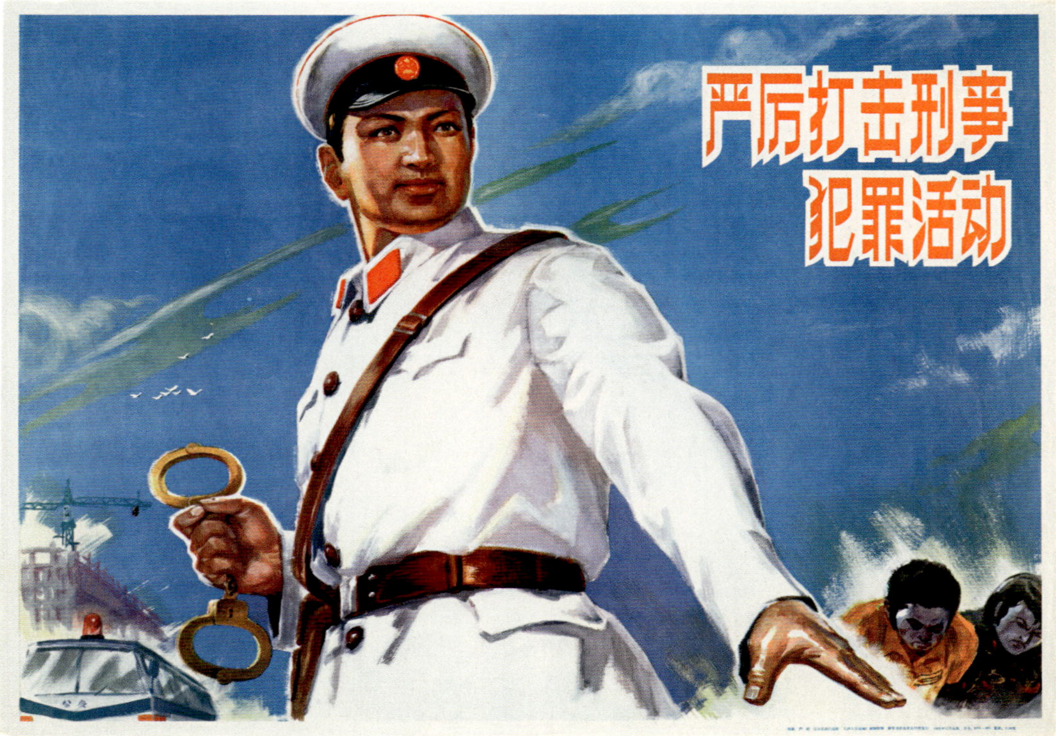

Sternly attack criminal activities, 1983.
Gehe hart gegen kriminelle Machenschaften vor, 1983.

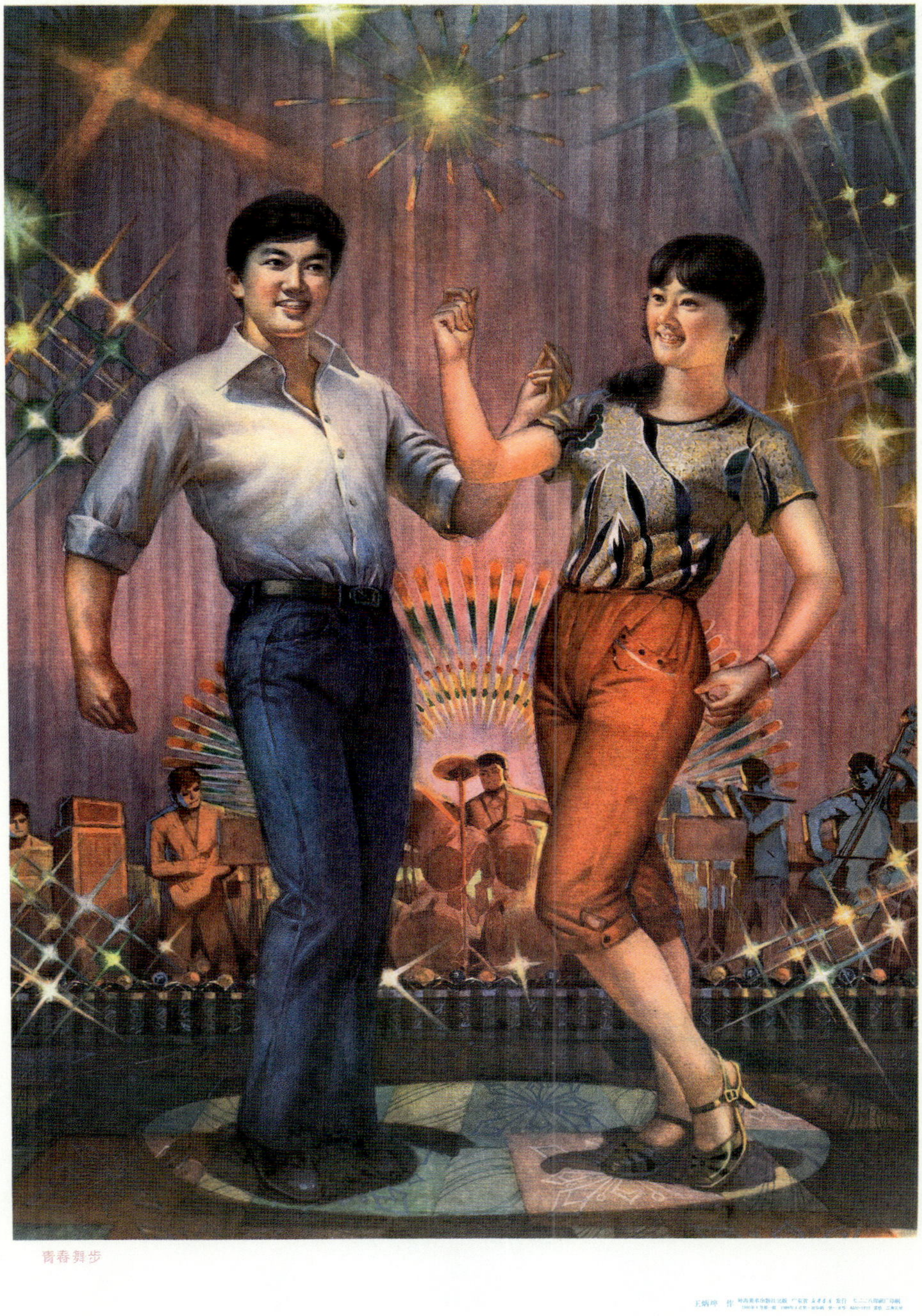

Youthful dance steps, 1986.
Jugendliche Tanzschritte, 1986.

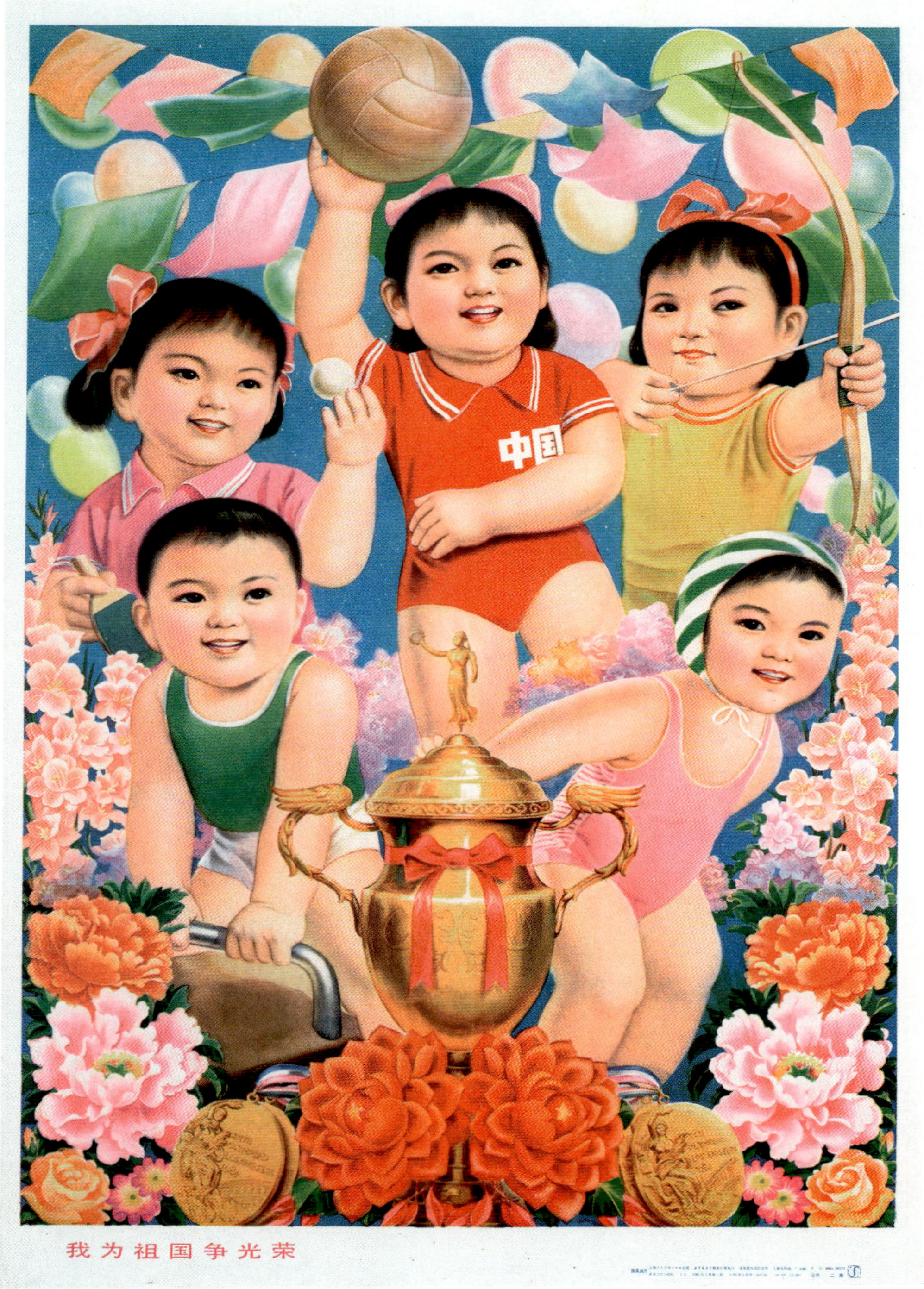

I strive to bring glory to the mother country, 1986.
Ich bemühe mich, dem Vaterland Ruhm zu bringen, 1986.

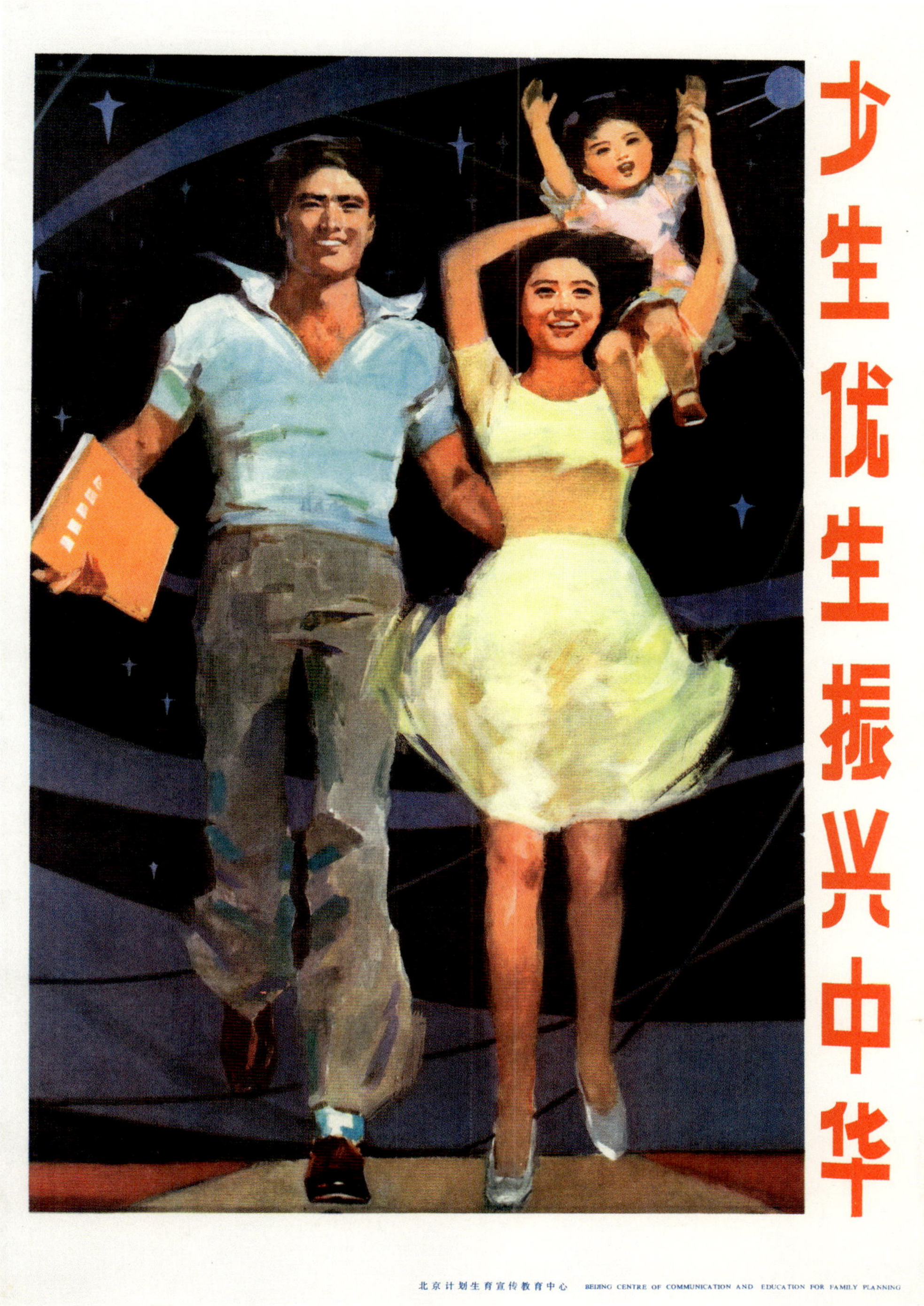

Fewer births, better births, to develop a strong China, 1987.
Weniger Geburten, gesündere Geburten, um ein starkes China zu erschaffen, 1987.

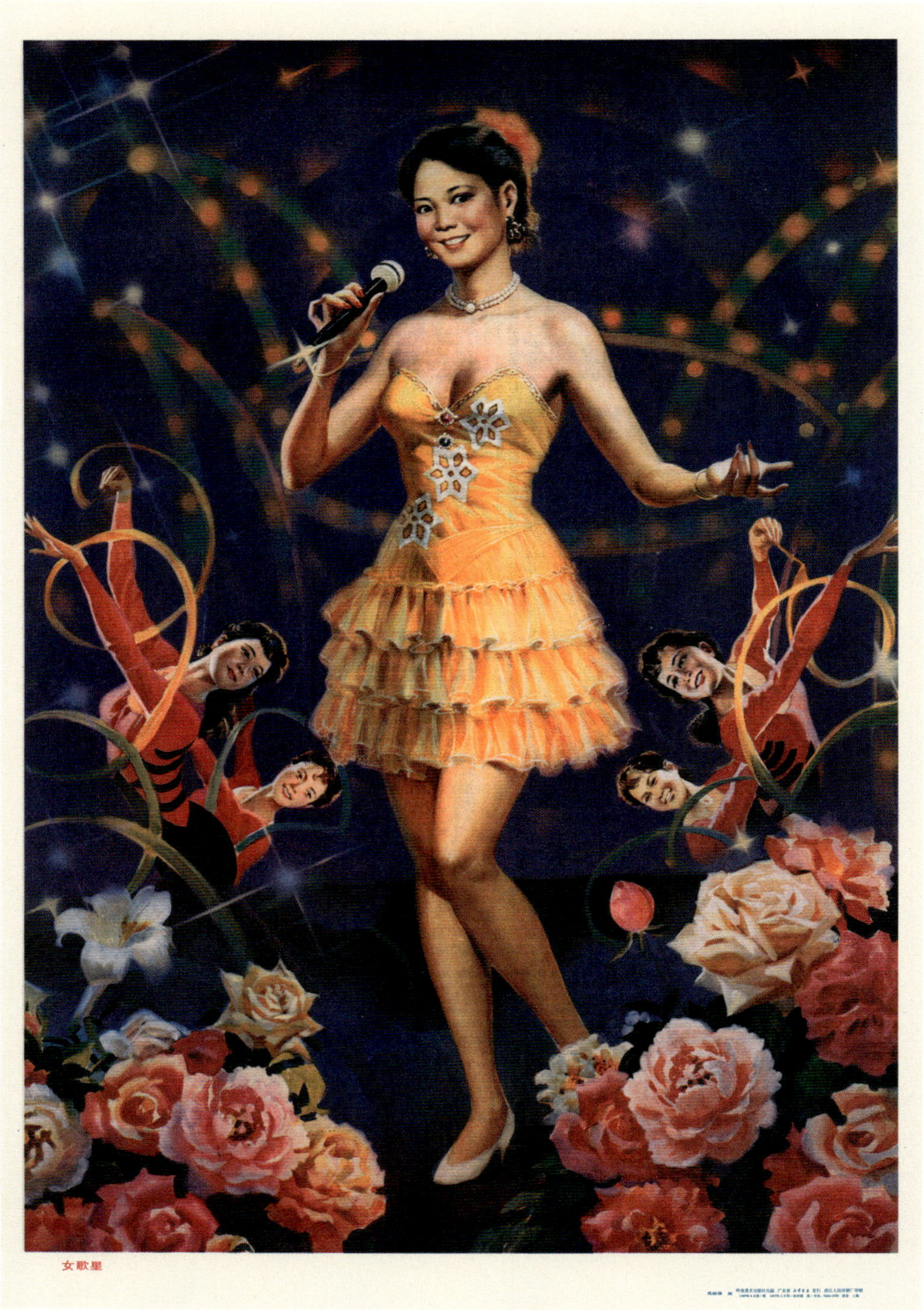

Pop star, 1987.
Popstar, 1987.

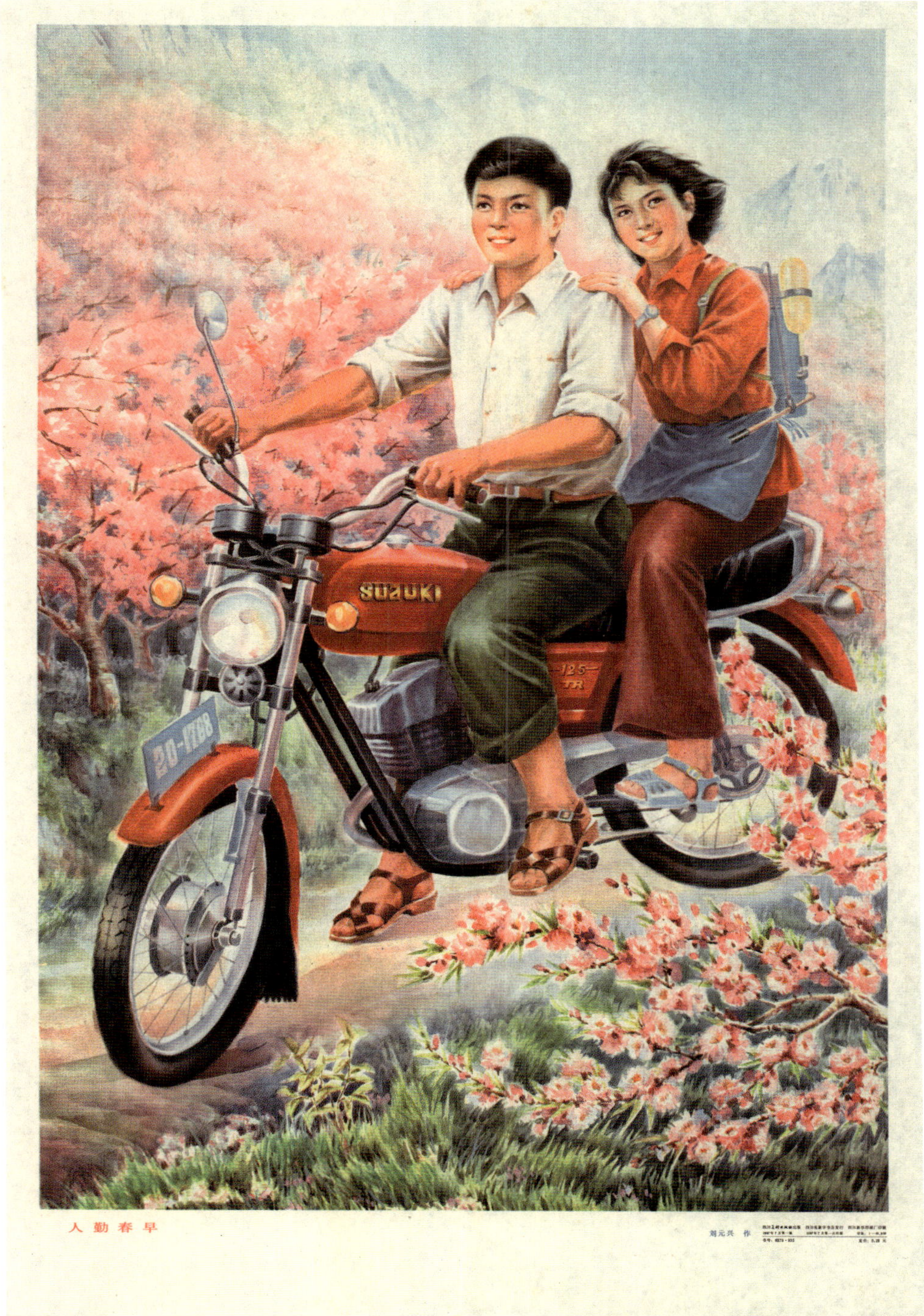

The people are industrious; spring is early, 1987.
Die Menschen sind arbeitsam, der Frühling ist da, 1987.

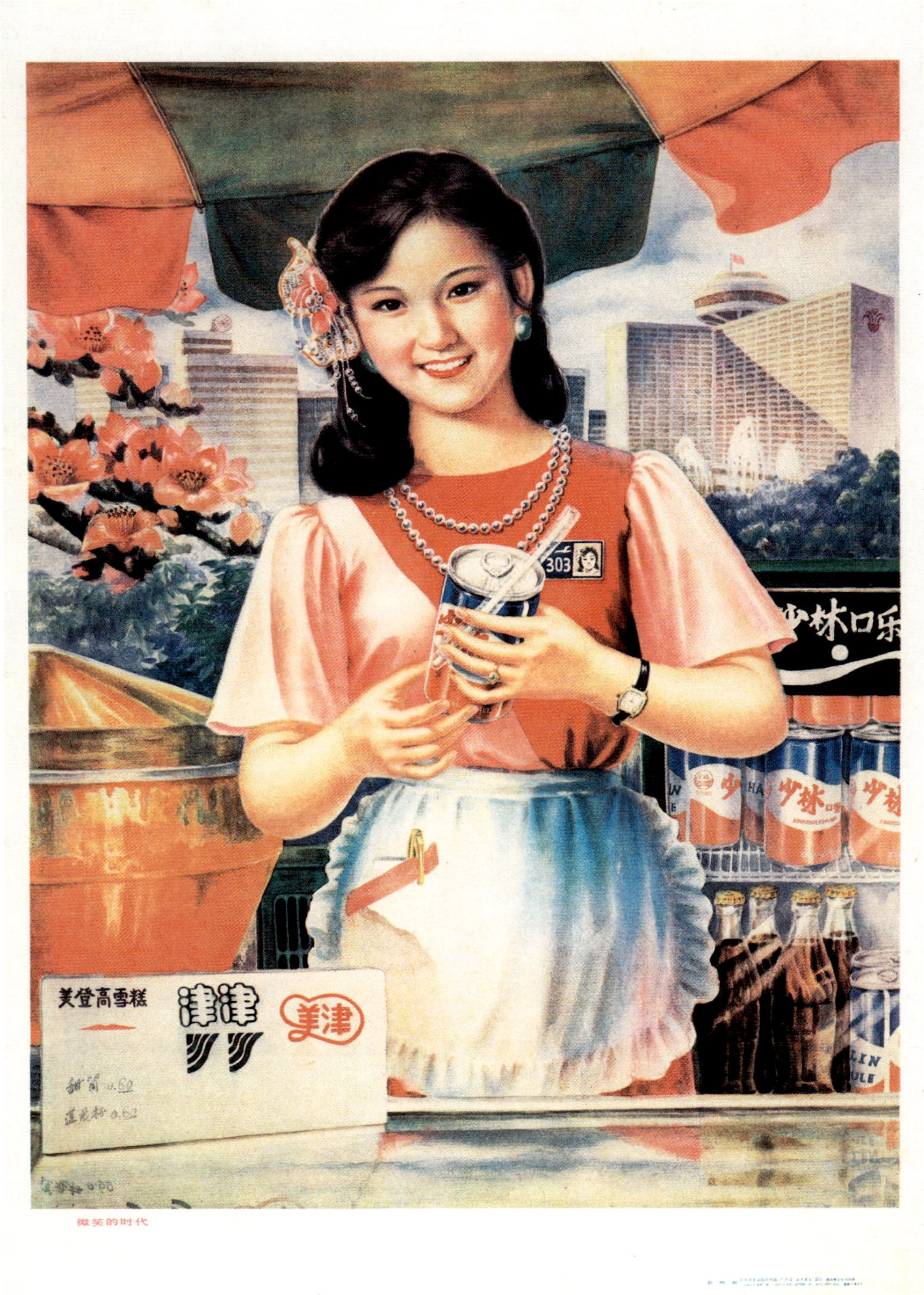

The age of smiling, 1988.
Die Ära des Lächelns, 1988.

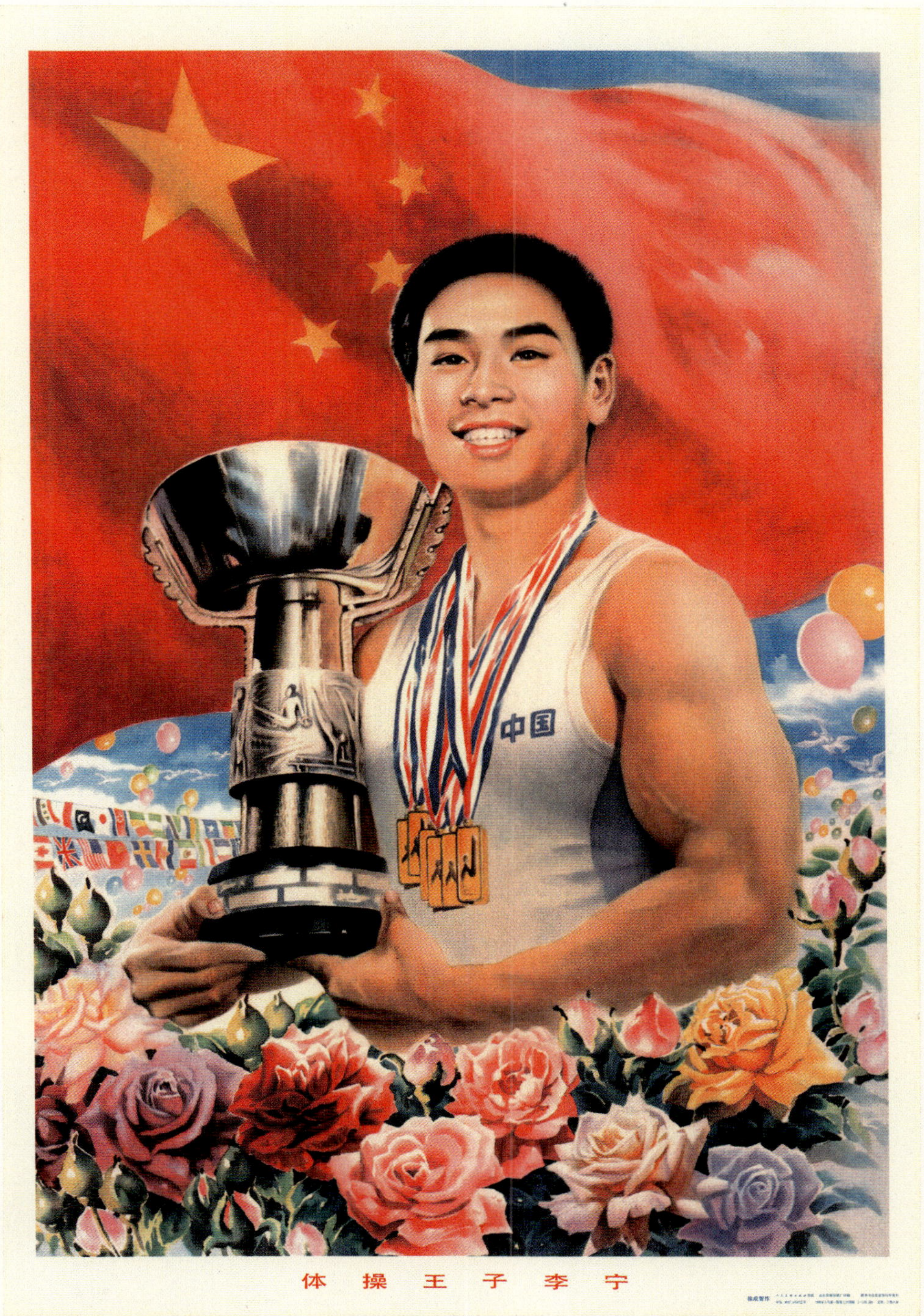

The king of gymnastics Li Ning, 1988.
Der König der Turner Li Ning, 1988.

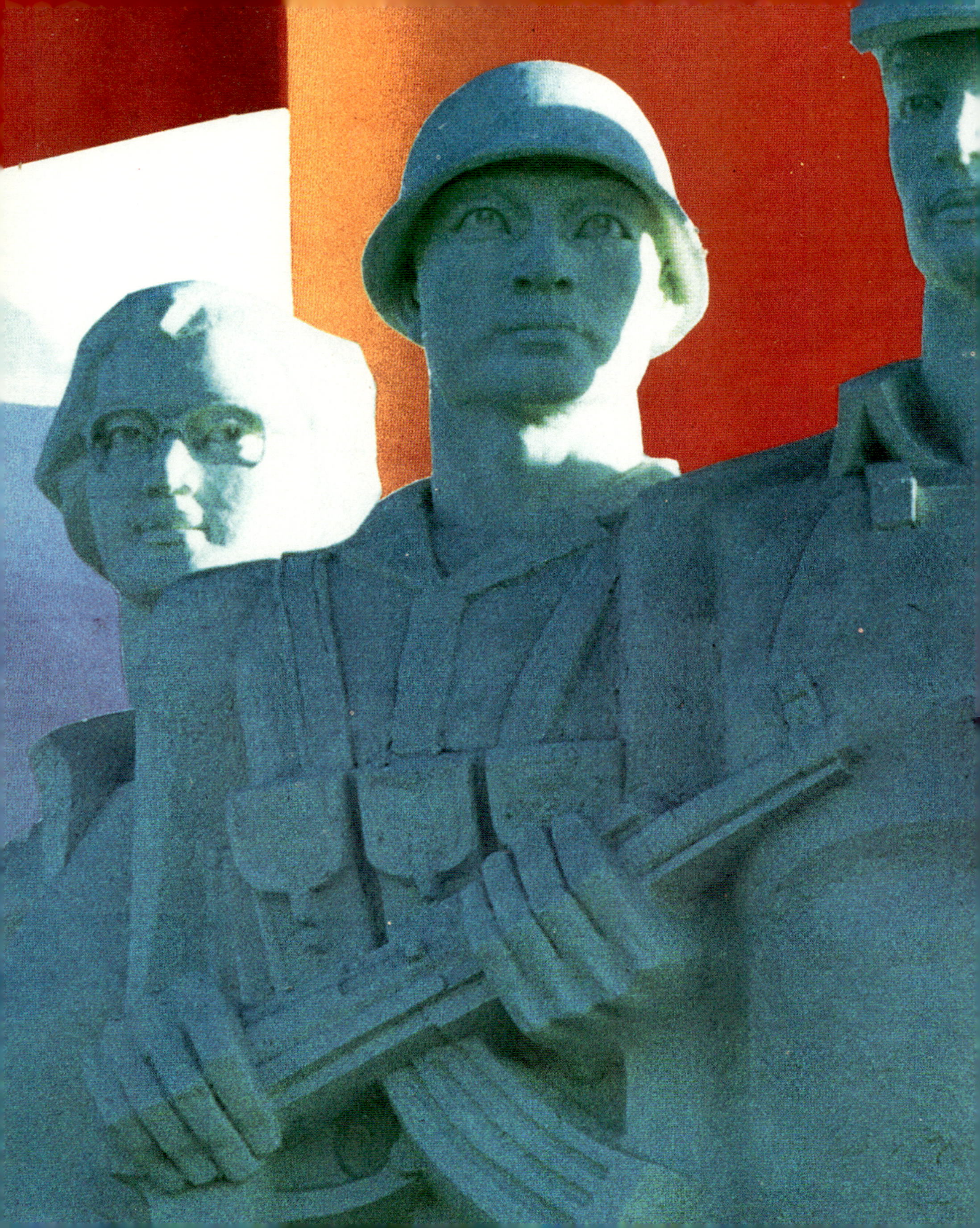

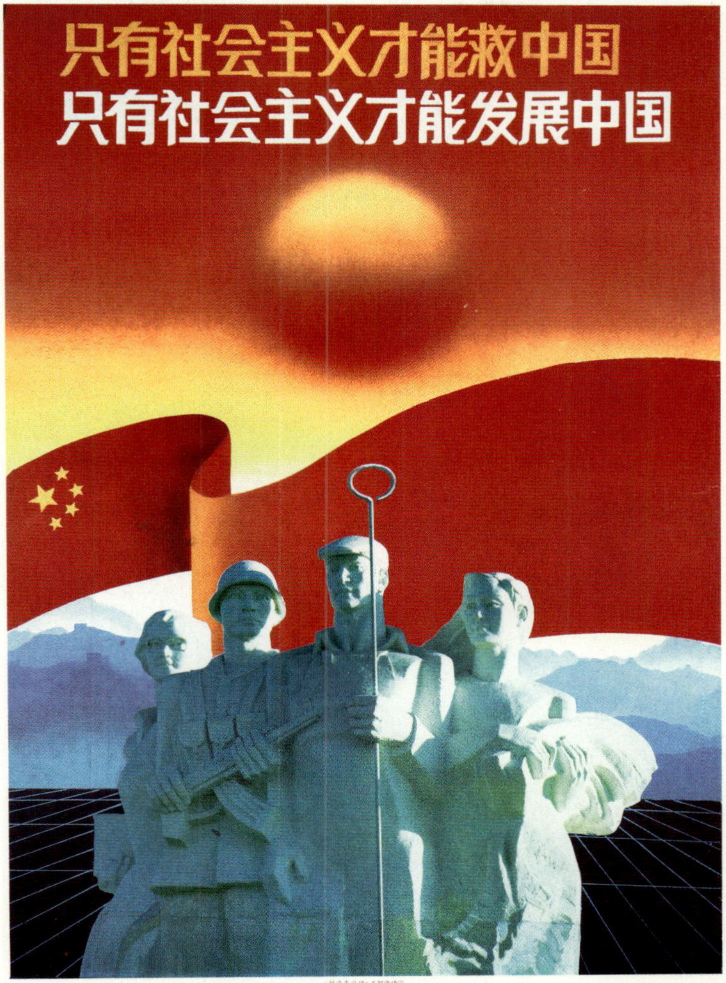

Only socialism can save China, only socialism can develop China, 1989.
Nur der Sozialismus kann China retten, nur durch den Sozialismus kann China wachsen, 1989.

During the student demonstrations on Tian'anmen square in Beijing in 1989, a white statue of the "Goddess of Democracy" was erected. After the crushing of the demonstrations, the authorities put this statue in its place.

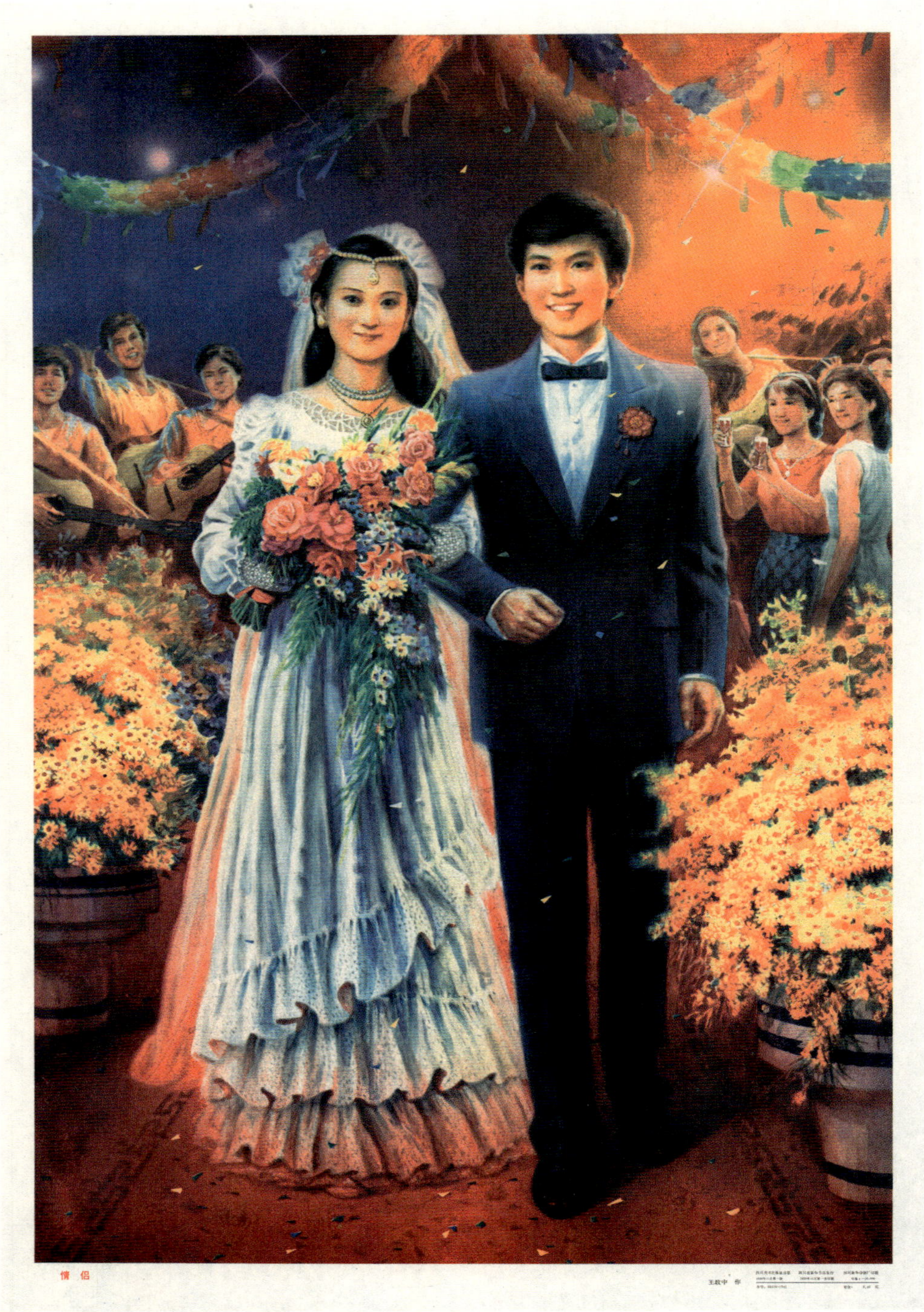

Sweethearts, 1990.
Die Liebsten, 1990.

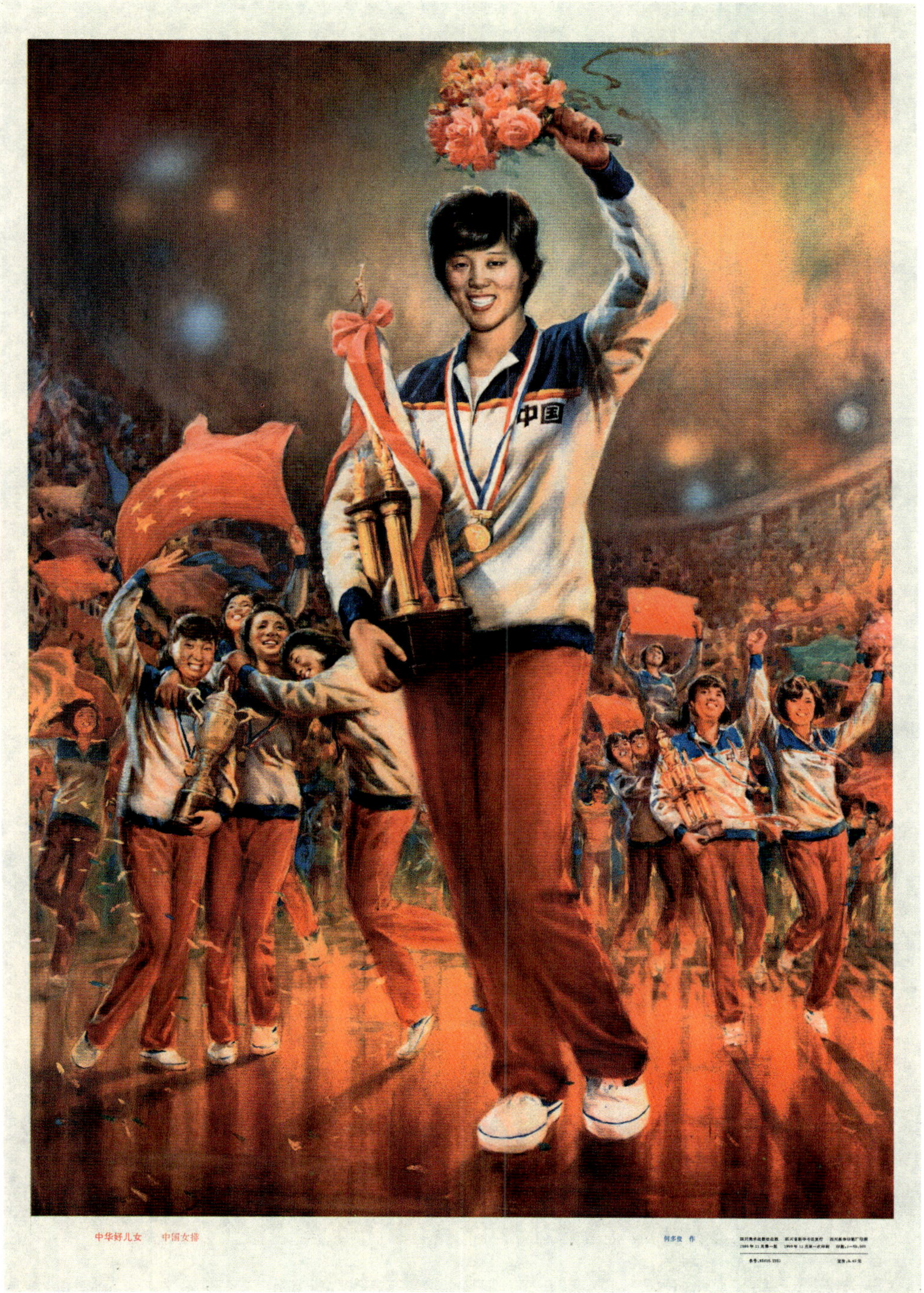

Chinese women's volleyball team, 1990.
Das chinesische Volleyball Damen-Team, 1990.

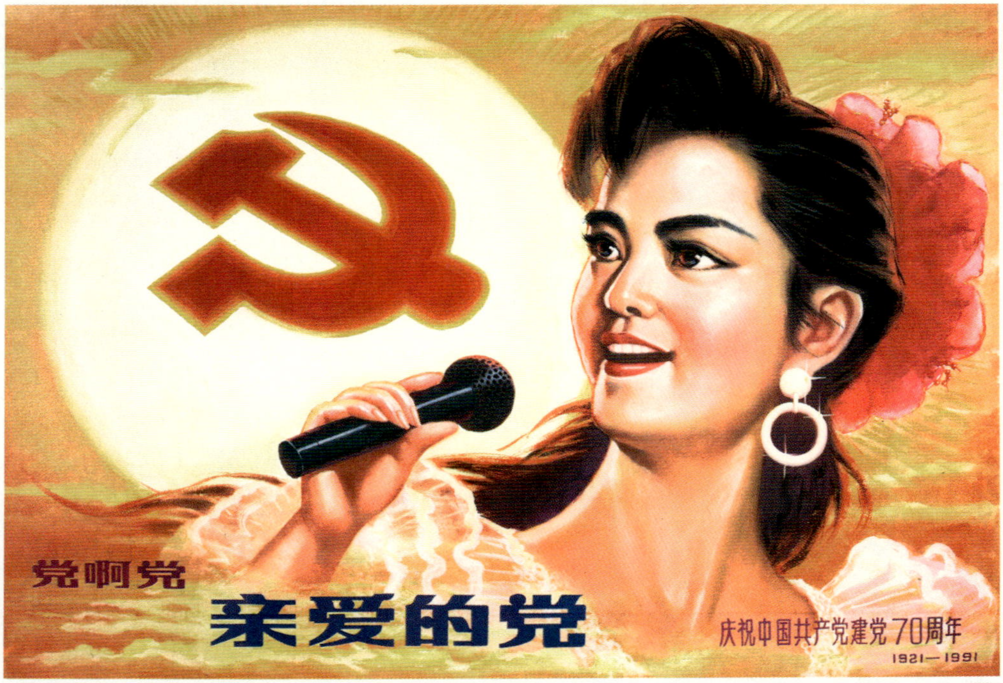

Party, oh party, beloved party, 1991.
Partei, oh Partei, geliebte Partei, 1991.

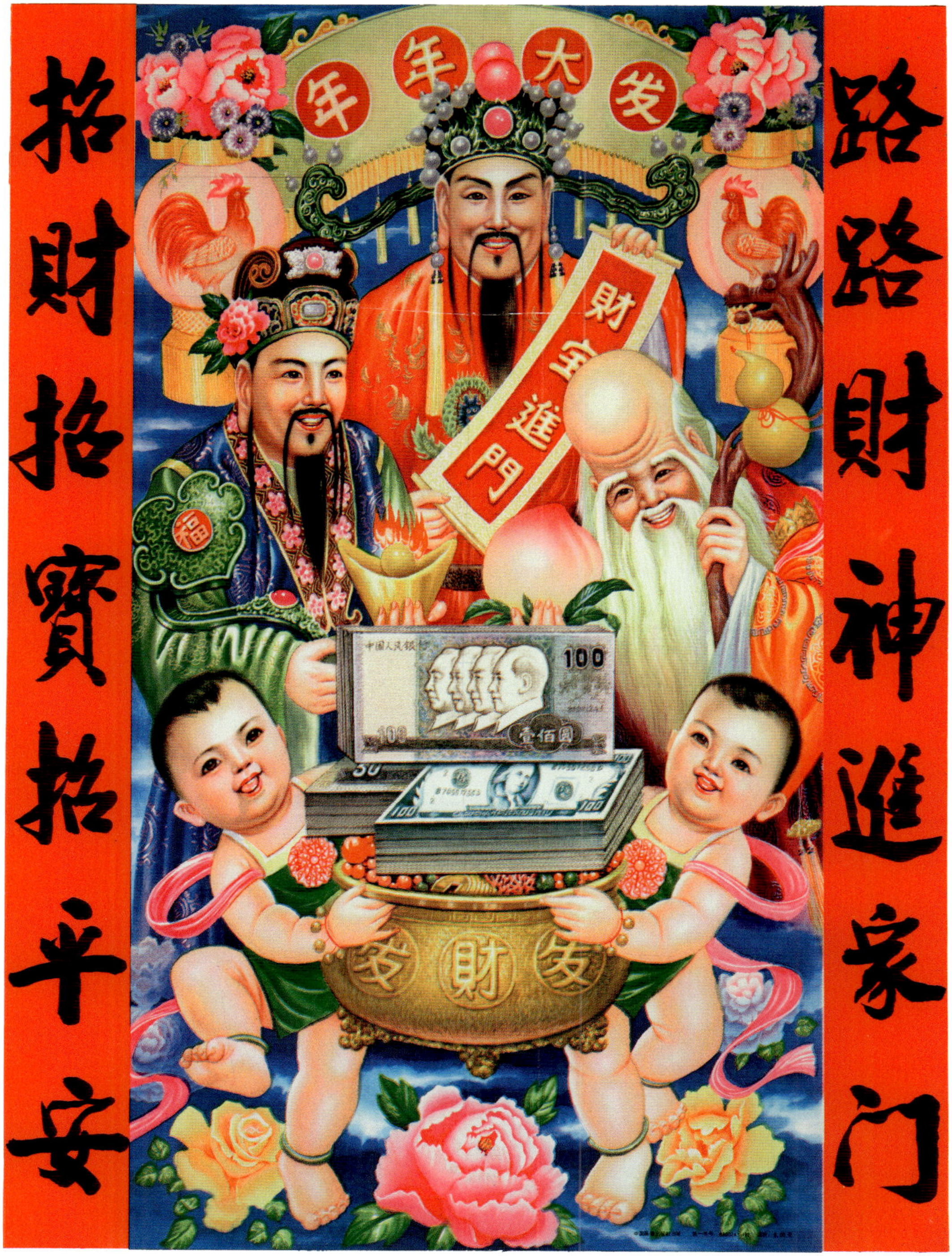

The Gods of wealth enter the home from everywhere:
wealth, treasures and peace beckon, 1993.
Die Götter des Reichtums kommen von überall her ins Haus:
Reichtum, Schätze und Frieden winken, 1993.

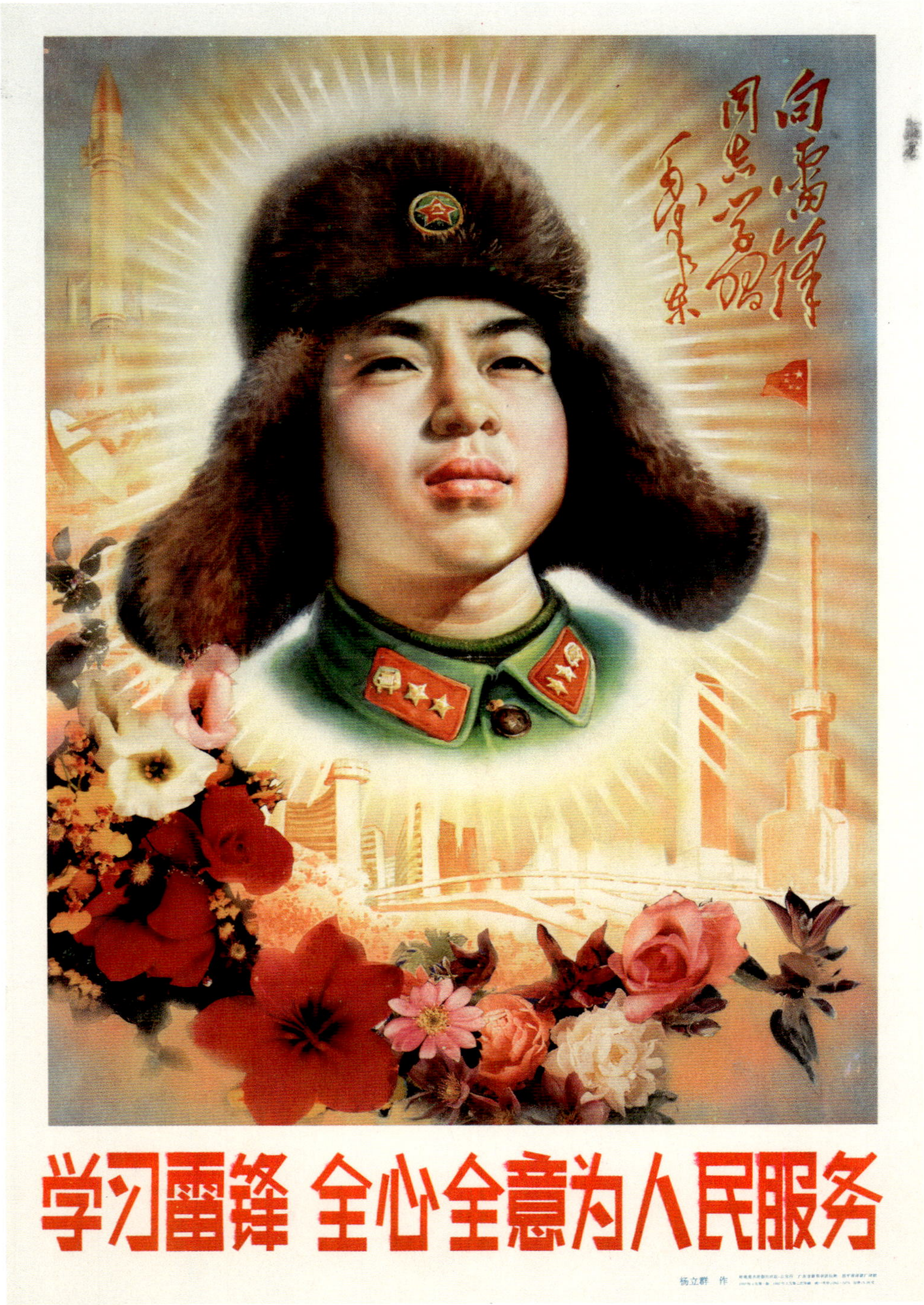

Study Lei Feng: serve the people wholeheartedly, 1995.
Studiert Lei Feng: Dient dem Volk aus ganzem Herzen, 1995.

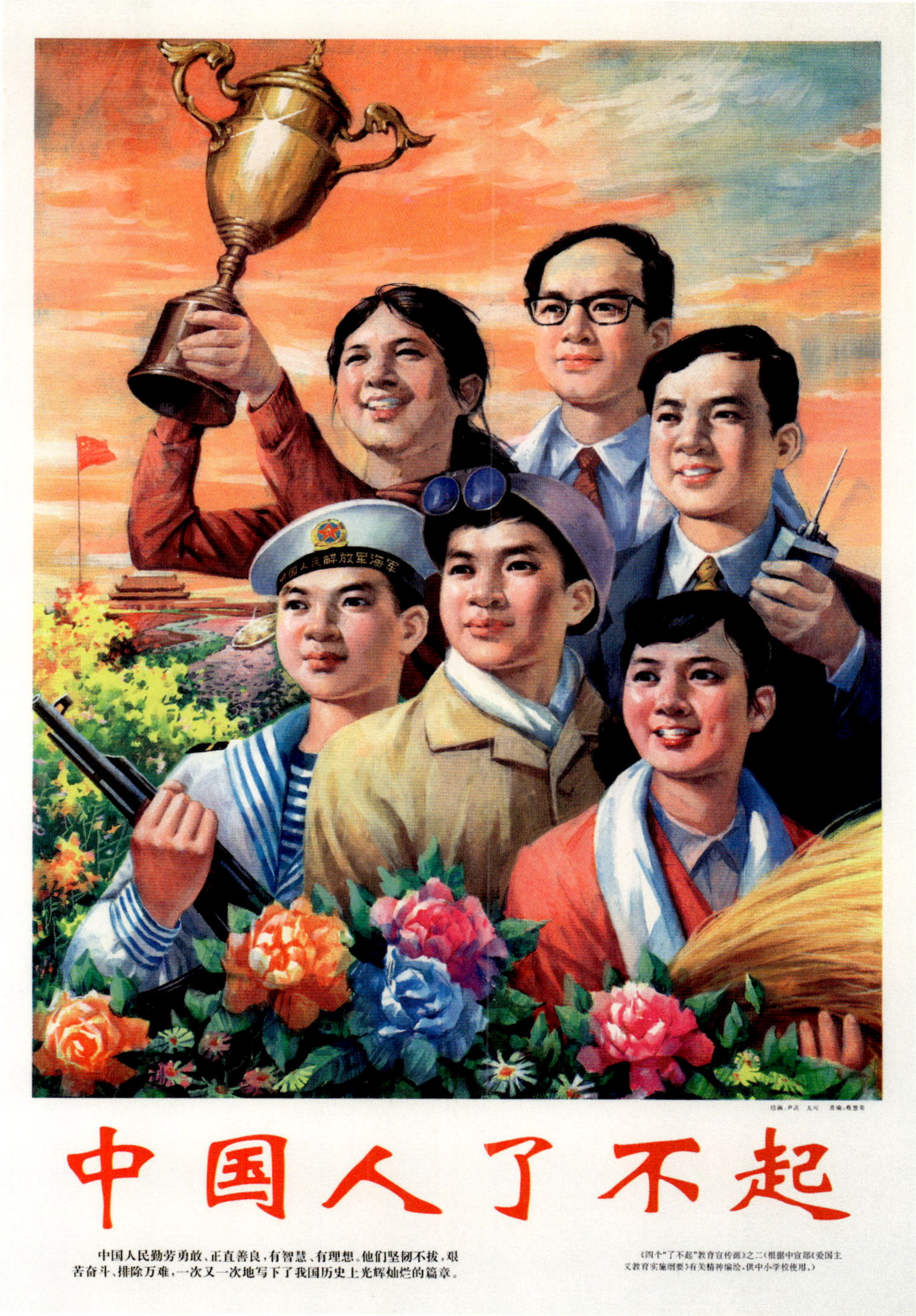

The Chinese are amazing, 1996.
Die Chinesen sind fantastisch, 1996.

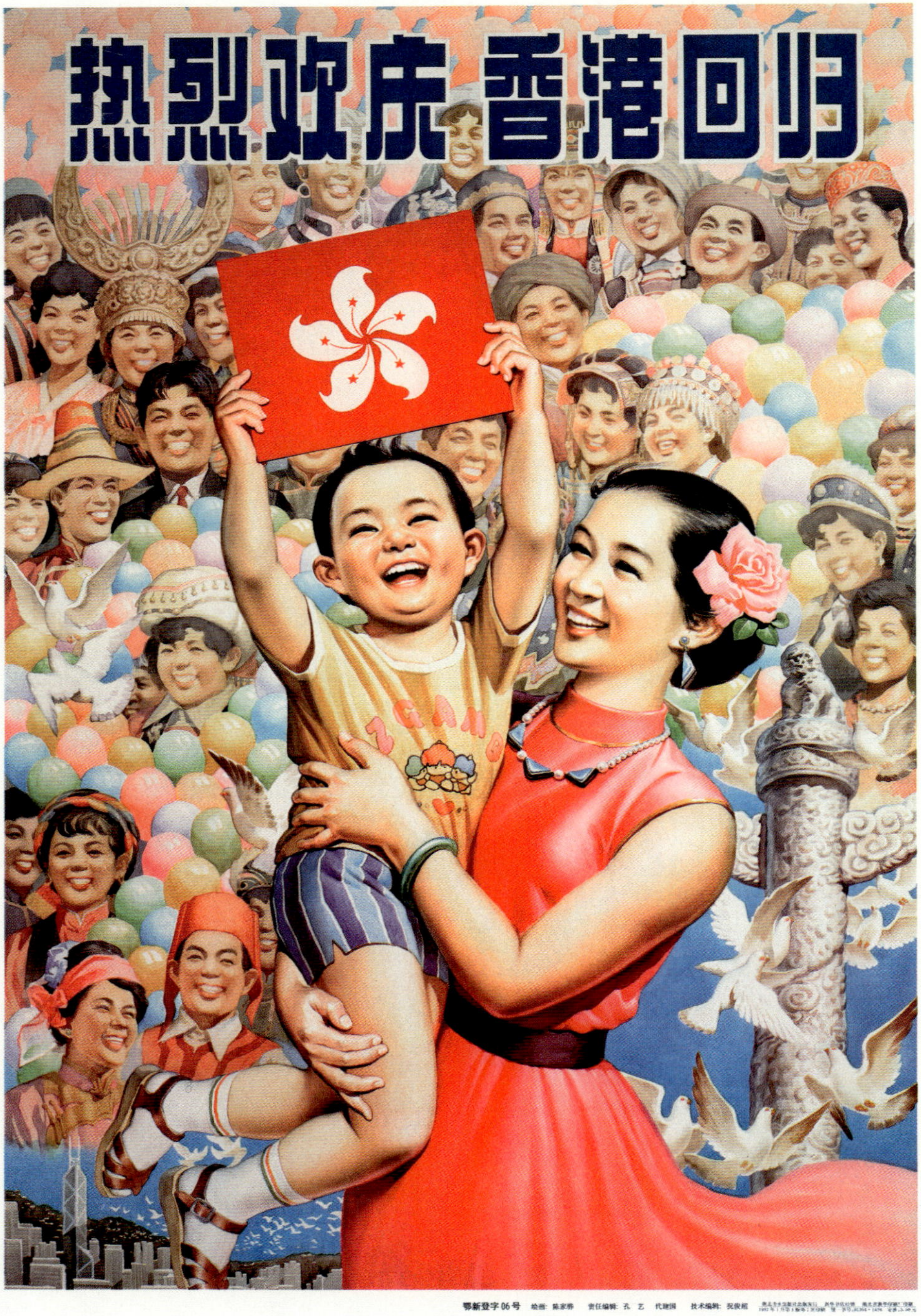

Enthusiastically celebrate the return of Hong Kong, 1997.
Feiert begeistert die Rückkehr von Hongkong, 1997.

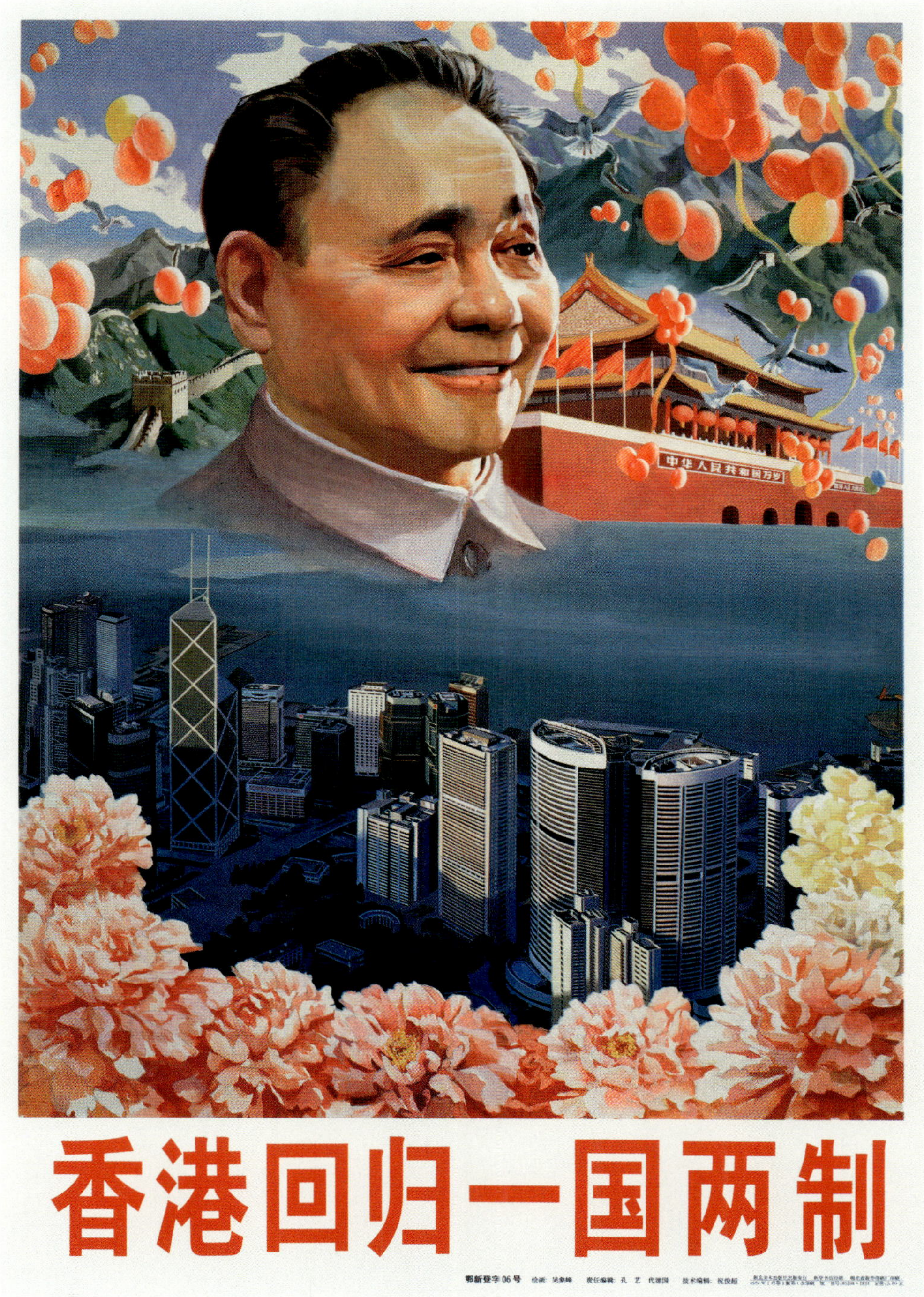

The return of Hong Kong. One country – two systems, 1997.
Die Rückkehr von Hongkong. Ein Land – zwei Systeme, 1997.

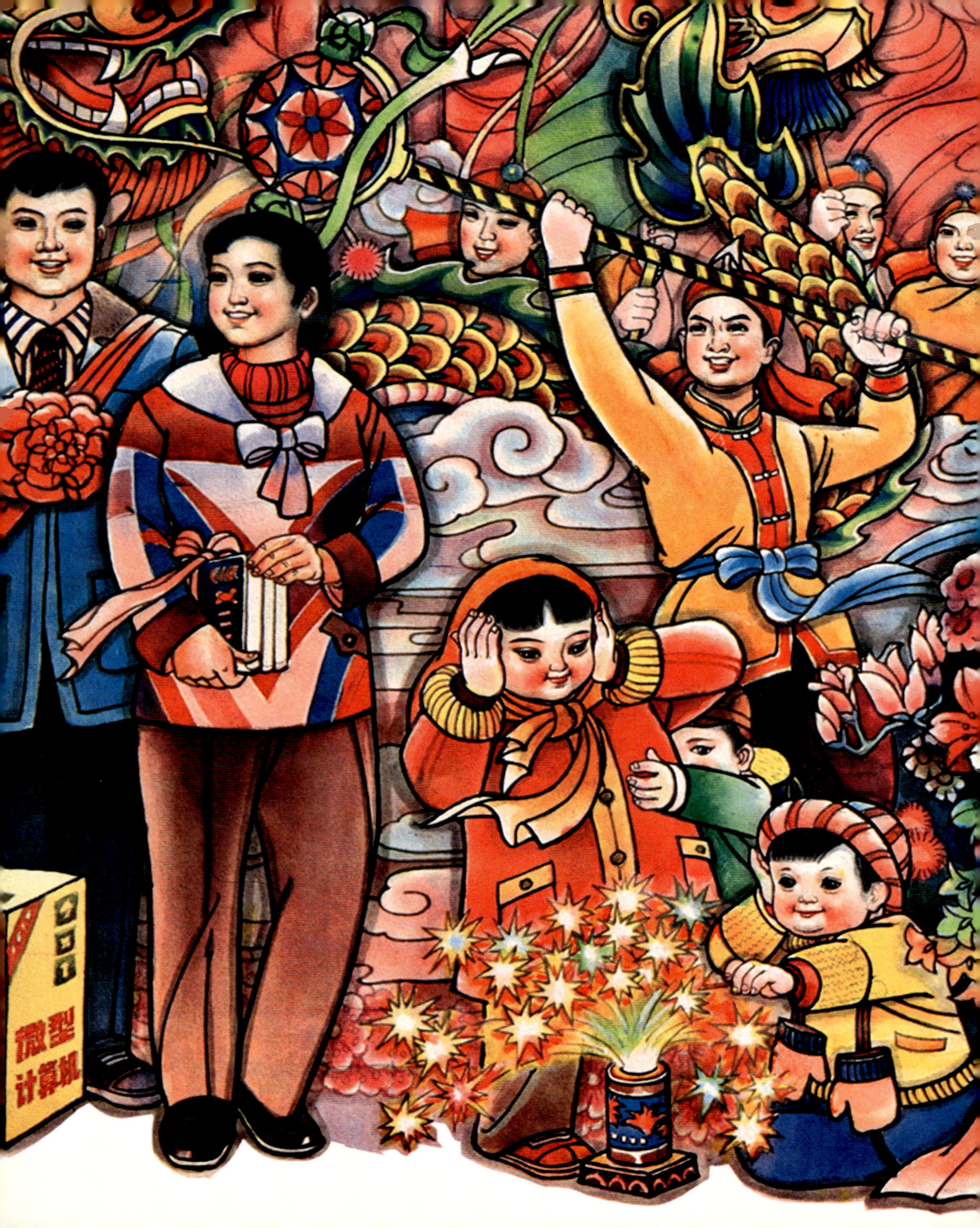
微型
计算机

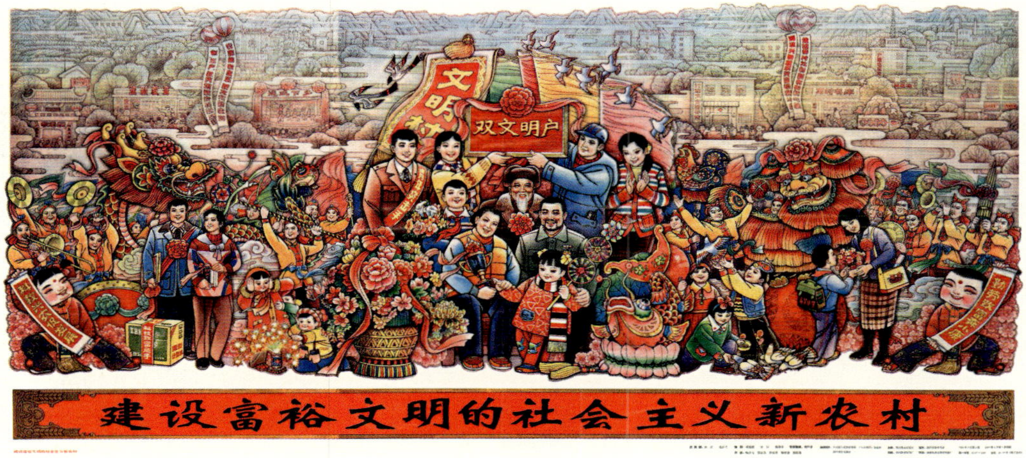

Build a prosperous and cultured new socialist countryside, 1997.
Erschafft ein blühendes und kultiviertes neues sozialistisches Land, 1997.

Prosperity in the countryside: material abundance, plenty of food, good facilities for all age groups, ranging from schools, libraries and hospitals to offices where media companies operate. Note the box with an IBM computer on the left.

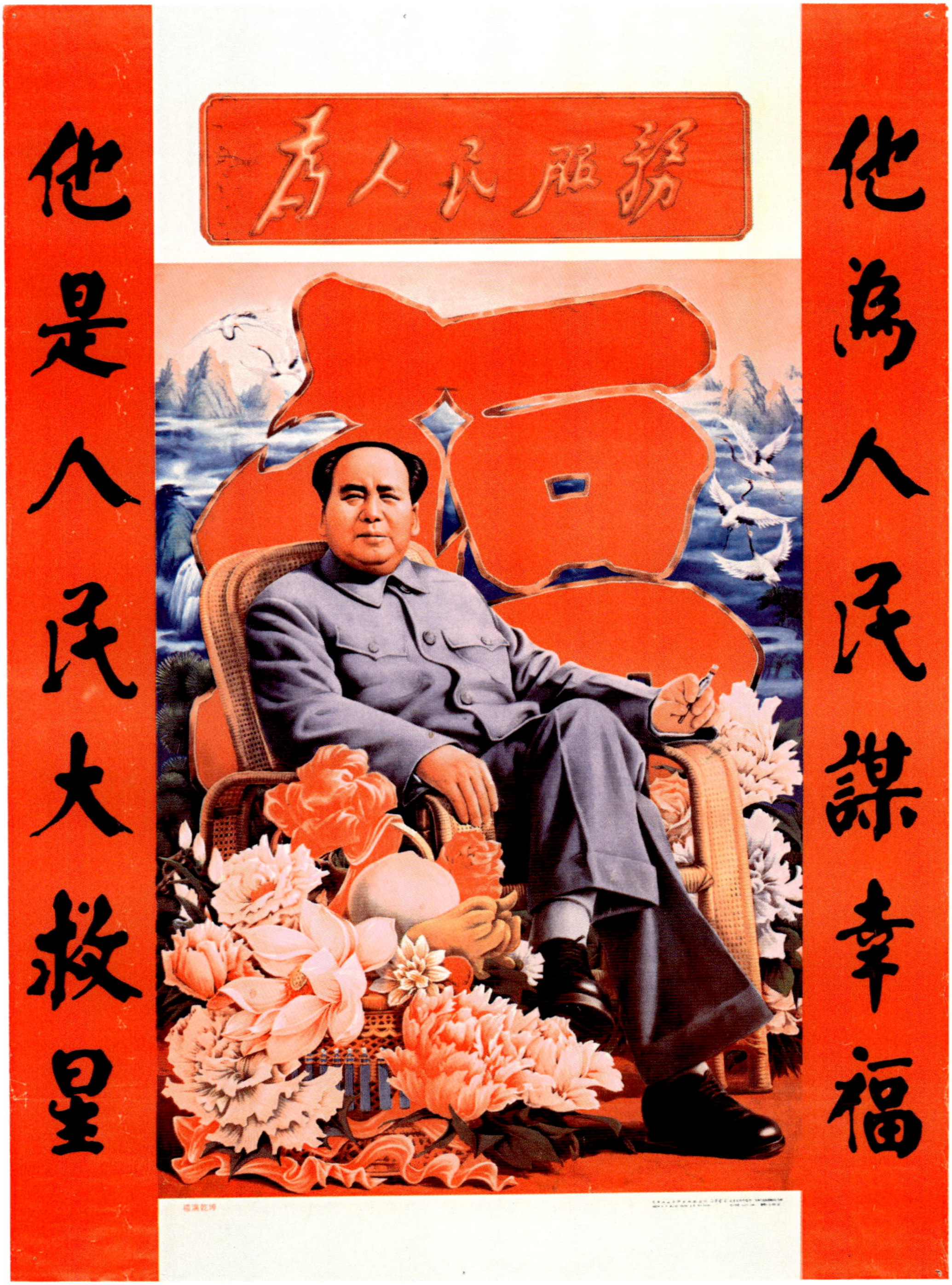

Happy Universe, 1997.
Glückliches Universum, 1997.

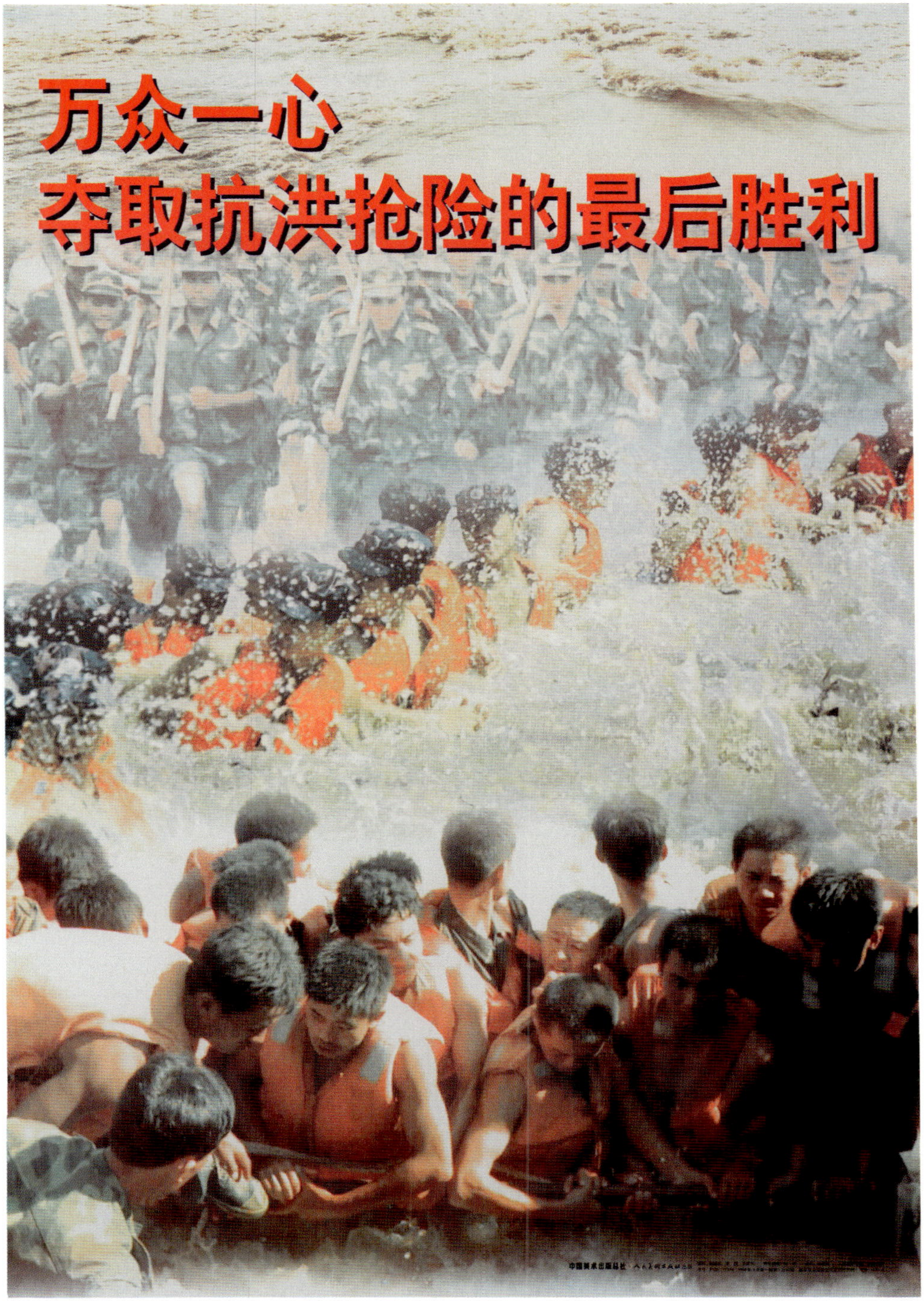

Millions of people all of one mind strive for the ultimate victory in combating floods and dealing with emergencies, 1998.
Millionen von Menschen streben im Geiste vereint für den großen Sieg, indem sie Fluten bekämpfen und Katastrophen bewältigen, 1998.

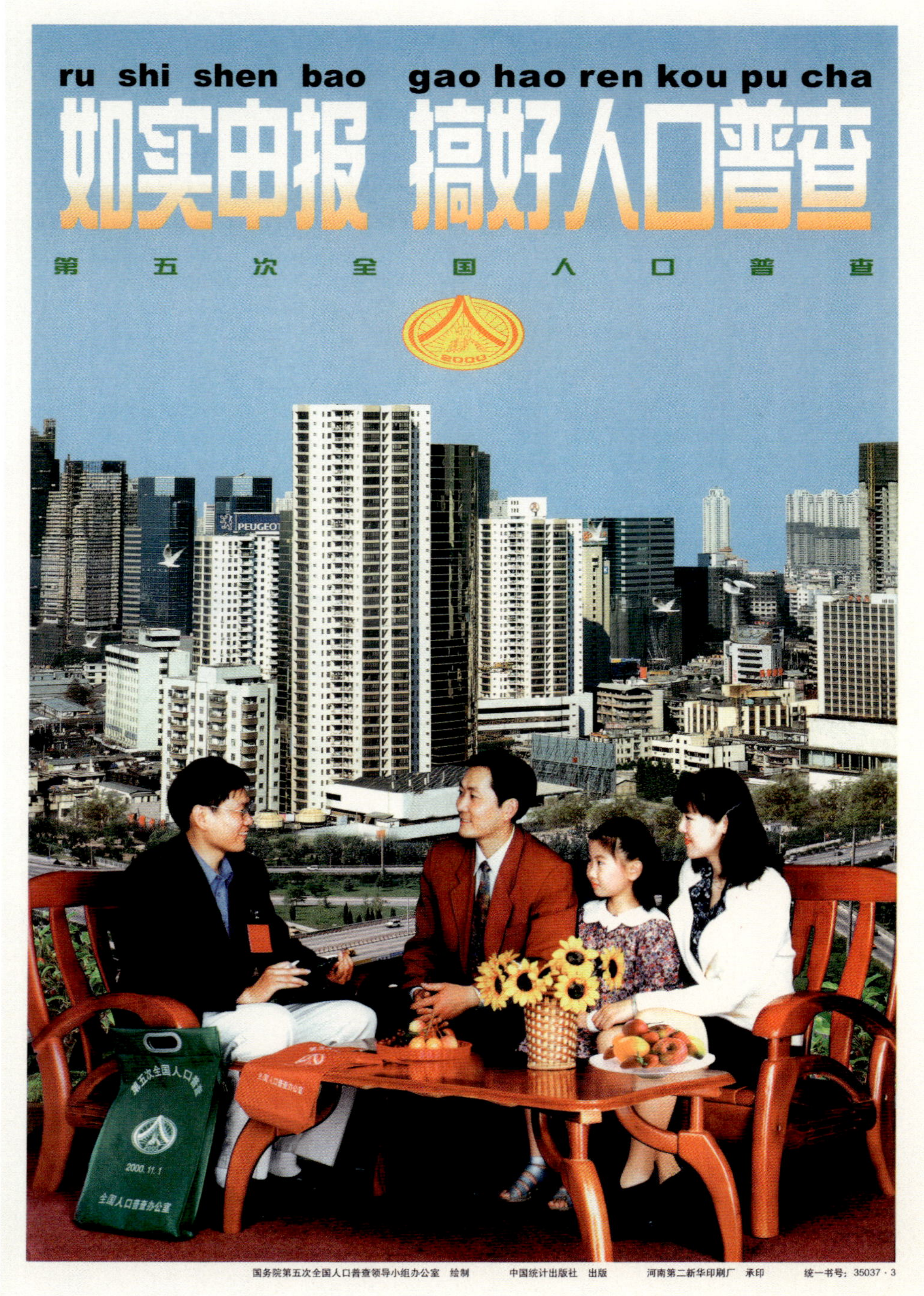

Report things as they really are, do a good job in the national census, 2000.
Berichtet die Dinge, so wie sie wirklich sind, leistet gute Arbeit für die Volkszählung, 2000.

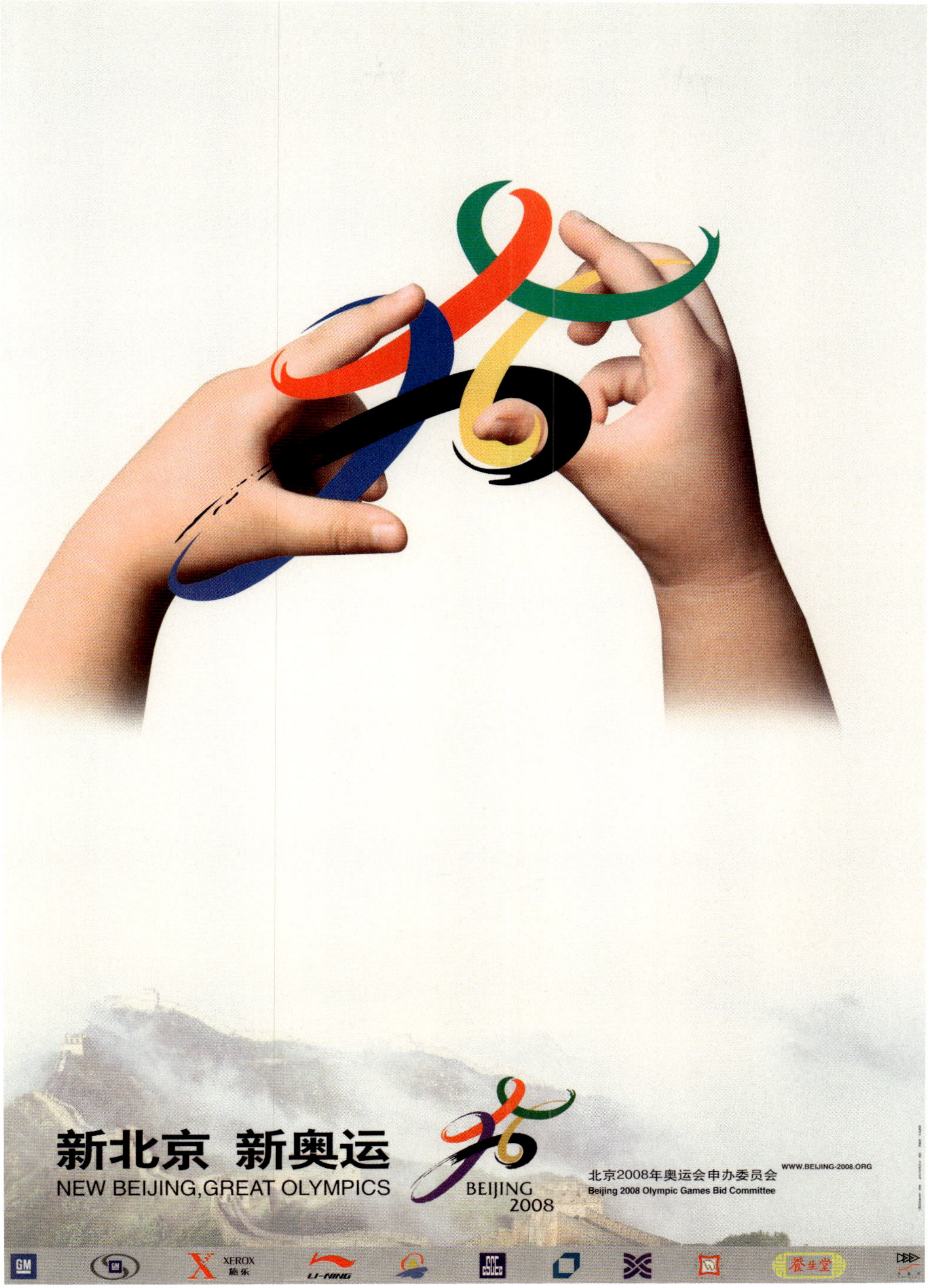

New Beijing, Great Olympics. Beijing 2008, 2000.
Neues Peking, Großartige Olympische Spiele. Peking 2008, 2000.

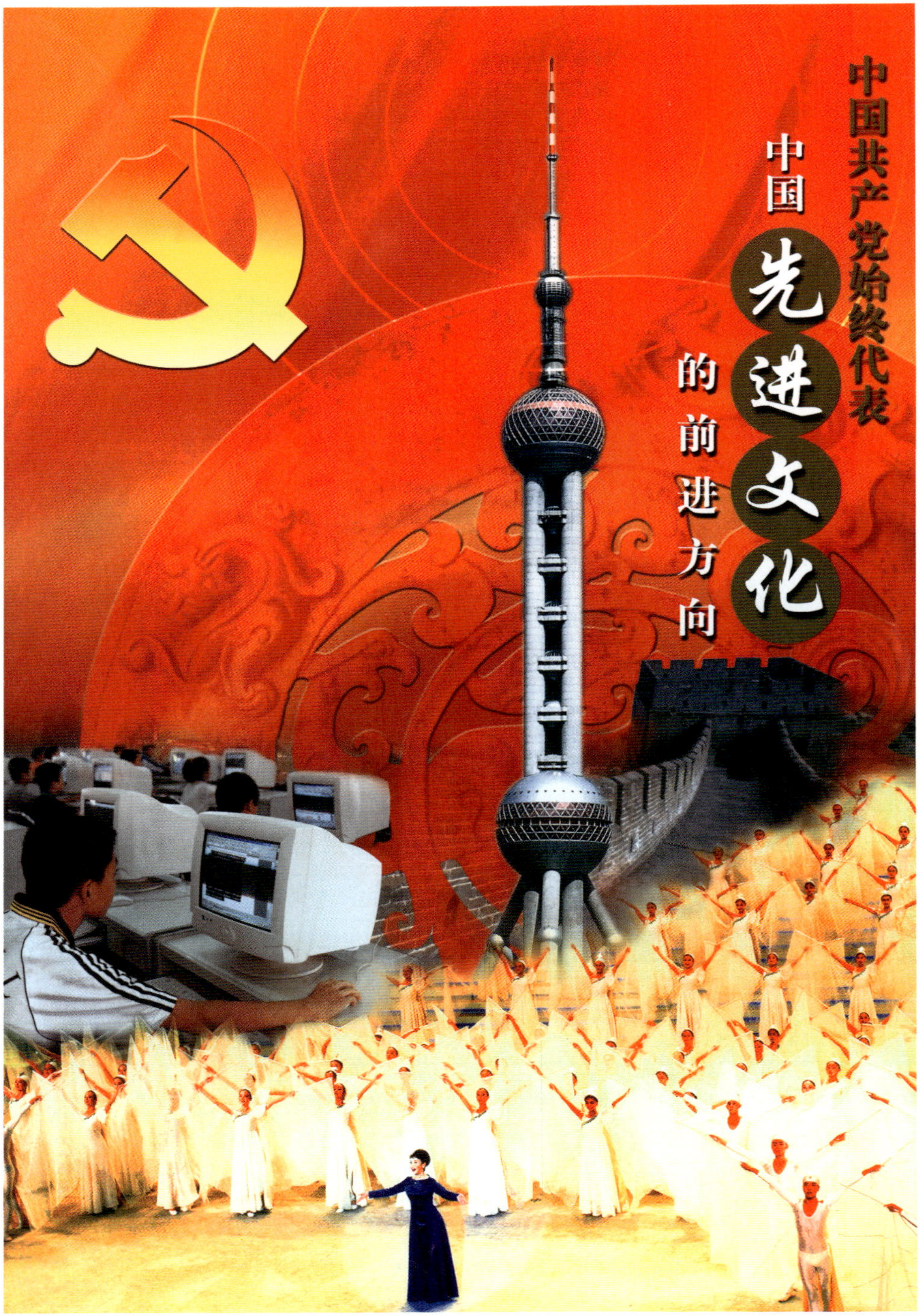

The Chinese Communist Party fully represents
the progressive orientation of China's progressive culture, 2002.
Die Kommunistische Partei Chinas steht für die
fortschrittliche Orientierung der progressiven Kultur Chinas, 2002.

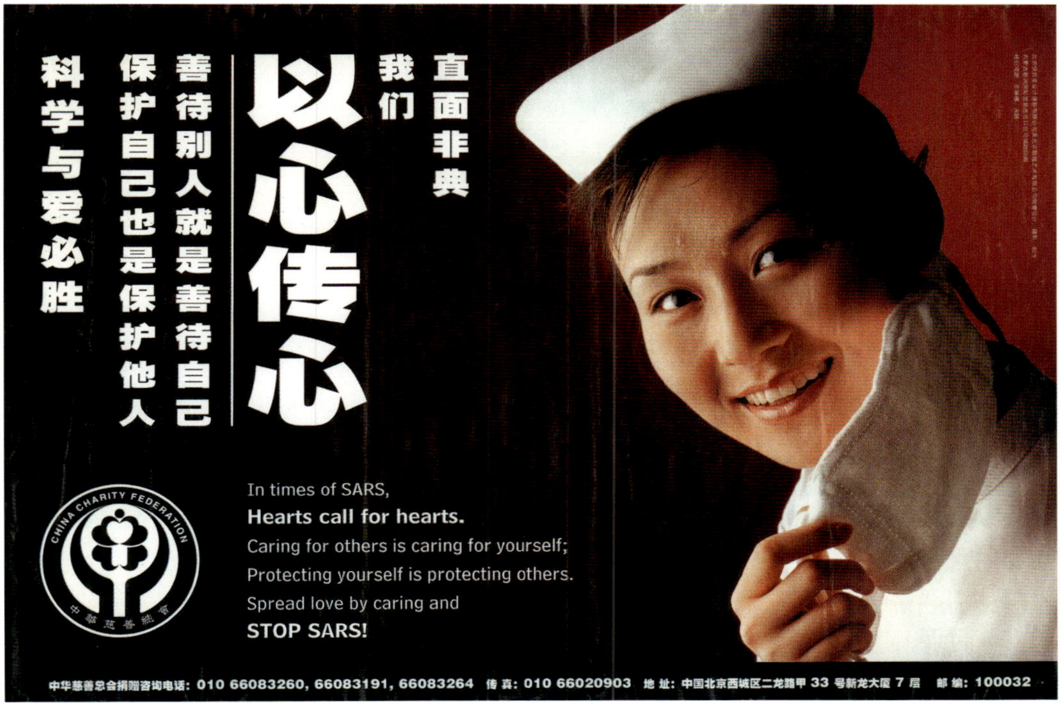

In times of SARS, hearts call for hearts, 2003.
"Herzen brauchen Herzen" – in Zeiten von SARS, 2003.

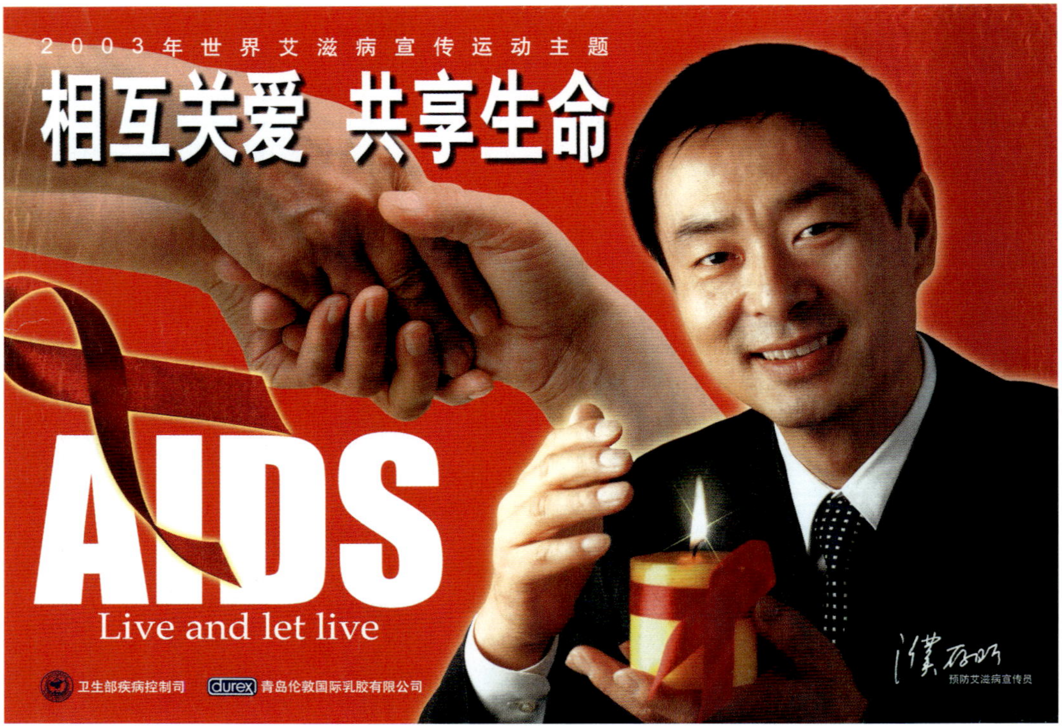

Mutual care and love, share life. The main topic of the 2003 International Aids Movement, c. 2003.

Gegenseitige Fürsorge und Liebe - teilt Euer Leben. Das Hauptthema des International AIDS Movement 2003, um 2003.

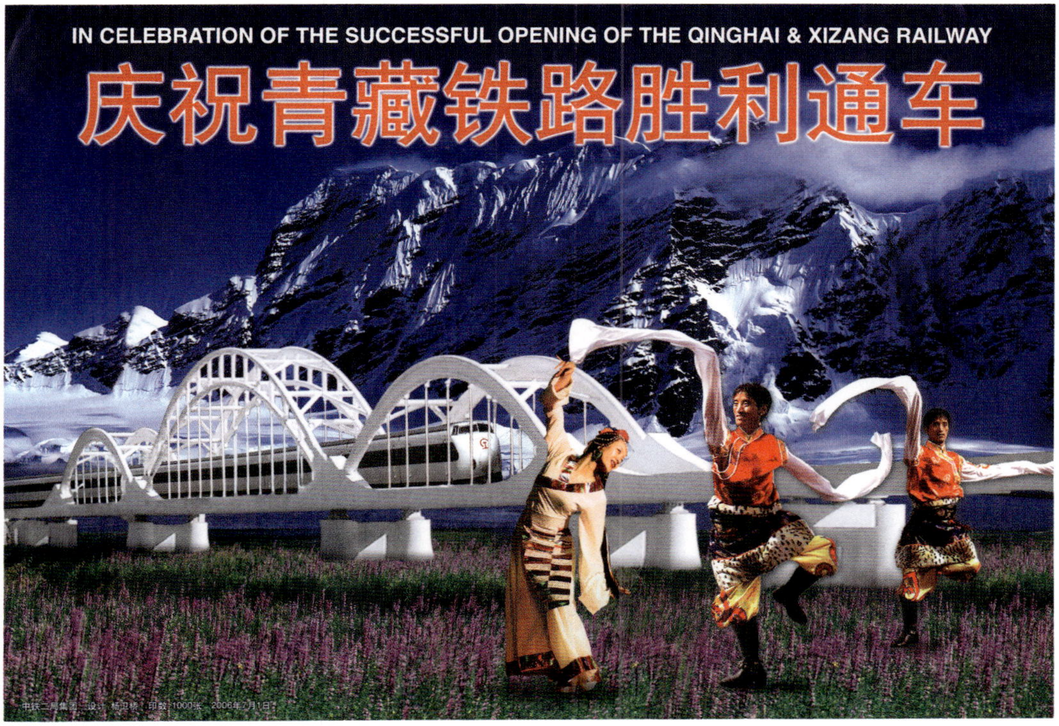

In celebration of the successful opening of the Qinghai and Xizang railway, 2006.
Feierlichkeiten zur erfolgreichen Eröffnung der Qinghai-Tibet-Bahn, 2006.

LIST OF POSTERS

page 24
DESIGNER UNKNOWN
Defeat Japanese imperialism.
Dadao Riben diguozhuyi.
c. 1937; 64.5 x 39 cm
Junshi weiyuanhui zhengxunchu
D25/197

page 25
DESIGNER UNKNOWN
Step up general mobilization, towards total militarization.
Jiajin zong dongyuan, yiqie junshihua.
c. 1937; 64.5 x 39 cm
Junshi weiyuanhui zhengxunchu
D25/199

page 26
DESIGNER UNKNOWN
Everybody must hate the enemy, defenses must be constructed step-by-step, fortifications must be strengthened, the enemy must be exterminated.
Renren dikai, bubu shefang, jianqiang bilei, zhidi siming.
c. 1937; 64.5 x 39 cm
PC01-1938-004

page 27 (detail on pages 22–23)
DESIGNER UNKNOWN
Millions of people all of one mind vow to exterminate the Japanese enemy.
Wanzhong yixin shimie Wokou.
c. 1937; 64.5 x 39 cm
Junshi weiyuanhui zhengxunchu
PC01-1938-011

page 28
DESIGNER UNKNOWN
Swear to defend the nation to the death.
Shiyu guotu gong cun wang.
c. 1937; 80 x 52 cm
Junweihui zhengzhibu
E15/687

page 29
DESIGNER UNKNOWN
[no title]
Some of the slogans: Oppose Communism; Long Live North-China; Forward China Japan Manchuko; Peace in East Asia; Down with the Communist Party; Have full confidence in the Japanese Army; Peace and happiness; A bright North China; Down with the Guomindang.
1938; 74 x 52 cm
Published by Japanese authorities
E27/165

pages 30–31
DESIGNER UNKNOWN
Look ! Look ! The cruel injustice of the Communist Party.
Kan ! Kan ! Gongchandang zhi canhai.
1938; 76 x 104 cm
Published by Japanese authorities
E27/166

page 34
NANJING PEOPLE'S MEETING FOR THE COMMEMORATION OF THE TWELFTH ANNIVERSARY OF THE "JULY THE SEVENTH" WAR OF RESISTANCE
Advance under the banner of Mao Zedong!

Zai Mao Zedong qizhixia qianjin!
1949; 55 x 39 cm
Publisher unknown
D29/876

page 35 (detail on pages 32–33)
DESIGNER UNKNOWN
The central people's government constitutes the only legitimate government of all the people of the People's Republic of China.
Zhongyang renmin zhengfu wei daibiao Zhonghua renmin gongheguo quanguo renminde weiyi hefa zhengfu.
c. 1950; 78.5 x 54.5 cm
Political Department of the Third Field Army of the East China Military Region
E11/968

page 36 (detail on page 21)
SU GUOJING
Celebrating the People's Republic of China's National Day.
Qingzhu Zhonghua Renmin Gongheguo Guoqingjie.
December, 1950; 42 x 57 cm
Xinhua shudian
D29/685

page 37
ZHAO YU (1926-1980)
Distributing land.
Fadizhao.
c. 1948; 38.5 x 53.5 cm
Dongbei huabaoshe
D25/190

page 38
HUANG JUN
Emulate the Patriotic production campaign.
Kaizhan aiguozhuyi shengchan jingsai.
December, 1950; 39 x 54 cm
Renmin meishu chubanshe
D29/709

page 39
JING XIAOHU
Sending off the People's Liberation Army to overthrow Taiwan! Carry out the revolutionary war to the end!
Huansong renmin jiefang jun, dadao Taiwan qu!
Ba geming zhanzheng jinxing daodi!
c. 1950; 42 x 55 cm
Dazhong Meishu chubanshe
D29/878

page 40
XU LING
The Chinese people absolutely cannot condone the encroachment of other countries, and cannot listen to any imperialist who thinks that it can wantonly encroach on its own neighbors without action.
Zhongguo renmin jue bu neng rongren waiguode qinlüe, ye bu neng ting ren diguo zhuyizhe dui ziji linren sixing qinlüe.
c. 1950; 77 x 106 cm
Publisher unknown
E27/169

page 41
FANG LING
The justified noose awaits them!
Zhengyide jiaosuo zai dengdaizhe tamen!
1951; 78.5 x 58.5 cm
Renmin meishu chubanshe
PC01-1950

page 42
DESIGNER UNKNOWN
Resolutely cut off the bloody and criminal hand of the American aggressor that spreads germs!
Jianjue zhanduan Meiguo qinluezhe sabu xijunde zui'e xueshou!
c. 1951; 77 x 53 cm
Publisher unknown
E15/833

page 43
QIAN DAXIN (1922)
Produce more! Contribute more!
Duo shengchan! Duo juanxian!
c. 1951; 77.5 x 53.5 cm
Shanghai Lushan huapian tushu chubanshe
E13/807

pages 44–45
ZHANG BIWU (1905-1987)
It's glorious to participate, to oppose America, to support Korea, and to protect the home and the nation.
Guangrong can'gan, kang Mei yuan Chao, baojia weiguo.
January, 1951; 53.5 x 76.5 cm
Haojiu heji huapian chubanshe
E15/474

page 46
JIN MEISHENG (1902-1989)
The life of peasants is good after the Land Reform.
Tugai wancheng nongmin shenghuo hao.
c. 1951; 53 x 77 cm
Huamei Huapian chubanshe
E15/595

page 47
YE SHANLU
Everybody must take precautions against epidemics to smash the germ warfare of American imperialism!
Renren fangyi, fensui Mei diguo zhuyide xijunzhan!
June, 1952 ; 77 x 53.5 cm
Renmin meishu chubanshe
E13/964

page 48
DESIGNER UNKNOWN
Stamp out the flames of war, save the peace!
Pumie zhanhuo, zhengjiu heping!
September, 1952; 78 x 54 cm
Beijing Renmin meishu chubanshe
E14/988

page 49
ZHANG DANIAN
Regularly wash clothes and bedding, bathe often, and maintain cleanliness for good health.
Chang, xi yi bei chang xizao, baochi qingjie shenti hao.
c. 1952; 77 x 53.5 cm
Shanghai Hygiene Department of the East China Military Region Logistics Department
E13/711

page 50
YANG ZIQIANG; HUANG NAIYUAN (1931); SUN YISHENG; LIU PING
Building the Tianlan railwa.
Xiutong Tianlan tiel.
November, 1952; 55 x 73 cm
Xibei Renmin chubanshe
E16/633

page 51
XIN LILIANG (1912)
A new view of the rural villag.
Nongcun fengguang.
1953; 53.5 x 77.5 cm
Sanyi Printers
E12/527

page 52
JIANG FENG (1910-1982)
A happy marriage.
Xingfude hunyin.
February, 1953; 53.5 x 77.5 cm
Shanghai Xu Shengji Printing Factory
E15/472

page 53
ZHAO YU (1926-1980)
Go participate in the elections!
Canjia xuanju qu!
July, 1953; 54 x 78 cm
Renmin meishu chubanshe
E16/640

pages 54–55
DING HAO (1917)
Study the Soviet Union's advanced economy to build up our nation.
Xuexi Sulian xianjin jingji jianshe womende guojia.
June, 1953; 53 x 77 cm
Shanghai Huadong renmin meishu chubanshe
E15/334

page 56
ZUO YAO
Participate in the elections to build up a great motherland!

Weile jianshe weidade zuguo, canjia xuanju qu!
August, 1953; 77 x 53 cm
Renmin meishu chubanshe
E15/380

page 57
CHEN XINGHUA (1924)
Create our eternal happiness!
Chuangzao women yongyuande xingfu!
1950s; 77 x 54 cm
Renmin huabaoshe
E15/302

page 58
XIE ZHIGUANG; SHAO JINGYUN; XIE MULIAN (1918–1985)
Moving into a new house.
Banjin xin fangzi.
November, 1953; 39 x 54 cm
Shanghai Huadong renmin meishu chubanshe
D29/682

page 59
TAO TIANEN; LÜ PIN
The kindergarten at the factory.
Gongchang tuo'ersuo.
November, 1953; 54 x 78 cm
Xinmeishu chubanshe
E16/630

page 60
AN LIN
For projects of vital importance, quality is number one.
Bainian daji zhiliang diyi.
December, 1953; 77.5 x 52 cm
Beijing Renmin meishu chubanshe
E12/362

page 61
NING HAO
We are proud of participating in the founding of our country's industrialization.
Women wei canjia guojia gongyehua jianshe er zihao.
February, 1954; 78 x 54 cm
Shanghai Huadong renmin meishu chubanshe
E16/17

page 62
ZHAO YANNIAN (1924)
Make the nation rich and strong and the people happy.
Weile guojia de fuqiang he renminde xing fu.
March, 1954; 53 x 77 cm
Shanghai Huadong renmin meishu chubanshe
E13/700

page 63
XIN LILIANG (1912)
Chairman Mao gives us a happy life.
Mao zhuxi gei womende xingfu shenghuo.
March, 1954; 78 x 53 cm
Publisher unknown
E16/269

page 64
ZHANG HUAIJIANG (1922–1990)
Sing about victory ! Sing about our beloved nation!
Gechang shengli ! Gechang women qin'aide zuguo!
March, 1954; 78 x 53 cm
Shanghai Huadong renmin meishu chubanshe
E15/589

page 65
FANG JING (1909)
I want to make a dove of peace.
Wo yuanyi zuo yige hepingge.
May, 1954; 78 x 54 cm
Chao [?] meishu chubanshe
E16/18

page 66
JIN ZHAOFANG
A glorious production model
Guangrongde shengchan mofan!
July, 1954; 78 x 54 cm
Publisher unknown
E16/627

page 67
ZHU PEILIN
Daddy, mummy see you tonight.
Baba mama wanshang jian.
September, 1954; 78 x 53 cm
Shanghai Huapian chubanshe
E16/629

page 68
XIE ZHIGUANG
A morning off.
Jiaride zaochen.
September, 1954; 53.5 x 77.5 cm
Xinmeishu chubanshe
PC01-1954

page 69
NING HAO
After work.
Xia ban yihou.
November, 1954; 53 x 77 cm
Huadong Renmin meishu chubanshe
E16/632

page 70
HU JINYE (1928)
Resolutely liberate Taiwan, save the Taiwanese people from their misery!
Jianjue jiefang Taiwan, zhengjiu ku'nan zhongde Taiwan renmin!
January, 1955; 54 x 78 cm
Political Department of the Third Field Army of the East China Military Region
E15/609

page 71
ZHANG YUQING (1909-1993)
New China's female parachuters.
Xin Zhongguode nü tiaosanyuan.
1955; 55 x 79 cm
Shanghai Huapian chubanshe
E15/27

page 72
XIE ZHIGUANG
Lots of love for Chairman Mao.
Reai Mao zhuxi.
May, 1955; 77.5 x 54 cm
Shanghai Huapian chubanshe
E12/601

page 73
ZHU LIN
On the Karzang plateau.
Zai Karzang gaoyuanshang.
November , 1955; 79 x 54 cm
Shanghai Huapian chubanshe
E15/577

pages 74–75
CHEN FEI
Shanghai's no. 1 Department Store.
Shanghaishi Diyi baihuo shangdian.
July, 1955; 53.5 x 77.5 cm
Shanghai Huapian chubanshe
PC01-1955

page 76
YU YUNJIE (1917-1992)
Helping mama study culture.
Bangzhu mama xue wenhua.
April, 1956; 77 x 53 cm
Shanghai Renmin meishu chubanshe
E15/382

page 77
YANG JUNSHANG
Long live the great unity of all the people of the whole nation.
Quanguo ge minzu da tuanjie wansui.
January, 195; 53 x 77 cm
Shanghai Renmin meishu chubanshe
E15/355

page 80
YANG FURU (1918)
Walk along the road to cooperativization.
Zuo kezuohuade daolu.

March, 1956; 53.5 x 77.5 cm
Shanghai Huapian chubanshe
E12/476

page 81
WENG YIZHI (1921-1995)
The hogs of the commune must be raised to be fat and big!Yao ba shelide zhu yangde you fei you da!
May, 1956; 53 x 77.5 cm
Shanghai Renmin meishu chubanshe
E15/450

page 82
BI CHEN
Everybody comes to beat sparrows.
Dajia dou lai da maque.
September, 1956; 76.5 x 52.5 cm
Chao [?] meishu chubanshe
E12/901

page 83
HA QIONGWEN (1925)
In fifteen years we will certainly have surpassed England
Shiwu nian hou yiding chaoguo yingguo!
April, 1958; 77 x 53 cm
Shanghai Renmin meishu chubanshe
E16/337

pages 84-85
RUI GUANGTING
The people's communes are good.
Renmin gongshe hao.
1958; 77.5 x 108.5 cm
Shanghai Educational publishing house
G1/959

page 86
LI LIANG
Study the Soviet Union, to advance to world-class levels of science.
Xuexi Sulian, xiang shijie kexue shuizhun jinjun.
August, 1958; 53 x 76 cm
Shanghai Renmin meishu chubanshe
E15/427

page 87
DENG KE (1936)
Transform seas and rivers, temper yourself.
Gaizao haihe duanlian ziji.
August, 1958; 78 x 53 cm
Tianjin Meishu chubanshe
E15/826

page 88
ZHANG YUQING (1909-1993)
Installing electric lights in the cooperative.
Hezuosheli zhuang diandeng.
August, 1958; 77.5 x 53 cm
Shanghai Tupian chubanshe
E13/714

page 89
ZHANG RUJI (1931); WANG SHUHUI; SHAO GUOHUAN
Go all out and aim high. The East leaps forward; the West is worried.
Guzu ganjin zheng shang you. Dongfang yuejin xifang you.
September, 1958; 53 x 78 cm
Renmin meishu chubanshe
E16/33

page 90
JIN MEISHENG (1902-1989)
A high pile of winter gourds.
Donggua shang gaolou.
1959; 77 x 53 cm
Shanghai Renmin meishu chubanshe
E12/528

page 91
JIN MEISHENG (1902-1989)
The vegetables are green, the cucumbers plump, the yield is abundant.
Cailü guafei chanliang duo.
February, 1959; 77 x 53 cm
Shanghai Renmin meishu chubanshe
E11/992

pages 92-93
HU YUELONG
When the dining hall is well-run, the spirit of production will rise.
Shitang bande hao shengchan jintou gao.
February, 1959; 53 x 77 cm
Shanghai Renmin meishu chubanshe
E15/829

page 94
SHAO WENJIN (1931)
Strike the battle drum of the Great Leap Forward ever louder.
Ba dayuejinde zhangu qiaode geng xiang.
February, 1959; 75 x 52 cm
Tianjin Meishu chubanshe
E13/557

page 95
JIANG SHU
Prosperity brought by the dragon and the phoenix.
Long feng cheng xiang.
February, 1959; 77 x 53 cm
Chongqing Renmin chubanshe
E16/340

page 96
ZHAO WENFA
Everybody studies science, everybody does experiments.
Renren xue kexue gege gao shiyan.
August, 1959; 78 x 53 cm
Tianjin Meishu chubanshe
E15/968

page 97
BEI YINGREN; ZHANG LINGZHI
Celebrate the 10th anniversary of the founding of our great nation.
Qingzhu women weidade zuguo jianguo 10 zhounian.
1959; 77 x 106.5 cm
Renmin meishu chubanshe
G1/958

page 98
CAO HUILU; ZHAO YI
Ten gloriously bright years.
Guanghui canlande shinian.
September, 1959; 77 x 54 cm
Sichuan Renmin chubanshe
E15/907

page 99
HAN HEPING
To catch up with England in the output of industrial products in about ten years time, we bravely forge ahead!
Wei zhengqu zai shinian zuoyoude shijiannei zai zhuyao gongye chanpin chanliang fangmian ganshang!
September, 1959; 77 x 53 cm
Shanghai Renmin meishu chubanshe
E16/330

page 100
QIAN DAXIN (1922)
Study culture and realise the Four Modernizations.
Xuexi wenhua shixian Sihua.
December, 1959; 78 x 54 cm
Shanghai Renmin meishu chubanshe
E16/36

page 101 (detail on pages 78–79)
JIANG NANCHUN (1925); HAN MIN (1929)
Ride the wind and part waves to realize a leap forward in all fields.
Chengfeng polang quanmian yueyin.
1960; 76.5 x 105.5 cm
Shanghai Renmin meishu chubanshe
G1/961

page 102
DESIGNER UNKNOWN
Be indomitable in training, to strengthen the physique of officers and soldiers.
Wanqiang duanlian, zengqiang guanbing tizhi.
1960; 77.5 x 53.5 cm
Jiefangjun huabaoshe
E15/488

page 103
DESIGNER UNKNOWN
The people's commune is good; happiness will last for ten thousand years.
Renmin gongshe hao xingfu wannian chang.
c. 1960; 75 x 54 cm
Publisher unknown
E16/40page 104

SHEN LIN; ZHANG HANYI; LU XINGCHEN
Getting organized is boundlessly good. Collective life brings a lot of happiness.
Zuzhi qilai wuxian hao. Jiti shenghuo xingfu duo.
May, 1960; 77 x 54 cm
Shanghai Renmin meishu chubanshe
E16/41

page 105
A ZHI
Chairman Mao loves children (1). Chairman Mao visits a peasant village.
Mao zhuxi ai ertong (1).
September, 1960; 39 x 54 cm
Liaoning Meishu chubanshe
D29/715

page 106
A ZHI
Chairman Mao loves children (2). A mother is unable to come and see the Chairman; her child is ill. Another child urges the mother to go and see Mao.
Mao zhuxi ai ertong (2).
September, 1960; 39 x 54 cm
Liaoning Meishu chubanshe
D29/714

page 107
A ZHI
Chairman Mao loves children (3). Mao is informed of the situation.
Mao zhuxi ai ertong (3).
September, 1960; 39 x 54 cm
Liaoning Meishu chubanshe
D29/712

page 108
A ZHI
Chairman Mao loves children (4). Mao sends mother and child to a hospital in his car.
Mao zhuxi ai ertong (4).
September, 1960; 39 x 54 cm
Liaoning Meishu chubanshe
D29/712

page 109
A ZHI
Chairman Mao loves children (5). The child recovers and tells the story of his salvation to the people of the village.
Mao zhuxi ai ertong (5).
September, 1960; 39 x 54 cm
Liaoning Meishu chubanshe
D29/711

page 110
ZHANG YUQING (1909-1993)
The new center of the commune.
Gongshe xincun tu.
1961; 53 x 77 cm
Shanghai Renmin meishu chubanshe
E12/531

page 111
HA QIONGWEN (1925)
Long live the Yan'an spirit.
Yan'an zuofeng wansui.
May, 1961; 107 x 74 cm
Shanghai Renmin meishu chubanshe
G2/53

page 112
HA QIONGWEN (1925)
Study the spirit of Daqing.
Xue Daqing jingshen.
June, 1965; 77 x 50.5 cm
Shanghai Renmin chubanshe
E13/950

page 113
QIAN DAXIN (1922)
Walk the road of Dazhai.
Zou Dazhai zhi lu.
April, 1965; 107 x 76 cm
Shanghai Renmin meishu chubanshe
G2/52

page 114
ZHANG YUQING (1909-1993)
Anti-American wave of rage next to the Huangpu river.
Huangpujiangbiande fanmei nuchao.
October, 1961; 54 x 78 cm
Shanghai Renmin meishu chubanshe
E14/990

page 115
LI MUBAI (1913-1991);
JIN XUECHEN (1904-1997)
Man works hard; flowers are fragrant.
Ren qin hua xiang.
October, 1962; 77 x 52 cm
Shanghai Renmin meishu chubanshe
E16/47

page 116
HA QIONGWEN (1925);
YANG WENXIU (1929)
Long live the General Line, long live the Great Leap Forward, long live the People's Communes.
Zongluxian wansui Dayuejin wansui Renmin gong-she wansui.
April, 1963; 76 x 107 cm
Shanghai Renmin meishu chubanshe
G2/722

page 117
ZHANG RUJI (1931)
Hold high the banner of the General Line, the Great Leap Forward and the three aspects of the people's commune, and advance bravely!
Gaoju zongluxian, da yuejin, renmin gongshe san-mian hongqi fenyong qianjin!
September, 1963; 77 x 108 cm
Beijing Renmin meishu chubanshe
G2/680

page 118
WEN BING (1932)
Awakened peoples, you will certainly attain the ultimate victory!
Juexinglede renmin, bi jiang dedao zuihoude shengli!
September, 1963; 53 x 77 cm
Renmin meishu chubanshe
E15/879

page 119
ZHOU RUIZHUANG (1930)
Vigorously support the anti-imperialist struggle of the peoples of Asia, Africa, and Latin America.
Jianjue zhichi Yazhou Feishou Lading Meizhou renminde fandi douzheng.
1964; 53 x 77.5 cm
Shanghai Renmin meishu chubanshe
E3/724

pages 120–121
HA QIONGWEN (1925)
Long live Chairman Mao.
Mao zhuxi wansui.
January, 1964; 76.5 x 53 cm
Shanghai Renmin meishu chubanshe
E12/605

page 122
YAO ZHONGYU
Long live the General Line, long live the Great Leap Forward, long live the People's Communes.
Zongluxian wansui Dayuejin wansui Renmin gong-she wansui.
September, 1964; 76.5 x 53 cm
Shanghai Renmin meishu chubanshe
E13/985

page 123
DESIGNER UNKNOWN
Resting between the fields.
Tianjian xiuxi.
November, 1964; 53 x 77 cm
Lianong Meishu chubanshe
E12/591

page 124
XU JIPING; WANG LIUYING
New village (1, 2).
Xin nongcun (yi, er).
November, 1964; 76 x 53 cm
Hebei Renmin meishu chubanshe
E16/205

page 125
XU JIPING; WANG LIUYING
New village (3, 4).
Xin nongcun (san, si).
November, 1964; 76 x 53 cm
Hebei Renmin meishu chubanshe
E16/206

page 126
WU ZHEFU; YANG YUHUA
Uncle Lei Feng tells revolutionary stories.
Lei Feng shushu jiang geming gushi.
February, 1965; 76.5 x 53 cm
Publisher unknown
E13/884

page 127
LI MUBAI (1913–1991);
JIN XUECHEN (1904–1997)
Little anti-imperialist warriors.
Fandi xiao zhansi.
1965; 77 x 53 cm
Shanghai Renmin meishu chubanshe
E12/620

pages 128–129
HA QIONGWEN (1925); QIAN DAXIN (1922); ZHOU RUIZHUANG (1930); YANG WENXIU (1929)
Fully engage in the movement to increase production and to practise economy to set off a new upsurge in industrial production.
Guangfan shenrude kaizhan zengchan jieyue yundong xianqi gongye shengchan xin gaochao.
April, 1965; 77 x 159 cm
Shanghai Renmin meishu chubanshe
E15/127-129

page 130
HA QIONGWEN (1925)
American imperialists, get out of South Korea!
Meidi cong Nanchaoxian gunchuqu!
July, 1965; 77 x 105 cm
Shanghai Renmin meishu chubanshe
G2/684

page 131
ZHANG YUQING (1909–1993)
The East is red.
Dongfang hong.
October, 1965; 76.5 x 53.5 cm
Zhejiang Renmin chubanshe
E12/606

page 132
WEI KUIZHONG (1940)
Miraculous soldiers on the shallow lake.
Dianshang shenbing.
January, 1966; 53.5 x 77 cm
Hebei Renmin meishu chubanshe
E13/865

page 133
ZHANG YUQING (1909–1993)
The new look of traffic.
Jiaotong xinmao tu.
February, 1966; 77 x 53.5 cm
Shanghai Renmin meishu chubanshe
E13/883

page 134
CHAO YOUCHENG (1928);
MENG GUANG (1921)
Resolutely support the American people in their resistance against American imperialist aggression in Vietnam.
Jianjue zhichi Meiguo renmin fandui Mei diguozhuyi qinlue Yuenan.
February, 1966; 107 x 77 cm
Shanghai Renmin meishu chubanshe
E15/838

page 135
XIN LILIANG (1912); WU QINGXUN
The projectionist of the village.
Nongcun fangyinyuan.
June, 1966; 77 x 53 cm
Shanghai Renmin meishu chubanshe
E13/870

page 138
DESIGNER UNKNOWN
Criticize the old world and build a new world with "Mao Zedong Thought" as a weapon.
Yi Mao Zedong sixiang wei wuqi pipan jiu shijie jianshe xin shijie.
September, 1966; 108 x 77 cm
Shanghai Renmin meishu chubanshe
E15/699

page 139
DESIGNER UNKNOWN
Hold high the great red flag of "Mao Zedong Thought"; thoroughly smash the reactionary line of Liu and Deng.
Gaoju Mao Zedong sixiang weida hongqi, chedi fensui Liu Dengde fandong luxian.
c. 1966; 77 x 54 cm
Publisher unknown
E15/183

pages 140–141
DESIGNER UNKNOWN
Completely smash the capitalist class and the reactionary line of Liu an d Deng!
Chedi zalan Liu Deng zichan jieji fandong luxian!
c. 1967; 52 x 65 cm
Publisher unknown
E16/338

page 142
TIANJIN GEMING GONGREN DAIBIAO HUIYI. CHOUBEICHU
Carry out the revolutionary "integration of three," take the power from Tianjin's black municipal Party committee.
Shixian gemingde "san jiehe" duo Tianjin hei shiweide quan.
c. 1967; 54 x 78 cm
Publisher unknown
E12/627

page 143
WORKERS-PEASANT-SOLDIERS PRINTING HOUSE; WORKERS REVOLUTIONARY REBEL GROUP
Take up a pen as a weapon and concentrate fire to hit Liu and Deng.
Naqi bi zuo daoqiang jizhong huoli da Liu Deng.
c. 1967; 54 x 78 cm
Publisher unknown
E16/354

page 144
DESIGNER UNKNOWN
Overthrow Peng Dehuai, Luo Ruiqing, Chen Zaidao, Liao Laotan!
Dada Peng Dehuai, Luo Ruiqing, Chen Zaidao, Liao Laotan!
c. 1967; 78.5 x 53.5 cm
Publisher unknown
E12/626

page 145
DESIGNER UNKNOWN
Thoroughly smash the dynastic Li family!
Chedi cuihui Lijia wangchao!
c. 1967; 77 x 54 cm
Publisher unknown
E16/109

page 146
DESIGNER UNKNOWN
Oppose economism: destroy the new counter-offensive of the capitalist class reactionary line.
Fandui jingjizhuyi: fencui zichan jieji fangdong luxiande xin fanpu.
January, 1967; 53 x 77 cm
Shanghai Renmin chubanshe
E12/610

page 147

DESIGNER UNKNOWN

Fully criticize the Chinese Khrushchev from a political, ideological, and theoretical perspective.
Cong zhengzhishang sixiangshang lilunshang chedi pidao pixiu Zhongguode Heluxiaofu.
November, 1967; 53 x 76 cm
Shanghai Renmin chubanshe
E3/763

page 148

ZHENG SHENGTIAN; ZHOU RUIWEN; XU JUNXUAN; ZHEJIANG GONG NONG BING MEISHU DAXUE

The correct way among the people is bringing great change to the world.
Renjian zhengdao shi cangsang.
December, 1967; 51.5 x 76.5 cm
Zhejiang Renmin meishu
E3/704

page 149 (detail on pages 136–137)

DESIGNER UNKNOWN

With regard to the great teacher Chairman Mao, cherish the word "loyalty." With regard to the great "Mao Zedong Thought", vigorously stress the word "usefulness."
Dui weida daoshi Mao zhuxi xinhuai yige "zhong" zi, dui weida Mao Zedong sixiang hen zhua yige "yong" zi.
April, 1968; 77 x 106 cm
Shanghai Renmin meishu chubanshe
E3/705

pages 150–151

DESIGNER UNKNOWN

Advance victoriously while following Chairman Mao's revolutionary line in literature and the arts.
Yanzhe Mao zhuxide geming wenyi luxian shengli qianjin.
c. 1968; 76.5 x 154 cm
Beijing Central Industrial Arts College
E13/632-4

page 152

DESIGNER UNKNOWN

Chairman Mao is the great liberator of the world's revolutionary people.
Mao zhuxi shi shijie geming renminde da jiuxing.
April, 1968; 77 x 53 cm
Shanghai Renmin meishu chubanshe
E16/339

page 153

LIU CHUNHUA (1944)

Chairman Mao going to Anyuan.
Mao zhuxi qu Anyuan.
July, 1968; 106 x 76 cm
Hebei Renmin meishu chubanshe
E12/703

page 154

PROPAGANDA GROUP OF THE REVOLUTIONARY COMMITTEE OF THE SHANGHAI NO. 3 INK FACTORY

Firmly grasp large-scale revolutionary criticism.
Zhuajin geming da pipan.
1969; 78 x 104 cm
Shanghai Renmin meishu chubanshe
G1/957

page 155

DESIGNER UNKNOWN

Forging ahead courageously while following the great leader Chairman Mao!
Jingen weida lingxiu Mao zhuxi fenyong qianjin!
April, 1969; 72 x 106.5 cm
Shanghai Renmin meishu chubanshe
E12/631

page 156

DESIGNER UNKNOWN

The invincible thought of Mao Zedong illuminates the stage of revolutionary art!
Zhan wubushengde Mao Zedong sixiang zhaoliang-le geming yishu wutai!
May, 1969; Zhejiang Renmin meishu chubanshe
E15/573

page 157

DESIGNER UNKNOWN

Prepare for struggle, prepare for famine, for the people.
Bei zhan, bei huang, wei renmin.
1970; 53 x 77 cm
Shanghai Renmin meishu chubanshe
E12/532

page 158

DESIGNER UNKNOWN

Go among the workers, peasants and soldiers and into the thick of struggle!
Dao gong nong bing qunzhongzhong qu, dao huore-de douzhengzhong qu.
c. 1970; 106 x 77 cm
Shanghai Renmin meishu chubanshe
E3/733

page 159

DESIGNER UNKNOWN

Keep the country in heart and the whole world in mind!
Xionghai zuguo, fangyan shijie.
c. 1970; 106 x 77 cm
Shanghai Renmin chubanshe
E3/734

page 160

DESIGNER UNKNOWN

Greet the 1970s with the new victories of revolution and production!
Yong geming he shengchande xin shengli yingjie qishi niandai!
January, 1970; 53 x 77 cm
Shanghai Renmin meishu chubanshe
E12/744

page 161

DESIGNER UNKNOWN

To villages we go, to the borders we go, to places in the fatherland where we are most needed, we go.
Dao nongcun qu dao bianjiang qu dao zuguo zui xuyaode difang qu.
February, 1970; 77 x 53 cm
Shanghaishi Gemingzu
E16/331

page 162

DESIGNER UNKNOWN

Fully carrry out the revolution on the line of thought and cultural struggle.
Ba sixiang wenhua zhanxianshangde geming jinxing daodi.
June, 1970; 53 x 70.5 cm
Shanghaishi Chuban Gemingzu
E12/611

page 163

DESIGNER UNKNOWN

Win honor for our great leader Chairman Mao, bring credit to our socialist motherland.
Wei weida lingxiu Mao zhuxi zhengguang, wei weida shehui zhuyi zuguo zhengguang.
July, 1970; 106 x 77 cm
Zhongyang gongyi meishu xueyuan
E13/566

page 164

THE PROTECTING EAGLES OF THE AIR-FORCE (SHANGHAI)

Stand in combat readiness, be always prepared to eliminate the aggressor.
Yanzhen yi dai suishi zhunbei xiamomie qinlüezhe.
August, 1970; 53 x 77 cm
Shanghaishi Chuban Gemingzu
E13/638

page 165

DESIGNER UNKNOWN

Long live Chairman Mao! Long long life!
Mao zhuxi wansui! Wanwansui!
October, 1970; 53 x 77 cm
Shanghai Renmin chubanshe
E13/701

page 166

DESIGNER UNKNOWN

March a distance of a thousand miles to temper a red heart.
Qianli yeying lian hongxin.
January, 1971; 53 x 77 cm
Shanghai Renmin chubanshe
E13/708

page 167
RED EAGLE CORPS OF THE AIR FORCE (NANJING)
We will definitely free Taiwan!
Yiding yao jiefang Taiwan!
January, 1971; 53 x 77 cm
Shanghai Renmin meishu chubanshe
E12/613

page 168
QI SHUYAN
Use and study Chairman Mao's glorious philosophical thought in a big way.
Daxue dayong Mao zhuxi guanghui zhexue sixiang.
April, 1971; 77 x 97.5 cm
Beijing renmin chubanshe
E13/854

page 169
BEIJING NO. 76 MIDDLE SCHOOL COLLECTIVE
Turn philosophy into a sharp weapon in the hands of the masses.
Rang zhexue bian wei qunzhong shoulide jianrui wuqi.
April, 1971; 77 x 97.5 cm
Beijing renmin chubanshe
E13/854

page 170
DESIGNER UNKNOWN
The industry learns from Daqing, agriculture learns from the village of Dazhai and the whole country learns from the People's Liberation Army.
Gongye xue daqing nongye xue dagong quanguoxue renmin jiefangjun.
May, 1971; 53 x 77 cm
Shanghai Renmin chubanshe
E12/604

page 171
REVOLUTIONARY COMMITTEE OF JILIN PROVINCE MOVIE DISTRIBUTION COMPANY COLLECTIVE
Advance victoriously while following Chairman Mao's revolutionary line.
Yanzhe Mao zhuxi geming luxian shengli qianjin.
June, 1971; 53.5 x 75 cm
Jilin Renmin chubanshe
E13/622

page 172
REVOLUTIONARY COMMITTEE OF THE SHANGHAI NATIONAL COTTON FACTORY NR. 21
Thoroughly criticize the "theory of human nature" of the landlord and capitalist classes.
Chedi pipan dizhu zichan jieji "renxinglun".
December, 1971; 107 x 77 cm
Shanghai Renmin chubanshe
G2/37

page 173
LITERACY OFFICE OF THE POLITICAL WORK GROUP OF THE REVOLUTIONARY COMMITTEE OF THE SHANXI PROVINCE COLLECTIVE
Study the village of Dazhai; we must rely on self sufficiency to wage the bitter struggle.
Xue Dazhai, bixu zili gengsheng jianku fendou.
c. 1972; 53.5 x 76.5 cm
Shanxi Renmin chubanshe
E15/496

page 174
DESIGNER UNKNOWN
Socialism is fine.
Shehuizhuyi hao.
c. 1972; 53 x 77 cm
Shanghai Renmin chubanshe
E13/450

page 175
DESIGNER UNKNOWN
Happy that pulling up seedlings no longer means bending down.
Xikan bayang bu wanyao.
c. 1972; 53 x 77 cm
Shanghai Renmin chubanshe
E11/989

page 176
ZHANG YUQING (1909-1993)
The Yangzi River Bridge at Nanjing.
Nanjing Changjiang daqiao.
c. 1972; 53 x 77 cm
Shanghai Renmin chubanshe
E3/731

page 177
CHANGZHOUSHI GONGNONGBING MEISHU CHUANGZUO XUEXIBAN GONGGAO
The feelings of friendship between the peoples of China and Africa run deep.
Zhong, Fei renmin qingyi shen.
May, 1972 ; 78 x 106 cm
Shanghai Renmin chubanshe
E15/837

page 178
ZHAO DAWU
Unite to achieve an even greater victory!
Tuanjie qilai, zhengqu gengdade shengli!
1973; 106 x 77 cm
Renmin meishu chubanshe
G1/962

page 179
LIU ZHIDE (1939)
Old party secretary (Selected from the Huxian peasant painting exhibition).
Lao shuji (Xuan zi Huxian nongmin huazhan).
1973; 77 x 53 cm
Shanghai Renmin chubanshe
E13/344

pages 180-181
DONG ZHENGYI
The commune's fishpond.
Gongshe yutang.
1973; 53 x 77 cm
Renmin meishu chubanshe
E13/353

page 182
LI ZHENHUA
The brigade's ducks.
Dadui yaqun.
March, 1973; 53 x 77 cm
Shanghai Renmin meishu chubanshe
E13/352

page 183
SHANGHAI RENMIN CHUBANSHE PROPAGANDA POSTER CREATION GROUP
Go all out, aim high, and achieve greater, faster, better, and more economical results in building socialism.
Guzu ganjin lizheng shangyou duo kuai hao sheng-de jianshe shehui zhuyi.
April, 1973; 107 x 76.5 cm
Shanghai Renmin chubanshe
E15/629

page 184
ZHANG HERONG (1932); CAI XU
Our commune has constructed a well drilling machine.
Anshe chuangzaole dajingji.
June, 1973; 53.5 x 77 cm
Renmin meishu chubanshe
E15/94

page 185
HU BOYA
The factory is small, the aspirations high, striving to make great contributions.
Chang xiao zhiqi gao, zhengzuo da gongxian.
July, 1973; 54 x 77 cm
Jiangsu Renmin chubanshe
E12/738

page 186
XIANG YANG
Carry out birth planning for the revolution.
Wei geming shixing jihua shengyu.
March, 1974; 53 x 76.5 cm
Shanghai Renmin chubanshe
E12/608

page 187
LI FENGLAN (1933)
Spring hoeing.
Chun chu.
June, 1974; 53 x 77 cm
Shanghai Renmin chubanshe
E13/56

page 188
KANG ZUOTIAN (1942)
The glow of the red sun warms ten thousand generations.
Hong taiyang guanghui nuan wandai.
June, 1974; 53.5 x 77 cm
Renmin meishu chubanshe
E13/827

page 189
XIN LILIANG (1912)
Little Red Guard tea stop.
Hongxiaobing chashuizhan.
June, 1974; 54 x 77 cm
Shanghai Renmin chubanshe
E15/346

page 190
WANG WEIXIN; WANG LIGUO
A life of combat produces art; the working people are in charge.
Douzheng shenghuo chu yishu laodong renmin shi zhuren.
July, 1974; 77 x 106 cm
Shanghai Renmin chubanshe
G2/808

page 191
LIU ZHIGUI (1945)
After the bumper harvest.
Fengshou zhi hou.
July, 1974; 53 x 77.5 cm
Liaoning Renmin chubanshe
E13/932

page 192
SONG HOUCHENG
Hold the gun tight in one's hand.
Jinwo shouzhong qiang.
August, 1974; 54 x 77 cm
Renmin meishu chubanshe
E15/75

page 193
LIU ZHIGUI (1945)
The red electromagnetic wave brings good news.
Hongse dianbo chuan xixun.
August, 1974; 53.5 x 77 cm
Beijing Renmin meishu chubanshe
E12/742

page 194
DESIGNER UNKNOWN
The construction of the bridge over the Yangzi River at Nanjing is a great victory for "Mao Zedong Thought"!
Nanjing Changjiang daqiaode jiancheng shi Mao Zedong sixiangde weida shengli!
c. 1975; 38.5 x 98.5 cm
Jiangsusheng Geming Weiyuanhui
E12/617

page 195
ZHAO KUNHAN
The production brigade's reading room (selected from the Huxian peasant painting exhibition).
Dadui tushushi (Xuan zi Huxian nongmin huazhan).
January, 1975; 53 x 77 cm
Shanghai Renmin chubanshe
E12/124

page 196
LU JUDING (1940)
Study well and grasp the theory of the dictatorship of the proletariat.
Xuehao nongtong wuchan jieji zhuanzhengde lilun.
May, 1975; 77 x 106 cm
Renmin meishu chubanshe
E13/619

page 197
DESIGNER UNKNOWN
Set the record of history straight.
Ba diandaode lishi zai diandao guolai.
July, 1975; 53 x 76.5 cm
Tianjin Renmin meishu chubanshe
E13/951

page 198
ZHAO KUNHAN
Develop physical education activities in peasant villages.
Guangfan kaizhan nongcun tiyu huodong.
July, 1975; 106.5 x 74 cm
Beijing Renmin tiyu chubanshe
E3/751

page 199
ZHOU SHUQIAO (1938)
Spring breeze in Yangliu.
Chunfeng Yangliu.
July, 1975; 54 x 78 cm
Renmin meishu chubanshe
E15/178

page 200
ZHANG WENXU; NANJING TROOPS COLLECTIVE WORK
Reconnoitering the enemy's advance.
Di qian zhencha.
August, 1975; 52.5 x 76 cm
Shanghai Renmin chubanshe
E13/945

page 201
LU ZHONGDE; CHEN YUNQING; COLLECTIVE WORK
New songs on the battlefield.
Zhandi xin'ge.
September, 1975 ; 53 x 77 cm
Shanghai Renmin chubanshe
E13/652

page 202
WEI YANG (1928)
Crossing the 10,000-li long Yangzi River.
Wanli Changjiang hengdu.
1976; 76 x 106.5 cm
Renmin tiyu chubanshe
E13/855

page 203
GUO ZHIMING
Our brigade leader.
Ni duizhang.
March, 1976; 53.5 x 77 cm
Shanghai Renmin chubanshe
E15/93

page 204
WU QIZHONG (1944)
Deepen the criticism of Deng Xiaoping, strike against the right deviatonist wind of overturned verdicts.
Shenru pipan Deng Xiaoping, fanji youqing fan'an feng.
May, 1976; 76.5 x 51 cm
Guangdong Renmin chubanshe
E13/967

page 205
YU ZHENLI (1946)
We must grasp revolution and increase production, increase work, increase preparation for struggle, to do an even better job.
Yao zhua geming cu shengchan, cu gongzuo, cu zhanbei, ba gefangmiande gongzuo zuode geng hao.
May, 1976; 77 x 212 cm
Renmin meishu chubanshe
G2/29-30

page 206
SHANG TAO (1938)
Before the contest.
Sai qian.
June, 1976; 53 x 77 cm
Renmin tiyu chubanshe
E13/337

page 207
WANG MINGYU
Prosperity.
Xinxin xiang rong.
June, 1976; 54 x 78 cm
Liaoning Renmin chubanshe
E15/479

pages 208–209
CHEN RUPENG
The loving care of the mother country.
Zuguode guanhuai.
July, 1976; 53.5 x 76.5 cm
Renmin meishu chubanshe
E13/972

page 210
LU YIFEI (1931–1997); ZHANG GUIMING (1939); XU ZHIWEN
A spring breeze in a snowy night.
Xue ye chun feng.
July, 1976; 53.5 x 77 cm
Shanghai Renmin chubanshe
E15/98

page 211
CULTURAL REVOLUTION COLLECTIVE PAINTING CREATIVE GROUP
Bombard the capitalist headquarters.
Paoda zichan jieji silingbu.
August, 1976; 54 x 78 cm
Shanghai Renmin chubanshe
E15/125

page 212
NANHUI DISTRICT SPARE TIME ART GROUP
Four scrolls about not having to bend down (1, 2).
Si bu wan yao bing.
August, 1976; 77 x 53 cm
Shanghai Renmin chubanshe
E15/103

page 213
NANHUI DISTRICT SPARE TIME ART GROUP
Four scrolls about not having to bend down (3, 4).
Si bu wan yao bing.
August, 1976; 77 x 53 cm
Shanghai Renmin chubanshe
E15/104

page 214
CAO ZIQIANG
A new scene in Xiangyangyuan.
Xiangyangyuanli qixiang xin.
September, 1976; 54 x 77 cm
Shanghai Renmin chubanshe
E15/132

page 215
CHEN YI
Training the body for the revolution.
Wei geming lianhao shenti.
May, 1977; 77 x 53 cm
Shanghai Renmin chubanshe
E16/525

pages 218–219
SHANGHAI RENMIN CHUBANSHE PROPAGANDA POSTER GROUP
Turn grief into strength, carry out Chairman Mao's behests, and carry the proletarian revolutionary cause through to the end.
Hua beitong wei liliang jicheng Mao zhuxi yizhi ba wuchan jieji geming shiye jinxing daodi.
September, 1976; 77.5 x 106 cm
Shanghai Renmin chubanshe
PC01-1976

page 220
YIN RONGSHENG (1930); MA CHANGLI (1931); YANG XIANRANG (1930); ART ACADEMY OF THE CENTRAL 7 MAY UNIVERSITY
Carry out Chairman Mao's behests and carry the proletarian revolutionary cause through to the end!

Jicheng Mao zhuxide yizhi, ba wuchan jieji geming shiye jinxing daodi!
September, 1976; 76 x 106 cm
Renmin meishu chubanshe
G2/679

page 221
WANG YONGQIANG (1945)
Relentlessly criticize the Gang of Four, set off a new upsurge of industry studying Daqing and agriculture studying Dazhai.
Henpi "Sirenbang", xianqi gongye xue Daqing nongye xue Dazhai xin gaochao.
January, 1977; 77 x 106 cm
Shanghai Renmin chubanshe
G2/36

page 222
SUN QUAN (1942)
Thoroughly expose and criticize the Gang of Four.
Chedi jiefa pipan "Sirenbang".
March, 1977; 77 x 53 cm
Renmin meishu chubanshe
E15/965

page 223
WANG BAOGUANG
Smash the Gang of Four.
Da "Sirenbang".
September, 1978; 53 x 77 cm
Tianjin Yangliuqing huadian
E13/418

page 224
WANG YIDING
Chairman Hua waves his hand, we advance victoriously.
Hua zhuxi huishou women shengli qianjin.
September, 1977; 53 x 76 cm
Zhejiang Renmin chubanshe
E15/279

page 225
LUO DE'AN (1940)
Ordinary worker (Hua Guofeng).
Putong laodongzhe.
c. 1977; 77 x 53 cm
Tianjinshi Weisheng xuanchuan jiaoyusuo
E13/627

page 226
XIE MULIAN (1918–1985)
Selling the fruits of a bumper harvest in a friendly manner.
Xishou fengshou guo.
April, 1978; 77 x 53 cm
Shanghai Renmin meishu chubanshe
E13/417

page 227
WANG MEIFANG (1949); ZHAO GUOJING (1950)
Song of Friendship.
Youyi zhi ge.
March, 1979; 52 x 75 cm
Tianjin Renmin meishu chubanshe
E13/868

pages 228–229
GAO QUAN (1936); YANG KESHAN (1944)
Long live the People's Republic of China.
Zhonghua renmin gongheguo wansui.
June, 1979; 77 x 211 cm
Renmin meishu chubanshe
E13/492-3

page 230
NINGXIA HUI AUTONOMOUS REGION PATRIOTIC HYGIENE MOVEMENT COMMITTEE; NINGXIA HUI AUTONOMOUS REGION HYGIENE OFFICE
Keep the environment clean, create spiritual civilization.

Baochi huanjing zhengjie jianshe jingshen wenming.
c. 1980; 78 x 54 cm
Publisher unknown
E15/606

page 231
JIANG JIANZHANG (1925)
Foster a correct spirit, resist the evil spirit, resist corruption, never get involved with it.
Fuzhi zhengqi, dizhi waiqi, ju fushi, yong buzhan.
January, 1983; 77 x 53 cm
Renmin meishu chubanshe
E13/413

page 232
XU WENHUA (1941)
Love the people.
Ai renmin.
February, 1983; 77 x 53 cm
Shanghai Renmin meishu chubanshe
E12/128

page 233
WEI ZHIGANG
Celebrate a festival with jubilation.
Huandu jiajie.
August, 1983; 105 x 57 cm
Tianjin Renmin meishu chubanshe
E13/363

page 234
YAN MING
Sternly attack criminal activities.
Yanli daji xingshi fanzui huodong.
December, 1983; 77 x 105 cm
Falü chubanshe
E13/370

page 235
WANG BINGKUN
Youthful dance steps.
Qingchun wubu.
April, 1986; 77 x 53 cm
Lingnan Meishu chubanshe
E13/441

page 236
WEI YINGZHOU
I strive to bring glory to the mother country.
Wo wei zuguo zheng guangrong.
June, 1986; 77 x 53 cm
Shanghai Renmin meishu chubanshe
E13/85

page 237 (detail on pages 216–217)
DESIGNER UNKNOWN
Fewer births, better births, to develop a strong China.
Shaosheng yousheng zhenxing Zhonghua.
1987; 77 x 53 cm
Beijing Centre of Communiciation and Education for Family Planning
E13/871

page 238
XI LIJIANG
Pop star.
Nü gexing.
April, 1987; 75 x 52 cm
Lingnan Meishu chubanshe
E15/50

page 239
LIU YUANXING
The people are industrious; spring is early.
Ren qin chun zao.
July, 1987; 77 x 52 cm
Sichuan Meishu chubanshe
E15/518

page 240
PENG MING (1953)
The age of smiling.
Weixiaode shidai.
April, 1988; 77 x 53 cm
Lingnan Meishu chubanshe
E13/437

page 241
XU CHENGZHI
The king of gymnastics Li Ning.

Ticao wangzi Li Ning.
September, 1988; 77 x 53 cm
Renmin meishu chubanshe
E16/302

pages 242–243
CENTRAL INDUSTRIAL ARTS COLLEGE
Only socialism can save China, only socialism can develop China.
Zhi you shehui zhuyi cai neng qiu Zhongguo, zhi you shehui zhuyi cai neng fazhan Zhongguo.
December, 1989; 77 x 53 cm
Renmin jiaoyu chubanshe
E13/460

page 244
WANG ZHENGZHONG
Sweethearts.
Qinglu.
October, 1990; 77 x 53 cm
Sichuan Meishu chubanshe
E15/933

page 245
HE DUOJUN
Chinese women's volleyball team.
Zhongguo nüpai.
November, 1990; 77 x 53 cm
Sichuan Meishu chubanshe
E13/471

page 246
ZHENG NIAN
Party, oh party, beloved party.
Dang ah dang, qin'aide dang.
May, 1991; 53 x 77 cm
Chongqing chubanshe
E13/448

page 247
DESIGNER UNKNOWN
The Gods of wealth enter the home from everywhere: wealth, treasures and peace beckon.
Lulu caishen jin jiamen, zhao cai zhao bao zhao ping'an.
1993; 82 x 68 cm
Zhongguo huabao chubanshe
E13/491

page 248
YANG LIQUN
Study Lei Feng: serve the people wholeheartedly.
Xuexi Lei Feng, quanxin quanyi wei renmin fuwu.
July, 1995; 75 x 51.5 cm
Lingnan Meishu chubanshe
E13/643

page 249
YIN HONG; DA KE
The Chinese are amazing.
Zhongguo ren liaobuqi.
September, 1996; 76.5 x 52 cm
Hubei Meishu chubanshe
E13/747

page 250
CHEN JIAHUA
Enthusiastically celebrate the return of Hong Kong.
Relie huanqing Xianggang huigui.
January, 1997; 76 x 52 cm
Hubei Meishu chubanshe
E13/558

page 251
WU XIANGFENG
The return of Hong Kong. One country – two systems.
Xianggang huigui, yiguo liangzhi.
January, 1997; 76 x 52 cm
Hubei Meishu chubanshe
E13/559

pages 252–253
DU JIANG
Build a prosperous and cultured new socialist countryside.
Jianshe fuyu wenmingde shehui zhuyi xin nongcun.
February, 1997; 106.5 x 229 cm
Sichuan Meishu chubanshe
E15/892-894

page 254
DESIGNER UNKNOWN
Happy Universe.
Fuman Qiankun.
June, 1997; 106 x 76 cm
Tianjin Renmin meishu
E12/704

page 255
ZHAO JIANWEI; LI GANG (1951); WANG JIANMIN
Millions of people all of one mind strive for the ultimate victory in combating floods and dealing with emergencies.
Wanzhong yixin duoqu kanghong qiangxiande zuihou shengli.
August, 1998; 76 x 52.5 cm
Zhongguo meishu chuban zongshe
E13/739

page 256
OFFICE OF THE STATE COUNCIL FIFTH CENSUS LEADING SMALL GROUP
Report things as they really are, do a good job in the national census.
Rushi shenbo gaohao renkou pucha.
2000; 77 x 53 cm
China Statistics Publishing House
E15/1

page 257
HAO XUELI
New Beijing, Great Olympics. Beijing 2008.
Xin Beijing xin Aoyun - Beijing 2008.
2000; 100 x 70 cm
Publisher unknown
E15/20

page 258
BEIJING ZHONGTONG SHI'AO TUWEN SHEJI ZHONGXIN
The Chinese Communist Party fully represents the progressive orientation of China's progressive culture.
Zhongguo gongchandang shizhong daibiao Zhongguo xianjin wenhuade qianjin fangxiang.
2002; 78 x 53 cm
Zhongguo huabao chubanshe
E15/322

page 259
DESIGNER UNKNOWN
In times of SARS, hearts call for hearts.
Zhimian feidian women yi xin chuan xin.
2003; 57 x 83 cm
Publisher unknown
E15/759

page 260
DESIGNER UNKNOWN
Mutual care and love, share life. The main topic of the 2003 International Aids Movement.
Xianghu guanai gongxiang shengming-2003 nian shijie aizibing xuanchuan yundong zhuti.
c. 2003; 74 x 52 cm
Weishengbu yibing kongzhisi Durex
E15/498

page 261
YANG WEIQIAO
In celebration of the successful opening of the Qinghai and Xizang railway.
Qingzhu Qing-Zang tielu shengli tongche.
July, 2006; 51.5 x 73 cm
Zhongtie erju jituan
PC01-2006

STEFAN R. LANDSBERGER is Olfert Dapper Professor of Contemporary Chinese Culture at the University of Amsterdam and Lecturer in Contemporary Chinese History at Leiden University, The Netherlands. Fascinated by totalitarian propaganda, he started to collect Chinese propaganda posters in the 1970s. His collection has grown into one of the largest private collections in the world.

MARIEN VAN DER HEIJDEN has worked with the poster collection of the International Institute of Social History since 1984. He has organized exhibitions on social history and social art, and published on Dutch socially engaged artists, Russian revolutionary museums, and more.

KUIYI SHEN is Professor of Art History in the Department of Visual Arts, University of California, San Diego. He served as director of the art book department at the Shanghai People's Fine Arts Publishing House before relocating to the United States. He has published many books, exhibition catalogues, and articles on modern and contemporary Chinese art.

Prestel Verlag
Königinstrasse 9, D-80539 Munich
T +49 (0) 89 242 908 300
F +49 (0) 89 242 908 335
www.prestel.de

Prestel Publishing Ltd.
4, Bloomsbury Place, London WC1A 2QA
Tel. +44 (020) 7323-5004
Fax +44 (020) 7636-8004

Prestel Publishing
900 Broadway, Suite 603
New York, N.Y. 10003
Tel. +1 (212) 995-2720
Fax +1 (212) 995-2733
www.prestel.com

Library of Congress Control Number is available.

British Library Cataloguing-in-Publication Data: A catalogue record for this book is available from the British Library. The Deutsche Bibliothek holds a record of this publication in the Deutsche Nationalbibliographie; detailed bibliographical data can be found under: http://dnb.dde.de

Prestel books are available worldwide. Please contact your nearest bookseller or one of the addresses on the left for information concerning your local distributor.

Editorial direction: Philippa Hurd
Design: Liquid, Augsburg
Layout, typesetting: Fabian Kornher
Origination: Reproline mediateam, Munich
Printing and Binding:
Druckerei Uhl, Radolfzell
Printed in Germany on acid-free paper
ISBN 978-3-7913-4389-1

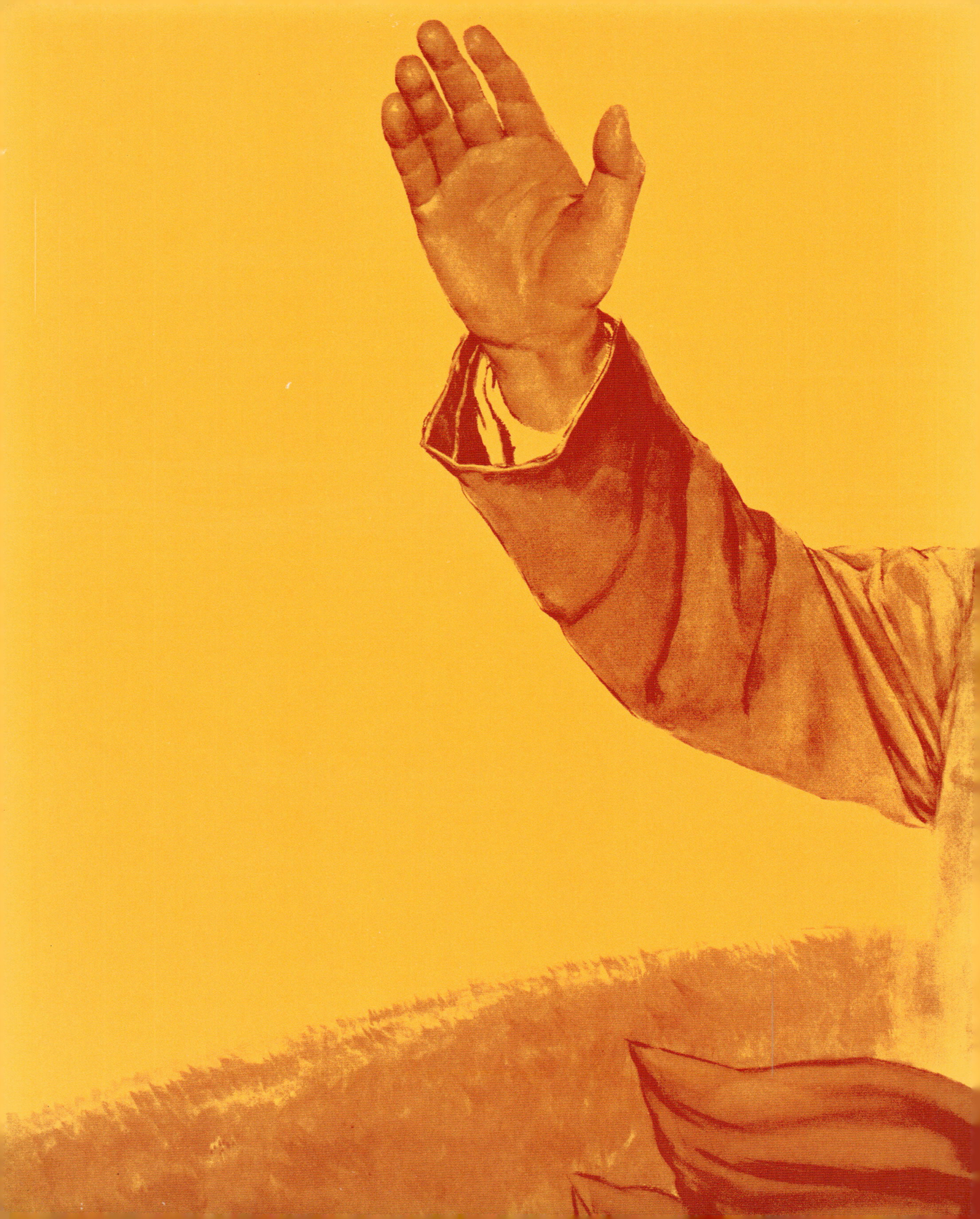

Claire Mclonghlin

Matisse Portraits

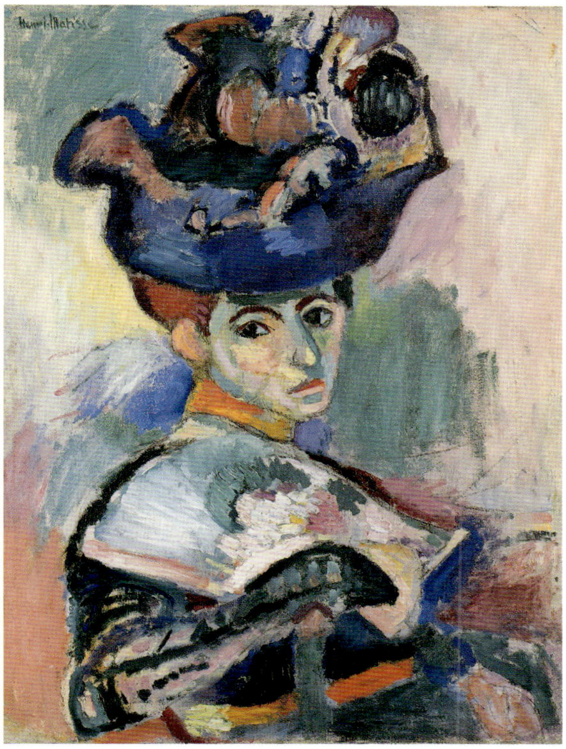

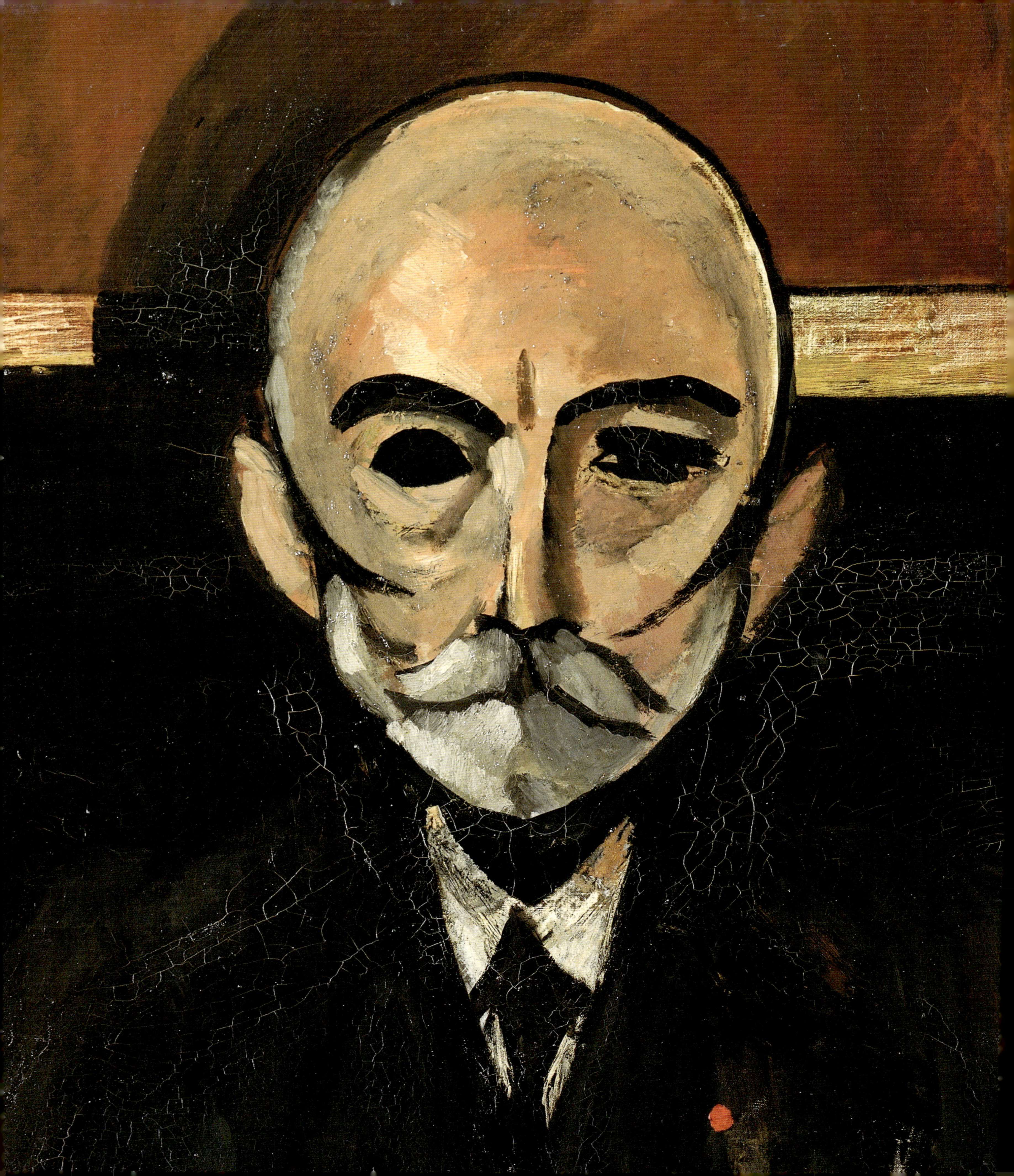

John Klein

Matisse Portraits

Yale University Press
New Haven and London

Designed by Gillian Malpass

Printed in Singapore

Library of Congress Cataloging-in-Publication Data

Klein, John, 1953–
Matisse portraits / John Klein.
p. cm.
Includes bibliographical references and index.
ISBN 0-300-08100-6 (cloth : alk. paper)
1. Matisse, Henri, 1869–1954 – Criticism and interpretation.
2. Portrait painting, French – 20th century. I. Title.
ND533.M37 K57 2001
759.4 – dc21

2001023738

A catalogue record for this book is available from The British Library

PAGE i *Woman with the Hat*, 1905. Oil on canvas, 80.6 × 59.7 cm.
San Francisco Museum of Modern Art, bequest of Elise S. Haas.

FRONTISPIECE *Auguste Pellerin II* (detail), 1917. Oil on canvas, 150.2 × 96.2 cm.
Paris, Musée National d'Art Moderne, Centre Georges Pompidou.

Contents

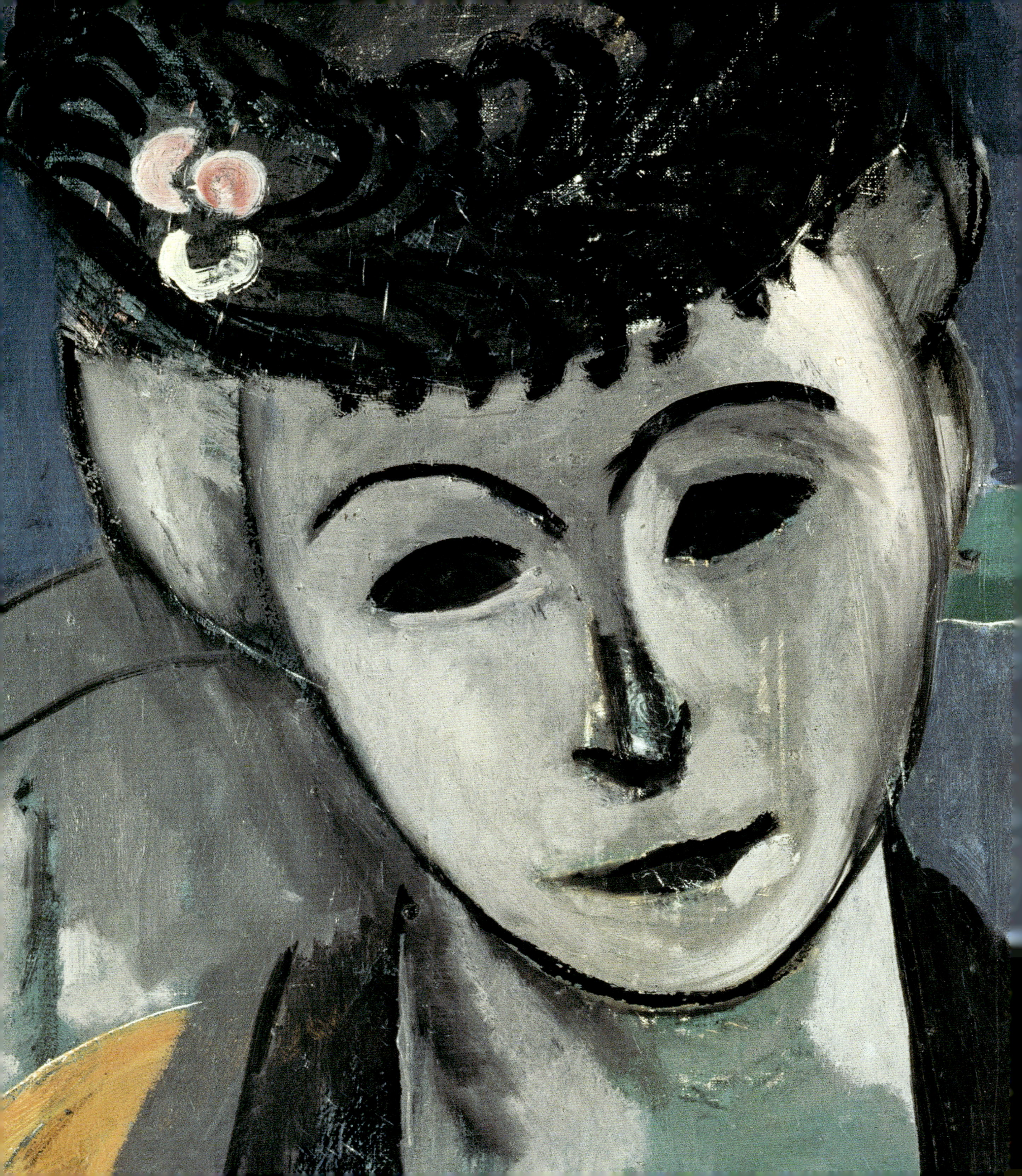

Acknowledgments

Like Matisse's portraiture, this book originated in family. First are my parents, John and Juliet Klein, who have supported my efforts over many years and in ways that cannot easily be put into words, but all born of faith and love. I dedicate the book to them. My wife, Elizabeth Childs, has been my closest reader and most thorough critic. She has made key intellectual contributions at every stage. She and my son, Willy Childs-Klein, have also sustained me in other ways during the writing and revision, sometimes through pleasurable distraction, sometimes by leaving me alone. I have been profoundly grateful for their presence, and their sacrifices. Other family members – Rick Klein and Carol Bishop, Orlo and Libby Childs, Brad and Barry Childs – have been most supportive, and I thank them.

I have incurred many debts in the community of scholars. Among the most important of these people were my advisors at Columbia University, Theodore Reff and Allen Staley, who guided the dissertation that has evolved into this book. Kirk Varnedoe also made important intellectual contributions at that time. I am grateful for their formative influence. Many others who contributed to my work on the dissertation are acknowledged there. Since then, those who have been helpful in so many ways include Roger Benjamin, Catherine Bock-Weiss, Yve-Alain Bois, Eric Carlson, Eric de Chassey, John Elderfield, Dominique Fourcade, Judi Freeman, the late Sir Lawrence Gowing, Lewis Kachur, Paul Kaplan, Rémi Labrusse, Isabelle Monod-Fontaine, Kasper Monrad, John Neff, Marc Restellini, Sabine Rewald, Pierre Schneider, Gerald Silk, Hilary Spurling, and especially Jack Flam, who encouraged me when I first had the idea to work seriously on Matisse's portraiture, and whose support has been unmatched since; and the late Edward Fry, who urged me to have a good idea in the first place. Kirsten Hoving at Middlebury College, Janet Bishop at the San Francisco Museum of Modern Art, Caroline Turner at the Queensland Art Gallery, Brisbane, and Cornelia Homburg at the St. Louis Art Museum kindly extended invitations to lecture or publish on Matisse's portraiture, and I profited greatly from these public tests of some of my arguments.

The help of several members of the Matisse family has been essential to the completion of this book. I thank Georges Matisse, Marie Matisse, the late Pierre Matisse, Jacqueline Matisse Monnier, and especially Claude and Barbara Duthuit for their generosity over the years. At the Archives Matisse in Paris, I have received crucial support from Wanda de Guébriant in matters large and small. Her intelligence and acumen about all matters relating to Matisse's work have made significant contributions.

One of my greatest debts is to my friend Dominique Szymusiak, director of the Musée Matisse, Le Cateau-Cambrésis. From our initial meeting on a stifling July day, when her first gesture upon welcoming me to her museum after my walk from the train station was to offer me a beer, she has given me unexpected and

Detail of fig. 55.

unstinting support, including invitations to collaborate with her on two wonderful exhibitions. She has repeatedly put the considerable research resources of the Musée Matisse at my disposal, and she and her family, Yves-Marie, Samuel, and Grégoire, have ensured that the Nord-Pas de Calais region is my favorite part of France. I am deeply grateful to them all. Elsewhere in France I have been helped by Xavier Girard, former director, and Marie-Thérèse Pulvenis de Séligny, current director, Musée Matisse, Nice, and their staffs; Jacqueline Besson, Paule Caen, Dina Vierny, and especially Lydia Delectorskaya, who was highly informative about Matisse's work with models.

In the United States I should like to thank Janet Hicks at Artists Rights Society, New York; Sylvie Merian and the rest of the staff at the Reading Room, Pierpont Morgan Library, New York; Rona Roob and Michelle Elligott at the Museum of Modern Art Archives; and Olive Bragazzi at the Pierre Matisse Foundation, New York.

For their willingness to help me to obtain photographs and transparencies I thank Frédérique Barret, Fereshteh Daftari, Carol Eliel, Stephen Hahn, Beatrice Kernan, Albert Kostenevich, Nathalie Lavarenne, Jean-Pierre Manguin, Sandrine Polvent, Bertha Saunders, Richard Smooke, Robert Stoppenbach, and Daniel Wildenstein.

Some special friends deserve to be mentioned. I thank Bob Zuber for his generosity and companionship during concentrated research trips to New York, and Hope Hanafin for her help with my work at the CBS Archives there. In France I was often sustained by the hospitality of Caroline Boyle-Turner, Nana Gregory, Nancy Keeler, and John Smith. By Judy Meighan and Shirley Blum I have been reminded of what is really important.

At the University of Missouri-Columbia I have received help from many colleagues. I am especially grateful to my department chairs, Kathleen Slane, Howard Marshall, and Marcus Rautman, for their support. Daffany Hood provided timely logistical help. Joe and Françoise Bien, Haskell Hinnant, Ozzie Overby, and Anne and Stephen Stanton offered important encouragement. The members of my graduate seminar in modern portraiture, Debra Byrne, Alex Huff, and Lisa Moore, repeatedly challenged and augmented my thinking about my subject. Work on the book was aided by a grant from the Research Board of the University of Missouri System, and essential subvention of the costs of the illustration program was provided by the Research Council of my campus. I am thankful for this enlightened institutional help.

It has been a real pleasure to work with Yale University Press, London, on the book's evolution. I thank Katharine Ridler for her careful and astute editing of my manuscript. The two anonymous readers helped me to tighten my arguments; the book is much better for their help. At the Press itself, I should like to thank Elizabeth McWilliams and especially Sandy Chapman and Gillian Malpass. Sandy Chapman was instrumental in obtaining much of the book's illustrative material and keeping it in order, for which I am grateful. My editor and designer, Gillian Malpass, has been a dream collaborator. In having her commitment, I am a fortunate author.

John Klein
St. Louis, 2001

Introduction The Social Agency of Portraiture

In the art of Henri Matisse we have one of the great sustained responses to some of the strongest challenges to painting during the last two hundred years. His art, though innovative, was also fiercely resistant to things outside its scope. Against the call to political engagement he created private worlds of sensation. To the apparently mechanistic photograph he responded with a carefully governed personal expression. In answer to modernism's rejection of traditional practice he insisted on the importance of drawing. Abstraction's threat to the regime of representation met in Matisse an artist resolved to work every day from the model.

Few challenges, however, gave him more trouble than one from within the compass of his own ambitions – the challenge of portraiture. As an artist who wished to innovate within traditional media and formats, and who sought accomplishment in a wide range of genres, Matisse embraced the portrait as one of the ways to manifest his devotion to working from the human figure. This commitment was not always repaid with satisfaction. It is well known that his expressive responses to his sitters often met with disapproval from those who felt them to be ugly, aggressive, inhuman, and so on. For the portrait in modern art, this is the same old story, told through countless tales of conflict between artist and sitter for control of how the sitter should be represented. We are long past following the same old story with the same old laments about the philistinism of patrons, critics, and other viewers unable to embrace the new. Instead we need to consider the differences in values that fed such disagreements about how identity should be expressed in a portrait. These values concern differences in perception about the role of art, but also differences in perception of what constitutes the self. Change in these areas redefined the portrait.

Disagreement about how the self should be represented was also played out on a much larger field of which artistic representation was but one part. New concepts of identity changed the way people thought about themselves and others, their place in society, and their claims to how their identity could or should be expressed.[1] Matisse trained as an artist and matured as a man in an age that philosophically understood the self as a unified entity, constituted politically and socially as male. During the sixty-year span of his career, ending at his death in 1954, this unitary idea of the self was broadened on many fronts. The decline of religion, the rise of nationalism, and the increasing importance of the family, among other things, shifted the locus of individual identity. The horrors of the First World War and Freud's proposals about the power of the unconscious suggested deeper and darker habitations of the self. Gauguin's *Where do we come from? What are we? Where are we going?* represented his search and that of others for personal and collective origins. Novels such as Proust's *Remembrance of Things Past* and Joyce's *Ulysses* shattered narrative and thus the linear accumulation of personal experience. Suffragists and other advocates asserted public and private rights of women to selfhood. Research by Magnus Hirschfeld and others into homosexuality tried to elucidate and validate an expanded notion of human sexuality and its relation to identity. Salman Rushdie has summed up the modern expansion of the idea of the self and our implicit acceptance of this complex notion of identity:

> In the modern age, we have come to understand our own selves as composites, often contradictory, even internally incompatible. We have understood that each of us is many different people. Our younger selves differ from our older selves; we can be bold in the company of our lovers and timorous before our employers, principled when we instruct our children and corrupt when offered some secret temptation; we are serious and frivolous, loud and quiet, aggressive and easily abashed. The 19th century concept of the integrated self has been replaced by this jostling crowd of "I"s. And yet, unless we are damaged, or deranged, we usually have a relatively clear sense of *who we are*. I agree with my many selves to call all of them "me."[2]

Although Matisse was in his formation a product of the nineteenth century, and though he could be blinkered, he was not oblivious to the implications of philosophical and social change for the task of representing the human face and figure in art. At the same time he also wished to satisfy his need to make an art that expressed his own identity. The challenges he faced in representing the individuality of another in a portrait, his simultaneous need for self-expression, and the accommodations he made to reconcile the conflict between these two goals are the subject of this book.

What is a portrait?

Like many things, a portrait is easier to identify than to define. Underneath its acerbity, John Singer Sargent's quip about a portrait being "a likeness in which there is something wrong about the mouth" is structurally similar to most efforts to evade the pitfalls of definition.[3] Because of this difficulty, general studies of the portrait in art (there are many other kinds of portraits) usually shy from attempting to define the genre. Their inclusion and analysis of works are typically based on *a priori* acceptance of given images as portraits. Unspoken consensus governs these efforts. Such standard books as John Pope-Hennessy's *The Portrait in the Renaissance* and Max J. Friedländer's *Landscape, Portrait, Still Life*, which function as classics and virtual reference works, contain no defining rationale for classifying as portraits the works of art under discussion.[4]

In fact, it may be that in works of art history such as these a definition of portraiture is more likely to be taken for granted than in studies intended for a wide popular audience or in those with a specifically didactic purpose.[5] Philosophers, too, sometimes feel an obligation to construct specific categories prior to analysis of the conditions of portraiture.[6] Yet even in these efforts to delineate the field more precisely by paring away untenable premises for portraiture, an actual definition, as opposed to a system of classification, is rare.

Although definition and classification are their business, dictionary and encyclopedia entries are of little help either. Their definitions are either too narrow or too broad to be useful in discussing a wide range of works of art. Sometimes the two extremes are combined in one definition, as in that offered in the French *Grande*

Encyclopédie of about 1900, and thus contemporaneous with Matisse's artistic formation: "Portrait. 1. Fine Arts. – A portrait is the representation – line for line – in profile, or in bust- or full-length, of the specific exterior physiognomy of a man, a woman, or a child."[7] Besides having obvious and easily redressed omissions (such as group portraits), this definition is more fundamentally limited by its literal etymological approach to the word portrait (which in English, German, Italian, and Spanish, for instance, has the same derivation as in French). Portrait – "pour trait" – carries the connotation of exact copying after an object ("trait pour trait"). This etymology is the basis of nearly all definitions of the portrait.[8]

In the literature of art history, one of the best sustained efforts to define portraiture was made by James Breckenridge in *Likeness: A Conceptual History of Ancient Portraiture.*[9] From among several definitions proposed by others who had taken up this question, he offered these requirements of a "true" portrait:

> 1) It must represent a definite person, either living or of the past, with his distinctive human traits. 2) The person must be represented in such a manner that under no circumstances can his identity be confused with that of someone else. 3) As a work of art, a portrait must render the personality, i.e., the inner individuality, of the person represented in his outer form.[10]

Breckenridge then found that these terms were too restrictive and settled on a more expansive statement: a portrait is "the representation, intended to be like, of a definite individual."[11] Yet he ultimately judged this definition to be too broad, as it inappropriately encompassed images intended to have a "magic" function. When he modified this formulation so as to specify that the object of a portrait is shown "for his own sake," then Breckenridge concluded that he had arrived at a necessary and sufficient definition of the portrait: "a work of art which seeks to represent the totality of an individual, for the sake of his individuality."[12]

In these terms, then, a portrait is a likeness of an individual person represented for his or her own sake, such that the image cannot be mistaken to represent anyone else; this likeness also conveys something of the personality or character of that individual. So the portrait has a unique referent – the individual – and two necessary characteristics – likeness and character, both alleged to be attributes of the referent. Most discussions of portraiture accept these components as fundamental even if they do not articulate them. The unity of the individual in a portrait is seen to consist of the combination of outer individuality (the "likeness" part) and inner individuality (the "character" part).

Portraiture and society

Any discussion of likeness and character isolates the individual from society, and so a definition of the portrait that has only these as criteria misses the most important context for producing personal identity. The process itself of making a portrait must also be understood in social terms, as a negotiation of how the sitter's identity should be visualized in the portrait. Both artist and sitter have a great deal at stake, because each comes to the portrait transaction with the goal of furthering the cause of his or her identity. A portrait, then, should be understood as a transaction between two distinct but fluid identities – that of the subjective artist and that of the object of the portrait, the sitter, who also has an investment in subjectivity. This transaction should be characterized in social as much as in artistic terms: it negotiates a self-presentation even as it creates a representation of another individual.

Both the social component of portraiture and the traditional requirement of fidelity to appearance have given it a problematic status in the era of the modernist avant-garde, roughly since Manet. There are several good reasons for its discredit. First and most obvious are the recording and commemorative functions of the portrait, conventionally tied to representational goals of specificity, imitation, and likeness on one hand, and social status on the other. This material and social concreteness has often been anathema to the artist whose project is either expressive or abstract, or who consciously sought to deviate from conventional paths. The portrait had little role, for instance, in the work of Kandinsky, Malevich, or Pollock. Conversely, for artists professing belief in the collective, such as Léger or Stuart Davis, the validation of individual identity by the portrait may have seemed anachronistically elitist.

Other forces were marshaled against portraiture. Even when a recording function was still desirable in portrait painting, the photograph offered a viable and relatively inexpensive alternative. The apparent fidelity of the photograph to the way a person looks laid down a substantial challenge to the painter or sculptor of portraits. The tribute the portrait pays to its sitter compromises the modern artist's self-sufficiency and desire for control over a work of art's expressive content. The contraction of public and private systems of patronage and the inverse rise of the open art market reduced the role of the commissioned portrait as a means to fame and security for the artist. Even for artists awash in commissions, painting portraits could be a distracting task, as Ingres had famously expressed: "Damned portraits! They're always keeping me from getting on with more important things."[13] Later in the nineteenth century those who did find success as painters of society portraits often did so in the service of a clientèle whose values had been rejected by many independent-minded modernists. Finally, despite the portrait's lowly status in the classic hierarchy of genres, sometimes its practice seemed just too bound by tradition. These are but a few ways to account for the challenges to portraiture in the late nineteenth and early twentieth centuries.[14]

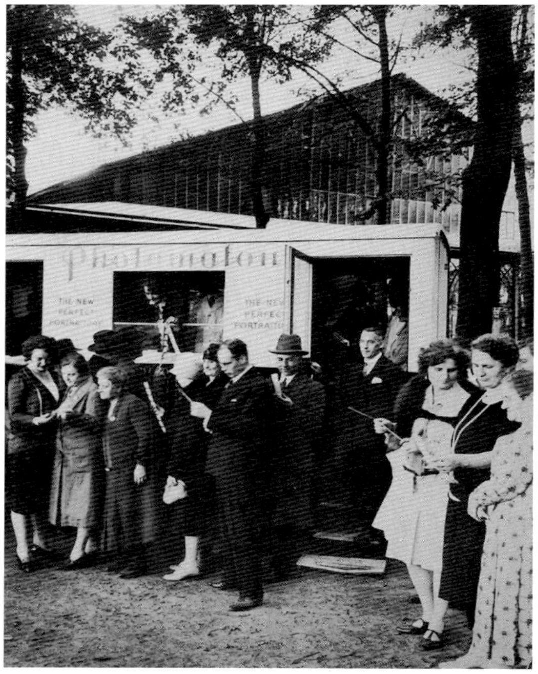

1 Photomaton, 1930s.

These factors may have been obstacles to the continued vitality of this genre across the spectrum of the art world, but they indicate important social functions that more generally govern the production and understanding of portraits.[15] A portrait publicly declares relationship and interdependence. It is therefore both a social artifact and a social agent. This tends to be true in all periods and for a great variety of portrait types and practices, from the splendor of Renaissance courtship portraits, which sometimes bore the weight of imperial consolidation (fig. 2), to the humble attractions of the Photomaton (fig. 1), an early instant photograph booth, whose artist-free portraits could be the object of lively, if more ephemeral, public discourse.[16]

Representing identity

Several important reciprocal relationships are implied in a portrait. The relationship of a portrait to its sitter, of the portrait to an audience, of the sitter to this audience, of the artist to the sitter, and of all of these to conventions for public presentation as well as artistic representation – each plays a part in negotiating identity in the portrait. Whatever other characteristics it may possess, a portrait should be

2 Peter Paul Rubens, *Henri IV Receiving the Portrait of Maria de' Medici*, 1622–5. Oil on canvas, 394 × 295 cm. Paris, Musée du Louvre.

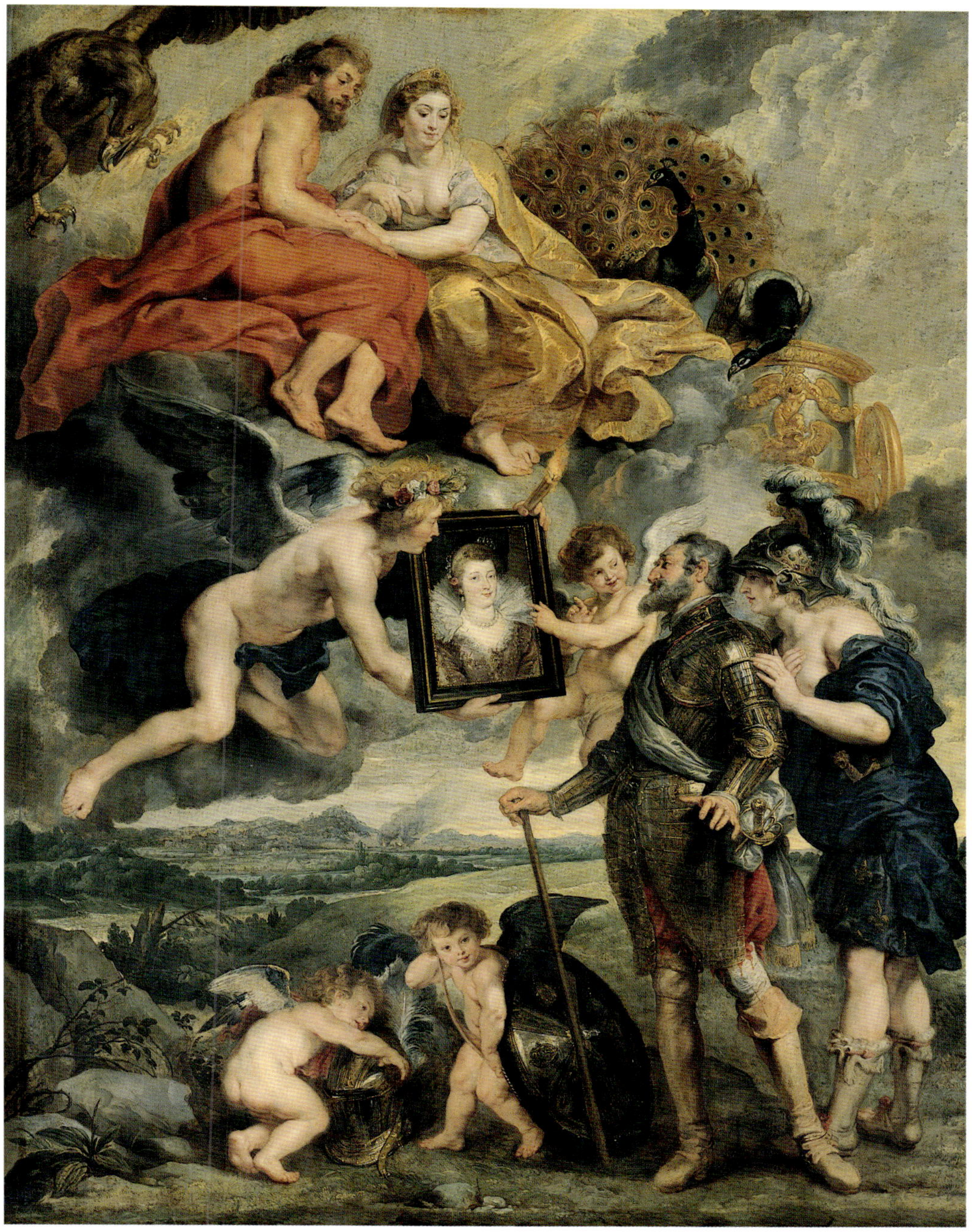

understood to be the site for a complicated transaction that produces and affirms some form of identity in a field of social relations. And this question of form in two senses – what form identity takes in society, and what form its representation takes in a portrait – is a contested one in the modern period. A portrait may look like its sitter; or it may not, as in Francis Picabia's machine personages or the poster portraits of Charles Demuth (fig. 3). A portrait may purport to "reveal" the character of its sitter; or it may not, as in Andy Warhol's repetitions of Marilyn Monroe and other celebrities. But what a portrait must do is to propose that it is authorized to represent an individual to his or her society. A portrait is as much a social representation of its sitter as it is a visual representation of that person.

3 Charles Demuth, *Poster Portrait: Marin*, 1926. Poster paint on pressed-paper board, 67.9 × 83.8 cm. New Haven, Conn., Beinecke Rare Book and Manuscript Library, Yale University, gift of Georgia O'Keeffe to the Collection of American Literature.

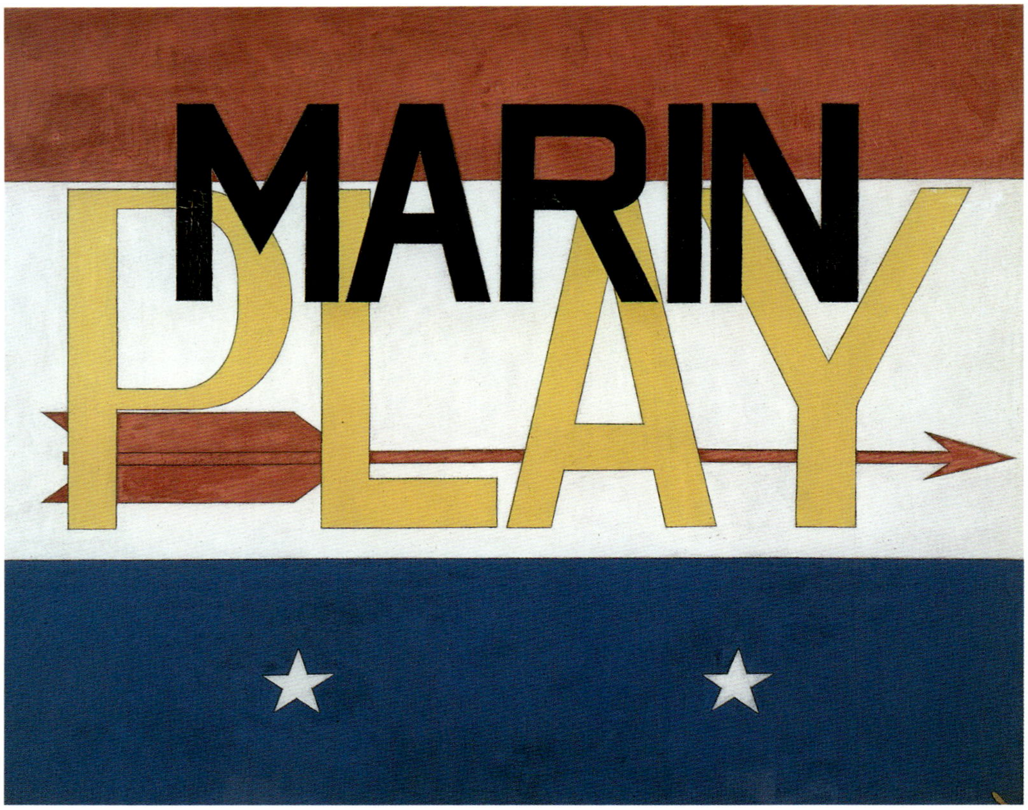

Matisse was one of the few modernist artists to embrace portraiture because of, not despite, its representational strictures and its associations with tradition. He struggled with the challenge that portraiture presented to self-expression in his art, his often-stated supreme goal. Yet his portrait practice also attests to his desire to be connected to a larger human world, and to anchor himself in its material and social specificity. In a period of rapid change in artistic practice and in the role of the artist in society, to which he contributed substantially, his attitude toward portraiture reflects the general ambivalence around this deceptively complex genre. His particular use and manipulation of it is worth an extended examination.

Self-portraiture, while often taken to be a subset of portraiture, has unique properties that warrant separate treatment. If the portrait seemed to compromise the self-sufficiency and expressive potential of the modern artist, the self-portrait could be seen to confirm them. Although not of course exclusively a modern genre, its questioning stance and ready-made self-consciousness offer an emblematic site of subjectivity. This subjectivity warns us not to accept the self-portrait as transparent or factual. The modern self-portrait is often invented for public consumption, abetting a myth of the self isolated from society. Thus the self-portrait, apparently a sincere and unmediated form of artistic expression, can at times be one of the most artificial and deceptive.

In my analysis of Matisse's self-portraits, I have sought to approach them in two distinct but related ways. On one hand, I consider self-portraiture in the context of his artistic development and goals. Early in his career the self-portrait was a private means for expanding his repertoire and establishing the modes of self-reference and subjectivity that are characteristic of his work as a whole. Later, he used this self-referring quality of the self-portrait as a tool in public relations, as a way of personalizing his art. On the other hand, self-portraiture may be related to more general issues of human development. Individuality predicates subjectivity, and it is useful to consider self-portraiture in the context of psychoanalytic theories of identity formation, in which the self builds its repertoire by testing its capacity for identifying with images of otherness. On the foundation of a sense of individual identity, to which self-portraiture may contribute, can then be balanced the needs of the self and the other that is part of the process of making a portrait in the modern period.

The portrait and self-portrait in modernism

Both likeness and character as fixed concepts come under assault from the modern artist and from modern society. It is clear that if a definition of the portrait is going to include such twentieth-century works as Demuth's poster portraits or Picabia's *portraits-machines*, and, more recently, Arman's *poubelles*, Felix Gonzalez-Torres's word portraits, or Byron Kim's visual cataloguing of the colors of his son's skin, the concept of likeness is exploded. But even if such modern abstractions or post-modern synecdoches of the unique individual did not exist, likeness as a necessary attribute of portraits should be rejected.[17] Works of art of any kind rarely deceive their viewers into believing they are in the presence of their referent. (The sculptures of Duane Hanson offer one example of an effort at such deception that is frequently successful, but these are proposed as generic types rather than portraits. The generic quality itself of Hanson's stereotypes underlies their success as trompe l'oeil representations.) It is futile to define likeness, and we should be aware of how conventional is our understanding of the concept, how much it is a matter of recognition rather than definition. Instead of speaking of likeness, it is more useful to say of a portrait that in the image we should recognize, for whatever reason, a unique human referent. This allows us to embrace the many kinds of displaced or symbolic portraits that characterize the efforts of modern artists such as Matisse, Picasso, Max Beckmann, and others who have found a challenge in adapting this traditional genre to the culture of rejecting tradition.

Character, too, is a troublesome concept in portraiture. Character is also implicit in the etymology of the word portrait: "trait pour trait" in this case refers also to elements of personality. But etymology again leaves us in too abstract a realm. Whose idea of character? That a great artist can "penetrate the character" of a sitter and reveal the "real" person in a portrait is one of the hoariest clichés of art history. Character is no more immanent than portraiture is a process of psychic divination. Character is not a fixed thing, embedded in a person, to be discovered by the special insight of an artist: it is produced in any social transaction, of which portraiture is one special kind. The "character" produced in a portrait is an annealed blend of the desires and projections of the two interested parties, artist and sitter.

What, in fact, we usually mean when we say that a portrait exhibits such and such an element of character of the individual represented is either that the portrait looks "characterful" – in which case we impute the aspect of character we perceive in the portrait back onto the sitter – or that the artist has understood the sitter in a particular way and has persuaded us that this expresses his or her character. We should not imagine that all of Sargent's sitters were insouciant and superficial, something that a critic recognized in 1888: "It is all surface and no soul with most of Mr. Sargent's portraits, and the fault must lie with him, not with his sitters, for it can hardly be that all of them are as flinty and impudent in character as they appear."[18] Nor should we believe that all of Alice Neel's were insecure, or that all of Chuck Close's act like deer caught in the headlights. In 1937 Picasso painted an extraordinary portrait of his friend the writer Paul Eluard dressed in women's clothing (fig. 4). If Eluard's character had such transgressive potential, it was not apparent to those who knew him; instead Picasso has transposed an imaginative (or projective) aspect of his relationship with Eluard onto the image of his friend. We should not conclude from this that Picasso thought Eluard womanly, or that Picasso treated Eluard in this portrait in the same way that he treated his female sitters.

One measure of the impact of any great work of art is its maker's ability to persuade in that instance, in that confrontation between the individual work of art and the viewer. At different times and in different cultures it is customary for the artist to seek to convince an audience of different things, but a portrait, like many other works of art, is a tool of persuasion. To make a persuasive portrait the artist must work within prevailing standards of expression of what is counted as character, but this expression of character should not be made at the expense of the uniqueness of the sitter, or the work of art becomes something else, such as a figure study or a genre scene, not a portrait. The acknowledgment of identity within cultural norms is the single most important element of a portrait.

Definition is not the only problem. Even at the level of recognition we are far from being on firm ground. We often judge whether or not an image is a portrait by deciding its primary purpose. It makes a difference to a viewer whether a painting of a boy among trees is a portrait in the open air or a landscape with a figure, even if the figure is not anonymous. This problem of recognizing the "portrait situation" will form part of the subject of Chapter 1.

The self-portrait has traditionally been less difficult to define because the impossibility of confusion with another individual seems self-evident. Most definitions of the self-portrait assume an anterior definition of the portrait; readers of dictionaries and encyclopedias are frequently referred to the term "portrait" for enlightenment, and "portrait of the artist by himself" is the most common independent formulation of the term self-portrait. In theory the apparently self-evident quality of self-portraiture is illusory, since the self-portrait is fashioned by the same subjective source as the portrait – by an artist. So we should be reminded that any seemingly transparent qualities of the self-portrait (for example, the "window onto the soul" idea) are also fictions. The theatrical performances of themselves by Picasso, Beckmann, Egon Schiele, and Frida Kahlo should be adequate reminders of this. Self-portraits are just as surely constructions by the artist, and tools of persuasion, as portraits of others are – and perhaps even more so, because the image is not tempered by a transaction with another person. The artist's freedom to manipulate often goes unchallenged. Sincerity and transparent expression are assumed only by the unwary viewer.[19]

In part because of its apparent autonomy and candor, self-portraiture has come to seem more pertinent than ever in the twentieth century, as it distills the emphasis on the subjectivity of all art. Modernism's celebration of the individual creating author has guaranteed the status of this supremely self-validating form of authorship. By making the self into the object of art, the artist makes most explicit the conviction that an artist's work expresses first and foremost the artist's personal responses. The self-portrait is the paradigm of the self-consciousness of modern art.

4 Pablo Picasso, *Woman with a Cat: Cryptic Portrait of Paul Eluard*, 1937. Oil on canvas, 81 × 65.5 cm. Private collection.

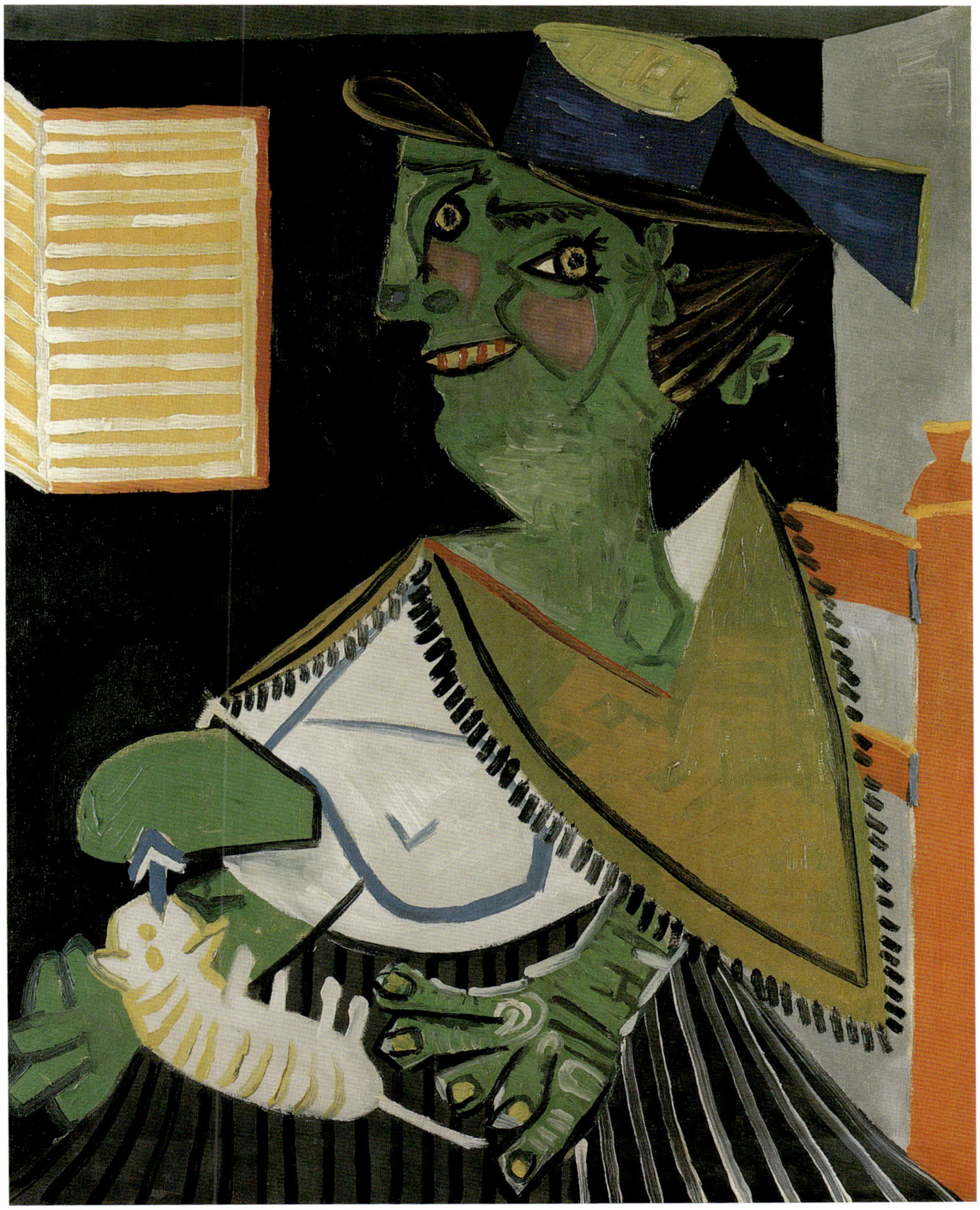

In recent decades, a different, less confident self-consciousness has arisen. The post-modern emphasis on the construction and politics of identity has brought the self-portrait and other forms of self-representation into renewed prominence, as in the work of Robert Mapplethorpe, Lorna Simpson, Cindy Sherman, or Lyle Ashton Harris.[20]

As I have implied, developments in modern art have placed considerable strain on traditional definitions of portraiture. Clearly, one of the key points of transition was brought about by the invention of photography. As photography became simpler, quicker, and more satisfying for making a permanent image of a person's physical features, the manual arts no longer provided the definitive means of recording empirical reality. So portrait painters sought to distinguish their art from what they viewed as the gross mechanical production of a mere likeness.[21] They pressed the idea that they offered more than a likeness, that through their art, they could disclose the real person behind the outward appearance. But this claim is revealed as problematic in the modern period. Increasing belief that a person's character is not what it seems, that deeply seated unconscious drives contribute strongly to behavior, made the concept of personality more fluid and multiple. The credibility of portraiture seemed more questionable than ever. Moreover, within the avant-garde an entire class of portraiture – the commissioned portrait – seemed to be in danger of disappearing. As artists sought to express themselves without constraint, the demands of a patron often came to seem too high a price to pay for the work and recognition that a commission could bring.[22]

Portraiture redefined

But the persistence of the genre in the practice of a broad range of artists must lead us to reconsider the traditional definitions.[23] As a way of addressing the conflict I have perceived between the portrait in Matisse's art and conventional ideas of the genre, I have sought to give a new definition of portraiture. As understood here, a portrait is a work of art whose principal object is any identifiable representation of a specific individual or individuals other than hired models. This definition is founded on the premise that the traditional visual and psychological components of portraiture are inadequate to an assessment of the avowed portrait practice of Matisse and many other modern artists.[24] I also believe that a substantial case can be made for all portraiture to be construed as social in origin.

This redefinition has several important virtues. Two thorny issues – the visual question of likeness and the psychological question of character – are rendered unnecessary to a sufficient definition of the portrait in Matisse's art. Visual analysis of Matisse's portrait images, and what they seem to reveal of the sitter, have been the objects of most studies of this area of his art. Visual considerations are extremely important, but I also want to emphasize what a portrait does, what role it takes in a network of social relations. In all but a few instances of the works by Matisse that I consider to be portraits, the sitter has been identified; that kind of investigation therefore has little place in this study. There is often a good reason why we lack the full names of Matisse's hired models – he (and many people since) did not feel any obligation to acknowledge their public claim to full identity as social beings. Thus we still do not know the surname of one of his most important models, Laurette, a woman who posed for some of Matisse's best-known compositions and also some riveting paintings of her head and her heavy features (see figs. 182–4). Merely to recognize a person in a work of art does not allow us to call that representation of the person a portrait. The viewer does not have complete control over the terms of definition any more than the artist does. To understand the portrait in Matisse's work as an artifact with a primary function beyond verisimilitude releases us from the traditional obligation to compare it with other images (usually photographs) of the sitter, or with witness accounts, an often fascinating but confounding procedure that is prone to inconclusion if such comparisons are made with responsible attention to the difficulties. This practice of comparison also offers a false sense of closure, as if we have done something satisfyingly systematic, by appearing to offer a "constant" against which to measure the "variable" of the artist's portrait.[25]

Detail of fig. 184 (larger than actual size).

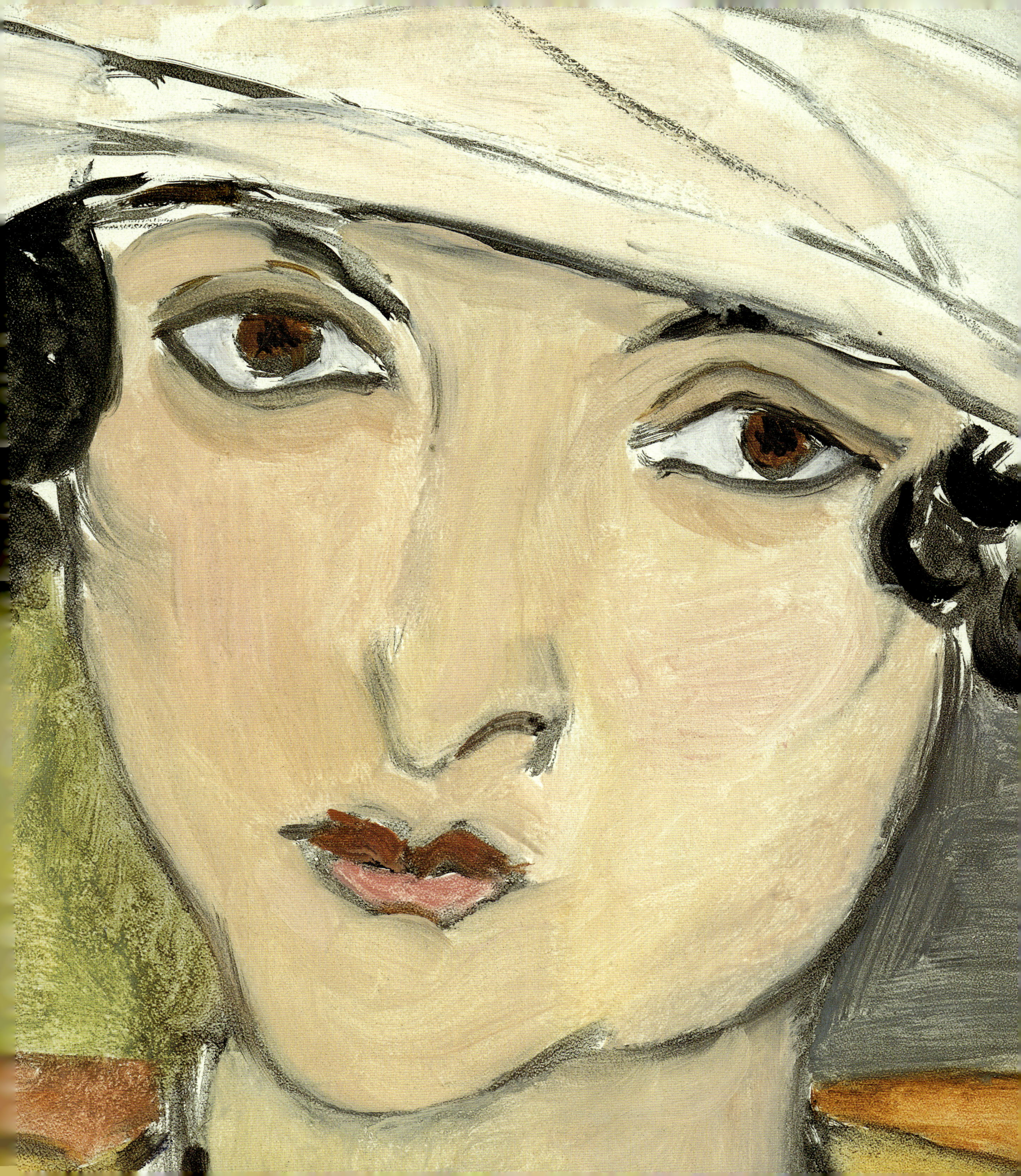

A key point in traditional definitions of the portrait is also central to what is proposed here – a concept of identity. The artist's respect for the identity of the sitter – not only the sitter's uniqueness and continuity of being, which is how identity is traditionally understood, but also his or her identity in a social context – is, I suggest, the determining factor in what makes a work of art by Matisse a portrait. This has led me to exclude from the realm of portraiture in Matisse's work what I consider to be portrait-like pictures (or sculptures) of hired models.

Representing the face and figure was fundamentally important to Matisse, as he emphatically said on a number of occasions, most famously in "Notes of a Painter" in 1908. In this formal statement of his artistic intentions he declared, "What interests me most is neither still life nor landscape, but the human figure. It is that which best permits me to express my so-to-speak religious feeling towards life."[26]

He never wavered in this commitment to the human figure as the principal motif of his art. But after 1918, a point less than midway through his long career, Matisse used hired models almost exclusively in his paintings of the figure (this dominance is less pronounced in the drawings). It is my contention that in his painting, the medium most important both to his practice and to his public image, Matisse virtually gave up portraiture. He grew tired of one of its central challenges, to balance the competing claims of the human integrity of the sitter with the artistic integrity of the painter. But he still needed the physical presence of the figure and did for many years after. In order to continue his emphasis on the figure, he substituted the economic transaction with a hired model for the social transaction with an individual from his own familial, social, or professional milieu. These individuals constitute what may be called class-equivalent sitters, whose identity made some claim on the artist. The nature of professional modeling released the artist from obligation to the individual identity of the model, since modeling was and is a socially acceptable exchange mechanism to this end. I would assert, therefore, that the depictions resulting from this transaction with a hired model are not portraits, because the relationships transacted and the identities proposed are not, or are not primarily, social. Works such as *Woman in Blue* of 1937 (see fig. 10) often look as if they might be or even must be portraits, but they cannot be. In paintings such as these, which Matisse made throughout the 1920s, '30s, and '40s, the hired model is made to look like a class-equivalent sitter for a portrait, following conventions for environment, costume, pose, and address. To put it another way, apparently individualized identities, and signs of recognized social status, are projected onto these models, who absorb them completely because that is what they have been hired to do. The hired model is a sanctioned vessel, positioned as a portrait sitter but ready to be filled with characteristics and attributes of the artist's choosing, a process that results in a simulacrum of identity and social marking. Since many of the works of art that fall into this category are among Matisse's best-known paintings and sculptures, and because many of them are readily thought of as portraits by most observers, my conviction about their separate and unequal status requires justification, which I undertake in Chapter 7.

To put it briefly here, when Matisse hired a model he bought not only access to a body to study but also freedom from obligation to the identity of another human being. By hiring a model the artist controls the economic terms, the social dynamics, and the representational possibilities in the work of art that is the outcome of their transaction. Furthermore, when the model is female and nude and the artist male and clothed, their relationship is sexualized in a one-sided way that Matisse often acknowledged both in his statements and in his art. The unilateral relationship that results from the redistribution of power by the artist–model exchange does not generally offer the possibility of the social transaction that I believe to be essential to portraiture.

The definition proposed here has some limitations. We must still recognize, without being able to define, what is the "principal object" of an image before we can call it a portrait. In my view this requirement is inherent in any definition of the portrait, and is thus unavoidable. More seriously, money paid by the artist to a sitter does not in all cases transform the sitter into a hired model, whose depiction would therefore (under my definition) not be a portrait. In 1914 Matisse paid Josette Gris, the wife of his friend Juan Gris, to sit for some small etchings and at least one drawing (figs. 95, 96). But he did this as a form of charity to relieve the precarious finances of the Gris family during the war. Benevolence toward friends was Matisse's principal motivation in this case, taking this particular relationship outside the normal transaction of professional modeling. Nor was every hired model always paid with money. Other forms of compensation, such as works of art – trade in kind – were certainly possible.[27] But Matisse's relationship with some of his models – and his artistic representations of these women – seems to have transcended the limitations of the modeling transaction, and I also consider this shifting status of some models, notably Lydia Delectorskaya.

Finally, even when we learn the name of a previously anonymous model – when, in other words, we can begin to give such a person a public identity and a social context – the status of his or her depiction might not change; it does not necessarily "become" a portrait when we learn who is represented. For instance, owing to the research of Sabine Rewald, we know the identity of the young man Matisse depicted in *Young Sailor I* (private collection) and *Young Sailor II* (New York, Metropolitan Museum of Art).[28] Germain Montargès was an eighteen-year-old fisherman. It is not known if Matisse paid the young man to sit, but it is clear that Matisse considered his model to be more significant as a type than as an individual. Despite the convincing relationship between the features of the boy in this painting and the features of his son as seen in a recent photograph of him as a middle-aged man, the paintings of the young sailor are no more portraits than the quasi-ethnographic generalizations Matisse made in his later depictions of Moroccans or Eskimos. In these instances Matisse was more interested in typicality than individuality.

In order to maintain the distinctions I have outlined here, I do not use the word model to refer to the sitter for a portrait, nor do I use the word portrait to refer to a depiction of a hired model. Thus a portrait is a restricted type of depiction, and a model is a restricted type of sitter.

The limits of self-portraiture

Many works in Matisse's oeuvre have generally been understood as surrogate or symbolic self-portraits, in which the subjective presence of the artist is implied through other personages or objects.[29] As fruitful as this approach is, a problem of limits arises when such works are considered in this way. The extreme position, absurdly unhelpful, is that, when dealing with the work of such a self-conscious artist as Matisse, every work is in some sense a self-portrait.[30] While clearly the concept of a symbolic self-portrait is connected to Matisse's expression of his self-consciousness, a hunt for them should not become a goal in itself. The self-conscious quality of certain themes in Matisse's art may be acknowledged without straining to call the expression of these themes self-portraiture. For example, the subject of the artist and model in the studio, which appears frequently throughout Matisse's career, will not generally be treated here as self-portraiture, despite an undeniable element of self-reference and sometimes self-representation.

In another class of paintings and drawings by Matisse the presence of the artist is implied through the surroundings, especially when they are viewed through a window or a door, or, in a few cases, from the interior of an automobile. When Tériade asked him in 1929 about the motif of the window in his art, Matisse replied that in such works he could represent space "from the horizon to myself, myself included. For very often I put myself in the picture, and I am aware of what exists behind me."[31] Although these compelling works cannot be considered as self-portraits, they testify to Matisse's desire for expression through other forms of self-representation, too.[32] Other paintings in which Matisse's presence is implied, such as *The Red Studio* (New York, Museum of Modern Art) and *The Painter's Family* (fig. 59), are central to an understanding of his attitude toward personal expression in his art and are specifically self-referential. Despite the absence of a recognizable effigy of the artist in paintings such as these, it seems appropriate to consider them as a kind of self-portraiture. Nevertheless, these images of surrogacy and implied self-representation will not receive the same attention as self-portraits in which it is clear that Matisse's intention to present his self-image through a direct representation of his face and body is paramount. These superficially uncomplicated images have received less attention than the apparently more complex symbolic works. One of the intentions of this book is to redress the prevailing emphasis on the symbolic side of Matisse's self-reference by concentrating on the allegedly straightforward, bodily self-images that may be referred to simply as self-portraits with no modifying idea of surrogacy or substitution.

Portraits and self-portraits in the Matisse literature

Writing about Matisse's portraits has, unsurprisingly, mirrored prevailing critical climates. The first study to consider the issue was *The Art of Henri-Matisse* by Albert Barnes and Violette de Mazia, published in 1933. In a chapter on portraiture, the authors perceptively but restrictively analyzed only the formal qualities of Matisse's depictions of individuals, who were understood as fields "for plastic, not psychological, exploration" by the artist.[33] Alfred Barr, in his landmark *Matisse: His Art and His Public* of 1951, did not devote a special section to portraiture, but he did occasionally address concentrations of these works, especially in the 1910s. Some of his analyses of individual portraits remain compelling, but in many cases the terms of his interpretation were restricted because he was writing with the artist looking over his shoulder.[34] In 1954, the year of his death, Matisse himself wrote an important essay about his attitude to portraiture and his approach to making portraits, while saying nothing about individual works by him.[35]

Later books contain many fine passages on particular paintings, drawings, prints, and sculptures, as do several catalogues of important public collections of Matisse's work.[36] Of these authors, only Pierre Schneider made a sustained attempt to identify and analyze the special conditions of portraiture in Matisse's art. While notable, the value of Schneider's attention is compromised by his insistence on an overlay of spirituality, especially in Matisse's portraits of his family, that subordinates the more pressing issues of representation and social transaction in portraiture.

Matisse's self-portraits are less numerous than his other portraits and have received less attention in the literature (this is also partly because few of them are paintings). Jack Flam was the first to write about the self-portraits as separate and significant phenomena, in a short article of 1975 that was a part of his larger effort to decipher Matisse's personal iconography.[37] In 1988 Catherine Bock published a long article on Matisse's self-portraits, studying them in conjunction with photographs taken of the artist as alternative forms of self-presentation.[38] Also in that year Dominique Szymusiak organized the first exhibition devoted to Matisse's self-portraits.[39]

The seven chapters of the present book are organized to reflect the emphasis on the social basis of portraiture. In the first chapter I explore the problems posed by portraiture of other individuals to an artist who was resolute that the goal of his art was self-expression. The next three chapters trace a movement from private to public self-expression through the development of Matisse's portraiture and self-portraiture. Chapter 2 is devoted mainly to Matisse's early self-portraits and their role in his artistic and personal self-definition. Chapter 3 concerns portraits of his family and the peculiar combination of intimacy and manipulation in such representations of people with close emotional attachments to the artist. In his portraits of fellow artists and other creative figures Chapter 4 considers a site of portraiture outside the family but not completely public, a transitional circle of people who were sympathetic to his artistic concerns.

The next two chapters examine aspects of the public character of Matisse's mature production in portraiture and self-portraiture. Chapter 5 studies his patronage and portrait commissions, and the development of his public image as a portraitist. Chapter 6 surveys Matisse's self-portraiture during the period when he had attained a measure of fame and shows how the self-portrait contributed, in the form of personalizing publicity, to Matisse's reputation, as well as offering an outlet for private concerns about the self. Finally, in Chapter 7 I consider the phenomenon of the portrait-like depiction of a hired model in Matisse's work in answer to the problems that portraiture's social dimension posed. His avoidance of the social transaction that results in a portrait is in line with his development of sign-making as a means to avoid renewed observation and representation of familiar phenomena. The sign has the same relationship to the observed physical fact as the depiction of the hired model has to a portrait. By signifying the portrait Matisse could practice the form of this genre without having to deal with the content. In this way Matisse's artistic goals exceeded the capacity of the portrait genre to express them. It is also possible to say, however, that these goals were personal and limited, and that Matisse shrank from the real human and social meaning that characterizes portraiture throughout its history.

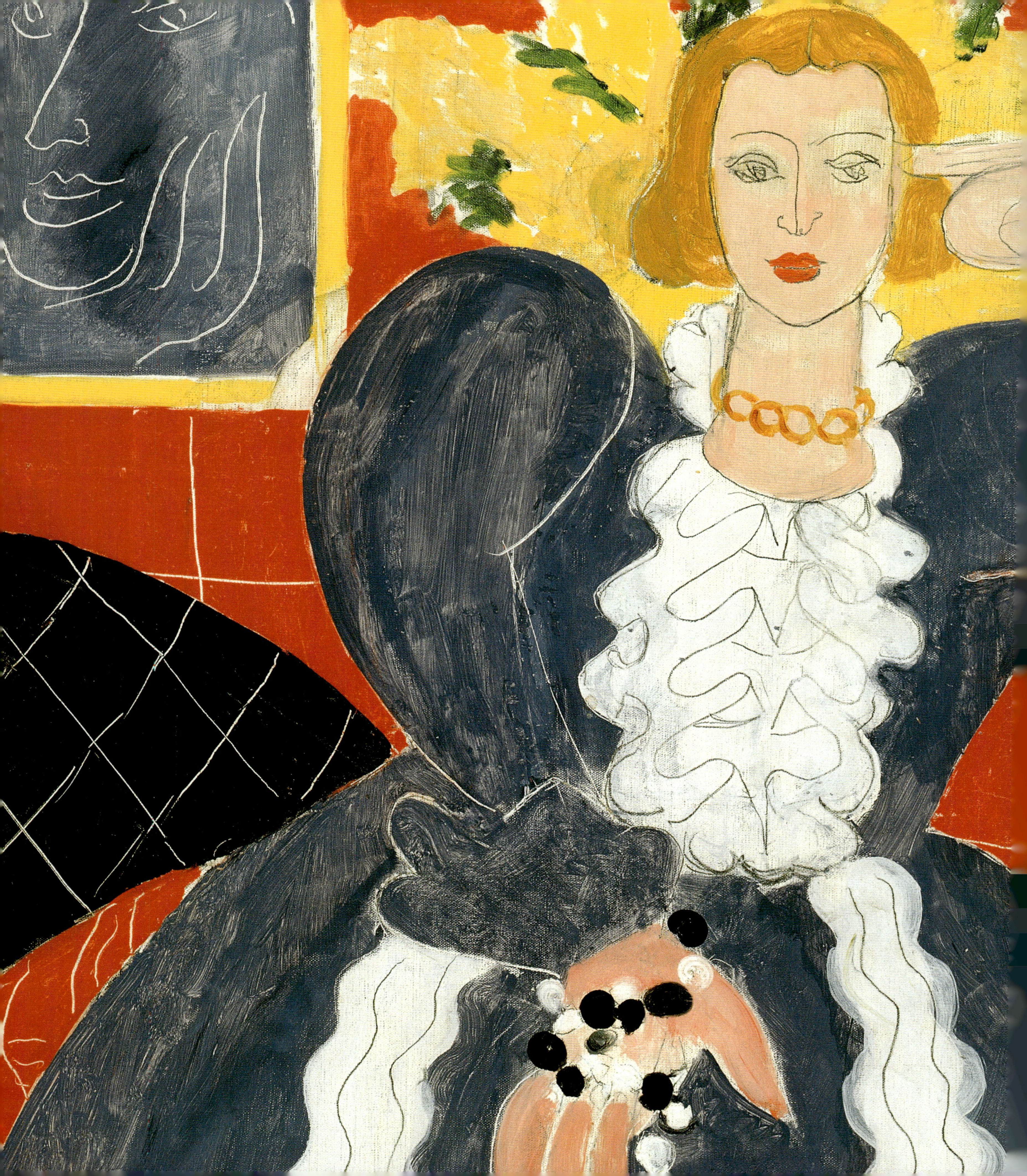

Chapter 1 The Eternal Conflict of Representation and Expression

The title of this chapter refers to one of Matisse's famous verbal formulations, in which he spoke of the importance of the "eternal conflict of drawing and color" in an artist. The possibility of resolving this conflict in his own work was, he said, what kept him going and gave him hope.[1] He believed that in his late paper cut-outs, a wholly new medium of his invention, he had finally found a way to reconcile color and line in a single work of art. He considered this to be one of his greatest achievements.

In framing this conflict within the context of differing basic artistic practices, Matisse echoed a nearly ceaseless debate about the purposes of art: should artists concern themselves with essence or appearance? Should they represent what is there or express what they see? Drawing and color have often been enlisted as convenient shorthand terms in this more complex dialogue about art's goal: *disegno* and *colore* in the Renaissance stood virtually for opposing world views. Debate continued through the seventeenth century between the *poussinistes* and the *rubénistes*. At other times the larger issues have been cast as intellect *vs.* senses, Classic *vs.* Romantic, academy *vs.* avant-garde, Realism *vs.* Impressionism, Impressionism *vs.* Symbolism, Cubism *vs.* Fauvism, and so forth. The need for dialogic struggle of this kind in contemporary art theory and criticism has rarely flagged.

Even by Matisse's time this set of oppositions, most consistently gathered under the labels of Classicism and Romanticism, was still forceful. Because he is so famous as an artist of vivid color and its associations with sensuality, Matisse is usually thought of as a more "romantic" than "classic" artist – occasionally he even referred to himself as a romantic; but on one occasion he quickly qualified this by asserting that he had "a good half of the scientist, the rationalist, which makes for the struggle from which I emerge sometimes victorious, but breathless."[2] There is certainly some justice to the romantic label applied to Matisse (and there are other reasons to think about him in this way), but Matisse himself usually hedged, and there is some indication that he did not want to be seen to take sides in this debate. If he was a romantic artist, he knew that becoming one had entailed close attention to the "classic." For instance, he approved of the heterodox tastes of his admired teacher, Gustave Moreau, who "one day . . . would affirm his admiration for Raphael, another, for Veronese" – embracing, in other words, Renaissance painters renowned, respectively, for their mastery of drawing and color, and standing in for the oppositional terms of the period.[3] Moreau, too, is usually considered more a romantic than a classic artist, but to Matisse he was an enlightened eclectic, capable of endorsing work of quality at any point on the ideological spectrum. Matisse's early homages seem catholic too. When he addressed himself to copying paintings

Detail of fig. 10.

enshrined in the Louvre, he favored eighteenth-century French models, and copied Delacroix and Annibale Carracci too, but also took on Poussin, Prud'hon, and, several years later, Raphael himself. In 1908, by which time he was well known as an expressive colorist, he nevertheless insisted that the students in his art school pay attention to their drawing. In Hans Purrmann's recollection, the emphasis in Matisse's instruction was on "adhering to nature and trying to portray it with exactness."[4] Certainly there is an element of "do as I say not as I do" counsel from the wise elder in this but, more importantly, he felt he had never renounced the fundamental role of drawing and design in his art, and he never would. Colorist, romantic, expressionist, Matisse nevertheless depended on drawing, a classical sense of order, and the reality check of observed things to act as a governor on the engine of imagination.

For Matisse, the more profound conflict, more complex than that between line and color, was between representation and expression. It was the principal artistic antinomy of his time, one that led eventually to non-objective art – the complete abandonment of representation – in the hands of Kandinsky, Dove, or Kupka. The centrality of this opposition at the time of Matisse's formation is indicated in the questionnaire of 1905 that the art critic Charles Morice distributed to contemporary artists in France. Morice's final question posed just this choice between representation and expression: "In your view, should the artist expect everything from nature or take from it only the plastic means to realize his own thought?"[5] The path of abstraction was obviously not for Matisse; he nearly always anchored his expressive extremes in his observation of material things, and never relinquished completely some vestige of their visual appearance. But Matisse is one of the artists of the end of the nineteenth and the beginning of the twentieth centuries for whom the weight of reference in the work of art shifted decisively, and with no recanting, from things in the world to the artist's sensibility, from object to subject. Still the object was necessary: based on his training and on his respect for tradition, as well as some innate conservatism, he sought in his art to attend to the world's appearance and to make a rendering of this appearance in his art. Yet he was also convinced that the higher purpose of art should be to use the things of the world and the means of the artist to express his emotional response, which is what gives the world meaning for each individual. The definitive statement in his major theoretical treatise "Notes of a Painter" (1908) – "What I am after, above all, is expression" – asserts this goal of art and serves as Matisse's response to Morice's question.[6] Whereas Matisse felt he could reconcile drawing and color, it was not possible to reconcile representation and expression. These goals of art are antithetical; all he could do was to try to hold them in balance so that he could be true to his personal drives without losing contact with observable reality. He sought this balance in all his art, but portraiture presented special problems in this regard.

History or fiction?

In his "Salon of 1846" Charles Baudelaire announced "two ways of understanding portraiture: history and fiction." The historical portrait, Baudelaire went on to explain, was more faithful to the sitter's physical qualities and mental attitudes; the method of the fictional portrait, by contrast, "consists in making a picture out of a portrait," which "is more difficult, because it is more ambitious."[7] For the artist who makes a picture out of a portrait, "imagination plays a greater part, and yet, just as fiction is often truer than history, so a sitter may be more clearly interpreted by the rich and skilful brush of a colourist than by the pencil of a draughtsman." As examples of portraitists who adhere to a historical approach Baudelaire cited David and Ingres – classicists and conspicuous masters of linear drawing. He identified as the leaders of the fictional method Rembrandt, Reynolds, and Lawrence – not Romantic artists, of course, but ones committed to the component of personal expression in their art. For Baudelaire, the artists who in this way used their imagination – what he famously called the "queen of the faculties" – were the modern artists.[8]

As traditionally understood, portrayal is a subset of representation, and portraiture is a part of the practice of representation with special claims on fidelity to appearance. Baudelaire turns this alignment around to assert that the portrait should answer primarily to the artist, not the sitter. In his view "a portrait is a model complicated by an artist," an aphorism worthy of Matisse.[9] Matisse's approach to portraiture was distinctly Baudelairean, as we shall see, but not without a fight with tradition (an opponent he could not, and did not want to, dismiss), and not without some contradiction in his statements about portraiture. Here it is worth surveying these statements to see how contradictory his expressed attitudes to the genre could be. His shifting expressions about the value and purpose of the portrait illuminate his ambivalence toward a genre he wished for many reasons to embrace but whose responsibilities in the social sphere he could not sustain.

What Matisse said about portraiture

Perhaps it is too much to ask of anyone that their statements about a given topic made over a long period of time be absolutely consistent. But there are different reasons for inconsistency, and with an artist as self-conscious and as adept in verbal expression as Matisse we should look beyond conventional allowances and consider deliberate as well as inadvertent changes in his posture. Moreover, most of his significant statements about portraiture are from late in his career, when he had a complete idea of his goals as an artist, even if new means of achieving these goals could still be discovered. Matisse's writings are full of paradoxes, and Jack Flam has argued persuasively that many of his statements about art were intended as deflections of matters that could be inferred from an examination of his art, matters of which he either was not aware or did not want to be admitted into its interpretation.[10] In writing he often took a defensive posture, responding to what he believed was misunderstanding of his work. This led him at times to adjust his rhetoric according to the demands of the occasion.

On two occasions, both late in his career, Matisse made extended statements about portraiture. In the earlier essay, "L'Exactitude n'est pas la vérité" (1947; Exactitude is not Truth), he meditates on the differences among four drawings he made of himself (fig. 5).[11] They are "portraits perhaps." He compares the drawings to forms in nature, such as fig leaves, which for all their individual variations have a common structure, an irreducible identity, that makes them fig leaves. Appearance alone cannot be used to judge similarity or difference: "there exists an essential truth that must be disengaged from the outward appearance of the objects to be represented. This is the only truth that matters." Likewise he goes on to examine the differences in expression among these self-portraits, but emphasizes the essential similarity of their internal relationships, concluding "that this ensemble of

5 *Four Self-Portraits*, 1939. Crayon on paper, each approx. 37.5 × 26.5 cm. Private collection. As reproduced in *Henri Matisse: Retrospective Exhibition of Paintings, Drawings, and Sculpture*, 1948.

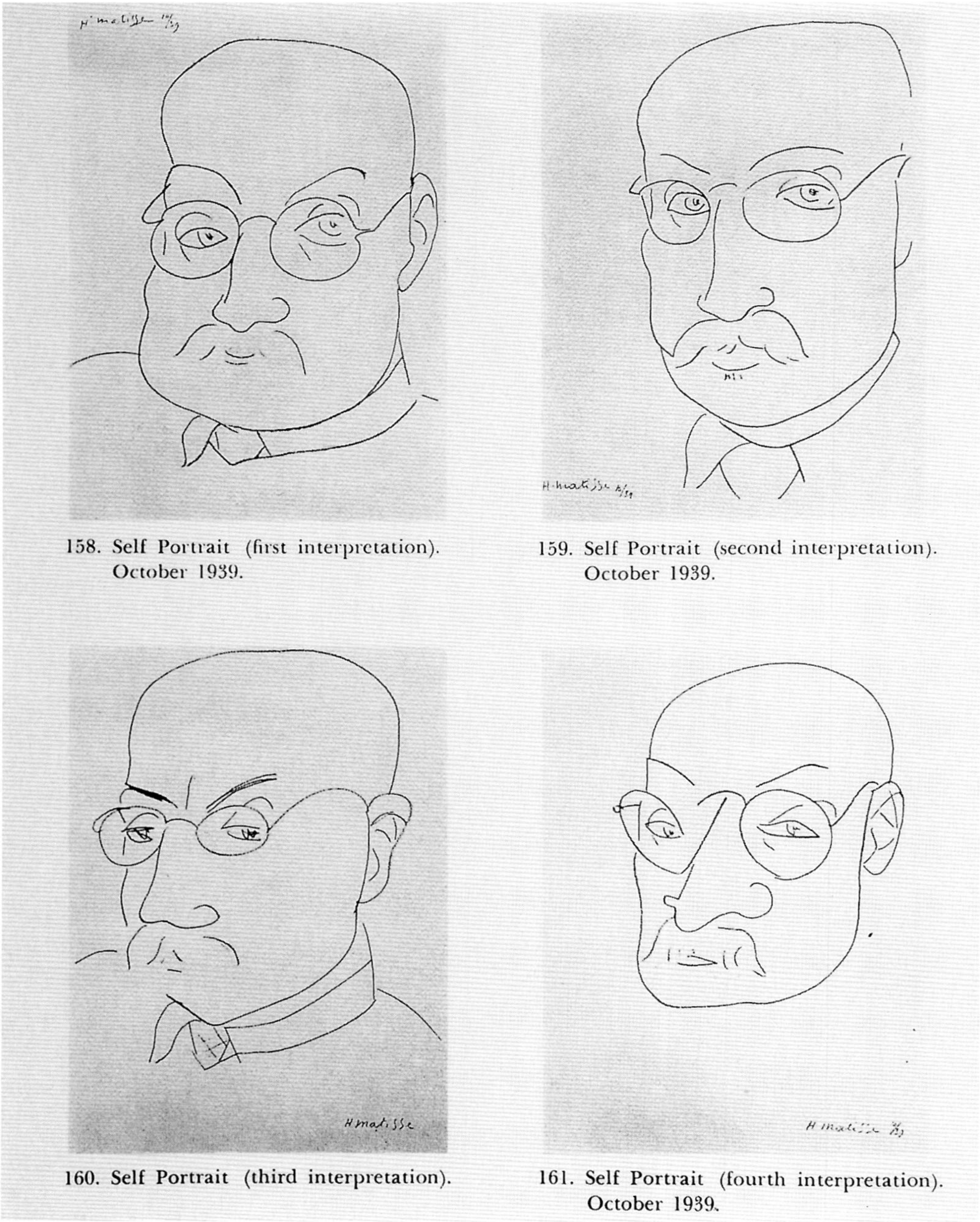

elements describes the same man, in terms of his character, his personality, his way of considering things, his reaction to life, and in terms of the reserve he displays in relation to life which keeps him from uncontrolled surrender to it. It is indeed the same man, who always remains an attentive spectator of life and of himself."

He then returns to the central question and asks rhetorically if the drawings are portraits or not; his indirect response makes it clear that he believes they are because they transcend the differences in detail to arrive at essential qualities. The artist has penetrated the contingencies of surface appearance to express the truth of the sitter, "the only truth that matters." Thus Matisse's Baudelairean assertion: "Exactitude is not truth."

On the second occasion he was less oblique. In 1954 he was asked to compose a text to accompany an album of reproductions published as *Portraits*.[12] This essay is a more thorough explication of his practice of and attitudes to portraiture. But it has in common with "L'Exactitude n'est pas la vérité" the idea that the artist making a portrait first works to clear away details in his or her mental image of the model, then finds and expresses the essence of the model, either in a single image or – as with the four self-portraits – in a series of drawings whose differing details do not prevent a structural truth from being evident. In both essays it is clear that Matisse describes a working procedure and proposes a theory of representation that apply more or less to all his late work but especially to his drawing practice along the lines of the "Thèmes et variations" he began to make in the 1930s. The basic procedure of the themes and variations was this: Matisse made one or more drawings in charcoal or pencil from the model, working on them heavily and over a period of perhaps several days. Such a drawing would be erased and begun again, scrubbed and adjusted until, as he said, "I am surprised to see an image that is a more or less precise likeness of the person with whom I am in contact gradually appear on my paper." Then, after an interval following the "meager result" of this analytic process, he either went on to make a painting from this model, or he rapidly made a series of drawings (the "variations") that "spring forth in one piece, constituted of elements without apparent coordination to the analysis that preceded them."[13] Saying little in these essays about the act of painting a portrait, Matisse concentrates on the practice of drawing from the model, a central part of his artistic activity for the last twenty years of his career.[14]

In these programmatic and self-conscious statements about his current working procedure at a time when his career was well advanced Matisse fashions an image of harmony and satisfaction: harmony between himself and his model; congruity between the model and the images he made of her; pleasure for Matisse himself in reaching a felicitous conclusion. Like most artists, he preferred to talk about fresh concerns and not old business. It is also not surprising that, especially when he was asked specifically to write about portraiture, he should present his practice of the genre as both satisfying and exemplary. Portraiture is presented here as a natural and representative part of his overall artistic practice of working from nature. But because he restricted his discussion to recent work using hired female models, which resulted principally in drawings, we learn nothing from these statements about Matisse's attitude to some of the more contested portrait transactions from earlier in his career, or about the circumstances under which he had agreed to make those portraits. No doubt his sense of discretion would have prevented him from talking out of school about a portrait transaction with a class-equivalent sitter that had not evolved as planned or had ended badly.[15] He also characteristically preferred to discuss general procedures rather than specific works of art. But it is significant that in these essays Matisse described an idealized activity, a Platonic version of the process of portraiture. He achieved this state of grace for the portrait transaction only through his deployment of the hired model. This was portraiture the way he liked it, without demands or conflicts, a process completely in his control.

A number of briefer comments about portraiture, however, reveal contradictory attitudes. Some of these remarks seem quite offhand, and it may be argued that at such moments Matisse was not saying what he really meant to say. But, as we know, the unguarded expression may be the most revealing. From some of these

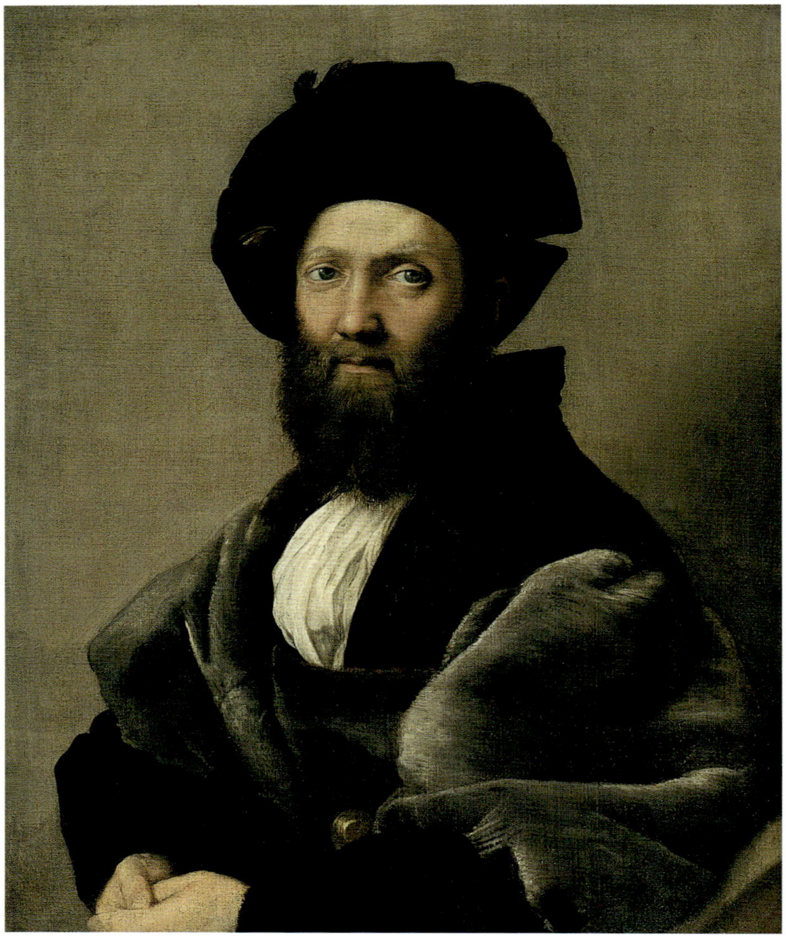

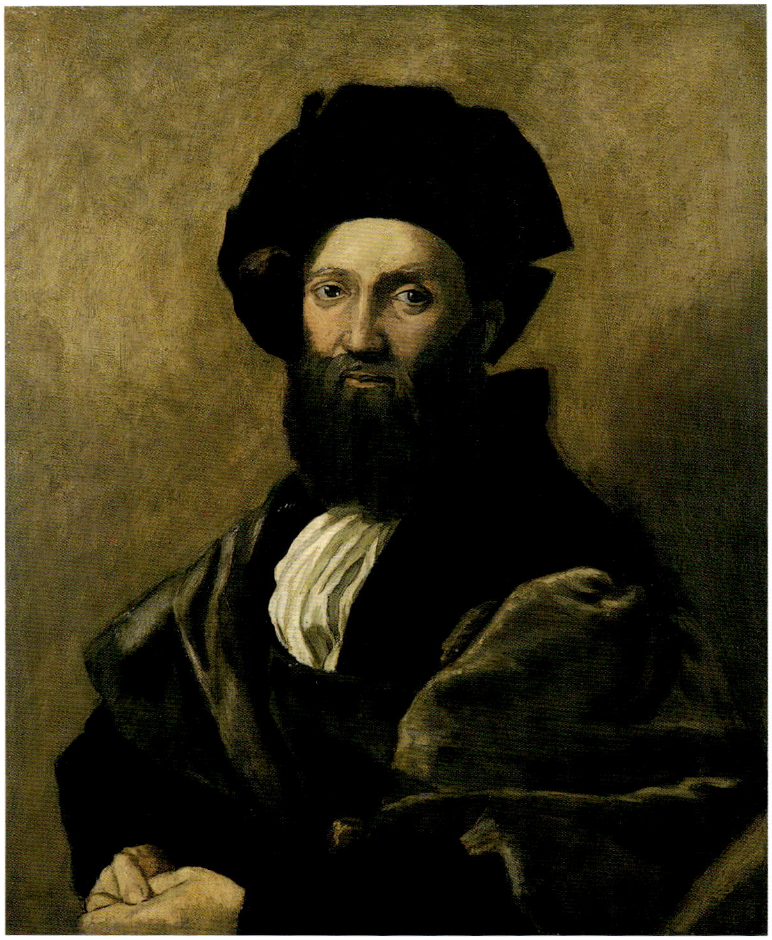

6 (*above left*) Raphael, *Baldassare Castiglione*, 1514–15. Oil on canvas, 82 × 67 cm. Paris, Musée du Louvre.

7 (*above right*) Copy after Raphael's *Baldassare Castiglione*, 1904. Oil on canvas, 82 × 67 cm. Bagnols-sur-Cèze, Musée Albert André.

comments it is clear that he pejoratively associated the practice of portraiture with niggling and self-defeating attention to detail, unworthy of an artist with the ambition to express himself in his work. He spoke in 1942 of "the painter who composes on the grand scale," by which he meant himself, who "cannot stop over details, paint each detail *as if it were a portrait*, make the portrait of a different hand each time . . ."[16] He went on to characterize "two sorts of artists, some who on each occasion paint the portrait of a hand, a new hand each time, Corot for instance, and the others who paint the sign for a hand, like Delacroix. With signs you can compose freely and ornamentally . . ."[17] According to this statement, a portrait of something pays too much attention to appearance, and it is preferable to devise a shorthand, a "sign" for the motif. But this process of sign-making accords with his statements in "Portraits" and "L'Exactitude n'est pas la vérité" about finding the essential structure of his sitter when making a portrait. Is such sign-making, then, consistent with portraiture or not?

Contradiction arises also in the way Matisse enlisted earlier artists in his discussions of portraiture. His invocation of Raphael is particularly significant. On one hand, for example, he said in the 1950s that Raphael's portrait of Baldassare Castiglione in the Louvre (fig. 6) had "revealed to him what the art of the portrait should be."[18] In need of money in 1904, Matisse had made a full-size copy of the painting for sale to the state (fig. 7).[19] It is a fine, lightly interpretive rendering, far from slavish but clearly the product of careful study. Raphael's painting of Castiglione has had a long history of admiring commentary and, although at the time of his statement Matisse was probably indulging in hyperbole, it is clear that he continued to think highly of this Renaissance essay in subtle color and rhyming form. On the other hand, in "L'Exactitude n'est pas la vérité" he dismissed Raphael's *Joanna of Aragon* (fig. 8), also familiar to Matisse from all his time spent in the Louvre, by implying with a sneering rhetorical question that this painting is not "really what can be called a portrait."[20] Although its stylizations were no more thorough than those of Castiglione's portrait (they may have been more obvious), Matisse's coy peevishness toward the portrait of Joanna of Aragon may reflect his distaste for Mannerism. In this late work by Raphael, largely executed in his workshop, can be found elements of the bizarre distortions that Matisse's nineteenth-century training warned against (but that were later cherished by the Surrealists). Still, there is reason to think Matisse a little disingenuous when we consider some of the mannerisms in his own late work, as in the stylized pose of the model in his painting *Woman in Blue* of 1937 (fig. 10). Here the arrangement of hands and body owes a debt to Ingres's *Madame Moitessier* (fig. 9), whose distended hands in turn are a direct descendant of the contrived pose of Raphael's sitter Joanna. Matisse's ludicrous costume piece is clearly part of the heritage, dubious though he thought it might be, of these late portraits, similarly excessive, by past masters.

About another artist he recruited in the name of portraiture, Rembrandt, Matisse was more consistent, but with some bizarre conclusions. Rembrandt was one of the artists of the past Matisse admired the most. In his statements he referred to him frequently, and he modestly likened the expressive goals of his own art to Rembrandt's mastery of suggestion and emotional expression. Even more than Delacroix, another artist Matisse respected highly, Rembrandt was "noble."[21] On at least two occasions he called attention to a statement he attributed to Rembrandt: "I have never painted anything but portraits."[22] Whatever this could have meant in Rembrandt's mind (if in fact Rembrandt ever said such a thing), for Matisse it was important to call on this most admired painter to validate his own exposition on portraiture. Associating Rembrandt with portraiture was a way of elevating the genre as well as enhancing by association Matisse's practice of it.[23]

Rembrandt is invoked in another comparison. Matisse sometimes made a distinction between ordinary portraits and what he called "true portraits." Along with Holbein, Dürer, Lucas Cranach, and Quentin de Latour, Northerners like Matisse himself, Rembrandt made "true portraits," attentive to the peculiarities – the details – of their sitters' faces. To these artists Matisse opposed "the Southerners who usually tend to consolidate everything into a regular type, a symmetrical structure." Here Matisse contrasts freshness and alertness to the particular with repeated formulas of the kind he associated with Raphael and Italian art.[24] But even here he was inconsistent. His favor toward the detail-oriented makers of "true portraits" contradicts his only slightly earlier criticism of those painters who "paint each detail as if it were a portrait."[25] He could not seem to reconcile the need for portraiture to individualize with his disdain for attention to the particular.

In a way, there was no need for consistency here. Both alternatives – the detailed and the formulaic – are insufficient in light of his belief that "the essential expression of the work depends almost entirely on the projection of the feeling of the artist in relation to his model rather than on the organic exactitude of the model."[26] For Matisse all art, portraiture included, required this projection of the artist's

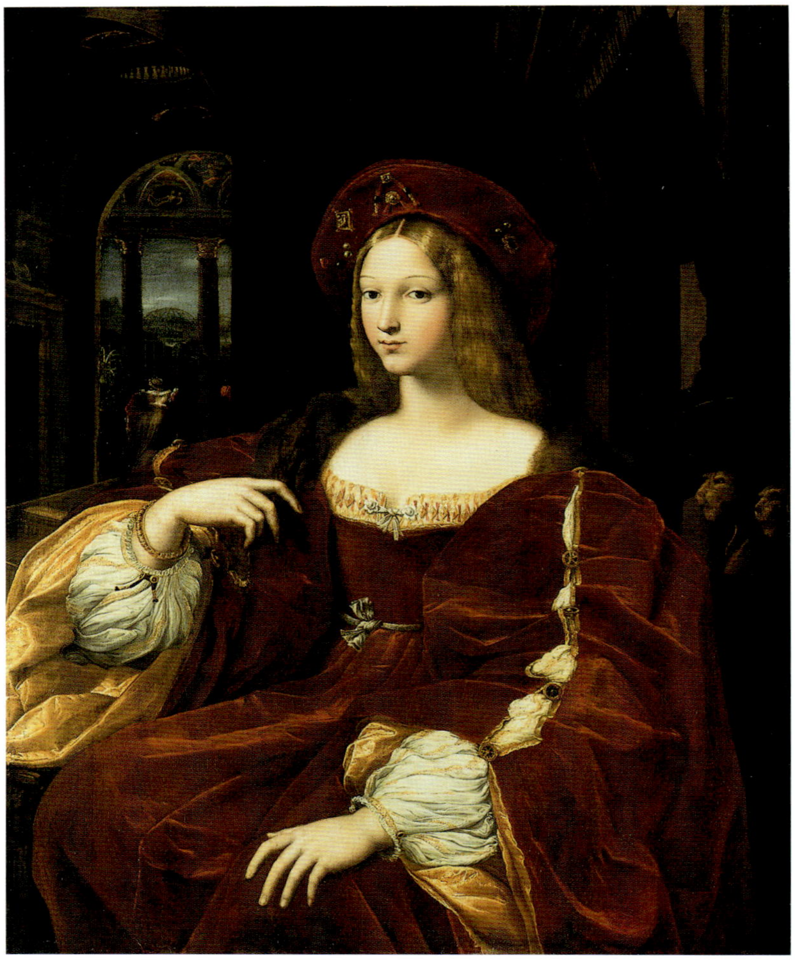

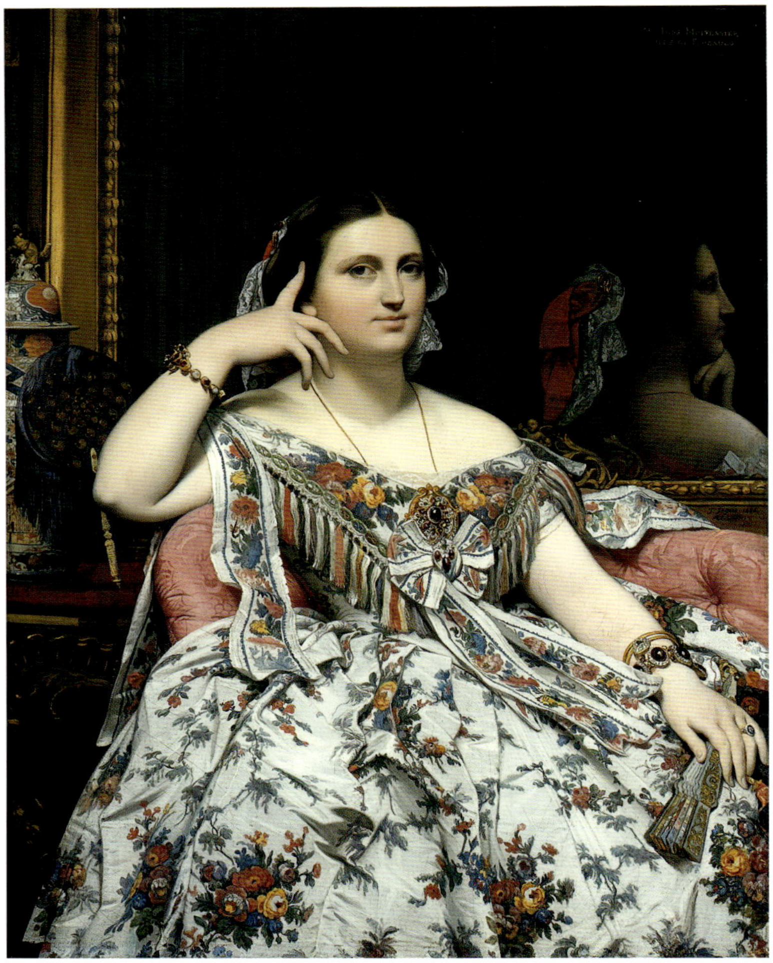

8 (*above left*) Raphael, *Joanna of Aragon*, ca. 1518. Oil on panel transferred to canvas, 120 × 95 cm. Paris, Musée du Louvre.

9 (*above right*) Jean-Auguste-Dominique Ingres, *Madame Moitessier*, 1856. Oil on canvas, 120 × 92 cm. London, The National Gallery.

sensibility, which at an early time he had characterized as the principal goal of artistic composition, "the art of arranging in a decorative manner the diverse elements at the painter's command to express his feelings."[27] Decoration and expression would be coincident.

Which brings us finally to Matisse's response to a question put to him in 1912 by an interviewer who asked if he painted portraits: "No; I seldom paint portraits, and if I do only in a decorative manner. I can see them in no other way."[28] Leaving aside the fact that in the two years preceding he had painted many portraits of family and friends, and that he had also undertaken a few portrait commissions, Matisse's statement asserted a priority for self-expression that was not to change. Composition, decoration, expression of feeling, these formulations became virtually synonymous in Matisse's mind, and their competition with the human element of his sitters was the central conflict in his portraiture. Most of his statements about portraiture indicate in one way or another his avowal to engage – or to be seen to engage – one of the grand artistic traditions. Yet Matisse also seems to have harbored for portraiture a special if veiled contempt. He once declared pithily that "a portrait is a feud."[29] He was clearly not referring to the harmonious ideal that he wrote about in "L'Exactitude n'est pas la vérité" and "Portraits," but to a contested transaction of the kind that he engaged in many times but did not relish. This deep and fruitful ambivalence resulted in some of his most striking and original works,

10 *Woman in Blue*, 1937. Oil on canvas, 92.7 × 73.6 cm. Philadelphia Museum of Art, gift of Mrs. John Wintersteen.

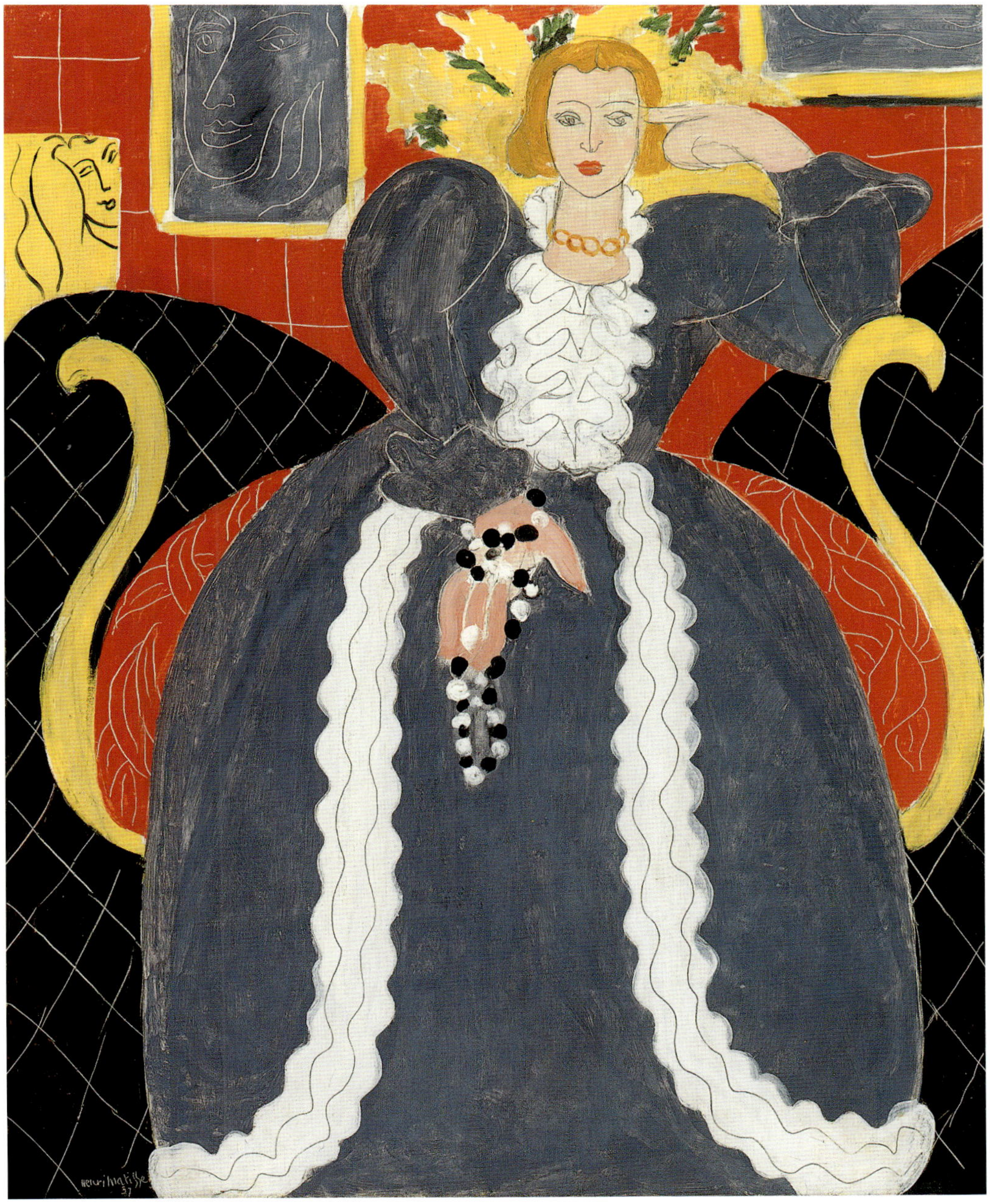

portraits that were products not of harmony and control, but of conflict, compromise, and consolidation.

Abstraction and archetype

In his essay of 1954 on portraits Matisse described an experience that left a lasting impression on him, calling it "the revelation at the post office." He found this curious episode significant to his understanding of portraiture. His framing of the incident is worth quoting at some length:

> The revelation of my life in the study of the portrait came to me in thinking of my mother. In a post office in Picardy, I was waiting for a telephone call. To

> pass the time I picked up a telegraph form lying on a table, and drew a woman's head on it with a pen. I drew without thinking of what I was doing, my pen going by itself, and I was surprised to recognize my mother's face with all its subtleties. My mother had a face with generous features, the highly distinctive traits of French Flanders.
>
> I was still a pupil occupied with "traditional" drawing, anxious to believe in the rules of the school, remnants of the teaching of the masters who came before us: in a word, the dead part of tradition, in which all that was not actually observed in nature, all that derived from feeling or memory was scorned and condemned as "bogus." I was struck by the revelations of my pen, and I understood that the mind which is composing should keep a sort of virginity in relation to certain chosen elements and reject what comes to it by reasoning.
>
> Before the revelation at the post office, I used to begin my study by a kind of schematic indication, coolly conscious, showing the reasons for the interest that had sparked my interpretation of the model. But after this experience, the preliminary indication I have just mentioned was modified right from the very beginning. Having cleansed and emptied my mind of all preconceived ideas, I drew this preliminary outline with a hand completely given over to my unconscious sensations, which sprang from the model. I was careful not to introduce any deliberate observation into this representation, or even to correct a physical error.[30]

Matisse's revelation is difficult to date precisely, but it took place early in his career, when he was, he says, "still a pupil occupied with 'traditional' drawing." A likely date is 1903, when he was living with his wife and children in Picardy where they were dependent on his parents for more than a year. (In these circumstances it is easy to imagine why he might have had his mother on his mind.[31])

But the meaning of this incident lies in psychic realms well beyond the circumstance of being temporarily in his family's neighborhood. Intending to draw a picture of a woman, Matisse found that when his mind was "cleansed and emptied . . . of all preconceived ideas," his hand unconsciously formed the image of his mother. The face that emerged in the absence of rational control was the very face that had confronted him when he had been inherently without mental preconceptions – in the first moments, hours, and days of life. The first face, the mother's face, the Ur-face for all others thereafter – in Matisse's discovery of this archetype lay the significance of the revelation at the post office.[32] He was using this unconscious emergence of an archetypal face as a way of talking about the process of abstraction in his work, a process that was integral to his portraiture.[33] But contrary to his assertion that, as a result of this incident, he began to reject the powers of "deliberate observation," direct contact and observation remained crucial to his method for many years, and his portraiture also required this confrontation.[34] His reliance on physical presence is in stark contrast to Picasso's practice in portraiture (as well as many other genres), in which his use of photographs frequently complemented or even supplanted direct contact with a sitter.[35]

Not a rejection of empiricism, Matisse's unbidden peek into his unconscious revealed to him the wider meaning of archetypes for his art-making. The revelation was that behind the face of any particular individual lay a more general model for a face. In this instance, his unconscious showed him that his mother's face was the lowest common denominator for the face of a – any – woman.[36] Something had intervened between the two faces, something outside Matisse's control. Such a deeply subconscious operation as that suggested by the revelation at the post office sets out the greatest possible extreme of displacement from conscious observation. In conscious procedures of representation, portraiture among them, the mind usually seeks a closer analogy, whether visual, symbolic, or otherwise, between depiction and what is depicted. Below the surface, anything may be possible, but consciousness generally seeks to narrow the possibilities available to it, not widen them.

Self-evidently, the conscious mind cannot direct itself to intervene passively, in the way that Matisse's unconscious had done at the post office: consciousness is active and self-aware. Nevertheless, Matisse, like the Surrealists, seemed to believe that the artist could, if properly disposed, harness the unconscious at will and make it serve his art. Here he is again on making portraits after the lesson he absorbed from his psychic experience: "Having cleansed and emptied my mind of all preconceived ideas, I drew this preliminary outline with a hand completely given over to my unconscious sensations, which sprang from the model." This initial drawing was then the basis for further, conscious, operations: "The almost unconscious transcription of the meaning of the model is the initial act of every work of art, particularly of a portrait. Following this, reason takes charge, holds things in check and makes it possible to have new ideas using the initial work as a springboard."[37] The artist wills himself to the state of a blank slate; in this condition of suspended consciousness he acts as a medium for the transmission of sensation; then his conscious mind returns to bring order to the image that his receptive state has led him to deposit on the canvas or page.

It is not necessary to question the quality of Matisse's belief in the power of the unconscious. But there may be a simpler and more compelling explanation for just how he used this power. Contrary to his statement that he wanted to avoid "preconceived ideas," a basic mode of preconception was at the heart of his approach to depicting the human face and figure. The mental process Matisse described permitted (or forced) him to develop a means of generalizing from the particular features of the person before him. This process of generalization became a routine. Early in his career Matisse had developed what became for him a useful habit – a habit of abstraction.

Habit is one of the most significant areas in which human activity is influenced by unconscious structures for conscious behavior. Habits can be consciously induced, but once established they can be difficult to will away or change. Gustave Moreau had seen the possibility of Matisse's habit of abstraction: "You are going to simplify painting," he had said to his student.[38] The general and theoretical nature of Matisse's most important writings indicate his tendency to abstraction in his thought about art. This will to abstraction was tantamount for Matisse to the expression of his emotion, "the profound feeling of the artist before the objects he has chosen," which allowed him to extract "an essential truth . . . from the outward appearance" of these objects.[39] Determining and giving visual form to this essential truth, as he understood it, was, as we have seen, his primary motivation in portraiture.

For although Matisse usually relied on close observation of a sitter, he did so to derive general laws from particular appearances. Such derivation is different from mere simplification, but depends on it. Simplification was the unconscious, habitual procedure on which he based his more concerted goal: determining an essence in things and people. To a great degree this goal is present in all his work, not only portraiture. Observed detail was a necessary stimulus, but making a work of art required a substructure so that detail would not simply bewilder or bore. To get the better of detail, Matisse sought the archetypal or essential in his subjects.

In his writings and statements we find many avowals of this process of moving from the particular to the general. From 1908 in "Notes of a Painter" ("I . . . condense the meaning of [a woman's] body by seeking its essential lines," its "truer, more essential character") to 1954, writing directly of his procedure in portraiture ("The conclusions made during the first confrontation fade away to reveal the most important features, the living substance of the work"), Matisse consistently emphasized this process of generalization that grounded his art.[40]

Particular and general

As we have seen, late in his career (1947), he devoted an entire essay to this idea. "L'Exactitude n'est pas la vérité" addresses the relationship between the particular and the general in art. In it Matisse asserts that exactitude corresponds to particular appearances, but that truth can be derived only from generalization. The particularities of appearance are contingent, but these particularities contain something in common, something intangible. This essence, extracted and expressed by the artist, is the truth lying beneath the surface. Whether the process of deriving this truth is called distillation, abstraction, or sign-formation (as Matisse eventually called it), it amounts to the same desire to generalize from visual appearance to arrive at a more profound expression both of the motif's fundamental structure and of Matisse's response to it. So this truth has two components, which only the artist can realize.

This brings us to the importance of the artist's response to a motif in the process of abstraction. Response itself is a process of generalization. Response abstracts. We see only selectively, and we respond only selectively to what we have seen.[41] We respond by incorporating the contingent experience into the total fund of past experiences for comparison. Our response to a thing or event results from a complicated process of such comparisons, by which we place the new in the context of the old. In this way the particularity of the new stimulus is made meaningful by being related to similar things we already know about – that is, by being compared and generalized. We do this with people as well as with sunsets or world records in sport.

The differing demands of the particular and the general, between detail and essence – even between stimulus and response – are not easy for the artist to reconcile in making a work of art. It is clear that in retrospect Matisse was aware of this conflict over most of his career, as when he spoke much later of the reason that drawing was so important to him at the turn of the century: "At this time I focused particularly on drawing – on exactness and inexactness. . . . The blending of these two things was the goal of my work."[42] To fuse in a single image "exactness and inexactness" – particularity and generalization or abstraction – was an elusive goal, and proved to be even more difficult to achieve in portraiture (which may be part of the reason that, toward the end of his career, Matisse wrote of these achievements with such satisfaction).

The conflict between the particular and the general is always difficult to reconcile in portraiture, especially when portraiture is construed primarily as a process of visual representation. In fact, this conflict is one of the central philosophical problems for the portrait artist, and it has far-reaching implications for portrait practice. In the peculiarities of visible physiognomy are found the signs by which we distinguish one individual from another. In other words, a person is seen as individual by virtue of his or her difference from other individuals. Matisse's way of saying this was that "the likeness of a portrait comes from the contrast that exists between the face of the model and other faces, in a word from its particular asymmetry."[43] But in portraiture there is a danger in being too specific, as well.

The portrait, the individual, and the group

Portraiture since the Renaissance calls on the viewer to recognize the sitter's individuality. To the extent that we do, we presume that the portrait is a "likeness" of the individual depicted. And yet if the depiction is too particularized, it may not persuade us of the sitter's individuality, because, in a seeming paradox, it is not characteristic – not general – enough. The danger of over-particularization may be present whether or not we are personally acquainted with the sitter. This is one reason why death masks, or even life masks, are not good likenesses.[44] How people look to us is instead based either on a composite of their appearance to us at numerous moments over time, sifted into an image that we take as typical, or on one attitude or "look" that comes to stand for the whole person. Satisfaction of the sense of recognition thus demands that the individual be presented in a manner that the viewer is convinced is typical of that individual.

Furthermore, in order to prompt the viewer's presumption that a depiction of a person may contain the qualities of visual resemblance that would link it to an individual, such a depiction must be recognized as a portrait in the first place. This need for the portrait to look like a portrait is the first key to its comprehension as a depiction of a unique individual, whether or not likeness is an issue.[45] To be understood as a portrait, it is first necessary for the image to conform to any number of conventions (social, psychological, pictorial, environmental) that help the viewer to recognize its type, the portrait type. A degree of typing is necessary for proper comprehension of the image and its messages about the sitter.

For instance, sometimes pictorial and psychological factors combine to encourage, or deny, identification of a picture as a portrait. Consider a figure in a landscape painting. The figure may be identifiable as a given person, but if our conventions for reading the picture (granted these are complicated) place it in the category of landscape, then the question of the likeness of the human depiction to its referent is less relevant. Whether or not we comprehend the depiction as a portrait will depend on such factors as the size and format of the picture, the scale of the figure in the pictorial field, lighting, distribution of emphasis across the picture surface, or, even more arbitrarily (because the artist's intention may no longer operate), how the picture is labeled, and the context in which it is displayed. Any judgment of the "portraitness" of a depiction will be subjective, because it is difficult to be precise about these distinctions.[46] But if we are inclined to understand a depiction as a portrait, then a judgment of resemblance may come into play, and the quality of individuality becomes pertinent.[47]

Consideration of likeness and individuality, and the kinds of typing necessary to their comprehension – the typing of the individual by the artist and the typing of the resulting depiction by the viewer – must not obscure another cardinal function of portraiture. A portrait may also align the depicted individual with a larger group.[48] Portraiture may confirm and validate the ways in which people are related to others, or may figure ways in which they wish to be so related. The values of the group are in this way attributed to the individual.[49] The ancestor portrait over the hearth assures the descendant-owner of his or (less often) her lineage, confirming the prerogatives of both heritage and ownership. Seventeenth-century Dutch corporation portraits gave image to the importance of business and guild relations. Roman funerary portraits symbolically reassured the living that their relations with the beloved deceased were not terminated. The pictorial tropes for Renaissance portraits of nobles likened their sitters to great personages of the ancient world. And so on.

Such a group does not necessarily have fixed criteria for membership. In fact, sometimes the group to which the sitter for a portrait belongs is little more than those people who have their portraits painted. This group, however otherwise ill-defined, embodies a set of values and assumptions that may nevertheless be easy to recognize, as the art dealer Ambroise Vollard illustrated with an anecdote. Vollard told of "a certain financier [who] owed his salvation to the portrait a famous artist painted of him." This banker had gotten an artist friend of his to ask Léon Bonnat, the accomplished and highly successful society portrait painter, to do a sketch of him – at a premium price. But the shrewd banker was certain that it would prove a good investment:

> I was literally at the end of my tether. I expected to go smash from one minute to the other, when the idea came to me of bluffing with that portrait by Bonnat. . . . *Coup de théâtre*: when they read in the *Figaro* and the *Gaulois* that the eminent painter of the Presidents and other big-wigs of the Republic was at work on a portrait of the "great banker," you can imagine it gave all the people who were preparing to hang me something to chew! I immediately found all the money I needed to set myself afloat again.

After the happy man of finance had gone, the artist said to Vollard: "Well, now you see the true uses of painting."[50] Not only can a portrait confirm status, it has the potential to create it by ascribing desirable characteristics and associations to its sitter.

Typicality in a portrait may therefore have two senses. The representation of an individual in a portrait may show the individual in a typical, or characteristic, attitude; and it may present him or her as the embodiment of the values of a group.

So the individual must be generalized – and perhaps on several levels – as well as particularized for the portrait to satisfy both requirements, of resemblance and typicality. Although this is always a great challenge to the artist, the dual project meets its greatest success in times when realism is highly valued and conventions (both for likeness and for typing) are clear. Certainly there have long been portraits when the convention for typing was everything, as in classical Greek portraits of warriors, or Roman portraits of statesmen. But generally speaking, since the Renaissance some sense of likeness, however ill-defined the concept of likeness might be, was regarded as a prerequisite for a portrait.

The progressive undermining of these conditions for artistic expression in the nineteenth century was the double-barreled threat to portraiture, as we have seen. One result was the blending of traditional genres in a single image.[51] But to preserve the portrait *per se* when both the traditional concept of likeness and traditional categories of interpretation had lost some credibility required the artist to contribute new criteria to the context for interpretation. While likeness may have been devalued in portraiture, individuality as a human attribute was not.

Artistic traditions and conventions of rank and privilege may have lost strength under attack, but the basic need to comprehend the individual in a larger context remained. More than ever, it was up to the artist to determine how the sitter's individuality was to be given an image. More than ever, the artist also determined the values for the interpretive context. Reconciling the particular and the general presented a different set of problems from those it had before, because selection and context both came under greater control of the portrait artist. Although likeness and conformity may no longer have been prerequisite to the condition of portraiture, both particularization and generalization in the service of individuality were still necessary.

Caricature *versus* collective identity

This new distribution of emphasis can have two results in portraiture, depending on whether individuality or typicality is stressed. Emphasis on individuality may move the portrait in the direction of caricature. It is not too much to say that the popularity of caricature in the nineteenth and twentieth centuries may be attributed in part to the gradual discrediting of likeness in portraiture alongside the promotion of individuality in many modern societies. Physical caricature of an individual works by targeting and exaggerating salient features, making a mockery of a person's individuality while crucially depending on it for its dual purpose of identification and critique. Particular features (Louis-Napoléon's nose, Hitler's moustache, George W. Bush's ears) can stand for the whole. The greater autonomy and powers of self-determination increasingly granted to the artist during the nineteenth century may also partly explain the enormous growth of caricature and, in the realm of portraiture, the popularity of the *portrait charge*.[52]

Several of Matisse's early self-portrait drawings approach caricature as he plays with the essence and the limits of his individuality. There are other examples,

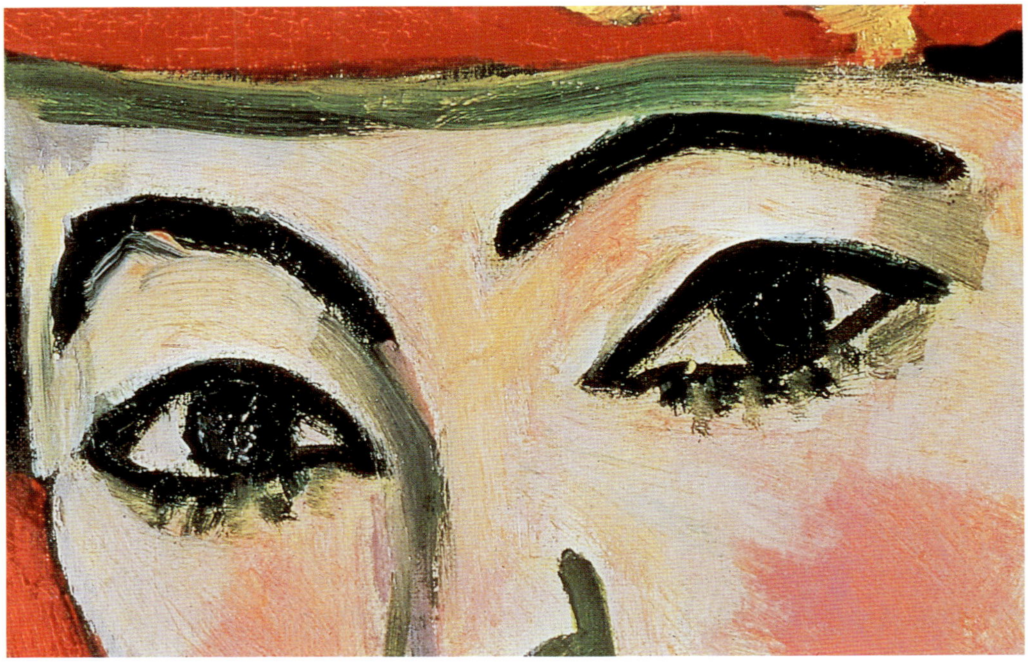

Detail of fig. 52.

including several portrait drawings, throughout his career.[53] But by and large he was not interested in summing up individuals by exaggerating features distinctive to them, any more than he would "copy" indiscriminately for the sake of a likeness. This did not prevent him from summarizing distinctive racial or ethnic features in a class of images that he made largely without concern for the individual, as in many late drawings of non-European models.

An encounter between Matisse and Picasso, opposite in spirit here as in so many ways, may illuminate Matisse's attitude. We can find a caricature-like procedure much more in the portraiture of Picasso, especially the Cubist portraits of 1909–11 and, later, the many portraits of Marie-Thérèse Walter, Dora Maar, and Françoise Gilot (or, for that matter, his dress-up portrait of Paul Eluard). In a painting such as Picasso's *Wilhelm Uhde* (1910; private collection), although the sitter's face is fragmented, certain key elements stand out, notably the puckered mouth and alert steady eyes. These clues permit the sense of "recognition" we may feel before the portrait (that is, what we may feel we would experience if we knew the sitter). But portraiture of this kind is risky. Sometimes the artist does not provide enough clues; and if a viewer is not prepared to see a key feature as a clue to identity, she may not recognize anything. The case in point: about 1913, Matisse paid a visit to Picasso's studio. Picasso showed him a Cubist painting and asked him if he understood what it represented. Matisse was at a loss, but when Picasso held a false moustache in a certain place on the picture, Matisse was able to recognize the portrait of a man.[54] He needed just that additional (and admittedly obvious) point of reference, the key that opened the door of recognition, for everything else to fall into place. Successful perception of a face under such challenging circumstances depends, as in the case of caricature, on our expectations of what we are going to see. It also depends on our familiarity with conventions for representation. In 1913 Matisse was skeptical of Cubism, and was unprepared to decode its pictorial language. A few years later he had become more familiar with Cubist syntax and more sympathetic to its possibilities, and he was himself making paintings in a Cubist manner, including a portrait, with a similar juxtaposition of abstract passages and recognizable motifs.[55]

Emphasis on typicality in portraiture of the modern period seemed to open a much wider range of possibilities, especially from the standpoint of the groups with which a sitter might be associated. The potential for greater social mobility might break down or reconfigure some of the traditional groups – national, social, professional, royal, even familial – for whose values portraiture was an exemplary vehicle. We might expect the result to have been a greater egalitarianism in portraiture. In one sector this was true: it was frequently a consequence of the burgeoning of portrait photography in the late nineteenth century.[56] This was the means of portraiture most accessible to the growing but amorphous middle class. But, if anything, portraiture in the manual arts became more restrictive with respect to the groups whose values it confirmed and conveyed. In part this was because élites, responding to the very populism of the portrait photograph, shunned photography and sought economic and expressive distinction in painting. But the artist who painted or sculpted portraits was also increasingly a source for the limitations on what values the portrait transmitted. As overt artistic expression became more acceptable as a goal in art, even in portraiture, pressure increased on the patron to share the values of the artist, or at least to accept their imposition on his or her image. With a portrait, and the sitter's hope of self-expression, let alone self-aggrandizement, this could be a difficult pill to swallow.

To comprehend the individual as a member of a larger group, rather than to attend to the sitter's uniqueness, was Matisse's preference in portraiture, in spite of his statements about the "particular asymmetry" of a sitter's face.[57] In a certain way the groups to which his sitters could be seen to belong were very restricted; the limiting factors were Matisse's own values and aspirations. I believe Matisse's portrait practice before 1919 exemplified to the fullest extent the tendency of the modern artist to determine the context of values expressed in a portrait, and in a way that was of the greatest potential service to him. He did not so much project his personality on his sitters (a conventional and overworked way to talk about the effects of modern portraits) as project his values on them. I believe he saw his sitters as members of the groups that were most important to him. These may not have coincided with how the sitters wished to see themselves and, in fact, it is frequently easy to see that these visions clashed. Matisse may have actually belonged to these groups, or he may have had aspirations to belong. I do not mean this too literally, and I use the concept of the group with some flexibility, in terms of shared values without fixed concepts of membership. For instance, his portraits from 1916 to 1917 of the businessman Auguste Pellerin (see figs. 129, 130) do not indicate that Matisse wanted to be a businessman (even though he was becoming in effect more entrepreneurial at this time, less dependent on "employment" by specific patrons). But at that time, in those circumstances, something of Pellerin's status appealed to Matisse, as did his splendid art collection, containing important paintings by Cézanne and Renoir, to which he thereby gained access. In other words, Matisse did not want to be like Pellerin, but he wanted some of the same things that Pellerin wanted and by virtue of his wealth and drive had accumulated. We shall see that such portraiture of others could be used, self-interestedly, to further Matisse's process of identification. But as with most artists, his first efforts in this process of forming his own identity were in images of himself.

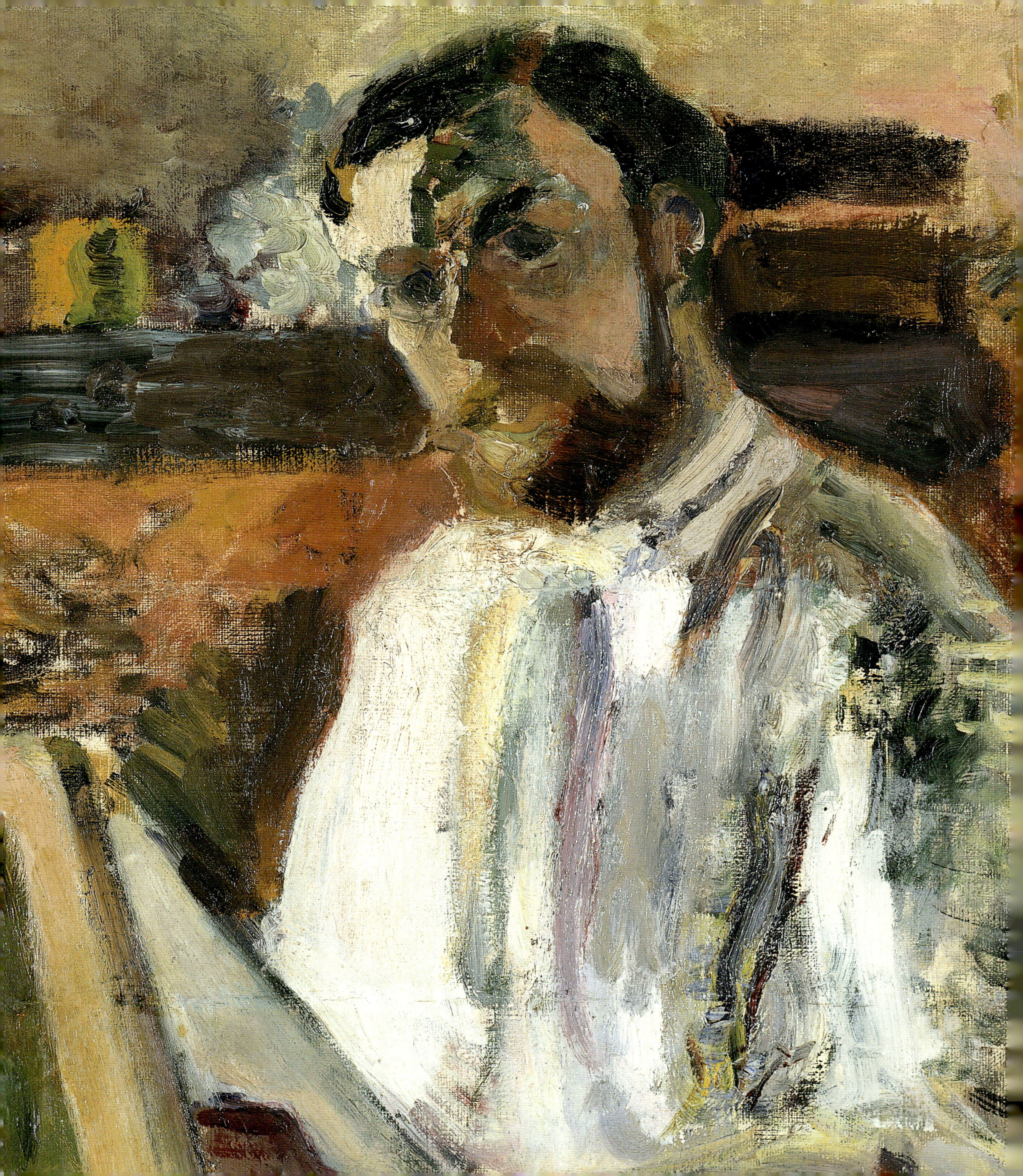

Chapter 2 Self before Other

Matisse made few portraits in the 1890s, the first decade of his career, when still life, landscape, and interior scenes dominated his art. Portraiture is not often a pursuit of youth. It is dutiful, and does not seem reflexive enough to interest the self-absorbed beginner. Nor was it part of the academic curriculum that Matisse's generation was one of the last to consume. For the young artist, other genres offer greater agency, or feature the artist's own environment, so they can be used to convey the urgency of personal circumstances. The youthful desire for control and intimacy does not yet extend into the larger social world that is the source and context of portraiture.[1] Becoming familiar with and achieving some sense of mastery over a more modest and immediate psychic space comes first.

So for Matisse, as for many modern artists, the social activity of making portraits was preceded by the more private inquiries of self-portraiture. The reasons are many. The most obvious derive from the harmonious convergence of energy, patience, and penury of sitter and artist. Narcissism is certainly also active – staring in the mirror, even preening, is validated by a higher pursuit. The self-portrait offers the most direct opportunity for self-centered expression. Underneath such a superficial indulgence, though, a young artist such as Matisse contributes to the process of forming his or her identity by examining and comparing different faces, attitudes, and costumes in the mirror. Changes on the surface mark deeper longings for integration and mastery. Self-portraiture becomes a metaphor for acquiring self-knowledge, for completeness.

But then we have to return to the surface, and the pose. In his early self-portraits, most of these clustered in the years 1898–1900, Matisse was not only coming into self-knowledge through a process of assuming different identities. He was also trying on public personas, imagining how he would look to others, even imagining how he would look as others, figuring his self-presentation in the safety of the space between face and mirror. By the end of this decade he knew that he would be an artist, but he did not seem to know yet what an artist would look like if it were he. A decision about professional identity does not come automatically with a visual form, and Matisse still had to work this out, which he did not do to his satisfaction for years to come.

Displacement

In a way, he could displace his unformed identity onto others. Most of Matisse's early portraits represent children – younger surrogates for the young artist, in the process of forming their own identities. These pictures allowed him to learn both about artistic techniques and conditions of becoming. Among the earliest is a

Detail of fig. 34.

12 *Marguerite*, 1901. Oil on canvas, 71.1 × 53.3 cm. Private collection.

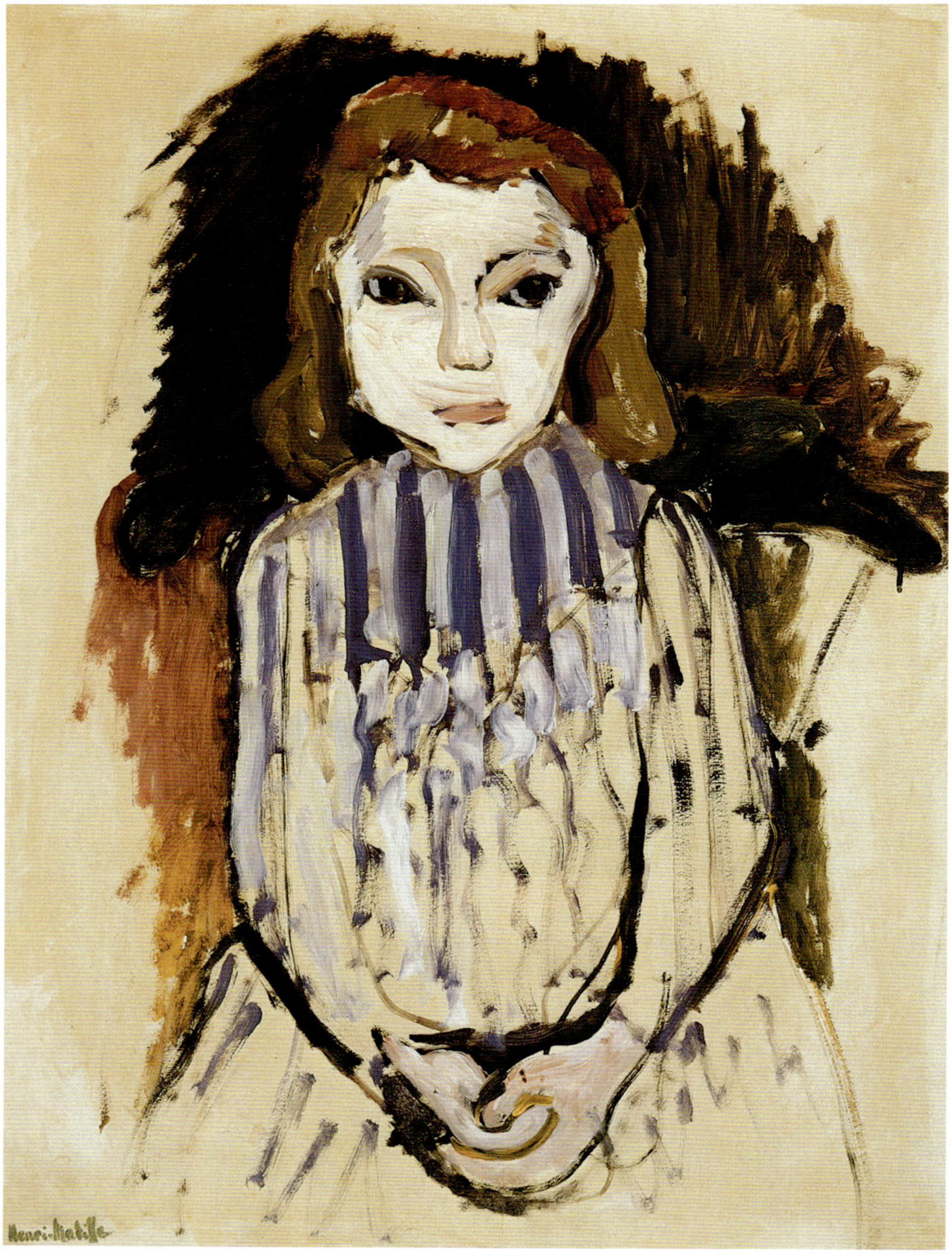

11 *The Little Breton Girl (Annie Pétron)*, 1896. Oil on wood, 54 × 40 cm. Private collection.

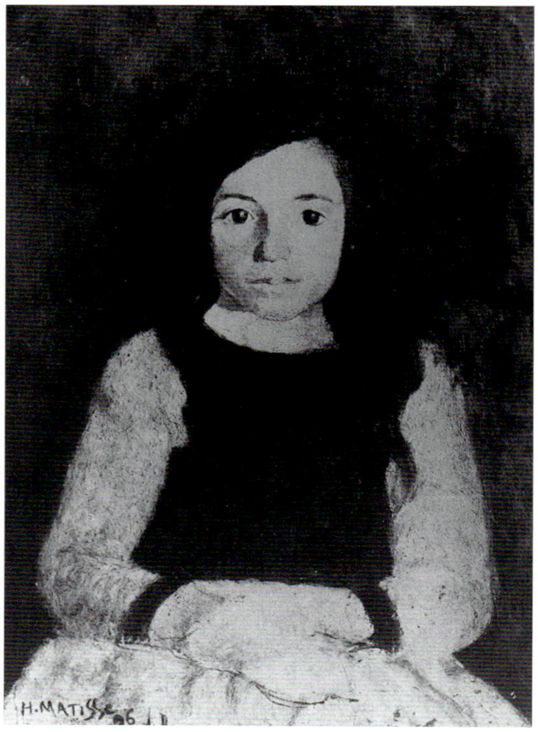

portrait of a young Breton girl (fig. 11). The sitter's identity has never been verified, and Matisse seems to have treated her more as a regional Breton type, a general interest of many artists of the time.[2] Piety, purity, and simplicity were thought to be Breton characteristics, but determination and physical brutishness could also be part of the type. Matisse's Breton girl, with a wide face and thick body, iconically posed with her hands folded before her, is a secular equivalent of Dagnan-Bouveret's women at pardons or Gauguin's *Belle Angèle*. His painterly treatment of the girl consists of a simplified chiaroscuro without nuance, concentrating on the expressive power of simple forms and bold features, all contributing to the effect of generalization.

Matisse apparently kept the portrait all his life, which was not in itself unusual for his early work if it had not been put on the market initially. More interestingly, *The Little Breton Girl* hung on the wall of his studio in the late 1940s, and Matisse chose the picture for inclusion in his late album of portraits.[3] Although he was always prone to look back over his early work, and never more than toward the end of his career, this painting seems to have had special and enduring significance for the artist – not, presumably, for the sake of its sitter, but because its strategy of generalization or typing suited Matisse's ultimate conclusions about the goal of portraiture as he expressed them in his late essays. The artist who eventually made portrait-like pictures of women entitled *Asia* or *Algerian Woman* had a penchant for surveying his earliest work and finding there early confirmation of his direction, a wholeness that could be discerned, or invented, only in retrospect.

A painting of greater ambition, although it was never finished, was his first portrait of his daughter, Marguerite, done in 1901 after an emergency tracheotomy that left her weakened and scarred (fig. 12).[4] Matisse had had to assist in the operation, and this joint trauma bound them closely thereafter. The strangely rubbery but riveting and memorable portrait is an essay in the vulnerability of the body and the persistence of the spirit in someone so young. Its sketchy qualities seem to create a loosely knit and malleable façade masking a forceful interior presence that is surely as much Matisse's projection of himself into his daughter's image as it is a reflection of her own considerable strength in testing circumstances.

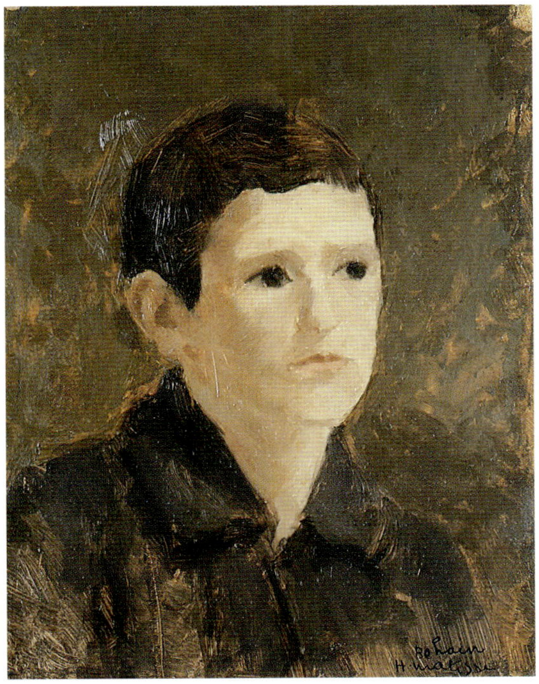

13 *Young Capella*, 1902–3. Oil on cardboard, 34 × 26 cm. Le Cateau-Cambrésis, Musée Matisse.

Inevitably less compelling is his portrait of a boy, *Young Capella* (1902–3; fig. 13), from Bohain-en-Vermandois, where Matisse spent much of his own youth. Tonally constructed, controlled, and modest in conception but with a richly textured paint surface, this picture is an attractive but unexceptional heir to a mixture of Northern traditions. His romanticized and somewhat vague rendering of the boy's face contributes to the generalized sense of potential that is a theme at least implicit in most portraits of children and adolescents. Important, too, for Matisse's work in this time of poverty for him and his family was that the Capella boy, whose family was even poorer, would pose for long periods for just a few sous.[5]

Secret agency

Matisse's early self-portraiture presented itself in less direct ways. Surreptitiously, in three domestic interior scenes from the mid 1890s, he inserted a framed image of himself into the décor, to blend in with other objects of his private surroundings. This long-lost drawing is Matisse's earliest known self-portrait. Despite its fugitive existence, the drawing has a key status in his work at this time, more important for the role it takes in these interiors than it would be as an isolated instance of self-representation (no other self-portraits before 1898 are known). As he used it in these interior scenes, this self-portrait is an index of his early assertion of subjectivity, and shows how he could translate this subjectivity into the pictorial terms of a traditional genre. We might not suspect this importance solely on the evidence of *Woman Reading*, 1895, in which the framed self-portrait takes a more or less natural place on a wall with other pictures (fig. 14). Matisse's painting seems benign enough, harmlessly *intimiste*, an updated Corot. It was one of his first public successes, as it was bought by the French government after its exhibition that year in the Salon of the Société Nationale des Beaux-Arts.[6] Presumably this was the sort of intelligent middle-of-the-road painting the state wished to encourage from its young artists. But its apparently bland accommodation is deceptive.

Certain works, sometimes, but not necessarily, at key moments in Matisse's career, are denser in ideas and potential than others. These are not the same as the periodic "summing-up" works he made to bring his interests, explored sometimes over a period of years, to a conclusion, usually in a large ambitious painting intended for public appraisal. His *Dinner Table* from 1897, a true reception piece, is an example of such a demonstration of mastery.[7] But there is another kind of picture, more private and disarmingly simple, whose density is not apparent without considering what issued from its potential. These paintings (and sometimes sculptures) held the seeds for many later works and introduced durable, sometimes obsessional themes to which Matisse returned over and over again.[8]

Woman Reading is one of these pictures. Its theme of absorption, of a woman in an interior lost in a private experience, unknowingly observed, would be pure Nabi if Matisse had not marked it with his self-consciousness and turned it into a display of artistic and psychological control. The framed self-portrait shares the crowded space with other objects of the library, the writing-desk, and the studio in a casual arrangement reminiscent of the Dutch seventeenth-century interior scenes and still lifes with which Matisse was familiar. The casualness is only superficial, however; this little drawing has a willed purpose here and in the other two paintings in which it is depicted. It is a portable effigy, a surrogate for the artist's presence and control, its mobility a sign of his omniscience. In another drama of gazes, *Still Life with Self-Portrait* of 1896 (fig. 15), he inserts the drawing into the jumble of books, jugs, and papers crowded onto a figured carpet that he has draped over a table or desk. Off the wall, the self-portrait becomes another object, but as an image it also figures in a furtive game, as if the artist is peeking at the viewer, implicating the voyeuristic inspection by an outsider. This positioning of the viewer as an object of surveillance is also generated in the third painting of this self-conscious triad, *Interior with a Top Hat* of the same year (fig. 16). Here the drawing is back on the wall, above the clutter. Matisse has hung a small empty frame across the lower right corner of his self-portrait. Unlike all the other objects on these angled walls, this pictureless enclosure does not follow pictorial conventions of foreshortening. Instead Matisse has depicted the frame as if it were hung on the picture surface itself, rectangle on rectangle, its boundaries an interior echo of the edges of our view into this room, its frontal address a signal that this view is presented to us for very specific artistic reasons.

Such reminders of artifice are rarely far away in these early paintings. Matisse makes the terms of engagement with his world and his means explicit. Still-life paintings are especially congenial to this. A fundamental theme in the European still-life tradition is the artist's control over the objects depicted, in analogy to the conception and composition of a picture. Art-making entails not acceptance but construction of a world. By explicitly incorporating a self-image into his composition Matisse redoubles the effect, asserting that the artist is a necessary presence within the work he creates. He composes from the inside of his subject because part of his subject is the creating self. Moreover, the self is self-observing, a witness to the creative act. Such indirect self-portrayal, creating a surrogate for the presence of the artist, a reminder of who is always in control, was a recurring motif in Matisse's work.

14 *Woman Reading*, 1895. Oil on wood, 61.5 × 48 cm. Paris, Musée National d'Art Moderne, Centre Georges Pompidou.

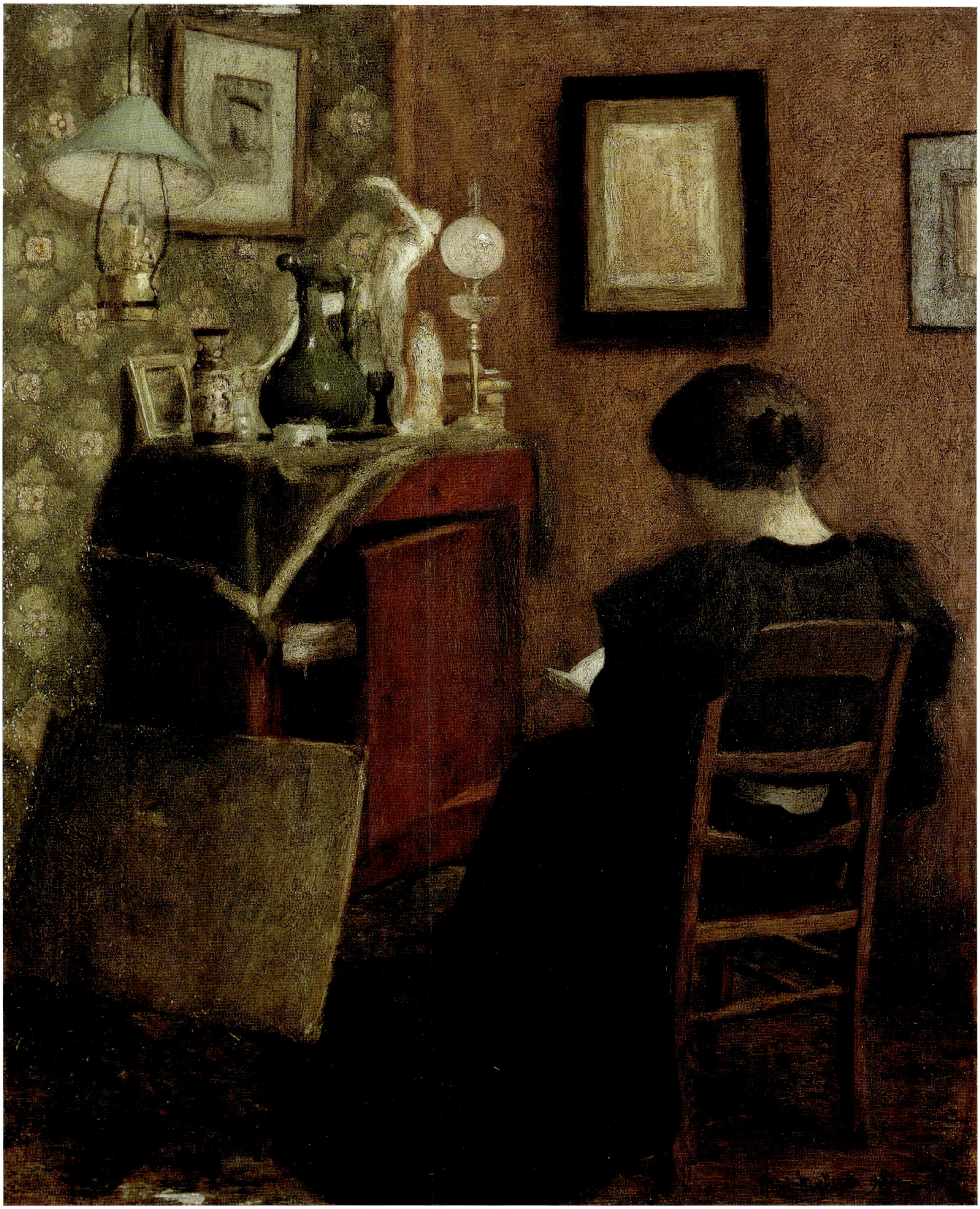

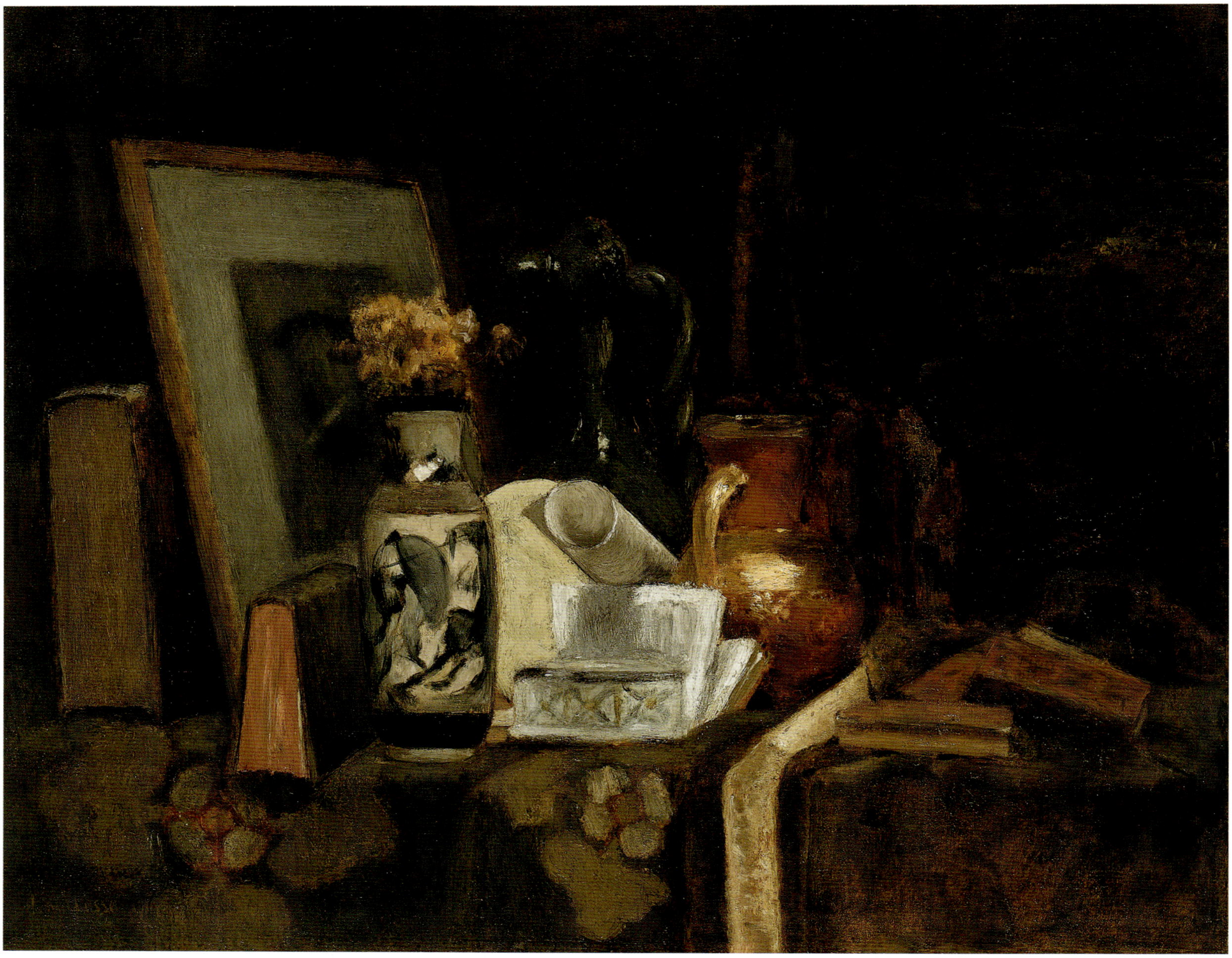

15 *Still Life with Self-Portrait*, 1896. Oil on canvas, 64.8 × 81.3 cm. Columbus Museum of Art, Ohio, gift of Howard D. and Babette L. Sirak, the Donors to the Campaign for Enduring Excellence, and the Derby Fund.

Passive reading, active looking

This cat-and-mouse game of observing and being observed, of visual power and blind passivity, is most pronounced in *Woman Reading*. The key to the picture's visuality is the confrontation between the woman and the artist's self-image. Matisse in his self-portrait is "looking" at the young woman bent over her book; she is oblivious to being observed either by him or by the viewer.[9] This woman is Caroline Joblaud, a clerk in a hatshop with whom he was then living, and the mother of Matisse's daughter Marguerite.[10] But the picture is less a portrait of Caroline – her individual identity is subsumed in her role as a reader and as the object of surveillance – than a probe into the relationship between active and passive entities, between the creating role of the artist and the receptive malleability of his model. Her role here is to provide an object of the gaze through an image of passive tran-

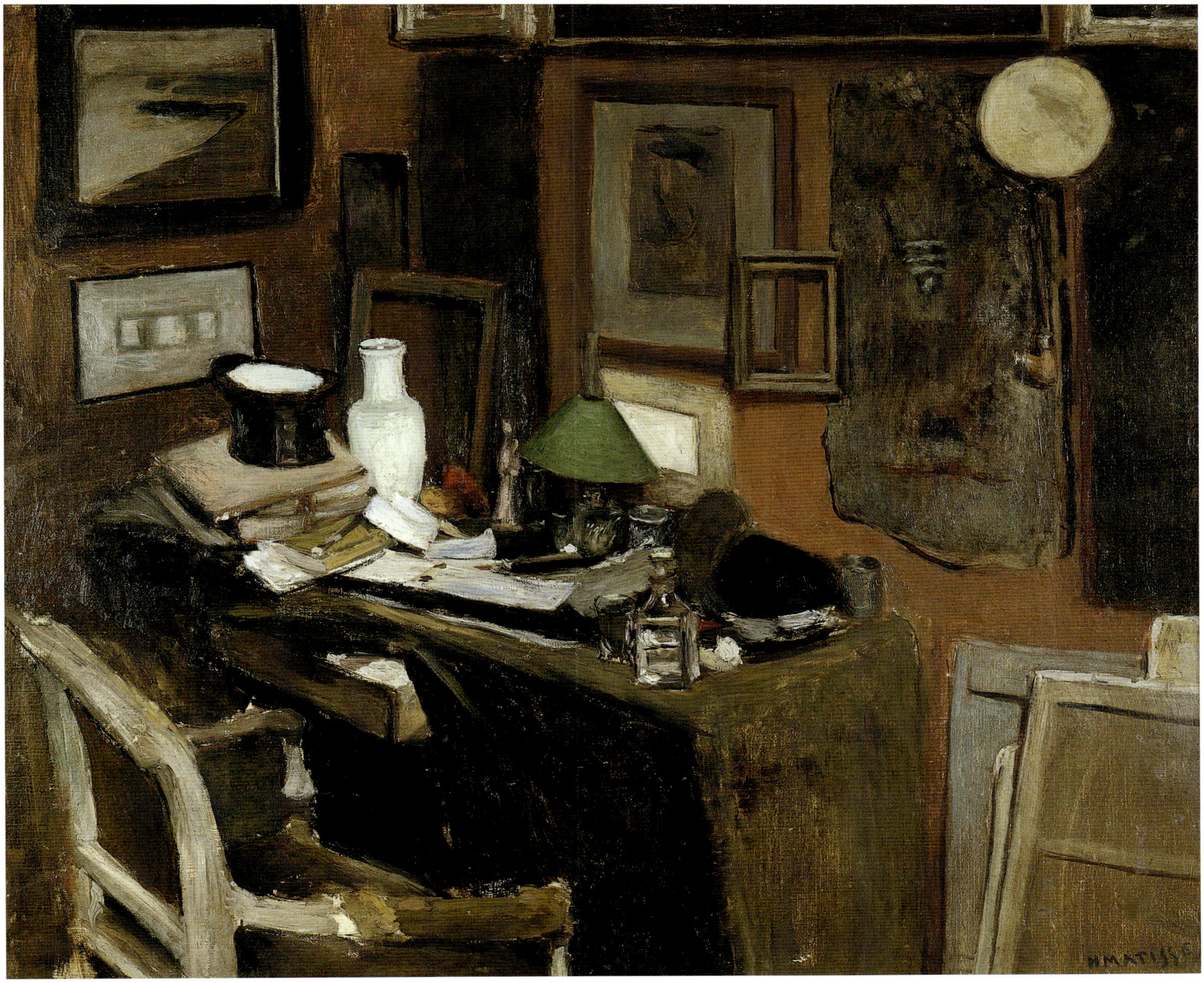

16 *Interior with a Top Hat*, 1896. Oil on canvas, 80 × 95 cm. Private collection.

quility.[11] A reader, whose occupation is necessarily visual, is thus transformed into an image of disempowered sight.

The confrontation between Matisse's self-portrait and the reader is complicated and contradictory. He, discarnate in a mere image, is nevertheless positioned as the active participant – he "looks" toward the preoccupied object of his gaze. By contrast, she, the living presence in the scene, is passive, absorbed. The highlights in this picture are concentrated in the bright areas of Caroline's neck and book (thus conventionally marking the "subject" of the painting), but the real visual hook is the area between the two human presences, where the confused clutter of disparate objects agitates the otherwise tranquil interior. These sculptures, vases, lamps, and frames suggest that many considerations come between the artist and the ostensibly natural and uncomplicated representation of his world.

Detail of fig. 14.

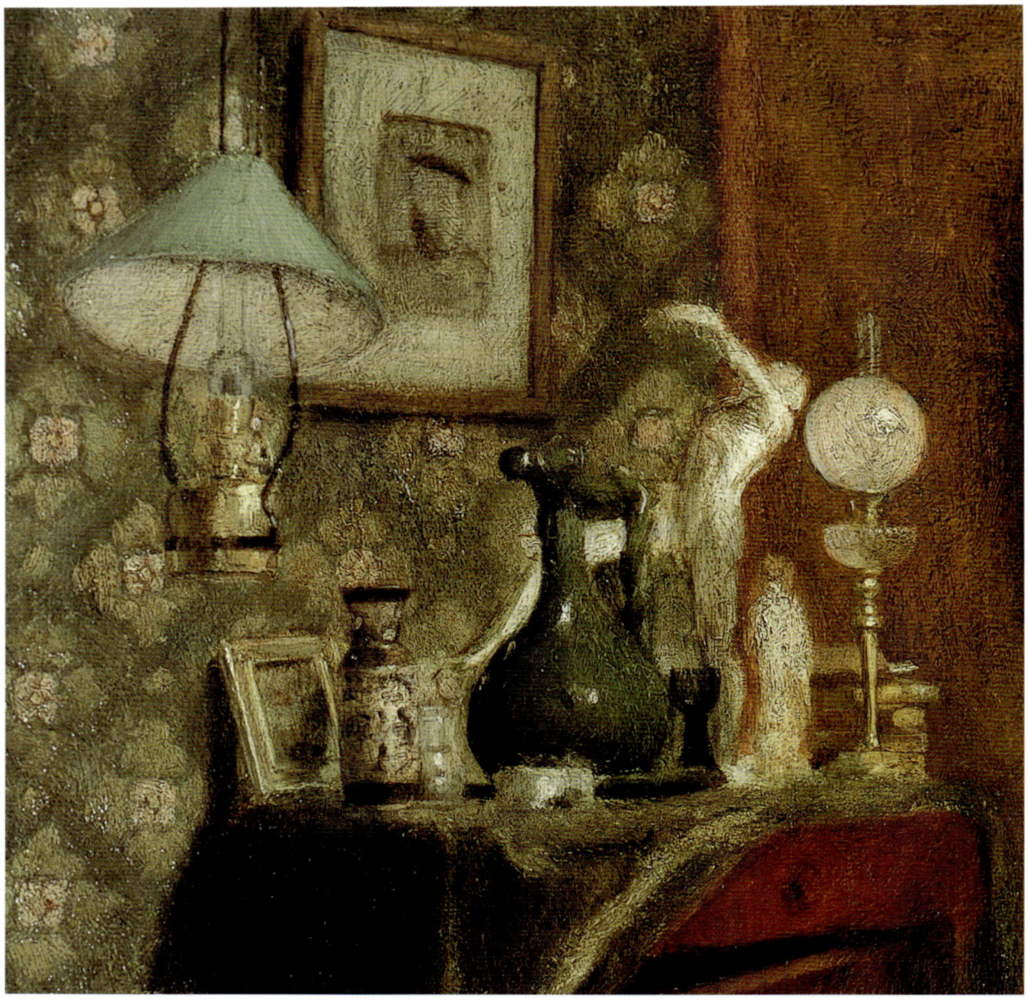

Another visual axis in the picture is less mediated but reveals more about Matisse's self-consciousness and about the claims he was beginning to make for his art. This secondary dialogue explores another relationship, that between the work of art – the image that includes a self-portrait – and the viewer. The unchanging perspective of two-dimensional imagery ensures that Matisse in his self-portrait obliquely "looks" at us as well as at Caroline. Artist and viewer both spy on the reader with apparent impunity. But the panoptic gaze of the artist from his vantage point on the wall, exchanged with ours, alters all that. The viewer is implicated along with the artist in the process by which this picture creates meaning in relationships of looking.[12] Such a circulation of gazes in works of art was anything but unique at this time; in a public setting, it was the concern of Mary Cassatt in her ironic visual essay on the empowering quality of vision, *Woman in Black at the Opera* (Boston, Museum of Fine Arts). But the complexities of this sort of exchange of looks were explored by Matisse for the first time in his work in *Woman Reading*. With its companion pictures it indicates at this early moment his particularly self-conscious turn of mind and the way he used self-portraiture as an agent to assert this subjectivity.

Matisse also welcomed complexity in the treatment of standard artistic genres. *Woman Reading* throws up obstacles to an easy understanding of its content partly

17 *Profile of a Woman, II*, 1894. Bronze, 24.7 cm diameter. Nice, Musée Matisse.

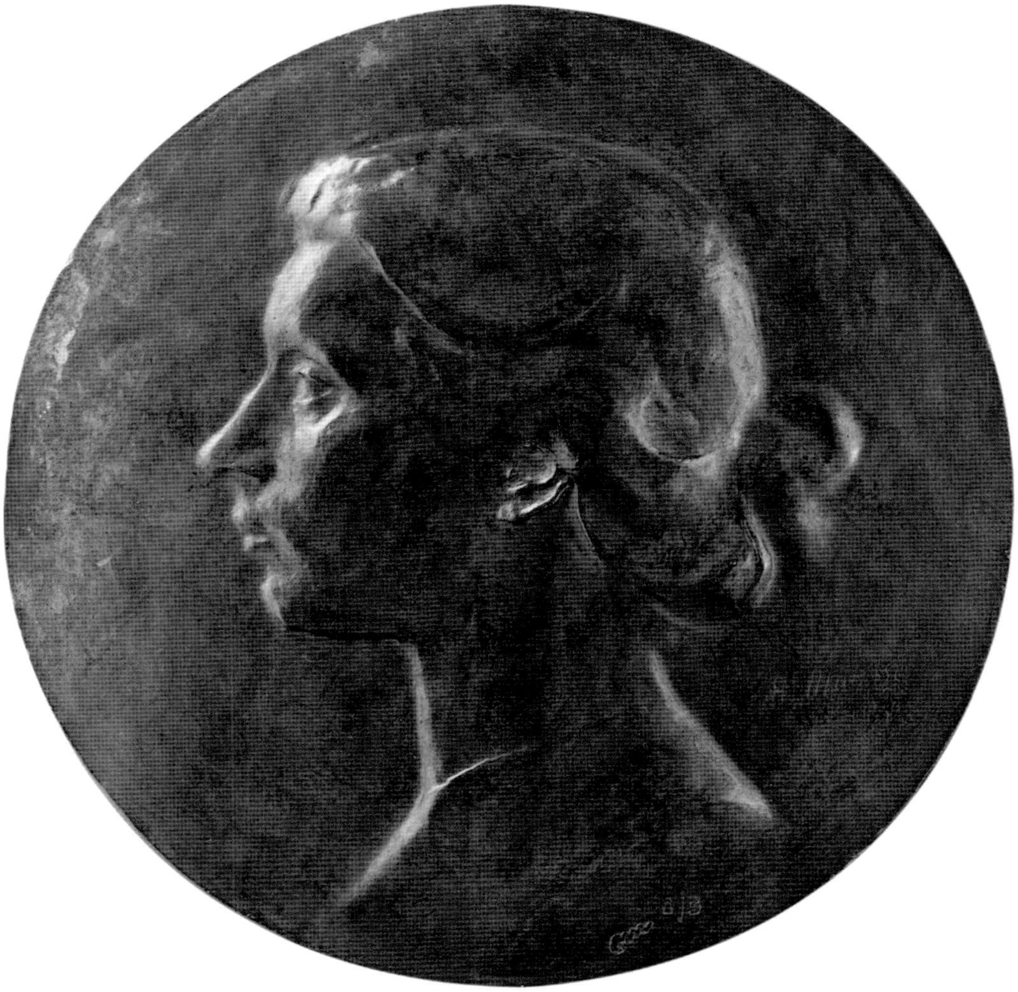

because it refuses to be pigeonholed into a traditional genre category. The intrusion of the self-portrait ensures this. Artists throughout the nineteenth century had challenged viewers' expectations by eroding strict genre categories. By the end of the century, audiences seem to have been prepared for this sort of thing, permitting a painting such as *Woman Reading* uncontroversially to gain official sanction. Although the very genreless character of such a picture may by then have become an acceptable pictorial mode, Matisse's self-portrait disturbs the easy complacency of the spectator's role by forcing his or her complicity in constructing the passivity of the sitter.

The model of Caroline Joblaud

This enforced passivity operates even in an apparently ennobling portrait of Joblaud. In 1894 she had borne Matisse's first child, their daughter Marguerite.[13] At that time the artist observed the advent of his new role as a father with two sculptures of Caroline (fig. 17).[14] These nearly life-size reliefs, in the general style of coins or Renaissance portrait medallions, are Matisse's first known sculptures. They were also his first portraits of someone who had special meaning for the artist. But despite the intimacy of his relationship with Caroline Joblaud, the traditional form here supplies a doubly distancing mechanism. There seems little question that these works are portraits, but they are oddly dry and documentary. For this quality of detachment they are exceptional in Matisse's portraiture (and they are among his few portraits in profile, another neutralizing feature).

Furthermore, their commemorative function locates the motive for these portraits outside their sitter, who is here more pretext than honoree. Matisse's use of a commemorative mode is ironic given his later repudiation of Caroline. But the profile format is also a mechanism for placing full control of the dynamics of the relationship between image and viewer in the hands of the artist, and producing collusion between artist and viewer: once more, active viewer, passive sitter. Matisse uses this control here to suppress the individuality of the sitter, which was less important to him than was her role as the mother of his daughter.[15] Marguerite was intensely special to Matisse, and he later made many portraits of her that demonstrate both his affection and the ways in which she stimulated his imagination. As for Caroline, Matisse thereafter cast her as a servant in *The Dinner Table*; then, long after they had parted, he distantly evoked her subordinate status in almost mocking manner in *Harmony in Red*.[16]

Although Matisse nowhere else offers Caroline Joblaud to the viewer for inspection so collusively as in *Woman Reading*, she is in his work always subordinated to us by being always available to our gaze while having no power to return it. Matisse never positions her to engage the viewer and thus to assert her claims on us (or him) for equivalence. Bound by her class, she is also subordinated by the modes of representation he reserves for her.[17] His manipulation and sometimes effacement of her identity anticipates the kind of role-assignment he later performed with his wife Amélie, whom he married in 1898. Caroline's passive performances became the model for Matisse's efforts to control the representation of Amélie Matisse, with much more contested results.

Determining the self in art

During the period through 1900, Matisse made many more self-portraits than portraits. This concentration on himself as the object of his art is fully in keeping with the reflexive qualities of much of his early work. But these early self-images are not evenly distributed throughout this period. Except for the ghostly, mobile effigy he put to such insistent use in the three interior scenes from 1895–96, his known self-portraits from this time are bunched in the final three years of the decade, with most of these clustered in 1900, including two important paintings. This concentration indicates more than routine self-consciousness. It also signifies a process of consolidation, an effort at a reckoning. At the end of his student years, a long apprenticeship with many masters living and dead, Matisse was coming into his own as an artist. He was pushed a little: his beloved teacher Gustave Moreau died in 1898, and in the following year Matisse was forced to leave the Ecole des Beaux-Arts because he had reached the maximum age (thirty) for a student. The clutch of self-portraits culminating in 1900 shows us an artist newly isolated and forced into independence, and locates Matisse's investment in a process of self-assertion. He was a mature person and an artist of growing confidence, but he was without a fully developed persona as an artist. The production of self-imagery helped Matisse to define himself. Once outside the supporting frame of apprenticeship, greater self-

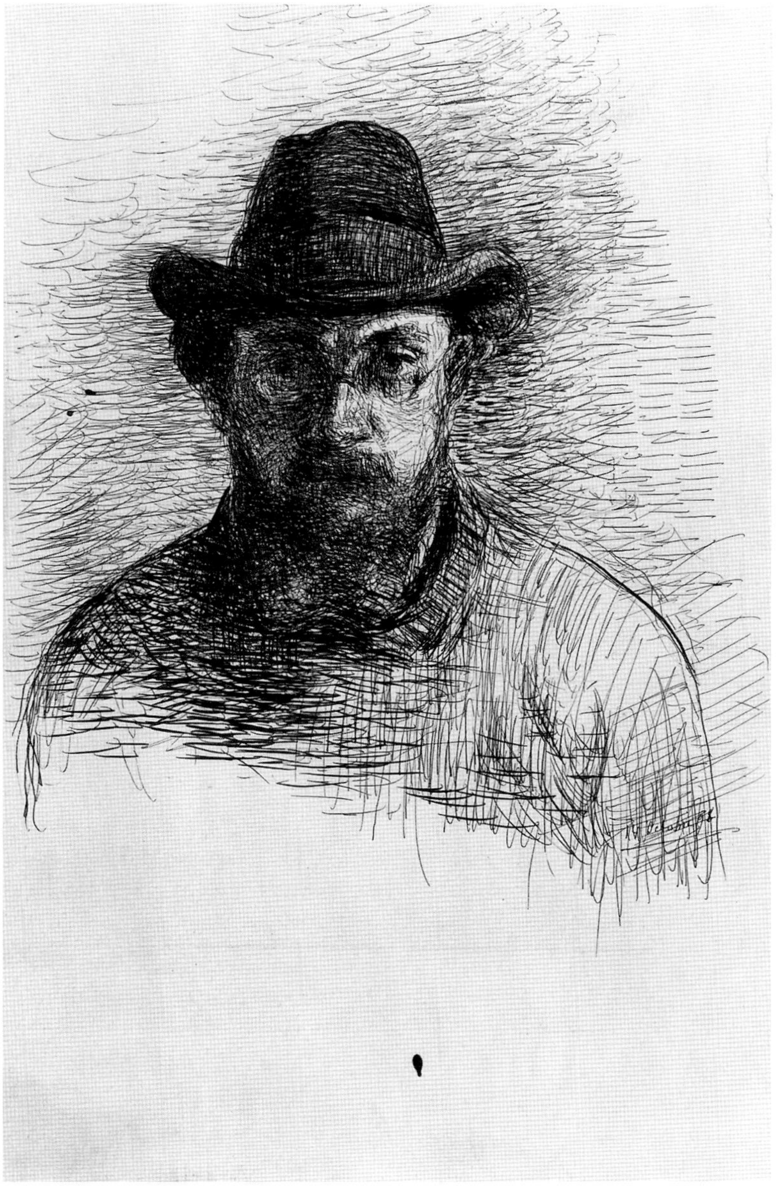

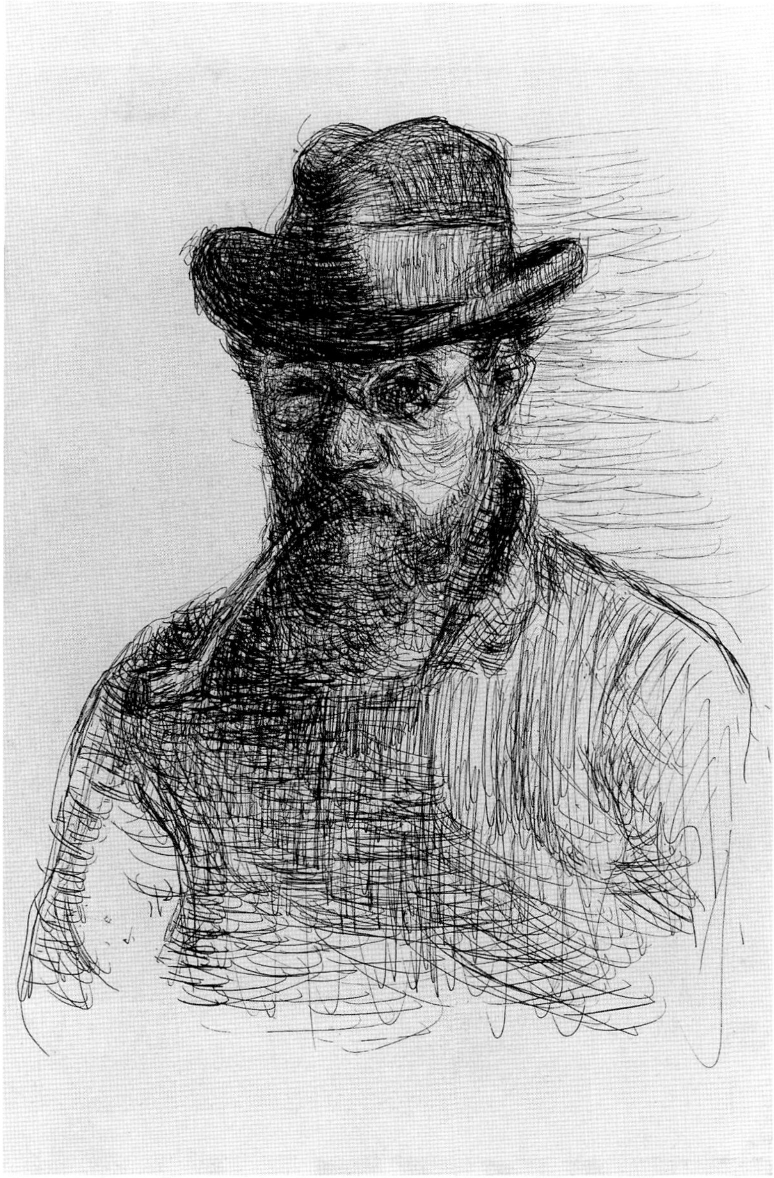

18 (*above left*) *Self-Portrait*, 1898. Pen and ink on paper, 31 × 20 cm. Private collection.

19 (*above right*) *Self-Portrait with Pipe*, 1898. Pen and ink on paper, 31 × 20 cm. Private collection.

knowledge is necessary to understand one's relationship to the world and to assert a distinct place in it (Matisse later spoke of himself at this time as open to influences, but only as forces to be mastered).[18]

When his work is discussed in terms of his innovations in color as a response to nature, his stay in Corsica and Toulouse in 1898–9 is usually cited as his first revelation of the possibilities for constructing paintings by color rather than by tone.[19] When his discovery of modern art is held to be a turning point in his career, Matisse's friendship with Camille Pissarro and their visits to the Impressionist paintings in the Caillebotte bequest in 1897 are offered as the keys.[20] But when we consider his maturity and his confidence in his vocation, his self-fashioning as an artist, the year 1900 should be understood as a time when Matisse's sense of himself as an artist came to have a look, a mode of address that he could at last begin to formulate as an image.[21] In these self-portraits we are seeing him in the process of

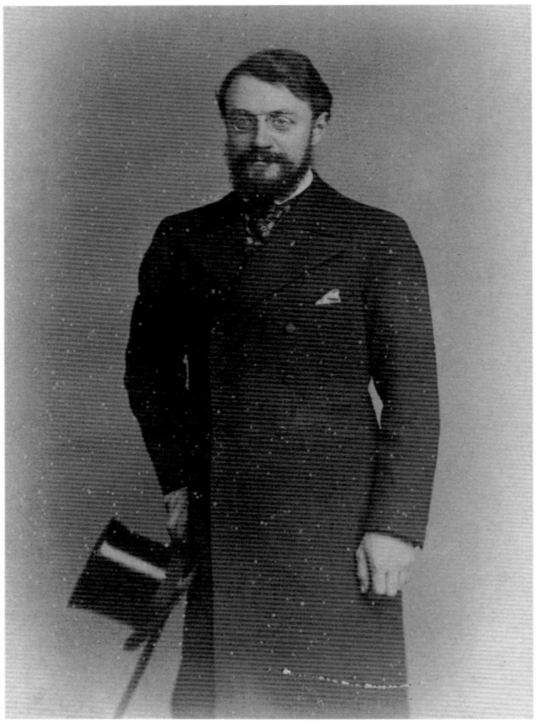

20 Photograph of Matisse at the time of his marriage, 1898.

imagining his professional identity alongside other aspects of his adult character, realizing perhaps at this time that there was no single way to think about himself. In the 1950s, reflecting on this early period, he acknowledged this divided self, saying that he had been "pushed on by I know not what, by a force that I see today is quite alien to my normal life as a man."[22] Becoming an artist entailed the fostering and acceptance of different orders of being within himself, something he could admit later in statements about himself and his development, but that about 1900 was expressed visually, through the medium of the self-portrait.[23]

Other artists helped Matisse in his process of determining what form he would give to his own identity as an artist. In two meticulously rendered pen and ink drawings from 1898 (figs. 18, 19), he enlisted Rembrandt and Degas as a lineage for a concentrated rendition of quiet seriousness in soigné black and white.[24] In one, full face, the artist stares gravely out from a fine mesh of rapidly drawn but carefully accumulated pen strokes, producing the effect that the figure is made from the same shadowy stuff that forms the background. In the other, head tilted down and slightly to one side, a long clay pipe in his mouth evokes the Dutch traditions of observation and realistic depiction so important to his formation. His bearing here and in a contemporaneous photograph (fig. 20) recalls his nickname, "the Doctor," given to him a few years later by his contemporaries. Matisse presents himself here with consistency and control, the careful, gradual build-up of spidery lines suggesting prudence and calculation, as does the calibrated variation of his address from one drawing to the other. In the first drawing – it is the only one dated, it is more direct in presentation, and more thoroughly finished, all suggesting precedence – he introduces the theme in an iconic, formal, and deeply probing statement. The more casual variation lightens the mood a bit. Now he detaches his image from the background, suggesting alertness and greater psychological freedom. The face and shoulders, turned, invite the perception of movement. Light and dark play haphazardly over his face in contrast to the tyrannical certainty of their effects in the earlier image. These drawings suggest careful steps in a tentative process.

Performing an artist

The lid came off in the next two years. In several dozen self-portrait drawings and two paintings, Matisse significantly increased his expressive range and adopted both a more selective and a more synoptic approach to the features of his face. This development accords with his general way of working, or at least with his self-perception as an artist, in reaction to a visit to Auguste Rodin's studio at this time. At the suggestion of a friend, Matisse took some of his drawings to Rodin for commentary and was put off by the great sculptor's insistence on pursuing seemingly trivial details. "Already," Matisse said later, "I could envision my work only as a general architecture, replacing explanatory details with a living and suggestive synthesis."[25] While it would be natural for Matisse, looking back from a distance of many years, to dissociate himself from Rodin's powerful influence, his claim to the pursuit of a "living and suggestive synthesis" is borne out in the self-portraits executed in a variety of media and expressing a wide spectrum of moods from gravity to mania.[26] Not that these could all be records of emotions Matisse felt as he drew. We should be cautious about reading these self-portraits as reflex actions imaging actual states of mind caught at the time of their (facial) expres-

21 (*facing page top left*) *Self-Portrait*, 1899. Pen, brush, and ink on paper, 31 × 20 cm. Private collection.

22 (*facing page top right*) *Four Self-Portraits*, 1899. Pen and ink on paper, 20 × 31 cm. Private collection.

23 (*facing page bottom*) *Self-Portrait Smoking a Pipe*, 1900. Pen, brush, and ink on paper, 30.8 × 19.9 cm. Private collection.

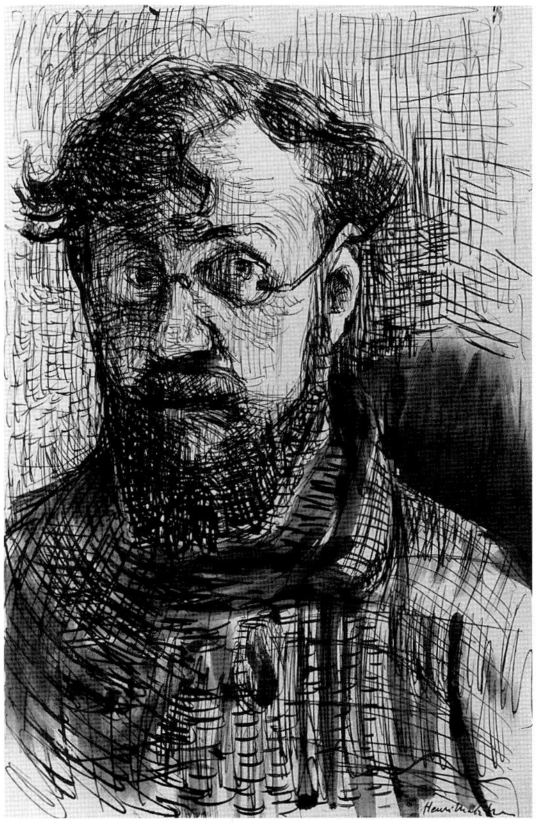

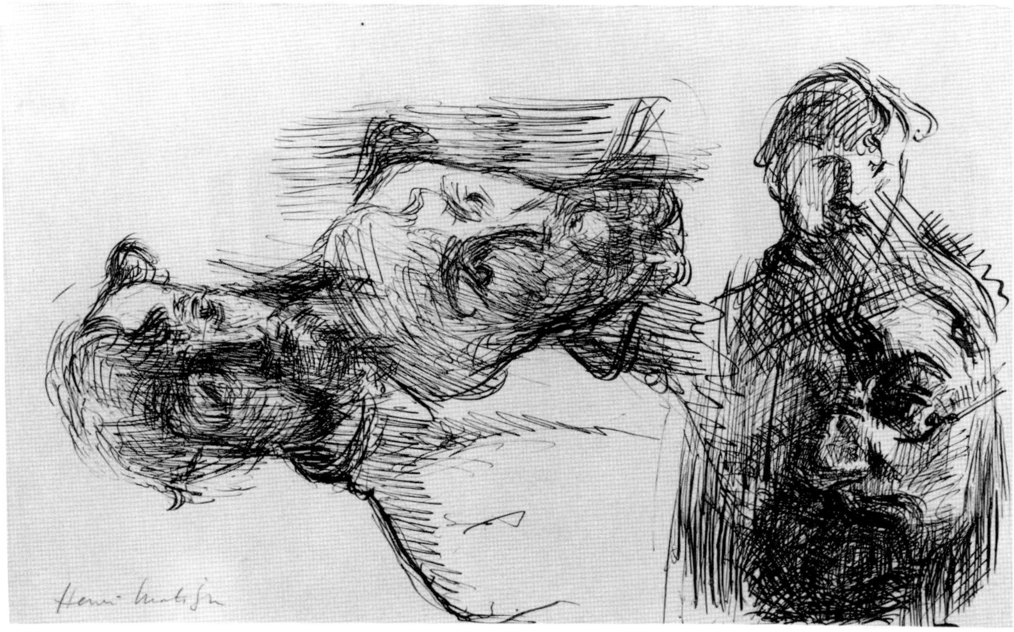

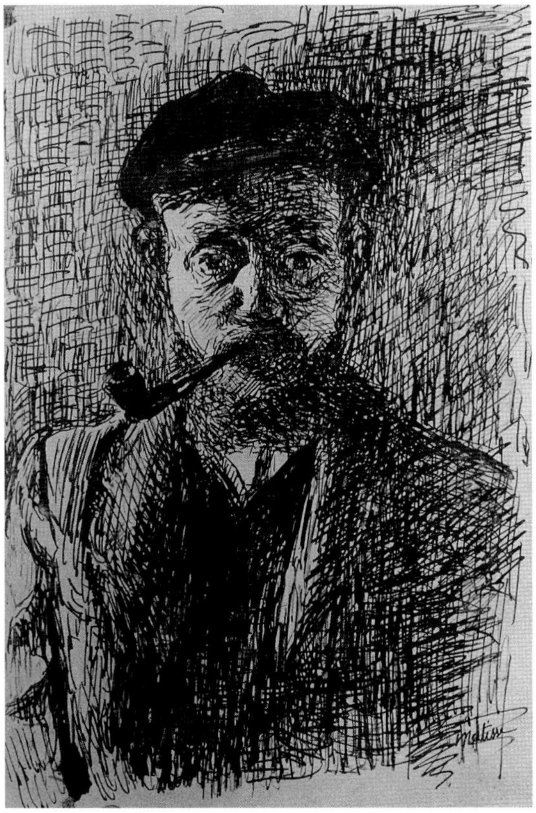

sion. It is certainly true that the turn of the century was a critical time in his life. Marriage, more children, straitened finances, and doubts about his artistic direction mark this period. It seems appropriate that Matisse literally looked to himself more than he had done and expressed his uncertainties, even his mood swings, in his self-portraits. But however compelling, personal circumstances and emotional turns can only partly explain his investment in self-imagery at this time and in the diverse self-images he produced. What is taking place is primarily a psychological and artistic process with two components: self-determination and self-presentation. Such self-portraiture is both a means to self-construction and a way of exhibiting public behavior while alone.

Testing identities, fashioning and refashioning himself, he offered anything but a unified persona in these self-portraits from 1899 to 1900 (see figs. 21–9, 31, 34). His self-staging runs the full theatrical range from melodrama to burlesque. In some of the more highly worked images, he seems to play it straight, his careful attention to feature, texture, and tone extending the labors of his meticulous essays from 1898. In the largest and most elaborated of the drawings (fig. 24), patiently constructed with varied strokes, flecks, and smudges of charcoal, he projected a chiseled gravity striking for a young man. In others (figs. 25, 26), he worked more quickly, creating characters who project more active emotions, rapid technique seeming to well up from unbridled feeling. His most painterly drawings of this time, done in brush and ink, share a moody intensity with the feverish palette and dense application of pigment in one of his two self-portrait paintings of this year (see fig. 29).

As great as the range is, it never seriously strains plausibility. None of the roles, none of the modes, seems too far a stretch for the sense of Matisse that emerges from all the biographical sources, or from his other art of this time. All the parts he plays on the stage of the self-portrait could "be" Matisse. In some ways, perhaps, he was an artist of limited imagination, without the mercurial transformative qualities of Picasso in the same period (Picasso was also younger and had not gone

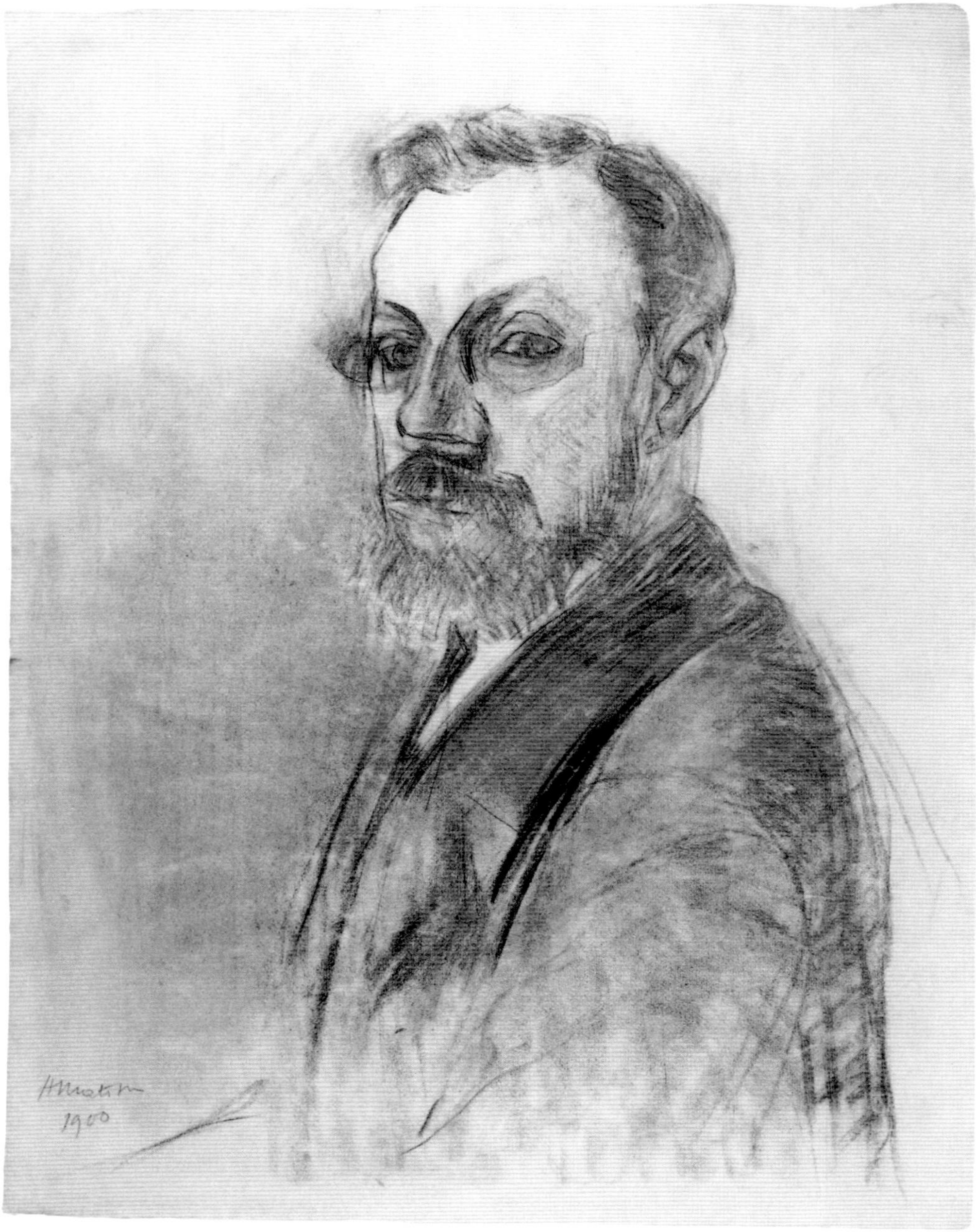

24 *Self-Portrait*, 1900. Charcoal on paper, 62.5 × 48 cm. Le Cateau-Cambrésis, Musée Matisse.

through a long period of academic training). Although he altered the rendering of his hair to project various emotional states, Matisse did not use wigs (see fig. 30). He also never figured himself as an urban dandy or a harlequin, or a creature of simian instincts, as Picasso sometimes did in self-mocking caricature.[27] The limitations in Matisse's self-projection may have been governed by a kind of "moral gravity," to use Jack Flam's phrase for the artist's seriousness and his sense of responsibility to himself and to his art.[28] It just did not allow him to be a monkey. Seen another way, Matisse was practicing a more rigorous form of "impression management" than Picasso was, monitoring and controlling his self-images even when he had no one but himself for an audience.[29]

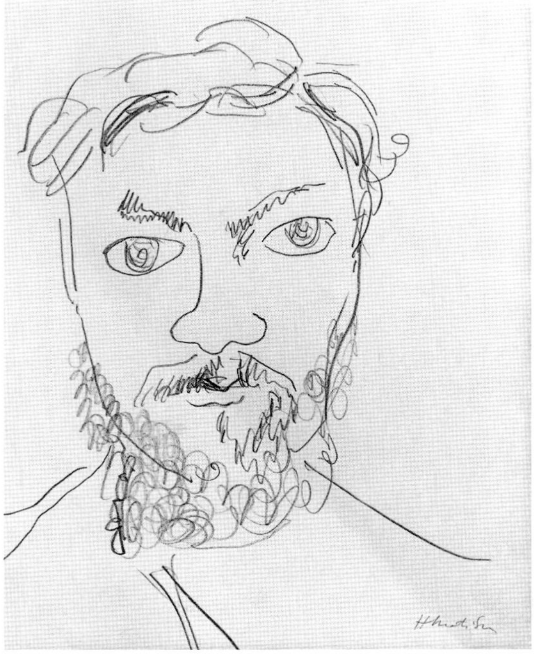

25 *Self-Portrait*, 1900. Crayon on paper, 30 × 23.6 cm. Private collection.

26 *Self-Portrait*, 1900. Brush and ink on paper, 24 × 19 cm. Private collection.

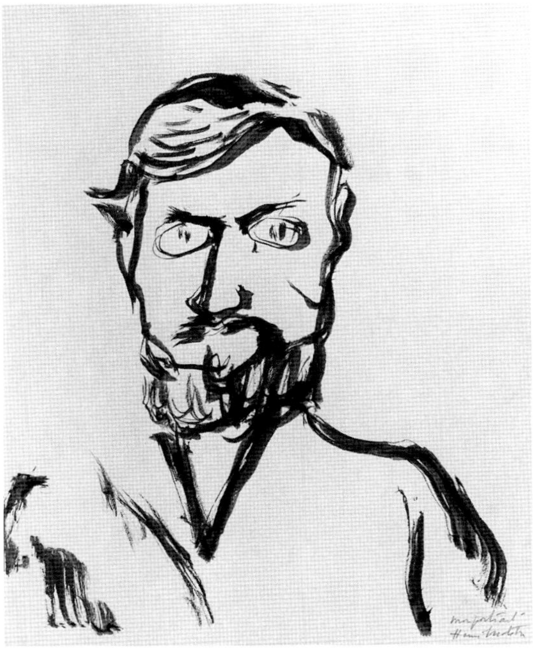

No animals, but props – plausible props – play a liberal role. Hats jaunty and sober come and go. He turns his head this way and that. His eyeglasses (Matisse was extremely nearsighted) come off; they go back on (figs. 21–3). When he drew himself with his glasses he used them to mark structure and space: the connection of sidepiece to lens becomes an evident reference point, anchoring the turn from the side of the head to the face. This stability allows for impression: he scrawls on the paper at the hair and beard, enjoying the analogy between cursive pen line and springy curls, then elsewhere concentrates on overall contours. In some drawings (see fig. 23), he modifies the patient accretive technique of the drawings from 1898 so that thread becomes wire, activating the surface without sacrificing precision effects, tensing the relationship between solid form and vibrating envelope. In another (fig. 21), impatience seems to put a brush in his hand so he can lay in shadow more rapidly. The eyes are, for seemingly obvious reasons, the center of attention in many of these works (figs. 25, 26, 29); in others they recede (figs. 24, 34), divert (fig. 22), are obscured by a hat (fig. 27), or even disappear (fig. 28). He plays other games with the eyes. Contrast the focused, searching quality of the eyes in some of the highly worked drawings and paintings (figs. 21, 24, 29) with their near-parody (fig. 25). In this drawing – perhaps the most Picasso-like – the effect of the wide eyes, so riveting elsewhere, is utterly undercut by the coiling tangles of beard, the unruly mat of hair, the stylized and flattened nose, and the little jolts of eyebrows scrawled in black crayon. Sometimes Matisse's technique seems crude, as in the lack of subtlety in his drawing of beard and jawline. Other details such as the assured and synoptic rendering of the nose, mouth, and hair show that his powers of condensation are impressive, as is the detachment required to pull off this sendup of his soul-searching mode. Here speed of execution is the natural result of hasty and concentrated observation – as well as playfulness – not the wellhead of intense feeling.

Calm or crazed, diffident or demanding, the images in these works allege a man of acute powers of observation and synthesis, as well as invention. What Matisse invents in these drawings, as so many artists do in self-portraiture, is a fiction of transparency. This transparency consists in the elimination of device and intention from the image, creating a performance of spontaneity, of the self suddenly apparent. Some of the drawings (figs. 21, 24, 25, 26) defy localization, the isolation of the image releasing it from anchorage in any place or circumstance. So thoroughly does Matisse form a sense of self-identification that these self-portraits seem to obliterate the distance between subject and object, so in looking at them we may well forget that an ordinary mirror has intervened, and that bodily action and conscious decision have occurred in real time and space.

In at least two ways, however, his self-portraits from this period also disclose the artifice of the transparent self to assert the factual conditions of self-portraiture, the physical and psychological separation of artist from image. The site of disclosure, appropriately, is the eyes, but eyes averted or occluded. Sometimes Matisse apparently tried to draw himself as if he were not looking at the mirror, as if he were not looking at himself, as if the drawing were of someone else; in other images this effect may be more apparent than intended (figs. 22, 24, 27, 28). Intended or not, distance is produced, the artist divorced from his image as it seems to offer the possibility of representing another man and not an artist making his own image, making the image of an artist. In assuming a range of identities from encounter to encounter Matisse was of course trying to render himself as though he were

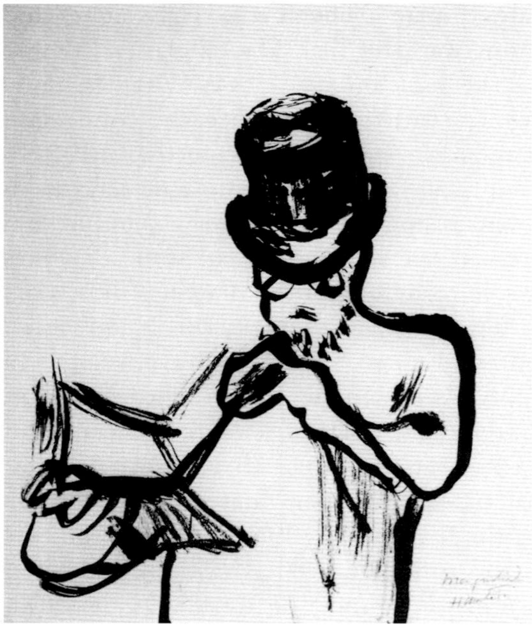

27 *Self-Portrait, Sketching*, 1900. Brush and ink on paper, 23.9 × 18.9 cm. Private collection.

28 *Self-Portrait, Sketching*, 1900. Pen and ink on paper, 33 × 22 cm. Private collection.

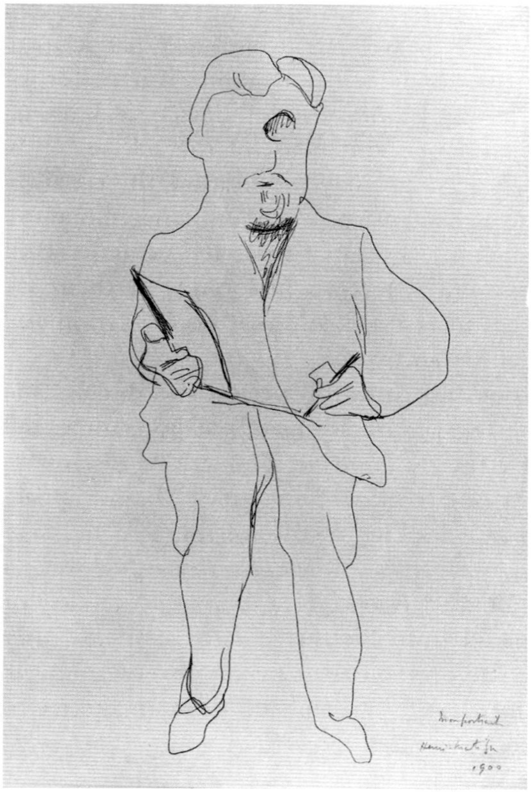

someone else, as if he could escape the constraints imposed when a person sits deliberately in front of a mirror and looks back and forth between it and a drawing pad or canvas. Yet it is the very act of assuming those constraints, of accepting them for the sake of making art, that produces the consciousness that in the act of creation the artist is also an other, an "alien" to ordinary life, as Matisse said of his own driven creative self. Cézanne had also acknowledged this duality of the artist at work (fig. 32) when he said: "Every time I face my easel, I am another man, yet I am still Cézanne."[30] The uncertain focus of Cézanne's eyes in his self-portrait indicates this division of the self that artists experience because they must address themselves as an other. Artists who show themselves at work provide another reminder to us and to themselves that history and fiction can sometimes make an uneasy alliance.

Matisse also accepted the duality of the identity of the artist by giving it a visual form, showing himself at work with brush or pen (figs. 27, 28, 34). Self-portrait as an artist making a self-portrait as an artist – evoking this infinite regress is the second way in which Matisse included the mechanics of self-portraiture in the image, cutting through the fiction of the transparency of the self, the notion that the relationship between artist and self-image – between subject and object – is indexical, a simple reflexive imprint with no intervention. But this move to show himself as an artist at work also has a reportorial quality about it, and a certain candor, a way for him to say that this, frankly, is what happens and how it looks when I do this. Thus a new transparency is produced, this one non-fictional, about the conditions of artistic production. In these images Matisse specifies the conditions and the tools of self-portraiture and expresses the vital energy of the artist at work.

Some of these images (figs. 31, 34) identify the studio as the site of this activity. Several (figs. 28, 29) imply other, indeterminate settings. In the interest of inoculating his students against artifice and mannerism in their work, Gustave Moreau had encouraged Matisse and his cohorts to learn from encounters with real life outside the studio, sketching cabaret singers, street sweepers, omnibuses – and themselves, sketching. In several full-length self-portraits (fig. 28), Matisse drew himself with sweeping lines, indicating only the general contours of his body and a few salient facial features.[31] Notebook grasped in one hand, he shows himself in this act of hit-and-run sketching. Here and in several related drawings his face is dominated by a single cyclopean eye socket, but the sensory organ itself, normally such a prominent feature of self-portraits, is obscured, even effaced. Paradoxically, suppressing the eyes, the visual hinge linking object and image, could also be a way to call attention to the transformative process of making the self-portrait. This suggests a third way in which Matisse's images of himself expose the fiction of transparency in self-portraiture. By combining an image of the artist at work with the suppression of the evidence of sight, these drawings deny in yet another way that the artist is a simple recorder of his own physical and mental state when he makes a self-portrait. He is not a mirror of nature any more than the mirror is merely a reflective device.

Between the two images of himself he painted in 1900 Matisse offers the same vision of a plural self. In a frenzy of brushwork (fig. 29), his varied, not to say chaotic technique agitates the surface and creates a mood of tentativeness and even anxiety. The bust-length format limits the evidence of his surroundings, although he is clearly posing himself in an interior, where rectangular forms suggest anything from door frames to paintings. Stark lighting contrasts convey a dramatic pres-

29 *Self-Portrait*, 1900. Oil on canvas, 55 × 46 cm. Paris, Musée National d'Art Moderne, Centre Georges Pompidou.

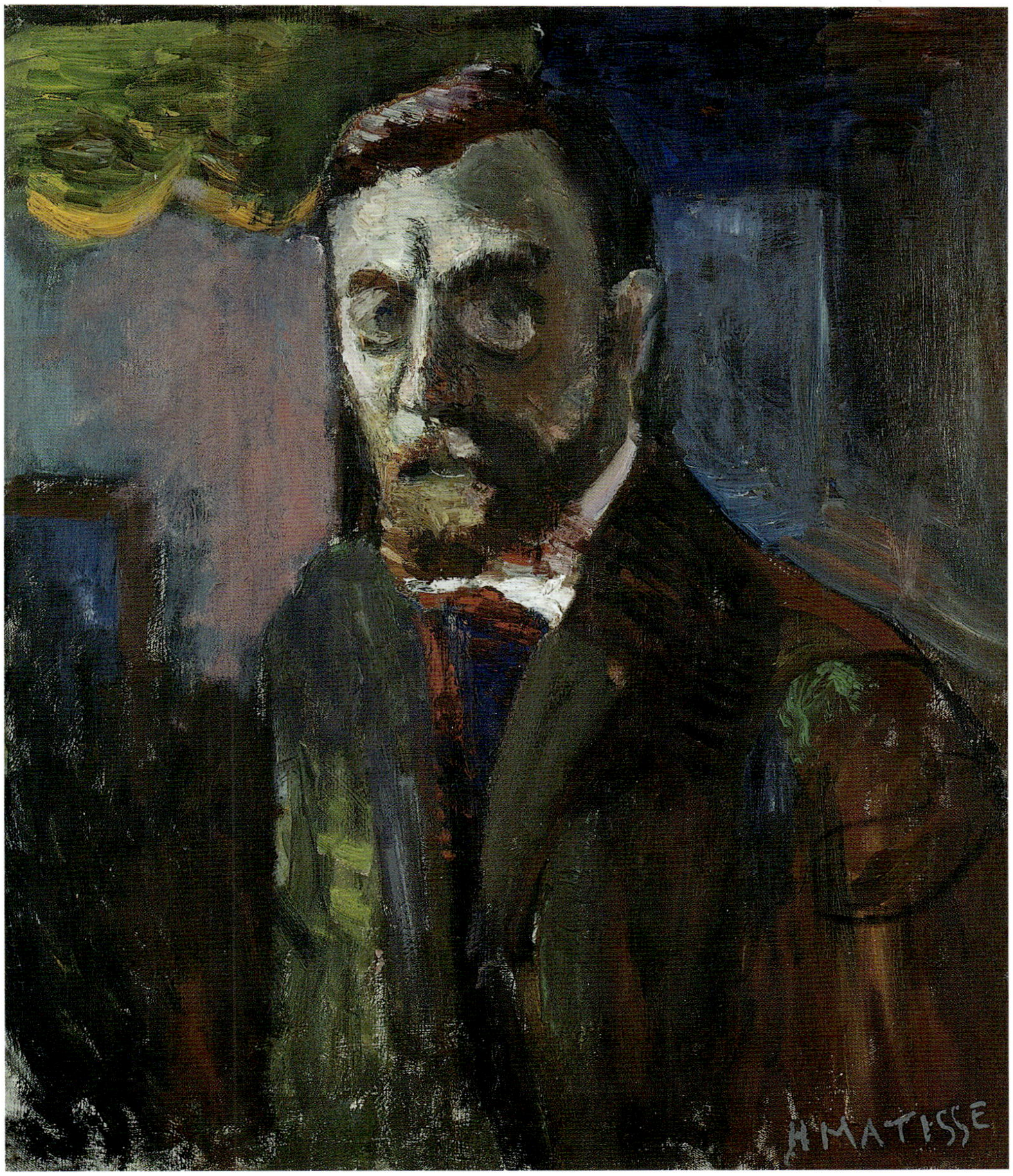

30 Pablo Picasso, *Self-Portrait in a Wig*, ca. 1897. Oil on canvas, 55.8 × 46 cm. Barcelona, Museu Picasso.

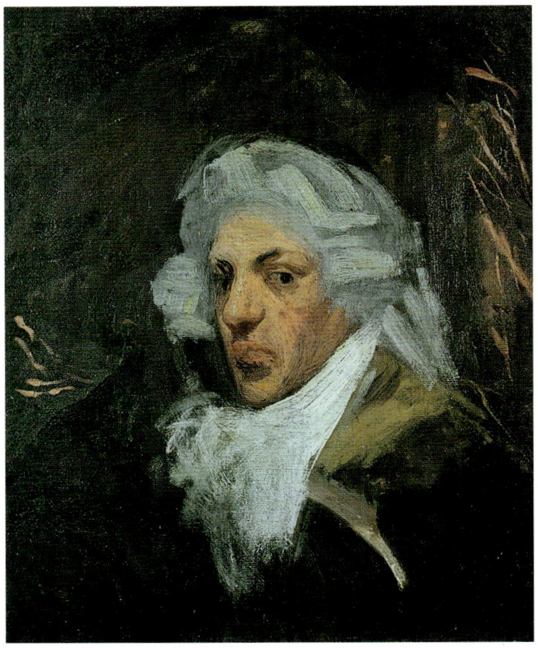

ence, a rhetorical flourish. The expressive use of color in this painting is allied to the landscape paintings he had recently made in the South that communicate excitement and unbridled pleasure in the possibilities of color freely handled. This self-image is charged with the intensity of the new. In the other painting, *Self-Portrait at the Easel* (fig. 34), everything is more restrained. Although it is a colorful canvas, the hues are more localized and generally do not run roughshod over contours (there is one exception to the restrained color: the orange aura with which Matisse surrounds himself). In palette, technique, and mood this is a more conservative painting and presents quite a different self-image. The environment is explicit, his occupation out in front. Now Matisse is clearly at work, not only on a self-portrait but on a programmatic statement of intention to declare himself an artist. In effect, these two paintings propose two sides of Matisse, what might be called the expressionist and the professional. The bold, unleashed, personal quality of one

31 (*right*) *Self-Portrait as an Etcher*, 1900–03. 4th state. Drypoint, 15.1 × 20.1 cm. The Museum of Modern Art, New York. Gift of Mrs. Bertram Smith.

34 (*facing page*) *Self-Portrait at the Easel*, 1900. Oil on canvas, 64 × 45.1 cm. Private collection.

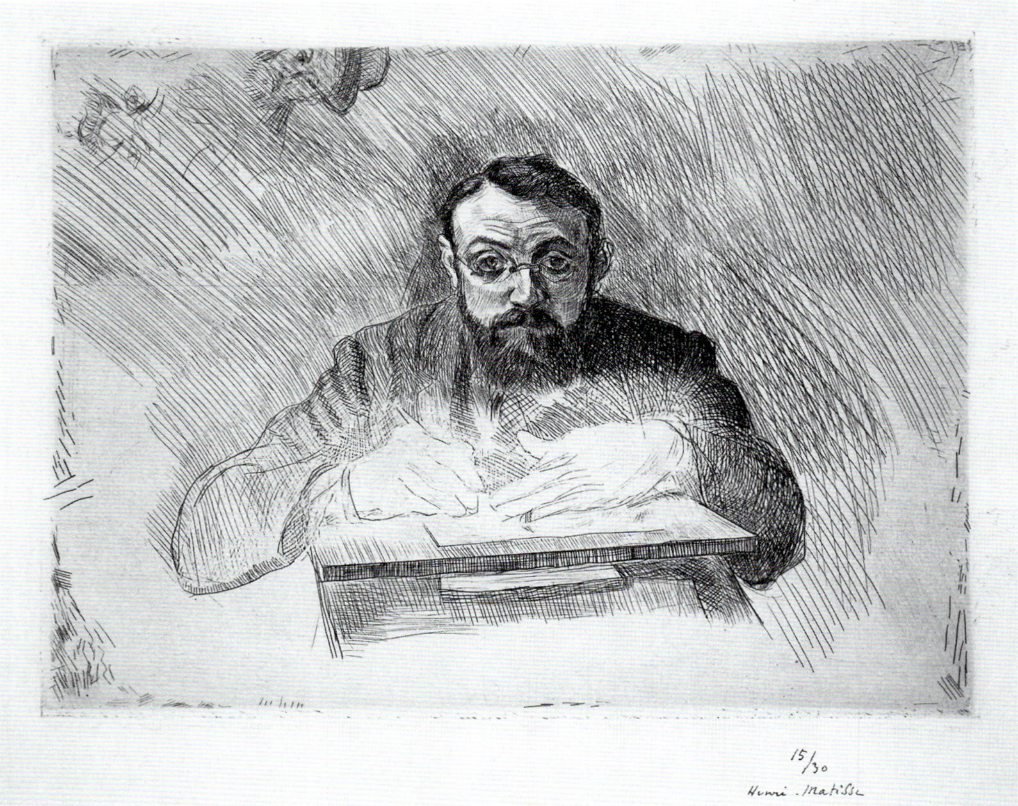

32 (*below left*) Paul Cézanne, *Self-Portrait with Palette*, ca. 1890. Oil on canvas, 92 × 73 cm. Zürich, Foundation E. G. Bührle Collection.

33 (*below right*) Rembrandt van Rijn, *Self-Portrait at the Easel*, 1660. Oil on canvas, 111 × 90 cm. Paris, Musée du Louvre.

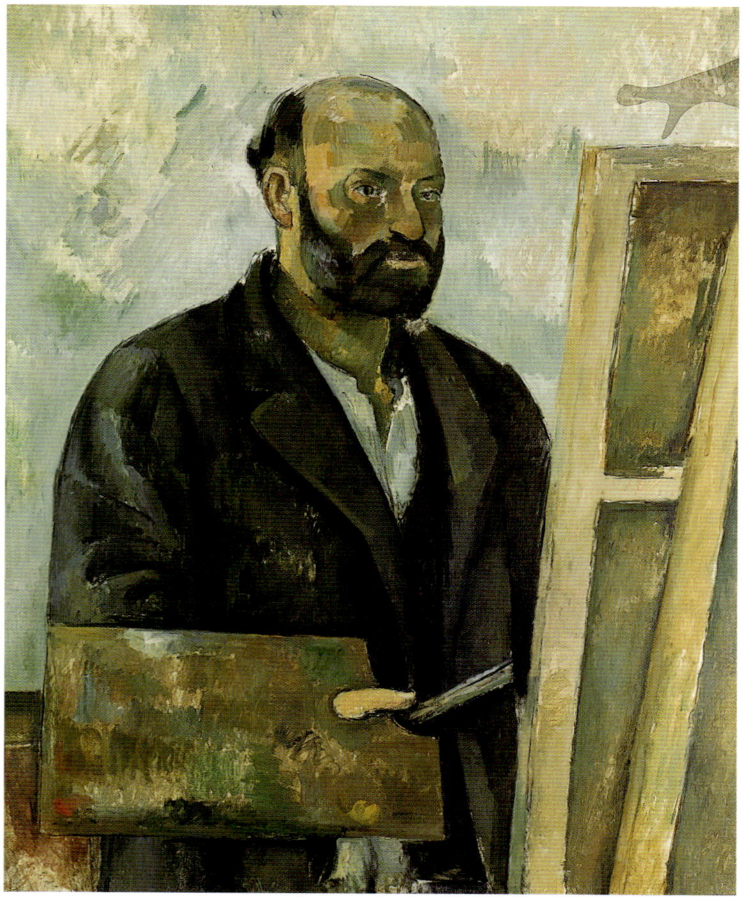

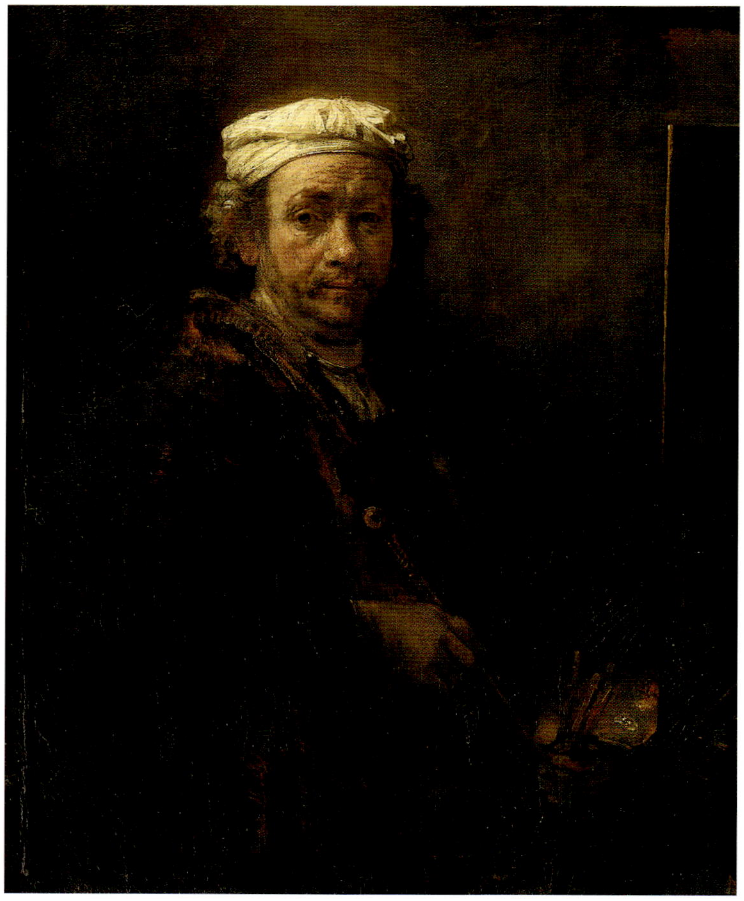

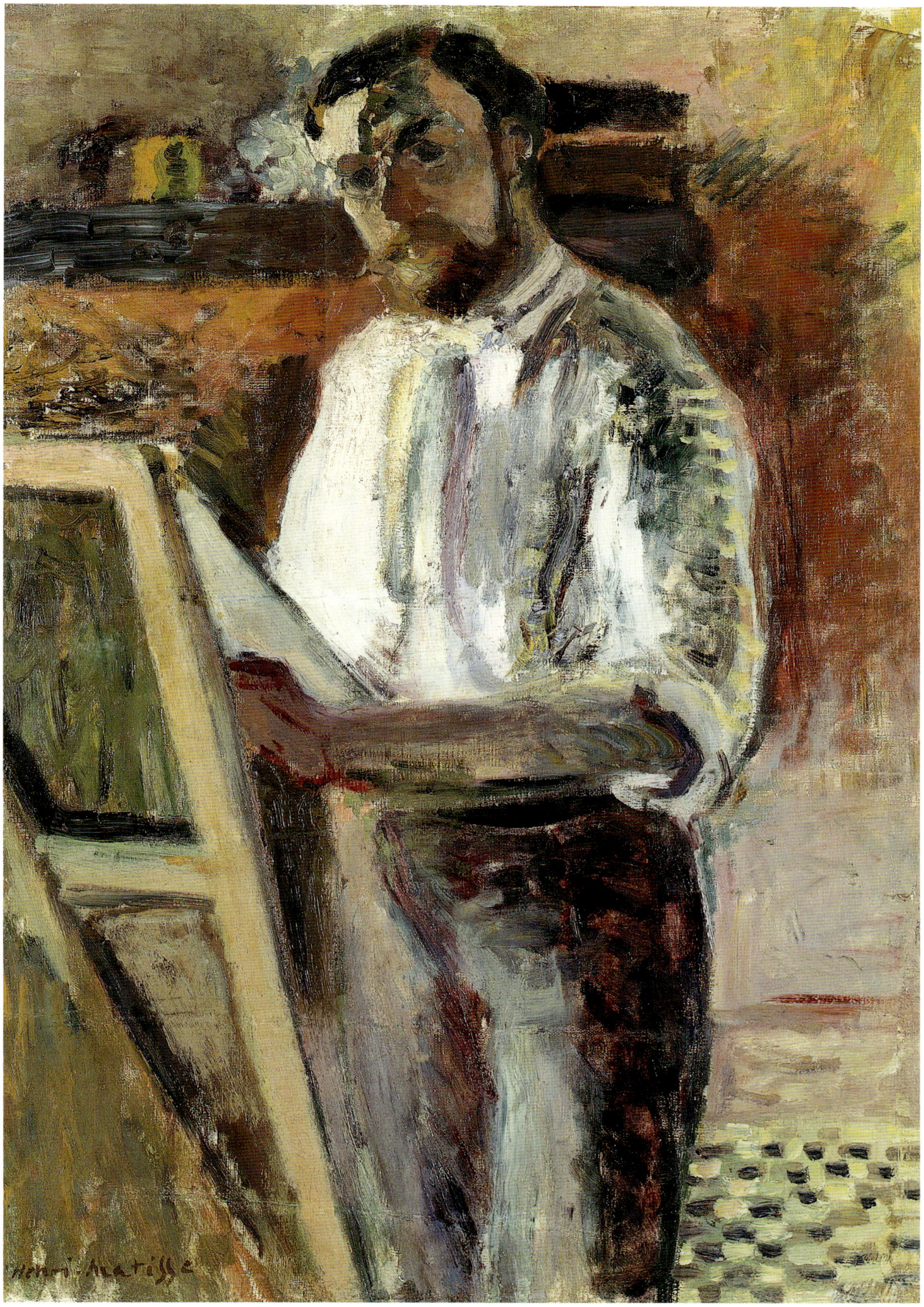
Henri-Matisse

is the flip side of the cool, assessing detachment of the other. In one a man; in the other an artist.[32] To these oppositions may be added another: a site of private contemplation and expression in contrast to a public declaration of *métier*. But it should be emphasized that Matisse apparently did not intend either of these paintings to become public; they were not exhibited or published until decades later.[33] His declarations, whether bold or tentative, of self or selves, were made largely in private.

For a personal, "expressionist" self, Matisse could rely on observation of his mirror image and his newly found sense of freedom with color to create an appropriate image. For the professional image, he sometimes sought a model, which he found in artists' self-portraits from the past, most clearly those of Rembrandt, of which a moving example was to be found in the Louvre (fig. 33). More recent artists had also enlisted Rembrandt for their occupational declarations, notably Van Gogh and Cézanne (see fig. 32).[34] Like Van Gogh and Cézanne before him at the easel, Matisse shows his desire both to ally himself with a distinguished lineage and to declare his investment in his profession. Tradition and practice fuse in such images, the past validating the present. Matisse made a similar declaration of commitment and professionalism in *Self-Portrait as an Etcher* (fig. 31), begun at the same time, showing him at work on the etching plate that would bear the matrix of the image we see. Unexperimental in technique and conventional in composition, this image seems to re-engage the conservatism of the self-portraits of 1898. Perhaps this can be explained as a natural tentativeness in a new medium. It was his first effort in printmaking, heralding a large graphic oeuvre (with *The Serf*, he was also learning sculpture at this time, and with a doggedness that characterizes also *Self-Portrait as an Etcher*). Like the studio painting, this work is indebted to Rembrandt, as the practice of etching was virtually indivisible from Rembrandt's reputation in the nineteenth century.

Matisse's plate (the technique is actually drypoint) seems to recapitulate on a small scale the duality of the self offered in the two painted self-portraits. He began, in what is now the upper left corner of the print, by drawing his head in small, almost caricatural doodles. Such offhandedness of placement and treatment, diffident and marginalizing, gives way to a more serious consideration of himself and his new medium.[35] Even more calm and watchful than in *Self-Portrait at the Easel*, the artist seems to be performing a stock-taking. In a new medium, he could make a further assertion: the artist himself has different identities – painter, sculptor, printmaker – with a range of tools at his disposal for his self-expression.[36] Already reflexively inclined, Matisse may have been attracted to printmaking at this time by its reversal of the image when the plate is printed. Reflexiveness (remember the mirror) is redoubled. It is also notable that of the several hundred etchings and drypoints he made in his career, this first print was the most carefully developed and thoroughly worked, evolving to its final form through several revisions. Finally Matisse left the hands incomplete. Their absence contrasted with the assured and complete drawing of the head suggests, maybe fortuitously, that the seat of art lies in the mental realm rather than in manual facility.

The self-portrait as a beginning text

The professional self comprises respect for and a thorough assimilation of traditional practices of making art; a desire to identify himself with the practitioners of the past; a tenuous hold on supportive material circumstances; insecurity about his new isolation, forced out of the shadow of student status; an ambitious need to break rules and innovate. Making self-portraits offered a comforting field of control for the self split by competing demands, both internal and external. All of the self-portraits just discussed – and many other works too – are part of Matisse's efforts at this juncture to define himself through the act of making art, creating himself along with his works. The real subject of these self-portraits is the process of self-definition in the creative act and in the work of art, made explicit and programmatic in such works as *Self-Portrait at the Easel*. After years of successful imitation and emulation of the certified artistic achievements of the past, after assimilating newer, less stable but potentially more exciting styles, Matisse was just at the point of reaching a horizon – but one within himself. The self is not found, as if it already exists, only to be discovered. The artist creates herself. Realizing this, and working from the need to undertake this process of self-definition, is the beginning of a career.

Edward Said has identified a tendency in the work of young writers that is pertinent to a consideration of the early development of Matisse's career, and perhaps other artists' careers as well. Said finds that the early writing of many authors is not only barely disguised autobiography, as is often obvious and expected, but is more significantly and subtly concerned with the process itself of becoming a serious creator. It is well known that young writers' novels are often about the self-questioning of characters who are uncertain of their path, but who know they want to get somewhere and persevere in this effort, even if somewhat blindly. Speaking in terms of literature, Said approaches the problem of why it is sometimes difficult for a writer, especially at the beginning of a career, to produce a text – that is, to begin and finish a distinctive personal effort that sets its author apart from others and marks the way to future expression. What can hinder this process, Said proposes, is a writer's inability "to distinguish adequately between the author as a human being . . . the author as a producing writer, and his production."[37] Separating these entities may result in the detachment and the consciousness of the self that are often necessary to wrest the "beginning text" – the opening gambit in artistic development – from the continuing process of human development.

The issue is the same for a painter as for a writer. To recast the problem: where does an author's, or an artist's, identity reside? In the self, in the act of creation, or in what is created? How does the artist decide? This "exemplary uncertainty" about what the self is binds Matisse's various self-portraits at the turn of the century into a common effort at self-definition. Individually considered, each self-portrait asserts something, or at least proposes a self. But taken as a group these self-images force these questions about the very source of the self for the artist. In the collective of these images some are commanding but none authoritative: they do not speak with one voice. If they had been unified – if they had projected a confident, unitary self – they would not have been necessary.

Asserting that distinctive personal voice is also a process of distinguishing oneself from everyone else, of staking out what is unique about oneself. In Matisse's case, it is precisely because his relationship to traditional art practice was so filial and extended, was a long artistic childhood of a kind, that his need to pose the question of his identity and work it over in many variations was so concentrated at this time. In speaking of his early career he characterized the necessity of self-assertion in terms of competing with and mastering his influences: "I believe that the personality of the artist develops and asserts itself through the struggles it has to go through when pitted against other personalities. If the fight is fatal and the personality succumbs, it means that this was bound to be its fate."[38] He said this to Guillaume Apollinaire in 1907, a time when he could speak with assurance, an assurance projected also in his assertive self-portrait painting of the previous year (see fig. 90). In 1900, the decisive year in his early career, Matisse's voice still echoed those of other creators. But by 1907 he was intent on fashioning for himself an identity that would resist the influence of others so that he could emerge master of them and of himself.

A second mirror stage

At this point we should note several obvious things that, taken together, may contribute to a deeper understanding of the psychology of self-portraiture, and its importance to young artists. First, an artist usually makes a self-portrait by looking in a mirror and creating a picture with reference to the reflected facial or bodily image.[39] Even more mundanely than this, nearly every person in Western culture is familiar with his or her image in the mirror; Matisse certainly was. The image we see in a mirror is basic to our understanding of how we look to ourselves. It is also the foundation of our sense of how we look to others, but there is a paradox here. We not only see ourselves (in the figurative sense) – that is, understand ourselves – uniquely, but the image of ourselves that we perceive in a mirror is different from what all other people see when they look at us. This difference between perception of self and others' perception of us is due, first of all, to the left-right reversal of our features in the mirror's reflection (certainly the increasing ease of studying photographs of ourselves reduces this element of the sense of difference). This much is obvious, and the difference may be trivial if it is considered in day-to-day terms, as a kind of operative procedure, as if we were to ask, "How do I really look to them?" But at an early age we learn how we look to ourselves before we are able to imagine how we look to others, and this may be significant. The circumstances, early in our lives, of one way in which we come to know about ourselves, and its implications for self-portraiture, are worth some consideration.

We take our mirror image for granted, but there is a point in the development of an individual when he or she is not aware of its existence and significance. Research into the process by which an infant gradually develops the awareness of its own reflection in the mirror was the basis for Jacques Lacan's "mirror stage" theory.[40] Lacan conducted a comparative study of the behavior of infant chimpanzees and human babies in the presence of a mirror. He observed that in their first months neither chimpanzee nor human had any awareness of its mirror image. The developing chimpanzee never attains this awareness of the mirrored self. The mirror image is eventually apprehended as if it were another chimpanzee.

As early as six months, though, the human infant begins to identify the connection between the mirror image and its body. This realization that the self and the mirror image are connected is a source of delight, what Lacan describes as a "jubilant assumption" by the child of its image, a pleasurable identification with a spectacle of wholeness before it. Before full mobility, before learning to talk, the child begins to perceive its body as a whole, as integrated and independent. Its identification of this image of wholeness with the actual body of which it has yet only fragmentary knowledge (what Lacan calls the *corps morcelé*, the "body in pieces") is the key to the child's symbolic understanding of its wholeness, its uniqueness – in short, its identity. This sense of wholeness is, however, premature, "tied to the temporal dialectic by which she appears *already* to be what she will *only later become*."[41] The perception of a whole self is located in an imaginary space, the space of the mirror, something the child also discovers in a later phase of the mirror stage. The resulting disillusionment – the disintegration of the illusion of wholeness by the realization that the child's skills are insufficient to attain autonomy – leads to frustration and desire (Lacan goes so far as to present this as an alienating process). Thus the mirror stage contains both an anticipation of future wholeness and a revelation of present inadequacy. For Lacan, the mirror does not simply reflect the self, despite any literal visual correspondence between bodily appearance and mirror image. The mirror is an agent of self-construction used in the creation of an ideal that cannot yet be realized. Eventually the child "grows into" the image of wholeness and mastery that produced the initial pleasure.

But before this mastery of the body and of language, the child learns control over an image. This mirror image is possibly one of the first things a child is able to control. Children learn to control themselves by learning to control an image, an other.[42] The assumption of the mirror image is a process of seeing the self in an other, of making an identification. Identification is possible through, but perhaps at the price of, detachment. This detachment, acknowledging the other, begins the individual's process of socialization.

By now a suggestive parallel between Lacan's mirror stage theory of developing identity and Matisse's process of self-determination in early self-portraiture should be clear. A young artist who had had a long apprenticeship under several teachers, and whose ultimate frame of reference was the example of Western artistic tradition, makes a focused effort to assert himself by drawing and painting after his image in a mirror. He proposes various images of himself, posing, staring, shifting, mugging, and he achieves a wide range of effects, a series of others outside himself, some of which he decides may represent him. It is tempting to believe that this process is an adult version of the stage in infancy when such activity before a mirror is first found by its performer to have meaning.[43]

Matisse was not merely recording his actions, as of course he consciously was, but was asserting the fundamental importance of his own subjectivity. I am not suggesting that the process of invention in the act of portraying the self is entirely a conscious activity. A desire or urge to make self-portraits surely has some basis in needs that cannot always be articulated. But as in the mirror stage, the artist forms the subject by treating it as an object outside the subjective self. Identification and detachment are mingled in the creative process as the self creates possibly assimilable others.[44] Perhaps without full awareness of its implications, Matisse determined his artistic identity in the three-way intersection of the subjective self, the act of creating, and the objects he created.

Lacan's mirror-stage model has limitations for illuminating this kind of self-portraiture. The infant's mirror stage is a process of self-discovery, albeit an illusory self-discovery. As I have suggested, self-portraiture at an early point in an artist's career is not a means of discovery but of self-determination, a process of making the self through the activity of art, not of finding or discovering the self, as the infant does in its identification. As a corollary, this difference between making and finding can be found also in the realm of images. The infant gradually finds and identifies its image in the mirror; the artist seeks the specular self-image as a stimulus to her creation of a further and more productive kind of self-image as an artist. Lacan proposed that the child does not attain "sufficiency" as a result of the mirror stage, but reaches only a state of anticipation of sufficiency: that is, the illusory wholeness of the mirror image would continually elicit the desire for sufficiency that the infant cannot attain until full motor and linguistic skills develop. For Matisse, by contrast, the second mirror stage resulted precisely in the kind of sufficiency he sought – that of an artist with the confidence to pursue his individual vision, using what he needed from his training and the example of traditional practice, but making his own path by first constructing his image as an artist.[45]

Willed fragments

After 1900 Matisse made self-portraits only sporadically for the next thirty-five years, although they do include two important paintings done at key moments in his career. In the early years of the century Matisse greatly increased his public activity as an artist by showing work in exhibitions and by selling both privately and through gallery representation. His self-assertion was now a more public affair and began, tentatively, to take the form of career management. His employment of careful strategies for public exposure is a notable aspect of his overall development at this time.[46] The more private mode of expression and self-assessment characteristic of the self-portrait, not intended for public consumption, did not fit into his needs.

Yet he had certainly not relinquished his earlier insistence on representing his subjectivity pictorially. As an alternative to depicting his face and body in his work, he began to assert himself without this presence that signals wholeness. Instead, he devised ways to insert himself subtly, or partially, or even invisibly, by inference. One of the ways to do this was to paint and draw his immediate environment, especially his studio, as he did in several paintings in 1902 and 1903.[47] In some of these the presence of the artist is implicit; the studio acts as an extension, both conceptual and spatial, of the artist and his practice. (These works were echoed later by such paintings as *The Red Studio*, the ultimate in the animistic studio.) In others he reprised another self-referring theme from his earlier work – the self-image incorporated into a larger composition. *Carmelina* (fig. 35) and *Still Life with Red-Checkered Tablecloth*, both from 1903, look back to *Woman Reading* (see fig. 14) and the other reflexive paintings of the 1890s that blend genres together to form a hybrid that calls attention to the manipulative role of the artist.[48] In both paintings the image of Matisse's face now appears in a mirror, not as a movable image. Marginalized in *Still Life with Red-Checkered Tablecloth*, at a regressive remove in *Carmelina*, Matisse's self-image is fragmentary but understood to represent his full command over everything around him. Whereas the relationship between the creating artist and his studio world is slyly disclosed in *Woman Reading*, in *Carmelina* it is displayed as a bold confrontation, even a kind of competition. The presence of the eponymous subject – a robust nude woman – is lively and assertive. But the artist, though small and partial in his mirror image, is in complete control, the arresting red of his shirt set in opposition to the blue jug signaling his importance to all physical properties of the picture.[49] Nominally an attractive, alluring presence, the richly modeled nude is no match for the seductiveness of the specular image of the artist, which spreads from its disembodied post throughout the picture as the viewer realizes that everything is just so because of him. This sense of control characterized Matisse's work for several years, not as a pictorial subtext, as here, but in the willful character of his formal invention and manipulation in works of art

35 *Carmelina*, 1903. Oil on canvas, 81.3 × 59 cm. Museum of Fine Arts, Boston. Tompkins Collection.

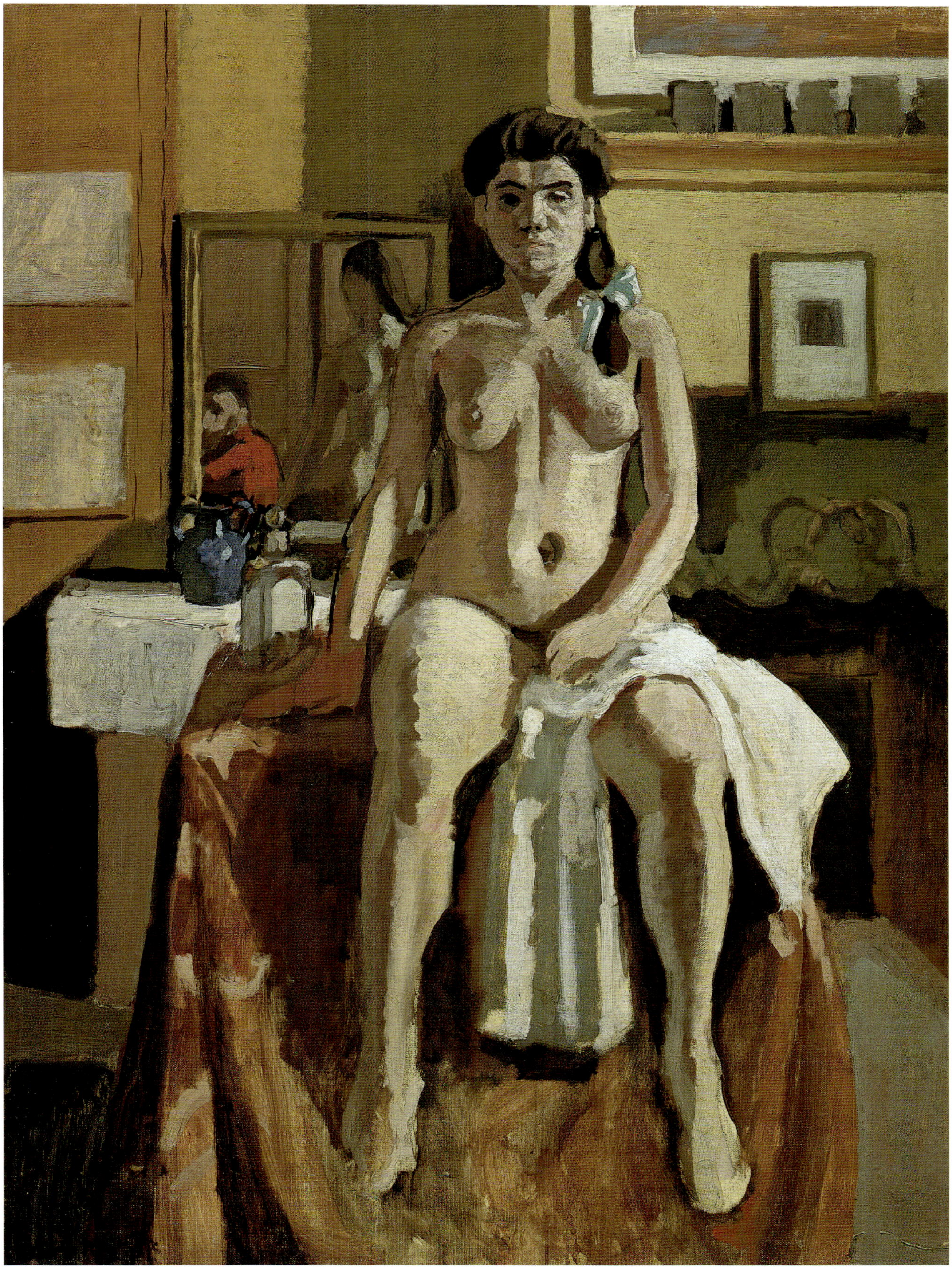

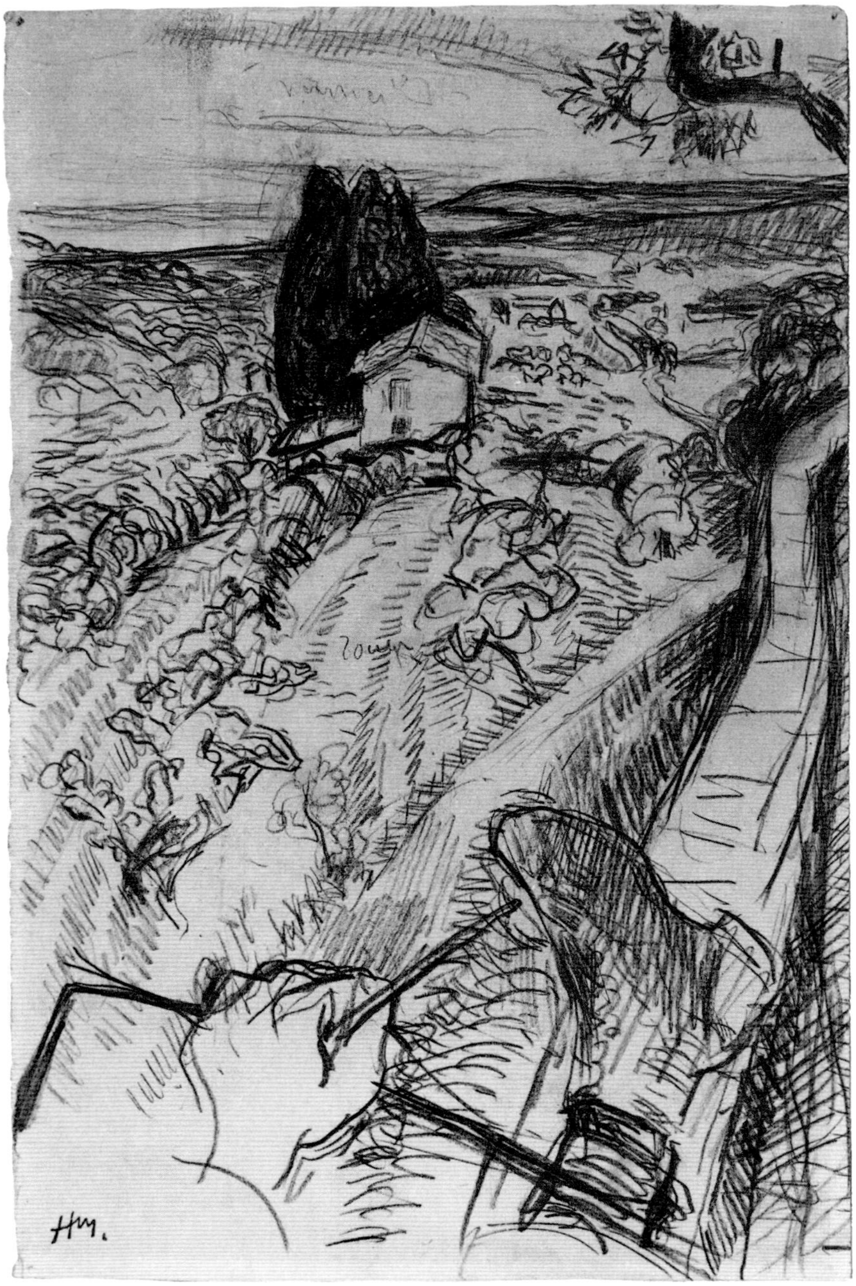

36 *Landscape, Saint-Tropez*, 1904. Pencil on paper, 31 × 20 cm. Nice, Musée Matisse.

without the element of self-portrayal, as well as in his public challenges to convention.

A final self-image here, another fragment, specifically does not lend itself to closure or completion. Partial and marginalized also is the artist's presence in *Landscape, Saint-Tropez* (fig. 36). In a strange composition, he has shown a landscape, a landscape that he is drawing, one that also contains the image of him drawing. Fragments of his body are part of his view, as is the drawing pad he addresses. Having, around 1900, realized a totalizing image through a conscious process of self-portrayal, Matisse can now confidently make a partial image – an image of a piece of his body, two disconnected pieces, in fact – without anxiety, playfully, masterfully.[50] The image of the *corps morcelé* when made by the artist himself is not a threat to self-perception of wholeness; in fact, it is a demonstration of self-command as well as an expression of wit. Part of the playfulness is in the conundrum of Matisse's representation of himself drawing. If he is drawing himself drawing, then his drawing hand should address the pad of paper at the lower left, not the foot extended before him. Yet of course he is drawing this booted foot too. Here Matisse halts the potential for infinite regress (a drawing of a hand drawing a hand drawing, and so on) and brings the image up short, returning it to the real, in apparent uncertainty about how to resolve this exercise.[51] Finally, there is an additional irresolution, this in the right-handed Matisse's apparent depiction of his left hand in the act of drawing: a whimsical coda to the intensity and reflexiveness of mirrored self-construction a few years earlier.

The next self-portrait Matisse made was the true master image, resolutely whole and self-sufficient, of 1906 (see fig. 90). During this decade the portrait, so marginal in his work of the 1890s, emerged as a central concern both in the realms of formal invention and as a means of personal expression. Of Matisse's portraits from this period, none figure so prominently in both these areas as the many images of the members of his family. If the origins of the self-portrait as a process of self-definition may be found in early stages of the development of the individual, it may be possible to locate the genesis of Matisse's portraiture in those who initially meant the most to the artist, and who provided the most ready extension and confirmation of his values. In the family the self is reflected and transmitted into others: after the second mirror stage the specular I can (again) become a social I.

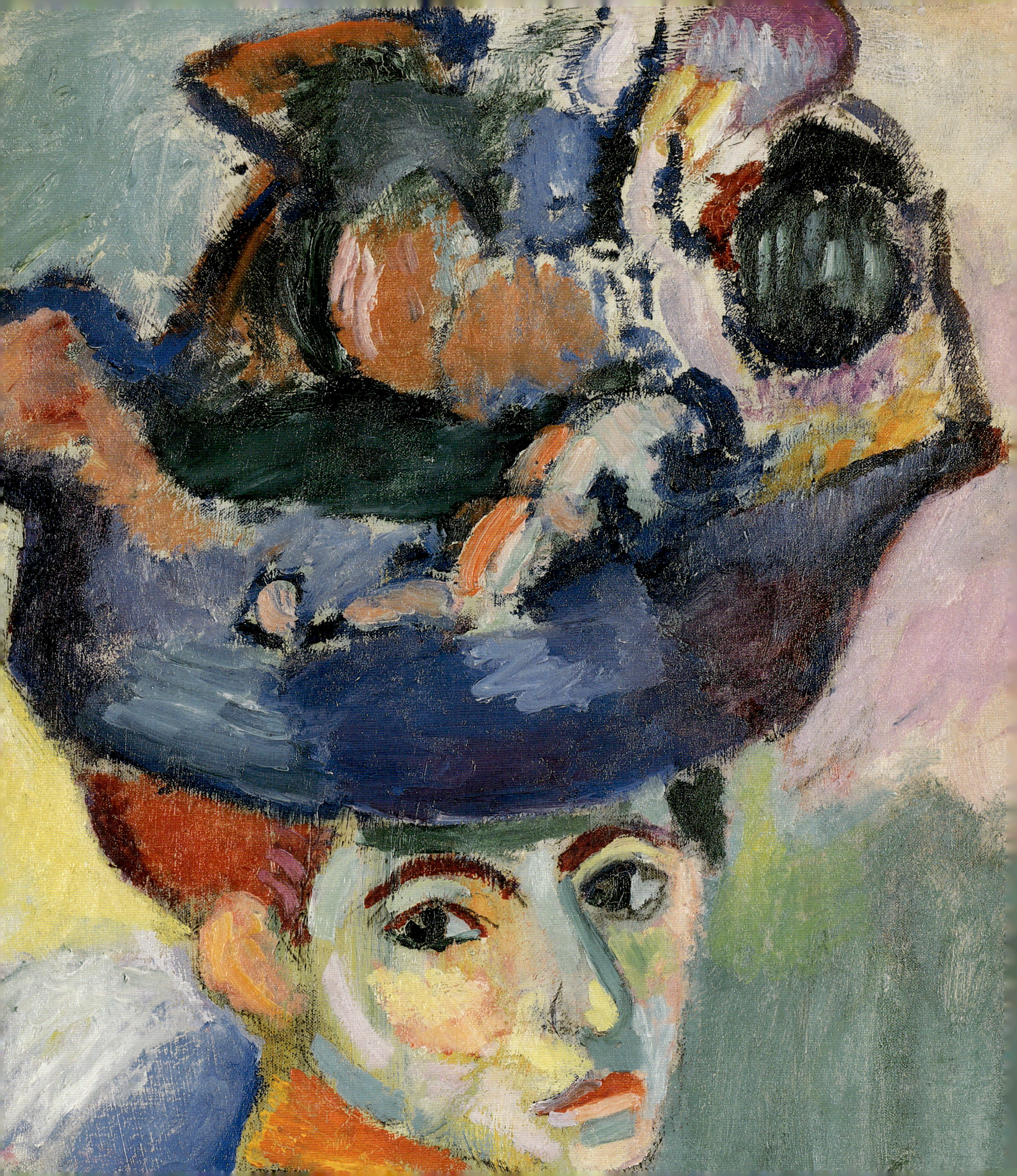

Chapter 3 Private Lives in Public Spaces

We have seen the analogy Matisse made between artistic and genetic creation, and it should be no surprise that his principal field of inscription for this analogy was his own family. Although the drawing of his mother that prompted the "revelation at the post office" has not survived, and he apparently made no other portraits of his parents, the role in his art of the family he created testifies to the importance of this affinity between two modes of creation. In an interview near the end of his life, Matisse himself acknowledged a link between artistic and genetic legacies. When asked, "Does the work reflect the artist?" he replied: "The work is the emanation, the projection of self. My drawings and my canvases are pieces of myself. Their totality constitutes Henri Matisse. The work represents, expresses, perpetuates. I could also say that my drawings and my canvases are my real children."[1]

While this may be passed off as casual hyperbole, more than a figure of speech animates that last, sad, sentence. By then, his actual children, Marguerite, Jean, and Pierre, had for many years all been adult creators themselves, both in artistic and genetic terms.[2] Perhaps partly because of these marks of maturity and independence, for the most part they had long ceased to be of interest to Matisse as the object of his own art, and obviously his own recent artistic creations were more vital to him. But his grandchildren were cherished sitters late in his career, as we shall see: Matisse was fascinated by their youthful development, as he had been by that of his children.

Expanding the field of identity

Portraits within the family circle overwhelm in number all others by Matisse until 1908, when the cachet of being painted by the king of the Fauves began to increase his opportunities for representing people in the public sphere. While they were often for private consumption only, his portraits of his family cannot be thought of merely as dry runs leading up to more public efforts. His goals in these family portraits were distinct and were governed in part by his sense of his family as an extension of himself; nevertheless, they may have conditioned his later approach to portraits of friends, colleagues, patrons, and others. Once Matisse had undergone the process, through the self-portrait, of establishing a field for the image of his own identity, he then used his family and his images of them to extend his sense of himself in his art as well as in his life. His wife and children were the raw human material that contributed to the shape of his attitude to the portrait. In both fields – portraiture and family – Amélie, Marguerite, Jean, and Pierre Matisse served as means to further his own artistic concerns more than to represent his sitters' claims to identity and expression.

Detail of fig. 46.

Matisse's new interest in the human figure around 1900 should also be associated with his feelings toward his family, completed in that year with the birth of Pierre, the last of three children. From this nucleus he derived the greater part of his portraits and figure studies over the next five years, the crucial period of his maturity into an artist of conviction. His principal sitter of 1900, himself, whose availability was limited only by that of a mirror, was followed closely by his family, whose availability was conditioned by traditional deference to patriarchal will. He wanted them to sit, and they sat.

There is more to it than this, of course. Between 1900 and 1906 Matisse made very few self-portraits. It is not coincidental that he shifted his attention from overt depictions of himself. In this period he became a far more public figure, a frequent exhibitor in Paris, an object of critical scrutiny. Furthermore, the move away from the mode of overt self-representation that characterized the period before 1900 is not as definitive as it seems. The family is an extension of the self, genetically, psychologically, and socially. Consequently, portraits of family members extend and develop self-imagery into a new realm. They explore and express an aspect of the self that did not exist before being created, through marriage and parenthood, by the artist. It would be vain to propose rigorous parallels between the creation of works of art and human procreation, but some of the interest for an artist in portraying his children may lie in their extension of his own genetic identity (this could of course be expected to apply equally to an artist who is also a mother). Thus the artist's inquiry into the forms of the self may continue with his dependents. The limitation of the artist's self-expression in a single image can be transcended by family portraiture.

A portrait, I have already asserted, is a site of transaction between an artist and a sitter. It gives an image to a process of negotiated representation and self-representation. A portrait brings to the surface – and onto a surface – the trace of a personal relationship that is not ordinarily given such a fixed form. When a portrait is exhibited or otherwise published, the struggle for control of the representation of identity that a portrait records takes place in a much larger public arena, where the response of others to this struggle enters the life of the portrait. If a portrait of a family member, and the intimate transactions to which the portrait gives an image, enters the public sphere, the revelation to an audience of what had been held as private can cause acute discomfort. As Matisse attained notoriety and then fame, portraits of his family were key instruments both in his artistic development and in the formation of his public reputation. The link between Matisse's use of his family in the service of his art and his use of that art in creating his public persona is the subject of this chapter.

Self-portraiture and autobiography

The relationship between the self-portrait and literary autobiography bears on the transition from private domain to public sphere in portraiture. The flourishing of the autobiographical novel is a well-known phenomenon in the nineteenth and twentieth centuries.[3] The genre also became more explicitly self-referential. I have suggested in the Introduction reasons for the rise of the artist's self-portrait in the same period as an explicit statement of the validity of self-expression. The parallel between the self-portrait and the autobiography is on many counts incomplete and, for that matter, the two self-referring genres are not comparable in several respects. This incommensurability has a great deal to do with how an artist can use portraiture, especially family portraits, to compensate for the limits of the self-portrait as a vehicle of self-expression. In addition to having a temporal structure normal for most works of literature, autobiography has what we might call a spatial, or environmental, structure as well. The story of a life, in all but the most recondite cases, is also, maybe even mainly, the story of the intersection of the life of the author with the lives of others. Family, friends, influential figures, nemeses, all go in. The social component of autobiography is taken for granted because it is usually so central.

The self-portrait is limited in this respect. It does not typically convey the intersection of lives, as the autobiography does. Its constraint in the temporal sphere is effectively absolute. The autobiography combines memory and invention; the self-portrait observation and invention. In self-portraiture, since the act of observation and the thing observed are both in the present, the self-portrait seems more verifiable, seems to offer more of a reality check. Writers and students of autobiography have long accepted the necessary component of invention in an allegedly candid genre. The same caution must accompany the interpretation of self-portraiture.

Although expansion of the environmental aspect of the self-portrait is possible, most artists have not usually undertaken this. Some exceptions, of course, arose in the last two centuries. Occasionally an artist may pose with a friend (Degas, Vuillard), a lover (Courbet, Tissot, Picasso), or with spouse or children, especially among the apparently more family-oriented Northern artists (Corinth, Thoma, Lenbach, among many others) – Matisse's *Conversation* (see fig. 57), a double portrait of himself and his wife, is an exceptional instance in his work. By and large, though, the self-portrait isolates the self – after all, this is so often the point of such imagery. And this is where much of the invention in self-portraiture is accomplished: the artist creates a myth of a self isolated from society and unaffected by it. The expansiveness of the sphere of the self so fundamental to autobiography must in the visual arts spill over into other traditional genre categories, most obviously and conveniently the portrayal of others. Thus portraits of Matisse's intimates may be understood as expressions of himself inasmuch as they extend the scope of thought, emotion, and action of the self. The artist projects himself onto those close to him. This may be true even without an artist's overt manipulation of the images of friends, lovers, children, and others in a close circle.

One can easily imagine that such an enterprise for the use of the family is as demanding as it is appealing to an artist. When the family situation is less than harmonious, as was often the case in the Matisse household, one might also expect tensions to be expressed in the imagery, not, again, in the interest of realism, but of expression. But beyond any link between emotional cause and artistic effect, I propose that the act of portrayal itself came to have too much emotional freight for Matisse, deriving in part from his experiences in making portraits of the members of his family. These experiences had an archetypal relationship to his later efforts in portraiture. He was attracted by what he saw of himself in the members of his family, and by the consequent opportunity for self-expression, but was challenged by conflicting emotions, especially toward his wife Amélie. When he made portraits he could not avoid a certain frustration that filled the resulting gulf between his respect for the sitter and for the conventions of the genre, on one hand, and his desire for complete self-expression, on the other.

Sincerity was a central element in Matisse's mentality and in his projection of a public self-image. He insisted that he was sincere to himself and that his work was unimpeachable as an expression of his emotional response to his motifs.[4] Portraiture came to seem a compromised activity for him not because he needed to "lie" to make a portrait, but because the honest results of his investigation of his sitters sometimes did violence to the conventions by which the portrait could be recognized as a portrait. Decorum could not hold against the assault of private forces. Such violation became clear only when private responses were put on public display. There they were unacceptably candid. What can be said at home cannot necessarily be repeated outside the family circle.

Amélie Matisse, wife and mother

Early in 1898, Matisse married Amélie-Noémie-Alexandrine Parayre (born 1872), from Toulouse. In the previous year he had broken off with Caroline Joblaud and had taken the legal steps to recognize officially his illegitimate daughter, Marguerite. He may have wished to stabilize Marguerite's status in anticipation of the end of this unsanctioned relationship.[5] His legal action with regard to his daughter was not directly related to his marriage since he had not yet even met his future wife.

By most accounts, Amélie Matisse was the model wife of an artist. "Among the many admirable wives of great artists very few have been more generously self-sacrificing and at the same time effectively practical as Amélie Matisse" was Alfred Barr's assessment, and it is typical.[6] She was industrious and highly resourceful, and was frequently responsible for keeping the family finances together. For several years she was the only one who brought in any money, from her milliner's business, an index of her ability to take charge and do what was necessary. At home she generated the necessary support that insulated her artist husband from distraction. She was almost universally acknowledged for the sacrifices she made for the sake of her husband's art, and we can imagine that her lot was often hard, and that she might not always have borne these burdens lightly, as some anecdotes confirm. Barr's statement that "Mme Matisse found time too to pose for many of her husband's paintings" makes her time-consuming and tedious labors as a model – while still being the main provider – sound voluntary and amiable, but this seems an unlikely construction, a product of Barr's discretion as he worked under the authority of the artist himself.[7]

Nearly a year after their marriage, Matisse made a seated half-length drawing of Amélie (fig. 37).[8] It is like a belated wedding portrait (or perhaps he made it to observe their first anniversary), traditional in pose, formal, removed from daily life. In its bold mixture of techniques it corresponds to his contemporaneous self-portrait (see fig. 21) and, although these two drawings are not the same size, they have the quality of being pendants. Here as in his self-portrait, Matisse primarily used the brush to lay in areas of costume and background, reserving the finer pen lines for delineating facial features. Those of his wife seem less fluid, more firmly incised than his own. While the atmosphere in the self-portrait is tentative or inquisitive, in the face of Amélie there is sharpness and resolve. Matisse's approach here is far from the documentary tone of the bas-reliefs of Caroline Joblaud – the draftsmanship in this drawing is decidedly expressive – but this portrait of Amélie nonetheless has an obligatory quality. Despite its interest on both a

37 *Amélie Matisse*, 1899. Pen, brush, and ink on paper, 32.2 × 24.6 cm. Private collection.

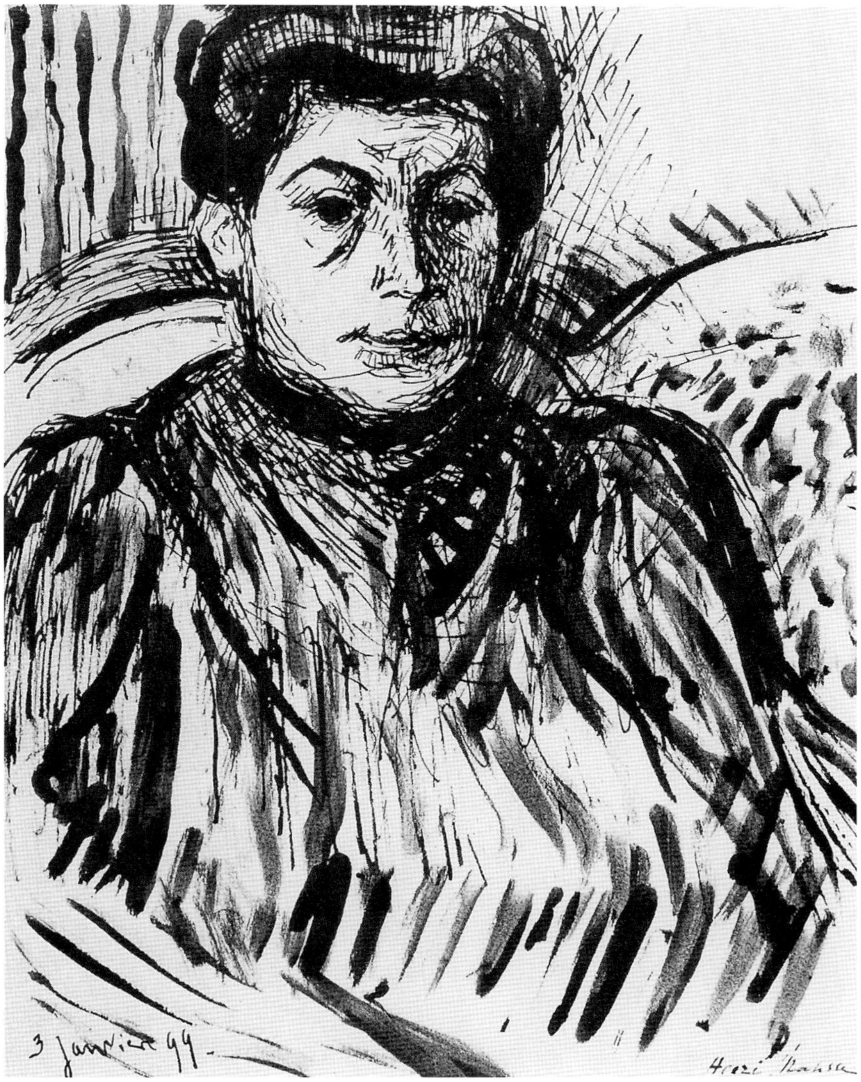

38 *Madame Matisse Feeding Jean*, ca. 1901. Pen and ink on paper, 29.6 × 23.8 cm. Private collection.

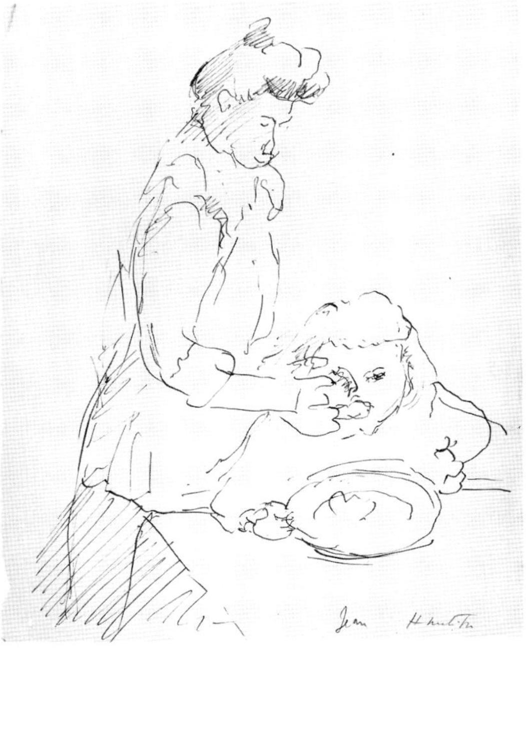

technical and psychological level, as a portrait of a bride it strikes a discordant note.[9]

Other early depictions of Amélie seem also to involve a ritual recognition of her new part in his life. Step by step, in the world created by Matisse's brushes and pen as in actual life, she replaced Caroline Joblaud, assuming the domestic roles formerly played by his lover. First came the reader, the generic inhabitant of the quiet interior, in *Woman Reading* of 1898 (Musée de Reims), in which Matisse recreated the setting of his earlier painting (see fig. 14), placing Amélie in the same position as that once occupied by Caroline. Then he showed her as the caretaker of the children: the theme of the painting *Breton Serving Girl* (1896) was echoed in *Madame Matisse with Jean in his Cradle*, of 1899, with Matisse's newborn son.[10] Amélie's motherhood role was explicitly repeated in a drawing of a few years later (fig. 38), showing her placidly feeding baby Jean at the table. Her half-smile of contentment conveys her pleasure in the task – or perhaps Matisse's pleasure that he had someone to take this role, as well as all the others in the arrangement of domestic order. He may have preferred to figure her as a happy mother because the image of that performance was necessary to the order that served his needs.[11]

Amélie as a model

Seen another way, these are natural enough themes for a new husband and father to incorporate into his art, as countless other artists have done. Matisse, it might be said, simply depicted his wife in roles that were natural to the domestic situation at the time. As I have suggested, he also in this way continued the project of self-expression through the representation of family intimacy. Increasingly, however, Amélie's "natural" roles in the marriage gave way to more contrived ones as Matisse removed his wife from the domestic context and gave her new parts to play. She had a variable identity for the purposes of Matisse's art, and the relationship between her roles in the family and in his art changed with time. Although she appeared regularly in his work during the first decade of the century, her identity as wife and mother diminished sharply. Her interest to him as material for his art became less and less connected to the real and essential roles she played in his life. On the contrary, her usefulness to his art was increasingly linked to her flexibility in role-playing. To put the matter differently, he took greater license in manipulating her identity so that its representation in his art expressed her identity less and his concerns more. Much later, when Matisse depicted Amélie in a domestic role in paintings such as *Conversation* (1908–12) and *The Music Lesson* (1917; see fig. 60), it usually expressed an uncomfortable irony that reflected a marriage, in fact an entire family, in distress.

Even early in their marriage Matisse did not paint and draw his wife with the intimate attention Bonnard, Corinth, Vallotton, Manguin, or even Cézanne – to cite some of his contemporaries whose wives were frequent sitters – gave to theirs in their work. Matisse's vision of Amélie as projected in his representations of her is rarely attractive. She was more obviously exploited as a model to be supplied with an identity than were most artist's wives.[12] This arrangement, relying on Amélie's enforced abeyance of her identity in the service of her husband's art, did not always produce satisfactory results, either in terms of Matisse's artistic development or as an index of their negotiation of whose identity would take precedence in the representation. Amélie appears to have assumed the various roles Matisse assigned her grudgingly and sullenly, to judge from the pictures themselves and from accounts of her posing.

A painting such as *Madame Matisse en japonaise* of 1901 (fig. 39) hovers in a vague terrain between portrait and costume piece. Matisse's uncertainty about just what to do with this picture seems to be reflected in the dull-toned, sketchily defined interior and the unstable pose of its pallid, diffident inhabitant. On all levels this is an entirely unappealing painting. Significantly, there is a stronger suggestion of both physical presence and mental activity, as well as greater formal interest, in Matisse's contemporaneous study of the hired model Bevilacqua. Rendered with "Dostoevskian intensity," in Lawrence Gowing's apt phrase, Bevilacqua's face is riveted by a more aggressive and eccentric framing, within which his shifting glance suggests a more active mental state than Matisse has attributed to his wife.[13]

At other times Matisse's depictions of his wife in costume and genre pieces are marked with more open tension. Forced by her husband to pose interminably, she occasionally became rebellious. While sitting for *The Guitarist* (fig. 40), for which he required her to assume an uncomfortable position, Amélie's patience snapped. Her subsequent deliberate irritation of her husband nearly brought disaster to the work in progress, although the story (at least as related by the artist) had a cathartic happy ending. Even Alfred Barr, ever polite, acknowledged that the inci-

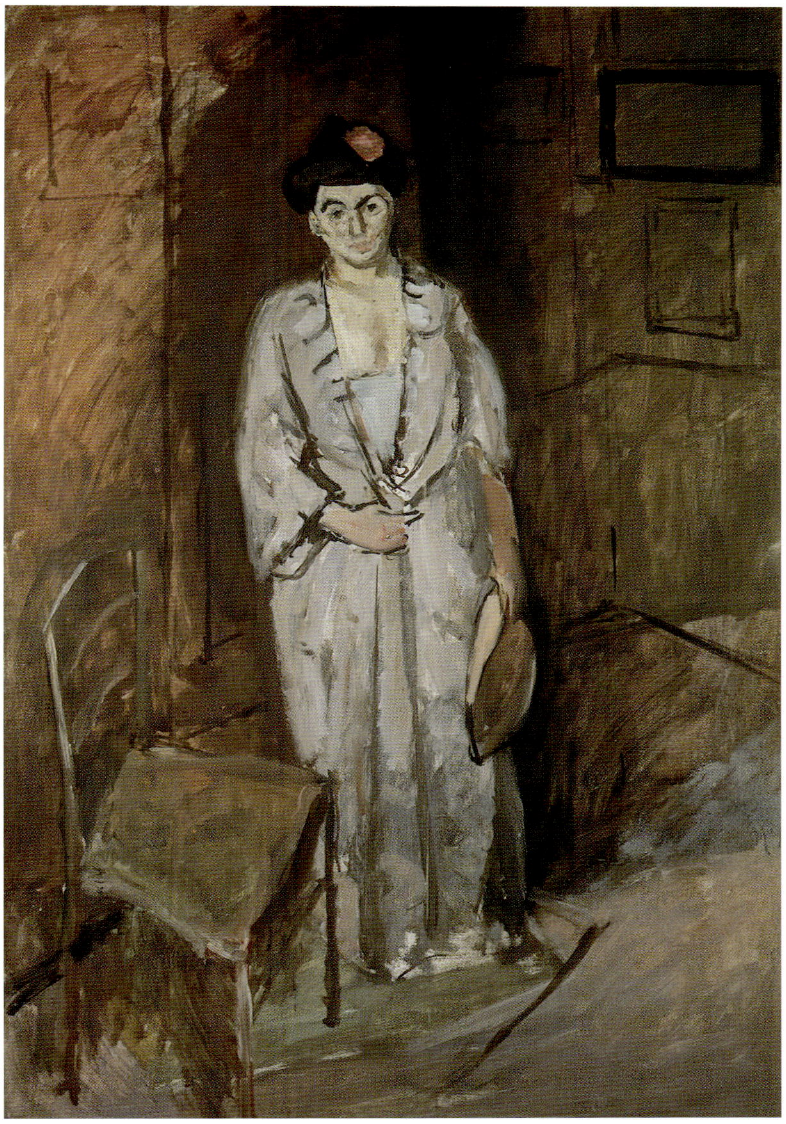

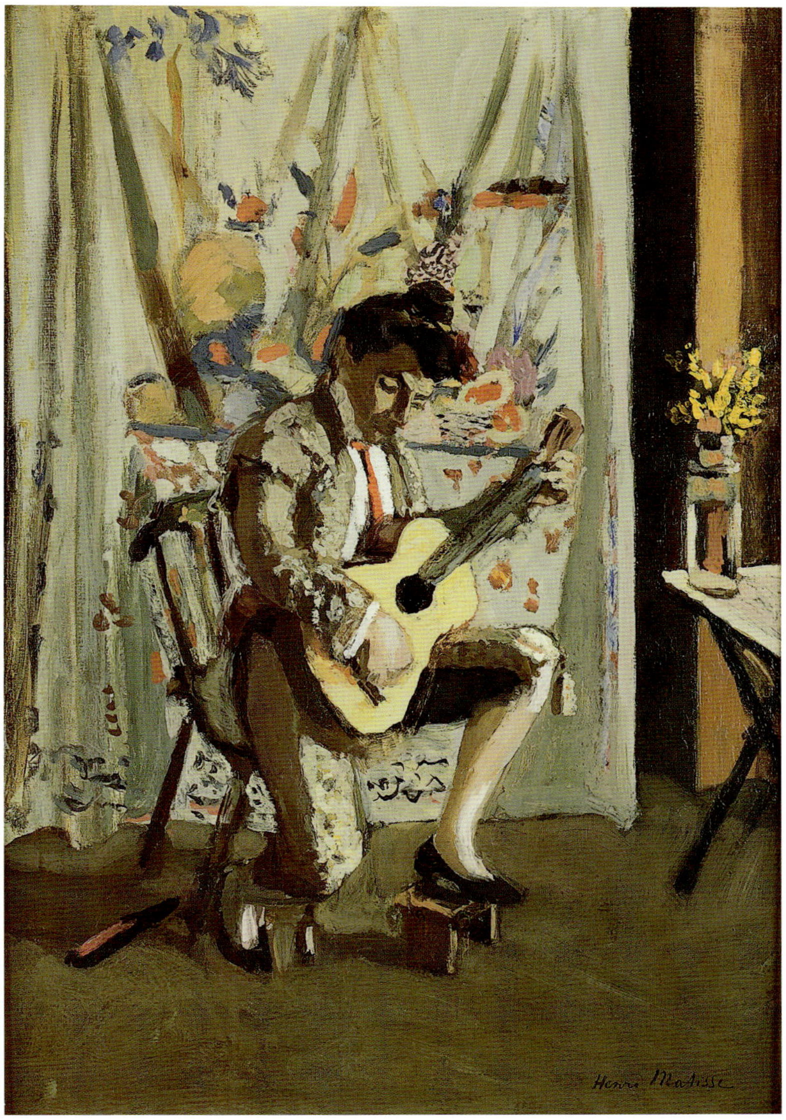

39 (*above left*) *Madame Matisse en japonaise (Japanese Lady)*, 1901. Oil on canvas, 116.8 × 80 cm. Private collection.

40 (*above right*) *The Guitarist*, 1902–3. Oil on canvas, 54.6 × 38.1 cm. Private collection.

dent "reveals something of the strain under which he and Mme Matisse worked" at this time, although he implies that their tension was due solely to economic straits.[14] This is not to suggest that Amélie Matisse was a particularly difficult woman or that other artists' wives posed more graciously. But the tension in, for example, Cézanne's portraits of his wife seems to be less interpersonal than reflexive: it is the artist's own inner gnashings that are played out on the field of his wife's image. The conflicts in these portraits by Cézanne seem to be his alone, not theirs. In Matisse's images of his wife, however, the impression of mutual and unresolved difficulty in the working relationship of two forceful personalities can be very strong.

It may be objected that I am reading meaning back into pictures dating to early in the century from Matisse's and his wife's later estrangement, which was a long time in coming but which devolved into final separation only in the 1940s. I am of course doing this to some extent, but the implications in the pictures themselves and the evidence of witness accounts is so compelling as to force acknowledgment of what has remained largely unsaid: Matisse's wife was a necessary presence in his life and her efforts ensured that he could keep working, but in that work she was important almost exclusively in the service of his art, not as a function of her independent identity or of her importance in his family life.[15] The representation of her identity is not the object of these works of art: Matisse's response to her, and the resultant construction of her in a role, always takes precedence. He apparently regarded *The Guitarist* as representative of his efforts when he made it. Another painting of a guitarist, this one male (and posed by the model Bevilacqua), was exhibited by Matisse both at the Salon d'Automne of 1904 and his one-man show at Vollard's gallery earlier that year. Both paintings were entitled simply *Le Guitariste*: where his art was concerned, his wife and the hired model were on equal terms.[16]

Ironically, when he chose in painting Amélie to suppress overtly the main visible outlet for personality – the face – the result could be quite sensitive, both pictorially and in the psychological realm. This is the case with *La Coiffure* (1901; Washington, D.C., National Gallery of Art). Amélie's semi-nude body, bright and substantial, is seen from behind as she is posed in the simple endearing act of putting up her hair in its characteristic bun. Beyond, the mirror reflects her face, dark and indistinct. This device suggests, as with Ingres, another, more complex side to the simple beauty of an intimate scene.

In another setting, out of doors in the fresh air, Matisse sometimes enlisted Amélie in the creation of scenes of idyllic beauty and gentle repose. Beginning in 1904 and continuing for several years, he made a significant group of landscape pictures – oil paintings, watercolors, and drawings – that include her as the main figural element. She can be identified in most of them by varying combinations of her costume, her distinctive hairstyle, and the circumstances in which the works were made, at Saint-Tropez or Collioure in the summers, when the Matisse family was together in these attractive surroundings. In some she is the principal element in the overall composition, as in the costume pictures *Woman with a Parasol* (Nice, Musée Matisse) and *Woman in a Japanese Robe beside the Water* (fig. 42), both painted at Collioure in the summer of 1905. Among other things, these two paintings show the transition Matisse made in the course of this summer between a Neo-Impressionist style and a more personal, less systematic approach to marking the canvas. But this makes no difference in terms of representing the individuality of the model. In *Woman with a Parasol*, Amélie's identity is screened by the regular system of a dominating style; in *Woman in a Japanese Robe* the bold pattern of the garment is absorbed into the even more freely brushed rendering of the landscape, and the slabs of color denoting her face carry no more connotation of individuality than other similar marks elsewhere in the picture.[17]

By contrast, when André Derain painted Amélie Matisse in the same Japanese robe (fig. 41), he gave the figure much greater importance, and the features of her face come into play in establishing the picture's serene mood. Perhaps this is no more than might have been accomplished with an anonymous model, but Derain has treated this class-equivalent woman taking on a temporary role as much more than a prop or a receptacle for stylistic experiment. The index – the imprint – of Matisse's personal manner forces out any iconic relationship, based on resemblance or identification, between image and referent, between figure study and the actual woman who posed, mitigating the transaction necessary for portraiture. In one sense there should be no surprise in this: Matisse's formal concerns in this period of stylistic invention were paramount, and he seemed willing to ignore the real human content of these works. A contrary view would, of course, see in Matisse's greater

41 André Derain, *Woman with a Shawl*, 1905. Oil on canvas, 80 × 65 cm. Formerly Paris, Collection Boris Fize.

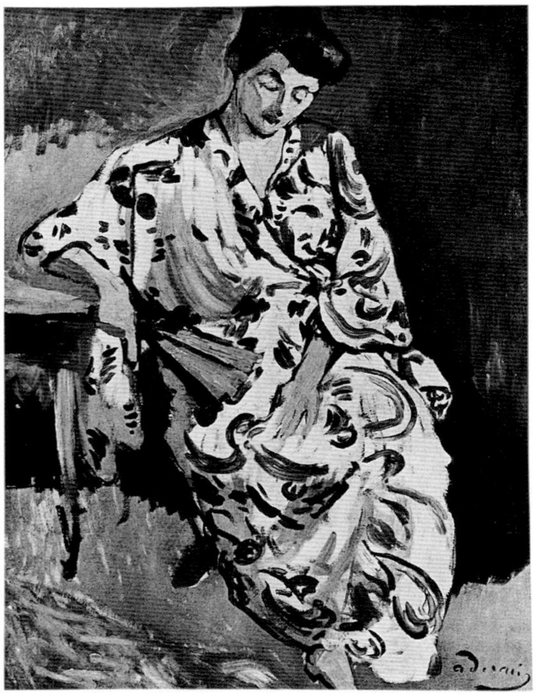

42 *Woman in a Japanese Robe beside the Water*, 1905. Oil on canvas, 35.2 × 28.2 cm. The Museum of Modern Art, New York. Purchase and partial anonymous gift.

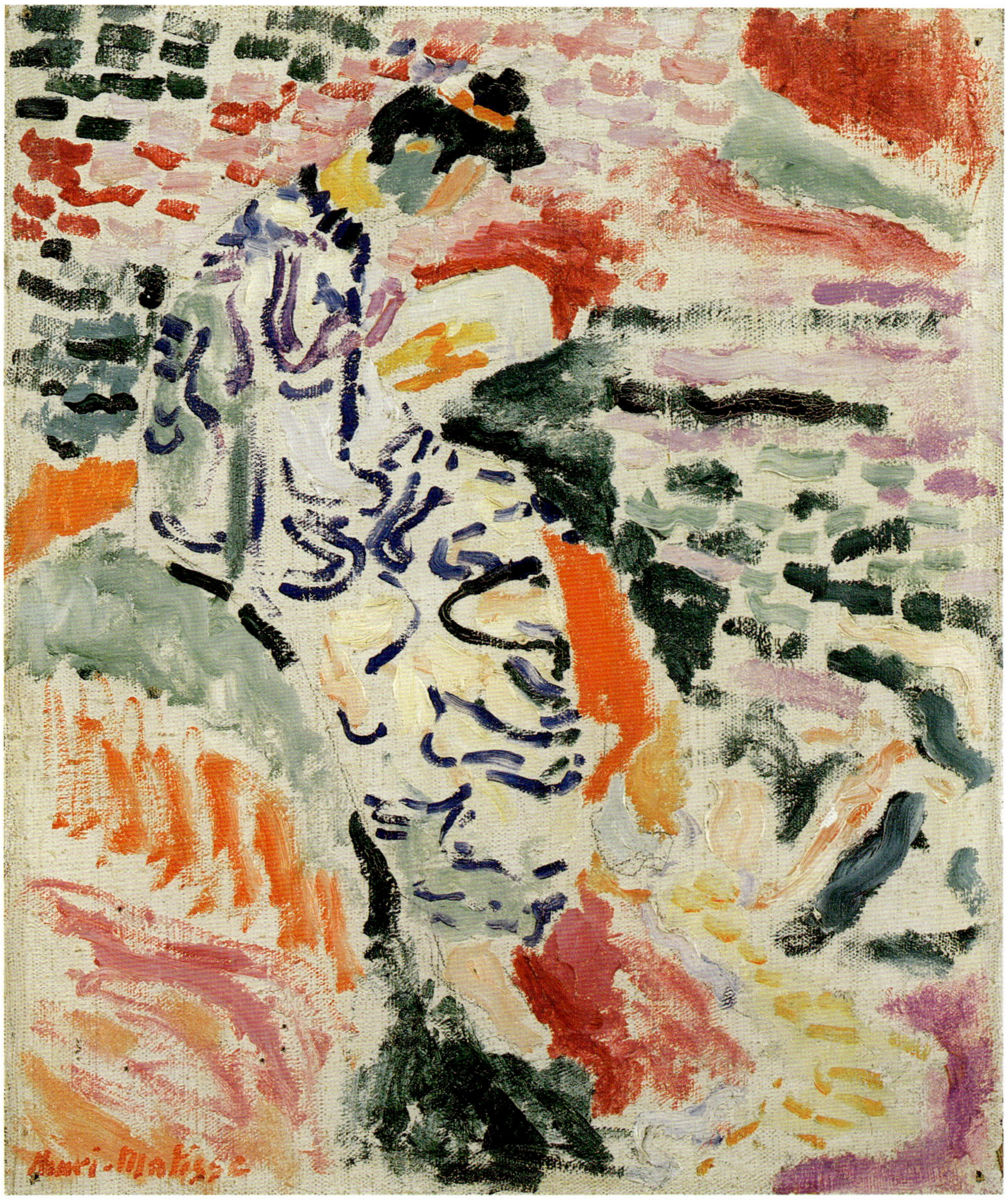

disregard for the individuality of the model a higher modernity and a more dedicated concern with problems of pure painting – an explanation as insufficient as it is dated. In any case, the trade-off between Matisse's artistic needs and his obligations to those he enlisted in satisfying those needs became the governing calculus of his portraiture over the next decade.

Amélie Matisse's roles are even more complicated when we consider the paintings that Matisse made combining real landscape settings with invented figure compositions, a development that culminated in *Le Bonheur de vivre* (1905–6). And yet in other paintings from the time the representation of Amélie Matisse provides a touchstone with reality that anchors a flight of fantasy and artistic experiment. The major outcome of his painting campaign in the South in the winter of 1904–5, *Luxe, calme et volupté*, was preceded by studies which in turn derived from a painting of Amélie and Pierre Matisse seated by the seashore. The image in this origin picture, *The Gulf of Saint-Tropez* (1904), was developed into Matisse's first painting done from imagination.[18] In *Luxe, calme et volupté* the figure of Pierre is no longer recognizable but has become a specter. By contrast, the now much more generalized depiction of Amélie is still sufficiently specified to act as a worldly counterbalance to the fantastic landscape and its variously occupied nude women.

In the context of all these depictions of leisure by the sea in which Matisse's wife does next to nothing it should be remembered that during this period and earlier Amélie Matisse had a profession. The income from her work as a milliner and tapestry maker had been essential to the freedom that her husband enjoyed to paint as he wished. The only time Matisse had ever labored for a living, he lasted a week; he had little experience of the rigors of day-to-day work for hire, and so perhaps little appreciation of them.[19] Despite the crucial contribution Amélie made to Matisse's art by utilizing her own abilities and acumen in a business enterprise, Matisse never depicted her in this role of her own making. Interestingly, Matisse's fellow painters Albert Marquet and Charles Camoin did show her at work on a tapestry.[20] Perhaps it was easier for them to acknowledge Amélie's identity and self-image in her work than it was for her husband – as a patriarch of his time he may have resented being displaced as the family provider. Then again, as she assumed a relatively fixed posture in this work, the possibility must be admitted that the two artist friends were simply opportunistic and recognized a free model when they saw one.

Although we can identify his wife in these and other paintings and drawings by Matisse in the first years of the century, despite the lack of identifiable facial features in most of them, they are not portraits. I have devoted some attention to these pictures in order to show the range of his use of his wife in his painting, which is another way of saying the variety of identities she was made to assume in the service of his art. In giving Amélie new and unfamiliar parts to play, Matisse crossed the line between the portrait and the figure study as the role became more important than the person who played it. Even though the protagonist in these genre scenes and costume pictures was known to him, and was a class-equivalent sitter and therefore should have enjoyed some control over the representation of her identity, she takes on the attributes of the hired model. Her individuality suppressed, Amélie is presented by Matisse in these pictures as the passive effect of his emotions and mentality, not their cause or the vehicle of her own. In these works the psychodynamics of their relationship do not intrude because the structures and conventions Matisse employed are for artist and model, not husband and wife.

Portrait or caricature?

Matisse's more direct representations of Amélie from this time in 1904 and early 1905 – his portraits of her – embody curious tensions and animadversions. These drawings in pen and ink are not so obviously sites of formal invention for Matisse, and they lay bare what is often overshadowed by the overt experimentation in his painting at this time. In a drawing from 1905, *Madame Matisse Seated (Collioure)* (fig. 44), Amélie sits on the ground, turned away from the viewer. All landscape details are suppressed and the figure, seen from above and filling the pictorial field, receives full concentration, in contrast to her submergence in waves of color in *Woman in*

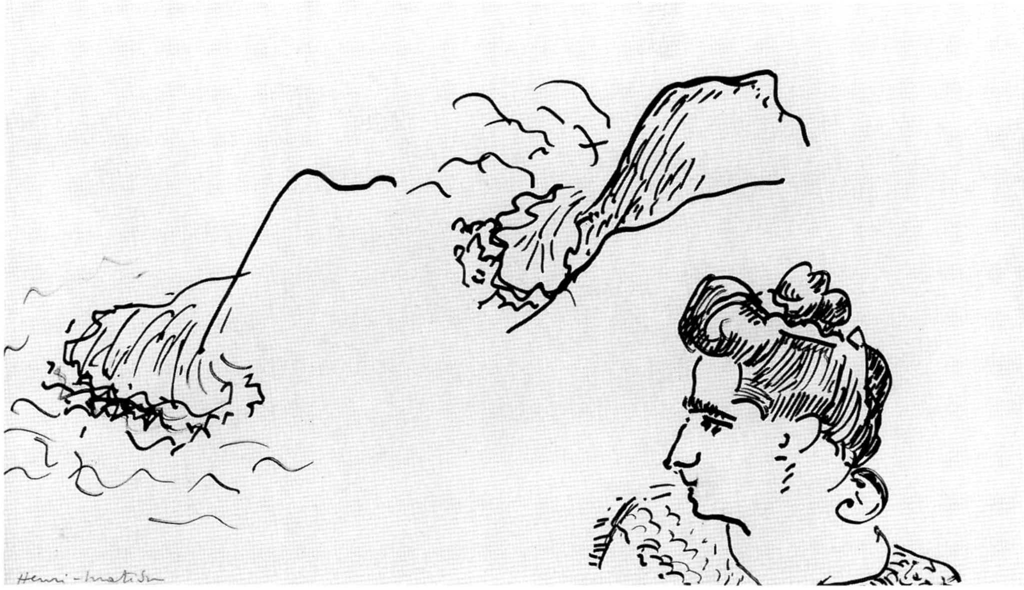

43 *Madame Matisse, Rocks*, 1905. Pen and ink on paper, 18 × 30 cm. Céret, Musée d'Art Moderne.

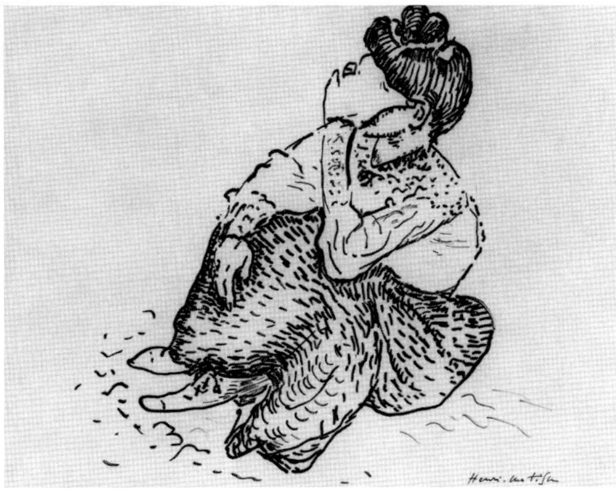

44 *Madame Matisse Seated (Collioure)*, 1905. Pen and ink on paper mounted on card, 19.3 × 23.8 cm. Paris, Musée National d'Art Moderne, Centre Georges Pompidou.

a Japanese Robe beside the Water. The sense of Amélie's individuality here, and the particularity of Matisse's response to her, are quite strong. Her left hand awkwardly and conspicuously covers her face as she shields her eyes from the sun. On another level, the drawing of this gesture is a sign of aversion and denial, signaled in the expressive exaggeration of the covering hand. From the same time is the drawing *Madame Matisse, Rocks* (fig. 43), in which Amélie's beaky profile is isolated and likened to the rough rocks and turbulent sea. The analogy is stressed through similarities in the quality of the pen line between the rocks and her profile, on one hand, and between the waves and foam and Amélie's hair, on the other.

The deployment of exaggeration and analogy in these drawings strongly suggests the method of caricature, and in this connection there is additional meaning in Matisse's observations in a letter to Henri Manguin from September 1904. In despair about his work, Matisse said to his friend: "I think that painting will drive me crazy, and I'm going to try to get out of it as soon as possible. . . . I am sketching the proprietor of a café [here he included a profile sketch of the woman], who until now I had thought very pretty, and I realize that in drawing her I've caught only what is ugly about her. If you look closely, she is frightening; I've exaggerated everything ugly about her. You see how I must be a pain to be around right now."[21] Leave aside the slight similarity between the profile in this sketch and Amélie's features in *Madame Matisse, Rocks*, probably a function of reducing the features of individuals to a lowest common denominator. More to the point is Matisse's apparent inclination at this time to simplify and exaggerate by the means of caricature the bodies and features of people when he represented them within the terms of their own identities. In costume pieces and genre scenes Matisse used these role-playing scenarios as occasions to render conventional subjects in unconventional form. The individuality of a model or the identity of Matisse's wife when treated like a model was not at issue in such paintings. But when he turned his attention to making portraits – works of art that embodied the identity of the sitter and made some claim to his or her self-representation to society – his use of the strategies of caricature resulted in considerable tension between expression and decorum.

Woman with the Hat and the risks of social instability

In painting the stakes were much higher than in drawing. They were raised higher still on occasions of public exhibition of his efforts. There the social component of portraiture received a severe proof. Matisse learned just how contested could be the social ground on which portraiture was based when he exhibited a portrait of his wife in 1905. In *Woman with the Hat* (fig. 46) Matisse pushed his stylistic experimentation beyond anything he had previously done. And by doing this in a portrait he took a risk that he had not anticipated. He threatened to alienate not a sitter, not a patron, but an entire social register whose values came implicitly under attack from within.

Femme au chapeau is a seated half-length portrait of Amélie Matisse. She sits in a chair, not facing the viewer directly but from a three-quarters pose, turning her body and head to engage our look. A gloved arm, extended out toward the viewer and resting on the back of the chair, holds a fan spread across her chest and shoulders, covering them entirely. A hat worthy of Carmen Miranda perches on her head and draws attention by its visual dominance and its precarious position. No setting is specified, and it is even difficult to determine the position of the chair because the background is indefinite if not neutral, consisting of swirls and scumbles of multicolored paint. The sitter's only attributes are the fan and the hat.

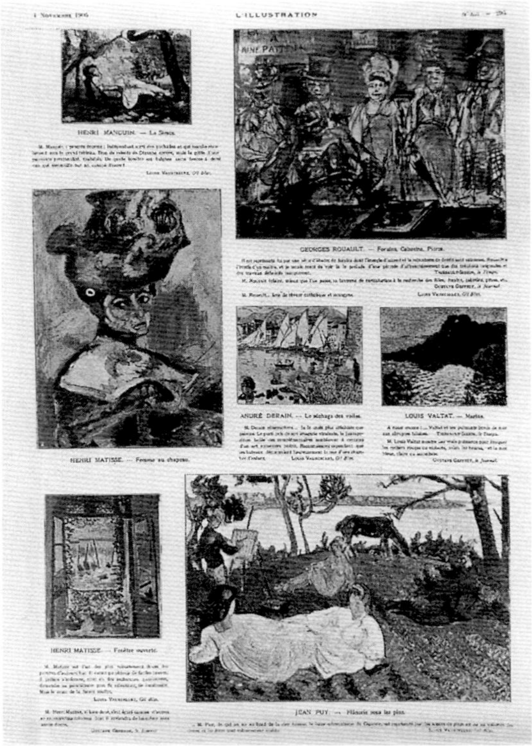
L'ILLUSTRATION

HENRI MANGUIN. — La Sieste.

GEORGES ROUAULT. — Forains, Cabotins, Pitres.

HENRI MATISSE. — Femme au chapeau.

ANDRÉ DERAIN. — Le séchage des voiles.

LOUIS VALTAT. — Marine.

HENRI MATISSE. — Fenêtre ouverte.

JEAN PUY. — Flânerie sous les pins.

45 *L'Illustration*, November 4, 1905.

The story of the exhibition of *Woman with the Hat*, the scandal it created, and its subsequent purchase by Leo and Gertrude Stein has been told many times but may be reprised briefly.[22] Fresh from the easel, Matisse put the painting on show at the Salon d'Automne in Paris in October 1905. He had originally planned to submit the large Neo-Impressionist landscape called *Le Port d'Avall*, a panoramic view of Collioure. He had spent the summer there and this landscape painting was his major effort, an apparently programmatic expression of his allegiance to Paul Signac and the older artist's color theories. But the program changed dramatically. Even with an extension from the Salon jury Matisse could not finish the exacting painting on time, and nearly at the last minute he substituted *Woman with the Hat*. He may even have painted it expressly for this purpose: more than one account asserts that he did it rapidly, after he and his family returned to Paris from Collioure in early September, and that it was finished by mid-October, just before the opening.[23]

Of his ten entries in the Salon, *Woman with the Hat* was the largest and drew most of the attention from viewers, mainly though not exclusively critical and some of it outraged. Criticism in the press was forceful. The painting featured prominently in both written accounts and pictorial spreads in the popular press (fig. 45). Even fiercer responses, some strongly physical, came from members of the visiting public. According to Gertrude Stein, people laughed at the picture and even scratched it, as if attacking the image on the canvas was, *ad hominem*, an act of aggression against the artist himself.[24] The scorn generated by the painting seemed to fulfill the worst fears of the president of the Salon d'Automne, the relatively liberal Frantz Jourdain, who had urged the jury not to accept the painting, fearing that the public response would damage Matisse's reputation.[25] Matisse was already highly regarded by progressive critics, many of whom were beginning to see him as the leader of new tendencies in art.[26] Among these generally sympathetic observers was Louis Vauxcelles, the art critic for the daily newspaper *Gil Blas* and the writer who named Fauvism. A Quattrocentesque figure by the sculptor Albert Marque had been placed in Salle VII with the brightly colored canvases of Matisse, Camoin, Marquet, and Manguin. To Vauxcelles the sculpture was incongruous

46 (*facing page*) *Woman with the Hat*, 1905. Oil on canvas, 80.6 × 59.7 cm. San Francisco Museum of Modern Art, bequest of Elise S. Haas.

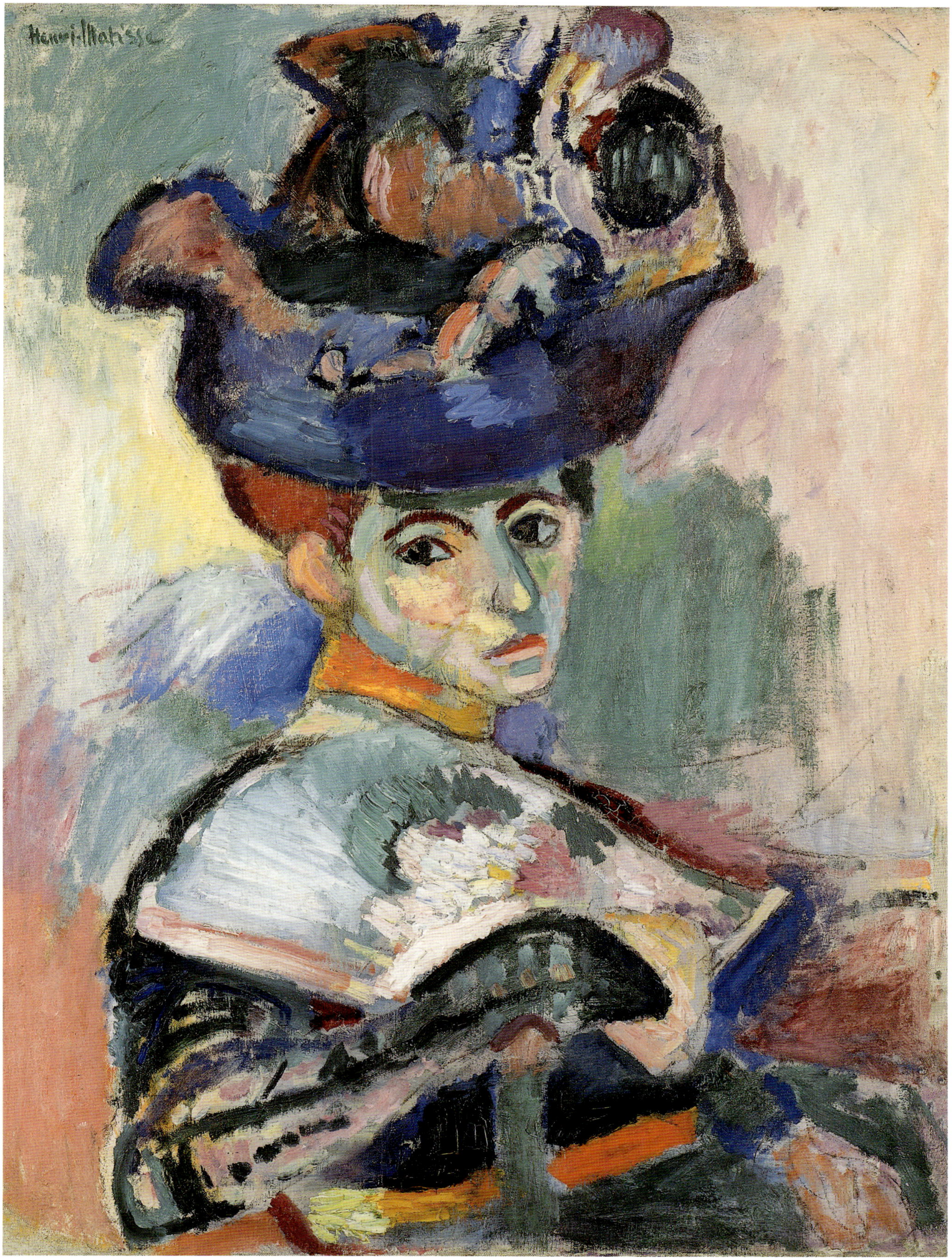
Henri-Matisse

"amidst the orgy of pure tones: Donatello among the wild beasts [Donatello chez les fauves]." Thus was the term "fauves" inaugurated to characterize Matisse and the young painters who were frequently associated with him.[27] Vauxcelles's quip, taken in the context of his entire review, reflected an element of admiration. But his was among the mildest comments on the inhabitants of the "cage centrale" at the Salon.

It is inconceivable that the furor brought on by the exhibition of *Woman with the Hat* would have been occasioned by a landscape or a still life. In fact, Matisse's other contributions to the autumn salon in these genres were not the objects of such withering criticism. Much of the attention was directed at the way Matisse had put the paint on the canvas, with a bright palette and loose, seemingly haphazard application. Painting together in Collioure in the summer of 1905, Matisse and Derain had experimented with a freer, sketchier painting technique as a vehicle for directly translating their personal responses to nature into their paintings. Portraiture was another matter entirely, and part of Matisse's assault on convention in *Woman with the Hat* was to introduce the sketch aesthetic and the overt personal response of the artist into a genre that demanded greater consistency, finish, and neutrality. While much of the criticism was of Matisse's artistry, the terms in which these criticisms were voiced suggest the recognition that his transgression was more serious than rejection of accepted artistic form. The genre of portraiture itself seemed to be under attack, and by implication the class of people who had their portraits painted.[28]

Woman with the Hat positions itself as a society portrait in terms of size, format, pose, and costume. It may be compared in these terms with any number of ingratiating images of women by an international corps of portrait painters in this period, such as Jacques-Emile Blanche, William Orpen, John Singer Sargent, or Giovanni Boldini. Even less well-known practitioners competently delivered on the promise of a pleasing and suitable self-representation for a sitter with a claim (or aspiration) to such an image (fig. 47). Most of these artists adapted the loosely organized Impressionist brushstroke to the portrait genre, readily conveying informality and fashionable contemporaneity without violating the terms of flattery and grace so essential to this subset of the portrait genre. Portraits of women by such painters as these and many others openly mark and confirm status, situating the sitter with some precision in the social field.

Social status and representation

Matisse's startling portrait of his wife interrogates this social class by sending mixed signals. *Woman with the Hat* frames itself to validate its sitter in a social context, but then undermines both artistic and social convention for the genre (this may have been an attraction for the unconventional Steins). And because this is a portrait of a woman, this transgression was easily accomplished. An oblique, turning pose in a portrait of a man is usually a gesture indicating casual ease and self-confidence, as it is in many portraits by Frans Hals (fig. 48). In Matisse's painting the pose becomes suggestive and tense, a sign of the ambiguity of the social position of the sitter. A steady look, which in a male sitter is usually taken as a mark of confidence and self-possession, could seem aggressive when borne by a woman in a portrait, as it is in *Woman with the Hat*. In the nineteenth and early twentieth centuries, codes for representing women as public figures were less well defined than for men. The

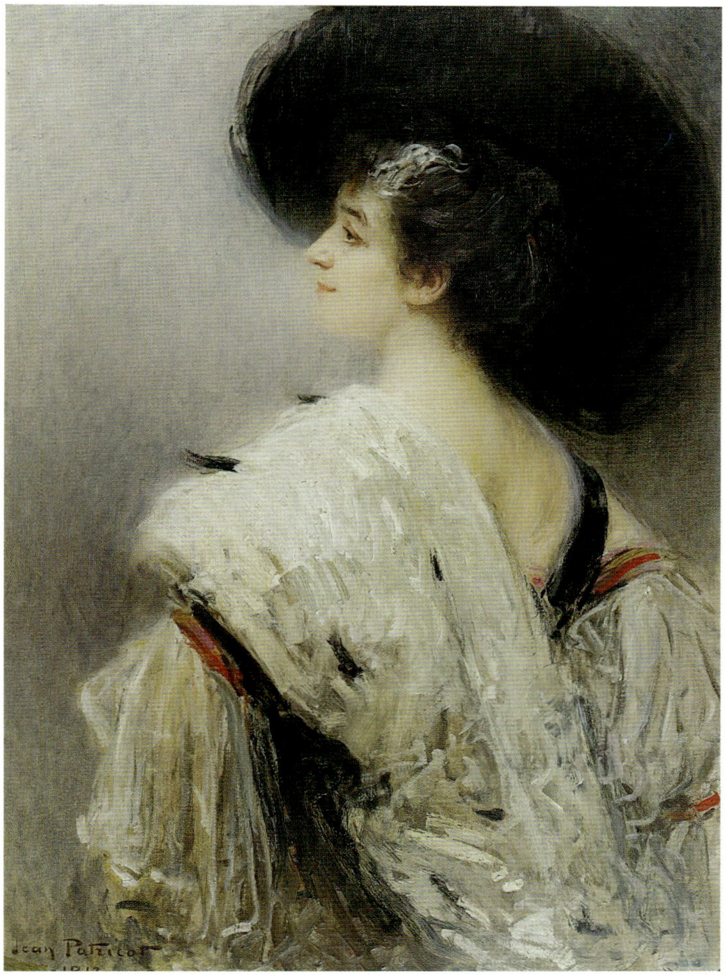

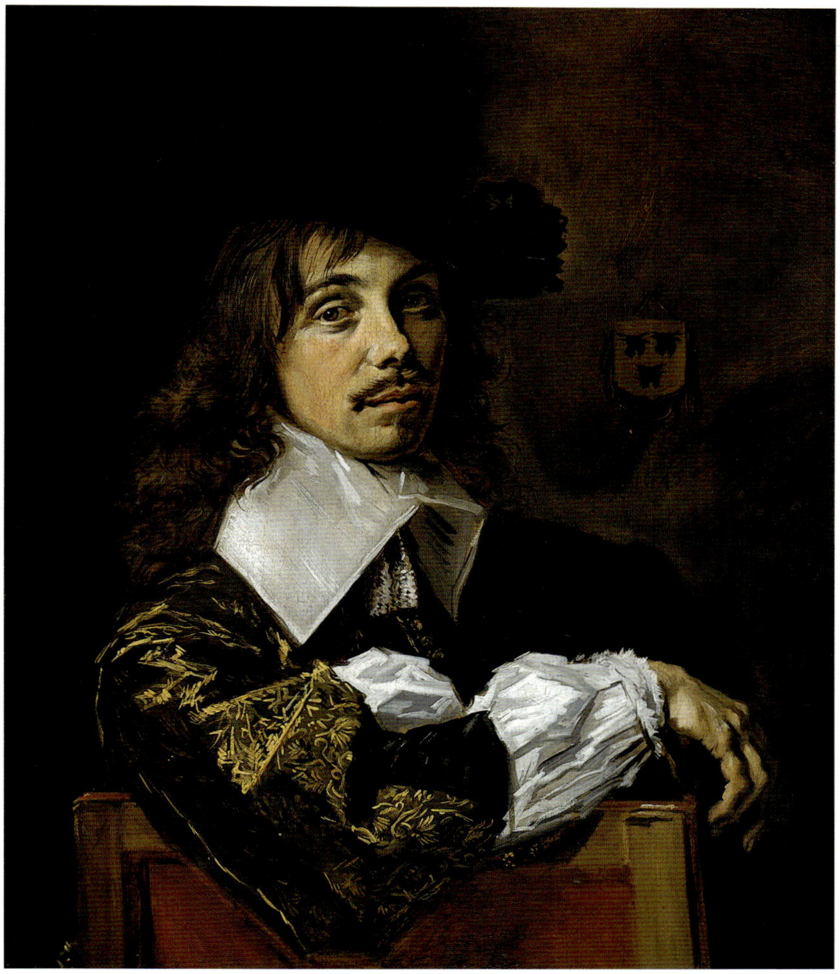

47 (*above left*) Jean Patricot, *The Countess of Noidans*, 1912. Oil on canvas, 100 × 70 cm. Nice, Musée des Beaux-Arts Jules Chéret.

48 (*above right*) Frans Hals, *Willem Coymans*, 1645. Oil on canvas, 76.8 × 63.5 cm. Washington, D.C., National Gallery of Art, Andrew W. Mellon Collection.

domestic sphere that was the generally accepted context for women lent itself to genre subjects, not portraiture. As a public art, portraiture was largely the domain of men, whose positions in public life had always given the portrait – even the portrait of a woman, often conceived and seen in pendant – its functional context. Without a well established set of conventions for representing women independent of men, there was more room for slippage into other genres. The portrait could be confused with other kinds of representations. The class and social status of the woman represented was too easy to misconstrue.[29]

By undermining the flattering, self-justifying terms of expression that characterized the society portrait, Matisse challenged this social class (to which, however, he clearly aspired) and its image of itself. The threat to social values is central to the ruckus *Woman with the Hat* caused in 1905. The magnitude of Matisse's assault on convention may be measured in a comparison of the painting with a portrait by Louis Valtat, Matisse's exact contemporary (Valtat even exhibited at the Salon d'Automne in 1905, but outside the "cage aux fauves"). His *Madame Valtat* of 1906 (fig. 49) is identical in premise to (and shares an outsized hat with) *Woman with the Hat*, but the differences between them are obvious and crucial. Valtat has cast his wife as the natural bearer of the middle-class attributes she displays. She is portrayed as direct and confident without being aggressive. Valtat's application of paint, though free and expressive, is sensuous and calculated to be pleasing. Its fluidity

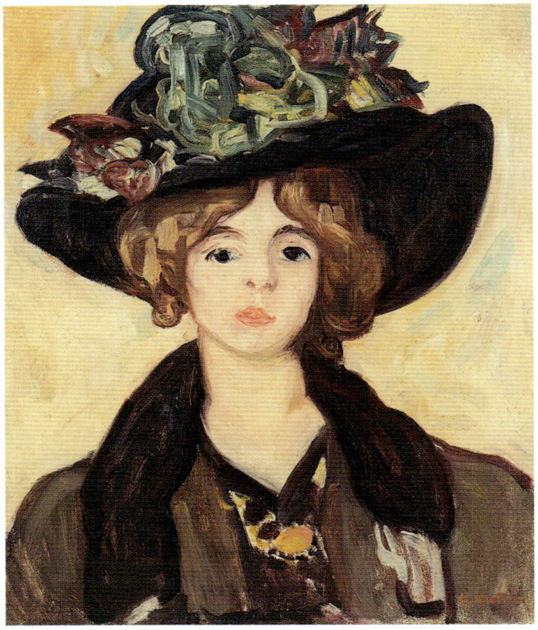

49 Louis Valtat, *Madame Valtat*, 1906. Oil on canvas, 55 × 46 cm. Geneva, Petit Palais, Musée d'Art Moderne.

facing page Detail of fig. 46.

50 Maurice de Vlaminck, *Woman at the Rat Mort*, 1905–6. Oil on wood, 59 × 43.2 cm. Los Angeles, Nathan and Marion Smooke Collection.

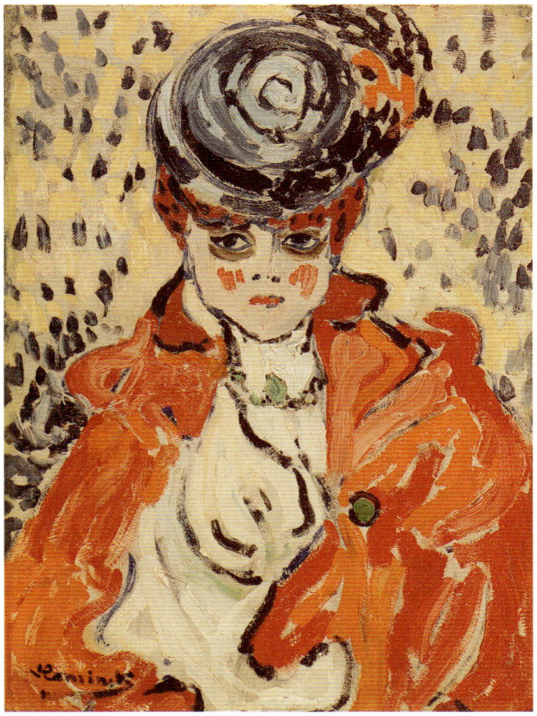

enhances the classic appeal of abundant hair, the softened, generalized features of the woman's face and a mobile mouth. The rich but neutral background accords her the quiet prominence she is so clearly figured to deserve. By contrast, Amélie Matisse is posed uncomfortably and self-consciously, shielded behind the wide spread of fan, usually a symbol of gentility but in her hands a kind of protective coloration. Here an oblique pose – so often indicating casual ease in portraiture – is a sign of the ambiguity of Madame Matisse's social position, the uncertainty of her status.[30]

A contemporaneous painting by Maurice de Vlaminck, Matisse's fellow Fauve, suggests an alternative context for representing an independent woman in the public sphere (fig. 50). His image of a woman at a Paris *boîte*, garishly made up, with disheveled dress and cheeky hat, figures her as a *demimondaine*, a woman of questionable respectability. Matisse's *Woman with the Hat* made a risky association with this world. Some art students seemed to understand this transgressive possibility when, in mock tribute, they sent to Matisse a real woman colored in garish hues from head to toe – a literally painted woman.[31] Challenging the boundaries between acceptable and transgressive representation could bring about great anxiety. This had also been so forty years previously when Edouard Manet exhibited his *Olympia*, a painting that equally flouts convention for its class of representation, in its case pushing against acceptable ways of representing a prostitute. I am certainly not suggesting that Matisse meant to represent Amélie as a prostitute, an implication made by Marcelin Pleynet, and possibly by the rambunctious art students in 1905.[32] But some of the uproar caused by this portrait may have been due to the appearance – even if unintended or subliminal – of a prostitute being elevated to the social level implied by the bourgeois portrait. Or even worse, the staining of middle-class society by association with the *demimonde*. In either case, Matisse's portrait of his wife is made to bear a freight of ambiguity it could not handle within the contemporary social context. To portray someone is to introduce their image into a public space. Portraits are less ambiguous when they can be readily accommodated to public life; when matters deemed private are inappropriately made public, an uncomfortable burden to acknowledge these matters is placed on the spectator.[33] In such a case the portrait may fail to persuade an audience of the sitter's implicit claim to public representation. Even within the avant-garde, *Woman with the Hat* was an aggressive challenge to the affirmative social construction of portraiture.

"*The Green Line*" and the assertion of coherence

Matisse was stung by the uncomprehending criticism of *Woman with the Hat*, the accusations of formlessness and lack of unity in his painting, and he complained that all he had tried to do was to express his feelings in his art.[34] Soon he set to work on another portrait of Amélie Matisse (fig. 51), possibly while *Woman with the Hat* was still hanging at the Salon d'Automne. In *Madame Matisse (The Green Line)* Matisse employed a completely different expressive system from that in the earlier portrait, and it seems clear that his work on this new picture was in reaction to the public controversy over his painting.[35] The new portrait was in part also his response to *Woman with the Hat* itself: the two portraits may be understood as one of the many pairs of paintings Matisse made of the same subject, in which the first combines stylistic heterogeneity and a wide color range with a free touch,

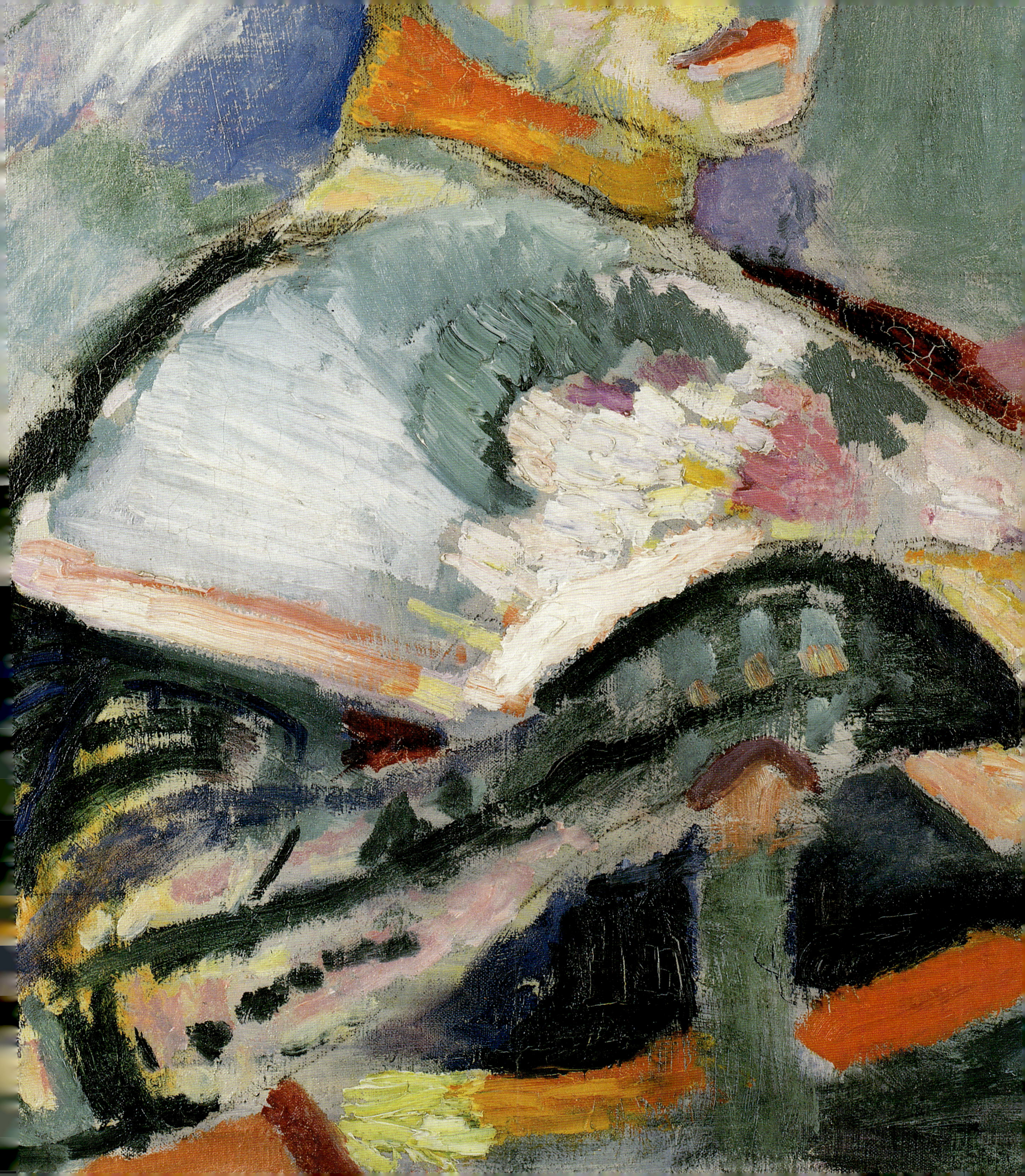

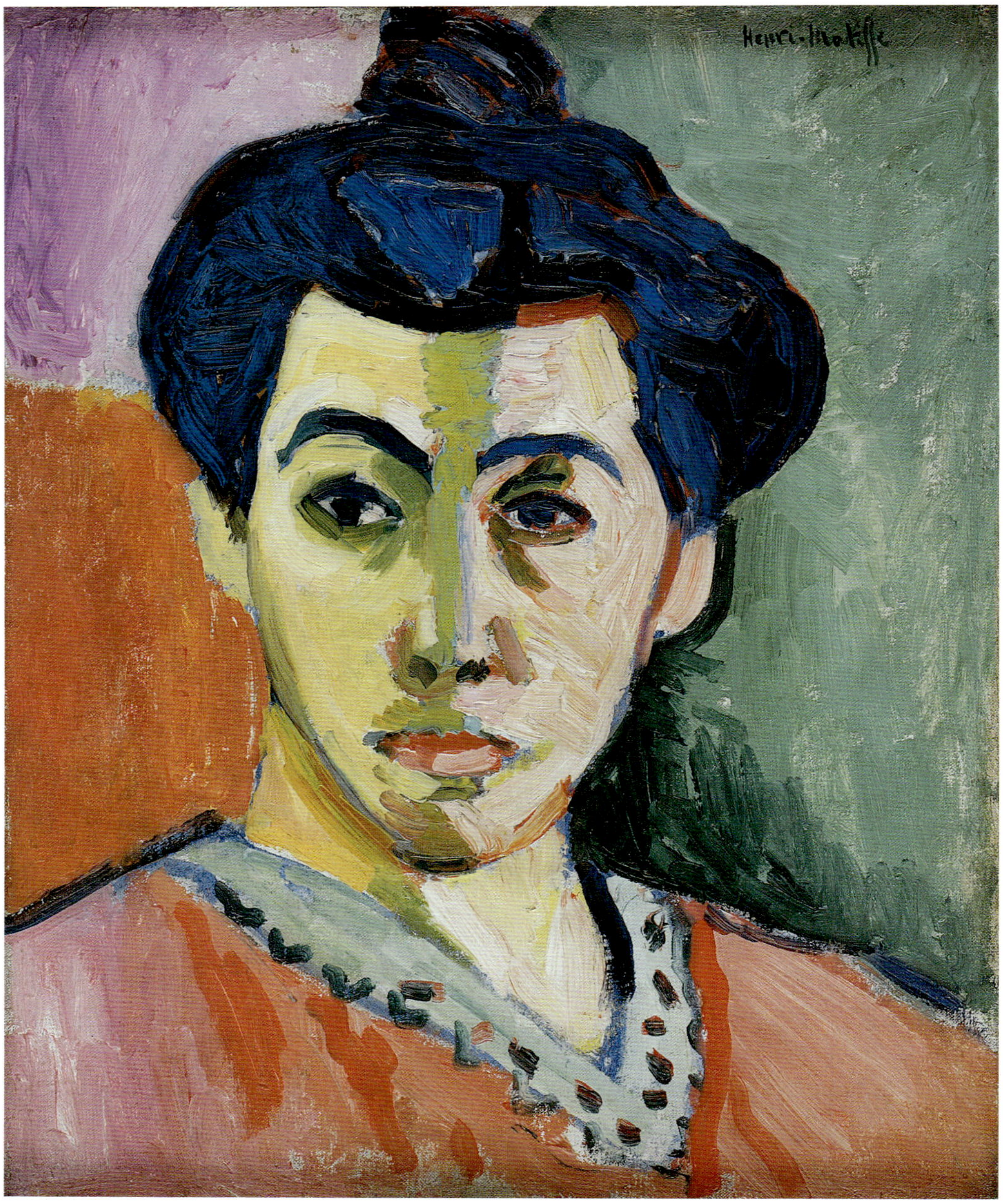

51 *Madame Matisse (The Green Line)*, 1905. Oil on canvas, 40.5 × 32.5 cm. Copenhagen, Statens Museum for Kunst, J. Rump Collection.

and the second simplifies the premise of the first, brings structure to apparent chaos, and synthesizes his responses into an ordered, decorative whole.

There is no sense that the second portrait was painted directly from *Woman with the Hat*, and thus at a remove from the sitter; if anything, the human presence of Amélie Matisse is more strongly conveyed in the second portrait than in the first. Costume is less important. The mode of presentation is more direct. Color is reduced to a few strong hues applied in large areas. Although the picture is smaller by half in each dimension than *Woman with the Hat* the scale is much greater and in fact the head is close to life size. Here we find none of the effects of informality, temporality, instability, and atmosphere that characterize the earlier portrait. The hermetic, mask-like appearance of *Madame Matisse* counters and closes off the open-ended but troubling personal qualities of the earlier painting. Attention is relentlessly focused on Amélie's face, producing an iconic image in sharp contrast to the worldly associations of *Woman with the Hat*. The feeling of intense confrontation with this specific individual is, however, parried by Matisse's presentation of her as an obdurate mask. In this contrast between the intimate and the impersonal lies some of the tension – tension of quite a different sort from that generated by *Woman with the Hat* – that so many observers have detected in this picture. A woman, Amélie Matisse, is there but at the same time she is absented because abstracted.

Equally direct formal means – bold contrasts of strong colors and a harnessed vigor in the handling of the paint – reinforce the focus.[36] So strong are the formal elements that discussion of them has dominated the discourse surrounding the painting. Its nickname, "The Green Line" or "The Green Stripe," is an implicit homage to the defining power of Matisse's paintbrush. Once again, though, as with *Woman with the Hat*, such powerful formal qualities would be less compelling in a landscape composition: they are so forceful because they are applied to and shape the image of an individual human being. And so their dominance has a human dimension too, performing a kind of coercion of the individual that has distinct interpersonal implications. *Woman with the Hat* and *Madame Matisse (The Green Line)* are only the most famous of Matisse's many representations of his wife that compromise her individuality in the service of his artistic goals. Her identity is not the primary object of these representations; Matisse's response to her, and the resultant construction of her in a role of his choosing, take precedence. There is also some evidence, and much to suggest, that the marital union of Henri and Amélie Matisse was uneasy. It had begun on an uncertain footing, was always subject to tension, and was all but dissolved by the late 1910s, when Matisse moved more or less permanently from Paris to the south of France. Matisse's portraits of his wife are sometimes marked quite clearly by animus – a quality noted by the American writer Gelett Burgess in 1910 in writing about *Madame Matisse*. Burgess found it to be Matisse's "punishment" of Amélie, teaching the viewer "to see in her a strange and terrible aspect."[37] Annette Rosenshine, a friend of the Steins who saw the painting when Michael and Sarah Stein brought it to San Francisco in 1906, later called it "a demented caricature of a portrait."[38] Less strong but no less perceptive about the dominance of the artist's concerns are the comments of Matisse's friend Francis Carco, writing some years later about first seeing *Woman with the Hat*: "The painting is a portrait of Madame Matisse, and I remember what a strange effect it had on me. . . . There was nothing physically human about it. The artist must have been more preoccupied with his own personality than with his sitter's."[39] The attack on artistic convention at the heart of Fauvism, and the attack on social convention as represented by the bourgeois portrait, is also in Matisse's portraits of his wife an assault on an individual. And this is surely pertinent to the anxiety and the exaggerated response of many of the original viewers of these paintings. To see such a "strange and terrible aspect" of a specific person on public display produced discomfort. Matisse went too deep and said too much, and no amount of formal invention can hide, or should excuse, the personal disaffection expressed in his construction of her.

* * *

"The entire arrangement of my picture is expressive"

At the Salon d'Automne of 1907 Matisse exhibited a recent picture that he called *Tête d'expression*. This is the portrait of Amélie now known as *The Red Madras Headdress* (fig. 52).[41] In it she wears a dress similar to that in *Madame Matisse (The Green Line)*, but now she sports the brightly colored scarf of the title. Altogether the painting is bold in color, simplified in drawing and design, and flatly painted – in a word, decorative, in the positive sense toward which Matisse was moving in his work at this time. From this period dates the beginning of the conflict that Matisse experienced in portrait painting until he abandoned the endeavor – the conflict between the representation of individuality and the overall decorative qualities he sought in all his art.

The face of this portrait of Amélie Matisse is the most simplified part of all, which makes the title under which it was exhibited, *Tête d'expression*, seem anomalous. This portrait is surely not in the tradition of expressive heads, demonstrating human emotions, implied in its stock title. And yet the concept of the *tête d'expression* is fully in keeping with the generalized nature of this portrait, its approach to an impersonal type. Matisse may have meant this designation as a witticism, since he seems so deliberately to have wanted to drain the picture of the kind of tension that had brought him such criticism for *Woman with the Hat*. Instead, *The Red Madras Headdress* seems made to illustrate the passage in Matisse's "Notes of a Painter," written the following year, in which he distinguished expression in art from human emotion: "Expression, for me, does not reside in passion bursting from a human face or manifested by violent movement. The entire arrangement of my picture is expressive." And: "Composition is the art of arranging in a decorative manner the diverse elements at the painter's command to express his feelings."[41] Matisse evidently believed that *The Red Madras Headdress* represented his new intention to simplify his art; an illustration of it accompanied his interview with Guillaume Apollinaire that appeared in December 1907.[42] The interview is significant for presenting Matisse's first public statements about his art, at a time when he and his work seemed almost constantly to be under attack. This painting, and the three others reproduced there, exemplified the image of greater seriousness and purpose that Matisse wished to foster in the face of criticism of the incoherence of his art.

The strategy backfired, at least with regard to *The Red Madras Headdress*. Although the painting seems to defuse the tensions expressed in the two previous portraits of Amélie Matisse, the simplifications and the firm handling of drawing and color proved risible to some observers. When it was exhibited in 1907, several critics, perhaps mindful of Matisse's growing reputation, made an effort to take it seriously, but in the end judged that there was something ridiculous about the painting. Although Vauxcelles appreciated its "decorative merits," he was put off by the "caricature-like effigy of a woman," this "bizarre face." Michel Puy likewise found that it "did not avoid a certain comic effect."[43] When *The Red Madras Headdress* was exhibited in New York in 1913 in the Armory Show, it was one of the most remarked exhibits by Matisse, prompting one reviewer, Frank Jewett Mather, Jr., to brand it for its "wilful if powerful distortions, a childish symbolism, fairly appalling ugliness."[44] For these critics, Matisse's simplified drawing, abstracting the features of the sitter, and bright color scheme and bold patterning resulted in caricature of the sitter, and of the art of painting.

52 *The Red Madras Headdress*, 1907. Oil on canvas, 99.4 × 80.5 cm. Merion, Pa., The Barnes Foundation.

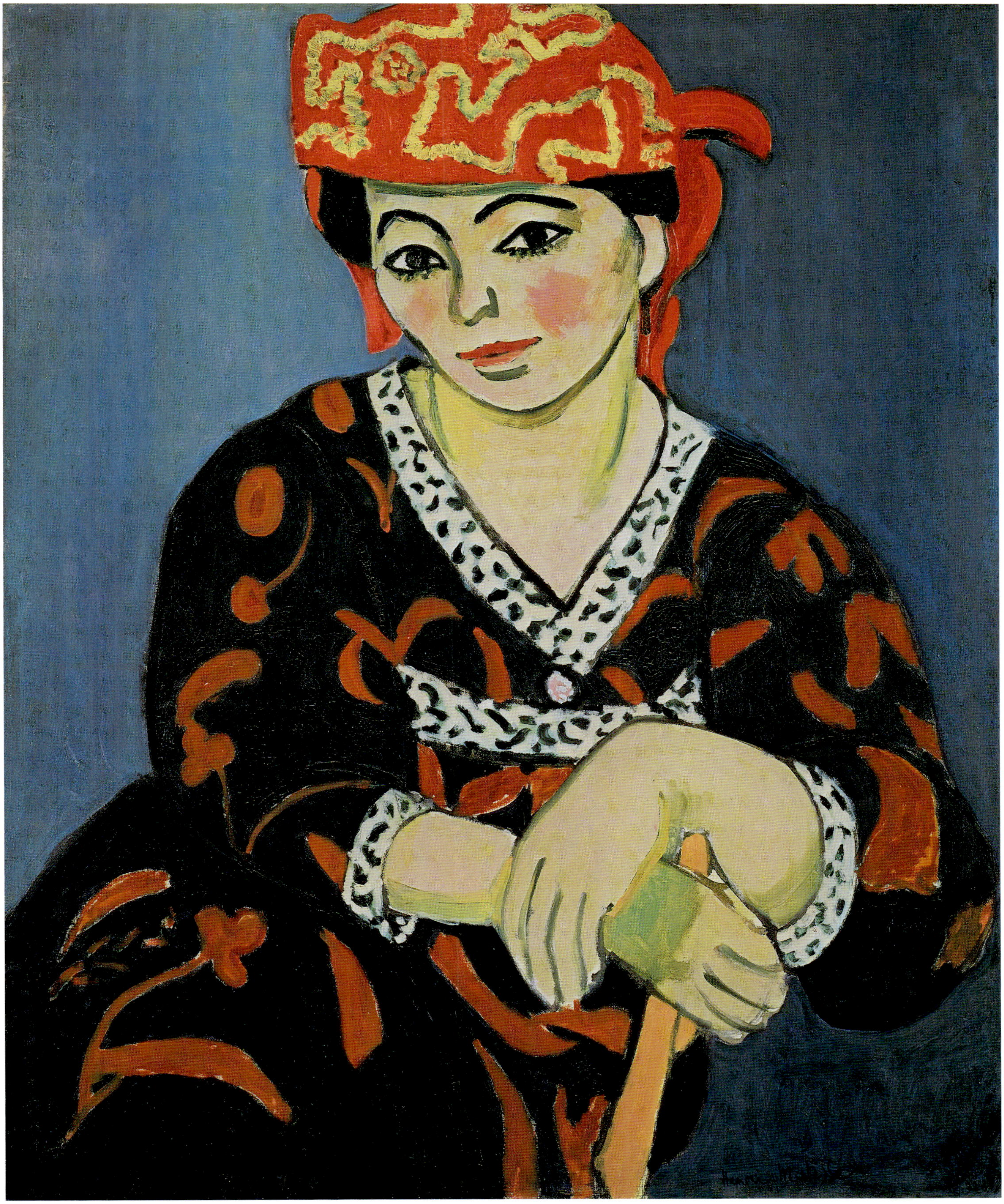

I have juxtaposed the two sets of responses to portraits of Amélie Matisse – the two paintings from 1905 on one hand, *The Red Madras Headdress* on the other – to indicate Matisse's dilemma in portraiture at this time. When he honestly translated his emotions into painted expression, he was lacerated for being violent and barbarous. When he consciously avowed a goal to suppress the contingency and messiness of actual human emotion, he was then accused of caricature – in other words, of being dishonest.[45] Portraits of his wife, fraught with personal concerns and private emotions, were not the appropriate site for Matisse to express himself and to expect these expressions to find a sympathetic public audience.

Masking individuality

This stymied state of affairs changed within a few years. Matisse continued to exhibit paintings that depicted Amélie, believing them to represent his achievement. Their creation and exhibition continued to be central to his goal of self-expression in his art. But these paintings have some flavor of the costume piece, and they did not call into question the values that animated portraiture and made their violation so controversial. Critical response to *The Manila Shawl* (1911; Basel, Kunstmuseum) and to *Portrait of Madame Matisse* from 1913 (fig. 55) was considerably more favorable. Both paintings deflect the human expressive content of portraiture: the former through the emphasis on costume and pose; the latter through the device of turning the face into a mask, more resolutely impersonal than anything Matisse had imposed on a class-equivalent sitter, and the feature of the painting that attracted the most attention.

Portrait of Madame Matisse was the only painting Matisse sent to the Salon d'Automne in 1913. There it was identified simply as *Portrait*, but it was concurrently illustrated in a review with its present title.[46] Apollinaire was enthusiastic, calling the canvas "the best thing in the Salon"; moreover, he believed it was, "with the *Woman with the Hat* in the Stein collection, the artist's masterpiece . . ."[47] There was adverse criticism of the portrait, as we shall see, but even Matisse seemed to be pleased with the general response. In one respect times had clearly changed: there was general critical acceptance and Apollinaire could credibly link in one sentence *Portrait of Madame Matisse* and *Woman with the Hat*, only eight years before one of the most reviled works of art in Paris. The development of Cubism had undoubtedly made *Woman with the Hat* seem tame, perhaps even old-fashioned. Cubism may also have prepared viewers for the sketchiness and abstraction of the later portrait, which may in fact reveal Matisse's efforts to understand Cubism and to assimilate to his own art some of its formal characteristics.

Connected to these formal developments in his work is a progressive denaturing of Amélie in the portraits from the 1910s, a process that had begun earlier with *The Red Madras Headdress*. She is reduced to a mannequin in *The Manila Shawl*, then to a mask in the St. Petersburg *Portrait of Madame Matisse*. Amélie Matisse is said to have wept as Matisse's progress on this portrait removed the image farther and farther from natural appearances.[48] Each of these portraits from 1907 to 1913 in its way abstracts the specificity of Amélie's face and removes the emotional impact of direct confrontation that had been such a powerful feature of the portraits of 1905.[49] Louis Vauxcelles felt this etiolation in 1913, finding *Portrait of Madame Matisse* lifeless and schematic. André Salmon was more specific and lurid:

"his woman in blue wears a wooden mask smeared with chalk . . . a figure in a nightmare," allowing though that it was "quite a harmonious nightmare."[50]

Apollinaire may have been thinking of the color scheme – a striking mixture of green, orange, and violet, with bright pink accents – when he called the same painting "voluptuous," and likened this quality in it to what he admired in the late paintings of Renoir.[51] It is difficult to imagine that Apollinaire considered Matisse's rendering of the figure to be highly sensual (although he must have had more stringent Cubist paintings in mind as a contrast). The portrait would be an austere conception of any human being, let alone the artist's own wife. His masking of Amélie nullifies her individuality; the jet black of the eyes robs her of being the bearer of vision, of her power to engage others.[52] Any "alertness and elegance" that Alfred Barr could see in her could only be imputed to the trope of the tilted head, a limp sign of vitality, perhaps even an ironic one, in light of the blank mask and of Matisse's sketchy treatment of those other chief vehicles of expression in the human figure, the hands. Matisse never painted hands easily, and rarely satisfactorily, but in this portrait they are particularly cursory and uncertain.

The masks through which Matisse represented Amélie were both modern and "primitive." Cézanne's portraits of his wife Hortense provided one way of imagining a woman seated in a chair; Matisse had recently seen one of these paintings by Cézanne, and he owned two of the artist's bust-length portraits of his wife.[53] It is not a question of influence (Cézanne's influence on Matisse had already been profound) but rather that Matisse was in this portrait seeing Amélie through Cézanne, even perhaps identifying more with Cézanne than with his wife in the process of making the portrait.[54] He was also approaching Cézanne in a new way, through the more recent model of Cubism, trying to assimilate both, but completely on his own terms, through radical substitution rather than expressive representation. Both Cubist collage and Cubist portraiture as practised by Picasso in the years 1909–11 are relevant here for the domination of the sitter by a sign.[55] But Matisse was striving not for double meaning or secret code but for something more direct and visceral, more relentless than diverting.

André Salmon identified the other sign that Matisse substituted for Amélie. His "wooden mask smeared with chalk" may have been derived from Matisse's familiarity with actual West African masks, especially Fang masks from Gabon that were held to represent spirits. Such a Fang mask (fig. 54) was then in the collection of Derain, who had bought it from Vlaminck, and it seems likely that Matisse derived his conception of the face in his portrait from this or another example.[56] More important than any specific source is the process of masking in the first place, of covering up what is not to be seen or engaged, but Matisse has also substituted an exotic "other" for the face of his wife. A more dramatic but finally less egregious example of such substitution is Picasso's *Gertrude Stein* of 1906 (fig. 53). The story of the many sittings, of Picasso's frustration over the picture, and of his final imposition, out of Stein's presence, of a mask-like face perhaps derived from ancient Iberian sculpture, is well known.[57] Despite similarities in the making of the two portraits (Matisse's painting also evolved through many sittings), Picasso's device for masking a strong personality is finally more fitting, and less damaging to the individuality of his sitter. In fact, this portrait, which Gertrude Stein kept for many years before donating it to the Metropolitan Museum of Art, has ultimately contributed to her identity and maintained it in the visual sphere.[58] By contrast, Matisse's obliteration of the markers of Amélie's individuality is more thorough. Despite her strength, despite her resistance to erasure, she was no match for her

53 *(right)* Pablo Picasso, *Gertrude Stein*, 1906. Oil on canvas, 100.7 × 82.6 cm. New York, The Metropolitan Museum of Art, bequest of Gertrude Stein, 1946.

55 *(facing page)* *Portrait of Madame Matisse*, 1913. Oil on canvas, 145 × 97 cm. St. Petersburg, Hermitage Museum.

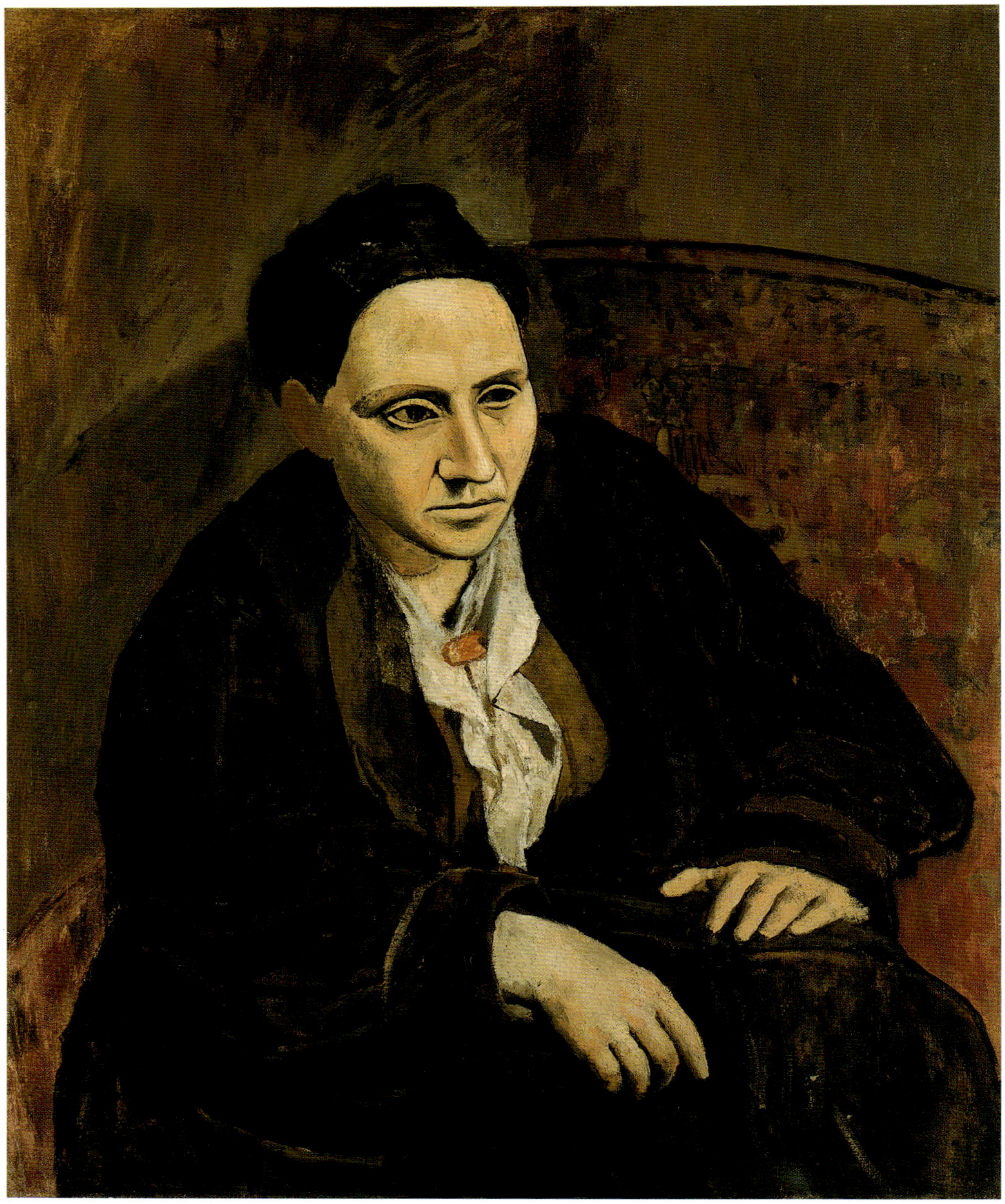

54 Fang mask, Gabon. Painted wood, 48 cm high. Paris, Musée National d'Art Moderne, Centre Georges Pompidou.

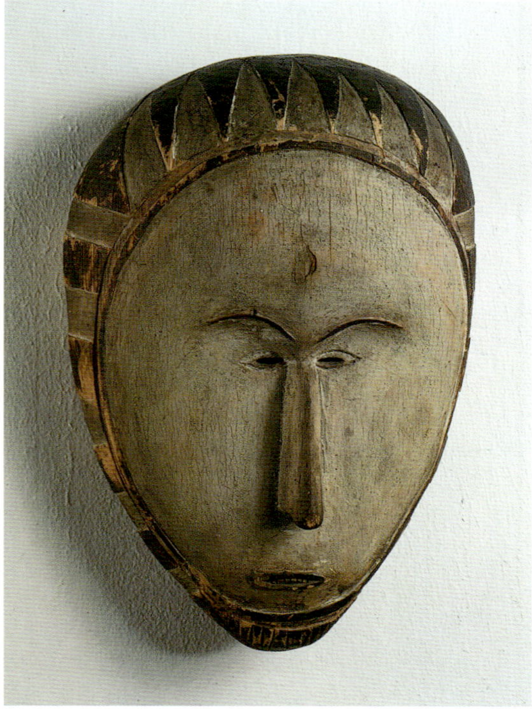

husband in the contest of wills over who would be represented by this portrait.[59] This was the last drama Matisse acted out in a portrait of his wife, and the last time he put the results into the public arena. The few subsequent portraits of Amélie are more subdued, and they are all drawings and prints, where less was at stake artistically. *Portrait of Madame Matisse* represents one of the great struggles in Matisse's portraiture, and one in which the individuality of the sitter was most thoroughly re-imagined in terms of the artist's desires, willfully carried out in representation.

* * *

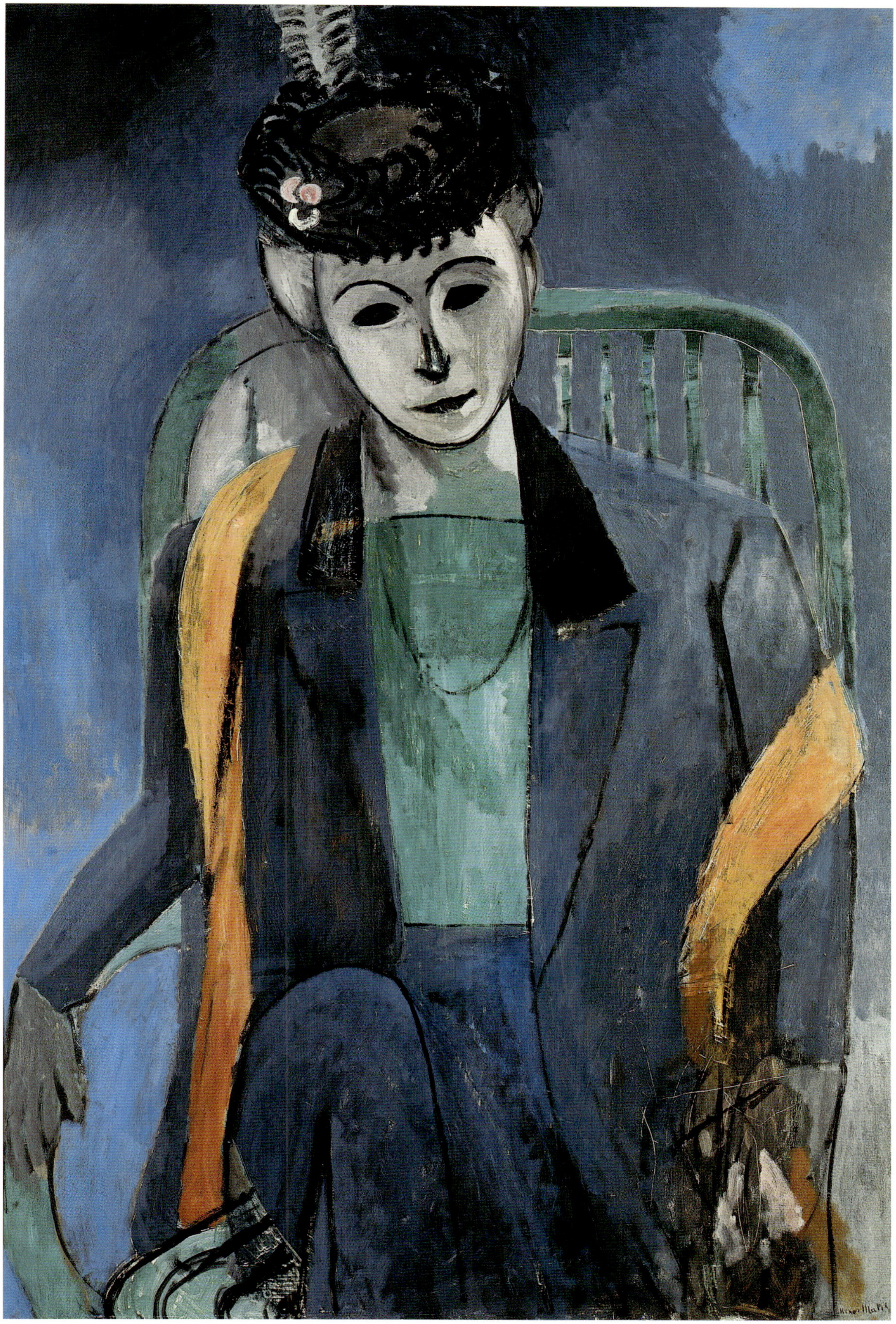

Family portraits and "the sense of assimilated secrets"

One of the last times Amélie Matisse appeared in her husband's painting was in *The Music Lesson* of 1917 (see fig. 60). This large and important canvas was also the last of a small number of family portraits. Together these pictures tell a great deal about the state of his family at various junctures, about Matisse's attitudes and position within the family, and about his decisions to depict his family in works that strive for a decorative unity.[60]

Unity in the Matisse family itself, both literal and emotional, seems to have been elusive. Due to economic conditions and constraints of space early in Matisse's career, the two boys, Pierre and Jean, were sent for long periods of time to live with their grandparents. When it came to school, they boarded first at *collège*, then at *lycée*. Marguerite, the only daughter, stayed at home. The boys returned to the family home only once the Matisses had settled in Issy-les-Moulineaux, a near suburb of Paris.[61] The artist's growing financial security enabled him first to rent a house with a large garden there in 1909, then to buy it a few years later. The American journalist Clara MacChesney, interviewing Matisse in this house in the summer of 1912, asked him about his family:

> "How many children do you have?"
> "Four."
> "What are their names?"
> "Let's see. There's Marguerite and Jean and Pierre – no, I have three."[62]

This curious error suggests that perhaps he thought of Amélie as a dependent in the same way as his children were. Other explanations would be less charitable.

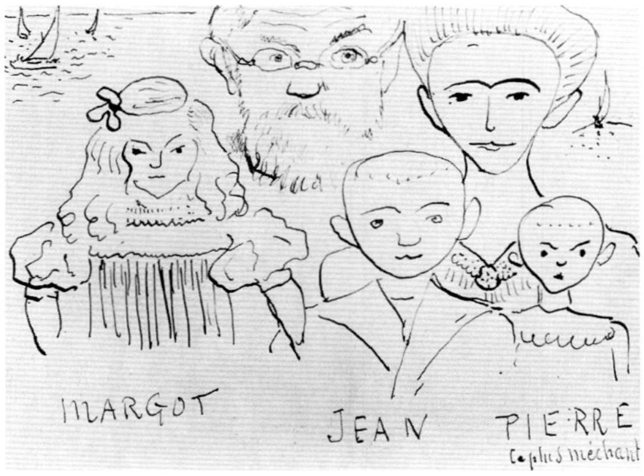

56 *The Artist's Family, Collioure*, 1906. Pen and ink on paper, 9 × 11.5 cm. New York, Cary Lochtenberg collection.

When the boys had been away at school, they could all be together in the summers, and the family sometimes went south with Matisse to Collioure or Cavalière on the Mediterranean coast. At Collioure in 1906 Matisse made an amusing drawing of the family arrayed before the sailboat-dotted sea (fig. 56). The children are labeled; Pierre, frowning, is further identified as "the naughtiest." Marguerite (affectionately called Margot) is aligned with her father; Amélie overlooks the two boys. Allegiances are implied.

The drawing is on a plain postcard. Matisse sent the card on July 4 to Allan Stein, the young son of Michael and Sarah Stein, Matisse's most important patrons at this time. The back of the card is inscribed: "De Henri Matisse à Allain [sic] Stein Cordial souvenir de toute la famille Matisse de vous et de vos chers parents." This amiable and amusing gesture may have had a self-serving purpose for Matisse. His exceptional portrayal of his family together was intended for the consumption of another family whose good favor toward him was desirable.[63] He may have felt it important to express in this apparently offhand little picture the values he perceived in the personal lives of his patrons, affirming an image of family harmony.

The same could not be said for *Conversation*, a double portrait of Matisse and his wife, which he began two years later, in 1908 (fig. 57).[64] Nevertheless, Sergei Shchukin, who by 1912 had surpassed the Steins as Matisse's main source of patronage, was eager to own it. Shchukin was impressed with the magnificent blue that dominates the color scheme, which together with the gravity of mood and rigidity of composition reminded him of the treasured icons of his native Russia.[65]

Matisse portrayed himself and his wife in their night clothes in the master bedroom of the house at Issy; the view through the window is of the front garden and the inside front wall of the property, with a gate.[66] The site is private, the

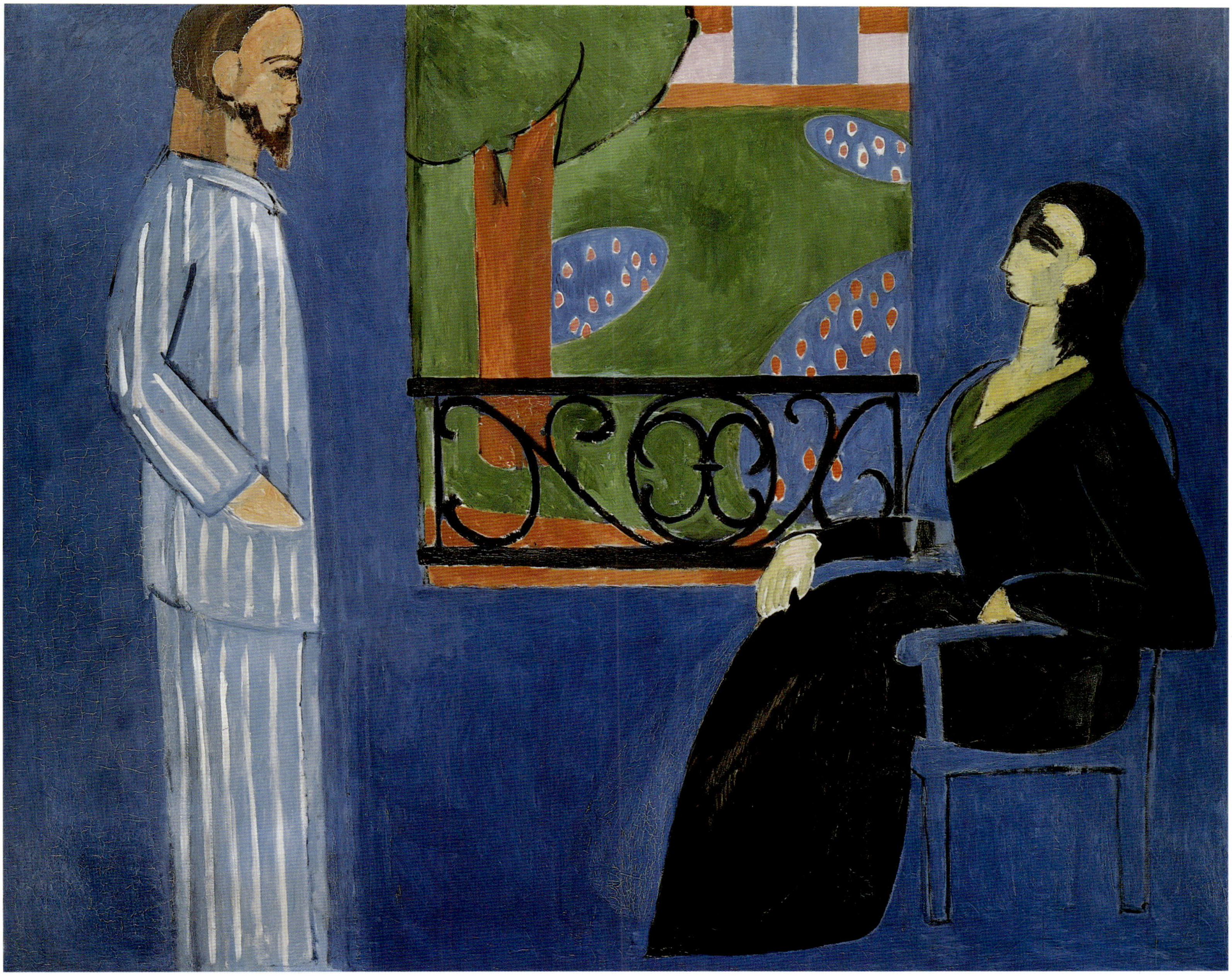

57 *Conversation*, 1908–12. Oil on canvas, 177 × 217 cm. St. Petersburg, Hermitage Museum.

couple's dress is intimate, but none of this speaks of close affection. The figures contrast in many ways (standing *vs.* seated, straight *vs.* curved, light *vs.* dark) but do not complement one another; rather they are positioned as terms of opposition. There is no conversation – ironic title – and no communication. More than one observer has pointed out that the grillwork at the window, whose elaborate pattern separates the two obdurate figures, spells out NON. Matisse and his wife are shown by him as if at a standoff.[67] Perhaps there was such a confrontation; when Matisse began the painting he was apparently having an affair with a young student who was modeling for him.[68]

For all its considerable formal interest and iconographic possibilities, *Conversation* is an image of entirely personal frustration, but painted on the scale of a public pronouncement. It seems incredible that Matisse could exhibit the painting (in

London in 1912) and sell it (to Shchukin in that year). But then again, both actions took it far from home (it was not seen again in Paris until 1970). Perhaps also, for Matisse, the painting abstracted the actual situation to an extent that public display (albeit at a distance) could do no further harm. But he could be discomfited when woman and picture were compared and the differences queried. Gertrude Stein recorded a conversation between her friend Nellie Jacot and Matisse, probably a few years later, during the war: "It was . . . Nellie who made Matisse blush by cross-questioning him about the different ways he saw Madame Matisse, how she looked to him as a wife and how she looked to him as a picture and how could he change from one to the other."[69] We have already seen that this split was relatively easy for Matisse to accomplish; *Conversation* is unique in his work, not least for the extent to which it acknowledges the difficulties in Matisse's marriage and finds a candid form in which to express them.

The decorative turn against intimacy

Less forceful and more appealing, but still insistent finally on a fragmented vision of domestic affairs, is *The Painter's Family*, 1911 (fig. 59). Amélie is set back on the margin on a banquette, where she works quietly on some embroidery. In the center, Jean and Pierre are linked to one another by their red outfits and their game of checkers. Marguerite, wearing a long black dress, stands at the right, holding a book at her side. She is the most prominent of the four in her size, position, and degree of contrast with the busy interior, a riot of patterned rugs, fabrics, and wallpaper. No one communicates save the boys, and that communication is adversarial and through the intermediary of their game. Marguerite is especially aloof, but she is linked by her standing pose to the sculpture on the mantelpiece, a representation by Matisse of his sculpture *The Serf*, a frequent surrogate for the artist. The awkward gravity of the painting recalls Henry James's comment on John Singer Sargent's *The Daughters of Edward Darley Boit* and its conspiratorial atmosphere, in which

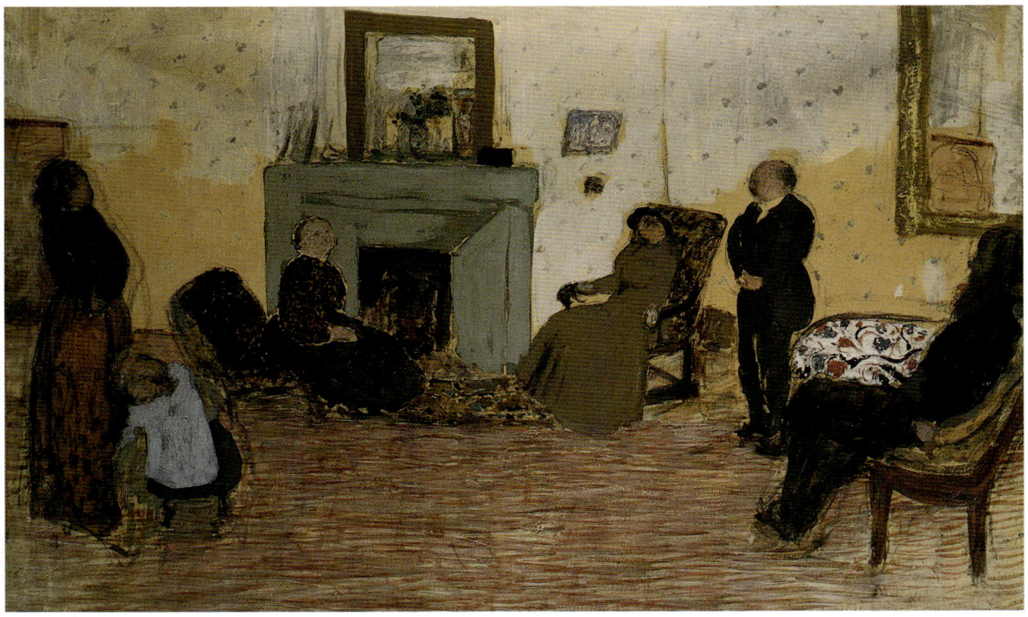

58 Edouard Vuillard, *The Family*, ca. 1901. Glue size on paper, 66 × 107 cm. Private collection.

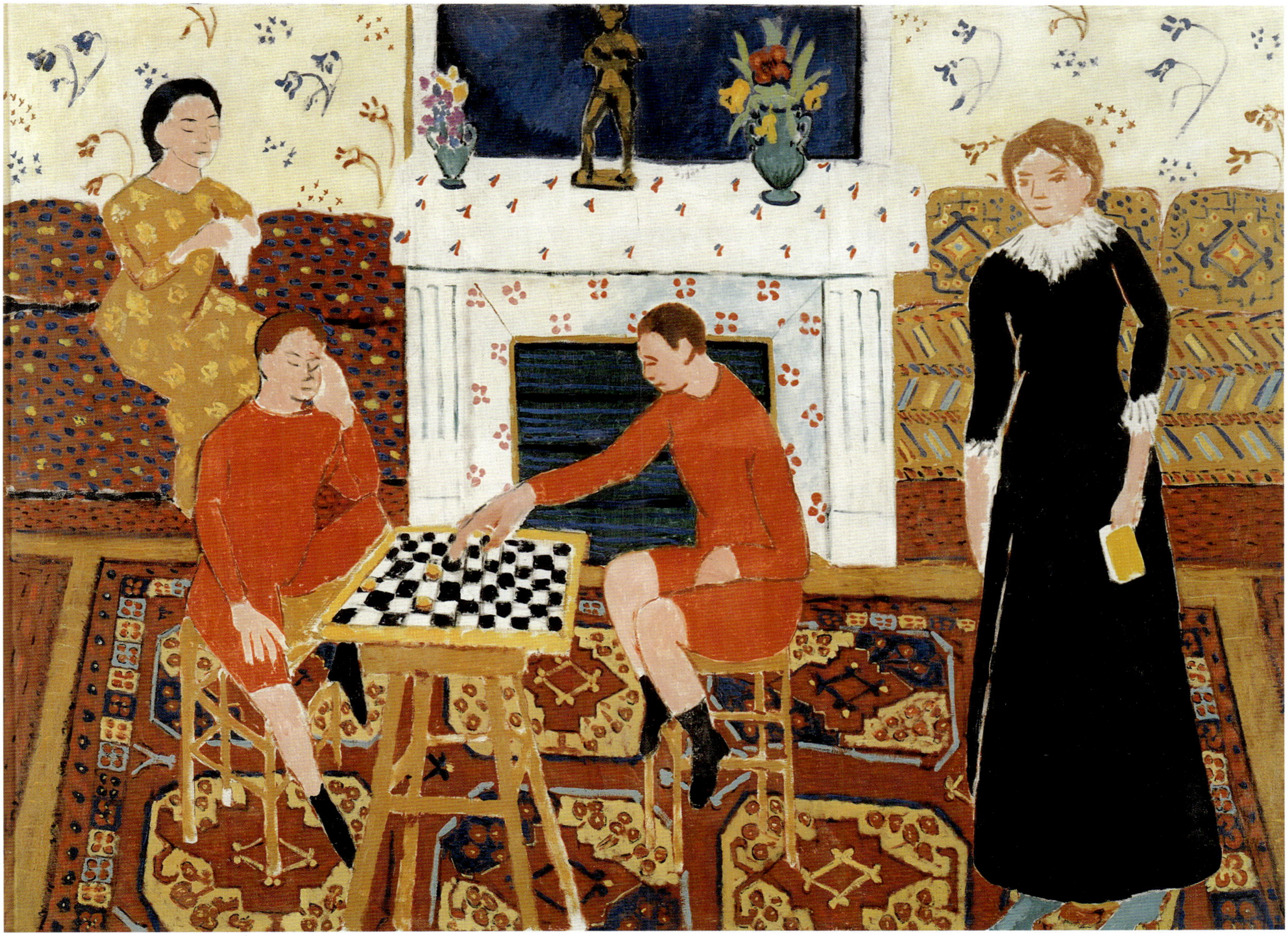

59 *The Painter's Family*, 1911. Oil on canvas, 143 × 194 cm. St. Petersburg, Hermitage Museum.

James felt "the sense . . . of assimilated secrets."[70] In *The Painter's Family* conflicts are muffled and contrasts are tensely balanced, not resolved.

Matisse tried to assimilate his family's secrets through decoration, but the calm, distributed expressiveness of a decorative aesthetic was difficult to reconcile with the pointed and urgent emotional concerns around him.[71] The elaborate interior setting of *The Painter's Family* at once diffuses and sets into relief the tension projected into this family representation. Matisse saw decoration as a solution to a pictorial problem and, perhaps, to a problem of emotional response and its representation in art. His experience of Persian miniature paintings, which he had seen in Munich the previous year, with their fiendishly intricate but boundless decorative patterns, helped him, he said later, "to get away from intimate painting."[72] Intimate painting ("la peinture d'intimité") should be understood to mean the closed domestic interior world of Bonnard's or especially Vuillard's art; Matisse's interest in the decorative is demonstrably different from theirs. In *The Painter's*

Family the figures are set in counterpoint to the buoyantly decorated interior, not in rhythm with it as in Vuillard's domestic tableaux. When Vuillard painted his family in an interior, as in *The Family* from about 1901 (fig. 58), he projected an atmosphere of extreme, even exaggerated casualness through the seemingly uncalculated distribution of the figures in the room, grouped around a deliberately unfocused expanse of space, and the eccentric and cropped framing of the scene. A willed informality of this kind was not Matisse's goal.

His desire to avoid a painting of intimacy was probably also a reflection of the estrangement within his family.[73] The stylizations of Persian art may have suggested to Matisse a way to paint his family as a decorative ensemble, a purely plastic expression in pattern and counterpoint.[74] Fascinatingly, he once again offered to the Steins a neatened version of Matisse family relations. This time it was with a postcard to Michael Stein, on which he sketched the work in progress and bemoaned the difficulties in its making. Another card sent the same day describes the figures. The sketch makes the home scene look more hospitable than the painting does, and perhaps *The Painter's Family* did evolve away from a more harmonious rendering of the family group. If a family may have a persona, Matisse again seems to have been doing his best to project his family persona in a favorable way to the Steins.[75]

This is apparently the theme of Matisse's final picture of his family, *The Music Lesson* (1917; fig. 60), but this painting also marks a breaking point leading to far-reaching transitions. The children are gathered in the living room of the house at Issy. Recalling *The Piano Lesson* of the previous year, to be discussed below, Pierre is at the piano; Marguerite supervises his efforts. Jean sits at the lower left reading a book. Separated from the children, Amélie is shown outside in the garden, sewing – again: apparently Matisse, having never represented her professional efforts in his art, did not mind depicting her doing domestic work of this sort. The immediate motive for Matisse to paint his family at this time was Jean's imminent departure that summer to serve in the army – his son, with a moustache and smoking a cigarette, was now a young man of eighteen years. The unusual speed with which Matisse painted this very large picture doubtless reflected his urgent desire to seize the moment, in the middle of a war that could disrupt the fabric of life at any time (as Matisse well knew: some of his relatives in the north of France were behind enemy lines).[76] He may also have been anticipating his own departure later in the year for the South, which, war or no war, marked the end of any sense of unity in the Matisse family as he took up a geographically and psychologically divided mode of living in two worlds.

This break – Matisse's flight from domestic responsibility – is signaled in the opposition formulated across the garden pond. A gigantic rendering in lifelike hues of Matisse's actually quite small bronze sculpture *Reclining Nude I* – emblem of sensuality for Matisse – looms over the passive figure of his wife – emblem of domesticity and in a rocking chair, no less.[77] The figure of Amélie embodies responsibility and stability, evidently confining to Matisse at the time, a constraint he was about to leave behind. His own part in the scene is represented by the open violin case containing the instrument he played as a pastime at home. Its surrogate status emphasizes Matisse's absence. Jack Flam perceptively interprets the activities engaged in by the family: "The music making, the sewing, the reading all represent the bourgeois consumption of art. The artist, in removing himself from the picture, is distancing himself from his family and his bourgeois past."[78] Soon Matisse left this conflicted reality behind in favor of a place – Nice – where he could produce a bourgeois art of another kind, of hedonistic fantasy.

60 *The Music Lesson*, 1917. Oil on canvas, 243.8 × 209.5 cm. Merion, Pa., The Barnes Foundation.

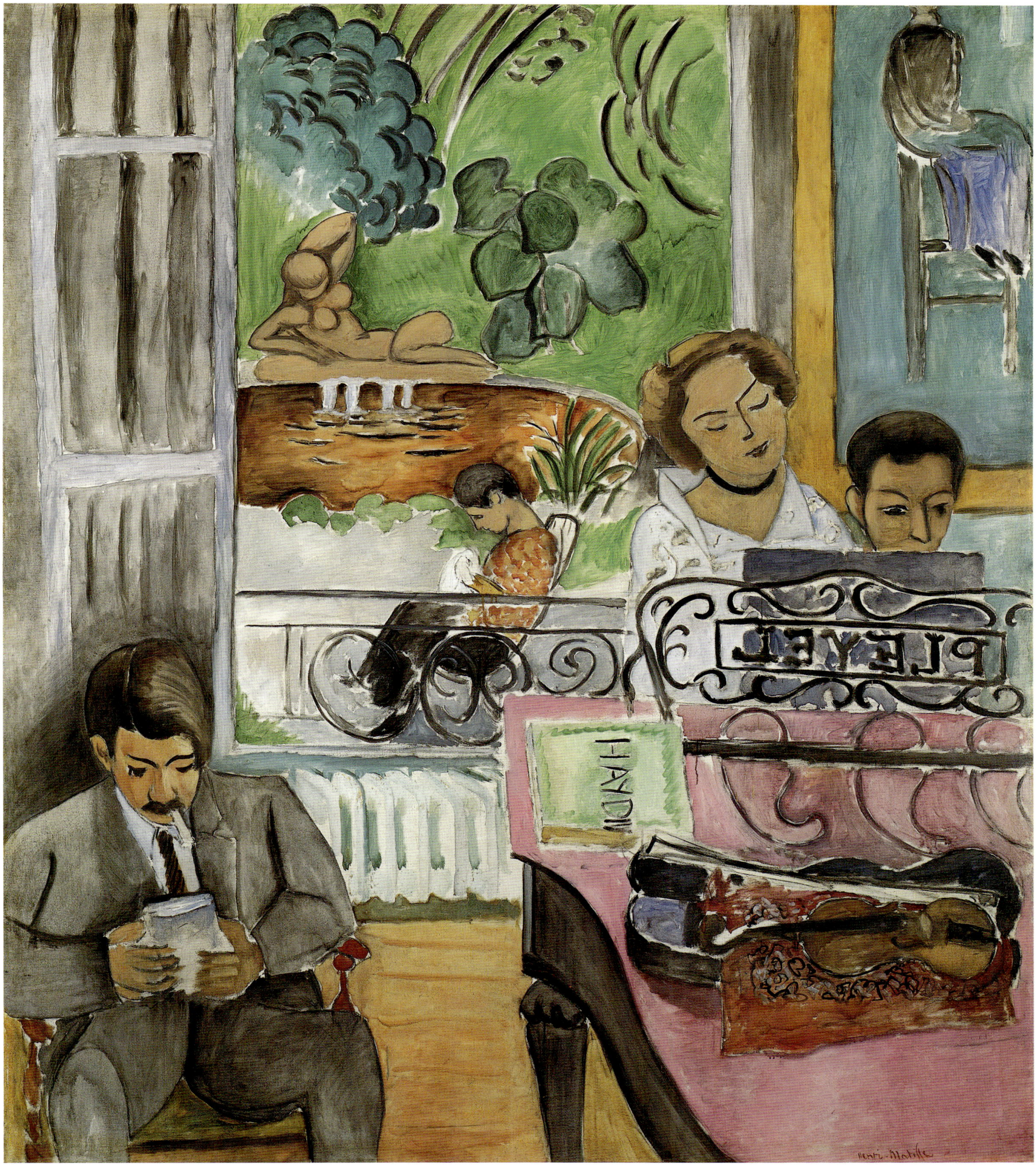
PLEYEL
HAYDN

Marguerite Matisse from *gosse d'atelier* to fashion plate

The portraits Matisse made of his children are considerably less conflicted than those of Amélie, or of combinations of the whole family. For the most part they are not "problem pictures" (or sculptures): they do not engage as many of the great themes and symbolic operations that are generally seen as such a rich aspect of Matisse's more obviously ambitious productions. In the images of Marguerite especially we often sense instead a simpler motivation – Matisse's undemanding delight in the uncompromised presence of those closest to him, and a desire to express this emotion in relatively direct terms, at least for a time. Yet in these portraits we may still see Matisse at work on the overall project of declaring and defining himself through extensions of his ego as well as his corporeal presence.

Matisse made many more portraits of Marguerite than of all the other members of the family together, and he did them in all the major media he employed during the first half of his career. The earliest portrait of Marguerite dates from 1901 (see fig. 12) the last from 1945. They are concentrated in two periods: around 1906 and a much larger number in the years 1914–1920 when, in a period of rapid and profound development in his work, and while family ties in general deteriorated, she was an element of constancy in his life and work, even as she developed into a chic and worldly young woman.

Marguerite was Matisse's favorite among his children. He painted her with the loving attention to her activities that characterizes Rembrandt's portraits of Titus or Lovis Corinth's many drawings of his son Thomas. Marguerite was not, of course, Amélie's child; a connection between this and Matisse's protective feelings toward his daughter seems unavoidable. In her turn, she remained loyal to her father and devoted to the cause of his work and the support of his reputation.[79] An example, a significant one: Marguerite was herself an artist and had a modest career in the 1920s, but when some of her paintings appeared on the French art market bearing her father's signature as a result of someone's attempt to pass her work as his, she destroyed nearly all her remaining canvases and gave up painting.[80] When she was young she was a self-described "studio kid"; as an adult she was responsible for the establishment of systematic house catalogues of her father's work. As already recounted, in 1901 she underwent a tracheotomy, assisted by her father. She covered the resulting scar with a high collar or, more usually, a black velvet ribbon, often with a decorative pendant, making a virtue of a necessity. She can be identified in many pictures by this distinctive and highly personal ornament, which was also a constant reminder of the bond between father and daughter.

In a certain way Matisse used Marguerite's face as a field for formal experiment no less than he did with Amélie. But much more often Marguerite is portrayed as herself, in possession of her own identity. She is almost never asked in these works to play a role alien to her natural status as a child and a growing young woman. Moreover, no hostility accrues to these images: Matisse never used her as the vehicle through which his conflicts could be expressed. It seems clear that he was more deeply respectful of his daughter than his wife. In one sense this is to be expected: as a child she would have been relatively guileless and susceptible to manipulation, and warranted protection, which her father provided both in life and in representation. Matisse undoubtedly saw more of himself reflected in Marguerite than he did in Amélie, or even Jean and Pierre. This leads naturally, I believe, to Matisse's tendency to portray Marguerite as a whole and independent being, even when his portraits of her were the site for radical stylistic moves, as in *Girl Reading* (fig. 61).

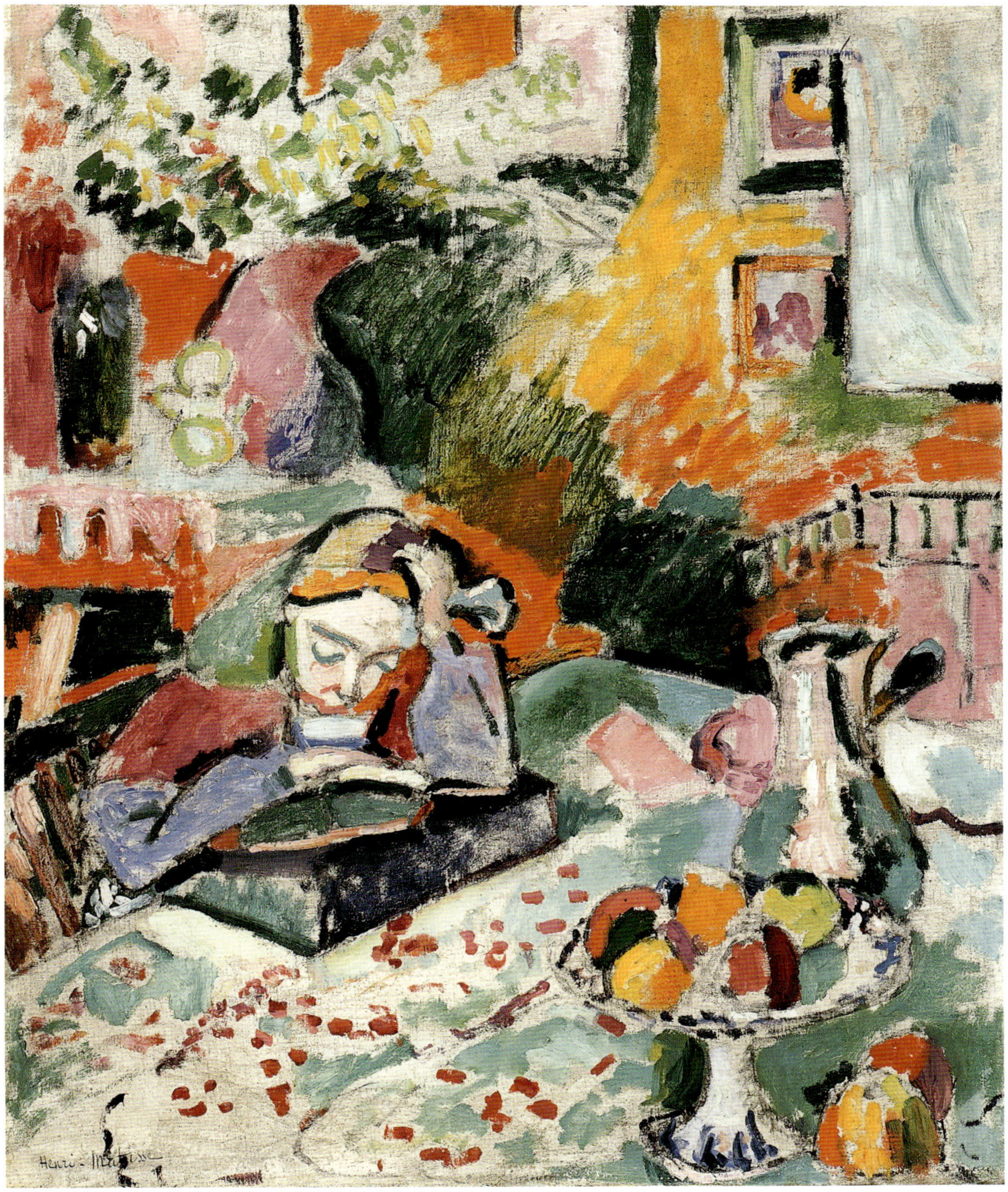

61 *Girl Reading*, 1906. Oil on canvas, 72.7 × 59.4 cm. Private collection.

With Amélie, Matisse's approach was much more to appropriate her and to shape her image to serve his self-expression; with Marguerite the independence and wholeness he accorded her may have worked equally well as a means for him to express himself.[81] Given the affinity he always felt for his daughter, it is as if he were exploring an aspect of himself by portraying her, as if she gave him access to something of himself that he could not apprehend more directly and could not express through self-portraiture whether direct or symbolic. By affirming her individuality he could also reflect on and amplify his own.

* * *

Learning and mastery

Before 1906 Matisse had made a few scattered portraits of his daughter, but the sudden concentration of images of her in that year is a striking development at a time when Matisse's career had taken an important turn. The shock waves from the Salon d'Automne of the previous year had not subsided, but as we have seen Matisse was already moving beyond the anarchic-seeming Fauve style that had made him so notorious. He seemed to want to broaden the scope of his work, and perhaps also to bring under control the style of painting that had produced such a problematic response. In portraiture, as we have seen, this move is signaled by *Madame Matisse (The Green Line)* as a synthesizing response to *Woman with the Hat*. In a pair of portraits from 1906 of Marguerite reading a book he continued this consolidation. The larger group of portraits of Marguerite extend his effort to work at once in a variety of styles, and furthermore in a variety of media, demonstrating mastery of another kind. Matisse's paintings, drawings, and sculptures of his daughter, among other figurative works at this time, establish and increase his range. These portraits of Marguerite are acts of self-projection as well as images deriving from Matisse's fascination with his beloved daughter.

Girl Reading, finished early in 1906, continues the fervid mixed-technique Fauve style Matisse used in *Woman with the Hat*, but most of the pyrotechnic effects are not directed at the figure of Marguerite but instead vitalize her surroundings. The lower part of the painting, where she sits at a table reading a book raised on a stand, is more solidly painted, with greater emphasis on contour and modeling.[82] In contrast, everything above is insubstantial, as if from another realm altogether.[83] Oblivious, absorbed in her book, Marguerite carries on a perfectly normal

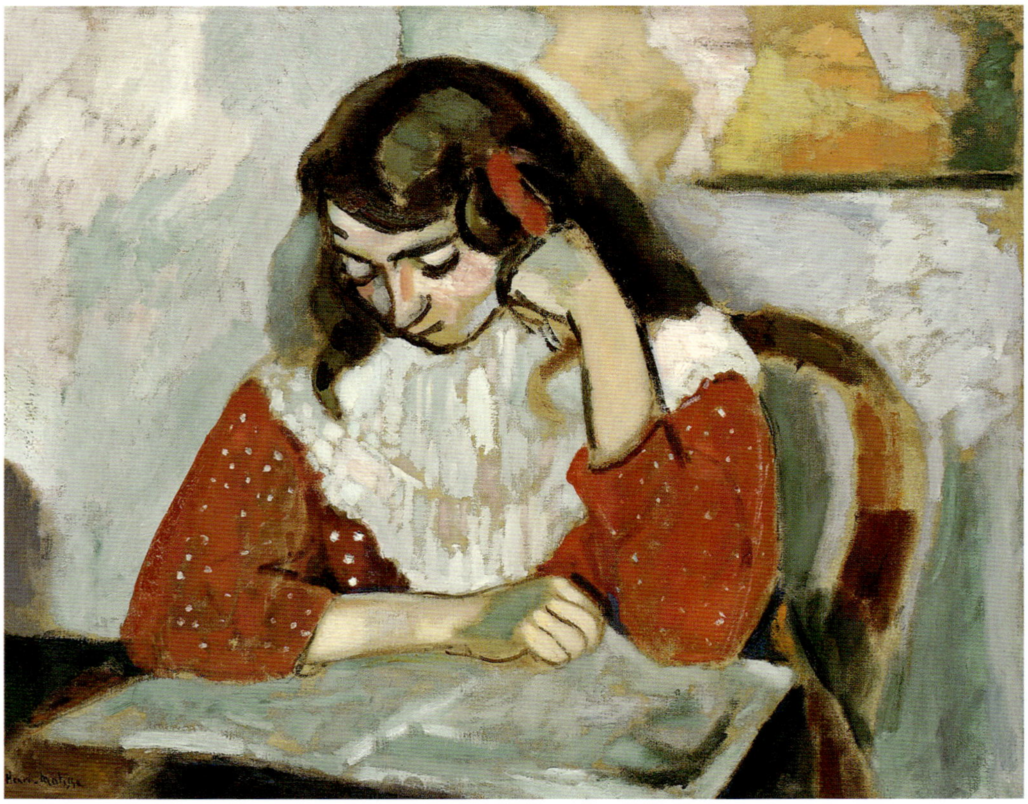

62 *Marguerite Reading*, 1906. Oil on canvas, 65 × 81 cm. Grenoble, Musée de Peinture et de Sculpture.

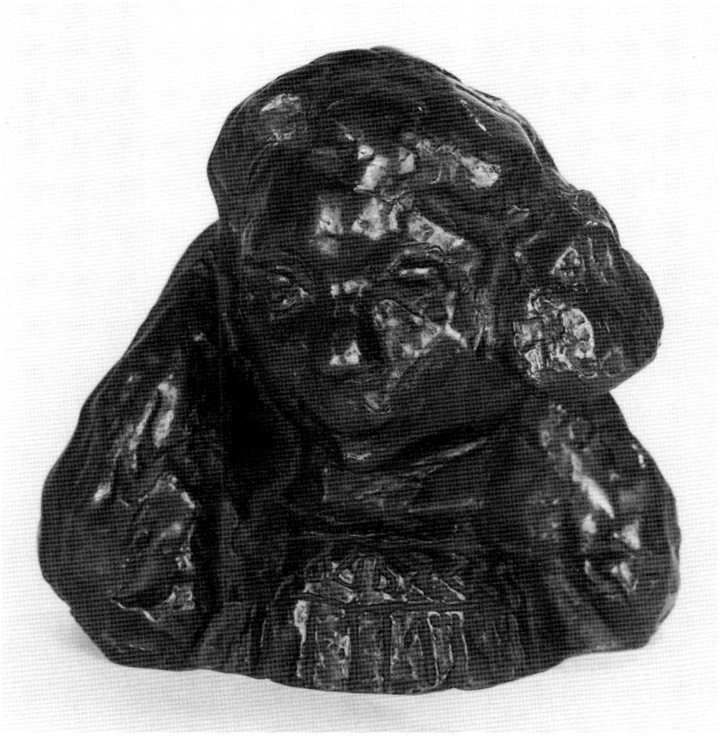

63 *Head of a Young Girl*, 1906. Bronze, 16 cm high. The Baltimore Museum of Art, The Cone Collection, formed by Dr. Claribel Cone and Miss Etta Cone of Baltimore, Maryland, BMA 1950.426.

activity for a young girl – her acquisition of knowledge (in *The Painter's Family* a book is still her attribute). A modern Education of the Virgin is suggested but should not be insisted upon. The theme of the girl reading also recalls Matisse's earlier paintings of readers, notably *Woman Reading* of 1895.[84] Possibly unconsciously, Matisse thus related his daughter to her mother Caroline Joblaud. Later in the year Matisse took up the subject again in *Marguerite Reading* (fig. 62). The theme of the reader is now more focused, as is the sense of individuality in how Matisse has represented the girl. As with the two portraits of his wife from 1905, here he brings into a more controlled and legible state a subject initially treated with apparent abandon.[85] Features are more delineated, costume is more specific, and her orientation more toward the viewer enhances her presence.[86] She is still absorbed in a book, but now it is a picture book – an education from images (art?), not text.[87]

Other portraits of Marguerite in this period – in painting, drawing, and sculpture – seem to embody the theme of the self in formation, all fluidity and potential. Sometimes Matisse treated her features as highly mobile indices of development. In the small sculpture *Head of a Young Girl* (fig. 63), the twelve-year-old Marguerite has the mouth of an infant, and her eyes are noticeably without definition. Portraits of children frequently express this theme of nascence, and the idea of a child's development can become a metaphor for other things in a state of formation, notably art itself. Figural sculpture particularly lends itself to the Pygmalion-like idea of an artist fashioning a new self from unpromising material, as in the heads of children by Medardo Rosso. Matisse at this time was certainly responding to the sense of potential in his own children – he also sculpted a small portrait of Pierre – but he was more widely interested in the general state of childhood, in analogy to the sense of innocence and delight in discovery that he believed animated his overall artistic project. The childlike sense of wonder and simplicity that he cherished is sometimes made explicit in these portraits, where it is also contrasted with signs of self-mastery as Matisse explored the contrast between Marguerite as a child and Marguerite as a potential adult.

Marguerite from the following year appears to spare nothing to simplification (fig. 64). The unmodeled face and summarized features have been likened to the drawings of children and "primitive" artisans. Both comparisons are apt given Matisse's growing interest in these forms of expression. Nevertheless, the painting is not as simple as it looks. Matisse used a sophisticated and fairly somber palette of close-valued greens, ochers, and blues, far more conservative and less brashly childlike than the vivid blues and reds of the similarly reductive *Red Madras Headdress* from the same year. Picasso appreciated this combination of simplification and subtlety in the portrait of Marguerite, and saw in it some parallels to his own direction; this was the painting he chose in an exchange of works with Matisse

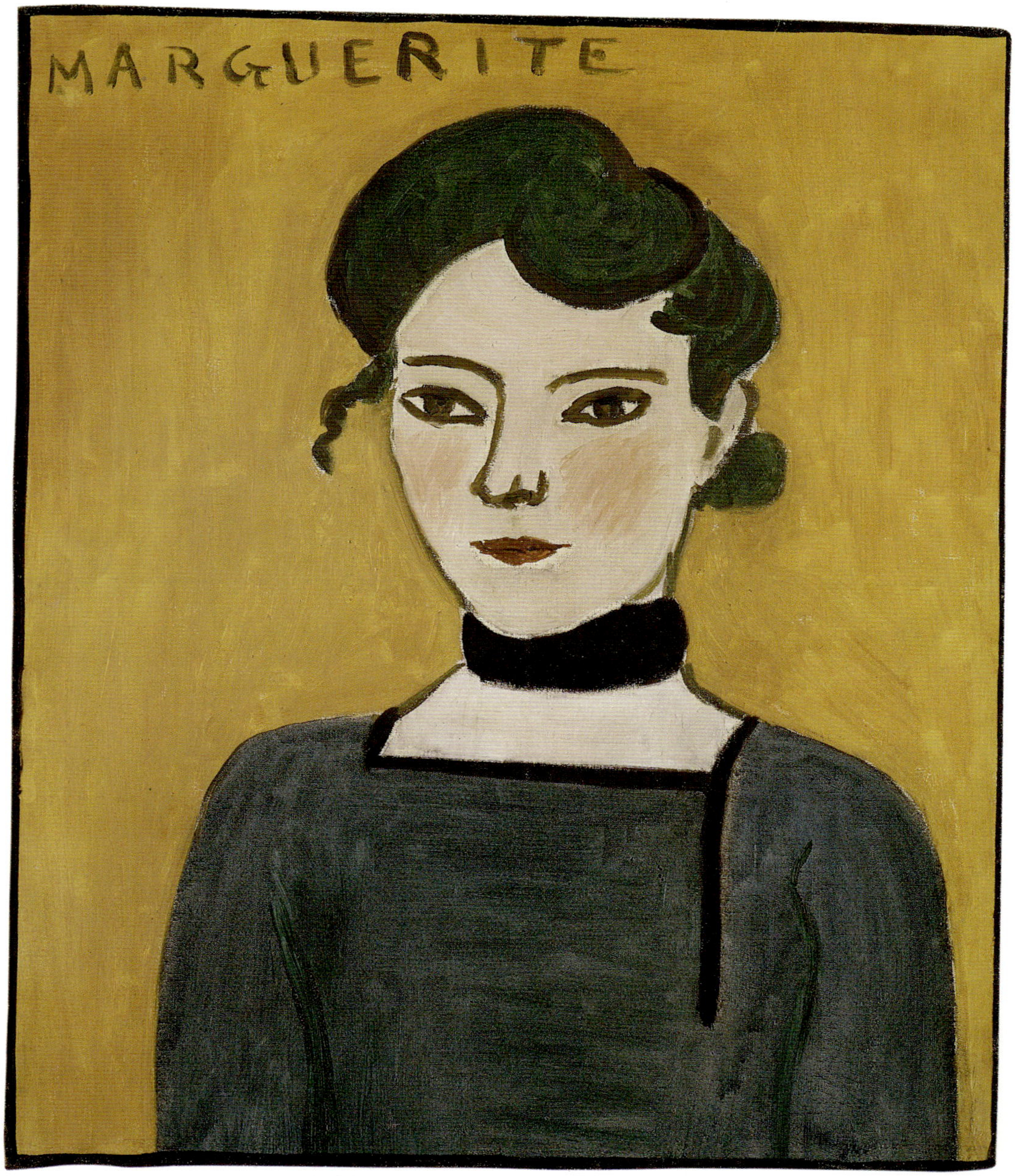

64 *Marguerite*, 1907. Oil on canvas, 65 × 54 cm. Paris, Musée Picasso.

65 *Marguerite with a Black Cat*, 1910. Oil on canvas, 94 × 64 cm. Private collection.

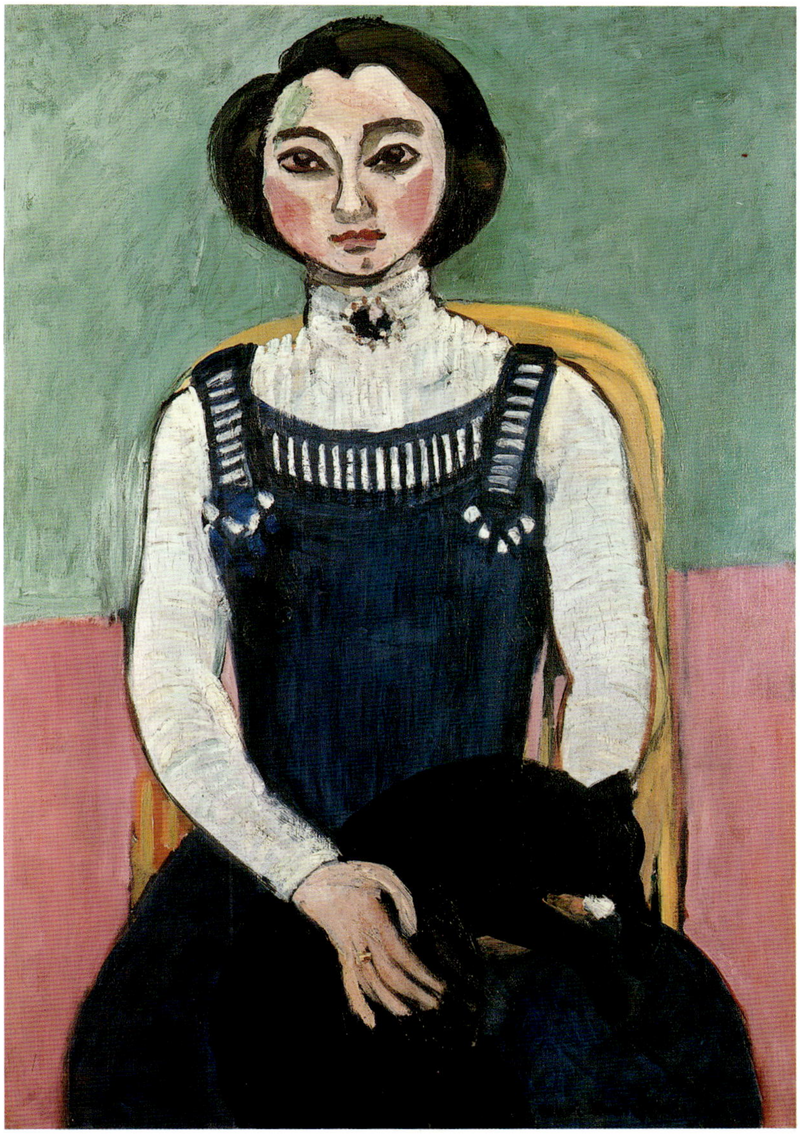

around the summer of 1907, at a time when Matisse told Picasso of his fascination with the art made by his own children.[88] According to André Salmon, Picasso's appreciation did not prevent him and his friends from using the portrait of Marguerite as a dartboard (the darts had suction cups).[89]

To the image Matisse added the crude lettering MARGUERITE to identify the figure, as if this were a self-representation by his daughter. Moreover, he did not sign the painting with his own name, perhaps with deliberate irony – this is an "artless" image. The label is the linguistic equivalent of the signifying image, and labels were of course common (and often necessary) adjuncts to portraits that did not depend on physiognomic accuracy in order to function. Face and name bear the same referent, each a sign, neither a substitute. Here Matisse distills the language of portraiture to its most reductive form in his work.

Grown up a bit more, Marguerite posed for a stately but also greatly simplified portrait in 1910, *Marguerite with a Black Cat* (fig. 65). It is as formal as *Conversation*, still in progress at this time, and, as with that painting, more than one observer has felt a quasi-religious echo of icons.[90] The rigid pose, frontal, nearly centered, is offset by subtle asymmetries in hair, chair, and cat, cradled in a lumpish hand that conveys adolescent clumsiness. The presumption of majesty in this large, three-quarter-length portrait contrasts poignantly with the awkwardness of the girl's age.

Another burst of interest in Marguerite's development is indicated by the large number of portraits Matisse made of her beginning in 1914 and continuing into the war years. The variety of poses and garments suggests not only a young woman establishing her identity through her personal modification of it but also the refreshment of direct observation Matisse may have needed as an alternative to his work increasingly from imagination. But he was still able to mix extreme stylistic experiment with his observations of her specificity. As he worked on one canvas he asked Marguerite: "This painting wants to take me somewhere else. Do you feel up to it?"[91] She did; the result was the severely architectonic, heavily worked *Tête blanche et rose* (fig. 66). Within the Cubist-influenced grid of pink, blue, and white – stripe-signs referring to Marguerite's jacket – several more descriptive details may be found. Curved red lips contrast oddly with the angular structure. The eyes, though not rendered descriptively, radiate life through touches of red, and with remarkable effect Matisse has made the eye on the light-struck side of her face smaller, vividly conveying its automatic response. Above the eyes are arched brows, echoed below the face by Marguerite's characteristic ribbon, from which hangs a sparkling gold pendant. Our attention is particularly drawn to this feature by its location and its facture, more varied than in the rest of the painting, signifying the glitter of a bauble.

Matisse's use of Cubist principles in *Tête blanche et rose* has often been noted, however superficial or imposed on his sitter they may be. Such discussion has usually concentrated on his desire for greater structure in his work at this time, and the friendship with Juan Gris that stimulated his interest in Cubism. This is certainly true, although the painting is also related to the analytic Cubist paintings of Picasso and Braque through Matisse's interest in signs in common with those painters. The outward appearance of objects and people in analytic Cubist paintings is disintegrated by space-penetrating *passage*, but a few signs always remain, preserving the visual link between the image and its referent. In a portrait, as here with Marguerite's ribbon and pendant, they are signs of individuality. The selection and exploitation of such signs is also a mark of caricature. Cubist portraiture (including *Tête blanche et rose*) does not exaggerate such signs out of proportion to achieve the desired effect, as caricature does, but in a field of disintegration of the individual, the importance of these signs is magnified. The selectivity identifies the sitter, as it does in caricature, but without the potential for mockery that goes with exaggeration. Thus this portrait of Marguerite may be a kind of caricature, but one that is witty and affectionate.[92]

Among his portraits of Marguerite from the war years, *Tête blanche et rose* is the most overtly radical in style, but what these many images have in common is Matisse's interest in exploring a variety of approaches to the same subject, while always preserving the integrity and individuality of his daughter. This sense of experiment with different modes of seeing Marguerite, explored through a variety of media, lasted only a few years. By the end of the war his portraits of her, while still reflecting his fascination with her image, also project a more consistent vision of her as a young adult coming into her own. When he had shown her with the whole family in *The Music Lesson*, in the summer of 1917, he had cast her as the attentive older sister. When he moved to Nice later that year he embarked on a

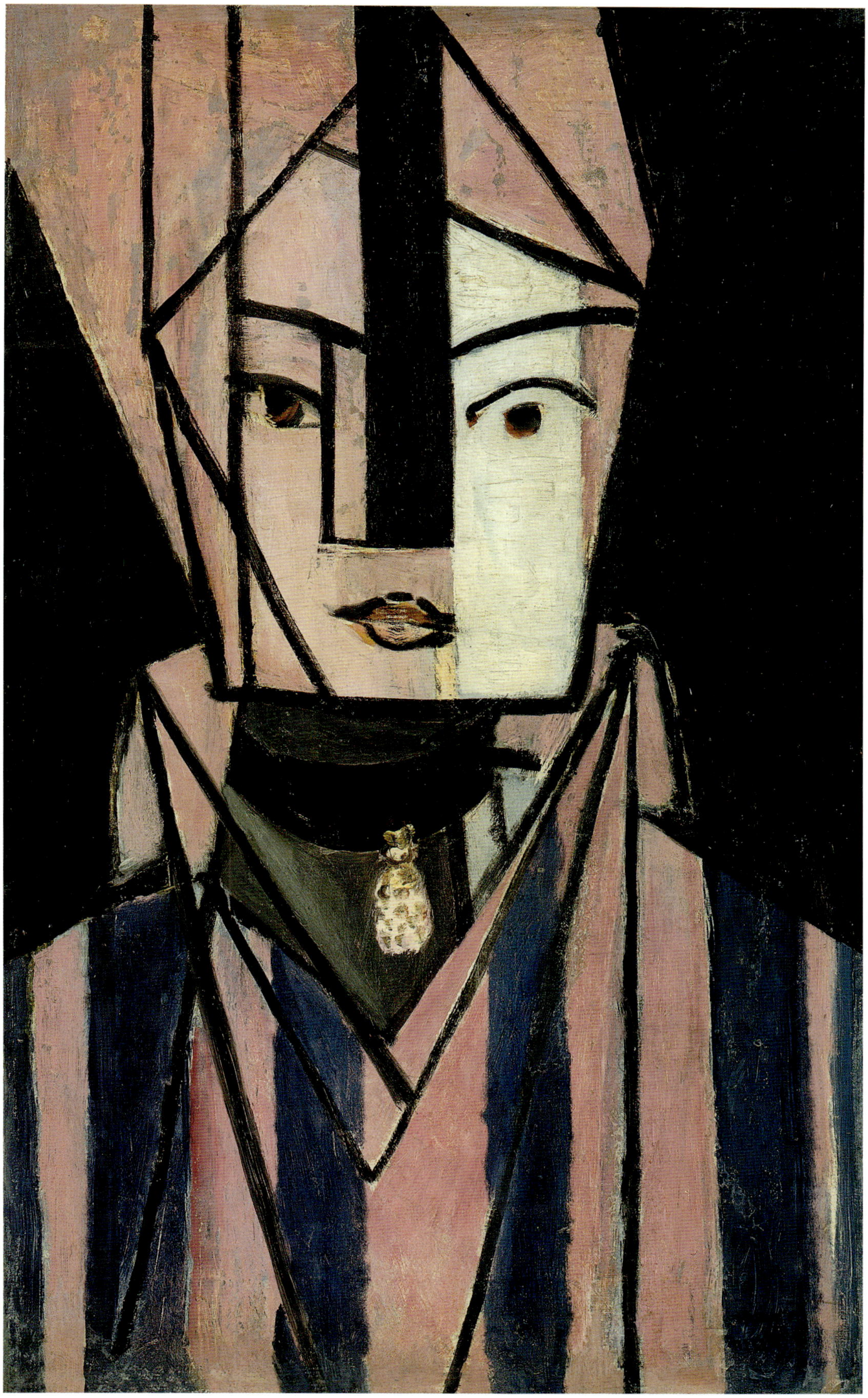

66 *Tête blanche et rose*, 1914. Oil on canvas, 75 × 47 cm. Paris, Musée National d'Art Moderne, Centre Georges Pompidou.

67 *Mlle Matisse in a Scotch Plaid Coat*, 1918. Oil on canvas, 95 × 75 cm. Private collection.

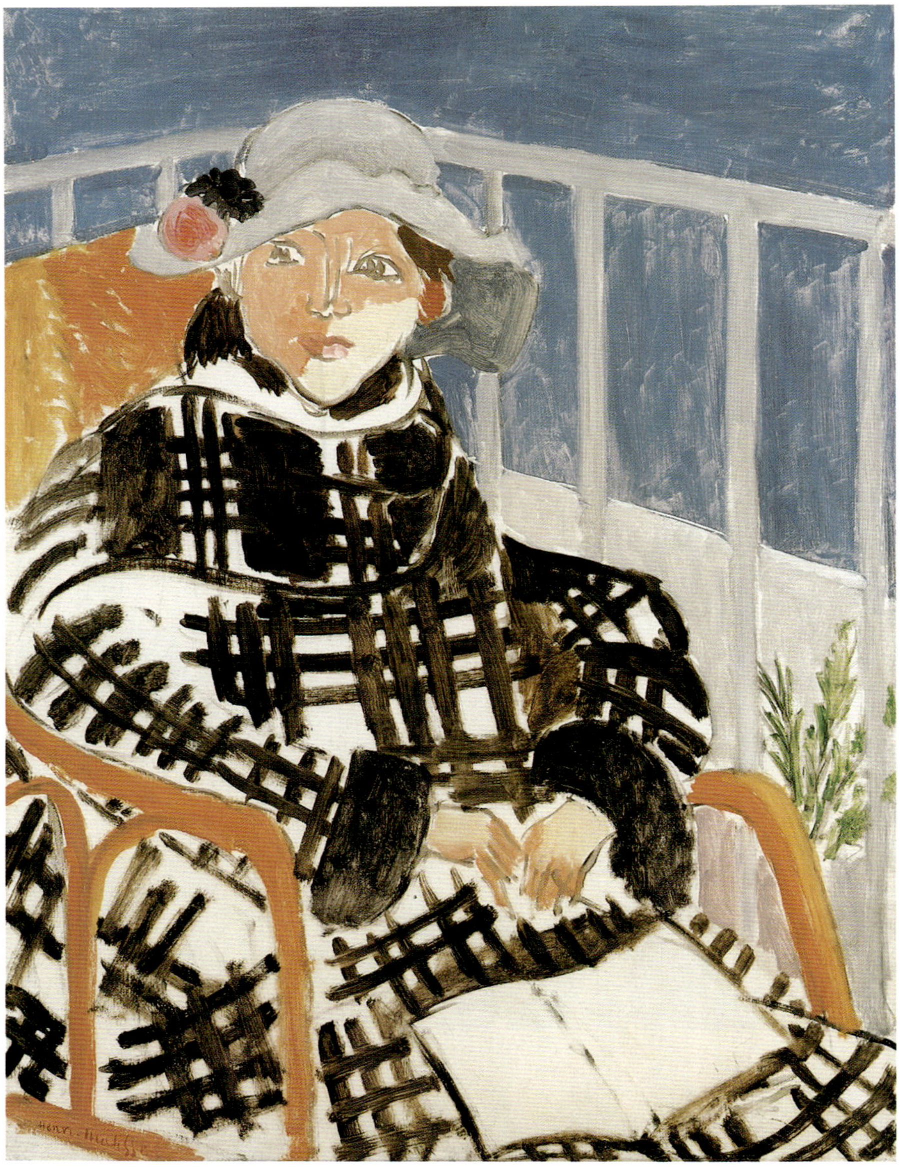

new life that did not include his former role in the family. During an Easter visit from her in 1918, he must have been struck by how different she had become, and by their altered relationship. The portraits from this time reaffirm Marguerite's importance to her father, while measuring her independence. In *Mlle Matisse in a Scotch Plaid Coat* (fig. 67) and other portraits of the young adult Marguerite, Matisse makes us feel that this is a confident woman with a strong sense of herself (the coat was designed by Matisse's friend Germaine Bongard, but Marguerite's taste in fabric was far removed from her father's). From this point it seems that his fascination with her diminished. Later portraits of Marguerite echo his prevailing, and general, concerns with the representation of the face and figure, concerns that could be served equally well by the hired models he used with increasing frequency (in some of these paintings, in fact, Marguerite shares an interior with a model). Although she always retained her father's favor, as a subject in his art she was now one young woman among many.

68 *Pierre Matisse*, 1909. Oil on canvas, 40.6 × 33 cm. Private collection.

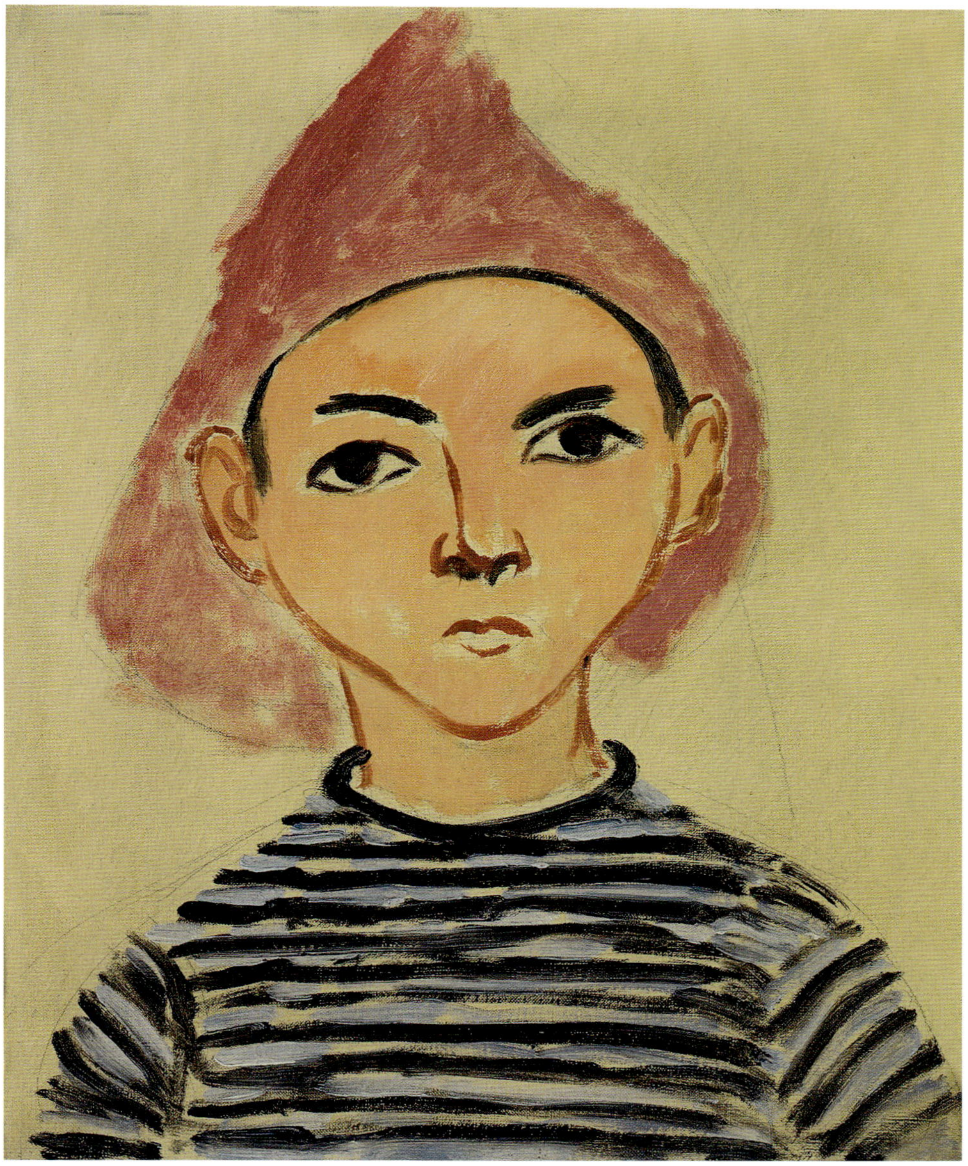

Pierre Matisse and the clock turned back

The independence Marguerite Matisse attained as an adult was forced much earlier on Jean and Pierre. As we have seen, they spent more time away from home and they were much less involved in Matisse's artistic concerns than was their sister. Matisse made many fewer portraits of the two boys, but several of Pierre stand out both for the way in which they mark his own development and for how they contribute to his father's meditations on the process of artistic creation. Like *The Red Madras Headdress* (see fig. 52) and *Marguerite* (see fig. 64), *Pierre Matisse* of 1909 (fig. 68) projects a childlike artlessness through the simplification of the boy's features, the elimination of modeling altogether, and the deliberate awkwardness of the drawing. As a group, these three paintings of his family members are Matisse's most reductive portraits from this period, and we may readily see the family as the laboratory for radical experiment in making portraiture without expressing

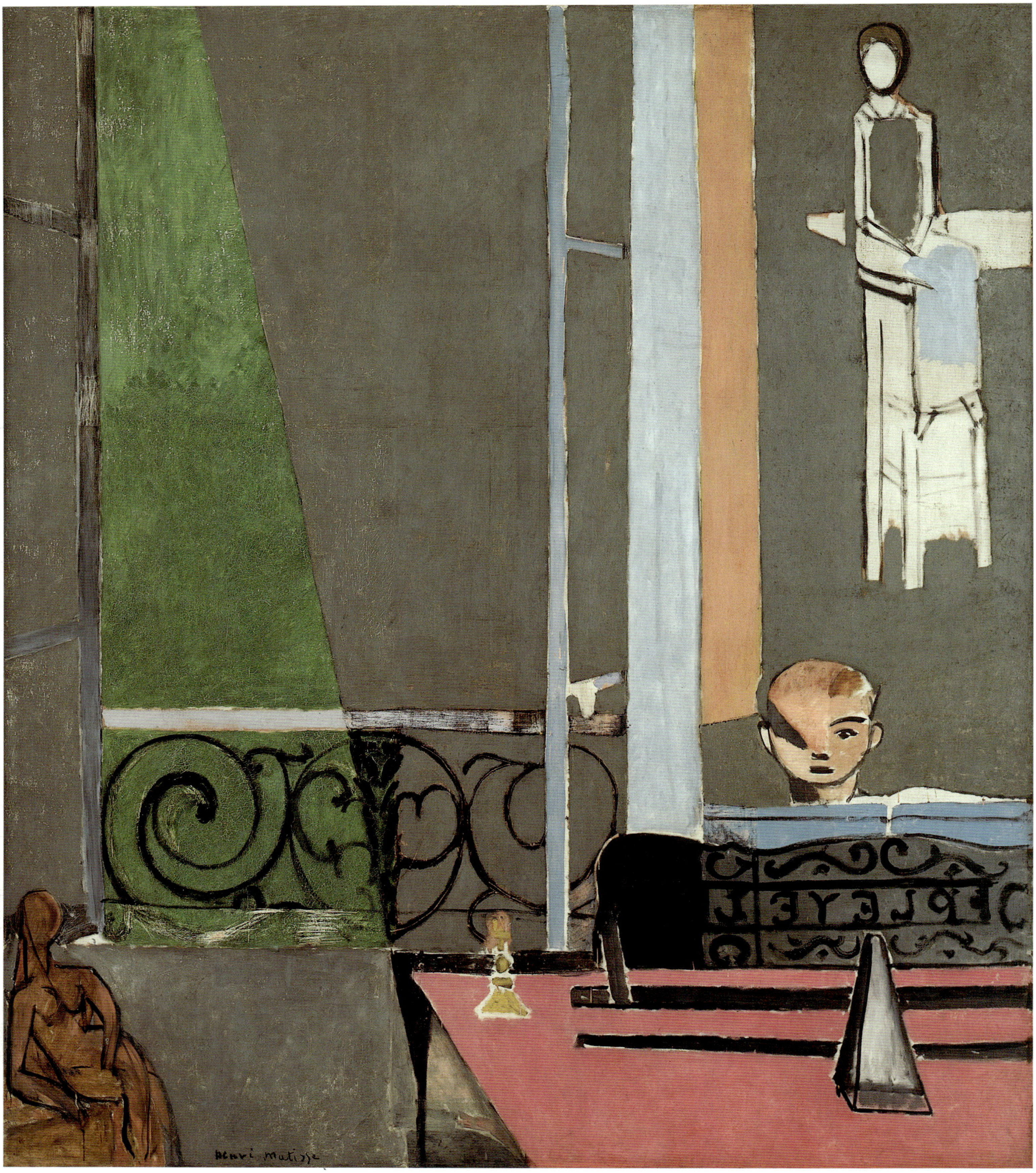
Henri Matisse

69 (*facing page*) *The Piano Lesson*, 1916. Oil on canvas, 245.1 × 212.7 cm. The Museum of Modern Art, New York. Mrs. Simon Guggenheim Fund.

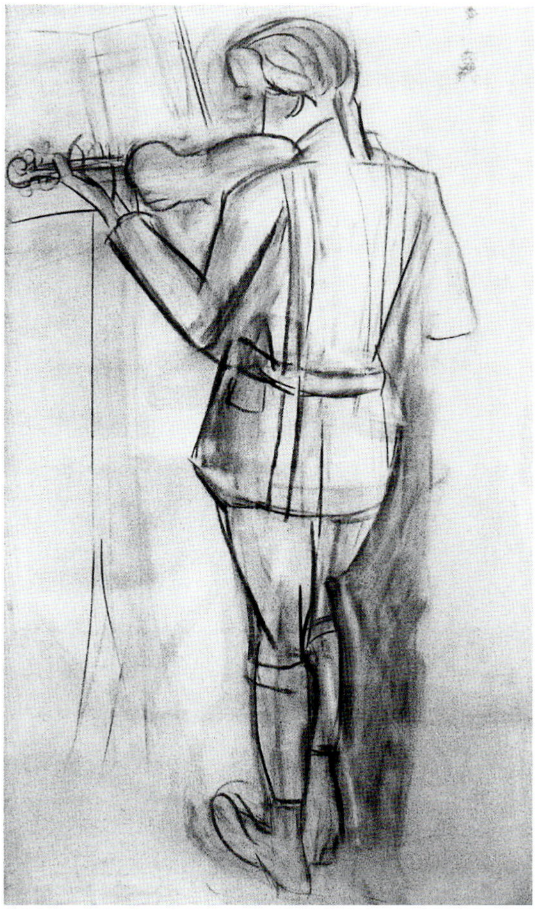

70 *Violinist*, 1918. Charcoal on canvas, 194 × 114 cm. Le Cateau-Cambrésis, Musée Matisse.

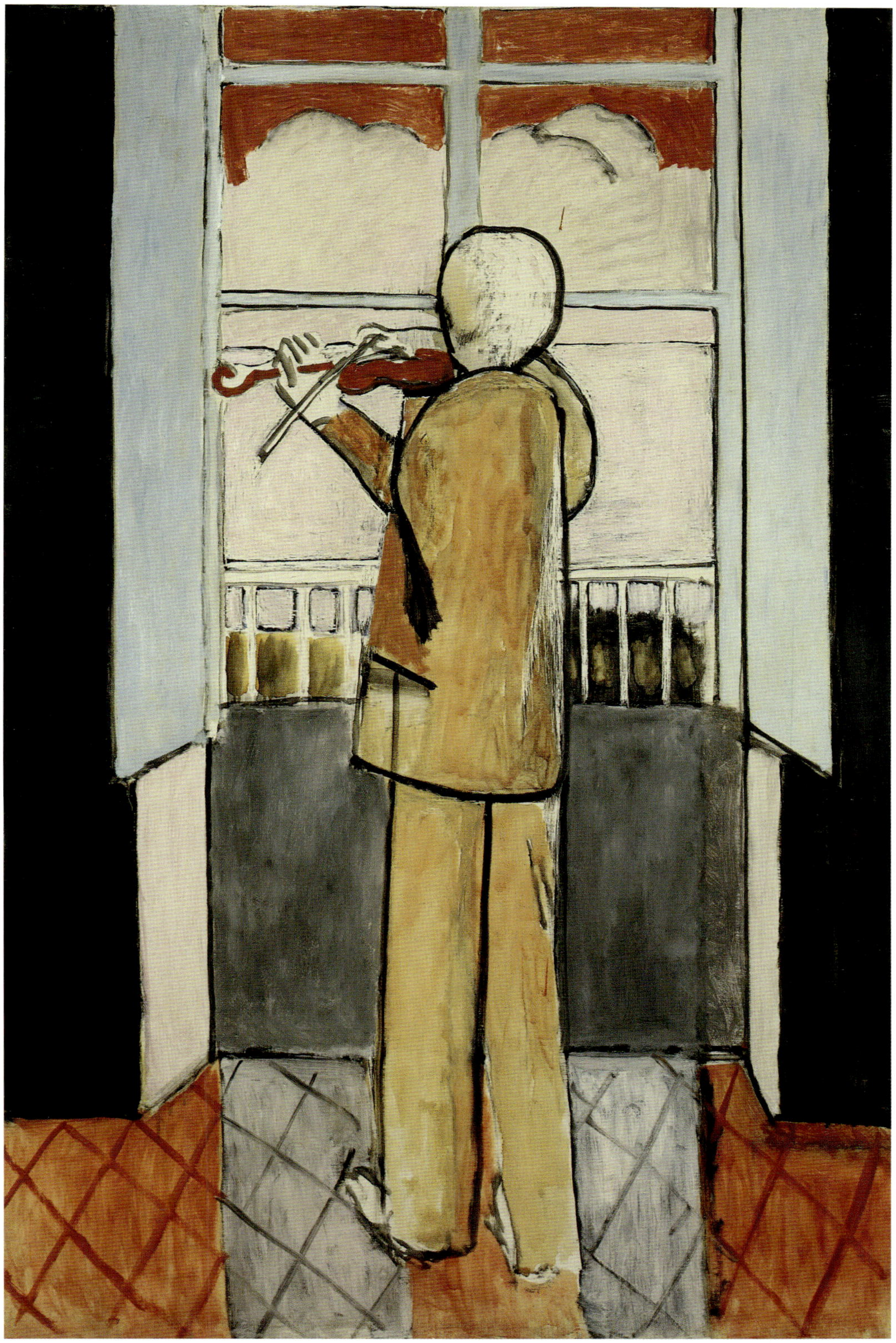

71 *Violinist at the Window*, 1918. Oil on canvas, 150 × 98 cm. Paris, Musée National d'Art Moderne, Centre Georges Pompidou.

individuality. In these portraits Matisse goes as far as possible to reduce the expression of personality to a minimum while retaining a visual connection with recognizable features. In all three, however, a vivid sense of alertness signals the human presence of the sitter. Matisse painted the portrait of Pierre in the summer of 1909 on the beach at Cavalière, an unusual site for an artist who preferred to make his portraits in the controlled conditions of the studio, because they usually took so long to do.[93] Thus this picture was probably painted quickly: the thinness and unevenness of the paint, and the unfussy treatment of the stripes of Pierre's shirt, speak of haste. Pierre is said to have been a cantankerous sitter, but Matisse has given him an implacable presence that reads in all ways like a younger version of his own self-portrait in a striped sailor's jersey from three years earlier (see fig. 90).

This desire to see a surrogate for himself in Pierre is expressed most elaborately in *The Piano Lesson* of 1916 (fig. 69). As in *The Music Lesson* from the following year, Pierre sits at the piano in the living room at Issy, but now alone – or almost. Symbolic female figures bracket his creative activity. This and the impression that Matisse has rewound the clock on his son – he looks much younger than his actual age then of sixteen – suggest an allegory. The painting is about the creative process, and the portrait of Pierre is a surrogate for his artist father, "a symbol for the artist surrounded by emblems of his craft." It thus "assumes an autobiographical and allegorical role telling of the history and character of Matisse's art."[94] In this role a portrait of his son is a heavily weighted vehicle for the artist to refer to himself and his own concerns. Even if he did manipulate the boy's age, Matisse has staged Pierre's presence in such a way as to keep him in his own character (his son did play the piano) as well as to allude reflexively to himself.

Similarly Matisse used his son, now playing the violin, as the starting point for the striking and enigmatic painting *Violinist at the Window* of 1918, which is another symbolic or surrogate self-portrait (fig. 71). The painting was preceded by an even larger drawing in charcoal showing Pierre playing before a music stand (fig. 70).[95] Both father and son actually did play the violin, and Matisse frequently used the instrument as a symbol of his implied presence (as in *The Music Lesson*). Violin and window view, often Matisse's symbol for painting, are combined to form an image of the solitary artist at work in the mode of similar images from German Romanticism. Through the same kind of imaginative displacement and abstraction that went into *The Piano Lesson*, Matisse has transformed a representation of Pierre (in military uniform – he had just been called to service) into an allusive image reflective of his own artistic meditations. These few symbolic images of Pierre operate in a different way from the more straightforward portraits of Marguerite. Although Matisse was closer to his daughter, he used the presence of Pierre for an expression more searching than affirmative. Matisse's construction of Pierre in his art is more abstract and symbolic, and is obviously related to the process of artistic creation. It would not be surprising if Matisse were simply able to imagine himself, as a creator of art, more through the agency of this male child. Portraits of Marguerite, on the other hand, show his more personal concern with an individual who simply by being herself – and by being represented as herself – would substantiate him as a person. Thus these two children, so different from one another, had distinct functions in Matisse's self-construction through family imagery.

* * *

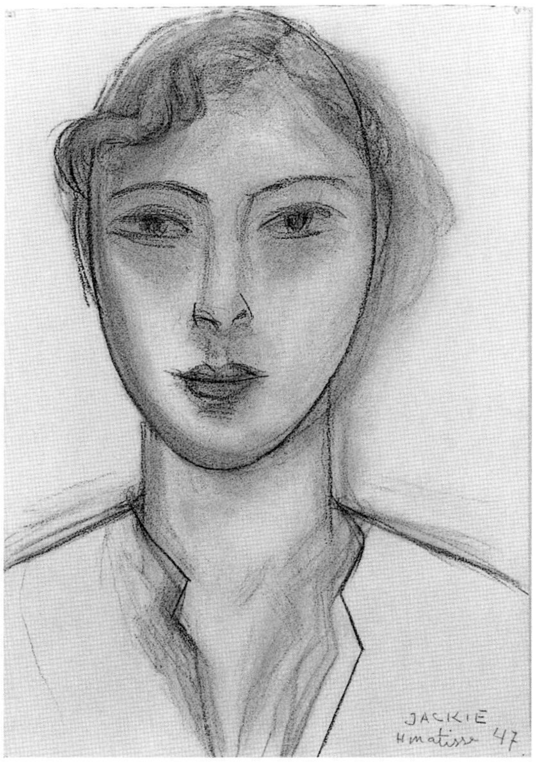

72 *Jackie*, 1947. Charcoal on paper, 56.8 × 38.3 cm. Private collection.

73 *Jacky*, 1947. Ink on paper, 49.4 × 37.4 cm. Private collection.

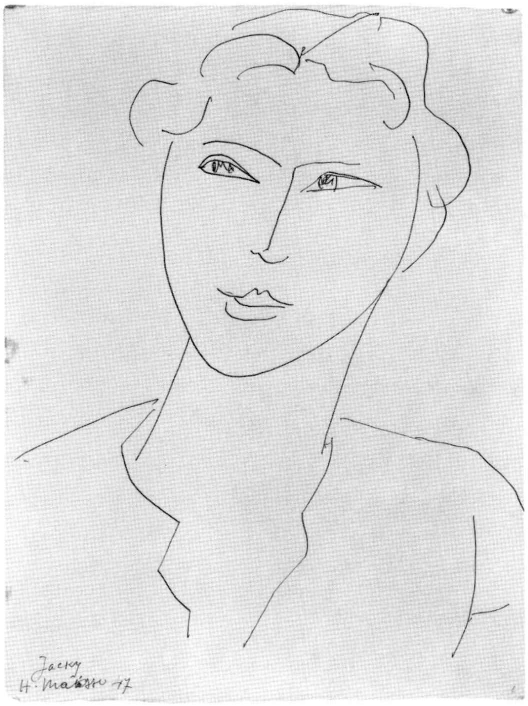

Coda: the next generation

In 1952 the German critic Gotthard Jedlicka visited Matisse in Nice. By this time the artist was confined to bed for long periods. On the ceiling above the bed in which Matisse lay, Jedlicka noticed several drawings, faces, done with a piece of charcoal attached to a shaft of bamboo (figs. 74a, b). Matisse explained:

> "Those are my grandchildren."
> "I see . . ."
> "I sleep badly. So I think of my grandchildren. I try to picture them to myself, and when I succeed I feel better. I drew them on the ceiling to be able to see them at a glance especially at night. In this way I feel less alone."[96]

This touching confession of the need to create companionship through portraiture also reveals the importance to Matisse of the next generation of his family. Not only were they his genetic legacy, but he saw in them an opportunity to make portraits, as he had done of their parents when they were young. He drew many images of his five grandchildren during the 1940s, in a variety of drawing media. But by this time Matisse had a fully developed sensibility and method for depicting the face, giving it the quality of an anonymous mask, with the barest hint of difference from other such masks, the difference that signaled individuality within continuity.

In the majority of these drawings he followed the procedure he had established in the series he called *Thèmes et variations*. With Jacqueline, for example, he drew from the sitter in charcoal, rubbing out, adjusting, erasing, and continuing to draw until he felt in the resulting distillation that he understood the essential features of the face before him: *thème* (fig. 72). Then, rapidly, he drew in ink or pencil a series of variations in pure line, with no correction, as he did in many synoptic drawings of his granddaughter (fig. 73). As a group these drawings make it clear what is physically distinctive about this young woman and, although he was intrigued by the face of Jacqueline, his treatment of her in each individual drawing did not vary from that of countless women he employed in these years. Artistic procedure had by this time superseded the search for individuality, and Matisse's practice in making portraits of his grandchildren had completely assimilated the method he had developed when making drawings from hired models.[97] This was not a sign of his indifference to their individuality; on the contrary, the process of drawing was part of Matisse's way of getting to know them, even (perhaps especially) when they were not physically present.[98]

It was essentially thus with all the portraits of his grandchildren, but an exception is worth noting. In the summer of 1940, with German troops threatening Paris, Matisse planned to leave France but then changed his mind. In Marseilles he met Marguerite, who was there to put her son Claude on a boat for New York, where he was to join his father Georges Duthuit. During the few days before Claude's departure, Matisse filled two small sketchbooks with pencil portraits of his nine-year-old grandson. One of the drawings (fig. 75) is different from the others in an important respect. Claude's features are quite altered, more mature, and inscribed on the sheet are the words "Claudi quand il aura 20 ans" – Claudi when he will be 20 years old. After many sketches, Matisse made a drawing in which he predicted how his grandson would look eleven years later, based on the knowledge he had acquired of the essential qualities of the boy's features. Matisse knew he would not see his grandson again for some time; he knew too that in a war

74a Matisse's bedroom at the Hôtel Régina, Nice, 1954.

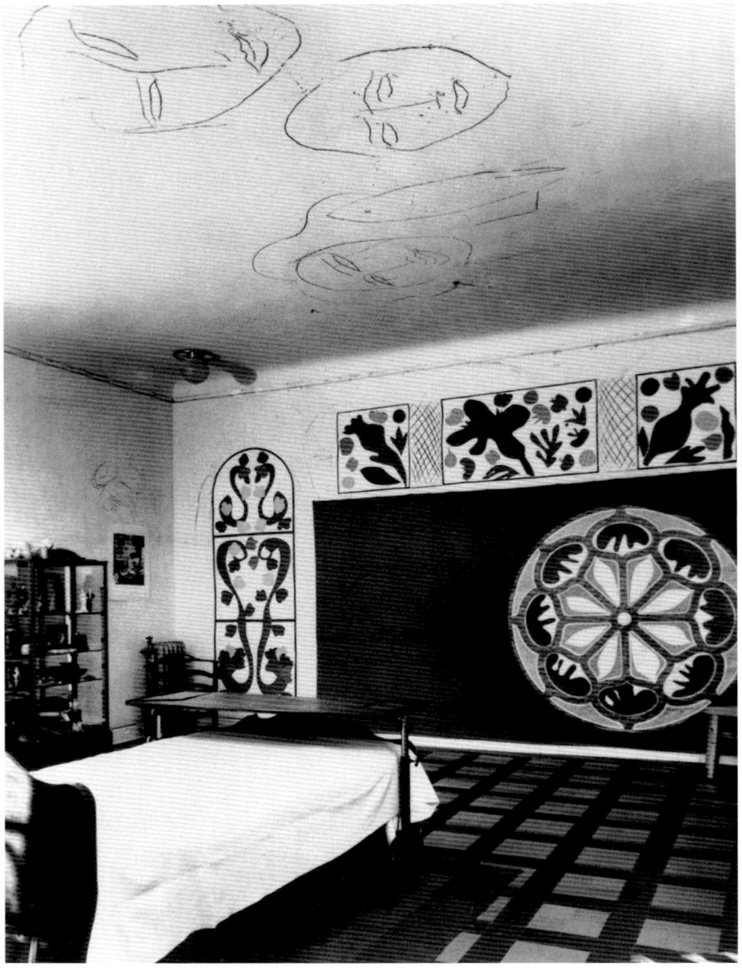

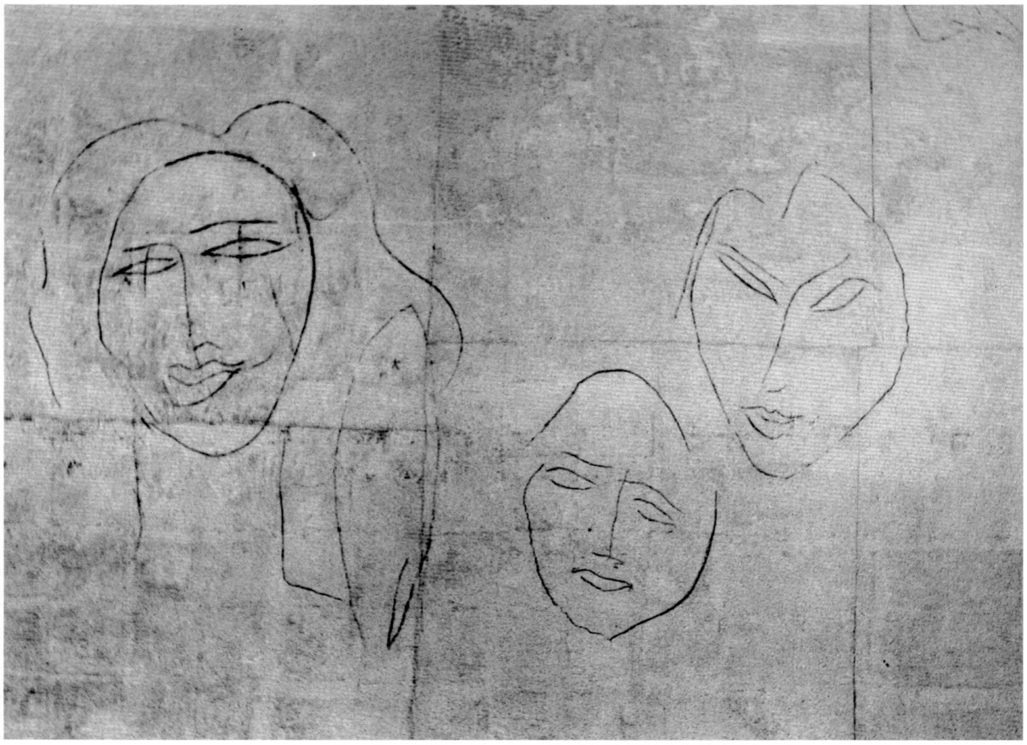

74b The ceiling of Matisse's bedroom at the Hôtel Régina with the portraits he made of three of his grandchildren in 1950. Charcoal on plaster, fixed to canvas, approx. 5 × 5 m. Musée Matisse, Le Cateau-Cambrésis.

75 *Claude*, 1940. Pencil on paper, 19 × 14 cm. Private collection.

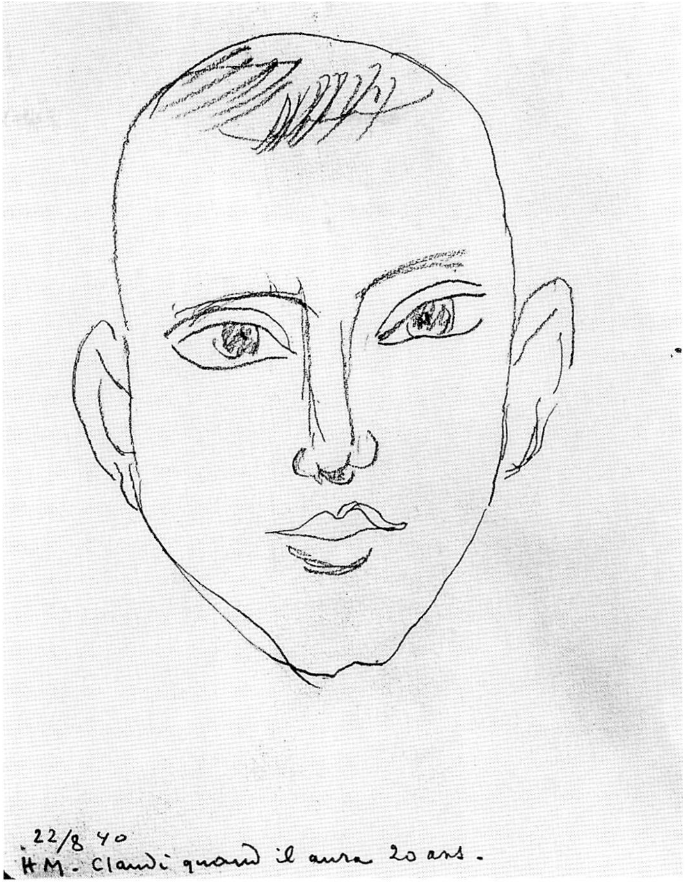

anything could happen and reunions were speculative. But he was also interested in the potential carried in this young boy's face, in how Claude would look as a young adult – in other words, what was continuous in his features – and in the larger idea of the continuity he saw with himself.[99] This state of grace could be broken, however. At age 19 Claude injured himself in an automobile accident, resulting in a scar over one eye. His innocence and freshness lost, he was no longer a desirable model. Saying to him "you have destroyed the symmetry of your face," Matisse never made any drawings of Claude again.[100]

If Matisse's portraits of his wife, children, and grandchildren could extend his self-presentation through the representation of his family, there is another class of portraits in his work that acts as a confirmation of the other major concern of his life, his development and career as an artist. Portraits of fellow creative figures in several fields form the subject of the next chapter. Most important among these are his portraits of the painters with whom he shared the aspiration of self-expression. In reciprocal acts of homage and confirmation, these members of the artistic avant-garde at the beginning of the century found in portraiture the means to express their sense of innovation.

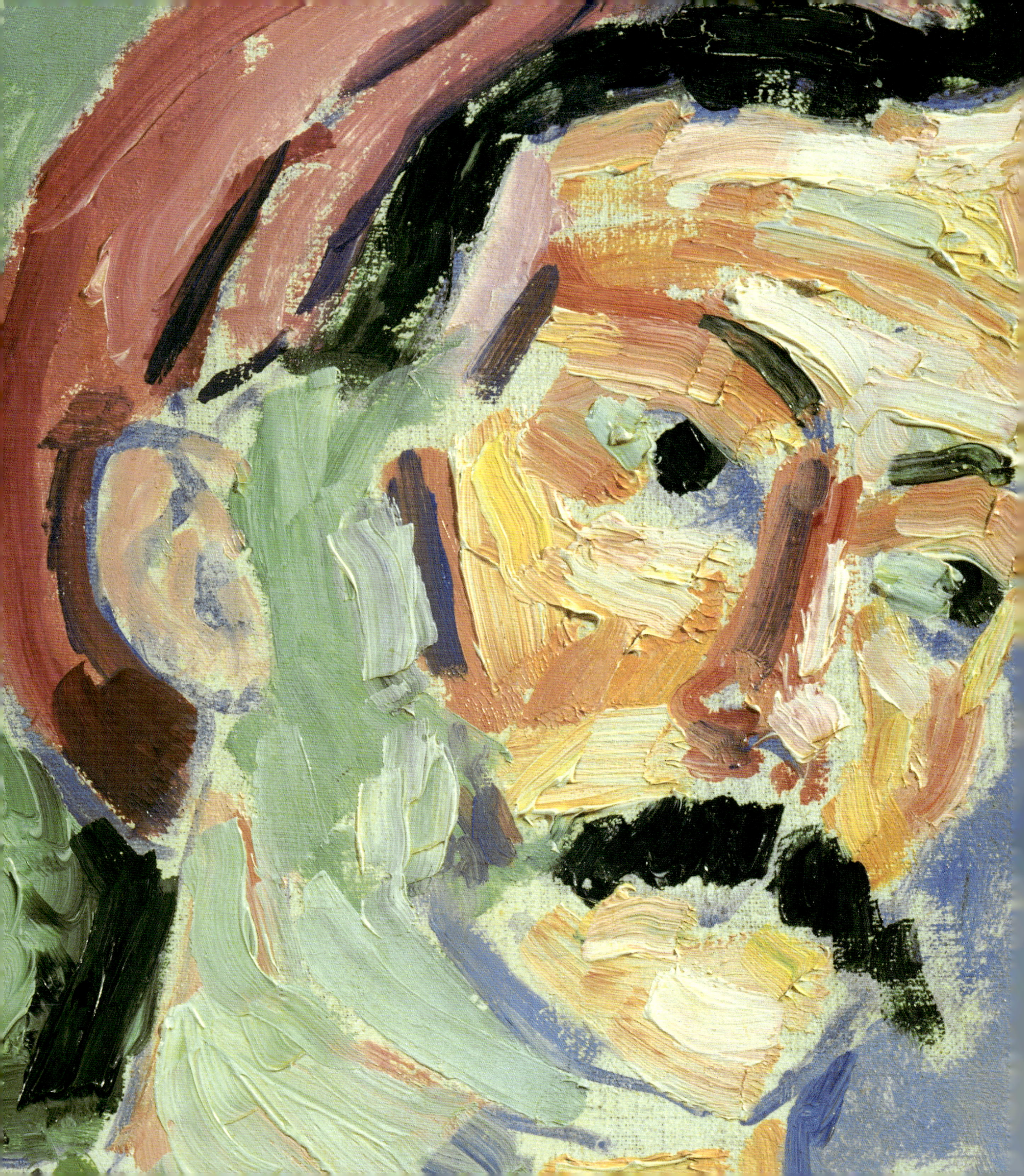

Chapter 4 The Image of Creativity

During the first five years of the century, when his family had become an important theme in his art, Matisse aligned himself with another key group, the avant-garde in France. His emerging consciousness of his position among his contemporaries was briefly but significantly expressed in portraiture, in striking images of fellow artists and in a magisterial self-portrait. In these works he identified and fashioned into facial and bodily images the artistic values he shared with highly sympathetic sitters, as part of a general process of negotiating artistic identity within rapidly changing practices and public debates. Some of these portraits of fellow artists were shown within an overall exhibition program, allowing both a public self-fashioning and a selective assertion of allegiance. But even when such portraits did not have a specific public destination, Matisse's use of the genre within the context of avant-garde practice signaled his intent to make the intersubjective element of a social activity a theme of his work.

Choosing friends

One might consequently expect that Matisse would make many portraits of artist friends to affirm his artistic values through the agency of others. But his portraits of fellow artists were made under very limited circumstances, at the only time when he could have been thought a member of an artistic group – the Fauves. And even then, Matisse made only a few portraits of his fellow artists, all in 1905–6: paintings of André Derain and Albert Marquet; and, in an even narrower context, several small drawings of the Provençal painter Etienne Terrus. These images of fellow artists are among the most sympathetic of all his portraits. For this reason they are rarities. Sympathy toward another individual – artist or not – was not one of Matisse's strong characteristics. His projection of himself generally did not extend into the realm of identification with another. But he was adept at identifying himself with an exemplar of values that he held, or wished to hold, himself. After the Fauve period, other artists met these criteria only occasionally (Matisse never, for instance, made portraits of the other influential artists of the century who were his acquaintances – Picasso, Rouault, Masson, Duchamp, and others). Instead, he gravitated in his later career to more minor figures, old friends such as Francisco Iturrino or Simon Bussy. They were not competitors for posterity and some were nearly acolytes. His few later portraits, always drawings, of fellow painters were certainly not damning, but many were obligatory in character, and in most cases they offered no more than faint praise of their sitters independent of Matisse's interest in them.

Detail of fig. 80 (larger than actual size).

I propose an explanation for the exceptional solidarity expressed by the portraits of Derain, Marquet, and Terrus, along with Matisse's self-portrait of 1906, and for the subsequent scarcity of portraits by Matisse of fellow painters and sculptors. But the group known as "artists" should not be confined to practitioners of these few means of creative expression. The notable rarity of portraits of other visual artists is partly compensated by the many portraits, almost all in various graphic media, of creative people in other arenas. With such men and women Matisse could feel affinity without conflict. For this reason, I shall also consider in this chapter his portraits of musicians, theatrical personages, and writers. By making a portrait (usually, it must be said, one that did not take too much time or effort) of a fellow creator in another artistic pursuit, Matisse chose to express his sense of shared values with his or her field of endeavor as well as with the individual sitter. These portraits, concentrated later in his career, lack the competitive aspect that may have prevented him from making more portraits of fellow painters.

In his portraits of the members of his family Matisse had at one and the same time expressed his belief in familial values and asserted his position of dominance in that group. His ambivalence with regard to his family, demanding but accessible, sometimes had problematic results, as we have seen. Here, by contrast, the old adage about being able to choose your friends applies to Matisse's portraits of artists with whom he had evident sympathy. But ambivalence also enters into his portraits of fellow visual artists. Although the portraits of Derain and Marquet from 1905 represent the culmination of Matisse's attachment to other artists, they also display his mixed feelings toward such an allegiance, his desire to deflect a direct expression of affinity with these contemporaries. Throughout most of his career Matisse positioned himself as a loner in his artistic goals, rarely expressing admiration for particular painters or sculptors unless they were dead.[1]

The fulcrum point in 1905 also marks Matisse's rapid assertion of independence from any artistic group or movement. Its fullest expression is the singular *Self-Portrait in a Striped Jersey* (see fig. 90), a strong bid for autonomy and disengagement. From then until the First World War he did not make another portrait of a fellow artist.[2] His priorities in this period lay elsewhere, as his portrait activity focused on commissions and other portraits related to his growing patronage. Then the extraordinary circumstances of the war led him again to a sense of affiliation with other artists, manifested in the large group of portrait etchings from 1914–15. Not until the next war did Matisse make another image of a fellow painter. Portraits of artists in other fields, such as literature and music, are slightly more numerous: a few isolated examples in the 1920s, when Matisse most consciously orchestrated his isolation from the Paris art world, as well as his family; a handful from the 1930s and 40s, mainly of writers of his acquaintance; and several drawings in the early 1950s, final homages to fellow creators.

To understand the importance of the artist portraits Matisse made in 1905, and the ways in which they express his sense of shared values at that time, we need to look briefly at some paintings that cannot be considered portraits but that set the stage for the sense of community expressed in Matisse's portraits of his painter friends. Through these works we can consider the contexts of two systems around the turn of the century that gave rise to these portraits – the artist's studio and artistic patronage.

* * *

The social studio

Matisse had worked in a number of studios by 1905. Most of them were steps in his long apprenticeship to various masters, beginning with Bouguereau in 1891 and not really ending until Matisse moved from under Signac's influence during 1905, a process culminating in *Le Bonheur de vivre*.[3] In Moreau's studio at the Ecole des Beaux-Arts, and at the so-called Académie Camillo where Eugène Carrière corrected students' efforts, Matisse as a student found encouraging working conditions and in these places he met most of the painters who became his fellow Fauves.[4] In the company of Henri Manguin, Marquet, Charles Camoin, Jean Puy and Derain, the older Matisse found sympathetic friends with whom he could share aspirations and discoveries, as well as models and other expenses – both the creative and the logistical needs of the artist's life.

From 1895 onward Matisse sought to make the conditions of artistic production in the studio a theme of his work. This epistemological approach, with the process of making expressed in the finished work of art, is consistent with his general self-consciousness at this time. We recall the series of three paintings from 1895–96 in which he included a self-portrait to assert his creative presence, indicating his desire to identify the object of his art with his subjective perception. *Carmelina*, in 1903 (see fig. 35), introduced another actor, the female model, over which the artist could assert control. The studio pictures from 1904–5 mark the expansion of Matisse's self-consciousness into an arena of peers. They show the initial conditions under which he was trying to integrate his desire for self-expression into a social setting: the world Matisse represented in the three domestic interiors was his alone, but the studio could be shared with others. Art-making was coming to have a social context. These studio pictures were the first steps toward the portraits of 1905 that he and his fellow Fauves made to assert both individual identity and group allegiance.

The most important studio for this sense of fellowship among the Fauves-to-be was Manguin's. In the winter of 1904/5, Manguin, Marquet, and Matisse made a series of paintings there that sum up their relationship to each other's art and emphasize the studio as the site of a shared endeavor. The similarity of these paintings brings to mind what Jean Puy later said of this time in Manguin's studio, that it was "l'époque d'émulation" for these artists.[5] Matisse's *Marquet Painting a Nude* (fig. 76), Marquet's *Matisse Painting in Manguin's Studio*, and a painting formerly attributed to Matisse but that may have been painted by Manguin, *Nude in the Studio (Marquet Painting a Nude)* show the same model in a standard pose.[6] Manguin at any rate painted another picture that is comparable to those by Matisse and Marquet, as did Puy about the same time, also in Manguin's studio; and Marquet painted Camoin at his easel, working from a seated model.[7] This constellation of studio scenes by like-minded artists demonstrates their interdependence, mutual regard, and self-consciousness over a period of time late in 1904 and early in 1905. Each painter shows another artist working, bound to him by their common model and their common concerns.

The idea of a social studio was well established in artistic iconography. For Rubens it had been the center of fashionable art world society. Courbet imagined an even larger universe turning around the axis of his efforts. The Impressionists' claims were more modest, but they still proposed a special sociological status for this environment, even if their "studios" were sometimes out of doors, as represented in paintings by Sargent and Manet of Monet in his *bateau-atelier*, or with

76 *Marquet Painting a Nude*, 1904–5. Oil on paper, 31 × 24 cm. Paris, Musée National d'Art Moderne, Centre Georges Pompidou.

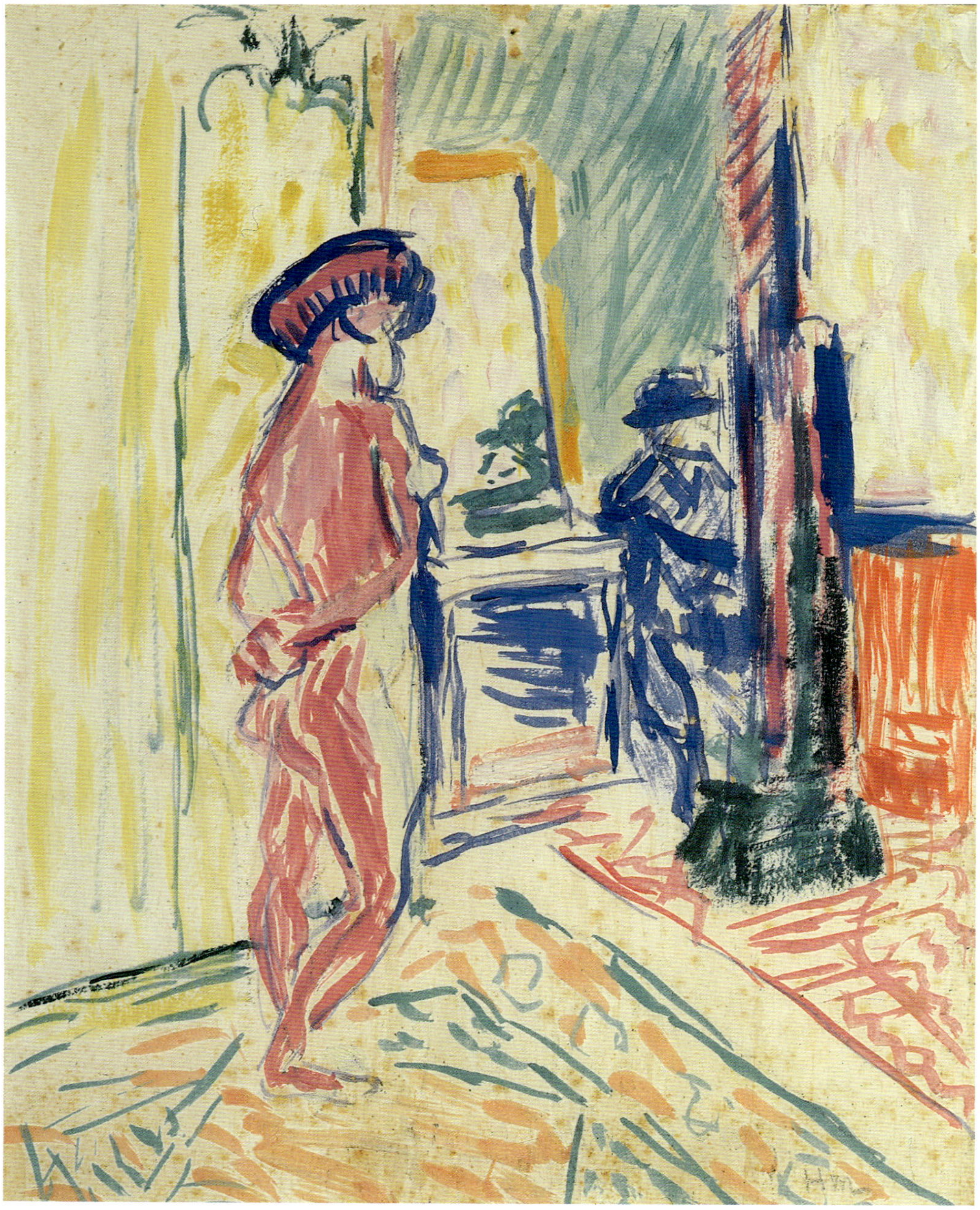

his easel set up in his tiny garden in Argenteuil. And the Neo-Impressionists often made portraits of each other at work – Luce of Seurat, Signac of Luce, Seurat of Aman-Jean and of Signac.

What distinguishes the Fauve studio scenes of 1904–5 from these earlier representations of artists at work is the strong mutuality, heightened by the reflexiveness signaled by the frequent presence of mirrors and mirror images. Not only does each painter depict another, or several others, but he depicts the others doing the same thing he is doing, in a shared activity. The reflexiveness is significant of their self-consciousness, a driving force of avant-garde developments at this time. Such self-consciousness is not always productive. There is something juvenile about the evident pleasure of the Fauve painters in the cleverness of these tropes of mutual support – the kind of cleverness we might feel when we take a photograph of someone else taking a photograph (of someone else, of us) – voyeuristic, somewhat unexpected (though done thousands of times before), self-justifying.

Competing individualities

The sense of mutuality did not last long. The communal studio scenes of the Fauve painters contained the seed for the eventual assertion of individualism, or in some cases shift of artistic allegiance, that they all made within a few years. For with the fellowship and the sharing went some friendly competition. Advances by one painter became something for another to aim at, even surpass in audacity – the ambitious side of Puy's "emulation." To varying degrees these studio scenes are painted in an advanced Neo-Impressionist style derived from Signac, so it is clear how much these younger artists were striving for a place on the leading edge of developments. Some kept pace; others, like Puy, confessed bewilderment at the most advanced of the advanced, Matisse, who "had no hesitation about introducing extreme and wholly artificial elements in his pictures."[8] Marquet too spoke of comparing his efforts with those of Matisse, and Puy later expressed regret about the rivalries in this episode.[9]

Both attitudes – the competitiveness as well as the fellowship – can be traced to the atmosphere in the studio of Gustave Moreau. By all accounts, Moreau showed a remarkable liberality in his instruction. His greatest contribution to the formation of his young students was that he urged Matisse, Marquet, and the others to develop individual, personal means of self-expression. This communal experience of becoming individuals bound the young Fauves together. United individualism, it may be noted here in passing, was also the basis for the rapid expansion by the turn of the century of the Société Nationale des Beaux-Arts and the proliferation of other artists' associations (notably the Société du Salon d'Automne), which offered alternatives to, and eventually superseded in importance, the orthodoxy of the established Société des Artistes Français. The dynamics of the Fauve group mirrored larger developments favoring collective nonconformity in the Paris art world.

In the Fauve group Matisse took the position of first among equals. He was acknowledged by his friends to be more experienced and serious – hence the "Doctor" tag he received, among other good-natured tokens of respect. Matisse preferred to be set apart, to be distinguished in some measure from his younger colleagues. The patriarch asserted himself here, too, and enjoyed taking a leading role. Years later he acknowledged that all of them had done important things together, but he couched the matter in terms of the others' confirmation of what he had already discovered.[10] Besides, he said in another context, the defining characteristics of a movement were limiting because they "militate against individual recognition" – the most important thing in the end.[11]

The public context

Public recognition of the Fauves' efforts was fitful and produced more notoriety than admiration. Private, mutual support was an alternative to the uncertain prospect of sales and commissions. This situation should be set out briefly. Before

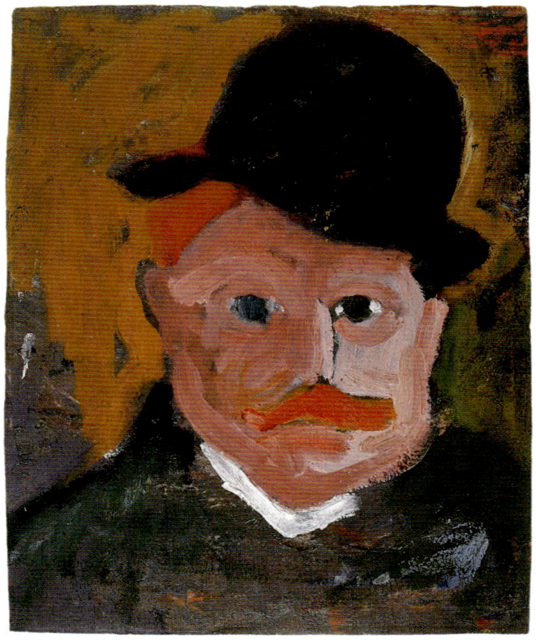

77 André Derain, *Maurice de Vlaminck*, 1905. Oil on canvas, 41 × 33 cm. Private collection, courtesy Musée des Beaux-Arts de Chartres.

78 Maurice de Vlaminck, *André Derain*, 1905. Oil on canvas, 27 × 22.2 cm. New York, The Metropolitan Museum of Art, The Jacques and Natasha Gelman Collection, 1998.

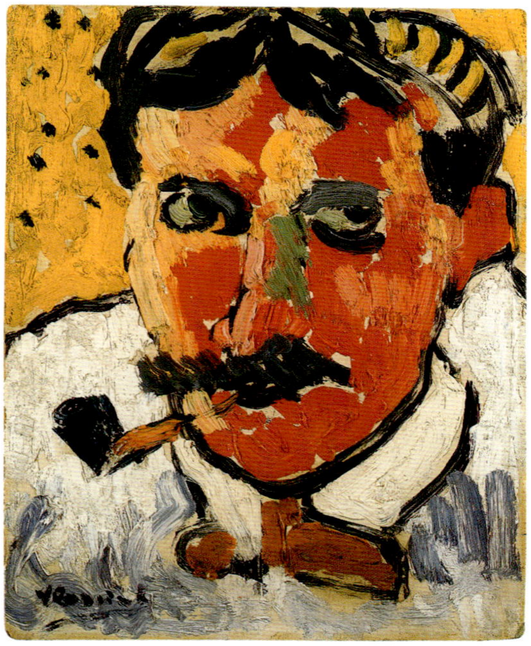

1904, the French state almost never bought works of art other than official entries at the Salon des Artistes Français, or copies after "old master" paintings. Copying paintings in the Louvre was another activity these young artists had undertaken together, partly at Moreau's urging, but also as a more general part of an artist's education. Between 1892 and 1896 Matisse made over a dozen copies of French and Dutch paintings, intended mainly for sale to the state.[12] Roger Marx, a prominent supporter of young artists, was instrumental in recommending purchases of the copies made by Matisse and others.[13] Some of them, including Marquet and Manguin, continued to sell their copies to the state well into the twentieth century.

In this context of a particular form of state patronage, Matisse made his copy of Raphael's portrait of Baldassare Castiglione in the Louvre (see figs. 6, 7). Roger Benjamin has established that Matisse painted the copy in the spring of 1904, not long before he left Paris for Saint-Tropez and a summer of experimentation in high-keyed color in the company of Signac.[14] The contrast between the sober, certified potboiler and the bright freewheeling Mediterranean landscapes he soon painted is amazing. In the contrast are embodied the poles between which he would move throughout his life and art: North *vs.* South; patronage *vs.* independence; responsibility *vs.* liberation; society *vs.* nature. His original work was not selling but, thanks to Roger Marx, the French state bought Matisse's copy after Raphael, providing him with a much needed 300 francs.

Matisse's rendering of Raphael's portrait is assured, but, understandably, it lacks the distinction that his independent painting had already possessed for some years. The copy is curiously both more painterly and less supple than its Renaissance model. Matisse's painting retains the general spirit of Raphael's conception of a man ennobled within an idealized form, a living embodiment of the Neoplatonic idea of perfection in the circle. But by hardening Castiglione's features Matisse denied the courtier and his portrait the quality of *sprezzatura* – the art that conceals art – so important to both Raphael and his patron. Nevertheless, at the time Matisse's work did the job it needed to and, as we have seen, the portrait may have had some lasting effect on his art – not in any narrow stylistic sense, but by opening his eyes to a genre that he had neglected. Matisse had by then undertaken few portraits, and this was the sole portrait copy he made. His later statement that the Raphael painting had been a revelation to him about the possibilities for portraiture makes more sense in the context of his work in 1904 than it did when it was believed that Matisse had made his copy ten years earlier.[15] Beginning in 1905, portraiture became an integral part of Matisse's practice, as well as an important social instrument, when he moved beyond the family circle to use the genre to establish elective artistic affinity.

Emulating patronage

Eventually portraiture also came to be linked with patronage, but for Matisse and other young artists early in the century sales were sporadic and security elusive. At its best, the government bought no more than one work by an artist each year. The open market for art, characterized by the new exhibiting associations and speculative dealers, offered the excitement of possibility but also uncertain and uneven returns. Some artists floated schemes to ensure a steady income. Matisse tried to form a syndicate with shareholders who would invest in his new production,

79 André Derain, *Henri Matisse*, 1905. Oil on canvas, 46 × 35 cm. London, The Tate Gallery.

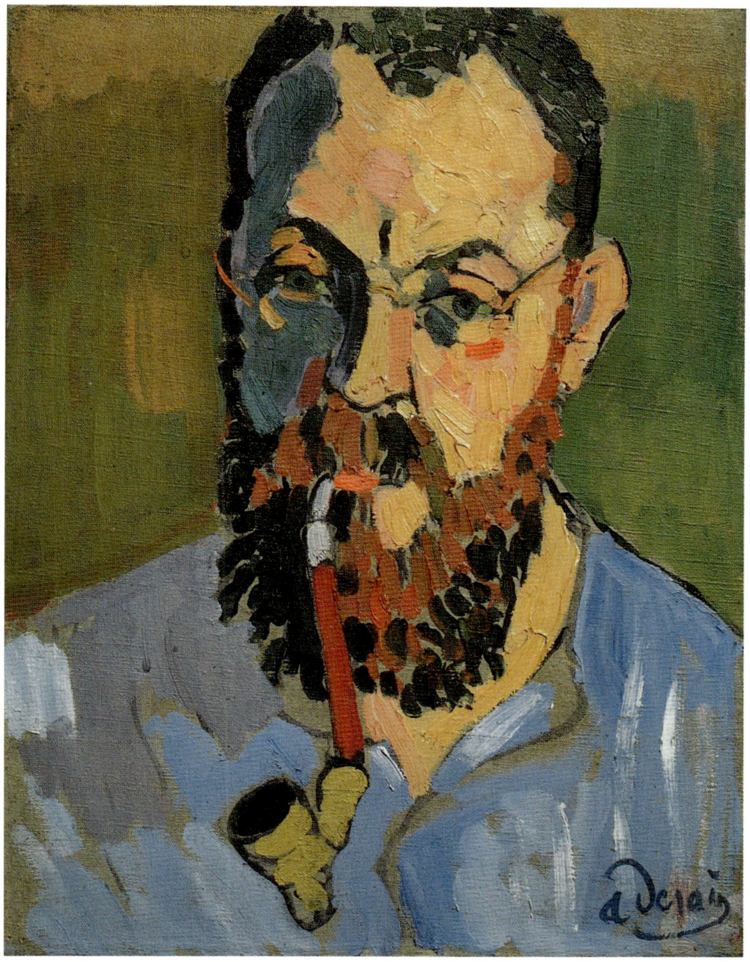

seeking in effect to create a collective patron. Dealers sometimes bought artists' production *en vrac* (in bulk), as Vollard did with Derain, Vlaminck, and Manguin in 1905 and 1906, but the unit price for these sales was very low. The private patron, sympathetic to the artists' aims and prepared by fair and regular financial commitment to back his or her taste, was rare. So the young Fauve artists used the portrait to create images of ideal patrons – themselves.

Matisse's portraits of Marquet and Derain (figs. 81, 80) are among the many portraits that the Fauves made of each other in and around 1905. Such reciprocation is a common practice among artists who are sympathetic to one another, and such reflexiveness can be understood as "part of the ritual of artistic life."[16] The Fauves' portraits are distinct from the studio scenes of the winter of 1904/5 in which they depicted each other at work, but the portraits often reflect the same relationships. Individuality is more strongly asserted. Selves are represented, not behaviors. Matisse painted Marquet and Derain, his closest friends in the group and those who shared most thoroughly his artistic aims. Derain painted a careful and respectful portrait of Matisse (fig. 79), and Marquet made an amusing drawing of the older artist sporting a pipe and top hat.[17] Derain also painted Vlaminck (fig. 77) and Vlaminck in turn made a drawing and a painting (fig. 78) of his Chatou mate. In a calmer, less jaunty vein, Manguin also painted a portrait of Jean Puy in 1905, and Charles Camoin painted a portrait of Marquet in 1904.[18] Matisse and

80 (*following page*) *André Derain*, 1905. Oil on canvas, 39.5 × 29 cm. London, The Tate Gallery, purchased with assistance from the Knapping Fund, the National Art Collections Fund and the Contemporary Art Society and private subscribers.

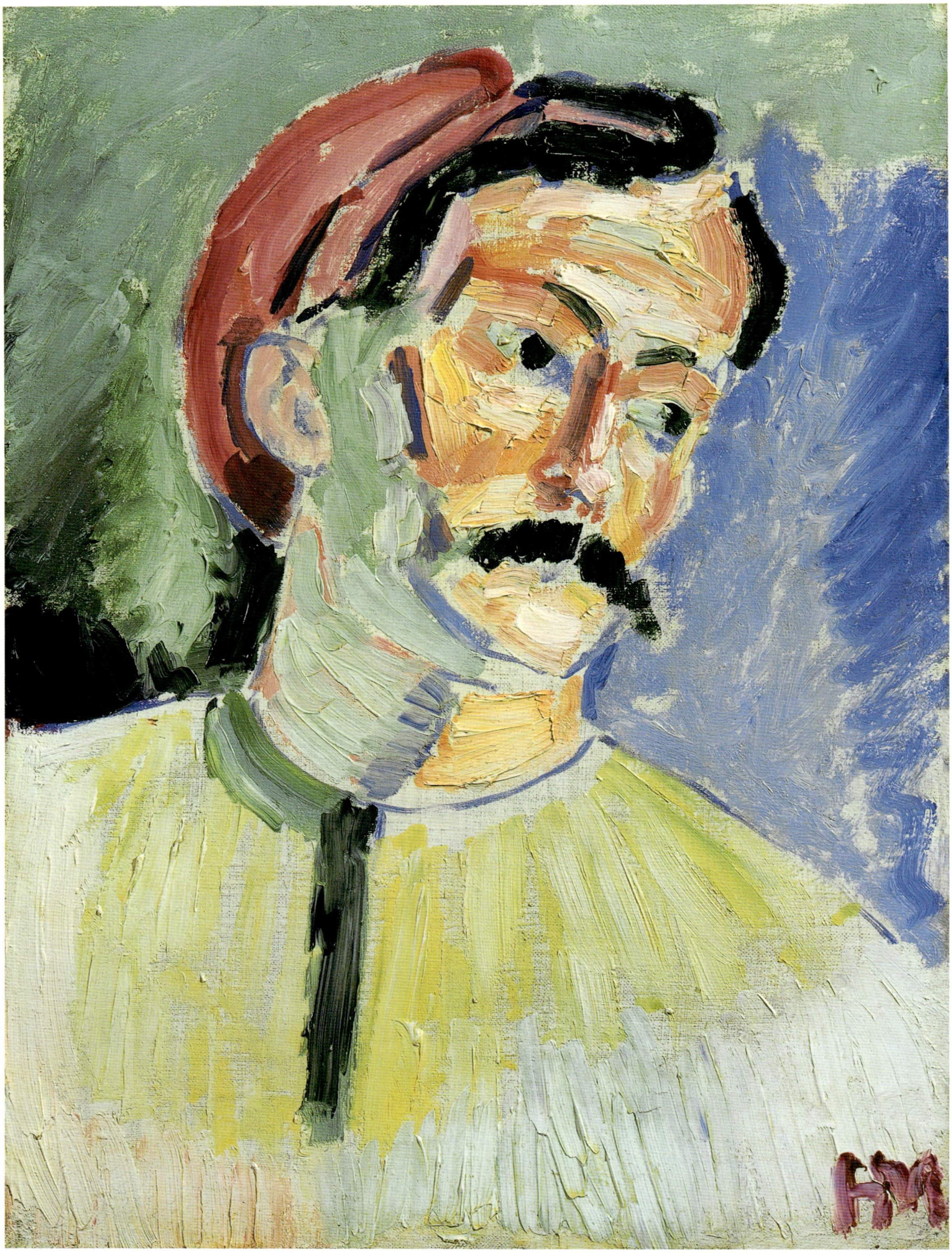

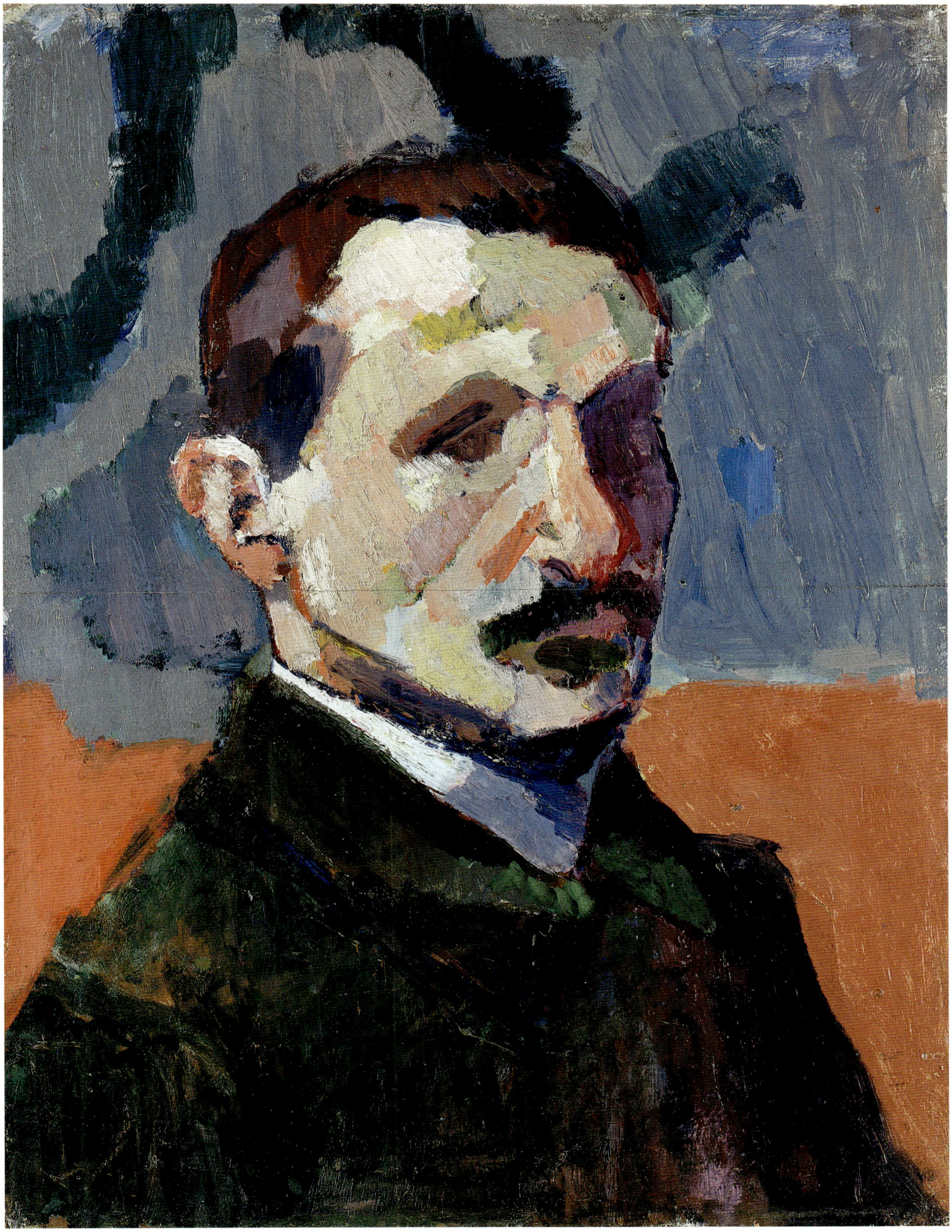

Vlaminck made no portraits of each other; although in some ways these two men were the most audacious painters of the Fauve group, they were not personally close, and they had different emotional approaches to painting. The absence of their interaction in this way is therefore not surprising.

On the most obvious level, then, these portraits acknowledge personal relationships. But to view them collectively as simple expressions of friendship and solidarity is to miss their fulfillment of one of the social functions of portraiture. Without intending it, these artists were asserting their masculine professional image as a cohesive identity, as well as declaiming their individuality and their mutual sympathy.[19] For the most part they used a traditional honorific genre, the bust-length portrait, for their tributes. In doing this they also liberated the genre from its traditional site in patronage. The portrait, classically one of the most remunerative but also one of the most odious undertakings for many artists (recall Ingres's expletive) is here seen to be free of both consequences.[20] The Fauve portraits are pure luxury items, indulgences, fantasies. Their creators had as yet no patrons who might commission portraits from them. Thus the series of portraits by Matisse, Derain, Marquet, Vlaminck, Manguin, and Camoin are a species of wish-fulfillment, creating patrons in fantasy. From one another they received the sympathy and psychological support that they desired from patronage. None of them, however, literally fulfilled the role: among the Fauves, there was no Bazille or Caillebotte, buying regularly from their friends. Manguin had means but apparently could not, or did not want to, extend his support of his friends into the realm of patronage. The other Fauves only rarely bought one another's paintings. These portraits created only the form of the patron-object out of the friend-object and the artist-object. By bringing this form of the patron into being, these artists displayed their aspirations to the content, to the material benefits of patronage.

Marquet and Derain (and Cézanne)

Matisse's portraits of Marquet and Derain were his only painted portraits of artist peers. After 1905, all of his portraits of friends and acquaintances who were artists were made in various graphic media. While the choice of medium does not determine the quality or value of a portrait, it is worth noting Matisse's brief, restricted use of oil paint in this context. For the people who mattered most to him at a time when his artistic identity was partly shared with others of the avant-garde, he used the means that really mattered.

With these flexible means, Matisse could tailor his expression to suit the roles these two close painter friends had in his artistic formation at this time. The portrait of Marquet (fig. 81) is by far the more conventional, a sober and solid construction all around. The painter is posed in three-quarters position against a background divided horizontally into two zones, the lower dull brick in color, the upper blue-gray with fragments of a darker blue arabesque. Marquet's head is smaller than life size; this combined with the subdued color scheme promotes a feeling of intimacy. The eyeglasses that Marquet wore are sacrificed to a simplified, distilled conception that would not tolerate such a distracting feature. Matisse's use here of a wood support ensures that the surface effects are entirely due to the working of the paint, and this surface, though far from uniform, has the glistening quality of highly crafted panel painting.

81 (*previous page*) *Albert Marquet*, 1905–6. Oil on wood, 41.5 × 31 cm. Oslo, Nasjonalgalleriet.

Matisse began the head by outlining it in blue paint, an academic procedure he had also used to lay in the main lines of the portraits of his wife (see figs. 46, 51). Marquet's face is built of overlapping slabs of color painted in a firm systematic stroke in the manner of Cézanne. In areas where Cézanne had trouble in his own paintings – the joins between forms – Matisse seems also to have faltered, to judge from the particularly thick paint around the mouth and the region where the jaw recedes into shadow. The background, too, in its working and reworking, recalls the dogged technique of Cézanne. The upper zone, originally a lighter blue that still leaks through the darker surface, especially evokes Cézanne's colorations, and the arabesque figure recalls the background decorations found frequently in his portraits. The thorough Cézannism of *Albert Marquet* has led some writers to date the painting to the first few years of the century, when Matisse's other works show Cézanne's influence most strongly.[21] The error is understandable, because it is an exceptional work for Matisse in the years 1905–6, tonal, harmonious, and carefully laid out, seemingly a dry patch in the lush Fauve jungle.

Of the Fauves, Marquet and Camoin shared with Matisse the most profound appreciation of the painting of Cézanne. In this portrait Marquet and Matisse show their affinity with Cézanne: Matisse pays tribute to both artists. But it is certainly a view of Marquet through Cézanne: Marquet's well-known jauntiness is nowhere to be seen here. At a time of stylistic innovation Matisse could also, when appropriate, turn for a model to an artist who was, after all, still alive and still a powerful force with the avant-garde.[22] Cézanne is the subtext of this portrait, the underpinning of Matisse's dual desire to identify with the recently honored master from Aix and to present himself in the vanguard of painting in his own time.

Matisse gave the portrait to Marquet; and although Matisse soon had recourse to Cézanne for a way out of Fauvism, this painting would not have been the right kind of touchstone for Matisse's simplifications of the figure in 1907–8. In 1916 Marquet sold the painting to the Nasjonalgalleriet in Oslo. By then Matisse had done another portrait of him, one of the many monotypes he made during the First World War (fig. 82). This is Marquet as figured in his own self-portraits – insouciant, hair and clothing awry, all conveyed by Matisse with a few winding white lines scratched into the black printing ground. Here is Matisse's friend, sketched breezily after Marquet's own manner; the earlier painted portrait had a more complicated agenda, a deeper relationship to shared values.

The portrait of Derain (fig. 80) has received much more attention in the Matisse literature than the painting of Marquet because it is easier to fit into the general picture of Matisse's development in 1905–6. And it is a spectacularly realized image of sympathetic vitality. It looks more like a characteristic painting of the Fauves – the high-keyed color, the energetic style – and it is a portrait of his close collaborator in the summer of 1905 in Collioure, the crucible of the movement. Cézanne is harder to invoke in this portrait (although the influence on Matisse of his technique can still be detected), and one of the appealing qualities of this painting is that it seems to have nothing to do with anything but Matisse, Derain, and paint. Their mutual experiments seem to unfold right here on this canvas, so that the portrait comes to represent their innovative efforts in a very direct way. The two artists began nearly on a master and protégé footing, but the older Matisse also profited from the relationship. Derain's stimulus to Matisse's efforts that summer was crucial, perhaps as much from the younger artist's energy and productivity as from the way his paintings looked.

82 *The Painter Albert Marquet*, 1914–15. Monotype, 14.5 × 10.5 cm. Private collection.

In the portrait Matisse seems to have made little effort to characterize Derain except in the generalized mode of a wistful romantic artist type, head inclined as if in thought, glance cast out of the picture field. This contemplative or introspective image is at odds with Matisse's paint handling, in sharp strokes of bright color. Where Matisse's construction of Marquet is stable and ordered, Derain in paint is a product of flux and imbalance. Derain was possibly an unsettling influence on Matisse, sometimes even more daring in his painting than the "roi des Fauves." The brilliant portrait of Derain is also a summer canvas from the Mediterranean, the dark portrait of Marquet a winter picture done in Paris, but the differences in conception and tone are explained more by what was reinforced in Matisse by each artist. Marquet was an old comforting *camarade*; Derain was a fresh challenge. With Marquet he looked to the reassurance of Cézanne's structure; with Derain ahead into uncharted territory. Raymond Escholier spoke fittingly of the "affectionate violence" with which Matisse made this portrait.[23] Certainly there was affection, but there was also serious rivalry, a dynamic never found between Marquet and Matisse.

The color and the activity of the paint are the two most striking features of Derain's portrait. Although most of the colors are pleasing pastels, their contrasts are sharp. Red and green – Matisse's main color opposition that summer, and a driving force in *Woman with the Hat* (see fig. 46) – are vigorously juxtaposed at the upper left. The most varied color activity and brushstrokes animate the face. Colors are blended everywhere, the result of new strokes over and through still-wet paint. Everything lightens in both color and texture toward the edges, but the creamy strokes at the bottom add stabilizing weight to this part of the image. Matisse then boldly marked the canvas with an outsized monogram in the lower right corner.

The portrait of Derain is frequently compared with Derain's corresponding portrait of Matisse (fig. 79). This is usually done so that Matisse's work may be declared more daring.[24] The truth of this should not obscure the greater significance of the reciprocal activity and the projection of each artist's fixations on the other. Derain saw in Matisse an older figure of stability and support, and the pose and construction of his portrait reflects this sense of homage. For Matisse, Derain represented liberation from tradition. Matisse's Derain was more of a *tabula rasa* than he was himself, and Matisse's projection onto Derain is deeply tied to Derain's youth and freedom from convention. In a sense, in this portrait Matisse is assuming Derain for himself, ascribing to the young painter the qualities he found valuable for his own development at this time.[25]

Derain gave his portrait of Matisse to the sitter, presumably in friendship and homage. Matisse kept his painting of Derain for himself, perhaps because there was more of him than of his sitter in it.[26] Before long, though, the portrait became more important to him as one example among others of his work than as a document of an extraordinary relationship and as a marker of his stylistic development. By 1908 he had sold the painting to his new patrons Michael and Sarah Stein, the most important supporters of his work after the Fauve period. The Steins had no special feeling for Derain (they did not collect his work); for both buyer and seller at this point, the portrait was significant because Matisse had painted it at a key moment in his development.[27]

Terrus and the telluric drive

Matisse's portraits of the painter Etienne Terrus complete a triad of artist images from this time, portraits in which Matisse singles out meaningful elements of the identities of the sitters that represent both these men and his own search for an artistic identity. The images of Terrus (see fig. 83) are of a different order, and not merely because they are drawings and not oil paintings.[28] Matisse and Terrus were not close friends, and it cannot even be said that they had similar artistic goals. Even more than the portrait of Derain, these small drawings are the product of particular circumstances. These circumstances are revealing about some of Matisse's aspirations at this time.

Terrus came from Elne, just inland from Collioure in the Pyrénées-Orientales. He painted mainly landscapes of the Midi, which he exhibited at the Salon des Indépendants from 1908. The sculptor Aristide Maillol, also a man of the Midi, was his close friend. Terrus was responsible for introducing Matisse to Maillol in the summer of 1905, when the two painters helped Maillol cast his important bronze *La Méditerranée*.[29] Both Terrus and Maillol were somewhat older than Matisse, and Matisse may have seen Terrus in much the same way that Derain regarded Matisse himself, as an experienced, stabilizing influence.

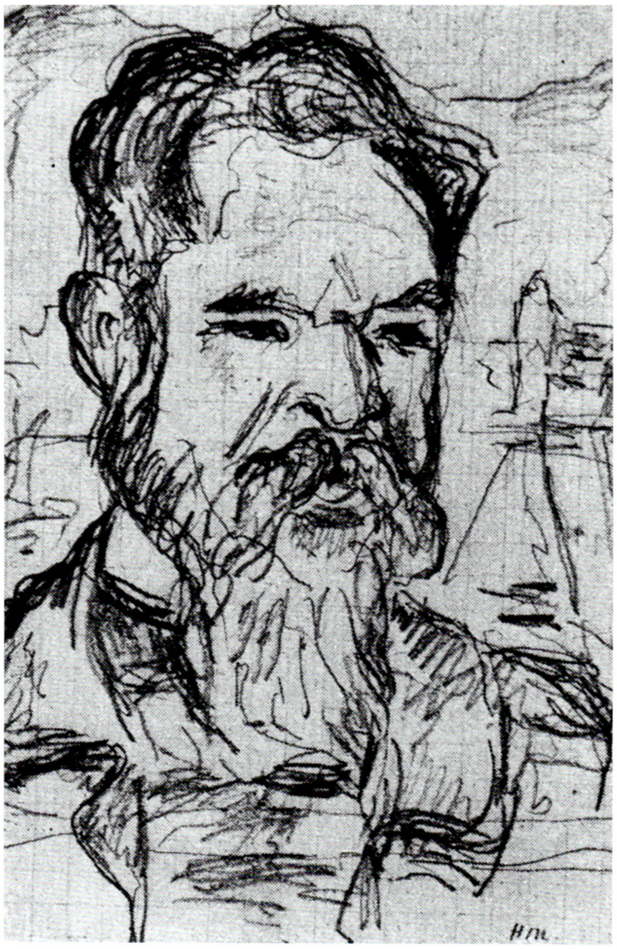

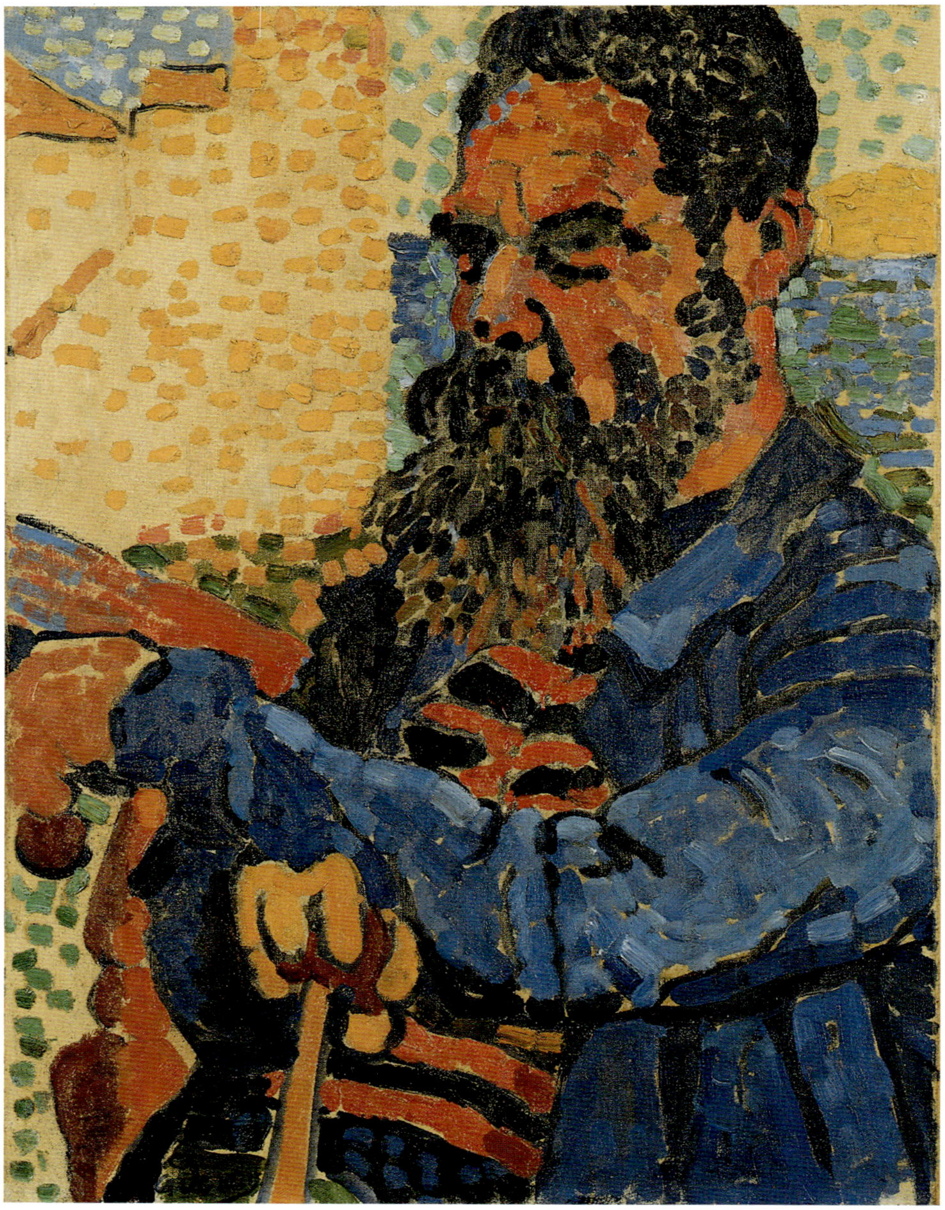

83 (*above left*) *Terrus at Collioure*, 1905. Pencil on paper, 13.8 × 8.7 cm. Private collection.

84 (*above right*) André Derain, *The Painter Etienne Terrus*, 1905. Oil on canvas, 65 × 49 cm. Columbus Museum of Art, Ohio, gift of Howard D. and Babette L. Sirak, the Donors to the Campaign for Enduring Excellence, and the Derby Fund.

Matisse depicted the rough-hewn Terrus against the backdrop of Collioure's harbor with its distinctive round belltower to the right. This contextualization – unusual in Matisse's portraits, as is the outdoor setting – has everything to do with the conjunction of Terrus's regional identity and Matisse's admiration of the culture of the Midi during his first summer in this region, as well as the predominance of landscape painting in his work then. Another unusual feature of Matisse's drawing, his use of squared paper, may indicate that this was a study for a larger painted portrait that was never realized. Support for this possibility is found in a portrait of identical conception, with the rugged artist set against the distinctive architectural features of Collioure, that Derain made of Terrus at this time (fig. 84). The northern artists were clearly impressed with this imposing character and his aura of enduring values, linked to the features of his *pays*.[30] Both Terrus and Maillol were proud men of the southwest who wore their provincialism on their sleeves.

In the words of one who knew him, Terrus "would have liked to remain rooted in his native soil like a gnarled olive-tree," and Maillol said of him after his death that "he represented for us [the artists and writers of the region] the people, the land itself. His name alone expresses it: Terrus."[31] This rootedness was the basis of his appeal for Matisse at a time when he sought to express a new Mediterranean spirit in his art, a solidity and durability, associated with stone and soil, to support the wild experiments in color that were in part instigated by the light of this region.[32]

Family matters

Between 1905 and 1908 Matisse also made several portraits of family members of his artist friends. At one level these are natural extensions of his expanding social and artistic relations. They also parallel some of Matisse's portraits within his own family, and similarly the sitters may have been a ready pool for his new interest in the problems of representing a particular face and attending to another's identity in the context of his desire for self-expression in his art. Moreover, in the families of friends he seems to have found confirmation of some of his attitudes within his own family. In certain cases the parallels, and their paternalistic implications, are quite specific.

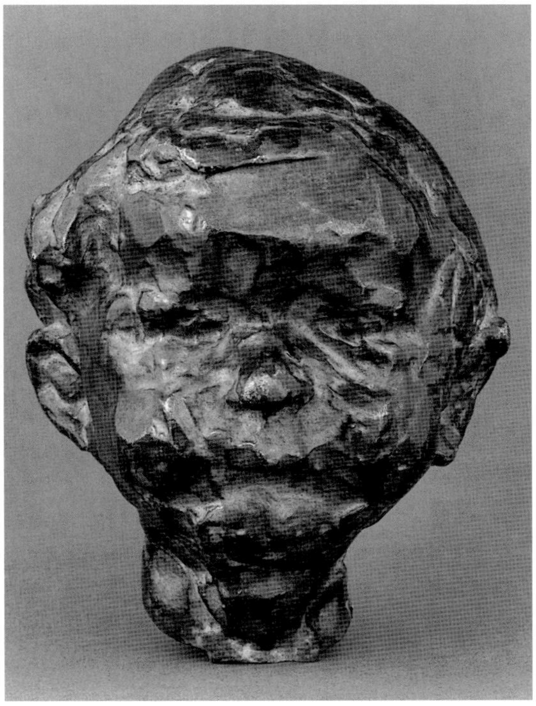

85 *Head of a Child (Pierre Manguin)*, 1903–5. Bronze, 13 cm high. Private collection.

Among several small bronze sculptures of his children he made around 1905 (see fig. 63), Matisse also fashioned a portrait of Pierre Manguin (fig. 85), the young son of Henri Manguin. He probably formed these sculptures in his hand rather than on a sculpture stand.[33] That procedure clearly suggests the Pygmalionesque process of transforming the formless into something vital and meaningful, one of Rodin's favorite sculptural themes. The intimacy of Matisse's method also suggests the formative relationship between a parental figure and a child. As with the head of his son Pierre, made the same year, Matisse has made an analogy between the emerging personality and the indefiniteness of form in one so young. In these busts, in fact, the formlessness of youth is exaggerated to emphasize this potential. The heads are certainly differentiated from one another, but the qualities they share – formal and psychological generalization – seem to be more important than the distinctions among individuals that constitute one of the fundamental principles of portraiture. While acknowledging that the stakes were different for these heads from those for a commissioned portrait, for example, it is significant and consistent that Matisse's expressive concerns have priority over the individuality of the sitter.[34]

Jeanne Manguin, the wife and mother in the Manguin family, was the sitter for one of Matisse's most celebrated drawings (fig. 86). In the image of this woman there is no question of an absence of individualization. The portrait is unusual among his Fauve drawings because it matches his paintings of the time in variety and energy of mark-making. Matisse's mixed-technique method is most evident in Mme Manguin's elaborate costume, including a big hat. He has summed up her face in a small number of lines. Although these have the effect of synopsis rather than exaggeration, the drawing indicates Matisse's continuing flirtation with caricature in some of his portraits.

In Matisse's drawing, Jeanne Manguin's carriage mirrors the pose of the portrait of Baldassare Castiglione (see fig. 7), so his recent exercise in copying may indeed have had a direct impact on his approach to other portraits. The drawing of Jeanne

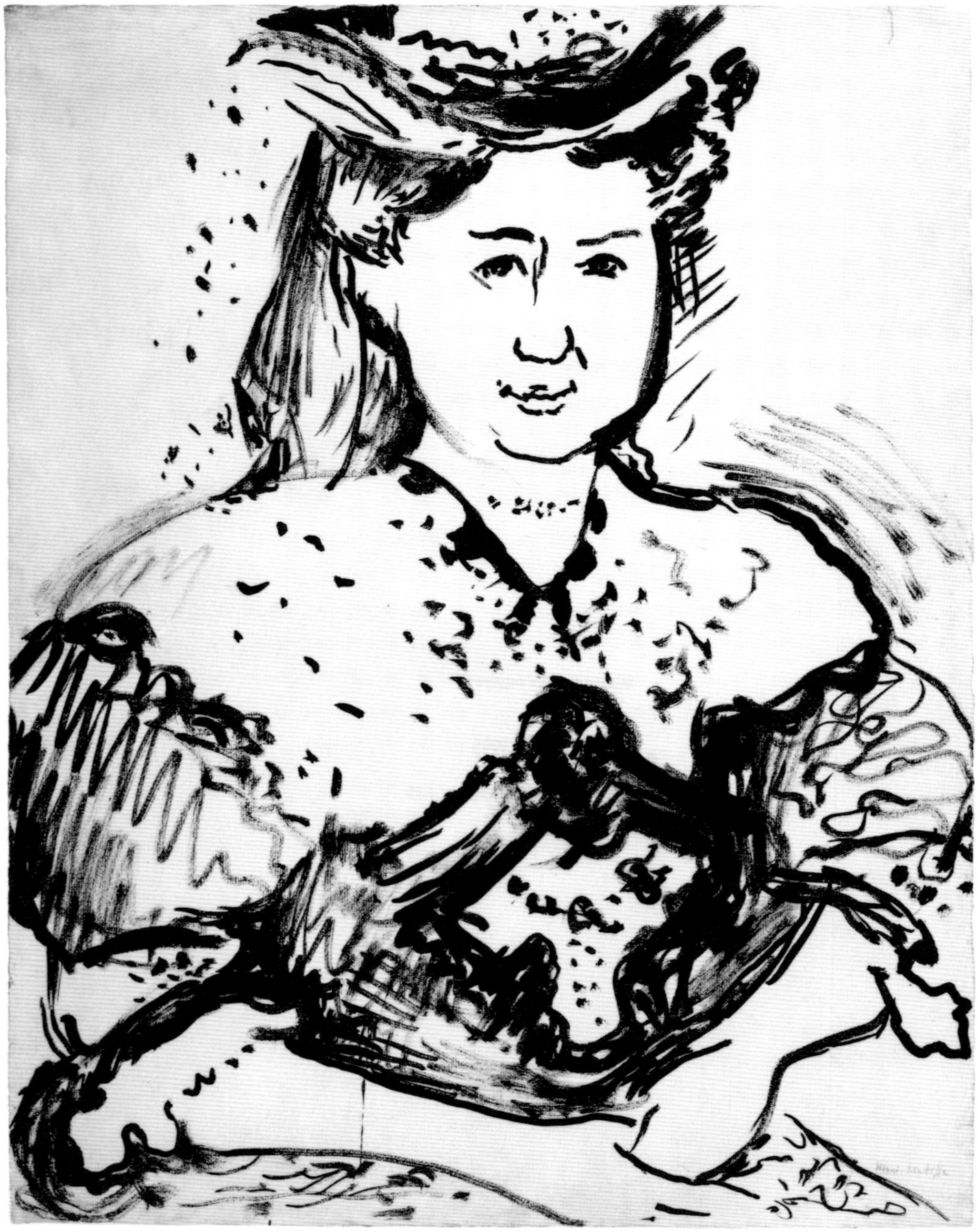

86 *Jeanne Manguin*, 1906. Brush and ink on paper, 62.2 × 46.9 cm. The Museum of Modern Art, New York. Given anonymously.

Manguin also shows how adaptable this portrait convention was in Matisse's hands. And so, more than the individual is parodied. The forms of society portraiture are also sent up here.[35] The critique of this mode of class expression links the drawing to *Woman with the Hat* of the previous year, but at the personal level, there is at least amusement and affection in Matisse's rendering of the wife of his friend. The contrast between his more severe portraits of Amélie from 1905 and the drawing of Jeanne Manguin is telling. In *Woman with the Hat* Amélie Matisse appears thin and sharp; Jeanne Manguin in her portrait is ample and buoyant. Mme Manguin dominates the space Matisse has given her, pressing out against the drawing's edge at all sides; Mme Matisse seems to submit to her surroundings, particularly her

87 *Nono (Mlle Lebasque)*, 1908. Oil on canvas, 54.9 × 45.7 cm. New York, The Metropolitan Museum of Art, bequest of Miss Adelaide Milton de Groot (1876–1967), 1967.

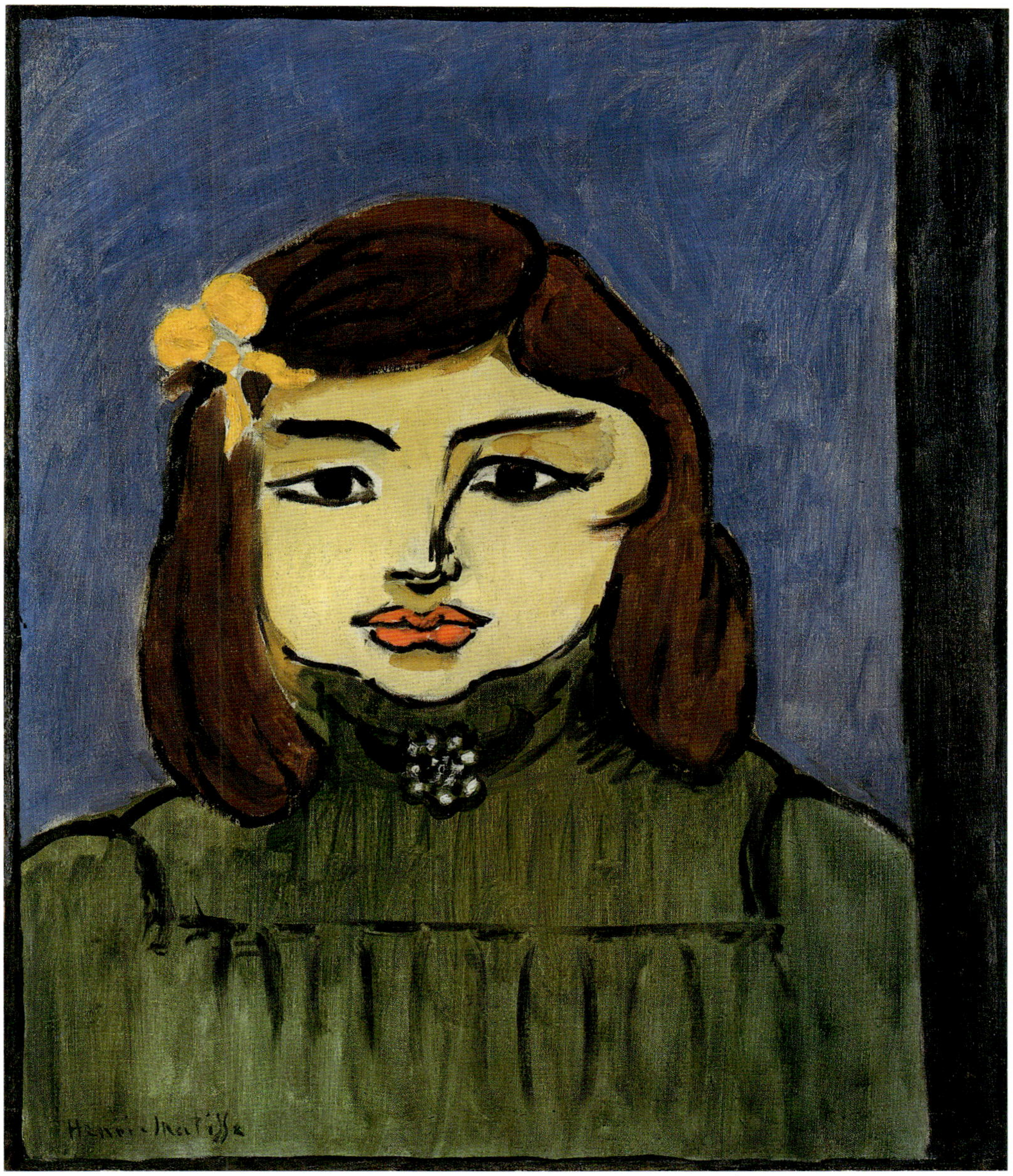

aggressive adornment. Although the formal elements of caricature are more explicit in the drawing of Jeanne Manguin, finally this is a more sanguine and sympathetic portrait.[36]

A combination of awkwardness and sympathy also characterizes Matisse's portrait of Nono Lebasque of 1908 (fig. 87). Nono was the daughter of Matisse's friend Henri Lebasque, a slightly older contemporary and a painter of landscapes in a heightened Impressionist style. Her real name was Hélène, and she was a childhood playmate of Pierre Matisse.[37] Matisse's conception of the girl in this portrait is strikingly in tune with how he painted his own daughter Marguerite and his son Pierre in this period (see figs. 64, 68). As in the portrait of Marguerite, Matisse has inscribed the sitter's name in bold letters directly on the canvas (though why he halved Hélène's nickname to "NO" is unknown). As in both portraits of his children, Matisse has presented Nono Lebasque with a frank directness in the

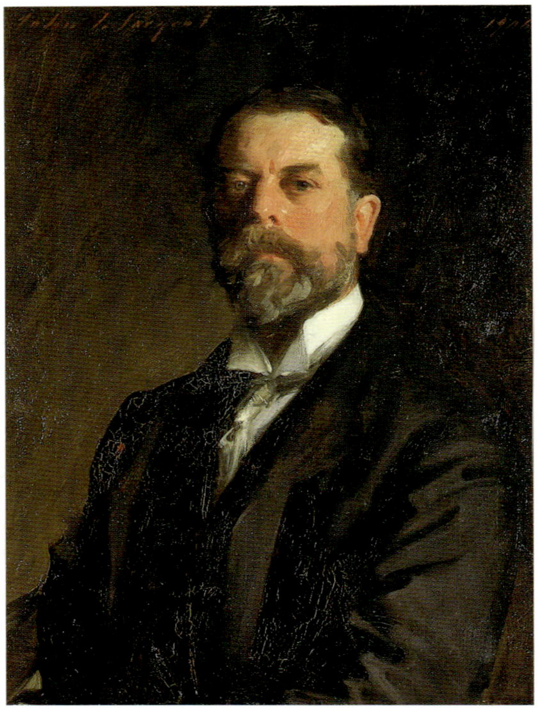

88 John Singer Sargent, *Self-Portrait*, 1907. Oil on canvas, 76.2 × 63.5 cm. Florence, Galleria degli Uffizi.

89 Pablo Picasso, *Self-Portrait with Palette*, 1906. Oil on canvas, 92 × 73 cm. Philadelphia Museum of Art, A. E. Gallatin Collection.

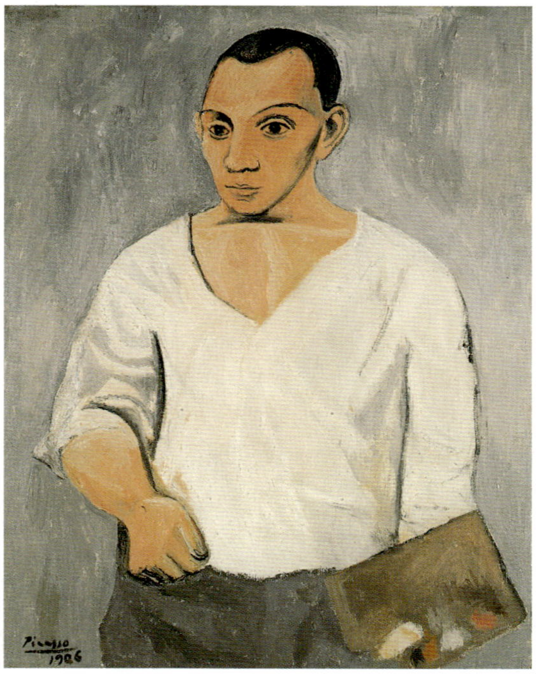

bust-length frontal format, producing a telling contrast between the formality of the pose and the childlike attributes of the face, executed with a minimum of modeling. The contrast between these three paintings and the contemporaneous portrait of Greta Moll (see fig. 113), a commission with an elaborate development, shows how Matisse took the occasion in portraits of children to project on them his desires for simplicity and directness of expression. Style is adjusted to the sitter in ways that suggest both the sitter's attributes and their intersection with Matisse's own growing interest in more simplified means in his portraits.

Yet sophistication is not entirely absent in this painting. The subtle asymmetry of the composition, accentuated by the uneven vertical band along the right side of the canvas, evokes the *japonisme* of some of Van Gogh's portraits. The flat areas of fairly uniform color – also a feature of the portrait of Marguerite of 1907 – and the simplified system of one-tone modeling in the face suggest the technique of the *ukiyo-e* woodcut. The vertically oriented inscription within the band at the right again alludes to the conventions of Japanese art. Thus another form of expression outside the Western tradition, along with the aura of naïveté found in children's art, is an appropriate mode of presentation for the young sitter in this portrait.

Declaration of independence

As though to declaim a position, Matisse in 1906 made the most intense and confrontational self-portrait of his career. *Self-Portrait in a Striped Jersey* (fig. 90) has none of the feeling of searching self-determination associated with his many self-portraits from about 1900. It was instead a confident announcement of what he had become. The boldness of the image is reinforced by its over-life size and by the bust-length format. The large size is particularly striking in a genre based on the diminished size of the mirror image of the artist making the self-portrait. Moreover, Matisse addresses the viewer without his characteristic eyeglasses. He is simultaneously exposed and bolder as a result, a trope of honesty and directness. Nor does informal clothing make for an informal presentation.[38] All here is hard, unflinching confidence and will.

Matisse rhetorically constructs himself as an adventurous explorer, a toughened sailor of the most violent seas. His calm self-assurance, verging on arrogance, is expressed in the eyes and the set of the mouth within the imposing frame of his beard. Around these implacable features he has applied the paint thickly and apparently in haste (there is a great deal of cracking). Energy radiates from the centrally placed eye in the manner of some of Van Gogh's self-portraits, fixing the viewer with a challenging stare. The color is vivid and arbitrary, providing other marks of self-assertiveness. At the same time, the head is also strongly sculptural, a dense and durable-looking presence.[39] While for many viewers the self-portrait has evoked art of the past, both distant and recent (Roman mosaics, Byzantine icons, the portraits of Cézanne), in this powerful self-performance Matisse declares himself to be his own artist, self-sufficient and confident in the extreme. Cézanne is certainly there, but Cézanne's famous doubt is nowhere to be seen in Matisse's self-fashioning.

Performance aside, he had good reason to be confident at this time. By the summer of 1906 he had a much higher public profile than just a year earlier. He had exhibited some of his most innovative work and endured vehement criticism. But he had become admired as well as notorious, and he had gained support from several important sources. The Galerie Druet held a moderate-sized exhibition

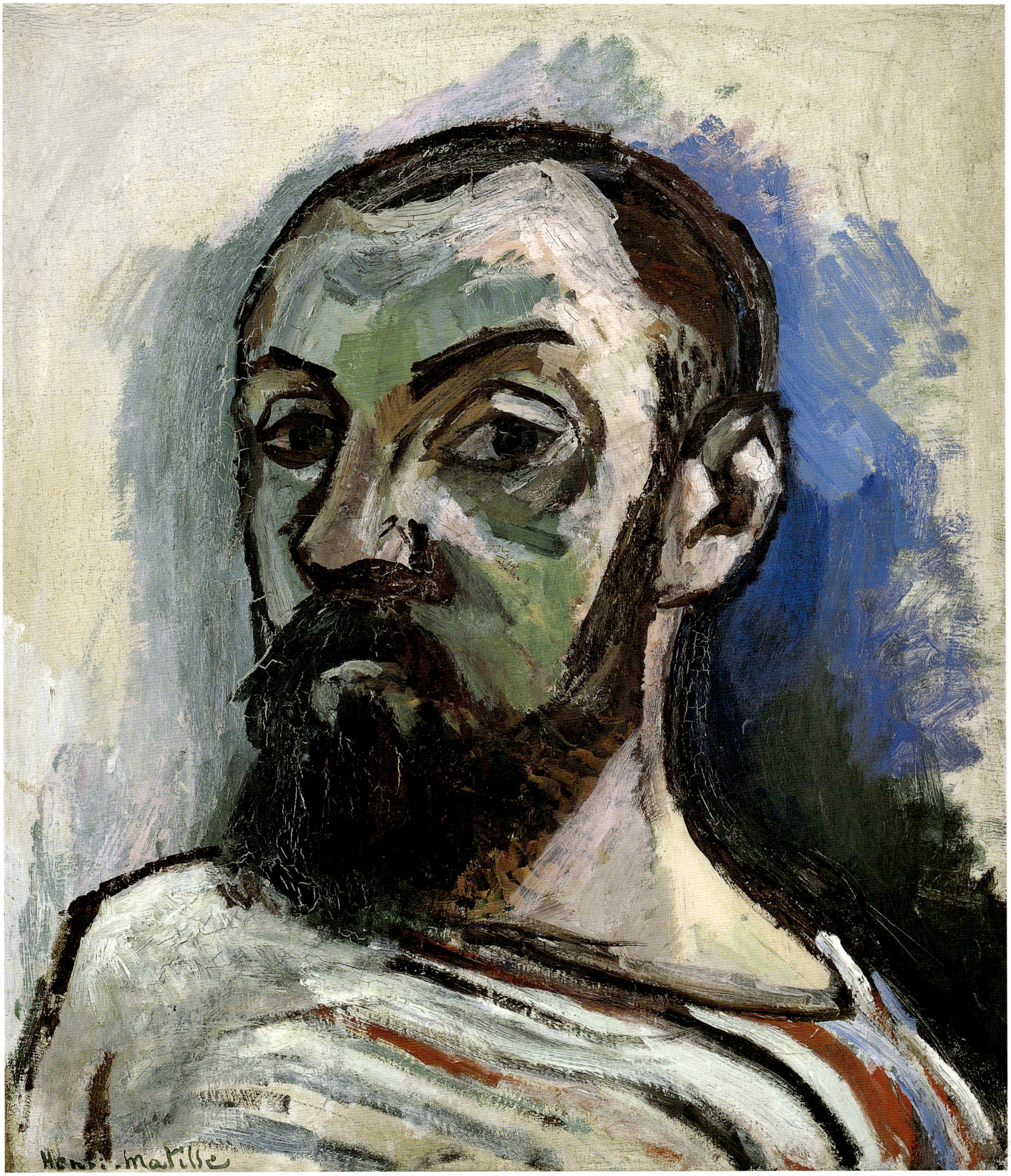

90 *Self-Portrait in a Striped Jersey*, 1906. Oil on canvas, 55 × 46 cm. Copenhagen, Statens Museum for Kunst.

of his work, mainly recent paintings from Collioure, in the spring of 1906. More importantly, his work was selling. The patronage he had sought was beginning to materialize, especially from several members of the Stein family.

Gertrude Stein is said to have believed that *Self-Portrait in a Striped Jersey* was "too intimate to be shown publicly."[40] In this she understood the character of the portrait but mistook its purpose. Before long she grasped better the "brutal egotism" that in 1906 Matisse displayed in this painting.[41] Michael and Sarah Stein bought it and hung it in their Paris apartment, where it presided over a room dominated by the display of Matisse's recent work.

He did in fact show it publicly, as his sole entry in a group exhibition in 1907 at Bernheim-Jeune called "Portraits d'hommes."[42] Furthermore, he chose it as one of four of his works to illustrate (as *Portrait de l'artiste*) Guillaume Apollinaire's interview with him, published that year. These public deployments of the painting soon after he made it indicate that Matisse felt strongly enough about its declarative nature to let it represent him in these two important contexts, especially since the interview with Apollinaire constituted his first public statements about his art. For Matisse and some of the other artists formerly of the Fauve circle, the "*Portraits d'hommes*" show was little more than an excuse to exhibit a self-portrait and nothing else: Marquet, Jean Puy, and Louis Valtat also showed self-portraits as their only exhibits.[43] What compelled Matisse to make this singular statement of individuality and self-command may also have motivated other artists to do the same, in a more general trend to self-assertion following the dissipation of the short-lived but intense Fauve movement. By this time it was every man for himself.

For all its formal innovation, on its own Matisse's painting offers neither a distinctly new conception of the self nor a radically new artistic self-conception. A stylistically more traditional self-portrait such as the contemporaneous painting by John Singer Sargent (fig. 88) shares Matisse's proud posture (the body is turned in both cases to give the figure greater volume and movement back into space), and the same arrogant stare, punctuated by the challenge of the slightly raised brow and romantically accented by a light that illuminates one side of the face and leaves the other in shadow, suggesting psychological complexity. But Matisse's image also shares with some of the self-portraits of his contemporaries the programmatic and modernist assertion of the independence of the artist from tradition, as in Picasso's *Self-Portrait with Palette*, also of 1906 (fig. 89). Both Matisse and Picasso figure themselves as laborers in the service of art, hard honest workers without artifice, in images hewn as if from stone. Both artists have built these solid edifices on the foundation of Cézanne, even as each in his way asserts a new, singular direction with "the solid heft of a planned statement."[44]

Portraiture, mortality, and collective consciousness

After the painted portrait of Marquet, the next time Matisse made a portrait of another artist was at the beginning of the First World War. Then he made over fifty small portraits of a variety of sitters – several painters among them – in etching or drypoint, media he had hardly used since *Self-Portrait as an Etcher* of 1903 (see fig. 31). He had recently bought an intaglio press and possibly made these simple prints as a convenient distraction from the increasing rigors he imposed on himself in his painting.[45] He printed the plates with Marguerite's help, and liked the speed and ease with which this could be done.[46] Most of the prints have a fine even line

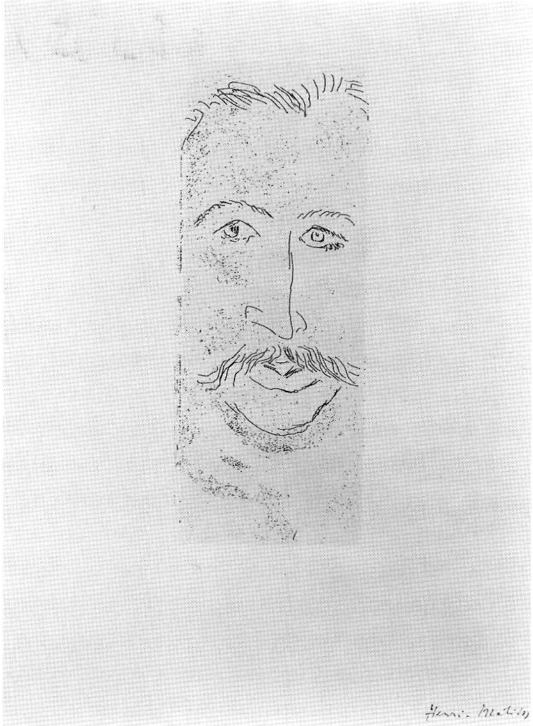

91 *Walter Pach*, 1914. Etching, 16.1 × 6 cm. The Museum of Modern Art, New York. Purchase Fund.

92 *Marguerite Matisse* (known as *Utamaro*), 1914. Etching, 17.8 × 12.9 cm. Private collection.

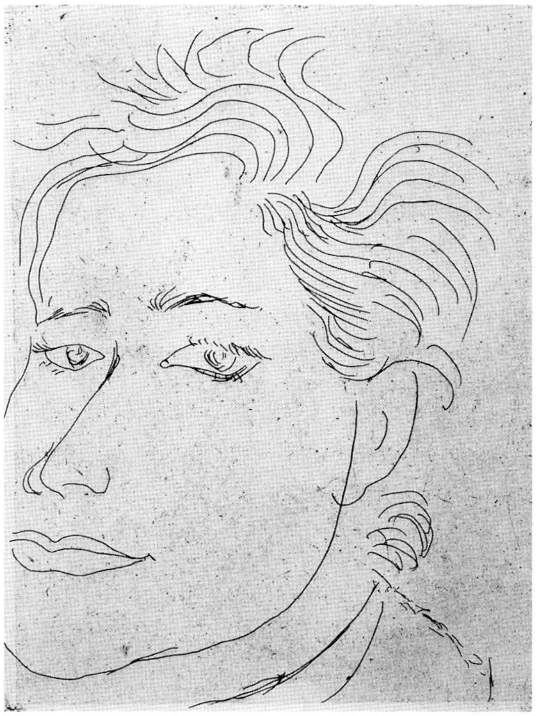

with a minimum of inflection or modeling. In many of them the narrow vertical format into which Matisse fitted the image – *japonisme* again – emphasizes their restrained and concentrated simplicity.

The American painter Walter Pach gave the best account of Matisse's work on these etchings, disclosing both his procedure and his attitude in making them. One day in 1914 Matisse asked Pach to pose at short notice. He had a small plate ready and in five minutes he produced a portrait (fig. 91) that he initially downplayed as too casual. Later, with more time, he drew several more elaborated images of Pach on additional plates. Matisse seems to have been sympathetic to the younger American, who, like himself in a more modest way, was a writer as well as a painter. Pach was an ardent supporter of modern European art and in fact was in Paris to make the arrangements for Matisse's exhibition to be held the following year at the Montross Gallery in New York. Both artists agreed that the more summary first effort was preferable because livelier. Matisse effaced the portraits he had worked up more completely without biting the plates, and no other etching of Pach is known.[47]

The general characteristics of the etching of Pach may be found in most of Matisse's other portraits of this time.[48] Pach is pressed between the borders of the image in a markedly vertical format, creating the amusing effect of a face seen framed by an opened door. Although his face is centered and frontally oriented, asymmetry is introduced in the eyes, in the line of the nose, and in his bushy moustache. In this plate, foul biting creates a kind of fortuitous modeling, but Matisse appears to have been more careful with the biting of the others.

Concision in the etchings is coupled with subtle wit. Like so many of Matisse's drawn and painted portraits, the etchings track a fine line near caricature but do not quite cross it. In fact, some would fail as caricatures of an individual for a fundamental reason: it is sometimes difficult to identify the sitter in this highly unified series of prints. Their unity under the sign of Japonism is indicated in the traditional title of one of them, *Utamaro*, without reference to a sitter – in fact Marguerite Matisse, identifiable by the ribbon around her neck (fig. 92).[49] In another example, the etching known as *Bourgeat looking like Vassaux*, Matisse seems to have figured his sitter (the printmaker Charles Bourgeat, who had been in Moreau's studio with Matisse) in terms of his memory of another person (the absent Léon Vassaux, another old cohort).[50] Doubtless one of Bourgeat's personas crossed over with Vassaux, at least in Matisse's mind, but given that, Matisse has wrested control of the sitter's identity from him in making this little picture.

The point of this transference is that Matisse occasionally failed in these etchings to make a portrait incorporating the signal prerequisite of portraiture – a coherent individual identity; in others he was exquisitely successful. The explanation for this inconsistency in characterization lies, without paradox, in the consistency of Matisse's technique and procedure. The technique is limited; the procedure was predicated on speed. Furthermore, and most importantly, the style of each etching is not oriented toward an individual sitter but is fairly uniform throughout the group. Matisse imposed something resembling a formula on a diverse group of people, a comprehensive liberty he did not take in his portrait paintings or drawings. He used an overtly childlike simplicity of conception for Marguerite or Nono; for Greta Moll (see fig. 113), sophisticated art-historical references; for Sarah Stein (see fig. 127), an ethereal aura; for his wife, sharp aggression; shared stylistic innovation with Derain; for Marquet, the sober solidity of their mutually admired Cézanne.

In the etched portraits, although individual identity may be attributed to each, the overall concept of individuality is subordinate to the sense of community. This collective idea was appropriate to the time. In extraordinary circumstances, people will draw together in unaccustomed ways, as they did during the First World War. In the war Matisse saw a much wider range of people than he had normally done since moving from Paris into his suburban house. The temporary, circumstantial diversity of his society is directly reflected in these individually slight but collectively compelling portraits. Not all of these people may have known each other, but Matisse knew them all, and has in spirit formed them into a community in a body of work uniform in style and conception.

He had other plans for the portraits. As he imagined it, this community of his own making in his art would contribute to the war effort. Distressed by the confinement of his parents and other relatives behind German lines in the North of France and especially by the capture and imprisonment of his brother, Matisse proposed to sell some of these etchings to raise money for "the civilian prisoners of Bohain-en-Vermandois," where his parents lived.[51] An album of eleven prints was planned; these would be issued in an edition of fifteen. Ten of the prints were to be small etched portraits; the eleventh, a lithograph, was to depict a full-length figure. For reasons unkown the project was never realized.

Kenneth Silver has noted the favor with which this humanitarian gesture was received in official circles, not so much because of its purpose – though there was no argument there – or the dominance of portraiture, but for the simplicity and purity of Matisse's style in these etchings, which one critic likened approvingly to the work of Ingres.[52] To this writer and others these modest portraits were a relief after the difficulty of Matisse's stylistic development before the war, especially in his painting. Perhaps, it was thought, Matisse had finally come to value the great French traditions and was seeking a place within them with his new work. In this way, according to the writer's view, he would serve his country best. Certainly these portraits are an important step toward the changes Matisse made in his style in the 1920s, toward a more widely appealing mode of representation that rapidly gained for him the status of a national asset.

The same critic observed that the etchings were appropriate wartime art despite not having war as their theme. Their style – sober, simple, direct – redeems them above all. But portraiture specifically was sometimes hailed as the exemplary art of war.[53] Moreover, portraits executed in a neutral style, without reference to any context, past or present, as in Matisse's prints, placed the maximum emphasis on the individual outside history. Decontextualizing the portrait may have been a form of resistance to the war, a way of asserting the value of the individual in the face of the collective horror.[54] Whatever may have been his intentions in making them (as separate from his intention to market them for the war effort), Matisse's wartime portrait etchings do participate in this spirit, but with qualification. The portraits have the character of individuality, but their common conception and style are what truly distinguish them as a rare, unified group – a collective, social portrait – in his work.

In addition to Walter Pach, other artists of whom Matisse made etched portraits included Charles Bourgeat, mentioned above; Francisco Iturrino, a Spaniard and another Moreau student with Matisse; and Demetrius Galanis, a Greek whom Matisse had probably met in Cormon's studio in 1900. They are not identified with their profession in these etchings any more than most of the musicians or other personages are. The high proportion of foreigners is explained by the circumstances of the war. The predominance of minor artistic figures in his portraits at this time is a trickier matter. Although he was in contact with Picasso, Gino Severini, and especially Juan Gris during the war, Matisse never made portraits of these artists, at this or any other time. Except for the early Fauve portraits with their strength-to-strength equation, their feeling of reciprocal respect, the absence of portraits of major artists in Matisse's work overall suggests that he preferred to record in portraits the fellowship of old studio comrades without the rivalry that might accompany a relationship with an avant-garde figure of more recent acquaintance.

Music and war

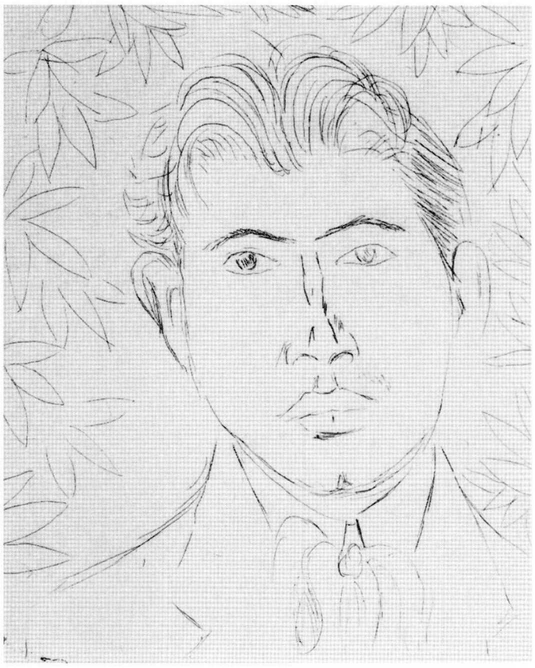

93 *Massia with Flowered Background*, 1914. Etching, 24.8 × 19.4 cm. Private collection.

During the war Matisse found special solace in music and took up the violin, which he had learned as a child, with renewed dedication. Among those in the diverse group of people who passed through Paris and Issy were several musicians with whom Matisse played occasionally. Of some of these he made the type of small etched portrait that so aptly expressed the ephemerality of these associations, producing true souvenirs. Among them, Joan Massia, a Spanish violinist, was the sitter for three portrait etchings and one of the beautiful and delicate monotypes Matisse made during the war. In the etchings Matisse sequentially moved from a descriptive conception of Massia's face, framed by a characteristic decorative border (fig. 93), to a more abstract mask rendered with a minimum of lines. In all three the sitter's mane of thick hair assumes central importance as the principal "Massia-sign" (see also fig. 202). Matisse reduced the sitter even further in the monotype, eliminating this distinctive feature. Now the image lacks enough information to be identified as a distinct individual; Massia's name is the only sign that can give identity to this mask. Despite the over-reduction in that particular print, Massia is the only man among the entire group of prints in this period to receive in his portraits the variety of treatment Matisse lavished on several of his female sitters.

Another violinist, Eva Mudocci, occasioned exercises in abstraction on a completely different path. In the best-known and most striking of three charcoal drawings of Mudocci (fig. 94), Matisse drew, erased, and redrew, expanding and contracting the image as he worked, finishing with nearly all straight lines that hover seemingly at random over their faded origins. In the progressive abstraction of this individual, the process through which the image has been distilled is stated directly and physically, not implied as in the more conceptual abstraction in the etchings of Massia. This difference is in part due to technical considerations that distinguish the two media; and in fact Matisse made more stylized portraits of Mudocci in etching and drypoint, in which it is clearer that this is the same woman who had sat for Edvard Munch decades earlier. But in Matisse's prints, too, variety can be found: in two of the plates Matisse shows her playing; in the third her isolated face tends toward the generic, collective mask. One conception of this sitter is physical and temporal, the other disembodied and elusive.

Just as in the Fauve period Matisse had made a few portraits of the family members of his artist friends, now during the war he had the wives and daughters of painters sit for small etched portraits. The men of these families were engaged or were otherwise constrained by the conflict. Portrait etchings of Mme Galanis (her husband enlisted in the Foreign Legion), Mme Derain (husband at the front), and Mme Gris (Juan Gris was gravely ill, without funds, and unable to leave the South) are direct results of wartime circumstances. In another medium, charcoal,

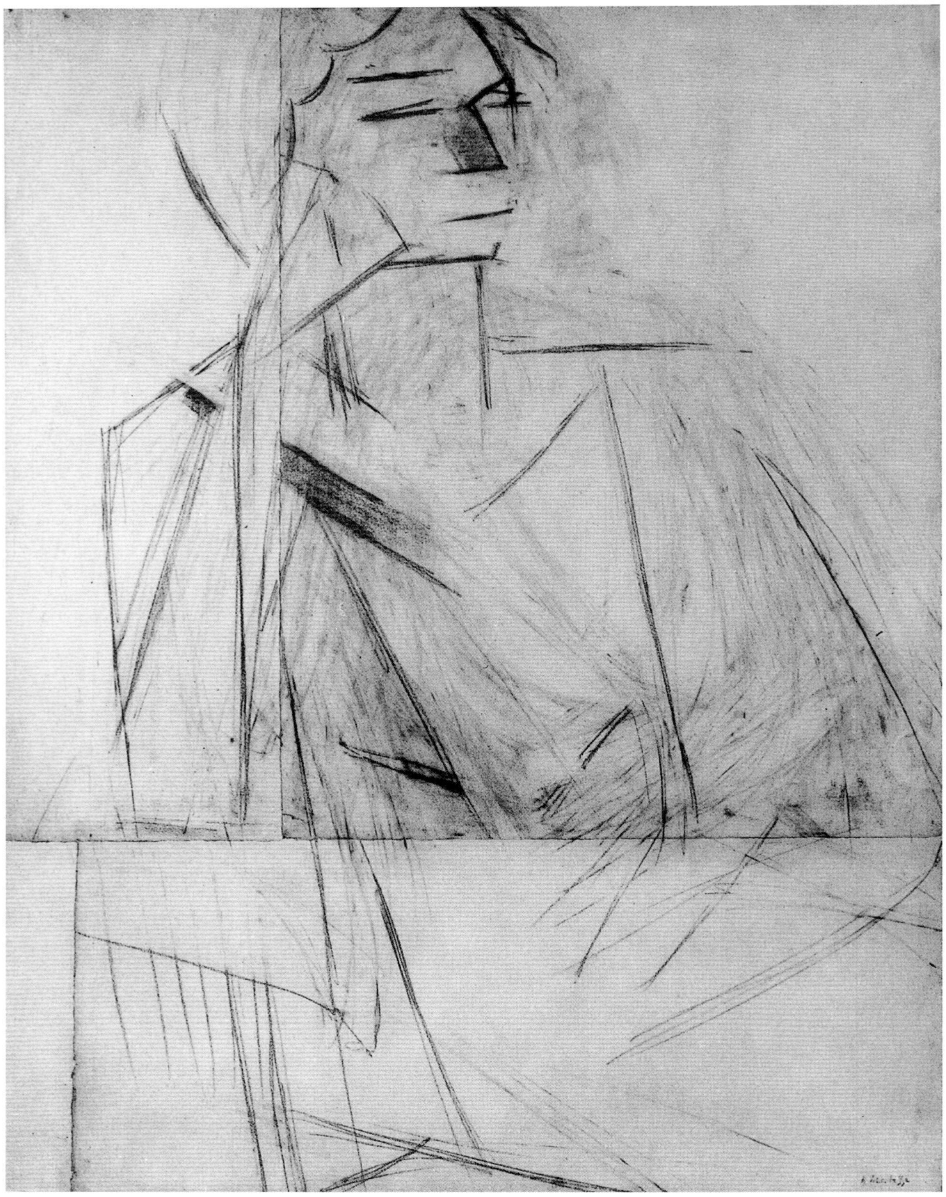

94 *Eva Mudocci*, 1915. Crayon on paper, 92.6 × 70.5 cm. Private collection.

he made several drawings of the daughter, Janine, of his Issy neighbor Jean Chaurand-Naurac, who had been in Moreau's studio in 1897 and who was now at the front.

The portraits of Josette Gris are the most numerous and the most interesting. Owing to the poor financial state of the Gris family, Matisse paid Mme Gris to model for him in Collioure. He may have exchanged this gesture of kindness for the license to make seven etchings and at least one drawing of her, a majestic, heavily worked portrait in pencil (fig. 95). As in his portrait of Eva Mudocci, Matisse has thoroughly revised this image, in the process distilling the sitter's features to the point of masklike abstraction. The contrast between his renderings of this sitter in the two media demonstrates his changing priorities in favor of carefully considered stylization. The pencil drawing is a startling departure from the informality of the etchings. In its intractable symmetry and flatness of effect it resembles nothing so

95 *Josette Gris*, 1915. Pencil on paper, 29.3 × 24 cm. Private collection.

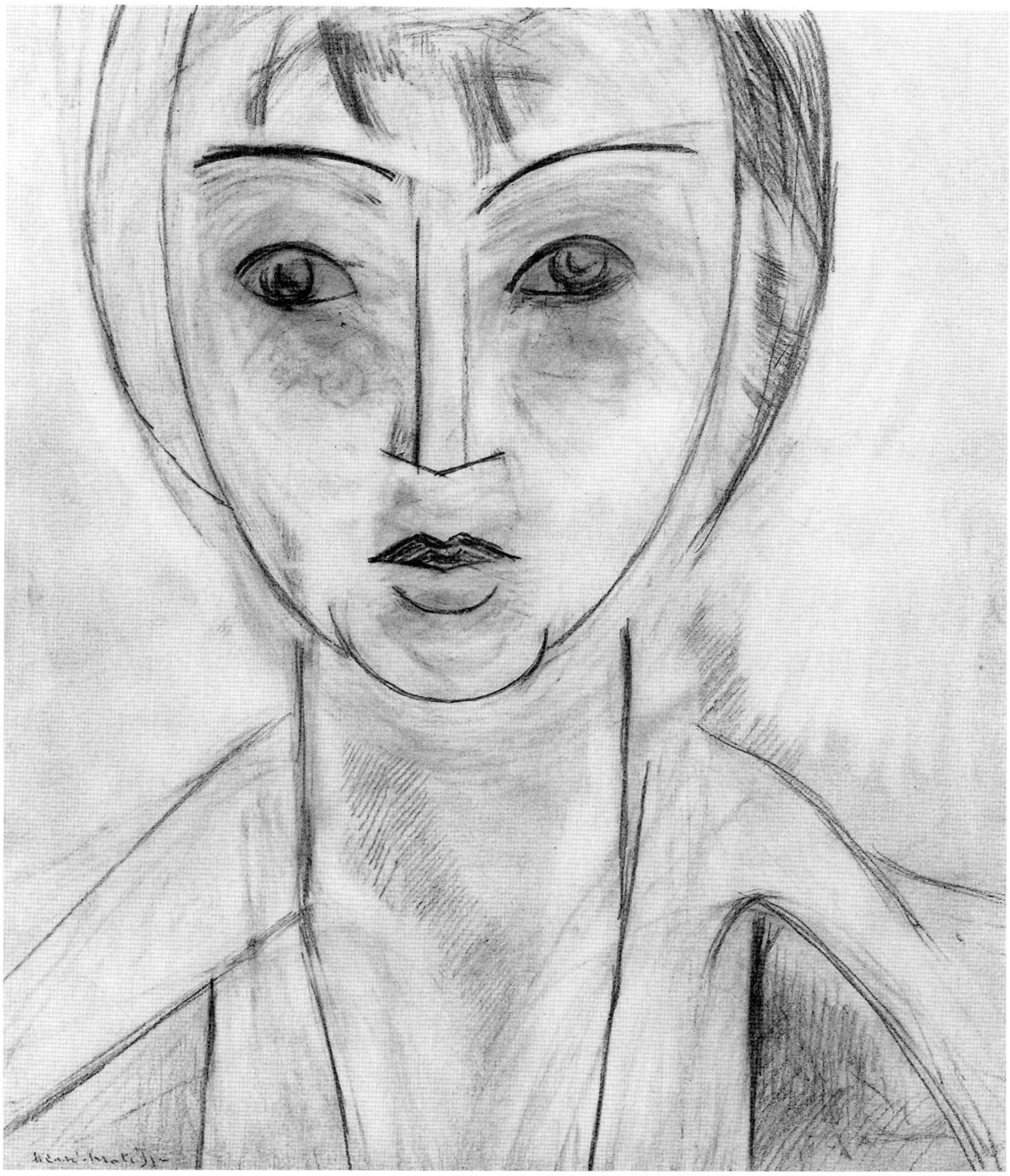

much as the several paintings Matisse made the following year of a bowl of apples on a pedestal table.[55] This procedure of abstraction reflects his general concerns in painting at this time. In the etchings he playfully turns Josette Gris this way and that, studying her face from several angles, a nearly physical manipulation he performed with other female sitters. In one double portrait (fig. 96), Mme Gris is presented in different poses, an implication of narrative that is antithetical to the rigid durability of the pencil drawing. The process of distillation to essential features in the pencil portrait and the free play and informal technique of the etchings anticipate Matisse's later procedure of "theme and variations" in drawing, flourishing in the 1940s (but: in the Gris portraits it appears that the simpler etchings may have come first, though this is not certain).

The war over, Matisse was engaged by the ballet impresario Serge Diaghilev in 1919 to design the sets and costumes for *Le Chant du rossignol*. In the course of

96 *Double Portrait of Josette Gris*, 1915. Etching, 13.1 × 18.1 cm. The Museum of Modern Art, New York. Abby Aldrich Rockefeller Purchase Fund.

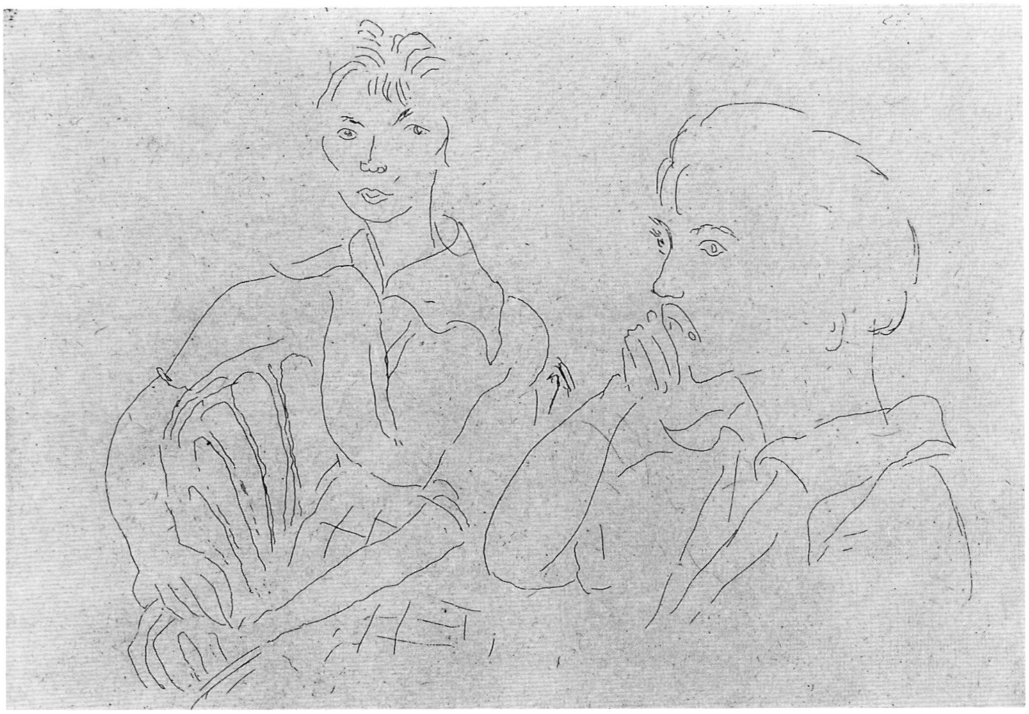

97 *Léonide Massine*, 1920. Pencil on paper, 39 × 28.5 cm. The Art Institute of Chicago, Samuel A. Marx Purchase Fund, 1972.427.

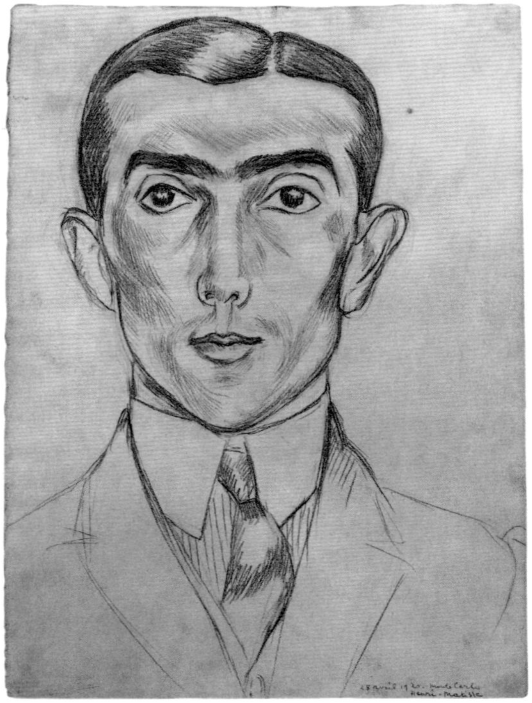

this commission he made the acquaintance of Léonide Massine, the principal dancer and choreographer for Diaghilev's Ballets Russes, and in effect Matisse's collaborator for this ballet. Matisse made at least five pencil drawings of Massine in Monte Carlo in April 1920. In the most assertive of them (from both parties' points of view), Matisse's meticulous modeling with a fine pencil has produced a head of precisely defined volumes and contours (fig. 97).[56] Like the simple etchings from the first years of the war, these drawings invoke a past master of the pencil line. A strong *ingrisme* in Matisse's work had already been apparent in several studies in pencil of the model Antoinette Arnoux beginning in 1919 (see figs. 186, 203). Like many artists in France after the war, Matisse was following the *rappel à l'ordre*, the call to order, that pointedly revived interest in one of the great figures in the French tradition.

These drawings of Massine also strongly resemble a number of portrait drawings by Picasso from the late 1910s. Picasso, less secure as a foreign national than many of his French counterparts, had even anticipated the *rappel à l'ordre*, finding Ingres in his pencil as early as 1914. The diversification of Picasso's styles did not obligate him to abandon the avant-garde completely, however, and in 1917 he agreed to design the costumes and sets for Diaghilev's Ballets Russes production of *Parade*. Léonide Massine was the choreographer, and Picasso made some delicate pencil portraits of him in Rome in 1917 and in London in 1919. One wonders whether, during the work on *Le Chant du rossignol*, Massine showed Matisse one of the finely drawn heads Picasso had recently done of him. Was Matisse not already trying to keep step with the younger member of the pre-war avant-garde by turning his hand to stage and costume design in the first place?

★ ★ ★

Vieux camarades

It was a long time before Matisse again made a portrait of an artist peer. When he did, in 1940 and then again in 1952, he was also reaching back in time to his student experience, the all-important years in Moreau's studio, where he had made so many of the friends to whom he remained loyal throughout his life. Théodor Pallady and Simon Bussy were minor but moderately successful artists, and both were highly cultivated and cosmopolitan individuals with whom Matisse enjoyed conversation on a wide variety of topics. Again, there are no portraits of the truly strong painters of the time with whom Matisse had some contact – Bonnard, Masson, Picasso. Matisse preferred to express in portraiture relationships that were comfortable and self-confirming, and that had fixed parameters that did not challenge his own artistic concerns.

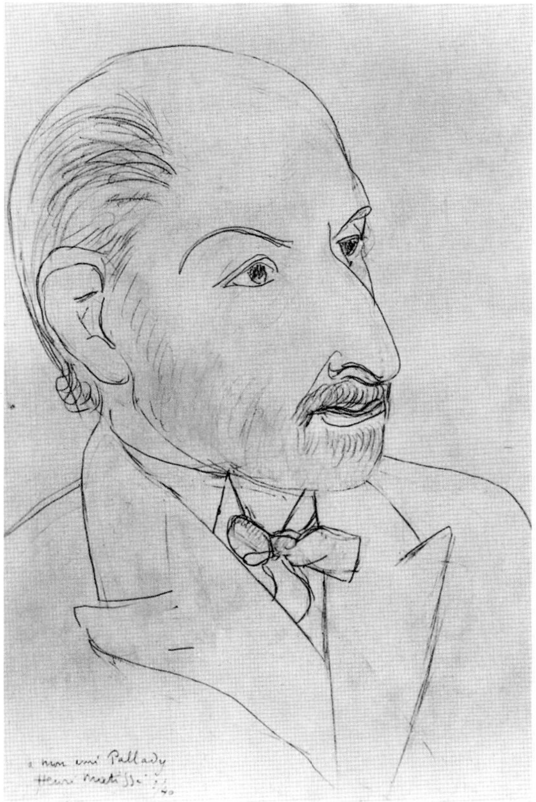

98 *The Painter Pallady*, 1940. Pencil on paper, dimensions unknown. Present location unknown.

Pallady was a Romanian who had come to Paris as a young man and attended the Ecole des Beaux-Arts from 1891 to 1900. He was a painter of landscape, still life, and the figure whose style was much influenced by Matisse. After his return to Romania in 1940 under the stress of the Second World War, he and Matisse carried on a substantial correspondence in which they discussed problems of painting.[57] Matisse especially seems to have used his letters to talk through his current work, sometimes including little sketches for precision. He complained of being misunderstood, confident that his friend would support him.[58] He probably made his well-known painting *The Rumanian Blouse* (1940; Paris, Musée National d'Art Moderne) with Pallady in mind. While Pallady was still in France Matisse made several portrait drawings of him in a variety of media (fig. 98).[59] They communicate the affinity each felt with the other. Carefully dressed, with a noble balding head and neatly trimmed beard, Pallady displays a well-kept appearance and alert countenance that were also distinctive characteristics of Matisse himself. In a difficult time both were defending themselves in the best way they could – with expressions of their civilized cultivation – now that war had returned to Europe. In a letter from later in 1940, during a dark time in France's history and self-image, Matisse wrote to Pallady of the "vague, collective anxiety, formulated by the misfortunes of all kinds that overwhelm everybody, I believe, without exception."[60] The earlier world war had generated a similar anxiety, but this time Matisse was not surrounded with a buffering community. With few exceptions he saw old friends infrequently now. So there were fewer portraits to mark such occasions.

Matisse turned for help more regularly to Simon Bussy, especially when the crises were personal. In 1903 he had written to Bussy to tell him of his poverty and to ask for help with the syndicate plan. When things were going badly with the Barnes murals in 1931, he appealed to his old friend to come and rescue him from his difficulties. Similarly, he confided to Bussy his troubles in 1934 in planning the illustrations for Joyce's *Ulysses*. Finally and most personally, Matisse depended on the Bussy household heavily during the 1930s for relief from the growing conflict between him and Amélie.[61] He called on Bussy because he could be sure that his friend would respond; many of his relationships seem to have operated in this way. Nicholas Watkins has aptly characterized the nature of Matisse's friendships with men: "His men friends tended to be divided between those whose talent, intelligence, and integrity he respected, and those whom he had known for most of his adult life and could call upon whenever he needed them."[62] Bussy may have been both.

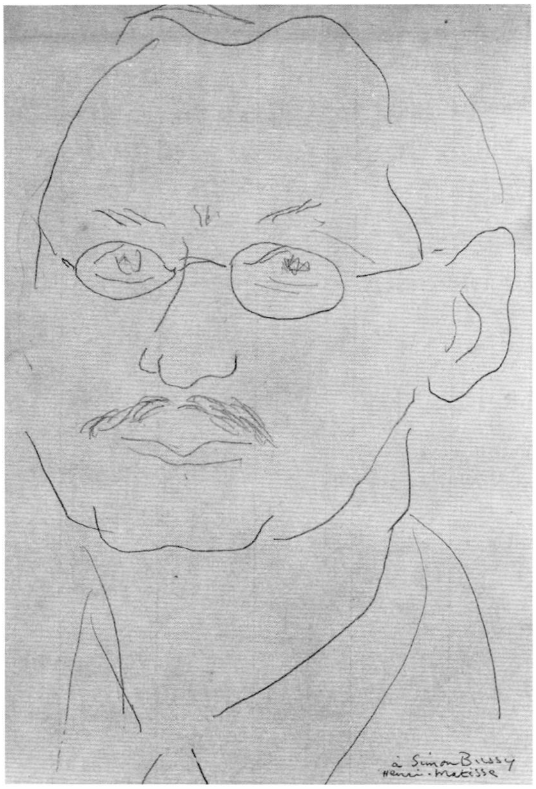

99 *Simon Bussy*, 1952. Pencil on paper, 22 × 15 cm. Present location unknown.

100 *André Rouveyre*, 1912. Charcoal on paper, 41 × 28 cm. Paris, Musée d'Art Moderne, Centre Georges Pompidou.

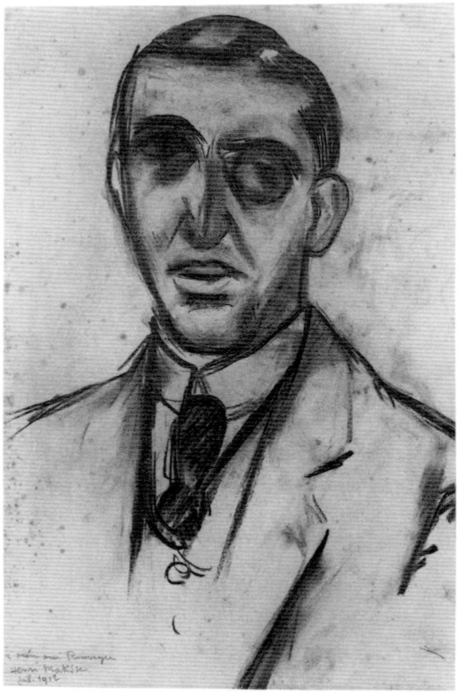

Matisse's pencil portrait of Bussy shows a serious man with no frills (fig. 99). Although his art had developed in an entirely different direction from Matisse's (he specialized in stylized, almost heraldic depictions of birds and reptiles), Bussy shared with Matisse the desire that in his work, "resemblance is detached from the accidental more cleanly, more precisely, more purely."[63] In his portrait Matisse seems to have stripped away some of the "accidental" features of age: this image does not look like a man of eighty-two years, as Bussy was in 1952 when Matisse made the portrait. Age and infirmity could be staved off, as Matisse thoroughly believed, by work. And, exaggerating to the young side, Matisse was recalling the younger man on whom he had depended so heavily so often.[64]

Literary homages

"To write you have to be a writer!" Matisse declared to Wassily Kandinsky in 1911 in response to a request that he contribute something to *Der Blaue Reiter*. And in 1934 he asked an interviewer with some exasperation: "What do you want me to say? A painter shouldn't have anything to say, his painting speaks for him."[65] Such demurral was a posture he maintained when he was satisfied that his art was reaching the audience he wanted to reach and he had no need to intervene with verbal gloss. Of course, Matisse was a writer, and his major theoretical statements, "Notes of a Painter" (1908) and "Notes of a Painter on his Drawing" (1939), were direct responses to perceived misunderstanding of his work by other writers. He wrote about what he had already done, to clarify, to explicate; only occasionally, as in *Jazz*, did he write as a parallel creative expression alongside his plastic and graphic art.[66]

Matisse became most involved with the world of books and writing in the 1940s, and it was at this time that his friendships with some of the leading authors of his day were strongest and most interesting. His contacts with the literary world were not always to his liking: he complained to his son Pierre in 1940 that the circle of writers around Simon Bussy was "quite a strange crowd to me . . . I cannot chat and be intimate in their circle in which one does not understand painting" (he also seems to have preferred one-on-one encounters in any case); but he had several rewarding friendships with authors.[67] His portraits of some of the poets and novelists he knew express the vital connections between the literary and artistic worlds in France, a link in tradition that Matisse was concerned to make in his own work in book illustration at this time.

The destination of his first portrait of a writer, decades earlier, set a precedent for many of his later depictions of authors. In 1912 he had made a few charcoal drawings of his old friend André Rouveyre, yet another cohort from the Moreau studio, for the frontispiece of a book devoted to the sitter. Rouveyre had sharp facial contours and wore a monocle, which might easily have lent his face to a caricatural treatment. But Matisse's rendering is straightforward and respectful (fig. 100). Heavily worked in the manner of the nearly contemporaneous portrait of Sergei Shchukin (see fig. 118), this drawing is a fitting homage despite the awkward arrangement of Rouveyre's eyes, which does not immediately force itself on the viewer's attention.

It is ironic that Matisse's sober tribute was not for a book about Rouveyre's literary accomplishments but for an account of his notorious career as a caricaturist. Until the First World War Rouveyre was a fierce parodist of the upper-crust social

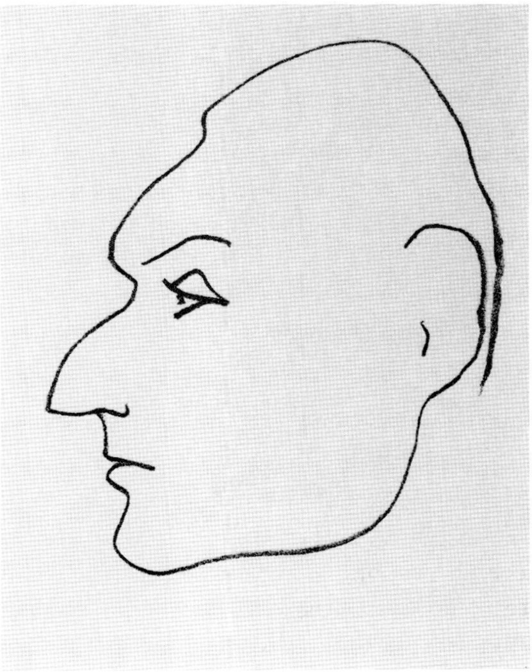

101 *Henry de Montherlant*, 1937. Lithograph, 19.2 × 16.7 cm. Private collection.

102 *Henry de Montherlant*, 1937. Charcoal on paper, 57 × 38.5 cm. Nice, Musée Matisse.

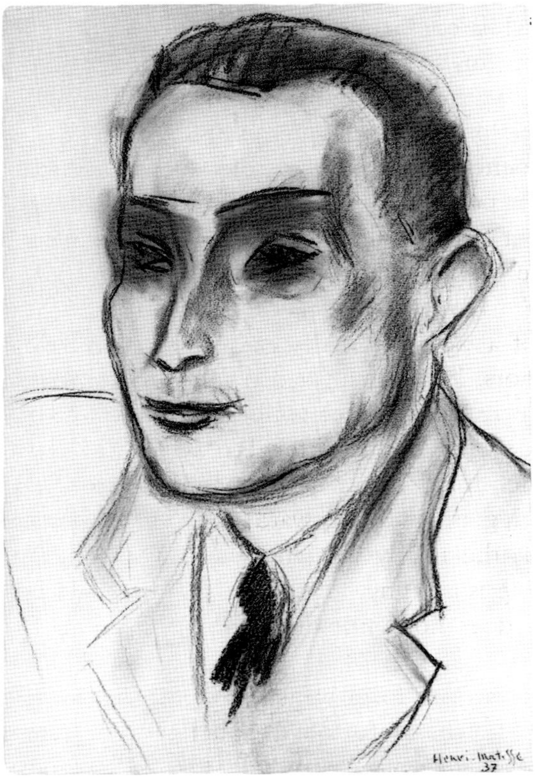

manners of the day.[68] In addition he was a world-class misogynist, as his book of drawings *La Gynécée* demonstrates liberally. His later writings were often in the same vein. He and Matisse maintained a close friendship, often largely by correspondence, throughout the last decades of Matisse's life.[69] Matisse also made several more groups of drawings of Rouveyre, grown fleshy with indulgence, in 1936 and 1944. In execution they lack completely the sharpness of the charcoal of 1912. Both parties had softened. For Rouveyre's novel *Repli*, published in 1947, Matisse made six lithographic portraits of the author, all in the same simple linear style to which he had become devoted in his prints.

In the same spirit of homage Matisse made a portrait, in profile, of the novelist and playwright Henry de Montherlant (fig. 101) for the cover of his short book *Sur les femmes*.[70] Montherlant was not one of Matisse's *amis fidèles* from the old days; they had first met in 1936 in Nice. Matisse admired Montherlant's work and later illustrated his meditative play on Minoan myths, *Pasiphaé*. *Sur les femmes* was only one expression – and a mild one – of Montherlant's sustained antipathy toward women. It may seem remarkable that Matisse, fabled lover of the female figure in his work and his life, should have maintained friendships with such misogynists as Rouveyre and Montherlant. But it is consistent with the less obvious expressions of dominance in his own work.

Matisse had also made some charcoal drawings of Montherlant in 1937 (fig. 102). At that time he spoke revealingly of the process of making these portraits:

> Interested by Montherlant's face, I asked him to pose for me, and during seven sessions I was able to make some drawings that were simply responses inspired by this face. An artist must be able to forget everything about the life and work of whoever poses for him. . . . The whole time Montherlant posed, my reading of his work, which I love, was far from my mind; I took into account only the original life in his expression in making his portrait. Our conversation was mainly commonplace. But we did talk about work – everyone who works as we do knows that it always goes this way. When Pasteur and Rodin met at a party, they understood that they had exactly the same discipline in their work.
>
> At the eighth session, it was impossible for me to see anything at all in Montherlant. I couldn't grasp him; he wasn't there. Today, I have in front of me another Montherlant, who is also unyielding. I have to stop after two wasted hours. Then I learned from him that at the carnival, he had had an experience that became for him, in his extreme imagination, a thing of the greatest importance and took over him completely. So I consoled myself about my lost session by thinking that since he creates out of his life, even a banal adventure would give us some beautiful pages.[71]

We note first Matisse's stated goal of mentally removing the sitter from the context of his life, and distancing himself from his knowledge of the author's work. This is done in order to isolate how the expression in the face reveals the essence of the self. This proves to be impossible – there are many Montherlants, some more accessible, more yielding than others. Matisse's charcoal drawing of Montherlant expresses some of this elusiveness in the vague features and the blank expression in the eyes. Smudging out and redrawing was insufficient in this case for Matisse to find the specificity of Montherlant's face. He did better in the lithographs for *Sur les femmes*, showing in each incisive profile a face of greater distinction. But one is left with the feeling that this was the easy way out, this reliance on the writer's distinctive hooked nose to confer identity on the portrait. Here Matisse

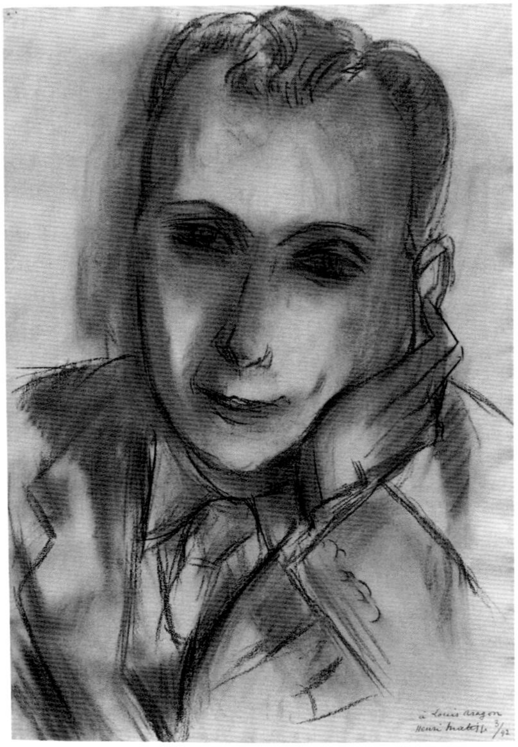

103 *Louis Aragon*, 1942. Charcoal on paper, 61 × 40.5 cm. Private collection.

104 *Paul Léautaud*, 1946. Lithograph, 21.7 × 13.9 cm. Private collection.

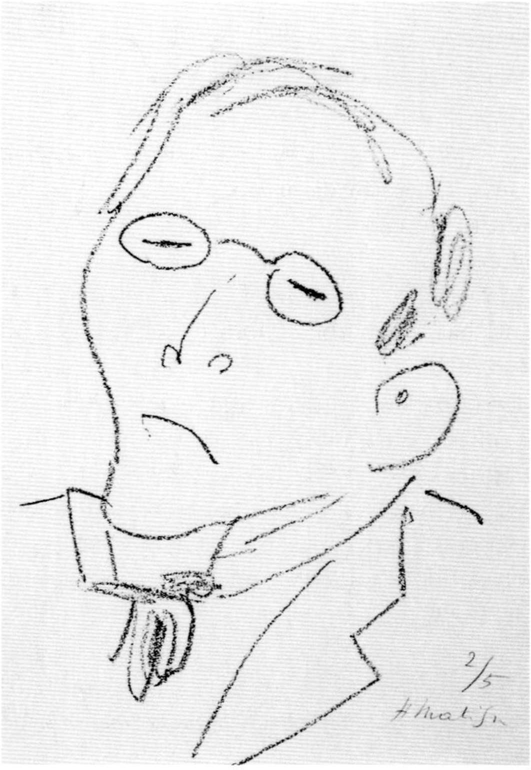

has settled for targeting a physiognomic feature, resorting, as he did so often, to the methods (if not here the spirit) of caricature, and forfeiting his stated goal of a more profound expression of interior life through his response to the sitter's face.

A related contradiction should also be remarked. Matisse's respect for professionalism is clear from his account of Montherlant's posing; indeed, their professional identities are what brought them together in the first place. Professional concerns are also the source of Matisse's exasperation in feeling unable to penetrate the spirit of someone who may be as preoccupied with his own affairs as he, Matisse, is with the task before him. The "real" Montherlant is not elusive; he is right there, caught up in the very process of defining himself through his work – hence Matisse's respect, for he too defines himself in this way. It is Matisse's oversimplified goal in such a portrait – to find in a person his or her one essential identity – that is vain.

Aragon and signs

Matisse may soon have realized the futility of fixing the identity of a complex person in a single drawing. In his portraits of the young writer Louis Aragon of 1942, he used the elaborate "theme and variations" method to do justice to the complexity of the sitter as well as the multiformity of the artist's response.[72] He had intensively exploited this procedure in the previous year, in series of drawings of still life motifs and studies of models, later published as *Dessins: Thèmes et variations*.[73] Aragon wrote a sympathetic preface to the album, "Matisse-en-France," in which he claimed the modernist artist for the great French traditions. Matisse's approach to the portraits of Aragon derive directly from the theme and variations project.

In one of several charcoal portraits (fig. 103), Matisse depicted Aragon with something of the bland, muffled quality of the charcoal drawings of Montherlant. In the pen and ink "variations," Aragon unfolds in the kind of "floraison" that Matisse felt characterized his drawing at this time.[74] When seen in series (fig. 105), these drawings express what he called the "cinema of my sensibility," as he also referred to his rapid procedure.[75] Changes of expression, pose, and gesture by Aragon animate his character through a remarkable range in demeanor, from aquiline suavity to rubbery goofiness (here Matisse could indulge in caricature without being limited by a single outcome). Aragon's accessibility and humanity come through in all of them, overcoming his sense of self-importance, which was considerable.

Nevertheless, the range expressed in these drawings may even exceed Aragon's own impressive complexity. Surrealist poet, realist novelist, essayist, and dedicated member of the French Communist Party as the editor of its weekly *Les Lettres françaises*, he was a prominent voice on the literary left. He wrote copiously on Matisse in a series of highly personal essays, collected under the telling title *Henri Matisse, roman*.[76] Where is the connection? What did Matisse and Aragon have in common? Matisse was studiously nonpolitical and was certainly not a Communist. Aragon was not notably a champion of modern art in general. The link is linguistic. Aragon, deeply concerned with the primacy of the word as the foundation not only of language but of thought, found a counterpart in Matisse and his development of the elements of visual shorthand he called plastic signs. Aragon approved immensely of Matisse's transcendence of detail by the sign, and he seems to have understood that they both wanted to augment their respective languages

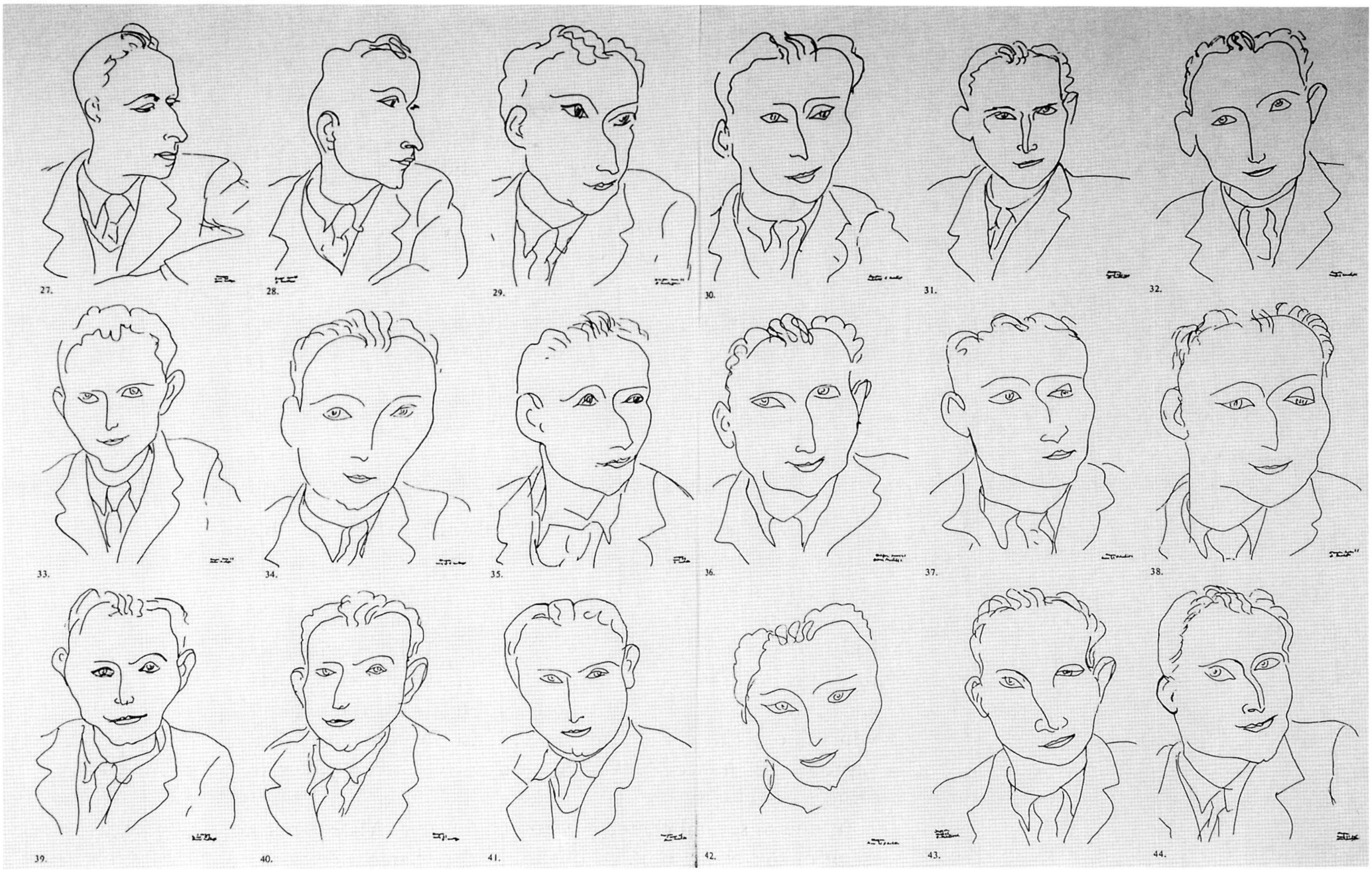

105 Portraits of Louis Aragon, 1942. Pen on paper, each approx. 53 × 40 cm. From Aragon, *Henri Matisse, roman*, 1971.

with personal signs by which they might respond consistently to the particularities of the world. In the drawings of Aragon, we have one of Matisse's most sustained efforts to apply the sign to the portrait. But as these brilliant drawings also demonstrate, the essence of a facial feature proved to be easier to signify in a single image than the complexity of a person's character.

Several other portraits of writers by Matisse deserve a brief consideration. Paul Léautaud was a journalist and essayist and had been the drama critic for various Paris literary journals. He had attained a reputation for sarcastic misanthropy in his writing as in his personal relations. In 1946 Rouveyre, who was preparing an edition of Léautaud's writings, asked Matisse to make a portrait of Léautaud for the book.[77] Several sittings took place in August 1946. Matisse gave the choleric sitter one of the charcoal drawings preparatory to the lithographs for the book. Léautaud promptly sold it, obviously realizing its value as a work by Matisse even though he himself thought it the product of the artist's "illusion, blindness, and aberration."[78] The twelve lithographs consistently express Matisse's sense of a pinched and dour presence before him (fig. 104). All of Léautaud's philistinism and narrowness is in these drawings. But significantly, in one thing at least Léautaud was in full accord with Matisse; the writer was also capable of saying: "Moi seul m'intéresse."[79] One egotist seems to have recognized another.

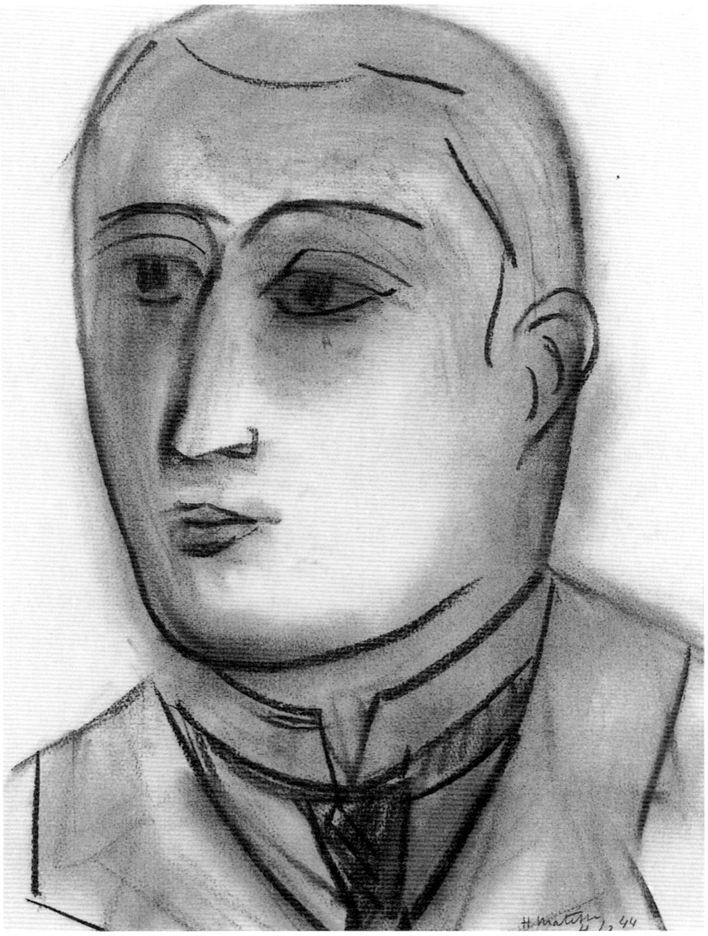

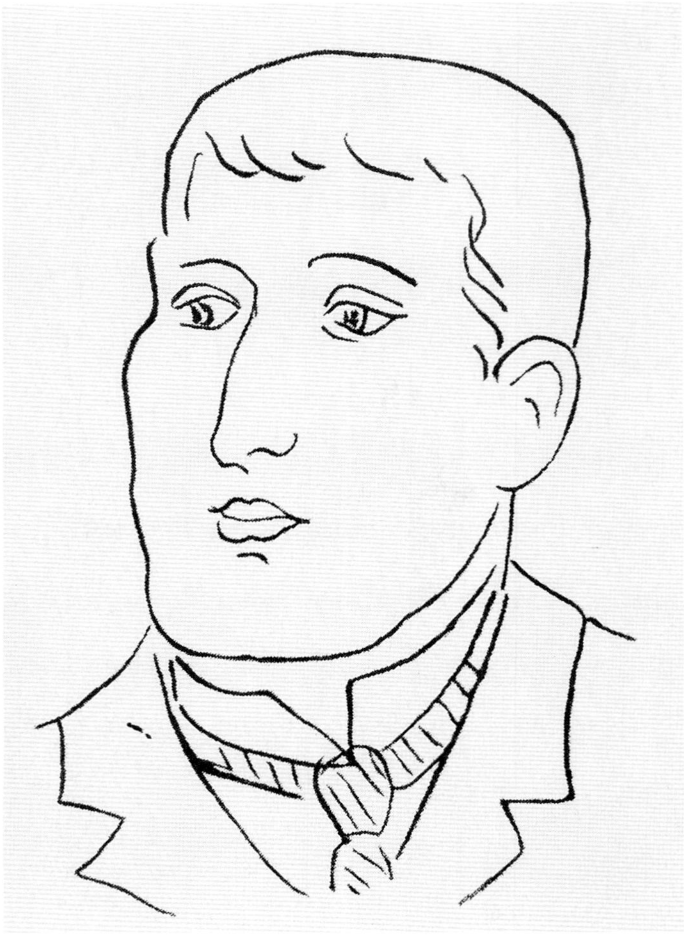

Portraits and immortality

One of the classic functions of portraiture is to fix for eternity an image of a living person: *ars longa, vita brevis*. There is also the portrait that revives the deceased, restoring life, and the portrait that turns back the clock, that rejuvenates. Concern with mortality and the continuity of the self had occasionally informed Matisse's attitude and procedure when making a portrait but, as we might expect, never so much as in his old age. This concern is especially reflected in some of his portraits of authors already dead – Poe, Baudelaire, Rabelais.

Among several such portraits, Matisse's homages to Guillaume Apollinaire stand out. Throughout the 1940s, Rouveyre as author and Matisse as illustrator collaborated on a book about the poet who had been their friend before the First World War, in which Apollinaire had been mortally wounded.[80] Apollinaire had been one of Matisse's earliest supporters in the press, and now Matisse could pay him homage in kind. For his charcoal "theme" portrait (fig. 106), Matisse relied on a small identity photograph of Apollinaire, taken about 1899 and supplied by Rouveyre.[81] Thus Matisse gave Apollinaire's youth back to him.[82] Six lithographic portraits derived from the charcoal were used in illustrating Rouveyre's book (fig. 107). They make the poet into an even nattier character than is figured in the charcoal drawing; and these products of line drawing distill the features of the writer in the way that by now had become standard procedure in Matisse's work.

108 (*right*) *Three Heads ("To Friendship")*, 1951–2. Aquatint, 43.6 × 34.8 cm. Le Cateau-Cambrésis, Musée Matisse.

106 (*facing page left*) Study for *Guillaume Apollinaire*, 1944. Charcoal on paper, 40.2 × 33 cm. Paris, Musée National d'Art Moderne, Centre Georges Pompidou.

107 (*facing page right*) *Guillaume Apollinaire*, 1944. From André Rouveyre, *Apollinaire*, 1952.

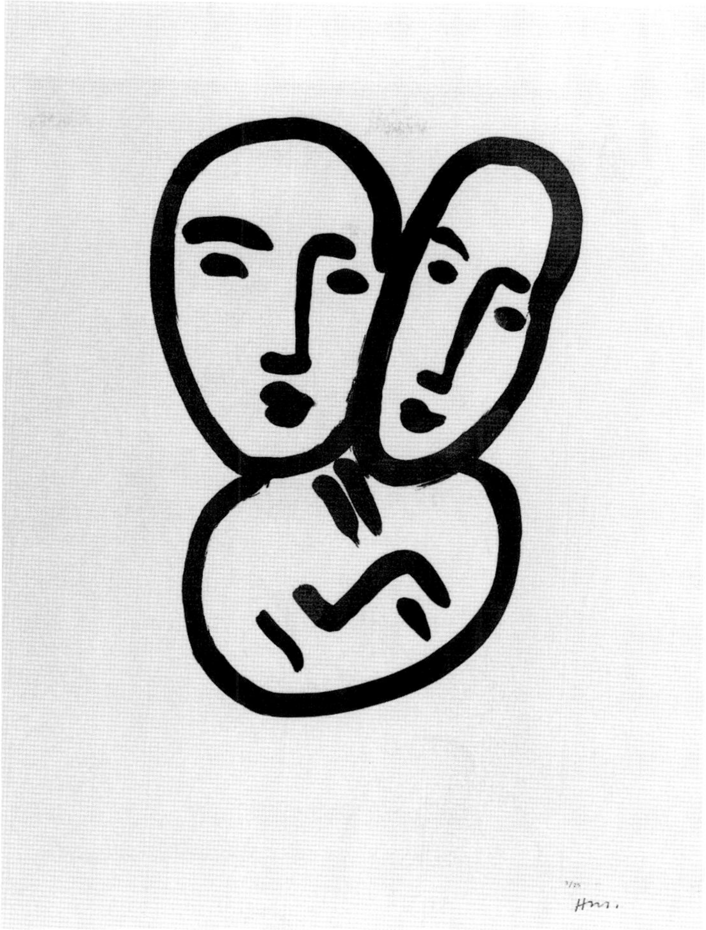

Still more reduced were the images he made for the frontispiece of the book. Matisse first made several linogravures of Rouveyre and Apollinaire; then, not wishing to leave himself out, in aquatint he made a series of triple portraits (fig. 108). Apollinaire, long dead; Rouveyre, who lived many years more; and Matisse, by then nearing the end – three old friends, each distilled by Matisse's brush to a mask, poignantly reunited in his art. Rarely has portraiture seemed less concrete, material, and specific; never more ethereal and haunting.

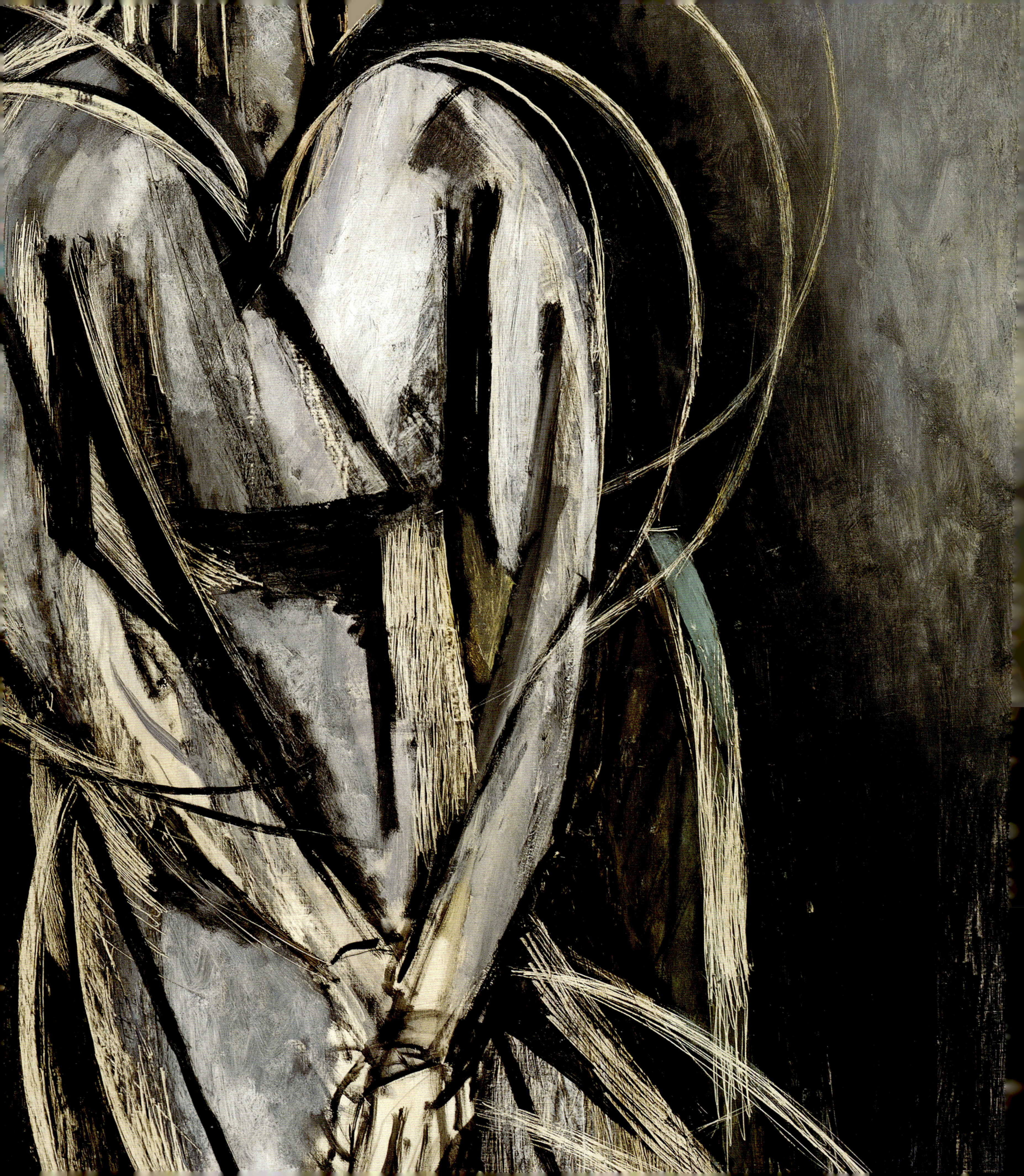

Chapter 5 Negotiating Identity

Unlike family members or sympathetic fellow artists, all with ready-made allegiances, portrait sitters with a more detached professional or social relationship to the artist implicitly make greater demands for themselves. This challenge to his autonomy was felt acutely by Matisse. In the transaction of portraits with strangers, or with other persons who have independent claims to personal and social identity, the artist needs to balance the desire of the sitter for an exemplary image, incorporating his or her own values, with the artist's own creative or expressive concerns. This class of transaction, in other words, cannot operate in one direction only. When imposing on a wife, daughter, or son for the service of sitting for a portrait, there is not necessarily any expectation of indebtedness – family members are constantly, fluidly in debt to one another, and no tally can or needs to be kept. Moreover, imbalance is built in when the family is governed by patriarchal prerogatives, as Matisse's family was. When asking another artist to sit, a sense of reciprocation should operate, but it may be only implied. Matisse paints Derain; Derain paints Matisse: they each get something and their common interest is strengthened. But even if the favor is not returned in kind, it could be, and the sense of shared purpose among like-minded artists may right any actual imbalance. It is certainly unrealistic to think that this is a matter of all for one and one for all, but nevertheless a collective atmosphere often disallows protocols of obligation. And, with family and friends, artistic license is more or less a given.

From private life to the public sphere

In the world beyond these close associations, whether the artist is drawn to a given portrait transaction for social reasons – the person's status matters – or artistic compulsion – something about the appearance of the person intrigues or attracts – the dialogic relationship between these sitters and the artist limits the artist's freedom of expression and changes the terms of engagement. Of course artists of the twentieth century responded to this structural abridgement of their freedom in various ways. Picasso, for example, made portraits but sometimes avoided personal confrontation, long trivial conversations, or the tedium of the actual process of posing a sitter by using photographs (with some notable exceptions, he also worked quickly with sitters, and he undertook very few commissions). Other artists disavowed portraiture in the public sphere altogether when the social cost of artistic freedom could be so high (Cézanne was probably one of these). Still others, such as Vuillard, Kees van Dongen, or Félix Vallotton, accepted and thrived on the society portrait as a natural outcome of success and a means to further their worldly ambitions.

Detail of fig. 122.

As we have seen, Matisse felt compelled to make art in a wide range of the traditional genres, even if he elided standard categories, as he ultimately did in portraiture. He embraced portraiture for a significant part of his career, and during the period of his greatest innovation. It is clear that he was attracted to faces and was interested in their peculiarities. This was not just a matter of finding a way to render interesting forms artistically. The human side of portraiture did not escape him, and the making of a portrait could be a gratifying social occasion. It seems that he welcomed the challenge of finding an area of satisfaction for both himself and his sitters, working within the sometimes narrow zone of mutual needs. He did not always meet this challenge, and sometimes one party or the other found themselves giving way. Matisse recognized the strong chance of such an outcome when making portraits either through his own initiative or on commission, and he often gave portraits a separate status when establishing terms with clients or dealers. He was also careful to protect his artistic concerns when entering into an agreement to make a portrait with someone over whom he had little influence other than as a function of his own reputation. The sitter was not merely a pretext for his artistic manipulations, but once he was engaged in the portrait his own concerns took precedence. This is shown in the arrangements he sometimes preferred when accepting a portrait commission, offering the client the right of first refusal, which gave him greater control over the process and at the same time allowed his sitters to reject the result with grace if it was not to their liking (which occurred a few times). Matisse often found things in his sitters that intrigued him and reflected his own interests, but these interests were not necessarily shared with the clients. He also used portraiture to express his own values by identifying something in the sitter's circumstances that he shared. And in terms of his general desire to work in the direction from analysis to synthesis, he sometimes made pairs of portraits to fulfill these larger artistic goals.

Portraits were also an important element in the public presentation of his work and the development of his reputation, but here too they were set apart from the rest of his production. When he signed his first contract with the Bernheim-Jeune Gallery in 1909, a conspicuous clause exempted direct portrait commissions from the financial arrangements with his new dealer, a clause maintained through four subsequent contracts over a period totalling fifteen years, ending in 1926.[1] This term of his contract acknowledged that portraits were not like other pictures, that their origin was not in the artist's desires alone but arose also from the wishes of another party. The exemption also had the effect of allowing Matisse to initiate portrait transactions without financial disadvantage, acknowledging a social component of portraiture that remained outside the business of being an artist. Portraits of friends and acquaintances were not amenable to negotiation through a dealer contract. This flexibility surely simplified the relationship between the artist and his sitters when producing a portrait, and left Matisse in a position of greater control over the outcome than if the commission had been engaged through the intermediary of his dealer. In other words, he remained free to use his own social and entrepreneurial skills in the building of his reputation and the fostering of his patronage, and he could make the artwork he wanted. He also evidently recognized that the portrait was problematic from the point of view of the market, its value not so easily determined as a landscape could be with a standard calculus of canvas area. His own prices for some private commissions – some well below, some above the contractual norms – bear out the portrait's anomalous status in the marketplace.

However they came about, the commissions entailed the greatest constraints on the artist, but they also led to some of Matisse's most memorable portraits, images that bear fully his mark and that also express significance in the sitter. This balance was hard to achieve. Eventually the difficulty was too great and there was no longer any need for special terms. But before he relinquished this social component of his art, he produced portraits that fully embody the challenges faced by an artist who wanted to reconcile the generic and the specific, the abstract and the concrete, the typical and the individual. This chapter addresses this more public side of Matisse's portraiture – portraits he created of and for patrons, potential patrons, or more casual, occasional clients. Together with Matisse's exhibition and publication of portraits, these works constitute the public sphere of Matisse's portrait practice.

The social transaction of portraiture

The values embodied in the family and in shared artistic concerns are not, it should be stressed, completely absent from the realm of Matisse's "public" patronage. In fact, these values inform the relationships between Matisse and some of the most important collectors of his work. Although with his own family the traditional unity of the family structure was threatened on several fronts – by the presence of an illegitimate daughter in the home, by the absence of the boys away at school, by Matisse's own travels, and his eventual departure from the family home – and eventually broken, by marital tensions, Matisse greatly admired the coherence of other people's families. He was also keenly interested in family resemblance and genetic legacy, as we have seen in his portraits of his own grandchildren, and he sometimes sought to apply these concepts to his portraits of people outside his family. The individual, though unique, can be generalized through these relationships, and Matisse sometimes found this to be a useful approach when making a portrait of someone who was a comparative stranger.

With regard to exhibition as a way of introducing his portraits to a wider public, this is not the place to compile an exhibition history of Matisse's portraits. But I do want to indicate how important the genre of portraiture was within his overall exhibition strategy. I shall return to this issue from time to time, at certain points in what might be called the social history of Matisse's artistic development and career path. The exhibition of his portraits, as much as his making them, reveals his awareness of the social dimension of portraiture, and his attitudes toward the class of people whose members have their portraits painted.

For the most part, however, this chapter will be concerned with specific portraits by Matisse and their sitters, and the class of people they make up. These include mainly collectors, art dealers, and members of the general system of art-world patronage. I have proposed to call these individuals class-equivalent sitters. By this term I mean individuals of social status comparable to the artist's. This equivalence is not necessarily expressed explicitly in the portrait. But what is always expressed is the area where the value systems of artist and sitter intersect or become aligned. Between any of these sitters and the artist there is no fixed axis of superiority and subordination. The category of fellow artistic creators studied in Chapter 4 overlaps to some degree with the group of sitters based on a concept of class identity, and many of Matisse's later portrait sitters in that area fall readily under the idea of class equivalence. Writers and musicians such as Louis Aragon and Eva

Mudocci were evidently respected by Matisse as his counterparts in other creative fields, and vice versa. For this reason, in the social context defined by portraiture, these individuals may be considered to be of the same class as Matisse – a class of individuals who conceive their class identity in terms of their creative acts and products. Hence my use of the term class equivalence to describe the relationship between individuals who may conceive their identities in different ways, but who can nevertheless lay claim to full-partner status in a process of mutual confirmation of values.

Here is what happens when an artist makes a portrait of a class-equivalent sitter. Two independent adults whose class identities allow them, even if they come from different walks of life, to relate more or less as equals within socially prescribed situations, come together, for whatever reason, for a transaction that results in a portrait. We might say that these independent individuals are known to each other, perhaps not (or not initially) as individuals, but by virtue of their individuality itself. So the equivalence I propose between such sitters and the artist is not exactly an equality between their social or economic positions (though it is usually related to these positions). It also cannot necessarily be accounted for by the reciprocity of friendship, but is based on a shared concept of identity. In an increasingly meritocratic modern society, an emphasis on ability and achievement rewards and affirms individuality. Thus a concept of shared identity between individuals in the modern world may be based on a sense of shared achievement; such a sense may supersede class identity. This recognition of ability has increasingly challenged class position as the determining social structure. The vitality of modern portraiture depends on it just as surely as portraiture in the *ancien régime* was bound to the court and its subsidiaries.

In the twentieth century this equivalence between artist and sitter holds true even in the case of portrait commissions when they are transacted with the most prominent artists. The traditional relationship of controlling patron to resentfully cooperative artist is completely transformed when the portraits of Matisse, Picasso, Kokoschka, Corinth, Modigliani, Munch, Giacometti, or Dix (and even – or perhaps especially – Giovanni Boldini, Giuseppe La Gandara, or Jacques-Emile Blanche), artists of this century who had a substantial output as portrait painters, are brought under consideration. Modern patrons who commissioned portraits often so strongly desired to act as benevolent champions of new ideas that they would forfeit the traditional satisfaction of flattery in favor of the cachet conferred by having initiated, through a portrait, a collaboration with a celebrated artist. To be recognized for sharing the values of such an artist could be a means both of confirming status and affirming the self.[2]

Challenging tradition

The event that assured Matisse's notoriety and subsequent fame was the public exhibition of a portrait. We have already seen the impact of the display of *Woman with the Hat* (see fig. 46) in the Salon d'Automne of 1905. Whatever discomfort Matisse may have suffered as a result of the public outcry was alleviated by the sale of the painting to the Steins, which led directly to most of Matisse's early patronage. But Matisse seems to have understood the significance of exhibiting the portrait even before the public saw it. That *Woman with the Hat* is a portrait is central to the meaning of Matisse's move – both to paint it and to exhibit it – in a way that no landscape painting could be. That it is, furthermore, a portrait of his wife invested the painting with personal resonance beyond the capacity of his portraits of other sitters. His project at this time in 1905 was to find a way to express his personal response to the object of his representation. He had spent the summer of that year making small landscape paintings and casual figure studies, some of Amélie, out of doors. By contrast, *Woman with the Hat* is a large, formal studio portrait, and it was the first portrait he exhibited. Thus its exhibition was an extraordinary step in several ways. It was a public declaration of the extent to which Matisse wished to invest his painting with his personal responses to the world, and to make it known that this was an essential component of his art. His disappointment at the critical reception was acute, personal, and a little petulant; he was "saddened . . . a great deal," he said, "for my things may not be very important but they have the merit of expressing my feelings in a very pure way."[3]

In exhibiting *Woman with the Hat*, Matisse also sought to identify himself with a more important genre, cloaked in heavier layers of history and significance, than landscape painting. Because he was so well versed in the art of the past, Matisse must have had a sense that he had raised the stakes in his decision to exhibit the portrait. He was, in fact, trying for more than a simple display of self-expression. In the context of tradition represented by portraiture, self-expression was a greater challenge, because it had to be mediated by convention. This mediating context, in turn, made his formal innovations more disturbing, as we have seen. Casting the traditional content of a genre in an original and personal form proved to be a greater trespass than sheer violation of formal norms without such a context of tradition, as in the relatively fluid and neutral genre of landscape painting.

Thus, through the portrait and its exhibition Matisse had not only taken on a genre deeply ingrained with social meaning, he had also used the occasion to assert the artist's freedom of self-expression. He did not stop there, either. There is no better way for an artist to make a public statement of the priority of the self than to exhibit a self-portrait, as Matisse did with *Self-Portrait in a Striped Jersey* (see fig. 90) in the Bernheim-Jeune exhibition "Portraits d'hommes" in 1907. As we have seen, several other artists also showed self-images in this exhibition, so we may discern a trend to self-display. The exhibition itself may also have been designed to elicit such reflections of and on the artistic process and artistic identity. But in addition Matisse was taking the logical course to complete a process begun with his exhibition of *Woman with the Hat*. With that painting he had made his first major public statement of self-assertion; *Self-Portrait in a Striped Jersey* was the definitive projection of his artistic identity into the public sphere.

The Steins and family values

In this self-portrait Matisse constructed himself as calm, tough, and self-sufficient. Yet like all artists of ambition he was dependent on the network of opportunity, promotion, and acclaim of the art world. And the flinty image was only one aspect of his self-projection at this time. In other, less exposed contexts, he welcomed the personal sympathy that sometimes went along with appreciation of his work. In this overlapping area between his public and private personas, none were more sympathetic than the American collectors, the Steins. As we have seen, members of the Stein family owned both *Woman with the Hat* and *Self-Portrait in a Striped Jersey*; the former, bought in 1905, was their first Matisse; with the latter, acquired by

1908, they added another important portrait to their growing collection of the artist's work. As a group the Steins – Gertrude, Leo, Michael, and Michael's wife Sarah – were among the most enthusiastic and perceptive collectors of modern art in Paris in the first decade of the century, and especially in the first years of their activity their judgments had a collective flavor. The patronage of each was vital to Matisse at one time or another, and Michael and Sarah Stein were lifelong supporters. Each member of the family eventually went his or her own way with regard to the artist's work, and in time Matisse and Gertrude Stein formed a pungent dislike for one another. But in the decade before the First World War, both the patronage and the friendship of this close-knit family of American expatriates was crucial to Matisse.[4]

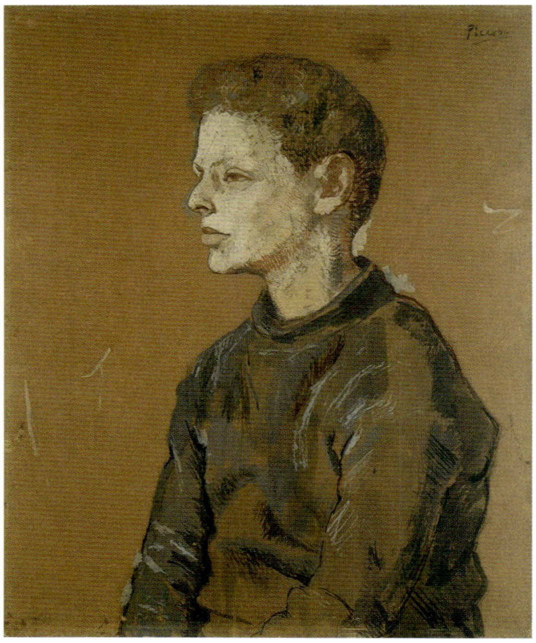

109 Pablo Picasso, *Allan Stein*, 1906. Gouache on cardboard, 74 × 59.7 cm. The Baltimore Museum of Art, The Cone Collection, formed by Dr. Claribel Cone and Miss Etta Cone of Baltimore, Maryland, BMA 1950.275.

It seems, in fact, that the Matisses and the Steins related strongly to each other as families, as well as friend to friend, artist to patron. It should not be surprising that Michael and Sarah Stein identified most strongly with the Matisses, as the two families clearly shared middle-class values: both couples were married and had children, for instance. Similarly, the more individualistic Gertrude and Leo Stein soon cast their lots with Picasso: all three were less conventional expatriates. Michael and Sarah Stein clearly liked Amélie Matisse (Gertrude just as clearly did not, but she showed Matisse's wife a grudging admiration), and although they had bought *Woman with the Hat* without knowing who the sitter was (Sarah Stein said that the portrait reminded her of her mother), it cannot be coincidental that they acquired, in short order, two more portraits of Amélie (see figs. 51, 52). Moreover, they bought several portraits of two of the Matisse children – at least two paintings and two sculptures. And we have already seen the amusing drawing of his own family that Matisse sent to Michael and Sarah's son Allan in 1906 (see fig. 56). With money and sympathy as well as through friendship, the Steins thus gathered a surrogate Matisse family in their apartment on the rue Madame.[5]

In the summer of 1907 Matisse and his wife spent a month in the flesh with the Steins at their villa in Fiesole, near Florence. One of the direct artistic results of this visit was his portrait of Allan Stein (fig. 110), probably painted in Collioure later that year. Among all the Steins, Allan seems to have been the object of Matisse's greatest affection. In addition to the family drawing Matisse sent him, at about the time he painted the boy's portrait he dedicated another drawing to him.[6]

Boy with a Butterfly Net (Allan Stein) is the largest and most impressive of the group of striking portraits of children Matisse painted from 1905 to 1909 (see figs. 64, 68, 87). The eleven-year-old boy is standing on a path leading through a hilly landscape, holding in his hands a butterfly net, as if he had been walking down the path and had stopped to survey his quarry. The intensity of the painting's Tuscan color scheme – dense blue sky, deep green for the hills, terracotta in the path – recalls the forceful color contrasts in some of Matisse's contemporary portraits, while the colors themselves and the pose of the figure against the landscape were echoed later by the saturated hues and indeterminate settings of the *Dance* and *Music* paintings of 1909–10.

110 (*facing page*) *Boy with a Butterfly Net (Allan Stein)*, 1907. Oil on canvas, 177.2 × 115.1 cm. The Minneapolis Institute of Arts, Ethel Morrison Van Derlip Fund.

The portrait is permeated by a solemnity that belies the image of a child at play. This gravity has been noted as a mark of Matisse's interest at this time in the painting of the early Italian Renaissance, which he studied that summer in Florence, Padua, and Arezzo, especially the work of Giotto, for whom he expressed keen admiration.[7] The impact of this Italian art on Matisse was a key factor in his shift of attention away from landscape toward the depiction of the human figure in the post-Fauve years. As a reaction against the ephemerality of his Fauve pictorial

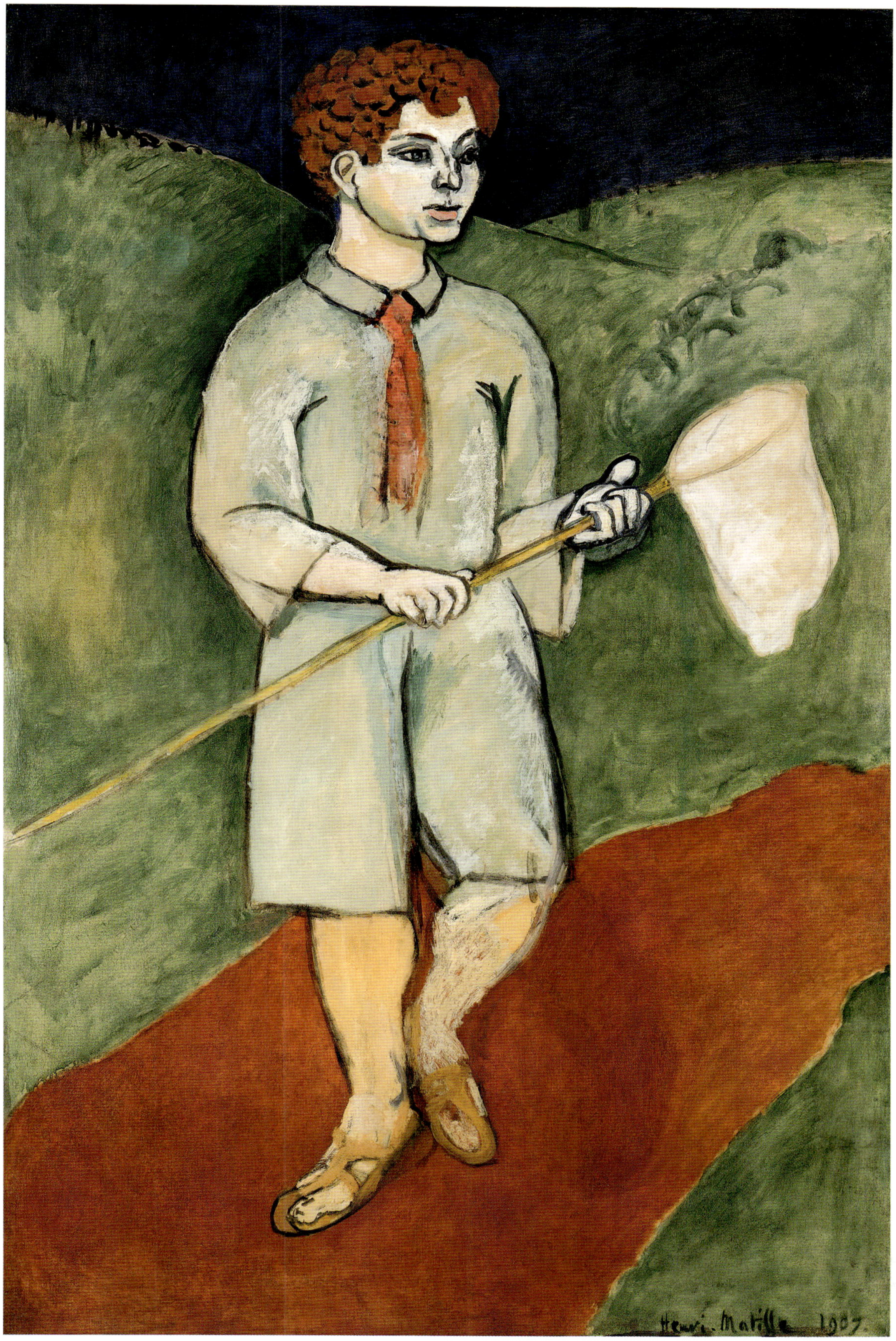
Henri-Matisse 1907

effects, he was also seeking the kind of stability and seriousness in his art that he found in the Italian painters.

The stylized features and awkward address of Allan Stein in the portrait also relate it to the generalized figure paintings Matisse made in these years, culminating in the ultimate ritual images of *Dance* and *Music*. This is especially clear when an earlier version on the canvas, as revealed in an x-ray photograph, is considered.[8] Originally Matisse had shown the boy walking along the path, resulting in a more dynamic twist of the body. But in that early rendition the face was more simplified, with an open mouth, smoother features, a straight nose, and smaller and more regular, almost almond-shaped eyes. In fact, this original face comes from the same family as the generic, mask-like faces in such figure compositions as *Le Luxe I* and *Le Luxe II*, or *Music (Sketch)*, begun at about the same time as Allan Stein's portrait. It has been suggested that the pose in the portrait derives from the enigmatic standing figure in the two versions of *Le Luxe*.[9] This may well be so; and a painting of a boy out to catch butterflies also has a thematic relationship to other compositions of stylized figures at play or leisure out of doors – the recent *Bathers* and the two versions of *Le Luxe*, as well as *Bathers with a Turtle* and *The Game of Bowls* (both 1908).[10]

I would go even farther and suggest that the portrait of Allan Stein was not originally conceived as a portrait but began life as one of these enigmatic figure paintings. Full length – rare for a portrait in Matisse's work – and over fifty percent larger than any other portrait by him up to this time, its size and scale accord well with these new types of imaginary figure compositions on which he had been focusing his energies. Probably, his developing relationship with the Steins then prompted Matisse to make the original generic features of a boy's face more specific in order to make a portrait of their son.[11] Was Matisse thus trying to ingratiate himself with the Steins? Very likely, but it may not have been necessary; they did not buy the portrait and remained loyal.[12] More importantly, if Matisse did transform one of his new figure compositions into this portrait, he may have been making an associative, if not causal, link between his experience in Italy and his relationship with the Steins, each a sponsor of new directions in his art.

Another triangulation was taking shape here, too – Matisse, the Steins, and Picasso. Picasso had painted a half-length portrait of Allan Stein in the previous year (fig. 109). In making his portrait of Allan Stein, Matisse may have responded to Picasso's own classicizing tendencies at this time.[13] It also seems that Allan Stein became one locus of the competitiveness that marked the relations between the two artists, especially where the Steins as patrons were concerned. This would make it all the more plausible that Matisse would change course in making this painting, transforming an existing composition into the portrait of the boy. Whatever its evolution, *Boy with a Butterfly Net* should be counted among the impressive large-scale figurative works he made in 1907–8. In these compositions Matisse made the definitive shifts from landscape to the human figure in his work, and from the desire for momentary effects to the satisfactions of solidity.

★ ★ ★

Greta Moll and Veronese's arms

It was Sarah Stein who in 1908 urged Matisse to open an art school, and to take on formally the role of a master.[14] He modeled his school on the independent academies in which he himself had received vital training and encouragement. Once again the Steins functioned as Matisse's patrons, putting up finance for the venture. Although their patronage was in the process of being overtaken by the greater resources of the Russians Shchukin and Morosov, Michael and Sarah Stein were still making important purchases, and they were still bringing new collectors, such as Claribel and Etta Cone, to the cause of Matisse's work.

Among the original students in Matisse's school were the Germans Oskar and Margareta Moll. He was a painter, she was a sculptor; Matisse taught in both media. Greta Moll had been a student of Lovis Corinth in Berlin, and the famous German artist had painted her portrait the previous year (fig. 111). Shown a photograph of this portrait, Matisse declared his dislike of it, saying that Corinth had not evoked her youthfulness (she was then twenty-three years old), and offered to paint her portrait himself (fig. 113). Thus again Matisse's competitiveness with another (though very different) artist led to a major portrait. Matisse and the Molls settled on a price of 1000 francs – a little on the low side of Matisse's scale – and also agreed that if the Molls did not like the result, Matisse would keep the painting.[15] By picking up the gauntlet of Corinth's painting Matisse got his first portrait commission. With it he initiated the arrangement of the patron's right of first refusal that he often followed thereafter. His preference for these kinds of terms indicate two things. He was aware that his work was not to everyone's liking, and that it might be prudent to offer an inducement to purchase. He was also just as happy to keep such a work as to sell it, seeing that he was arranging things so that he could paint it on his own terms, and offer it at a price well below market value.[16] Furthermore, in the Molls' case, as in others where collectors were concerned, Matisse may have had the dual goals of painting a challenging picture and gaining access to potentially important patrons. Indeed, Oskar and Greta Moll went on to build the finest collection of Matisse's work in Germany.[17]

Moll sat long and patiently for her portrait. Her account of its progress is one of the most valuable reports on Matisse's working method:

> For the portrait I sat ten times, three hours each. When I came for the eleventh time it was finished. At first we tried out various things: with the white blouse and the large patterned blue-white cloth, "ça prend une grandeur merveilleuse" he assured me. He then told me that he was placing the canvas so that I could not watch him, since he wanted to show me the picture only at the end. . . . Although I could not see the picture I watched his palette and since I knew what he was painting I found it very interesting to watch how always when he altered one color he felt forced to change the whole color scheme. The blouse which ended up greenish was at one time lavender-white. Even the black skirt was once colored yellow or greenish. . . .

The "patterned blue-white cloth" was Matisse's length of *toile de Jouy*, a large-figured French fabric that was a stock prop in many of his paintings, usually still lifes. This fabric re-oriented his approach to the portrait. Then at the end Matisse did an extraordinary thing to the image. Only after the tenth sitting, Moll continued,

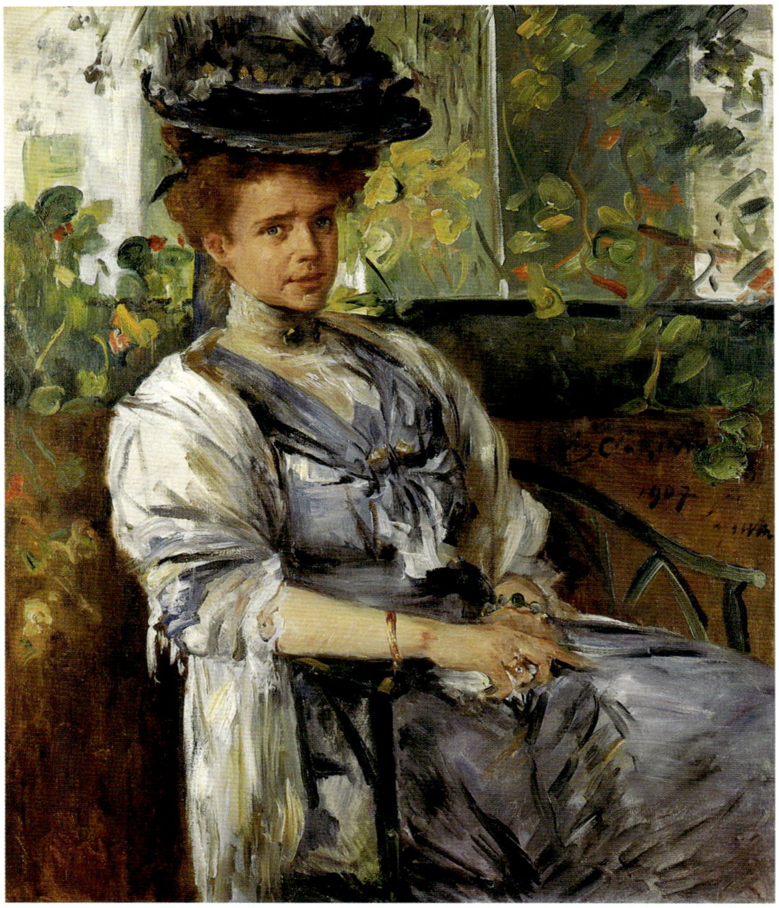

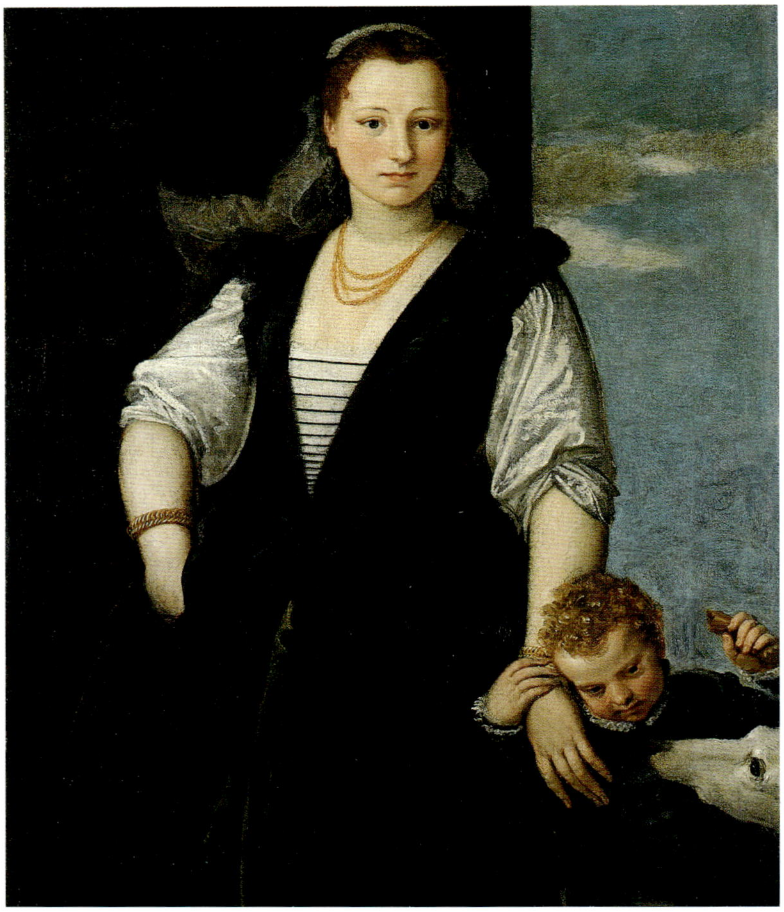

111 (*above left*) Lovis Corinth, *Greta Moll*, 1907. Oil on canvas, 120 × 100 cm. Darmstadt, Hessisches Landesmuseum.

112 (*above right*) Paolo Veronese, *Woman and Child with a Dog*, 1565–70. Oil on canvas, 115 × 95 cm. Paris, Musée du Louvre.

113 *Greta Moll*, 1908. Oil on canvas, 92.7 × 73 cm. London, The National Gallery.

did it receive its final vigor and form. Matisse was not satisfied. For consolation and to receive new inspiration he went to the Louvre and we had a few days' rest. There he found the Veronese portrait (not with a white blouse, that is not true). But the lady had her arms in front of her the same way I did, though her arms were rather full and round. He took them over for my portrait so that as usual he had to change the entire picture. . . .[18]

We note two things from Moll's account: first, whenever Matisse changed one part of the painting, he changed all parts in the effort to achieve an all-over decoration. Second, he found his way out of a pictorial dilemma by studying a distinguished Renaissance painting, delighting in the robust forearms of the woman in the Veronese portrait. Returning to his canvas, and in the absence of his sitter, he changed all the other parts again to achieve the harmony he sought, a harmony having little to do with the appearance of the sitter. Greta Moll witnessed the central struggle Matisse faced in his portraiture, his effort to reconcile incompatible goals: at once to paint his sitter in a sympathetic way that expressed an inner truth; and to consider all parts of his painting in concert, so that nothing stood out. This required a solution outside the picture and outside his sitter, a solution he found in other art. Having appropriated something from Veronese, and from the forms and pose of the beautiful Venetian sitter, he then had to make these elements thoroughly his own.

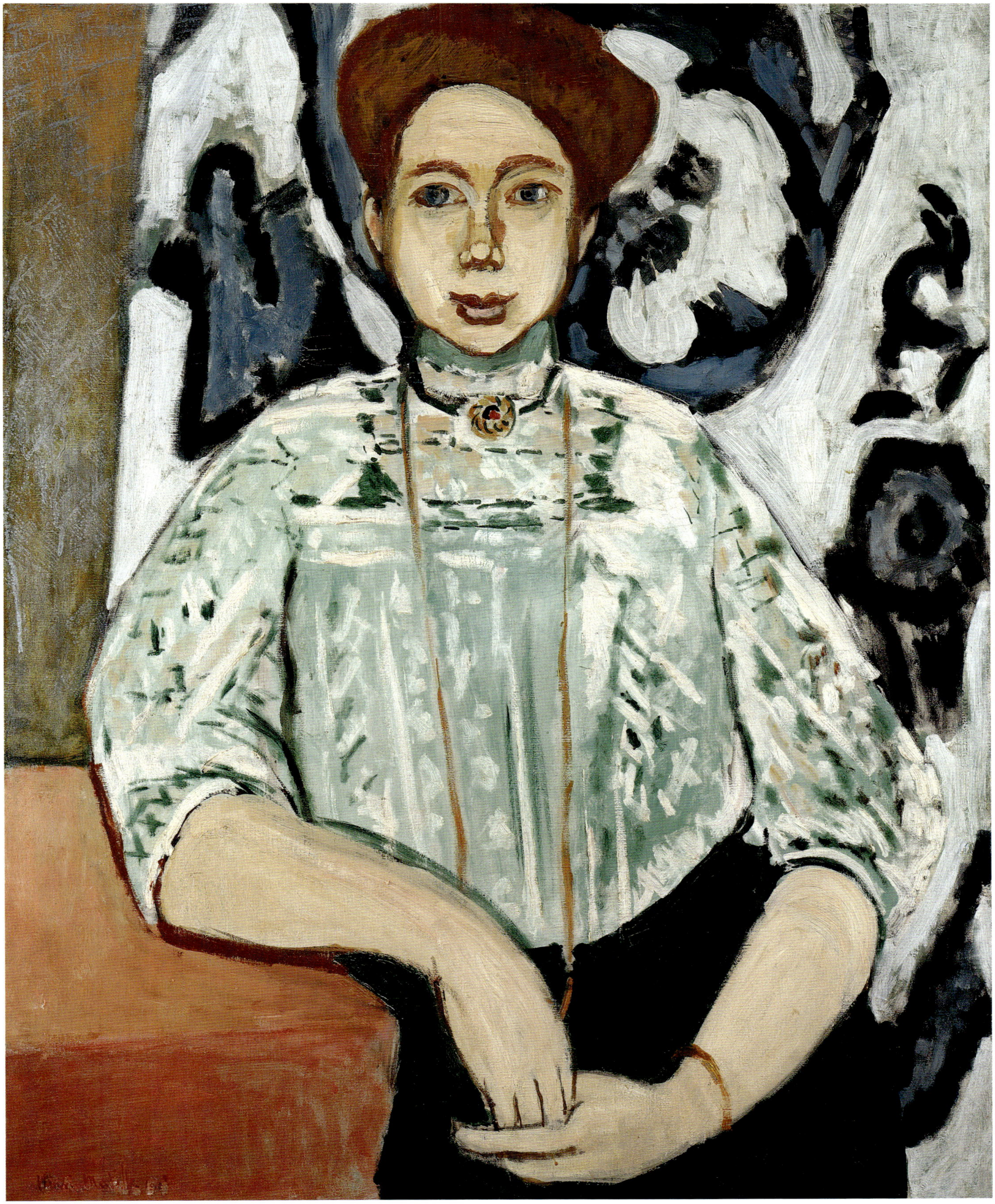

Another, less familiar report of Matisse painting the *Greta Moll* was given by Hans Purrmann:

> [Matisse's] relation to old masters was alive in a most peculiar way. He once painted the portrait of a German lady. During the sittings he wanted to know everything: how she judged herself, what head shape, placement of the eyes, what colors, clothing and fashions she considered suitable and chose for herself. The picture was excellent in its first state, and then moved on to a second, uncertain, over-painted state – a procession which repeats itself almost regularly with every painter in this form. Before the painting came into the third, final state, of which he said that only few painters reached it because most of them are satisfied with the first state, he went to the Louvre to get advice and courage from the old masters. He found there a portrait by Veronese of a blond woman in a white dress with too small a head but voluptuous body forms and light reddish skin color, everything exactly like his model. After thoroughly studying this painting he hurried back to his studio and painted this time from memory like obsessed, and united his painting into an expressive unity, put down his paintbrushes and nobody – not even the disappointed lady who commissioned the painting and who sorrowfully looked back to the first version, which was more amiable and had more portrait likeness – could persuade Matisse to change one stroke. For him the painting was finished and the subject closed.[19]

The account makes it clear that Matisse was more interested in his picture than in the portrait. Purrmann characterizes a three-stage process that may be likened to a procedure of description ("more portrait likeness"); analysis ("uncertain, overpainted"); and finally synthesis ("expressive unity"). These are terms that Matisse himself might have used generally of the process of painting from the motif. Matisse's careful inquiries of Moll, as described by Purrmann, were intended more to put the sitter at ease and to establish a dialogue than to elicit crucial information about her that could then be given pictorial expression. The ostensible effort to learn more about her was also perhaps a form of distraction from the truth of the changes he was making in her image. Even with this knowledge, he did not have everything he needed there before him, or in him: his visit to the Louvre gave him an inspiration and a brutal solution to a dilemma, the conflict between picture and portrait. And yet finally the contradiction between the all-over unity Matisse sought and his quotation from a Renaissance painting points up the impossibility of his quest when faced with the specificity and substance of a class-equivalent sitter such as Greta Moll. He could not have it both ways; a gorgeous, limpidly painted result – which this painting emphatically is – does not necessarily solve the problem of representing a sitter's identity when the artist's real goals differ so clearly from his stated intentions.

Matisse himself said of the painting's state before the final *dénouement*:

> Despite my efforts I had not gotten beyond the charming features which were not lacking in my model, but I had not been able to capture her statuesque quality. I was nearly completely discouraged about it, but I knew about a portrait of similar character that already existed. It was to be found in the Louvre, in the long gallery along the Seine, and was signed Veronese. In it you could see the same development of the body of an Italian girl on the verge of blossoming in all her beauty. The proportions of the model were very like those of Mme O. Moll. So I decided to make a special trip to the Louvre to see the Veronese

again. It penetrated me with its clarity, which had remained firmly in my mind, and without letting myself be distracted by other paintings I hurried to my studio at the convent. I remember that it was about 5 or 7 o'clock in the evening and that I locked myself in so I wouldn't be disturbed. Under the force of the revelation of the Veronese I took up my portrait again. Throwing caution to the winds, I worked on it an hour, maybe two, then I felt that I had done my very best. The next day when Mme O. Moll came back to pose I told her that her portrait was finished and she was overwhelmed by the result and asked me if she could go get her husband. I saw them completely dumbfounded in front of the result of my work, which seemed to them a disaster. They missed all the blond curls and the varied colors of the portrait. After I reminded them of one of the conditions of our agreement I told them that they were not obligated to take it and I left them. Only the following day they told me via our mutual friend Hans Purrmann that they would take it. This portrait was later very much admired, even by them, and I said to myself once more that Bonnard was right to declare that a portrait always ends up being a likeness.[20]

If anything, Matisse's account makes the "revelation" of the Veronese portrait more dramatic than Moll's and Purrmann's do. It also reveals his satisfaction at his solution and the eventually favorable reception of his artistry.

The painting in the Louvre that inspired Matisse to finish his own picture was Veronese's *Woman and Child with a Dog* (fig. 112).[21] The informal spirit in the Veronese portrait lent itself naturally to Matisse's conception of Greta Moll in a standing, hipshot pose; conversely, Matisse said that he wanted to give the portrait of his student the same "grandeur" he found in the Veronese.[22] But the arms of Veronese's unnamed sitter were the key – generous, richly modeled arms that Matisse translated into thick undifferentiated tubes, "like rolls of clay," that link together in a pattern as assertive as the *toile de Jouy* that dominates the background of the portrait.[23] Matisse had taught his students, Greta Moll among them, that "an arm is always first of all a round form, whatever its shades of particular character."[24] In other words, he emphasized the typical over the specific in this limb, in keeping with his tendency to generalization. Even so, appropriating the arms of Veronese's sitter compelled Matisse to overhaul his entire painting. Perhaps it is no coincidence that Cézanne apparently felt the same way about the all-over unity of a portrait, and similarly went to the Louvre to gain distance from his task when he was painting his portrait of Ambroise Vollard, a tactic Matisse cited with approval.[25]

Matisse thought highly of the portrait and believed that it represented his effort well at that time, because on two occasions he gave it a prominent role in the public presentation of his work. *Greta Moll* was entered as *Portrait de Mme M . . .* among his entries in the Salon d'Automne of 1908. More significantly, Matisse chose the picture as one of six illustrations – one of two portraits, and the more recent one – to his theoretical exposition "Notes of a Painter," published in the widely read *Grande Revue* in late 1908. All six illustrated works were figure paintings, exemplifying Matisse's emphasis on the figure in his essay. Moll and the "Notes" were deeply connected: she translated Matisse's article for publication in Germany in 1909; and her accounts of how Matisse painted her portrait describe exactly the concept and the goal of decoration that Matisse attempted to put across in this explanation of the new direction in his work.[26]

A comparison with the way Picasso finished his portrait of Gertrude Stein (see fig. 53) is revealing. Other art helped Picasso, too, to complete his portrait, but whereas Picasso's imposition of its forms produced a definitive result, for Matisse the introduction of the outside elements was only a prelude to a more thoroughgoing solution, albeit one achieved rapidly. Significantly, also, Picasso's source – the African and ancient Iberian sculpture to which he had recently become attracted – was outside the Western tradition and in a different medium. Matisse's, by contrast, was firmly in the heart of Italian Renaissance portrait painting. Picasso the outsider and *bricoleur*; Matisse the great synthesizer, respecting tradition: in each portrait is summed up a key methodological strength of its maker.

Yet the solution each found to the problem of their portraits reveals their own concerns and expresses their own experiences and desires more than those of their sitters. Both artists expressed their satisfaction through statements claiming victory for the portraits over their sitters: Picasso saying "Everybody thinks [Stein] is not at all like her portrait," but "never mind, in the end she will manage to look just like it"; and Matisse similarly asserting that "a portrait always ends up being a likeness."[27] Picasso created the more forceful and memorable image of his sitter, which he correctly predicted would represent Gertrude Stein long after she was gone. Matisse created the more beautiful picture, a graceful and serene composition that nevertheless subsumes its sitter within the grander overall conception, as the artist intended.

Portrait and pattern

Greta Moll, as the sitter herself well recognized, suppressed her identity within Matisse's self-expressive composition. Another portrait of 1908 that displays in full Matisse's decorative impulse at this time is *The Girl with Green Eyes* (fig. 114).[28] Its rigid structure makes for a striking contrast with the considered casualness and serpentine lines of the portrait of Greta Moll, but this painting too is all about the play between volumes and surface pattern, here arrayed into distinct and well-ordered zones. *The Girl with Green Eyes* presents a dazzling mixture of patterns and colors – the woman wears a turquoise, violet, and ocher hat and a vivid red tunic with a Chinese design, and her face is marked by deep red lips and riveting blue (not green!) eyes. She stands against a mantelpiece draped with several printed fabrics and laden with objects; behind these are more patterns of bold hues. East and West mix freely in a cultural bazaar characteristic of Matisse's catholic attitude to useful sources of motifs and approaches to decoration. This attraction to bold patterning surfaced again a few years later in the dizzying clashes of carpets and fabrics in *The Painter's Family* (see fig. 59), a painting that similarly engulfs its protagonists in powerful currents of decorative exuberance.

The woman in *The Girl with Green Eyes* has not been identified; she may have been a friend of Harriet Lane Levy, who bought the portrait soon after it was finished.[29] The equivalence Matisse proposes between the woman's irregularly framed face and the patterned vessels and sculpture behind her is striking. Her collar is like a pedestal on which rests a work of sculpture, to be compared with the plaster cast of a river god from the Parthenon pediment; alternatively, we are invited to see the collar as the footing of a vessel that takes its place with the ceramic vases displayed alongside. These formal analogies and elisions of space are characteristic of many paintings by Matisse at this time, especially the large interiors and still lifes in which he juxtaposed brightly patterned fabrics or carpets

114 *The Girl with Green Eyes*, 1908. Oil on canvas, 66 × 50.8 cm. San Francisco Museum of Modern Art. Bequest of Harriet Lane Levy.

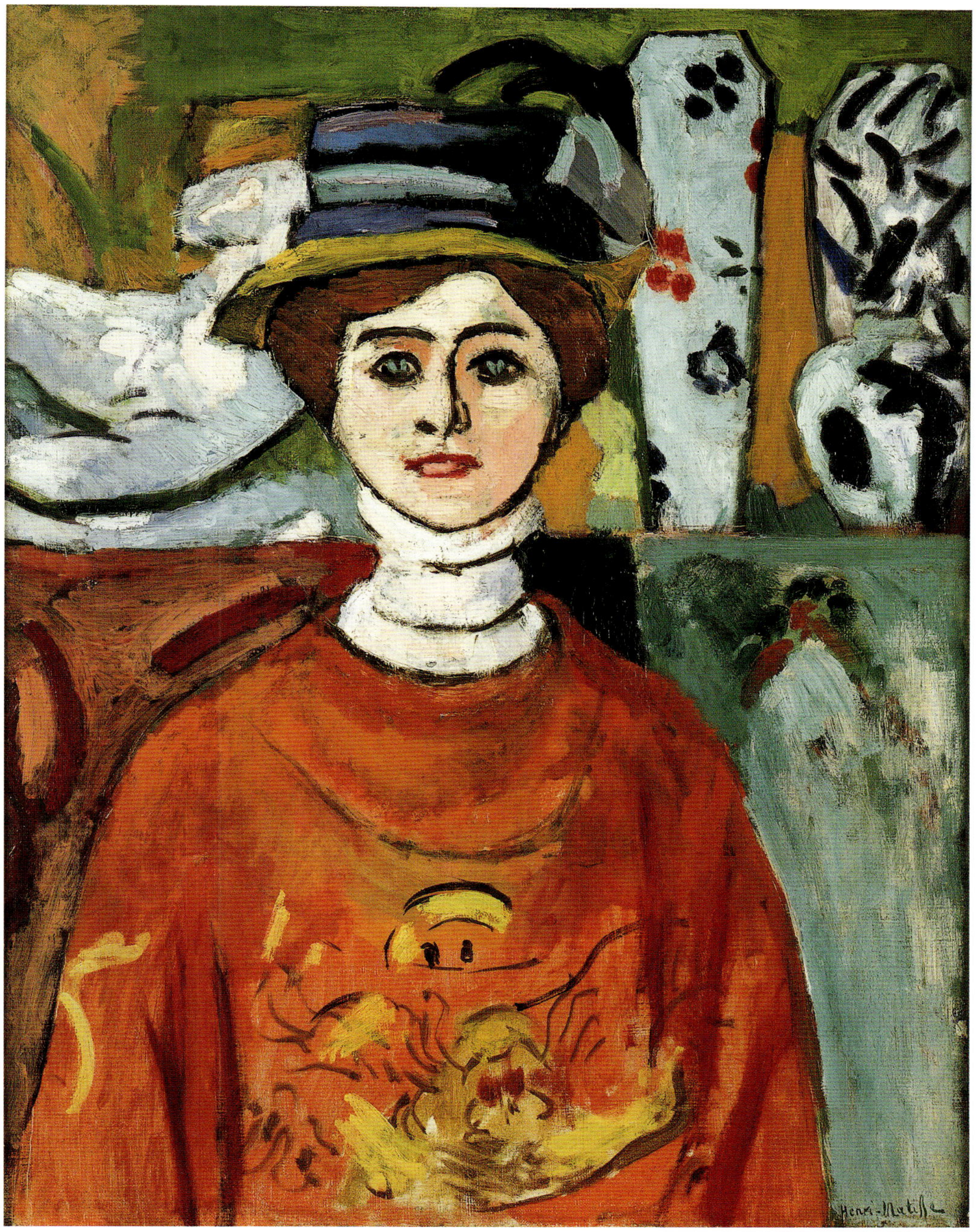

with his own sculpture, to explore the decorative possibilities in such mixtures of the flat and the volumetric.

Like *Greta Moll*, *The Girl with Green Eyes* represented Matisse's most advanced work in the realm of decorative painting, and he exhibited it three times within two years of making it.[30] When it was shown in London in 1910 an English critic, C. J. Holmes, recognized the provisional temper of Matisse's explorations, his "experiment in simplification." Sniffing at the "cleverness" of Matisse's "performance," Holmes suggested that "such experiments will be precious to their maker if from them he can learn how to build up a method of expression more complete," showing "the power which unites isolated things into a significant and harmonious design." This was Matisse's intent: one man's harmony is another man's chaos. For Holmes, Matisse had made a "noisy poster" with "common outward effectiveness."[31] In a more restrained sense, Holmes was exactly right. The painting is clever and self-conscious about forcing the issue of decoration in the context of a portrait among diverse objects, a conceit Matisse did not use again until the portrait of the Baroness Gourgaud over fifteen years later (see fig. 188), in the ebb of his portrait practice.

Themes of process and growth

But as the simplified portraits of his children Marguerite and Pierre from this time (see figs. 64, 68) make clear, Matisse did not confine his experiments in portraiture to essays in allover decoration. His treatment of each sitter was individualized, if not apparently tailored to the individual in question. In contrast to the environmental specificity of *The Girl with Green Eyes* and the decorative lushness of *Greta Moll*, Matisse's *Olga Merson* (fig. 115) is restrained and even austere.[32] Merson was a young Russian woman who had entered Matisse's school in 1908. By the time he painted the portrait in Collioure in 1911, the artist and his student were having an affair.[33] Thus there may have been several reasons that the portrait is not a graceful picture. Matisse has presented Merson as a seated figure, but we cannot see what she is sitting on so her body seems at first to hover uncertainly in space. However, conditions within the picture itself firmly control her position. The composition fixes her within the complementary opposition of the two zones of background color. Her elbows bend precisely at the junction of these background planes, suggesting a further interlocking of bodily position with compositional structure. Pentimenti indicate that Matisse had altered her contours significantly, finally making her image smaller. Seated demurely, hands clasped on her lap, this figure would project an unexceptional persona were it not for the way she fixes us disturbingly with the one eye that was not obscured when Matisse scraped away the paint on half her face, leaving it scarred and incomplete. He then applied slashes of black paint, cutting across the reduced but otherwise self-contained body, giving it an arbitrary extension into the surrounding space but also pinning the figure definitively in two dimensions. The way Matisse has structured the formal elements of the painting so that they take control of the sitter forcefully illustrates the tension between pictorial and human needs in his portraits.[34]

We have already seen how prominent the theme of growth and development was in Matisse's portraits of children. It also seems that he wished to advance such ideas into a larger arena by using portraits of adults to explore a more general expression of change over time. In the portrait of Olga Merson the changes expressed were partly those made in the process itself of painting the portrait. Despite the clear visual differences between this painting and his portrait of Greta Moll, perhaps here too in his portrait of one of his students Matisse felt he had a sitter who would be sympathetic – or at least acquiescent – to his experiments.

The bold black arcs, which Alfred Barr timidly characterized as gestures of "impatience" and "dissatisfaction," are more than mere arbitrary formal devices with which Matisse finished off the portrait.[35] In these scything strokes may be inferred the tension and perhaps the passion that went with Matisse's liaison, terminated, it is said, when Amélie Matisse threw the young woman out in a display of passion

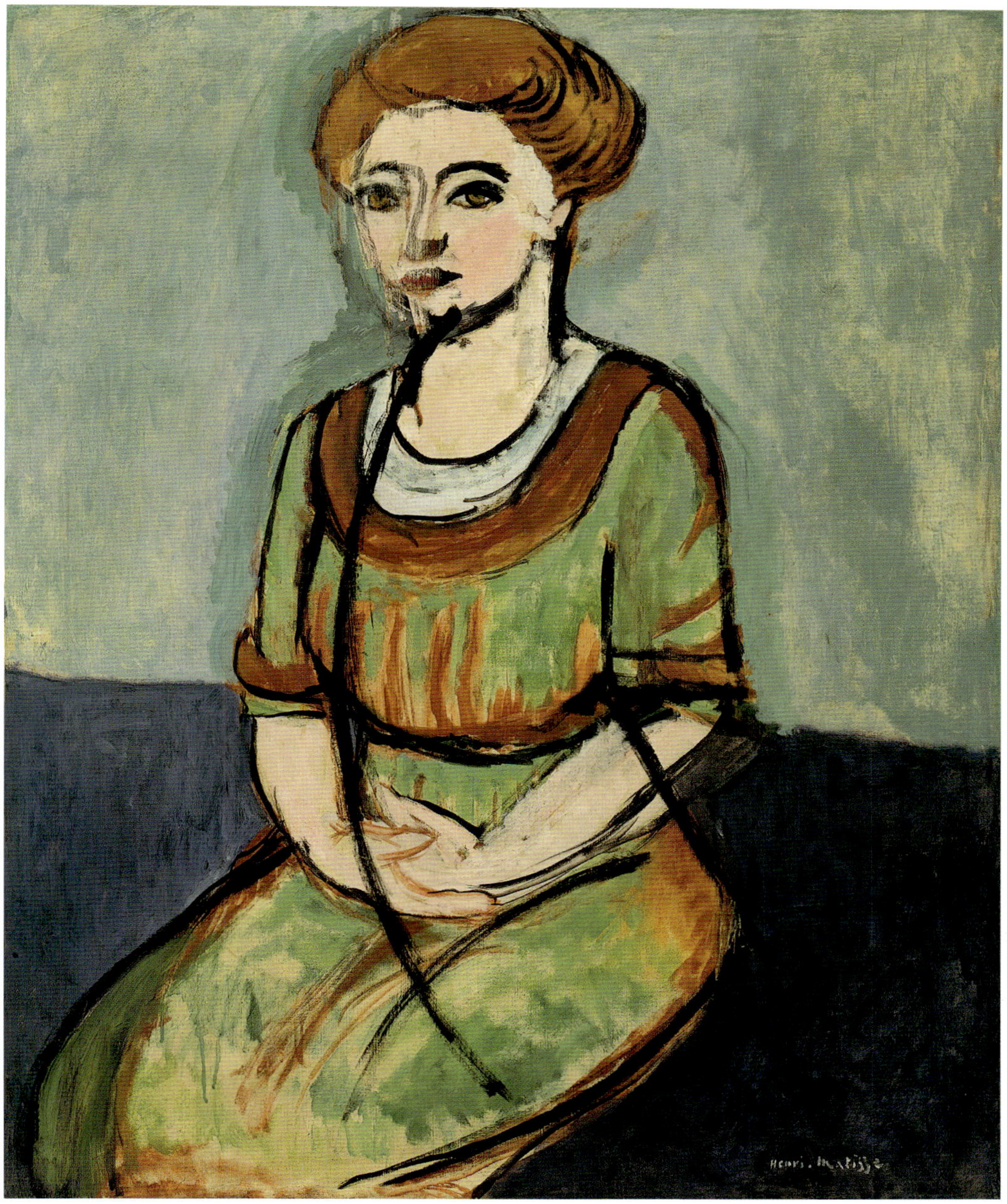

115 *Olga Merson*, 1911. Oil on canvas, 99.7 × 80.6 cm. The Museum of Fine Arts, Houston; Museum purchase with funds provided by the Agnes Cullen Arnold Endowment Fund.

of her own.[36] More than characterizing Olga Merson, Matisse has given a severe and memorable form to his ill-fated relationship with her.

The association in art between women and flowers is age-old, but is nevertheless prominent in modern art as well and occurs with some frequency in Matisse's work. He deployed it in his portrait of Jeanne Vaderin, a young woman who was a neighbor in Issy-les-Moulineaux, while she was convalescing from illness (Matisse always believed that his art could help the sick). In *Girl with Tulips (Jeanne Vaderin)* (fig. 117), the process of growth and change is presented more as a metaphor for the sitter than as a residue of pictorial transformation, as in the portrait of Olga Merson. But the two paintings are linked by the programmatic simplicity of a two-part background, which is also a feature of the contemporaneous *Marguerite with a Black Cat* (see fig. 65).[37] Matisse began with a preparatory drawing (fig. 116) in

116 *Girl with Tulips (Jeanne Vaderin)*, 1910. Charcoal on paper, 73 × 58.4 cm. The Museum of Modern Art, New York. Acquired through the Lillie P. Bliss Bequest.

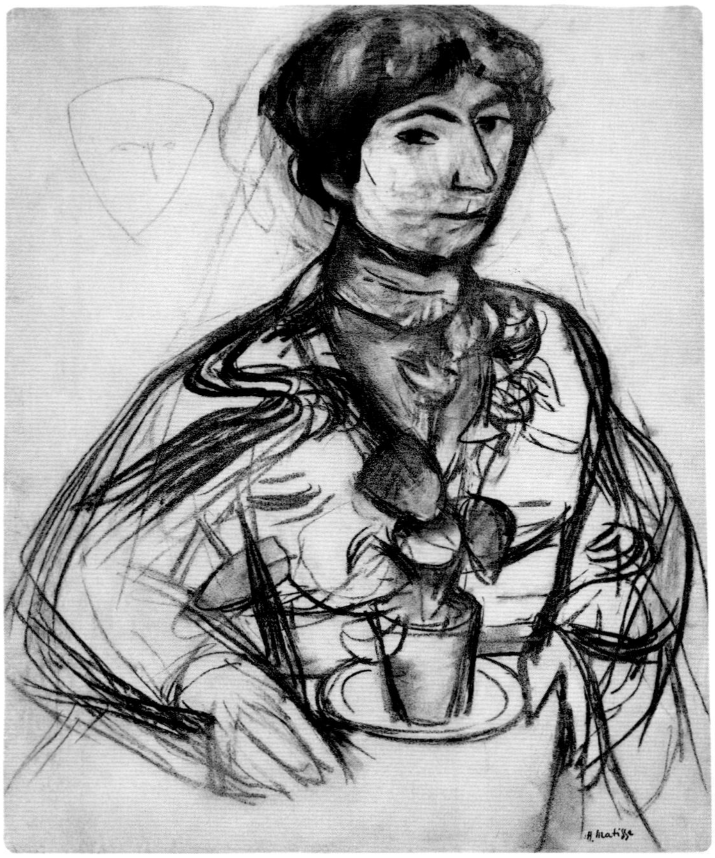

which the analogy between women and flowers is made explicit to a fault. In this first essay Jeanne Vaderin embraces a single pot of flowers (which don't in fact appear to be tulips) whose blossoms are superimposed on her body. The "ingratiating" qualities (Barr's term) of the painting are absent in the drawing as Matisse evidently struggled to construct this image. Thus while the flower metaphor is emphatic, so too is the record of process in this drawing, of Matisse's simultaneous building up and simplification of the forms of the young woman and the placement of her body in space, in repeated rhythms based on a single form like a rounded triangle.[38]

In the painted portrait Jeanne Vaderin stands with clasped hands behind a table with two pots of tulips. Her self-referring gesture of containment is reiterated by the tulip stems, which bow toward each other in suggestive sympathy at the point of their flowering. The budding itself is the most telling metaphorical language, suggesting the girl's own physical development. Her figure emerges from an ocher ground into a blue field, completing the analogy with growth in nature in the coloring of the entire composition, as well as a spring recovery in vibrant hues from the dun color of her winter illness. The analogy between human and plant forms has another function. Combining them was a further means by which Matisse tried to attain a decorative condition in his art. By making the human figure more plant-like, he rendered it more amenable to transformation into an element of decoration, as in the Islamic traditions that interested him so keenly at this time. The analogy that could individuate his portrait by suggesting personal qualities of his sitter could also universalize it, transcending the category entirely.

117 *Girl with Tulips (Jeanne Vaderin)*, 1910. Oil on canvas, 92 × 73.5 cm. St. Petersburg, Hermitage Museum.

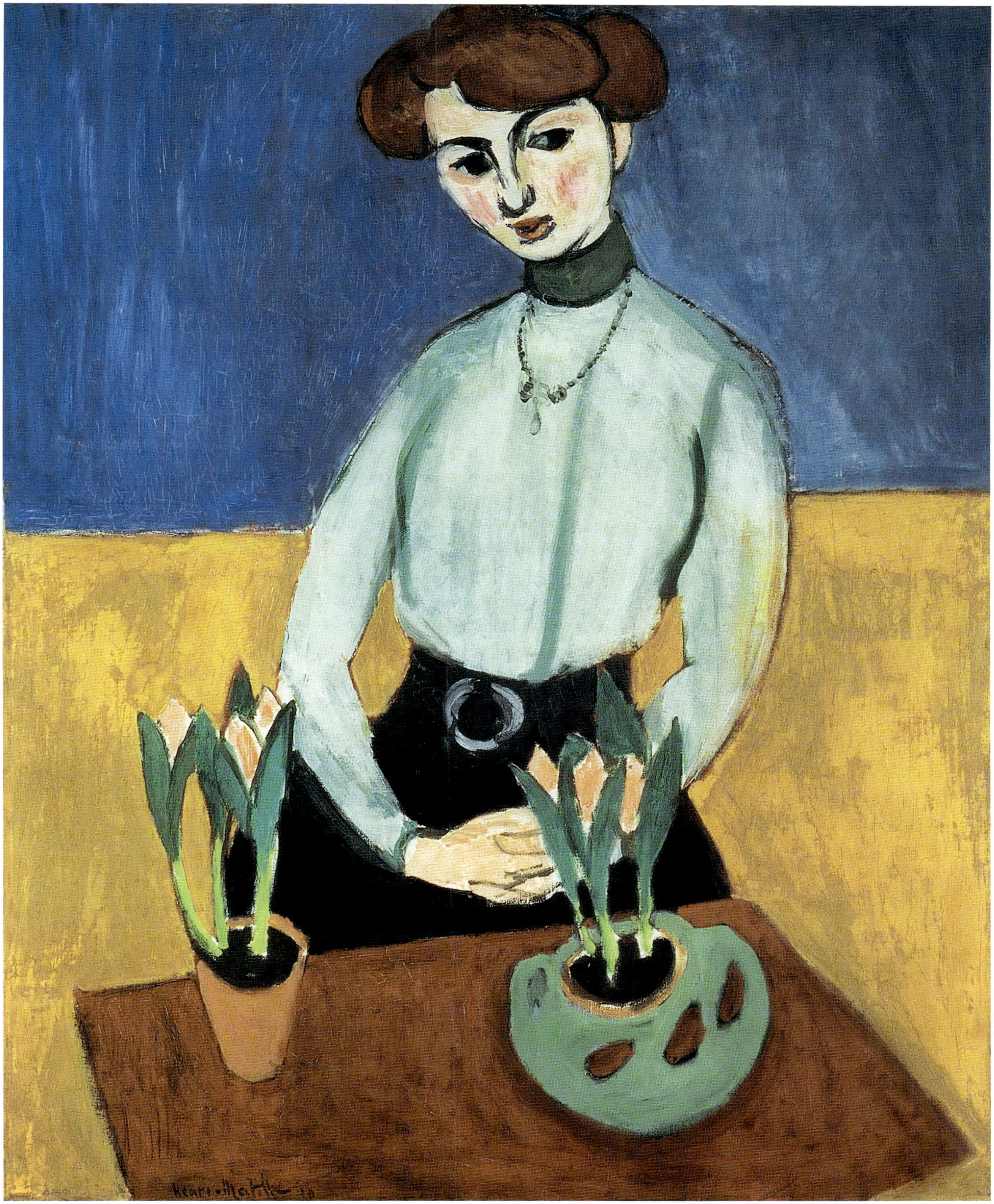

Patrons from East and West

Matisse certainly did not use such metaphoric language in all of his portraits from this time, and he never did it in his portraits of men, nor did his portraits of men express his urge toward the decorative. With men his approach was more straightforward. So it is with the distinctive portrait drawing Matisse made in Paris in 1912 of Sergei Shchukin, the dominant collector of his work at the time and a vital patron (fig. 118). After Shchukin's bold commission of the murals *Dance* and *Music* for his Moscow home, the Russian textile merchant requested that Matisse paint his portrait, but before Matisse could make this painting – his second portrait commission – Shchukin returned to Moscow. The painting was never executed and Matisse retained the charcoal drawing he had made in preparation. It is a great shame that he never had the chance to paint Shchukin's portrait. It might have revealed a deeper element of this relationship between a great artist and his great patron than we now have.[39]

As it is, the drawing is of considerable interest. The heavy charcoal with which Matisse had wrapped Jeanne Vaderin in repeating looping arabesques is here used with at once greater delicacy and decision. He focused only on Shchukin's head, which according to one witness was disproportionately large for his body.[40] The format Matisse chose minimizes this effect. The sitter's head is nestled in the upper left corner of the sheet, and the slight turn of his torso activates the unused area of paper to the right by implying a deeper space. In general the mask-like treatment of the almond form of Shchukin's head is early evidence of Matisse's interest in African art as a vital form-giving source – or an expedient – in his portraiture, as it was for *Portrait of Madame Matisse* (see fig. 55) the following year. Perhaps, also, Matisse found in the otherness of a non-European form an appropriate cultural language for representing a sitter who, however sympathetic and enthusiastic about his art, may have seemed quite foreign to him. When, years later, Pierre Courthion asked him about the strangeness of the portrait of Shchukin, the artist replied: "I brought out his Asiatic character, and I think that annoyed him." Matisse also considered Moscow, which he had visited late the previous year, to be Asian, so he may have been predisposed to cast Shchukin as a type. Yet he believed in the resemblance between the portrait and its sitter, asserting to Courthion, as he had done for the portrait of Greta Moll, that, "as Bonnard says: a portrait always ends up being a likeness."[41] Such was his faith in his skill to create a portrait that would represent the sitter in ways perhaps unforeseen.

In the drawing, the potentially sinister blankness of the dense black eyes and the bristling aggressiveness Matisse has imputed to his patron (who was in fact often indecisive) contrast curiously with the prissiness of Shchukin's pursed lips. But overall, Matisse attributes to Shchukin an impression of forcefulness. One may understand the annoyance of the bold collector of Western art coming from conservative circumstances, but once again Matisse created a memorable if not entirely flattering representation.

Shchukin was Matisse's greatest but not his only major patron in the years just before the First World War. In addition to the Steins, several Americans bought his work and spread his reputation beyond the borders of France. In 1912–14 Matisse made a small group of portrait drawings of such Americans of passage: patrons, potential patrons, and other supporters. From the point of view of patronage, the most significant of these figures was Harriet Lane Levy, who as we have already seen was the early purchaser of Matisse's *Girl with Green Eyes*. An amusing and

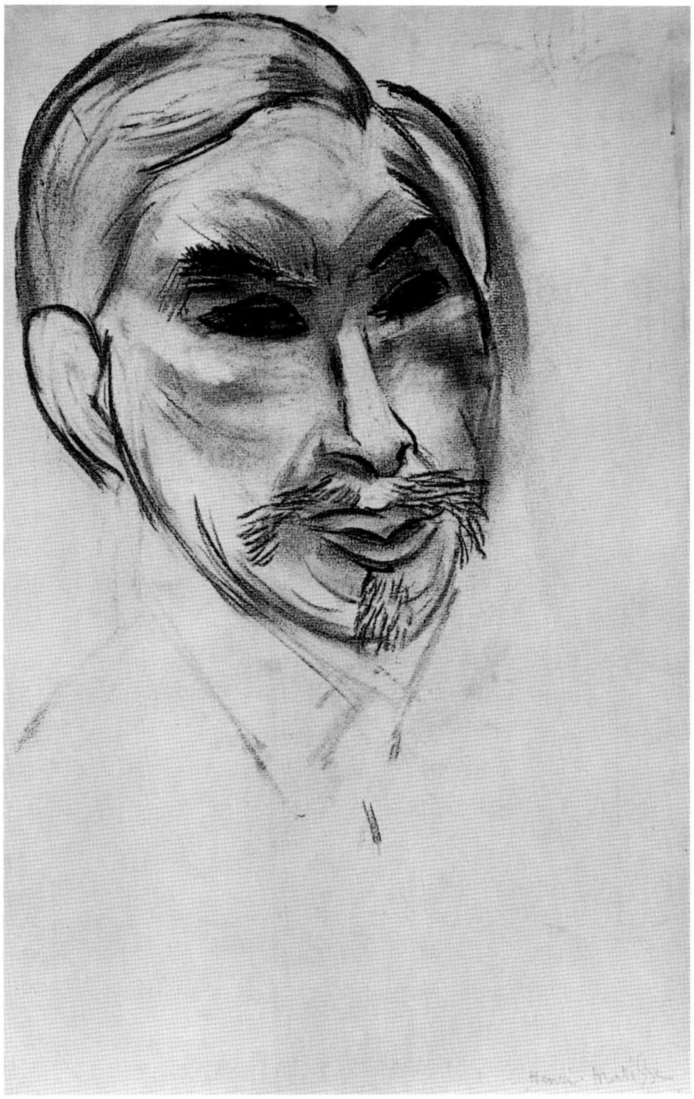

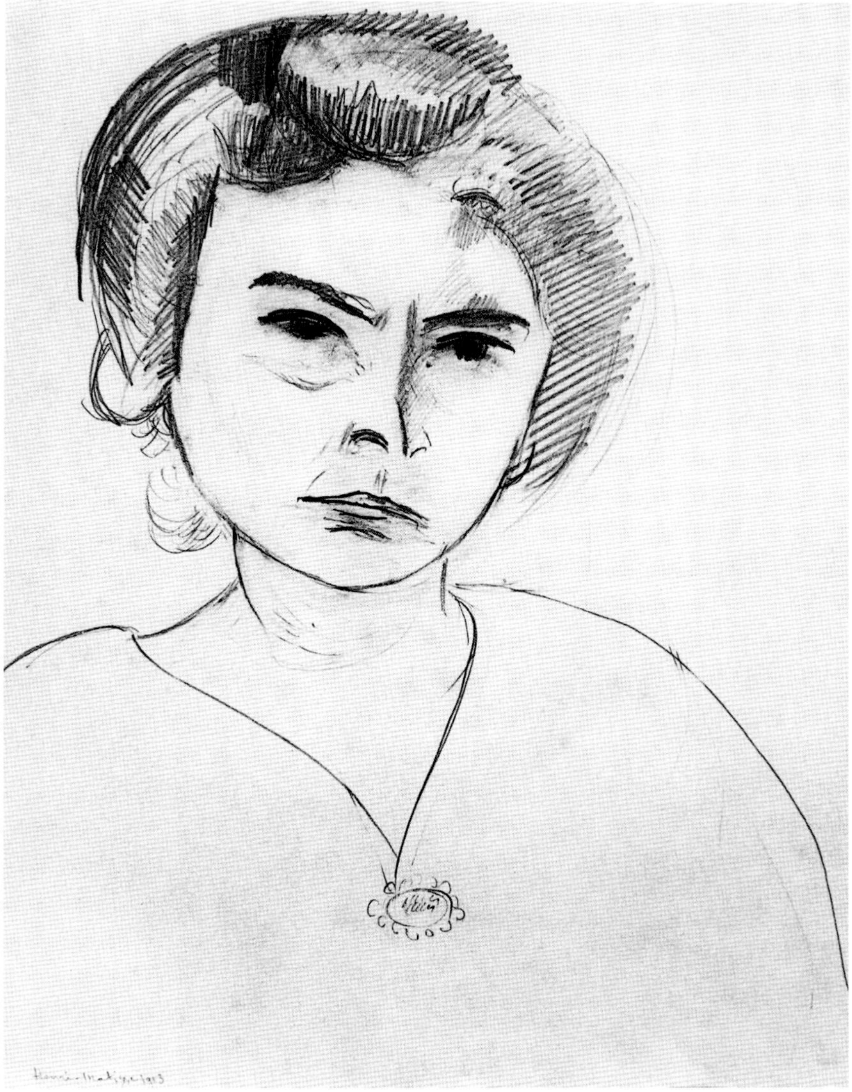

118 (*above left*) *Sergei I. Shchukin*, 1912. Charcoal on paper, 49.5 × 30.5 cm. Private collection.

119 (*above right*) *Harriet Lane Levy*, 1913. Pencil on paper, 27.6 × 21.3 cm. San Francisco Museum of Modern Art. Bequest of Harriet Lane Levy.

revealing drawing Matisse made in Cavalière in 1909 and sent to Levy sums up his aspirations for the relationship between artist and patron. On a sketch of a man diving from a boat into the water he inscribed "Bonjour Mademoiselle Lewy" [sic] in an obvious reference to Gustave Courbet's *The Meeting (Bonjour Monsieur Courbet)* (Montpellier, Musée Fabre), whose theme is the relationship the arrogant Courbet enjoyed with his patron Alfred Bruyas.[42] Matisse's drawing is superficially more flippant but at the same time more respectful toward Levy. His hopes were realized: Levy went on to amass a distinguished collection of the artist's work.

The sour and unflattering drawing Matisse made of Levy in 1913 (fig. 119) is therefore surprising. It seems that with this drawing he did not seek to ingratiate himself with his patron any more than with Greta Moll or the Landsbergs. A softer, more sympathetic representation of Levy in the same pose, in pen and ink, was probably a study for this drawing in pencil, based on an inference of initial hesitancy leading toward a sharp incisiveness.[43] The pencil drawing does not indicate a particular sense of certainty on Matisse's part (there is much erasure and redrawing), but it does have a quality of finality that the weaker portrait in ink lacks.

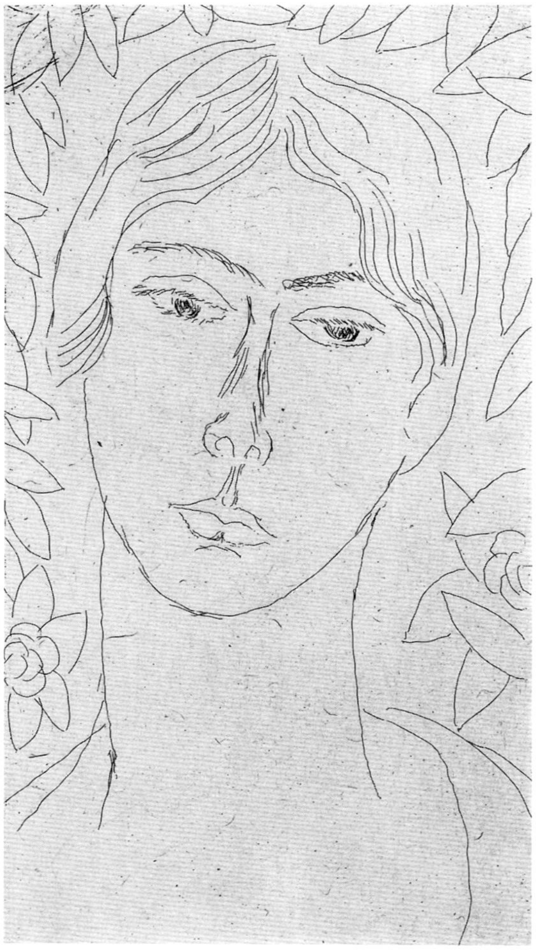

120 *Yvonne Landsberg*, 1914. Etching, 20.1 × 11 cm. The Museum of Modern Art, New York. Gift of Mr. and Mrs. E. Powis Jones.

121 *Yvonne Landsberg*, 1914. Pen and ink on paper, approx. 21 × 27 cm. Present location unknown.

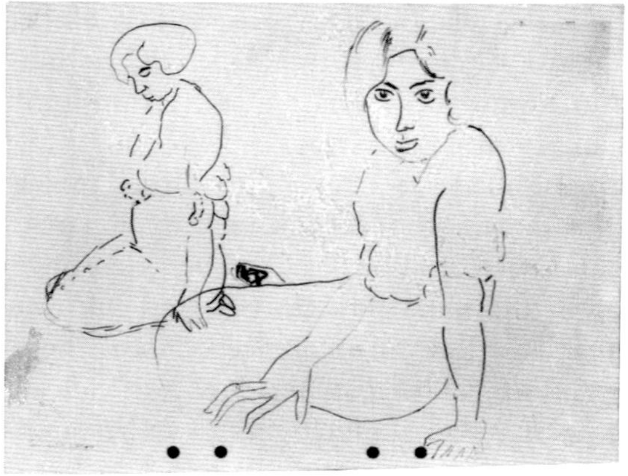

Shy sitter, ruthless artist

The most extraordinary metaphor of becoming in Matisse's portraiture is in the image of a modest young woman with whom the artist felt an exceptional sympathy. Yvonne Landsberg was the daughter in a Brazilian family temporarily resident in Paris. Her brother Albert commissioned Matisse to make a portrait drawing of Yvonne, then twenty years old, which the family apparently believed would improve her confidence. Matisse did this drawing; the family was pleased with it, and Albert and Yvonne's mother paid for it on the agreed terms (which have never been reported).

Of the several extant drawings by Matisse of Yvonne Landsberg, none seems to be the original portrait in question, to judge from a tracing of it that had been made by Albert Landsberg. Matisse's rendering of his sitter (via Landsberg's tracing) has the same synoptic quality found in his pencil portraits of Levy and Elsa Glaser (Art Institute of Chicago) of about this time. Matisse has regularized and softened Yvonne Landsberg's features, bringing them into a constructed balance, making of the whole a pleasing simple shape. Albert Landsberg did another tracing of a drawing his sister made of herself, which shows in full awkward force the young woman's receding chin, small mouth, and widely spaced, slightly bulging eyes.[44] If Yvonne Landsberg was being even moderately frank in her self-perception, Matisse was a blatant flatterer. No wonder the Landsbergs were pleased with a superficially appealing, innocuous depiction of Yvonne.

But they did not know what they had gotten themselves into. Matisse, too, expressed satisfaction with the drawing but then proposed to make a painting, a portrait of Yvonne Landsberg for his own interest (actions would speak louder than words), and exactly as he wanted to do it. The Landsbergs would be free to buy the portrait if they liked it, but they would be under no obligation. Once again Matisse shrewdly offered this right of first refusal in order to gain the freedom to work as he wished. Landsberg *mère* agreed to these terms. The painting that resulted from Matisse's initiative was the anomalous and innovative *Mlle Yvonne Landsberg* (fig. 122).

Apart from the two spectacular images of his wife from nearly a decade earlier, Matisse's *Mlle Yvonne Landsberg* is his most celebrated portrait, and one of the most discussed in his entire oeuvre, owing largely to the extraordinary arcs Matisse incised around the figure in the final stages.[45] Albert Landsberg later stated that the artist began the painting in the spring of 1914.[46] Their friend Matthew Stewart Prichard reported in mid-July that the portrait, arcs and all, was finished.[47] This extended period of evolution, and the intensive labor suggested by the appearance – scraped, rubbed, scumbled – of the painting itself, exemplify the difficulty Matisse sometimes encountered, or made for himself, in this period in constructing the image that would express his responses most completely. This was true to some degree of his work in all genres at this time. But as with the *Portrait of Madame Matisse* of the previous year, the difficulty was greatest in portraiture – that is, when Matisse's desire to objectify and synthesize was most firmly resisted by the identity of a unique individual, even one without his wife's formidable powers of self-assertion.

During the painting's long development, Matisse also made three etchings, two drypoints, and at least ten drawings of his sitter. The variety in the presentation of the young woman is instructive. Matisse was clearly giving Yvonne different personae, from the aloof and iconic (fig. 120) to the casual and winsome (fig. 121).

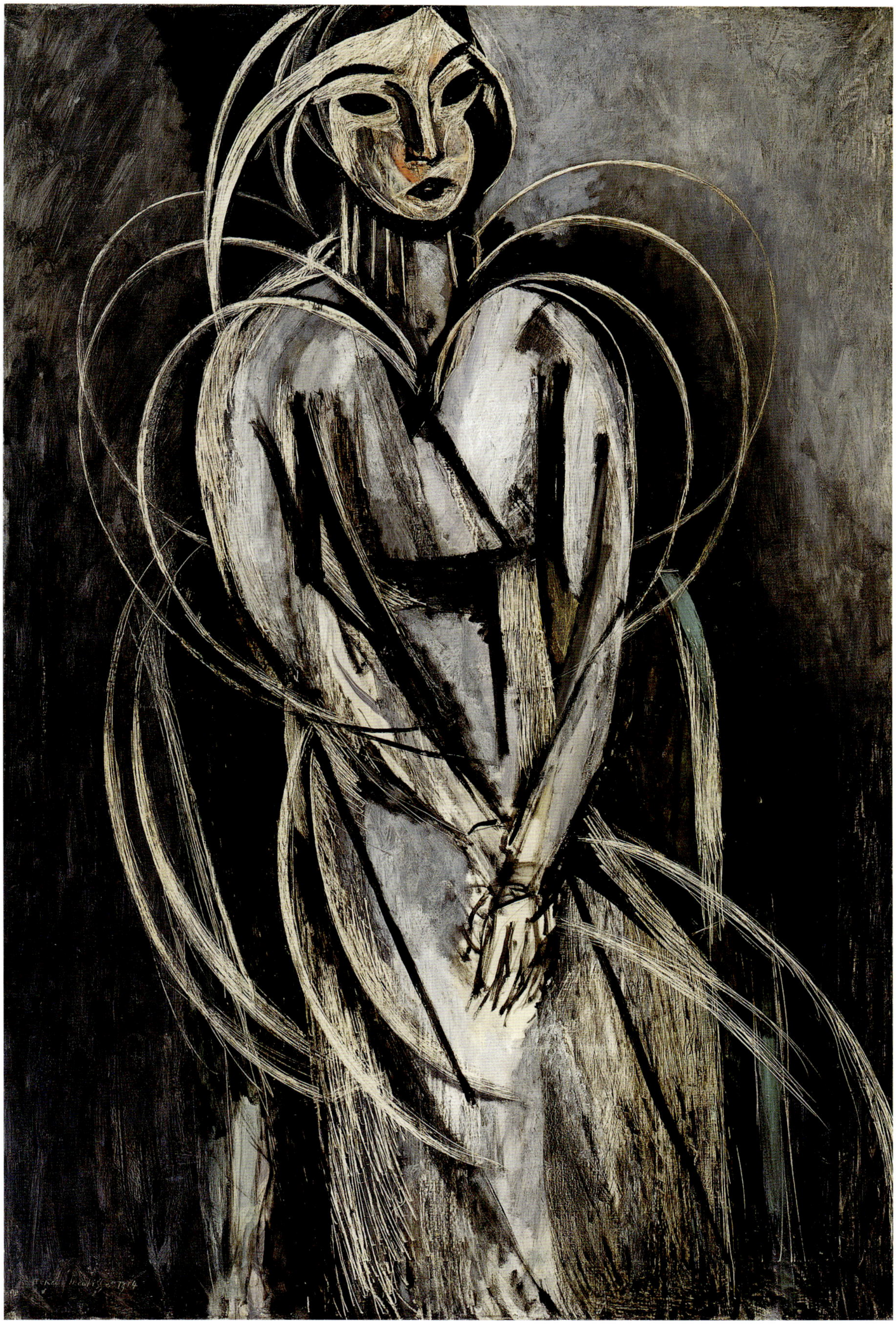

122 *Mlle Yvonne Landsberg*, 1914. Oil on canvas, 146.5 × 95.5 cm. Philadelphia Museum of Art, The Louise and Walter Arensberg Collection.

The latter sketch encompasses a range of self-images, from concern about her appearance to a more engaging boldness, that seemed to characterize the young woman. An air of seductiveness even floats off some of the drawings. Matisse clearly was not trying out different possibilities for his painted portrait, but was exploring independent alternatives, because the painting's basic conception of a seated, full-length pose changed little from beginning to end.[48]

As in other portraits of women, Matisse introduced an association with flowers. In preparation for the first sitting for the painting, he had made drawings of blossoming magnolia buds, finding in them an analogy for Yvonne's tender potential. In one of the prints (see fig. 120), the analogy is proposed explicitly, as if for comparison (in two others she wears a flowered hat). But this sense of correspondence is made more complex when, in the painted portrait, Matisse pursued the organic analogy right to the edge of abstraction. What was tentative about the process of artistic creation in the portrait of Olga Merson is here made explicit and fused with the organic analogies of the other female portraits, making of Yvonne's representation a pure sign of growth and change. And in the process, what happened to the portrait of the shy Brazilian girl?

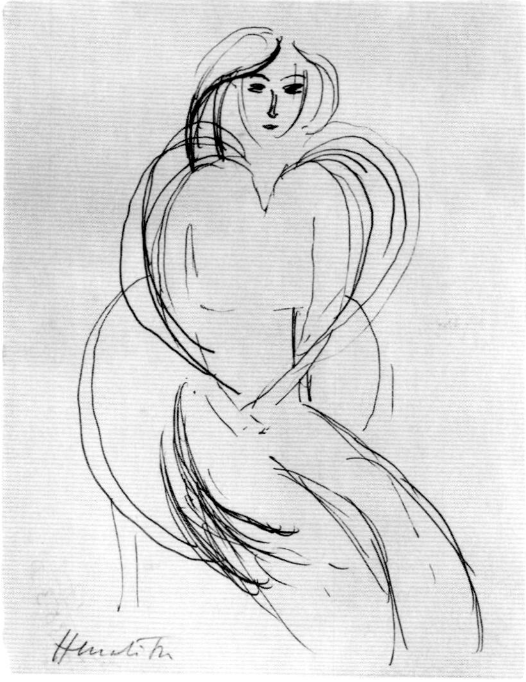

123 *Yvonne Landsberg*, 1914. Pen and ink on paper, 22 × 16 cm. Private collection.

Albert Landsberg, who was present at each sitting, told Barr that the painting began as a "strikingly recognizable portrait" of Yvonne, but that it moved farther and farther from physical appearances until it no longer seemed to depict her at all. In this process of abstraction from her appearance, however, he felt that "possibly" her spirit was increasingly present in the painting.[49] Prichard had also imagined this progression, and said further that the portrait returned "a little toward like-ness at the end."[50] Landsberg stated, however, that Matisse's final touch was to add the arcs by incising them in the still-wet paint either with the butt end of his brush or with a palette knife. This unusual act has led some writers to understand Matisse's gesture as spontaneous.[51] But there are too many lines, and they are incised too precisely and repeated too carefully, to be acts of spontaneity. Furthermore, another drawing of Yvonne (fig. 123), made before the painting was finished, suggests that Matisse was already considering his sitter in terms of these abstractions.[52]

Asked in 1951 by Alfred Barr about the scratches, Matisse explained simply that they were "lines of construction which I put in around the figure in such a way as to give it greater amplitude [*plus d'ampleur*] in space." In other words, Matisse used this device to make the retiring Yvonne look bigger than she was, to give her a firmer presence.[53] He also said in an interview at the time that the lines corresponded to the overtones of a musical note, implying a rich harmony added to the single tone.[54] A structural explanation and a musical metaphor: Matisse would not be pinned to a single interpretation, nor should we. The signs are so pure, and at the same time so ambiguous, that they force the process of interpretation to be flexible. It needs to be pointed out here that Matisse's statements are themselves posterior interpretations: when he finished the portrait the artist himself was shocked and unsettled by the effect.[55]

Two parallels with *Greta Moll* indicate a certain continuity in Matisse's method in portraiture, though the results look entirely different. As he had with Moll's portrait, Matisse completely repainted his large canvas with every sitting.[56] This has the effect of making the results of a deliberate procedure look spontaneous (an effect Matisse often sought), because each stage presents a wholly new image. It also reveals that in *Mlle Yvonne Landsberg* Matisse was just as concerned with an overall decorative concept as he had been in the portrait of Greta Moll, even if "decorative" does not seem to apply easily to this brittle, insectile construction.

Furthermore, as with the portrait of Greta Moll, there is some suggestion that Matisse had come to an impasse and needed an expedient to get out of it, "something drastic – something his conscious reason could not help him with."[57] He had indeed become somewhat obsessed with this portrait, and he was also under time pressure, facing the Landsbergs' return to Brazil.[58] But in some way he seemed to know what he was doing as he struggled to express through pictorial means his overall response to this sitter. This time he did not feel compelled to repaint the entire picture once more to accommodate the changes brought to his decorative scheme by the introduction of these fantastic lines. He did add, as his final efforts, the heavy straight black strokes, which straighten and fetter the body and so make a counterpoint to the filament-thin swooping arcs. Both kinds of marks depart so radically from natural appearances that they justify Lawrence Gowing's characterization of Matisse's mood at this time as "extraordinarily ruthless and reckless."[59] Too ruthless for the Landsbergs: they declined to purchase the portrait.[60]

An expressive Parisian actress

In early 1916 Matisse undertook a large painting of Greta Prozor, the daughter of a Lithuanian diplomat in Paris (fig. 125).[61] Greta Prozor was an actress, a theater director, and a celebrated reader of poetry. She was married to a former student in Matisse's studio, the Norwegian Walter Halvorsen, who had become an art dealer, and she and Matisse may have met through him. She was thirty-one years old when she sat for her portrait.[62] There is no evidence of a commission, and Matisse seems to have undertaken the portrait purely for his own interest.[63]

As with the portrait of Yvonne Landsberg, Matisse made a number of drawings of his sitter, but Prozor herself said later that they were all done in advance of the painting, not integrated with its progress as they had been with Landsberg's portrait. While Matisse worked, he asked Prozor questions about the theater, to which she responded with characteristic animation. When she assumed a pose or made an interesting gesture, he called on her to be still while he drew. With this procedure he made many drawings (not all of which may have come down to us). She then sat for the painting. After a few sessions of posing, Matisse told her that he was dissatisfied with how the painting was going. He apologized for having caused her any inconvenience, terminated the sittings, and at that point apparently abandoned the portrait. A decade later Prozor was astonished to see the painting hanging in a large group exhibition in Paris. Either Matisse (who had retained the painting) had had a change of heart about the picture or he had continued to work on it in the absence of the sitter; we cannot know which. In either case he had produced one of his most astringent visions of an individual. It is clear, despite his apparent dissatisfaction with the picture at the time he painted it, that later he valued it highly as an example of his art, showing it in several exhibitions and giving it a prominent place among his own works of art on display in his various apartments over the years.

For a portrait of an actress, it is remarkably untheatrical, even inexpressive when one considers the modern history of portraits of actors, a history that includes Manet's *Faure as Hamlet* (Hamburg, Kunsthalle) and Matisse's own portrait of Lucien Guitry as Cyrano de Bergerac from 1903 (New York, Museum of Modern Art). Prozor plays no role but neither does she seem to project a personality of her own. Some of the half-dozen known drawings and two prints are more animated than

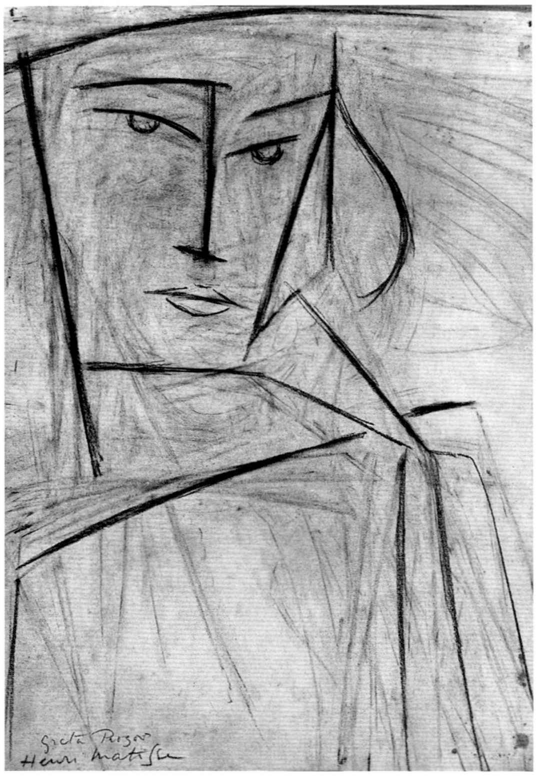

124 *Greta Prozor*, 1915–16. Pencil on paper, 55 × 36 cm. Private collection.

the painting, but in general they project a collective gravity that makes the portraits of Yvonne Landsberg look almost whimsical. Yet, although as an image of a human being *Greta Prozor* seems to lack spirit, as a painted surface it has unexpected life. The background is divided on a rough diagonal into zones of gray and ocher, painted with a rich texture. Prozor's cobalt blue dress makes an assertive swathe of bright color against these earth hues, a vivid formal accent much more striking than the occasional flashes of bright green against gray that is the sole coloristic enlivenment of *Mlle Yvonne Landsberg*.

The comparison between these paintings may be extended fruitfully. Whereas with the Landsberg portrait the final state of the painting was the most abstract conception of the sitter, in the case of Greta Prozor Matisse reached his most austere treatment of her in one of the preparatory drawings (fig. 124), with its sparing complement of curves which were then more thoroughly, and perhaps more weakly, realized in the painting. This greater elaboration from study to final work had also characterized the evolution from drawing to painting for his portrait of Sarah Stein (see figs. 127, 128). If in some sense the spirit of Yvonne Landsberg had been made to emanate from the contours of her body in the form of Matisse's arced incisions, in the portrait of Greta Prozor Matisse exteriorizes the body itself, as if the lower half of Prozor's dress were transparent. Matisse's characterization of her awkwardness may have reflected how she felt under his scrutiny, but it is just as likely that it indicates the artist's irresolution when faced with the task of reconciling the image he had produced with the woman before him. Only in retrospect could he leave the portrait behind and appreciate the picture.

The self in others

Nearly a decade after making the portrait of Allan Stein and under quite different circumstances, Matisse painted portraits of his parents Michael and Sarah (figs. 126, 127). It is not known if the portraits were a commission; Alfred Barr implied that they were not, saying Matisse's efforts here were "labors of affection."[64] In any case, it is clear that the two paintings were conceived together and as pendants, even though their dimensions do not match. Such a pair of related portraits of different sitters is a unique conception in Matisse's work, evidence of the respect he felt toward both. Although he is reported to have said in admiration of Sarah Stein that "she knows more about my paintings than I do," he also thought highly enough of Michael Stein to involve him in the progress of his work by sending him postcards with a description and sketch of *The Painter's Family*, as we have seen.[65] Why Matisse had not made portraits of Michael and Sarah Stein earlier, when their patronage was more critical, is not known. But in 1916 he was taking up portraiture with renewed interest. With regard to the Steins in particular, Matisse may have been doing them a favor and also assuaging his own guilt. At his request, in 1914 Michael and Sarah Stein had lent nineteen of his paintings to an exhibition at the Galerie Gurlitt in Berlin. Once the war began, the Steins' property was sequestered. For several years the fate of these canvases, the heart of the Steins' collection, was uncertain.[66] Matisse likely painted his friends' portraits as much in compensation as for any other reason, and he could do this more directly through portraiture than with paintings of other subjects since under his contract with Bernheim-Jeune he was free to make his own arrangements with respect to portraits.

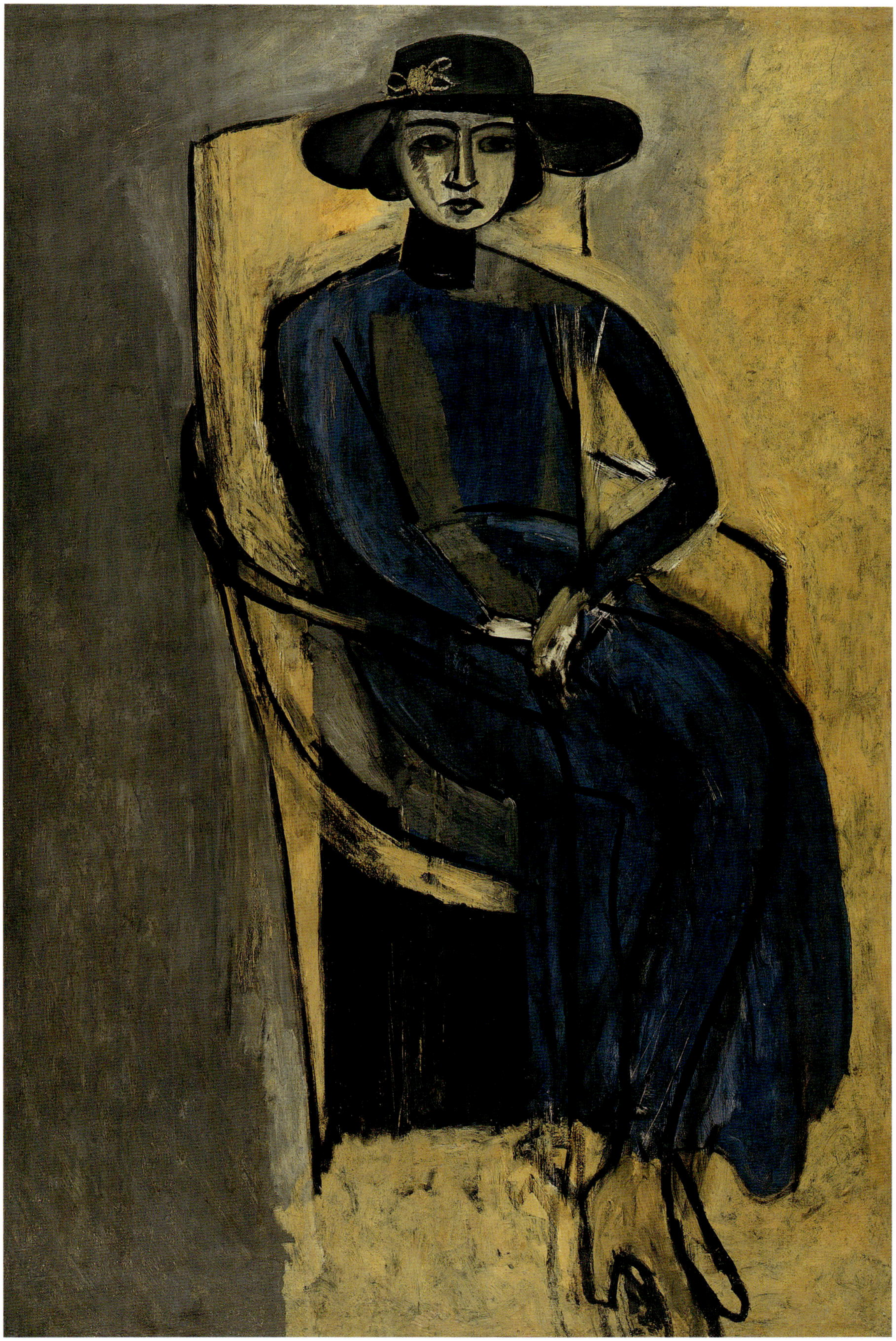

125 *Greta Prozor*, 1916. Oil on canvas, 146 × 96 cm. Paris, Musée National d'Art Moderne, Centre Georges Pompidou, gift of the Scaler Foundation.

126 (*following page*) *Michael Stein*, 1916. Oil on canvas, 67.3 × 50.5 cm. San Francisco Museum of Modern Art, Sarah and Michael Stein Memorial Collection. Gift of Nathan Cummings.

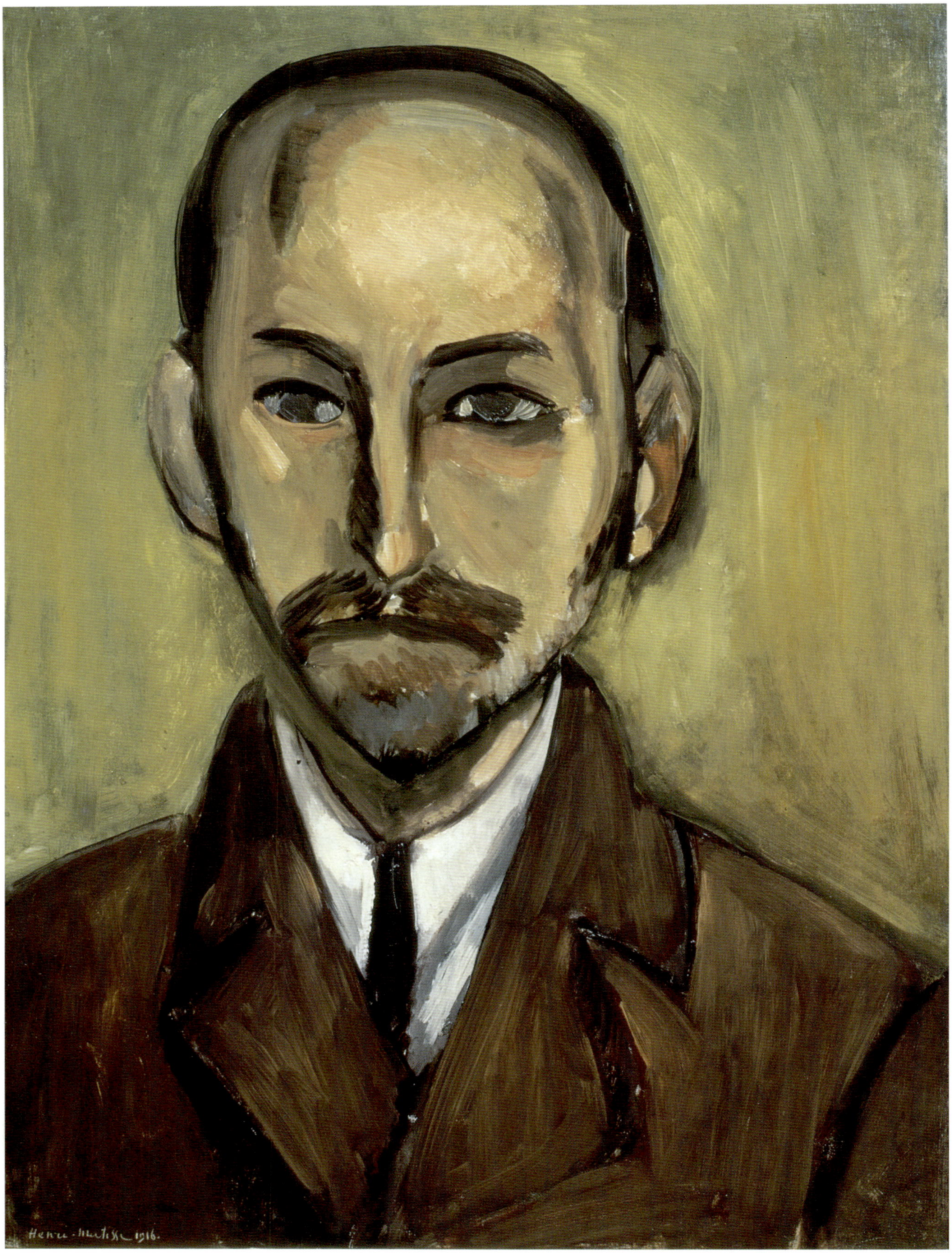
Henri-Matisse 1916.

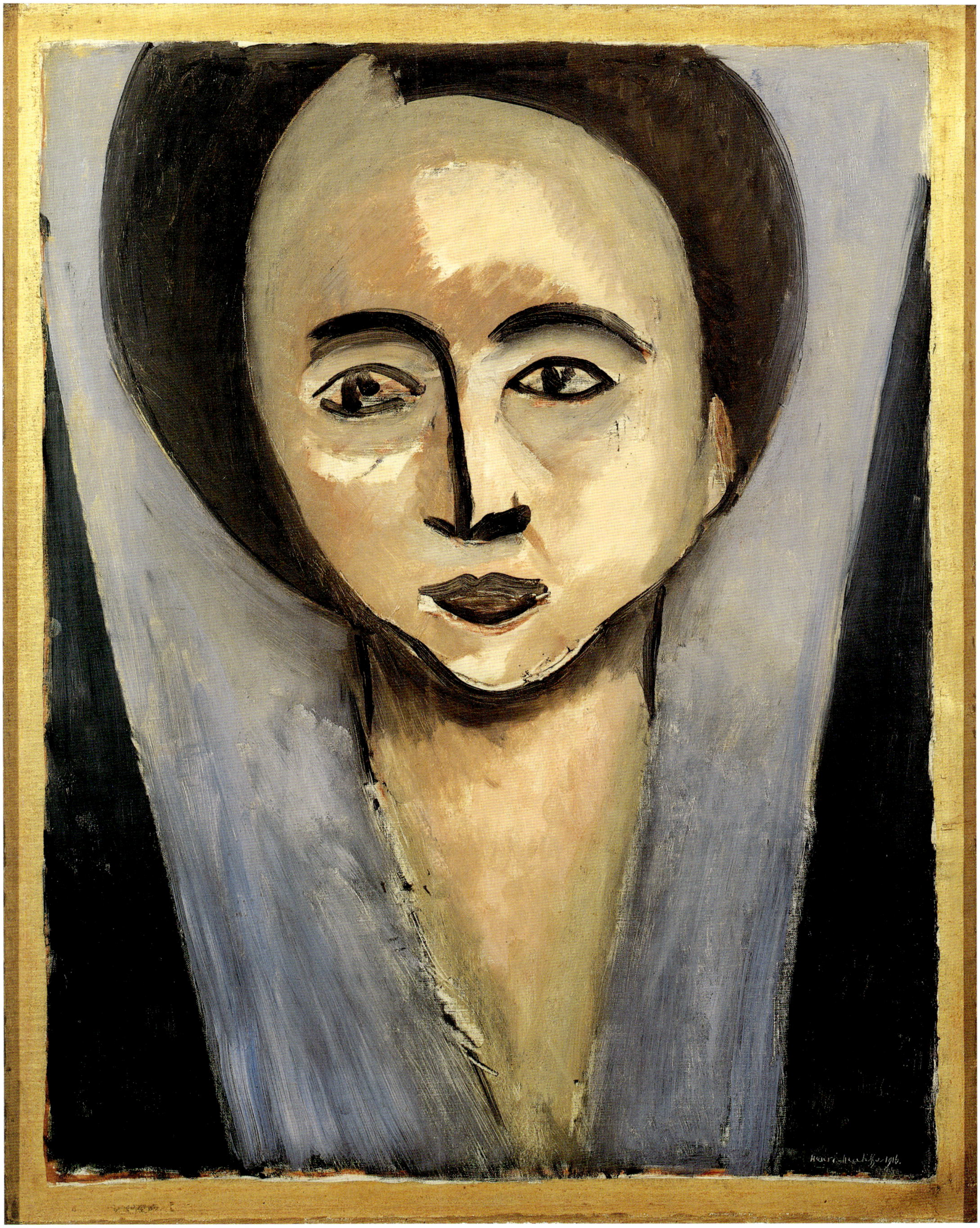

Photographs from 1916 demonstrate that the Stein portraits were probably finished late in that year, but they do not indicate which one was done first.[67] It has been implied that the portrait of Michael Stein is merely a businesslike portrait of a businessman, yielding a blander, more conventional result than the portrait of his less materially occupied, more artistic wife.[68] But he was certainly not a typical *homme d'affaires*: he had in fact retired prematurely in 1903 from his position as the superintendent of the streetcar system in San Francisco, and thereafter devoted himself, along with Sarah, to travel and collecting art.[69] Still, it does seem that Matisse completed the portrait of Michael Stein with little trouble. The thin paint surface overall and the loose brushwork indicate a rapid execution. Matisse concentrated on Stein's forehead, giving it an emphatic roundness not found elsewhere in the portrait, where the emphasis is on things that are sharp and pointed – ears, nose, chin, and the tie and suit lapels of the businessman's uniform.[70] Blank eyes (though an intense blue) and a nearly frontal pose contribute to the feeling of mask-like abstraction. Abstract but far from inert: an alert, sharp intelligence is conveyed in the intensity of those blue eyes, as well as through the movement and fluidity of the entire painted surface.

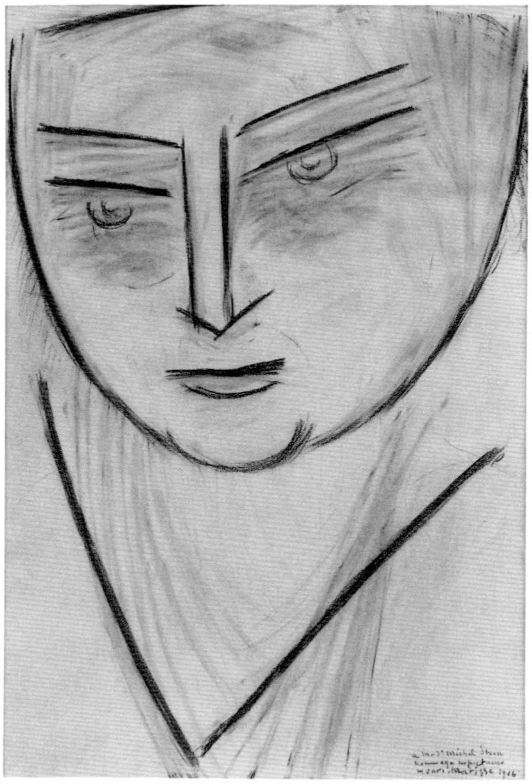

128 Study for *Sarah Stein*, 1916. Charcoal on paper, 48.5 × 32.1 cm. San Francisco Museum of Modern Art. Gift of Mr. and Mrs. Walter A. Haas.

127 (*previous page*) *Sarah Stein*, 1916. Oil on canvas, 72.4 × 56.5 cm. San Francisco Museum of Modern Art, Sarah and Michael Stein Memorial Collection. Gift of Elise S. Haas.

The portrait of Sarah Stein clearly went through more changes as Matisse altered his conception of her. The sense of reduction to an abstract sign of this person is evident, especially when the painting is compared to a drawing made in preparation for the portrait (fig. 128). In this charcoal drawing Matisse erased and redrew each contour repeatedly, beginning with a more natural transcription of Stein's features but progressively distilling them into fewer and fewer lines. The collar of her dress, which went through several stages of declension, finished as a broad v to frame the face. Meanwhile Matisse moved the sitter's eyes steadily upward on the sheet, where they finally came to rest under simple parallel brow lines on either side of an angular nose. The effect of these changes was to press the face up and forward, crowding the top of the sheet, increasing the feeling of intimacy even as the image grew more abstract under Matisse's hand. Then, a last touch of the specific: a slight inflection in the generous curve of the jawline indicates the double chin of the ample woman, one of the few distinctive physical traits to remain in this portrait.[71]

She was then further and more remarkably transformed in the painting. Matisse retained the buoyancy developed in the rising forms of the drawing and enhanced this effect by making Stein's head seem to hover in space. This he achieved by imaginative extension of the collar of her dress into the background, creating a wedge shape against which is set her contrastingly rounded, slightly inclined head with its penumbra of dark hair, which is now withdrawn physically and psychologically from its looming position in the preparatory drawing. The elision of spatial zones here is characteristic of other works Matisse made around this time, as in *The Piano Lesson* (see fig. 69) from the same year or the landscape painting *Trivaux Pond* of 1916–17 (London, Tate Gallery), in which areas of local color are made to spring from their contours to bridge spatial gaps in a fusion of near and distant areas. In Sarah Stein's portrait the effect of this device is to flatten and dematerialize the masses of the sitter's head and body. Several writers have believed that in doing this, Matisse emphasized a spiritual dimension in Sarah Stein (and correspondingly deflected attention from her heavy body and features).[72] The spectral quality of the portrait is enhanced by the gold-painted border that surrounds the portrait, and this feature may have influenced a spiritualizing reading of the image of Sarah Stein. But the border is not original and Matisse did not paint it. It was apparently added (by the Steins?) when the painting was first framed.[73] Yet the device, evoking the gold ground of icons, would have been in keeping with Matisse's desire for very simple framing arrangements for his paintings, and it may have been added at his suggestion. He did not like the violent distraction of the traditional carved picture frame, and in another case, the portrait of Yvonne Landsberg of two years earlier, he had advocated a simple gold strip as a border, feeling that this best permitted the "expansion" of the image into the space around it.[74] This may have been his hope also for the portrait of Sarah Stein, since the entire image implies extension beyond the frame, beyond the physical, beyond the individual.

Certainly Matisse was painting these pictures in homage to his patrons and probably to compensate them for their missing collection, but in the way he has differentiated his sitters Matisse was also expressing the opposing sides of his own character. We see the artist through the no-nonsense presentation of the businessman Michael and also through Sarah the aesthete and romantic. Matisse remained close to the Steins for many years, favoring them with such gestures as a wedding portrait of Allan Stein's bride, Yvonne Daunt, and with gifts of his work that he felt would complement their already highly personal collection. To Matisse, the Steins were second in importance only to his own family, and while the artist's responses to his wife and children may have been mixed, his sympathy for the Steins, as expressed in his portraits of them, was unalloyed.

Pellerin between Renoir and Cézanne

Although not as celebrated as the portrait of Yvonne Landsberg, the two versions of Matisse's portrait of Auguste Pellerin (figs. 129, 130) deploy a mode of symbolic reference nearly as complex and personal; and *Auguste Pellerin II* deserves recognition as Matisse's most commanding image of another human being and one of the greatest portraits of the twentieth century, delivered with an authority matched only by his self-portrait from a decade earlier (see fig. 90).

A Parisian businessman who had made a fortune in the manufacture of margarine, Pellerin had been directing his wealth into collecting art for some years. The board of directors of his company commissioned Matisse to make Pellerin's portrait with the intention of giving it to the sitter.[75] It is not known why these business associates of Pellerin chose Matisse. The artist and the margarine king may have been acquainted through Greta Prozor and her Norwegian husband; Pellerin had considerable business interests in Scandinavia and was the Norwegian consul-general in Paris.[76] But the outcome of the Prozor portrait would have been a risky recommendation. In any case, at least one aspect of the businessman's interest for Matisse is clear: Pellerin was one of the major collectors of modern French art in France, with substantial groups of works by Manet (forty paintings alone) and Cézanne (at least ninety canvases).[77] The Pellerin commission coincided with Matisse's renewed interest in the work of Cézanne, as evidenced by his taking up two earlier works, the *Bathers by a Stream* (Art Institute of Chicago) and the *Back* sculptures, and giving them Cézannian structural features. Some of the highlights of Pellerin's Cézanne collection were the several compositions of bathers; that Matisse too owned a Cézanne bathers canvas, the jewel of his own collection, immediately signaled a shared passion.

129 *Auguste Pellerin I*, 1916. Oil on canvas, 92.3 × 78.5 cm. Private collection.

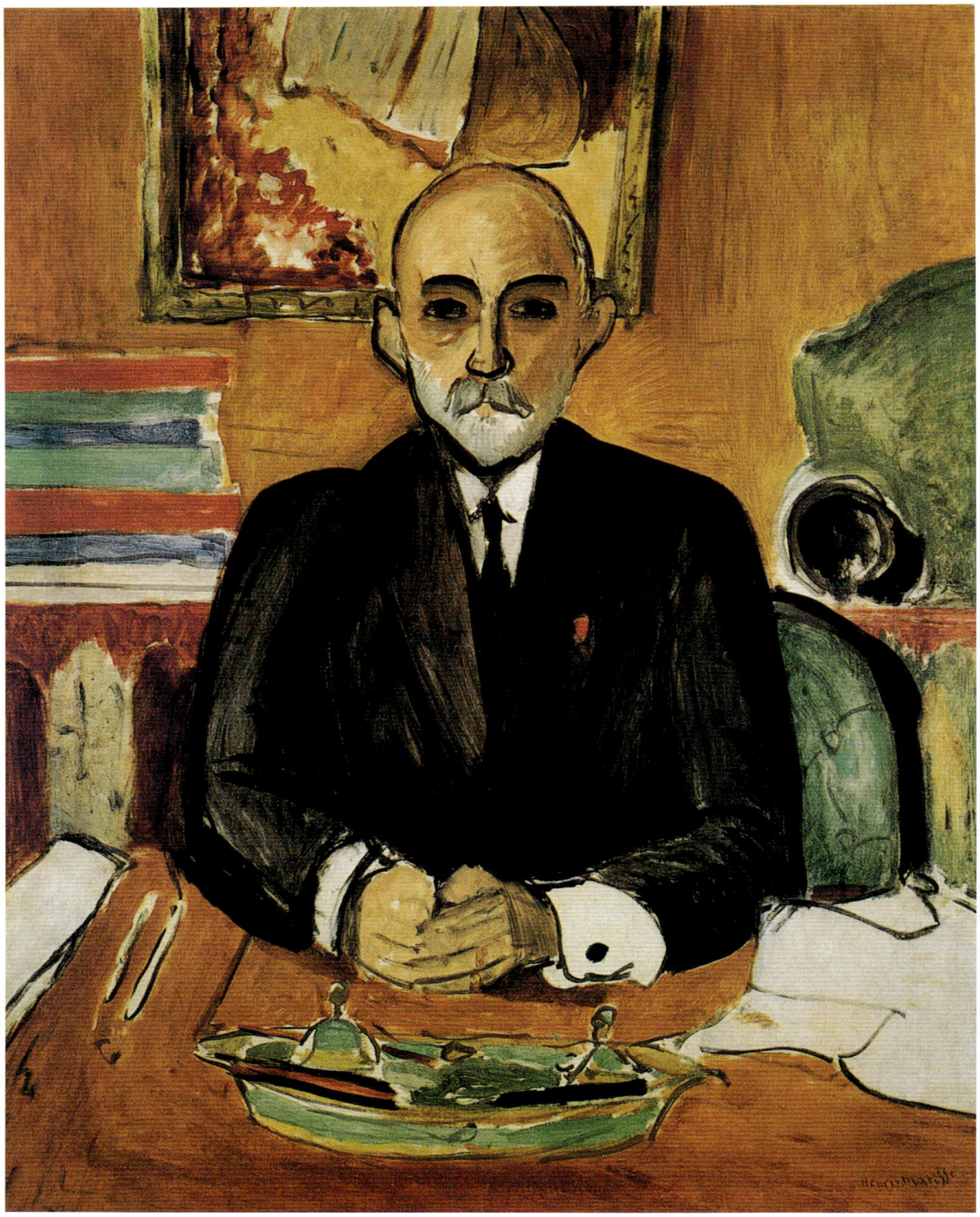

Pellerin did not like the portrait Matisse made of him. It seems that he then took matters into his own hands: instead of rejecting the painting outright he asked Matisse to paint another. When this second portrait was finished, Pellerin decided that the first one was acceptable (perhaps in light of the outcome of the second), but he proposed that he should receive both for the original price. In the end Matisse insisted on the full price for each painting, and Pellerin took both on these terms.[78]

The pair of portraits offers a classic instance in Matisse's work of analysis leading to synthesis as he developed the image of his sitter. *Auguste Pellerin I* seems a weak human characterization by comparison with the focused intensity of the second

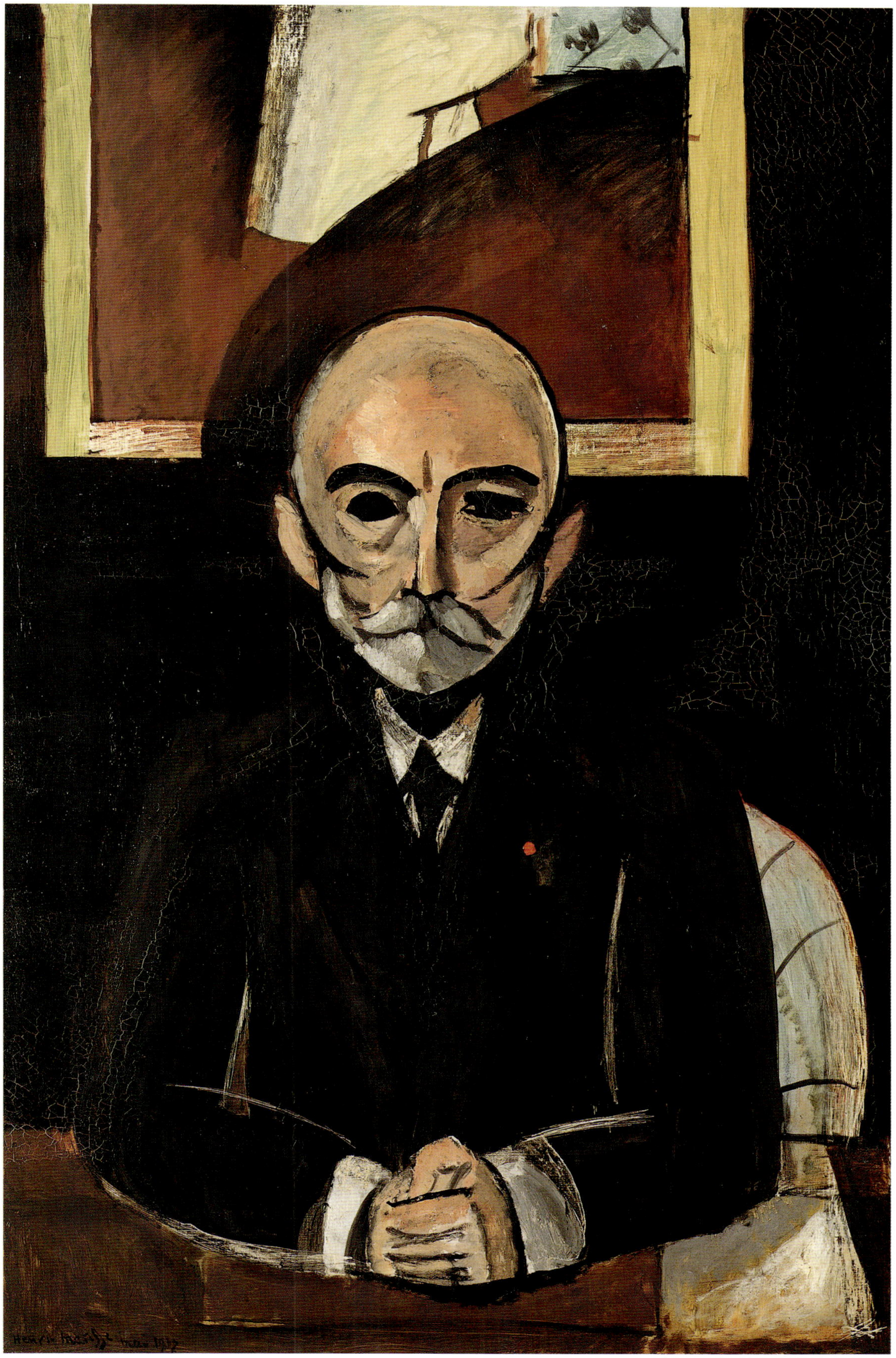

130 *Auguste Pellerin II*, 1917. Oil on canvas, 150.2 × 96.2 cm. Paris, Musée National d'Art Moderne, Centre Georges Pompidou.

131 Paul Cézanne, *Gustave Geffroy*, 1895. Oil on canvas, 116.2 × 89.9 cm. Paris, Musée d'Orsay.

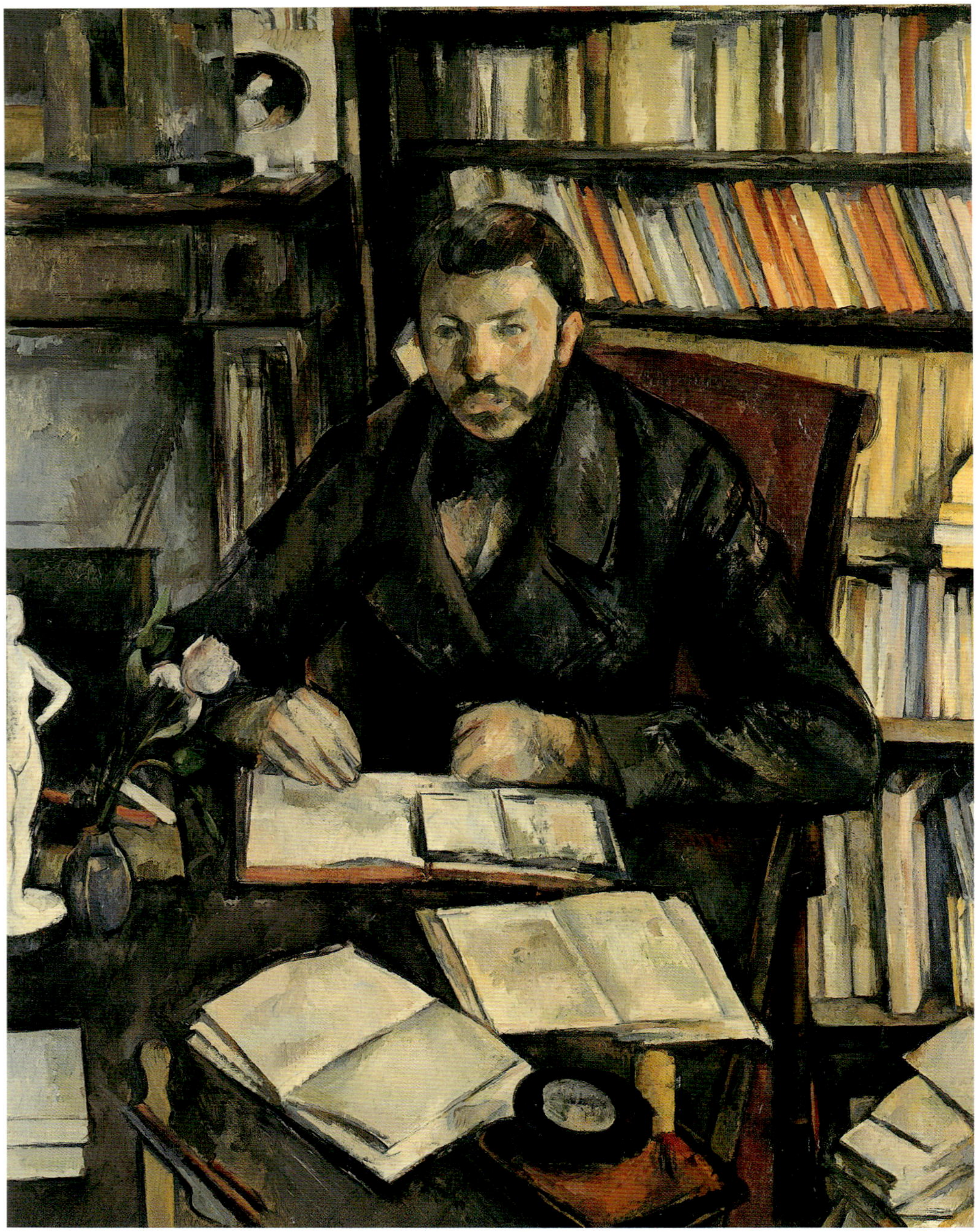

version. However, Pellerin's dissatisfaction with the first portrait was probably a matter of the painting's sketchy appearance, like unfinished business. Matisse's general conception should have been pleasing. This image of a professional man in his office is typical of the modern environmental portrait in the recent tradition of Manet's Zola, Degas's Duranty, or Cézanne's portrait of Gustave Geffroy (fig. 131), a painting in Pellerin's own collection, which may well have been in Matisse's mind when he painted the portrait of its owner. Geffroy, a writer, is surrounded by emblems and products of his craft. Pellerin, captain of industry and collector, is bracketed by a desk set and a painting on the wall behind his chair. It is interesting that this is not a painting by Cézanne, as has usually been believed, but

Renoir's portrait of Rapha Maître, recently acquired by Pellerin.[79] There is a key difference between Matisse's portrait and its predecessors: those works had been portraits of empathy, depicting in all cases the artist's supporters; Pellerin's portrait transaction with Matisse was more confrontational, a process of negotiation between two mature (Pellerin was sixty-four), strong-willed men. But the compositional stability of Cézanne's portrait of Geffroy may have had a particular attraction for Matisse in his quest for a suitably assertive representation of Pellerin. Matisse hoped for further patronage from the collector, and therefore he sought to cast Pellerin in Geffroy's solid, sympathetic image.

Even in the milder first version the direct gaze of the sitter, quite unlike the more elusive appearance of Yvonne Landsberg, Greta Prozor, and Sarah and even Michael Stein in their portraits, conveys Pellerin's self-possession. Yet the effect of this first portrait pales in comparison to the second version, which Matisse completed in May 1917.[80] On a much larger canvas, and with more vertical proportions, Matisse tightened the composition and eliminated the objects and thus much of the "environment" of the first picture. He reduced the color range, and the whole is dominated by the black of Pellerin's coat and the surrounding wall surface, punctuated by the riveting red spot of the sitter's Legion of Honor pin. At the center of it all is Pellerin's face, stylized, sharp, and hardened into a carapace. From this psychological fortress Pellerin's blank, black eyes project both enigma and a disturbing aggressiveness. The blankness may have another aspect. It was not for nothing that Georges Duthuit considered this portrait, along with that of Michael Stein, as the "definitive dismissal" of man in Matisse's portraiture, likening the heads in these portraits to those of the mannequin-like figures of de Chirico.[81] But the second portrait of Pellerin – drained of human sympathy, perhaps – has few equals as an iconic image of masculine authority, among them Ingres's portrait of the publisher Bertin or Eduard Steichen's photograph of the banker J. P. Morgan.

One area of black fuses with another as Pellerin seems locked into his surroundings, dominating his environment but inextricable from it. As he had in the portrait of Yvonne Landsberg, Matisse inscribed the interior contours around Pellerin's arms into the canvas surface with long scratches in the paint. But here, instead of the metaphoric expansion of form in the Landsberg portrait, Pellerin's body is brought right back to the surface of the painting, even as the white lines detach arms from torso, allowing the arms to assert their own spatial position. In formal terms the most striking aspect of the painting is the elision of spatial zones through the melding of different areas of black, even more effective in the sweeping arbitrary shape that seems to emerge from this dark field and cross the frame of Renoir's painting, so that one fictive painted space is linked with another. We can find this kind of elision of figure and ground in the slightly earlier *Italian Woman* (fig. 182), where the blend is even more radically conceived. In the Pellerin portrait it is endowed with greater potential meaning: the phantasmal curving shape implicitly links the man with his collection, a completely abstract sign for Matisse's interest in this sitter.

As depicted in the second version, Pellerin looked strikingly like Cézanne late in his life (see fig. 132). It is probably not possible to determine how much Pellerin actually did look like Cézanne (perhaps through a process of identification with his favorite artist) and how much Matisse has made him resemble Cézanne. Or the resemblance may be a coincidence.[82] But another striking resemblance – this one between painted images – probably cannot be coincidental. Ten years earlier, Leo Stein had painted several portraits of his brother Michael, two of which can be

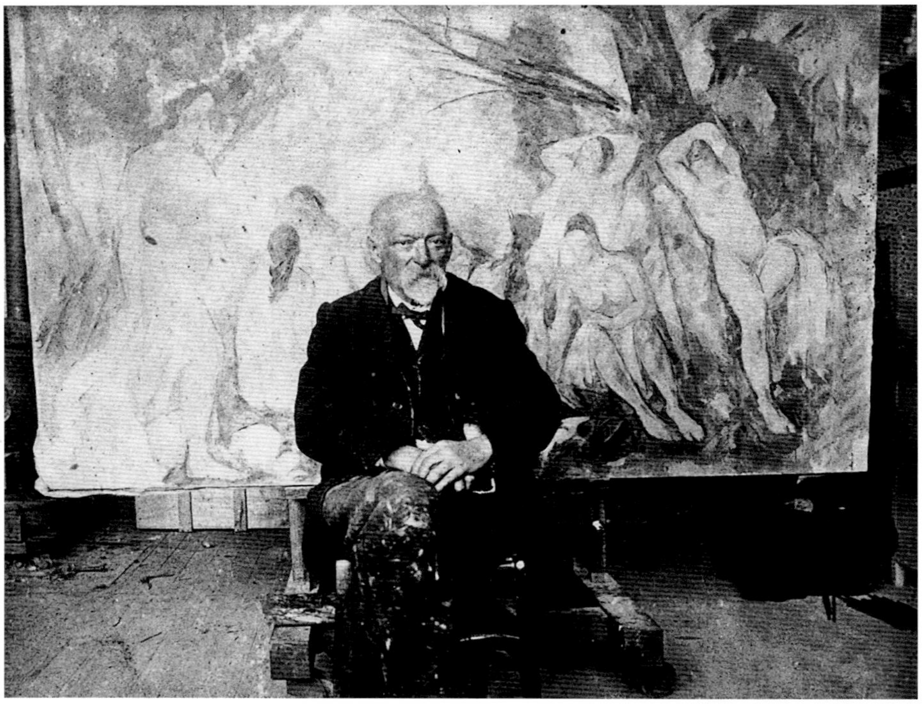

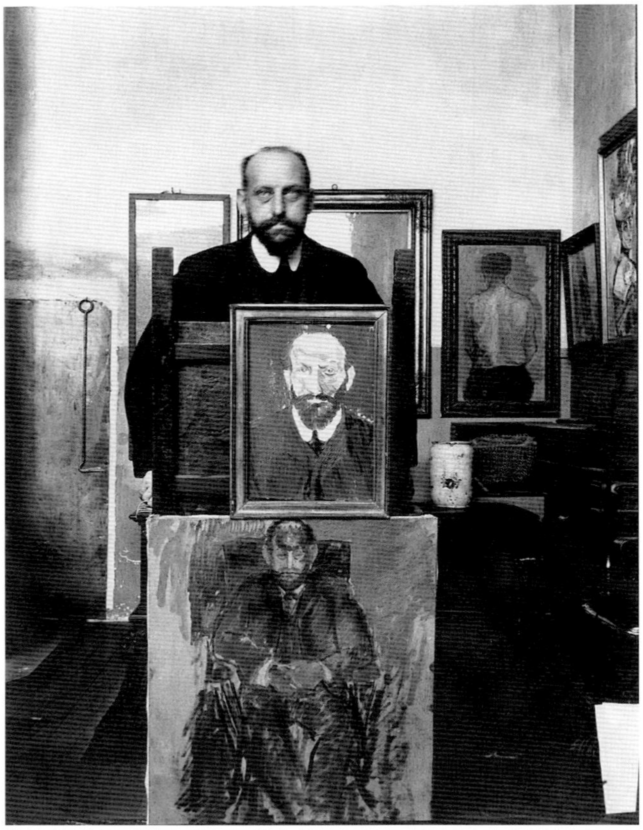

132 (*above left*) Photograph of Cézanne taken by Emile Bernard in 1904 in front of Cézanne's painting *Grandes baigneuses*.

133 (*above right*) Photograph of Michael Stein, ca. 1906, with portraits of him painted by Leo Stein. The Baltimore Museum of Art, The Cone Archives.

seen in a photograph from about 1906 (fig. 133). The lower of these two paintings is of considerable interest, for in it Michael Stein, businessman, is depicted in precisely the pose of Matisse's Pellerin (though without the protective desk). Whether or not Matisse was recalling this portrait, the Cézanne connection must have linked the Steins and Pellerin in his mind, as he had also recently finished his portraits of Michael and Sarah Stein. A bathers painting by Cézanne in the Stein collection, closely related in composition to Matisse's own precious Cézanne, had once belonged to Pellerin.[83] And the similarity between Matisse's portrait of Sarah Stein and a portrait by Cézanne of his wife in the Pellerin collection (fig. 134), as well as the generic relationship between Sarah Stein's portrait and two portraits by Cézanne of his wife in Matisse's collection, all suggest a complex of interests at this time with Matisse, the great collectors of his work that the Steins had been, and the great collector of his work that Matisse must have hoped Pellerin would become.[84] We recall that the Stein collection of Matisse's works was in jeopardy at this time. Was Matisse displacing Michael Stein onto the image of Pellerin, hoping that the French collector would offer the same kind of patronage that the Americans had bestowed on him until their change in fortunes?

It is usually asserted that Matisse resented the constraints imposed upon him when making a commissioned portrait.[85] This was often true but it is not the whole truth, and it was not necessarily to the detriment of his art. At this point in his career he had no financial motivation to undertake commissions since he was enjoying a comfortable standard of living. Why bother? If money was not the issue, what was? Surely Matisse welcomed the challenge, the unexpected benefits that sometimes accompanied constraint and opposition, as in the transaction of a portrait commission with a strong personality. He was attracted to strong personalities, especially in men, and was challenged to make an appropriate image that would do justice to the strength to which he responded. It seems clear too that Matisse accepted the challenge of portraiture along with the benefits of patronage, and used the portrait to gain access to private collections – Pellerin had his Manets and Cézannes, Shchukin had his great collection of modern French art. But Matisse did not merely want to study these collections, he wanted to be included in them, as a way of assuming a place in the modern tradition. In both of these collections, Matisse's work would form the contemporary manifestation of the great post-Impressionist trends. With Pellerin, Matisse was surely hoping to reap some benefit from his sacrifice of absolute artistic freedom in making his portrait.

As it turned out, Pellerin's patronage of Matisse began and ended with the portraits, and it seems that he did not value Matisse's work for its own sake.[86] Matisse's strategy – if it had been a strategy – had failed. But even though he may not have been at his ease when working at the behest of this demanding individual, in the case of the monumental second portrait of Pellerin, he was certainly at his best.

Portraits and career advancement

In October 1917 Matisse made a momentous journey to the South of France. He went first to Marseilles, where he met his old friend Albert Marquet. The two painters spent some time in the company of George Besson, a young art critic and collector. Besson had a wide range of contacts in the Midi, and one of the first introductions he made for Matisse was to Auguste Renoir, who lived in nearby Cagnes.[87] This young man seems to have had a considerable role in helping Matisse to become accustomed to what became effectively his home for the next twenty years. Besson was thus present for one of the most important transitions in Matisse's life, when he left the Paris art scene and its social and professional complexities in favor of a world in which he could exert greater control over his environment.

134 Paul Cézanne, *Mme Cézanne*, 1885–7. Oil on canvas, 46 × 38 cm. Paris, Musée d'Orsay.

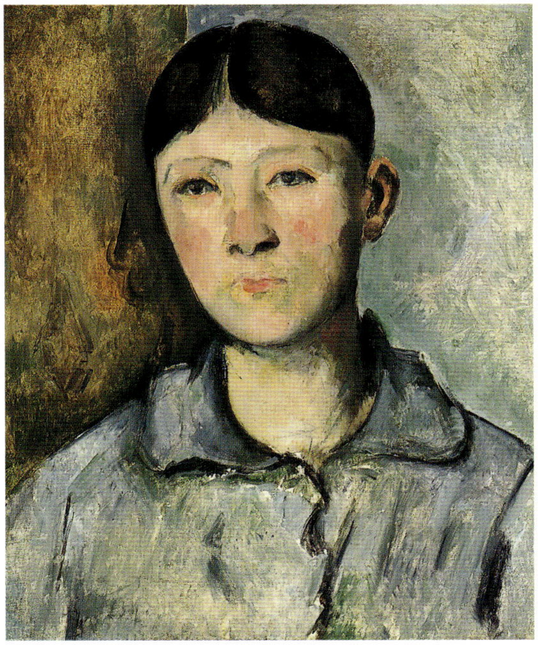

In his hotel room in Marseilles, Matisse painted a tiny portrait of Besson in December 1917 (fig. 135). Besson reported that Matisse did the portrait in one sitting.[88] Painted in a narrow range of colors from straw to gray, the surface shows a lively freshness reflecting a rapid execution. Besson's head nearly fills the vertical format, leaving room only for his neat collar and tie. Through his pince-nez we see the kind of small dark eyes that by now seem characteristic of Matisse's portraits. Not to paint the eyes is a form of negation, but this device may have had a decorative function too: by suppressing the most important center of attention in a face, Matisse forces attention to the ensemble: "the entire arrangement of my picture is expressive."[89] Or expressively inexpressive, in this case. As with so many of Matisse's portraits from the 1910s, he offers no insight into the personality of the sitter through the way he presents his new acquaintance. Here as in most of Matisse's portraiture in the public sphere the sitter's personality, social standing, relationship to the artist, and so on, are reflected more in the decision to make the portrait than in the specific visual properties of the portrait itself.

From Marseilles Matisse went to Nice, where he settled temporarily in the Hôtel Beau-Rivage. There he made another portrait of Besson, in January 1918 (fig. 136).[90] This second portrait is almost identical in size to the first and, like it, is exceptionally painted on a wood panel, possibly the top or bottom of a cigar box. This support may emphasize the occasionality of these portraits (both Matisse and Besson

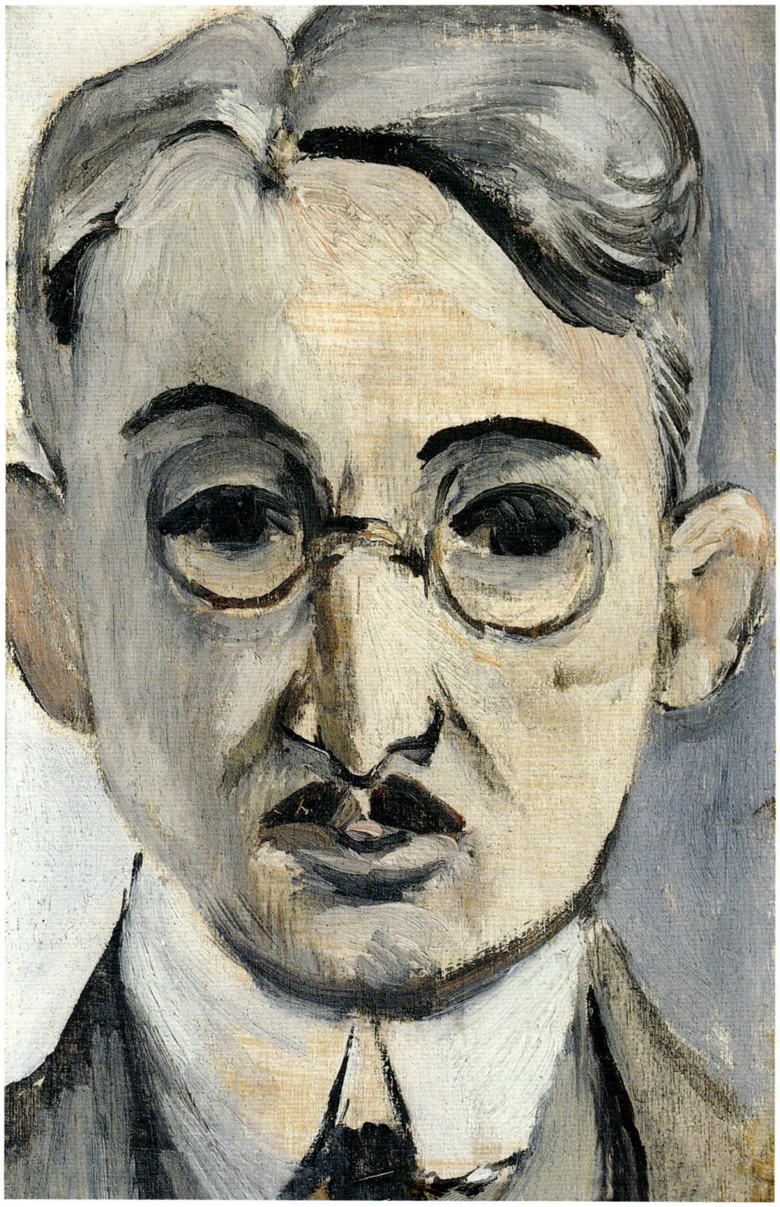

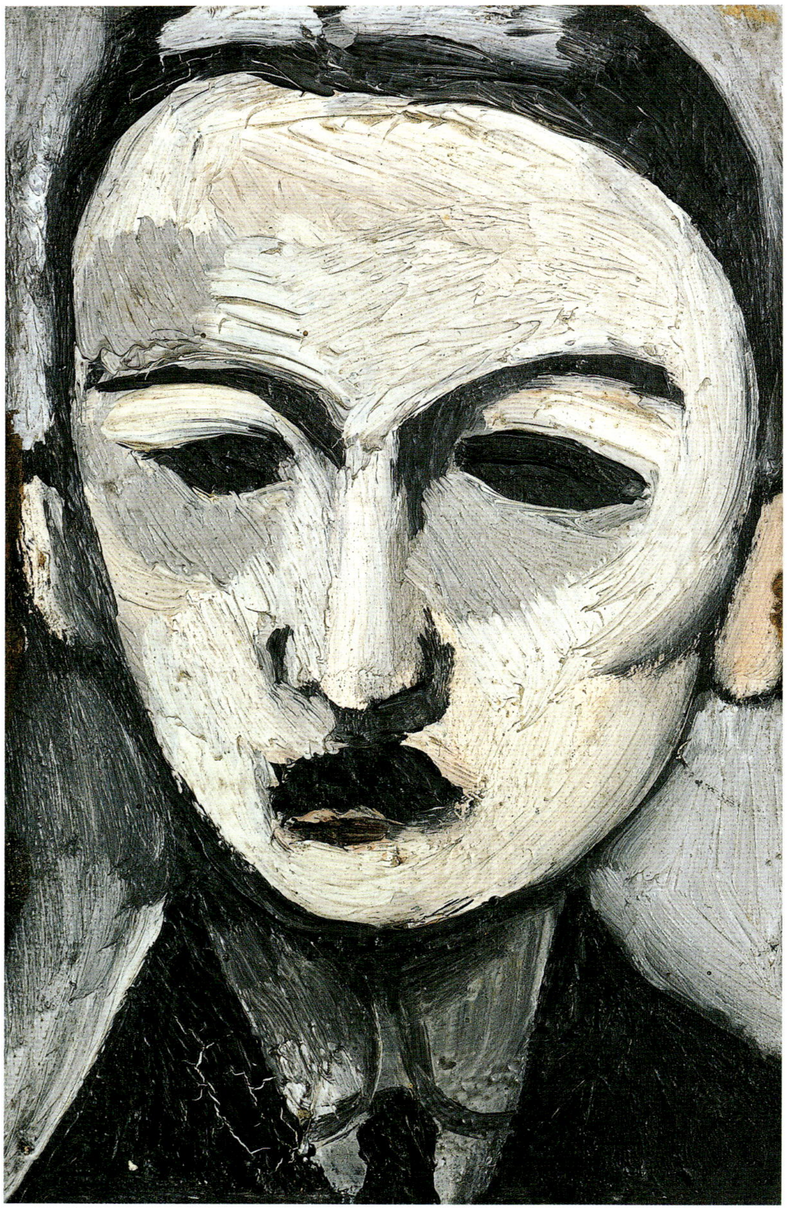

135 (*above left*) *George Besson I*, 1917. Oil on panel, 14 × 8 cm. Bagnols-sur-Cèze, Musée Albert André, gift of George and Adèle Besson.

136 (*above right*) *George Besson II*, 1918. Oil on panel, 14 × 9 cm. Besançon, Musée des Beaux-Arts et d'Archéologie.

enjoyed a good cigar) as well as the difficulty of obtaining art materials. Besson reported that he sat fourteen times for the second version.[91] Matisse's extra attention shows: this portrait has a much more considered surface, having been worked and reworked, almost modeled, so dense is the paint. All the complicated and inflected lines, and most of the nuances found in the first portrait have been simplified in the second. Besson has also lost his moustache and eyeglasses, which he wore at all times.[92] These were but details, contingent and inconsequential.

For Matisse's goal was larger. He told Besson while he worked on this portrait that he was trying to think about the sitter's family, despite not knowing what any of these people looked like, or anything else about them for that matter.[93] "I want this portrait to look like your ancestors and your descendants," he said to his sitter.[94] This second effort is another expression of Matisse's desire to make this kind of meaningful extrapolation from the particular appearance of a sitter. From the tension of the Pellerin commission and the monumentality of his second portrait to the elfin delicacy of the two images of his sympathetic new friend is psychologically a long way, but the basic procedure with both sitters, moving from the blandness of observed fact to the sharp focus of a synthetic construction, was the same.

The movement from observation to synthesis in the Besson and Pellerin portraits should also be understood in terms of Matisse's renewed fascination with Impressionism in the late 1910s, set in dialogue with his deeper dependence on the example of Cézanne, a dialogue apparent in Matisse's painting generally at this time.[95] Matisse himself put the point on the relevant differences between Renoir and Cézanne, stressing the spontaneity and effortlessness in Renoir's example that "rescues" the artist devoted to Cézanne – himself – from "the more arid aspects of pure abstraction" and from the dangers of "continuous tension."[96] It is certainly true that, superficially at least, Matisse did incline toward Impressionist engagement with nature and the spontaneous effect in the following decade. Not only had he met Renoir, and gone back to visit him several times, he had made the pilgrimage to Giverny to meet Monet in May 1917; and, suiting action to homage, he bought an automobile in 1917 so he could take his painting materials into the woods to work *en plein air*, leading him to renewed interest in landscape painting.[97] In the years 1916–18, however, the dialogue with Cézanne was still active and would prove to be the dominant element in his portraiture. This can be seen in the Besson and Pellerin portraits. The first portrait of Besson is the "Renoir" version, the second the "Cézanne" version; the same is true of the portraits of Pellerin (even the Renoir painting behind the sitter is subject to transformation by Cézannian *passage*). Matisse might have preferred an easy road to completing a portrait, but chose in these cases, as he had done with Greta Prozor and Yvonne Landsberg, to work through the state of "continuous tension" to a resolution in a lasting image that assimilated the sitter completely to the artist.

In the end the adventuresome Besson preferred the pinched and ugly but more "Matissian" appearance of the second portrait to the mild manner of the first. When he had had his portrait painted by Bonnard (in 1909), and portraits of his wife made by Kees van Dongen and Renoir, he had paid these artists, but Matisse made a gift of both of his little portraits to the sitter.[98] On one hand, Matisse seems to have made them for his own interest, as we have seen him do before. On the other, it seems likely that he hoped for other forms of compensation from his well-connected sitter, which he was amply to receive – extensive publicity for himself and his work due to Besson's new enthusiasm, and his energy and contacts in the publishing industry. In 1918 Besson was a figure of increasing importance in the French art world. Early in his journalistic career he had been a stringer for Alfred Stieglitz's journal *Camera Work*, and in this capacity he had interviewed Matisse for a special issue on painters' views about photography.[99] At about this time also Besson began to collect art in a modest way, and the contents of his collection closely mirrored his contacts among artists: he tended to acquire the work of friends. His collection was thus strong in Renoir, Bonnard, Matisse, and especially Marquet, all of whom he knew well.[100]

Besson's real contribution, however, was in the growing field of popular art journalism and publishing, in which he was a key figure. In 1912 he founded the journal *Les Cahiers d'aujourd'hui*, which he built into a publishing firm; under his imprint Besson published one of the first books on Matisse.[101] He went on to direct the art division of the publishing giant Braun et Cie in Mulhouse. In addition to holding these positions, Besson wrote many articles and books and was a major contributor to the early literature on Matisse. Small portraits; big impact.

Forming a professional image

In times of transition the help of friends may be welcome but it is also necessary to rely on oneself. Self-examination seems natural at such moments, and the self-portrait is often the tool of artists in the throes of adjustment. One of the works that best summarizes the changes in Matisse's life and art after the First World War is the painted *Self-Portrait* of 1918 (fig. 137). Of modest size but monumental in proportion to its dimensions, this picture expresses the artist's transition between very different aspects of his life and artistic practice. Immediately after the most experimental period of his career, which had been characterized by daring formal invention and astringent vision, he shifted rapidly toward apparently more luxurious subjects and naturalistic, even seductive pictorial treatment. Although this small painting still embodies much of the austerity and reserve of the previous decade, it also marks out a new direction in his attitude to himself and to the relationship between his personal and professional identity.

He painted the picture during his first extended sojourn in the South of France. During that winter of 1917/18, Matisse stayed temporarily in the Hôtel Beau-Rivage in Nice; his room there was the setting for the picture.[102] Much has been made in the literature of the transient quality of Matisse's surroundings at this time and of how this painting testifies to his readiness to leave at a moment's notice.[103] But his status may not have been as unsettled as it is usually believed to be. His residence in a hotel in itself is no evidence of his transience – he preferred hotels and their conveniences. At the Beau-Rivage he immediately resumed the same regular habits and daily schedule of work that he had followed at Issy.[104] He apparently wished to pick up where he had left off and get on with his new situation.

The canvas itself is the best demonstration of this desire for stability and of the confidence with which it was expressed. Matisse's last painted self-portrait, it is also a symbolic manifestation of a new direction. For the first time since the drypoint of 1900–03 (see fig. 31), he showed himself at work, and without the elaborate triple dialogue of the more recent *The Painter and His Model* (1916; Paris, Musée National d'Art Moderne). To state the obvious, Matisse's self-portrait of 1918 is a classic image of the artist playing the role he scripted for himself, and does not emphasize the more abstract issues in the process of making art, as some of his representations of his studio do. The sense of tangibility and temporality in the self-portrait is heightened by the mundane quality of his surroundings and the specificity with which they are described in paint.

Although the painting embodies a phase of transition, there is little hesitation or ambiguity in it. It is as solid in composition as the most rigorously constructed paintings of the decade – its composition strongly resembles, in fact, that of the Cubist-influenced *Interior with Goldfish* of 1914 (Paris, Musée National d'Art Moderne). The paint is firmly and soberly applied, in accord with the artist's dour self-projection here. The color scheme is dominated by the browns, blacks, and ochers that characterized some of his portraits and landscapes of the time. If anything, it is more sober than most of his other work of the 1910s. It is certainly more conservative. The only relief is found in the pastel accents in orange-pink, ice blue, and lemon yellow, a mild flirtation with the kinds of colors that came to

137 *Self-Portrait*, 1918. Oil on canvas, 65 × 54 cm. Le Cateau-Cambrésis, Musée Matisse.

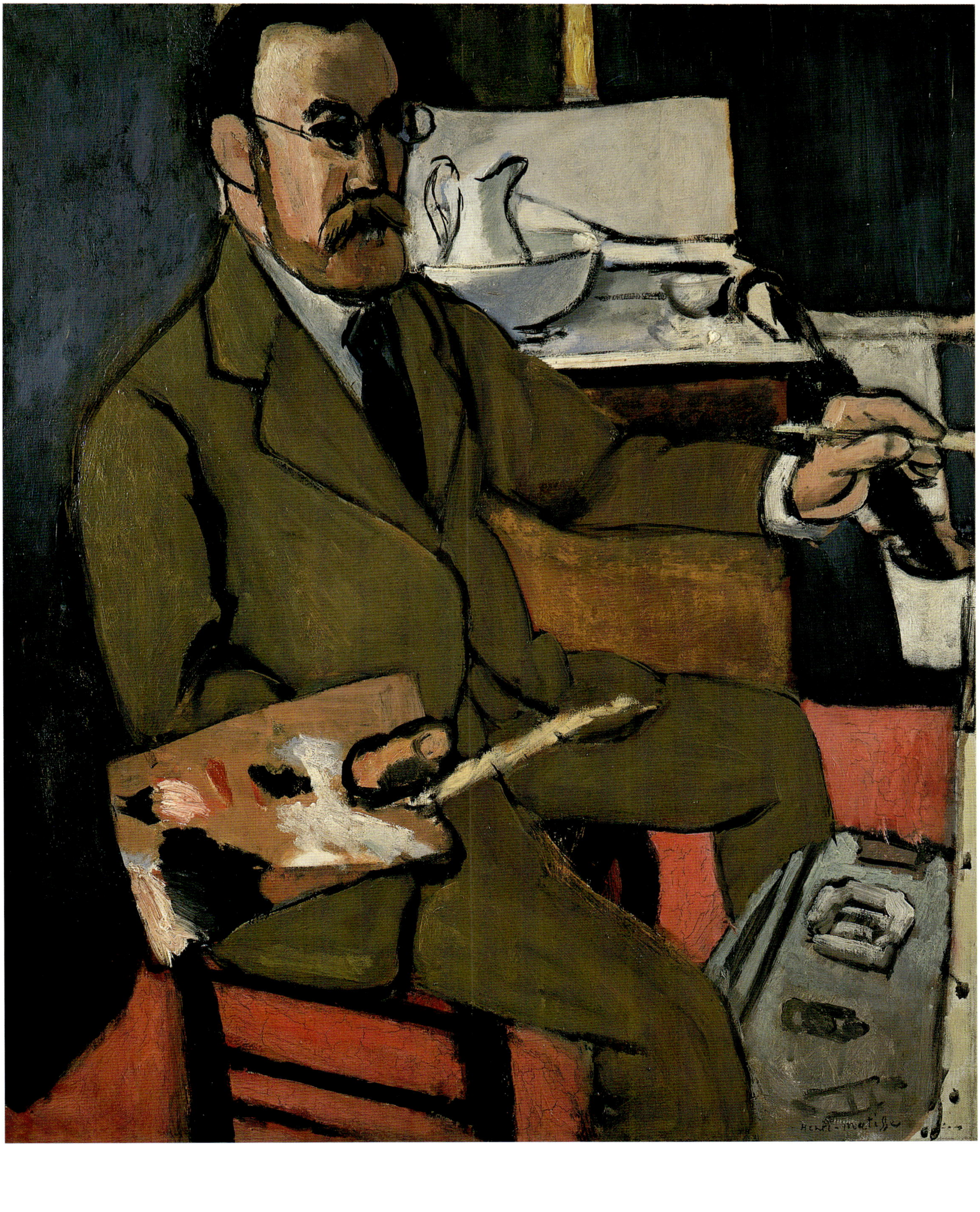
Henri-Matisse

stand for the artificiality and supposed lightweight quality of the paintings of the first Nice period. Here they are anything but frivolous: they assert the artist's prerogative to arbitrariness even in a painting that seems to exemplify Matisse's renewed embrace of realist painting.

This realism, however, was combined with, and indeed was at the heart of, a specific rhetorical stance taken by Matisse at this moment. With this picture he made a pledge to traditional values while still asserting the central role of the artist. Dressed in a vested suit (assuredly not his painting clothes, but consistent with his everyday costume when not at work), he holds his palette before him like an emblem. The image is a demand by Matisse to be taken seriously, and in the service of this desire he allies himself with a long lineage of self-images of the artist as a confident and highly qualified practitioner. Among the archetypes for this kind of professional self-imagery are the self-portraits of Poussin, Largillière, and Labille-Guiard. Matisse's painting is less obviously a rhetorical construction than these, but its rhetoric is the same in essence, allowing for the differences in artistic and cultural temperaments between eras.

His construction of himself as a dedicated professional artist was far from isolated in his own time. This rhetorical position had many other adherents at the end of and immediately following the First World War as a reassertion of stability was foremost in the minds of many artists. Artists as diverse as Lovis Corinth and Roger Fry, Amédée Ozenfant, Max Liebermann, and Piet Mondrian all painted self-portraits with much the same basic conception as Matisse's, all in this year, 1918.[105] At this particular time, these various painters shared the same serious outlook, the same attitude toward themselves, and the way in which they exemplify their profession. In a general sense, this conception of the artist as a conservative professional arose with the postwar *rappel à l'ordre* that had also been evident in France and elsewhere before the armistice.[106] Matisse obliquely referred to the political situation and its relation to his work in a letter to Camoin a few months after painting his self-portrait: "Here [Nice] I am working hard all day, and with passion. I feel that that is the only good and certain thing to do. I don't get into politics, as regrettably nearly everyone else is. So to compensate I am making solid and sensible canvases."[107] Whatever brand of politics he may have been referring to, Matisse believed he could steer clear of it. But in making "solid and sensible canvases," he was in fact participating, along with so many other artists, in the dominant political and artistic conservatism of the time. His isolation was not as complete as he might have liked it to be. Whether singular or part of the crowd, though, his newly constructed aura of respectability was a significant departure from that of the self-conscious innovator of the previous two decades.

The image is quite different from the one he had projected in 1906, and the contrast is worth a brief examination. As befits a Fauve painting, *Self-Portrait in a Striped Jersey* (see fig. 90) is far more vivid in color and more energetic and arbitrary in application of paint; much cracking of the surface implies a hasty and impatient execution. Although slightly smaller in each dimension than the later self-portrait, it is much larger in scale – the head is greater than life-size. The fixing eye in the center, unmediated by eyeglasses, is the focus of the confrontational stance of the image; by contrast, the eyes in the Nice self-portrait, obscure behind spectacles, do not engage the viewer. In the later picture, Matisse situated his figure naturally in his workaday surroundings; in Collioure, the artist had isolated his head and shoulders, projecting them outward against an indefinite and atmospheric background. Matisse's earlier rhetorical construction of himself as an adventurous sailor gave way in the later picture to the creature of regular habits. Both men are self-assured, but the younger expressed this confidence through defiance, the older in quiet satisfaction. Bold *vs.* detached; outdoors and informal *vs.* roombound and proper; searching amateur *vs.* confirmed professional – the differences between these two pictures do not account completely for the changes that took place between two different phases in Matisse's long career, but they focus and symbolize his aspirations and accomplishments at each period.

I have discussed the self-portrait of 1918 at this length as much because of the position it takes within Matisse's career as for its intrinsic qualities. For while its rhetorical construction is matter-of-fact, it is Matisse's businesslike assumption of his own importance that drove his growing interest in an advantageous public presentation of himself and his work. His sense of himself not only informs much of his self-imaging, but it also affects how the relationship between him and his work is construed – by Matisse himself and by all others who stood to benefit from a greater general appreciation of his work. Further consideration of the relationship between Matisse's self-portraits and publicity will be the subject of Chapter 6.

Drawings for patrons old and new

In 1924 Matisse made his last painting that can unequivocally be called a portrait. *The Baroness Gourgaud* (fig. 188) will be discussed in Chapter 7, as it occupies a symptomatic place in the decline of the portrait in Matisse's work. Not until the 1930s did he make in any medium another portrait related to patronage of his work. Thereafter until the end of his career he made a handful of such portraits, all drawings, in themselves private endeavors but even so having some public role in the spread of the artist's reputation and knowledge of his work.

Most of his drawings from the 1930s in the sphere of commissioned portraiture were aligned with American patronage. In this decade he became an international celebrity, and American museums and private collections led the way in the acquisition of his work.[108] Numerous publications and exhibitions, including the first American retrospective of Matisse's work, organized by Alfred Barr in 1931 at the Museum of Modern Art in New York, brought his art to the attention of a worldwide public. Matisse received an increasing number of commissions for an ever greater variety of projects, including stage and costume design, book illustration, and mural decoration.

His most substantial commission of the 1930s, and the one most fraught with difficulties, was the decoration of the central hall at Albert Barnes's Foundation in suburban Philadelphia with his *Dance* mural. Barnes at this time was the most important collector of Matisse's work in the United States. While in the country to discuss the commission in 1930, Matisse was introduced by Barnes to the philosopher and educator John Dewey, one of the irascible collector's few friends. Barnes had been much influenced by Dewey's writings about art and education, and a few years before had appointed him Educational Director of the Barnes Foundation.

Dewey had just retired after twenty-six years of teaching at Columbia University; possibly this was why Barnes suggested to Matisse that he make a commemorative portrait of the seventy-one-year-old philosopher. The original proposal was for a lithograph, to serve perhaps as a frontispiece to one of Dewey's books.[109] Matisse made at least three charcoal drawings in New York in preparation for the print,

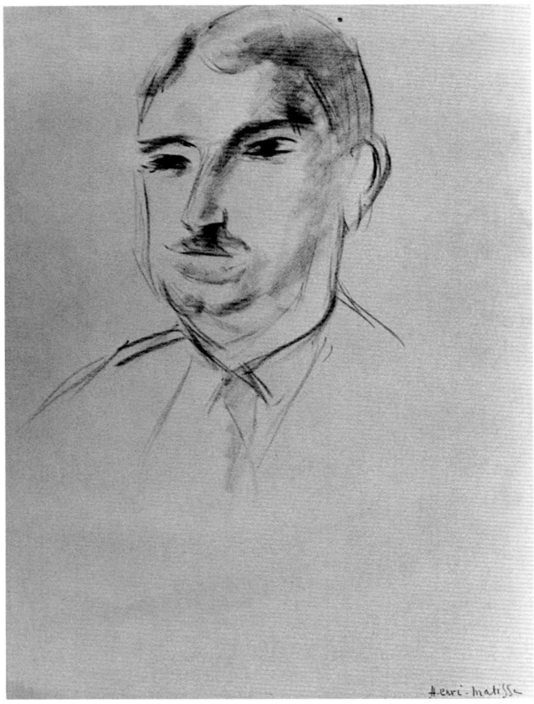

138 *John Dewey*, 1930. Charcoal on paper, 57 × 48 cm. New York, Columbia University, gift of Pierre Matisse.

139 *Dr. Claribel Cone*, 1933–4. Pencil on paper, 31.4 × 24.8 cm. The Baltimore Museum of Art, Cone Collection, formed by Dr. Claribel Cone and Miss Etta Cone of Baltimore, Maryland, BMA 1950.12.72.

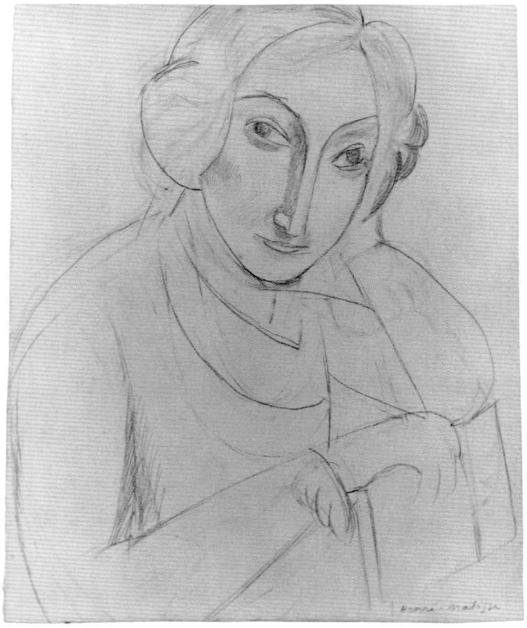

which was never carried out. The portrait of John Dewey (fig. 138) in the collection of Columbia University is not the worst of them, but they are all dull and vague, and convey neither the specificities of the sitter's mature age nor his creative powers as a teacher and thinker.[110] One suspects that Matisse felt himself to be working under duress at the behest of the demanding Barnes. The technique of the portraits is soft and tentative, with no resolution, no sense that trials were followed by firm results as in most of Matisse's other series of drawings in the 1930s. Little of Dewey therefore emerges from these smudgings, and little of Matisse. These portraits are instructive examples of the collapse of the portrait transaction when neither side is prepared to offer much.[111]

On the same trip to the United States in 1930 Matisse traveled to Baltimore to visit Etta Cone, who together with her sister Claribel had amassed, over a period of twenty-five years, the second most extensive collection of Matisse's work in the United States after Barnes's. And unlike Barnes, whose commission from Matisse for the murals in Merion was his final acquisition of the artist's work, Etta Cone continued to be an important patron and supporter of his work in the United States.

Claribel Cone had died the previous year and Etta asked Matisse to make a memorial portrait drawing of her sister.[112] He was to work from memory with the aid of a photograph that Etta gave him, an unusual instance of his use of photography in this way. Matisse began to work on the portrait of Claribel as early as February 1931.[113] Other projects intervened, notably the Barnes mural and his illustrations for a new edition of Mallarmé's *Poésies*, and Matisse let the portrait commission lapse. On a visit to Paris in 1933, Etta took up the matter again and Matisse promised to finish the portrait right away. Even then it was nearly a year before he presented Etta Cone with a portrait of her sister (fig. 140), as well as her own portrait (see fig. 141), apparently also done from a photograph. The delay has been characterized as evidence of Matisse's "personal integrity and artistic rigor," but it seems likely that he procrastinated for a while in the face of a task that, however good his intentions, was far removed in spirit from his current work.[114] The portrait of Etta was a handsome gesture; he may also have done it in compensation for running the risk of letting Claribel's memory grow cold.

Once he got down to serious work, Matisse felt pleased by the challenge, as he told his old friend Simon Bussy in a letter written shortly before he finished the drawings:

> I'm still on my portraits from photographs of my two Baltimore ladies, whom you perhaps don't remember. I'm finishing them – somewhat arduous work (what work isn't?), particularly so because imagination, memory and the precision of the photograph must join forces to produce the truth, but all the same very interesting because it's based on two opposing characters, yet from the same family because they are sisters. One of them [Claribel] is beautiful, a great beauty, noble and glorious, lovely hair with ample waves in the old style, contented and dominant, the other [Etta] with the majesty of a Queen of Israel but with a less obvious beauty, with straight hair which, however, falls in beautiful lines like those of her face, but with a touching depth of expression, always submissive to her glorious sister, but attentive to everything. Simplified means, paper and charcoal. The second portrait is finished, I'm on the first, of which you've already seen the pencil studies. I've been working on them every morning for nearly a month now – it's hard but I'm learning a lot.[115]

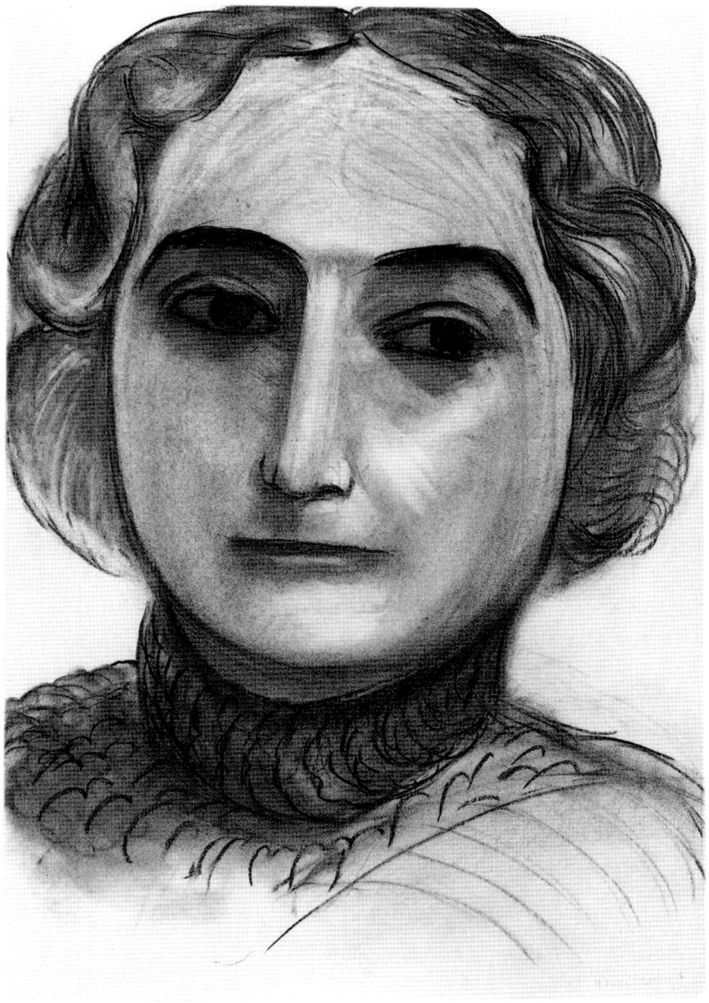 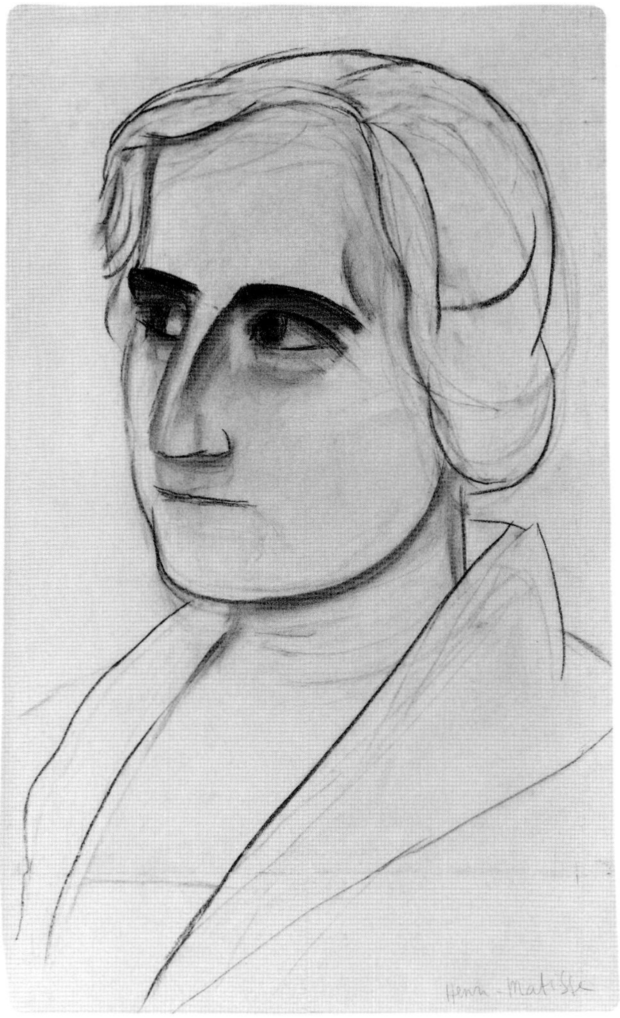

140 (*above left*) *Dr. Claribel Cone*, 1933–4. Charcoal on paper, 59 × 40.6 cm. The Baltimore Museum of Art, Cone Collection, formed by Dr. Claribel Cone and Miss Etta Cone of Baltimore, Maryland, BMA 1950.12.71.

141 (*above right*) *Etta Cone*, 1934. Charcoal on paper, 70.5 × 40.6 cm. The Baltimore Museum of Art, Cone Collection, formed by Dr. Claribel Cone and Miss Etta Cone of Baltimore, Maryland, BMA 1950.12.69.

He had shown Bussy some studies in pencil he had done for the portrait of Claribel. These, three in number, he sent to Etta with the final portrait, along with six drawings of Etta herself: ten drawings in all, received just in time for them all to be reproduced in a deluxe catalogue of the Cone Collection being prepared in Switzerland for Etta.[116] Matisse considered the three pencil drawings of Claribel to be states leading to the fourth and definitive portrait (see fig. 140), which formed the frontispiece of the Cone catalogue. Of the six drawings of Etta, the fifth in the chronological sequence was, he insisted, to be regarded as the final portrait (fig. 141).[117]

Matisse had begun the portrait of Claribel from the photograph he had been given, showing her seated and posed with a book (see fig. 139). He reworked each drawing several times, erasing and changing contours, simplifying features, making minor adjustments in the expression of the face. For the final portrait he took a different approach in a nearly frontal bust-length pose that departs completely from the photographic model. Now more a product of Matisse's memory, the image takes on a more youthful appearance while still retaining the sense of self-command for which the sitter was known. Her impressive waves of hair (as he had described them to Bussy) push against the borders of the sheet and frame a calm oval face.

The drawing is simple, sensitive, and extremely beautiful, and in both conception and realization far more majestic than the somewhat horsey appearance Claribel takes on in the preliminary states.

By comparison to the memorial to Claribel the definitive drawing of the living Etta is wanting in vivacity. Matisse had begun with a bare outline of her head, emphasizing eyes looking as if heavenward. Through several drawings he refined Etta's features and added subtlety to the topography of her face. Still, in the three-quarter pose her prominent nose stands out, a problem Matisse avoided in the nearly frontal view of Claribel. The genetic affinity of the two women – something of characteristic interest to Matisse – can be seen in this bold nose, as well as in the dark eyebrows and the set of the eyes in both portraits. Between the fifth and sixth in the Etta sequence there is little to choose – except, obviously, in the eyes of the artist, who may have preferred the more elegant contour of the cheek in the penultimate version to the more volumetric modeling of the last.[118]

Matisse's procedure in these portraits is one of the first instances of his development of a definitive version of a drawing through a series of studies that in themselves may look no less finished than the definitive version. At the time, Matisse was also pursuing this approach in painting, most famously in the *Large Reclining Nude* of 1935, whose progress he had documented in a state-by-state photographic record. It may not be coincidental that Etta Cone bought this painting in 1936, Matisse having already sent her the accumulated photographic account of its evolution.[119] Several years earlier, Etta had bought from the artist all the working drawings and proofs for his illustrations to Mallarmé's *Poésies*, comprising some 250 items, a rich record of Matisse's working procedure in this project. She was manifestly interested in the creative process of his art; for this reason he may have felt she would have a special interest in works, such as the *Large Reclining Nude*, whose progress was so well documented.

142 Fernand Léger, *Maud Dale*, 1935. Oil on canvas, 100 × 80 cm. Washington, D.C., National Gallery of Art, Chester Dale Collection, 1962.

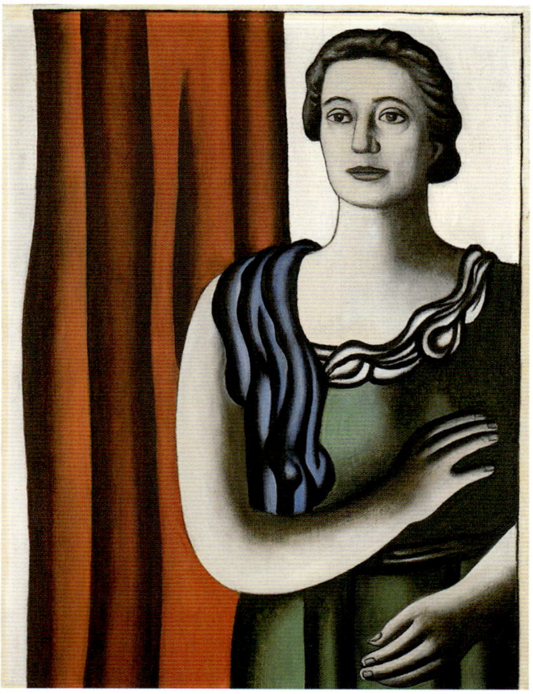

Conversely, perhaps Etta's acquisition of the Mallarmé studies and Matisse's work on the portrait drawings of the sisters together prompted him to realize how interesting and useful it would be to document the evolution of unique works such as paintings, which he began to do in 1935. This realization governed his working methods in countless paintings, drawings, and decorative projects over the rest of his career. His deliberated development of the images of the Cone sisters may have had a deep impact on his attitude toward process, and how knowledge of it could shape understanding of the final work of art, an application taken well beyond portraiture or even the rendering of the human figure in his art.

The portraits of Claribel and Etta Cone also have a place within a wider frame of reference than Matisse's own work. Both final portraits are distinctive in being very large for portrait drawings, and vaguely classicizing. This monumental classicism can be found in other commissioned portraits of American patrons by French artists, such as Fernand Léger's *Maud Dale* (fig. 142), painted in the following year, 1935. This coincidence should remind us of the proliferation in the 1930s, for better and for worse, of "a new Classicism that is entirely modern."[120]

Whereas the Cones had been collecting Matisse's work for decades, William Paley and his wife, Dorothy, were newcomers in the 1930s. After buying two of Matisse's Nice period paintings in 1936, the Columbia Broadcasting System executive commissioned Matisse to paint a portrait of his wife. In early September of that year, the Paleys visited Matisse at his studio in Paris, where he made at least eight charcoal drawings and an unknown number in pen and ink.[121] Any of the charcoal drawings (see fig. 143) is typical of the group. Among them there is little change

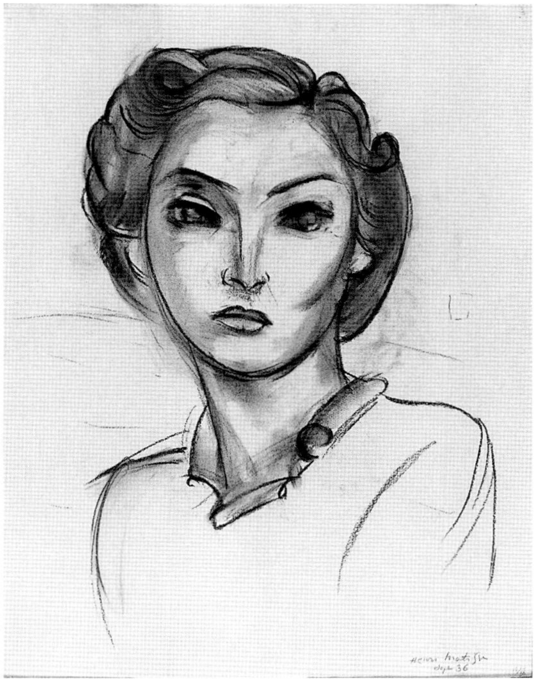

143 *Dorothy Paley*, 1936. Charcoal on paper, 66.5 × 57 cm. Le Cateau-Cambrésis, Musée Matisse.

in pose, coiffure, and placement in space, in contrast to Matisse's procedure in the drawings of the Cone sisters. What is clear in the portraits of Dorothy Paley is how Matisse concentrated on her eyes, as if he isolated this feature in order to study them specially, making them wider then narrower, sharpening then obscuring their gaze, calibrating their effect on the entire expression of the portrait.

Paley said later that Matisse fell ill when he was about to begin the painting, and they put off the work until the following year, when the Paleys would be back in France.[122] In the spring of 1937 Matisse wrote to Paley requesting the loan of his *Nude with a Tambourine* without mentioning the portrait project.[123] Paley agreed and took the opportunity to express his eagerness for Matisse to proceed with the portrait of Mrs. Paley. He proposed two periods, in early July and late August, when the Paleys would be in Paris.[124] In his reply Matisse expressed a preference for the first period, implying (in an indulgence of his recurrent hypochondria) that that would be better because of the possibility that he might be sick later on. He went on to estimate that the portrait would require ten or twelve sittings.[125] Paley confirmed these arrangements.[126] The portrait was never done: the Paleys arrived two weeks late for their appointment, Matisse had gotten busy in the meantime on other things, and he was displeased enough to refuse to take up the project again.[127] Apparently, he would endure only so much inconvenience from people whom he may have perceived as American *arrivistes*. On this unsatisfying outcome Paley is silent in his memoir. Perhaps in the ill-fated Paley transaction Matisse's worst fears about the nature of the give and take in a portrait commission were confirmed. Real portraits, forged in a dialogic relationship, had long been marginalized, pushed aside by the more easily controlled transaction of hiring a model.

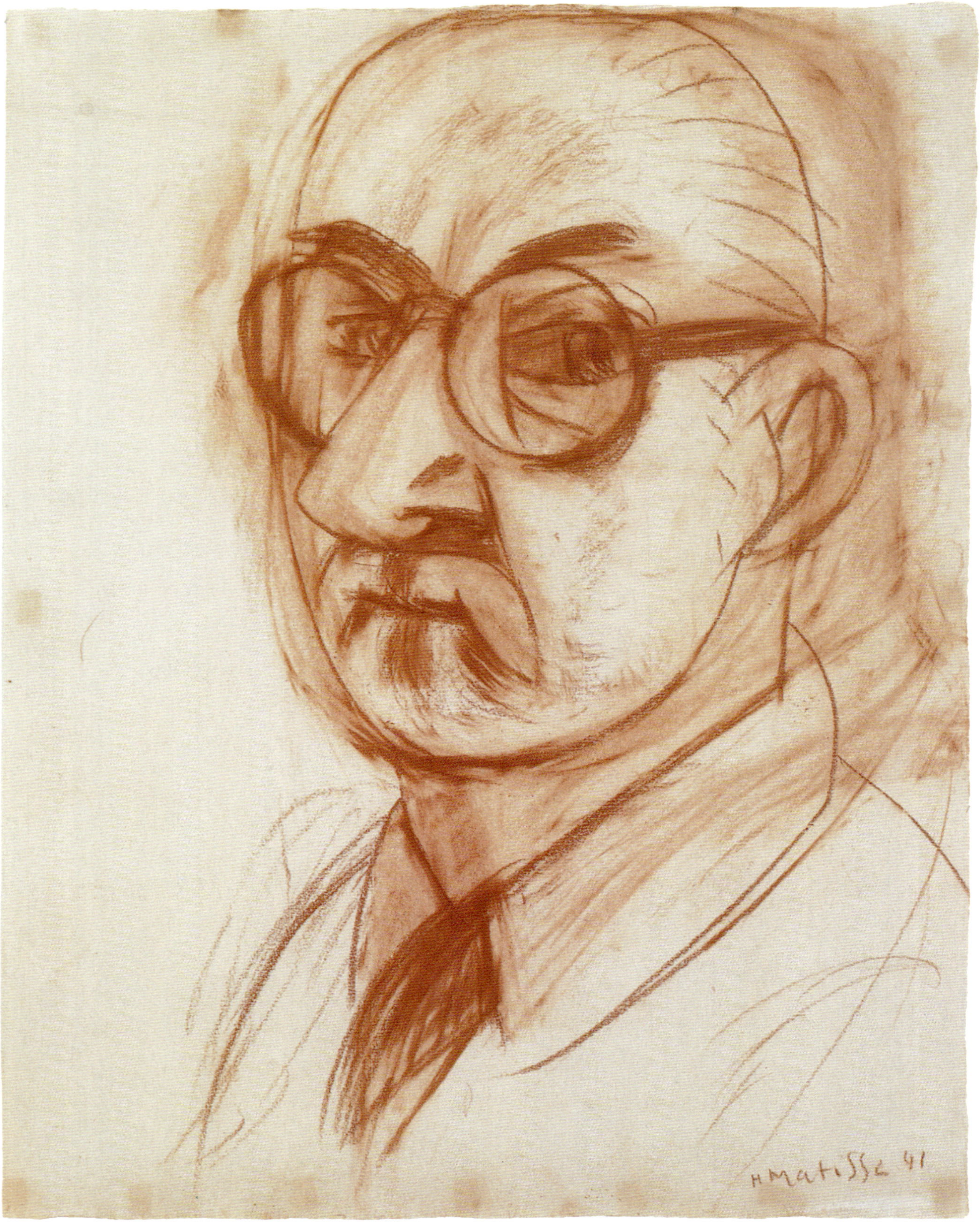
H Matisse 41

Chapter 6 Self-Portraiture and Self-Promotion

In Chapter 2, I considered traditional modes of self-portraiture and the way in which Matisse's early works in this genre fulfill many conventional expectations even as they reveal a singular and probing artistic personality. Most of these works – those grouped around 1900 – may be understood as a collective act of self-determination as Matisse formed his mature artistic identity through the process of their making. They may be considered as the first deeply felt essays in a career of personal investment in creative work.

Then during his early artistic maturity, beginning at the end of his apprenticeship and continuing with the Copenhagen self-portrait of 1906 (see fig. 90) and a few self-portrait drawings during the 1910s, Matisse's self-image became more assertive and definitive, as is to be expected. In this chapter I shall consider the self-portraits he made after 1906 in a different set of contexts, more from the standpoint of how he used them after he made them than as artifacts of an internal process. These portraits were at once reprises of self-images developed early in his career and tools of self-assessment, usually at crucial times in his life; but they were also deliberate projections used to enhance his growing reputation.

Private withdrawal, public recognition

These functions derive from a shift in Matisse's understanding of the role of the self-portrait in relation to his other work and to his life. After the First World War he treated the self-portrait more as a public instrument – though there were some significant exceptions. In general, his self-images at this time assert an idea of his personality that is consistent with the values apparently embodied in the works themselves. The image of relaxation, sensuality, and material well-being that is often imputed especially to Matisse's paintings of the 1920s has usually set the tone of response to the artist as a vital creative force, though this older view of unself-conscious ease has been seriously revised.[1] In the works from the Nice period and beyond, there is little difficulty or conflict implied in the process of artistic creation, and during this time, as we have seen, Matisse began to construct himself as a professional artist doing his job well and doing well by it. Here I shall be concerned with how Matisse presented himself in these self-portraits; how he and his work were then publicized through exhibitions, books, and articles; and in this process how one and the other, the man and his creations, were consciously and successfully linked in a way that they were not in the first decades of his career.

The change, like all such fundamental shifts, was not sudden. Its antecedents may be tentatively marked in the years leading up to a phase of transition, at the end of the 1910s, to his new way of life. By living at least half of the year in the South

144 *Self-Portrait*, 1941. Sanguine chalk on paper, 48 × 37.5 cm. Private collection.

of France, away from his family (which had nurtured him in one way and then ceased to) and away from the Paris art world (which had nurtured him in others, then similarly had outgrown its function as a direct context for his practice), he withdrew into conditions of greater intimacy and privacy. There he could both shield himself and offer of himself what he chose for public inspection. What he did disclose must be regarded as selective and calculated, as a guide to a properly informed critical and public reception of his art. He was also projecting a withdrawal from the avant-garde in this period, a deferral that ultimately promoted the collecting of his work and the development of his reputation in this conservative period in France.

In the 1920s Matisse's reputation began to be molded in earnest, then to solidify into the stuff of legend. The first book on the artist, by his early supporter Marcel Sembat, was published in 1920. In 1921 the French government bought the painting *Odalisque with Red Trousers*, the first state purchase of one of Matisse's works since the acquisition of some of his copies of "old masters" culminating in 1904, potboilers that were destined for distribution to the provinces. Also in 1921 Elie Faure's landmark *Histoire de l'art: l'art moderne* canonized Matisse as one of the leading moderns. Further official recognition in France came in 1925 when he was made a Commander of the Legion of Honor. He achieved a wider international reputation in 1927 with the award of the first prize in the Carnegie International Exhibition in Pittsburgh. By the end of the decade scores of books and articles on his work had been published in half a dozen countries, and paintings, drawings, and sculpture by Matisse had been exhibited in cities throughout Europe and the United States.

Many people of course were deeply invested in these developments, first of all Matisse himself. The members of his family were strongly affected; at this time his children made their career choices, each in a fairly clear relationship to their father's forceful personality and formidable public successes (see Chapter 3, note 2). Art dealers and publishers of books and journals had a great deal at stake in the promotion, sale, and distribution of the artist's work. Their strategies, together with Matisse's evidently sincere desire that his aims be understood by as wide an audience as possible, played a major role in determining how his work was perceived by specialists and the educated public alike.

A distinct image of Matisse, the man as well as the artist, was projected into the public domain during the 1920s. The image had been in formation earlier, but in this decade the man and his work were linked more persistently and were seen to be in greater accord than before. Matisse was certainly not alone in this respect, and it may be possible to detect a general interest during the postwar period – possibly from humanizing motives – in the personal lives of prominent artists.[2]

The first interview with Matisse that consisted largely of personal reminiscences, as opposed to statements of his artistic aims, was conducted by Jacques Guenne in 1925.[3] Its emphasis differed significantly from Matisse's major theoretical statement, "Notes of a Painter" of 1908, which, even while speaking of expression and the role of the artist, had been notably impersonal. The process of personalizing his work had begun in his interview with Clara MacChesney, published in 1912, in which he expressed concern about his public image and was eager to emphasize his human side.[4] But the construction of Matisse's humanity in the MacChesney interview was made to provide a contrast with the apparently anarchic character of the work. The set piece of the bourgeois in pleased possession of his house, his garden, and his senses was meant to be reassuring, but there is also an element of the relish of paradox here.[5] By 1925 and the Guenne interview, however, the image had become seamless. The work was now perfectly the product of the man and it was implicit that knowledge of that man, especially of his personal history and formation, would enhance appreciation of the work.

This approach to Matisse's work through his personality as a man had substantial recent precedent in the study of art in France. The genre of the art-historical biography – an encompassing "Life and Works" – came into its own in the last quarter of the nineteenth century.[6] Persons close to an artist in life became valued for the alleged authority of their reminiscences after his death. Millet had his Sensier; Manet his Antonin Proust; Cézanne his Vollard. But Matisse (like Picasso) had a significant advantage: he was alive when several of his acquaintances published their books of anecdotes and personal memories – Pierre Courthion in 1934 and 1942; Raymond Escholier in 1937; and Francis Carco in 1953.[7] Obviously, an artist cannot be everywhere at once in the enterprise of producing and defending his or her reputation. But Matisse's penchant for control is well known, and from an early time he fed apologists and hagiographers their lines when he could.[8] His opportunities to do this could only multiply as he was increasingly solicited for statements on his art and for complementary information that would help to enlighten an occasionally befuddled but clearly malleable audience. Matisse understood how his pronouncements could shape critical and public understanding, and he further understood the call for his personal contribution to satisfy an increasing need for evidence of a human element in an art that may have seemed ever more divorced from ordinary experience.

His work after the First World War should be seen in this context of greater public attention. Of course the work itself also underwent radical changes in the years of his transition from the north to the south. This is not a case of Matisse's pandering to a certain market for his painting, but it is inevitable that he would be increasingly conscious of his status, the power of his wishes, and the need to preserve his interests. There is not a chance connection between the obdurate difficulty of his paintings of the 1910s and their critical and public reception on one hand, and, on the other, the greater accessibility and the marketability of the work of the 1920s. If he did not divine a trend, at least he was willing to participate actively in a climate of more favorable reception and the advantages this could bring.

The way in which Matisse's self-image was produced and distributed after the First World War also differed considerably from how this was done earlier. The change was intimately connected with the new conditions in his personal life and artistic outlook. Among his works (as opposed to his statements about them), Matisse's contribution to his self-image is seen most literally in the large number of self-portraits, mainly drawings, often grouped at significant junctures in the latter two-thirds of his career. The traditionally private discoveries and determinations of the self-portrait were increasingly made a matter of record for other, more public purposes. The transfer of Matisse's self-image from the private realm to the public arena is remarkable for its success, in stark contrast to the retreat he made in this period from the public expression of shared values in his portraits of other people.

* * *

Limited release

Despite the general surge of interest in artists' portraits of themselves late in the nineteenth and early in the twentieth centuries, the traditionally private character of self-portraiture was accepted largely intact by Matisse through the First World War. The two painted self-portraits of 1900 (see figs. 29, 34) were never made public during this time. Neither was exhibited or published until after the Second World War, and until recently neither left the possession of the Matisse family.[9]

Self-Portrait in a Striped Jersey of 1906 was not cloistered in this way. As we have seen, Matisse offered the painting as his sole exhibit in the group show at Bernheim-Jeune entitled "Portrait d'hommes" in 1907. In the same year it was one of the four recent paintings chosen to illustrate Apollinaire's long magazine piece about the artist.[10] Matisse probably prompted Apollinaire's statements in this article, and possibly the artist chose the illustrations through which his work would be represented, as he did a year later with those for the publication of "Notes of a Painter." It is significant that in Apollinaire's article and in his shorter "Médaillon: un fauve," written in 1909 but not published during the author's lifetime, he showed himself to be the rare early writer on Matisse who concerned himself with the artist's personality and private life.[11] This was, however, Apollinaire's general approach with artists whose work he discussed, and in many cases he wrote more about personal matters than about their paintings. His eliciting of such details from Matisse says more about his own brand of criticism than about Matisse's desire for his work to be perceived through the lens of his private life at this time.

By 1909 *Self-Portrait in a Striped Jersey* was in the collection of Michael and Sarah Stein. Matisse borrowed it from them in 1914 for his major show at the Galerie Gurlitt in Berlin. This particular painting was therefore a notable exception to the withholding of Matisse's early self-portraits; it has indeed remained his most celebrated self-image.

The early exhibition and publication record of Matisse's drawings is much more difficult to ascertain and in many cases it is probably impossible. In the catalogues for the large annual exhibitions, as in those for the solo shows of Matisse's work at Vollard, Druet, and Bernheim-Jeune, his drawings were almost never identified by subject, dimensions, or owner – standard practice in such publications. As often as not they were not even listed individually. Thus perhaps no general statement about the public exhibition of Matisse's self-portrait drawings during the first two decades of the century can be authoritative.[12] The same is true for the only self-portraits of the period in printmaking media: the etching of 1900–03 and a monotype of 1914–15.[13] These works in black and white thus also seem to conform, in the circumstances of their origin and use, to the generally private character of Matisse's self-imagery during the years of his formation and early maturity.

One measure of the separate status of self-portraits in Matisse's work may be found in an article of his first contract with Bernheim-Jeune, who remained his exclusive dealers for over seventeen years. In this agreement of 1909, Bernheim-Jeune engaged to buy from Matisse all the pictures he would produce with certain exceptions detailed in Article VIII, including commissions already in progress and "son propre portrait."[14] Some works were clearly not going to go on the market, including those whose object was most personal.[15]

Such reticence about his personal image is consistent with the position Matisse adopted in his most important public statement of this period, "Notes of a Painter" of 1908. In this exposition of his artistic theory and practice there is no element of autobiography. He writes about his feelings and beliefs as they relate to the creation of his art, but on other aspects of his personality he is silent. "Notes of a Painter" is an exceptionally reasoned and coherent effort by Matisse to defend his artistic aims in the public arena, and from the same platform as his critics. In addition to offering a theoretical framework for his painting, his essay is a finely calculated work of public relations. But while Matisse took a big step in "Notes of a Painter" away from letting his work speak for itself, his defense of his ideas is conspicuously detached from their human underpinnings.

Special delivery

Although possibly none of the early self-portrait drawings was exhibited or published during this period, a few were made public in other ways and in a more limited sense. Some of them, drawn in letters or on postcards and mailed to correspondents, were destined for particular audiences. In these self-portraits Matisse's human side comes to the surface with humor and occasionally with a sense of sympathetic vulnerability. We recall, for example, the small drawing of the Matisse family the artist sent to Allan Stein in 1906, clearly meant for the entire Stein family (see fig. 56). In a more focused and deliberated way, Matisse sometimes gave or posted, to friends and acquaintances who were actual or potential patrons, self-portrait drawings as a form of souvenir – or salesman's calling card.

In sending these drawings he could communicate a particularly personal message about his state of mind and body. In a letter of January 4, 1916 to Gustave Kahn, a collector and the influential art critic for the *Mercure de France*, Matisse made a drawing of himself taken ill, very similar to the drawing illustrated here (fig. 145). Seeing himself in this state had reminded him of Morocco, and he said to Kahn of his drawing: "Over here you can see my fluey noggin . . . I think I look a bit Moroccan with my towel on my head – that's what gave me the idea to sketch myself."[16] Nearly the entire letter is about his illness in one form or another (Matisse often complained about his health to his friends and family), and in one sense the drawing he included in the letter to Kahn is a succinct illustration to enliven a monotonous text.

It is egocentric, to say the least, to write so much about the state of one's health. The two related self-portraits may also be understood in this light, but there is more at work here than self-centeredness. At another level the self-image in the letter to Kahn was a way for Matisse to communicate something about himself – most superficially how he looked, and in this case under a particular circumstance of ill health – and more rapidly and concisely than words could have done.

Seeing himself in this condition also triggered a memory of a place – Morocco – of high significance to him and to his art.[17] He chose to record this moment of remembrance with a self-portrait, which he then sent to a friend. At the time he made these drawings there was good reason for Morocco to be on Matisse's mind, because he had recently begun his ambitious painting *The Moroccans* (New York, Museum of Modern Art), a work of imagination based on his experiences in North Africa several years earlier.

At that time, in 1912, he had made several self-portrait drawings in which he distinctly contrasted his bourgeois European identity to the exotic land in which he traveled. The contrast in a drawing entitled *H. Matisse by Himself* (fig. 146) is

145 *Self-Portrait*, 1916. Pen and ink on paper, 21 × 13.5 cm. Private collection.

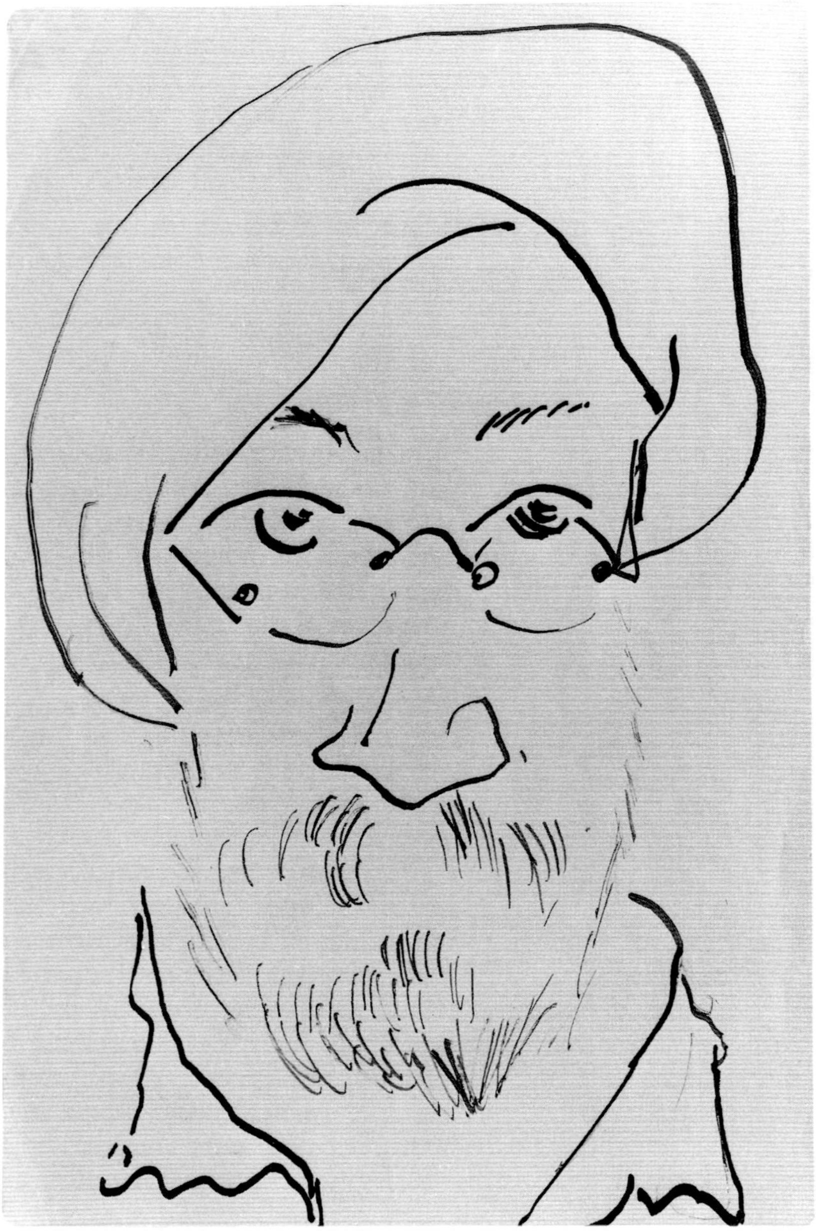

particularly vivid and amusing. Obviously drawing from imagination, Matisse depicted himself dressed formally but nevertheless at work painting, seated awkwardly before his motif and looking as out of place as possible, the observer in turn observed by a local woman standing nearby. In another drawing from this time (fig. 147) he juxtaposed two self-images in suit and dashing touring cap with a study drawing for the painting *Acanthus* (Stockholm, Moderna Museet), a lush Moroccan landscape. Back in France in 1916, he imaginatively projected himself, "going native" in his study, back into the exotic land in which he had previously been a self-conscious European stranger. In both types of self-portraits – "Moroccan" in France, Frenchman in Morocco – Matisse dealt with the foreignness of his associations and memories by distancing himself from his immediate surroundings through his appearance when making these self-images.

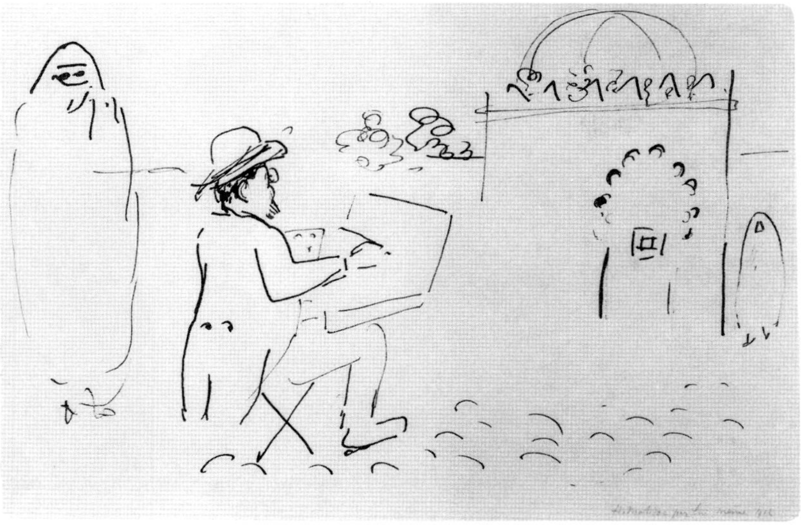

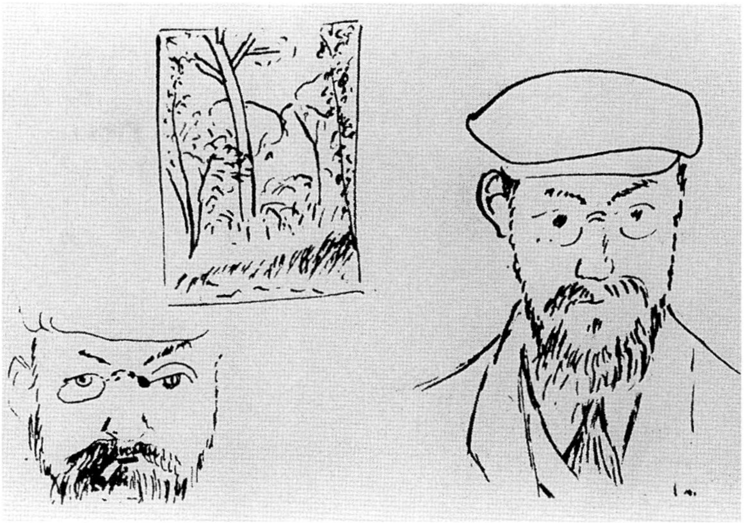

146 (*above left*) *H. Matisse by Himself*, 1912. Pen and ink on paper, 19.3 × 25.3 cm. Private collection.

147 (*above right*) *Two Self-Portraits and a Moroccan Landscape*, 1912. Pen and ink on paper, 22.3 × 32 cm. Private collection.

Reflections on loss of wholeness

Something else is being communicated in the Kahn letter, even if it is not clear that Matisse was fully aware of it. This is the kind of direct, visual association between himself and his work that he had not made since the three interiors of 1895–96 containing a framed self-portrait drawing, when it was obvious that he was highly conscious of the implications of such self-projection (see figs. 14, 15, 16). Moments of self-involvement, as when one is sick, can often have the effect of inducing us to stand outside our normal relationship to ourselves. Stressful circumstances such as illness breach the assumed wholeness that we usually live with and that allows us to conduct our lives in a consistent fashion. When this integrity is compromised, the need to affirm the self is often much greater than normal. Sickness is in fact a common premise for self-portraiture, in the modern era as at other times – Rembrandt, Van Gogh, Kollwitz, Munch, Modersohn-Becker, Schiele, Kahlo, and Mapplethorpe come to mind as examples of artists whose physical (or mental) impairment was a source of their own fascination and of striking imagery.

Whether the artist is sick or well, the link between his or her appearance and the work is a reminder that that work is not disembodied from the concerns of an actual person and from the vicissitudes of human frailty. It is unlikely that Matisse would have consciously formulated the matter in this way. Yet these and other drawings have a distinct flavor of an appeal to human concerns in the context of Matisse's development of a clientele for his work. If this is true, he showed himself to be a shrewd judge of what sticks in the mind. An artist's persona can be a more lasting and identifiable entity than any individual work of art.

With variations, Matisse repeated this practice of including self-portraits in letters many times in his life.[18] Perhaps he also felt that his own image, quickly recorded while in distant communion with his correspondent, could convey his state of mind and body in complement to his words. Sometimes a little self-portrait sketch replaced words entirely, as on a picture postcard of the town of Blois addressed but never sent to the chocolate manufacturer Georges Menier (fig. 148), whose fortune had enabled him to buy the nearby chateau of Chenonceaux. Menier owned several of Matisse's paintings, and he was a potentially important patron in the business community of Paris that also included Auguste Pellerin. Following the war, Matisse

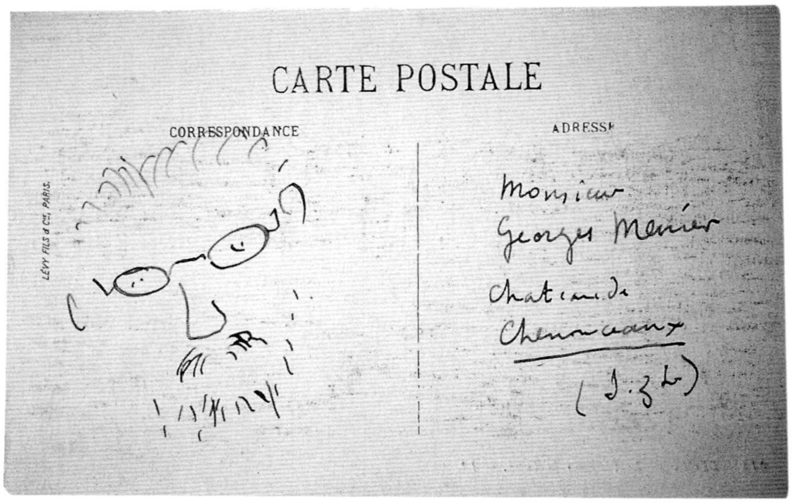

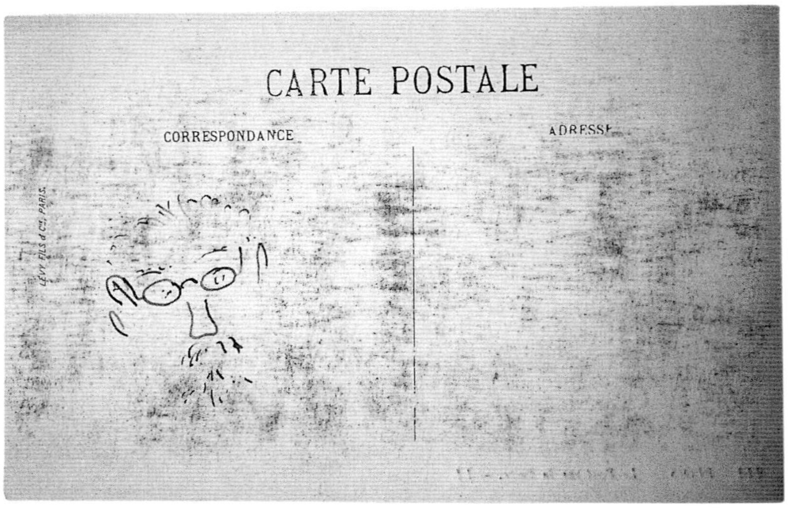

148 (*above left*) Postcard of Blois with self-portrait by Matisse, 1919. Pen and ink on paper, approx. 10.5 × 15 cm. Private collection.

149 (*above right*) Postcard of Blois with self-portrait by Matisse, 1919. Pen and ink on paper, approx. 10.5 × 15 cm. Private collection.

had begun to cultivate an entirely new group of collectors, including Menier, to replace those whose activities had been curtailed in one way or another by war and revolution – the Steins, Marcel Sembat, and especially Morosov and Shchukin.

Another postcard of Blois (fig. 149) with a self-portrait sketch on the reverse was never addressed, as if Matisse knew in advance what his "message" would be, no matter who the recipient of it.[19] These little sketches are appropriately slight for the ephemeral purpose, but even their abbreviated style is unusual among Matisse's drawings at this time. The self-portraits are also lively and amusing, and in that respect they differ from most of his other work in painting and drawing of the moment. The light touch and the ingratiating manner are in contrast with the sobriety of the recent painted self-portrait (see fig. 137). The drawings suggest a different image of the artist for those whom Matisse hoped would buy his work from the self-image for those whom he wished would understand it – a different persona for Renoir, to whom he specially showed the painted self-portrait just after he had finished it, from the persona for the businessman patron. The concision, humor, and consistency of the self-portraits on these postcards testify to Matisse's desire at this time to construct a legible and appealing projection of himself for a new audience.

The face of public relations

In fact, at this time Matisse was becoming actively engaged in the promotion of his own work. He chose and directed the publication of a group of drawings that appeared in 1920 under the title of *Cinquante dessins*, a visual manifesto of the new direction his work had taken since the war.[20] For his large exhibition at Bernheim-Jeune in the same year, he selected a small group of pictures from early in his career to function as antecedents for his recent production in Nice and Etretat. And he enlisted the help of his friends – Marcel Sembat, George Besson, Jules Romains – in writing and publishing the articles and books that began to proliferate at this time. Not merely a result of the time being ripe for this swell of publicity, the new and more favorable public standing of Matisse's work was closely integrated with his efforts on his own behalf.

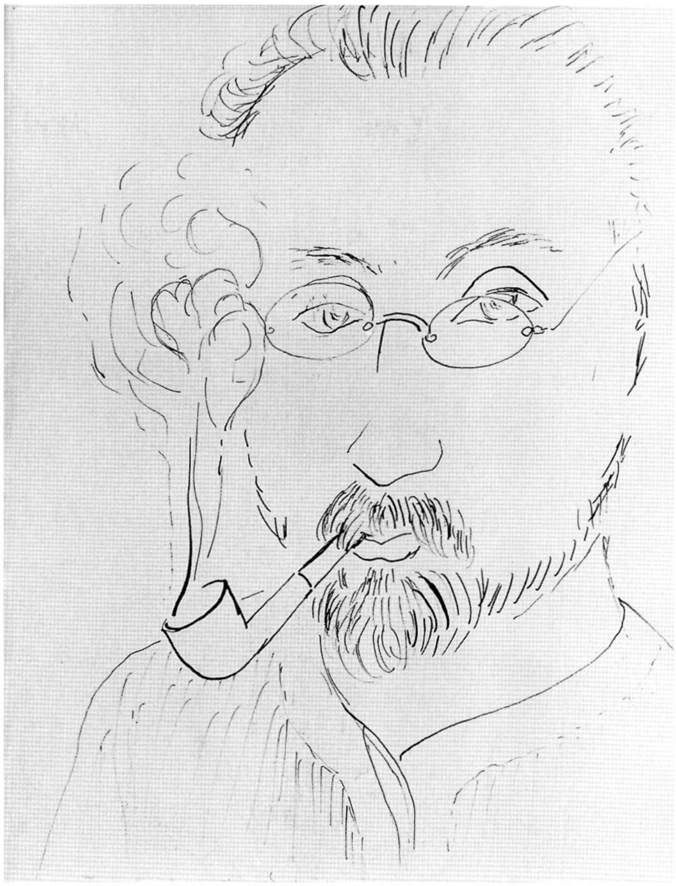

150 *Self-Portrait*, 1919. Pen and ink on paper, 37 × 26 cm. Besançon, Musée des Beaux-Arts et d'Archéologie.

In conjunction with his growing interest in self-promotion, Matisse developed a new attitude toward the self-portrait. After regarding self-portraiture as a largely private activity for many years (with important exceptions, as we have seen), he began to see how the artist's construction of his image could take a more public and pragmatic role. Increasingly in the 1920s and beyond he made self-portraits as instruments of publicity, as means of making a link for his growing audience between his work and himself.[21]

George Besson was probably the most important figure in spreading public knowledge of and promoting critical favor for Matisse's art during the 1920s, and in fact his role was substantial throughout Matisse's career. As an editor for several publishing houses, and as the publisher of Editions Georges Crès, he was also responsible for the publication of many books and articles on art, including a considerable number about Matisse. Besson and Matisse were not extremely close friends, but they were companionable, and Besson was certainly sympathetic to Matisse's work (see figs. 135, 136). They might be characterized as working in a cordial and mutually fulfilling business partnership.

Matisse dedicated a self-portrait drawing in 1919 to Besson (fig. 150). It is a firmly drawn pen and ink sketch only slightly more elaborated than the contemporaneous postal portraits. Its apparent casualness is, however, belied by the willful and even slightly perverse detail of the frame of Matisse's spectacles cutting through his right eye. He puffs on a pipe, probably one that Besson gave him – Besson's father was a pipe-maker and the writer himself was a great fancier of them.[22]

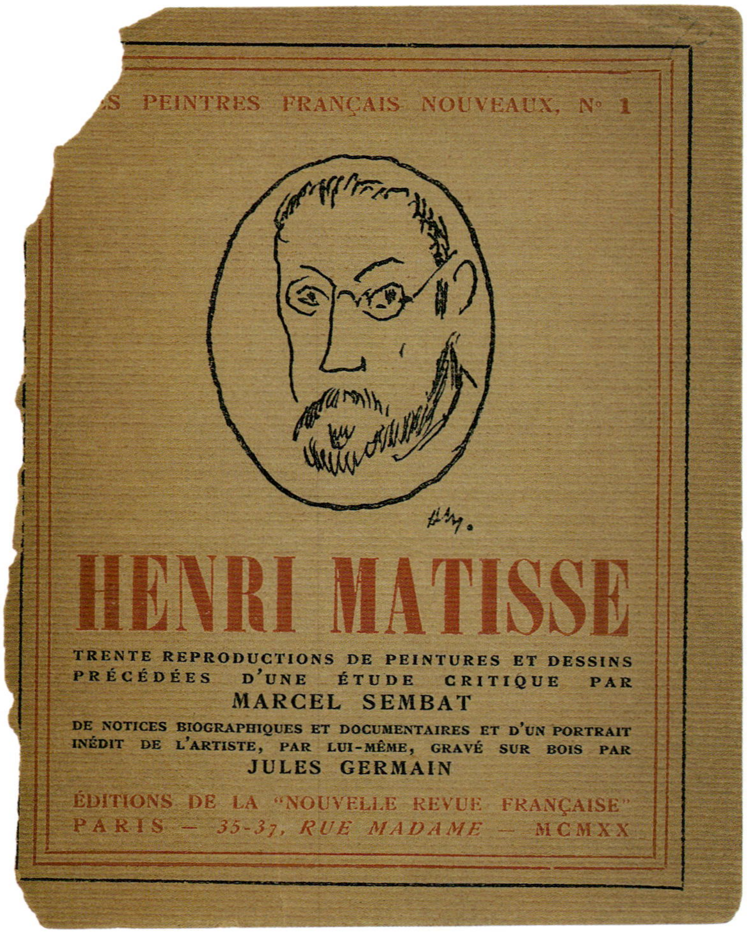

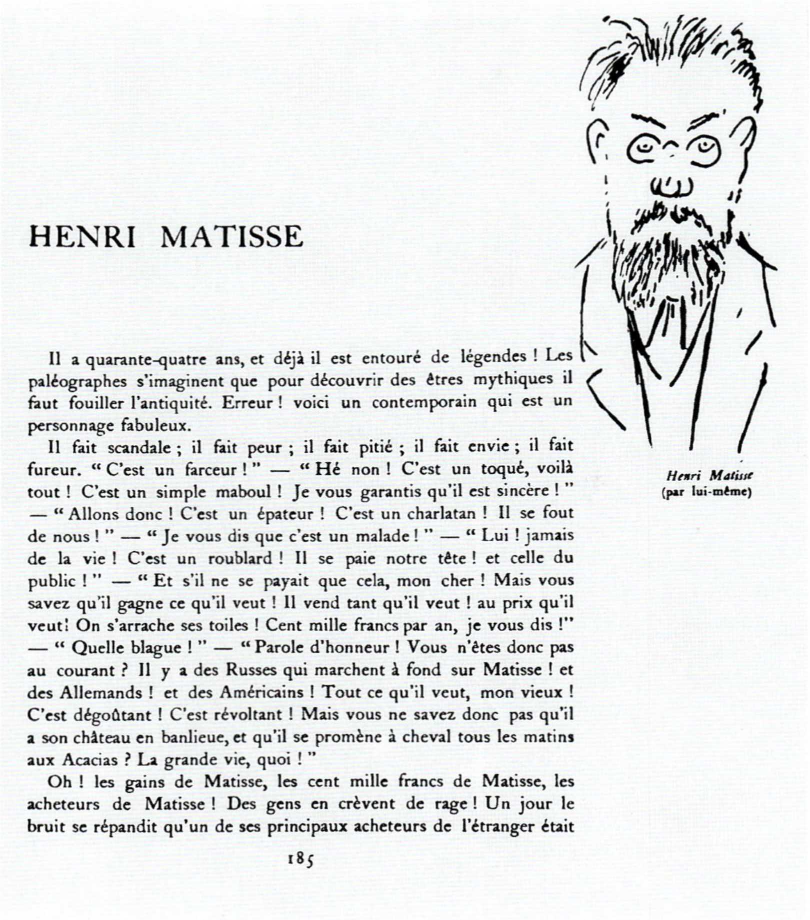

HENRI MATISSE

Henri Matisse
(par lui-même)

Il a quarante-quatre ans, et déjà il est entouré de légendes ! Les paléographes s'imaginent que pour découvrir des êtres mythiques il faut fouiller l'antiquité. Erreur ! voici un contemporain qui est un personnage fabuleux.

Il fait scandale ; il fait peur ; il fait pitié ; il fait envie ; il fait fureur. « C'est un farceur ! » — « Hé non ! C'est un toqué, voilà tout ! C'est un simple maboul ! Je vous garantis qu'il est sincère ! » — « Allons donc ! C'est un épateur ! C'est un charlatan ! Il se fout de nous ! » — « Je vous dis que c'est un malade ! » — « Lui ! jamais de la vie ! C'est un roublard ! Il se paie notre tête ! et celle du public ! » — « Et s'il ne se payait que cela, mon cher ! Mais vous savez qu'il gagne ce qu'il veut ! Il vend tant qu'il veut ! au prix qu'il veut! On s'arrache ses toiles ! Cent mille francs par an, je vous dis ! » — « Quelle blague ! » — « Parole d'honneur ! Vous n'êtes donc pas au courant ? Il y a des Russes qui marchent à fond sur Matisse ! et des Allemands ! et des Américains ! Tout ce qu'il veut, mon vieux ! C'est dégoûtant ! C'est révoltant ! Mais vous ne savez donc pas qu'il a son château en banlieue, et qu'il se promène à cheval tous les matins aux Acacias ? La grande vie, quoi ! »

Oh ! les gains de Matisse, les cent mille francs de Matisse, les acheteurs de Matisse ! Des gens en crèvent de rage ! Un jour le bruit se répandit qu'un de ses principaux acheteurs de l'étranger était

185

151 (*above left*) *Self-Portrait*, 1920. Wood-engraving by Jules Germain for cover and title page of Marcel Sembat, *Henri Matisse*, 1920.

152 (*above right*) Marcel Sembat, "Henri Matisse," *Les Cahiers d'aujourd'hui*, no. 4 (April 1913), with self-portrait by Matisse.

Perhaps Matisse even offered the drawing in exchange. Besson and Matisse both got good mileage from this self-portrait: it figured among the illustrations in the book of essays (by Elie Faure and others) and reproductions brought out under Besson's direction in 1920, and Besson used it as an illustration in a number of his journal *Les Cahiers d'aujourd'hui* in 1921.[23]

Another self-portrait drawing was reproduced in wood-engraving on the cover and title page of a book on the artist by Marcel Sembat, one of Matisse's earliest and most ardent supporters in France (fig. 151).[24] The book was the first in a new series of slim low-priced volumes on contemporary artists, "Les Peintres français nouveaux." The series was a great success, clearly filling a market niche for a new kind of inexpensive popular publication on modern art. Each book had such an image of its artist on the cover, most, like this one, in an honorific cameo format. Most were self-portraits, and each volume reinforced the identification between the artist's self and work.

The texts in the series were generally adulatory and flamboyant, and Sembat's is no exception. But Sembat purported to speak of the "real" Matisse, of the man behind the reputation, to show how much the work is an extension of the man and inseparable from him. This posture offers much the same line as he had taken in his first essay on Matisse's work, seven years earlier, which had also been accompanied by a Matisse self-portrait (fig. 152).[25] In this ink drawing, the neat, sporty-looking bourgeois of the double self-portrait of the same time (see fig. 147) is

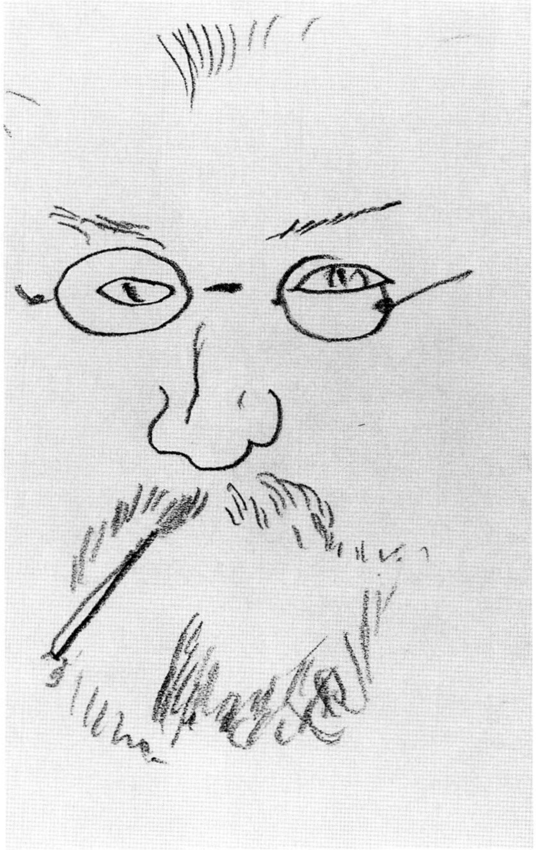

153 *Self-Portrait*, ca. 1920. Crayon on paper, 16 × 9.5 cm. Private collection.

unravelling a little: he stares with wild eyes, his hair springs up like a weedy garden now that the cover of the natty hat has been removed, and the image hovers at one edge. The sense that he is an absent-minded professor is very strong (Sembat even characterized him as a "professeur allemand" – this in 1913), and the drawing expresses enough vulnerability to modify the perception of the artist conveyed by his commanding and difficult canvases of this time. Their creator is, after all, only too human.

Matisse also drew self-portraits that may have had no overt purpose other than to amuse himself. These too reveal a human, and sometimes whimsical, side of the artist. He made several in crayon, a drawing instrument he had not used regularly for years. In one acute, tart little sketch (fig. 153), he zoomed in on the central features of his face to vignette them within the rectangular frame of the sheet from a tiny sketchbook. Matisse's crayon in these drawings produced a line that varied greatly with the artist's touch, giving sometimes a solid contour (the eyeglasses and nose reliably provided this opportunity), sometimes a diffuse texture, as in passages of beard and hair. Always in these drawings Matisse abbreviated and synopsized, producing a visual shorthand that is not characteristic of his paintings or his drawings of other subjects, both more elaborate at this time. The condensation seems elemental, sometimes even crude, and approaches the state of caricature, not only of the subject but of technique, at a time when his other work reached a high point of suavity and seductiveness.

In a few other pen drawings (figs. 154, 155), using stationery from the Savoy Hotel in London where he stayed briefly during the summer of 1920, Matisse drew his own frame, creating charming little oval portraits. Their size, format, and medium suggest that he did these in preparation for the cover of the Sembat book, and indeed maybe the final choice was made from a small group of such sketches, numbered in a way that suggests a series or ranking.

Alternatively, and this purpose notwithstanding, it may not be difficult to imagine the artist in London, passing the time by sketching himself while waiting to go out for an evening performance of *Le Chant du rossignol*, the Diaghilev ballet for which

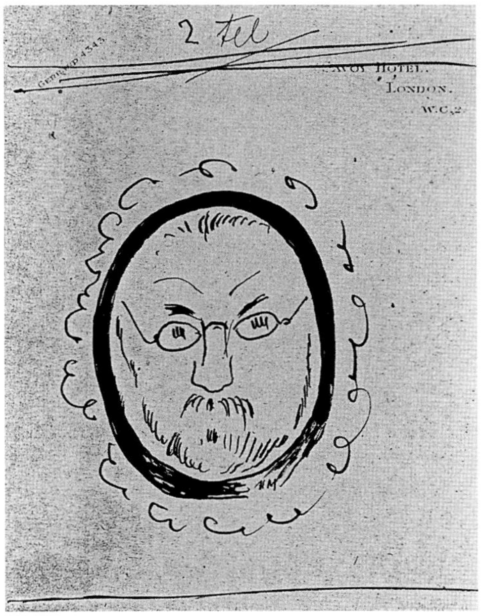

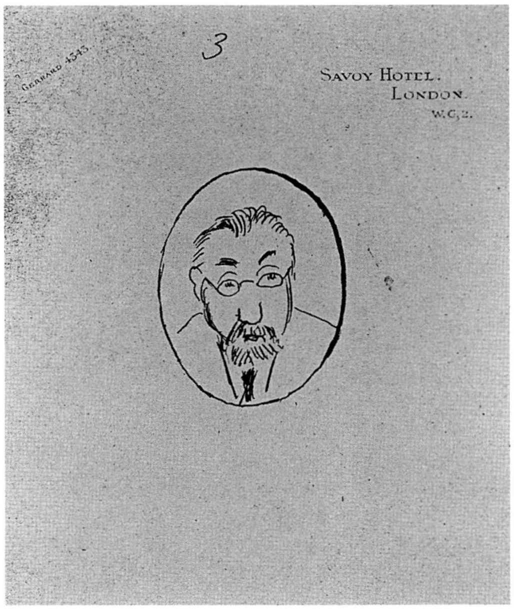

154 *(right)* *Self-Portrait*, 1920. Pen and ink on paper, 14.8 × 12 cm. Private collection.

155 *(far right)* *Self-Portrait*, 1920. Pen and ink on paper, 20 × 15.8 cm. Private collection.

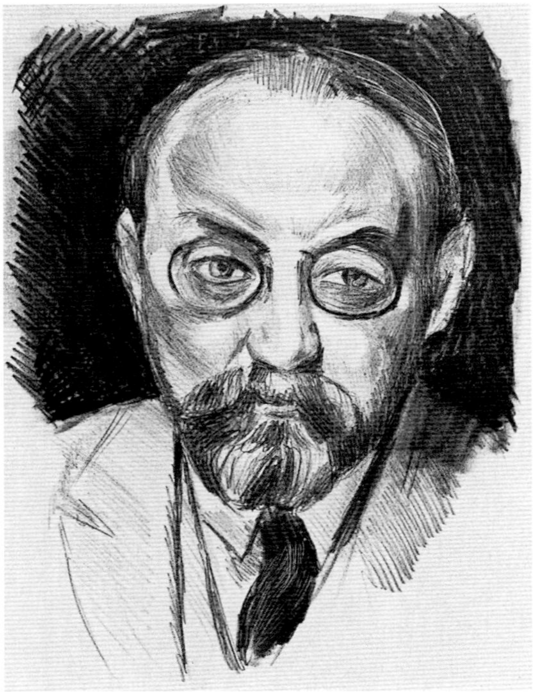

156 *Self-Portrait,* 1923. Lithograph, 32.5 × 25.5 cm. Private collection.

he had designed the scenery. Self-scrutiny need not always be serious business, even for an artist in demand. And in this London context the faintly Rococo preciousness of the cameo format and the whimsical decorative border nudged around one of them accord well with his designs for the post-avant-garde Diaghilev revival. To some extent, Matisse's self-portraits from this time seem to go their own way without any consistent relationship to the style and intentions of his other work early in the Nice years, even as the images were often enlisted in the promotion of that work.

In any case, he made few self-portraits for the remainder of the 1920s. It may be possible to ascribe this to the certainty of purpose that soon characterized his first Nice period. More typical of this time are the many paintings of artist and model in which the figure of the artist is generalized to the point that the works express a generic theme of the creative process. The painting *Interior with Phonograph* of 1924 (fig. 157), in which Matisse was explicit about his identity, summarized his attitude to the relation between himself and his work in the 1920s. The curtain of revelation, closed in his other depictions of this interior, is here drawn back to permit a glimpse, through two elaborately decorated rooms, of the artist in a mirror on the distant wall. Although his image is small and discreet, Matisse has placed himself at the center of a world of order and contrivance. His controlling presence – recalling that in the early *Carmelina* (see fig. 35) – not usually in evidence in his work at this time, is nevertheless asserted as necessary to the effect. This is just the point in his work of the Nice period generally: he was more interested in securing the right theatrical effect than in examining the director who caused it.[26]

Each of the few self-portraits he did make before the close of the decade followed in its own way the new conservative line proposed by the painted self-portrait of 1918. In a lithograph of 1923 (fig. 156), Matisse made the most carefully finished image of himself since the finely drawn ink self-portraits of 1898 (see figs. 18, 19). The velvety tones of the crayon and the emphasis on modeling over contour came to dominate his lithographic production for several years. This print is so beautifully finished and the conception and pose are so formal, and its position so isolated in Matisse's work at this time, that it may appear to be a specific occasion for public self-presentation. But there is no evidence that he had any such intentions for it, especially since it was printed in a much smaller edition than his other lithographs of the time.

The self-portrait in the age of mechanical reproduction

By 1929 Matisse was showing a greater interest in bolder and simpler graphic techniques, as demonstrated by the large group of line etchings from this year. It does not seem coincidental that in the same year Matisse was involved in the production of several books and catalogues devoted to his work, and that he was also becoming re-engaged with the self-portrait. For his interest both in graphic means and in making self-portraits should be understood in the context of these publications. He made these self-portraits mainly for cover and frontispiece illustrations for books and catalogues, part of the publicity machine for his reputation, which was beginning to assume a worldwide scope.

In most cases he seems to have done only a single drawing, perhaps made expressly for the purpose, as for the catalogue cover of one of several retrospective exhibitions held in 1930–31 (fig. 158).[27] This highly schematic and slightly eerie

157 *Interior with a Phonograph*, 1924. Oil on canvas, 100.5 × 80 cm. Private collection.

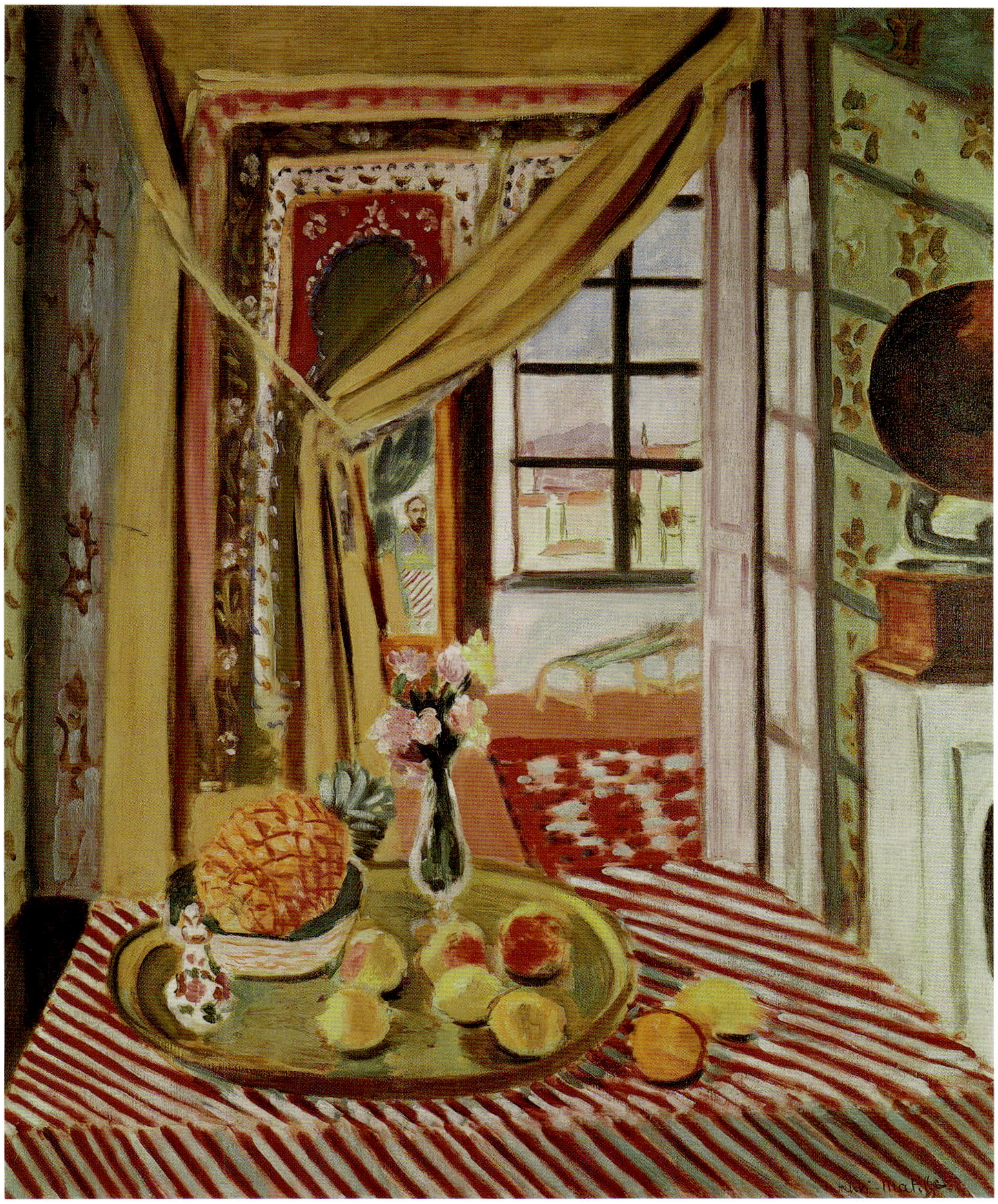

drawing certainly made for a riveting cover illustration, as if the reader were challenged by Matisse himself to confront the work presented within. Another, drawn in ink with the brush, was reproduced on the covers of concurrent books from the same publisher with texts written by Florent Fels, Roger Fry, and Gotthard Jedlicka (fig. 160).[28] Matisse's presentation of himself in these drawings, and especially in the latter, is far removed from the painted self-portrait of 1918. Now his self-image is of a forcefully intelligent artist more than a dedicated practitioner. The leveled, penetrating stare behind owlish eyeglasses combined with the broad expanse of forehead proposes an idea of a stronger mental presence than is conveyed by his self-portraits from the previous two decades. In greatly intensified fashion, it recalls the more matter-of-fact drypoint from the beginning of the century (see fig. 31), an early assertion of Matisse's belief in the mental component of his art.

Not all of his self-portraits from 1930 were so purposeful and professional. His extraordinary trip to Tahiti in that year elicited a kind of self-examination and desire for orientation that is unsurprising on a venture into an unfamiliar and exotic place.[29] Reprising the format of *Carmelina* and *Interior with a Phonograph* but without adopting the controlling stance, Matisse sketched himself en route to (or returning from) Tahiti in his ship's quarters among bed, brush, and bottles (fig. 159). However modest, this drawing thus aligns itself with the painted *Self-Portrait* of 1918 (see fig. 137) as a document of new circumstances and a means of self-assessment at a moment of transition.[30] Such private explorations were in the minority in this period of increasing public attention to himself and his work, but they may have been no less necessary to his equilibrium in changing conditions.[31]

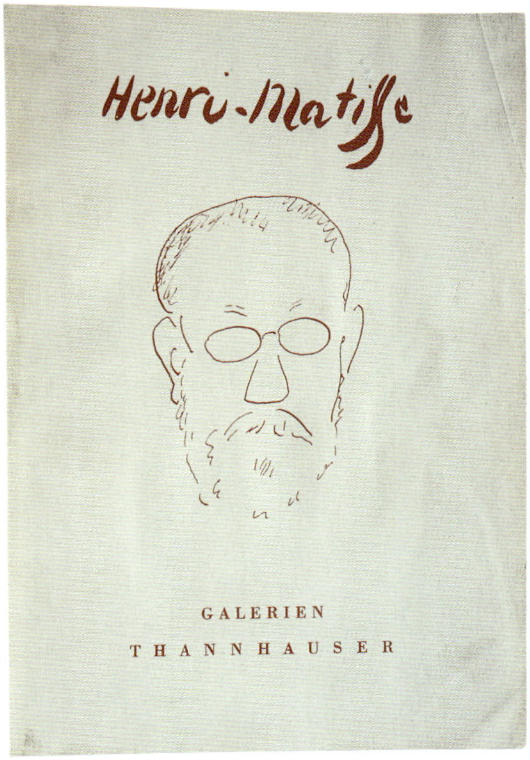

158 Galerien Thannhauser, *Henri-Matisse*, 1930, cover with self-portrait by Matisse.

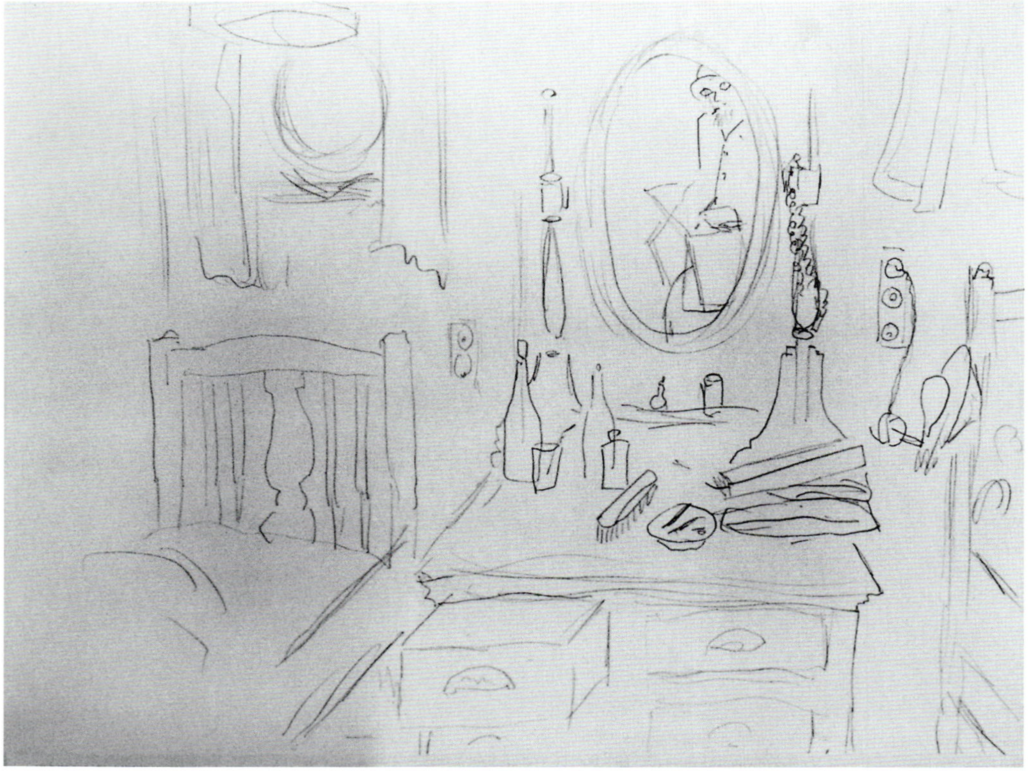

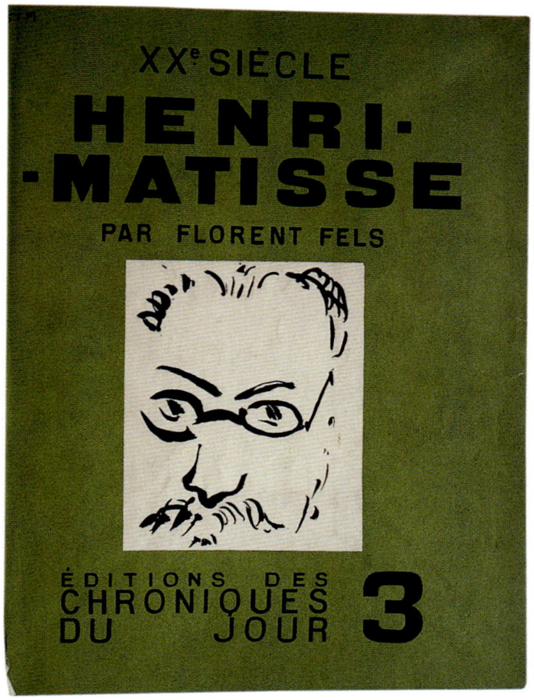

160 Florent Fels, *Henri-Matisse*, 1929, cover with self-portrait by Matisse.

Assertiveness more than orientation is the effect of a related group of at least five self-portrait drawings in brush and ink from 1934 to 1935 (fig. 161). One from this group was chosen for the cover of the new French and American editions of Roger Fry's book of 1930 (fig. 162).[32] In these drawings Matisse handled the brush with great restraint and precision. His exacting manner of laying down the strokes of black ink has a distinctly calligraphic quality, as if the least inflection could change the proportions and the overall effect. This sense of subtle condensation especially characterizes the drawing chosen for publication. Compressed into the cramped horizontal space of the sheet, the features of Matisse's face, rendered in a few strokes of the brush, gain an immediacy lacking in the other drawings. Although in his hands the inked brush is quite subtle in its ability to convey expression so economically, it is likely that Matisse also specifically chose this medium, now and

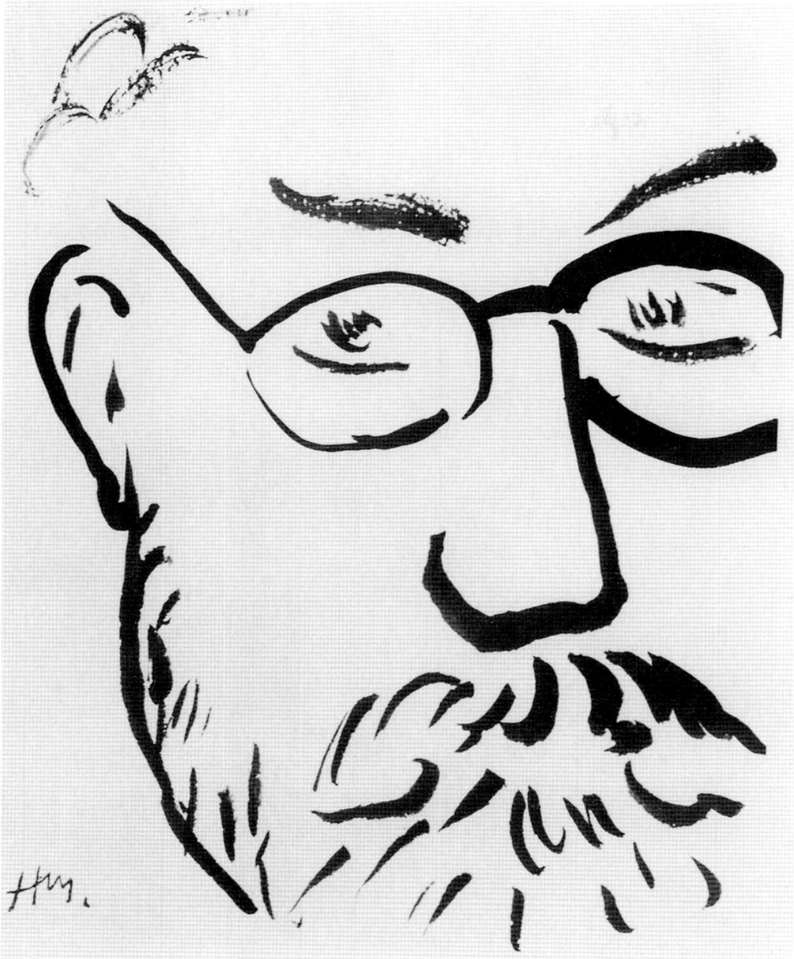

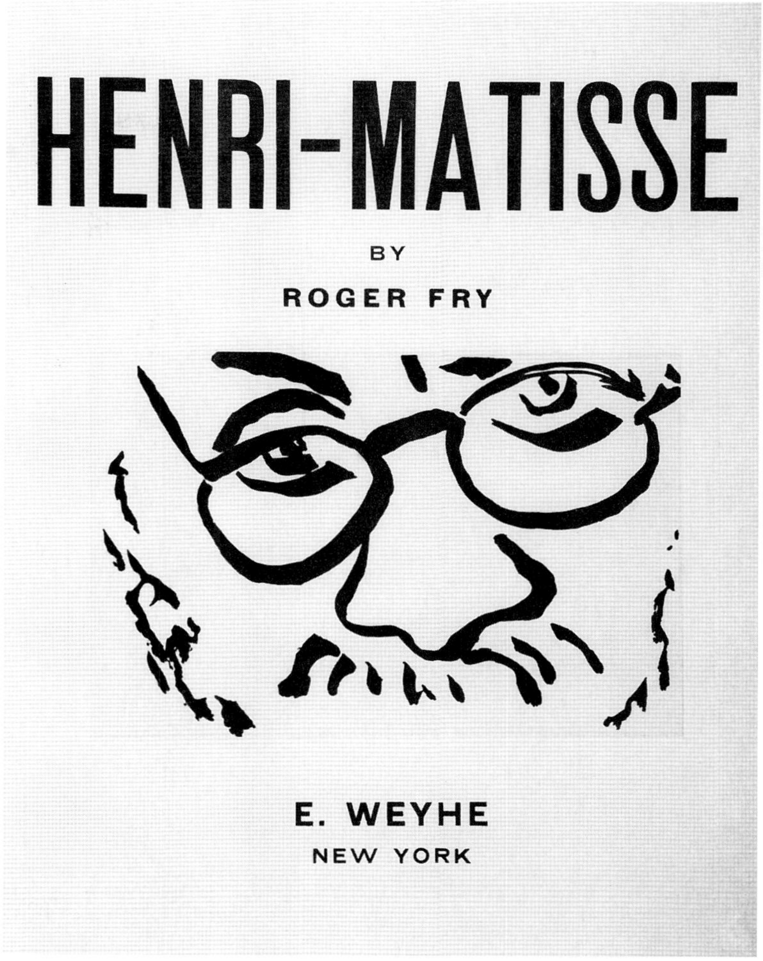

161 (*above left*) *Self-Portrait*, 1934–5. Brush and ink on paper, 14.6 × 12 cm. New York, Cary Lochtenberg collection.

162 (*above right*) Roger Fry, *Henri-Matisse*, 1935, cover with self-portrait by Matisse.

159 (*facing page right*) *Interior with Self-Portrait*, 1930. Pencil on paper, 25 × 32.5 cm. Private collection.

for the earlier books, for its particular graphic qualities of assertiveness and contrast. Bold strokes of black ink were easy to reproduce by commercial printing techniques, in contrast with the finer tonal gradations of charcoal or the lightness of pencil, both more elusive in reproduction. When employed as a cover illustration the ink drawings would also produce the desired eye-catching effect among other publications competing for a buyer's attention. In this medium Matisse found an especially effective combination of disciplined execution and shelf appeal.

When not working for publication Matisse used charcoal to make some of his best-known self-portrait drawings from this decade. It was a drawing instrument he favored generally in the 1920s and 1930s for the fine nuances of tonal modeling it could give. In several self-portraits of 1937, however, he manipulated the charcoal with great emphasis (fig. 163). His forceful technique here also made these drawings more susceptible to reproduction; one of them (fig. 164) was used in that year on the cover of Raymond Escholier's book on the artist.[33] In both drawings, lines laid down with the end of the charcoal were smudged and modified, as Matisse changed the contours and proportions of the head with each addition and erasure. The process of obliteration itself produced a kind of fortuitous modeling of the main planes of the face. Although his procedure was sometimes slow and painstaking, and seems to border on indecisiveness, the results in the case of these self-portraits are firm and resolved. In fact, the three-quarters pose and domineering

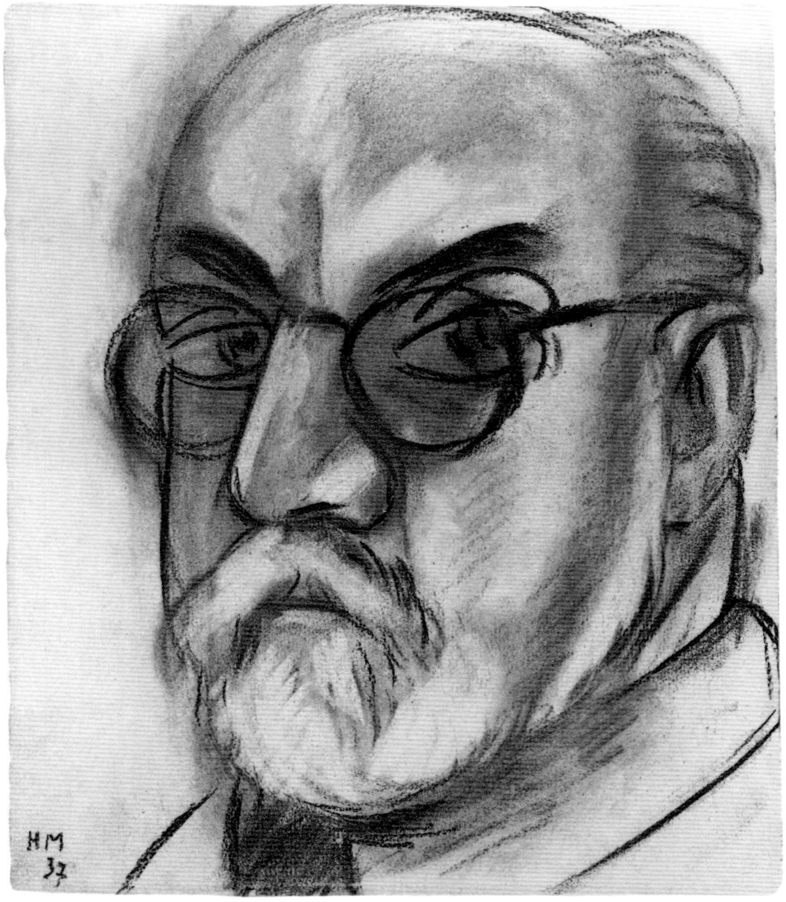

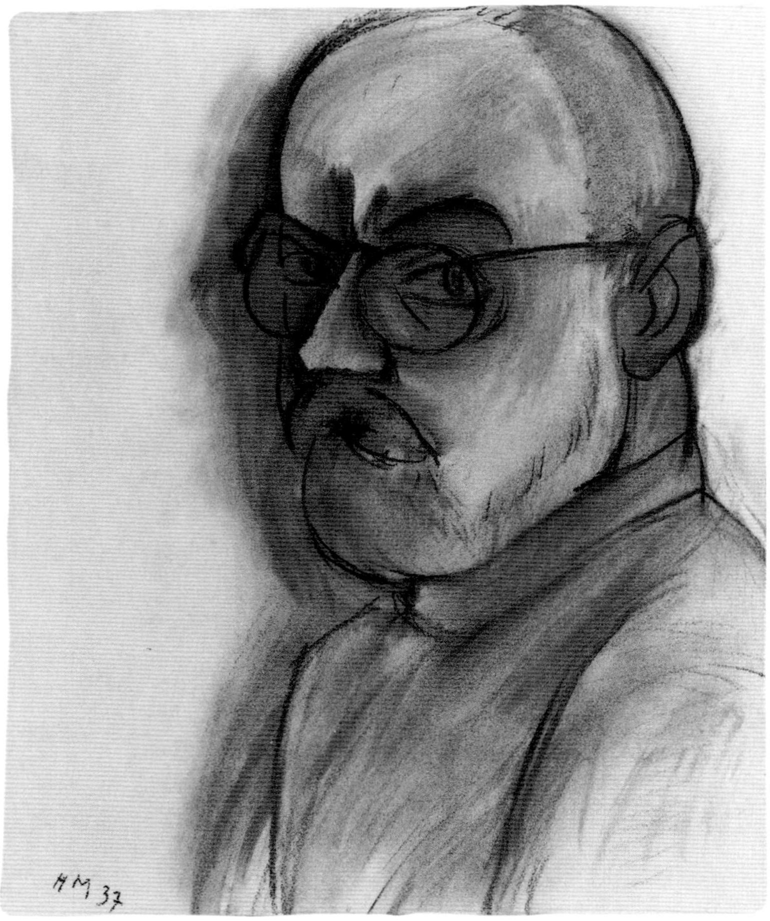

163 (*above left*) *Self-Portrait*, 1937. Charcoal on paper, 34 × 28.5 cm. Washington, D.C., National Gallery of Art. Collection of Mr. and Mrs. Paul Mellon.

164 (*above right*) *Self-Portrait*, 1937. Charcoal on paper, 47.3 × 39.1 cm. The Baltimore Museum of Art, The Cone Collection, formed by Dr. Claribel Cone and Miss Etta Cone of Baltimore, Maryland, BMA 1950.12.61.

stare of both drawings are so similar to the painting from Collioure of 1906 that these drawings are virtual restatements of that earlier assertion of confidence – and Matisse was certainly a more intimidating presence thirty years later.

The way in which he expanded the scale to fill the page with his head in some of these drawings implies yet another shift of self-image in this decade, toward a more forceful, physical conception of himself. This is ironic, perhaps even compensatory, because for years his health had been uncertain and he had recently suffered an attack of influenza that he thought would kill him. He would never again be in complete good health, but at the moment he made these self-portraits (he was 67), both his paintings and drawings generally showed an exceptional vigor.

Preface to *Thèmes et variations*

The method of the charcoal drawings is also important because it prefigures Matisse's procedure in the most significant and elaborate group of drawings from the following decade, the several series of *Thèmes et variations*, which Matisse considered to be one of his greatest achievements in drawing. He never made himself the object of such a designated series, but if the technique of the charcoal drawings looks forward to the "themes," another group of self-portraits from two years later precisely anticipates the purpose of the "variations." When the Second World

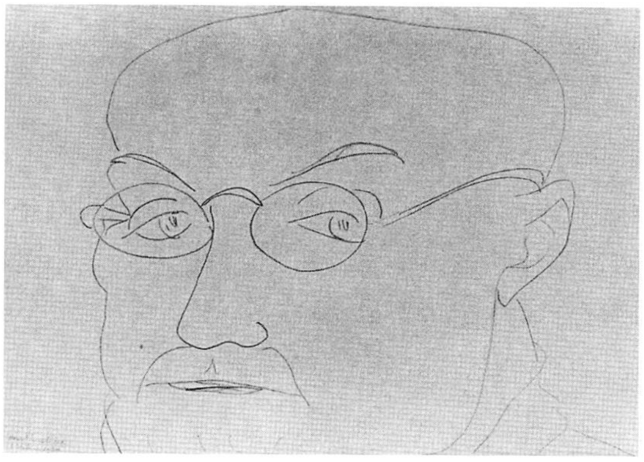

165 *Self-Portrait,* 1939. Crayon on paper, 26.5 × 37.5 cm. Private collection.

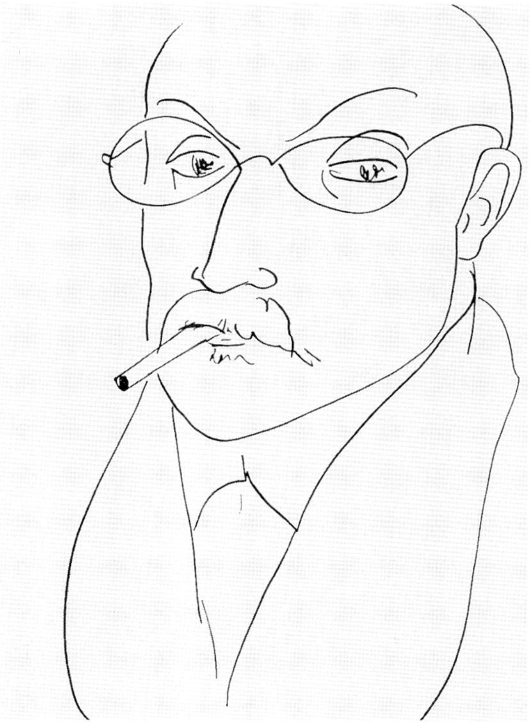

166 *Self-Portrait,* 1939. Crayon on paper, 37.5 × 26.5 cm. Private collection.

War broke out in September 1939, Matisse left Paris for Rochefort-en-Yvelines, near Rambouillet. In a time of growing crisis he painted little but made many drawings from nature and at least fifteen self-portraits in crayon (figs. 165, 166).[34] This large group of drawings was apparently done within a short time, each executed rapidly and with confidence, and each quite different from the others. But all have a certain recognizable essence that derives more from relations between lines than from the character of the individual lines themselves or the specific anatomical features they denote. Since nearly all the lines have an equal weight (an index of Matisse's great discipline), the spaces they bound take on greater importance, swelling or receding according to the slightest inflections of contour.

In the brush and ink drawings of 1934–5, to take a contrasting example, the thick lines were disposed within a pre-existing space whose arbitrary boundaries were crucial compositional elements. In the later crayon drawings, space is much more fluid and extensive, much more at the service of the line that controls it. In their purity of line and lack of overt texture, these are highly conceptual drawings. They are examples of the rapid and practiced signification by the mind and hand of what the eye sees at a given moment under particular conditions.

Matisse himself made this point in his essay "L'Exactitude n'est pas la vérité" (Exactitude is not Truth), which he wrote for an exhibition of his drawings in Liège in 1947. Accompanying the essay were illustrations of four drawings of his own head (see fig. 5).[35] Of them he said that they "sum up, in my opinion, observations that I have made for many years about the character of drawing, a character that does not depend on forms being copied exactly as they are in nature or on the patient assembling of exact details, but on the profound feeling of the artist before the objects that he has chosen, on which his attention is focused, and whose spirit he has penetrated."[36] Evidently Matisse used the drawings of himself to make these didactic observations because his own face was the best example of something studied repeatedly and with care, which could therefore most effectively illustrate the underlying principles of his art as he had come to understand them over the course of long commitment to self-expression.

The drawings are also another example of the way in which Matisse came to personalize his art by referring to himself not only as its creator but as its principal point of interest. And more than at any time since 1900, this concentration on the self produces a great variety of perceptions or constructions of it. Psychological focus shifts along with spatial point of view. Anchored by the indefinable essence – as well as the constant of ocular inspection – a fluid persona emerges in each drawing. Suave and reserved; distracted and pensive; haughty and distant; heavy with fatigue; or looming and wary – he has freed himself to see himself in many different guises and temperaments. This exploratory urge is also characteristic of the "Themes and variations" in which an object or array of objects is turned and shifted, pushed back or pulled right up to the picture plane. Indeed, it may be ventured that in these self-portraits Matisse is treating his head like an object, so much does he manipulate it. The sense is very strong that he has stepped outside himself for observation and analysis. This impression was increasingly apparent in the following decade. But it is worth noting that for his exposition in "L'Exactitude n'est pas la vérité" he chose four similar drawings from a larger and more diverse group. This is surprising because with a greater variety he could have illustrated his point – that essential qualities are what counts – more effectively. Did he lose his nerve about his thesis, or did he just want to project the most consistent image possible for these important international presentations of his work?[37]

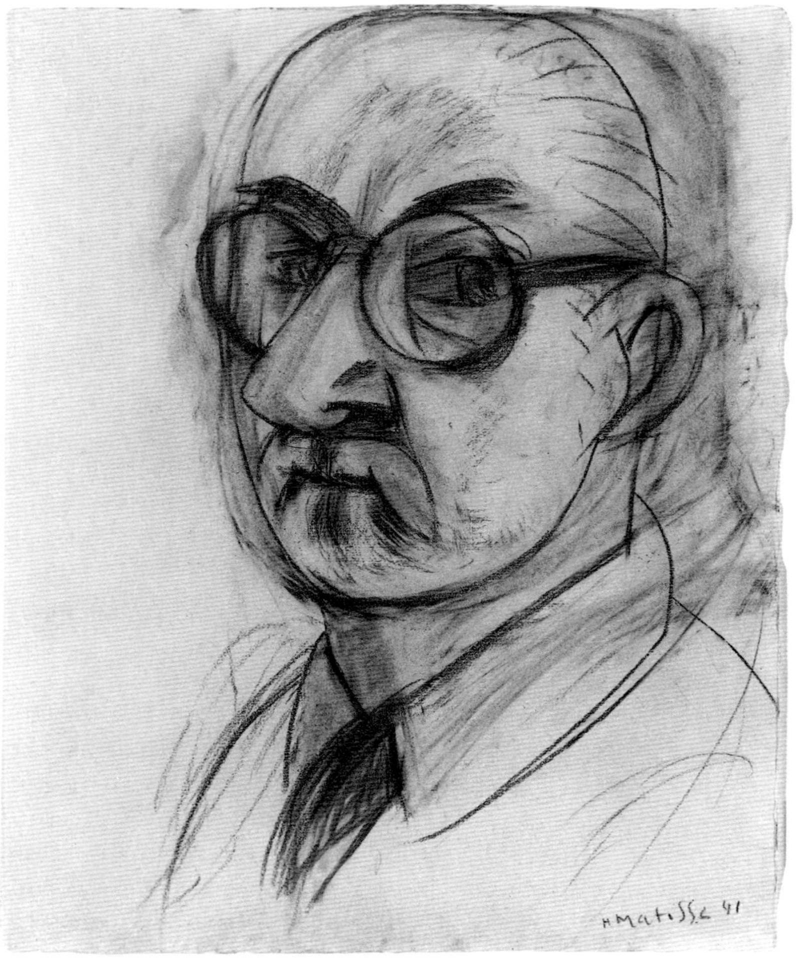

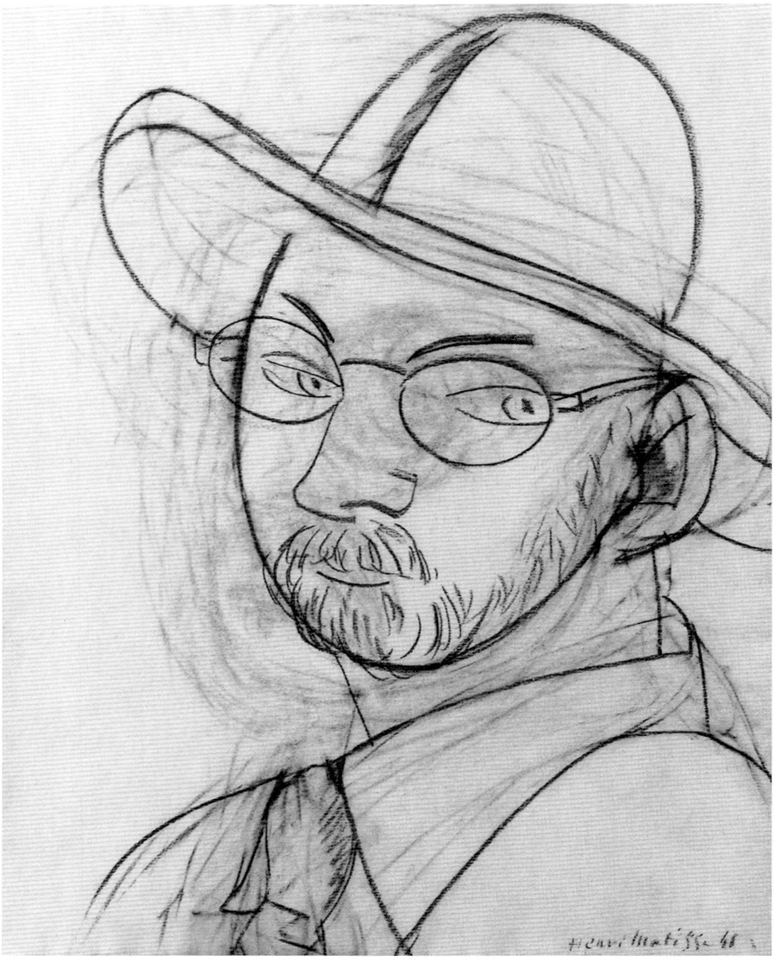

167 (*above left*) *Self-Portrait*, 1941. Sanguine chalk on paper, 48 × 37.5 cm. Private collection.

168 (*above right*) *Self-Portrait with Straw Hat*, 1941. Sanguine chalk on paper, 48 × 37.5 cm. Private collection.

Drawing and diagnostics

Matisse's next self-portraits followed closely his most serious health crisis, which provoked deep self-inspection on all fronts. In early 1941, at the age of 71, he endured surgery for intestinal cancer and suffered severe post-operative complications. His convalescence was long but he worked as actively as his health allowed. Among the first things he made in this period of recovery were several drawings of himself in his weakened state (figs. 144, 167, 168). These moving portraits in sanguine follow the method of the drawings in charcoal from four years earlier – draw, smudge, find a new line, efface, adjust – but with greater hesitation than certainty. Not like the shrewd self-advertising of the drawings of the early and late 1920s or the bold and bravura display of easy powers in the images from the 1930s, these self-portraits have a stubborn and resolute quality that is directly expressed through his technique and the record of process in the final image. In these drawings, one feels strongly the vulnerability of the man but also the triumph of the artist over physical adversity.

Matisse did not ignore the potential benefit to his artistic knowledge in these sessions of self-examination. On both of these sheets of paper one can see the intermediary stages underlying the final image, but in the case of the second drawing Matisse deliberately revealed the exact nature of this step-by-step process. He made

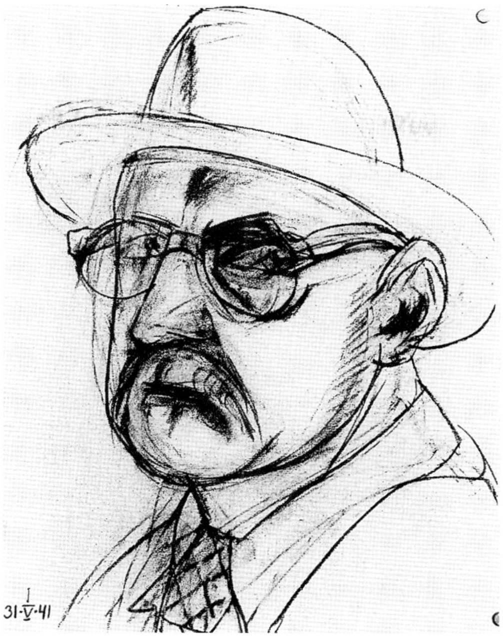

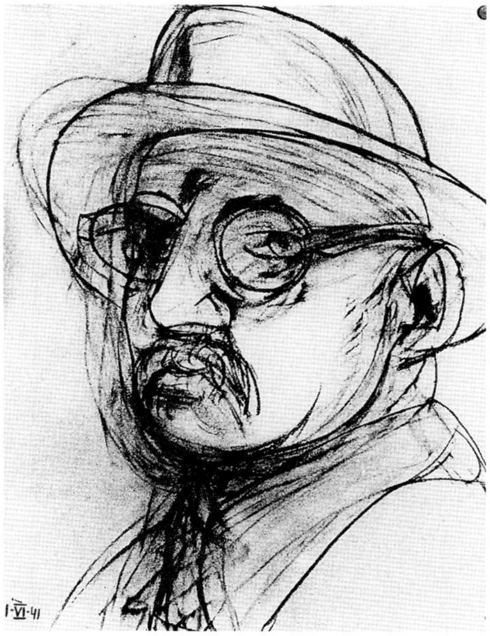

169a (*right*) Photograph of the first state of fig. 168. Archives Matisse, Paris.

169b (*far right*) Photograph of the second state of fig. 168. Archives Matisse, Paris.

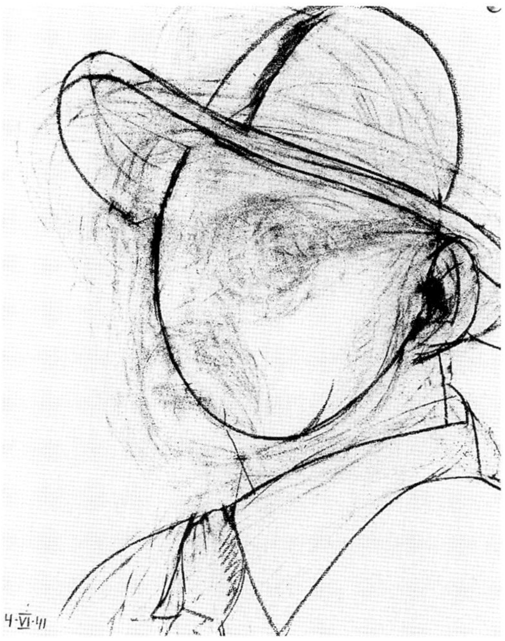

170 Photograph of the third state of fig. 168. Archives Matisse, Paris.

the drawing over a period of several days in late May and early June just after he returned to Nice from Lyons, the site of his operation and recovery. When he finished a day's session of work, he attached to the sheet a small label with the date and had it photographed to record the states of his progress (see figs. 168–70). It is thus easier to see the movement from the particular toward the general, the simplification of form that was for him analogous to finding the essence of spirit.

He began with a jowly, scowling face on May 31 (fig. 169a), picking up where he had left off in the other drawing, completed two days earlier (see fig. 167).[38] By the end of the following day (fig. 169b), he had streamlined the contours of his jaw to make himself look less corpulent, which also had the effect of lessening the severity that is such a marked characteristic of the first state. In the next, on June 4, he effaced most of this work. Over these erasures he redrew the head (fig. 170), but only in outline, forming an elegant oval bisected by the brim of his hat, to which he also gave a new look (probably by changing hats). Finally on June 6 he drew in facial features, eyeglasses, and beard (see fig. 168). Matisse's transformation of this drawing had moved from a harsh but possibly candid self-image toward a more positive expression. Slimmed down, unified, hat brim turned up in a jaunty flip, he seems almost to have performed an act of healing – or of hopeful projection of good health – through his synthetic procedure.[39]

Matisse's self-consciousness about his working method in this drawing, and his desire to learn from each successive state, recall his use of photography to record the stages of work on some of his most important paintings of the time, such as *The Rumanian Blouse* of 1940 (Paris, Musée National d'Art Moderne). He preserved the appearance of the states of these canvases for his own study, but after finishing the painting he also used the photograph to demonstrate to others that a result that looks as if it had been easily gained is in fact the product of long and exacting work. He wished to counter the perception that his art sprang fully formed in an effortless display of natural ability, which had been the substance of the image constructed by many of the writers on him during the 1920s and the 1930s. Matisse showed here that his paintings were created in time, with careful thought, and through hard work.

In making the self-portraits during his convalescence, it is likely that he was also interested in his own physical progress. Certainly the drawings were meant as private diagnoses of himself and his drawing practice – they were not made public during his lifetime, and even now the photographs of the stages are not well known. But he did show his works in progress – body and art – to an old friend. On June 4 he wrote to André Rouveyre, enclosing a few of the just-taken photographs: "I am back at work and I've begun with some drawings of myself. I'm sending you some photos of them so you can tell me whether or not I've lost too much energy . . ."[40] The artist's anxiety is clear. He had been under expert medical care and had made a remarkable recovery, but perhaps in these drawings he needed to make his own assessment of the state of his artistic as well as physical health. Doctors have their tools; so do artists. Rouveyre's response to Matisse's appeal assured the artist that he had not lost his powers.[41]

Role-playing and humor

During and just after the Second World War, Matisse made many other self-portrait drawings, the first in a large group in Vence in July 1944 (fig. 171). At the same time he made two similar lithographic self-portraits and four more self-portraits on lithographic transfer paper (fig. 172). These four were never transferred onto stones or plates, and their purpose is unknown, although Matisse may have conceived them as a series.[42]

Eight of the drawings (including fig. 171) were published the following year in a special number of *Verve*, "De la couleur."[43] These black and white drawings in pure line were clearly not in keeping with the theme of the issue. But juxtaposed as they are to his intensely colored paintings of the time, they extend the idea of Matisse's public use of his self-portraits in the 1920s to identify himself with his work. In doing this he fortified again the idea of the directly personal qualities of his art, its self-expressive foundation. And these drawings do seem to be very personal in character: he is dressed informally in working clothes, not his usual made-to-measure image for public consumption.

In both the drawings and the lithographs Matisse projected a wide range of expression, from stolid to amused to slightly deranged. It is interesting to note, however, that the limited selection of drawings published in *Verve* shows a more uniformly benign personage. This conservatism about his public image anticipates the uniformity of the choices he made in 1948 of his earlier self-portraits, as we have already seen. Furthermore, as in the drawings from 1939, which he used to show that truth lies in essence not detail, his publication in *Verve* of the later works has a strong flavor of such an instructive exercise, as if he were fascinated by how the same person can look so different under identical exterior conditions. The object does not change, except to move. Sometimes he does not even do that: among several of these drawings of precisely the same point of view, in some he appears extremely feeble, in others (such as fig. 171) amused and confident (this is naturally the one he gave to an acquaintance and collector).[44] But the object moves only because the subject does, changing slightly his point of view of himself. Thus it is implied that the artist projects difference onto the object of his study.

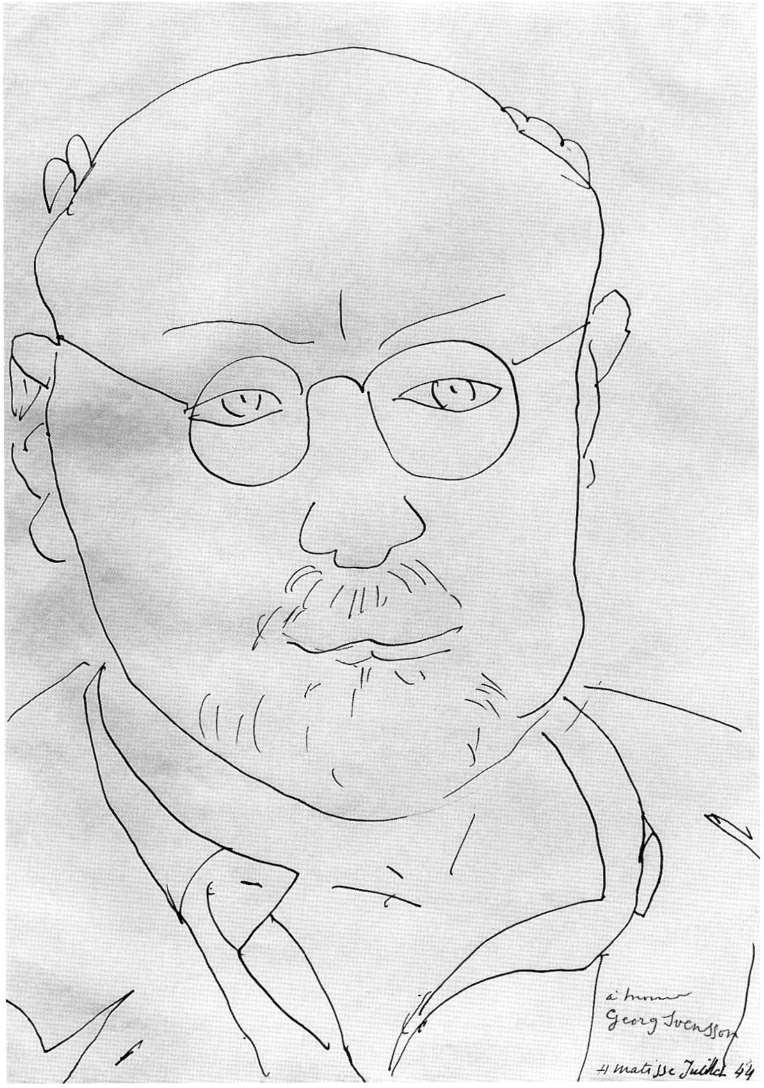

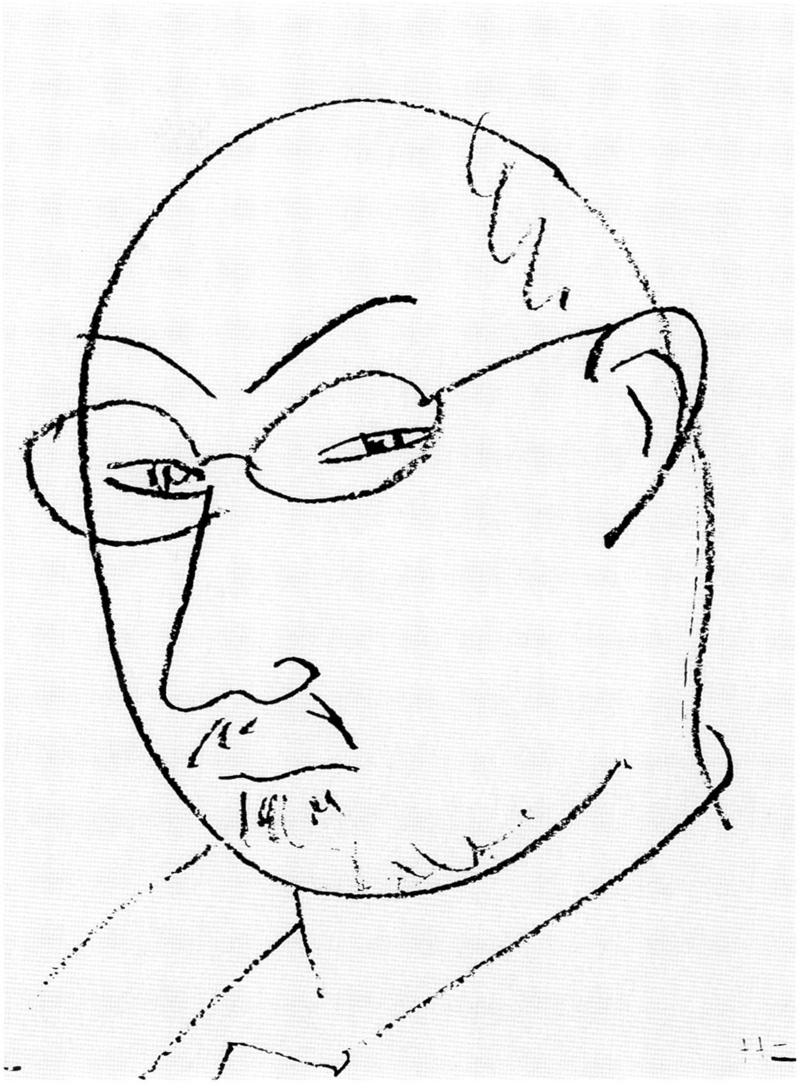

171 (*above left*) *Self-Portrait*, 1944. Pen and ink on paper, 40 × 26 cm. Stockholm, Nationalmuseum.

172 (*above right*) *Self-Portrait*, ca. 1944. Lithographic crayon on transfer paper, 29 × 21 cm. Private collection.

Never more concisely expressed than here is the combination of reflexive and self-projecting qualities that characterize so much of his art.

We should recall that the Second World War had for years taken a severe toll on everyone in France, even those seemingly most removed from it. This was a time of great uncertainty in Matisse's life: he lived in Vichy France; his health was uncertain; and he feared for the safety of his wife and daughter, who were captured and imprisoned for their roles in the Resistance. Certainly his art suffered from these multiple concerns, as he said frequently to close friends. His discontent or discomfort is plain in some of his wartime self-portraits, but in others from 1945 (figs. 173–6) his mood also seems to vary from expectant watchfulness to plain silliness as he proposes diverse personages, much as he had done about 1900. Three or four different hats, a pipe, a scarf knotted casually around his neck, and various drawing instruments are his props in these little performances of himself. They are among the most light-hearted works of his career; but in another way they have a serious implication.

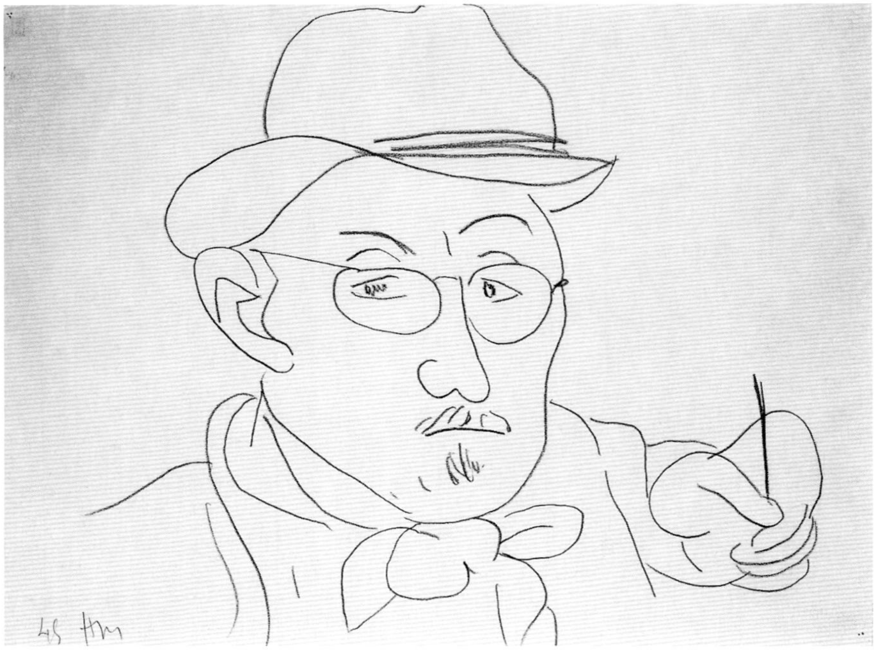

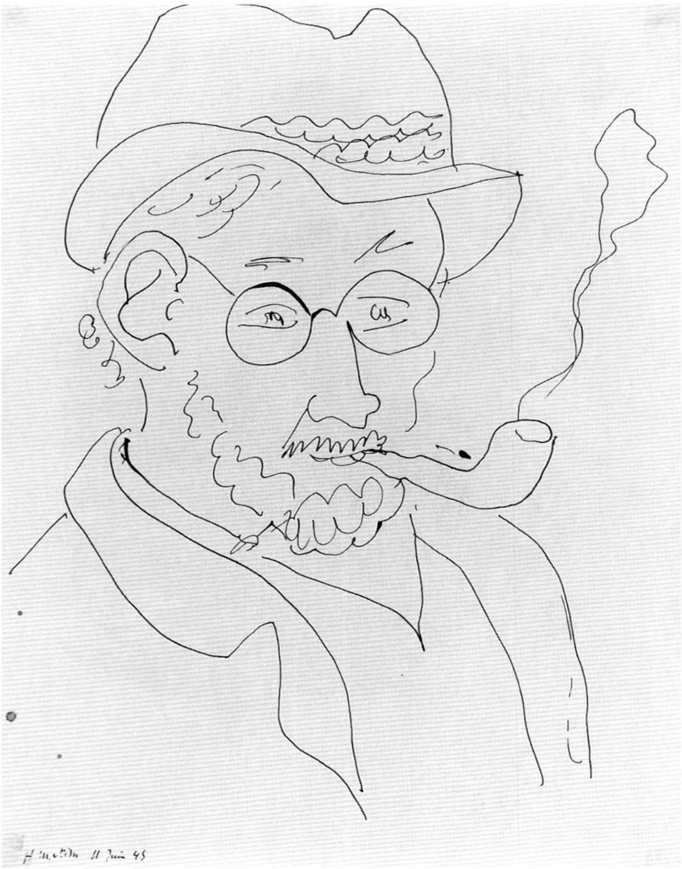

173 *(above left)* *Self-Portrait*, 1945. Crayon on paper, 40.5 × 52.5 cm. The Museum of Modern Art, New York. John S. Newberry Fund.

174 *(above right)* *Self-Portrait with a Straw Hat*, 1945. Pen and ink on paper, 52 × 40 cm. The Museum of Modern Art, New York. Gift of Philip Johnson (by exchange).

177 *(facing page bottom)* Letter from Matisse to George Besson, August 10, 1949, with a self-portrait by Matisse. Paris, Jacqueline George Besson.

175 *(facing page top left)* *Self-Portrait ("Masque")*, 1945. Lithograph, 22.2 × 15.7 cm. Private collection.

176 *(facing page top right)* *Self-Portrait*, ca. 1945. Pen and ink on paper affixed to board, 28.3 × 22 cm. Nice, Musée Matisse. Gift of Madame Albert Marquet, 1964.

On a drawing of himself in his night clothes (fig. 176) he wryly asked his old friend Albert Marquet: "Would you have recognized, my dear Albert, the young fellow who used to kick up such a ruckus [?]"[45] During those frequent times when he suffered from insomnia, Matisse's thoughts often turned to the friends of his youth: his amusement at his appearance is mixed with the poignancy of his isolation in the middle of the night. In the only lithograph in the group (fig. 175) he enclosed his features in an irregular contour punctuated by a bristly point of beard. The vignette effect emphasizes the pure sign value of the lines used to denote nose, brows, lips, and so forth, and the encircling border turns his face into a mask – immobile, schematic, symbolic. Yet a slight smile and lively eyes belie the mask-like implications of his formal decisions. The result is a fitting paradox, for its combination of telling specificity and typifying abstraction was one of Matisse's highest goals in portraiture.

It may seem contradictory that Matisse, who often regarded himself and his art with self-righteous seriousness, clearly could have fun drawing himself. These late drawings have a candor that he may have found possible only in self-portraiture. The self-portrait, especially the quickly drawn, unmediated kind, may have been an outlet for what he usually suppressed in the more deliberated realm of his public life – his humility and sense of humor. And in fact these expressions seem to have been made largely in private; apparently the works were never exhibited during Matisse's lifetime, although a few of the drawings were published.[46]

After the war Matisse was frequently occupied with illustrated books, large-scale decorative projects, a new and fruitful medium in the form of the innovative paper

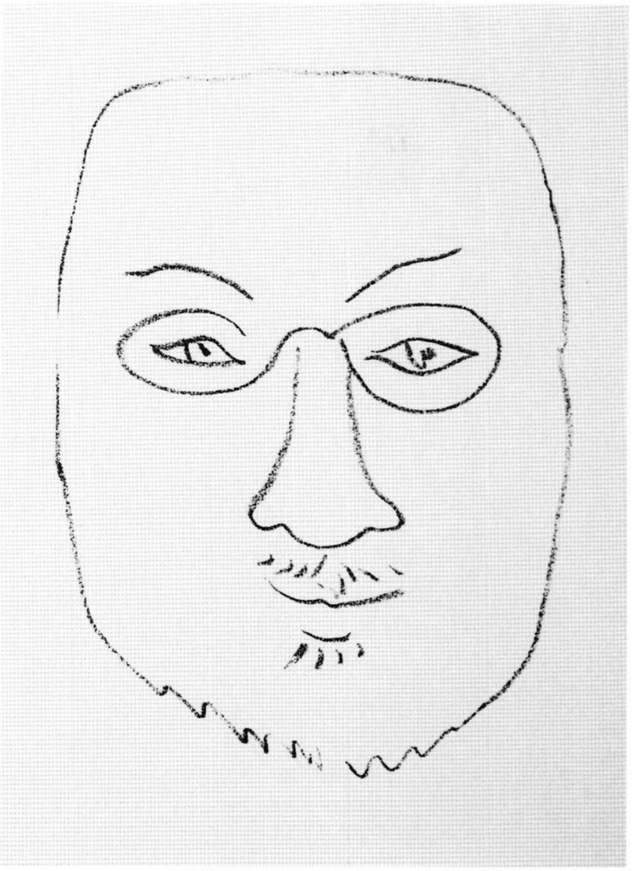

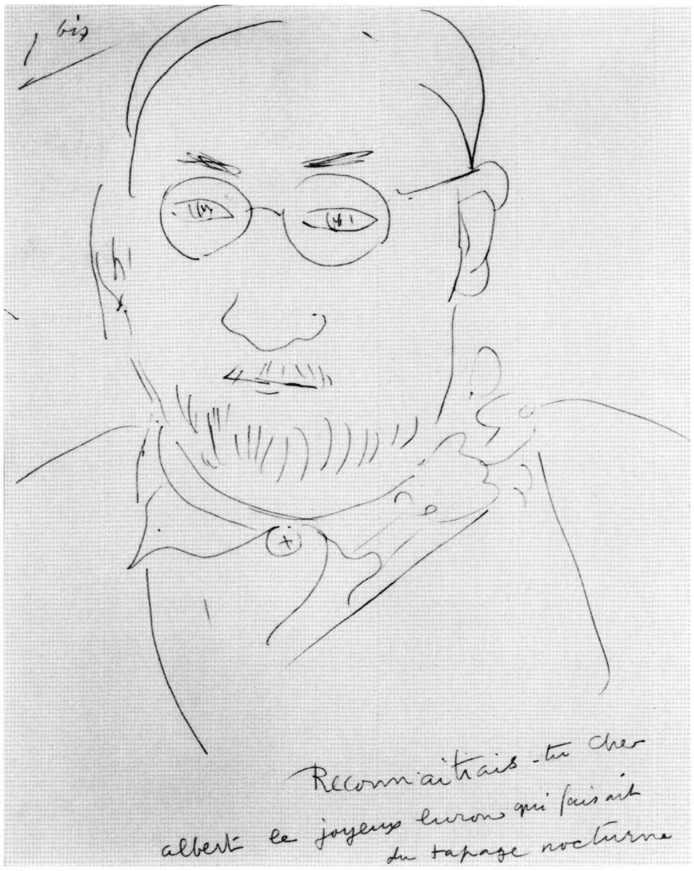

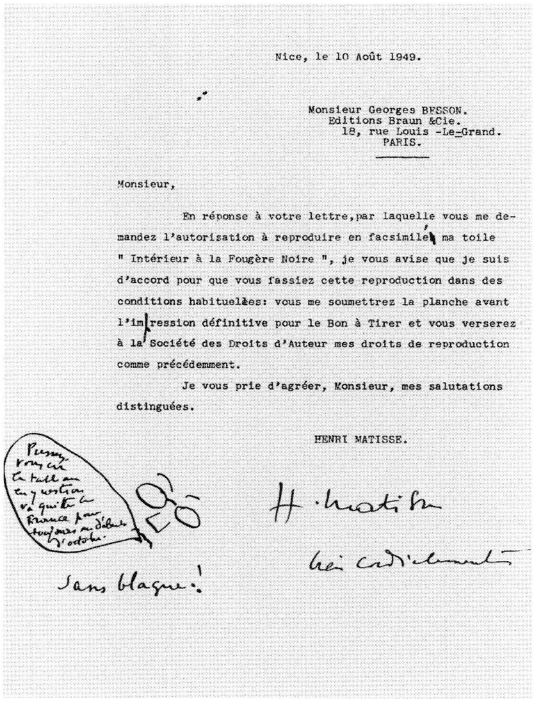

Nice, le 10 Août 1949.

Monsieur Georges BESSON.
Editions Braun &Cie.
18, rue Louis -Le-Grand.
PARIS.

Monsieur,

En réponse à votre lettre, par laquelle vous me demandez l'autorisation à reproduire en facsimilé ma toile " Intérieur à la Fougère Noire ", je vous avise que je suis d'accord pour que vous fassiez cette reproduction dans des conditions habituelàes: vous me soumettrez la planche avant l'impression définitive pour le Bon à Tirer et vous verserez à la Société des Droits d'Auteur mes droits de reproduction comme précédemment.

Je vous prie d'agréer, Monsieur, mes salutations distinguées.

HENRI MATISSE.

H. Matisse

Sans blague!

cut-outs, and the many importunities that arose from his position as the most famous French artist. Drawing – and therefore, for the past thirty years or so, self-portraiture – seemed to give way to these concerns; in fact, he said to Rouveyre in 1947: "I've devoted myself definitively to color because drawings don't interest me any longer."[47] He made hardly any self-portraits at this time, but some display the same comic spirit of a few years earlier combined with a new awareness that his time was limited. Beginning with the drawings from 1945, even when Matisse's line is firm the expression in his eyes, once unfailingly sharp and penetrating, is frequently diffuse.

In these years self-portraiture often formed part of his correspondence, and not only of the most private kind, as we can see in a letter to George Besson formally granting him the right to reproduce one of his paintings: a little self-portrait image barks orders at the publisher (fig. 177). Here in this minimal, highly amusing self-image, Matisse literalizes in a poignant and effective way the function of portraiture as a surrogate for the absent referent. It is at once a profound acknowledgment of the power of portraiture and a clever jape with a distinctly limited and practical purpose.

By the 1950s the eyes in his self-portraits were reduced to largely indifferent scrawls (fig. 178), and in some cases he did not draw them at all, eliminating that crucial instrument in an artist's creative process. In the same years he spoke in a tone of wonder to some of his old friends of his mood as he felt himself approaching an unknown place that was as yet beyond his understanding and that he could not share with others. His consciousness of impending death is not easily discernible

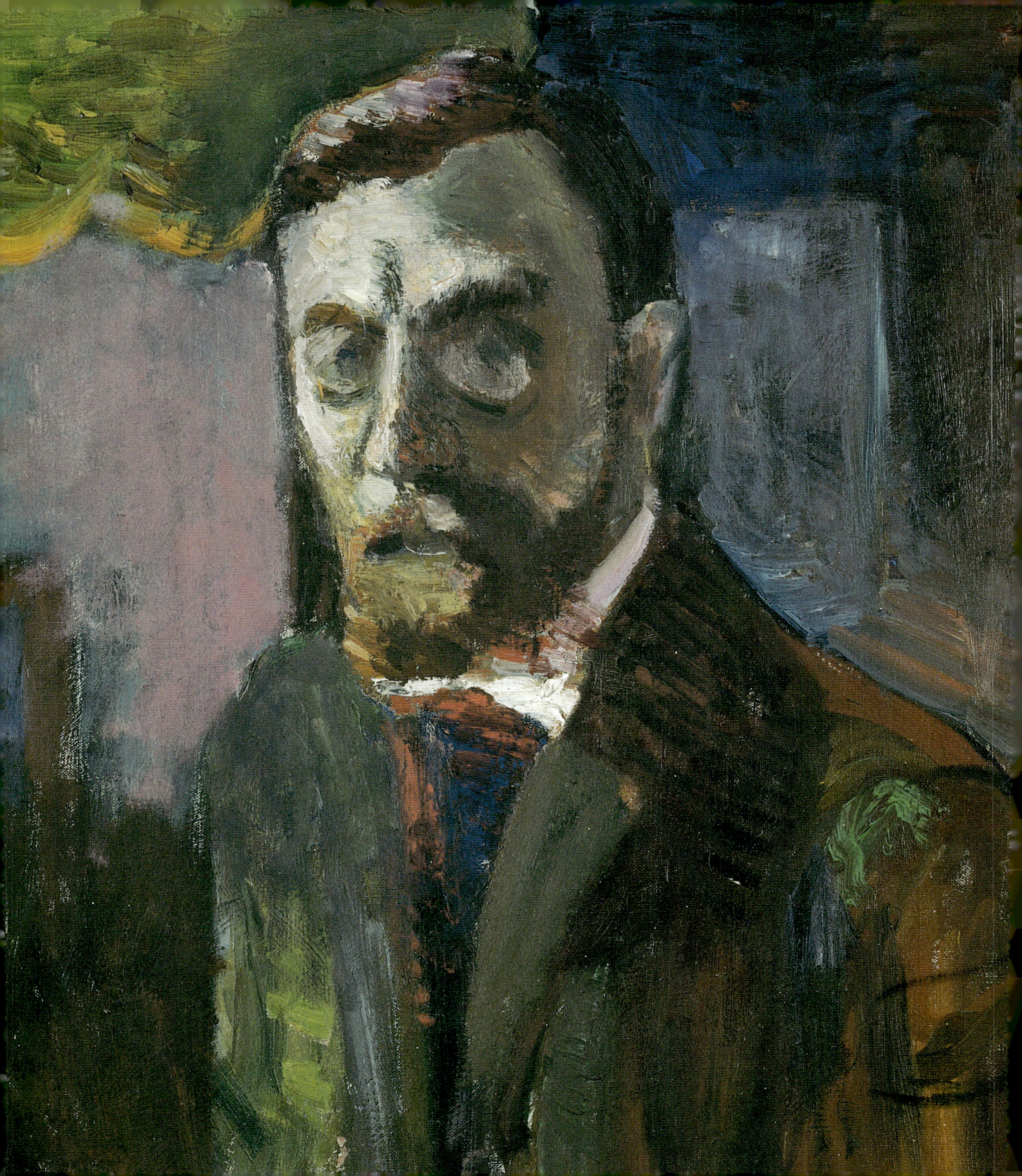

178 *Self-Portrait*, 1951. Lithograph, 31 × 21.2 cm. Le Cateau-Cambrésis, Musée Matisse.

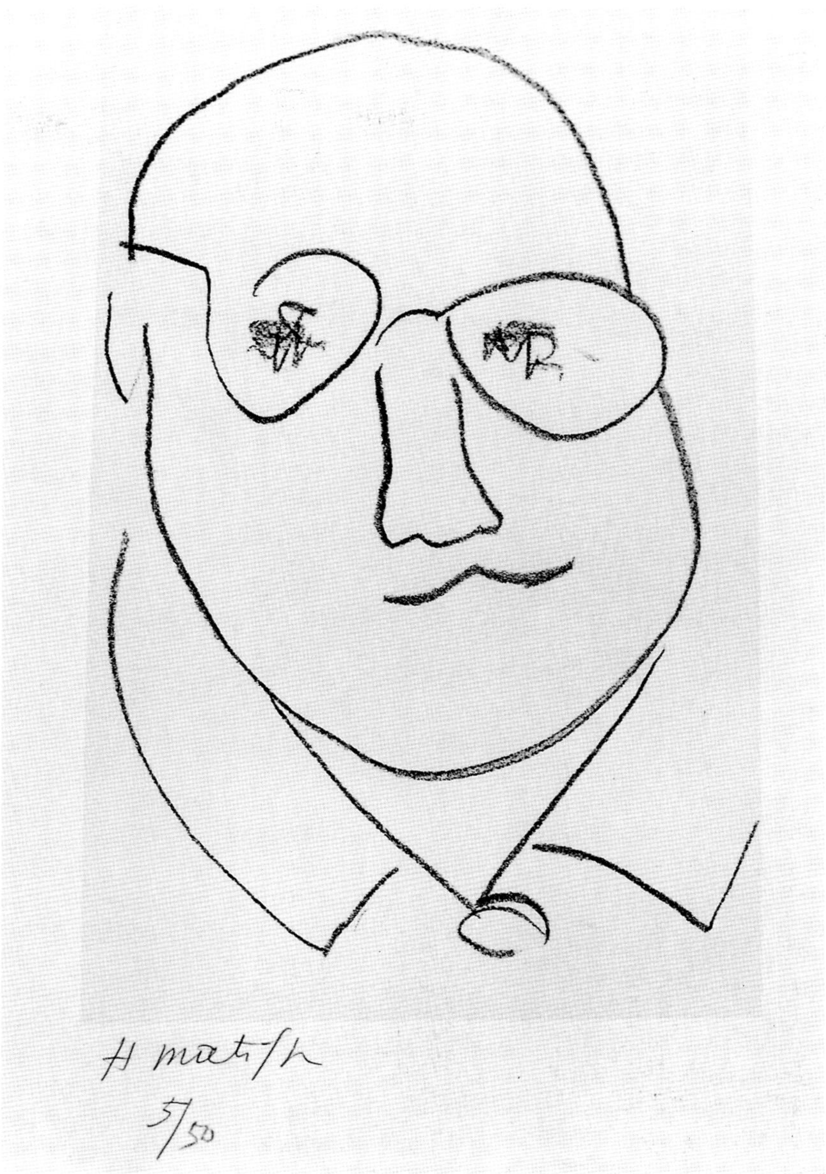

in the vivid paper cut-outs, which brought him ever greater acclaim, but it is clear in his last desolated self-images. They are among our very few means of access to the private refuge into which he withdrew in the final years of a long life. After a career of concern about his public image, these offhand graphic works reassert private values and the intimacy of the individual, vulnerable soul. Following Matisse's lifelong, resolutely isolated exploration of himself in his art, a parabola had been completed, the corresponding coordinates located before 1900 in the tentative, searching self-portraits of his beginnings.

Detail of fig. 29.

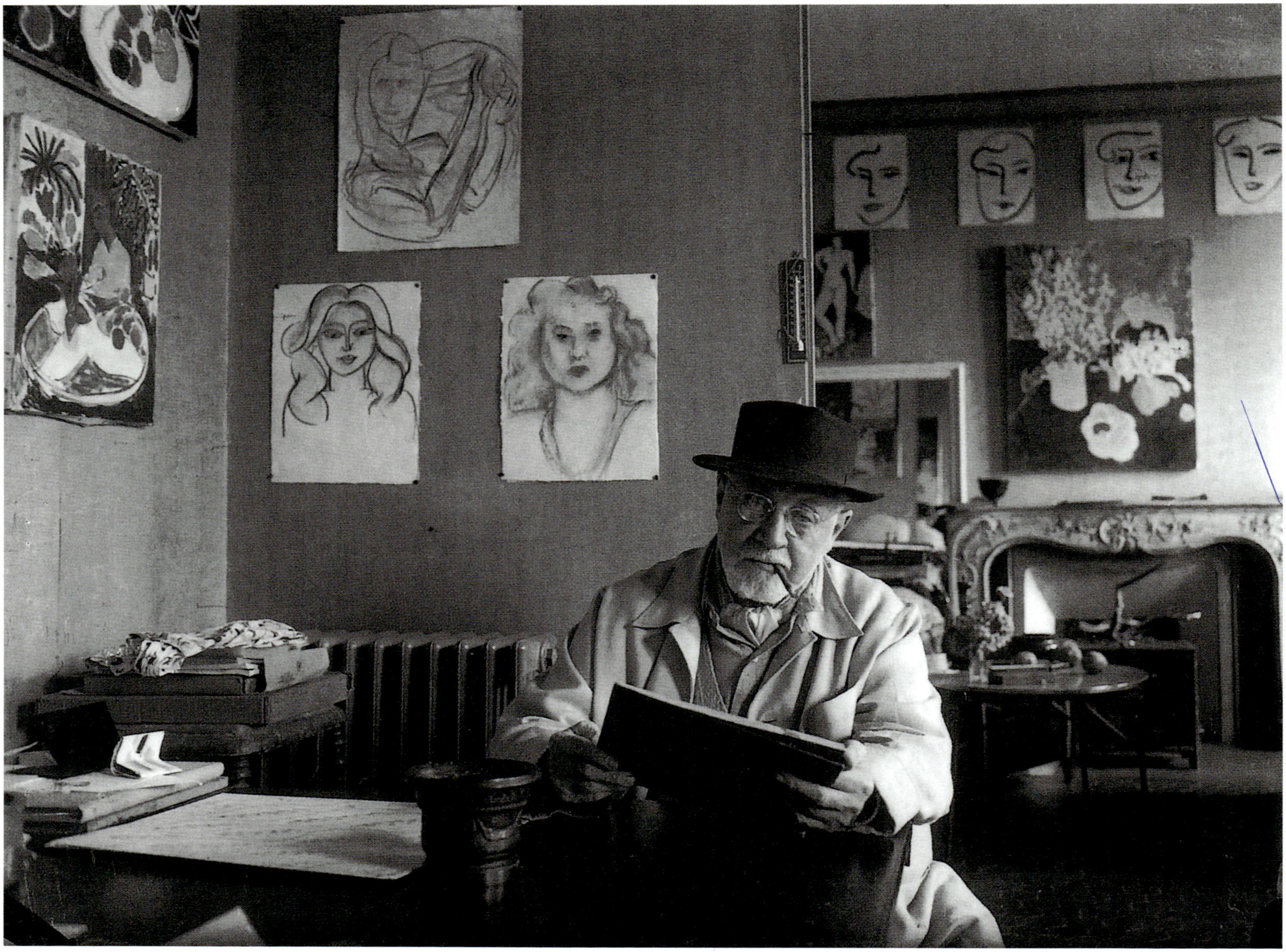

Chapter 7 The Problem of the Model

The portrait of Georges Demotte (fig. 179) from 1918 occupies a transitional place in Matisse's portraiture overall, but it nearly brought to a close his activity as a portrait painter. In technique and style it is far more sober and traditional than any other portrait from the decade, with none of the extensive formal manipulations that characterized his most radical departures from the appearance of his sitters. Embedded in a brown ground that seems to absorb the figure, the sitter's bright, balding head and impressive beard, which widens as it descends, create together a simple sign of stability that is rare in Matisse's work until this moment, when it can also be found in the self-portrait he made earlier that year in Nice (see fig. 137). Even the spots of brighter color in the portrait of Demotte – red in the mouth, blue in the eyes – appear also as accents in the self-portrait. The tendency to abstraction that led to the definitive versions of the portraits of Yvonne Landsberg, Auguste Pellerin, and George Besson is absent here. Matisse's stamp unmistakably marks this representation, but, even so, it was his most realistic portrait in nearly twenty years.[1]

Leaving the social

In terms of the function of Matisse's portraiture, a transition more momentous than stylistic change was in progress. When he went to Marseilles and Nice in late 1917, he made the first step in what became a decisive escape from his troublesome family situation and a more gradual break with the art world in Paris. The portraits of Demotte and the art critic Besson, Parisians both, were vestiges of one of the main roles of portraiture in Matisse's work until then: to affirm and extend the values of the societies in which he had participated to this point, and from which he gradually detached himself with his move to the South of France. In the place of those societies he substituted a world largely of his own creation, with little reference, especially in the 1920s, to values other than artistic ones. The importance – the pleasures and difficulties – of making art became his obsession in painting for the next decade. The themes of his work from this period in Nice – luxury, self-absorption, sensuality, tension, unfocused longing – derive their meaning outside any context of social transaction. And the greater realism of his work beginning especially in 1918 did not mean that he had abandoned his desire to internalize his motifs and express his responses through decoration. But he did so in a less abstract way, as he became more a stage director of elaborate scenarios in his studios and apartments. The metaphor of the theater to describe his ambiguous pictorial dramas is apt (and has been invoked many times, including by Matisse himself),

Matisse in his studio, Villa Le Rêve, Vence, 1948.
Photograph © Michel Sima. All rights reserved.

179 *Georges Demotte*, 1918. Oil on panel, 54 × 45 cm. Lyons, Musée des Beaux-Arts.

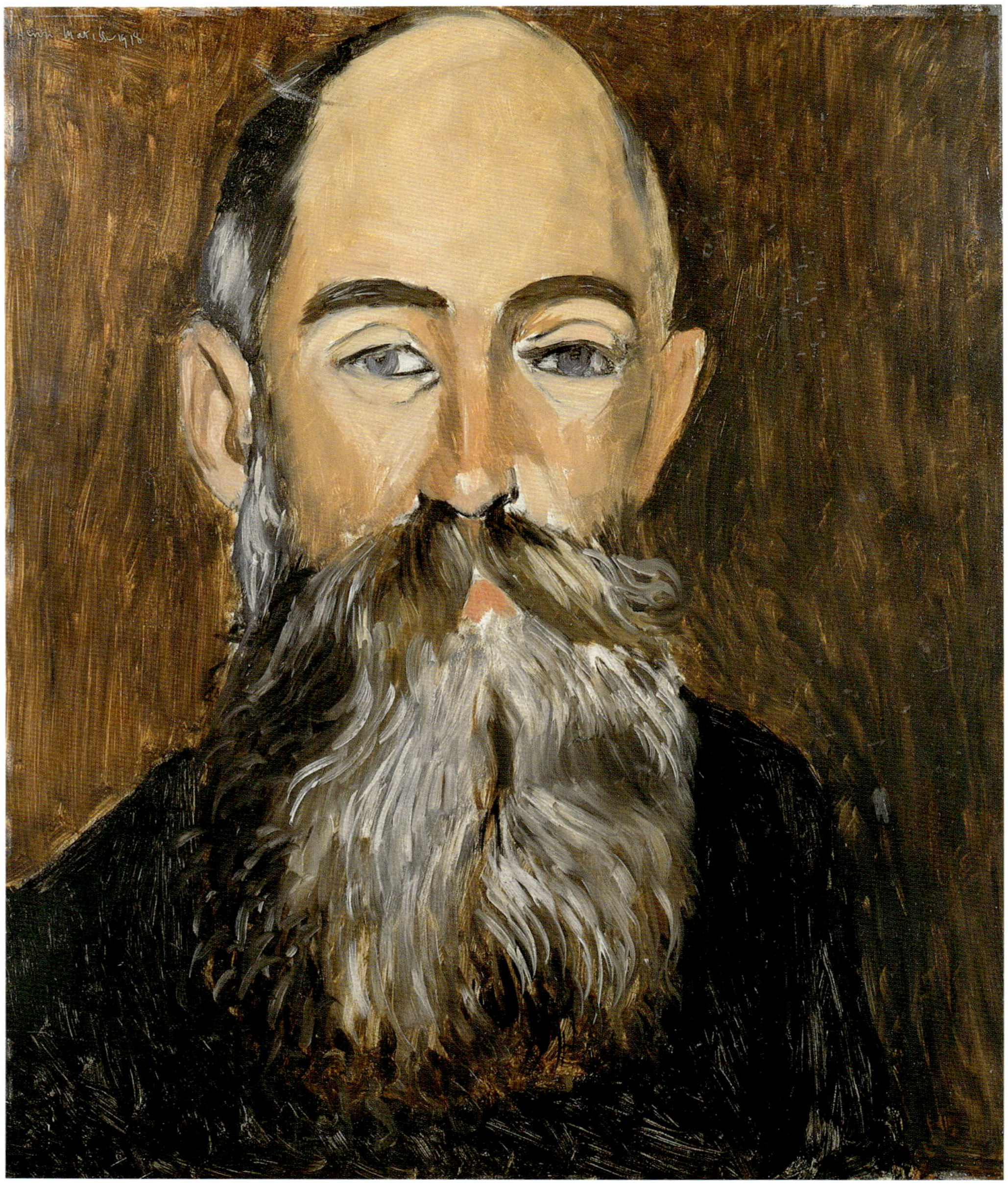

especially considering that almost invariably when the human figure appears in his work it is to act a role of his invention.

After 1918 Matisse painted only one portrait, *The Baroness Gourgaud* in 1924 (see fig. 188). He executed no commissions for portrait paintings and he did not paint a single family member, friend, or acquaintance.[2] From 1920 to the end of his life he did make many portrait drawings and some prints: of family members, as we have seen in Chapter 3; of friends and acquaintances among artists, writers, and musicians, considered in Chapter 4; and of collectors, dealers, publishers, and museum officials. But he ceased to paint images of class-equivalent sitters. Instead of taking commissions, or asking a friend or family member to sit for a portrait painting, when Matisse wanted to paint from the human face or figure – and this is to say, invariably, the female face or figure – he hired a model for the job.

In finally abandoning the painting of portraits in the 1920s Matisse was observing (or sharpening) two distinctions. The lesser of these in itself is an artistic concern, the distinction between painting and drawing. Although on several occasions Matisse held that drawing was the foundation of his art, painting was what really mattered to him, as it would to nearly any modern artist concerned with his place in the great European traditions. This concern on his part was particularly focused in the 1920s, when he showed renewed interest in the history of French figure painting from Poussin to Courbet. Drawing of course has a practical advantage over painting, which should not be underestimated. Drawings are generally easier and faster to make than paintings, and increasingly Matisse was reluctant to synthesize his responses to any individual – hired model or not – in a single painting; hence his increasing satisfaction with his drawings in the 1930s and the later proliferation of themes and variations beginning in his drawing practice but also carrying over into his painting on the scale both of the easel and of the wall. And in general there is little question that drawing was more central to Matisse's artistic practice than that of any other major twentieth-century artist with the exception of Picasso.

The second distinction, which subsumes the first, is primarily social. Matisse's artistic and social values had diverged once he had determined to make a kind of art that was intensively, definitively, self-referential. Portraits, especially painted portraits, were no longer a major component of his art consequent to his withdrawal from the societies in which such portraiture functions. Portrait drawing, though, still had a role in Matisse's new order of values. In fact, drawing generally assumed a greater importance in his work beginning in the late 1920s.[3] Drawing was a more private medium, more given to occasional uses, as when an old friend paid a visit. Sometimes the occasion was a commemoration, as in several frontispiece portraits, where the greater graphic clarity of a drawing was an advantage in book production. When he drew the portraits of fellow artists, it was either to honor an old friendship or a new accomplishment, not to delineate a community of shared interests as it had been in the Fauve period. When he made drawings of his daughter Marguerite in the 1940s, he did so to celebrate her safe deliverance from wartime danger; when he sketched his grandchildren, it was to observe youthful rites of passage and to mark his sense of personal and biological continuity, not to promote the family structure. All that had gone into portraiture as a social agent in his work was now to be subordinate to his artistic needs, which would be more efficiently served by hiring models.

The hybrid family

An important symptom of Matisse's transition from his bourgeois world in Paris to a less regulated life in Nice are the paintings that combine model and family. *Tea* of 1919 (fig. 180) is the best known of these. This large painting completes a symbolic triptych of family portraits at the Matisse house in suburban Issy-les-Moulineaux.[4] The first, *The Piano Lesson* of 1916 (see fig. 69), is an essay in structure, discipline, denial, and the assertion of the symbolic law of the father. The second is *The Music Lesson* of 1917 (see fig. 60), gathering the whole family before his sons left home, but banishing Amélie Matisse to the garden. *Tea* moves outdoors to the garden itself and indicates new domestic protocols. Of the family only Marguerite remains. But in this setting she is accompanied by Matisse's favorite

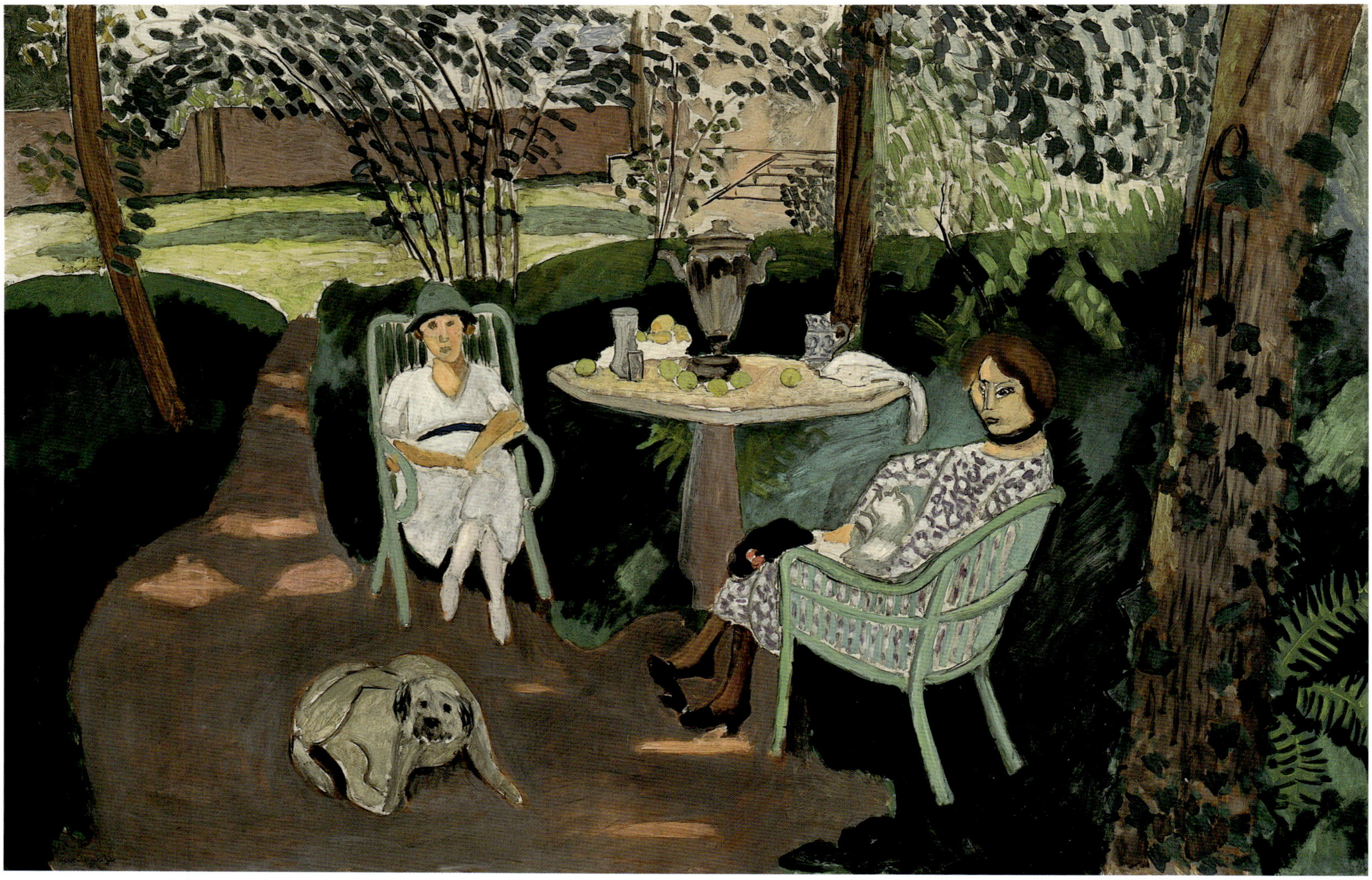

180 *Tea*, 1919. Oil on canvas, 140.3 × 211.3 cm. Los Angeles County Museum of Art, Bequest of David L. Loew in memory of his father, Marcus Loew.

professional model of the moment, Antoinette Arnoux, whom he had brought north from Nice so he would not have to deny himself the chance to work with her while he visited his family. On the ground before these young female counterpoints a scratching dog adds a vulgar and humorous note. Matisse has painted Marguerite's face in a severe and fractured manner, reminiscent of the painting of Pierre in *The Piano Lesson* or her own *Tête blanche et rose* (see fig. 66), harking back to a recent time of experimentation and bold advance in his art, letting his labor on the face show on its surface. By contrast, he rendered the model Antoinette in a soft and hazy style that is in keeping with the new manner of painting he had adopted in the South. Worlds combine here as Matisse uses the occasion to look both back and forward.

In *Young Women in the Garden* (fig. 181), painted about the same time, Matisse compares old and new worlds even more explicitly. Now dominating the foreground, Antoinette Arnoux lounges on a sofa that has been brought into the garden and covered with the kind of figured fabric or carpet that enlivened the interior in *The Painter's Family* (see fig. 59), a family portrait from the beginning of the decade. Her dynamic pose and bright dress against bold pattern outshine the figures of Marguerite and Amélie Matisse in the background, faces blank, bodies inert,

181 *Young Women in the Garden*, 1919. Oil on canvas, 54.5 × 65 cm. La Chaux-de-Fonds, Switzerland, Musée des Beaux-Arts, collection René and Madeleine Junod.

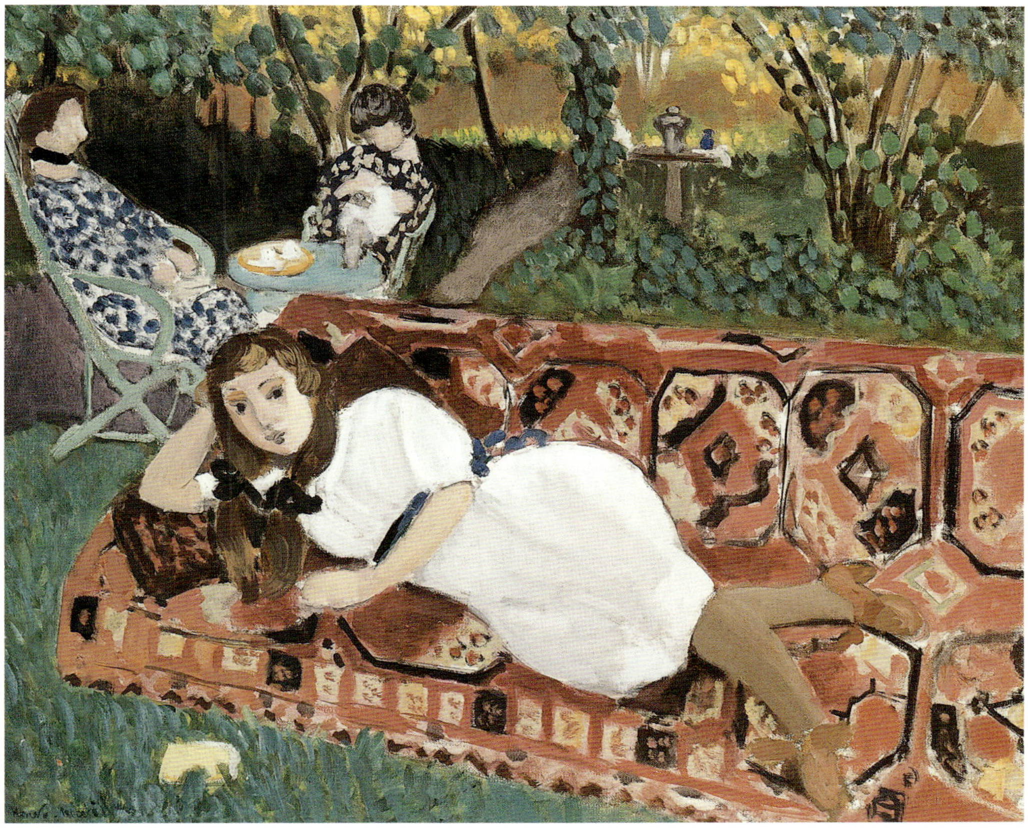

slumped or mannequin-like, even dressed to match, a collective presence. In giving his model the larger, more alert, and more distinctive figuration Matisse again expresses what now holds his attention. Back in Nice he went further in this direction of symbolically reconstituting his fragmented family. A few years later, with the model Henriette Darricarrère and her two brothers, he recreated in his studio past scenes from his own family life, in which surrogate daughter and sons play the piano, read, or sit down to checkers.[5] On one hand, it seems that Matisse missed his family, or at least reminisced about the past with them, and re-enacted these family scenes with his models. On the other, the family is replaced by these pliant surrogates in the new setting as Matisse mimics the form and activities of the family structure without depending on the content: sociable images drawn from transient relations eclipse the expressions of the more permanent bonds of his life.

Back to the future

The shift from the society of portrait sitters, family members or otherwise, to the hired model deployed in portrait-like settings had in fact been under way well before he went to Nice. Matisse made a "return to the model" in 1916–17 to explore a dialogue between architectonic and organic approaches to the human figure, specifically the female form.[6] Over a period of a year he made several dozen paintings (but strangely few drawings) of a dark-haired model named Laurette (or Lorette; her surname is not known), not only alone but sometimes with one or two other women in simulated family groupings which, while not as explicit as

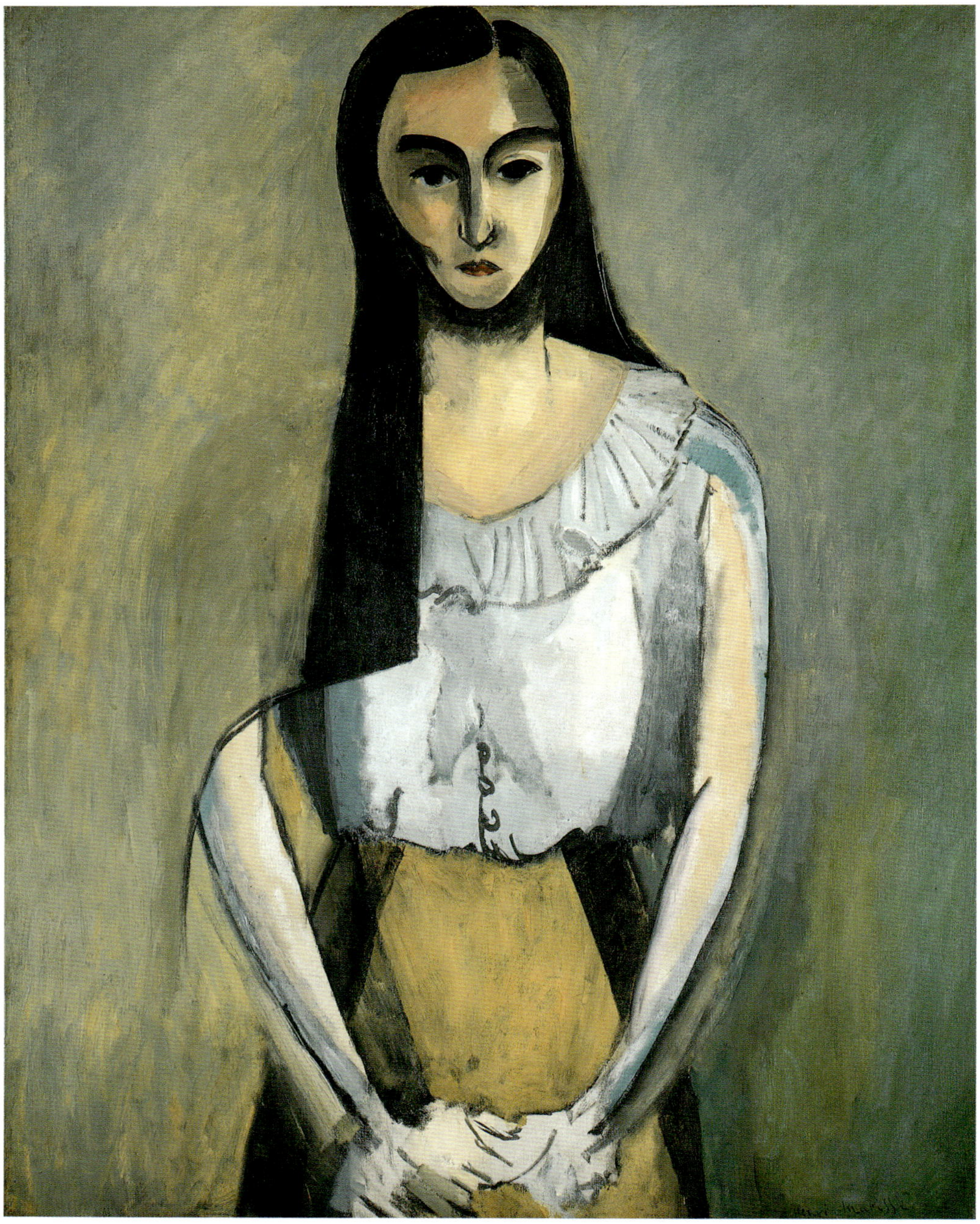

182 *The Italian Woman*, 1916. Oil on canvas, 116.7 × 89.5 cm. New York, Solomon R. Guggenheim Museum, by exchange, 1982.

the surrogate family groups of the 1920s, indicate an interest in filial attachment but also a desire to express the relationship between genetic affinity and formal similarity.[7]

From the first painting of Laurette, the severe and enigmatic *Italian Woman* of 1916 (fig. 182), Matisse went on to paint a startling variety of images of this woman's face, often filling the picture field in tight-focus scrutiny, loaded with psychological intensity (see fig. 183). The austerity and experimentalism of *The Italian Woman* gives way to abundance of both paint and flesh in the image, conveying pleasure in the physicality of these things for the artist. Laurette is imaged in a multitude of imputed characters, no one stylization sufficient to express the artist's responses to this model. Although this variety has been characterized as a function

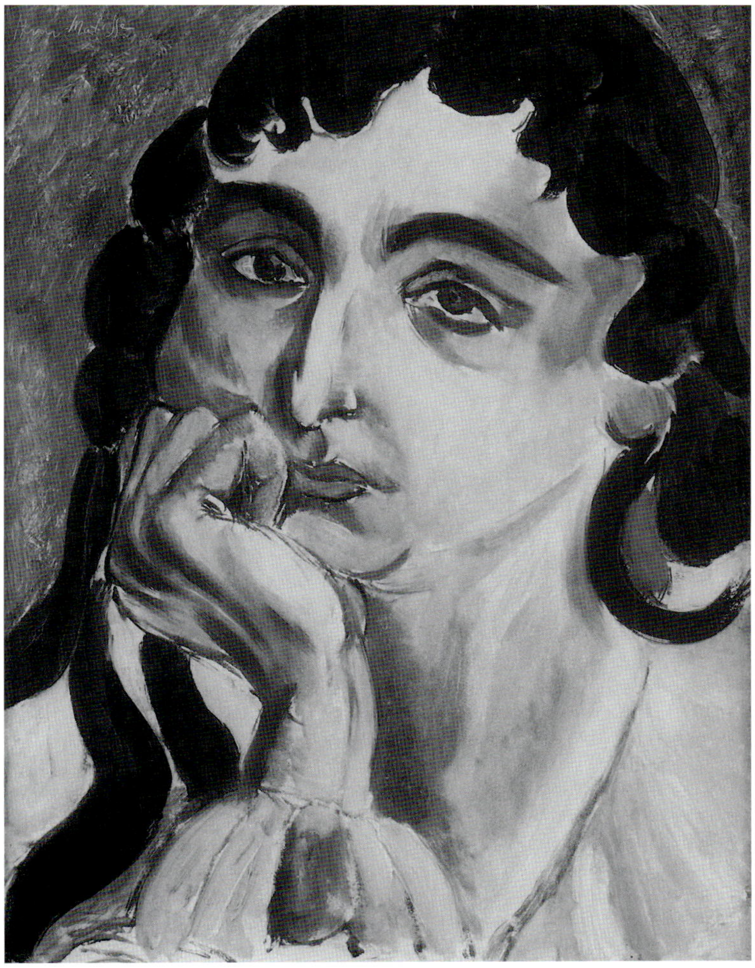

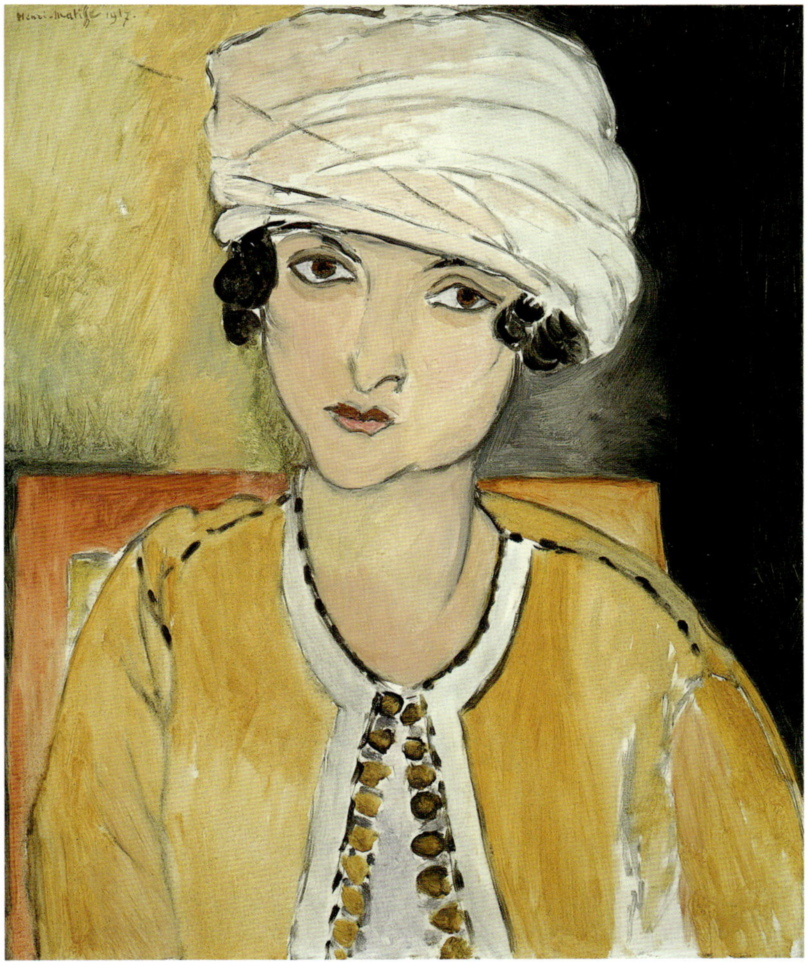

183 (*above left*) *Laurette*, 1917. Oil on wood, 35 × 26.7 cm. Private collection.

184 (*above right*) *Laurette with Turban, Yellow Jacket*, 1917. Oil on canvas, 61.3 × 49.4 cm. Washington, D.C., National Gallery of Art, Chester Dale Collection.

of Matisse's indecisiveness, it is surely also a mark of a renewed engagement with and confidence in the craft of painting, stimulated by the repeated encounters with this sensuous model.[8] The depictions of her that approach more nearly the visual conventions of portraiture (see fig. 184) seem less assured, as if the artist was in fact uncertain about how he should deploy her on these occasions, and what kind of identity she should have. Having hired her, Matisse was obliged to make all these decisions for her image since he controlled entirely the transaction now taking place. And so perhaps irresolution is at the heart of this proliferation of identities for Laurette. The person before him did not offer the same resistance, the same force of ego, that a person in a portrait transaction does. He did not have to do battle with Laurette as he did in the same period with Auguste Pellerin; did not have to show her the respect and solicitude he accorded his cherished patrons the Steins. Less resistance led to uncertainty as Matisse experimented with a new, ambiguous genre that was neither portraiture nor a mere still life of the human form.

Even more than with Laurette, Matisse reveled in the heavy, luxurious physicality of the model Antoinette Arnoux.[9] She appears nude in conventionally posed ways in his work many times, but also in situations of greater ambiguity, both by herself and, as we have seen, in the fanciful family groupings of *Tea* and *Young Women in the Garden*. Many of his paintings and drawings of her convey the

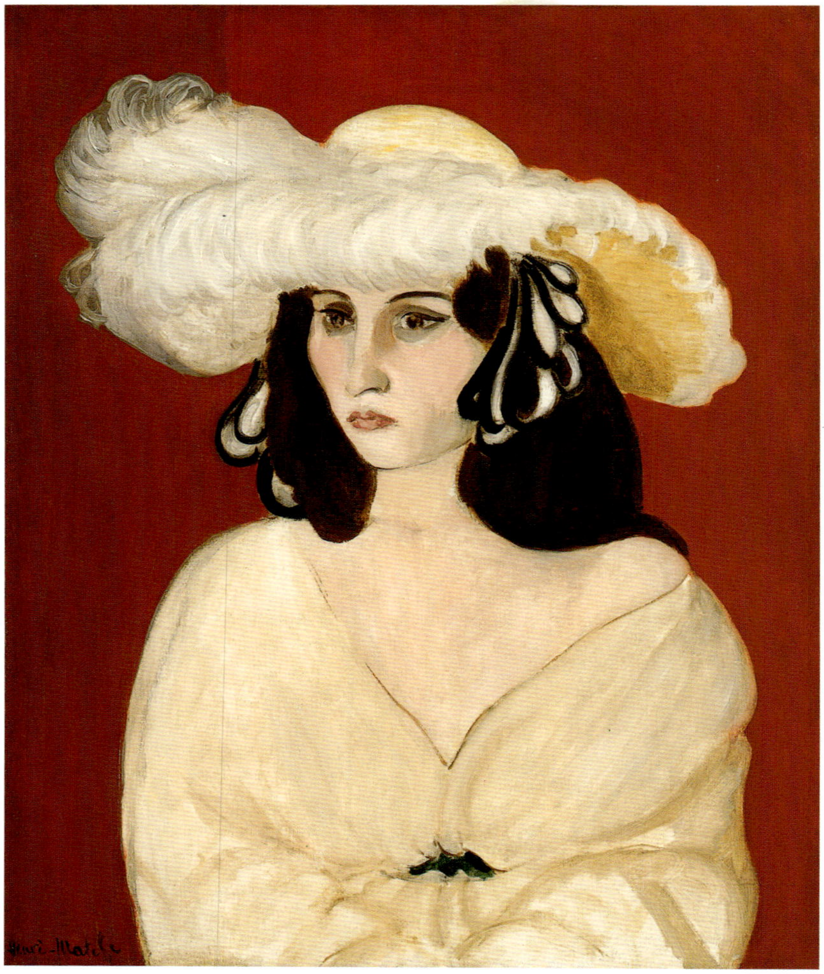

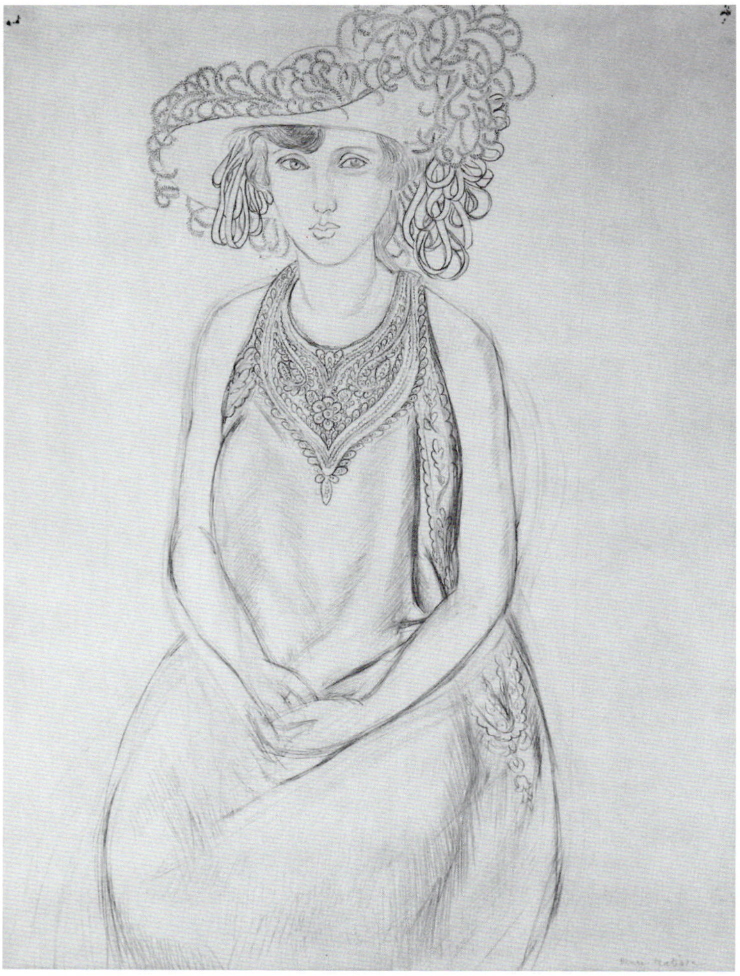

185 (*above left*) *The White Plumes*, 1919. Oil on linen, 73 × 60.3 cm. The Minneapolis Institute of Arts, William Hood Dunwoody Fund.

186 (*above right*) *The Plumed Hat*, 1919. Pencil on paper, 49 × 37 cm. Washington, D.C., National Gallery of Art, Collection of Mr. and Mrs. Paul Mellon.

sensibility of portraiture without the sense, notably the series in both media sometimes called the "White Plumes" (see figs. 185, 186).[10] The large number of elaborate drawings of her face and body allege periods of careful study. Still, Matisse seems to have been less intrigued by Antoinette Arnoux than he had been by Laurette, less compelled to cast her in different roles. In his images of Laurette, Matisse created a more complicated and active sensuality; Antoinette is more often passively on display. She was also younger than Laurette and may have been more timid, but Matisse's constructions of these women should be understood to express his images of them more than their own self-images. It is possible that he was coming to understand better what he wanted from these models.

His next principal model, beginning in 1920, was another young and voluptuous woman, Henriette Darricarrère. Her principal role was to pose nude as well, and with her Matisse added an overlay of luxuriousness associated with Orientalism that lasted through most of the 1920s as she became the main odalisque figure in his painting.[11] Matisse used her solidity to lend gravity to these highly artificial scenes, and often even melancholy (compared to Antoinette Arnoux, Henriette is more an anchor than a balloon). But he also depicted her many times as a young worldly woman decked out in contemporary fashion (fig. 187). In this mode Matisse sometimes paired her with his daughter Marguerite in an ersatz social situation.[12] He may even be comparing them, as two sides or elements of the same person. Matisse's

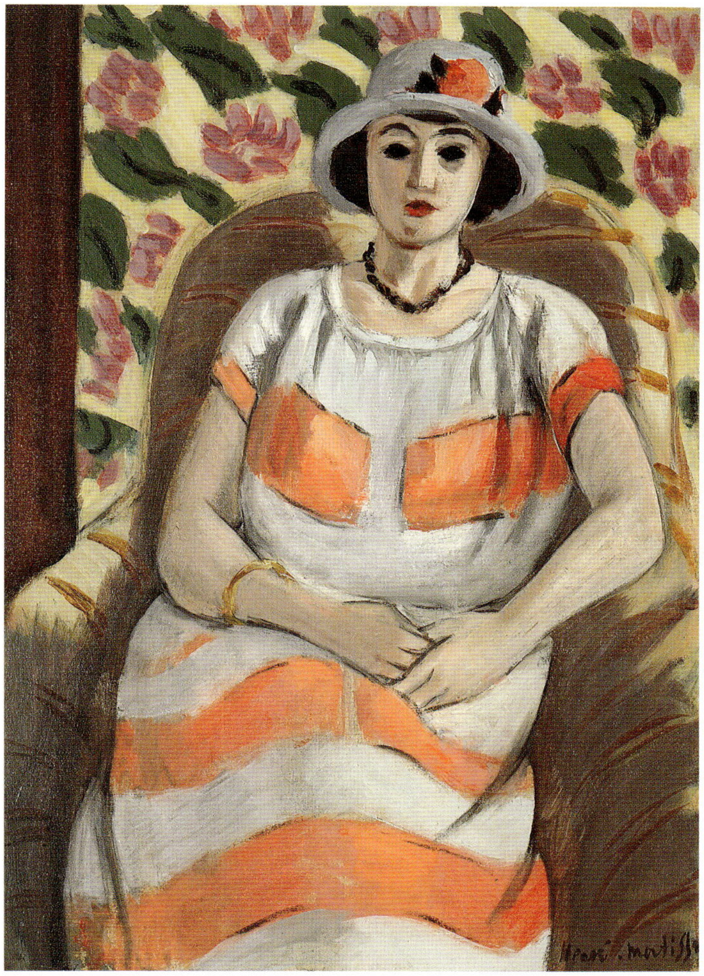

187 *Young Woman in Pink*, 1923. Oil on canvas, 55 × 38 cm. The Fine Arts · Museums of San Francisco, Memorial Gift from Dr. T. Edward and Tullah Hanley, Bradford, Pa., 69.30.134.

identification of Henriette Darricarrère with his daughter suggests once again a way in which he was seeking to create in a displaced version the forms and attachments of family life.[13]

The conflict between portrait and decoration

Matisse's models became extraordinarily important for him as the means to act out human dramas, social conventions, and artistic allegories; he was particular when choosing them, as we shall see, and faithful to ones he favored. Models were the agency for his freedom, and he seems to have viewed them as a form of protection from the social world. This desire for complete freedom from the constraints posed by the individuality of another person and the obligations to acknowledge his or her social identity is embarrassingly clear in his final painted portrait, *The Baroness Gourgaud* (fig. 188). It is difficult to tell with this portrait to what extent Matisse was fully engaged with his project or whether the informality, even vacuity, of the image reflects his prevailing interests at the time. The Baron Gourgaud commissioned Matisse in 1924 to paint his wife, an American, born Eva Gebhard. The Gourgauds were adventurous collectors of modern art; other Matisses in their collection included the austere, Cubist-influenced *Interior with Goldfish* (Paris, Musée National d'Art Moderne).

Matisse painted the portrait in Cannes, at the Hôtel Carlton (in the South, he could not entirely avoid collectors). Pierre Matisse reported that his father undertook the commission with reluctance.[14] Matisse exacted his familiar terms for these occasions, with an additional requirement that ensured some continuity with his current endeavors. Michel Dauberville of Galerie Bernheim-Jeune later described the artist's efforts to guarantee that he would not be fettered by this commission: "To make a portrait, said Matisse, is vexing . . . He described the conditions he placed on doing this one: his usual model would take an equal part in the picture, no one would be allowed to see the painting while it was in progress; if in the end the portrait was unacceptable, Matisse would take it back. In this way he sought to preserve his friendly ties with the Gourgaud family."[15] His ties with the Gourgauds were certainly friendlier than those with Auguste Pellerin had been; but Matisse may have seen in them something in common that attracted him: they both were collectors of Cézanne.

It was an extraordinary act of deflection to give such a prominent place to a hired model in a commissioned portrait. Pierre Matisse credited his father's choice to purely artistic needs, claiming that Matisse included Henriette Darricarrère "to complete the picture."[16] This can be only a partial explanation. We have already seen that it was one of the artist's conditions for doing the portrait. Matisse was clearly pushing at the outer limits of credibility of the portrait as a vehicle for the values of the sitter. The artist's own values overwhelm. Despite the intrusion of the model and the banality of the image of the sitter, the Gourgauds accepted the portrait, which they eventually donated, along with many other works from their collection, to the French national museum.[17]

In the portrait Matisse made use of the time-honored device, beloved of Ingres, of a doubled view of a sitter in a mirror located behind her. But instead of psychological complication through an alternate image, the only effect is an empty echo of the rear view of Henriette Darricarrère's head as the hired model is likened formally and socially with the baroness through this play of mirroring and miming. The mirror has the additional effect, as it does in many of his interior scenes of the 1920s, of initiating a complicated game of expanding and collapsing space in this lavishly decorated suites of rooms, a private, if temporary, world of his own creation.

Despite the sence of calm, even ennui, the entire surface of the painting is activated by an abundance of objects, patterns, and abstractions. Matisse has given the baroness her prominence by emptying her of vivacity; he has treated her as a precisely drawn, solid volume amid the profusion of active but flattened decorative elements. It is a backhanded attention – his real concerns here are indicated by a copy of the journal *Art et décoration* placed on the table at the junction of the two figures, where their hands awkwardly converge. No matter that the cover of the journal, devoted to both the decorative arts and the concept of painting as decoration, looked nothing like this. Not a literal object, Matisse's centerpiece is an abstraction, a pure sign of his motive for bringing together patron and model in this lavish interior – the motive to create an expressive and satisfying decorative art no matter what the occasion.[18] Darricarrère's awkwardly projecting arm, linking the pattern of the tablecloth, the shorthand manifesto, and the figure of the baroness, acts as a surrogate for the form of the artist painting the canvas. This sign of artistic control and unification declares Matisse's willingness to construct a painting, even a commissioned portrait for desirable patrons, on his own terms. The baroness's status, collection, character, physical presence – all of this was no match

188 *The Baroness Gourgaud*, 1924. Oil on canvas, 81 × 65 cm. Paris, Musée National d'Art Moderne, Centre Georges Pompidou.

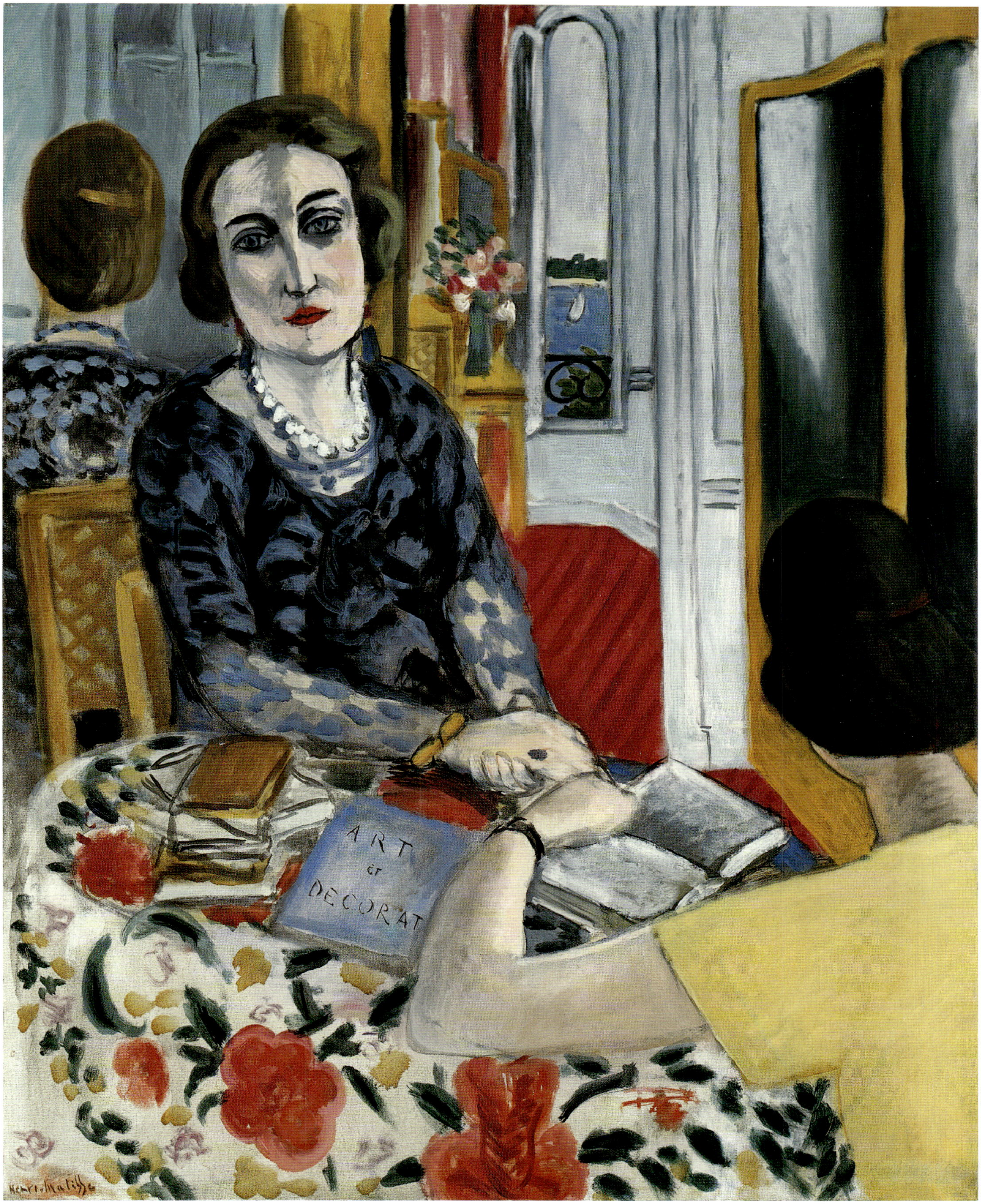
ART
ET
DECORAT

for Matisse's domination of the portrait transaction. What chance could a hired model have?

The Baroness Gourgaud is only the most egregious – and publicly played out – example of Matisse's willingness to stack the deck in his favor in a portrait transaction. This ultimate expression of disregard for the socially constituted identity of a sitter had, as I have already implied, its origin long before this impasse. He had previously identified the essentials of the problem and set out the terms of engagement. We return to his response to Clara MacChesney's question about portraiture in 1912: "No; I seldom paint portraits, and if I do only in a decorative manner. I can see them in no other way."[19] Four years earlier, in his public declaration of purpose, the essay "Notes of a Painter," he had written about the vital links between expression, composition, and decoration: "The entire arrangement of my picture is expressive: the place occupied by the figures, the empty spaces around them, the proportions, all of that has its share. Composition is the art of arranging in a decorative manner the diverse elements at the painter's command to express his feelings. . . . A work of art must be harmonious in its entirety: any superfluous detail would replace some other essential detail in the mind of the spectator."[20] Also in 1908, to the students in his newly formed art school, he declared that everything in a painting "must be considered in interrelation during the process – nothing can be added," and that it was necessary to "stop from time to time to consider the subject . . . in its ensemble." Finally: "What you are aiming for, above all, is unity."[21] Even earlier than this, before formulating practice as theory, he had begun combining the human body with strongly patterned environments, seeking to unify these disparate elements.[22]

In his statements about his art Matisse was more consistent about this idea of unity, harmony, and the interrelatedness of all parts of a work of art than about any other issue. And this is the issue at the heart of decoration. For Matisse, decoration was overall, interrelated composition that would permit the most complete expression of his feelings. A completely unified painting represented the whole artist. There was room for nothing else. Decoration as conceived by Matisse was antithetical to portraiture if by a portrait we mean a representation of a sitter – not merely a depiction – as well as an expression of the artist.[23] Taking into consideration the point of view of the spectator, portraiture presented to Matisse this problem, too: faced with an iconic portrait image, the viewer would identify too strongly with the human subject, his or her attention would be too focused, not permitting the dispersal of attention that is one of the things Matisse valued in decoration.[24] Writing in the 1930s about his recently completed mural decoration *Dance*, he was explicit about this conflict between his goals and the attraction for the spectator of "the human character" of his subject: "the spectator's mind shouldn't be arrested by this human character, with which he would identify, and which, in immobilizing him, would keep him apart from the harmonious, living, and animated association" that he sought within his painting, and between his painting and the environment.[25] In a portrait the effect would be magnified; the attraction to faces is innate. The human element would "immobilize" the viewer in a one-to-one confrontation, like a distorted mirror image. An old and familiar pleasure, the viewer's sensation of recognition, would become an obstacle to a new pleasure, the pleasure produced by Matisse's ability to seduce the viewer to his point of view through the indirect process of diffusion.

Yet he spoke of painting portraits in a decorative manner, and doing it only in this way. How would this be accomplished? How could the prerogatives of the sitter, premise for the portrait, be reconciled with the subjugation of part to whole required in decoration? And how could Matisse keep the attention of a spectator who expected a portrait to emphasize the fundamental human element of its sitter? This was the delicate balance Matisse sought to achieve. He came close to this goal only rarely – with Greta Moll, with Sarah Stein, with Auguste Pellerin in his second portrait. The cost of striving for this balance was unacceptably high, however. It was impossible to reconcile these opposing forces except under the most specific conditions: either when the sitter, whose ego was partly invested in Matisse's aims, was in evident sympathy, such as Moll or Sarah Stein; or when the sitter could stand up to Matisse and resist assimilation, as with Amélie Matisse or Pellerin. Even with these supreme examples of Matisse's success as a portraitist there are problems. The portrait of Greta Moll is a considerable decorative achievement, but it falls short of rendering the complexity of the woman. By contrast, the portrait of Sarah Stein and the second Pellerin portrait are strong images of their sitters, but they are more iconic than decorative. We recall the eternal, intractable conflict in Matisse's work between representation and expression. He could not resolve this conflict. He also could not reconcile the opposition of portraiture and decoration. Instead, he could evade it. He was able to do this by painting women.

The portraits Matisse did "in a decorative manner," with an evident goal of allover composition, are all of women. In them women are compared with other things, merged with other things, or characterized through abstract concepts. The portraits do this in a variety of ways, but they have in common Matisse's introduction into the portrait of a framing or completing device that has a significant impact on how the sitter's identity is projected. These decorative portraits, including *The Girl with Green Eyes* and his portraits of Greta Moll and Jeanne Vaderin (see figs. 114, 113, 116), offer a variety of strategies in the service of their common goal to construct identities that emerge more from his artistic concerns than from any claims these women had to an independent and self-validating representation. Matisse's portraits of women seem to be the pictorial fulfillment of the art critic Camille Mauclair's declaration in an article of 1899 about portraiture: "A feminine portrait was . . . always a decorative work. . . . a stylized landscape of which the woman's body, invisible and central, was the driving force and the prisoner of the whole ensemble."[26]

Clothes make the woman

As we have seen, an ambiguity about a sitter's identity sometimes characterized Matisse's portraits of his wife. Befitting ambiguity, this is not always entirely obvious. The remarkable portrait of 1913 (see fig. 55) presents Amélie Matisse as an apparently self-possessed adult, free of things to be compared to or merged with. Her alert pose and especially the slight tilt of her head imply energy, as several observers have noted.[27] But the blank eyes and the final mask-like face impoverish her individuality. The sitter herself seems to have recognized this loss – we recall she is said to have wept as the image under construction came to seem less and less related to her, more and more an expression of his artistic needs.[28] The many sittings attest to the sitter's resistance to erasure, but in the end she was no match for Matisse's will. This is another portrait of Amélie Matisse – remember the furor over *Woman with the Hat* – that sends mixed signals about status and identity.

189 *The Embroidered Dark Blouse (Woman in a Red Chair)*, 1936. Oil on canvas, 35.3 × 24.1 cm. The Baltimore Museum of Art, The Cone Collection, formed by Dr. Claribel Cone and Miss Etta Cone of Baltimore, Maryland, BMA 1950.260.

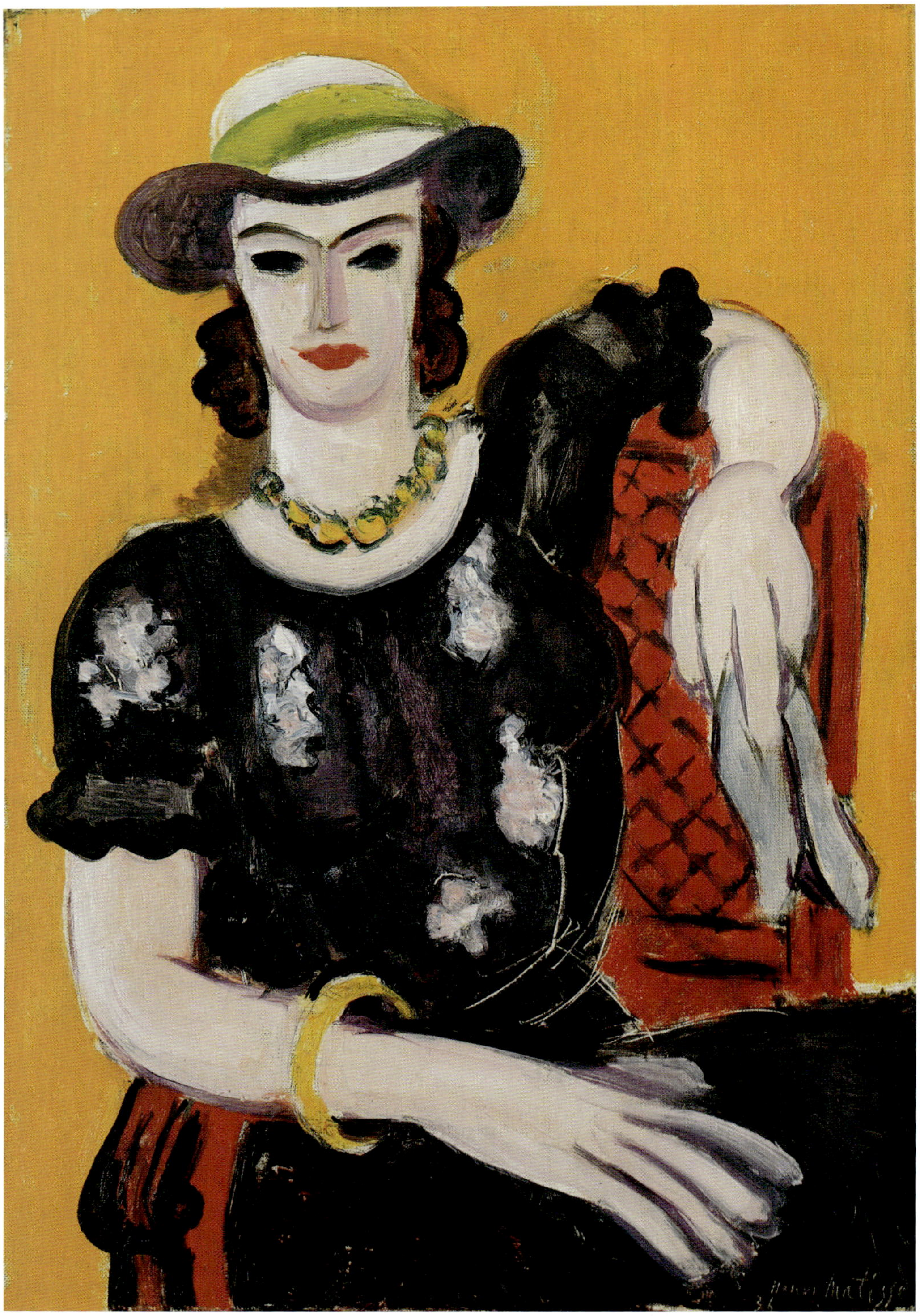

Such a tension between presence and erasure may also be found in many of Matisse's portrait-like depictions of hired models, in which the model, also dressed out in up-to-date style, has similarly had her identity compromised by the blackening or other disfigurement of her eyes (fig. 189). And these models are attired in a way that implies the importance to them, as ersatz portrait sitters, of their fashionable clothes as an element of self-presentation – which is really to say, their importance to Matisse, who kept closets full of dresses on hand for his models. This emphasis on fashion in Matisse's portraits of women and in his portrait-like depictions of hired female models is a common feature of some significance.[29]

In the way that the costumes of these women dominate how their images present them, they recall the tribute to women and fashion made by Charles Baudelaire in the 1860s in *The Painter of Modern Life*. According to Baudelaire, women's identity in the public sphere is not intrinsic, nor is their power to enthrall men. Women require fashion to complete them. These are Baudelaire's words: "All the things that adorn woman, all the things that go to enhance her beauty, are part of herself; and the artists who have made a special study of this enigmatic being are just as enchanted by the whole *mundus muliebris* [world of women] as by woman herself. . . . above all, she is a harmonious whole, not only in her carriage and in the movement of her limbs, but also in the muslins and the gauzes, in the vast and iridescent clouds of draperies in which she envelops herself, and which are, so to speak, the attributes and the pedestal of her divinity," and so on in this manner.[30] Here we see Baudelaire, who formulated so many of the premises of modernity for subsequent generations, setting out the terms of engagement that Matisse followed in his portraits of women – terms that led to the eclipse of the individual, leaving free signifiers of femininity, portraiture, and social position unattached to any individual to whom the artist would feel obliged to show some personal or social responsibility.

Man and the sufficient self

In his portraits of men, although Matisse employed conventional formats and typologies for male portraiture he manipulated them less freely than in his portraits of women. Working within a more established tradition of public representation, he imposed fewer external frames on his sitters who were men, fewer analogies of form or theme. In his portrait of Albert Marquet of 1905–6 (see fig. 81), it is true that we may find an effort to interlock figure and ground, as was the case in *Olga Merson* of a few years later (see fig. 115). But in the portrait of Marquet, the formal structure does not control the image of the sitter; on the contrary, it expresses Marquet's own identity as a painter. Matisse's construction of this painting by muted color and tonal contrasts indicates the respect both painters felt for the work of Cézanne, whose technique this painting emulates. And the color scale even seems to be a tribute to Marquet's own palette, dark for Matisse in 1905 but perfectly in keeping with Marquet's own preference for somber, close-valued hues. The format – an uncomplicated bust-length representation – is thus relatively neutral and allows the sitter to stand for himself, while the style forms an affinity with the sitter rather than a template for reshaping him. The portrait of André Derain from the same time (see fig. 80) offers a strikingly different palette but this similarly seems designed to express respect for the identity of the sitter. It had been the young and energetic Derain who helped Matisse liberate his own sense of color and paint handling. The fresh-looking and vital image of Derain acknowledges that contribution, as well as his youth and mercurial romanticism. In both paintings, formal concerns reinforce defining attributes of the sitters themselves. The identities of these men as painters are expressed and validated in Matisse's treatment of them in their portraits.

He also employed the simple bust-length format against a neutral background in one of his most assured masculine representations – his own self-portrait of 1906, an image of conspicuous independence and command (see fig. 90). This projection of self-determination is the principal quality of Matisse's portraits of men that distinguishes them from his portraits of women – though once again, the great exception is *Madame Matisse (The Green Line)* (see fig. 51). In itself this is unsurprising but some analysis is nevertheless warranted. In most of his portraits of men, masculinity is a sufficient sign for itself. Its attributes are adequately and unstrenuously borne in the carriage and physiognomy of the male sitter. There is thus a kind of essentialism in Matisse's portraits of men, but not strictly speaking a biological essentialism, as is clearly the case in depictions of the female nude, where identity is entirely borne by anatomy, and anything that might further identify the model is largely suppressed by conventional agreement. Rather, the essentialism in Matisse's portraits is in their public identities as men. They are figured as social and professional beings, directly addressed, without contingency or modifying devices, and acknowledging their equal partnership and equivalence of class position with the artist in a social as well as artistic transaction.

Environments subsume women in Matisse's decorative portraits, but when a man in Matisse's portraiture appears in an environment he typically dominates it, as in his second portrait of Pellerin (see fig. 130). We saw that in the development from first to second version, the final image attains a remarkable intensity that results in part from the artist's ability to distill incidental detail into an image of unity and controlled power. But it is due in part also to Pellerin's own resistance, his strength as Matisse struggled to construct an appropriate image of him. The tension gives the portrait a vitality that recalls Matisse's portrait of his wife from a few years before (see fig. 55). In that painting the struggle between artist and sitter – which may also have been a struggle between husband and wife – seemed in part to erase the sitter, canceling her identity between the mantle of fashion and the blankness of her mask-like face. But Matisse presents Pellerin as fully alive, active, even sinister.

Reading the gender of portraiture

Here a caveat needs to be introduced. It must be allowed that the contrast I have drawn between portraits of men and women may have been produced not by Matisse, or not only by Matisse, but by a gendered reading of the two paintings, in which characteristics shared by a painting of a man and a painting of a woman are seen to support contrary interpretations. To the extent that this might be true, it indicates the challenge for the viewer today – this viewer and writer, any viewer or writer or reader – to imagine contemporary or earlier public representations of women that build a convention for the portrait of Amélie Matisse in the same way that, for instance, Ingres's Bertin provides the authoritarian type for the portrait of Pellerin. For Greta Moll's portrait, Matisse had appropriated some particularly seductive arms; for Pellerin's, he invoked an entire cultural ethos of patriarchy and control.

This challenge to find appropriate models for the modern female portrait is not the viewer's alone. It may be that the problem of the artist and the problem of the interpreter – this problem of gendered reading – are the same. Recall Baudelaire's assertion that women in modern public life cannot bear their entire identity intrinsically. Therefore painting portraits of such women would require a commensurate attention to the form in which a woman presents herself. This formulation was given a significant twist in 1906 by Camille Mauclair. Writing again about contemporary portraiture, Mauclair was participating in a gendered discourse on both the creation and reception of the portrait. According to Mauclair, the interest in a woman, for the artist, is found completely in her surface appearance. A woman can be contained entirely within the image of her. By contrast, Mauclair says, "the likeness of a man, in effect, is always *social*. The portrait of a man," he continues, "seems to come to the viewer, to impose a will on him; the portrait of a woman waits for him to come to her. [A woman's portrait] is an impersonal form, the object of a desire, a motif of lines, of tonalities, of ornaments. . . . [In the portrait of a woman], the artist has not pursued the investigation of an idea, but rather of the secrets of form."[31] Mauclair's opposed characterization of male and female portraiture clearly positions the viewer of any portrait as male, and gives some indication that in the period when Matisse was active in portraiture, the position of the artist and the position of the interpreter were the same with regard to this kind of gendered reading. Mauclair's gendered distinction, with man as a social being and woman as spectacle, offers a contemporary framework for addressing Matisse's portraiture as itself a gendered activity.

With the possibility of this kind of gendered reading in mind, let us return to Matisse's portraits of Michael and Sarah Stein (see figs. 126, 127). They do not produce the kind of high drama of the portrait of the artist's wife or the second portrait of Pellerin. Nor do they evoke such a rich complex of personal struggle or historical reference. They do not even seem to offer much of an interpretive challenge. As we have seen, it has been standard practice (and my own view) to say of the portrait of Sarah Stein, a sensitive woman with whom Matisse felt a great empathy, that her face is the locus of a marvelous rising field of spiritual energy. By contrast (for a contrast is needed to follow this dialogic tack), the portrait of Michael Stein is a little boring, his presentation more quotidian than that of his exceptional and sympathetic wife. With Sarah, exotic color contrasts shimmer; with Michael, hue is dull and muddy. As we have seen, several preparatory drawings showing Matisse's transformations of her appearance indicate that he worked hard to produce an appropriate image of Sarah. His execution in Michael's portrait, on the other hand, was cursory; this portrait was not a labor of love, but of obligation, completing the pair. And so on in like fashion.

Consider now these paintings along the lines I have already suggested as general terms of contrast between Matisse's portraits of women and men. Thus: Sarah's dematerialization is spectacular, not a sign of inner spirituality. The imposition is a striking metaphor devised by the artist, willfully imposed upon the actual woman Sarah Stein. Michael Stein, however, is presented simply as himself, without elaboration, even if this public persona might seem unimaginative. To continue along these lines: Matisse struggled with his portrait of Sarah Stein less because he sought an appropriate form for the most complete expression of her identity than because in a portrait of a woman he assumed greater control, and he could allow his emotional and formal concerns to dominate the portrait transaction. If the portrait of Michael Stein seemed to proceed more smoothly, this ease was not due to Matisse's indifference, but instead because the terms in which this man's image could be expressed were less flexible, less open to intervention – and invention – by the artist. This inversion of conventional interpretive strategies could be extended further. Whichever set of interpretations seems more suitable (and we may even allow that both sets can co-exist), the difficulty of working on the edge of representational possibilities and social responsibilities in these high points of Matisse's portraiture contributed to the decline of the portrait in his work.

Within Matisse's concept of the decorative portrait there are also distinct differences in how men and women are handled. The overall decorative conception he sought in his portraits of Greta Moll, Jeanne Vaderin, and *The Girl with Green Eyes* – abetted by his manipulations of the figure–ground relationship in these paintings – would not be acceptable in a portrait of a man. In his portraits of men, the figure never struggles for predominance against an active, competing background. Their faces are always the dominant element in the representation of their figures; Matisse employs the traditional iconic mode of portraiture more with men. Even within a sometimes abstracted treatment, the features of his male sitters are always stressed to a point that seems to allow recognition of the sitters, or they are at least rendered with enough specificity that they present the illusion of an accurate transcription of identifying visual marks. Whatever distortion or abstraction Matisse performed on his male sitters, men in his work always retain integrity and identity, indeed frequently a sense of mastery, both over themselves and over their environment. They are at once self-possessed and incipiently active. In his painting women are more often rendered so that their image visually struggles with their environment, or alternatively blends with it or is even subsumed by it. Questions of social equivalency aside, women in his portraits are generally more passive or withdrawn, men are characterized more actively or at least with greater autonomy and individuality. Actual sitters, of course – real social beings – do not position themselves so easily on one side or the other of this gendered division. That is why all of Matisse's hired models in the Nice period and after were women.

Study of a model, or portrait?

The only hired male model of any importance to Matisse's work after his student years was the Italian Bevilacqua, who posed for him in the first few years of the century. Between then and 1916 he hired numerous female models, none for very long; some of them appear in such generic portrait-like pictures as *The Idol* (1905–6) and *The Algerian Woman* (1909).[32] Then, as we have seen, he quickened his use of hired models with the succession of Laurette, Antoinette Arnoux, and Henriette Darricarrère, employing them intensively to make a great variety of paintings, drawings, prints, and sculptures. In 1932 Lydia Delectorskaya, a young Russian student in Paris, began working for Matisse as a studio assistant and secretary. She was his favorite model for the rest of his career, though she also transcended this role by becoming his secretary, closest confidant, and companion to the end of his life.

These are only the best known of Matisse's models from the period 1916–54. He hired untold dozens of others for periods long and short. For an empiricist like Matisse, who rarely worked entirely from imagination until near the end of his career, models were essential to his procedure of painting from the human figure. We know that he paid his models well, keeping careful accounts.[33] He always paid them for each session of posing, despite his intimacy with some of them when they were not at work. This indicates a sense of fairness, of course, but perhaps it was also a distancing mechanism, a protection from personal obligation. In the economy of exchange, these women, whatever other status they may have had, were always hired models.

His attitude toward his models was distinctly different from his attitude toward sitters whom he did not pay to pose, who came from one of the societies to which Matisse himself belonged. The class position of these sitters vis à vis Matisse's was not determined by the exchange of money for service, though money may have changed hands. The class-equivalent sitter retained his or her identity and integrity, despite pictorial distortion. Models were far more manipulable as pictorial tokens, and this of course is why Matisse came to prefer working with them: their identity and integrity could be subject to compromise in the service of his artistic desires.[34]

There are many reports of his demanding ways with the models he hired, his insistence on punctuality, his exasperation on Sundays and holidays when the young women had other plans, his expectation of service without stint. One will suffice here. In 1940 a beautiful Turkish woman, Nézy-Hamidé Chawkat, had begun posing for him. After about a year of periodic modeling,

> Possibly irritated to see Matisse becoming interested in other subjects for his work, to not work with her as frequently, as a provocation Nézy Chawkat announced to him on August 31, 1941, that she was going to leave in two months to get married in Albania. Despite his extreme delight with this model, now, his enthusiasm broken, it came to pass that Matisse didn't work with her any more, disturbed by this deadline that bridled him.[35]

This woman tried to assert her identity in the context of the modeling transaction, and it was too much for Matisse. Was he simply petulant? Was his enchantment truly disrupted? It hardly matters: his requirements were not met in the way he expected them to be.

In addition to the erotic connotations of many of his paintings of models nude and clothed, Matisse has left a wealth of evidence of how he eroticized his relationships with his hired models. His copious statements about his art and its making abound with erotic references to these women and within his general procedure of working from the model. He certainly always wanted them to be young and attractive. Especially interesting are the analogies he made between pictorial and sexual consummation in the context of working from an anonymous and ultimately dispensable female model, this one in a letter to his son Pierre in 1940:

> I have arranged with some motion picture agents to send me their prettiest girls – if I don't keep them I give them ten francs. And thus I have three or four young and pretty models whom I have pose separately for drawing, three hours in the morning, three hours in the afternoon. This keeps me in the midst of my flowers and my fruits with which I can get in touch gradually without being aware of it. Sometimes I stop in front of a motif, a corner of my studio which I find expressive, yet quite beyond myself and my strength and I await the thunderbolt which cannot fail to come. This saps all my vitality.[36]

And in the previous year, in his essay "Notes of a Painter on his Drawing," in a passage which, curiously, has sometimes been cited as evidence of Matisse's humanity:

> My models, human figures, are never just "extras" in an interior. They are the principal themes in my work. I depend entirely on my model, whom I observe at liberty, and then I decide on the pose which best suits *her nature* . . . and then I become the slave of that pose. I often keep those girls several years, until my interest is exhausted.[37]

While he says that he determined poses suitable for each particular woman, he then goes on to characterize the relationship between himself and the model as a kind of mutual bondage whose duration he nevertheless controls. Then, picture finished (Matisse went on to say in the same passage), the composition resulting from "the emotional interest aroused [in him by the models]" may express his "sublimated sensual pleasure."[38] Elsewhere, more outrageously, he spoke of his relationship with the model as "a flirtation that results in a rape."[39] Despite much of what has been written about the matter (and still is being written), Matisse did not treat the nude figure of a female model as an eye-pleasing but otherwise neutral form.

That he eroticized his models is not surprising when it is considered that he broke the pact of family unity with his new calendar divided between Paris and the South of France, beginning in 1917. In his consequent freedom from bourgeois constraints in the Midi he had affairs with some of the models whom he hired to pose.[40] A parallel with prostitution is unavoidable but should not be insisted on. Nevertheless, a historical relation between modeling and prostitution is well established, often forming a pattern for survival for young single women in large cities.[41] It is improbable – and irrelevant – that any of Matisse's models could have been a prostitute, nor should we imagine that he hired models so that he could have sex with them. Yet the potential for the parallel would not be entirely beside the point. Like many male artists, Matisse paid young, attractive women to take off their clothes and perform as models under his direction. He paid them for their compliance as well as their time: in hiring them for this service to his art he guaranteed his control and dominance of them. Loss of integrity and identity was the price that these models – any model – paid in return. This loss is part of the nature of the transaction in modeling.[42] The works of art that result from this particular transaction, no matter how resemblant, no matter what emotional content they seem to carry, no matter how insightful they may seem, are of a completely different order from portraits that result from the meeting of two people with mutual obligations in a social context. By paying a model Matisse controlled completely his representation of her, without the need either to preserve her individuality or to be accountable to the social interdependence that is a crucial component of the portrait transaction.

In Chapter 5 I touched on the phenomenon, more important in the modern period than in earlier times, of the patron or sitter who was willing to forego the satisfactions of flattery in order to participate in an avant-garde artist's creative project. This subordination of one ego to another has important consequences for the study of modern portraits. The impact of such brand-name recognition extends well beyond the relationship between artist and sitter at the time of the portrait transaction. Its logical outcome is our own recognition of these sitters as worthy objects of study, as in my consideration of Matisse's sitters in this book. We know with few exceptions the full names of this type of sitter. They have this degree of recognition at least.[43] By contrast, we know the full names of only the most prominent and persistent of Matisse's hired female models; some of these have been gleaned only through assiduous research.[44] And even then some of these identities have proved elusive, as with Laurette, whose visual presence in his art is remarkably intense. His only important male model, Bevilacqua, has at least a surname, conferring a patrilineal and thus societal identity. A great many of Matisse's female models have until very recently been distinguished only by the comparative anonymity and diminishment of a first name.[45]

* * *

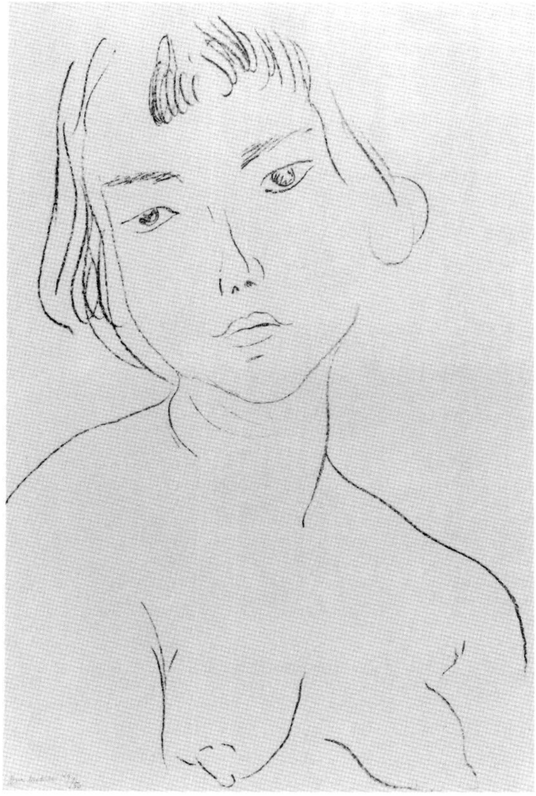

190 *Head Tilted Slightly to the Left*, 1913. Lithograph, 49 × 32.2 cm. The Baltimore Museum of Art, The Cone Collection, formed by Dr. Claribel Cone and Miss Etta Cone of Baltimore, Maryland, BMA 1950.12.144.

Shifters

We have seen that hired models may play multiple roles in Matisse's work: in some cases they are used for their bodies alone, as an object of visual consumption and a gloss on conventional representations of the female nude; in others Matisse's depictions of them look like portraits because the figures are alert and dressed and posed in such a way as to suggest self-possession and therefore identity. There are also several cases of class-equivalent sitters whose status seems to change according to the purpose for Matisse's representation of them. It is worth considering here some that are not clear-cut, occupying border territory that includes both portrait and figure study, both the representation of a unique individual and the use of a model as a site for artistic exploration. Three examples, all of women (there are none of men) will illustrate the possibility of a shift in the identity of a portrait sitter when Matisse used such a person in the same way that he used his models. Then an example, the most significant and complex of all, of a hired model whose status clearly merits a special consideration.

During the First World War, in conditions of extraordinary stress and deprivation for many, Matisse paid Josette Gris, the wife of Juan Gris, to sit for several etched portraits (see figs. 95, 96). As I suggested in the Introduction, this should be understood as a thinly veiled form of charity to a class-equivalent sitter (and her husband) temporarily down at heel, not a transaction with a model. Under similar circumstances, Germaine Raynal, whose husband the art critic Maurice Raynal had been called into military service, posed for Matisse, but she did so nude or partly nude (fig. 190).[46] Matisse paid Mme Raynal to pose, as he had Mme Gris. As with Gris also, Matisse's motivation with Raynal seems to have been charitable. Does the fact that Matisse made a nude representation of this woman place her in the same class as his hired models? Or has he made a nude portrait of Mme Raynal? Is it any less a portrait than the painting *Woman on a High Stool (Germaine Raynal)* (fig. 191), which Matisse made at the same time? Both lithograph and painting are ambiguous about what genre they should belong to, and these questions are not easily answered. The difficulty is especially acute because Matisse's project at this time included blurring the boundaries of genres, as he interrogated the difference between a sitter for a portrait and a hired model.

Another instance of a sitter who posed both clothed for a portrait and nude for a figure study is Olga Merson, whose portrait Matisse painted in 1911 (see fig. 115). At about the same time she posed for the sculpture *Seated Nude (Olga)* (fig. 192). In modeling the face Matisse has smoothed out any specificity in the features, so the sitter is hardly recognizable in them. Even if she clearly were, what could be the status of a fully nude representation of a female sitter? Here it seems safe to say that Matisse was not aiming for representation of Merson's individuality, despite the inclusion of at least her first name in the conventional forms of the title for this sculpture. So this work should not be considered a portrait, despite the personal and class-equivalent relationship between Merson and Matisse. The nude portrait is a specialized and periodic phenomenon, arising from very particular circumstances. Matisse's sculpture is too generic and too much in keeping with his other figures of female nudes of the time to be a portrait of Merson. Here she becomes as a model by being nude: nudity has the nearly universal effect of stripping away markers of identity and social position with the clothing, although there are exceptions, from sixteenth-century Italy and France to Larry Rivers and Alice Neel in our own time. Such portraits have sometimes been justified on the

191 *Woman on a High Stool (Germaine Raynal)*, 1914. Oil on canvas, 147 × 95.5 cm. The Museum of Modern Art, New York. Gift of Florene M. Schoenborn and Samuel A. Marx (the former retaining a life interest).

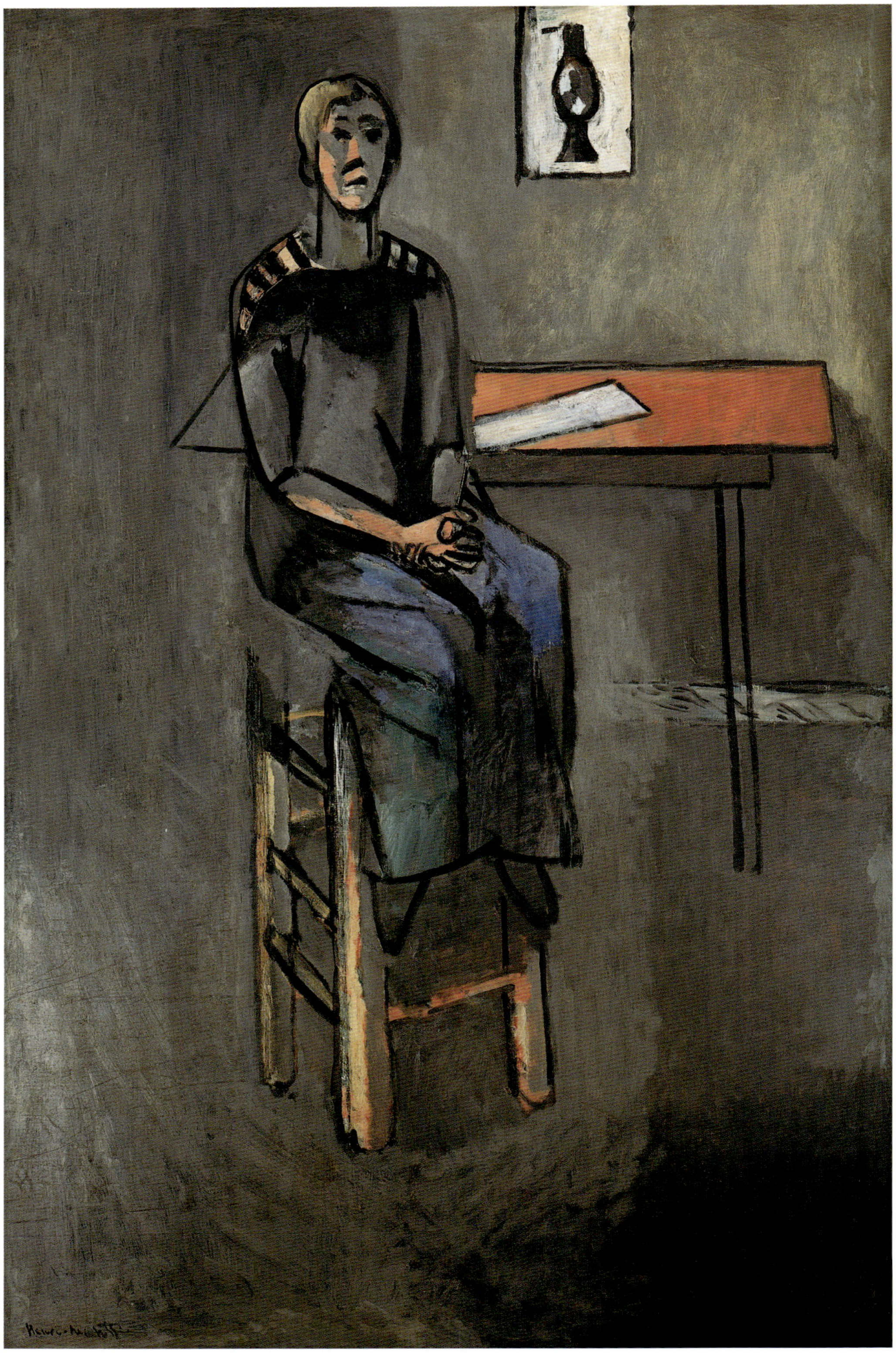

grounds of candor and the benefits of unmasking, but these representations could legitimately be portraits without this justification: the idea that taking off their clothes allows people "to reveal their true selves" is superficial and takes little account of the socially constructed element of identity.[47]

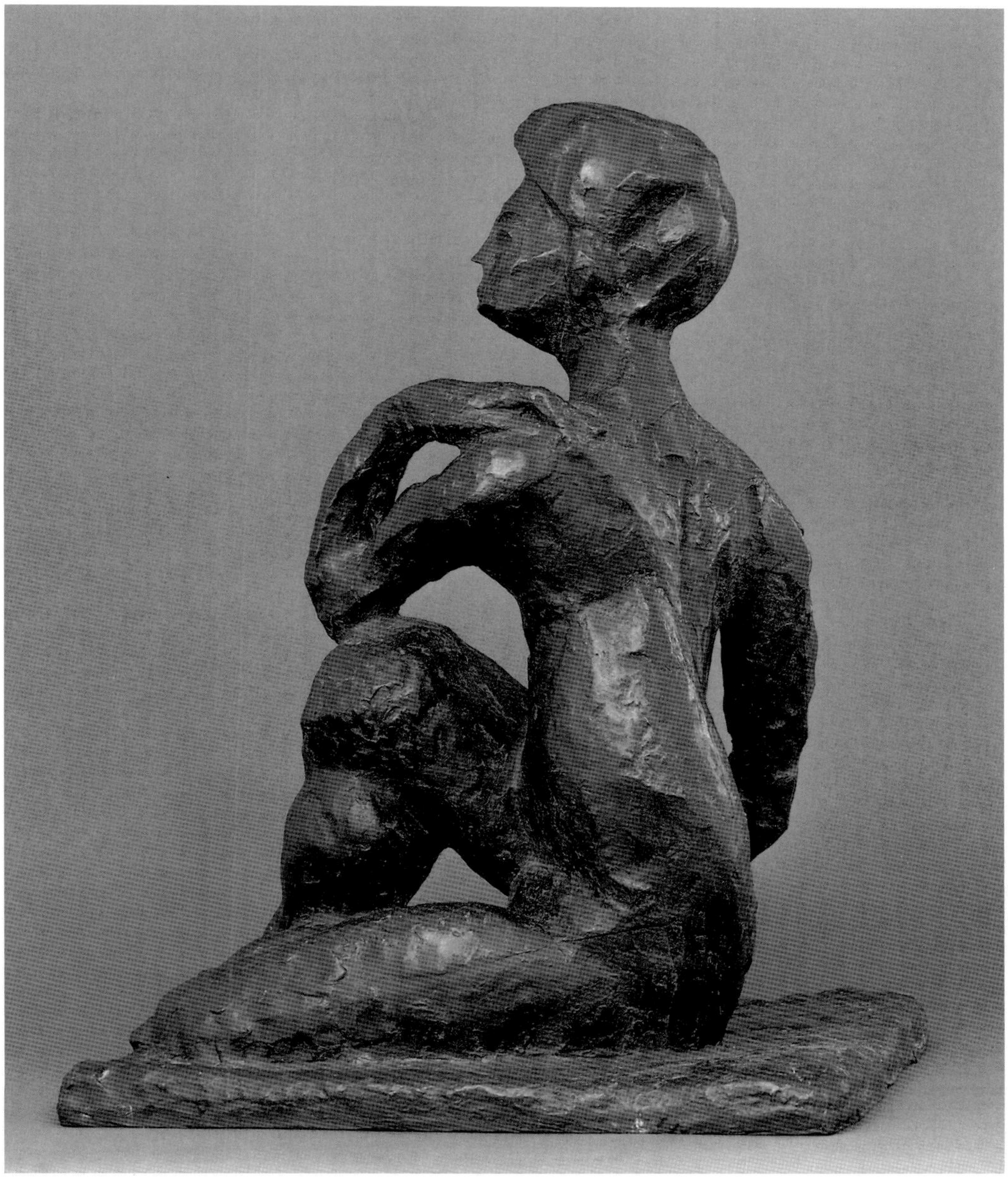

192 *Seated Nude (Olga)*, 1911. Bronze, 43.2 cm high. Private collection.

Jeanne Vaderin, who posed for *Girl with Tulips (Jeanne Vaderin)* (see fig. 117) was also the subject of some of Matisse's most celebrated sculptures, the five *Jeannette* heads (fig. 193), which he made between 1910 and 1916.[48] Taken together these five sculptures offer a spectacular range of conception of a single human head. They form a series – the first of several such series Matisse made in sculpture – moving from a naturalistic modeling of the young woman's features in *Jeannette I* to the abstracted organicism of *Jeannette V*, by which time Matisse was not working directly from his sitter but from the previous sculpted versions of her head. In the fifth sculpture he has attained, in effect, an imaginative blend of the animal (his human sitter) and the vegetable (the flower motif with which he had associated her in the earlier painting and drawing). Such a general organic conception anticipates the head–plant duality of his later sculpture *Tiare*, which he based both on a Tahitian woman and a Tahitian gardenia.

193 *Jeannette I-V*, 1910–16. Bronze, various heights. The Museum of Modern Art, New York.

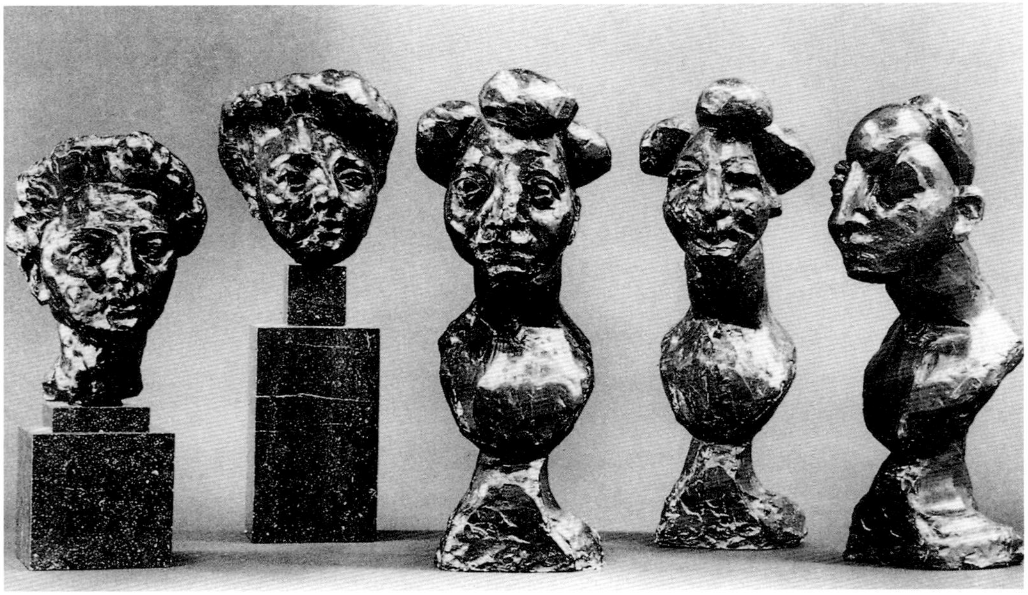

The greater abstraction of the final three renditions of the head of Jeannette, and the self-referring procedure through which Matisse made them, have led some writers to question whether they can be called portraits at all, so removed do they seem to be from the features of the sitter who inspired him, as well as her winsome youth.[49] These three sculptures also seem more aggressively independent of their source because of the massive socles that Matisse cast with the heads, implying a Brancusi-like integration of the object with its support. One scholar found *Jeannette IV* to be more a caricature than a portrait.[50] It has even been noticed that *Jeannette III* resembles Matisse's daughter Marguerite as much as it does Jeanne Vaderin.[51]

Taken together, these observations point to a problem with the integrity of the sitter in these sculptures, especially the final three of the series. No one factor is decisive – not the progressive abstraction, not likeness or its absence, not the compromise of identity by reason of resemblance to another individual, not the fact that in the final three sculptures Matisse worked from casts of previous versions rather than directly from Vaderin herself. But the equivocal status of Matisse's representations of her puts Jeanne Vaderin in the uncertain zone between the more clear-cut cases of the sitter whose identity – and thus whose representation in the social context of portraiture – is inviolable and the hired model, from whom the artist has bought the freedom to compromise, deny, or transform that identity. These portraits of Jeanne Vaderin are extreme examples of the general case of Matisse's greater manipulation of the features and uniqueness of his female sitters in his portraits of them. Jeanne Vaderin is the exception among Matisse's sitters that proves the rule of the greater license he took for himself when he painted, drew, and sculpted his representations of women.

Transcending the modeling transaction

The case of Lydia Delectorskaya merits a special consideration, because of the way many of Matisse's representations of her call into question my claims about the mutual exclusivity of models and portraiture. Matisse painted many pictures of the face and figure, clothed and nude, of this woman of particular importance to him. She can be seen in so many of Matisse's works, in such a variety of modes of representation, that we may come to feel that she is less anonymous than the other models, that more of her own personality is allowed to come through in Matisse's art.[52] She attains an intense, varied, and complex presence in his art that the other hired models (with the brief exception of Laurette in the 1910s) never do, and this presence may seem to reflect her importance to Matisse as a real individual with a relationship to him independent of her role as his preferred model and keeper of his agenda. More works depicting Lydia seem to aspire to portraiture than those of any other model, and she herself seems to approach more nearly the condition of social equivalence to the artist than any other of his models ever did.

And yet Matisse's insistence that he always pay her to model is striking, and its significance should not be underestimated.[53] Given their close and long-standing relationship, it seems that Matisse paid Delectorskaya not only from a sense of charity or even fairness (though she considered it an equitable arrangement) but also as a point of control, and possibly a means of distancing, not focusing, his emotions. He needed to comprehend this woman pictorially, and the mechanism of economic transaction could temporarily supersede the social transaction that characterized their normal relations. It is reasonable to suppose that Matisse understood the implication of not paying Lydia Delectorskaya to model, and did pay her in order to have complete freedom in his art, unfettered by a need to affirm his sitter's individuality and integrity in that site where professional modeling served his needs more effectively.

It is worthwhile considering one example of Matisse's portrait-like depictions of this hired model of undeniable special status to understand how they differ from his portraits. Among the works he included in his album of 1954 entitled *Portraits* are three paintings that depict Lydia Delectorskaya.[54] All are identified as "Madame L. D." modified by a descriptive or attributive phrase ("Les Yeux Bleus," "La Blouse bleue"). They share this characteristic of lack of identity with all the other depictions of hired models illustrated in the album. A model's full identity is not deemed to be important to understanding the painting; what she is wearing or what kind of chair she sits on is given greater significance.

One of the paintings of Lydia, *Madame L.D., Green, Blue, and Yellow Portrait* (1947; fig. 194), is actually identified as a portrait in its title. For this it is unique in the entire album – all of the family members, friends, and other class-equivalent sitters are identified simply by name. But this painting is not characterized as a portrait of this woman named Lydia Delectorskaya; it is instead a portrait of color relationships, as it were. Even so, this is the closest Matisse came to identifying a work of art as a portrait of a model.

In its vertical division of the face into two colored zones, the painting bears an eerie similarity to *Madame Matisse (The Green Line)* (see fig. 51) of more than forty years earlier. Its bland flatness and simplicity seem to mock the intensity of the portrait of Amélie Matisse: even the famous stripe down the bridge of the nose reappears in the painting of Lydia, here designated by a thin rillet of unpainted canvas. As in all of his work toward the end of his career, portraits (where the sitters are named, and thus their individuality preserved) included, this painting testifies to Matisse's general desire to simplify. In its reductive appearance the image may not seem to differ substantially from the many portrait drawings Matisse made of class-equivalent sitters in the last two decades of his life: the painting is, unequivocally, a depiction of Lydia Delectorskaya, just as the stylized portraits of

194 *Madame L. D., Green, Blue, and Yellow Portrait*, 1947. Oil on canvas, 64.3 × 49.7 cm. St. Petersburg, Hermitage Museum, gift of Lydia Delectorskaya.

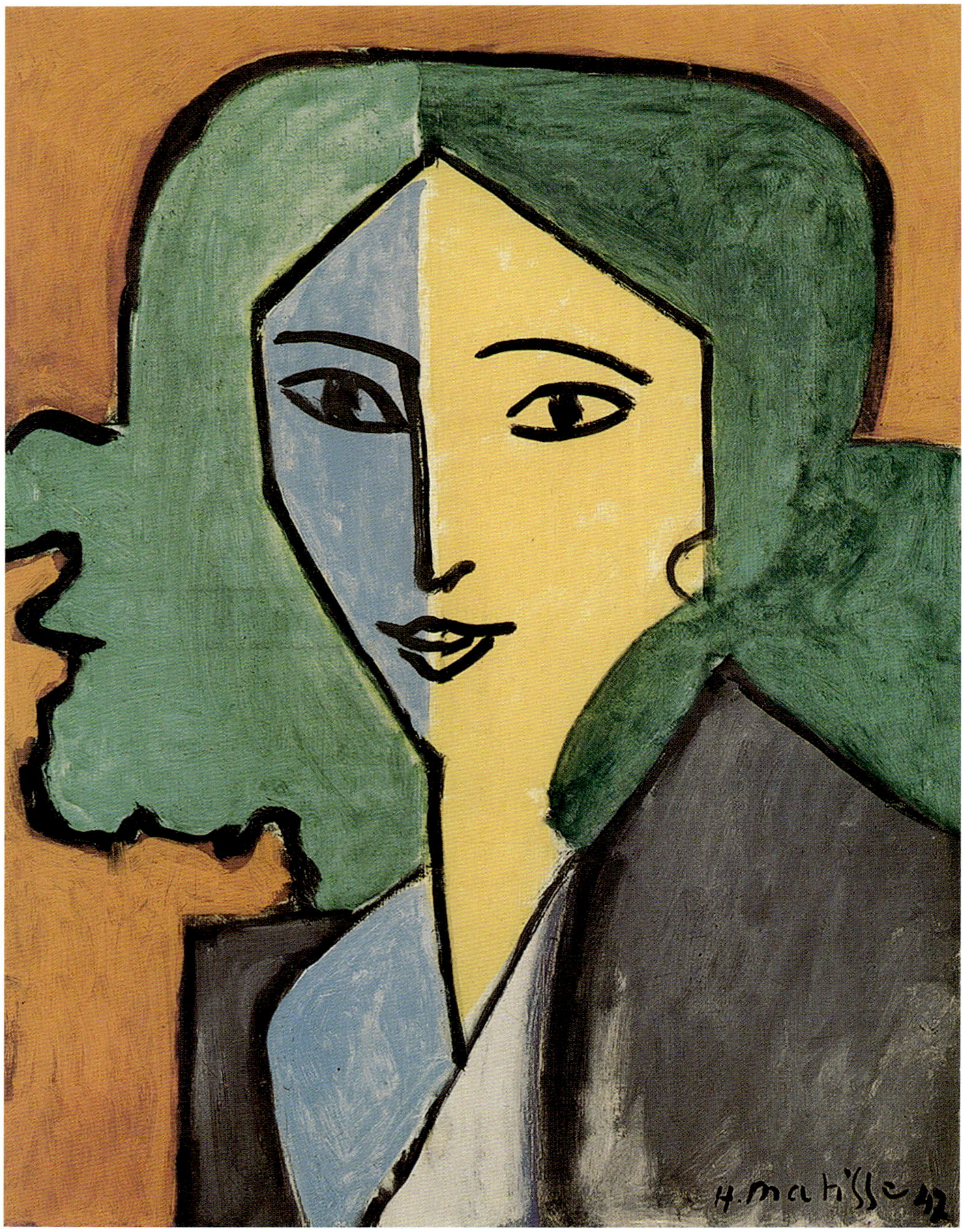

195 *Woman in a Hood*, 1939. Pencil on paper, 33.2 × 25.6 cm. St. Petersburg, Hermitage Museum.

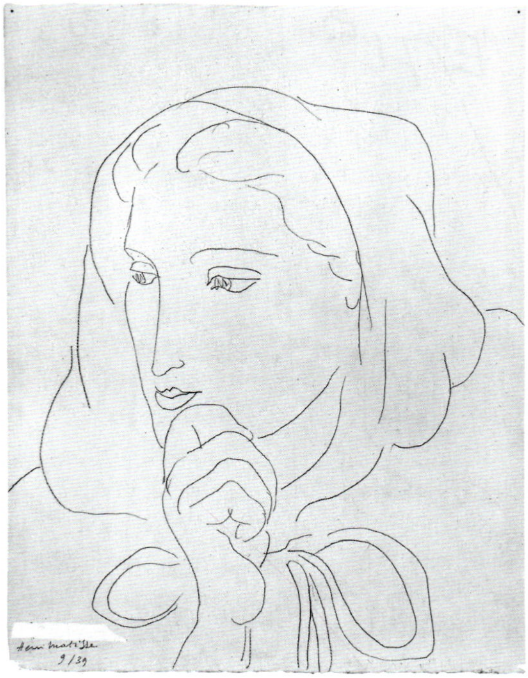

Louis Aragon or Henry de Montherlant are depictions of those persons. But the naming of those sitters by Matisse is telling – it is the index of their individuality, the individuality that is taken away through the economic transaction at the heart of modeling, that loss being signified by the suppression of the sitter's name. In this depiction of Lydia Delectorskaya, Matisse's personal and artistic concerns predominate; the identity of this woman is as subject to his pleasure at her appearance as are the color relationships.

Yet in other depictions of her face when she is not identified as the subject of a portrait, her living presence and individuality are nevertheless manifest, as in draw-

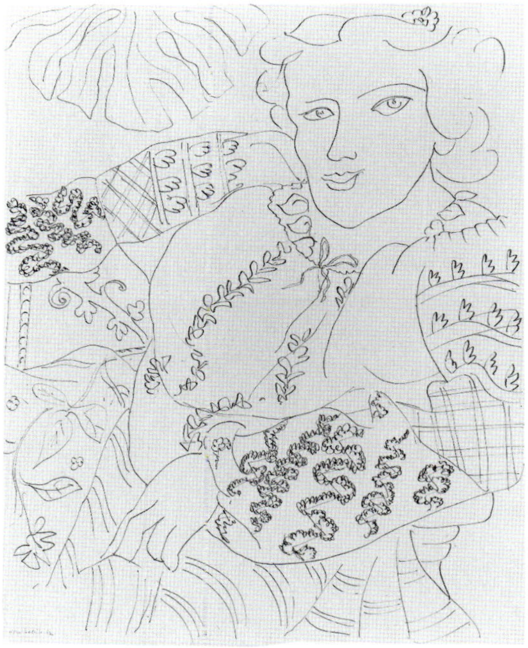

196 *The Rumanian Blouse*, 1937. Ink on paper, 63 × 50 cm. The Baltimore Museum of Art, The Cone Collection, formed by Dr. Claribel Cone and Miss Etta Cone of Baltimore, Maryland, BMA 1950.12.57.

197 Photograph of Lydia Delectorskaya in the "Harlequin" dress from Matisse's collection of dresses for models.

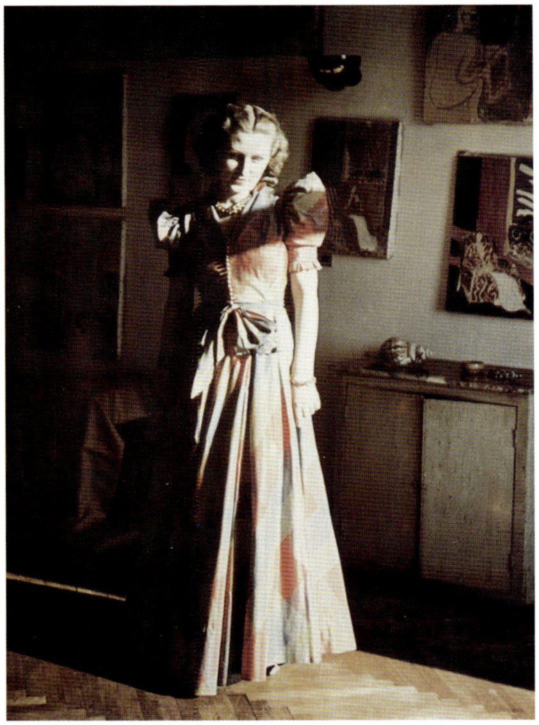

ings Matisse made of her (fig. 195) in the course of their flight from Paris together during the "phony war" in 1939, when he also made a series of self-portrait drawings (see figs. 165, 166). Delectorskaya's distinctive facial structure, her pensive expression, the garment suggestive of huddled protectiveness, and the uncertain circumstances combine to project an arresting image, both noble and vulnerable. In calmer times, too, Matisse's depictions of Lydia Delectorskaya seem to participate in more than the visual conventions of portraiture and allow this individual to respond to the artist and to the world and to maintain her individuality, as in some of the many amusing drawings he made of her in fanciful garments (fig. 196), reminiscent of the "White Plumes" drawings of Antoinette Arnoux but with considerably more spirit emanating from the image of the model. Yet we need to be reminded that in these and other works the model is playing a role, conceived and directed by the artist and even costumed by him from the several armoires of dresses and other women's clothes he kept explicitly to be worn by his models (fig. 197). The festiveness could be put on or taken off, according to the artist's desire.

If there is any doubt about the direction of the flow of will in the modeling transaction, the many drawings from 1935–37 showing the nude model in the studio before a mirror must remove it. Lydia Delectorskaya posed, too, for these; these drawings are her special domain, her theater. Matisse was evidently pleased with these productions, which are at once elaborate and surprising.[55] In many of the drawings the artist is reflected in the mirror along with a second view of the nude reclining model. Full display is linked to artistic control as Matisse pins the undulant body between the hard rectangular frames of his drawing pad and his hunched, intent mirror image (fig. 198), or dominates the model through the illusion of physical proximity as his head looms over her torso while he gestures as if to touch her (fig. 199). These meditations on the creative process in the artist's studio enlist the model to play in an allegory of nature that the artist manipulates through imagery.[56]

The status of Lydia Delectorskaya is even more complicated than this. Sometimes Matisse seemed to use her image as a surrogate for himself, acting the part of the artist, as in a drawing from 1941 that shows her before Matisse's easel, reaching toward the canvas upon it as if in a gesture of work (fig. 200). The image she addresses is an early version of the painting known as *Still Life with Magnolia* (Paris, Musée National d'Art Moderne); some of the objects depicted there are arrayed alongside. It takes a moment to realize that Delectorskaya is not shown as if in the act of painting the picture but rather that, with the aid of the bottle of spirits by her elbow, she is actually in the act of erasing it. This was one of her studio tasks. When Matisse worked on a painting over a long period, he often wished to start with a blank canvas each morning, retaining only in his memory (and in some cases by photograph) the work of the previous day. So at the end of the work day, his assistant performed this ritual cleansing. A photograph (fig. 201) taken by Matisse shows Lydia Delectorskaya wiping off the canvas on which the artist was painting *Large Reclining Nude* (1935; Baltimore Museum of Art), a painting for which she posed each day over its long evolution. Day after day as a model, she effaced herself to advance his work; then she effaced her own image in the same service. Although in the case of Lydia Delectorskaya the condition of modeling could be transcended, and was transcended in certain images of her, she was finally subject to the larger purposes of this transaction.

Gertrude Stein once expressed her surprise that modern painters seemed no longer to rely on the model, that "models were everything until the beginning of

198 *Artist and Model Reflected in the Mirror*, 1935. Ink on paper, 45 × 56 cm. St. Petersburg, Hermitage Museum.

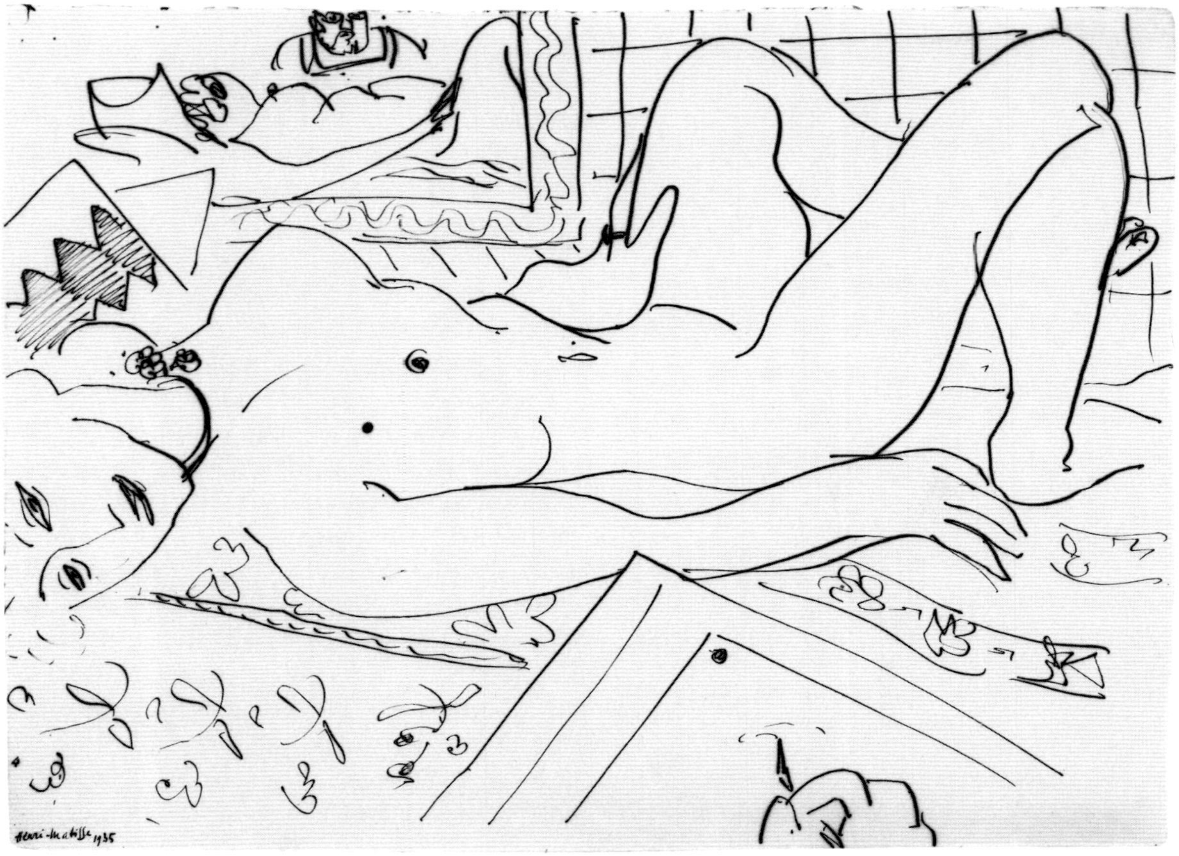

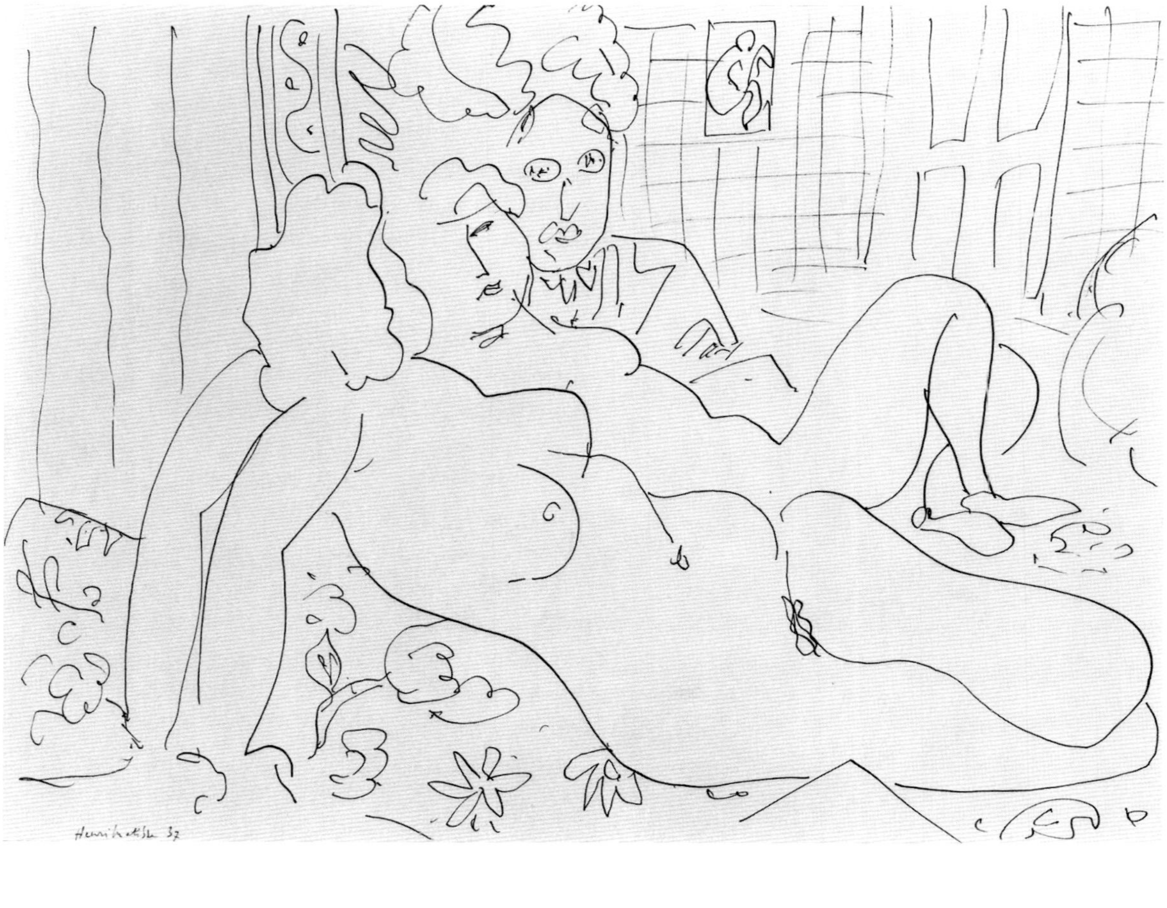

199 *Artist and Model Reflected in the Mirror*, 1937. Ink on paper, 28.2 × 38.2 cm. Private collection.

200 *L. D. at work*, 1941. Ink on paper, 52 × 40 cm. Private collection.

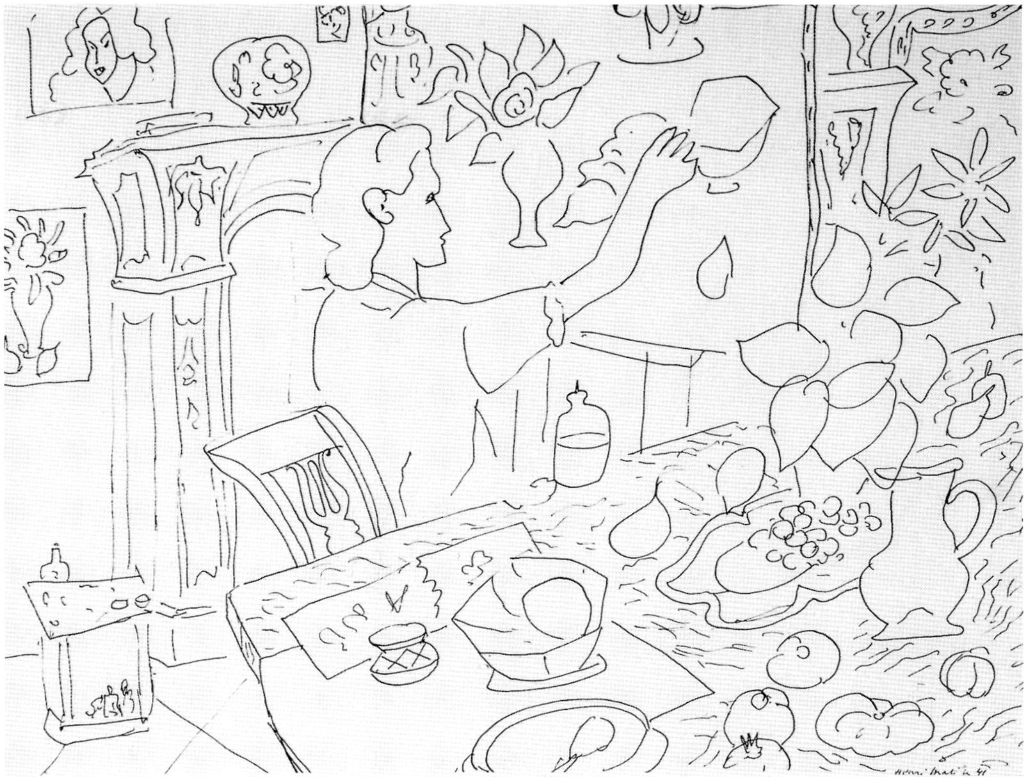

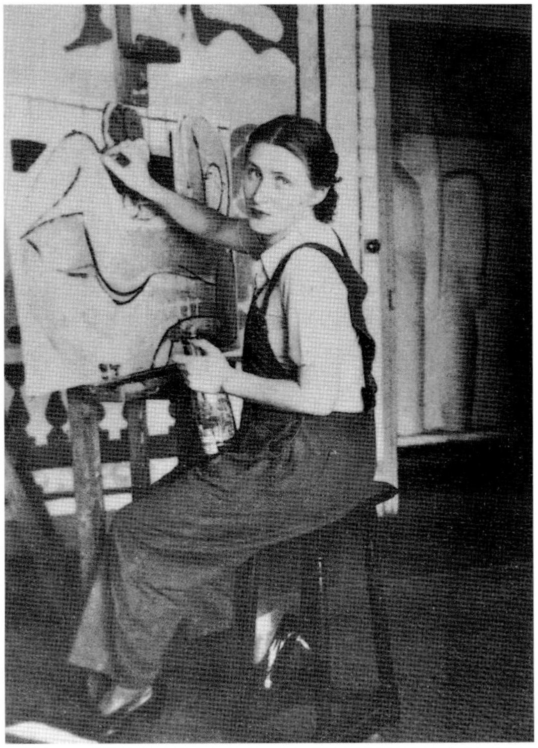

201 Photograph of Lydia Delectorskaya erasing an early state of *Large Reclining Nude*, 1935.

the twentieth century and now hardly any painter who interests anybody really has any realization that everybody used to have a model."[57] Dependence on the model had become problematic, in the eyes of some a sign of weakness, of outmoded fidelity to appearances, of want of imagination. Although in the final years of his life Matisse worked more from memory and imagination than ever before in his career, especially on the paper cut-outs, he never entirely gave up the model. In 1942, when he was beginning to use the medium of the paper cut-out as more than a maquette-making process, he expressed a longing for self-reliance: "I consider I have made some progress when I note in my work an increasingly evident independence from the support of the model. I should like to do without it completely one day – I don't expect to, because I haven't adequately trained myself to remember forms. Shall I still need forms?" Even earlier, in 1925, he spoke of a weaning process, a progressive move toward a state in which "one would have learned to do without the model."[58] But he always needed the forms of the model, and never more than when he displaced himself from the social world of portraiture. That world had become both aesthetically and socially problematic for him. Leaving it, he entered a world of his own construction, his imagination given a solid footing on the empirical and neutralized foundation of faces and bodies for hire. In an interpretation of Matisse's portraiture the model is a problem only for the interpreters. For Matisse it was not a problem, it was a solution. It was a solution to the problem of portraiture.

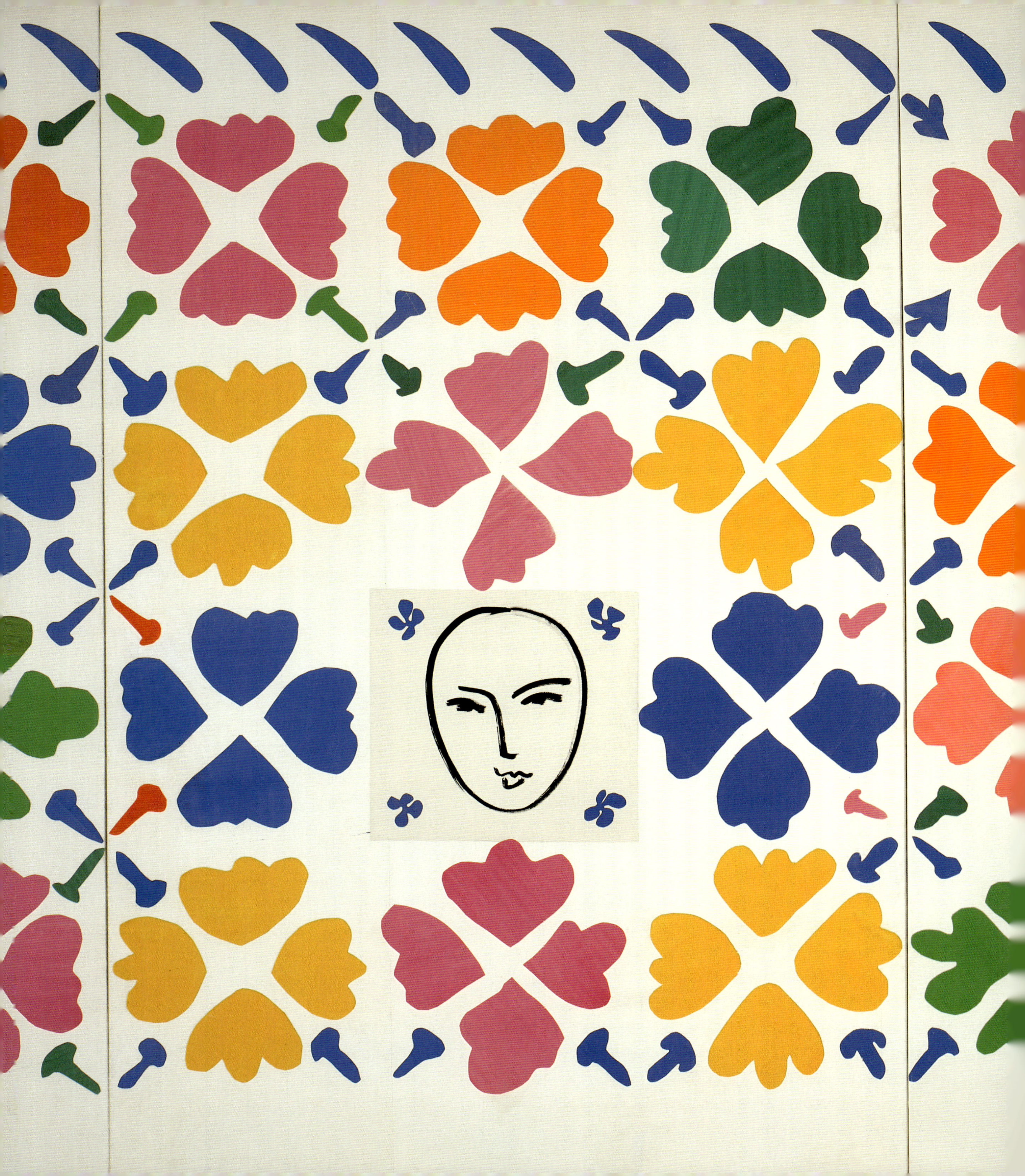

Conclusion Signing Off: The End of the Portrait

Variations on a theme

In his essay "Portraits" from 1954, written to accompany the selection of his paintings and drawings of the human face and figure published that year, Matisse gave the fullest description of his working procedure when drawing from the model:

> I find myself before a person who interests me and, pencil or charcoal in my hand, I set down her appearance on the paper, more or less freely. . . . After half-an-hour or an hour I am surprised to see an image that is a more or less precise likeness of the person with whom I am in contact gradually appear on my paper.
>
> This image is revealed to me as though each stroke of charcoal erased from a mirror some of the mist which until then had prevented me from seeing it.
>
> This generally is the meager result of a first sitting. It seems wise to me then to let one or two days intervene between this and the second sitting.
>
> During this interval there occurs a kind of unconscious mental fermentation process. And thanks to this fermentation, in conformity with the impressions I received from my subject during the first sitting, I mentally reorganize my drawing with more certainty than there was in the result of the first contact.
>
> [At the second sitting] the model is no longer more to me than a particular theme from which flow the forces of lines or values that broaden my limited horizon.

More sittings may follow, more labored drawings, or, more often, extended work on the same drawing, elaborated and erased and made again. Matisse then gets to the heart of the matter, describing the object of this method:

> I have gained a deep knowledge of my subject. After prolonged work in charcoal, made up of studies that are more or less interrelated, flashes of insight appear, which while seeming more or less cursory are the expression of the intimate exchange between the artist and his model. Drawings that contain all the subtleties of observations made during the work arise from a fermentation within, like bubbles in a pond.
>
> These drawings spring forth in one piece, constituted of elements without apparent coordination to the analysis that has preceded them; the multiplicity of the sensations expressed in each of them seems impossible to execute, so great is the speed with which they are all brought together. I am absolutely convinced that they represent the goal of my curiosity.[1]

Detail of fig. 206.

This procedure gave him a way, he believed, to approach each subject freshly and openly, but it just as surely allowed him to impose his vision on each model or other motif by providing him with a means to ensure that he synthesized his responses thoroughly. Matisse and those who speak for him describe an artistic ritual of attentive observation of a model accompanied by laborious construction of an initial impression, then the distillation of essential features in a single heavily worked image in pencil or charcoal.[2] This back-and-forth between the artist and his sheet of paper is accompanied by the social ritual of small talk, on one level a strategy of distraction to put the model at ease but on another a way to pretend that what is taking place is a social occasion. Nothing of real importance is communicated here; the artist learns nothing of significance about the model, nor surely did he want to while at work. Then this "bavardage" comes to an end. A threshold has been crossed. In silence, with a suddenness for which the artist and his assistant (armed with more pens and fresh paper) have prepared themselves well, the images pour forth in a cascade of "rapid drawings" (as he called them), variations on the theme.

Matisse is also describing a process of the assumption of the conscious by the unconscious, the replacement of artifice – his conscious labor – by a natural force over which the artist has no control. The observation and initial work of marking and erasure give way to the free flow of line drawings, done without hesitation or correction, spun out like spider's silk, or rising to the surface "like bubbles in a pond." This is the state of transcendence he wished to reach in his art, "the purest and most direct translation of my emotion."[3] He seemed most pleased when he could claim that he was a medium for a creative force that he could tap into through the performance of ritual. This allowed him to create what he called the sign, his visual shorthand that represented the distillation of sensation and the expression of emotion he sought to put into the work of art.

202 *Massia with an Elongated Face*, 1914. Etching, 13.6 × 10.1 cm. Private collection.

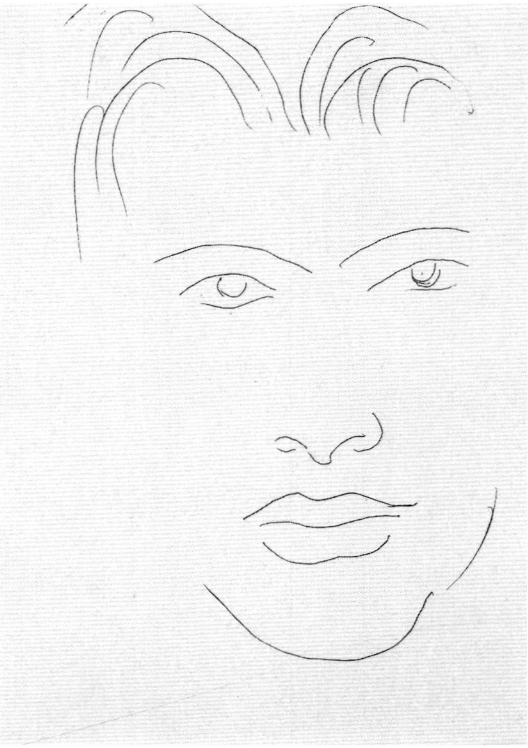

Typical and individual

His satisfaction at what he had wrought was a long time in coming. He had developed the germ of the idea as early as 1908 in "Notes of a Painter," in which he wrote about making marks or signs (*signes*) in the process of organizing a composition. These signs are determined, he implies, by a pictorial necessity, by the demands of the composition on him, not through his own conscious effort (he wrote of being "forced" to proceed in the way he describes).[4] In his painting, too, he was trying to develop this process of instinctive or demotic mark-making, but his main essays in this area were in graphic media. The group of small portrait etchings he made in 1914 during the First World War were one symptom of this effort. He did several of them in successive versions, seeking the minimum means to express the essential features of his sitter, as in his portrait of the Spanish violinist Joan Massia (fig. 202), where the distinctive waves of hair springing up from the sitter's forehead are distilled into a Massia-sign. This reduction borders on caricature, and Matisse seems to have recognized the danger to his expression of making the image too distinctively a function of personal features of the sitter (this could also be a problem in his portraits, such as *Tête blanche et rose* (fig. 66), of his daughter Marguerite, whose neck ribbon was like a saintly attribute and thus in a sense was non-negotiable). His goal, as we have seen, was a blend of the particular and the general. Too particular, and the sign would not bear his expression.

A few years later, the Swedish writer Ragnar Hoppe called on Matisse as he was deeply engaged in the "White Plumes" series of drawings of a hired model in a

203 *The Plumed Hat*, ca. 1919. Pencil on paper, 49 × 37 cm. The Baltimore Museum of Art, The Cone Collection, formed by Dr. Claribel Cone and Miss Etta Cone of Baltimore, Maryland, BMA 1950.12.58.

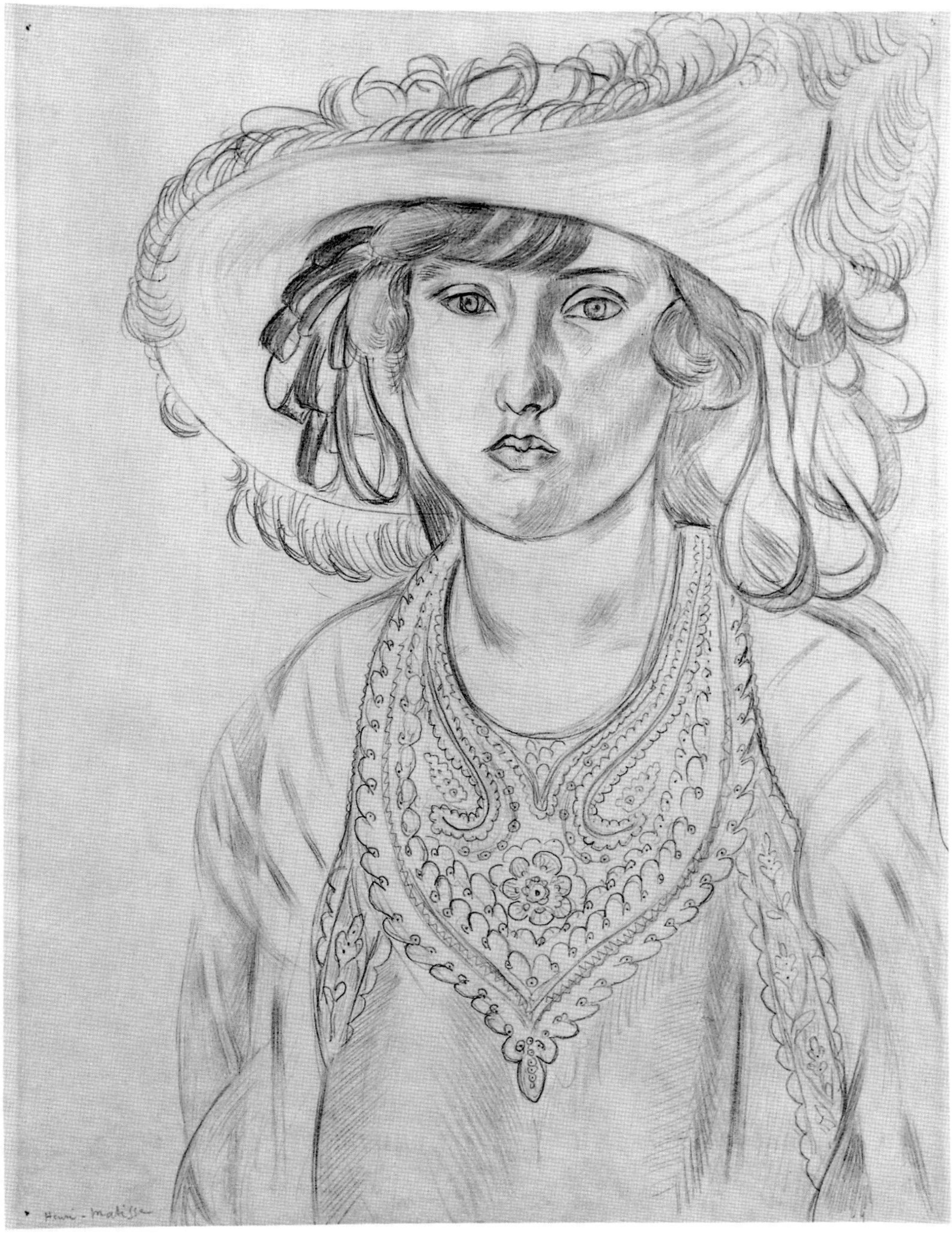

feathered hat. The artist told his visitor that he wanted "to depict the typical and the individual at the same time, a distillation of all I see and feel in a motif." He was hoping that his interviewer would recognize the dual purpose of his art: at once to represent and to express. To make his point, he showed Hoppe some of the many drawings he had made of the model Antoinette Arnoux in elaborate costumes (fig. 203), declaring that these were "a whole series of drawings that I did for one single detail, the lace collar around the young lady's neck. The very first ones are worked out minutely, each mesh, yes, almost each thread; then I could simplify more and more, and in this last one, when I knew the lace as if by heart, I was able to translate it with a few quickly drawn lines into an ornament, an

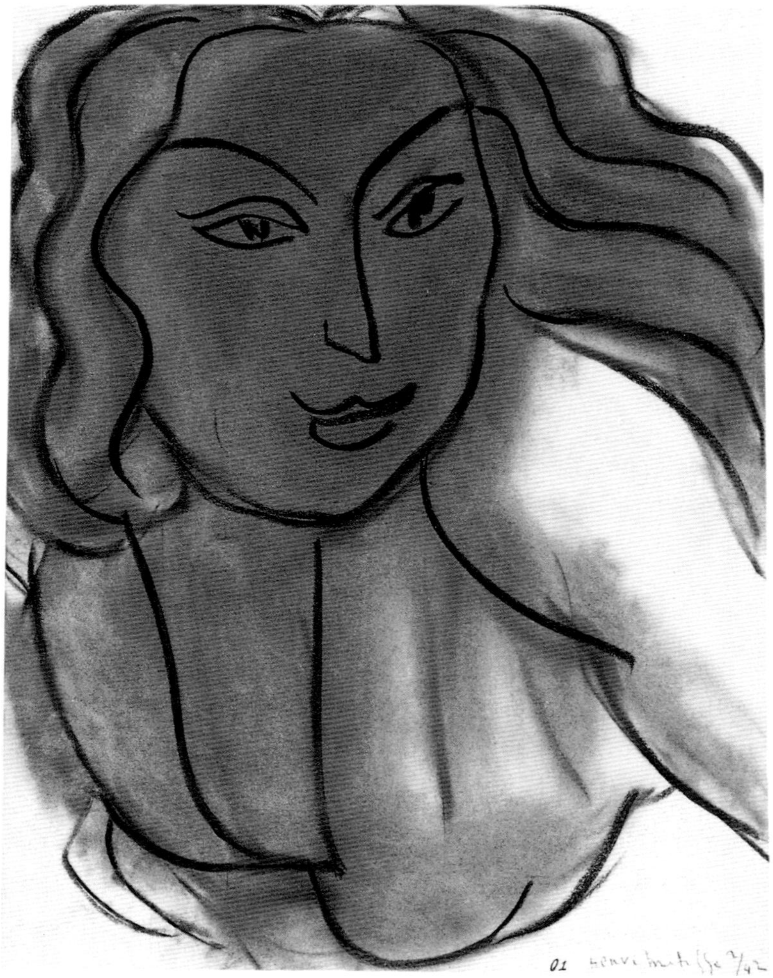

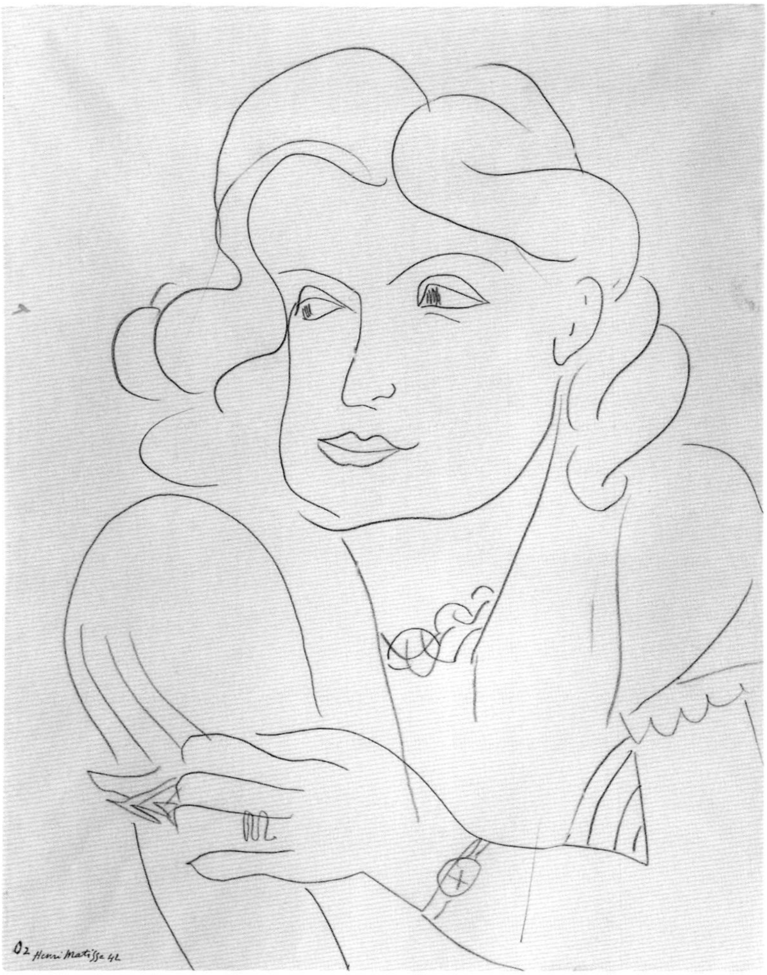

204 *(above left)* *Thèmes et variations: Series O, "dessin du thème"*, 1942. Charcoal on paper, 52.6 × 42.5 cm. Nice, Musée Matisse.

205 *(above right)* *Thèmes et variations, O 2*, 1942. Crayon on paper, 52.7 × 40.6 cm. The Menil Collection, Houston.

arabesque, without losing its character of being the lace, and of being that particular lace." Then, anxiously, he asked: "And at the same time, it is a complete Matisse, isn't it?" Finally, he assured Hoppe that he "worked the same way on the face, the hands, and all the other details . . ."[5]

Expressing himself in different language ("an ornament, an arabesque"), Matisse once again sought to create a decorative art out of the particularities of his motif, without severing the connection to these distinctive features. He worried that his transformations of the motif might render its features unrecognizable, but he worried even more about ensuring his presence in the image, and he was pleased that he seemed to have pulled off the balancing act he set for himself. To do this, however, required the discipline to equate the features of his living model with details of costume. This has obvious implications for the compromise of the human content in his depictions of these models, as we have seen in Matisse's efforts to reconcile portraiture and decoration.

In the 1930s he attacked the problem of finding the shared ground between individual and type with renewed force. Drawings such as his series of studies of Lydia Delectorskaya in the Romanian blouse (see fig. 196) and of the artist and his model in the studio (see figs. 198, 199) were part of Matisse's extended experiment to release from his accumulated perception of a motif a seemingly boundless array of variations on that subject, as he described later in his essay on portraits. By the early 1940s he believed that he had arrived at the key to this process of assimilation of the motif and the expression of the artist's work and emotion through the motif's essence. The publication in 1942 of several series of these light-fingered drawings, accompanied by their hard-won foundations in the statement of the theme (figs. 204, 205), is the definitive, even didactic, visual expression of Matisse's goals in drawing, indeed in all his art.

Transcending the portrait

Dessins: Thèmes et variations presents process as product, specifying the laborious means to the effortless end. The essence of the motif is discovered through careful observation and hard, draughtsmanly work, but the expression of that essence, Matisse believed, would not derive from the motif, but would instead be invented by the artist. A significant change has occurred in the relationship between the individual and the typical in his art. Previously he had been trying to balance the two, finding both particular and general in the motif and combining them in the work of art, an effort that characterized his portraiture in the 1910s and earlier. By the 1940s he was seeking the individual in the typical. He was trying first to create the typical in the sign rather than deriving it directly from the motif, then to use the sign like a pattern. We recall his approval of Delacroix's practice of drawing a claw-like appendage instead of a hand on each of his figures: this was Delacroix's hand-sign. Matisse deplored the idea that he might have to "make the portrait of a different hand each time."[6] Devising a sign for the hand was not only more efficient (but it was certainly that), it ensured that each hand in his work would be the expression of the artist more than a transcription of a motif, and it could be done as if unconsciously, because the artist had so thoroughly internalized the characteristics of a hand, just as when he was in the post office waiting for a telephone call he found that he was drawing the intimately familiar face of his mother without realizing it. The revelation at the post office was not only that drawing could give access to the unconscious, but also that drawing could be harnessed as a process for creating new archetypes, new unconscious structures, not just a medium for pre-existing ones. If he could create the typical, and have everything he painted or drew conform to its type, then the individual would not matter as much. This goal of governance by type was inimical to portraiture.

Louis Aragon recorded Matisse's thoughts about signs in "Matisse-en-France." In this essay Aragon also writes about portraiture, and tells a story about René, Duke of Anjou, who traveled a great distance to look upon Lady Anne, a renowned beauty. René does not know that she is dead and long buried. Discovering this, he wants to see her nevertheless, and her body is raised from its tomb. In spite of the depredations of her flesh, he finds her still so lovely that he insists on painting her portrait. Aragon:

> I like to imagine King René painting her, enraptured by her beauty and yet detached from it, because it had already shed all that was inessential, all mere *resemblance*, enabling him to rise above portraiture to attain something so pure and so lofty that no shadow of macabre delight still lingered there . . .[7]

If in the modernist regime of Aragon the best sitter is a dead sitter, at least Matisse agreed that in his own art the pure and lofty would not be attained through portraiture.

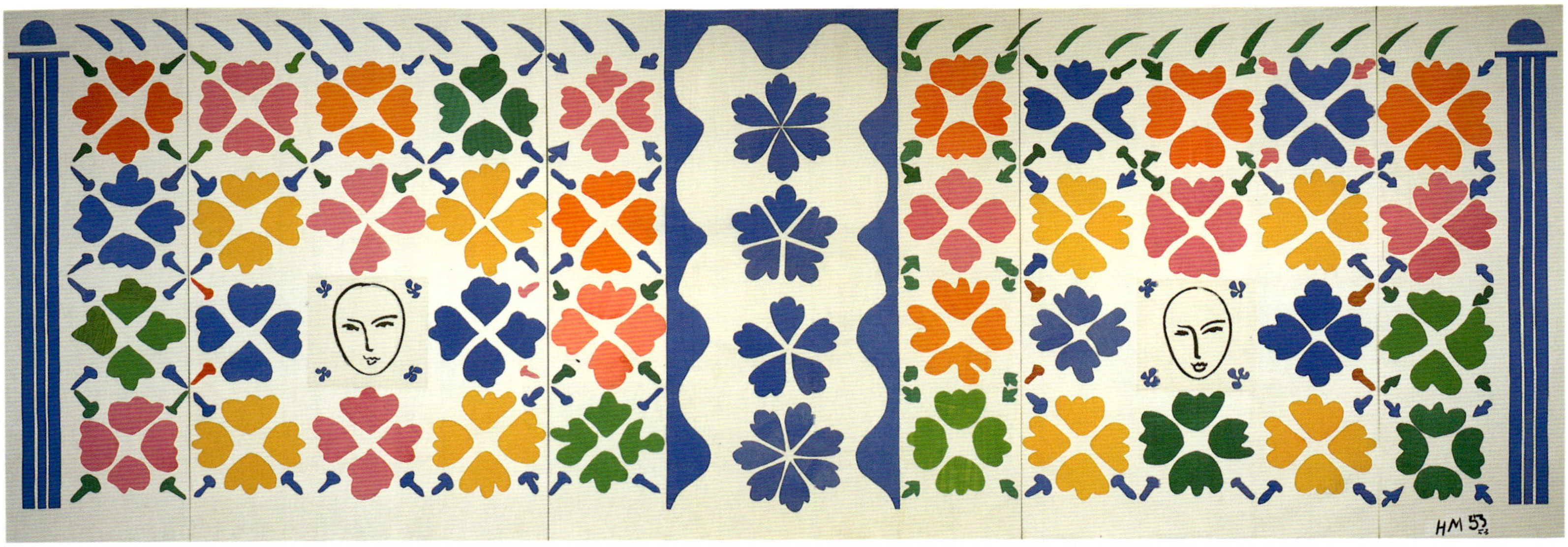

206 *Large Decoration with Masks*, 1953. Gouache on cut and pasted paper on canvas, 3.54 × 9.96 m. Washington, D.C., National Gallery of Art, Ailsa Mellon Bruce Fund.

It may be a loss that Matisse did not grapple longer and harder with the social content of portraiture, perhaps even a sign of weakness on his part, and turned instead to the compliant, and complacent, hired model. But the turn to the model was perfectly in keeping with the development of his idea of the sign. In Matisse's work the hired model is the sign for the socially constituted sitter for a portrait just as a cursive pencil mark can be a sign for an eye or hand. From this economy arose some of his lasting achievements. If the artist who made the memorable portraits of his wife, and of Yvonne Landsberg, Olga Merson, Auguste Pellerin, and others, had continued to paint portraits, he would never have made the paper cut-outs, innovative sign-making of a high order. Once he became thoroughly involved in his work in cut paper he could relinquish the empirical dependence on the model and work successfully from imagination. But it is significant that there are few faces in the cut-outs. The bodies there are non-specific, too, at once reduced to signs and elaborated into arabesques.

In the cut-outs, though, as in paintings and drawings from late in his career, there is the occasional mask, the sign for the face (fig. 206). They are innocuous generic visages, symmetrical like the florette motifs that surround them but with just enough inflection to carry the undulating rhythm across with neither pause nor monotony. Reconciling drawing and color, the cut-outs were the ultimate fulfillment of Matisse's desire to simplify and integrate his means in the creation of a decorative art, and they were the antithesis of portraiture in his work. When he shied from the social transaction of the portrait, and all the compromises that working with a sitter entailed, he may have realized that the only way for him to create an idealized art was to do it alone.

Notes

Introduction

1 See, among other studies of the development of modern notions of identity, Charles Taylor, *Sources of the Self: The Making of the Modern Identity* (Cambridge, Mass.: Harvard University Press, 1989), esp. chs. 22–4.

2 Salman Rushdie, "India at Five-o," *Time*, August 11, 1997, 42.

3 Quoted in Richard Brilliant, *Portraiture* (Cambridge, Mass.: Harvard University Press, 1991), p. 13.

4 John Pope-Hennessy, *The Portrait in the Renaissance* (London: Phaidon, 1966); Max J. Friedländer, *Landscape, Portrait, Still-Life: Their Origin and Development*, trans. R. F. C. Hull (Oxford: B. Cassirer, 1949).

5 For example, Malcolm Warner's *Portrait Painting* (New York: Mayflower Books, 1979), while clearly intended for the general public and part of a series of such introductory books, offers insightful assessments of what portraits were believed to be and to do in the history of painting since the Renaissance. Alistair Smith's chapter on portraits in Norbert Lynton, Alistair Smith, Robert Cumming, and Diané Collinson, *Looking Into Paintings* (London: Open University, 1985), part of the Open University's course series, is one of the most succinct historical and conceptual studies of portraiture.

6 F. David Martin, "On Portraiture: Some Distinctions," *Journal of Aesthetics and Art Criticism* 20 (Fall 1961): 61–72. Martin acknowledged the problematic nature of acclamation ("everyone agrees . . .") as a basis for studying the portrait, and strove for a system of classification. See also Risto Pitkänen, "The Resemblance View of Pictorial Representation," *British Journal of Aesthetics* 16 (Autumn 1976): 313–23, for a rigorous attempt to refute a definition of portraiture – among other forms of representation – in terms of resemblance.

7 *La Grande Encyclopédie* (Paris: H. Lamirault, [1886–1902]), vol. 27 (1900): 375: "Portrait. I. Beaux-Arts. – Le portrait est la représentation – trait pour trait – en médaillon, en buste ou en pied, de la physionomie extérieure et particulière d'un homme, d'une femme ou d'un enfant."

8 In his study of Renaissance portraiture, Lorne Campbell observes that the term "portrait" could also refer to artistic representations of things other than people; *Renaissance Portraits: European Portrait-Painting in the 14th, 15th, and 16th Centuries* (New Haven and London: Yale University Press, 1990), p. 1.

9 James D. Breckenridge, *Likeness: A Conceptual History of Ancient Portraiture* (Evanston, Ill.: Northwestern University Press, 1968). Although Breckenridge's book concerns ancient portraits, he intended it to begin a series encompassing the entire history of portraiture; hence his "conceptual" emphasis.

10 Ibid., p. 4, citing Bernhard Schweitzer, "Griechische Porträtkunst," *Acta Congressus Madvigiani Hafniae MDMLIV* (Copenhagen, 1957), III, *Portraiture*, trans. B.V. Bothmer, p. 8f.

11 Ibid., p. 7, citing Richard Delbrück, *Antike Porträts* (Bonn, 1912), p. vii.

12 Ibid., pp. 7, 266.

13 "Maudits portraits! ils m'empêchent toujours de marcher aux grandes choses." Quoted in Hélène Toussaint, *Les Portraits d'Ingres: Peintures des musées nationaux*, exh. cat. (Paris: Réunion des Musées Nationaux, 1985), p. 8.

14 An intelligent overview of this situation in the context of Impressionism is Colin B. Bailey, "Portrait of the Artist as a Portrait Painter," in Colin B. Bailey, ed., *Renoir's Portraits: Impressions of an Age*, exh. cat. (New Haven and London: Yale University Press and National Gallery of Canada, Ottawa, 1997), pp. 1–51. The recent literature on Impressionism has devoted much attention to portraiture. See also Linda Nochlin, "Impressionist Portraits and the Construction of Modern Identity," in *Renoir's Portraits*, pp. 53–86; and Sona Johnston, ed., *Faces of Impressionism: Portraits from American Collections* (New York: Rizzoli and Baltimore Museum of Art, 1999), esp. the essay by John House, "Impressionism and the Modern Portrait," pp. 11–35.

15 On various aspects of the social role of portraiture throughout history, see, for example, Alistair Smith, "Portraits," in Lynton et al., *Looking Into Paintings*; Richard Brilliant, *Portraiture*; and, briefly but suggestively, John Berger, "The Changing View of Man in the Portrait," in his *The Moment of Cubism and Other Essays* (New York: Pantheon-Random, 1969), pp. 41–7. For more specialized period studies that nevertheless have a broader application to this question of portraiture's social dimension, see Patricia Simons, "Women in Frames: The gaze, the eye, the profile in Renaissance portraiture," *History Workshop*, no. 25 (Spring 1988): 4–30, repr. in Norma Broude and Mary D. Garrard, eds., *The Expanding Discourse: Feminism and Art History* (New York: HarperCollins, 1992), pp. 39–57; Marcia Pointon, *Hanging the Head: Portraiture and Social Formation in Eighteenth-Century England* (New Haven and London: Yale University Press, 1993); and Andrew Wilton, *The Swagger Portrait: Grand Manner Portraiture in Britain from Van Dyck to Augustus John, 1630–1930*, exh. cat. (London: Tate Gallery, 1992). See also many of the essays in Joanna Woodall, ed., *Portraiture: Facing the Subject* (Manchester and New York: Manchester University Press, 1997).

16 See Nathalie Coupez, "Photomaton, le seul, le vrai," *Feuilles*, no. 11 (Winter 1985): 88–9.

17 Few art historians have challenged the relevance of likeness as a defining characteristic of portraiture. See Richard Brilliant, "Portraits: The Limitations of Likeness," in the special issue of the *Art Journal* devoted to this topic, *Art Journal* 46 (Fall 1987): 171–2. Brilliant expanded on the virtues and drawbacks of the concept of likeness in his book *Portraiture*, esp. ch. 1, "The Authority of Likeness." See also John Gage, "Photographic Likeness," in Woodall, *Portraiture*, pp. 119–30.

18 Quoted in Gary A. Reynolds, "Sargent's Late Portraits," in Patricia Hills, ed., *John Singer Sargent*, exh. cat. (New York: Whitney Museum of American Art, 1986), p. 162.

19 However, the reductive view that self-portraiture is transparent, simply self-registering, survives; for an example con-

cerning Matisse, see David Carrier, "Poussin's Cartesian Meditations: Self and Other in the Self-Portraits of Poussin and Matisse," *Source* 15 (Spring 1996): 28–35.

20 Some feminist writers have asserted that the tradition of using a mirror to make self-portraits is a masculine priority, and that feminist self-portraiture can avoid the mirror's "seeing is knowing" symbolism, taken to be central to male hegemony, by exploring other models for self-knowledge; see, for example, Luce Irigaray, *Speculum of the Other Woman*, trans. Gillian C. Gill (Ithaca: Cornell University Press, 1974), pp. 144–51, as applied by Marsha Meskimmon, *The Art of Reflection: Women Artists' Self-Portraiture in the Twentieth Century* (New York: Columbia University Press, 1996), p. 6. (On the other hand, some feminist writers are drawn to Jacques Lacan's "mirror stage" theory because it does not privilege the phallus and instead gives equal access to the symbolic order to both sexes.) While I have little doubt that Matisse participated in the full range of masculinist behaviors and projections in his day, I do not see any reason to peg the use of a mirror itself as an agent in the construction of a specifically masculine identity (although perhaps an interesting study might be made contrasting Matisse's "masculine" self-construction with the construal of his environment as "feminine"). For Matisse a mirror did not transparently convey information but was a manipulable tool in his process of constructing an image of himself; and so it could equally be for a woman artist who made, or makes, self-portraits. This could be true either despite or because of the traditional Western associations of women, mirrors, and vanity, precisely because the use of the mirror in self-portraiture is a metaphor, an act without fixed meaning: in self-portraiture, you are what you do with what you see.

21 I shall cite only two examples among many in the literature of aesthetics and art instruction at the end of the nineteenth century. The fashionable portrait painter Léon Bonnat claimed that the greatest portraits were made by the greatest painters, but that perhaps after all portrait painters had to have a special ability, which "consiste à découvrir le trait caractéristique du personnage" being portrayed. The "vérité" offered by a photograph "ne donne que très imparfaitement la ressemblance désirée. Le photographe n'a pas su découvrir le trait distinctif, le port du tête caractéristique, l'allure de son modèle; il a agi comme une machine"; cited in Ernest Hareux, *Cours complet de peinture à l'huile* (Paris: Henri Laurens, 1901), vol. 2, p. 23. Alfred Stevens, also a leading society portrait painter, likewise distanced his art from the photographic portrait: "La photographie donne la ressemblance banale que tout le monde peut voir; le peintre seul pénètre dans l'intimité du modèle et trouve le rayonnement de la physionomie"; Stevens, *Impressions sur la peinture* (Paris: Librairie des Bibliophiles, 1886), para. ccxlii.

22 One early twentieth-century observer lamented what he saw as one of the key reasons for portraiture's troubles: "Un admirable principe d'art est en train de se perdre. Celui-ci: soumission de l'artiste à l'oeuvre. A mesure que les peintres, pour ne parler que d'eux, s'éloignent de cette honnête et noble esthétique, ils ne font plus que peindre en pure perte; et leur talent n'importe guère. Mais ils sont misérables surtout dans le portrait. Ils croient indignes d'eux, probablement, d'asserver leur génie à la ressemblance de leur clientèle: les pauvres gens!"; André Beaunier, *L'Art de regarder les tableaux* (Paris: Librairie Centrale des Beaux-Arts, 1906), p. 104.

23 I am certainly not alone in such reconsiderations. A revised conception of portraiture is what William Rubin attempted in the exhibition and its accompanying catalogue *Picasso and Portraiture: Representation and Transformation* (New York: Museum of Modern Art, 1996). But Rubin hands all the responsibility to the artist: he would have us believe that Picasso's personal vision singlehandedly revised the genre of portraiture. Rubin's monolithic, modernist claim that Picasso "transformed" the portrait by "redefining [it] as a record of *the artist's personal responses* to the subject" ignores cultural forces and slights the social component of the portrait, giving no due whatsoever to the sitter's role in the portrait transaction (p. 13; italics in original). In the present book one of my aims is not to cede control of all the terms of representation to the artist. Portraiture is both more and less than what Picasso and Matisse said and made.

24 Richard Brilliant arrived at a similar conclusion in rejecting likeness and character as criteria for portraiture, but his definition is more general in that it includes all artistic representations of recognizable individuals; *Portraiture*, p. 8; also pp. 24–6. I am not the first to distinguish between hired models and portrait sitters; see Maurice Grosser, *The Painter's Eye* (New York: Reinhart, 1951), p. 90. As I do, Lorne Campbell in his *Renaissance Portraits* also bars likeness as a sufficient condition of a portrait, and excludes from consideration as portraits any depictions of hired or other models (pp. 2–6). This distinction between portraits and depictions of hired models has not often been applied to the art of Matisse and other modern artists, and it has never been subjected to the analysis I propose here. For two examples in the Matisse literature acknowledging the distinction, see Pierre Schneider, *Matisse*, trans. Michael Taylor and Bridget Strevens Romer (New York: Rizzoli, 1984), p. 330 (this does not prevent him from ignoring the difference elsewhere in his book); and Jean Leymarie, "The Painting of Matisse," in Jean Leymarie, Herbert Read, and William S. Lieberman, *Henri Matisse* (Berkeley and Los Angeles: University of California Press, 1966), p. 15, although Leymarie clearly sees this as a positive development, because a depiction of a hired model by Matisse "ceases to be *just a portrait* [my emphasis] and is assimilated into the rhythmic perfection of the composition."

25 This process of verification (but of what?) was the themed activity imposed on the visitor to the exhibition "Picasso and Portraiture" by wall labels containing not only the usual data for a work of art but also in many cases a photograph of the sitter. This tactic, apparently neutral and helpful to the viewer, served to undermine a dialogue between viewer and art in favor of one between two images, as well as to trivialize Picasso's transformative strategies by reducing them to greater or lesser distortions of specific interpretations of his sitters' physiognomies represented by each comparative photograph.

26 Henri Matisse, "Notes of a Painter," in Jack Flam, *Matisse on Art* (1973; rev. ed. Berkeley and Los Angeles: University of California Press, 1995), p. 41.

27 Matisse sometimes gave Lydia Delectorskaya, his secretary, principal model, and companion over many years, works of art in lieu of cash payment for modeling and as tokens of his respect for her (personal communication).

28 See Rewald's catalogue entry on *Young Sailor II* in William S. Lieberman, ed., *Twentieth-Century Modern Masters: The Jacques and Natasha Gelman Collection*, exh. cat. (New York: Metropolitan Museum of Art, 1989), pp. 88–91. Both paintings are illustrated there.

29 This is the focus of Jack Flam, "Some Observations on Matisse's Self-Portraits," *Arts Magazine* 49 (May 1975): 50–52. Symbolism of this kind also plays a large role in Flam's later, extremely important book, *Matisse: The Man and His Art, 1869–1918* (Ithaca and London: Cornell University Press, 1986).

30 For different reasons, this point was made recently with respect to Picasso by Kirk Varnedoe, "Picasso's Self-Portraits," in Rubin, *Picasso and Portraiture*, p. 111.

31 Matisse, "Statement to Tériade: On Fauvism and Color," in Flam, *Matisse on Art*, p. 86.

32 These works of implied self-representation are

perceptively analyzed by Yve-Alain Bois, "On Matisse: The Blinding," trans. Greg Sims, *October* 68 (Spring 1994): 61–121, here pp. 68–77.

33 Albert C. Barnes and Violette de Mazia, *The Art of Henri-Matisse* (New York: Scribner's, 1933), p. 184.

34 Alfred H. Barr, Jr., *Matisse: His Art and His Public* (New York: Museum of Modern Art, 1951).

35 Henri Matisse, *Portraits* (Monte Carlo: André Sauret, 1954).

36 See esp. Lawrence Gowing, *Matisse* (London: Thames and Hudson, 1979); John Elderfield, *The Drawings of Henri Matisse*, exh. cat., catalogue by Magdalena Dabrowski (London: Hayward Gallery and Thames and Hudson, 1984); Schneider, *Matisse*; Flam, *Matisse: The Man and His Art*; John Elderfield, *Henri Matisse: A Retrospective*, exh. cat. (New York: Museum of Modern Art, 1992). Collection catalogues: John Elderfield, *Matisse in the Collection of the Museum of Modern Art* (New York: Museum of Modern Art, 1978); Isabelle Monod-Fontaine, Anne Baldassari, and Claude Laugier, *Oeuvres de Henri Matisse* (Paris: Musée National d'Art Moderne, Centre Georges Pompidou, 1989).

37 Flam, "Some Observations on Matisse's Self-Portraits."

38 Catherine C. Bock, "Henri Matisse's Self-Portraits: Presentation and Representation," *Psychoanalytic Perspectives on Art* 3 (1988): 239–65.

39 Dominique Szymusiak and John Klein, *Henri Matisse: Autoportraits*, exh. cat. (Le Cateau-Cambrésis: Musée Matisse, 1988). My essay for this catalogue, "Matisse et l'autoportrait: démarche individuel et relation avec le public," pp. 9–28, has been the most comprehensive survey of this aspect of Matisse's art until now.

Chapter 1

1 Matisse, letter to André Rouveyre, 1941, in Dominique Fourcade, ed., *Henri Matisse: Ecrits et propos sur l'art* (Paris: Hermann, 1972), p. 188. For the view that there was in fact no such conflict, see Yve-Alain Bois, "Matisse and 'Arche-drawing'," in his *Painting as Model* (Cambridge, Mass., and London: MIT Press, 1990). But Matisse's saying that there was a conflict between drawing and color is the important thing here.

2 Matisse, letter to his friend Charles Camoin, 1914; see Danièle Giraudy, ed., "Correspondance Henri Matisse–Charles Camoin," *Revue de l'art* 12 (Summer 1971): 18.

3 Matisse said this in an interview in 1925, when his own attitudes along the Romantic–Classic axis may have been changing; Jack Flam, *Matisse on Art* (1973; rev. ed. Berkeley and Los Angeles: University of California Press, 1995), p. 79.

4 Hans Purrmann, cited in Flam, *Matisse on Art*, p. 45.

5 Originally published in the *Mercure de France*, August 1, 1905; see Philippe Dagen, ed., *La Peinture en 1905: "L'Enquête sur les tendances actuelles des arts plastiques" de Charles Morice*, Archives des arts modernes, no. 3, (Paris: Minard, 1986), p. 50. Matisse was sent the questionnaire but did not respond. For a subtle discussion of the general critical and theoretical context for the debate about representation and expression, see Richard Shiff, *Cézanne and the End of Impressionism: A Study of the Theory, Technique, and Critical Evaluation of Modern Art* (Chicago and London: University of Chicago Press, 1984), esp. chs. 4–6, the last focusing on Matisse.

6 Flam, *Matisse on Art*, p. 37.

7 Charles Baudelaire, *Selected Writings on Art and Artists*, trans. P. E. Charvet (Cambridge University Press, 1972), pp. 83–4.

8 Baudelaire, "Salon of 1859," in ibid., pp. 298–9.

9 Baudelaire, "Salon of 1846," in ibid., p. 78.

10 Flam, *Matisse on Art*, Introduction, pp. 8–9.

11 Matisse, "Exactitude is not Truth," in ibid., pp. 179–81, and for the quotes following.

12 Matisse, *Portraits* (Monte Carlo: André Sauret, 1954). See Flam, *Matisse on Art*, pp. 219–23, and for the quotes following.

13 The most comprehensive study of the "Thèmes et variations" series is Jack Flam, "Matisse's *Thèmes et variations*, a Book and a Method," in *Henri Matisse, Zeichnungen und Gouaches Découpées*, exh. cat. (Staatsgalerie Stuttgart, 1993), pp. 121–32.

14 It is therefore a source of regret that a series of "small anecdotal texts" that Matisse apparently wrote for *Portraits* was not included in the publication, at his direction. See Claude Duthuit, with the collaboration of Françoise Garnaud, *Henri Matisse: catalogue raisonné des ouvrages illustrés* (Paris: Claude Duthuit, 1988), p. 263. These texts, which had been delivered to the publisher before Matisse asked for their return, have been lost (information from Archives Matisse, Paris).

15 Some of his sitters were more candid, such as the writer Paul Léautaud, famously vituperative anyway, but adamant that the process of having Matisse draw his portrait had not been harmonious (see Chapter 4).

16 As recorded, with italics, by Louis Aragon, in "Conversations with Louis Aragon: On Signs," in Flam, *Matisse on Art*, p. 150; translation slightly modified.

17 Ibid., p. 151.

18 Matisse, cited in Raymond Escholier, *Matisse: A Portrait of the Artist and the Man*, trans. Geraldine and H. M. Colvile (New York: Praeger, 1960), p. 29. I have modified the translation for greater fidelity to the original sense.

19 See Roger Benjamin, "Une Copie par Matisse du *Balthazar Castiglione* de Raphaël," *La Revue du Louvre* 35, no. 4 (1985): 275–7.

20 Flam, *Matisse on Art*, p. 180. There is a legitimate doubt about whether this painting can really be called a Raphael, but it is unquestionably a portrait.

21 Giraudy, "Correspondance Henri Matisse–Charles Camoin," p. 18.

22 "Exactitude is not Truth," in Flam, *Matisse on Art*, p. 180; reiterated in "Portraits," in ibid., p. 220.

23 There is the intriguing possibility that Matisse picked up Rembrandt's putative "I have never painted anything but portraits" from Van Gogh. In a letter to Emile Bernard from July 1888 in which he discusses the portraiture of Frans Hals and Rembrandt, Van Gogh says of Hals: "He did portraits, and nothing, nothing else"; and of Rembrandt: "The same thing absolutely: a painter of portraits." A conflation of these declarations may have been Matisse's source for "Rembrandt's" statement. See *The Complete Letters of Vincent van Gogh* (Greenwich, Conn.: New York Graphic Society, 1959) vol. 1: 506 (letter B13). Van Gogh's letters to Bernard were published by Vollard in 1911, a likely source for Matisse's knowledge of them; *Lettres de Vincent van Gogh à Emile Bernard* (Paris: Ambroise Vollard, 1911), pp. 97–8 for letter B13.

24 Significantly, Baudelaire also contrasted Raphael, whom he saw as "pure" but "materialist," to Rembrandt, a "strong idealist" who makes us look beyond physical appearances; "Salon of 1846," in *Selected Writings on Art and Artists*, pp. 53–4.

25 Flam, *Matisse on Art*, p. 150.

26 "Portraits," in ibid., pp. 220–21.

27 "Notes of a Painter," in ibid., p. 38.

28 "Interview with Clara T. MacChesney," in ibid., p. 69.

29 "Un portrait . . . c'est une brouille." Quoted in Pierre Schneider, *Matisse*, trans. Michael Taylor and Bridget Strevens Romer (New York: Rizzoli, 1984), p. 406. Schneider told me that Marguerite Matisse Duthuit is the source for this statement by her father, and that she mimicked his voice when reporting it (personal communication, August 28, 1997).

30 "Portraits," in Flam, *Matisse on Art*, pp. 221–2.

31 Hilary Spurling's revelation about the financial scandal in which Matisse's parents were implicated at this time suggests a further

reason for the artist's preoccupation with his mother; see *The Unknown Matisse: A Life of Henri Matisse: The Early Years, 1869–1908* (London: Hamish Hamilton; New York: Knopf, 1998), ch. 8.

32 The incident so impressed Matisse that he apparently told Maurice Denis about it: Denis recounted Matisse's "revelation" in quite similar language in 1915. See Roger Benjamin, *Matisse's "Notes of a Painter": Criticism, Theory, and Context, 1891–1908* (Ann Arbor: UMI Research Press, 1987), pp. 19–20, 240 n. 51.

33 Here it should be clear that by abstraction I mean a process of generalization or simplification, not the non-objective art that is one potential outcome of the process – an outcome that Matisse never sought.

34 A very few of Matisse's portraits – the drawings of Claribel and Etta Cone from the 1930s (see figs. 139–41) – were based on photographs of the sitters, but this was because one was dead and the other was far away in the United States. He did another kind of commemorative portrait after photographs of Baudelaire, Poe, and other older writers, as frontispieces and other illustrations for books. There is obviously no irony in showing the similarity here between Matisse's expressed belief that "photography should register and give us documents" (1908; in Flam, *Matisse on Art*, p. 44) and Baudelaire's view that photography should be used strictly as a "secretary and record-keeper" (*Selected Writings on Art and Artists*, p. 297). Matisse was a thorough Baudelairean in this respect, too. Consistent with this attitude about photography – and with his ambivalence toward portraiture – is his statement that inferior portrait painters, those "who make complete likenesses," are "outdone by good photographers," who can simply play this game better (Flam, *Matisse on Art*, p. 145). When it came to photographs of himself as a form of public presentation, however, Matisse was predictably not so rigid or dismissive; see Catherine C. Bock, "Henri Matisse's Self-Portraits: Presentation and Representation," *Psychoanalytic Perspectives on Art* 3 (1988): 239–65. On Matisse's attitude to photography see also Jean-François Chevrier, "Matisse et la photographie," in Xavier Girard, ed., *Matisse: Photographies* (Cahiers Henri Matisse, no. 2), exh. cat. (Nice: Musée des Beaux-Arts Jules Cheret, 1986), pp. 8–18; and pp. 19–21 for statements by Matisse on the medium.

35 See Anne Baldassari, "'Heads Faces and Bodies': Picasso's Uses of Portrait Photographs," in William Rubin, ed., *Picasso and Portraiture: Representation and Transformation* (New York: Museum of Modern Art, 1996), pp. 203–23; and the three exhibition catalogues Baldassari has published at the Musée Picasso on Picasso and photography.

36 Another interpretation of the revelation at the post office is offered by Marcelin Pleynet. He relates the incident to Matisse's beginnings as an artist, when his mother gave him a box of colors as a pastime during recovery from illness in 1890. Pleynet asserts that these and other interventions by Matisse's mother in his artistic career substantiate an interpretation of much of his work as the result of unresolved Oedipal conflicts: see "Matisse's System" in his *Painting and System*, trans. Sima N. Godfrey (University of Chicago Press, 1984), pp. 39–50. Pleynet's argument is provocative, but even if it could be bolstered in any way it would unnecessarily limit the meaning of Matisse's discovery. John Elderfield has written perceptively about Matisse's "revelation" as it illuminates his drawing practice, without considering its implications for a practice of portraiture; *The Drawings of Henri Matisse*, exh. cat. (London: Hayward Gallery and Thames and Hudson; New York: Museum of Modern Art, 1984), pp. 19, 27–8.

37 "Portraits," in Flam, *Matisse on Art*, p. 222.

38 Matisse told this to an interviewer in 1925; see ibid., p. 79.

39 "Exactitude is not Truth," in ibid., pp. 179–80.

40 Ibid., pp. 38–9 and 223, respectively.

41 It may also be argued that seeing and responding are the same thing – that we cannot register any visual stimulus without simultaneously analyzing it somewhere in our inner universe of experience. On this affinity between perception and cognition as it relates to the problem of representation, see E. H. Gombrich, *Art and Illusion: A Study in the Psychology of Pictorial Representation* (1960; 2nd ed. Princeton University Press, 1972), pp. 26–8.

42 Recorded by Pierre Courthion in 1941; cited in Jack Flam, *Matisse: The Man and His Art, 1869–1918* (Ithaca and London: Cornell University Press, 1986), p. 74.

43 Flam, *Matisse on Art*, p. 221.

44 Other, more practical reasons for the distortions in death and life masks are vividly described in James D. Breckenridge, *Likeness: A Conceptual History of Ancient Portraiture* (Evanston, Ill.: Northwestern University Press, 1968), pp. 8–10. On another aspect of over-specificity as a hindrance to recognition, see Richard Brilliant, *Portraiture* (Cambridge, Mass.: Harvard University Press, 1991), p. 23.

45 In emphasizing the role of the viewer in recognizing a portrait as such, I differ from the emphasis that Brilliant gives to the artist's intention to make a work of art a portrait (*Portraiture*, pp. 7–8). A work of art may be a portrait, but if it is not recognized as such by a viewer, it has failed to convey its status, and has therefore not done its work as a portrait, that is, as a social agent.

46 Nevertheless this is sometimes attempted, as by the painter who asserted that "a portrait can be defined as a picture painted at a distance of four to eight feet of a person who is not paid to sit"; Maurice Grosser, *The Painter's Eye* (New York: Reinhart, 1951), p. 90. Perhaps such precision is not possible, but Grosser's general idea accords with the need for some kind of judgment by the viewer about the genre of the picture in question based on the relative size, thus importance, of its components, as well as the social status of the sitter.

47 On fundamental distinctions between "depiction" and "portrayal," see Risto Pitkänen, "The Resemblance View of Pictorial Representation," *British Journal of Aesthetics* 16 (Autumn 1976): 313–23.

48 See Breckenridge, *Likeness*, p. 5.

49 A recent and intelligent study of portraiture of a group of people with specific values and disciplinary identity is Ludmilla Jordanova, *Defining Features: Scientific and Medical Portraits, 1660–2000* (London: National Portrait Gallery and Reaktion Books, 2000).

50 Ambroise Vollard, *Recollections of a Picture Dealer*, trans. Violet M. MacDonald (1936; repr. New York: Dover, 1978), pp. 314–16. Possibly Vollard was not always an impeccable witness, but this story nonetheless speaks a great truth about social status and portraiture as a tool for manipulating public perception.

51 See Chapter 2 for a discussion of Matisse's manipulation of genre categories early in his career.

52 On caricature and the perception of faces, an issue germane to portraiture, see E. H. Gombrich, "The Mask and the Face: The Perception of Physiognomic Likeness in Life and in Art," in Gombrich, Julian Hochberg, and Max Black, *Art, Perception, and Reality* (Baltimore: Johns Hopkins University Press, 1972), pp. 1–46; and Gombrich, *Art and Illusion*, Introduction.

53 An interesting study might be made of caricature and portraiture within the avant-garde in the twentieth century. Along these lines, see the excellent article by Adam Gopnik, "High and Low: Caricature, Primitivism, and the Cubist Portrait," *Art Journal* 43 (Winter 1983): 371–6.

54 Christian Zervos, "Notes sur la formation et le développement de l'oeuvre de Henri-Matisse," *Cahiers d'Art* 5–6 (1931): 246, 248. We do not know which of Picasso's portraits was the subject of this exercise.

55 I shall discuss one of the few examples of caricatural exaggeration in Matisse's paint-

ing, in a Cubist portrait of his daughter Marguerite (see fig. 66), in Chapter 3.

56 On the popularity of the portrait photograph in this period, see Elizabeth Anne McCauley, *A. A. E. Disdéri and the Carte de Visite Portrait Photograph* (New Haven and London: Yale University Press, 1985).

57 "Portraits," in Flam, *Matisse on Art*, p. 221.

Chapter 2

1 A significant exception to this is the prolific and enormously talented young Picasso, who drew and painted many portraits, especially of his family, which offered a ready social sphere of the kind that Matisse did not exploit.

2 Her name has been variously spelled Pétron and Bétron; also Nina Betrou: see Pierre Schneider, *Matisse*, trans. Michael Taylor and Bridget Strevens Romer (New York: Rizzoli, 1984), p. 409. Hilary Spurling has suggested that the girl's name was Annie Betrou, as this surname was that of a family known to have lived then on Belle-Ile, where Matisse painted in the summer of 1896 (personal communication, February 9, 1996).

3 For photographs of Matisse's studio in the 1940s, see *Matisse*, exh. cat. (Paris: Galerie Dina Vierny, 1982), pp. 74, 75.

4 See Hilary Spurling, *The Unknown Matisse: A Life of Henri Matisse: The Early Years, 1869–1908* (London: Hamish Hamilton; New York: Knopf, 1998), p. 231 and p. 450 n. 173, for the persuasive redating of this painting from the traditionally accepted date of 1906.

5 Hilary Spurling, personal communication, September 22, 2000. See Spurling, with the collaboration of Georges Bourgeois, *Henri Matisse, homme du Nord* (Le Cateau-Cambrésis: Musée Matisse, 1999), pp. 34–6, for the identification and redating of this portrait, formerly known as *Portrait of a Boy* from 1891.

6 See Isabelle Monod-Fontaine, Anne Baldassari, and Claude Laugier, *Matisse*, Collections du Musée National d'Art Moderne (Paris: Editions du Centre Pompidou, 1989), p. 18.

7 As summations consider also *Le Bonheur de vivre* of 1905–6 (Merion, Penn., Barnes Foundation); *The Piano Lesson* (see fig. 69); or the Barnes *Dance* of 1932–33.

8 In the same period Matisse painted two other compositions that can be considered as seed images, with recurrent branching and fruition over the following decades: *Breton Serving Girl* of 1896 and *The Open Door, Brittany* of the same year (both private collection). Later works proposing themes that Matisse returned to repeatedly include *Carmelina* (see fig. 35); and *Still Life with "Dance"* (1909; St. Petersburg, Hermitage). To this may be added *Le Bonheur de vivre*, because this singular painting both summed up recent developments and proposed things to come.

9 On the nineteenth-century image of the *liseuse moderne* as a context for Matisse's representation of this female reader, see Janis Bergman-Carton, *The Woman of Ideas in French Art, 1830–1848* (New Haven and London: Yale University Press, 1995), ch. 4, esp. pp. 106–16, where the author also discusses a sub-category of idle domestic servants "caught" in the act of reading. I thank Liz Childs for this reference.

10 Caroline Joblaud (or Camille, as she was known) was not spoken of, nor was her identity certain to scholars, for many years, presumably in deference to Matisse's family (especially while Marguerite Matisse was alive). Much new information about Joblaud has been unearthed by Hilary Spurling; see *The Unknown Matisse*, pp. 77 ff.

11 Nicholas Watkins, *Matisse* (New York: Oxford University Press, 1985), p. 23.

12 It is certainly suggestive, but I think not mandatory, to imagine the idealized viewer of this painting as male; in this case the collusion between artist and viewer may take on an added, sexualized edge. But the painting is not otherwise inflected in a way to suggest such gendered collusion. On questions of the complicity of a male viewer to deny the importance of female looking, see Griselda Pollock, "Modernity and the Spaces of Femininity," in Norma Broude and Mary D. Garrard, eds., *The Expanding Discourse: Feminism and Art History* (New York: HarperCollins, 1992), pp. 261–5, with reference to the work of Mary Ann Doane.

13 Marguerite Matisse was born September 3, 1894 in Paris, although Matisse did not legally recognize her until early 1897; archival sources cited in Jack Flam, *Matisse: The Man and His Art, 1869–1918* (Ithaca and London: Cornell University Press, 1986), p. 485 n. 38. By this time, as Flam proposed (ibid., p. 486 n. 14), Matisse may have anticipated ending his relationship with Caroline Joblaud. In any case, his failure to acknowledge Marguerite as his legal daughter for over two years was probably due to the lower-class position of her mother. And although it was Joblaud who ended their relationship, Matisse's legal recognition of Marguerite amounted to a definitive dismissal of her mother; see Spurling, *The Unknown Matisse*, pp. 137, 140.

14 This was suggested by Flam, *Matisse: The Man and His Art*, p. 35. The other sculpture is identical in size and very similar in execution.

15 Patricia Simons has examined the Renaissance male artist's implied control over the image (and thus over the object of the image) in female profile portraits; "Women in Frames: The gaze, the eye, the profile in Renaissance portraiture," *History Workshop*, no. 25 (Spring 1988): 4–30.

16 Hilary Spurling has proposed that *Breton Serving Girl* represents a girl named Clotilde, a summer employee on Belle-Ile when Matisse was there in 1896, and that he may have used Caroline Joblaud to complete the figure later in the year; Hilary Spurling, "Matisse on Belle-Ile," *Burlington Magazine* 137 (October 1995): 664.

17 To compare *Woman Reading* with a nearly contemporary painting of a reader – complete with framed pictures on the wall and a plaster sculpture displayed on a sideboard, as in Matisse's picture – shows how differently the subject of the reader could be construed when the reader was a member of the same social class as the artist. Henri Evenepoel (1872–99), a Matisse cohort in Moreau's studio, painted a portrait of his father in 1893 (Brussels, Musées Royaux des Beaux-Arts de Belgique). Although absorbed in his book, Evenepoel senior faces the viewer, sharply increasing the implied possibility of his engagement with us, and thus lessening our sense of control of the situation (interestingly, though, the plaster bust in Evenepoel's painting performs a role similar to that of Matisse's self-portrait in *Woman Reading*, overlooking and "gazing" upon the preoccupied reader). Consider also Cézanne's *Portrait of Louis-Auguste Cézanne Reading "L'Evénement"* (1866; Washington, D.C., National Gallery of Art) for another portrait of a preoccupied reader who nevertheless seems capable of instant command. In these pictures both readers are male and it may be significant that these potentially vigilant figures are also the artists' fathers.

18 He first expressed this combative attitude to artistic influence in his interview with Guillaume Apollinaire, 1907; then this in 1925: "I have accepted influences but I think I have always known how to dominate them"; Jack Flam, *Matisse on Art* (1973; rev. ed. Berkeley and Los Angeles: University of California Press, 1995), pp. 29, 81.

19 See, for instance, John Elderfield, *Henri Matisse: A Retrospective*, exh. cat. (New York: Museum of Modern Art, 1992), p. 81.

20 As by Lawrence Gowing, *Matisse* (London: Thames and Hudson, 1979), pp. 18, 20.

21 I take the term self-fashioning from Stephen Greenblatt, *Renaissance Self-Fashioning from More to Shakespeare* (University of Chicago Press, 1980).

22 Matisse cited by Raymond Escholier, *Matisse: A Portrait of the Artist and the Man*, trans.

Geraldine and H. M. Colvile (New York: Praeger, 1960), p. 26.

23 He was aware of the various elements of his public reputation at different moments in his career. See also his famous exclamation to an American journalist in 1912 that, contrary to his reputation as a wild, undisciplined character, he was "a normal man," "a devoted husband and father," and that he enjoyed ordinary things "just like any man"; Flam, *Matisse on Art*, p. 69.

24 On Rembrandt as a reference for the nineteenth-century image of the artist, see Cornelia Homburg, *The Copy Turns Original: Vincent van Gogh and a New Approach to Traditional Art Practice* (Amsterdam and Philadelphia: John Benjamins, 1996), ch. 7; and Françoise Heilbrun and Philippe Néagu, *Portraits d'artistes*, exh. cat., Les Dossiers du Musée d'Orsay, no. 7 (Paris: Editions de la Réunion des Musées Nationaux, 1986), p. 20.

25 "Déjà, pour moi-même, je ne voyais qu'un travail d'architecture générale, remplaçant les détails explicatifs par une synthèse vivante et suggestive"; in Dominique Fourcade, ed., *Henri Matisse: Ecrits et propos sur l'art* (Paris: Hermann, 1972), p. 47 n. 12.

26 Several more not illustrated here were published in Dominique Szymusiak and John Klein, *Henri Matisse: Autoportraits*, exh. cat. (Le Cateau-Cambrésis: Musée Matisse, 1988). See also Schneider, *Matisse*, pp. 122, 408–9.

27 See Kirk Varnedoe, "Picasso's Self-Portraits," in William Rubin, ed., *Picasso and Portraiture: Representation and Transformation* (New York: Museum of Modern Art, 1996), pp. 113–31.

28 Flam, *Matisse on Art*, p. xvi.

29 The term "impression management" is from Erving Goffman, *The Presentation of Self in Everyday Life* (Garden City, N.Y.: Doubleday Anchor, 1959), ch. 6.

30 "Chaque fois que je me mets devant mon chevalet, je suis un autre homme, moi, et toujours Cézanne"; Cézanne quoted in Joaquim Gasquet, *Cézanne* (Paris: Editions Bernheim-Jeune, 1926), p. 196.

31 For other drawings in this series see Monod-Fontaine et al., *Matisse*, pp. 130–31.

32 Emphasizing the tension rather than the complementarity between these images, Catherine C. Bock also proposes this kind of duality in "Henri Matisse's Self-Portraits: Presentation and Representation," *Psychoanalytic Perspectives on Art* 3 (1988): 243–4.

33 *Self-Portrait at the Easel* was not exhibited or published until 1949; to my knowledge, the first public appearance of Matisse's other painted self-portrait was its reproduction in 1984 as the frontispiece of Schneider's *Matisse*. For that matter, the self-portrait drawings of 1898–1900 were rarely exhibited, and none at that time; many were first exhibited and published in 1988.

34 Jack Flam has pointed out the precedence of Rembrandt for these artists' self-conceptions at the end of the nineteenth century, remarking on the "associative resonance" among all these images; *Matisse: The Man and His Art*, p. 89. Van Gogh's self-portrait at the easel (Amsterdam, Rijksmuseum Vincent van Gogh) is reproduced in John Rewald, *Post-Impressionism from Van Gogh to Gauguin*, 3rd ed., rev. (New York: Museum of Modern Art, 1978), p. 70. It is unlikely that Matisse could have been familiar with either Cézanne's or Van Gogh's self-portrait; they remained in family hands until entering, much later, the public collections that house them today. The pervasiveness of the type is itself evidence of its usefulness as a model of professional assertiveness.

35 It is usually either stated or implied that Matisse began this plate around 1900 and completed it in 1903. See, for example, John Elderfield, *Matisse in the Collection of the Museum of Modern Art* (New York: Museum of Modern Art, 1978), p. 34; and Claude Duthuit and Marguerite Duthuit-Matisse, with the collaboration of Francoise Garnaud, *Henri Matisse, catalogue raisonné de l'oeuvre gravé*, 2 vols. (Paris: Claude Duthuit, 1983), vol. 1, no. 2. I am inclined to believe that the plate was substantially finished in 1900, and that only the scraping and burnishing of the hands was done in 1903 before the print was editioned.

36 On *The Serf*, also begun in 1900, as a displaced self-portrait (and thus, appropriately, as a counter-image to mastery), see Flam, *Matisse: The Man and His Art*, p. 88.

37 Edward Said, *Beginnings: Intention and Method* (New York: Basic Books, 1975), p. 224. See esp. ch. 4, "Beginning with a Text."

38 Flam, *Matisse on Art*, p. 29. The strong Darwinian flavor of Matisse's characterization of artistic development is strikingly echoed in his copy of Antoine Barye's (pre-Darwin) *Jaguar Devouring a Hare*, contemporaneous with these self-portraits and suggesting his preoccupation with the process of struggle and triumph.

39 The other principal ways in which an artist may make a self-portrait are to work from an already existing image, such as a photograph (or another self-portrait), or to create one entirely from imagination. The last method is rare. Re-imagining or inventing the self in a self-portrait seems to require a visual presence to react against. The inextricable link produced in mirroring, eye to eye, may provide a necessary stable component, which the artist may then alter (this act in itself is an imaginative process). Most self-portraits are in two dimensions; self-portrait sculpture is unusual and is generally derived from pre-existing imagery or performed from imagination. Although the sense of depth and volume in a mirror image is fundamentally the same as in direct perception, it is impossible to "move around," or fully scan with our vision the image in the mirror, as we can with objects in three dimensions. Vision is closely connected to the ability to move. This limits the feasibility of self-portrait sculpture. Conversely, our means of directly perceiving our bodies in three dimensions – looking down, essentially – yields an incomplete image that necessarily excludes the face, or at least the eyes. I say more about this below.

40 Lacan published his findings as "Le stade du miroir comme formateur de la fonction du Je" in 1949. See "The Mirror Stage as Formative of the Function of the I as Revealed in Psychoanalytic Experience," in Jacques Lacan, *Ecrits: A Selection*, trans. Alan Sheridan (New York: Norton, 1977), pp. 1–7 and for the quotes following.

41 Jane Gallop, *Reading Lacan* (Ithaca and London: Cornell University Press, 1985), p. 78 (italics in original).

42 There is also an analogy here to Freud's theory of the "fort-da" form of play by infants. Freud surmised that children learn mastery of other objects by making them disappear and reappear as a means of symbolic control over the mother-object. Anyone who has watched a year-old baby playing in front of a mirror may appreciate this analogy. When infants play a hide-and-seek game with their mirror image, moving to make it disappear, then bringing it back through direct confrontation, they are performing a fort-da exercise on the image they identify with themselves, enjoying control of themselves as independent actors.

43 Other aspects of Matisse's work have been discussed in the light of Lacan's mirror stage theory. John Elderfield likens Matisse's projection of himself into the figure of a child in his paintings as a desire for a return to a prelinguistic state of symbolic grace characterized by the mirror stage; thus the mirror stage is a lost paradise that Matisse recovers in paintings of idyllic, imaginary subjects that evoke the wondering state of childhood. See "Describing Matisse," in *Henri Matisse: A Retrospective*, p. 36. David Carrier takes an approach that is closer to mine, in that he is concerned with images of Matisse himself in his work, but Carrier construes as acts of self-definition Matisse's drawings from the 1930s in which he represents himself with a model; "Matisse: The End of Classical Art History and the Fictions of Early Modernism," in his

Principles of Art History Writing (University Park, Penn.: Pennsylvania State University Press, 1991), pp. 227–9. As these authors do also, I emphasize that Matisse probably knew nothing of Lacan's theories, and I do not suggest a causal relationship (nor does it appear that in his writings Lacan ever concerned himself with self-portraiture).

44 An interesting but limited analysis of self-portraits by another modern artist in the context of Lacanian theory is David Lomas, "Inscribing Alterity: Transactions of Self and Other in Miró Self-Portraits," in Joanna Woodall, ed., *Portraiture: Facing the Subject* (Manchester and New York: Manchester University Press, 1997), pp. 167–86.

45 As Richard Shiff has proposed, the modern artist concerned to be original – he is discussing Matisse here – values "finding" as a higher form of artistic creation than "making," although conscious making is still needed to control the adventitious effects of finding; see *Cézanne and the End of Impressionism: A Study of the Theory, Technique, and Critical Evaluation of Modern Art* (Chicago and London: University of Chicago Press, 1984), pp. 62, 68–9.

46 Flam comments on Matisse's exhibition strategies (*Matisse: The Man and His Art*, p. 109 and n. 3), and Schneider deals at length with Matisse's growing awareness of the economic forces in the art world and his efforts to form a marketing scheme to take advantage of them (*Matisse*, pp. 726–9).

47 As discussed by Flam, *Matisse: The Man and His Art*, pp. 103, 106.

48 *Still Life with Red-Checkered Tablecloth* is in a private collection; it is reproduced in Pierre Schneider, ed., with Tamara Préaud, *Henri Matisse: Exposition du centenaire*, exh. cat. (Paris: Grand Palais, 1970), p. 136.

49 The artist's control and the denial of female subjectivity in this painting is elaborated effectively by James D. Herbert, as is a similar strategy in Manet's *Bar at the Folies-Bergère*, whose composition *Carmelina* echoes; *Fauve Painting: The Making of Cultural Politics* (New Haven and London: Yale University Press, 1992), pp. 56–61.

50 This unusual drawing received some interesting attention in the 1990s. Unique in Matisse's work from this period as we know it today, it was apparently one of a group of such drawings including his feet, according to the witness account of Jean Puy; see Yve-Alain Bois, "On Matisse: The Blinding," trans. Greg Sims, *October* 68 (Spring 1994): 61–121, here pp. 74–6. Bois characterizes Matisse's self-referring gesture as a demonstration of the impossibility of totalizing – that is, for Matisse, Impressionist – vision. See also Elderfield, "Describing Matisse," in *Henri Matisse: A Retrospective*, p. 34, where the spatial discontinuity of the drawing is related to Matisse's painting *Luxe, calme et volupté* of the same year.

51 See Bois, "On Matisse: The Blinding," p. 76.

Chapter 3

1 From an interview with André Verdet (1952), in Jack Flam, *Matisse on Art* (1973; rev. ed. Berkeley and Los Angeles: University of California Press, 1995), p. 212.

2 All of Matisse's children had children of their own. With the encouragement of their father, all three also undertook serious artistic pursuits. Pierre, the youngest, was at one point pulled out of school to study the violin for three years: see Pierre Schneider, *Matisse*, trans. Michael Taylor and Bridget Strevens Romer (New York: Rizzoli, 1984), p. 339 n. 38. He also played the piano and had aspirations as a painter; he went on to be an art dealer in New York. Jean studied the cello and later became a professional sculptor of modest reputation. Marguerite, always the closest to her father, was also a painter – even, it is usually said, taking lessons from him. Both Marguerite and Pierre exhibited in the 1920s in the Salon des Indépendants; some of Marguerite's paintings are in the Cone Collection of the Baltimore Museum of Art, as are several sculptures by Jean Matisse. Both Marguerite and Pierre remained closely allied to Matisse's professional concerns, Marguerite by acting as his unofficial archivist, Pierre by handling his work in New York. Marguerite remained in closest contact with her father. Nevertheless, she did marry, in 1923, the art historian and critic Georges Duthuit, and had her own life.

3 An excellent discussion of this evolution is Paul Jay, *Being in the Text: Self-Representation from Wordsworth to Roland Barthes* (Ithaca and London: Cornell University Press, 1984), esp. the introduction.

4 For Matisse's frequent assertions of the importance of his sincerity, see Flam, *Matisse on Art*, pp. 158–9, 161–2, 195, 213, 215. The entire idea of the modern artist's sincerity is part of the larger context of the ascendance of the value of personal sincerity and candid self-representation in modern society; see Lionel Trilling, *Sincerity and Authenticity* (Cambridge, Mass: Harvard University Press, 1972).

5 See Jack Flam, *Matisse: The Man and His Art, 1869–1918* (Ithaca and London: Cornell University Press, 1986), p. 486 n. 14.

6 Alfred H. Barr, Jr., *Matisse: His Art and His Public* (New York: Museum of Modern Art, 1951), p. 37. Based on considerably more research, Hilary Spurling came to the same conclusion about Amélie Matisse's self-sacrificing and supportive nature; *The Unknown Matisse: A Life of Henri Matisse: The Early Years, 1869–1908* (London: Hamish Hamilton; New York: Knopf, 1998), esp. pp. 147–54, 205–7.

7 Barr, *Matisse*, pp. 41–2.

8 It should be understood that when I use the surname to refer to Henri Matisse and the first name to refer to Amélie Matisse, I do this for the dual reason of consistency in reference to the artist and convenience in distinguishing these two people who share a last name.

9 Other portraits of her from this time support this assessment. Two unflattering drawings – really caricatures – of a woman who appears to be Amélie Matisse, both from around 1900, are reproduced in Schneider, *Matisse*, pp. 124, 571.

10 Both paintings are reproduced in ibid., pp. 316, 113. Schneider was, I believe, the first to notice that in some pentimenti in *Breton Serving Girl* can be seen the head of a small child, and therefore to interpret the original subject of this painting to be a mother and daughter – Matisse's "family" of Caroline and Marguerite.

11 I am referring of course to Carol Duncan's essay on the French ideal of the woman at home, serving husband and children, reifying patriarchal order: "Happy Mothers and Other New Ideas in Eighteenth-Century French Art," in Norma Broude and Mary D. Garrard, eds., *Feminism and Art History: Questioning the Litany* (New York: Harper and Row, 1982), pp. 201–19.

12 Henri Manguin, a contemporary and friend of Matisse, is an especially interesting case. For a number of portraits and other pictures of his wife, maybe ultimately no less manipulative than Matisse's of Amélie but projecting a good deal more sympathy, see Denys Sutton, *Manguin in America*, exh. cat. (Tucson: University of Arizona Museum of Art, 1974).

13 Lawrence Gowing, *Matisse* (London: Thames and Hudson, 1979), p. 38. Matisse's painting of Bevilacqua is illustrated on p. 36.

14 Barr, *Matisse*, pp. 41–2. We now also know that the financial scandal in which Amélie's parents were falsely implicated brought considerable tension to the Matisse family at this time; see Spurling, *The Unknown Matisse*, pp. 234–42.

15 His friend Jean Puy, in "Souvenirs," *Le Point*, no. 21 (July 1939): p. 32, gives a retrospective account from about this time in which Matisse's attitude toward Amélie is even less charitable when getting his work done was at stake: "[Matisse] était tellement pris par ses recherches, qu'il nous dit crûment, comme un aveu pas très aimable pour sa femme, mais

c'était une boutade: 'Je voudrais vivre comme un moine dans une cellule pourvu que j'aie de quoi peindre sans souci ni dérangement.'"

16 Information from the Archives Matisse, Paris. He had also exhibited a *Guitarist* – it is not known which one – at the Salon des Indépendants of 1903.

17 One visitor to the Steins, who owned the canvas in 1908, could not tell landscape from figure, figure from landscape in this and other contemporary paintings by Matisse; see Dominique Fourcade and Isabelle Monod-Fontaine, *Henri Matisse 1904–1917*, exh. cat. (Paris: Centre Georges Pompidou, 1993), p. 425.

18 For a thorough analysis of these transformations, see Flam, *Matisse: The Man and His Art*, pp. 114–18, where these paintings are illustrated. More recently John Elderfield has discussed the "hallucinatory" quality of *Luxe, calme et volupté* as emblematic of a lost paradise; "Describing Matisse," in *Henri Matisse: A Retrospective*, exh. cat. (New York: Museum of Modern Art, 1993), pp. 35–6.

19 See Flam, *Matisse: The Man and His Art*, pp. 78–9.

20 Marquet and Camoin depicted Amélie Matisse in the process of making a tapestry that was based on Derain's painting (see fig. 42) of her. Her doing this is a curious act of recursive self-portrayal, perhaps expressing her desire to embody herself in her work as an indication of its importance to her. She subsequently exhibited the tapestry in the Salon des Indépendants of 1905, but this was the extent of her public career as an artist, possibly because her husband's star was rising so quickly and his career was to take precedence. See John Elderfield, *The "Wild Beasts": Fauvism and its Affinities*, exh. cat. (New York: Museum of Modern Art, 1976), p. 42, where Marquet's and Camoin's paintings are also illustrated.

21 "Je crois que la peinture me rendra fou, aussi je vais tâcher d'en sortir le plus tôt possible. . . . Je viens de croquer la patronne du café, qui jusqu'ici j'avais trouvée très jolie, et je remarque qu'en la dessinant je n'ai pris que tout ce qu'elle a de laid. A bien regarder, elle est affreuse; j'ai exagéré tout ce qu'elle a de laid. Tu vois comme je dois être pénible à fréquenter en ce moment." A page of the letter, including Matisse's sketch of the *patronne*, is reproduced in Pierre Gassier, ed., *Manguin parmi les Fauves*, exh. cat. (Martigny, Switzerland: Fondation Pierre Gianadda, 1983), p. 23.

22 For more complete accounts, see Barr, *Matisse*, pp. 55–8; Elderfield, *The "Wild Beasts"*, pp. 43–4; and Flam, *Matisse: The Man and His Art*, pp. 143–6. For a more extended study of the place of *Woman with the Hat* in Matisse's career, and of the critical response to it, see John Klein, "When Worlds Collide: Matisse's *Femme au chapeau* and the Politics of the Portrait," in *Matisse and Other Modern Masters: The Elise S. Haas Collection*, ed. Janet Bishop, exh. cat. (San Francisco Museum of Modern Art, 1993), pp. 7–18, on which the present account is based in part.

23 See, for example, Jean Leymarie, *Fauvism: Biographical and Critical Study*, trans. James Emmons (New York: Skira, 1959), p. 83. Catherine C. Bock [Bock-Weiss] wrote aptly of *Femme au chapeau* as "a kind of 'release' painting after the constraint of 'little dots'"; *Henri Matisse and Neo-Impressionism, 1898–1908* (Ann Arbor: UMI Research Press, 1981), p. 89.

24 Gertrude Stein, *The Autobiography of Alice B. Toklas* (1933; New York: Vintage, 1961), pp. 34–5. Stein may have exaggerated, but she did make this statement twice.

25 See Barr, *Matisse*, p. 56.

26 For the most thorough and astute analysis of Matisse criticism in the first decade of the century, on which I have relied for some of my characterizations of it, see Roger Benjamin, *Matisse's "Notes of a Painter": Criticism, Theory, and Context, 1891–1908* (Ann Arbor: UMI Research Press, 1987), esp. ch. 4.

27 Cited in Benjamin, *Matisse's "Notes of a Painter"*, p. 106. As with other aspects of the anecdotal history of *Woman with the Hat*, accounts differ: Vauxcelles himself said that before writing his review he had made his comment to Matisse directly as they toured the show together; Barr, *Matisse*, p. 56.

28 Pierre Schneider reached a similar conclusion about the challenge to middle-class values and to the privilege of the sitter's self-representation in this painting; *Matisse*, p. 729.

29 In the context of Van Gogh's portraiture of "modern types," Carol Zemel interestingly considers the problematic status of female representation in this period; *Van Gogh's Progress: Utopia, Modernity, and Late-Nineteenth-Century Art* (Berkeley and Los Angeles, University of California Press, 1997), pp. 110–15.

30 Thus I cannot agree with Hilary Spurling that this painting could be "a portrait of Amélie's courage, her will and her passionate, exacting faith in the painter"; *The Unknown Matisse*, p. 335.

31 See Barr, *Matisse*, p. 56. In this respect it may be significant that we know that Amélie Matisse characteristically dressed in monochrome, usually in deep browns and maroons, and in fact posed in such a dress for this portrait. I thank Claude Duthuit for this information about his grandmother's color preferences in her dress. Sarah Stein reported that Amélie posed in black for this portrait; see Marcelin Pleynet, *Painting and System*, trans. Sima Godfrey (Chicago and London: University of Chicago Press, 1984), p. 49. It has sometimes been asserted that Amélie Matisse dressed only in black. In any case, Matisse radically transformed the visual appearance of his sitter – not a very surprising realization about his work at this time.

In unpublished work on John Singer Sargent (presented in a lecture, "Painting Skin: Decay and Resistance in Sargent's *Madame X*," College Art Association Annual Conference, New York, 1997), Susan Sidlauskas offers provocative parallels to the transaction of Matisse's *Woman with the Hat*. "Madame X" – Virginie Gautreau – was a famous professional beauty who literally painted herself with make-up in a performance of a certain type of femininity. This pre-painting of her self-canvas offered a frustrating resistance to Sargent's efforts to control his representation of her, a challenge familiar to Matisse. Both portraits, in which "something inarticulated or invisible was exposed to view," and each with a sitter in a state of "restless immobility," produced public scandals on exhibition and memorable images of their sitters.

32 Pleynet, *Painting and System*, pp. 39–52, esp. 49.

33 A point made in the context of British portraiture by Ann Pullan, "Head to Head Encounters," *Oxford Art Journal* 17, no. 2 (1994): 105.

34 Matisse, letter to Paul Signac, quoted in Benjamin, *Matisse's "Notes of a Painter"*, p. 106.

35 See Barr, *Matisse*, pp. 62, 74; and Elderfield, *"The Wild Beasts"*, p. 61.

36 An excellent discussion of the painting's formal qualities is found in Flam, *Matisse: The Man and His Art*, pp. 145–6.

37 Gelett Burgess, "The Wild Men of Paris," *Architectural Record* 27 (May 1910): 401–14; quoted in Barr, *Matisse*, p. 74. Although the article was published in 1910, Burgess saw the works of art he wrote about in 1908.

38 Annette Rosenshine quoted in Spurling, *The Unknown Matisse*, p. 352.

39 Francis Carco quoted in Raymond Escholier, *Matisse: A Portrait of the Artist and the Man*, trans. Geraldine and H. M. Colvile (New York: Praeger, 1960), p. 61.

40 According to Greta Moll, a student in Matisse's school who later commissioned a portrait of her from him (see fig. 112), Matisse himself gave the title *Madras rouge* to the painting; Margarete Moll, "Erinnerungen an Henri Matisse," in *Matisse und seine deutschen Schüler*, exh. cat. (Kaiserslautern: Pfalzgalerie, 1988), p. 41.

41 Flam, *Matisse on Art*, p. 38. In its original pub-

lication in *La Grande revue* in 1908, Matisse used his comparable portrait of Greta Moll as an illustration of his desire to render all parts of a portrait expressive.

42 See Flam, *Matisse on Art*, pp. 27–30.

43 Flam, *Matisse: The Man and His Art*, pp. 212, 215.

44 See *Great French Paintings from the Barnes Foundation* (New York: Knopf, 1993), p. 308, entry for *The Red Madras Headdress*. Also in 1913, and perhaps for reasons not so far removed from this kind of adverse criticism of the painting, Apollinaire claimed that the exhibition of Matisse's *Tête d'expression* in 1907 gave rise to the terms *expressionisme* and *expressioniste* in France; see Flam, *Matisse on Art*, p. 32.

45 In the years 1907–9 Matisse was frequently accused of dishonesty and a kind of charlatanism in his painting. One of the best-known occasions was the review by Josephin Péladan that compelled Matisse to write his "Notes of a Painter"; see Benjamin, *Matisse's "Notes of a Painter"*, pp. 156–7 and, for examples of similar accusations by other critics, p. 286 n. 172; and Flam, *Matisse: The Man and His Art*, p. 293.

46 See *Les Soirées de Paris* (November 15, 1913), p. 19.

47 Guillaume Apollinaire quoted in Barr, *Matisse*, p. 183.

48 Flam, *Matisse: The Man and His Art*, p. 371. Years later, Dora Maar reacted with defiance to Picasso's equally radical abstractions from her appearance in his portraits of her: "They're all Picassos, not one is Dora Maar. . . . Do you think I care? Does Madame Cézanne care? Does Saskia Rembrandt care?"; quoted in Judi Freeman, *Picasso and the Weeping Women*, exh. cat. (Los Angeles County Museum of Art, 1994), p. 129.

49 On Matisse's self-expressive distortions of the appearance of his sitters in the context of this portrait as a form of "imitation," or internalization of them, see Richard Shiff, "Imitation of Matisse," in Caroline Turner and Roger Benjamin, eds., *Matisse*, exh. cat. (Brisbane: Queensland Art Gallery, 1995), pp. 42–3.

50 Vauxcelles and Salmon cited in Flam, *Matisse: The Man and His Art*, p. 372.

51 Apollinaire cited in Barr, *Matisse*, p. 183.

52 John Elderfield makes the contrasting claim that the blackness of the eyes in Matisse's portraits is a sign of preoccupation; "Describing Matisse," in *Henri Matisse: A Retrospective*, p. 41.

53 Flam, *Matisse: The Man and His Art*, p. 371.

54 This was suggested by Shiff, "Imitation of Matisse," p. 42.

55 In 1909–11, Rosalind Krauss implies, Picasso needed to make portraits because they belonged to "precisely that genre in which the image is understood to be transparent to a unique sitter who anchors the representation in the real world," allowing Picasso's substitution of verbal for visual representation. Rosalind E. Krauss, *The Picasso Papers* (New York: Farrar, Straus, and Giroux, 1998), p. 152 and p. 256 n. 50. In an interesting convergence, five Picasso collages were reproduced in the same issue of *Les Soirées de Paris* (November 1913) in which *Portrait of Madame Matisse* was illustrated.

56 Jack D. Flam, "Matisse and the Fauves," in William Rubin, ed., *"Primitivism" in 20th Century Art: Affinities of the Tribal and the Modern*, 2 vols. (New York: Museum of Modern Art, 1984), vol. 1: 214–15; also 230–31.

57 This process is related most recently and thoroughly by John Richardson (with the collaboration of Marilyn McCully), *A Life of Picasso*, vol. 1: *The Early Years, 1881–1906* (New York: Random House, 1991), ch. 26.

58 A different view of the stakes for both Stein and Picasso in the transaction of this portrait is expressed by Robert S. Lubar, "Unmasking Pablo's Gertrude: Queer Desire and the Subject of Portraiture," *Art Bulletin* 79 (March 1997): 57–84.

59 While *Portrait of Madame Matisse* was on view at the Salon d'Automne, Matisse wrote to his daughter, Marguerite, about how much effort it had cost him, but that he deserved the resulting success of the portrait; see Rémi Labrusse, ed., *Matisse: "La Révélation m'est venue de l'Orient,"* exh. cat. (Rome: Musei Capitolini, and Florence: Artificio, 1997), p. 160. I cannot go as far as Labrusse, who interprets Matisse's phrase about how the painting embodied his efforts ("Ceci est ma chair et mon sang") as the declaration of a kind of incarnation of himself in the portrait, but clearly Matisse felt he had given it his all and that this portrait of his wife represented him fully. I thank Rémi Labrusse for making the original French text of this publication available to me.

60 Although I certainly agree with Pierre Schneider about the importance of Matisse's family to his art, and despite the religious overtones in a few portraits of the artist's family members, I cannot follow him in seeing the family as Matisse's point of access to mythic sacred origins; *Matisse*, ch. 12, "The Family Prerogative." As I have made clear, I prefer to understand his portraits and other pictures of his family members as a staging ground for formal experiment and as a validation of his desire for self-representation outside the traditional formal limits of the self-portrait.

61 See ibid., p. 724.

62 See ibid., p. 24, where Schneider says that the exchange was omitted from the publication of the interview.

63 Despite Matisse's misspelling of his name, Allan Stein was a great favorite of the artist, and the following year he painted a large and important portrait of the boy (fig. 110) that is discussed in Chapter 5.

64 In response to a question from Alfred Barr, Matisse said that *Conversation* was not intended to represent specific personalities, but that the models were himself and his wife (Museum of Modern Art Archives, N.Y.: Alfred H. Barr, Jr. Papers, 11.I.B.1a.v). Despite his deflection, the self-referential qualities of *Conversation* are undeniable. Dating this painting has posed problems. Flam has argued that Matisse began it in 1908, resumed work on it in 1910, and may have finished it as late as 1912; *Matisse: The Man and His Art*, p. 249. The terminus date of 1912 has now been accepted by John Elderfield, *Henri Matisse: A Retrospective*, p. 184. Thus the painting was under work for a long time. Matisse's considerations and reconsiderations of the subject are reflected in the thick application of paint and in the prominent pentimenti.

65 Shchukin probably believed that Russian icons inspired Matisse here, but there is no evidence for this. Extensive discussion of many aspects of this painting may be found in several sources. There has been much effort at iconographic interpretation. In the long and fascinating "overture" to his book of 1984, Pierre Schneider, in addition to discussing Russian icons, likens the composition and grave atmosphere of *Conversation* to early Renaissance images of the Annunciation; *Matisse*, pp. 14–24. Flam gives the most complete and balanced assessment in *Matisse: The Man and His Art*, pp. 248–52, and proposes an intriguing compositional source, the stele of Hammurabi in the Louvre, which Matisse is likely to have known. Here I find Schneider's evocation of a more general iconographic tradition to be more enriching and compelling than Flam's interpretation, which, in imputing all the power in the "conversation" to Amélie (who, in Flam's words, "lays down the law"), distorts the reality of Matisse's dominance in his family.

66 On a visit to Matisse's house in Issy, I confirmed that this was the site of the painting. Some writers have incorrectly located the scene in a back room, overlooking Matisse's studio, which was at the rear limit of the property.

67 Although Elderfield apparently acknowledges the theme of marital discord in the painting, he does not recognize the "privileged" nature of the setting, the bedroom, as a reinforcement of the personal implications of this

representation; "Describing Matisse," in *Henri Matisse: A Retrospective*, p. 72 n. 89.

68 This was Olga Merson, who also sat for a portrait by Matisse (see Ch. 5, fig. 115). Flam implies, correctly in my view, that *Conversation*'s atmosphere of silent frustration presents a thematic contrast to Matisse's contemporaneous *Nymph and Satyr* (1908–9), an image of lustful sexuality that probably evoked his transgressive feelings toward Olga Merson; *Matisse: The Man and His Art*, pp. 248–9.

69 Stein, *Autobiography of Alice B. Toklas*, p. 150.

70 Henry James quoted in Robert Rosenblum and H. W. Janson, *19th-Century Art* (New York: Abrams, 1984), p. 379.

71 See Nicholas Watkins, *Matisse* (New York: Oxford University Press, 1985), p. 106.

72 Flam, *Matisse on Art*, p. 178.

73 Photographs of the Matisse family from this time and later reinforce this sense of estrangement and discomfort, as do witness accounts.

74 On these figures as "embodied ciphers" in the dominant decorative surroundings, see Deepak Ananth, "Frames within Frames: On Matisse and *The Orient*," in Paul Duro, ed., *The Rhetoric of the Frame: Essays on the Boundaries of the Artwork* (New York: Cambridge University Press, 1996), pp. 159–60.

75 Matisse also seems to have hoped that Michael Stein would buy the painting (he did not). The postcard with the sketch, and a related drawing of the boys playing checkers are reproduced in A. Izerghina et al., *Henri Matisse: Paintings and Sculptures in Soviet Museums*, trans. R. J. Rosengrant et al. (Leningrad: Aurora, 1978), pp. 159–60. Translations of the messages on the two cards may be found in Barr, *Matisse*, p. 152.

76 At this time Matisse was also taking an increased interest in the painting of Monet, which may have contributed to the relaxed and "impressionistic" rendering of *The Music Lesson*. See Paul Hayes Tucker, "The Revolution in the Garden: Monet in the Twentieth Century," in Paul Hayes Tucker and MaryAnne Stevens, eds., *Monet in the Twentieth Century* (New Haven and London: Yale University Press, 1998), p. 70. Yve-Alain Bois has also proposed, in the context of Matisse's fitful dialogue with Picasso, that in this painting Matisse was leaving Cubism behind; *Matisse and Picasso* (Paris: Flammarion, and Fort Worth: Kimbell Art Museum, 1999), p. 30.

77 On the sensual associations of this sculpture, related to the painting *Blue Nude* and Matisse's memories of exotic North Africa, see Theodore Reff, "Matisse: Meditations on a Statuette and Goldfish," *Arts Magazine* 51 (November 1976): 109–15.

78 Flam, *Matisse: The Man and His Art*, p. 452.

79 With the significant exception that, much later, Marguerite sided with Amélie Matisse in the matter of Henri and Amélie's marital problems.

80 Information from Archives Matisse, Paris.

81 See Jack D. Flam, "Some Observations on Matisse's Self-Portraits," *Arts Magazine* 49 (May 1975): 51.

82 The most extensive discussion of this painting, with special attention to its formal qualities, is John Elderfield, *Matisse in the Collection of the Museum of Modern Art* (New York: Museum of Modern Art, 1978), pp. 44–7.

83 In a brilliant analogy Pierre Schneider likens the disintegrated quality of the upper zone to consuming flames; *Matisse*, pp. 203–4.

84 Ibid., p. 203.

85 When *Marguerite Reading* was exhibited in the Salon d'Automne in 1906, critics noted an increase in intelligibility in Matisse's work; see Fourcade and Monod-Fontaine, *Henri Matisse 1904–1917*, p. 431.

86 An ink drawing of Marguerite's head and shoulders (New York, Museum of Modern Art) is usually said to be preparatory to this painting but is just as likely to have followed it, as it further refines and synthesizes the image.

87 Hilary Spurling emphasizes the strong visual sense of the Matisse children, especially Marguerite; *The Unknown Matisse*, p. 336.

88 See Richardson, *A Life of Picasso*, vol. 1, p. 417. Marguerite Duthuit told the photographer Brassaï that Picasso had chosen her portrait because he "was struck by its extreme simplicity"; Brassaï, *Conversations with Picasso* (1964), trans. Jane Marie Todd (Chicago and London: University of Chicago Press, 1999), p. 333.

89 See Spurling, *The Unknown Matisse*, p. 380.

90 Barr, *Matisse*, p. 131, described Marguerite as "in the rigid frontal pose of a Romanesque or Byzantine saint" and likened the black cat to a secular attribute. I cannot agree with Flam's proposal that the cat is a symbol of sexuality in this context; *Matisse: The Man and His Art*, p. 275.

91 Quoted in Flam, *Matisse: The Man and His Art*, p. 403.

92 Another anecdote about the development of *Tête blanche et rose*: Marguerite told her father that she thought an early version of the painting was "très jolie"; Matisse, in a rage, repainted it; Pierre Schneider in a lecture, "Matisse's *Italian Woman*," New York, Guggenheim Museum, November 22, 1982.

93 Pierre Matisse, personal communication. There is also the possibility that Pierre's portrait was based on a photograph; see John Russell, *Matisse: Father and Son* (New York: Abrams, 1999), p. 8, where a candidate for the photographic source is reproduced.

94 Elderfield, *Matisse in the Collection of the Museum of Modern Art*, p. 114.

95 A related photograph of Pierre playing the violin about 1916 is reproduced in Albert Kostenevich and Natalya Semyonova, *Collecting Matisse*, trans. Andrew Bromfield (Paris: Flammarion, 1993), p. 125.

96 Quoted in Schneider, *Matisse*, p. 334. The ceiling depicts Claude (Marguerite's son), Gérard (Jean's son), and Jacqueline (Pierre's daughter). The cousins were all nineteen years old when Matisse made the drawing in 1950. See Jackie Matisse Monnier, "Souvenirs," in Pierre Schneider, ed., *Matisse: Visages découverts, 1945–1954*, exh. cat. (Paris: Mona Bismarck Foundation and Adam Biro, 1996), p, 81.

97 Georges Duthuit, with typical candor, also identified this problem with individuation in Matisse's portraiture, noting that certain of Matisse's portraits "could well also be the portrait of a dozen other people"; Georges Duthuit, *Ecrits sur Matisse*, ed. Rémi Labrusse (Paris: Ecole Nationale Supérieur des Beaux-Arts, 1992), pp. 127–8.

98 In 1945, and perhaps at other times, Matisse made portraits of the absent children of Pierre Matisse from photographs: see Russell, *Matisse: Father and Son*, pp. 246–7.

99 Claude Duthuit, personal communication. For a selection of these drawings, see Schneider, *Matisse*, pp. 336–7.

100 Claude Duthuit, personal communication. See also Claude Duthuit, "Réflexions sur une séance de pose," in Schneider, ed., *Matisse: Visages découverts*, p. 73.

Chapter 4

1 Like many artists, Matisse had difficulty acknowledging the influence of others on his practice. To Apollinaire in 1907, in some of his first public statements, he claimed to "have never avoided the influence of others," but he also maintained that the best thing to do with influence was to subjugate it; Jack Flam, *Matisse on Art* (1973; rev. ed. Berkeley and Los Angeles: University of California Press, 1995), p. 29. While allowing that Cézanne, Van Gogh, and Gauguin had all been important influences on his early work, he believed the triumph of Fauvism to have been the rejection of all influences in favor of the pure expression of feeling; Dominique Fourcade, ed., *Henri Matisse: Ecrits et propos sur l'art* (Paris: Hermann, 1972), p. 98. Renoir was an exception – a living artist whom Matisse openly admired; but then, Matisse said of

Renoir that he was unusual because he was interesting for reasons other than his painting (ibid., p. 310). In any case, by then Renoir was no longer working.

2 Greta Moll, whose portrait Matisse painted in 1908 (see fig. 113), was an accomplished sculptor, but she was Matisse's student and admirer, and the portrait was a commission. Thus her independent status as an artist was not her principal identity in this portrait transaction.

3 On Matisse's relationship to Signac see Catherine C. Bock, *Henri Matisse and Neo-Impressionism, 1898–1908* (Ann Arbor: UMI Research Press, 1981). *Le Bonheur de vivre* was in a sense Matisse's third *chef d'oeuvre*: the first had been *The Dinner Table* (1897), his demonstration piece for Moreau; the second was *Luxe, calme et volupté*, his declaration of allegiance to Signac, a respected leader of the modernists. With *Le Bonheur de vive* (1905–6) Matisse became his own master.

4 Marquet was the main exception. Matisse met him at the Ecole des Arts Décoratifs in 1892, but their lasting friendship was strengthened when Marquet entered Moreau's studio in 1894.

5 Letter from Jean Puy to Charles Camoin, January 19, 1943, cited in Pierre Schneider, ed., *Henri Matisse: Exposition du centenaire*, exh. cat. (Paris: Grand Palais, 1970), p. 53.

6 See Isabelle Monod-Fontaine, Anne Baldassari, and Claude Laugier, *Oeuvres de Henri Matisse*, Collections du Musée National d'Art Moderne (Paris: Editions du Centre Georges Pompidou, 1989), p. 30, for reproductions of the last two paintings, and for the questions of attribution.

7 For the Manguin, see Bernard Dorival, "Nouvelles oeuvres de Matisse et Marquet au Musée national d'art moderne," *La Revue des arts* 7 (May–June 1957): 120; for the Puy, see William John Cowart III, "'Ecoliers' to 'Fauves': Matisse, Marquet, and Manguin Drawings, 1890–1906" (Ph.D. diss. Johns Hopkins University, 1972), fig. 245. For Marquet's *Camoin at his Easel* (1904), see Colette Audibert and Chuji Ikegami, eds., *Matisse et ses amis*, exh. cat. (Nishinomiya, Japan: Musée Otani des Beaux-Arts, 1981), no. 69.

8 Jean Puy quoted in John Elderfield, *The "Wild Beasts": Fauvism and its Affinities*, exh. cat. (New York: Museum of Modern Art, 1976), p. 20.

9 For Marquet, see ibid., p. 23; for Puy, see Schneider, *Henri Matisse: Exposition du centenaire*, p. 53.

10 To his son-in-law Georges Duthuit; in Fourcade, *Henri Matisse: Ecrits et propos sur l'art*, p. 95.

11 Flam, *Matisse on Art*, p. 121.

12 See Alfred H. Barr, Jr., *Matisse: His Art and His Public* (New York: Museum of Modern Art, 1951), p. 33; Jack Flam, *Matisse: The Man and His Art, 1869–1918* (Ithaca and London: Cornell University Press, 1986), pp. 34–5.

13 See Flam, *Matisse: The Man and His Art*, p. 109.

14 Roger Benjamin, "Une Copie par Matisse du *Balthazar Castiglione* de Raphaël," *La Revue du Louvre* 35, no. 4 (1985): 275–7. Matisse's copy was previously thought to date to the mid-1890s, when he made several other copies at the Louvre. Matisse himself probably generated the error by implying this; see Flam, *Matisse on Art*, pp. 106, 120, 201.

15 See Chapter 1, p. 22.

16 Françoise Heilbrun and Philippe Néagu, *Portraits d'artistes*, Les Dossiers du Musée d'Orsay, 7, exh. cat. (Paris: Editions de la Réunion des Musées Nationaux, 1986), p. 5.

17 See Cowart, "'Ecoliers' to 'Fauves'," fig. 161.

18 Manguin's portrait of Puy is in a private collection; Camoin's portrait of Marquet is in Paris, Musée National d'Art Moderne, Centre Georges Pompidou.

19 A point made more broadly about Fauvism by Gill Perry, *Women Artists and the Parisian Avant-Garde* (Manchester and New York: Manchester University Press, 1995), p. 49.

20 See Hélène Toussaint, *Les Portraits d'Ingres*, exh. cat. (Paris: Musée du Louvre, 1985), p. 8.

21 Lawrence Gowing, for instance, dated the painting to ca. 1900–02 in *Matisse* (London: Thames and Hudson, 1979), p. 37. Even so, he was uncomfortable with this date, finding it difficult to reconcile the Marquet portrait with the study from the model Bevilacqua (Gowing's fig. 22) as productions of the same time.

22 Camoin's earlier portrait of Marquet is also flavored strongly with Cézanne. Camoin alone among the Fauves knew Cézanne, and it seems likely that Camoin's exposure to some of Cézanne's portraits of Madame Cézanne or Joaquim Gasquet entered the conception of his own portrait of Marquet. Camoin figures Marquet as a man with the patience of Job, which one had to have to sit for Cézanne.

23 Raymond Escholier, *Matisse: A Portrait of the Artist and the Man*, trans. Geraldine and H. M. Colvile (New York: Praeger, 1960), p. 66.

24 As in Flam, *Matisse: The Man and His Art*, p. 124.

25 In this I agree with Marcelin Pleynet, who writes of Matisse's "appropriation" of Derain through the aggressive monogram in contrast to the more discreet signatures he affixed to the two portraits of Amélie that year; *Henri Matisse: Qui êtes-vous?* (Lyons: La Manufacture, 1988), pp. 83–4. But I contend that Matisse just as surely "appropriated" Amélie, albeit through other means.

26 See Ronald Alley, *The Tate Gallery's Collection of Modern Art other than Works by British Artists* (London: Tate Gallery, 1981), pp. 166, 493.

27 Its wildness even overshadowed the identity of the sitter at one point: after it left the Stein collection the portrait of Derain was exhibited in 1925 as a "Buste d'un Maroquin" [sic]; see Dominique Fourcade and Isabelle Monod-Fontaine, *Henri Matisse 1904–1917*, exh. cat. (Paris: Centre Georges Pompidou, 1993), p. 166.

28 Another drawing by Matisse of Terrus is in a French private collection.

29 See Escholier, *Matisse*, p. 65.

30 Apparently Derain also made a double portrait of Matisse and Terrus, "two solid fellows," which has not been traced; ibid, p. 66.

31 Marc Laforgue on Terrus quoted in ibid., p. 66; Maillol quoted in *Aristide Maillol*, exh. cat. (Buffalo: Albright Knox Art Gallery, 1945), p. 50.

32 Terrus was also the subject of a portrait sculpture by Maillol from 1905, reproduced in John Rewald, *Maillol* (London: Hyperion, 1939), no. 147. One of Maillol's few painted portraits was also of Terrus, and another was of Renoir, who in the early twentieth century also stood for the classical, Mediterranean spirit; see Denys Chevalier, *Maillol* (New York: Crown, 1978), p. 89. On Terrus and Matisse, see Hilary Spurling, *The Unknown Matisse: A Life of Henri Matisse: The Early Years, 1869–1908* (London: Hamish Hamilton; New York: Knopf, 1998), pp. 307–10; also Jean-Pierre Barou, *Matisse ou le miracle de Collioure* (Montpellier: Indigène, 1997), p. 45 – however, this book, an imaginative account of Matisse's summer in Collioure, must be used with caution.

33 See Albert E. Elsen, *The Sculpture of Henri Matisse* (New York: Abrams, 1972), p. 116. Matisse's bust of his son Pierre is illustrated on p. 117.

34 In emphasizing the general over the individual in these portrait heads I am at odds with Elsen's view of them as highly particularized.

35 See Victor I. Carlson, *Matisse as a Draughtsman*, exh. cat. (Baltimore Museum of Art, 1971), p. 48.

36 If, as some writers have suggested, the portrait of Jeanne Manguin dates to 1905, the differences between Matisse's conceptions of the two women would be even more striking and significant: see Elderfield, *The "Wild Beasts"*, p. 182 n. 14; Flam, *Matisse: The Man and His Art*, p. 148.

37 Pierre Matisse, personal communication.

38 Barr called attention to the contrast in this painting between the informal and the monumental; *Matisse*, p. 94.

39 Flam comments that this painting is at once

Matisse's most painterly and most sculptural self-portrait; *Matisse: The Man and His Art*, pp. 183–4.

40 Lucile M. Golson, "The Michael Steins of San Francisco: Art Patrons and Collectors," in Margaret Potter, ed., *Four Americans in Paris: The Collections of Gertrude Stein and Her Family*, exh. cat. (New York: Museum of Modern Art, 1970), p. 43.

41 Gertrude Stein said this of Matisse in 1909 when he raised his prices without giving her favored status; see Leon Katz, "Matisse, Picasso and Gertrude Stein," in ibid., p. 55.

42 *Son portrait* by Matisse is no. 84 in the catalogue, *Portraits d'hommes* (Paris: Galerie Bernheim-Jeune, 1907).

43 In addition Walter Sickert, Auguste Rodin, and Ker-Xavier Roussel exhibited nothing but a single self-portrait. The great modernist father figures Van Gogh, Gauguin, and Cézanne – all dead – were also represented by self-portraits. Thus the organizers of the show, who chose the latter paintings, seem to have sanctioned this focus by some of the living artists. See Donald E. Gordon, *Modern Art Exhibitions, 1900–1916*, 2 vols. (Munich: Prestel, 1974), vol. 2: 239–41.

44 As Kirk Varnedoe has characterized Picasso's picture; "Picasso's Self-Portraits," in William Rubin, ed., *Picasso and Portraiture: Representation and Transformation* (New York: Museum of Modern Art, 1996), p. 136.

45 See Flam, *Matisse: The Man and His Art*, p. 386.

46 Pierre Matisse, personal communication.

47 Walter Pach, *Queer Thing, Painting* (New York: Harper and Brothers, 1938), pp. 219–20.

48 For the ensemble of these portraits, see Claude Duthuit and Marguerite Duthuit-Matisse, with the collaboration of Françoise Garnaud, *Henri Matisse, catalogue raisonné de l'oeuvre gravé*, 2 vols. (Paris: Claude Duthuit, 1983), vol. 1, nos. 14–76.

49 Jack Flam also noted that the "Utamaro" etching is apparently a portrait of Marguerite (*Matisse: The Man and His Art*, p. 402).

50 Duthuit, *Henri Matisse, catalogue raisonné de l'oeuvre gravé*, vol. 1, no. 40.

51 See Kenneth E. Silver, *Esprit de Corps: The Art of the Parisian Avant-Garde and the First World War, 1914–1925* (Princeton University Press, 1989), pp. 59–61, for an extended discussion of Matisse's project within the author's general analysis of art during the war, to which I am indebted. For Matisse's expression of his aid efforts in the war, including the sale of these portrait prints, see letter of June 7, 1915 to Jacques Doucet, whose help in the cause he was soliciting, in Fourcade and Monod-Fontaine, *Henri Matisse 1904–1917*, p. 116.

52 Clément Janin admiringly compared Matisse's linear style with Ingres's and Rodin's; "Les Estampes et la guerre," *Gazette des Beaux-Arts* 59 (1917): 382, cited in Silver, *Esprit de Corps*, p. 60.

53 One critic, André Dezarrois, associated portraiture with heroism in battle; Silver, *Esprit de Corps*, pp. 417–18 n. 63.

54 Elizabeth Louise Kahn, *The Neglected Majority: "Les Camoufleurs," Art History, and World War I* (Lanham, Md.: University Press of America, 1984), pp. 40–45, discusses extensively the importance of neutral representational styles in the art of the war.

55 See Flam, *Matisse: The Man and His Art*, figs. 433, 434.

56 Three other pencil drawings of Massine are in the collection of the Bibliothèque Nationale de France, Paris.

57 Some of the Matisse–Pallady letters were published in the Romanian journal *Secolul* 20, no. 6 (1965).

58 See Pierre Schneider, *Matisse*, trans. Michael Taylor and Bridget Strevens Romer (New York: Rizzoli, 1984), p. 374.

59 For other portraits of Pallady, see Lydia Delectorskaya, *Henri Matisse: Contre vents et marées: Peinture et livres illustrés de 1939 à 1943* (Paris: Editions Irus et Vincent Hansma, 1996), pp. 40–43, 87.

60 Matisse, letter to Théodor Pallady (1940), quoted in Schneider, *Matisse*, p. 45.

61 Detailed in the tart memoir of Matisse written by Bussy's daughter Jane Simone Bussy, "A Great Man," *Burlington Magazine* 128 (February 1986): 80–84.

62 Nicholas Watkins, *Matisse* (New York: Oxford University Press, 1985), p. 10.

63 Simon Bussy quoted in François Fosca, *Simon Bussy* (Paris: Gallimard, 1930), p. 9.

64 Matisse's correspondence with Bussy extended over many years, beginning in 1903 and continuing until a few months before Matisse's death. Copies of Matisse's letters, most of them unpublished, are on deposit at the Courtauld Institute of Art, London, and at the National Gallery of Art, Washington, D.C.

65 Both cited in Fourcade, *Matisse: Écrits et propos sur l'art*, p. 309.

66 The best analysis of Matisse as a writer is Jack Flam's introduction to *Matisse on Art* (1995).

67 Letter of September 1, 1940, cited in Barr, *Matisse*, p. 256.

68 In Rouveyre's heyday as a satiric illustrator, Marquet had painted a full-length portrait of him as a rakish bohemian (1904; Paris, Musée National d'Art Moderne, Centre Georges Pompidou).

69 Matisse's letters to Rouveyre, numbering over five hundred, are in the collection of the Kongelige Bibliotek, Copenhagen.

70 Henry de Montherlant, *Sur les femmes* (Paris: Sagittaire, 1942).

71 Fourcade, *Henri Matisse: Ecrits et propos sur l'art*, p. 179.

72 Matisse erroneously dated many of the drawings of Aragon to March 1943. They all date from March 1942. See Dominique Fourcade, "65 Dessins de Matisse dans les collections du Musée national d'art moderne," *Cahiers du Musée National d'Art Moderne*, no. 13 (1984): 15.

73 Henri Matisse, *Dessins: Thèmes et variations* (Paris: Martin Fabiani, 1943).

74 See Barr, *Matisse*, p. 268.

75 Flam, *Matisse on Art*, p. 135.

76 Louis Aragon, *Henri Matisse, roman*, 2 vols. (Paris: Gallimard, 1971); published in English as *Henri Matisse: A Novel*, trans. Jean Stewart, 2 vols. (New York: Harcourt Brace Jovanovich, 1972). Four charcoal drawings of Aragon are reproduced in vol. 1: 171 and vol. 2: 15, 48, 49. Thirty-four of the pen-and-ink drawings are reproduced in vol. 2: 50–54. Twenty years later, Andy Warhol unwittingly paid homage to Matisse's "cinema" in such photo-booth multiple portraits as *Ethel Scull 36 Times* (1963; New York, Whitney Museum of American Art).

77 André Rouveyre, ed., *Choix de pages de Paul Léautaud* (Paris: Editions du Bélier, 1946).

78 Paul Léautaud quoted in Schneider, *Matisse*, p. 406, which contains an abbreviated account of the affair. For Léautaud's views on the matter see his *Journal littéraire*, 19 vols. (Paris: Mercure de France, 1954–66), vol. 16: 362–4; vol. 17: 73–4; vol. 18: 96, 194–5. A charcoal drawing of Léautaud with the Galerie Dina Vierny, Paris, in 1987, inscribed to the sitter, may be the drawing Matisse gave to him.

79 Léautaud quoted in André Rousseaux, "Le Journal de Paul Léautaud," *Le Figaro littéraire*, November 13, 1954, p. 2. Compare Matisse's confession, "Je ne m'intéresse qu'à moi," quoted in Bussy, "A Great Man," p. 81.

80 André Rouveyre, *Apollinaire* (Paris: Raisons d'Etre, 1952).

81 The photograph of Apollinaire is reproduced in Monod-Fontaine, *Oeuvres de Henri Matisse*, p. 274.

82 Matisse performed a similar process of rejuvenation two years later in two portraits of the Russian writer Ilya Ehrenburg: first he made a charcoal study of the writer's face; then another was made "d'après Ilya Ehrenbourg et après avoir vu le film *Notre Jeunesse*." Matisse included both drawings in his book *Portraits* (Monte Carlo: André Sauret, 1954), nos. 58, 59.

Chapter 5

1 From 1910 to 1926, with a hiatus in 1915–17. For the contracts, see Alfred H. Barr, Jr., *Matisse: His Art and His Public* (New York: Museum of Modern Art, 1951), pp. 553–5.

2 We have already seen Vollard's exemplary anecdote about the importance some people attributed to having their portrait painted by the right artist (Chapter 1, p. 30). To this may be added John Quinn's comments on the portrait of Jeanne Robert Foster that he commissioned from Derain. Quinn thought it "too sensual" – that is, too much like the woman herself. Derain's response: "I know Quinn's trouble. He doesn't want a portrait; he wants 'a Derain'." B. L. Reid, *The Man from New York: John Quinn and his Friends* (New York: Oxford University Press, 1968), p. 593.

3 Matisse quoted in Roger Benjamin, *Matisse's "Notes of a Painter:" Criticism, Theory and Context, 1891–1908* (Ann Arbor: UMI Research Press, 1987), p. 106.

4 On the rift between Matisse and Gertrude Stein, see Jack Flam, *Matisse: The Man and His Art, 1869–1918* (Ithaca and London: Cornell University Press, 1986), p. 394. On the Steins and their collecting, see Margaret Potter, ed., *Four Americans in Paris: The Collections of Gertrude Stein and Her Family*, exh. cat. (New York: Museum of Modern Art, 1970).

5 In May 1911 he mailed a sketch of his large canvas *The Painter's Family* (fig. 59) to Michael Stein. On another card Matisse told the Steins that he hoped "to have it still in September when you come back," which sounds like an overture to the Steins to buy the family portrait (Sergei Shchukin bought it that summer instead). For the postcards, see Barr, *Matisse*, pp. 152–3.

6 See Potter, *Four Americans in Paris*, p. 160.

7 See Michael P. Mezzatesta, *Henri Matisse, Sculptor/Painter: A Formal Analysis of Selected Works*, exh. cat. (Fort Worth: Kimbell Art Museum, 1984), p. 64. As a comparison Mezzatesta illustrates a standing figure from Giotto's Peruzzi Chapel in Santa Croce, Florence (his fig. 37).

8 I thank George Keyes, then at the Minneapolis Institute of Arts, for allowing me to examine the x-ray photographs of this painting in the museum's files.

9 Mezzatesta, *Henri Matisse, Sculptor/Painter*, p. 65.

10 *Boy with a Butterfly Net* also has a typological heritage in such paintings of children in adult guises as Velasquez's portraits of the six-year-old Prince Baltasar Carlos as a hunter (Madrid, Prado) or Manet's *Boy with a Sword* (New York, Metropolitan Museum of Art).

11 The sense of specificity found in the painted portrait is also present in drawings Matisse made of Allan Stein: one showing several heads is reproduced in Pierre Schneider, *Matisse*, trans. Michael Taylor and Bridget Strevens Romer (New York: Rizzoli, 1984), p. 733, as "studies" for the painted portrait; another, later, drawing is reproduced in Potter, *Four Americans in Paris*, p. 161.

12 Greta and Oskar Moll, soon to be two of Matisse's students, bought the painting, probably in early 1908. A statement by Pierre Matisse (born 1900) that he saw the portrait of Allan Stein in the Paris apartment of Michael and Sarah Stein is confusing but just possible, if the painting were with the Steins temporarily – on approval? – before being bought by the Molls (letter from Pierre Matisse, September 13, 1983, in the curatorial file for the painting at the Minneapolis Institute of Arts).

13 See Flam, *Matisse: The Man and His Art*, p. 217.

14 Sarah Stein's statements about Matisse's teaching methods form the most valuable account of this aspect of his career; see "Sarah Stein's Notes," in Jack Flam, *Matisse on Art* (1973; rev. ed. Berkeley and Los Angeles: University of California Press, 1995), pp. 44–52.

15 Letter from Greta Moll to Alfred Barr, April 20, 1951, in Barr, *Matisse*, p. 129.

16 The contract that Matisse signed with Galerie Bernheim-Jeune in the following year, 1909, specified a net price of 1500 francs for a canvas the size of *Greta Moll*. The retail price would have been about double this. As we have seen, however, under the terms of his contract Matisse was free to accept portrait commissions directly, with no obligation to the gallery. Hilary Spurling's assertion that the price of 1000 francs was "at the top of [Matisse's] price range" does not square with the prices set by the contract; see *The Unknown Matisse: A Life of Henri Matisse: The Early Years, 1869–1908* (New York: Knopf, 1998), p. 411.

17 On the Molls' collection of Matisse's work, see Peter Kropmanns, "Matisse und die Molls, seine bedeutendsten deutschen Sammler," in *Oskar Moll: Gemälde und Aquarelle*, exh. cat. (Mainz: Landesmuseum, 1997), pp. 76–92.

18 Greta Moll quoted in Barr, *Matisse*, p. 129.

19 Hans Purrmann, "Über Henri Matisse," *Werk* 3 (June 1946): 191; trans. in the Archives of The Museum of Modern Art, New York, Alfred H. Barr, Jr. Papers, 11. I.B. Ia. viii.

20 "Malgré mes efforts j'étais resté dans les sensations de charme dont mon modèle ne manquait pas, mais je n'avais pu obtenir son aspect de statue. J'en étais presque découragé, je savais pourtant qu'un portrait de caractère semblable existait déjà, il était placé au Louvre, dans le longue galerie de la Seine et signé Véronèse. On y voyait le même développement du corps d'une jeune fille italienne sur le point d'éclore dans toute sa beauté. Les proportions du modèle étaient presque semblable à celles de Mme O. Moll. Je décidai donc d'aller spécialement au Louvre pour revoir ce Véronèse. Il me pénétra par son évidence qui m'était bien restée dans l'esprit et sans me laisser distraire par d'autre peinture, je filais au plus vite à mon atelier du couvent. Je me souviens qu'il était à peu près 5 ou 7 heures du soir et que je m'enfermais sous clef avec la volonté de ne pas être dérangé. C'est sous le coup de cette révélation du Véronèse que je repris mon portrait. Sans aucune prudence, j'y travaillais une heure peut être deux j'avais le sentiment ensuite de m'être délivré de la meilleure façon. Le lendemain quand Mme O. Moll revient pour sa séance de travail je lui déclarai que son portrait était terminé et elle fut effondrée du résultat et me demanda la permission d'aller chercher son mari. Je les ai vus complètement anéantis devant le résultat de mon travail qui leur parut désastreux. Ils regrettaient toutes les boucles blondes et les colorations diverses du portrait. Après leur avoir rappelé une des conditions de notre accord je leurs dis qu'ils n'étaient pas obligés de le prendre et je les laissais. Ce n'est que le surlendemain qu'ils me firent dire par Hans Purrmann notre ami commun qu'ils acceptaient. Ce portrait fut par la suite très apprécié, même par eux et je me dis encore une fois que Bonnard avait raison de déclarer qu'un portrait finit toujours par être ressemblant." The translation is mine. Matisse's statement was previously translated into German in Kropmanns, "Matisse und die Molls," pp. 85–6. I have not been able to confirm the precise source of the statement, which Matisse apparently made in the 1940s. I am grateful to Wanda de Guébriant of the Archives Matisse, Paris, for making it available to me.

21 This is the only painting then attributed to Veronese in the Louvre that corresponds to Greta Moll's description, despite her denial, "not with a white blouse" (this was probably a response to Purrmann's description). While it is true that the position of the woman's arms in *Woman and Child with a Dog* is different from Moll's pose, the conception of the bare arms themselves as smooth boneless shapes is strikingly similar. It has sometimes been asserted that Veronese's well-known portrait of a woman called *La Bella Nani* is the painting that Matisse had in mind; see, among others, Pierre Schneider, *Matisse et l'Italie*, exh. cat. (Venice: Museo Correr, 1987), pp. 23–4; and Spurling, *The Unknown Matisse*, p. 410. This painting cannot have been Matisse's inspiration, however, because it was still in a private collection in 1908; it entered the Louvre in 1915; see Terisio Pignatti, *Veronese: l'opera completa*, 2 vols. (Venice: Alfieri, 1976), no. 104. Even had it been accessible to Matisse, *La Bella Nani* is an unlikely model, if only because her arms, which are the point of the relationship, are completely covered by her decorated sleeves. Independently, Peter

Kropmanns has also proposed *Woman and Child with a Dog* as the painting that helped Matisse complete his portrait; "Matisse und die Molls," p. 86.

22 Greta Moll stated this in another account of the portrait commission, which otherwise differs little from that in her letter to Alfred Barr; see Margarete Moll, "Erinnerungen an Henri Matisse," in *Matisse und seine deutschen Schüler*, exh. cat. (Kaiserslautern: Pfalzgalerie, 1988), p. 45. Letters from Matisse to the Molls were destroyed in the Second World War (letter to the author from Iris Filmer, granddaughter of Oskar and Greta Moll, September 3, 1986).

23 The quoted phrase occurs in a general discussion of arms in Sarah Stein's notes on Matisse's teaching; Flam, *Matisse on Art*, p. 47.

24 From Sarah Stein's notes; ibid., p. 48.

25 See Raymond Escholier, *Matisse: A Portrait of the Artist and the Man*, trans. Geraldine and H. M. Colvile (New York: Praeger, 1960), p. 33. Vollard reported that, during one of his many sittings for Cézanne's portrait of him (Paris, Petit Palais), he pointed out to the artist some unpainted spots; Cézanne replied that they must be very carefully considered so that he would not have to repaint the entire picture; Ambroise Vollard, *Cézanne* (Paris: the author, 1914); cited in William Rubin, ed., *Cézanne: The Late Work*, exh. cat. (New York: Museum of Modern Art, 1977), pp. 387–8. A substantial group of Cézanne's portraits was exhibited in the retrospective exhibition of his work in the Salon d'Automne of 1907, not many months before Matisse began his portrait of Greta Moll. It is clear from the changes in Matisse's work in general in the years 1907–9 that he was much influenced by Cézanne at this time.

26 See Flam, *Matisse on Art*, p. 40.

27 Picasso's statement is cited in John Richardson (with the collaboration of Marilyn McCully), *A Life of Picasso*, vol. 1: *The Early Years, 1881–1906* (New York: Random House, 1991), p. 455, quoting Roland Penrose. Penrose added his own confirmation of Picasso's claim: "And she did."

28 This painting has often been dated to 1909 (see, for instance, Flam, *Matisse: The Man and His Art*, p. 258), but a date of 1908 is confirmed by the bill of sale from Galerie Bernheim-Jeune dated November 23, 1908; see Diana C. duPont et al., *San Francisco Museum of Modern Art: The Painting and Sculpture Collection* (New York: Hudson Hills Press, 1985), p. 236.

29 Levy, a San Francisco friend of the Steins, paid 1950 francs for the picture. Considering that, under the terms of the contract Matisse signed in the following year with Bernheim-Jeune, the retail price for a painting of that size would be about 1500 francs, *The Girl with Green Eyes* was expensive. Although an acquaintance of Matisse or Levy may have been the sitter, it is possible that the painting depicts a hired model. Matisse included the work in his book *Portraits* as *Mlle X . . . La Femme aux yeux verts*. While not conclusive on this point, the designation "X" usually signifies one whose identity is known but is not disclosed for reasons of discretion; hired models had no identity in this sense.

30 At the Salon des Indépendants in Paris in 1909; in his exhibition at Bernheim-Jeune in 1910; and in London at the Grafton Galleries in the same year, in one of its groundbreaking exhibitions of Post-Impressionist art organized by Roger Fry.

31 C. J. Holmes, *Notes on the Post-Impressionist Painters, Grafton Galleries, 1910–11* (London: Philip Lee Warner, 1910), pp. 15–16, 31.

32 Jack Flam has convincingly dated this portrait to the summer of 1911 as against the traditional date of 1910; *Matisse: The Man and His Art*, p. 498 n. 35.

33 Ibid., pp. 314–15. Merson's "especial interest" in Matisse was noted at the time; see Alice B. Toklas, *What is Remembered* (New York: Holt, Rinehart and Winston, 1963), p. 38.

34 For another characterization of the way the black arcs mediate between the figure of Olga Merson and the picture that represents her, see Richard Shiff, "Imitation of Matisse," in Caroline Turner and Roger Benjamin, eds., *Matisse*, exh. cat. (Brisbane: Queensland Art Gallery, 1995), p. 47.

35 Barr, *Matisse*, p. 131.

36 Jack Flam, personal communication. Given these circumstances, it is not surprising that Matisse never exhibited the portrait, despite the obvious boldness of formal means that made it representative of his most advanced work. Rather than the arcs binding together sitter and picture (as Shiff and I suggest), perhaps they were part of Matisse's means of distancing himself, as an artist, from the bodily figure of Olga Merson, object of desire.

37 I cannot see, with Flam, even a covert flower metaphor in this portrait of Marguerite; *Matisse: The Man and His Art*, p. 275: "The girl's head . . . rests on her shoulders like a flower." Perhaps Matisse was making a different kind of thematic link between this painting and his portrait of Jeanne Vaderin from the same year – opposing animal and vegetable metaphors.

38 I am indebted to the focused discussion of this drawing in John Elderfield, *The Modern Drawing* (New York: Museum of Modern Art, 1983), p. 56.

39 The belief that Shchukin's reason for returning to Moscow was that he learned of his brother's suicide is corrected by Natalya Semyonova, "The Story of an Encounter," in Albert Kostenevich and Natalya Semyonova, *Collecting Matisse*, trans. Andrew Bromfield (Paris: Flammarion, 1993), p. 43. The terms of the commission – if formal terms were made – have never been reported. That the portrait was a commission has been questioned (ibid.), but this may be a moot point because Shchukin liked everything he saw by Matisse.

40 Fernande Olivier, *Picasso et ses amis* (Paris: Stock, 1933), p. 143; cited in Barr, *Matisse: His Art and His Public*, p. 106.

41 Typescript of conversations with Matisse by Courthion, 1941; Pierre Matisse Gallery Archives, Pierpont Morgan Library, New York, Box 192, File 20. Albert Kostenevich points out that in the drawing Matisse stressed Eastern, almost Mongol features that Shchukin did not have; "The Russian Collectors and Henri Matisse," in Jack Cowart and Pierre Schneider, *Matisse in Morocco: The Paintings and Drawings, 1912–1913*, exh. cat. (Washington, D.C.: National Gallery of Art, 1990), p. 251; Flam, *Matisse on Art*, p. 206. Whatever Matisse's particular cultural inspiration, or preconception, he exaggerated Shchukin's appearance to distance him from Western European norms.

42 Matisse's drawing is in the San Francisco Museum of Modern Art, Harriet Lane Levy Bequest. In these years when he was competing with Picasso for the attentions of American patrons, Matisse may have been familiar with Picasso's own gesture to Courbet, a drawing inscribed "Bonjour Mlle Cone" and sent to Etta Cone in 1907; illustrated in Potter, *Four Americans in Paris*, p. 77.

43 See Victor I. Carlson, *Matisse as a Draughtsman*, exh. cat. (Baltimore Museum of Art, 1971), p. 62. On the other hand, an argument could be made for the pen drawing as the final version, since Matisse inscribed it to Levy.

44 Both of Albert Landsberg's tracings are in the Alfred H. Barr, Jr. Papers, Archives of The Museum of Modern Art, New York.

45 The classic discussion of the portrait is by Alfred Barr, with its compact and solid speculations about the sources of Matisse's conception of the portrait in Futurist theory and Henri Bergson's philosophy of *élan vital*; *Matisse*, pp. 184–5. The most thorough and broadly considered study is the unpublished M.A. thesis (University of Pennsylvania, 1981) by Maud Lavin, "An Analysis of Henri Matisse's 1914 *Portrait of Mlle Yvonne Landsberg*." On the Bergsonian character of the form Matisse gave the portrait, see Mark Antliff, "The Rhythms of Duration: Bergson and the Art of Matisse," in John Mullarkey, ed., *The New Bergson* (Manchester and New

York: Manchester University Press, 1999), pp. 199–200. Antliff also gives a sophisticated analysis of Matisse's pencil drawings of Mabel Bayard Warren (1913; Boston, Museum of Fine Arts) in terms of how they express the Bergsonian "rhythmic duration" of the sitter (pp. 197–9). On the Warren portraits see also Flam, *Matisse: The Man and His Art*, pp. 373–5.

46 See Barr, *Matisse*, p. 184.

47 Flam, *Matisse: The Man and His Art*, p. 502 n. 15.

48 See Lavin, "An Analysis," pp. 7–8, based on her study of an x-ray photograph of the painting, which shows that although Matisse made many changes, he determined the basic pose early in the portrait's development.

49 Barr, *Matisse*, p. 184. Albert Landsberg also likened Matisse's rendering of his sister to a "chrysallis," an obvious parallel to the image of budding flowers; letter from Alert Landsberg to Alfred Barr, June 26, 1951, in MoMA Archives, N.Y., AHB, 11. I.A. 9.

50 See Flam, *Matisse: The Man and His Art*, p. 502 n. 22.

51 Barr hedged, calling the lines "only superficially spontaneous" but "probably not premeditated"; *Matisse*, p. 184.

52 See Lavin, "An Analysis," pp. 9–10. As Lavin pointed out, the drawing does not show Yvonne in the final posture she assumes in the painting, and it does not reflect Matisse's final addition of the thick black lines of paint marking interior contours. Albert Landsberg also stated that Matisse may have made the incisions both during the final sitting and immediately after it, further evidence against spontaneity; letter from Albert Landsberg to Alfred Barr, June 26, 1951, in MoMA Archives, N.Y., AHB, 11. I.A. 9.

53 Barr, *Matisse*, p. 184. Claude Duthuit made the similar suggestion that Matisse needed to create an armature for his image of Yvonne Landsberg; "La physionomie de la jeune fille manquait de force: pas un angle, pas une saillie pour lui permettre, selon sa propre expression, d' 'accrocher' son sujet!"; "Réflexions sur une Séance de pose," in Pierre Schneider, ed., *Matisse: Visages découverts, 1945–1954*, exh. cat. (Paris: Mona Bismarck Foundation and Adam Biro, 1996), p. 71.

54 Frank Trapp, "Form and Symbol in the Art of Matisse," *Arts Magazine* 49 (May 1975): 57.

55 In a letter of July 8, 1914 to Mrs. Frances Gordon Burton-Smith, Prichard relayed Matisse's response to *Mlle Yvonne Landsberg*, as reported to Prichard by "a friend" (probably Albert Landsberg): "Matisse dit lui-même que c'est un peu énorme et que son tableau le choque un peu lui-même, qu'il se sent mal à l'aise, un peu surpris." The letter was printed as part of an insert in some copies of *Henri Matisse Exhibition*, New York, Montross Gallery, 1915. My thanks to Jack Flam for a copy of this text.

56 See Barr, *Matisse*, p. 184.

57 Letter from Albert Landsberg to Alfred Barr, quoted in ibid., p. 184 n. 6.

58 According to a later statement by Georges Duthuit, Matisse's son-in-law; Fourcade and Monod-Fontaine, *Henri Matisse 1904–1917*, p. 500.

59 Lawrence Gowing, *Matisse* (London: Thames and Hudson, 1979), p. 127.

60 Matisse sold the portrait of Yvonne Landsberg at an "extremely reduced" price to Walter Arensberg; see John Cauman, "Henri Matisse's Letters to Walter Pach," *Archives of American Art Journal* 31, no. 3 (1991): 6.

61 A photograph showing Matisse in his Paris studio with finished portraits of Michael and Sarah Stein, and the unfinished portrait of Greta Prozor, has been convincingly dated by Jack Flam to late 1916; it is reproduced in *Matisse: The Man and His Art*, p. 434.

62 See Dominique Fourcade, "Greta Prozor d'Henri Matisse," *Cahiers du Musée National d'Art Moderne*, no. 11 (June 1983): 104. I am indebted to Fourcade's thorough study for the circumstances surrounding this portrait. See also Isabelle Monod-Fontaine, Anne Baldassari, and Claude Laugier, *Matisse*, Collections du Musée National d'Art Moderne (Paris: Editions du Centre Pompidou, 1989), pp. 53–7, and pp. 177–83 for related drawings of Prozor.

63 See Rémi Labrusse, ed., *Matisse: "La Révélation m'est venue de l'Orient,"* exh. cat. (Rome: Musei Capitolini and Florence: Artificio, 1997), p. 166.

64 Barr, *Matisse*, p. 189.

65 For Matisse's statement about Sarah Stein, see Lucile M. Golson, "The Michael Steins of San Francisco: Art Patrons and Collectors," in Potter, *Four Americans in Paris*, p. 35.

66 On this situation and its impact on Matisse's patronage see John Klein, "Objects of Desire and Irresistible Forces: Matisse Between Patrons, Collectors, and War," in *Henri Matisse: Four Great Collectors*, ed. Kasper Monrad, exh. cat. (Copenhagen: Statens Museum for Kunst, 1999), pp. 11–23.

67 Flam, *Matisse: The Man and His Art*, pp. 434–5.

68 Schneider, *Matisse*, p. 326.

69 See Golson in Potter, *Four Americans in Paris*, p. 38.

70 A photograph showing Michael Stein posing for Matisse is reproduced in Barr, *Matisse*, p. 26.

71 Another preparatory study for the painting, this on a canvas nearly as large as the finished portrait and evidently done after the charcoal, is reproduced in Schneider, *Matisse*, p. 326.

72 Barr, *Matisse*, p. 189; Schneider, *Matisse*, p. 326.

73 Note in the painting's file in the archives of the San Francisco Museum of Modern Art.

74 Letter from Matisse to Walter Pach, December 14, 1916, quoted in Dominique Fourcade and Isabelle Monod-Fontaine, *Henri Matisse 1904–1917*, exh. cat. (Paris: Centre Georges Pompidou, 1993), p. 500. Matisse wrote this letter at about the same time he finished the portraits of Michael and Sarah Stein.

75 See Fourcade and Monod-Fontaine, *Henri Matisse 1904–1917*, p. 396.

76 See Anne Distel, "Auguste Pellerin," in *Le Petit Larousse de la peinture* (Paris: Larousse, 1979), II: 1403–4.

77 See Sophie Monneret, *Impressionisme et son époque*, 2 vols. (Paris: Denoël, 1979), vol. 2: 114; also Sylvie Gache-Patin, "Douze oeuvres de Cézanne de l'ancienne collection Pellerin," *La Revue du Louvre* 34, no. 2 (1984): 128–46.

78 See Barr, *Matisse*, p. 189. It is not known who put up the extra money, but one presumes Pellerin himself.

79 The painting is illustrated in Colin B. Bailey, ed., *Renoir's Portraits: Impressions of an Age*, exh. cat. (New Haven and London: Yale University Press and National Gallery of Canada, Ottawa, 1997), p. 115.

80 Matisse did the first version in late 1916. The second version is dated May 1917 on the canvas. Matisse was in Nice from January to May of that year; this absence from Paris, where he made both portraits, accounts for the delay of several months between the first portrait and the second, although it is not known if Matisse began the second painting before going south. A bust-length drawing of Pellerin, tentative and probing but distilling the sitter's features to the essential lines of the second painted version, was probably done between the two paintings, perhaps as a way of getting back to the commission after the hiatus. Matisse kept this drawing; see Monod-Fontaine et al., *Matisse*, pp. 58–9, 184–5, where the drawing is illustrated.

81 Georges Duthuit, *Les Fauves* (Geneva: Éditions des Trois Collines, 1949), p. 229.

82 No photographs of Pellerin from this period, and no other portraits, have come to light.

83 Now at the Baltimore Museum of Art, the painting belonged to Leo Stein by 1905. See Rubin, *Cézanne: The Late Work*, p. 397.

84 Matisse's Cézannes are now in the collections of the Philadelphia Museum of Art and the Musée d'Orsay, Paris.

85 Here is Alfred Barr in the context of the Pellerin commission: "Matisse . . . rarely seems at his best or even at his ease when working on a commissioned portrait. He was determined to paint as he felt he had to without compromise"; *Matisse*, p. 189.

86 Schneider reports that Pellerin mistreated the second version of his portrait by folding the canvas back to hide unpainted portions; *Matisse*, p. 417 n. 64.

87 George Besson, "Arrivée de Matisse à Nice: Matisse et quelques personnages," *Le Point*, no. 21 (July 1939): 38–44. This article is the source of much of our information about Matisse's first trip to Nice.

88 See Jean Cassou, *Collection George et Adèle Besson*, exh. cat. (Paris: Musée du Louvre, 1964), p. 67. Besson also said that the first portrait was done in thirty minutes: see Pierre Schneider, *Henri Matisse: Exposition du centenaire*, exh. cat. (Paris: Grand Palais, 1970), p. 87.

89 From "Notes of a Painter"; Flam, *Matisse on Art*, p. 38.

90 Besson said the sittings for the second portrait began on January 10, 1918; Barr, *Matisse*, p. 196 n. 2.

91 See Cassou, *Collection George et Adèle Besson*, p. 67.

92 Interview with Jacqueline George Besson, Besson's second wife. I am grateful to Mme Besson for much helpful information and for access to documents in her possession.

93 Information from Jacqueline George Besson.

94 Quoted in Schneider, *Henri Matisse: Exposition du centenaire*, p. 87.

95 See Flam, *Matisse: The Man and His Art*, pp. 473–4.

96 Matisse in late 1917 or early 1918, quoted in Isabelle Monod-Fontaine, "A Black Light: Matisse (1914–1918)," in Turner and Benjamin, *Matisse*, p. 93.

97 See Monod-Fontaine, et al., *Matisse*, p. 60.

98 Information from Jacqueline George Besson.

99 "George Besson Conducts Interviews on Pictorial Photography," *Camera Work*, no. 24 (October 1908): 22; see Flam, *Matisse on Art*, pp. 43–4.

100 Besson left two-thirds of his and his first wife's collection to the Musée d'Art et d'Archéologie, Besançon, one-third to the Musée Albert André, Bagnols-sur-Cèze. Curiously, he left one of his Matisse portraits to each museum instead of keeping them together.

101 Elie Faure, Jules Romains, Charles Vildrac, and Léon Werth, *Henri-Matisse* (Paris: Editions des "Cahiers d'Aujourd'hui," 1920).

102 Two photographs by George Besson taken in January 1918 show Matisse in his hotel room beside the then unfinished self-portrait. Propped beside the artist in one of them is the second portrait of Besson, which was done during the month of January and which the photograph shows apparently finished. Later in the month Matisse took his self-portrait, among other paintings, to show to Renoir, so it too was presumably finished by this time. The main difference between the self-portrait as it appears in these photographs and its finished appearance is in the eyes, which Matisse seems to have left blank and unresolved until the last. In the finished picture, the orientation of the eyes is obscured by shadow, a deliberate ambiguity that substantiates the illusion of the artist regarding the work before him on the canvas, not himself in the mirror. For the photographs, see Besson, "Arrivée de Matisse à Nice," p. 38.

103 See Barr, *Matisse*, p. 195, and Schneider, *Matisse*, p. 735, for example. Such is Schneider's need to make this link that he has even proposed redating this picture earlier by one year, against the evidence in photographs and witness testimony, to account for the appearance of the umbrella that Matisse would have needed to battle against the excessive rains of the winter of 1916–17.

104 See Besson, "Arrivée de Matisse à Nice," p. 42.

105 If a few more years are taken into consideration, one may add the names of Otto Dix, Alberto Giacometti, Giorgio de Chirico, Cuno Amiet, and Félix Vallotton. It must be said, however, that both de Chirico and Vallotton nearly always appeared extremely sober in their self-portraits.

106 The classic study of the period from this point of view is Kenneth E. Silver, *Esprit de Corps: The Art of the Parisian Avant-Garde and the First World War, 1914–1925* (Princeton University Press, 1989).

107 "Ici [Nice] je travaille énormément toute la journée, et avec ardeur; je sens qu'il n'y a que ça de bon et sur. Je ne puis faire de politique, comme hélas presque tout le monde en fait. Aussi pour compenser il faut des toiles fermes et sensibles." Letter from Matisse to Camoin, April 10, 1918, in Danièle Giraudy, ed., "Correspondance Henri Matisse–Charles Camoin," *Revue de l'art*, no. 12 (1971): 7–34.

108 On this topic see John O'Brian, *Ruthless Hedonism: The American Reception of Matisse* (Chicago and London: University of Chicago Press, 1999).

109 See William S. Lieberman in John Elderfield, *Matisse in the Collection of The Museum of Modern Art* (New York: Museum of Modern Art, 1978), pp. 136–7.

110 The two other known drawings of Dewey are in the collection of the Museum of Modern Art and the Fleming Museum, University of Vermont. Another (present location unknown) was reproduced in Matisse's album *Portraits*, p. 38. Photographs of all four drawings are in the Pierre Matisse Gallery Archives, Pierpont Morgan Library, New York, Box 34, File 27.

111 Dewey is reported to have said of the drawing now in the Fleming Museum that it made him look like "something between a thug and a truckdriver" (I thank Pat Brennan of the Fleming Museum for this information). That Pierre Matisse gave one of the drawings to Columbia University indicates that the artist's son may have felt that the principal value of the portraits was documentary and commemorative.

112 Apparently these were not the first portraits Matisse made of the Cone sisters; see Potter, *Four Americans in Paris*, pp. 162–3, where a drawing of each from 1913 is mentioned. I have not located these drawings.

113 See Carlson, *Matisse as a Draughtsman*, p. 128.

114 The quoted phrase is from Brenda Richardson, *Dr. Claribel & Miss Etta: The Cone Collection of the Baltimore Museum of Art* (Baltimore Museum of Art, 1985), p. 124.

115 Letter from Matisse to Simon Bussy, May 25, 1934 (not May 24, as cited by Schneider, *Matisse*, p. 416 n. 52; and by Richardson, following Schneider). I have based my translation on that in Schneider's book, but with modifications for greater fidelity to the original letter.

116 *The Cone Collection of Baltimore, Maryland: Catalogue of Paintings – Drawings – Sculpture of the Nineteenth and Twentieth Centuries*, foreword by George Boas (Baltimore: Etta Cone, 1934). Matisse apparently made a gift of the ten drawings to Etta Cone. The original commission of a drawing of Claribel was probably not governed by formal terms.

117 See Richardson, *Dr. Claribel & Miss Etta*, p. 124; all ten drawings are reproduced here, pp. 122–3.

118 Curiously, when Matisse included two of the six states of the portrait of Etta Cone in *Portraits*, he chose the first and the fourth, not the definitive fifth. Claribel was represented in the album by the definitive charcoal.

119 See Richardson, *Dr. Claribel & Miss Etta*, p. 129. The twenty-two photographs are reproduced on pp. 136–7.

120 Maud Dale, in her introduction to *Twentieth Century Paintings and Sculpture of the French School in the Chester Dale Collection*, rev. ed. (Washington, D.C.: National Gallery of Art, 1965), p. 7.

121 Lydia Delectorskaya told me that Matisse made about fifteen ink drawings of Dorothy Paley in September 1936. One is reproduced in *Portraits* (1954), along with one of the charcoal drawings, where they are both misdated 1937. Seven of the charcoal drawings are in the collection of the Musée Matisse, Le Cateau; they are reproduced in Dominique Szymusiak, *Musée Matisse: Dessins de la dona-*

tion Matisse (Le Cateau-Cambrésis: Musée Matisse, 1988), pp. 74–6.

122 William S. Paley, *As it Happened: A Memoir* (New York: Doubleday 1979), p. 99. Paley may have exaggerated in saying that "[Matisse] must have done fifty sketches of her" (the businessman may also have been impatient).

123 Letter from Matisse to William Paley, March 15, 1937; William S. Paley Papers, CBS Archives, New York.

124 Letter from Paley to Matisse, April 1, 1937.

125 Letter from Matisse to Paley, April 10, 1937.

126 Letter from Paley to Matisse, May 5, 1937.

127 Related to me by Lydia Delectorskaya.

Chapter 6

1 Starting with Jack Cowart and Dominique Fourcade, *Henri Matisse: The Early Years in Nice, 1916–1930*, exh. cat. (Washington, D.C.: National Gallery of Art, 1986), and continuing, in diverse ways, with such publications as Kenneth E. Silver, "Matisse's Retour à l'ordre," *Art in America* 75 (June 1987): 110–23, 167–9, and John Elderfield, *Pleasuring Painting: Matisse's Feminine Representations* (London and New York: Thames and Hudson, 1995).

2 Consider the transformation of Picasso into a materially oriented bourgeois during the First World War, and the subsequent public attention to his daily affairs – nor has this interest ended: see Billy Klüver, *A Day with Picasso* (Cambridge, Mass. and London: MIT Press, 1997). Duchamp professed to give up art-making altogether in 1918, and allowed his chess playing and his iconoclastic personality to deflect critical discussion of his work. Other examples are the personality cults of the Surrealists, notably Breton. Each of these artists had reached a different stage in his life in the 1920s, so the emphasis on personality does not seem to be a function of age and possible greater retrospection.

3 Jacques Guenne, "Entretien avec Henri Matisse," *L'Art vivant* 18 (September 15, 1925): 1–6; also published in Guenne's *Portraits d'artistes* (Paris: Seheur, 1925), pp. 205–19. Trans. in Jack Flam, *Matisse on Art* (1973; rev. ed. Berkeley and Los Angeles: University of California Press, 1995), pp. 78–82.

4 See Matisse's famous plea: "Oh, do tell the American people that I am a normal man . . ." He was obviously conscious of the reputation his work had acquired and was concerned to dispel the sentiment that it must have been made by a madman or a bohemian; see Flam, *Matisse on Art*, pp. 64–9.

5 Indeed, Matisse had been aware that this was seen as a discrepancy in 1908 when he said in "Notes of a Painter": "M. Péladan in the *Revue Hébdomadaire* [reviewing the Salon d'Automne of 1908] reproaches a certain number of painters, amongst whom I think I should place myself, for calling themselves 'Fauves,' and yet dressing like everyone else, so that they are no more noticeable than the floor-walkers in a department store"; Flam, *Matisse on Art*, p. 43. Péladan's delicious crack ("Correct, elegant, one would take them for department store floor-walkers") is less a reproach for apparent inconsistency than a shrewd and sarcastic recognition of the slightly *arriviste* quality of Matisse and the other Fauve painters, fostered by their recent success.

6 This observation is made and developed in relation to Van Gogh by Nicholas Green in his review of Carol Zemel's *The Formation of a Legend: Van Gogh Criticism 1890–1920* in *Oxford Art Journal* 6, no. 2 (1983): 80–2; see also Green's "Dealing in Temperaments: Economic Transformation of the Artistic Field in France during the Second Half of the Nineteenth Century," *Art History* 10 (March 1987): 59–78.

7 Pierre Courthion, *Henri-Matisse* (Paris: Rieder, 1934) and especially *Le Visage de Matisse* (Lausanne: Marguerat, 1942); Raymond Escholier, *Henri Matisse* (Paris: Floury, 1937); Francis Carco, "Conversation avec Matisse," in *L'ami des peintres* (Paris: Gallimard, 1953).

8 This had certainly been true with two early supporters, Guillaume Apollinaire and Georges Desvallières; see also Flam, *Matisse on Art*, pp. 11–12 for a later example of Matisse's manipulation of spokesmen.

9 *Self-Portrait*, 1900 (fig. 29), was part of the *dation* from the estate of Pierre Matisse to the French national collections.

10 Guillaume Apollinaire, "Henri Matisse," *La Phalange* 2 (December 15, 1907): 481–5.

11 See Alfred H. Barr, Jr., *Matisse: His Art and His Public* (New York: Museum of Modern Art, 1951), p. 553.

12 I have nevertheless found no record of exhibition and little publication of his self-portrait drawings before the 1920s.

13 The monotype is still in the collection of the Matisse family and has apparently never been exhibited. It was published for the first time in Claude Duthuit and Marguerite Duthuit-Matisse, *Henri Matisse, catalogue raisonné de l'oeuvre gravé*, 2 vols. (Paris: Claude Duthuit, 1983), vol. 1, no. 328.

14 Matisse's five contracts with Bernheim-Jeune are reprinted in Raymonde Moulin, *Le Marché de la peinture en France* (Paris: Minuit, 1967), p. 546.

15 It is unclear from the wording of the article whether the phrase "son propre portrait" refers to a specific picture or to any self-portrait that Matisse might make. Alfred Barr, who published an English translation of the contract of 1909 (*Matisse*, pp. 553–4) opted (arbitrarily, I think) for the former, even formulating it as a title, *Self-Portrait*. This cannot, however, refer to the *Self-Portrait in a Striped Jersey*, which was already in the possession of the Steins; it is also unlikely that the phrase refers to the two painted self-portraits of 1900, far from the sort of thing Bernheim-Jeune would be interested in. It seems more reasonable to accept Matisse's designation in the contract as a reference to self-portraits generally.

16 "Vous verrez ci-contre ma bobine de grippé . . . je me suis trouvé un peu marocain avec ma serviette sur la tête, c'est ce qui m'a donné l'idée de me croquer." A photocopy of the letter is in the Archives Matisse, Paris; the self-portrait drawing that accompanied it is reproduced in Pierre Schneider, ed., *Henri Matisse: Exposition du centenaire*, exh. cat. (Paris: Grand Palais, 1970), p. 50.

17 For an assessment of the impact of Morocco on Matisse, see Jack Cowart and Pierre Schneider, *Matisse in Morocco: The Paintings and Drawings, 1912–1913*, exh. cat. (Washington, D.C.: National Gallery of Art, 1990), and *Le Maroc de Matisse*, exh. cat. (Paris: Institut du Monde Arabe, 1999).

18 For example, there are several letters to André Rouveyre containing self-portrait drawings (Copenhagen, Det Kongelige Bibliotek) and a few to George Besson (Paris, George Besson archives).

19 These drawings on postcards are datable to late 1919 on the basis of Matisse's trips to the Loire valley that year.

20 *Cinquante dessins par Henri Matisse*, preface by Charles Vildrac (Paris: published by the artist, 1920).

21 In this he had help: John Russell reports that in 1925 Pierre Matisse, newly in business in New York and preparing an exhibition of his father's work, requested from him a "tiny self-portrait" for the cover of the catalogue; John Russell, *Matisse: Father and Son* (New York: Abrams, 1999), p. 38.

22 Information from Jacqueline George Besson.

23 Elie Faure, Jules Romains, Charles Vildrac, and Léon Werth, *Henri-Matisse* (Paris: Georges Crès, 1920; rev. ed. 1923), p. 51; *Les Cahiers d'aujourd'hui*, n. s., no. 6 (September 1921): 256.

24 Marcel Sembat, *Henri Matisse*, Les Peintres français nouveaux, no. 1 (Paris: Editions de la Nouvelle Revue Française, 1920).

25 Marcel Sembat, "Henri Matisse," *Les Cahiers d'aujourd'hui*, no. 4 (April 1913): 185–94.

26 Compare *Interior with Phonograph* to the

closely related picture entitled *Interior, Flowers and Parrots* of the same year (Baltimore Museum of Art, Cone Collection). The interior is almost identical. A cage containing two parrots sits on the table, a source of noise as exotic as the phonograph it replaces (an observation made to me by Theodore Reff), and the viewpoint has changed slightly, but the overall effect is completely different. In large part this is due to the ways our knowledge of the artist's self-consciousness affects our relationship to the picture space. The little image of Matisse in the mirror in *Interior with Phonograph* wards off our participation, making it clear that we do not control the manipulation of this space; the illusion of our control is one of the seductive features of the Baltimore painting. On this problem of the viewer's "specular identification," discussed in the context of Matisse's drawings of 1935–7 of artist and model seen in a mirror (see figs. 198, 199), see Yve-Alain Bois, *Matisse and Picasso* (Paris: Flammarion, and Fort Worth: Kimbell Art Museum, 1998), pp. 105, 110.

27 *Henri Matisse*, exh. cat. (Berlin: Galerien Thannhauser, 1930).

28 In French: Florent Fels, *Henri-Matisse* (Paris: Editions des Chroniques du jour, 1929); in English: Roger Fry, *Henri-Matisse* (Paris: Editions des Chroniques du jour; New York: E. Weyhe, 1930); in German: Gotthard Jedlicka, *Henri-Matisse* (Paris: Editions des Chroniques du jour, 1929). The original drawing is lost. The format and illustrations of these three books are identical; only the text has been changed, as if what was said about Matisse's work did not matter as much as that something was said. Nevertheless, Fry's essay is one of the most perceptive pieces of criticism and explication of the work of the Nice period. The texts of the Fels and Jedlicka books do not correspond at all with the illustrations, suggesting that Fry's took precedence.

29 For an extended consideration of Matisse's trip to Tahiti, see John Klein, "Matisse After Tahiti: The Domestication of Exotic Memory," *Zeitschrift für Kunstgeschichte* 60, no. 1 (1997): 44–89.

30 Dominique Szymusiak pointed out to me the porthole that identifies Matisse's location. Another self-portrait drawing from his trip is reproduced in Szymusiak, ed., *Matisse et l'Océanie: le voyage à Tahiti*, exh. cat. (Le Cateau-Cambrésis: Musée Matisse, 1998), p. 131.

31 Also in private moments Matisse doodled some tiny, amusing self-portraits on several rejected etching plates for his illustrations to Mallarmé's poems (1930–32); see Claude Duthuit, with the collaboration of Françoise Garnaud, *Henri Matisse, catalogue raisonné des ouvrages illustrés* (Paris: Claude Duthuit, 1988), pp. 33–4.

32 Roger Fry, *Henri-Matisse* (Paris: Editions des Chroniques du jour, 1935). The book was published also in London by Zwemmer and in New York by E. Weyhe with Fry's English text. Matisse's original drawing was apparently mixed up with the reproductions of it and was pasted to the cover of one of the books (information from Archives Matisse, Paris). See also Dominique Szymusiak and John Klein, *Henri Matisse: Autoportraits*, exh. cat. (Le Cateau-Cambrésis: Musée Matisse, 1988), p. 84.

33 Escholier, *Henri Matisse*.

34 Personal communication with Lydia Delectorskaya, who was with Matisse in Rochefort-en-Yvelines. See also Lydia Delectorskaya, *Henri Matisse: Contre vents et marées: Peinture et livres illustrés de 1939 à 1943* (Paris: Editions Irus et Vincent Hansma, 1996), pp. 46–9.

35 *Henri Matisse, dessins*, exh. cat. (Liège: APIAW, 1947), nos. 13–16. The drawings were also shown the following year in Philadelphia, and the essay referring to them was translated for the catalogue, *Henri Matisse: Retrospective Exhibition of Paintings, Drawings, and Sculpture*, exh. cat. (Philadelphia Museum of Art, 1948). See also Chapter 1, pp. 19–20 here.

36 "Exactitude is not Truth" in Flam, *Matisse on Art*, p. 179.

37 These and more may have been the thirty-six self-portrait drawings that Matisse sent to his son Pierre in 1945 for the purpose of a book and exhibition at his gallery in New York. He emphasized to Pierre how much these drawings meant to him, saying that he did not want to sell them all, but that it "would be interesting to reproduce every one of them, unless you think that the public would think that there were too many and get bored." Although he did not write a text for this occasion, in this letter to Pierre he expressed the nub of the idea in "L'Exactitude n'est pas la vérité" that essence is more important than contingent detail. See Russell, *Matisse: Father and Son*, pp. 247–8. Only some of the drawings were shown in the gallery in 1945 and the book project never came to anything.

38 See Szymusiak and Klein, *Henri Matisse: Autoportraits*, p. 98.

39 Underlining the state of self-awareness and personal confession that accompanies illness and that occasioned these self-portraits, Matisse had also agreed to be interviewed by Pierre Courthion for the purpose of a memoir. Matisse had allowed similar interviews in 1938, when he was ill with influenza, and when he also made images of himself in his state of physical compromise.

40 "Je me suis remis au travail et j'ai commencé par des dessins d'après moi-même. Je t'en envoie quelques photos pour que tu me dises si je n'ai pas trop perdu d'énergie . . ."; André Rouveyre, "Matisse évoqué," *La Revue des arts* 6, no. 2 (June 1956): 69.

41 I owe this information to Lydia Delectorskaya.

42 The drawings are marked in series from 1 to 4. They are in a private collection.

43 "De la couleur," *Verve* 4, no. 13 (1945): 44–5.

44 Matisse dedicated this drawing to the Swedish collector Georg Svensson after its publication in *Verve*.

45 Matisse's inscription reads: "Reconnaitrais-tu cher Albert le joyeux luron qui faisait du tapage nocturne."

46 See *Art News Annual*, 21 (November 1951): 36, where one of the drawings from this time is illustrated with other self-portraits from throughout Matisse's life, signposts showing the biographical way along the path of his career. Here, in this case out of the artist's control, the use of the self-portrait as an identification tag for both the artist and his work is fully naturalized.

47 "Je suis engagé dans la couleur définitivement car les dessins ne m'intéressent plus"; Dominique Fourcade, ed., *Henri Matisse: Ecrits et propos sur l'art* (Paris: Hermann, 1972), p. 193.

Chapter 7

1 Georges Joseph Demotte was a dealer in antiquities who was eventually found to be faking pieces; see Dominique Brachlianoff, *Matisse dans les collections du Musée des Beaux-Arts de Lyon* (Lyon: Musée des Beaux-Arts, 1987), p. 12. Matisse painted his portrait on a fairly large wood panel, cut to a standard canvas size, possibly for ease of framing. Pierre Schneider, *Matisse*, trans. Michael Taylor and Bridget Strevens Romer (New York: Rizzoli, 1984), p. 417 n. 62, says that Matisse traded the portrait for a decorative bas-relief (this turned out to be of questionable authenticity), which suggests that he conceived this portrait transaction as trade in kind.

2 We recall (Chapter 5) that the commission in 1936 for a painted portrait of Dorothy Paley foundered.

3 On the increased importance of drawing for Matisse in the 1930s and 1940s, see John Elderfield, *The Drawings of Henri Matisse*, exh. cat. (London: Arts Council of Great Britain and Thames and Hudson; New York: Museum of Modern Art, 1984), pp. 101–34.

4 One could argue that this painting is not a portrait but a genre picture. This may be splitting hairs, as the same could be said of *The Piano Lesson* and *The Music Lesson*. In pictures of people engaged in characteristic activities, as opposed to frankly posing, the distinction necessarily blurs.

5 For several of these paintings from 1923–24, see Jack Cowart and Dominique Fourcade, *Henri Matisse: The Early Years in Nice, 1916–1930*, exh. cat. (Washington, DC: National Gallery of Art, 1986), pp. 197–9.

6 The phrase is used by Isabelle Monod-Fontaine, "A Black Light: Matisse (1914–1918)," in Caroline Turner and Roger Benjamin, eds., *Matisse*, exh. cat. (Brisbane: Queensland Art Gallery, 1995), p. 92.

7 See Jack Flam, *Matisse: The Man and His Art, 1869–1918* (Ithaca and London: Cornell University Press, 1986), pp. 444–57 for a number of paintings depicting Laurette; see also Jack Cowart, "The Place of Silvered Light," in Cowart and Fourcade, *Henri Matisse: The Early Years in Nice*, pp. 16–17 and plates 1–19.

8 John Elderfield calls the uncertain Matisse who painted all these pictures of Laurette "a kind of Hamlet of painting"; "Describing Matisse," in *Henri Matisse: A Retrospective*, exh. cat. (New York: Museum of Modern Art, 1992), p. 66.

9 On the sexuality in Matisse's paintings of women from this time, as well as a thoughtful exploration of Matisse's use of models, see John Elderfield, *Pleasuring Painting: Matisse's Feminine Representations* (London and New York: Thames and Hudson, 1995).

10 See Margaretta Salinger, "White Plumes with Variations," *Parnassus* 4 (December 1932): 9–10, and Elderfield, *The Drawings of Henri Matisse*, pp. 74–9; and for paintings depicting Antoinette, see Cowart and Fourcade, *Henri Matisse: The Early Years in Nice*, plates 28–9, 31–2, 73–6, 83–95.

11 On Henriette and the odalisque, see Elderfield, *Pleasuring Painting*, pp. 33–51.

12 As in, for instance, *Conversation under the Olive Trees*, 1921, illustrated in Cowart and Fourcade, *Henri Matisse: The Early Years in Nice*, plate 129. On Darricarrère, see Cowart, "The Place of Silvered Light," in ibid., pp. 26–42 and plates 147–72.

13 Elderfield, *Pleasuring Painting*, pp. 41–50 discusses the similarity between Henriette Darricarrère and Marguerite Matisse as something that enabled Matisse to remake the world of "the lost daughter," recently married to Georges Duthuit.

14 Pierre Matisse, personal communication.

15 Michel Dauberville cited in Isabelle Monod-Fontaine, Anne Baldassari, and Claude Laugier, *Matisse*, Collections du Musée National d'Art Moderne (Paris: Editions du Centre Pompidou, 1989), p. 72.

16 Pierre Matisse, personal communication.

17 See Bernard Dorival, "Musée d'Art Moderne," *Bulletin des Musées de France*, no. 4 (1947): 20–2.

18 Kenneth Silver has also pointed out that in this period Matisse, his friends, and such patrons as the Gourgauds all had a taste for the luxury decorative arts that marked one of France's efforts to reassert its national status following the First World War; "Matisse's Retour à l'ordre," *Art in America* 75 (June 1987): 117.

19 Jack Flam, *Matisse on Art* (1973; rev. ed. Berkeley and Los Angeles: University of California Press, 1995), p. 69.

20 Flam, *Matisse on Art*, p. 38.

21 Ibid., p. 50.

22 See Roger Benjamin, "The Body in Decoration," in his *Henri Matisse* (New York: Rizzoli, 1992), pp. 2–7.

23 This problem was also discussed with reference to any depiction of the human figure in Matisse's work by Nicholas Watkins, *Matisse* (New York: Oxford University Press, 1985), p. 79.

24 On the importance of inattention, or distraction, as a spectatorial response to Matisse's work, see Yve-Alain Bois, "L'Aveuglement," repr. as "On Matisse: The Blinding," trans. Greg Sims, *October* 68 (Spring 1994): 81–4.

25 Letter from Matisse to Alexander Romm, 1934, quoted in ibid., p. 82.

26 Camille Mauclair, "La Femme devant les peintres modernes," *La Nouvelle Revue*, n.s. 21 (November 1, 1899): 190–213, cited in Susan Sidlauskas, "Contesting Femininity: Vuillard's Family Pictures," *Art Bulletin* 79 (March 1997): 87. Mauclair went on to say, however, that due to the emergence of the "femme nouvelle," portraiture of women would move from the status of "tableau" to that of "document." Sidlauskas subtly argues a case for the ways in which Vuillard's "principal female subjects . . . resist some fundamental assumptions about how the feminine body should be represented" (p. 90), assumptions that, for the most part, its representation in Matisse's work does not resist. Some of his female sitters may well have been "femmes nouvelles," but with few exceptions (his daughter was sometimes one) this is not how Matisse represented them.

27 For example, Alfred H. Barr, Jr., *Matisse: His Art and His Public* (New York: Museum of Modern Art, 1951), p. 183.

28 Flam, *Matisse: The Man and His Art*, p. 371.

29 The role of fashion in Matisse's depictions of hired models is given a much needed consideration by Katherine M. Bourguignon, "'Un Viol de moi-même': Matisse and the Female Model," unpublished Ph.D. diss., University of Pennsylvania, 1998, esp. ch. 4. I am grateful to the author for making a copy of this work available to me.

30 Charles Baudelaire, *Selected Writings on Art and Artists*, trans. P. E. Charvet (Cambridge University Press, 1971), pp. 423–4.

31 Camille Mauclair, *Les Trois crises de la peinture actuelle* (Paris: Fasquelle, 1906), pp. 200–01; quoted in James D. Herbert, *Fauve Painting: The Making of Cultural Politics* (New Haven and London: Yale University Press, 1992), p. 61. Emphasis in original.

32 *Idol* is in a private collection; *Algerian Woman* is at the Musée National d'Art Moderne, Paris.

33 Lydia Delectorskaya, personal communication. She also affirmed that Matisse always paid her for each session of modeling, even while their relationship was considerably more intimate. See also Lydia Delectorskaya, *Henri Matisse: Contre vents et marées: Peinture et livres illustrés de 1939 à 1943* (Paris: Editions Irus et Vincent Hansma, 1996), p. 353, where she states that Matisse always paid his models at the top of the scale for such work.

34 Janet Hobhouse reached similar conclusions, but within a narrower, Orientalist frame of reference; "Odalisques: What did these sensuous images really mean to Matisse?" *Connoisseur*, no. 900 (January 1987): 60–7.

35 Delectorskaya, *Henri Matisse: Contre vents et marées*, p. 168.

36 Letter to Pierre Matisse, September 1, 1940; Barr, *Matisse*, p. 256.

37 See Flam, *Matisse on Art*, p. 131. Emphasis in original.

38 "L'intérêt émotif qu'elles m'inspirent ne se voit pas spécialement sur la représentation de leur corps. . . . C'est peut-être de la volupté sublimée . . ."; Dominique Fourcade, *Henri Matisse: Ecrits et propos sur l'art* (Paris: Hermann, 1972), pp. 162–3. Flam translates this as "The emotional interest they inspire in me is not particularly apparent in the representation of their bodies. . . . It is perhaps sublimated voluptuousness . . ."; *Matisse on Art*, p. 132.

39 After saying this, Matisse went on to ask, disingenuously, "Rape of whom? Of myself, of a certain sensitivity before a sympathetic object." And then, with transparent metaphors, he says of a model: "[She] is a springboard for me – she is a door that I have to break down [enfoncer] to get into the garden where I am alone and well – the model exists only so I can use her." See Fourcade, *Henri Matisse: Ecrits et propos sur l'art*, p. 162 n. 9 (my translation). Bourguignon,

"Matisse and the Female Model," p. vi cites Matisse's statement about flirtation and rape as evidence of his "disempower[ment]" and "self-effacement," a position with which I cannot agree in the light of so much evidence – anecdotal, documentary, pictorial – to the contrary.

40 This is of course a private matter that lends itself more easily to speculation than to historical confirmation. There is general agreement on this point among those who have worked on Matisse but, with few exceptions, such agreement may not be found in print. For one example see Flam, *Matisse: The Man and His Art*, p. 12. Flam has told me that he is convinced, through indirect evidence, that Matisse and the model Laurette had an intimate relationship during the time she posed for him, and that this explains in part the intensity of many of her images in his painting. If this is so, the split with his family in one sense was taking place before he went to the Midi.

41 On the model market in Paris, which resembled the "market" for prostitutes (e.g. the street), see John Milner, *The Studios of Paris: The Capital of Art in the Late Nineteenth Century* (New Haven and London: Yale University Press, 1988), p. 216. On the relationship between modeling and prostitution in the context of studio practice, see Linda Nochlin, "The Imaginary Orient," *Art in America* 71 (May 1983): 124–6.

42 It is noteworthy that Matisse preferred professional models to young women excited by the prospect of posing for a famous artist, and possibly seeking flattery and reflected celebrity; Delectorskaya, *Henri Matisse: Contre vents et marées*, p. 223.

43 In the case of a few of Matisse's sitters – Jeanne Vaderin and Nono Lebasque are examples – it is true that we can muster very little more information than the person's given name and surname, but the full name at least allows the possibility of acknowledging the sitter's social significance.

44 Only recently was the full name of one of Matisse's most important models discovered. Jack Cowart determined that the model Antoinette, depicted in such well-known paintings as *Tea* and *The Plumed Hat*, was Antoinette Arnoux (or perhaps Arnoud), an actress and sometime model in Nice. See Cowart, "The Place of Silvered Light," in Cowart and Fourcade, *Henri Matisse: The Early Years in Nice*, p. 24.

45 Thanks to Lydia Delectorskaya's journals we know the full names of the most important models Matisse employed in the period 1939–43; see Delectorskaya, *Henri Matisse: Contre vents et marées*. Delectorskaya was surely sympathetic to the models' agency, at least after the fact.

46 In another lithograph in precisely the same format and pose, Matisse omitted Mme Raynal's breasts. Significantly, those who have catalogued Matisse's prints have designated these lithographs with titles that either do not refer to the sitter or do so only with her initials, presumably out of discretion. But as we shall see, reducing a name to initials was often Matisse's own system of designating a hired model rather than openly acknowledging her identity by using her full name.

47 A modern expression of this trite equivalence between nudity and self-revelation is an article in *The New York Times Magazine* (January 11, 1998, p. 41) on celebrities who pose for nude photographs, where the quoted passage appears. Coincidentally on the following page, a landscape architect extols the appearance of gardens in winter, when "you're seeing things naked, in their true identity," indicating, if nothing else, that the idea of identity as something reducible to bare physical essentials is widespread and indiscriminate.

48 The *Jeannette* sculptures are analyzed in Flam, *Matisse: The Man and His Art*, pp. 315–18; the problematic question of their dates of execution is discussed on p. 498 n. 38.

49 See Schneider, *Matisse*, p. 562.

50 Robert Goldwater, "The Sculpture of Matisse," *Art in America* 60 (March–April 1972): 43.

51 Flam, *Matisse: The Man and His Art*, p. 316.

52 For a variety of images of Lydia that seem to approach the visual conditions of portraiture, see Elderfield, *The Drawings of Henri Matisse*, nos. 81, 83–84; Monod-Fontaine et al, *Oeuvres de Henri Matisse*, pp. 94–5; Brenda Richardson, *Dr. Claribel & Miss Etta: The Cone Collection of the Baltimore Museum of Art* (Baltimore Museum of Art, 1985), p. 132. In far more images of Lydia Delectorskaya, however, she is either depicted nude or as an accessory in an interior.

53 Lydia Delectorskaya, personal communication. Matisse also gave a number of works of art to Delectorskaya, but it seems that these were special signs of affection and respect. They may also have been Matisse's way of providing for her future, less crass than money in this context (she ultimately gave these works to the Hermitage Museum in St. Petersburg and the Pushkin Museum in Moscow, in recognition of her Russian heritage).

54 Henri Matisse, *Portraits* (Monte Carlo: André Sauret, 1954), pp. 135, 139, 147. Matisse chose and entitled the works in the album.

55 A selection of these drawings from 1935 and 1936 were published in a special issue of *Cahiers d'art* in 1936 devoted to Matisse's drawing.

56 These complex and fascinating drawings deserve an extended consideration, which I intend to give them in a future publication.

57 Gertrude Stein quoted in John Malcolm Brinnin, *The Third Rose: Gertrude Stein and Her World* (1959; Reading, Mass: Addison-Wesley, 1987), p. 148.

58 Both passages are quoted in Flam, *Matisse on Art*, p. 256 n. 18.

Conclusion

1 Jack Flam, *Matisse on Art* (1973; rev. ed. Berkeley and Los Angeles: University of California Press, 1995), p. 222. For the sake of brevity I have suppressed some parts of a much longer passage.

2 For a variant of his statement see Lydia Delectorskaya, *Henri Matisse: Contre vents et marées: Peinture et livres illustrés de 1939 à 1943*, (Paris: Editions Irus et Vincent Hansma, 1996), pp. 200–8. I have adapted some of Delectorskaya's observations from this text, and from personal communications with her, in my account here.

3 "Notes of a Painter on his Drawing" (1939) in Flam, *Matisse on Art*, p. 130.

4 "Notes of a Painter" (1908) in ibid., p. 40. Flam discusses Matisse's use of this primarily literary term in his Introduction, p. 16.

5 Ibid., p. 76.

6 Ibid., p. 150.

7 Louis Aragon, *Henri Matisse: A Novel*, 2 vols., trans. Jean Stewart (New York: Harcourt Brace Jovanovich, 1972), vol. 1, 57. Aragon's emphasis.

Select Bibliography

Archives

Archives Matisse, Paris.

Documentation, Musée Matisse, Le Cateau-Cambrésis.

Documentation, Musée Matisse, Nice.

Documentation, Musée National d'Art Moderne, Paris.

George Besson archives, Paris.

Alfred H. Barr, Jr. Papers, Archives of The Museum of Modern Art, New York.

Pierre Matisse Gallery Archives, Pierpont Morgan Library, New York.

William S. Paley Papers, CBS Archives, New York.

Books, Exhibition Catalogues, Articles

Antliff, Mark. "The Rhythms of Duration: Bergson and the Art of Matisse." In John Mullarkey, ed. *The New Bergson*. Manchester and New York: Manchester University Press, 1999.

Apollinaire, Guillaume. *Chroniques d'art, 1902–1918*. Ed. L.-C. Breunig. Paris: Gallimard, 1960.

Aragon, Louis. *Henri Matisse: A Novel*. 1971. 2 vols. Trans. Jean Stewart. New York: Harcourt Brace Jovanovich, 1972.

Bailey, Colin B., ed. *Renoir's Portraits: Impressions of an Age*. Exh. cat. New Haven and London: Yale University Press and National Gallery of Canada, Ottawa, 1997.

Barnes, Albert C. and Violette de Mazia. *The Art of Henri-Matisse*. New York: Scribner's, 1933.

Barr, Alfred H., Jr. *Matisse: His Art and His Public*. New York: Museum of Modern Art, 1951.

Baudelaire, Charles. *Selected Writings on Art and Artists*. Trans. P. E. Charvet. Cambridge University Press, 1972.

Benjamin, Roger. "Une Copie par Matisse du *Balthazar Castiglione* de Raphaël." *La Revue du Louvre* 35, no. 4 (1985): 275–7.

——. *Henri Matisse*. New York: Rizzoli, 1992.

——. *Matisse's "Notes of a Painter": Criticism, Theory, and Context, 1891–1908*. Ann Arbor: UMI Research Press, 1987.

Berger, Harry, Jr. "Fictions of the Pose: Facing the Gaze of Early Modern Portraiture," *Representations* 46 (Spring 1994): 87–120.

Berger, John. "The Changing View of Man in the Portrait." In *The Moment of Cubism and Other Essays*. New York: Pantheon-Random, 1969.

Besson, George. "Arrivée de Matisse à Nice: Matisse et quelques personnages." *Le Point*, no. 21 (July 1939): 38–44.

Billeter, Erika, ed. *L'Autoportrait à l'âge de la photographie: Peintres et photographes en dialogue avec leur propre image*. Exh. cat. Lausanne: Musée Cantonal des Beaux-Arts, 1985.

Bock, Catherine C. *Henri Matisse and Neo-Impressionism, 1898–1908*. Ann Arbor: UMI Research Press, 1981.

——. "Henri Matisse's Self-Portraits: Presentation and Representation." *Psychoanalytic Perspectives on Art* 3 (1988): 239–65.

Bock-Weiss, Catherine C. *Henri Matisse: A Guide to Research*. New York and London: Garland, 1996.

Bois, Yve-Alain. "L'Aveuglement." In Dominique Fourcade and Isabelle Monod-Fontaine, eds. *Henri Matisse 1904–1917*. Exh. cat. Paris: Editions du Centre Pompidou, 1993. Repr. as "On Matisse: The Blinding," trans. Greg Sims, *October* 68 (Spring 1994): 61–121.

——. "Matisse and 'Arche-Drawing'." In *Painting as Model*. Cambridge, Mass. and London: MIT Press, 1990.

——. *Matisse and Picasso*. Paris: Flammarion and Fort Worth: Kimbell Art Museum, 1998.

Bourguignon, Katherine M. "'Un viol de moi-même': Matisse and the Female Model." Ph.D. dissertation, University of Pennsylvania, 1998.

Brachlianoff, Dominique. *Matisse dans les collections du Musée des Beaux-Arts de Lyon*. Lyon: Musée des Beaux-Arts, 1987.

Breckenridge, James D. *Likeness: A Conceptual History of Ancient Portraiture*. Evanston, Ill: Northwestern University Press, 1968.

Brilliant, Richard, ed. *Art Journal* 46 (Fall 1987), special issue: "Portraits: The Limitations of Likeness."

——. *Portraiture*. Cambridge, Mass: Harvard University Press, 1991.

Brooks, Linda Marie, ed. *Alternative Identities: The Self in Literature, History, Theory*. New York and London: Garland, 1995.

Bussy, Jane Simone. "A Great Man." *Burlington Magazine* 128 (February 1986): 80–84.

Campbell, Lorne. *Renaissance Portraits: European Portrait-Painting in the 14th, 15th, and 16th Centuries*. New Haven and London: Yale University Press, 1990.

Carco, Francis. *L'ami des peintres*. Paris: Gallimard, 1953.

Carlson, Victor I. *Matisse as a Draughtsman*. Exh. cat. Baltimore Museum of Art, 1971.

Carrier, David. "Poussin's Cartesian Meditations: Self and Other in the Self-Portraits of Poussin and Matisse." *Source* 15 (Spring 1996): 28–35.

Cauman, John. "Henri Matisse's Letters to Walter Pach." *Archives of American Art Journal* 31, no. 3 (1991): 2–14.

The Cone Collection of Baltimore, Maryland: Catalogue of Paintings – Drawings – Sculpture of the Nineteenth and Twentieth Centuries. Foreword by George Boas. Baltimore: Etta Cone, 1934.

La Cote des antiquités, no. 9 (June 1988). Special issue: "L'Autoportrait: de l'approche esthétique à l'approche psychanalytique."

Courthion, Pierre. *Henri-Matisse*. Paris: Rieder, 1934.

——. *Le Visage de Matisse*. Lausanne: Marguerat, 1942.

Cowart, Jack and Dominique Fourcade. *Henri Matisse: The Early Years in Nice, 1916–1930*. Exh. cat. Washington, D.C.: National Gallery of Art, 1986.

Cowart, Jack and Pierre Schneider. *Matisse in Morocco: The Paintings and Drawings, 1912–1913*. Exh. cat. Washington, D.C.: National Gallery of Art, 1990.

Cowart, William John, III. "'Ecoliers' to 'Fauves': Matisse, Marquet, and Manguin Drawings, 1890–1906." Ph.D. dissertation, Johns Hopkins University, 1972.

Dauberville, Michel and Guy-Patrice. *Matisse: Henri Matisse chez Bernheim-Jeune*. 2 vols. Paris: Editions Bernheim-Jeune, 1995.

Dean, Carolyn J. *The Self and Its Pleasures: Bataille, Lacan, and the History of the Decentered Subject*. Ithaca and London: Cornell University Press, 1992.

Delectorskaya, Lydia. *L'Apparente facilité: Henri Matisse, peintures 1935–1939*. Introduction by Isabelle Monod-Fontaine. Paris: Editions Maeght, 1986.

——. *Henri Matisse: Contre vents et marées: Peinture et livres illustrés de 1939 à 1943*. Preface by Isabelle Monod-Fontaine. Paris: Editions Irus et Vincent Hansma, 1996.

Derrida, Jacques. *Memoirs of the Blind: The Self-Portrait and Other Ruins*. Trans. Pascale-Anne Brault and Michael Naas. Chicago and London: University of Chicago Press, 1993.

Dorival, Bernard. "Musée National d'Art Moderne: Le Legs Gourgaud." *La Revue du Louvre*, no. 2 (1967): 93–102.

Duthuit, Claude, and Marguerite Duthuit-Matisse, with the collaboration of Françoise Garnaud. *Henri Matisse, catalogue raisonné de l'oeuvre gravé*. Preface by Jean Guichard-Meili. 2 vols. Paris: Claude Duthuit, 1983.

——, with the collaboration of Françoise Garnaud. *Henri Matisse, catalogue raisonné des ouvrages illustrés*. Preface by Jean Guichard-Meili. Paris: Claude Duthuit, 1988.

——, with the collaboration of Wanda de Guébriant. *Henri Matisse, catalogue raisonné de l'oeuvre sculpté*. Preface by Yve-Alain Bois. Paris: Claude Duthuit, 1997.

Duthuit, Georges. *Ecrits sur Matisse*. Ed. Rémi Labrusse. Paris: Ecole Nationale Supérieure des Beaux-Arts, 1992.

——. *Les Fauves*. Geneva: Editions des Trois Collines, 1949.

Elderfield, John. *The Drawings of Henri Matisse*. Exh. cat. London: Arts Council of Great Britain and Thames and Hudson; New York: Museum of Modern Art, 1984.

——. *Henri Matisse: A Retrospective*. Exh. cat. New York: Museum of Modern Art, 1992.

——. *Matisse in the Collection of the Museum of Modern Art*. New York: Museum of Modern Art, 1978. Additional texts by William S. Lieberman and Riva Castelman.

——. *Pleasuring Painting: Matisse's Feminine Representations*. London and New York: Thames and Hudson, 1995.

——. *The "Wild Beasts": Fauvism and its Affinities*. Exh. cat. New York: Museum of Modern Art, 1976.

Elsen, Albert E. *The Sculpture of Henri Matisse*. New York: Abrams, 1972.

Escholier, Raymond. *Henri Matisse*. Paris: Floury, 1937.

——. *Matisse: A Portrait of the Artist and the Man*. Trans. Geraldine and H. M. Colvile. New York: Praeger, 1960.

Farr, Margaret F. "Identity and Subjectivity in Edgar Degas's *Mme Jeantaud Before a Mirror*." *Nineteenth-Century Contexts* 19, no. 3 (1996): 305–25.

Faure, Elie, Jules Romains, Charles Vildrac, and Léon Werth. *Henri-Matisse*. Paris: Editions des "Cahiers d'aujourd'hui," 1920.

Fels, Florent. *Henri-Matisse*. Paris: Editions des Chroniques du jour, 1929.

Fiedler-Bender, Gisela, ed. *Matisse und seine deutschen Schüler*. Exh. cat. Kaiserslautern: Pfalzgalerie, 1988.

Flam, Jack D. "Henri Matisse," catalogue entries in *Great French Paintings from the Barnes Foundation*. New York: Knopf, in association with Lincoln University Press, 1993.

——. "Matisse and the Fauves," in William Rubin, ed., *"Primitivism" in 20th Century Art: Affinities of the Tribal and the Modern*. 2 vols. New York: Museum of Modern Art, 1984. Vol. 1, 211–39.

——. "Matisse in Two Keys." *Art in America* 63 (July–August 1975): 83–6.

——. *Matisse on Art*. London: Phaidon, 1973. Rev. ed. Berkeley and Los Angeles: University of California Press, 1995.

——. *Matisse: The Man and His Art, 1869–1918*. Ithaca and London: Cornell University Press, 1986.

——. "Matisse's *Thèmes et variations*, a Book and a Method." In *Henri Matisse, Zeichnungen und Gouaches Découpées*. Exh. cat. Staatsgalerie Stuttgart, 1993.

——. "Some Observations on Matisse's Self-Portraits." *Arts Magazine* 49 (May 1975): 50–52.

Fourcade, Dominique. "Greta Prozor d'Henri Matisse." *Cahiers du Musée National d'Art Moderne*, no. 11 (June 1983): 100–7.

——. *Matisse au Musée de Grenoble*. Grenoble: Musée de Peinture et de Sculpture, 1975.

——. "65 Dessins de Matisse dans les collections du Musée national d'art moderne." *Cahiers du Musée National d'Art Moderne*, no. 13 (July 1984): 8–17.

——, ed. "Autres propos de Henri Matisse." *Macula*, no. 1 (1976): 92–115.

——. *Henri Matisse: Dessins et sculpture*. Exh. cat. Paris: Musée National d'Art Moderne, Editions du Centre Pompidou, 1975.

——. *Henri Matisse: Ecrits et propos sur l'art*. Paris: Hermann, 1972.

——and Isabelle Monod-Fontaine. *Henri Matisse 1904–1917*. Exh. cat. Paris: Editions du Centre Pompidou, 1993.

Friedländer, Max J. *Landscape, Portrait, Still-Life: Their Origin and Development*. Trans. R. F. C. Hull. Oxford: B. Cassirer, 1949.

Fry, Roger. *Henri-Matisse*. Paris: Editions des Chroniques du jour and New York: E. Weyhe, 1930.

——. *Henri-Matisse*. Paris: Editions des Chroniques du jour, 1935.

Furst, H. E. A. *Portrait Painting: Its Nature and Function*. London: Lane, 1927.

Galligan, Gregory. "The Self Pictured: Manet, the Mirror, and the Occupation of Realist Painting." *Art Bulletin* 80 (March 1998): 139–71.

Gallop, Jane. *Reading Lacan*. Ithaca and London: Cornell University Press, 1985.

Gassier, Pierre. *Manguin parmi les Fauves*. Exh. cat. Martigny, Switzerland: Fondation Pierre Gianadda, 1983.

Gedo, Mary Mathews. *Picasso: Art as Autobiography*. Chicago and London: University of Chicago Press, 1980.

Girard, Xavier, ed. *Henri Matisse: L'Art du livre*. Cahiers Henri Matisse, no. 3. Introduction by Yuri Russakov. Nice: Musée Matisse, 1986.

——. *Matisse: Photographies*. Cahiers Henri Matisse, no. 2. Exh. cat. Nice: Musée des Beaux-Arts Jules Cheret, 1986.

——and Christian Arthaud. *Henri Matisse Dessins: Collections du Musée Matisse [Nice]*. Cahiers Henri Matisse, no. 6. Paris: Adrien Maeght Editeur, 1989.

——and Alain Mousseigne, eds. *Matisse: Ajaccio-Toulouse, 1898–1899, une saison de peinture*. Exh. cat. Cahiers Henri Matisse, no. 4. Toulouse: Musée d'Art Moderne, 1986.

Giraudy, Daniéle, ed. "Correspondance Henri Matisse–Charles Camoin." *Revue de l'art*, no. 12 (1971): 7–34.

Golding, John. *Matisse and Cubism*. University of Glasgow Press, 1978.

Gombrich, E. H. *Art and Illusion: A Study in the Psychology of Pictorial Representation*. Princeton University Press, 1972.

——Julian Hochberg, and Max Black. *Art, Perception, and Reality*. Baltimore: The Johns Hopkins University Press, 1972.

Gopnik, Adam. "High and Low: Caricature, Primitivism, and the Cubist Portrait." *Art Journal* 43 (Winter 1983): 371–6.

Gowing, Lawrence. *Henri Matisse: Harmony in Red*. Washington, D.C.: National Gallery of Art, 1986.

——. *Matisse*. London: Thames and Hudson, 1979.

Grosser, Maurice. *The Painter's Eye*. New York: Reinhart, 1951.

Heilbrun, Françoise, and Philippe Néagu. *Portraits d'artistes*. Les Dossiers du Musée d'Orsay, 7. Exh. cat. Paris: Editions de la Réunion des Musées Nationaux, 1986.

Herbert, James D. *Fauve Painting: The Making of Cultural Politics*. New Haven and London: Yale University Press, 1992.

Hobhouse, Janet. "Odalisques: What did these sensuous images really mean to Matisse?" *Connoisseur*, no. 900 (January 1987): 60–67.

Holmes, C. J. *Notes on the Post-Impressionist Painters, Grafton Galleries, 1910–11*. London: Philip Lee Warner, 1910.

Hyslop, Francis E. *Henri Evenepoel: Belgian Painter in Paris, 1892–1899*. University Park, Pa: Pennsylvania State University Press, 1975.

Izerghina, A. et al. *Henri Matisse: Paintings and Sculptures in Soviet Museums*. Trans. R. J. Rosengrant et al. Leningrad: Aurora Art Publishers, 1978.

Jay, Paul. *Being in the Text: Self-Representation from Wordsworth to Roland Barthes*. Ithaca and London: Cornell University Press, 1984.

Jordanova, Ludmilla. *Defining Features: Scientific and Medical Portraits, 1660–2000*. London: National Portrait Gallery and Reaktion Books, 2000.

Klein, John. "Matisse et l'autoportrait: démarche individuel et relation avec le public." In Dominique Szymusiak and John Klein, *Henri Matisse: Autoportraits*. Exh. cat. Le Cateau-Cambrésis: Musée Matisse, 1988.

——. "Objects of Desire and Irresistible Forces: Matisse Between Patrons, Collectors, and War." In *Henri Matisse: Four Great Collectors*, ed. Kasper Monrad. Exh. cat. Copenhagen: Statens Museum for Kunst, 1999.

——. "Portraiture and Assimilation of the 'very singular Vallotton'." In *Félix Vallotton*, ed. Sasha Newman. Exh. cat. New Haven: Yale University Art Gallery, 1991.

——. "When Worlds Collide: Matisse's *Femme au chapeau* and the Politics of the Portrait." In *Matisse and Other Modern Masters: The Elise S. Haas Collection*, ed. Janet Bishop. Exh. cat. San Francisco Museum of Modern Art, 1993.

Koortbojian, Michael. *Self-Portraits*. London: Scala Books, 1992.

Kostenevich, Albert, and Natalya Semyonova. *Collecting Matisse*. Trans Andrew Bromfield. Paris: Flammarion, 1993.

Kropmanns, Peter. "Matisse und die Molls, seine bedeutendsten deutschen Sammler." In *Oskar Moll: Gemälde und Aquarelle*. Exh. cat. Mainz: Landesmuseum, 1997.

Labrusse, Rémi, ed. *Matisse: "La Révélation m'est venue de l'Orient."* Exh. cat. Rome: Musei Capitolini and Florence: Artificio, 1997.

Lacan, Jacques. *Ecrits: A Selection*. Trans. Alan Sheridan. New York: Norton, 1977.

Laude, Jean. "Les 'Ateliers' de Matisse." *Colóquio, artes* (Lisbon), no. 18 (June 1974): 16–25.

——. *La Peinture française (1905–1914) et "l'art nègre"*. Paris: Klincksieck, 1968.

Lavin, Maud. "An Analysis of Henri Matisse's 1914 *Portrait of Mlle Yvonne Landsberg*." M.A. thesis, University of Pennsylvania, Philadelphia, 1981.

Léautaud, Paul. *Journal littéraire*. 19 vols. Paris: Mercure de France, 1954–66.

Levey, Michael. *The Painter Depicted: Painters as a Subject in Painting*. London: Thames and Hudson, 1981.

Levine, Steven Z. *Monet, Narcissus, and Self-Reflection: The Modernist Myth of the Self*. Chicago and London: University of Chicago Press, 1994.

Leymarie, Jean, Herbert Read, and William S. Lieberman. *Henri Matisse*. Berkeley and Los Angeles: University of California Press, 1966.

Lieberman, William S., ed. *Twentieth-Century Modern Masters: The Jacques and Natasha Gelman Collection*. Exh. cat. New York: Metropolitan Museum of Art, 1989.

Livingston, Jane. "Matisse's *Tea*." *Los Angeles County Museum of Art Bulletin* 20, no. 2 (1974): 47–57.

Lubar, Robert S. "Unmasking Pablo's Gertrude: Queer Desire and the Subject of Portraiture." *Art Bulletin* 79 (March 1997): 57–84.

Lubin, David M. *Acts of Portrayal: Eakins, Sargent, James*. New Haven and London: Yale University Press, 1985.

Lynton, Norbert, Alistair Smith, Robert Cumming, and Diané Collinson. *Looking Into Pictures*. London: Open University, 1985.

Martin, F. David. "On Portraiture: Some Distinctions." *Journal of Aesthetics and Art Criticism* 20 (Fall 1961): 61–72.

Matisse, Henri. *Dessins: Thèmes et variations*. Preface by Louis Aragon. Paris: Martin Fabiani, 1943.

——. *Portraits*. Monte Carlo: André Sauret, 1954.

Henri-Matisse. Exh. cat. Berlin: Galerien Thannhauser, 1930.

Henri Matisse, dessins. Exh. cat. Liège: APIAW, 1947.

Henri Matisse: Retrospective Exhibition of Paintings, Drawings, and Sculpture. Exh. cat. Philadelphia Museum of Art, 1948.

Matisse, Marguerite, preface. *Henri Matisse: Lithographies rares*. Exh. cat. Paris: Berggruen, 1954.

——. "Marguerite Matisse: Les Drames de mon père." Interview with Gilbert Ganne. *Les Nouvelles littéraires* (April 23, 1970): D17–18.

Meskimmon, Marsha. *The Art of Reflection: Women Artists' Self-Portraiture in the Twentieth Century*. New York: Columbia University Press, 1996.

Mezzatasta, Michael P. *Henri Matisse, Painter/Sculptor: A Formal Analysis of Selected Works*. Exh. cat. Fort Worth: Kimbell Art Museum, 1984.

Milner, John. *The Studios of Paris: The Capital of Art in the Nineteenth Century*. New Haven and London: Yale University Press, 1988.

Monod-Fontaine, Isabelle. "A Black Light: Matisse (1914–1918)." In Caroline Turner and Roger Benjamin, eds. *Matisse*. Exh. cat. Brisbane: Queensland Art Gallery, 1995.

——. *The Sculpture of Henri Matisse*. Trans. David Macey. Exh. cat. London: Arts Council of Great Britain and Thames and Hudson, 1984.

——and Claude Laugier. *Dation Pierre Matisse*. Exh. cat. Paris: Editions du Centre Pompidou, 1992.

——, Anne Baldassari and Claude Laugier. *Matisse*. Collections du Musée National d'Art Moderne. Paris: Editions du Centre Pompidou, 1989.

Moulin, Raymonde. *Le Marché de la peinture en France*. Paris: Minuit, 1967.

Nochlin, Linda. "Impressionist Portraits and the Construction of Modern Identity." In Colin B. Bailey, ed. *Renoir's Portraits: Impressions of an Age*. Exh. cat. New Haven and London: Yale University Press and National Gallery of Canada, Ottawa, 1997.

O'Brian, John. *Ruthless Hedonism: The American Reception of Matisse*. Chicago and London: University of Chicago Press, 1999.

O'Connor, Francis V. "The Psychodynamics of the Frontal Self-Portrait." *Psychoanalytic Perspectives on Art* 1 (1985): 169–221.

Oppler, Ellen Charlotte. *Fauvism Reexamined*. New York: Garland, 1976.

Pach, Walter. *Queer Thing, Painting*. New York: Harper and Brothers, 1938.

Paley, William S. *As it Happened: A Memoir*. New York: Doubleday, 1979.

Pitkänen, Risto. "The Resemblance View of Pictorial Representation." *British Journal of Aesthetics* 16 (Autumn 1976): 313–23.

Pleynet, Marcelin. *Henri Matisse: Qui êtes-vous?* Lyon: La Manufacture, 1988.

——. *Painting and System*. Trans. Sima N. Godfrey. Chicago and London: University of Chicago Press, 1984.

Pointon, Marcia. *Hanging the Head: Portraiture and Social Formation in Eighteenth-Century England*. New Haven and London: Yale University Press, 1993.

Pollack, Barbara. *The Collectors: Dr. Claribel and Miss Etta Cone*. Indianapolis: Bobbs-Merrill, 1962.

Pope-Hennessy, John. *The Portrait in the Renaissance*. London: Phaidon, 1966.

Potter, Margaret, ed. *Four Americans in Paris: The Collections of Gertrude Stein and Her Family*. Exh. cat. New York: Museum of Modern Art, 1970.

Puy, Jean. "Souvenirs." *Le Point*, no. 21 (July 1939): 112–33.

Puy, Michel. *L'Effort des peintres modernes*. Paris: Messein, 1933.

Reff, Theodore. "Matisse: Meditations on a Statuette and Goldfish." *Arts Magazine* 51 (November 1976): 109–15.

Richardson, Brenda. *Dr. Claribel & Miss Etta: The Cone Collection of the Baltimore Museum of Art*. Baltimore Museum of Art, 1985.

Richardson, John, with the collaboration of Marilyn McCully. *A Life of Picasso*. Vol. 1: *The Early Years, 1881–1906*. New York: Random House, 1991.

Rouveyre, André. "Matisse évoqué." *La Revue des arts* 6, no. 2 (June 1956): 66–74.

Rubin, William, ed. *Picasso and Portraiture: Representation and Transformation*. Exh. cat. New York: Museum of Modern Art, 1996.

Russell, John. *Matisse: Father and Son*. New York: Abrams, 1999.

Said, Edward. *Beginnings: Intention and Method*. New York: Basic Books, 1975.

Salinger, Margaretta. "White Plumes with Variations." *Parnassus* 4 (December 1932): 9–10.

Schneider, Pierre. *Matisse*. Trans. Michael Taylor and Bridget Strevens Romer. New York: Rizzoli, 1984.

——. "The Striped Pajama Icon." *Art in America* 63 (July–August 1975): 76–82.

——, ed. *Matisse: Visages découverts, 1945–1954*. Exh. cat. Paris: Mona Bismarck Foundation and Adam Biro, 1996.

——, ed., with Tamara Préaud. *Henri Matisse: Exposition du centenaire*. Exh. cat. Paris: Grand Palais, 1970.

Sembat, Marcel. "Henri Matisse." *Les Cahiers d'aujourd'hui*, no. 4 (April 1913): 185–94.

——. *Henri Matisse*. Les Peintres français nouveaux, no. 1. Paris: Editions de la Nouvelle Revue Française, 1920.

Shackelford, George T. M. and Mary Tavener Holmes. *A Magic Mirror: The Portrait in France 1700–1900*. Exh. cat. Houston: Museum of Fine Arts, 1986.

Sheriff, Mary D. "Invention, Resemblance, and Fragonard's *Portraits de Fantaisie*." *Art Bulletin* 69 (March 1987): 77–87.

Shiff, Richard. *Cézanne and the End of Impressionism: A Study of the Theory, Technique, and Critical Evaluation of Modern Art*. Chicago and London: University of Chicago Press, 1984.

——. "Imitation of Matisse." In Caroline Turner and Roger Benjamin, eds. *Matisse*. Exh. cat. Brisbane: Queensland Art Gallery, 1995.

Shone, Richard. "Matisse in England and Two English Sitters." *Burlington Magazine* 135 (July 1993): 479–84.

Sidlauskas, Susan. "Contesting Femininity: Vuillard's Family Pictures." *Art Bulletin* 79 (March 1997): 85–111.

Silver, Kenneth E. *Esprit de Corps: The Art of the Parisian Avant-Garde and the First World War, 1914–1925*. Princeton University Press, 1989.

——. "Matisse's Retour à l'ordre." *Art in America* 75 (June 1987): 110–23, 167–9.

Simons, Patricia. "Women in Frames: The gaze, the eye, the profile in Renaissance portraiture." *History Workshop*, no. 25 (Spring 1988): 4–30. Repr. in Norma Broude and Mary D. Garrard, eds. *The Expanding Discourse: Feminism and Art History*. New York: HarperCollins, 1992.

Spurling, Hilary. "Matisse on Belle-Ile." *Burlington Magazine* 137 (October 1995): 661–71.

——. *The Unknown Matisse: A Life of Henri Matisse: The Early Years, 1869–1908*. New York: Knopf, 1998.

Stein, Gertrude. *The Autobiography of Alice B. Toklas* (1933). New York: Vintage, 1961.

Steiner, Wendy. *Exact Resemblance to Exact Resemblance: The Literary Portraiture of Gertrude Stein*. New Haven and London: Yale University Press, 1978.

Szymusiak, Dominique, ed. *Hommage à Lydia Delectorskaya*. Le Cateau-Cambrésis: Musée Matisse, 1999.

——. *Musée Matisse: Dessins de la donation Matisse*. Le Cateau-Cambrésis: Musée Matisse, 1988.

——and John Klein. *Henri Matisse: Autoportraits*. Exh. cat. Le Cateau-Cambrésis: Musée Matisse, 1988.

Taylor, Charles. *Sources of the Self: The Making of the Modern Identity*. Cambridge, Mass: Harvard University Press, 1989.

Terrasse, Antoine. "Matisse et Bonnard: Quarante ans d'amitié." *Revue de l'art*, no. 64 (1984): 77–84.

Toussaint, Hélène. *Les Portraits d'Ingres: Peintures des musées nationaux*. Monographies des Musées de France. Exh. cat. Paris: Réunion des Musées Nationaux, 1985.

Trapp, Frank. "Form and Symbol in the Art of Matisse." *Arts Magazine* 49 (May 1975): 56–8.

Trilling, Lionel. *Sincerity and Authenticity*. Cambridge, Mass: Harvard University Press, 1972.

Tucker, Paul Hayes and MaryAnne Stevens, eds. *Monet in the Twentieth Century*. New Haven and London: Yale University Press, 1998.

Turner, Caroline and Roger Benjamin, eds. *Matisse*. Exh. cat. Brisbane: Queensland Art Gallery, 1995.

Varnedoe, J. Kirk T., ed. *Modern Portraits: The Self and Others*. Exh. cat. New York: Columbia University, Department of Art History and Archaeology, 1976.

——. "Picasso's Self-Portraits." In William Rubin, ed. *Picasso and Portraiture: Representation and Transformation*. Exh. cat. New York: Museum of Modern Art, 1996.

Verve 4, no. 13 (1945). Special issue on Matisse: "De la couleur."

Vollard, Ambroise. *Recollections of a Picture Dealer*. Trans. Violet M. MacDonald. New York: Dover, 1978.

Warner, Malcolm. *Portrait Painting*. New York: Mayflower Books, 1979.

Watkins, Nicholas. *Matisse*. New York: Oxford University Press, 1985.

Wilton, Andrew. *The Swagger Portrait: Grand Manner Portraiture in Britain from Van Dyck to Augustus John, 1630–1930*. Exh. cat. London: Tate Gallery, 1992.

Woodall, Joanna, ed. *Portraiture: Facing the Subject*. Manchester and New York: Manchester University Press, 1997.

Woods-Marsden, Joanna. *Renaissance Self-Portraiture: The Visual Construction of Identity and the Social Status of the Artist*. New Haven and London: Yale University Press, 1998.

Zemel, Carol. *Van Gogh's Progress: Utopia, Modernity, and Late-Nineteenth-Century Art*. Berkeley and Los Angeles: University of California Press, 1997.

Zervos, Christian. "Notes sur la formation et le développement de l'oeuvre de Henri-Matisse." *Cahiers d'art* 5–6 (1931): 9–32.

Photograph Credits

In most cases photographs and transparencies have been provided by the owners or custodians of the works and are reproduced with their permission. Illustrations for which further credit is due are listed below. Every reasonable attempt has been made to identify owners of copyright. Errors or omissions will be corrected in subsequent editions.

2: © RMN–Jean/Lewandowski; 6: © RMN–J. G. Berizzi; 7, 135: © Daspet; 8, 33, 131, 134: © RMN–Hervé Lewandowski; 9, 113: Reproduced by courtesy of the Trustees, The National Gallery, London; 10, 89: Graydon Wood; 13, 137: Claude Gaspari; 16, 20, 22, 23, 25, 26, 28, 39, 65, 75, 94, 98, 118, 121, 123, 124, 145, 146, 153, 169a, 169b, 170, 195, 199: Archives Matisse; 17, 85, 192: Archives Matisse/Adam Rzepka; 18, 19, 21, 34: Archives Matisse/Jacqueline Hyde; 29, 125, 130: Philippe Migeat © Musée National d'Art Moderne, Centre G. Pompidou; 30: Arxiu Fotogràfic de Museus, Ajuntament de Barcelona; 31, 86, 91, 96, 116, 120, 173, 174, 193: © 1995 The Museum of Modern Art, New York; 35: Courtesy, Museum of Fine Arts, Boston. Reproduced with permission. © 2000 Museum of Fine Arts, Boston. All rights reserved; 36, 102, 176, 204: Ville de Nice, Service photographique; 40: Bob Whitfield; 42, 69, 191: © 2001 The Museum of Modern Art, New York; 43, 103: Archives Matisse/Marc Vaux; 44, 54, 66, 76, 100, 106, 188: Service photographique, Musée National d'Art Moderne, Centre G. Pompidou; 46, 126, 127, 128: Ben Blackwell; 47: Michel de Lorenzo; 48, 142, 184, 186, 206: Photograph © 2001 Board of Trustees, National Gallery of Art, Washington; 49: Monique Bernaz, Geneva; 51, 90: DOWIC Fotografi; 52: BF#448 © Reproduced with the permission of The Barnes Foundation™, All Rights Reserved; 53, 87: © 1996 The Metropolitan Museum of Art; 55, 57, 59: Art Resource, NY; 56: Ali Elai, Camerarts; 58: Wildenstein Institute; 60: BF#717 © Reproduced with the permission of The Barnes Foundation™, All Rights Reserved; 61, 78: Malcolm Varon, New York; 62: © Musée de Grenoble; 64: © RMN–R. G. Ojeda; 68: Archives Matisse/© G. Schiavinotto; 71: Adam Rzepka; 72, 73: Jacqueline Hyde; 74a, 74b: Musée Matisse, Le Cateau; 77: François Velard; 79, 80: John Webb © Tate, London 2000; 81: J. Lathion © Nasjonalgalleriet; 88: Scala; 95, 168: Archives Matisse/André Morain; 97: © 1995 The Art Institute of Chicago, All Rights Reserved; 99: Courtesy Robert Stoppenbach; 111: Sina Althöfer, Hessisches Landesmuseum Darmstadt; 112: © RMN–Daniel Arnaudet; 114: Don Myer; 115: J. Haggard; 117: The Bridgeman Art Library; 136, 150: Charles Choffet, Besançon; 138: Office of Art Properties, Columbia University; 171: Hans Thorwid, Statens Konstmuseer; 179: © Studio Basset; 180: © 2000 Museum Associates/LACMA; 181: Fernand Perret, La Chaux-de-Fonds; 182: David Heald © The Solomon R. Guggenheim Foundation, New York; 205: Hickey-Robertson, Houston.

Index

Boldface page numbers indicate illustrations.